THE BUILDINGS OF SCOTLAND

FOUNDING EDITORS:
NIKOLAUS PEVSNER & COLIN MCWILLIAM

ABERDEENSHIRE: NORTH AND MORAY

DAVID W. WALKER AND MATTHEW WOODWORTH

North Sea
Moray Firth
Lossiemouth
Burghead
Hopeman
Gordonstoun
Inverugie House
Duffus
Findrassie House
Burghead Bay
Findhorn Bay
Findhorn
Milton Brodie
Quarrywood
A96
Elgin
Spynie
Pitgaveny House
Leuchars House
Innes House
Urquhart
Lhanbryde
Kinloss
Grange
Alves
Aldroughty
The Bield
Coxton Tower
Kincorth House
Invererne House
Moy House
Grange Hall
Milton Duff
Dalvey House
Dyke
Forres
Burgie House
Birnie
Brodie Castle
Dallas Dhu
Rafford
Blervie Tower
Pluscarden
Darnaway Castle
Blervie House
Altyre House
Kellas
Lossie
A941
Dallas
MORAY
Logie House
Relugas
Dunphail House
Edinkillie
Findhorn
A940
Divie
Rothes Glen House
Auchinroath House
Rothes
Spey Bay
Kingston
Tugnet
Garmouth
Mosstodloch
Fochabers
Spey
Orton House
Mulben
Auchlunkart House
Arndilly House
Easter Elchies House
Craigellachie
Drummuir Castle
Drummuir
Isla
Kininvie House
Archiestown
Charlestown of Aberlour
Knockando
Carron
Dufftown
Auchindoun Castle
Deveron
Huntly
Portknockie
Scar Nose
Findochty
Portessie
Cullen
Buckie
Tochieneal Ho.
A98
Rathven
Birkenbog House
Portgordon
Letterfourie House
Preshome
Drybridge
Kirktown of Deskford
Tynet
Cairnfield House
Edingight House
Newmill
Grange
Knock
Keith
Milltown of Rothiemay
HIGHLAND
Cragganmore
Ballindalloch
Kilmaichlie House
Grantown-on-Spey
Glenlivet
Tomnavoulin
Livet
The Cabrach
A97
A95
Spey
Chapeltown of Glenlivet
Kylnadrochit Lodge
Tomintoul
Avon
The Lecht
Don
Inchrory
ABERDEENSHIRE
Dee
00
10
20
30
40
50
80
70
60

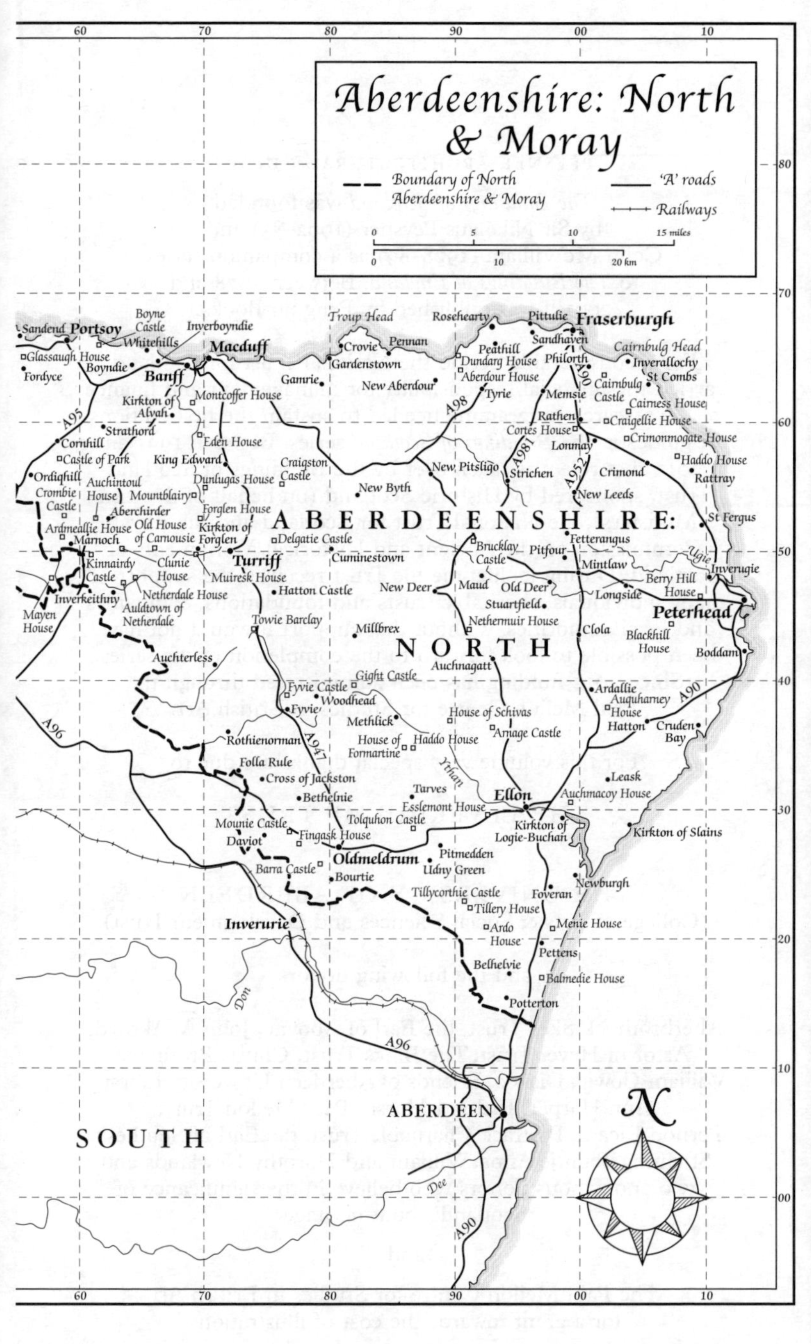

Aberdeenshire: North & Moray
Boundary of North Aberdeenshire & Moray
'A' roads
Railways
0 5 10 15 miles
0 10 20 km
60
70
80
90
00
10
80
70
60
50
40
30
20
10
00
ABERDEENSHIRE: NORTH
SOUTH
N
Sandend
Portsoy
Boyne Castle
Whitehills
Inverboyndie
Macduff
Glassaugh House
Fordyce
Boyndie
Banff
Kirkton of Alvah
Montcoffer House
A95
Strathord
Cornhill
Eden House
Castle of Park
King Edward
Ordiquhill
Auchintoul House
Mountblairy
Dunlugas House
Craigston Castle
Crombie Castle
Aberchirder
Forglen House
Ardmeallie House
Old House of Carnousie
Kirkton of Forglen
Marnoch
Kinnairdy Castle
Clunie House
Turriff
Delgatie Castle
Cuminestown
Muiresk House
Netherdale House
Inverkeithny
Auldtown of Netherdale
Mayen House
Hatton Castle
Towie Barclay
Millbrex
Auchterless
A96
Troup Head
Crovie
Pennan
Gardenstown
Gamrie
New Aberdour
Rosehearty
Peathill
Dundarg House
Aberdour House
Tyrie
A98
Pittulie
Sandhaven
Fraserburgh
Philorth
Memsie
A90
Cairnbulg Head
Inverallochy
St Combs
Cairnbulg Castle
Cairness House
Rathen
Cortes House
Craigellie House
Crimonmogate House
Lonmay
A981
A952
New Pitsligo
Strichen
Crimond
Haddo House
Rattray
New Byth
New Leeds
St Fergus
Fetterangus
Brucklay Castle
Pitfour
Mintlaw
Ugie
Inverugie
New Deer
Maud
Old Deer
Berry Hill House
Longside
Stuartfield
Peterhead
Nethermuir House
Clola
Blackhill House
Boddam
NORTH
Auchnagatt
Gight Castle
Fyvie Castle
Woodhead
Fyvie
Ardallie
Auquharney House
A90
House of Schivas
Methlick
Hatton
Cruden Bay
Arnage Castle
Rothienorman
A947
House of Formartine
Haddo House
Ythan
Folla Rule
Cross of Jackston
Leask
Bethelnie
Tarves
Ellon
Auchmacoy House
Esslemont House
Mounie Castle
Tolquhon Castle
Kirkton of Logie-Buchan
Kirkton of Slains
Fingask House
Daviot
Oldmeldrum
Pitmedden
Barra Castle
Udny Green
Bourtie
Newburgh
Tillycorthie Castle
Foveran
Tillery House
Inverurie
Menie House
Ardo House
Pettens
Belhelvie
Balmedie House
Don
Potterton
A96
ABERDEEN
Dee
A90

PEVSNER ARCHITECTURAL GUIDES

The Buildings of Scotland was founded by Sir Nikolaus Pevsner (1902–83) and Colin McWilliam (1928–89) as a companion series to *The Buildings of England*. Between 1978 and 2001 it was published by Penguin Books.

For a considerable period the National Trust for Scotland carried the financial responsibility for management and finance of the research programme needed to sustain the first editions of guides in the *Buildings of Scotland* series. Between 1991 and 2012 that role was taken over by the Buildings of Scotland Trust, sponsored by Historic Scotland (on behalf of Scottish Ministers), the National Trust for Scotland and the Royal Commission on the Ancient and Historical Monuments of Scotland. During its lifetime the Trust received the support of many individuals, charitable trusts and foundations, companies and local authorities. Without that support it would not have been possible to look forward to the completion of the series. Since 2012 funding has been administered through the Paul Mellon Centre for Studies in British Art.

For this volume very special thanks are due to

THE LEVERHULME TRUST

and

THE UNIVERSITY OF ABERDEEN
(College of Arts & Social Sciences and Development Trust)

and the following donors

Aberbrothock Skea Trust, the Earl of Aboyne, John A. Akroyd, Astor of Hever Trust, The Binks Trust, Chivas Brothers, William Cowie, Diageo, Friends of Aberdeen University Library, Ann Harper, Richard Marsh, Paul Mellon Trust, Pernod Ricard, Portrack Charitable Trust, the Earl of Southesk, Stichting Teuntje Anna, William and Dorothy Newlands and two anonymous donors who believe in the significance of Scotland's built heritage

and

The Paul Mellon Centre for Studies in British Art
for a grant towards the cost of illustrations

Aberdeenshire: North and Moray

BY

DAVID W. WALKER

AND

MATTHEW WOODWORTH

WITH CONTRIBUTIONS FROM

RICHARD FAWCETT

ANDREW A. MCMILLAN

AND

GORDON NOBLE

THE BUILDINGS OF SCOTLAND

YALE UNIVERSITY PRESS

NEW HAVEN AND LONDON

YALE UNIVERSITY PRESS
NEW HAVEN AND LONDON
302 Temple Street, New Haven CT 06511
47 Bedford Square, London WC1B 3DP
www.pevsner.co.uk
www.yalebooks.co.uk
www.yalebooks.com

Published by Yale University Press 2015
2 4 6 8 10 9 7 5 3 1

ISBN 978 0 300 20428 5

Printed in China
through World Print
Set in Monotype Plantin

IN MEMORY OF

JOHN GIFFORD

(1946–2013)

ACCESS TO BUILDINGS

Many of the buildings described in this book are public places, and in some obvious cases their interiors (at least the public sections of them) can be seen without formality. But it must be emphasized that the mention of buildings or lands does not imply any rights of public access to them, or the existence of any arrangements for visiting them.

Some churches are open within regular hours, and it is usually possible to see the interiors of others by arrangement with the minister, priest or church officer. Particulars of admission to Ancient Monuments and other buildings in the care of Scottish Ministers (free to the Friends of Historic Scotland) are available from Historic Scotland, Longmore House, Salisbury Place, Edinburgh EH9 1SH or its website, www.historic-scotland.gov.uk. Details of access to properties of the National Trust for Scotland are available from the Trust's head office at Hermiston Quay, 5 Cultins Road, Edinburgh, EH11 4DF or via its website, www.nts.org.uk. Admission is free to members, on whose subscriptions and donations the Trust's work depends.

Scotland's Gardens Scheme, 42a Castle Street, Edinburgh EH2 3BN, provides a list of gardens open to visitors, also available on the National Gardens Scheme website, www.gardensofscotland.org. Scotland's Churches Scheme, Dunedin, Holehouse Road, Eaglesham, Glasgow G76 0JF, has a searchable database (www.sacredscotland.org.uk) of churches in Scotland including details of opening arrangements and publishes a series of regional guides. *Hudson's Historic Houses, Castles and Gardens Open to the Public*, published annually, includes many private houses open to visitors.

Local Tourist Offices can advise the visitor on what properties in each area are open to the public and will usually give helpful directions as to how to get to them.

CONTENTS

LIST OF TEXT FIGURES AND MAPS

Every effort has been made to contact or trace all copyright holders. The publishers would be glad to make good any errors or omissions brought to our attention in future editions.

MORAY

MAPS

ACKNOWLEDGEMENTS FOR ILLUSTRATIONS

We are deeply indebted to Heather Stoddart of the Royal Commission on the Ancient and Historical Monuments of Scotland (RCAHMS) who redrew measured plans for this volume.

The plates are indexed in the indexes of names and places, and references to them are given by numbers in the margin of the text.

Photographs are copyright of RCAHMS with the exception of the following:

Austin-Smith:Lord (Architects) and Keith Hunter Photography: 130

Claire Herbert, Aberdeenshire Council Archaeology Service ©ACAS: 16, 37

© Country Life: 92

© Crown Copyright Historic Scotland reproduced courtesy of Historic Scotland. www.historicscotlandimages.gov.uk: 10, 15, 20, 56, 76, 77, 124

David Newlan: 6

David W. Walker: 3, 4, 5, 27, 42, 49, 66, 71, 75, 87, 114, 115, 117, 125

Courtesy of Mr and Mrs Mark Ellington: 65

Matthew Woodworth: 19, 50, 58, 79, 88

© National Trust for Scotland: 86, 93

© 2011 Ranjith Jim Box: 51

Richard Fawcett: 13, 14, 17

MAP REFERENCES

The numbers printed in italic type in the margin against the place names in the gazetteer indicate the position of the place in question on the area map (pages ii–iii), which are divided into sections by the 10-kilometre reference lines of the National Grid. The reference given here omits the two initial letters (formerly numbers), which in a full grid reference refer to the 100-kilometre squares into which the county is divided. The first two numbers indicate the western boundary, and the last two the southern boundary, of the 10-kilometre square in which the place is situated. For example, Aberchirder reference 6050 will be found in the 10-kilometre square bounded by grid lines 60 (on the *west*) and 70, and 50 (on the *south*) and 60; Urquhart, reference 2060 in the square bounded by grid lines 20 (on the *west*) and 30, and 60 (on the *south*) and 70.

EDITOR'S FOREWORD

This is the first of two volumes to be published covering the north-east of Scotland. The extent of the area covered is that of the historic counties of Aberdeenshire, Kincardineshire, Banffshire and Morayshire which were abolished in 1975 and replaced by the Grampian Region. This was itself succeeded in 1996 by Aberdeen City Council, Aberdeenshire Council and Moray Council and it is the boundaries of the areas administered by these authorities that are observed by the *Buildings of Scotland* guides. The whole of the Moray Council area is described in this volume but it has been necessary to divide the gazetteer for Aberdeenshire between this volume and its companion guide to *Aberdeenshire: South and Aberdeen*. The division follows the boundary between Aberdeenshire Council's committee districts of Banff, Buchan and Formartine (in the north) and Marr, Garioch and Kincardine & Mearns (in the south). Readers should also note that all places in the county of Banffshire before 1975 are described in this volume, although split between the gazetteers for *Moray* and *Aberdeenshire: North*. They are indicated by B next to the relevant gazetteer heading.

FOREWORD

That you are holding this book, the first of two volumes of the *Buildings of Scotland* series devoted to the north-east part of the country, and that the second is (at the time of writing) in an advanced state of preparation, is owed first and foremost to Professor Jane Geddes of the University of Aberdeen, and Charles O'Brien, Series Editor at Yale University Press. Ian Shepherd had commenced research before his untimely death in 2009. Therefore, in conjunction with Ian Riches of the Buildings of Scotland Trust and Graeme Benvie of the University's Development Trust, an approach was made to the Leverhulme Trust for funding so that these two books could be researched and compiled. We as authors are profoundly grateful to Jane, Charles, Ian and Graeme, to the University and Yale, to the Leverhulme Trust and to all our other sponsors for their support, moral as well as financial, in the pursuit of this substantial undertaking over the past six years.

Equally fundamental to the successful outcome of this project has been the generosity of many individual people who with the courtesy typical of north-east Scotland took time to show us the buildings which interested us on our travels, and who were often able to provide us with background information or to point out details which we might otherwise have missed. Countless occasions remain vivid and delightful to the memory, and we hope that those we met will derive interest and pleasure from the portrait we have painted of the world in which they live.

Like all historians we have, to a considerable extent, been dependent on our predecessors. David MacGibbon and Thomas Ross's two magisterial surveys – *The Castellated & Domestic Architecture of Scotland* (1887–92) and *The Baronial & Ecclesiastical Antiquities of Scotland* (1896–7) – represented a quantum leap in scholarship in their time and for many buildings still provide the most useful information available today. But within Aberdeenshire, the meticulous studies by Dr W. Douglas Simpson (1896–1968), lecturer and Librarian at Aberdeen University, provide the bedrock of analysis for many of the castles discussed within this book. Most of these studies were originally published in the *Proceedings of the Society of Antiquaries of Scotland* and the *Aberdeen University Review*. Further detailed studies were produced after Simpson's death by Harry Gordon Slade in *P.S.A.S.* and *Château Gaillard*.

For a more wide-ranging survey of the north-east we have relied on the Lists of Buildings of Architectural and Historic Interest, supplemented by our own fieldwork. Although since revised and augmented by Historic Scotland, the original survey and documentary research for Aberdeenshire, together with the towns of Banff and Portsoy, were carried out by David M. Walker, then of the Historic Buildings Branch of the Scottish Development Department, while those for Moray and the remainder of Banffshire were the work of Elizabeth Beaton. We have of course often referred to Sir Howard Colvin's *Biographical Dictionary of British Architects 1600–1840* and to the online *Dictionary of Scottish Architects* of which David Walker was – as Professor at St Andrews University – the Founding Editor, almost all of the major biographical entries and lists of jobs for the period 1840–1940 being written by him on the basis of his research over the past sixty-plus years. Canmore, the database of the Royal Commission on the Ancient & Historical Monuments of Scotland, has also been invaluable, particularly for detailed information on early and medieval sites and for industrial archaeology, and we have made good use of the online *Inventory of Gardens & Designed Landscapes*. Special mention should be made, too, of the astonishingly extensive research notes prepared chiefly by John Gifford, Head of the Buildings of Scotland Research Unit, for the north-east as for the rest of the country, which with the publication of our two volumes will be deposited at the Royal Commission for general reference.

The north-east has always been blessed with fine local historians whose love of their subject matter comes through so richly (and infectiously) in their writing. We are very grateful to all the librarians and archivists who have introduced us to their collections and directed us towards publications of interest, in particular Michelle Gait, June Ellner, Jan Smith, Mary Sabiston and Paul Logie in the Special Collections Centre of Aberdeen University Library.

In helping us to prepare the text, Charles O'Brien has drawn on nearly twenty years' experience as a Pevsner author and editor to ensure that what we wrote came out at a reasonable length and conformed to the prescribed format. But the preparation of *Aberdeenshire: North*, in particular, has benefited considerably from the help of those with specialist knowledge. Professor Walker read the draft script in its entirety, as did Professor Peter Davidson of the University of Aberdeen, while Professor Jane Stevenson, also of Aberdeen, and Professor Jane Geddes read it in substantial part. Dr David Bertie, until recently Director of the Aberdeenshire Museums Service, reviewed the entries for Fraserburgh and Peterhead, and Dr Alistair Mason, of the Banff Preservation & Heritage Society, that for the Royal & Ancient Burgh. Further help with Banff was provided by Julian Watson, who has also carried out extensive research into the history of the town. Thomas Addyman, of Addyman Associates, provided the archaeological reports he had prepared in respect of Crombie Castle and Pitmedden House and Garden, while Dr Shannon Fraser of the National Trust for Scotland shared her latest discoveries at Fyvie Castle and Lorraine Hesketh-Campbell checked the entry for Haddo. Information in respect of several N.T.S. properties was provided by Ian Gow, Professor Alistair Mutch, of Nottingham Trent University, discussed with us the more important farm buildings, while Moira Greig kindly allowed us to see the final draft of her chapter on Cullykhan even before its publication by the Society of Antiquaries. A visit to Delgatie Castle with Professor Charles McKean, of Dundee University, shortly before he died proved – as always – both revelatory and very thought-provoking.

Across both North Aberdeenshire and Moray we have received much help from Alison Robertson and Canon Jeffrey Hopewell in respect of stained glass. In Moray, the text has benefited considerably from the assistance and research of Andrew Wright, PPRIAS, now of the Scottish Civic Trust and formerly of Law & Dunbar Nasmith. Other helpful information has been compiled by Gemma Wild, also of the Trust. Another fount of wisdom has been Bruce Bishop, late of Gordonstoun School and author of the two magisterial series, *The Lands and People of Moray* and *Banffshire: The People and Lands*. Stephen Leitch of Lossiemouth Library was efficient and very friendly, while Panny Laing arranged access to a number of houses that would have otherwise remained closed.

The section of the introduction covering Geology has been written by Andrew McMillan, lately of the British Geological Survey, and that covering Archaeology by Dr Gordon Noble, of the University of Aberdeen, who has also contributed many of the entries for the oldest sites and monuments. In addition, Professor Richard Fawcett of St Andrews University has written the entries for a number of the more important medieval churches. We are most grateful to them for all their contributions.

The completed text of *Aberdeenshire: North and Moray* has been copy-edited for us by Dr Hester Higton. The town plans and area map have been skilfully prepared by Martin Brown. Many other illustrations were provided by the Royal Commission's drawing office, particularly by Heather Stoddart, while the Commission's photographic department, chiefly in the form of Steve Wallace, was responsible for most of the colour plates. As longstanding admirers of the Commission's expertise in these fields we are extremely grateful to them, to Clare Sorensen who has acted as intermediary between us, and also to Kristina Watson, Neil Fraser and Kyle Watson. The Royal Commission photographed a number of Professor Walker's sketches made during his field surveys, but he has also prepared some new ones especially for this book. Further illustrations from antiquarian sources have been provided by Aberdeen University Library and the Aberdeenshire Museums Service.

Finally we would very much like to thank Phoebe Lowndes, Production Editor at Yale, and Alice Winborn, our Picture Editor, for successfully turning all our hopes and prayers as authors into the tangible reality of the present bound volume.

David W. Walker
Matthew Woodworth
King's College, Aberdeen: July 2014

NORTH-EAST SCOTLAND

INTRODUCTION

The north-east is like a country in itself: it is quite distinct from other parts of Scotland. The present-day counties of Aberdeenshire and Moray have expanded to embrace two other historic counties, Banffshire and Kincardineshire, which in the minds of local people retain a strong sense of separate identity.

Aberdeen lies relatively near the south-east corner of this great land mass, between the river-mouths of the Don and the Dee. Banff, the former county town of Banffshire, and Elgin, the capital of Moray, were both founded on the northern coast. That the town of Kincardine ceased to exist, with Stonehaven now the provincial capital, and that almost all the other important towns are ports with large harbours reflects the primary importance not just of fishing but of communication, the exchange of trade and culture, in the world of Northern Europe, centred and dependent on the sea.

But beyond its coast the north-east is chiefly comprised of a deep hinterland, some of it very sparse but much of it verdant and even luscious. It is separated and sheltered from the rest of Scotland by the Grampian and Cairngorm Mountains, but the hinterland itself is a low-lying, undulating country with only a few landmark peaks, among them Tap O'Noth, Bennachie, the Bin Hill of Cullen, Clachnaben and Mormond. Cutting through the landscape are the rivers Bervie, Esk, Dee, Don, Ythan, Ugie,
Deveron, Spey, Lossie and Findhorn, each with its tributary 1
burns and waters.

The names are Pictish or – progressively, from the C9 – Gaelic: when those languages were spoken here, the hills and rivers were lines of defence and communication and sacred places. Change comes gradually to the north-east. The Old Order suffered a seismic shock after the collapse of the Jacobite Rising of 1745, but unravelled only so far as it needed to; and afterwards the Improvers drained, cleared and enclosed the low ground, dotted it with farmhouses and steadings, planted shelterbelts and, in doing so, within a surprisingly propitious climate created the best agricultural land anywhere in Scotland. Their roads and bridges fall naturally into the folds of that land, interrupted by occasional villages, and the low horizons often result in skies which dazzle travellers with their vastness: sometimes brilliant pale blues reflected off the sea which bathe the countryside in gentle colours, at other times magnificent dark grey cloudscapes which harden those colours into very sharp focus. In such a land as this life, death and the divine seem close.

The north-east faces challenges from the modern world, both of change and neglect. It preserves and expresses its identity through its deep-rooted, vibrant culture – the Doric language both spoken and sung, instrumental music and dance, the narrative folklore of ferm-toun and fisher-toun, a sense of history intuitively understood: it is at heart a rural community which honours traditional values. That culture finds its most tangible, everyday form in the places described in this book, churches, castles and country houses, towns and villages, isolated mills, farm-steadings and bothies, and monoliths and carved stones set into the landscape. The authors extend their thanks to previous historians of the north-east, as well as to all those who helped them on their travels, who proved to be – in the words of the *Statistical Accounts* – 'sober, industrious and hospitable to strangers'.

LANDSCAPE, GEOLOGY AND BUILDING STONES

BY ANDREW A. MCMILLAN

The expansive LANDSCAPE of Aberdeenshire and Moray is one of many contrasts. In the south-west of the district, the Cairngorm massif, a dissected granite plateau, generally lies over 1,000 m. above sea level. Notable summits include Cairn Toul (1,291 m.), Braeriach (1,296 m.), Ben Macdui (1,309 m.) and Cairn Gorm (1,245 m.); with the exception of Ben Nevis these are the highest mountains in Britain. Eastwards, and south of Deeside, are Lochnagar (1,155 m.), Mount Keen (939 m.) and the lower rounded hills of the Mounth. The elevation of the land decreases eastwards and northwards towards the undulating coastal agricultural lowlands of Moray, Buchan, Aberdeen and Strathmore. In Buchan and Moray the lowlands are characterized by a series of ancient plateau surfaces eroded across a wide variety of rock types. Overlooked on its south-western margin by the tor-capped hill of Bennachie (528 m.), a granite landmark steeped in local folklore, the rolling Buchan plateau lies between 60 and 150 m. above sea level. Punctuating the Buchan landscape are small hills composed of the most resistant rock types, for example the quartzite of Mormond Hill (234 m.) between Fraserburgh and Peterhead and the Hill of Dudwick (174 m.), NE of Ellon. In Moray, Ben Rinnes (840 m.), a granite hill SW of Dufftown, dominates the scenery of the fertile countryside of the Speyside whisky industry. The rivers Findhorn, Lossie, Spey and Deveron all flow northwards to the Moray Firth by the coastal settlements of Findhorn, Lossiemouth, Garmouth and Banff respectively. The principal easterly flowing rivers of Aberdeenshire are the Dee, rising within the heart of the Cairngorms, and the much shorter Don, which meet the North Sea in the city of Aberdeen, while the lowlands of Buchan are drained by the River Ythan through Ellon and the River Ugie at Peterhead.

The lowland plateau landscape has been moulded by successive Quaternary ice sheets which moved broadly eastwards along the Moray Firth from a centre of ice accumulation in the northern Highlands, and north-eastwards across the district from the Cairngorms. The tip of Buchan and the E coast has been impinged

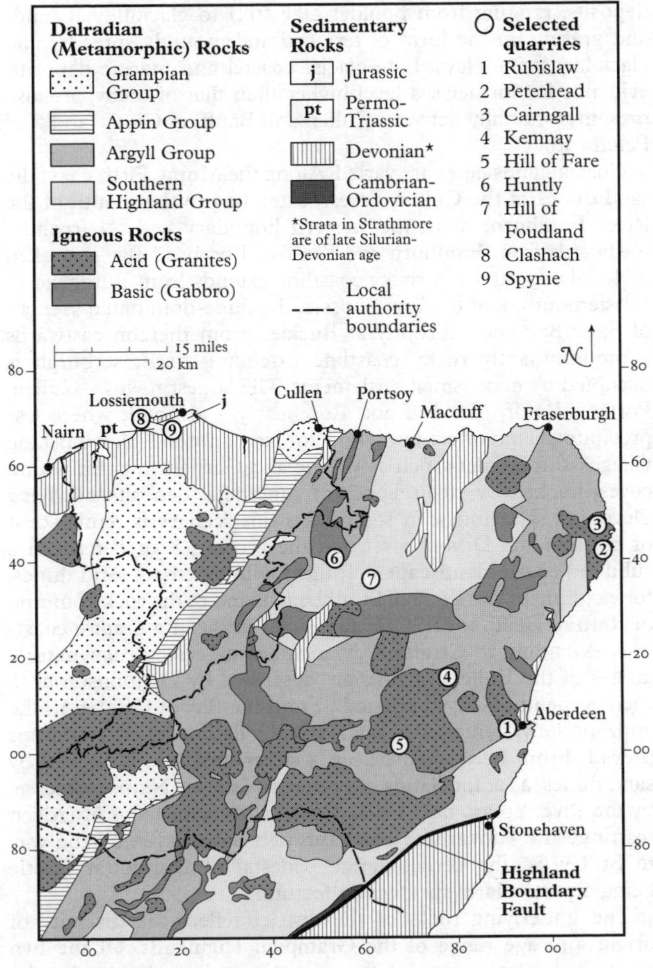

Geological map of North Aberdeenshire and Moray.

by ice of Scandinavian origin locally diverting Scottish ice south-eastwards. The form of today's landscape can be attributed to pre-glacial, glacial and post-glacial erosion of a wide variety of sedimentary, igneous and metamorphic rock types. From Troup Head above Gardenstown on the N coast the Buchan Plateau is crossed by a broad, undulating south-westward trending ridge developed on both slates and Old Red Sandstone lithologies. From the rugged Moray coast between Banff and Portknockie a similar series of broad south-westward trending ridges, developed on steeply dipping quartzite at elevations between 220 and 310 m. above sea level, extend westwards towards the N-flowing River Spey, where they merge into a dissected plateau, between 180 and 265 m. above sea level, developed across a range of lithologies. The ice sheets also left a succession of superficial deposits, ranging from boulder clay (till) to glaciofluvial sands and gravels (in the form of terraced and moundy spreads) and glaciolacustrine clays. Late glacial coastal and marine deposits, evidence for former sea level higher than that of today, are also present, especially between Cullen and Banff, at Crovie and N of Peterhead.

Coastal landscapes are varied. Along the Moray Firth coast the sand dunes of the Culbin Forest, extending to the mouth of the River Findhorn, mark the western boundary with Nairnshire. Eastwards from Findhorn and Kinloss, Burghead Bay is backed by low-lying dunes. A rocky coastline extends from Burghead to Lossiemouth. E of the River Lossie, the dune-dominated scenery of Spey Bay ends abruptly at Buckie. From thereon eastwards a predominantly rocky coastline extending to Fraserburgh is occupied by many small settlements. The largest towns – Cullen, Portsoy, Banff, Macduff and Rosehearty – are built where less precipitous land offered potential for larger ports. Isolated fishing villages and hamlets such as Crovie and Gardenstown sit within coves, backed by steep slopes of superficial deposits overlying Devonian sandstones: in some ways this scenery is reminiscent of parts of the Devon coast. On the E coast, N of Peterhead a subdued coastal landscape is fringed with extensive sand dunes, for example by the Loch of Strathbeg, inland of the rocky outcrop of Rattray Head, N of St Fergus. S of Peterhead a granite coastline, extending to Cruden Bay, includes the spectacular natural arches of the Bullers of Buchan, described by Dr Johnson as 'a rock perpendicularly tubulated'. From the Bay of Cruden to the appropriately named Rockend S of Collieston rocky outcrops prevail. From here to Aberdeen a softer coastline is backed by sand dunes, as at the Sands of Forvie, a National Nature Reserve, by the River Ythan, near Ellon. Rocky cliffs return S of Aberdeen to fringe the Kincardine coast through Stonehaven all the way to St Cyrus, the conglomerate pedestal of Dunnottar Castle being a particularly spectacular feature.

The underlying rocks of the district reflect the diversity of origin and age range of the Grampian Highlands. Of the two major boundaries that define the Grampian Highlands, the Great Glen and the Highland Boundary Faults, only the latter is present within the district. Here, it spectacularly defines the Highland edge along the N side of Strathmore and makes its appearance in the coastal cliffs N of Stonehaven. The oldest rocks of the district belong to the DALRADIAN SUPERGROUP, the term 'Dalradian' being introduced by Sir Archibald Geikie in 1891 for the varied assemblage of metamorphic rocks lying E of the Great Glen. Many of these rock types were employed locally as sources of rubble stone but were generally not used more widely, either because of their tendency to split too much or because of their intractability.

In the main, the original rocks of the Dalradian Supergroup were of sedimentary origin, formed between about 730 and 470 million years ago (Ma) (Late Neoproterozoic to Early Ordovician). The Dalradian Basin developed on the edge of a continental mass known as Laurentia as it broke away from the supercontinent of Rodinia and drifted off, opening up the Iapetus Ocean. After reaching its maximum width in the Early Ordovician (490 Ma) the ocean began to close. Evidence of the resultant collision of a volcanic arc system with the Laurentian margin can be traced from North America through Ireland and Scotland. In Scotland the collision (resulting in the 'Grampian Event') started around 470 Ma ago, during the Ordovician, and as it progressed the volcanic arc became buried under the leading edge of the continent and the Dalradian succession was progressively deformed and metamorphosed. In most of the Grampian Highlands the early deformation resulted in major, flat-lying recumbent folds, in which, on a regional scale, beds on the lower limb are overturned. However, in the north-east the deformation was less intense and the strata remained right way up. This area is known as the 'Buchan Block', bounded to the W and S by two shear zones, the Portsoy–Duchray Hill Lineament and the Deeside Lineament respectively. This area is also notable for relatively high heat flow during metamorphism, accompanied by the intrusion of gabbroic and granitic suites.

The Dalradian sequence is subdivided into five Groups. From oldest to youngest, rocks of the Grampian, Appin, Argyll and Southern Highland groups underlie much of Aberdeenshire and Moray. The Trossachs Group is confined to the Highland Boundary Fault zone. The surface geographical distribution of the Dalradian rocks is controlled by the geological structure of the district, and locally they are concealed by younger strata. Across much of the Grampians the orientation of major fold axes is NE–SW. In contrast, Buchan is dominated by broad, open upright folds, synclines and anticlines, with axes trending N and NNE. Notable structures include the Turriff Syncline and Buchan Anticline. The GRAMPIAN GROUP crops out in the coastal zone W of Cullen, where it is represented by the Cullen Quartzite (e.g. Bow Fiddle Rock). Inland, between Rothes and the N side of the Cairngorm Granite, the Grampian Group consists of interbedded quartzites and metamorphosed micaceous sandstones. APPIN GROUP rocks, also cropping out from the coast at Cullen but extending south-westwards, consist of thinly bedded successions of metamorphosed sandstones, with quartzites, metamorphosed mudstones (now represented by mica-schists) and several important limestones. The group includes the Findlater Flags, once a source of roofing material much used in Tomintoul, which crop out near Keith. The ARGYLL GROUP, which underlies much of eastern Buchan and southern Aberdeenshire including Donside and Deeside, comprises a mixed succession beginning with mainly quartzite and passing up into metasandstone and schist. The group includes some thin lava successions in the Tomintoul area, and, between Tomintoul and the Banffshire coast, numerous limestones including the Portsoy Limestone and Boyne Limestone. The limestones were exploited for agricultural purposes and roadstone and in the C19 were used in the walls of many houses in Banffshire. The SOUTHERN HIGHLAND GROUP forms much of the coastal outcrop between Banff and Fraserburgh and extends southwards under Buchan to Maud, New Deer and Turriff. Schists and locally coarse metasandstone predominate. The group also includes MacDuff Slate Formation, which in the C19 yielded a good resource of dark purple-grey slate for roofing from quarries lying SE of Huntly at Hill of Kirkney, Corskie, Hill of Foudland and Hill of Tillymorgan. Along the Highland Boundary Fault, metamorphosed sandstones, limestones and black mudstones of the Trossachs Group (Cambrian to Ordovician) mark the end of Dalradian sedimentation.

Cutting through the Dalradian sequence are numerous bodies of igneous and meta-igneous plutonic rocks which were emplaced prior to, and during and following, the 'Grampian Event'. These, generally coarsely crystalline rocks, range from acid (silica-rich) varieties such as granite to basic (silica-poor) varieties such as gabbro. Generally the older intrusions, intruded during the waning stages of deformation, exhibit a mineral foliation which is absent in the post-deformation younger rocks.

The Aberdeenshire GRANITES are famed for their exploitation, most notably in Donside where John Fyfe began his industry in the mid C19, in Deeside and in Buchan. Early uses are medieval rubble constructions and unworked granite, in the form of boulders gathered from the fields and rivers, may be seen in numerous places including the castles of Crathes, Drum, Midmar and Fraser. The earliest known use in mortar-built masonry is the late C12 tower of Monymusk church. But the working of granite was not well understood until much later and the early buildings of Old Aberdeen and King's College employed softer, more easily worked, imported sandstone. Only from the C18 do Aberdeen's buildings use granite ashlar from its numerous quarries for houses, public buildings, bridges, docks, lighthouses and monumental work.

Many of the granites were capable of taking a beautiful polish. The principal quarries supplied a range of grey granites, their colour and texture dependent on the proportion of the minerals quartz, feldspar (orthoclase and plagioclase) and mica (muscovite and biotite). Rubislaw (opened *c.* 1741; quarry workers were wont to say that 'Nearly half o'Aiberdeen has come oot o'

Rubislaw'), Sclattie, Dyce and Tillyfourie produced a greyish-blue variety; Kemnay and Toms Forest worked silver-grey granite for building and monumental purposes (best seen in Marischal College, Aberdeen); Persley and Cairncry produced finer, light grey granite; and Dancing Cairns yielded light grey-blue granite (as in the façade and gateway, of 1830, in front of the E and W churches of St Nicholas). The silver-grey of Invergelder, Deeside (not unlike Kemnay but with a tinge of brown), was used for Balmoral Castle and building on the royal estates.

Coloured granites owe their hue to the presence of coloured feldspars, notably to small quantities of iron oxides in the orthoclase crystals. The salmon pink of Corrennie, near Kemnay, was much used for polished work and Aberdeen Art Gallery is a fine example. Other coloured granites include, in Buchan, the reddish-brown Peterhead granite, not only used for the building of Peterhead and Fraserburgh but also worldwide for monumental and heavy engineering work. Blue-grey granite from Cairngall, N of Peterhead, was in great demand for major engineering works (e.g. the foundations of the Bell Rock Lighthouse, the foundations of Old London Bridge and the pier walls of the Houses of Parliament). Elsewhere, in the S, formerly Kincardineshire, dark grey granite was worked at Cove and Nigg. The Hill of Fare quarries, N of Banchory, yielded a fine dark red granite (finer than Peterhead or Corrennie). In Banffshire, smaller bodies of granite were worked for building, including the distinctively foliated Keith Granite seen in many local buildings.

Generally hard and compact basic and meta-basic plutonic igneous rocks, colloquially referred to as 'whinstone', are present in several masses including those of Belhelvie, Insch, Kennethmount, Boganclogh, Huntly and Morven-Cabrach. A principal constituent rock type in many of these plutons is GABBRO, a coarsely crystalline black igneous rock. Capable of being roughly worked, squared blocks of gabbro were used as local building stone in various parts of Aberdeenshire. Huntly Castle is a fine example, where the C17 reconstructed main wall is of Huntly Gabbro with the heraldic doorway in Old Red Sandstone. At Kennethmont, cottages display the typical use of basic igneous rocks with squared blocks and courses made up with snecks of gabbro, and door and window surrounds in pink sandstone. Ultramafic rocks including red and green serpentinite, were worked at Portsoy from the early C18 for ornamental and decorative purposes, and exported by sea to Europe (e.g. for use in the Palace of Versailles).

The principal building stone of the north-east is SANDSTONE. Several small basins or outliers, including those at Tomintoul, Rhynie, Cabrach, Turriff and Aberdeen, are considered to be remnants of a once more extensive development of the Lower Old Red Sandstone (Lower Devonian), and several of these outcrops are important as former sources of stone. These basins represent irregular sedimentary infills on the southern margin of the Orcadian Basin. At Tomintoul and Cabrach basal breccias are overlain by conglomerates and red and grey sandstones. The

Rhynie Outlier, a succession of conglomerates, sandstones and mudstones, is internationally recognized for the occurrence near the top of the sequence of the Rhynie Chert (formed as siliceous sinter by hot springs during contemporary volcanic activity), which contains exquisitely preserved fossils of early land plants. In the Turriff Basin, Lower Devonian sediments of the Crovie Group are, in the main, sandstones and conglomerates formed on river flood plains and alluvial fans. Well exposed at Crovie, New Aberdour and Gardenstown, the strata rest unconformably on the Macduff Slate Formation and are in turn unconformably overlain by conglomerates of the Findon Group (Middle Devonian), which notably contains the grey and red mudstones of the Gamrie Fish Bed, a correlative of the Achanarras Fish Bed in Caithness. Local red sandstone has been used
3 for many of Turriff's buildings and for many of the coastal villages. Conglomerates of the Inverness Sandstone Group (Middle Devonian) are seen E and SE of Elgin, where they are overlain by red-brown and purple-brown flaggy sandstones of the Fochabers Sandstone Formation. NW of Elgin these are succeeded by brownish-grey, yellow and red sandstones of the Alves and Rosebrae Beds (Upper Devonian). Quarries at Rosebrae, Alves and Pluscarden once yielded good building sandstone.

S of the Highland Boundary Fault, the northern extension of Strathmore is underlain by a thick sequence (several kilometres) of late Silurian to early Devonian fluviatile sediments, mainly sandstones and conglomerates with interbedded andesite lava flows. They belong to six groups, named, from oldest to youngest, the Stonehaven, Dunnottar, Crawton, Arbuthnott, Garvock and Strathmore groups. The older part of this succession is well exposed in coastal sections between St Cyrus and Stonehaven. Local red-brown sandstones supplied much building stone, as can be seen in Stonehaven and Inverbervie. Inland, local coarse-grained brown sandstones of the Strathmore Group were used in many villages, for example Fettercairn.

Mesozoic (Permian and Triassic) sedimentary rocks which developed within the mainly offshore Moray Firth Basin extend onto the land and are preserved in a coastal strip between Lossiemouth and Burghead. The Upper Permian to Lower Triassic Cutties Hillock and Hopeman Sandstones comprise yellow to buff to white aeolian sandstones with large-scale dune bedding and sparse fluviatile deposits. The strata are notable for having yielded a reptilian fossil fauna, fine examples of which may be seen in the excellent geological exhibitions of the Elgin Museum. The overlying fluviatile sandstones and conglomerates of the Burghead Beds are succeeded by the Upper Triassic Lossiemouth Sandstone, of aeolian origin. Many of these sandstones have been worked for building, particularly in Forres and Elgin. Notable quarries include Cutties Hillock, Knock of Alves, Burghead, Greenbrae, Clashach, Newton, Lossiemouth and Spynie. Of these, only Clashach, worked by Moray Stone Cutters, continues in full production to supply both local and national building projects.

Jurassic rocks (mainly calcareous mudstones and sandstones) of the Moray Firth Basin crop out just S of Lossiemouth. Rocks of Cretaceous age do not crop out in the district although there is indirect evidence that, during this period, parts of Buchan were inundated by the sea. Relict gravel deposits of possible Neogene age, containing flint pebbles and boulders, are present at Fyvie and on the Moss of Cruden, W of Peterhead. At Den of Boddam flints were mined in prehistoric times.

CLAYS suitable for BRICK AND TILE-MAKING are widely distributed within the Quaternary deposits of north-east Scotland. Nearly twenty sites were exploited, mainly along the coast of Moray and Aberdeenshire over the last 200 years. Both boulder clay (till) and glaciolacustrine clays have been used. The most recent brick production congregated between Peterhead and Aberdeen, where reddish-brown laminated clays were worked for brickmaking until the mid 1980s at the Cruden Bay Brick and Tile Works at Errolston and Tipperty. Numerous SAND AND GRAVEL pits have exploited the moundy and flat-topped glaciofluvial deposits of the district, principally for concrete products and also for mortaring and plastering sand. The best resources flank the valleys of the major rivers and lie on the coastal lowlands between Forres and Elgin.

PREHISTORIC, ROMAN AND EARLY MEDIEVAL ABERDEENSHIRE AND MORAY*

BY GORDON NOBLE

The prehistoric

The diverse landscapes of north-east Scotland, stretching from the coastal plains of the eastern lowlands to the eastern Grampian Mountains and the southern Cairngorms, supported substantial settlement in the prehistoric and early medieval periods. The earliest settlers were the hunter-gatherers of the MESOLITHIC, who colonized the early landscapes of Scotland after the end of the last Ice Age. Settlement during the Mesolithic in Scotland (*c.* 9000–4000 B.C.) stretches back to at least the 9th millennium B.C. (over 10,000 years ago), dating to a period a few thousand years after the end of the Ice Age. Mesolithic settlement in north-east Scotland is represented primarily by scatters of stone tools found in modern ploughed fields and along the coasts and rivers – the residues of a hunting-gathering-fishing lifestyle. Excavated sites can reveal tantalizing traces of settlement in the form of pits and postholes, while coastal sites can be represented by significant accumulations of shells, traces of shell middens where Mesolithic people gathered the bounty of the coast and the sea. These sites are only fragmentary traces of lives that may have

*Sites in *Aberdeenshire: South and Aberdeen* are denoted (S).

been relatively mobile, following the herds of wild animals and occupying the ever-changing riverine landscapes and coasts of the north-east. After the ice this would have been a relatively barren landscape, but by the end of the Mesolithic period, in the late fifth millennium B.C., the north-east would have been cloaked by a thick woodland dominated by oak. Mesolithic sites in the north-east are concentrated along the banks of the rivers Dee and Don, and the Ythan and tributaries, and these rivers would have formed the main routes through the wooded landscape. Traces of the Mesolithic can be found from Aberdeen, where excavations on the medieval parts of the city have uncovered prehistoric layers containing Mesolithic flints, to upland landscapes at the foot of the Grampians. However, little remains in the landscape to identify these sites – those most intensively studied are along the Dee in Southern Aberdeenshire and consist of extensive scatters of stone tools. A site at Nethermills, Banchory (S), was excavated in the 1980s and more than 20,000 stone tools were found, along with possible traces of Mesolithic timber dwellings. Slightly upriver at Warren Field, Crathes, giant pits dug from the 8th millennium onwards have been found – these may have been animal traps or may have had more ritualized roles in prehistoric life. In Northern Aberdeenshire, extensive scatters of Mesolithic stone tools have been found along the banks and at the mouth of the Ythan estuary at the Sands of Forvie.

A significant transformation occurred in the landscapes of north-east Scotland in the centuries after 4000 B.C. At this time the fringes of western Europe, including Scotland, came in contact with new ways of life associated with communities that practised the agricultural routines of crop-growing and animal husbandry. This period of prehistory is known as the NEOLITHIC or New Stone Age. In Scotland, as in the rest of Britain and Ireland, this era lasted for over 1,500 years (*c.* 4000–2500 B.C.). The Neolithic is generally recognized as the period when domesticated animals and crops such as cattle, sheep and barley and new technologies such as pottery and stone axes to clear woodland for crops and animal grazing were introduced. The Neolithic is not merely about the spread of new types of animals and technologies but also documents the spread of new ideas about life, death and the world around.

Many Neolithic sites and artefacts lie buried and are discovered only through excavation, but the most visible remains of the period in the Scottish landscape are monuments for burial and ceremony. In the earlier Neolithic period (4000–3300 B.C.) large stone-built cairns were constructed. Few of these have been excavated in north-east Scotland, but those that have been comprise massive mounds of earth or stone known as LONG BARROWS or LONG CAIRNS. The construction of these monuments was connected with the disposal, display and curation of the remains of the dead, but may also have marked land and territory among the early agricultural societies of the north-east. Elsewhere in Scotland at this time, chambered cairns were built to hold multiple human bodies – these were perhaps family or lineage monuments. In the north-east less is known about the long mounds or cairns, but these may have covered the remains of fewer individuals – perhaps important members of the community or individuals who represented the collective ancestral dead. The only well-excavated example in the north-east was dug at Dalladies, Fettercairn (S), excavated in advance of its destruction through quarrying. The mound at Dalladies was around 70 m. long and stood to a height of over 2 m. and dated to around 3700 B.C. The turf-built mound was found to cover a timber setting defined by a split tree trunk and a stone-built chamber. Inside the stone chamber a fragment of human skull and a flint knife was found. In Northern Aberdeenshire there are two long mounds at Knapperty Hillock (Old Deer) and Longman Hill (Macduff), and the long cairn at Cairn Catto (Longside) is an impressive trapezoidal mound of stones almost 50 m. long. All of these cairns and mounds are unexcavated, but are likely to overlie mortuary structures and deposits of human remains. Two stone axes were found at Cairn Catto in the C19.

SETTLEMENTS belonging to the Neolithic period in north-east Scotland are harder to identify than some of the monumental structures. At present we have only a very basic understanding of the settlement patterns and economy of the Neolithic. Investigations of prehistoric life more generally are hampered by the generally acidic nature of soils in Scotland, which is detrimental to the survival of bone and organic material. In the Neolithic the emphasis may have been on herding cattle with cereal farming probably undertaken as part of small-scale garden agriculture. The period has long been assumed to have been accompanied by a sedentary lifestyle, yet in north-east Scotland and in much of lowland Scotland generally we only have sporadic occurrences of what could be interpreted as Neolithic domestic structures. It has been suggested by some archaeologists that Neolithic people may have retained a large degree of settlement mobility, despite the uptake of agriculture. In this respect, there may have been a continuation of some of the lifestyles and settlement practices that occurred in the Mesolithic period. However, two Neolithic structures that had at least some role in domestic life are worth mentioning here: the 'TIMBER HALLS' at Crathes and Balbridie on the Dee (both S). These were monumental buildings over 20 m. long, constructed with large oak timbers, radiocarbon-dated to the period *c.* 3800–3600 B.C. Neither building had surviving floor surfaces, but traces of cereals including naked barley and emmer wheat were recovered from the hall at Crathes, along with fragments of Neolithic pottery vessels and stone tools. Over 20,000 carbonized cereal grains were found at Balbridie. There has been great debate about the role of these structures in Neolithic life: were they the houses of extended families of early Neolithic incomers to the area or were they more specialized and perhaps ritualized structures for communal gatherings? Unfortunately the evidence is ambiguous at present, but these structures reveal rare insights into the nature of Neolithic life in the north-east of Scotland. Settlement more generally is harder to identify and consists of very rare timber building of more modest proportions and pits and post-holes of more ephemeral (or less well-preserved) settlements. Northern Aberdeenshire also preserves a unique insight into the more mundane aspects of life in the later Neolithic. The flint-working site at Den of Boddam is Scotland's only flint mine and the only major inland source of flint in northern Britain. The flint dug out of the gravel deposits would have been an invaluable resource in earlier prehistory that could be traded and used to make stone tools. The outlines of some of the hundreds of pits dug can still be seen at the site today.

Around the middle of the third millennium B.C. (*c.* 2400 B.C.) there was a transformation of Stone Age society to societies that increasingly adopted new metalworking technologies, along with traditions and practices that found their ultimate origin in Continental Europe. Recently, the term 'Chalcolithic' has been used to describe a transitional period between the Late Neolithic and the BRONZE AGE. The Chalcolithic (*c.* 2450–2150 B.C.) is characterized by the appearance of new cultural practices and novel objects, including the first metal objects, new traditions of pottery (finely decorated Beakers) and new burial practices. These changes are most obvious in funerary traditions, with the increased visibility of burial – predominately inhumation in stone cist graves, with grave goods much more common than in Neolithic burial traditions. Some Bronze Age graves were covered by monumental earthen barrows or ROUND CAIRNS, as survives at Memsie. The burials of the Chalcolithic and Bronze Age can include grave goods such as Beaker pots, archery equipment (arrowheads, belt rings and wristguards) and more rarely modest metal objects such as copper knives or gold objects. North-east Scotland swiftly adopted the new practices associated with metalworking and from the end of the third millennium this area was an important region in the spread of full bronze-working traditions from the C22 B.C. onwards across Britain and Ireland. Many of the stone moulds for early bronze metalworking are concentrated here, despite the fact that the materials for bronze itself came from Ireland (copper) and south-west England (tin).

New traditions of megalithic and monumental architecture emerged in the later Neolithic and Early Bronze Age and include some of north-east Scotland's most famous monuments – the RECUMBENT STONE CIRCLES, a distinctive type of stone circle found exclusively in this part of Scotland and defined by a ring of standing stones with a massive recumbent stone on the S flanked by two tall standing stones. These circles enclosed central cairns which covered pyres used for cremating the dead. The dating for this tradition of architecture is uncertain, but the presence of Beaker pottery at a number of these monuments implies at least some were in use in the Chalcolithic/Early Bronze Age and their construction may have been closely linked to the importance of this area in the new era of metal and Beakers. The most extensively studied Recumbent Stone Circle is that at Tomnaverie near Tarland (S), which has been the subject of

detailed investigation and reconstruction. The excavations at
Tomnaverie showed that the first episode of activity on the hill
was the use of the hilltop for pyres: cremated bone, ashes and
burnt soil survived as a low mound under the later central cairn.
Over these pyres a polygonal cairn was constructed, the hill-slope
was revetted and a low platform of stones was built to support
the cairn. A secondary phase of construction involved encircling
the cairn with thirteen standing stones and a recumbent measuring over 3 m. in length, arranged in a circle 17 m. in diameter.
The stones were graded in height towards the SW, emphasizing
the recumbent setting. Sherds of Beaker pottery were found
beneath the outer platform at the foot of the kerb of the central
cairn. Radiocarbon-dating suggests construction in the C26–C25
B.C. Examples in northern Aberdeenshire include circles at Aikey
Brae (Old Deer), Loanhead of Daviot (Daviot), Strichen and
Berrybrae (Lonmay). Loanhead of Daviot was excavated by 8
Kilbride-Jones in the 1930s and has been restored, with the
central cairn, ring of orthostats and recumbent stone all well
displayed. The circle at Aikey Brae is a good example of a Buchan
variant of the Recumbent Stone Circle tradition where a stone-
kerbed bank linking the ring of monoliths can be found in place
of a central cairn. A number of other forms of later Neolithic/
Early Bronze Age monuments survive in the north-east, including a small number of HENGE MONUMENTS – enclosures defined
by ditches with external banks enclosing burials or settings of
timbers or megaliths within. The henge at Broomend of Crichie
(S) is the most investigated example of its type, built to enclose
an area that was used for burial in the Bronze Age. In Moray the
example at Quarry Wood is preserved in woodland to the W of
Elgin.

We have even fewer settlements dating to the Chalcolithic and Early Bronze Age than we do from the Neolithic in north-east Scotland, but from the mid second millennium B.C. onwards there is a change in the character of the archaeological evidence. Rather than landscapes of ritual monuments and burial we have landscapes dominated by evidence relating to the patterns of settlement and agricultural practices. A bewildering diversity of settlement forms emerged, but most were based on a tradition of architecture that came to dominate the settlement record for the next two thousand years in the later Bronze Age and IRON AGE: the ROUNDHOUSE. In the lowlands and in north-east Scotland these roundhouses were made of timber and turf and few survive above ground today. Some would have been monumental in their own right, using hundreds of trees in their construction and requiring a wide community to build and maintain them. These circular buildings measured from around 5 m. to 20 m. in diameter, based on a radial layout with a central hearth and wattle-and-daub timber partitions marking areas around the periphery of the roundhouse for sleeping, storage or keeping animals. One of the most common forms of north-east roundhouse was the ring ditch house, which included a sunken area (the ring ditch) between the inner roof-bearing posts and the outer wall that may have been used for the over-wintering of animals. People may have slept above on a raised floor constructed in the eaves of the house.

We are missing much of the detail of later Bronze Age and Iron Age lifestyles, which would have been defined by the routines of the household. Floor levels rarely survive in roundhouses and the architecture has largely decayed away, leaving little evidence for internal furniture, décor and economy. These would have been mixed farming economies in the main, and one of the more curious forms of archaeological monuments dating to the Iron Age are stone-built underground chambers known as SOUTERRAINS which were probably built in association with roundhouse settlements and may have been used for storing agricultural produce such as milk, cheese, meat and grain. A rare example of roundhouses and field systems survives at New Kinord (S) and good examples of souterrains can be seen at Culsh, Clova and Glenkindle House (all S). Certain forms of roundhouse endured for centuries and this conservatism in architecture characterized communities where status and identity may have been closely tied to the house and household.

Status and community identity in the late Bronze Age and Iron Age was also expressed in more monumental constructions that have been labelled with the descriptive, yet at times unhelpful, name HILL-FORT. In north-east Scotland these can range from modest sites defined by low stone banks and/or ditches (perhaps defining areas for settlement) to huge hilltop enclosures defined by massive stone- and timber-laced ramparts. Traditionally these enclosures have been linked to increasing tensions in prehistoric society where warfare became endemic, but undoubtedly they had multiple roles in prehistoric life, and some of these hill-forts, such as Tap O'Noth near Rhynie (S), may have been large-scale communal settlements. Tap O'Noth includes roughly a hundred house platforms on the slopes between an Iron Age oval fort and an undated lower stone rampart found towards the base of the hill. It is uncertain if all of the house platforms at such sites were in contemporary use and whether this was a permanent settlement or one used for periodic gatherings – perhaps summer fairs or important religious ceremonies. Indeed, the religious or ceremonial role of forts has been emphasized in recent scholarship and, while some may have had roles to play in Iron Age warfare and as markers of the status of powerful groups, others may have had more spiritual roles to play in prehistoric life. Oval Iron Age forts such as Tap O'Noth and Dunnideer (S), for example, did not have defined entranceways through the ramparts and some simply contain features such as wells or ephemeral remains that give little away regarding function – these may have been as much symbolic or ritual enclosures as they were defensive. Highlighting the potential symbolic and ritual role of forts is not to deny that warfare and conflict occurred in this period: cattle-raiding and inter-family feuds may have been a common part of later prehistoric life and at times enclosures such as hill-forts may have played a role in inter-community conflict and violence. Whatever the case, whether defensive or ritual enclosures, those who orchestrated the construction of these sites undoubtedly drew on the labour of a large community or workforce and would have ultimately relied on developed networks of power and social status. Hill-forts may have been the ultimate expression of power in Iron Age landscapes, whether spiritually or militarily ordained. Iron Age forts in northern Aberdeenshire include the fort at Cullykhan, situated on a dramatic coastal promontory near Pennan, and the fort at Barra Hill overlooking Oldmeldrum. 7

The Romans

In 79 A.D. the ROMAN army, under the command of Agricola, the governor of Britain, entered Scotland. The expansion into northern Britain originally came at the behest of Emperor Vespasian, who had participated in the Roman invasion of Britain in 43 A.D. and who was keen to expand the empire northwards. In the first year of campaigning Agricola and his army got as far N as the River Tay. Tacitus records that the Iron Age tribes of south Scotland disintegrated into warring factions, with some pro-Roman, others not. Over the next four years the Roman army proceeded to consolidate their control over south Scotland with the construction of a series of forts, roads and outposts securing the area between the Forth and the Clyde and routes into the Highland glens. The Roman military presence stretched up to north-east Scotland with forts constructed towards the Mounth, with the most northerly fort at Stracathro in Angus. In the following years there were subsequent seasons of campaigning northwards, culminating in 83 A.D. in the Battle of Mons Graupius. Tacitus records 30,000 natives under the leadership of Calgacus the Swordsman succumbed to a disastrous defeat to the Romans at the battle with a third of the native force decimated. Shortly afterwards Agricola's tenure as governor ended and he was recalled to Rome. The Roman army also suffered defeats on the Continent, leading to a withdrawal from the north. By the later C1 the Tyne–Solway line in northern England was reconsolidated as the northern frontier of the province of Britain.

The Roman archaeology for north-east Scotland is limited to the presence of a number of MARCHING CAMPS that stretch from the Mounth into the north-east following the Don and up towards the Moray coast. The camps almost certainly date to Agricola's campaign of 83 A.D. They were temporary fortifications that marked the lines of advance of the Roman army and were generally spaced at distances of a day's march, being defined by a rapidly constructed rampart and ditch that marked out a secure area in which the army pitched its tents. Ancient military manuals suggest camp space was ordered in much the same way as forts, with roads or paths through the camp and a hierarchy of settlement and tent location. The camps were generally defined by a V-section ditch and a turf and earth internal bank. Each *contubernium*, or messing unit of eight soldiers, occupied a tent; there were also areas for draught animals, the baggage train and cooking. In Aberdeenshire the Roman camps have largely been destroyed by ploughing, with the exception of some upstanding remains at Raedykes camp at Fetteresso (S) that may have marked Agricola's first foray into the north-east. Many of the camps in the north-east were discovered by the archaeologist J. K. St Joseph through aerial photography. There are now known to be at least six large camps of probable C1 date and two smaller ones extending towards the Spey from Angus. At Logie Durno (S) in the shadow of Bennachie in central Aberdeenshire, St Joseph discovered the largest camp in the north. He argued that, at 57 hectares, this was the mustering point for Agricola's troops during the battle of Mons Graupius and archaeologists estimate that it may have held a force of up to 30,000 troops (a number much bigger than Tacitus records). Our understanding of Roman marching camps has been hampered by lack of excavation and because many were assumed to be largely empty, but at Kintore (S), just to the S of Logie Durno, a 45-hectare camp has been the subject of extensive excavation: over 180 field ovens and 60 rubbish pits have been revealed – features that would have been essential for keeping the Roman army fed and the camp maintained during the brief occupation of the north-east.

The effect of the Romans on the region is much debated: was the presence of the Roman army a brief inconsequential interlude or something more substantial and long-lasting? Direct Roman presence in the north-east was probably restricted to Agricola's campaign and possibly an equally brief interlude in the early C3, when Emperor Severus came to Scotland to quell the troublesome natives N of the border. This was the last major Roman campaign in Scotland N of the Forth.

Ptolemy's C2 map of Britain records the Taexali tribe occupying the area of north-east Scotland. Cassius Dio, the Roman historian, records that tribes in eastern Scotland did not abide by their promises to keep the peace and were accused of conspiring against Rome. He notes that, in the previous decades, governor Virius Lupus had been compelled to buy peace for a large sum from these tribes. Severus arrived in the north in 208 A.D. to conduct a punitive campaign. This appears to have focused on the tribes of the Calidones and the Maiatai, who lived a little to the S, but may also have proceeded northwards, perhaps as far as the Moray Firth. The Romans decimated the countryside, burning crops and houses, but the campaign was undermined by the death of Severus in 211. His son Caracalla subsequently agreed treaties with the natives. The Roman marching camp at Kintore may have been reoccupied during Severus' war against the natives, and Roman coin hoards at native settlements in Moray, such as at Birnie, near Elgin, are evidence of the ways in which the Romans 'bought' peace.

Native settlement changed little during the first centuries of the Roman Iron Age, but from the C3 onwards settlement becomes much harder to identify. Other traditions of architecture such as hill-fort construction also seems to cease by this period and may have ended prior to the Roman occupation.

The Picts

In the late C3 A.D. Roman writers started to record renewed attacks on Britain's northern frontier. They called the aggressors *Picti*, or 'painted people', and throughout the C4 Roman military campaigns were waged against the Picts as they caused repeated trouble N and S of Hadrian's Wall. After the Roman withdrawal, during the early medieval period from the C4 to the C9, the kingdoms of the Picts became among the most powerful social and political groups in northern Britain. Their territories encompassed the entirety of north-east Scotland and at their height the Pictish kingdoms stretched from the Firth of Forth in the S to Shetland in the N. They, along with the Scots, the Britons, the Anglo-Saxons and latterly the Vikings, rivalled one another for control over northern Britain. Our knowledge of the social and political landscape of the Picts is vague, but in the north-east, the area of Aberdeenshire appears to equate to the Pictish territory known as Cé, while Moray may have made up the heartland of the most powerful Pictish kingdom, called Fortriu.

The political changes that occurred in the early medieval period in Scotland were part of a wider trend in northern Europe during the second half of the first millennium A.D. towards more centralized authority and power over increasingly large territories. This period formed the foundations for the medieval nation-state of Scotland; yet it was also a time of constant flux in power structures and social and political alliances. Native historical documents for the Picts, like those of many of the early medieval kingdoms of northern Britain at this time, are scarce. These changes also occured when the archaeological record becomes more diffuse and difficult to interpret. Pictish settlements are notoriously difficult to identify – everyday houses may have been largely built from turf and non-earthfast timber structures. No certain Pictish farms or everyday domestic sites are known from the north-east.

A little more is known about higher-status Pictish sites, but our knowledge is still limited. Accompanying the rise of new forms of social and political authority was a renewed focus on the construction and use of HILL-FORTS. The scant historical record mentions the use of forts as seats of kingship and their role in conflict, but few have been excavated on any scale. In the north-east one of the most important Pictish sites appears to have been a fort constructed on top of Bennachie (S). The historian Margaret Dobbs suggested in 1949 that the place name may originally have been *Benne Cé*, the 'mountain of the people of Cé'. In the Pictish king-lists, Cé is recorded in an origin myth as one of the seven sons of Cruithne, the father of Pictland; as noted above, Cé appears to have equated to the area of modern Aberdeenshire. The fort on the summit of Mither Tap, Bennachie, has long been thought to resemble other early medieval complex hill-forts (known as nuclear hill-forts) in Scotland. It comprises two massive ramparts defining an upper and lower fort; traces of collapsed walling around the prominent granitic tor of Mither Tap suggests that there may have been a third dramatic enclosure on top of the tor itself. The lower rampart was at least 8 m. thick and shows traces of a parapet and wall-head walk. Recent dating of occupation deposits within the hill-fort has confirmed occupation between the C5 and the C8, supporting the long-standing view that Bennachie is likely to have been a high-status Pictish centre.

In Moray the most impressive Pictish site is the massive fort at Burghead, the largest Pictish fort known and probable royal site of Fortriu. Its complex defences included a triple rampart defining a distinctive promontory that juts into the Moray Firth. Within the fort there are upper and lower citadel enclosures. Excavations and radiocarbon-dating suggest that it was in use from the C4 to the C9. Within the fort lies an impressive rock-cut well. Other excavations have identified more modest defended enclosures dating to the Pictish period. In Moray this includes a small promontory fort at Portknockie. The Iron Age forts at
7 Cullykhan and Barra Hill in Aberdeenshire were also refortified in this period.

Undoubtedly one of the most remarkable Pictish discoveries in the north-east in recent years has been a high-status settlement at Rhynie (S). Rhynie was previously known for its collection of eight Pictish carved stones found in the village and around from the earlier C19 (see below). Excavations in 2011–12 around the only stone now *in situ*, the Craw Stane, have shown that this stone was originally part of a very high-status settlement and fort, defined by both earthen ramparts and ditches and timber outworks. Centuries of agriculture mean that now only the Craw Stane is visible above ground, but aerial photography revealed the presence of significant buried remains here. The settlement would have been enclosed by a monumental timber rampart and wall-walk perhaps 4 or 5 m. high; inside, traces of timber buildings built of squared oak beams have been located. The settlement was a centre for the production of metalwork and finds have included bronze and iron pins and, more remarkably, wine amphorae imported from the Mediterranean and glass drinking beakers from France. The finds are of the type found on early royal sites in western Britain and Ireland, but are the first of their type to be excavated in Pictland. Rhynie contains the placename element *rīg*, early Celtic for 'King', and suggests that Rhynie may have been one of the early royal centres of the Picts in north-east Scotland.

The most iconic monument associated with the Picts are carved stones, generally known as PICTISH STONES. Symbol stones have been traditionally classified into types: Class I with animal and abstract symbols on generally unworked stones, as found at Rhynie; Class II with Christian iconography, which can be carved on much more finely worked and shaped stones; Class III, relief crosses without symbols and Class IV, stones with incised crosses. The usefulness of such a scheme is now questioned by some but provides a basic framework for the study of these monuments. The difference between Class I and the other forms of stones may be partly chronological, with the symbol-bearing slabs earlier (perhaps emerging in the c5 or c6) and the more elaborate cross-slabs and relief crosses later. Simple incised crosses may have a wider chronological range. It has been argued that Pictish stones may have emerged as a commemorative tradition associated with the dead. This commemorative role has been supported by a supposed association between symbol stones and burials; however a direct association between burial monument and symbol stone has rarely been unequivocally demonstrated. Sculptured stones obviously had other roles to play: six stones incised with bulls survive from Burghead from a much larger group found in the c19, and may have been displayed within the fort or on the ramparts. Similarly at Rhynie, the Craw Stane stood at the entrance of an elaborate fortified settlement. The symbols on Pictish stones also occasionally appear on metalwork and other more portable material culture, as well as on the walls of caves – clearly the symbols played diverse roles. Around thirty different symbols were in common usage and included abstract symbols such as crescents, double discs (many with V or Z-rods, a design resembling a broken arrow or spear) and objects such as mirrors and combs, as well as animal symbols depicting real and mythical beasts. North-east Scotland has a distinct concentration of the earlier stones that do not display Christian iconography.

In the c7 or c8 Pictish stones became more elaborate and monumental and the symbols appear alongside the Christian cross, marking the increasing influence of CHRISTIANITY. Some of the later sculpture gives further clues to what the symbols represent. The stones can include occasional depictions of individuals apparently 'labelled' with symbols and this strongly suggests that the symbols on these stones conveyed names or identities of some kind. The more elaborate monuments represent incredible investments in skill and resources and the hunting and other elite activities depicted on some stones suggest that these monuments were strongly implicated in the emergence of new forms of rulership that characterized the rise of the early Pictish kingdoms in a post-Roman context. Northern Aberdeenshire has an impressive array of Pictish carved stone monuments. The most imposing symbol stones include those at Inveravon and Fyvie, in both cases at church sites. Pictish symbols have also been found in Moray carved in the sandstone walls of the Sculptor's Cave, Covesea (Duffus), where remains of Iron Age and Roman Iron Age human sacrifices have been found, along with extensive deposits of metalwork, coins and jewellery. Impressive Class II stones include those at Brodie and Elgin Cathedral. The Brodie example, called Rodney's Stone, stands in the grounds of Brodie Castle; the back of the slab is decorated with an interlaced Pictish beast and double disc and Z-rod. A long ogham inscription (an early form of script) is the longest in Pictland and occupies the sides and back of the stone, but sadly, like most of the Pictish oghams, its meaning is unclear. On the front of the stone there is a majestic interlaced cross with pairs of interlaced beasts on each side. The Elgin cross-slab also shows the Four Evangelists and interlaced beasts to the sides and on the back a hunting scene, crescent and V-rod, and double disc and Z-rod.

Other than carved stone crosses we know very little about the Pictish church; there are no identified church buildings from this period. Sculpture from Burghead in Moray includes fragments of a cross-slab and shrine which suggest that an important Christian chapel was present in or near the Pictish fort here in the C8–C9. Other sites such as Tullich and Dyce (both S) that have impressive collections of carved stones may have been important early church sites or monasteries. Kinneddar

Forres, Sueno's Stone.
Engraving

(Lossiemouth), which has an important collection of sculpture was the site of the bishopric in Moray in the C12, while Mortlach (Dufftown), where an unusual cross-slab and Pictish stone can be seen, may also have been an episcopal see of the north-east before it was transferred to Aberdeen in the same century. The number and range of sculptures from Kinneddar is particularly impressive. Now in Elgin Museum, the collection is fragmentary but includes numerous examples of relief sculpture probably dating from the C7–C8. With one or two exceptions the stones are mainly fragments of interlaced cross-slabs without symbols, but there is at least one slab decorated with a crescent and V-rod. There are also slabs from shrines or sarcophagi, including a fragment showing Daniel rending the jaws of a lion – a very close match for the magnificent St Andrews sarcophagus in Fife, a more complete example of a royal shrine or burial monument. The Kinneddar sculpture includes unfinished pieces showing that sculpture was produced on site, underlining its importance as an uninvestigated location of an early church that almost certainly attracted royal patronage.

By the C9 or C10 the Picts were absorbed in the expanding Gaelic kingdom of Alba. Increasing Viking impact on northern Scotland from the C9 onwards appears to have weakened the powerful northern Pictish kingdoms, leading to the amalgamation of the Picts and the Scots. The forts that characterized the earlier Pictish kingdoms ceased to be constructed by the C9 and some, such as Burghead, may have been destroyed by Viking attacks. The carving of stone sculpture largely ceased, but some of the carved stone monuments, such as the remarkable Sueno's Stone at Forres in Moray, may continue into the C10. In many ways the period from the C10 to the C13 is more of a 'dark age' than the Pictish period: settlement and material culture from this period are even more difficult to identify and are poorly represented in north-east Scotland. Yet this period was when the medieval kingdom of Scotland truly took shape. Aberdeenshire appears to have been part of Alba, but Moray continued to have important, and at times competing, roles to play in the rulership of early Scotland. The slaying of Mac Bethad mac Findláich (Macbeth) at Lumphanan and his son Lulach at Essie (S) by Malcolm III and his followers, however, allowed the kingship of Alba to expand. The defeat of Macbeth and his son, whose power base lay in the north, marked the consolidation of royal power in central Scotland to the south.

ABERDEENSHIRE: NORTH

BY DAVID W. WALKER

The rest of this introduction relates to the area covered by the *Aberdeenshire: North* gazetteer. For the introduction to the buildings of Moray see p. 425.

CHURCHES

A see was founded at Mortlach (see Dufftown, Moray, p. 541) but the episcopal seat was transferred to Aberdeen *c.* 1131. In sharp contrast to Moray, surprisingly few MEDIEVAL CHURCHES survive in north Aberdeenshire, although they were certainly more numerous than the remains imply: Old Fordyce (existing by 1272) and Old St Mary, Banff (rebuilt 1471) have been substantially demolished, while Deer Old Parish Church (pre-1219),
18, 16 Deer Abbey (*c.* 1219), and St Mary, Rattray (earlier C13) have survived so far as they have done only through C18–C19 consolidation. Foveran contains a grave-slab of *c.* 1400, and two medieval effigies are now sheltered in Bourtie Parish Church. There are only two important medieval monuments, an ogee-arched
23 canopied tomb to James Ogilvy of Deskford of *c.* 1510 and another slightly earlier to an Ogilvy of Findlater, both at Fordyce.

The earliest POST-REFORMATION CHURCHES were mostly adapted from medieval predecessors or stood on their sites. Only three are known to have been built anew, all for new parishes: Longside (1619–20), Strichen (*c.* 1620) and Pitsligo (Peathill, *c.* 1632–4). Layout generally followed medieval precedent in being a long narrow rectangle, orientated E–W but with the pulpit centred in one long flank – preferably S – and lofts at both gables often accommodating the local landowners' families. Wealthier landowners usually had their own transept-like 'aisle' opposite the pulpit, sometimes adapting a medieval transeptal chapel but more often new-built to provide a retiring room behind the family pew and sometimes the family burial vault beneath: this bestows on many Scottish churches their familiar T-plan, as seen in the shell of Pitsligo (Peathill). Because they were maintained as burial vaults the aisles have often fared better than the churches. The oldest is probably Aberdour's (C16, reconstructed 1764) followed by the Ogilvie Aisle at Old St Mary, Banff (1580) with its three-light mullioned and transomed window. Other survivors vary in interest, but the Errol Aisle at Slains dates from 1599, and Rathen from 1633, its length rivalling Aberdour's. The aisle at Strichen (*c.* 1620), where the church is altogether lost, is two-storey with a curved external forestair to the loft, as is more common in southern Scotland. The resited Forbes Pew at the former Pitsligo New Church (Peathill) of 1634, a magnificent piece of Renaissance woodcarving – perhaps the finest in Scotland – is a rare survivor of the furnishings associated with such aisles.

Only Fordyce and Old St Peter's, Peterhead have towers; while these have a mid C17–early C18 character, both are probably of medieval origin. Bellcotes are frequently the best feature of post-Reformation churches, perhaps acknowledging the cost of the bell, which was sometimes imported from England or the Netherlands. Most common is the birdcage bellcote: good dateable examples are King Edward (1619), Longside (1620), Inverkeithny (1638), St Fergus (1644), Alvah (1645) and Fordyce (1661), St Fergus being re-erected on the successor church. But
the best are St Congan, Turriff (1635), with double pendant 22
arches and ogee top, and Pitsligo (Peathill 1635), of Dutch 27
Renaissance character with clustered columns and pilasters, the two finest surviving examples anywhere in Scotland.

The long period of religious tension and turbulence beginning with the Civil Wars in 1638 and concluding with the Jacobite Rebellion of 1745 resulted in very few if any churches being built in Banff, Buchan and Formartine throughout that time, and none has survived intact. Indeed, of GEORGIAN CHURCHES the earliest extant is that at Pettens (1762), a T-plan of which only the W gable remains. But then *c.* 1770–1820 comes a series of preaching-boxes, their building coinciding with the Agricultural Revolution with its rationalization of land-holding patterns, establishment of new weaving and fishing settlements, and the wars with America and France with their underlying political ideologies which threatened the Establishment order. In general, these are simple rectangles with a birdcage bellcote on the W gable, a doorway and gallery light in each end, and tall windows across the S flank with the N flank blind; inside, as in earlier churches, the pulpit was centred on the S wall with a gallery extending round three sides. Remarkably, six out of the twelve such churches built in northern Aberdeenshire between 1775 and 1800 stand within Ellon Presbytery (Ellon, Cruden, Methlick, Logie-Buchan, Foveran and Tarves) where evidence of agricultural unrest is made clear by an inscription on the farmhouse of Nether Ardgrain: 'How happy would the husbandman be if he knew his own good. Let Improvements and Liberty flow.' The smartest of this group are Cruden (1776) executed in finely squared masonry, the 15th Earl of Erroll apparently willing to spend more on his rural tenants than the six heritors of Ellon combined, and Tarves (1798), which is an equivalent expression of the 3rd Earl of Aberdeen's largesse. Outwith Ellon Presbytery, the T-plan Lonmay (1787) is the only mid-Georgian church surviving intact; its interior is very elegant, with two tiers of Doric columns and arcades at its E and W galleries, as well as its original pulpit.

Although simple, Ellon church by *William Littlejohn*, built in 1777, is the first of the 'Muckle Kirks' – the big burgh churches – notable for their enormous roof-spans which required timber rafters of exceptional length and section that sometimes threatened to push out the walls. At Ellon the roof-span was 12.25 m.;
34 at St Mary Banff, designed by *Andrew Wilson* in 1780 and built in 1789–90, the span was a remarkable 15.25 m. Banff, along with nearby Macduff (1805, afterwards rebuilt, *see* below), was also the first church in northern Aberdeenshire to be designed with a tower and spire, but the Episcopalian heritors' lack of enthusiasm ensured that it remained uncompleted until 1849. Fraserburgh Old Church by *James Littlejohn* of Aberdeen (1802–3) is a plain hip-roofed rectangle with the entrance tower in ashlar projecting only slightly from the harled gable front before rising into an octagonal belfry and stone spire. Peterhead, Fraserburgh's ancient rival, was clearly making a point with St Peter's parish church by *Alexander Laing* of Edinburgh, 1804–6. It is a far more sophisticated composition, built wholly in ashlar with a broad pedimented porch supporting its tall and elegant tower, the octagonal belfry and spire serving to make the comparison explicit.*

In the rural parishes, Ordiquhill (1805) is unusual in having its belfry raised over a gable in the centre of its long flank. It also has tall round-arched windows with stone Y-tracery, an indicator of the return of Gothic styles in the early C19. Bourtie (1807) is more truly Gothick and is the only Late Georgian church to have been unaffected by Victorian and early C20 reordering. Fyvie (1806–8), although a much larger church, adopts the same idiom, its W gable with twin doorways in a slightly projected centre, indicating the nave-and-aisles layout within: it cannot be coincidence that the principal heritor was Gen. William Gordon, who had reconstructed Fyvie Castle. Inside, however, it is still classical, with segmentally arched arcades on Doric columns at gallery level. *Robert Mitchell* was responsible for the first fully Gothic interior in north Aberdeenshire at St Peter (Episcopal), Peterhead, of 1813–14. Gothic in its Tudor form is first encountered at Aberdour in 1818, perhaps by *William Robertson* of Elgin. After that a more up-to-date Neo-Perpendicular idiom came into vogue with the churches of *John Smith I*, who had gained London experience before returning to Aberdeen in 1804. Smith was the architect of Udny (1821) planned on the English model, with an entrance tower (subsequently heightened) fronting the liturgical W gable of a longitudinally planned four-bay rectangle with its pulpit at the E end. Its tracery is in timber rather than in stone. Smith's church at New Deer (1839–41; its tower added more or less to his designs in 1864–5) is similar, but on a much larger scale with more scholarly tracery, again still in timber with small-paned glazing.

Archibald Simpson, also London-trained, built St Andrew (Episcopal), Banff in 1833–4. Its style is late Decorated, like a college chapel. Portsoy Episcopal by Simpson's former assistant *James Ross* (1840–1) is a perfectly miniaturized Gothic cruciform,

*Laing was also responsible for the Muckle Kirk at Huntly (S), his design of 1804 superseding an earlier scheme by George Burn of 1802.

standing very tall for its small size, the projected centre of its gable front rising into a slim, elongated belfry and stone spirelet to form a token tower. Peterhead East (later Free, now Trinity Parish Church) of 1842 is the last Tudor Gothic church, very severe externally, although adopting a nave-and-aisles frontage which expresses its galleried interior with tall arcades of four-centred arches on cast-iron columns. Of particular historic significance is the architect-bishop *James Kyle*'s Roman Catholic church for Portsoy built in 1829, the year of emancipation. It is a charming Gothick design, its gable front divided into 'nave' and 'aisles' by plain pilaster-buttresses rising into pinnacles above battlemented skews, a pointed-arch doorway and windows with basket-weave tracery. The addition of a presbytery shortly afterwards creates Kyle's trademark L-plan layout; it occurs right up to the end of his long church-building career at St Mary, Peterhead, 1850–1. (See Moray, p. 433 for other examples.)

In the DISRUPTION of 1843 about one-third of the Church of Scotland's ministers and one-third of parishioners walked out over the right of congregations, rather than heritors, to choose their ministers. Generally it was the energetic and evangelical (including some of the heritors themselves) who left, their departure resulting in the hasty erection of many simple 'Free' churches in 1843–4. Most in northern Aberdeenshire were by *James Henderson* of Aberdeen and a few survive, including Rosehearty and Potterton, both of which were originally plain rectangles, their towers added decades later. Henderson's Methlick (1847) was a little more ambitious, a simple tall gable front with applied buttresses and bellcote doing their best to suggest a tower. James's elder brother *William Henderson* and William's son *William Low Henderson* were also Free church builders, responsible for Ellon's of 1855–6. Easily the most distinguished of the immediate post-Disruption churches, however, is Banff, by *James & Robert Raeburn* of Edinburgh, built in 1843–4 with an impressive Ionic temple front.

If the Church of Scotland felt bereft after the Disruption, the Episcopalians responded with vigour, building several churches of notable quality. Cruden (1842–3), very tall and austere Early English, has a six-bay nave with slender tower and spire. It was the first ecclesiastical commission of the Peterhead-born *William Hay*, who returned to enlarge it over thirty years later. In 1847
Hay built St John, Longside, cruciform with a tall saddleback- 40
roofed tower over its crossing: it is very accomplished, reflecting his experience with George Gilbert Scott building St John's Cathedral in Newfoundland. *John Henderson* (not to be confused with the Free Church Hendersons) was the leading Scottish exponent of the Oxford Movement. He built the small and very simple church in the approved Early English (or First Pointed) style at Cuminestown (1844) and the delightful and very Tractarian Woodhead (1848–9), which gained its skilfully matched tower and spire courtesy of *James Matthews* in 1870. Pitfour (1850–1), very simple Gothic with a bold battlemented tower, was built as an English Episcopal Continuing church after Admiral Ferguson fell out with the incumbent at Old Deer. Ferguson's rival, James Russell of Aden, granted a site for a new

Episcopal church in Old Deer which was built to designs by *Matthews* in 1850–1. It is very similar in character to his partner *Thomas Mackenzie*'s Early English-style church at Huntly (S) but substitutes a bellcote for its spirelet. Turriff (1862–3) is the work of Simpson's successor, *William Ramage*, as is the smaller and simpler Strichen (1861), much altered by *Arthur Clyne* in 1891. Both of these were Tractarian in planning like the Hay and Henderson churches, but idiosyncratic and imaginative in their details.

When the Church of Scotland presbyteries began to build again after the Disruption, they too adopted C13 Gothic styles: *A. & W. Reid* of Elgin were responsible for King Edward (1848) with a square belfry spirelet and the very similar New Byth (1851–2) where the belfry is reduced to a bellcote, but their most accomplished design is Inverkeithny, built in 1880–2. *Brown & Wardrop*'s Methlick Parish Church of 1865–7, T-plan with a saddleback-roofed tower set into the angle, was built for the 6th Earl of Aberdeen and is comparable in quality with the best Episcopal churches of that time. The original fittings survive, although rearranged.

The Episcopalians stepped up their response with two new churches by *George Edmund Street*, who became the diocese's preferred architect after Henderson and Ramage had died.*
42 These are the powerfully composed St Mary on the Rock, Ellon, and St John, New Pitsligo, both built in 1870–1 and both eloquent of the greater landowners' predominantly Episcopalian sympathies; Street also built the private chapel for the 7th Earl of Aberdeen at Haddo House in 1876–81. Ellon – its W gable with a buttressed narthex and five-light window beneath a steeply pitched roof, four-bay nave with a square pencil tower set well back on one side, and chancel with a semicircular apse – is Early Middle Pointed in style; New Pitsligo – its W gable with a four-light window and neat side aisles, slim square bell-tower, short transepts and again a semicircular apse – was Early English, the interiors, as usual with Episcopalian churches, being exceptionally fine. St Mary's reredos was carved by *Thomas Earp*; at St John the *Davidsons* were the carvers. In 1875 *William Hay* returned to St John, Longside, to design the magnificent Caen stone reredos, richly embellished with marbles, and from 1896 at St Drostan, Old Deer, *J. Ninian Comper* provided fine furnishings along with his extension to the church. The furnishings designed by *John Kinross* for St Peter, Fraserburgh, are relatively restrained but scholarly and of fine quality, made by *Scott Morton & Co.* Of considerable splendour is the carved pulpit at St Congan, Turriff (1893), but the designer and carver are still to be traced, while at St Luke, Cuminestown there is a rather good Early Italian triptych by *Rachel (Edith) Ainslie Grant-Duff* (*c.* 1900).

Throughout the C19 Roman Catholic church-building in Buchan and Formartine was much less well funded, there being relatively few Catholic landed families there, but there was a stronger following in Banffshire, as seen at Our Lady of Mount Carmel in Banff by *Ellis & Wilson* (1870). Its elaborate Gothic

*Street had initially been brought to Aberdeenshire to enlarge Dunecht House (S) for the scholarly Alexander Lord Lindsay, son of the Earl of Crawford & Balcarres.

reredos is Flemish (1914); the Gothic fittings at Our Lady and St Drostan, Fraserburgh, are by *Beyaert* of Bruges (1895–6).

The Church of Scotland's building programme gathered pace from the later 1860s onwards, at least partly because of the ever-growing ambitions of the Free Church. Financial responsibility for parish churches still lay with the heritors, but after the Education Act of 1872 they had only the church and manse to pay for. The Smiths – now represented by the London-trained *William Smith* and his son *John Smith II* – were still the Aberdeenshire presbyteries' preferred architects but the style of their practice had become Early English or Decorated Gothic with occasional polychromy, e.g. Rathen (1867), Belhelvie (1876–8) and Auchterless (1877–9, its tower and spire completed by *Arthur H. L. Mackinnon* in 1894–9 but transepts there from the start). These churches were remarkably ambitious for the country parishes they served, even allowing for a rural population much bigger then than now; the Smiths' Gothic fittings at Belhelvie and Auchterless are relatively undisturbed. In the burghs, *James Souttar* adopted an idiosyncratic Gothic at Peterhead East Free (now St Andrew) in 1868–70, its broad gable front with large triple windows distinguished by proto-Art Nouveau tracery and Souttar's characteristic motif of parabolic voussoirs, the entrance porches on either side broaching into octagonal buttress-towers with spirelets. Equally idiosyncratic is *James Matthews*' complete remodelling of Macduff Parish Church (1865–7) with a Franco-Italianate tower (and, curiously, parabolic voussoirs like Souttar's) while his Monquhitter Parish Church (Cuminestown, 1866–8) presents a tall entrance gable expressed as nave and aisles with crowning bellcote and Quattrocento Renaissance details. Both have impressive furnishings, still largely intact.

In the fishing towns the Herring Boom encouraged the building of several Free Churches in the late 1870s and early 1880s. Peterhead and Fraserburgh again went head to head: Peterhead Free by *William Hay* (1878–9) is Geometric Gothic, a large simple gable front now diminished by reduction of its corner spire to a turret stump, but this time Fraserburgh came out on top with its magnificent Gothic gable front and soaring tower and spire by a young *John Bridgeford Pirie* in 1878–80 (now Fraserburgh South). This church – Pirie's first in independent 44
practice – lays fair claim to be the finest Presbyterian church throughout all northern Aberdeenshire, although unfortunately the ground-floor pews have been removed; Pirie's very original pulpit survives however, along with the gallery pews with their distinctive bench-ends. In rural areas, some early Free Churches were replaced or improved, e.g. Pitmedden (1865) by *William Knox*. An indication of the remarkable growth in power of Free Church congregations in just twenty years is the choice of *Campbell Douglas & Stevenson* of Glasgow to rebuild Clola (1863–4) with its square tower and pyramidal spire, and *John Russell Mackenzie* to rebuild Portsoy (1869–70) with its broach spire and big wheel window. Thereafter the Free Church's preferred architects were *D. & J.R. McMillan*, who succeeded to Mackenzie's practice after he emigrated to Johannesburg. Their work includes

Strichen (1893–4, now the parish church) of characteristically late Victorian robustness, the still more ambitious tall and spired Turriff (1898–1900, now St Andrew) and the smaller but more scholarly Cornhill (a remodelling of 1903–5).

During the late C19 and early C20 worship in the Church of Scotland and the Free Church changed radically as a result of the formation of the Church Service Society (1865) and the Aberdeen Ecclesiological Society (1886). The former resulted in the introduction of organs – 'kists o'fussils' (i.e. whistles) – and the Late Georgian Muckle Kirks had to be replanned or extended by an apse in order to accommodate them. The Aberdeen Ecclesiological Society was primarily interested in scholarship and in liturgical arrangements that were at least partly concerned with competing with Episcopalian forms of worship. Nearly all the older churches were radically reordered, sometimes producing impressive furnishings, notably by *John Robertson* of Inverness at Newburgh (1906–9) and by *Alexander Marshall Mackenzie*, a prominent member of the Ecclesiological Society, at Fyvie (1901–2, with Laird's Pew modelled on that at Pitsligo), Fraserburgh (1898–9) and Turriff (1913–14). Fyvie, Pitsligo (1889–90) and the Gardner Memorial Church, Macduff (1897–9), all have tracery modelled on Aberdeen's Greyfriars Church, which the Society was then campaigning to preserve. The last major project in this programme was *Waddell & Young*'s reconstruction of St Mary, Banff in 1927–8, in which the C18 and C19 interior was reordered to face a new chancel and apse; the classical furnishings here are of considerable opulence. *George Bennett Mitchell*'s Rothienorman Parish Church, late Arts and Crafts of 1935–6, is the only significant new church of the C20 in north Aberdeenshire. For the period since the Second World War a few furnishings may be noted: Daviot Parish Church has a 'Festival of Britain' pulpit and font and St Peter, Peterhead, has an oak pulpit of 1966–7 by *John Herdman Reid*. Since the Millennium there have been two more churches: Fraserburgh United Reformed by *Jeffrey Smith* (of *Davidson & Smith*, 2003) and Rehoboth Free Presbyterian near Gardenstown by the *Rev. Noël Hughes* (2004), both of which reinterpret earlier models of church design in a contemporary idiom, with a continuing emphasis on fine craftsmanship in their interiors.

Many churches contain good STAINED GLASS but too often the artists and glass-stainers have still to be identified. The Episcopalians led the way with glass from English firms for their new churches, beginning in 1853 at St John, Longside with windows by *Chance* of Birmingham, and the E window of St Drostan, Old Deer by *John Hardman*, who also provided glass for St Matthew & St George, Oldmeldrum in 1863. At Street's St Mary on the Rock, Ellon the earliest glass is by *Lavers & Barraud*, 1871, followed by *Clayton & Bell*, who also provided glass at St John, New Pitsligo and St George, Folla Rule. Other leading English glass-makers whose work is represented are *William Wailes* of Newcastle at St Congan, Turriff, 1867, *Heaton, Butler & Bayne* at St Peter, Fraserburgh, 1884, and *Ward &*

Hughes at St John, Longside. Presbyterian congregations were
generally much slower off the mark but by the later C19 could
take advantage of the revival in Scottish stained glass, e.g. by
James Ballantine & Son of Edinburgh, who installed two windows
at St Mary, Banff, during its reconstruction in 1877. Much the
most famous window in northern Aberdeenshire is the E
window of Fyvie Parish Church by *Louis Comfort Tiffany* (1901–2), 52
a rare example of that maker's work in Britain; it was quickly
followed by important *Douglas Strachan* glass at Fraserburgh Old 49
(1906) and St Fergus (*c.* 1898). Less well known are *George Donald
& Sons* who provided good glass at St Andrew, Peterhead (1908);
the *City Glass Window Co.* of Glasgow at Macduff Parish Church
(1922); and *Walter Pearce* of Manchester at Fordyce Parish
(former Free) Church, Portsoy (1938). Of the leading Scottish
stained-glass artists of the mid C20 *John Aiken* is represented at
St John, Longside, 1951; *Marjorie Kemp* at Tarves Parish Church,
1954; *Gordon Webster* at Meldrum Parish Church, 1957; *Brother
Gilbert Taylor* of Pluscarden Abbey at St Peter, Peterhead, in the
1960s; *Sadie McLellan* at Daviot Parish Church, 1973; and *Brother
Martin Farrelly* (again of Pluscarden Abbey) at Methlick Parish
Church, 1982. The glass at Maud Parish Church, 1977, was also
produced at Pluscarden. In recent times *Jennifer-Jayne Bayliss* has
undertaken a number of commissions, including windows at
St Mary on the Rock, Ellon in 1996, Macduff Parish Church in
2000, and the United Reformed church, Fraserburgh, *c.* 2003.

Because of the abandonment of medieval, C17 and earlier C18
churches in the late C18 and C19, most of the earlier MONUMENTS
are either now in churchyards or within surviving aisles
or burial enclosures, retained as free-standing structures by the
greater landowners after new parish churches had been built. Of
special note is the monument in the Tolquhon aisle at Tarves for 25
William Forbes, erected in 1589, with Renaissance decoration
and an elaborately cusped arch over its tomb-chest, attributed to
Thomas Leiper; King Edward churchyard has a fine round-arched
wall recess which once contained an effigy of Beatrice Innes
(†1590). The canopied tomb of the Bairds of Auchmedden in
the surviving aisle of Old St Mary, Banff, is dated 1636 but distinctly
conservative with an effigy under an ogee arch. There are
many later C18 or earlier C19 monuments, the most notable of
which are the splendid Ionic aedicule to Gen. James Abercromby
(†1781) in the Abercromby aisle at Fordyce and the Udny portrait
memorial within Foveran Parish Church, the latter by *John
Bacon* (1794). Among late C19 monuments, that of the Chalmers
family at Fyvie by *J. Pittendrigh MacGillivray* (1898) and two
commemorating Capt. Beauchamp Colclough Urquhart (†1898)
at St Matthew's & St George's Episcopal Church, Oldmeldrum
and New Byth Parish Church are particularly memorable.
Virtually all churchyards have good C17–C18 GRAVE-SLABS,
TABLE TOMBS AND MONUMENTS, those of the Annands at
Ellon, the Gordons of Gight at Fyvie, the Crudens at Lonmay
and the Cumines at Monquhitter having classical detail. Bishop
Meldrum's monument at Marnoch, a great Baroque aedicule 31

framing a portrait-bust recessed within a cartouche, challenges comparison with anything in central or southern Scotland. Purpose-built MAUSOLEA are rare, the only important examples within a churchyard being the Saltoun Mausoleum (1803) at Fraserburgh and *A. & W. Reid*'s Grant-Duff mausoleum formed within the ruins of the old church, King Edward, when it was abandoned in 1850. The most important of the later sepulchral monuments is the Forbes-Leith enclosure at Fyvie by *A. Marshall Mackenzie* (1901–2).

Five churchyards retain early GATEWAYS. Those of the old churchyard within Fraserburgh Cemetery (C16–C17), Old St Peter, King Edward (1621), and St Fergus (1751) are all very simple with moulded round-arched openings, St Peter having a superimposed carved gablet. St Congan, Turriff, has a very handsome C17 pilastered archway, while Longside has a barrel-vaulted lychgate, perhaps built with the Old Parish Church in 1619–20 although dated 1705. A few churchyards have MORT HOUSES, Udny's (1832) being circular.

CASTLES AND TOWER HOUSES

Of the early castles in northern Aberdeenshire little remains visible. Excavation of the promontory castle at Dundarg has shown that it was occupied by the C2–C3, but the fragmentary surviving masonry looks mostly C16. The promontory sites at Findlater and Boddam were probably also occupied from fairly early on: at Findlater the lower storeys of a C16 palace-block remain clinging to the cliffside and at Boddam a C16 tower house and its subsidiary buildings survived into the 1780s, their general appearance recorded in an engraving by Charles Cordiner. Cairnbulg Castle stands on a motte raised by the Celtic mormaers or the Comyn Earls of Buchan to defend against Viking raids, the mound on which Kinnairdy stands may also have been a former motte, and there are two other prominent examples near Auchterless and Inverugie. King Edward Castle existed by the C13 but the present remains are of the castle licensed in 1509.

As first built these early castles must mainly have been of timber. Those with the earliest surviving masonry are the royal castles at Banff and Fyvie. Banff is believed to have existed by the reign of David I (1124–53), a square-plan castle of enclosure surrounded by a ditch at the edge of a raised beach: the surviving N and E walls apparently date from Alexander III's strengthening of its defences *c.* 1250–75, but the details of the blocked sally-port
66 look C16. Fyvie was built as the Thanage of Formartine's *capital messuage*: it existed by 1214 and was at least partly masonry from the beginning. Rather less than half this castle survives within the present structure's S and W elevations. It was near-square on plan at 38 m. by 40 m. with angle towers 7 m. square and a gatehouse centred on its S side enlarged by drum towers *c.* 1290. Of similar date may have been the polygonal castle of enclosure built by the Cheynes at Esslemont, where the angle towers were circular.

By the mid C14 the characteristic Scottish tower house had emerged as a building type. Old Slains built by the Hays after 1308 was apparently four storeys and 35 m. high; the lower two storeys at least were vaulted, as can be seen from the three surviving storeys of the SE corner, all that was left standing after James VI blew it up in 1594. Cairnbulg's great tower was begun *c.* 1375 and as first built was a plain rectangle 12.5 m. by 9 m., but it was reconstructed in four-storey form with a caphouse within its corbelled parapet during the C15. Embedded within the great C16 and C17 courtyard castle of Pitsligo is the tower house built by Sir William Forbes shortly after 1424, again a rectangle, but rather larger in footprint at 16 m. by 11 m. with simple barrel-vaults over its lower two floors; the upper floors have gone.

All these simple rectangular towers had a single large room on each floor, that at first floor being the great hall, and small chambers within walls 2–3 m. thick augmenting the living accommodation. But in the very late C14 or earliest C15 the Gordons built the 'Auld Wark' at Huntly (S), a giant L-plan tower house with a main block 17 m. by 10 m. and a square-plan jamb 8.5 m. wide, the latter providing a private apartment or solar at first floor. James VI blew it up in 1594 and what remained was demolished in 1731 so little is known of its plan, but the stump of a tower house of similar date and block plan survives within the *enceinte* at Esslemont, rather smaller at 13 m. by 11 m. with a jamb 8 m. wide; it probably provided similar accommodation, as its walls were 2 m. thick rather than 3 m. as at Huntly.* As in central and southern Scottish tower houses of this type, the entrance was in the main block at the re-entrant angle with a 2 m. wide turnpike stair close by in the external angle. The ground floor of the main block was however vaulted in two compartments rather than one as was more usual in central and southern Scottish houses, and the kitchen was in the jamb, providing warmth for the solar above. By far the largest L-plan tower house in Aberdeenshire was Ravenscraig (Inverugie), licensed in 1491 but perhaps built in two phases and completed in the 1530s. It has a three-storey-and-attic main block and a four-storey jamb, its long walls 22 m. and 25 m. in extent. If it is of one build, its sheer size and unusual internal arrangements would imply a master-mason from outwith north-east Scotland, probably associated with the royal court.

More akin to the planning of Esslemont is an important group of closely related L-plan tower houses built in Aberdeenshire during the Reformation period, first identified by Dr Douglas Simpson in 1929.[‡] The defining features of these tower houses were a ground-floor corridor from the entrance to a generous turnpike in the centre of the long back wall, a jamb more often than not 8.5 m. wide containing the kitchen with solar above, and rib-vaults wherever the clients could be persuaded to pay for them. They are probably the work of the *Conns* of Auchry, a staunchly Roman Catholic landowning family of masons with a

*This was the predecessor of the late C16 tower house clearly visible from the road (for which *see* below).

[‡]See W. Douglas Simpson, 'Craig Castle and the Kirk of Auchindoir', *Proceedings of the Society of Antiquaries of Scotland* 64, 1929–30.

predominantly Catholic clientele. Of these Craig Castle (S) is the plainest but perhaps also the oldest, dated 1548 with a thinner-walled jamb only 7.25 m. wide. The entrance is in the main block and only the vestibule is rib-vaulted; it is the only tower house in this group to survive complete, albeit refitted internally in the late C17. Colquhonnie (S) may be about the same date, as a charter records the transfer of the estate in 1546. Fedderate of 1557 is next in seniority and, for what were doubtless good reasons relating to its vanished forecourt, the doorway was not in the re-entrant angle but adjacent to the stair under the solar window; only the much earlier Auchindoun (*see* Moray) had a similar though not identical arrangement. As at Craig the parapets were plain but Fedderate may have introduced the concept of a set-off in the walls above the hall vault. Gight, perhaps built *c.* 1564, was the largest of the group, with a main block 16 m. by 11 m. and a jamb 8.5 m. square, but only the ground floor and part of the first floor survive; only the vestibule seems to have been rib-vaulted. Knockhall (Newburgh), dated 1565, would appear to be of the same family. Its smaller scale required the entrance to be in the jamb as at Colquhonnie and its stair extruded into a square projection: it has no rib-vaults and the upper floors were reconstructed in the later C17. Delgatie, built *c.* 1570–9 with an unusually long jamb has rib-vaults at the vestibule, the solar and what was probably an oratory; it may well have had another rib-vault over its hall. At Towie Barclay (date uncertain) the hall retains its two-bay rib-vault, reminiscent of that at Auchindoun (Moray) a century earlier.

62 At Delgatie the jamb has survived largely unaltered to show what these later C16 L-plan tower houses looked like when complete. The upper floors were slightly intaken as at Fedderate and the wall-head had a corbelled ashlar parapet with angle rounds, a feature absent at Craig where the parapet is plain. These features suggest that two equally conservative rectangular tower houses may belong to the same group. Udny, 13 m. by 10.5 m., has the same rounded angles and intaken upper floor as Fedderate and was built for the same family as Knockhall, although its present upperworks are early C17. The position of its large winding stair at one corner might suggest that a jamb was
96 intended at a later date. Kinnaird Head Castle, Fraserburgh, built 1570–2 and slightly smaller at 12 m. by 9 m., has a corbelled ashlar parapet similar to that at Delgatie. Its interior has been gutted but a number of sculptured pendants similar to those in the rib-vaults of the Simpson group are preserved in the associated 'Wine Tower'.

In his study of Craig, Gight, Delgatie and Towie Barclay, Dr Douglas Simpson accepted the dates on these houses at face value but Dr Joachim Zeune has reassigned all four to the period 1540–50 from an analysis of their gunloops and other details, discounting the dates at Delgatie and Towie as subsequent heraldic décor.* At Towie the recorded datestone of 1593 appears

*See Joachim Zeune, *The Last Scottish Castles* (1992).

very late for the original date of construction, but the present writer is inclined to accept those at Delgatie as accurate. All these tower houses were deliberately conservative for their date, designed to withstand any sudden localized attack arising from their owners' predominantly Counter-Reformation sympathies.

The alternative solution to the provision of hall and solar at first-floor level was the *palatium* or palace-block, in which both these principal apartments were contained within a single long rectangle, and it was from the palace-block that the plan-types of the larger late C16 houses developed. The earliest palace-block in northern Aberdeenshire seems to be the W range – perhaps C15 – built within the C13 enclosure at Fyvie, where the SW tower provided a separate bedchamber. Rather more sophisticated were the palace-block of Druminnor (S) built in the 1430s and the closely related Huntly (S) built *c.* 1452 and recast in 1551–4. At Huntly the main block is 23 m. by 11 m. with a circular bedchamber tower 10.5 m. in diameter at its SW angle. Both these houses have lost their original stairs, but it can safely be assumed that Huntly was a very early instance of the Z-plan, with the stair in a NE jamb. Very similar to the 'New Wark' at Huntly was the closely contemporary work at Cairnbulg, where the original tower was extended as the entrance jamb of an otherwise completely new house, its main block almost exactly the same length as Huntly's but rather narrower at 9 m. At the Earl Marischal's Inverugie, now sadly reduced to a ruin, and at Glenbervie (S), the main block had a hall occupying the whole of the first floor and two circular angle towers providing private apartments in a near-symmetrical rather than a Z-plan arrangement; both Glenbervie and Inverugie date from the 1530s.

All of these houses probably had corbelled parapets as first built. By the late 1550s, however, in parallel with developments in central and southern Scotland, such parapets were generally given up in favour of simple roofs with dormers, enclosed pepperpot turrets instead of open bartizans, and Scots Renaissance rather than late medieval detail, while planning became more compact: the unturreted Terpersie (S) of 1561, where both the entrance tower and bedchamber tower were circular, was perhaps the pioneer. It introduces us to the master-mason *Thomas Leiper*, whose hand has been identified either by his characteristic triple gunloops or by his initials at Tolquhon (1584–9), the nearby 63 Schivas (*c.* 1582), Barra (*c.* 1614–18) and Arnage and Esslemont (neither securely dated). Similar in general appearance to Terpersie is the rather later and larger Carnousie (1577) where the entrance jamb is square, its unusual arrangement of entrance corridor and stair suggesting to Harry Gordon Slade that it might be a less martial work of the *Conns* of Auchry (*see* p. 31).

Except for the stepped L-plan Esslemont and Barra – a remodelling – both of which have single wide turnpike stairs right to the top as in the Conn houses, Leiper's later houses follow the same general arrangement as contemporary examples of similar scale in central and southern Scotland: a square or rectangular entrance jamb containing a big stair to the hall at first-floor level, and a smaller turnpike to the floors above, either contained within the jamb as at Tolquhon or corbelled out in the re-entrant angle as at Schivas and Arnage. Beyond the hall Leiper's planning varied: the long palace-blocks of Tolquhon and Schivas have private stairs to the upper floors at the internal gable between the hall and the private apartments, a similar arrangement being found at the idiosyncratically detailed Pittulie; at the Z-plan Arnage a comparable degree of privacy for the family apartments was achieved by the second jamb having its own stair, again an arrangement common in central and southern Scotland.

63 Much the largest of this group of castles was Tolquhon, where the palace-block was but one side of a courtyard castle with galleries over cellarage around the other three, the frontal range containing the entrance pend flanked by drum towers with sculptured figures. A still grander courtyard castle, now sadly fragmentary, was the château-like Boyne built rather earlier, probably from 1566 by Alexander Ogilvie for his wife, Mary Bethune, a prominent member of Queen Mary's entourage. It had buildings on three sides of its court with drum towers at all four angles and a smaller pair of towers flanking the entrance in the near-symmetrical S front, as at Dudhope (Dundee) and Rowallan (Ayrshire). The palace-block was on the W; the purpose of the slightly lower corresponding block containing the kitchen on the E is not known. Boyne may have formed the model for Lord Chancellor Seton's reconstruction of Fyvie – perhaps by *William Schaw* or the *Bell* family – in 1599–1603, by far the grandest castle in northern Aberdeenshire, where the general arrangement was predetermined by the existing structure. As at Boyne, Fyvie's palace-block was in the W range, replanned with a magnificent winding stair, but the symmetrical S front with its arch-linked entrance towers had now become a show frontage for its walled formal garden; the actual entrance was in the E range, which has since been demolished. The planning differed from Boyne's, the S range consisting of a rather narrow long gallery linking the accommodation in the towers and perhaps two further galleries above.

Related in symmetry and style to Fyvie is the giant tower house
67 built by John Urquhart at Craigston in 1604–7, 17.5 m. square and again with an arched recess over the entrance, here 3.5 m. wide and slightly off-centre in the W front. Craigston is actually an L-plan scheme developed into a U rather than a Z, the jambs being for what were doubtless good practical reasons 6 m. wide on the S and 7.5 m. wide on the N. The design's great glory is its sculptured parapet over the central arch, divided into five portrait roundels, a richer display than anything to be found at Fyvie and one which suggested to Harry Gordon Slade that it was the work of the *Bells*, discounting the tradition recorded in Jervise's *Epitaphs and Inscriptions* (1879) that it was the work of the *Conns*. What sort of forecourt Craigston presided over can only be guessed as it had seemingly disappeared without record by 1733.

Three more great courtyard castles of this vintage survive within northern Aberdeenshire but all are ruined and none had quite the same ambition as architecture. At Pitsligo the C15 tower referred to earlier became part of the S range of a great quadrangular castle of enclosure built by the Forbes from 1577 onwards, the palace-block being on the E with a gallery range on the N and a frontal range on the W. Unlike Fyvie the buildings were relatively low and unturreted with a single drum tower at the outer NE corner, the splendour reserved for the interiors and the very handsome square entrance tower within the NE angle of the court. Enough of the surrounding layout survives to give a picture of what has been swept away elsewhere. Inverugie was also predominantly low-rise but bigger, with two courts on the W and a great garden on the E; the 1530s palace-block referred to earlier was modernized *c.* 1600 and stood high above the remainder on the E side of the S court, the private apartments in the NE and SE drum towers overlooking the garden.

Finally mention must be made of two remarkable one-off houses. At Inchdrewer the plan of the court was much less regular than at Pitsligo because of the hillside site. Its nucleus is a small C15 or early C16 L-plan tower house with a main block only 10.5 m. by 6 m. and a 6 m.-wide jamb of very short projection, perhaps originally of the Colquhonnie–Knockhall type but so altered when remodelled in two phases to its present form during the late C16 that it is difficult to categorize. To this was added a long S forecourt range 20.5 m. long but only 4.25 m. wide with a circular SW tower, evidently similar to the courtyard ranges at Castle Fraser (S) and indeed with *Leiper*'s distinctive triple shot-holes. This wing lies at an angle of about 105 degrees to the original tower; a shorter almost parallel range occupies the forecourt's N side with a gateway to the W of it. Another exceptional house, seemingly also the work of *Leiper*, is Fordyce, built 64
in 1592 as an occasional residence with a main block not much more than square on plan, but with an entrance jamb and triple gunloops of the Leiper type and diagonally opposite angle turrets. It has no close parallel in the north-east, its kin being the smaller tower houses at Braikie and Flemington in Angus.

COUNTRY HOUSES

The transition of Scottish lairds from fortified houses to country houses is perfectly represented by Mounie Castle, mid-C17, a long two-storey rectangular block with small windows broadly spaced and a central circular stair-tower rising into a gabled attic caphouse. Perhaps it was a remodelling and extension of a late C16 tower house but it is consistent with central and southern Scottish T-plans of the same vintage. Within northern Aberdeenshire Mounie is, however, an isolated phenomenon. No other country house of this kind is known to have been built during the mid C17, and even the simmering religious tensions of the time do not seem to fully explain the reasons why.

Faichfield House.
Drawing by David M. Walker

Very regrettably, much the best country house built *c.* 1700 of which we have any knowledge, Faichfield House near Longside, was demolished as recently as 1969. It had a three-storey six-bay frontage, near-symmetrical but with its ground-floor entrance off-centre; the four central windows on its second floor rose into small dormerheads beneath a tall gabled roof with end stacks. It was only one room deep but it had a projecting stair at the rear resulting in a T-plan, and until the late C19 it had service offices extending forward from its l. bay, so forming a forecourt. Internally its wood panelling had survived unaltered. Although simple, Faichfield was an early example of the fusion of classical with vernacular architecture and its loss – wholly avoidable – was a disaster, not only in north-east but in wider Scottish terms.

In Faichfield's absence we must witness the development of north-east country houses through surviving two-storey examples. Dunlugas (1680) now forms the back wing of a larger house built a century later (for which see p. 39). Its windows in dressed surrounds against a background of harl appear originally to have been relatively small, and most have been enlarged, but it retains a strongly vernacular character. Birkenbog (1693) is rather taller two-storey, built as the wing of a tower house. Its fenestration, which is probably original, is broadly symmetrical in layout with a central doorway, only two ground-floor windows – one at each end – for security, but five evenly spaced windows lighting the first-floor principal apartments. It retains a l. forecourt wing like that at Faichfield although this has been much rebuilt. Hatton (1694; *see* Auchterless) has been altered and extended, but its doorway has been central, suggesting symmetrical fenestration, with first-floor principal apartments taller than ground floor although their windows may have been enlarged during the mid C18; inside they retain wood panelling such as Faichfield once had, while at the rear the stair is projected out in a half-moon bay. Hatton formerly had a l. wing which was demolished in the early C20, although the sense of a forecourt is preserved by the later extension on the r. side. Culvie House (Aberchirder), with irregular fenestration which appears to be original, also belongs to this early group; so once did Glack (*c.* 1723) and Nether Ardgrain, but their main blocks were enlarged later on in the C18.*

The development of north-east country houses can be seen at Auchiries, where two ruined examples dated 1715 and (reputedly) 1726 stand next to each other at right-angles. The 1715 house is two-storey with its doorway off-centre and four bays irregularly spaced; the 1726 house is two-storey five-bay symmetrical, its openings in raised margins, but it still has a forecourt wing. Much more sophisticated was the Old House of Auchmacoy (1722), now mostly demolished. This was three-storey, five windows wide and harled with a gabled roof; its low ground floor lit by square windows was however devoted to services and formed a plinth for the principal accommodation at first floor, with steps leading up to the doorway. Flanking quadrants linked it to square pavilions, single-storey and attic with hipped roofs which embraced a forecourt.

Such were the seats of the north-east gentry when *William Adam* built Haddo House (1728–36) for the 2nd Earl of Aberdeen 75
and then the still grander and more sophisticated Duff House 76
(begun 1735) for Lord Braco. Adam responded not to local traditions but followed Sir William Bruce and his successors who had pioneered Scottish classicism during the later C17 and early C18, and at Duff to Baroque English and Continental architecture. Haddo and Duff were much bigger houses than their predecessors, very deep on plan with formal suites of rooms for much larger households. They were built of expensive polished ashlar masonry, in Duff's case shipped up by sea from South Queensferry, rather than local harled rubble; they were self-evidently much more sophisticated designs, with hipped roofs and handsome pediments rather than homely wall-head gables; their detailing was far more elaborate and conspicuously expensive, with their owners' heredity boldly expressed in magnificent carving. Their main entrances at first-floor *piano nobile* were approached by balustraded external staircases and their interiors – doorcases, fireplaces and ceiling plasterwork – were, or in the case of Duff were intended to be, as splendid as their exteriors, awash with fine craftsmanship.

*Also belonging to this group is Auchlossan (S) built before 1709. Balnacraig (S) is dated 1735, and Janefield (Aberchirder) is *c.* 1740; Techmuiry, originally a seven-bay frontage, is *c.* 1744. Inverernan (S) 1764, Bellabeg (S) 1765, and Muiresk *c.* 1784 all follow the same formula but with central attic gables, suggesting that that at Balnacraig has been a later addition. Occasional examples are also to be found in the towns: the pattern served for inns as well as private houses.

The influence of such masterworks on the vernacular classical house – i.e. the classical house adapted to the means of more modest landowners – is subtle but can be discerned in the seg-
78 mentally pedimented doorpiece of Haddo House near Crimond which otherwise followed the T-plan model established at Faichfield. This house is a particularly good example of its type, a tall two-storey seven-bay frontage with a central first-floor roundel and a more generous eaves line than at Hatton, Birkenbog or Auchiries which provides for spacious attics. It retains excellent panelling and a splendid stair with reeded columns in its gabled outshot at the rear. Its offices are at the back, and its garden layout has survived virtually unaltered. Similar but plainer and only five windows wide is Kininmonth (New Leeds, dated 1740) with the same detail at the stair.

At Aberdour, also built in 1740, the development of the vernacular classical style is much more evident. Facing the garden, the main front is three-storey and seven windows wide with its central bay slightly advanced under a wall-head gable suggesting a pediment: this has a blind octagonal opening in its field, a detail borrowed from *Adam*'s Haddo. The doorway, which is itself pedimented, is at ground-floor level but the first-floor rooms' importance is stressed by their relative height. Aberdour is built in harled rubble rather than ashlar, but there is an attempt at mathematical proportions in the three bays on each side of the centre, which are perfectly square; the house is a single room deep like its predecessors but a simple rectangle rather than a T. Both plan and elevations are however quite different from those of Adam's houses and there is a charming touch of old Scottish traditions in the crowstepped end gables. The main block has quadrants and symmetrical pavilions embracing the service court, but these are at the back framing a near-blind rear elevation rising into a wall-head gable. Mains of Pittendrum (Sandhaven), built in 1734, is much more compact – a simple three-storey three-bay block with its upper-floor windows breaking through the eaves as swept dormers, and projecting single-storey-and-attic side wings, the lugged doorpiece with a heraldic
78 segmental pediment like that at Haddo House near Crimond.

Much more classical, simple but perfectly proportioned, was *John Adam*'s new Banff Castle built for Lord Deskford *c.* 1749–52. Three storeys and five windows wide, its walls are harled with ashlar dressings and a tall hipped roof; its two-storey pavilions and lodge houses are hip-roofed to match. Similar in profile was Troup designed by *John Jeans* in 1754 and built by 1772, perhaps with advice from *John Adam*. It was three equal storeys high and seven windows wide, and although now demolished echoes of it can be found at Auquhorthies (S) and Rannieston, both built at the end of the C18. Bourtie House (Kirkton of Bourtie) of 1754 represents another step in development, a three-storey five-bay front mostly in squared rubble with its projecting centre rising into a pediment. It was designed to be entered by a stair at its *piano nobile* as at Auchmacoy, although its present doorway is at ground floor. It has quite sophisticated interior work but it still

adopts the old-fashioned T-plan. Several mid-C18 houses have central wall-head gables in lieu of the great houses' pediments. World's End, Fraserburgh (traditionally ascribed to *c.* 1767) is 102
three-storey three bays broad in squared masonry, its centre breaking into a curvilinear wall-head gable with an arched attic window. But the centre is not projected: rather it is emphasized by its pedimented first-floor doorway approached by a railed stair, the detailing in general being of a notably high standard. At the charming Memsie of about the same date, two-storey five bays with its slightly projecting centre rising into a similar gable, the forecourt is flanked by tall hip-roofed pavilions, miniature versions of those formerly at Glassaugh House. At Glassaugh the W façade of 1770 was markedly English Palladian, suggesting that Gen. Abercromby obtained its designs from London; it is three storeys and five windows wide with advanced end bays which once rose into towers.

The immediate model for future developments was however the much simpler Auchry (built 1767, dem. 1967), the first country house in northern Aberdeenshire built for a lesser landowner to adopt the much deeper plan-forms found in southern Scotland, and perhaps the first truly classical – rather than vernacular classical – house of this scale in this part of the world, although its northern lilt remained clear in its ground-floor entrance, absence of sunk basement, and high gabled roof with broad end stacks. Its three-storey five-bay frontage was distinguished by its ashlar masonry and its quiet understatement, the only ornament being a heraldic panel over its doorway; its two-storey wings projecting to the rear were built in coursed masonry for picturesque contrast.

The vernacular classical house reaches its peak in the late C18 in two different ways. The first is the very simple and solid Orrok (Pettens *c.* 1781–2), deep-planned like Auchry. Its three-storey five-bay frontage with small flanking pavilions makes its statement solely through the good craftsmanship and sense of proportion possessed by local mason-builders. But the zenith of the style is represented in the much more sophisticated Dunlugas (1793) in which those builders at last achieved complete mastery of a more architectural style of house design with which they could mount some sort of convincing reply to *William Adam*'s work of fifty years previously. Dunlugas is a finely proportioned two-storey five-bay house raised over a basement, its centre bay slightly advanced and crowned by a low pediment. It is rubble-built but with copious use of ashlar dressings; approached by a railed horseshoe stair its tripartite doorway is framed by fluted Doric pilasters supporting an entablature. The wall-head pediment is finely moulded with an oval oculus, and the double-pile plan is neatly expressed by twin stacks at the end gables.

Thus far we have not mentioned much the largest country house project in northern Aberdeenshire in the later C18, Ellon Castle, which was hugely enlarged from the old House of Ardgirth by *John Baxter* for the 3rd Earl of Aberdeen in 1781–5. This vast U-plan house was plain and old-fashioned in style with a Baroque broken-pedimented doorpiece preserved at the present house. It fell into ruin after the earl's death in 1801, but its S elevation and garden remain almost intact.

Hardly any country houses were built in northern Aberdeenshire during the French Revolutionary and Napoleonic wars. But French Revolutionary thought – in Neoclassical architecture rather than politics – resulted in one house which, responding directly to the ideas of Boullée and Ledoux, was exceptionally important not only to Scottish or even British architecture but
81 to European architecture as a whole. Cairness by *James Playfair* (1791–7) is a unique composition, a two-storey-and-basement main block flanked by taller three-storey-and-basement end pavilions, its doorway framed by a tetrastyle pedimented portico, and with a hemicycle court at the rear. Beautifully constructed, its fabric nevertheless bears witness to changes of mind on Playfair's part as the latest architectural thinking progressed, and on that of his client, Charles Gordon of Buthlaw, whose meteoric rise to riches and vaulting ambition resonate deeply in undertones throughout the house. Pitfour by *John Smith I* (*c.* 1809, demolished) and Cortes, perhaps also by *Smith* (*c.* 1810), both post-date the Battle of Trafalgar, after which invasion seemed much less likely.

Construction of country houses began again in earnest even before the wars had quite ended, the landowners' prosperity ensured by the Agricultural Revolution and the Corn Laws. Hatton Castle, remodelled *c.* 1814 in the castellated idiom associated with *John Paterson*, is a delightful 'toy fort', not remotely defensible. Indeed the post-bellum witnessed a boom in country house-building, although classicism remained the rule and nearly all the houses were astylar, notably *John Smith I*'s Strichen (1818–21, ruinous) with its impressive eleven-bay frontage and nine-bay flanks, and Mountblairy (demolished), first completed in 1791 but extended in 1825, probably by *Smith*, who was responsible for a further enlargement in 1835. Pitfour was also extended by 1828, again by *Smith*.

Much the most sophisticated of the Aberdeen architects of this period, however, was *Archibald Simpson* who like Smith was London-trained and whose classical country houses challenged
84 comparison with W. H. Playfair's. His Crimonmogate (*c.* 1825) has a Greek Doric hexastyle portico framed between two-storey projecting pavilions, all in polished ashlar granite. Like Cairness and several other houses it was funded by a substantial fortune made overseas, but at home the banking crisis of 1825–6 brought the post-war building boom to an end and thereafter architects had to design new houses or remodel existing ones in more modest but still handsome styles. Thus *Simpson* remodelled Tillery with a Greek Doric portico in 1826; *William Robertson* – the most important practitioner north of Aberdeen – enlarged Eden House with a Greek Doric entrance front in 1828 and probably built Clunie House, a very sophisticated single-storey and basement villa of about the same date; while *John Smith I* refronted Aden House (Old Deer) with a Roman Doric porte

cochère and peristyled bow in 1832–3. Aden and the main block of Tillery are reduced to shells but Eden and Clunie still survive intact. A notable group of country villas around Peterhead includes Blackhill House (*c.* 1830), its three-bay porticoed centre block with flanking two-storey pavilions, and Berryhill House, single-storeyed three bays broad with a pilastered doorpiece raised up over a semi-sunk basement.

Then in 1825–7 *Simpson* built a simple but very handsome broad-eaved Italianate villa at House of Leask, apparently his first work in that idiom. Later (*c.* 1835–40) he completed the rebuilding of Glassaugh, its impressive palazzo-like s façade three-storey seven bays broad with a ground-floor portico and windows fitted with Continental casements rather than sashes as a cosmopolitan touch. *Simpson*'s still larger and even more sophisticated Italianate house at Carnousie (late 1830s) has all but disappeared. Also Italianate but asymmetrical and in a lower key was *John Smith I*'s enlargement of Buchanness (Boddam) as a marine villa for the 4th Earl of Aberdeen from 1840; his Italianate Craigellie (1840–1) adopted the balanced but asymmetrical entrance front arrangement of his Neo-Tudor and Neo-Jacobean houses. As an elegant inexpensive solution to country-house design Italianate would have a lasting vogue, culminating in *A. & W. Reid*'s Knockleith of 1864.

Until the mid 1830s it could not have been obvious that the universal adoption of classicism for country houses should be coming to an abrupt end in northern Aberdeenshire, to be largely superseded by historicist styles which were at first predominantly English rather than C16–C17 Scottish. Why the change? Perhaps the occasional outbursts of Gothick – adopted as distinctly 'British' – during the French wars provide a clue. For many years Continental travel had been severely circumscribed, and during that period Romantic literature had reinforced a sense of British identity, life and culture, Sir Walter Scott himself building the proto-Baronial Abbotsford (Borders) in the 1810s and 1820s. However the traditional Scots tower house appeared quite unsuited to contemporary life and for the next thirty years historical English styles were much better understood than Scottish ones, largely as the result of scholarly publications, in particular John Britton's *Architectural Antiquities of Great Britain* (1805–14).

Thus Auchmacoy, a Scots Elizabethan mansion designed in 85
1831 by *William Burn*, one of the leading London-trained practitioners in Edinburgh, was radically different from anything previously seen in Aberdeenshire. Burn was an innovative architect in many styles, and a pioneer (and throughout his long life the acknowledged master) of mid-C19 country house-planning. But somehow to his severe annoyance *John Smith I* managed to intervene and complete the construction of both Auchmacoy and Fintray (S, 1827, demolished) and by doing so he learnt much of Burn's compositional skill and particularly his planning. Auchmacoy serves as the model for *Smith*'s own Menie (*c.* 1836); he then designed the much bigger Slains Castle (1836–7),

87 incorporating earlier fabric. At Forglen (*c.* 1840), on plan the progenitor of Balmoral (S) which Smith's son William would design with the Prince Consort, his Tudor is much bolder – an impressive three-storey courtyard plan, its elevations enlivened with an asymmetrical arrangement of bay windows and gables, and its angles all treated differently, with a lantern tower over the stair. Almost as large and in the same idiom but more symmetrical was *Simpson*'s stylish reconstruction of Meldrum House in 1836–40, sadly reduced in 1934–7.

The deaths of Robertson (†1841), Simpson (†1847) and Smith (†1852) marked the passing of the first generation of famous north-east architects. With them went the dependence on English historical styles, for Burn, recognizing the need for a comparable understanding of Scottish historical precedents, financed Robert W. Billings to produce *The Baronial and Ecclesiastical Antiquities of Scotland* from 1846. On his travels north Billings struck up a friendship with *Thomas Mackenzie*, resident in Elgin (Moray) who seemingly worked briefly in Smith's office before moving to first Simpson's and then to Robertson's. In 1848 *Mackenzie* remodelled Brucklay Castle in the Scottish Baronial idiom but he died in 1854 and his partner *James Matthews*, also from Simpson's office, succeeded him. If the Baronial style as a means of architectural expression was developed chiefly by Burn's partner David Bryce – who had absorbed to the full Burn's mastery of planning, which he wrapped up in a magnificent series of Franco-Scottish country house designs – then Matthews, with the same access to Billings's engravings, retained his own distinct style and local patronage. Thus Matthews remodelled Arnage, a late C16 Z-plan tower house, as a Baronial mansion in 1860, and the classical Rothienorman in a similar idiom *c.* 1862–4 (now ruinous); he extended Philorth (since gutted by fire) in 1858–60 and 1873–4 and built New House of Glack (Daviot) in 1875–6. In parallel *John Russell Mackenzie,* who had been articled to Matthews,
90 rebuilt Esslemont in 1865–6, a substantial house very picturesque in appearance with lively modelling of its elevations, and yet still a tightly disciplined, clear composition of which Bryce would have approved. Such was the north-east architects' grip on their home territory that only one of Bryce's circle – *Charles Kinnear*, who had designed the City & County Buildings, Aberdeen – seems to have secured a country-house commission, to enlarge and Baronialize Balmedie in 1878.

The agricultural depression after 1870, the industrial recession from 1873 and the financial crisis of the early 1880s precipitated by the City of Glasgow Bank crash resulted in a twenty-five year moratorium on country house-building in northern Aberdeenshire. On the rare occasions that new building took place at all it was very different in style, such as *James Souttar*'s Tillymaud (1885), a polychrome granite villa in the Italianate style for a wealthy clergyman. Most clients were now successful industrialists with no centuries-old lineage to prove, but their understanding of historic Scots architecture would run much deeper as a consequence of MacGibbon & Ross's *Castellated & Domestic Architecture of Scotland* (1887–92). The long drought was eventually broken not by the construction or enlargement of a house but by the restoration of a castle – Cairnbulg Castle, which had been stripped to a shell in 1782 and suffered a disastrous collapse in 1806. Even the Duthie family of shipbuilders who had bought it in 1862 could not afford to rebuild it, but marriage to a stone-merchant's daughter produced a dowry of Corennie granite, enabling its reconstruction by *Jenkins & Marr* in 1896–7. Such indeed were the circumstances of the world by then that the next country house after Cairnbulg would be a diametric opposite. Tillycorthie Castle by *John Cameron* (1911–12), built anew for a Bolivian tin magnate, was described as 'a Spanish villa' but was actually a mischievous amalgam of Tudor and Franco-Scottish styles with disproportionate details, built in Hennebique concrete around a central winter garden large enough to turn around a Rolls Royce: perhaps a flat rejection by a successful outsider of academic ideals and Establishment values, yet also fun, boldly accepting of the modern world and modern materials – a true one-off.

The interwar period saw further tower house restorations by more scholarly architects – Kinnairdy by *George Bennett Mitchell* (1927–35) with *H.M. Office of Works*, and House of Schivas by *Fenton Wyness* (1934–7). House of Glennie, a late Arts and Crafts fishing lodge with C17 Scots influences, was built in 1936, while *David Vaughan Carnegie* seemingly designed his own house, Dundarg of 1937–8, really a Baronial villa built from recycled stonework. After the Second World War, however, no new country houses were built for fifty years. Only in recent times has light appeared at the end of the tunnel, the House of Formartine by 95
Morris & Steedman (1994–5) and House of Tifty, Fyvie, by *Law & Dunbar-Nasmith* (*c.* 2008) marking the welcome rebirth of old traditions – original design, elegance and fine craftsmanship.

Estate buildings etc.

STEADINGS AND STABLES. From the mid C18 the great houses' outer courts were cleared away and replaced by large quadrangular home farm steadings, although separate stable and coach-house blocks did not become common until nearer 1800. Aberdour House, built anew in 1740, illustrates the transition: a large steading with a pend tower was built flanking its outer court in that year, supplemented in 1795 by a separate stable block. More typical are unpretentious examples at Ardo (1756), and Craigston (1766 onwards). The earliest instance of architectural distinction is the Home Farm Steading at Delgatie, 1768, with a near-Palladian entrance tower. Such a tower also appears at Mains of Carnousie, dated 1797, although the courtyard there is probably earlier and still adheres to joint provision of farmstead-ing with coachhouse and stables. So does that at Auchintoul, again late C18, with plainer tower. The tower at Mountblairy,

1791–1800, is similar and it seems notable that Delgatie, Carnousie and Mountblairy were all either owned or had recent associations with the Hay family. Fyvie, begun 1777, is also extensive, but rather vernacular in character. Aden (Old Deer) has a rare and very handsome example of a 'round square', built in 1800.

During the earlier C19 several stylish stable blocks were built, all by *John Smith I*: Pitfour, U-plan with anta-pilasters, and Strichen, with arcaded elevations, both *c.* 1820; Brucklay, Tudor-classical, about the same date; and Mountblairy, a Greek Doric façade of 1835 grafted on to an earlier farmstead. Farmsteadings themselves also became more architectural, notably at Inverquhomery on the Pitfour Estate where a long, low, slightly irregular elevation was pulled together by a pedimented centre, and at the more symmetrical Shevado on the Brucklay Estate. By mid-Victorian times the supreme master of steading design was *James Duncan* of Turriff, responsible for the magnificent symmetrical steading at Bethelnie (1872) and for remodelling that at Towie Barclay with a very grand meeting room for the Aberdeen Guildry, *c.* 1874.

DOOCOTS. The earliest surviving doocot to remain reasonably intact is apparently that at Findlater, a C16 'beehive' type in three tiers with a funnel at the top; Glassaugh nearby, in four tiers, is *c.* 1600. Auchmacoy's was similar, but was remodelled in 1638, the uppermost tier corbelled to take a gabled caphouse. Again essentially similar, but of a slimmer telescopic form with battered sides, are Auchry and Delgatie, both presumably by the *Conns* of Auchry. Boyne is a big rectangular doocot of the type common in central and southern Scotland, and Mounie a smaller rectangular example dated 1694, although seemingly no others survive, later examples in general being circular with rat courses and conical roofs. Similarly proportioned but square-plan with pyramidal roofs are House of Leask (mid-C18, transferred from Pitlurg) and Hilton of Turnerhall (1787), while Crimonmogate is octagonal with a prismatic roof. Of the later examples much the most architectural is Mounthooley (Peathill, 1800), tall octagonal with a ball-finialled parapet.

Of the once extensive walled forecourts and GARDENS of the
greater C16 and early C17 houses the most complete surviving
63 layouts are at the ruined castles of Pitsligo and Tolquhon, those
at continuously occupied houses having largely disappeared in
later C18 landscape-gardening programmes. Much the most
important of the symmetrical late Stuart formal gardens is
71 Pitmedden, reflecting Continental examples as well as the work
of Sir William Bruce. Begun in 1675 it is on two levels with handsome stairs, gates and square ogee-roofed pavilions. Circular-plan pavilions survive from what was apparently a similar scheme at Meldrum House, and at Ellon Castle there is another particularly fine garden (1715) with a large two-storey garden house integrated into the terraces. Both Pitmedden and Ellon have exceptional SUNDIALS.

In the 1730s *William Adam* planned major formal layouts at Haddo, Duff and Craigston. Haddo's was carried out but fell into neglect. At Duff where *William Boutcher* was also consulted, the Deveron influenced the layout by precluding anything quite so axial. Elements of Adam and Boutcher's LANDSCAPING scheme remain, notably the Temple of Venus (1737) and the Fishing Temple (*c.* 1740), both circular on plan. From 1765 the greater part of the Duff landscape was remodelled on picturesque principles by *William Bowie*. At its Bridge of Alvah end a Gothic 103
tower, an ornamental bridge and a garden temple were provided. Bowie's work was seemingly restyled by *Thomas White* in the 1780s, a Gothick mausoleum being built as part of that programme in 1790. Upriver at Forglen, Lord Banff had a rather denser scheme of planting carried out from 1740, and at Fyvie the C17 layout was cleared away *c.* 1777, new steadings and a kitchen garden built and the parkland replanted on picturesque principles with an artificial loch, probably by *Robert Robinson*.

Artificial lakes were to be important features of the major landscape-gardening programmes of the earlier C19. *William Sawrey Gilpin* was consulted at Strichen built by *John Smith I* in 1818–21; Gilpin's planting has gone but his lake with two islets remains. He was probably responsible for the much more ambitious landscape at Pitfour, again built anew by *Smith* from *c.* 1809. This included an artificial lake spanned by a low-rise three-arched bridge and over the following decades it was provided with a racecourse, a Greek Doric temple, an octagonal observatory tower and a private Episcopalian chapel. Artificial lakes with islets were also included in the restyled park at Delgatie carried out by *Mr Johnstone* in 1814, at Brucklay Castle (probably during the house's remodelling in 1814) and at Hatton Castle (also remodelled in 1814), but the most ambitious among these later schemes was the reformation of Adam's park at Haddo. This was carried out in two phases: extensive replanting *c.* 1805, followed by remodelling and architectural embellishment by *James Giles R.S.A.* from 1830, culminating in *J. & W. Smith*'s Golden Gates and giant urn in 1847. Such major works of landscaping were probably driven by a wish on the part of landowners to re-employ tenants dispossessed by the Agricultural Revolution and soldiers returning home from the French wars.

Nearly all the larger estates had GATES AND LODGES of some quality. The Duff House gates on the Banff Bridge axis (1779) were probably the earliest but only a single Serlian lodge house remains. More sophisticated Neoclassical in design were *James Playfair*'s at Cairness (designed 1790, built 1891), and very exceptional indeed was Fyvie's towered North Gate, Scottish Baronial Revival of 1819. Good Neo-Greek lodges by *John Smith I* were features of the Pitfour, Aden and Strichen Estates, but the finest is Duff House's Collie Lodge of 1836, a Greek Doric temple now divorced from its park. At
Crimonmogate *Archibald Simpson* adopted a classical Italianate 84
idiom which also features at Haddo, where both he and *Smith* were employed.

Victorian lodges tended to be simple vernacular or cottagey, much the finest examples being *J.* and *H. M. Wardrop*'s at Udny. Scottish Baronial lodges of quite exceptional size were provided at Brucklay by *James Matthews c.* 1860, and Greengate Lodge, Delgatie Castle, by *A. & W. Reid* 1854, who almost certainly also designed Eastside Lodge at Forglen *c.* 1865. A very few of the larger estates have Victorian Gothic MAUSOLEA within their parks, all rather similar with low buttressed walls and big roofs: Mountblairy (*c.* 1860) and Hatton (1861) are perhaps by *A. & W. Reid*, while Forglen is certainly their work, consecrated in 1868; Auchmacoy differs in being Neo-Tudor to complement the house, *c.* 1866. By late Victorian times the fashion for such buildings had passed, *Alfred Waterhouse* providing a simple Gothic burial enclosure at Haddo in 1884.

BURGH, VILLAGE AND RURAL ARCHITECTURE

Of the six most important BURGHS of northern Aberdeenshire
– Peterhead, Fraserburgh, Banff, Macduff, Ellon and Turriff – it
is no coincidence that the first four are all on the coast, while
Ellon was the lowest fordable point on the Ythan, leaving only
Turriff landlocked in its rich agricultural hinterland in the remote
west of Buchan but on the road between Aberdeen and Banff.
Peterhead and Fraserburgh have long been much the largest
settlements and both grew considerably in the later C20, Peterhead
in particular driven by the oil industry. Banff, a royal burgh and
a county town, faces the upstart Macduff across Banff Bay with
4 its far superior harbour. Over the last hundred years, none has
grown so much as Ellon, its good communications to Aberdeen
resulting in what is effectively a second town on the Ythan's S
bank, while Banff's population has halved, and Turriff has always
enjoyed quiet yet sustained success.

All six towns have recognizable historic cores, the parish church, market place, public buildings and domestic accommodation closely bound together, with considerable variety not only of architectural purpose but of scale, date and a sense of patchwork accumulated over the centuries.

Ellon and Turriff date from very early times, whereas Banff is
3 probably early medieval. Turriff is focused on its long, gently
undulating, charmingly provincial High Street which, starting
from near St Congan's Church, wanders along the valley contours until it meets the axis of Schoolhill and Main Street rising
relentlessly up to the top of the hill. Banff developed along High
101 Street and later Low Street nearer the water's edge, with further
100 streets around Old St Mary's church, High Shore and Low
Shore. From the later C16 Peterhead was promoted by the Earls
Marischal, and Fraserburgh by the Frasers of Philorth, who
secured for them encouragement and advantages in trade as

burghs of barony granted by the King, then in their turn granted feuars special privileges and rights of self-government; in addition, Fraserburgh challenged Aberdeen as a free port. Two hundred years later the Earls Fife secured burgh of barony status for Macduff in 1783, when the history of that town formally began.

Peterhead's development began in Marischal Street, Broad Street, Longate and Back Street during the late C16 and early C17, with the Spa Town – rows of mid to Late Georgian terraced houses – running down towards the coast from the later C18. Fraserburgh, by contrast, was a very early example of a planned town, laid out by Alexander Fraser, 8th of Philorth *c.* 1600, which developed according to a preset pattern for the next 250 years before breaking out of its bounds during the later C19: the layout of the original grid can still be discerned quite clearly. Macduff's Shore Street following the serpentine curve of the bay is magnifi- 4
cent in townscape terms with the parish church on higher ground at one far end very much its dominant feature: seen from Banff across the water, it presents a picturesque appearance even if its late C18 houses are much neglected and the backstreets more workaday in nature, though not without character. Only Ellon's historic centre seems disparate: the old and new bridges across the Ythan give it a clear entrance, but it is not immediately obvious that Market Street, rising steeply to the E, is the pleasant approach to the market square on higher ground, with the parish church off it to one side, and the ruined Ellon Castle overlooking it from a higher situation still.

VILLAGES divide into three types: early kirktouns or estate villages, fisher-touns and late C18 and early C19 improvement villages. The early hinterland villages developed where clean water, farmland and peat for fuel were to be found, sometimes along communication lines such as river valleys; they were often associated with saints whose followers established religious settlements. During the C12 the feudal system with the parish as basic administrative unit resulted in churches across the countryside, and some villages remained just a kirktoun, a church with perhaps a manse and school, and a few simple houses along a roughly trodden path.

Chains of fisher-touns developed wherever the coastline provided shelter for boats. One chain on the east coast, beginning with Newburgh, extends as far N as Peterhead; the other chain on the N coast begins with St Combs and extends W to Kingston in Moray. The fisher-touns' natural layout was for cottages lining the shore: sheltered in a bay if possible, facing the sea if not, and often built at right angles to the waterfront so that only their end gables faced the storm while their long flanks faced each other for protection, extending back two, three, four, even five deep wherever the shore allowed. Sometimes a village expanded further on gently rising ground or as an associated cliff-top settlement. Like Fraserburgh the nearby villages of St Combs, Inverallochy and Cairnbulg developed on roughly grid-like plans;
Boddam near Peterhead developed on a unique triangular plan 128

dictated by a sheltering stump of rock just off its shore. Collieston and Gardenstown are unusually picturesque in that their cottages rise up the sides of a bay, Collieston's a beautiful crescent, Gardenstown clinging to the ledges of its vertiginous cliff face. During the 1860s the N coast was ravaged by cholera, after which the villages were rebuilt to much better standards. As fishing vessels grew larger, the fleets concentrated in fewer, deeper harbours, but the small villages remained populated by
5 fisher-folk, Crovie and Pennan still looking much as they did during the early C19.

Improvement villages were originally a mid-C18 phenomenon, an attempt by landowners to diversify rural economies from agriculture into small-scale industries such as textiles and distilling and to provide a market for tenant farmers at a time when road transport was still impracticably slow. The need for diversity grew ever more pressing as the Agricultural Revolution took hold, driven by the terrible Highland famine of 1782–3 and the need to support a growing population as well as British forces fighting overseas. Improvement villages were planned by the same surveyors who reordered the estates into larger and more efficient farms. Often built on the sunny aspects of hillsides to preserve agricultural land and ensure good drainage, they are particularly concentrated in northern Buchan, the pioneer example being James Ferguson of Pitfour's Fetterangus of 1752–3. Cuminestown (1763), promoted by Joseph Cumine inspired Strichen, Aberchirder, New Byth and The Garmond (Cuminestown) within a few years. Stuartfield was begun *c.* 1772, New Pitsligo in 1787 and New Aberdour and New Leeds in 1798. Such villages developed into four main plan-types. The Garmond got no further than a single street; Cuminestown, New Byth and New Aberdour developed into two main streets arranged in an L-plan. Fetterangus and Stuartfield were laid out on crossroad plans, one street being much longer than the other with a central market area, while New Leeds also had a crossroads plan but was not nearly so successful. The more prosperous villages developed into small grid-plan towns, Strichen with three parallel streets and Aberchirder ultimately with five. The most successful of all was New Pitsligo, its site topography resulting in an irregular grid-plan intersected by a burn.

The two exceptions to these standard village plan-types were both promoted by the Fergusons of Pitfour. Newton (St Fergus) was laid out on a hillside on a remarkable Vitruvian plan, with three concentric streets scarped into the slopes and a central axial street rising to the summit between them, while Longside was laid out by the surveyor *William Whyte c.* 1801 on English picturesque principles. The French wars seemingly forestalled further improvement villages, the last being Mintlaw of *c.* 1813.

Communications

Old ROADS usually followed high ground, avoiding bogs and agricultural land. In general they were poorly maintained despite

the introduction of tolls in the late C16 and Parliamentary Acts in 1617, 1669 and 1686, and not until the later C18 did they witness any significant improvement. A Turnpike & Commutation Road Bill was passed after thirty years' prevarication in 1795, resulting in new roads in the north-east, much better engineered and following more convenient routes: they were laid out by Scotland's first great road-builder, *Charles Abercrombie*. These turnpikes opened up the countryside, not only encouraging communication and trade but making the Agricultural Revolution a practical possibility through the import of fertilizer and the export of produce. Several TOLL HOUSES (which remained in operation until 1866) still exist, including very distinctive examples at Longside and the Deveron Bridge at Turriff. Among the ROAD BRIDGES themselves, the earliest in northern Aberdeenshire is Rora, probably built as a result of the late C17
Acts, although reconstructed and widened in 1860. Banff Bridge 104
across the Deveron was designed by *John Smeaton*, built by *James Robertson* in 1779; Robertson also built bridges at Inverurie (S,
1791, demolished) and Ellon (1793), as well as the Bridge of 103
Alvah (1771–3). The Deveron Bridge, which opened up a new route between Aberdeenshire and Banffshire, was probably designed by *William Minto* and built by *William Smith* in 1824–6.

HARBOURS began as natural havens. The N coast seems always to have offered better anchorages than the E coast, Newburgh having no manmade harbour until at least the late C18. Fraserburgh's harbours have their origin in that built for Faithlie village by Alexander Fraser, 7th of Philorth, *c.* 1540; it was overlooked by the 'Wine Tower', really just an observation post signalling to the Frasers' castle at Cairnbulg. Harbour development was closely linked to the development of towns, and when Alexander Fraser, 8th of Philorth, began the present Fraserburgh Harbour in association with his new town there, he built the tower house on Kinnaird Head (*see also* p. 32) as a base to oversee progress and ensure that duties were paid; later the Frasers built town lodgings where the Saltoun Arms now stands. Similarly Port Henry, the earliest of the basins forming the present Peterhead Harbour, was begun *c.* 1593 by the 4th Earl Marischal, again in association with his burgh's development and the construction of a tower house on Keith Inch, which was a more convenient base for its supervision than Inverugie Castle. The great length of Broad Street, the market square near the harbour, is echoed by that of Broad Street, Rosehearty, once also an important port; Rosehearty probably also had a small tower house of which the building called The Jam survives (*see* town houses below). Banff Harbour beneath the medieval castle was formed from Guthrie's Haven in 1625. Portsoy's Old Harbour, 1680–93, was protected by the tower house at Durn as a satellite
of Sir Patrick Ogilvie's principal seat at Boyne. Macduff is a 4
latecomer, developed from *c.* 1760 by the Duffs, who recognized that Banff Harbour, while convenient for vessels pursued by northerly winds, was shallow and impeded by a sandbar. Their new burgh was protected not by a castle but by Duff House, with

their factor's house – the oldest in town – establishing their presence in lieu of a lodging.

The development of primitive harbours into much larger complexes from the mid C18 depended not only on water depth and ease of access, but the ability of the burghs' economies to diversify and attract funding beyond what even the wealthiest individuals could afford, growth being encouraged through related industries such as shipbuilding and subsidiary trades including rope-making and sail-making. The efforts of Alexander Fraser, 8th of Philorth, and Sir Patrick Ogilvie at burgh and harbour development resulted in crippling debts to relatives: in the latter's case such indebtedness may have prompted his son to become heavily involved in the attempted Jacobite invasion of 1708. George Keith, 9th Earl Marischal, through loyalty to the Stuarts was likewise deeply implicated in the Fifteen, and his estates were forfeited; the Frasers, with strong Presbyterian leanings, were canny enough not to become involved in doomed rebellions and retained control of their town late into the C19.

Harbour development was driven during the C18 by grants from the Convention of Royal Burghs, and from the early C19 by grants and later loans from central government. Applications for government funds were led, in the case of Fraserburgh and Peterhead, by their harbour commissioners and trustees, the greatest civil engineers of the age – including *Smeaton*, *Rennie*, *Telford* and the *Stevensons* – being involved in north-east harbours' construction. During the late C19, when *David & Thomas Stevenson*, together with the Aberdeen-based *John Willet* and *James Barron*, were the leading civil engineers working in the north-east, fishing vessels grew so large that only the deepest harbours were able to accommodate them, and as the fleets concentrated in Fraserburgh, Peterhead, Macduff and Buckie, so Rosehearty, Portsoy, Whitehills and other smaller villages dropped out of contention. Such considerations led Alexander Duff, Duke of Fife, after over a century of family investment, to give Macduff Harbour to the town so that it too could compete for funding.

Indeed, the survival of working harbours has been that of the fittest, a vigorous determination to maintain facilities to the best possible standards and finding the money to pay for them. WAREHOUSES, many of them very impressive, survive near the harbours of Banff, Gardenstown, Macduff, Newburgh, Peterhead, Portsoy and Whitehills, their dates ranging from the mid C18 to the early C20. *Thomas Smith*, who converted Kinnaird Head
96 Castle as the north-east's first lighthouse in 1787, was the father-in-law of *Robert Stevenson*, progenitor of the famous Stevenson family who were synonymous with LIGHTHOUSES for over a
128 century, including those at Buchanness (Boddam, 1825–7) and Rattray Head (1891–5).

RAILWAYS directly affected every aspect of town development in the north-east, particularly the growth of suburbs; they allowed local goods, including fresh fish and livestock, to be transported rapidly across the whole of Britain, and they made tourism a practical possibility. After the First World War, however, the lines running through northern Aberdeenshire proved uneconomic in the face of road transport. They were lifted in the later C20, although a number of station buildings have survived: Maud as a museum, Macduff as a private house, Portsoy as a park pavilion and Oldmeldrum within an industrial estate. The most impressive infrastructure is the viaduct on the Formartine & Buchan line designed by *Alexander Gibb* and built in 1860 on the outskirts of Ellon.

Public and commercial buildings and housing before c. 1840

No tolbooths survive in northern Aberdeenshire but there are
two old MARKET CROSSES, Banff's and Fraserburgh's, their 98
cross-heads probably dating from the C16 and early C17 respectively.* The tolbooths were succeeded by the TOWN AND COUNTY
HALLS. At the top of Broad Street, Peterhead's Town House by 105
the Edinburgh architect *John Baxter* (1788) is classical, three-storey and five bays in granite ashlar with a central pediment supporting a clock tower and stone spire, its pedimented porch added in 1881; the ground floor was once an open arcade providing a market, with grand external stairs rising to the council
chamber and school on the upper levels. Banff's Town House by 100
James Reid (1795–1800) is simpler, reflecting a smaller budget and a local architect, a big three-storey five-bay block also ashlar-
built; its contrast in scale with the surviving tolbooth steeple by 100
John Adam (1764–7) seems very marked. Among smaller town
halls, Strichen's, probably by *John Smith I* (1816), is a charming 109
invocation of historical styles to suggest civic authority: a square tower with tall stone spire, standing at one end of a two-storey three-bay block, part traditional Scots tolbooth, part Tudor, part classical, at a time when the characteristics of Scottish building styles had still not been properly understood. It is nevertheless a design of real quality, again built in ashlar. The earliest PUBLIC HALL in northern Aberdeenshire is Shore House (1776–7) on Fraserburgh's harbour-side, very plain three-storey rubble-built with an attic gable at one far end; it contained a ground-floor warehouse to help cover its costs. Banff's status as a county town resulted in several important buildings constructed by the MASONS AND GUILDS. In High Street, Shoemakers' House was built by the Incorporated Trades in 1710 and remodelled by the Shoemakers in 1787. A belated example of a classic Scottish building type, this harled three-storey block with ground-floor pend and shops rises into a central attic gable.

Among HOSTELRIES Banff's Market Arms claims origins 100
from 1585 but was evidently rebuilt during the C17 or early C18.

*Both heads are in fact replicas: the originals are preserved in Banff Museum and Fraserburgh Public Library. Turriff's Market Cross is much more recent, erected in 1865–6 to designs by *James Duncan* with sculpture by *Thomas Goodwillie*. It replaced a cross of 1512 which had been repaired in 1842.

Simple vernacular, three storeys with comparatively few windows on its seaward side, it has a round-arched pend leading from High Shore and Old St Mary's churchyard into the New Market Place. Morris's Hotel in Oldmeldrum was established in 1673, eleven years before the parish church was transferred from its ancient seat at Bethelnie in response to the growing importance of this little town on the junction of two important drove roads; the Meldrum Arms was also reputedly founded in the 1670s, although its central block is mid-C18 and has been extended at each end. In Portsoy the Old Star Inn (1727), built in North High Street near the Old Harbour, is quite exceptional, and not just within its regional context. A very long and tall three-storey eight-bay range, its windows regularly laid out in slim ashlar dressings against a background of harl, the off-centre first-floor doorway is approached by a forestair, and a ground-floor pend forms a cut-through to Low Street. The largest building in this once-thriving seaport established only forty years earlier – it considerably predates the harbour warehouses and church – the inn reflects the importance of sea travel and makes an interesting contrast with contemporary country houses such as Haddo
78 House (Crimond), Kininmonth or even Aberdour. In The Square the Boyne Hotel also reflects up-to-date country house design of *c.* 1750–60, its entrance front two-storey three-bay with gabled centre slightly projected being similar to Aldie or Nether Ardgrain, and its fine lugged doorpiece with cornice and railed basement only adding to its distinction.

In Fraserburgh's newly formed Saltoun Square, the Saltoun Arms by *Alexander Morice* was completed in 1801, predating the reconstruction of the parish church in 1802–3. Its classical vernacular style, not dissimilar to a house such as Orrok – three storeys, five bays broad in whinstone rubble with pale granite dressings and a distyle Doric portico – still manages to evoke, however faintly, the atmosphere of a Late Georgian hostelry. The Tolbooth Hotel in Banff was built in 1802. Inland, the largest C18 inn was the Fife Arms at Turriff, progressively extended to an L-plan seven bays by five. Surprisingly, the late C18 and early C19 turnpikes did not encourage hotel-building, the only significant example being the Commercial Hotel in Portsoy.*

SCHOOLS display great variety and the contrast between the two earliest survivors could hardly be more striking. In Old Market Place, Banff Grammar adopts the same two-storey scale and rubble construction as the neighbouring mid-C18 houses although it was built as late as 1805. After the town received a substantial legacy from James Wilson in the 1830s, however, its
113 citizens decided to build Wilson's Institution (1836–8) as a magnificent temple of learning. They engaged *William Robertson*,

*The Waverley Hotel in Merchant Street, Peterhead, while probably built in the early C19 during the later years of the spa town, did not become a hotel until the mid C20. Like other large houses in Peterhead it may have been built as an upmarket boarding house.

whose hexastyle Doric portico with its flanking wings and end pavilions is a masterwork of the Scottish Greek Revival, comparable with William Burn's Edinburgh Academy (1823–4) and John Watson's School in the same city (1825–8), now the Scottish National Gallery of Modern Art. Wilson's Institution accommodated the grammar, free and infant schools, a library and lecture room, and a museum within its central hall. The classical temple proved a natural means of expression for educational institutions, the much more modest Peterhead Parish School in Prince Street, 1838, following the same formula – a Doric pedimented centre distyle-*in-antis*, with crowning belfry and very plain wings, still built in ashlar. In Macduff, the little temple-fronted building in High Shore was perhaps also a school: dated 1837, stylistically it suggests *William Robertson* and although neglected it is one of the best buildings in the town. In rural areas a simple vernacular prevailed for parish schools, but the *Smiths* built several more architectural examples. The Episcopal School, Chapel Hill (Cruden Bay; 1834) may be by *John Smith I*, who with his son *William* built New Deer (1844, extended by *James Matthews* 1874) and the near-identical twins Auchiries (Cruden Bay; 1847–9) and Bogbrae (1848–9).

During the C19, BANKS operated mainly through respectable local agents of substantial means – usually solicitors – who lent depositors' money at their own risk and received in return a consideration from the bank including the use of handsome living quarters built in association with the banking offices. On the junction of High Street and Frithside Street in Fraserburgh stands the present-day Bank of Scotland, a remarkable bow-fronted building two storeys and basement with an Ionic colonnade extending across the ground floor between square pavilions at the ends. It was built for Lewis Chalmers, Fraserburgh's baron-baillie, and its exceptionally sophisticated Neoclassical style has long been attributed to *Archibald Simpson c.* 1820–35. Simpson was responsible for two Neoclassical branches of the North of Scotland Bank immediately after its foundation in 1836, Broad Street, Peterhead, and the rather richer Low Street, Banff (now Clydesdale), symmetrical two-storey four bays with doorways at either end for the bank offices and bank agent's house. On Low Street's opposite side, the former Aberdeen Town & County Bank, *c.* 1840, is like a handsome two-storey villa with a hipped roof.

The older burghs all had major TOWN HOUSES built by the great landowners and wealthier merchants. The earliest survivor, The Jam in Rosehearty (1573), is now reduced to a shell. Its name – *jamb* – implies that it was once the wing of a larger structure, probably the palace-block of a small tower house. Banff is particularly rich in such houses but most of the early examples have gone. Much the earliest is No. 1 High Shore, dated 1675, a very 100
precious survivor – a three-storey harled L-plan with a small corner turret at its external angle marking the junction with Carmelite Street; its stair-tower is within its re-entrant angle, making it a miniature tower house in town. When first built it

seemingly stood on the outskirts of the walled burgh; its present entrance front facing High Shore was not the most important, but rather the inner angled elevation facing into its courtyard. Close to the harbour, it was possibly built by a merchant. It forms part of an attractive group, No. 3 next to it *c.* 1740 with a distinctive doorpiece probably built for Thomas Forbes the silversmith,
100 and then the Market Arms looking C17 or early C18 (*see* Hostelries above). Around the corner is Ingleneuk House, its name deriving from the massive hearth in its kitchen.

Also impressive is the row of tall houses at Nos. 1–5 High Street. No. 5, Lord Banff's town house of *c.* 1720–30, is simple vernacular classical, three-storey five-bay, its unusually narrow doorway and windows in ashlar surrounds almost a trademark of that decade. It stands slightly taller than its neighbours but is otherwise surprisingly demure for a nobleman's house. In Peterhead, Robert Arbuthnot's house dated 1730, much altered at its ground floor, is three-storey and seven bays broad but in the same simple idiom. Boyndie House, Boyndie Street, Banff, was built *c.* 1740, but seems old-fashioned because its three-storey four-bay front rises into a curvilinear gable. A more convincing sign of development is Carmelite House, Low Street, for Admiral William Gordon *c.* 1753 – vernacular classical, two-storey and five windows wide, raised slightly over a railed semi-sunk basement with stairs leading to a Gibbsian doorpiece; set well back in its garden, it might almost be a country house built in the town. The same could be said of the much grander St Brandon's, High Street (1790) which before its mid-Victorian transformation was a vernacular classical house of three storeys and basement with a broad three-window bow at the rear. In Portsoy, Soye House, Church Street, was begun in 1694 and extended in the later C18. Also surviving in the same town are two classic early C18 merchant's houses, Alexander Bremner's giant house-*cum*-warehouse of 1726 facing the Old Harbour, and Nos. 23–27 North High Street, a Dutch-gabled house of *c.* 1720–30.*

Several important baillies and provosts' houses were built *c.* 1770. In Peterhead, Baillie Ellis's House overlooking the Harbour where Broad Street meets Seagate was in direct competition with James Arbuthnot's house (now the Municipal Chambers) which stood immediately across the road at the E foot of Broad Street facing the Town Hall at the W end. The entrance front of Arbuthnot's house is two-storey and five bays in ashlar, raised over a railed basement with a Gibbsian doorway between ball-finialled gatepiers and a pedimented wall-head gable. But *c.* 1805 James's son George Arbuthnot formed a new and much smarter three-storey entrance front facing the Harbour, symmetrical with its doorway framed by three-window bows; and probably about the same time Baillie Ellis's House was remodelled into a broad three-storey four-bay pedimented frontage – although with seven bays at ground floor – also ashlar-built and with bowed returns.

*The building history of this house warrants more detailed investigation.

Another step-change in aspirations between father and son can be seen in Banff, where Provost George Robinson acquired No. 11 Boyndie Street, a three-storey vernacular house with central wall-head gable standing next to his factory, adding to it in 1772 a rear wing distinguished by a first-floor Serlian window overlooking a court. It has an impressive interior with a fine stair hall and since 1884 it has served as Banff's Town & County Club. Robinson's son George Garden Robinson, with whom he continuously alternated in the Provostship over a period of decades, seemingly built a smart new house – now the County Hotel – in 1778, following what had become a familiar pattern: a two-storey, five-bay ashlar front, raised over a semi-sunk railed basement and set back from the road in a garden; its handsome porch with doorway framed by sidelights and fanlight was added *c.* 1825, the interior representing work of both periods. Particularly fine is St Catherine's House in St Catherine Street, Banff – Greek Revival, two-storey and five bays over a basement in pale granite ashlar, with a stair leading up to a tetrastyle Doric portico; built *c.* 1830, its style suggests *Archibald Simpson*. Internally, a Doric-columned entrance hall with classical statues opens onto an imperial stair. Across Banff Bay in Macduff, No. 41 Duff Street is a neat two-storey three-bay villa with Roman Doric portico, Georgian Survival by *A. & W. Reid* of 1851; although relatively small, it is exceptional within the context of that particular town. Seafield House, Castle Street, Banff, by *Thomas Mackenzie* (1853–4), is more up-to-date, an Italianate version of the two-storey-and-basement five-bay formula with tetrastyle Doric portico which was already familiar from St Catherine's nearby.

No early Church of Scotland MANSES survive in the rural parishes; even mid-C18 examples have become the back wings of later manses if they survive at all. These mid-C18 manses were seemingly two modestly scaled storeys high and three windows wide, shallow on plan with a tall gabled roof, the attic space sometimes being augmented by a central wall-head gable. Secession manses, now best represented by Shiels (Belhelvie, 1784), were apparently similar but on a slightly smaller scale. By the early C19 Church of Scotland manses, like the better class of urban villas, had begun to be bigger in scale, deeper on plan and sometimes with basements, and were more classical in their treatment, although big gabled roofs remained common. The humbler scale of C18 manses persisted for SCHOOL HOUSES, however, reflecting the dominie's lower emoluments and social status. About 1820 a peculiarly Aberdonian type of villa came into vogue: deep-planned, single-storey-and-basement with a capacious gabled roof. Although probably adopted to economize on granite masonry, it rapidly developed considerable sophistication and was sometimes adopted for Free Church manses, farmhouses and even small country houses.

The oldest FARMHOUSES lie near the N coast. The very earliest is seemingly that forming the rear wing of Kininmonth House (New Leeds), probably built in the C17. Dipplebrae (Crimond) is dated 1735 or 1755; Lower Inchdrewer (Kirkton of Alvah) and

Mains of Melrose are early to mid C18. Among later examples, Howford (Strichen) is an early C19 Gothic *cottage orné*, and Strocherie (King Edward) is interesting for rooms added *c.* 1860 to accommodate the Earl Fife when visiting his Banffshire estates.

Of rural industry before 1840 there are a number of MILLS. Sandhaven meal mill, early C19, has been preserved as a museum. An excellent group of three textile mills remains in and around Stuartfield, the water-powered flax mill known as The Dyesters (established 1783) which is still in working order, Crichie Mill (early to mid C19) which also retains its machinery although non-operational, and Milladen begun in 1789, which remains an ongoing business concern. Strichen, another planned village, has two late C18 examples, one now the Anderson & Woodman Institute and the other the Mill of Strichen built 1791. WINDMILLS (albeit without sails) include Sandend's 'cup-and-saucer', perhaps 1761; early to mid-C19 examples survive in or near Fraserburgh, Macduff and Crovie; Hilton of Turnerhall's is very late, 1849. Banff has a large mid-C18 former BREWERY; the earliest fabric of the Glengarioch DISTILLERY at Oldmeldrum dates from *c.* 1830. There are three SALMON BOTHIES, Peterhead's rebuilt *c.* 1801, Portsoy's of 1834 and Macduff, also early C19.

Public and commercial buildings and housing c. 1840 to the present day

The Burgh Reform Act which overhauled Scottish municipal administration was passed in 1833, but twenty years would elapse before *Thomas Mackenzie*'s Fraserburgh Burgh Chambers were built in 1852–5, their Quattrocento style reminiscent of the Italian city-states although the handsome corner tower with its tall peristyle and dome is unmistakably Early Victorian. The Court Houses Act was passed in 1860 and *James Matthews*'s Court & County Buildings in Banff (1868) are also Italianate, a grand two-storey seven-bay palazzo with its centre slightly projected and a ground-floor Corinthian portico. By contrast, Peterhead Sheriff Court by *W. & J. Smith* (1869–71), superseding a grander towered scheme by *Peddie & Kinnear*, is like a simple villa; both the Banff and Peterhead buildings were partly financed by central government. In *Pirie & Clyne*'s robust Macduff Town Hall (1884–5) historical conventions are deliberately subverted: a two-storey three-bay block with bulbous first-floor oriels and central token tower, its spired turrets framing a carved gablet, and the masonry being in whinstone with stylized ashlar details. The Burgh Police (Scotland) Act passed in 1892 endowed larger communities with more extensive powers and, in marked contrast to Macduff, the Turriff Council Chambers by that town's principal architect, *William Liddle Duncan* (1907–8), are typical of the municipal architecture which it encouraged. A model of propriety, single-storey Neo-Baroque, its central pedimented doorway is framed by broad slightly projecting gabled bays with tripartite windows divided by Doric columns, all in the local red sandstone.

Macduff, Town Hall.
Engraving, 1893

Among PUBLIC HALLS, Fraserburgh's Dalrymple Hall by *Jenkins & Marr* (1881–3) is a big three-storey Baronial block with a quadrant corner and wall-head gables announcing a crenellated tower with spired corner turret, formerly serving a wide range of purposes from cultural facilities through baths to sheriff courts. The catalyst for its construction was no doubt Peterhead's Music Hall by *William Hay* of 1872 (burnt in 1936) which also included a range of cultural facilities. The Victoria Hall in Ellon, again by *Jenkins & Marr* with the Burgh Surveyor *William Davidson* (1897–1901), has a Tudor Gothic gable front with slim clock tower to one side rising into battlements: this too was a multi-purpose building with a Volunteers' armoury.

Buildings for MASONS AND GUILDS include St Andrew's Masonic Hall (now Town Hall) in Banff, a sophisticated Italianate palazzo by *Thomas Mackenzie* 1851–4. Its impressive hall with a coffered ceiling borne by six pairs of caryatids hosted the cream of society. Nearby in Braeheads, St John's Masonic Hall met the needs of practising stonemasons and tradesmen, a simple two-storey three-bay building, harled with its upper floor rising into attic gables; built in 1798, it was altered in the later C19 and again in 1914. Banff's Trades Hall in Low Street was built in 1781, but its original Palladian form is recorded only in photographs; it was remodelled into its present Neo-Baroque appearance *c.* 1900, perhaps by *Robert Gordon Wilson*.

During the mid C19, tourism prompted the building of HOTELS even before the railways reached Aberdeen. In Banff the 4th Earl Fife went to the Edinburgh practice of *Burn & Bryce* for the Fife
114 Arms, Low Street (1843–5), an exceptionally sophisticated three-storey five-bay Italianate palazzo in golden ashlar sandstone with its entrance porch framed by paired Doric columns like a London clubhouse. In marked contrast, Ellon's New Inn was reconstructed by *James Matthews* in 1853. His two-storey open courtyard scheme, suggesting an establishment built in phases, was dictated by a desire not only to retain a late C18 wing housing the burgh chambers but also to evoke the spirit of tradition and comfort which was always part of the appeal of such places. Rather less subtle was the Royal Hotel, Broad Street, Peterhead (1854), a big four-storey block with ground-floor shops and broad central pend defended by outsized battlements over its wall-head.

In Turriff High Street the mid-C19 White Heather Hotel (No. 14) is simple classical, two-storey in local red ashlar crowned with a pediment, probably by *James Duncan* who was the town's leading practitioner. With his son *William Liddle Duncan* he rebuilt a Late Georgian house as the Commercial Hotel (now Royal British Legion) in 1896–7; simultaneously the Union Hotel was being built in Main Street, while the villa-like George Temperance Hotel opened in 1906 near to the railway station. Equally villa-like was Ellon's Station Hotel of *c.* 1891–4: stations had a direct bearing on hotel provision as indeed on towns' development more generally. Fraserburgh's terminus near the Harbour encouraged the development of that end of town, including two hotels, the Royal in Broad Street being reconstructed by *William Wilson* in 1909–11.*

From the mid C19 SCHOOLS built by churches or philanthropists adopted a variety of styles, the Privy Council's Committee on Education meeting half the costs for approved schemes. St Peter's Episcopal School in Victoria Street, Fraserburgh, is a particularly good example by *William Ramage* of 1859. It has a

*Much the most magnificent hotel in northern Aberdeenshire is lost. The Cruden Bay Hotel built by the *Great North of Scotland Railway's Architect's Department* opened in 1899 to promote the coastal town as a first-rate tourist destination. Scottish Baronial, palatial in scale and the quality of its accommodation, its three-storey-and-attic centre block with tall central tower was framed between broad gabled end bays, the entrance sheltered by an awning to protect guests as they alighted from trams which brought them from the station. It was demolished in 1952; for photographs, *see* Jim Buchan, *Old Cruden Bay and Port Erroll* (2008), pp. 20, 21, 24.

Neo-Jacobean central classroom block with pairs of pointed-arch windows lighting the boys' and girls' classrooms beneath a tall gable, and mirror-image schoolmaster's and schoolmistress's villas on either side. The philanthropic Chalmers' Infants School in Banff Road, Turriff, was designed by *James Matthews c.* 1862 in a delightful villa-cottage style. Strachan's Industrial School in Fraserburgh's High Street, 1863, was very plain in rough rubble to provide a practical education for poor girls, while the simple Gothic Ramsay's School in Seafield Street, Banff, was built in 1888–9.

The Education (Scotland) Act of 1872 introduced compulsory schooling for all children between five and twelve. It provided for elected School Boards and large new ratepayer-funded schools all designed with a beady eye to cost. Although all were robustly constructed, some were much more successful than others in architectural terms. Macduff Board School, Shand Street (1872) is a simple repetitive composition of tall gabled bays, but Peterhead's North School in King Street (1877) shows a rare sense of fancy in its small-scale, lively composition with gables and tiny Germanic tower and spire like something out of a fairy story. Also very successful but much larger was St Andrew's Primary, Charlotte Street, Fraserburgh by *Matthews & Mackenzie* (1880–2), handsome Baronial, built for relatively little extra cost over a standard barrack-block. It is a two-storey courtyard building in granite ashlar, distinguished at one corner by a strong square three-storey tower which rises into a caphouse; set into one angle of the tower is a slim round turret rising into a belvedere and conical spirelet. Peterhead Central School, St Peter Street, was originally single-storey, *c.* 1838–40, but subsequently increased to two storeys in an austere classical idiom by *Arthur Clyne c.* 1905–6; Fraserburgh Academy in Finlayson Street, by *D. & J.R. McMillan* (1903–9) is a big, robust and boldly detailed version of the same barrack-like formula.

Education was reorganized under the Education Act (1918) when the county councils took over the School Boards' responsibilities. Peterhead Academy, York Street, by *J.A. Ogg Allan* (1922–4) presents a stripped classical palace front, its tall two-storey centre block with blocking course and flanking wings relying solely on good proportions and materials rather than on any applied ornament.

New MUSEUMS AND LIBRARIES were made possible by the Museums Act (1845) and Public Libraries (Scotland) Act (1854) but only the unprecedented generosity of Andrew Carnegie from the late C19 onwards made their adoption by the municipalities practical. Peterhead's Public Library & Arbuthnot Museum by *D. & J.R. McMillan* (1891–3) is a substantial two-storey Free Renaissance building with its big square corner tower rising into an octagonal clock stage and dome. Fraserburgh's Library by *William Wilson* (1904–5) is smaller two-storey Edwardian Neo-Baroque with its octagonal corner tower entered through a pedimented doorway and rising into a slim conical spire. Banff's Museum & Library is a plain palazzo by *Charles Cosser* (1902–3), while Strichen has its pretty Woodman Institute, a three-storey mill building of the C18 converted to a museum and library in 1923.

The first large HOSPITALS – and the most important public buildings outwith the towns – were the poorhouses built under the Poor Law (Scotland) Amendment Act (1845) and mental asylums built under the Lunacy (Scotland) Act (1857). These were enclosed, largely self-sufficient communities, but by no means without architectural dignity. The only poorhouse in Banff, Buchan and Formartine is *Alexander Ellis*'s Buchan Combination Poorhouse at Maud (1866–8), a long and rather attractive two-storeyed frontage of eclectic detail. Banff District Lunatic Asylum at Boyndie (1861–5) by *A. & W. Reid* is an immensely long Tudor frontage dramatically situated on a hill-side, two-storeyed over a raised basement, its boldly projecting centre block and intermediate day-room pavilions crowned by gables.

Among conventional establishments, the outstanding example
118 is Chalmers' Hospital in Banff, a Jacobean palace front by *W. L. Moffat* (*c.* 1860–6). Its two-storey centre block is distinguished by curvilinear attic gables and a peristyle cupola; its flanking bays rise into dormer gablets and its end pavilions also rise into gables and French mansard roofs. The central block of the Ugie Hospital at Peterhead, by the Burgh Surveyor *T.H. Scott* (1905–7), is of the homely 'villa' type, while Turriff by *James Duncan & Son* (1895–6) is cottagey both in scale and style.

No BANKS were built in northern Aberdeenshire for almost twenty years after 1840. The first were two very large bank houses erected in Broad Street, Peterhead, more or less opposite Simpson's North of Scotland Bank. The Union Bank of Scotland's simple Italianate three-storey building (now the Bank of Scotland) was by *William Smith*, 1858; then in 1863–5 the Commercial Bank engaged *David Rhind* to build a very handsome three-storey five-bay palazzo (now the Scottish Building Society) in which the end bays were set well back behind entrance porches, one for the bank and one for the bank agent's house. *Rhind* was the Commercial Bank's appointed architect and was almost certainly responsible for the highly impressive branch – now the police station – in Banff's High Shore, a three-storey five-bay palazzo with single-storey side wings. Its central entrance has massive scrolls supporting a balustraded balcony at first floor where console-cornices distinguish the tall windows of the bank agent's '*piano nobile*', the second-floor windows being smaller beneath a deep eaves cornice and wall-head parapet.

In Fraserburgh's Broad Street, the Aberdeen Town & County Bank (now Clydesdale Bank) by *J. R. Mackenzie*, 1875, is an early example of the austere Neoclassical which would become much more common for such buildings at the beginning of the C20. About the same time, however, the Town & County approached *James Duncan* for a modest two-storey Cinquecento palazzo (now the Scottish Building Society) with fine sculpture at the W end of Turriff High Street, while at the E end, the North of Scotland (now Clydesdale) Bank, two-storey with its crowstepped corner tower rising into a French spirelet with brattishing over the junction, was built *c.* 1873–5, probably by *James Matthews*. Matthews was the North of Scotland's preferred architect, building its branch in High Shore, Macduff as a Baronial villa with pepperpot turrets (1868). Villa-type banks continued to be built in smaller towns, including Ellon's Town and County Bank (now Bank of Scotland) in The Square 1845–7, and the North of Scotland Bank (now Clydesdale Bank) in Market Street by *Matthews & Mackenzie*, dated 1877. During the late C19 the Union Bank – which had absorbed the Aberdeen Bank – engaged in an expansion which resulted in three new branches each in a different style: Low Street, Banff, a handsome two-storey classical villa built 1891; High Shore, Macduff, two-storey and three bays with a tall central attic gable honouring Scots buildings of the mid C18; and Turriff High Street, Free Renaissance by *James Duncan & Son*, 1897–8. All are still in use as Bank of Scotland branches.

The dominance of the Neoclassical style for bank branches from the early C20 – such as *W.L. Duncan*'s Aberdeen Savings Bank in Balmellie Street, Turriff, built in the prescription grey granite ashlar *c.* 1910 – is perhaps indicative not just of shifts in architectural fashion but of a move away from resident agents to salaried managers working office hours and living elsewhere. It is very different from the Union Bank which Duncan had built only a decade earlier. He was also responsible for the Neoclassical British Linen Bank (now TSB) in Main Street, *c.* 1926, returning to alter it ten years later.

The National Commercial Bank (now Royal Bank) in Castlegate, Banff, was designed in a Scottish Renaissance idiom by *W.J. Walker Todd* with the bank's master-of-works *James McCallum* in 1937. Two storeys, it is built predominantly in golden sandstone, partly polished, partly in coursed rubble and partly harled with a black marble base course and a steep slated roof: it incorporates both contemporary sculpture and fragments from the much-altered Ogilvie house previously on the site. In an era when all bank interiors are homogenized and sanitized its telling hall with woodwork by *Scott Morton* and plasterwork by *Finnie* is a true delight.

From the mid C19 onwards TOWN HOUSES, like country houses, adopted non-classical styles. In Banff High Street, St Brandon's (*see* above) was transformed by a Baronial tower added against its front elevation in 1867, perhaps by *James Matthews*. Thereafter, however, SUBURBAN VILLAS were the norm. In 1897, having built much of Turriff as we know it, *James Duncan* purchased Hallhill House, a two-storey villa, and remodelled it for his own use. Much larger in scale is Auchtercrag in Ellon's Commercial Street, a Baronial country house with a square entrance tower standing in an urban environment, and looking *c.* 1870 although actually 1894; its owner's boot factory once stood immediately nearby. Ramornie in Craigs Road is C16–C17

Scots style akin to Robert Lorimer, but actually by *J. Girtrig Young*, 1914. Still more suburban is the Manor House in Skene Street, Macduff, English half-timbered by *A. Marshall Mackenzie*, 1905.

The Disruption of 1843 resulted in Free Church MANSES, often designed by *William* and *James Henderson*, being built in almost every parish. Most follow the simple vernacular classical of Church of Scotland manses, but a few adopted the single-storey, attic and basement model. From *c.* 1840 the heritors embarked on a programme of building bigger Church of Scotland manses or enlarging existing ones. A fine cubical example, two-storey over a raised basement with a Neoclassical doorpiece and a hipped roof, was built at Boyndie in 1841–2, perhaps by *William Robertson*, but most were in the hands of *J. & W. Smith* who built very grand English Tudor rectories for the 4th Earl of Aberdeen at Methlick (1860–1) and Tarves in 1847; *Thomas Mackenzie*'s stylish Italianate manse at Strichen, 1853, provides an attractive contrast but is basically similar on plan. The best of the later examples is the Lorimerian St Ninian's Manse, Turriff, by *W. L. Duncan*, 1924–5.

A survey of town and village buildings after *c.* 1920 need only be brief. Particularly notable among the WAR MEMORIALS are Macduff's octagonal tower (1921–2) designed by *John Fowlie* as a navigational landmark and Fraserburgh's bronze figures of Justice Guiding Valour by *Alexander Carrick*. A few buildings stand out from the interwar years, including the Male Ward
125 Buildings added to Daviot Hospital, and the swimming pool at Tarlair, Macduff. For much of the POST-WAR period the best architecture was the work of the public and charitable sectors – fine social housing and excellent schools, particularly Fraserburgh Academy in Dennyduff Road by *Alexander McGall*, 1951–62, and Banff Academy by *A. Milne Wilson*, completed in 1969, together with Peterhead's Community Leisure Centre, 1978, and
128 Peterhead Power Station, by *RMJM*, 1973–80. The work of Portsoy's Burgh Council in rehabilitating the Old Town for housing purposes also deserves special praise. Most recently, the
129 Museum of Scottish Lighthouses in Fraserburgh is a conversion by *Morris & Steedman* in 1995, while the Macduff Marine Aquarium opened in 1996.

GAZETTEER*

Places with B against their name lie in the historic county of Banffshire.

ABERCHIRDER B 6050

A planned village, still known by its original name of Foggieloan, on the road between Huntly and Banff. It was founded in 1764 by Alexander Gordon near his seat of Auchintoul (q.v.). Development was gradual but from *c.* 1800 it became a weaving centre: a factory was established but fell out of use after trade declined during the mid C19.

MARNOCH CHURCH HALL, Main Street. Built *c.* 1899 as a Church of Scotland mission hall. Simple Romanesque details.

MARNOCH NEW PARISH CHURCH, Main Street. By *James* 39
Henderson, 1841–2, built after the congregation at Marnoch (q.v.) walked out in protest at a minister imposed by the Court of Session. Handsome square classical box with finely detailed entrance tower centred against its S gable, rising in four stages from a half-octagon of polished granite ashlar to a fully octagonal belfry with an ogee-domed roof. Tall round-arched windows with lying-pane glazing. Vestry against rear gable *c.* 1900. Simple interior, its U-plan gallery with panelled front supported on cast-iron columns. – Large platform PULPIT, *c.* 1890 in dark-stained wood with approach stair and arcaded front, tall pilastered back rising into a deep cornice, dwarf arcade above. – FONT. Marble. From Westbourne Free Church, Glasgow, 1900. – STAINED GLASS. Two in the N wall. Probably early C20 – l., the Holy Family with Faith, r., the Good Shepherd with Hope. – MEMORIAL. Rev. David Hendry, the congregation's first minister. Neoclassical, with his portrait. – Outside, the WAR MEMORIAL, *c.* 1920. A tall tapering shaft of rock-faced granite with a low-relief lion rampant at its head. Pedestal carved with crossed sword and baton.

ST MARNAN (Episcopal), Main Street. Built 1824, remodelled by *Alexander Ross* in 1875–6. Entrance (N) gable has a small

*Places marked (S) have entries in the gazetteer for *Buildings of Scotland: Aberdeenshire: South and Aberdeen*.

wheel window and ogee-domed birdcage bellcote of 1824; its gabled porch with trefoil-headed windows is an addition. Three-bay flanks with two-light windows; S gable has a three-light window with timber tracery. The W organ loft was added perhaps during the remodelling, when the interior was recast. – STAINED GLASS. Above the reredos, a Crucifixion signed by *Jones & Willis*, 1896. – W wall, two-light window (St Margaret and St Marnan) by *Powells*, 1916. – E wall, two of *c.* 1920, Our Lord as Good Shepherd and as Light of the World by *W. Glasby*. – RECTORY, to S, *c.* 1868; SCHOOL, to N, of 1877, twice extended before becoming a hall in the 1940s.

Former UNITED PRESBYTERIAN CHURCH, Cornhill Road. Derelict. Built as the Secession church in 1839, but so substantially reconstructed by *Duncan McMillan* in 1892–3 as to be 'almost a new building'. E gable with original birdcage bellcote; the large depressed-arch window and entrance bay adjoining to the S are McMillan's work.

Aberchirder is laid out on a grid-plan with THE SQUARE at its centre. On its N side a broad two-storey four-bay block (now BREMNER'S) with a central attic clock gable built in fine pale ashlar is evidently early, *c.* 1770. Otherwise minor two-storey houses here and in MAIN STREET (originally Mid Street), which crosses The Square and runs for 800 m. falling W to E from the Episcopal church to the Free Church. Most houses, from the single-storey cottages to some respectable C19 villas, are built from one of the two village quarries at Causewayend and Knockorth.* SOUTH STREET was formed *c.* 1808 when John Morison of Bognie, then proprietor of Auchintoul, arranged for the new turnpike between Huntly and Banff to run immediately beneath Main Street. This with Main Street and North Street formed the grid's classic three-thoroughfare plan. The houses in South Street are along one side only. No. 23 is particularly notable: early C19 with a concave-splayed round-arched doorway and first-floor Serlian window.

JANEFIELD, 1.7 km. SW. Built *c.* 1740, perhaps for the Auchintoul Estate's factor (q.v.). Two-storey, five bays, white-harled with ashlar dressings, gabled roof with moulded skewputts and coped ashlar chimneystacks. Entrance concealed by large modern porch.

CULVIE HOUSE, 3.6 km. WNW. Vernacular, looks early to mid C18, but reputedly C17 with additions, so perhaps incorporates an earlier house. Main block long two-storey with moulded stone doorway slightly off-centre, four windows on each floor asymmetrically arranged, their slim grey margin-surrounds contrasting against the white harl. Moulded skewputts and gabled roof with coped end stacks. Low single-storey wing with tall roof on l. Rear elevation has large L-plan wing forming a courtyard, the main block with a central wall-head stack. Coped rubble walls enclose the front garden. WALLED GARDEN

*Knockorth stone is used for lintels as far afield as Banff and Buckie (qq.v.).

with C18 wrought-iron gates, and octagonal pavilion in the S wall.

AUCHINTOUL HOUSE. *See* p. 69.
CLUNIE HOUSE. *See* p. 128.
CROMBIE CASTLE. *See* p. 141.
NETHERDALE HOUSE. *See* p. 296.

ABERDOUR HOUSE

9060

2.6 km. ENE of New Aberdour

An imposing country house in the vernacular classical style, dated 1740 on its rear, and bearing the initials of Samuel Forbes and Margaret Chalmers. Quadrants link it to wings which enclose a rear court. Aberdour is the largest of the several houses of this type and date in Buchan, with the original formal layout very completely preserved.

The main block's principal front facing S over the gardens is three-storey and seven bays broad, symmetrical with its slightly projected centre bay rising into a pedimental gablet over the wall-head. A mid-C19 porch largely conceals the original pedimented doorway. Sash-and-case windows set in tooled margins against the harl: at ground floor of modest size, plate-glazed; first floor rather taller signifying the principal accommodation, with astragals; second floor with small square windows beneath an eaves cornice. Within the central bay, the first-floor window lintel has a mock acanthus key-block and moulded cornice; above, the gablet has a blind octagonal oculus, and moulded skews crowned by a ball finial; the three bays on each side of the centre are perfectly square in proportion. Small skylights for attic servants' rooms, crowstepped end gables rising into coped chimneystacks. Shallow single-pile plan, the end gables two windows broad, some dummies. Rear elevation almost wholly blind with later single-storey lean-to outshot.

The quadrants are very low single-storey with tall roofs. Rear wings near-identical: two-storey and attic, three generously spaced windows wide, harled with small windows in tooled margins, straight skews, moulded skewputts and coped chimneystacks. The E wing's ground-floor centre window was formerly a doorway; one of its stacks is unusually tall. The N side of the court, by which the house is approached, is partially enclosed by two short single-storey ranges flanking the entrance. Flanking the approach drive on either side, an outer court: on the E side, the STABLES, dated 1795; on the W, the much larger FARMSTEADING, its low tower with a pyramidal roof, built *c.* 1740, enlarged late C18 and early C19. Plain square GATEPIERS and low screen-wall to inner court.

The house enters directly into the stair hall, which has a timber stair with turned balusters and rails elegantly scrolled at the ends; the stair has probably been altered on the ground-floor l. side, where the square column supporting the first floor appears *c.* 1900. Two principal apartments on the ground floor, one with moulded cornice, the other a compartmented ceiling with gilt palmettes. On the first floor, one apartment with a Neoclassical cornice, the other with a Neoclassical patterned ceiling in papier mâché, both mid-C19. The fireplaces are replacements of different periods and styles.

WALLED GARDEN, immediately SW of the house, square with rubble walls, once divided into four compartments.

ADEN HOUSE *see* OLD DEER

ALDIE HOUSE *see* HATTON

0030 ARDALLIE

Former ARDALLIE CHURCH. Georgian Gothic Survival by *William Clarke*, 1857–8. Closed *c.* 1971. Gable-fronted, with its narrow centre slightly projecting as a token tower of diminishing stages rising into a bellcote with spirelet. Y-traceried windows. Session house, 1874.

MANSE, 1859, also by *Clarke*, but its character transformed by remodelling by *Keith Hart* since *c.* 1975, e.g. gabled porch and canted dormers. The doorway and sidelights are from the Episcopal rectory at Ellon (q.v.), and the Art Nouveau glass from an Aberdeen villa. The original porch is now at the side. Small steading with gig house.

SCHOOL and SCHOOL HOUSE by *G. & G. Marr* of Ellon, *c.* 1874, with TOTEM POLE *c.* 2005 by *Kenny Grieve* of Ladybank.

ARDGRAIN *see* ELLON

ARDLETHEN *see* ELLON

5050 ARDMEALLIE HOUSE B

0.8 km. NW of Marnoch

Vernacular classical country house built *c.* 1750. Two-storey, five windows wide with a distyle Corinthian portico, approached by a splayed railed forestair over a semi-sunk basement. Mostly of dark whinstone rubble, with basement harled, the slim window surrounds and long-and-short quoins in granite ashlar.

Modillion eaves cornice, elegant hipped bellcast roof extending into the end gables with tall ashlar stacks. The windows, with astragals in upper sashes only, are as altered by *A. Marshall Mackenzie*, who added the neat wings in 1900. These are slightly set back, a low single storey and basement, two bays broad with hipped roofs, the end stacks originally taller. Internally, a tripartite plan, with some fireplaces and plasterwork surviving; the stone turnpike stair is accommodated within a polygonal tower at the rear. A steading projecting from the E wing forms a rear court, with the COACHHOUSE to the N. The approach is by a fine tree-lined driveway some 600 m. long; the WALLED GARDEN immediately W of the house with its two-storey Gothick summerhouse is sheltered on all sides by a dense tree belt planted in the C20.

ARDO HOUSE 9020

5 km. NNW of Belhelvie

Ardo's main block was built for Peter Harvey *c.* 1850, perhaps by *J. F. Beattie* who laid out the grounds. Its entrance (S) elevation, two storeys and three windows wide, is clean-cut in granite ashlar, with plain eaves course, skews and end stacks. Its breadth and simplicity lend themselves to a Neo-Greek porch, with anta-pilasters and attached square Doric columns on the flanks, added in 1921. Against the E flank is the gable of an earlier house, built *c.* 1756 for the Dingwalls of Rannieston, also two-storey but lower, softer, in squared golden masonry; next to it again the long timber-framed greenhouse was built in 1913. Hidden behind this, a large square office courtyard, of various dates from *c.* 1756 onwards and much reconstructed for domestic use, N and W ranges two-storey, E range single-storey; the granary to the rear is a very broad gabled structure with external stair leading to a suspended loft floor. Large garden with rubble walls on two sides.

ARNAGE CASTLE 9030

4.8 km. S of Auchnagatt

A Baronial country house by *James Matthews*, 1860, for John Leith-Ross, remodelling a Z-plan tower house built in the late C16 for the Cheyne family, perhaps by *Thomas Leiper*. The site has reputedly been in occupation since 1210, so may incorporate medieval fabric.

The Z-plan TOWER HOUSE orientated roughly N–S comprised a two-storey main block 13.8 m. long by 8.8 m. wide. At ground floor it contained a passage on the E side opening onto two vaulted cellars, that at the S end possibly once a kitchen. The smaller SE jamb, 5.5 m. square, formerly contained the entrance at ground floor, its relieving arch still clearly visible in the rubble masonry with empty field-panels for heraldry above; this entrance opened onto a broad wheel stair leading up to the first floor. The NW jamb is larger at 6.8 m. by 7.5 m., its ground floor vaulted. The first floor comprised the principal apartments – in the main block, the great hall, and opening off this the laird's chamber in the NW jamb. Small stair-turrets within the angles then rose to the upper storey, the rooms in the main block rising up into the tall roof, with smaller rooms in the jambs. A unique peculiarity of Arnage is that both turnpike stairs link into smaller turrets embedded in the roofs at attic level. Leiper's authorship would appear to be confirmed by his distinctive gunloops, sometimes triplicated as at Tolquhon and Schivas (qq.v.). A courtyard which once existed on the E side of the house contained the large well which still survives. In the late C17 or C18, after Arnage had been acquired by the Forbes-Leiths, the entrance was transferred to the S end of the main block passage, the first-floor windows of the great hall were enlarged, the gable skews' appearance was simplified and a long wing was added at the N end, although at that time it was single-storey only.

In Matthews' remodelling a new ENTRANCE TOWER was built abutting the SE jamb, three storeys with a segment-headed doorway and sidelights supporting the Ross coat of arms, the corners at ground floor being rounded; at first and second floor angle-turrets rise into small fish-scale slated spirelets framing the crowstepped chimney gable. Matthews also increased the height of the Forbes-Leiths' N wing to two storeys, balancing it with a two-storey S wing, diagonal angle turret and conservatory, the upper-floor windows rising into dormer gablets. His alterations are clearly recognizable from

Arnage Castle.
Drawing by David M. Walker

their granite dressings, the earlier ones being sandstone. On the rear (W) elevation he enlarged the first-floor windows, but the small crowstepped porch towards the N end was added in 1964 by the flamboyant philanthropist *Donald Charles Stewart* (of the house-builders, *D.C. Stewart*), who purchased Arnage in the 1930s. The conically roofed tower towards the S end was added as recently as 2000 as part of a restoration begun four years earlier, which has also resulted in recreation of the great hall's fine panelling. Square WALLED GARDEN, 170 m. SSW.

ARTROCHIE *see* KIRKTON OF LOGIE-BUCHAN

AUCHINTOUL HOUSE B 6050

1.25 km. WSW of Aberchirder

A late C16 tower house extended into a courtyard U-plan, then much reconstructed by Major-Gen. Alexander Gordon, of the Imperial Russian Army, after he inherited the estate in 1711. He raised a sizeable contingent for the Jacobite cause and commanded the rebel forces at Sheriffmuir in 1715. He was attainted and went into exile, but apparently through Russian influence was allowed to return to Auchintoul in 1727.

The house's large E RANGE was rebuilt *c.* 1711–12, three storeys and four bays broad in random rubble, harled with ashlar dressings; tall ground and first floors, the second floor rising through the eaves into splayed hip-roofed dormerheads. The main roof is gabled at one end and hipped at the other, with moulded skewputts and coped ashlar chimneystacks. The E range also extends for two bays on the S side as an L-plan jamb, and within the angle on the courtyard side there is a circular C17 stair with a conical spirelet.

The S RANGE is lower and has also been much reconstructed in recent years. Its ground floor is *c.* 1711–12 with modern first-floor dormers matching those of the E range. The W RANGE survives only as foundations of the C16 tower house: its walls were immensely solid, as much as 3.5 m. thick within the basement at the SW corner, which comprises a dungeon or cellar divided into several pitch-dark compartments. The C18 superstructure which replaced the tower house was demolished after a fire in the 1970s. The N WALL with a segmental archway, giving entry to the courtyard, and the former washhouse and coal store were built during the mid C19 for William Aitken, proprietor at that time. Further alterations made by him, including a porte cochère tower on the S side, were demolished after the fire, and the fireplaces removed. Consolidation of the surviving structure began in the 1980s.

The large square WALLED GARDEN, 200 m. NNE, was reputedly laid out by *Major-Gen. Alexander Gordon*, although the granite ashlar walls with their pointed archway seem early C19. Polyhedron SUNDIAL on a square base.

COURTYARD STEADING, 300 m. NNE. Square-plan, built by John Morison of Bognie just after he purchased Auchintoul *c.* 1798. Tall two-storey ashlar pedimented centre with depressed-arch pend and pointed first-floor Gothic window, openings for attic doocot, moulded pediment with clock face and gabled bellcote. – SAWMILL, 1848, two-storey, five bays, built into rising ground. It had an overshot wheel on its N side.

SOUTH LODGE, 400 m. S., *c.* 1825. Single-storey octagon, white-harled with ashlar dressings and margins, low polyhedral roof with oversailing eaves and central chimneystack (cf. the toll house, Deveron Bridge, Turriff (q.v.)).

AUCHIRIES *see* RATHEN

9030

AUCHMACOY HOUSE

1 km. NNE of Kirkton of Logie-Buchan

85 Scots Elizabethan by *William Burn*, 1831, for James Buchan, completed by *John Smith I*, 1833, and the precursor of Smith's own houses in that style.

Auchmacoy is a finely judged balance between joyous movement and stately composure across consistently two-storey frontages, its square-based plan carefully meeting the needs of social entertaining on a grand scale and the private needs of a family. Its entrance elevation, facing W, is asymmetric but clearly structured: it steps down progressively from a tall broad gable with a canted bay at its S end, through a smaller Dutch entrance gable and pencil tower with conical roof, to two lower bays with dormers on the N. While attention focuses on the doorway with its stepped armorial hoodmould, the uniform quality of detail with mullioned and transomed windows, ball-finialled parapets, spike finials and diagonally shafted chimneystacks ensures coherence throughout its length.

The S front to the garden is five-bay symmetrical with the classic Burn arrangement of drawing room, library and dining room laid out *en filade*, the library lit by a canted bay beneath a projected central gable. The family apartments were at the NW and provided with a bathroom, and the service area was on the N side, laid out around a court, and extending into a wing at the NE which provided further accommodation for family use, probably the nursery. At the centre of the house is a spacious hall-staircase, lit by a big four-light window. The details are Neo-Grec: one room has original oak graining, now a rare survival of a treatment once common in Burn houses (cf. Brodie Castle, Moray, q.v.). Fine chimneypieces, some perhaps reused from the earlier classical house of which part survives nearby.

ESTATE OFFICE, 100 m. NE, incorporating the remains of the Old House of Auchmacoy, built 1722 (*see* p. 37). – DOOCOT, 0.6 km. NNW. Dated 1638, remodelled from a C16 'beehive' type; a tapered drum of pinned split boulder rubble with double rat courses, which corbels to the square beneath a crowstep-gabled caphouse. – MAUSOLEUM, 300 km. SSE. Tudor style, in stugged ashlar. For Thomas Buchan †1866.

AUCHNAGATT 9040

A small village, once part of the Haddo Estate, on the junction where the road from Ellon divides for Old Deer and New Deer (qq.v.). Within the junction, on the Ebrie Burn's W bank, the Formartine & Buchan Railway built a STATION *c.* 1861 serving a then densely populated agricultural hinterland. This resulted in a string of simple villas and a post office along the New Deer Road; the cottages on the junction itself were originally a CORN MILL. The former BARON'S INN on the Old Deer road is by *Jenkins & Marr* *c.* 1880, two storeys and three bays in rust-tinted granite with darker pinnings, and silver-grey dressings and margins. Development on the Old Deer road only began in earnest however in the mid C20. The SCHOOL by *A. Buchanan Gardner* was designed in 1952; the semi-detached cottages in MITCHELL PLACE with polychrome entrance recesses suggest the lingering influence of the pre-war years. The PUBLIC HALL is the former East Independent Church, Stuartfield (q.v.), originally built *c.* 1892, transported here and much altered since.

Former SAVOCH CHAPEL OF EASE, 1.8 km. S. Preaching-box of 1834, in squared and pinned blue whinstone with granite dressings. Four round-headed windows in its S flank, two in its N. The original W gable is concealed by the hall built out in front of it by *William Clarke* in 1897, the hall's Gothick gable-front now facing nearest the road. The hall replaced a predecessor of 1881–3, also the date when the E gable's birdcage bellcote was erected. The small N outshot is later but before 1900. S organ chamber by *James Cobban*, architect of the Haddo Estate, 1906. – U-plan gallery of 1834 with panelled fronts, mounted on cast-iron columns, but the church was 'extensively renovated' in 1897. Pews are probably of this date but the PLATFORM PULPIT on the S side in front of the arched organ recess may be either 1897 or 1906. All other furnishings have gone, and only the organ pipes are left. – STAINED GLASS. Three of 1897, all non-figurative, with the rich subtle colouring distinctive of their period: on either side of the pulpit, 'I am the Vine, Ye are the Branches', donated, despite the Haddo connection, by Mrs Udny of Udny, and 'Lo I am with You

Always Even to the End of the World', with palm leaves. In the E gable, 'I am the Good Shepherd', with motifs of Cross and Crown, and Lamp for the Holy Spirit. – Terraced CHURCHYARD formed 1877. – WAR MEMORIAL of 1920, a simple tall and handsome obelisk.

Former INKHORN SECESSION CHURCH, 2.4 km. SSW. Dated 1828. Two bays, rubble-built with dressings and margins, tall round-headed windows with replacement basket-tracery glazing. E gable with ground-floor windows and round-arched light, perhaps for a gallery. Manse built against length of W gable, single-storey with attic, three windows wide.

ARNAGE CASTLE. *See* p. 67.

7040

AUCHTERLESS

A church was reputedly founded at Auchterless by St Donan in the late C6; his miraculous staff was preserved here until the Reformation. 'Ocktirles' first appears in documents in 1157; an independent barony granted direct from the Crown, with a motte-and-bailey castle of which the motte still survives, Auchterless was held by the Dempsters from at least the mid C13 to the C17.

AUCHTERLESS PARISH CHURCH. Plans by *John Smith II* of *J. & W. Smith*, 1876, built by *A. Fordyce & Son*, masons, in 1877–9. Tower and spire by *A. H. L. Mackinnon*, 1894–9. Early Gothic, impressive in scale for a rural community. Entrance front strongly vertical, the gabled centre with twin doorways boldly stepped forward to suggest a tall slim nave, flanked S by the tower and N by the polygonal porch with prismatic roof. Behind, the main roof sweeps down steeply over the full breadth of the church, with slightly lower transepts at the E end. Mostly in squared red rubble, coursed and pinned, with ashlar dressings. Plate-traceried triple-light W window, but with a cusped-traceried rose, a hybrid arrangement; cruciform finial over the apex. Three-stage tower with angle buttresses, louvred belfry openings and stone octagonal spire, flanked by clock-face gablets and angle pinnacles, with dummy lucarnes and banded decoration just beneath the weathervane. Lancets in the flanks, the transepts with cusped circular windows, and the E window with mincer plate tracery. – Fine dark-stained hammerbeam roof, supported on slim cast-iron columns where it crosses the transepts. Deep W gallery with panelled front extends over the entrance vestibule and the inner hall formed in more recent times. – Raised and canopied PULPIT, in front of the fine ORGAN by *Wadsworth Bros* of 1904, with decorated pipes (rebuilt by *Robert Smith* of Cleish, 1974). – SCULPTURED FRAGMENTS. A grotesque head, and sundial, presumably from the Old Church (*see* below). – STAINED GLASS. Two in the transepts, by *James Garvie & Sons*, 1904 and 1906. Brilliantly coloured, very much of their period, and good quality, both taking as their theme Christ and the Family.

ST DONAN'S OLD PARISH CHURCH, 70 m. NE. Built after 1560. By 1780 it was ruinous and it was probably substantially rebuilt on a wider plan shortly afterwards. New aisle 1835, ruined again now. W gable's C17 finialled birdcage bellcote survives intact although much overgrown; its bell is by *Peter Jansen*, 1644. – WALL MONUMENTS mostly to Duffs of Hatton (q.v.). DUFF MAUSOLEUM, probably 1877, but incorporating earlier fabric. Small rectangular structure, built in rubble formerly harled, with slim door and window margins and big roughly dressed quoins. Tall central blocking course displaying coat of arms, low gabled roof with funereal urns, some of them reused.

WAR MEMORIAL. By *W.L. Duncan* and *Garden & Co.*, 1920. Rock-faced Kemnay granite obelisk.

Former FREE CHURCH, 0.8 km. SSW, 1862. Artisan Gothic with Y-tracery and a classical gable bellcote. Gutted. STAINED GLASS. Two small windows by *Edward Copland* of Aberdeen, 1898.

MANSE, opposite the parish church. By *A. & W. Reid*, 1862–4. Large two-storey villa with L-plan frontage, r. bay gabled and slightly stepped forward. Cream-harled with dressed work in red ashlar freestone. Central doorpiece has scrolled cresting; ground-floor bay windows front and flank, with first-floor windows breaking into dormer gablets.

HATTON MANOR, 0.6 km. W. A very early country house, begun in 1694, one of a group also including Birkenbog House (q.v.). Subsequently altered and extended in the mid C18. The N range, harled with dark red ashlar dressings, is the oldest part (dated skewputts). Its entrance (S) front has relatively few and small ground-floor windows; the first floor may have been heightened when the house was enlarged. As built it was probably semi-symmetrical, six bays broad with a central doorway before the two r. bays were obscured by the later E range. The W end of the roof is gabled with moulded skewputts, one on the entrance front initialled W.M. Almost blind rear elevation with semicircular stair off-centre. Single-pile plan, the bolection-moulded fireplaces and some early panelling and window shutters (either original or mid-C18) have survived. There was a W range of offices, forming a forecourt from the beginning, but its ruins were demolished in the early C20. The mid-C19 E range survives. It presents a four-window frontage to the court, with ground-floor windows again smaller than first, but its main elevation is its external, i.e., E front. This new entrance front is two-storey and seven bays broad, harled with sandstone dressings, its later date immediately evident in tall ground-floor windows similar in height to the first floor; it is however asymmetrical, the fifth bay blind because of an internal wall which contains the fireplace chimney flues, and the present doorway is off-centre, with the scar of a later porch. It is single-pile, the roof hipped at its N end where it joins the original range, and gabled at its S end where an oval oculus lights the attic, the skewputts being roll-moulded and the chimneystacks coped. – WALLED GARDEN on the N side.

KNOCKLEITH HOUSE, 1.2 km. SSW. 1864, probably by *A. & W. Reid* who designed Cobairdy (S) in the same relaxed Italianate style which had come into vogue some thirty years earlier. Entrance front two storeys and five bays facing S with off-centre round-arched porch, ground-floor windows tall and slim with low ashlar aprons and elegant glazing, small near-square windows on bedroom floor above. E flank four-bay symmetrical with the centre bays slightly projected under a gable, its main feature a semicircular bay window with prismatic roof; absolutely regular four-bay N front. Cream-harled, with flush quoins and thin margins in red freestone, low hipped roofs with oversailing eaves, coped chimney-stacks. W front containing service accommodation is smaller, almost cottage-scale, and may be partly earlier. Simple interior.

6040 AULDTOWN OF NETHERDALE B

1.25 km. NE of Inverkeithny

An Italianate villa by *A. & W. Reid* for Miss Rose-Innes, 1853, similar in concept to nearby Clunie House (q.v.). Entrance front single-storey, five bays broad with Doric pedimented portico distyle-*in-antis* approached across a railed basement area. Very tall ground-floor windows resting on apron panels above an ashlar band course, the walls otherwise harled, slim cornice with consoles at each corner and long low hipped roof with oversailing eaves. Deep three-bay flanks with slightly projected centres: in the basement area, a small service court on one side. Fall in the ground exposes basement at the rear. Interior with central hall lit from above through a coved ceiling. COACHHOUSE immediately W, three bays with two coach openings and small loft windows above. STEADING, 170 m. W. A long ten-bay range, perhaps extended, with off-centre tower containing ground-floor pend, first-floor Venetian window and doocot in the gable.

0030 AUQUHARNEY HOUSE

2.5 km. WNW of Hatton

Simple classical, style of *John Smith I*, *c.* 1840. Entrance (S) elevation two-storey, three windows wide in coursed granite with anta-pilastered porch in polished ashlar. Oversailing roof, low coped chimneystacks. Gables three windows deep but mostly blind. Small two-storey wing set back on E with ground-floor bay window. – LODGE of *c.* 1875. Porch set diagonally in the angle between its two wings, forming an attractive flourish of broad-eaved gables towards the drive.

BALMEDIE 9010

The estate village of Balmedie House, a place of modest consequence until the oil boom, when its proximity to Aberdeen on the A90 and ready access to the Sands of Forvie resulted in its development as a commuter village.

BALMEDIE HOUSE (Eventide Home). A Scottish Baronial country house for W.H. Lumsden, dated 1878, perhaps by *C. Kinnear* of *Peddie & Kinnear*, but incorporating a Regency house. Entrance elevation, facing W, comprises a strong square tower of four storeys with porte cochère and an angle tourelle at the far l. end, the main two-storey four-bay frontage being slightly set back and rising into paired central crowstepped gables. The porte cochère in ashlar masonry is boldly detailed: banded pilasters framing its shouldered openings rise into obelisks on either side of Lumsden's coat of arms. The tourelle rises from within the angle between the tower and the main frontage on deep corbelling and breaks above the tower's crenellated and bartizaned wall-head parapet into a fish-scale slated spirelet. The S front overlooking the gardens is two-storey over a raised basement, the ground level falling on this side; a single broad crowstep-gabled bay at one end is balanced by smaller paired crowstepped bays at the other, with ball-finialled canted bays introducing additional variety. On the N side, the service court with its own small clock tower. Attractive golden brown granite throughout. – Rich oak staircase with twisted balusters and panelled posts crowned by decorative finials; good ceilings in the drawing rooms, including a marble chimneypiece from the previous house. Dining room with panelled and arcaded dado, bold fireplace with baluster columns and arcaded overmantel, finely carved doorcases and compartmented ceiling with fretwork panels. Some Aesthetic Movement leaded and coloured lights in both the principal apartments and the porch.

BANFF B 6060

Standing on the Deveron's W bank where it discharges into the Moray Firth, with two natural havens and close to a ford which placed it on the main medieval route linking Aberdeen with Elgin (q.v.) and Inverness, Banff was created a royal burgh at the end of the C12, and the county town of a prosperous agricultural hinterland surrounded by the royal forest of Boyne. Banff Castle was probably established at the N end of the High Street sometime between the C11 and C13, a Carmelite friary was founded by King Alexander II in the late C13 and the Knights Templar also held property here. Banff prospered through North Sea trade in the later Middle Ages, and markets moved to Low Street where a tolbooth was erected. A burgh council is first recorded in 1541, controlling the town with the Guildry and the Six Incorporated Trades, but by the Reformation the Carmelite friary had fallen into terminal decline and it sold its lands mostly to Sir Walter Ogilvie of Dunlugas and his son Sir George Ogilvie of Castletoun. Banff's first manmade harbour was seemingly formed in Guthrie's Haven in 1625. During the Civil Wars the George Ogilvie of that time supported King Charles I and his fine Lodging in Low Street (built 1538) was destroyed by Gen. Munro in 1640, but the King recognized Ogilvie's loyalty and created him Lord Banff in 1642.

It was during the mid C18, however, that Banff really came into its own. William Duff, 1st Lord Braco, built Duff House (*see* p. 94) to designs by *William Adam* in 1735–40. From 1737 a military garrison was stationed in Banff to protect the seaport from French incursions and after the 'Forty-five to quell any further Jacobite uprisings. Although often an uncomfortable presence, nevertheless the garrison transformed the town. From the mid 1740s the value of trade began to increase exponentially, led by the Robinson family who were textile manufacturers and shipowners, George Robinson Sen. as provost driving through many civic improvements during the later C18. In 1750 High Street was linked to the Seatown by the formation of Castle Street and the present Banff Castle, a classical town house, was completed by James Ogilvie, Lord Deskford, to designs by *John Adam c.* 1749–52; from 1762 the burgh council developed the Seatown to promote the growth of the fishing community. The first military bridge over the Deveron built in 1763–5 collapsed in 1768, but Bridge Street was formed as a new entry to the town in 1769. Markets were transferred to the shoreline shortly afterwards, and the present bridge designed by *John Smeaton* was completed in 1779; Banff was connected to the turnpike system in the early C19. *Smeaton* also rebuilt the harbour in 1770–5, then a brief foray into whaling and the herring industry's rapid development from *c.* 1815 encouraged the harbour's further enlargement by *Thomas Telford* in 1818–28. In 1826 ambitious proposals were put forward to double the burgh's size by developing a large New Town on a grid-plan over Lord Findlater's lands to the W, but these came to nought.

The Banff, Portsoy & Strathisla Railway opened in 1859, and the Banff, Macduff & Turriff Railway reached the opposite end of Banff Bridge in 1860. The transformation of land communications had a profound effect on the harbour, but a still more

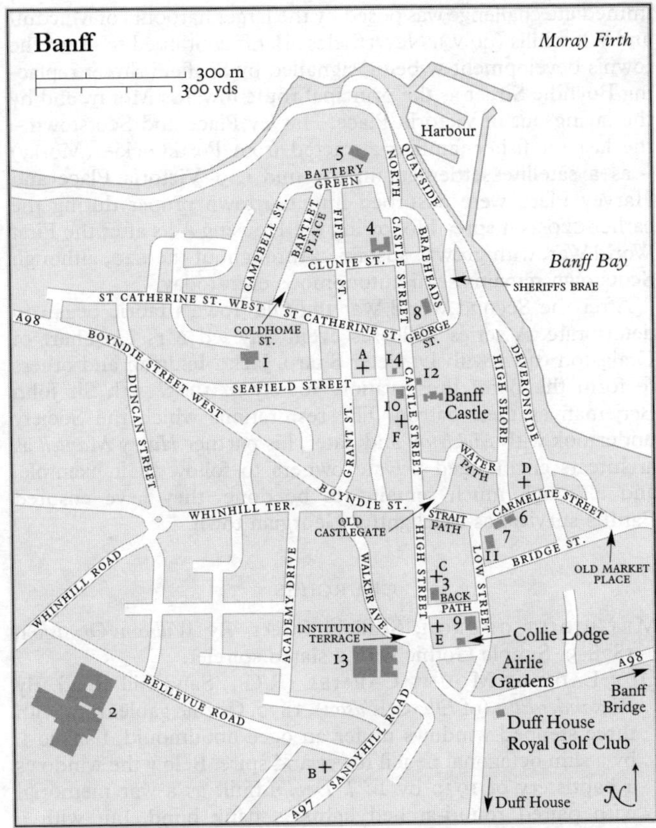

A Methodist Church
B Our Lady of Mount Carmel (R.C.)
C St Andrew (Episcopal)
D St Mary's Old Church
E St Mary
F Harvest Centre (former Free Church)

1 Former Adam Ramsay School (Nursery)
2 Banff Academy
3 Banff Museum and Library
4 Chalmers' Hospital
5 Coastguard Station
6 Old Police Station
7 Post Office (former)
8 St John's Masonic Hall
9 Sheriff Court
10 Town Hall (St Andrew's Masonic Hall)
11 Town House
12 War Memorial
13 Wilson's Institution (Banff Primary School)
14 Y.M.C.A.

immediate challenge was posed by the larger harbours of Macduff and Whitehills (qq.v.). Nevertheless Banff continued to grow, the town's development W being signalled by Seafield Street replacing Boyndie Street as the principal route towards Moray, and by the laying-out of Victoria Place, Harvey Place and Scotstown – the last for fisher-families attracted from Portknockie (Moray) – as a satellite settlement in the mid C19. Victoria Place and Harvey Place were absorbed into the town proper during the earlier C20 as it spread following the Housing Acts after the First World War, with growth sustained throughout the C20, although Scotstown remains semi-autonomous even today.

After the Second World War the Old Town's fabric began to deteriorate. A series of losses eventually led Mrs Urquhart of Craigston (q.v.) with Dr Peter Sharp, Jack Meldrum and others to form the Banff Preservation Society in 1965, with Sir John Betjeman as their patron. The restorations which the Society undertook with *Meldrum* and, later, his partner *Harry Mantell* as architects encouraged private owners to follow their example, and although much remains to be done, they have ensured Banff's survival as a delightful Georgian town.

CHURCHES

METHODIST CHURCH, Seafield Street. By *William Ormiston*, 1878–9. Simple Gothic with a slated spirelet.

OUR LADY OF MOUNT CARMEL (R.C.), Sandyhill Road. By *Alexander Ellis* (of *Ellis & Wilson*), 1870. Gothic gable front with three stepped windows under an ogee hoodmould, flanked l. by a slim octagonal pencil tower and spire. Below the windows a baptistery of 1920 by *W. J. Devlin* built as a war memorial with paired round-arched lights. S flank blind, but with a gabled porch; in the N flank, three paired lights. Simple nave interior, with a small gallery above the entrance lobby (now converted to an ante-chapel) and a rib-vaulted ceiling, quite unusual in style. – HIGH ALTAR. Of purple and white Italian marble, green marble from Greece and red marble from Belgium. Elaborate Gothic oak REREDOS, Flemish, with four carved angels, 1914. – Raised oak PULPIT with canted front and Gothic panelling. – Modern LECTERN, CANDLESTICKS and CHAIRS, all with good low-relief carving. – Adjoining PRESBYTERY, also 1870, with *Ellis*'s monogram. Its canted l. bay rises into a spirelet, and there are some idiosyncratic details.

ST ANDREW (Episcopal), High Street. By *Archibald Simpson*, 1833–4. Dec W front with pointed doorway and three-light curvilinear traceried window framed between giant octagonal buttresses which rise into crocketed pinnacles, all in pale ashlar sandstone. Behind it, a slightly broader nave, harled four-bay flanks with pointed windows. Chancel added 1913–14 (with original E window re-set), built over a large basement hall within the fall of the ground. The church was seriously damaged but restored after a fire in 1951–2. Internally, the nave has a W gallery and a panelled ceiling; its dark woodwork contributes to a rich, slightly subdued atmosphere. – REREDOS. Pale marble, triple-arched and gabled, with dwarf columns in darker material. – Octagonal pedestal PULPIT in oak with panelled sides. – FONT, beneath the W gallery. An octagonal basin nicely carved and lettered. – ORGAN by *Forster & Andrews*, 1871, rebuilt by *Andrew Watt & Son* and again by *Henry Hilsdon*, has pipes facing into both the nave and chancel. – STAINED GLASS. Richly coloured full-length figures of saints – S wall, St Matthias with an axe (1884) by *W.G. Boss*; then St Paul with book and sword (1875) and St Andrew with his Cross (1881), both by *James Ballantine*. – N wall, St Luke (1895) by *Alexander Ballantine*. – In the chancel, a triple-light Transfiguration window of SS Peter, James and John, again by *James Ballantine*, 1876.

The RECTORY is by *A. & W. Reid*, 1853. Tudor Gothic perfectly answering the church. Incorporated within its walls a carved stone representing a crowned hammer – a symbol of the Hammermen, one of Banff's Six Incorporated Trades.

ST MARY'S OLD CHURCH, High Shore.* The core of the medieval church was an extended rectangle, said to have been rebuilt in 1471 when Sir James Ogilvy of Deskford was the burgh's provost. It was abandoned after construction of the new church in 1789–90 (*see* below), and largely dismantled in 1797. A view by the Rev. Charles Cordiner, when much of the shell remained, shows the S flank with a sequence from W to E of a canopied tomb, a crowstepped porch and the Ogilvie Aisle near the mid-point. (Was the canopied tomb that of Provost Baird of Auchmedden †1663, which was removed to the Duff House mausoleum *c.* 1790 as part of the 2nd Earl Fife's quest for ancestors?) The OGILVIE AISLE remains in place; it contains an inscription stating that it was built in 1580 by Sir George Ogilvie of Dunlugas, ancestor of the Lords Banff, for his parents, Walter and Alison. Like the medieval chaplainry chapels that provided a model for many post-Reformation laird's aisles, it projected laterally from the church flank, opening into the church through a wide arch, and there are reminiscences of medieval prototypes – such as that at Arbuthnott (S) – in its polygonal apsidal plan. It has a three-sided crowstepped S gable, a pointed S window with a grid of two mullions and two transoms, and a round-arched doorway with a pair of continuous roll mouldings in its SW face. The arch into the church is framed by a triplet of roll mouldings and the aisle is covered by a barrel-vault, with a ridge rib and boss with the royal arms. Restored by the 8th Lord Banff (†1803), and again by *Mantell Ritchie* in 2001–3. Inside, below the S window, the MONUMENT for Alison and Walter Ogilvie (†1557 and 1558), dated 1577, and therefore presumably relocated to the aisle in 1580. The tomb-chest has an arcade of ogee arches, below an arched recess with an inscription to

*This entry has been contributed by Richard Fawcett.

the rear. The recess is framed by a round arch with paired filleted rolls, and flanked by triple-rolled shafts with mid-height shaft-rings and shields on their upper parts. Within the spandrels below the cornice are shields with the initials of those commemorated.

CHURCHYARD. A busy and unusually interesting concentration of enclosures, headstones and a strikingly high concentration of TABLE TOMBS. The CANOPIED TOMB of the Bairds of Auchmedden, dated 1636, survives in a retained fragment of the N chancel wall. It is a conservative design looking back to medieval prototypes, with an armoured effigy resting its head on a pillow and its feet on a lion. The chest is decorated with three panels of *memento mori*. The ogee-shaped canopy, which rises from dies flanking the chest, is framed by a ribbon-like moulding decorated with relief lozenges and ovals. Within the canopy a rectangular inscription is set within a strapwork cartouche. The apex of the canopy is flanked by volutes and surmounted by a large oval heraldic cartouche.

In the SE corner is a large Corinthian aedicular MEMORIAL capped by a shaped pediment with ball finials, framing an ogee-headed tablet flanked by obelisks; a high-relief skeleton is carved on the plinth. The inscription is now indecipherable, but among those commemorated are said to be Janet Abercromby, wife of Robert Sharp (†1667). There are re-set gablets to the rear; a later enclosing balustrade is composed of openwork intersecting circles. – N of the church, Admiral William Gordon †1769; a rectangular base with an inset panel decorated with naval trophies, supporting a large pyramid with inscribed tablet (re-cut 2006). – S of the church, John Mclean (†1738) and Jane Beaton (†1758), a pedimented headstone showing a death-bed flanked by angels, with *memento mori*. – CHURCHYARD WALL. 1772. Above the gate a re-set heraldic gablet commemorates Janet Abercromby (†1667). To the r. of the gate a heraldic tablet commemorates Dr Alexander Douglas, dated 1658.

34 ST MARY, High Street. A 'Muckle Kirk', designed by *Andrew Wilson* of Banff but not built until 1789–90, the plans based, as requested by the heritors, on St Andrew's Parish Church, Dundee. The outstanding feature is the W entrance tower, four stages and 40 m. high in golden ashlar. Wilson's design for it was left incomplete above the second stage in 1790, the Episcopalian heritors demurring to pay for its completion. Giant order Roman Doric pilasters frame the round-headed arches which span across the pavement; at second stage the round-arched windows have basket-weave glazing bars, with a triglyph frieze and Diocletian openings above. The Gibbsian upper stages and fine spire pierced by oculi were redesigned by *William Robertson* in 1829–30 and executed by his former assistant, *Thomas Mackenzie* (of *Mackenzie & Matthews*) in 1849. The nave itself is 15.3 m. wide and very tall, its cream-harled walls with slim ashlar dressings and margins. The three arched two-light windows on the S flank date from a

refurnishing of 1877 by *Ellis & Wilson*: Andrew Wilson's original elevation had two very tall arched windows flanking a central roundel. The interior was reordered and refurnished again in 1927–8 when, through the generosity of the Misses Martin of St Catherine's House (*see* p. 93), the original S-facing U-plan gallery was stripped out and the pulpit was transferred to the E end, *Waddell & Young* building an apsidal chancel and organ chamber. The large SESSION HALL, also given by the Martins, is by *George Bennett Mitchell & Son*, 1937–9.

The chancel has a sumptuous marble floor and high-backed SEDILIA, PULPIT, COMMUNION TABLE, FONT and LECTERN all of 1927–8 and lavishly classical. – ORGAN. Rebuilt 1928 by *Henry Hilsdon*. – STAINED GLASS. S wall centre, 1877 by *James Ballantine & Son*. The Good Sower and Angels gathering up sheaves with their sickles. – Three early C20 windows in late Pre-Raphaelite style: the Good Shepherd, the Risen Christ and Faith as a young woman carrying a Cross of Gold. Another of Hope, 1929, by *St Enoch Stained Glass Works*. – Apse windows. Given by the Martins in 1927–8. Scenes from the Life of Christ by the *Stephen Adam Studio*, reusing cartoons by *Alfred Webster* (†1915). – MONUMENTS. S wall. Fine Neoclassical white marble TABLET for Lt Peter Lawtie, killed in Nepal in 1815. – John Cruickshank, long-serving Rector of Banff Academy, erected 1834, with a boy mourning by an urn. – Under the gallery, Dr Henry Milne, general practitioner and surgeon, †1887. Gothic aedicule with handsome bas-relief medallion portrait.

HARVEST CENTRE (Riverside Christian Church), Castle Street. Built as the Free Church in 1843–4 to designs by *James & Robert Raeburn*, and unusually grand for so soon after the Disruption. A classical five-bay front with giant Ionic distyle-*in-antis* portico between single-bay ends, the portico's entablature with pediment and clock-dial oculus bearing the base of a small circular tower. Within the portico, three tall round-arched doorways, and niches in the flanks. Smaller windows almost square at gallery level. The low tower rises from its plinth in three stages, two pilastered drums – the upper drum with a blind arcade – then the taller belfry with louvred openings again framed between pilasters, and the ogee dome crowned by a peristyle. Originally a shallow Greek cross plan, the transepts were altered by *Ellis & Wilson* in 1875–7 to increase capacity, with three segment-headed windows at ground floor and gallery level. – CHURCH HALL AND SCHOOL by *A. & W. Reid*, 1845. Like a small classical villa, its centre slightly projected under a pedimental gable with a bellcote. Former MANSE, also by the *Reids*, 1845; canted bay windows added later.

BANFF CASTLE

Castle Street

A vernacular classical house of *c.* 1749–52, built for James Ogilvie, Lord Deskford, son of the 6th Earl of Findlater, to designs of

John Adam. It stands on the site of the medieval castle, thought to have been established between the C11 and C13, and is still enclosed by the remains of its enceinte walls.

The MAIN BLOCK entrance front, facing S, is three-storey and five bays broad with the windows of its *piano nobile* much taller than those at ground floor and second floor. It is harled in bright yellow with a tall bellcast roof punctuated by tall coped chimneystacks, and flanked by pavilions.* The ground floor entrance is concealed by a porch, with ball finials, added *c*. 1890. Two-bay flanks. The rear elevation is lit by small windows in an irregular layout; it has a two-storey wing of *c*. 1820 with an oriel in its E elevation, together with other later and smaller outshots. Inside, the entrance hall leads to a cantilevered scale-and-platt stair, now infilled at ground floor. One of the ground-floor rooms contains a carved timber fireplace with Dutch tiles; then at first floor two more fireplaces, one painted white with elaborate supporting scrolls, a central mask and deeply moulded overmantel, its threshold tiled to look like Roman mosaic; the other in stone with ribbed and shaped jambs, a female mask and foliate carving. Throughout the house the original woodwork and plasterwork has survived.

The PAVILIONS present an initial appearance of near-symmetry, square on plan, again harled in yellow, with ground and low first floors beneath pyramid roofs, and set at a little distance from the main block on each side. Within the rear court, however, enclosed by the enceinte walls of the old castle, the service ranges extend back in a less regular fashion: on the W side, what appear to be the erstwhile stables. The ENCEINTE WALLS themselves perhaps of the mid C13 and later survive on the N side and partly on the E and W sides: they stand some 3.2 m. high, the roll-moulding of a sally-port in the N wall suggesting alterations in the C16. Behind the house, part of the DRY MOAT and RAMPARTS survived Adam's re-landscaping of the grounds. In front of the entrance porch is the CASTLE WELL, a circular enclosure with low walls and columns supporting an ogee-domed roof, by *W. L. Duncan*, 1926. – Adam's LODGES are both two-storey, square and harled in yellow with hipped roofs. Both have round-arched recesses to the street but the windows in the N lodge are seemingly mid- to late C19. Behind the N lodge, and attached to it by a short link bay, a mid- to late C19 PAVILION, also hip-roofed. Ashlar GATEPIERS with low pyramidal copes and lanterns; the GATES themselves used to open onto the *clair-voyée* approach to Duff House, flanked by the pavilions at the W end of Banff Bridge (*see* below, p. 86).

*It is notably similar to Moffat House, Dumfriesshire, designed by Adam for the 2nd Earl of Hopetoun in 1762–7, even down to its first-floor band course.

Banff, Chalmers' Hospital.
Engraving, 1862

PUBLIC BUILDINGS

Former ADAM RAMSAY SCHOOL, Seafield Street. Now a nursery. 1888–9. Simple Gothic single-storey T-plan. Separate porches for boys and girls.

BANFF ACADEMY, Bellevue Road. The first purpose-built comprehensive school in the north of Scotland; *A. Milne Wilson*, Banffshire County Architect, completed 1969. The main block is a simple but well-executed cuboid form, four storeys, the long flank elevations a grid of glass contrasting with bright red and blue enamelled panels, with the stair bays expressed by continuous glazing; the solid ends are rendered in pale grey and a rich pinky-brown. The SE end is linked to a dining hall/gymnasium block on the S and a two-storey courtyard block of classrooms on the N. SWIMMING POOL of similar date on Whinhill Road junction.

BANFF MUSEUM & LIBRARY, High Street. By *Charles Cosser*, 1902–3. A very simple two-storey five-bay palazzo.*

BANFF PRIMARY SCHOOL, Academy Drive. *See* Wilson's Institution.

CHALMERS' HOSPITAL, Clunie Street. Built with a bequest granted by the merchant and shipowner Alexander Chalmers of Clunie (q.v.); by *W.L. Moffat*, *c.* 1860–6. Predominantly Neo-Jacobean, a large and impressive symmetrical design, constructed in local dark whinstone with contrastingly lighter dressings. Central block two storeys and three bays broad with depressed-arch entrance, mullioned and transomed windows, curvilinear attic gables and arcaded peristyle cupola with ogee roof; this is flanked by two-storey four-bay ward-blocks with 118

*It stands on the site of Lord Banff's Lodging known as 'The Turrets', for an illustration of which *see* David MacGibbon and Thomas Ross, *The Castellated and Domestic Architecture of Scotland* (1887–92).

triangular wall-head gablets and projecting end-pavilions with brattished French roofs, again with curvilinear gables and also once with peristyles. The flank elevations enclose a rear court. The new hospital is of 2008–12 by *Robertson Construction (Northern) Ltd.**

COASTGUARD STATION, Battery Green. *c.* 1882. Long two-storey with projecting gabled bay at its far r. end.

DUFF HOUSE ROYAL GOLF CLUB. Opened 1909 on land gifted by the Duke of Fife: the present eighteen-hole course was set out by the leading golf architects *A. & C. J. MacKenzie* in 1923–4. CLUBHOUSE mostly 1971–4.

OLD POLICE STATION, Carmelite Street. Mid-C19 classical, probably by *A. & W. Reid* of Elgin. Two-storey, five-bay frontage in granite ashlar with a sixth bay on the l. slightly set back. Round-headed central doorway and slightly broader windows each side, the outermost bays at ground floor are segmentally arched, with the one on the r. a pend. Above a gateway on its l., a re-set HERALDIC PLAQUE dated 1675 from the previous building on the site, known as Saunders' Heritage, with initials of John Gordon and Janet Saunders.

POLICE STATION, High Shore. *See* Description, former Commercial Bank.

Former POST OFFICE, Carmelite Street. By *W. T. Oldrieve* of *H.M. Office of Works*, 1906. Edwardian Baroque. Single-storey asymmetric in granite ashlar. Central doorway, its stylized console-cornice with Art Nouveau-influenced details. The broad r. bay is slightly projected with a Doric columnar tripartite window, cartouche and pedimental gable.

PUMPING STATION, High Shore. By *Douglas Forrest* of *Acanthus Architects df.* Paired gable front in random rubble, harled circular tower adjoining, its glazed clearstorey rising into an ogee dome.

ST JOHN'S MASONIC HALL (Lodge St John Operative No. 92), Braeheads. Originally a single-storey rubble structure of 1798, raised to two storeys in the late C19 with further alterations in 1914. Pedimented doorway, four small ground-floor windows in ashlar surrounds. Gabled wall-head dormers.

119 SHERIFF COURT, Low Street. Originally designed as the Court & County Buildings in 1868 by *James Matthews* (of *Matthews & Lawrie*) with *J. B. Pirie* as his leading draughtsman, opened 1871. A big and stylish Italianate palazzo grandly set back from the street in its own grounds. Its entrance front is two-storey, seven bays broad, the centre three bays slightly advanced with a deep ground-floor portico of coupled Corinthian columns. The ground-floor windows are segment-headed and set in moulded key-blocked surrounds with panelled aprons. Round-headed first-floor windows with their architraved and key-blocked arches linked by a frieze of sculpted decoration; those in the centre bays opening onto the balustraded balcony over

*This stands on the site of the Nurses' Home, by *George Bennett Mitchell & Son* *c.* 1930, and the Maternity Block by *James Wood*, 1952.

the portico. Channelled giant-order Doric pilasters at the angles, a plain frieze and slim mutuled cornice, wall-head balustrade with tall central panel. Inside, a large central Court Room with coffered ceiling; the former County Hall at first floor is approached by a stair with decorative cast-iron balusters.

TOWN HALL, Castle Street. Built as St Andrew's Masonic Hall. By *Thomas Mackenzie* of *Mackenzie & Matthews*, 1851–4. Italianate two-storey five-bay palazzo in coursed dark whinstone with dressings in pale polished sandstone. Central Doric doorcase with columns *in antis* and pilastered shopfronts to either side. Taller pedimented first-floor windows with balustraded aprons and pilasters with queen's-head capitals. To Seafield Street, a tripartite window with Corinthian pilasters and shell pediment. Inside the first-floor Masons' Hall, six pairs of draped angels carrying the coffered ceiling.

TOWN HOUSE, Low Street. Designed by *James Reid* 1795, completed by *John Rhind*, *James Robertson* and *James Nicol*, masons, by 1800.* Very tall but simple three-storey five-bay classical design in golden Covesea freestone with channelled ashlar ground floor and long-and-short quoins. Inside, a broad if simple stair with cast-iron balustered rail. Abutting to the r. and slightly set back, the TOLBOOTH STEEPLE of 1764–7 by *John Adam*, the contractors *John Marr* and *James Rhind*. First stage with a doorway set beneath a roundel within a tall round-headed arch, then a blind Diocletian window above; second stage taken in slightly comprises the town clock beneath an open pediment, then the belfry under the wall-head parapet with urn finials; octagonal stone spire with concave sides, oval oculi and a crowning ball finial and weathervane.

WAR MEMORIAL, Castle Street. By *William Kelly* (of *Kelly & Nicol*), 1920–1. A cenotaph of pale granite ashlar, set in front of a low curved wall, partly ashlar and partly hammer-dressed blocks with inset name panels.

WILSON'S INSTITUTION, Institution Terrace. Built with a 113
bequest granted by James Wilson, a Banff merchant who had made a fortune in Grenada; it was designed by *William Robertson* in 1836 and built in 1837–8. A splendid Greek Revival Temple of Learning. Broad Ionic hexastyle portico with pedimental gable is flanked by tall single-storey four-bay classrooms and pilastered end-pavilions which extend back to enclose a rear court, all in fine sandstone ashlar. Within the portico the main entrance is itself pedimented; the lying-pane glazing in the wings and pavilions is characteristic of the period. The portico steps are approached between two pedestals supporting lanterns. The Institution rehoused the Grammar School as well as providing a Free School 'for moral and religious instruction of labouring poorer classes', an infant school, a lecture room, a library and a museum in its central

*It was partly built with a legacy from George Smith of Bombay, who also provided for Fordyce Academy (q.v.).

hall. *A. Marshall Mackenzie* filled in the rear court in 1897–8, but the school was severely damaged by fire in 1921 and thereafter deepened on plan by *James Wood*, Banffshire County Architect, between 1923 and 1934 to provide additional accommodation: his rear extension is almost totally concealed but its long low roof reads very neatly with the portico of Robertson's original front. To the W new buildings for the PRIMARY SCHOOL, off Academy Drive, of 2002 by the *Holmes Partnership* (on the site of a secondary school of 1909–10 by *J. B. Pirie*). A long single-storey asymmetric entrance front, mostly sheltered beneath a broad symmetrical gable with boldly projecting eaves.

Former YMCA HALL, Seafield Street. By *James Duncan*, dated 1866. Single-storey with console-corniced doorway flanked by tripartite windows, also corniced. Contained hall, drawing room, library and reading room.

HARBOUR

The Harbour probably dates from 1625 when *James McKen* of Fraserburgh was engaged to remove rocks from Guthrie's Haven: although shallow it was unusually easy of access for ships being pursued by northerly winds. It was continually modified but in its present three-basin form dates chiefly from the late C18 and early C19, the INNER HARBOUR formed by *John Smeaton* in 1770–5 and the OUTER HARBOUR for larger vessels by *Thomas Telford* in 1818–28. Further alterations were made in 1840–51 but from the mid C19 onwards the fishing and mercantile fleets increasingly favoured the more generous harbours at Macduff and Whitehills (qq.v.). Restored 1983, partly converted to a marina in 2006–7.

DESCRIPTION

1. High Street, Low Street and the riverside

Banff and its much younger sibling Macduff (q.v.) are linked
104 together by BANFF BRIDGE across the Deveron, its seven segmental arches, each of 15.3 m. span, designed by *John Smeaton* and completed by master-mason *James Robertson* in 1779 to replace an earlier bridge which had been washed away. Widened on each side by *John Willet* in 1881, his arches spring higher from the piers and are consequently shallower so that the original arches can still be seen beneath them, and the effect is most graceful. At the bridge's W end a pedimented Palladian LODGE of *c.* 1766, the survivor of a pair which once flanked the *clair-voyée* gates to Duff House (*see* also Banff Castle, above), is probably also by *Robertson*.

Until 1960 the main route into Banff took a sharp turn N into Bridge Road along the Deveron's W bank and thence into Old Market Place, Bridge Street and Carmelite Street. Now it continues W straight through Duff House's former park, past the remains on the N side of its walled gardens. These incorporate a castellated TOWER, reputedly all that survives of Banff's Lodging (destroyed 1640), with half-hidden beyond them the attractive AIRLIE GARDENS housing scheme by *G.R.M. Kennedy & Partners*, 1985. At the top of the road, marooned in a car-park, COLLIE LODGE (Tourist Information Office), formerly the entrance from Low Street to the Duff House policies – a delightful Greek Doric temple probably of *c.* 1836 by *William Robertson*, complementing his design for Wilson's Institution further uphill (*see* Public Buildings); near the Lodge, a SCULPTURE, the Sea Tree by *Frances Pelly*, 1992.

HIGH STREET with the later Castle Street constitutes Banff's principal axis, extending absolutely broad level and straight for over 800 m. N from St Mary's Parish Church (*see* Churches), and separating the old town built on the riverbank below from the later town spreading further W up the slope. It begins at its S end on the corner with Institution Terrace with one of the many charming groups of houses which distinguish Banff as a town primarily of the Georgian era. Set back in its garden, No. 1 is dated 1764, three-storey three bays in squared rubble, its doorway set in a lugged architrave with small rosettes under a pulvinated frieze and cornice. No. 5 was Lord Banff's town-house, built *c.* 1720–30, taller than its neighbours and with windows of narrower proportions which unfortunately have lost their astragalled sashes-and-cases. Across the road, N of St Mary, a view down BACK PATH of more good C18 houses with harled and painted fronts and exposed margins to doors and windows. No. 8 at the top, dated 1739, has one sundial in its front and another in its crowstep-gabled flank. Closing the vista, the handsome Neoclassical Fife Arms (*see* Low Street, below). Further along High Street's W side, a long row of early C18 vernacular houses (Nos. 29–35) restored by the Banff Preservation Society. Two-storey, harled with doors and windows in roll-moulded surrounds, and with a tall wall-head chimneystack rising between the first pair, decorated with exposed quoins like a Battenburg cake. In the pend of Nos. 33–35 two re-set lintels inscribed J.M. V.F. and 17James M . . . & Violet Fraser28. Then a little further along the SHOEMAKERS' HOUSE, restored by the Society in 1975; it was founded as a charitable institution by John Murray, Convener of the Six Incorporated Trades in 1710, and reconstructed by the Shoemakers (the wealthiest of the Trades) in 1787, as its inscriptions make clear. It is a classic – if belated – example of an Early to mid-Georgian type found in most of the larger Scottish burghs, three storeys, five windows wide with a broad segment-headed and key-blocked pend and its wall-head gable rising into a chimneystack. Within the pend leading to a U-plan rear court, another stone 'Iohn Murray Iean Gray 1693.'

Opposite, between the Public Library (*see* Public Buildings) and St Andrew's Episcopal Church (*see* Churches) is ST BRANDON'S, a three-storey Georgian house of 1790, almost concealed by the massive three-storey Baronial tower added against its front in 1867, perhaps by *James Matthews*: the unity is in its rubble construction – originally harled with dressed angle quoins – rather than its style. An additional bay to the r., slightly set back, is probably early C19, its basement pend formed during restoration and reconstruction into flats by *Jack Meldrum* in 1969–72. The very tall rubble rear elevation has a big three-window bow forming a railed balcony for the top-floor Diocletian window. S of the pend, No. 1, St Brandon's Close, late C17 also restored, with a crowstepped E gable.

Beyond St Andrew, the COUNTY HOTEL. Reputedly built in 1778 as the house of George Garden Robinson, of Banff's linen- and thread-making family, who alternated with his father as provost for many years. Handsome classical, two-storey, five windows wide in silver tooled ashlar over a semi-sunk basement; its very large pilastered porch with a tripartite doorway and elegant fanlight was added *c.* 1825–30. The windows are set in painted ashlar surrounds and the wall-head crowned by a deep blocking course partly screening the big gabled roof with end stacks. The harled rear elevation, also five bays, rises a storey higher in the slope; its stairway is later. The interior dates from both the late C18 and *c.* 1825–30, the detail of the latter suggesting the hand of *Archibald Simpson* or *William Robertson*. The High Street's N end has been significantly altered by rebuilding and the insertion of shopfronts, including at Nos. 77–81 (W side) the former town house of the Forbes of Boyndie, built in 1741 but perhaps incorporating earlier fabric; its crowstepped gable to Boyndie Street has a cavetto rear skewputt carved with a grotesque mask.

There are more good houses in BOYNDIE STREET itself, which was the main route out of town until the mid C19. Of particular note are BOYNDIE HOUSE, three storeys and four bays with a heraldic panel dated 1740 and a very wide curvilinear gable, and the BANFF TOWN & COUNTY CLUB (No. 11), which formerly belonged to George Robinson Sen. and was reconstructed by him in 1772. Its street elevation is fairly plain, again three storeys and four bays broad but with the centre pair widely spaced (was there once a pend between them?) and the doorway curiously offset to the r. The main entrance front of Robinson's house, however, was in the rear wing standing in a courtyard off Kingswell Lane. It is a tripartite design with a pedimented centre in ashlar slightly stepped forward between the harled side bays, and with a Serlian window lighting a handsome interior. The adjoining premises in Boyndie Street (No. 13), mid-C18 but much altered, were the Robinsons' linen and thread factory. George Robinson (1713–98) was to establish the world's first steam textile mill in Nottinghamshire in 1786.

Before Castle Street was formed, High Street continued at an angle into OLD CASTLEGATE. At the junction is the ROYAL BANK OF SCOTLAND, built 1937 as the National Commercial Bank by *W. J. Walker Todd* with the bank's master of works

James McCallum. Two tall storeys in golden sandstone ashlar, rubble, brick and harl above a deep black marble base course, its slightly advanced ends are asymmetrically treated, that on the r. with a bellcast roof displaying the Bank's coat of arms over the main doorway, and the entrance bay to the upstairs offices on the l. also finely sculpted. In the end gable to High Street, five carved stones, at least three of them including a pedimented coat of arms from the house of Thomas and Eliza Ogilvie (1669, much altered) which previously stood on the site. The internal joinery is by *Scott Morton & Tynecastle*, with *Finnie* responsible for the plasterwork; the brass tellers' screen is distinguished by its carved lions and unicorn.

Beyond the bank, Old Castlegate is a delightful enclave. No. 2 is a very grand mid-C18 house with later alterations – three-storey three bays, a round-arched doorway with its late Georgian pilastered door-frame deeply recessed; tall tripartite windows in the first-floor outer bays and small second-floor windows hard under the eaves enjoying fine views over Banff Bay to the rear. No. 8, St Ninian's, of *c.* 1840–50 is an even taller three-storey house set back from the street with a simple pilastered and corniced doorway. Then No. 14 a two-storey house dated 1759 with an interesting distinction in its glazing, its ground-floor windows twelve-pane sash-and-case, first-floor Early Victorian lying-pane, and canted attic dormers of the late C19. At the High Street end of Old Castlegate, STRAIT PATH descends steeply towards Low Street, Nos. 5–7 incorporating two old carved stones, one of them dated 1669.

LOW STREET is the real heart of the old town: markets were 101
held here until *c.* 1770. In the NW corner on the 'Plainstones', a raised area E of the main street, is the Tolbooth Steeple and Town House (*see* Public Buildings) and a three-storey five-bay block harled with ashlar margins by *John Marr* built in 1764–7. The MARKET CROSS is a replica of 1994, the original now in Banff Museum. Its cross-head, probably dating from the C16, displays the Virgin and Child on one side and the Crucifixion on the other, a remarkable post-Reformation survival. The cross was removed from Low Street in 1767 but returned here in 1900, albeit without its base, which is still in Doo'cot Park. By that time its original site had been occupied by the BIGGAR FOUNTAIN (*John Rhind*, 1878), an elaborate late Gothic design in Binny ashlar freestone with much finely carved detail. It has a square base with clustered columns at each corner, and four flying buttresses with pinnacles supporting a central stem which rises into a crown spire. The backdrop to the fountain, on the W, is the neglected TOLBOOTH HOTEL dated 1801, with a blind Serlian window at first floor. On the N stands a good early C19 house, and to the r. of this the NEW MARKET ARCH, dated 1831, with its tall vehicular archway in rusticated masonry flanked by side arches in polished ashlar. On the W side, Nos. 43–47 is the former Trades Hall of 1781, originally Palladian but refronted in the Neo-Baroque style *c.* 1900, perhaps by *R. G. Wilson*. Three storeys, five bays broad with a

curvilinear wall-head gable, it has a broad semi-elliptical entrance arch with oversized keyblock and brackets, and plate-glazed shopfronts to either side. Next to it, the CLYDESDALE BANK (originally North of Scotland Bank), the earliest of three which have slugged it out for business near to the market place, was built by *Archibald Simpson* immediately after the bank's foundation in 1837. Neoclassical, two-storey with four bays in pale golden ashlar, its doorways are lugged and moulded with distinctive radial transom-lights; the ground-floor windows are pedimented, while the first-floor windows have console-cornices beneath a blocking course which is raised at its centre and flanked by scroll consoles. Directly opposite, next to the Tolbooth Steeple, is the former Aberdeen Town & County Bank, a neat little ashlar pavilion of *c.* 1840. Re-set in its N wall three SCULPTURAL FRAGMENTS: a Virgin and Child of 1628, the royal arms dated 1634, and a third figurative sculpture now severely eroded, perhaps also the Virgin and Child.

The Union Bank on Low Street's W side, now BANK OF SCOTLAND, 1891, is very much like a smart suburban villa of that date. CARMELITE HOUSE, set well back in the centre of Low Street's E side, was built for Admiral William Gordon *c.* 1753. Vernacular classical, two-storey and five windows wide over a semi-sunk basement with the charmingly modest proportions of that period, its central doorway is set in a Gibbsian surround; construction is in squared whinstone rubble with contrasting golden dressings, and the canted dormers in the tall gabled roof are *c.* 1900. Further down, on the opposite side, Nos. 15–17, built for William Robinson and dated 1745 on its dormer, still retains its chamfered doorway with a bolection-
114 moulded lintel. At the far end is the former FIFE ARMS, designed for the 4th Earl Fife by *Burn & Bryce* and built in 1843–5 as a genteel hotel for visitors to Duff House (*see* p. 94). Like the Sheriff Court opposite (*see* Public Buildings), in architectural terms it would have been grand enough for any large city in Scotland. It is three-storey and five windows wide over a slightly raised basement, with a shallow ground-floor portico of coupled Roman Doric columns supporting a triglyph entablature. Construction is in pale ashlar sandstone, the ground- and first-floor windows very tall with second-floor rather lower; at the angles long-and-short quoins, a mutuled wall-head cornice and a crowning balustrade, the wall-head chimneystacks at the gables being supported by scrolls. The two-storey wings are matching but non-identical, the N wing containing the broad semi-elliptical pend to the stables court between original shopfronts.

BRIDGE STREET, E from Low Street, was formed as the principal entrance into town in 1769. From the mid C19 its houses were converted into shops (e.g. No. 49, distinguished by smart pilasters with anthemion capitals) but many are disused and some have been demolished. Bridge Street leads into OLD MARKET PLACE near the riverside where markets were held from *c.* 1770 to 1831, after which they removed to the New Market following severe flooding in 1829. The former Masonic Lodge (later St Andrew's Hotel) built *c.* 1800 has a naïve Gibbsian doorway; then comes the late C18 Panton House, harled in white with doorway and windows in painted surrounds, and a small pend at its far r. On the Bridge Road junction's N side, Crown Court, social housing by *Baxter, Clark & Paul* replacing Castle Panton, a tall early C18 house summarily demolished after a fire in 1981 (a re-set datestone is incorporated); on the S side, the old Meal-houses, a triple-gabled frontage, the centre and W gables of 1793–6 and the E gable C20. The fine bellcote is reputedly that of the old grammar school of 1780: the former Grammar School which succeeded it in 1805 still honours the mid-C18 vernacular, with round-arched key-blocked doorway off-centre. The skewputts are its predecessor's, dated on the Church Street side. Following the curve of the road leads us to the S end of Carmelite Street and Old St Mary's churchyard (*see* Churches).

Continuing into High Shore, one of Banff's most excep- 100
tional groups of houses. No. 1 is a three-storey merchant's house dated 1675. Its small doorway and windows in moulded or chamfered surrounds are semi-regular in arrangement, there is a datestone at ground-floor level and small sundial at first, the second floor rising into hipped dormerheads with a corbelled pepperpot turret overlooking the junction beneath a tall steeply pitched roof. In the rear elevation a stair-tower once contained the main entrance, its canted corners rising into a caphouse. No. 3 is vernacular classical, with charmingly naïve proportions: its doorway framed by hefty long-and-short quoins and a contrastingly delicate bracket cornice, the windows in tooled ashlar surrounds probably C19 enlargements of the originals with those at ground floor nearly touching the pavement. The doorway lintel is carved with a lion's or gargoyle's head, the date is given as 1740, and the initials are probably Thomas Forbes the silversmith's. The Market Arms looks C17 or early C18, three-storey with only one bay of windows to the l. and two to the r. flanking a central pend leading to the rear court. Within this court a carved mask of a moustachioed man with date 1585 suggests the incorporation of earlier fabric.

Round the corner in Water Path, Ingleneuk is two-storey with a late C17 crowstepped gable. Its name derives from the massive hearth recess – reputedly medieval – in its kitchen; one of its other rooms has early C18 panelling. The adjoining No. 3, early C18, has a broad pend with initials I.D. E.D. leading into a court; No. 4 on the High Shore junction is again early C18 with a small chamfered doorway. The road continues up the steep slope to Path House, a tall three-storey-and-attic gable front with its owners' initials and date 1756 carved into its skewputts, with behind it on the l. a simple two-storey three-bay gabled frontage of the earlier C19 linking to Path Cottage – probably older than Path House – at the rear.

A little further on in High Shore, the former Commercial Bank (now POLICE STATION) of 1869, very characteristic of *David Rhind*, who designed nearly all of the Bank's branches. It is a handsomely proportioned three-storey five-bay palazzo, conspicuously robust in coursed hammer-dressed whinstone with lighter polished sandstone dressings and bold but refined detailing. Its entrance has very big console scrolls which support a balustraded balcony. The tall ground-floor windows of the bank office are set in simple architraved surrounds with slim cornices; the first-floor windows expressing the principal apartments of the bank agent's residence rest on a deep ashlar band course; and the second-floor windows are set in simple lugged surrounds. The wall-head is distinguished by a modillioned and mutuled cornice with panelled parapet graced by ball and urn finials, and there are corniced chimneystacks over the roof ridge and end gables. Inside, the broad staircase to the agent's residence with its cast-iron barley-twist balusters survives, together with the heavy metal door and window shutters and safes.

Opposite, the former GORDON'S GRANARIES, late C18, built as a three-storey U-plan, converted to flats in 2012. Originally they stood at the edge of the old quays near the mouth of the Deveron, before construction of the present sea-wall. In DEVERONSIDE, No. 11 is mid-C18, its rear stair-tower carved with the names of the merchant and baillie James Philip and his wife Janet Mitchie and the date 1744. The present HARBOUR (*see* p. 86) lies 250 m. further N; near to it stands a pair of converted three-storey WAREHOUSES with large round-headed pends, built for Philip *c.* 1763.

2. *Castle Street and the Seatown*

CASTLE STREET, linking High Street to the Seatown, was formed in 1750 while Banff Castle (*see* p. 81) was under construction. No. 6, tall two-storey four bays with a segmental pend, is *c.* 1760. Nos. 8–10 of the same height but with different floor levels, three-storey five bays with a pilastered doorway and segment-headed pend, is *c.* 1770. After the former Free Church (*see* Harvest Centre, above), some good mid- to later C19 blocks, then further along two two-storey villas, Nos. 23–25 of *c.* 1830–40 and No. 29 *c.* 1850. N of the Town Hall (*see* Public Buildings), SEAFIELD HOUSE also by *Thomas Mackenzie*, 1853–4 for Mr Grant, and in the same whinstone as the Hall. Distinctively proportioned Italianate, two storeys and five bays with a portico of paired Roman Doric columns crowned by a balustrade. Its tall ground-floor windows have console-cornices and blind apron panels; the smaller first-floor windows are set in architraved surrounds under a plain frieze and mutuled cornice. Inside, the entrance hall opens through a Doric screen to the stair which has decorative cast-iron balusters with rich foliate details.

SEAFIELD STREET was formed in the mid C19 as the new main road westwards to Moray. It was gradually built up with solid detached and semi-detached villas of good quality, its chief landmarks the former YMCA (*see* Public Buildings) and Methodist church (*see* Churches). ST CATHERINE STREET begins with ST CATHERINE'S HOUSE, austere Greek Revival in the style of Archibald Simpson, *c.* 1830 in granite ashlar. It is two-storey, five bays broad, with giant anta-pilasters at each corner and a portico of paired fluted Greek Doric columns over a railed semi-sunk rock-faced basement. Elegant tripartite doorpiece. Ground-floor windows with twelve-pane sashes and lying-pane casements at first floor; the low hipped and platformed roof has mutules supporting the eaves and broad coped chimneystacks. Inside, the entrance hall opens through a Doric columnar screen into the stair hall with an imperial stair. Two STATUES on plinths: a woman with a ewer and a basin, and a man with grapes and a vine. Beyond St Catherine's House the street continues on its N side with a short row of early C19 vernacular classical houses.

NORTH CASTLE STREET is much more modest in character, mostly two-storey houses but all different in proportion, No. 76 with a pilastered doorpiece and No. 78 of *c.* 1830–40 with its doorway consoled and pedimented. Then beyond Chalmers' Hospital (*see* Public Buildings), Castle Street ends with the mid-C18 BREWERY. This is a long three-storey sixteen-bay frontage, rough, gaunt and monumental, with two double-height round-arched portals (one at the S end and the other not quite central), its small square windows almost regular in arrangement. The portals give entry to a courtyard, enclosed by a lower two-storey return range on BATTERY GREEN, which takes its name from the gun battery established as a precaution against French warships and privateers in 1781; it was also used as a public park. The front to Battery Green retains an empty case for the harbour's FitzRoy barometer: at the instigation of Vice-Admiral Robert FitzRoy, the Board of Trade issued all harbours with barometers from 1858 (cf. Portsoy). The battery was dismantled in 1815; the Coastguard Station is *c.* 1882 (*see* Public Buildings).

The development of Castle Street linking the Old Town with the Seatown encouraged the construction of smart two-storey villas next to the single-storey fisher-cottages from the late C18. In GEORGE STREET, developed on its N side only to enjoy views of Castle Hill, No. 1 is a two-storey four-bay house of *c.* 1830–40 in dark squared whinstone, Nos. 2, 3 and 4 form an attractive row of late C18 houses, while No. 5 was perhaps rebuilt during the early C19. Continuing round the corner into BRAEHEADS, Nos. 1 and 2 are late C18, with St John's Masonic Hall (*see* Public Buildings) beyond.

On Castle Street's W side, Clunie Street (originally Back Street) running E–W and Fife Street running N–S were laid out on a crossroads plan in 1762. CLUNIE STREET begins, on its N side, with Chalmers' Hospital (*see* Public Buildings). On the other side, the former PIRIE'S FREE SCHOOL, T-plan two-storey with its steep gabled wing facing the street and crowned by a bellcote dated 1805. Further away from Castle Street, Clunie Street reduces to a charming fisher-cottage scale, with net lofts under their roofs.

FIFE STREET is lined on the E side, mostly by single-storey cottages, with taller two-storey houses on the W looking over their roofs to the sea – all very simple, but with an attractive variety of proportion, colour and texture.

In BELLEVUE ROAD, BELLEVUE of *c.* 1830 is a two-storey villa of three bays, raised over a tall basement; its doorway and ground-floor windows are framed by round-headed arches, their approach stair and flanking balconies with fine cast-iron balusters. Nearby, ST ANN'S HILL. Originally built before 1823, but remodelled by *A. & W. Reid* in 1846. Neat two-storey Tudoresque with central ground-floor porch framed by octagonal piers rising into ogival finials, mullioned and transomed first-floor windows, and the r. side slightly advanced with a canted bay under a tall gable; the roofs generally low-pitched with octagonally shafted chimneystacks.

DUFF HOUSE

76 Duff House is the last major country house to have been built by *William Adam* and one of the great masterpieces of British Baroque architecture, a richly detailed cube rising high above its flat riverside landscape into a triumphant staccato profile of domed towers, urns and chimneystacks. It is the work of a thoroughly accomplished designer, able not only to express himself in the language of contemporary architecture but also to develop that language in new ways. Adam's client, William Duff, had inherited substantial estates in Morayshire and Banffshire from his father, had made further acquisitions of his own, and possessed a large sum in ready money. He had already commissioned James Gibbs to build a new house at Balvenie (*see* Dufftown, Moray) from 1724, and in autumn 1730 made contact with Adam about the improvement of the House of Airlie, his existing seat in Banff. Duff retired from politics as M.P. for Banffshire in 1734 and work was about to begin to Adam's designs when he was elevated to the Irish peerage as Baron Braco of Kilbryde in 1735; and following a meeting – in his own words – with 'ane honourable person of great Judgement and taste in Architecture as well as other more usefull things', he decided to build a new house worthy of his lordly wealth and status at a greater distance from the town.

The plans were finalized and Adam commissioned on 20 May 1735. 'And a very handsome plan it was,' Lord Braco wrote, 'consisting of a body of a house seven windows in front to the north and south, besides a closet projecting at each angle; and the height of the house is four storeys reckoning the ground storey and the attick, of which the lowest was to be rustick work on the outside and the two middle or principal storeys adorned with Corinthian pilasters with their Capitals, Cornick, etc., and suitable ornaments on the attick storey; and in the middle of each front a pediment on which was to be carved a coat of arms, and on top of all a balustrade adorned with vases of stone.' As at Hopetoun, the S front of which Adam remodelled *c.* 1720–44 (*see* Lothian), the main block of the house was to be linked by giant quadrant colonnades to a library and kitchen wing (W) and a servants' and stables wing (E). The foundation stone was laid on 11 June, the construction being supervised by *John Burt*, the clerk of works.

Lord Braco's confidence then began to waver and he asked Adam to reduce the house from four storeys to three, only to conclude in May 1737 that it would not appear complete without its attic. Adam did not make his customary annual visit to inspect progress in 1738, perhaps a sign of rift between architect and client, although he was present when the shell was roofed over in 1739. But thereafter Braco's anxieties focused on the expense of the masonry, much of which was shipped from the quarries which Adam leased in South Queensferry, Lothian. This allowed him to oversee the carving of the fine details by *Charles* (or *John*?) *Burn* of Maxtoun but the charge for this carving – approximately £2,500, a substantial proportion of the house's cost – proved too much for Braco to bear. Work stopped with the ram's-horn stairs to the main entrance still unconstructed. Adam was obliged to resort to the Court of Session for costs due in respect of materials and workmanship in 1743 but offered a compromise shortly before he died in 1748. Braco accepted the offer but remained exceptionally bitter and resentful, and reputedly pulled the blinds of his carriage down every time he passed the house on his way into town.

The house's fitting-out did not proceed until 1754, the year after the death of Lord Braco's eldest son and the succession of his second son, James, as the Master of Braco. James commissioned *Thomas Dott*, wright and cabinet-maker in Edinburgh, to fit out the first-floor entrance vestibule and family apartments and part of the attic floor as bedrooms, although the second or principal floor remained as a shell. The work was spurred on by James's marriage to Lady Dorothea Sinclair, sole heir of the 9th Earl of Caithness, in 1759. William Duff became 1st Earl Fife and Viscount Macduff that year and James succeeded to the titles in 1763, but his marriage was not a success and latterly he lived at Duff House alone. He fitted out the library in the attic in 1774–6, his books transferred from Rothiemay Castle (*see* Moray). From *c.* 1790 he completed the principal floor to a different style of decoration from that proposed by Adam, chiefly as galleries for his many historical portraits, of which he was a pioneer collector.

James Duff, 4th Earl Fife who succeeded in 1811 was a hero of the Peninsular War and a favourite of the Prince Regent. He had acquired a collection of Spanish paintings and engaged on a further programme of furnishing and decoration seemingly under the guidance of *James Gillespie* (later *James Gillespie*

Graham) but financial embarrassment as a result of legal complications forced a major sale in 1824 and the family's fortunes were never the same again. Duff passed out of their ownership in 1906 when the 1st Duke and Duchess of Fife – who had focused their attention on the newly built Mar Lodge (S) – decided to offer the house with 55 hectares of ground as a gift to the Burghs of Banff and Macduff. Duff subsequently became an upmarket hotel, then a sanatorium for nutritional disorders, then a hotel again. During the Second World War it was requisitioned as a P.O.W. camp, after which it became a base for Polish and Norwegian troops. By the early post-war years it had fallen into a severe state of decline but its architectural importance was recognized by Stewart Cruden, Principal Inspector of Ancient Monuments at the Ministry of Works. He persuaded the Ministry to take it into care in 1956, and it was gradually restored under the supervision of *William Boal*, two rooms being redecorated and opened to the public. From 1992–5, however, work was undertaken in partnership with the National Galleries of Scotland to restore Duff's interior to something closer to its character in the heyday of the 4th Earl, with loans of pictures similar to those which had once hung in the house, as well as appropriate furnishings, including the only suite of furniture known to have been designed by *Robert Adam* and made by *Thomas Chippendale*.

Exterior

What makes Duff so distinctive among other Baroque houses is its strong vertical emphasis. It is four storeys high, rising from a rectangular footprint only 27.5 m. by 20.75 m.; its 5.5 m.-square angle towers take the overall dimensions to 30 m. by 24.5 m. It is thus relatively small for such a major country house, a tightly composed, well-disciplined design set off by its excellent construction in creamy Queensferry freestone for its principal elevations and magnificent carved details, and a very similar but slightly more golden Morayshire freestone for its flanks.

The ENTRANCE FRONT is nine bays broad with its windows closely spaced. Its three central bays are slightly advanced with a balustraded ram's-horn stair sweeping out in front of the adjoining bays. The single-bay angle towers are more boldly advanced, and rise into square 'tea-caddy' pavilions above the main cornice. Beneath the central platt of the stairs, three round-headed arches open into a porch sheltering the wet-weather entrance at ground floor. This level is faced in channelled ashlar with shouldered windows in the end bays, but the upper floors are all in polished ashlar. At the first and principal floors the centrepiece and angle towers are articulated by giant-order pilasters 9.8 m. high with fluted shafts and deeply undercut Corinthian capitals. The main doorway and windows within the centrepiece are all round-headed, those at first floor with distinctly Baroque moulded key-blocks, while those at principal floor have balustraded aprons and consoled key-blocks. Within the flanking bays and angle towers the windows are set in moulded lugged architraves with panelled aprons and pulvinated friezes; the first-floor windows are crowned by triangular and segmental pediments to distinguish the main family apartments, while the principal-floor windows have cornices. The Corinthian pilasters support a massive entablature, its architrave subtly moulded, a plain frieze and deep cornice elaborately dentilled and mutuled. The three-bay centre is crowned by a great pediment, deeply undercut with the Duff of Braco coat of arms, and its corners filled out with luxuriant foliage; die-blocks support lead figures of Apollo over the apex with Mars and Minerva at the ends.*

Above the cornice and behind the pediment extends the relatively low attic floor, with a wall-head balustrade punctuated by urn finials concealing the main roof. At this level the tall tea-caddy pavilions crowning the towers have Composite angle-pilasters and their round-headed windows are set beneath swags and blank panels which were intended for carving. They are capped by shallow square-domed roofs, again with urn finials at each corner, and crowned not by cupolae as might be expected but by short octagonal chimneystacks.

It is quite remarkable that so rich an entrance front should have been replicated almost exactly in the N ELEVATION. This is constructed in the same Queensferry freestone with its three-bay centre and towered ends framed by Corinthian and Composite pilasters identical to those of the main front, the pediment in front of the attic floor carved with Lord Braco's arms quartered with those of his wife, Jean Grant of Grant, and statues of Diana, Mercury and Bacchus. The only omission is that the smaller ram's-horn stair which Adam had intended for this side was never built, the shouldered windows now extending right across the channelled masonry of the basement.

Some inspiration for these principal elevations may derive from Powis House in London (1714) which had been published by Colen Campbell in *Vitruvius Britannicus* (1715–22) and which likewise had a three-bay centrepiece, two-bay links and single-bay ends framed by giant-order pilasters. Another source – as was suggested at the time – is Vanbrugh's garden front at Castle Howard, Yorkshire (1699–1737), which has very similar round-arched key-blocked doorways and windows and giant-order Corinthian pilasters. The effect of the first-floor main entrance approached by its balustraded ram's-horn stair above a full-height ground floor is exceptionally grand and, in particular, the neatly integrated angle towers – which most certainly are *not* Palladian towers – seem without any precedent. If anything they are closer in spirit to the C17

*The Mars and Minerva are fibreglass; the lead originals are now displayed in the main stair hall.

George Heriot's Hospital in Edinburgh or perhaps even Robert Smythson's Hardwick Hall in Derbyshire, built 1590–7, or Wollaton Hall, Nottinghamshire, built 1580–8 and also attributed to Smythson. But perhaps the simple truth was that Adam and Duff recognized that, as in tower houses, height as well as breadth could make a powerful impression. Challenging comparison with all but the very largest English palaces, Duff House may well be the pre-eminent example of what their Scottish contemporaries would have called 'a High Modern Castle'.

The W ELEVATION consists of a tight six-bay frontage between the angle towers, the two centre bays being very slightly projected and lit by round-arched windows expressing the main stair. In this elevation and the E ELEVATION the fenestration varies from the general pattern with much slimmer and smaller windows at the first and principal floors to accommodate Adam's use of servants' mezzanines over the corner bedchambers.

The exposed rubble at ground-floor level on both flanks relates to the unbuilt quadrant colonnades and pavilions. The quadrants were to have been of two-storey height with a giant Ionic order, and the pavilions an identical two storeys and three bays broad with central Serlian windows, balustraded parapets and hipped roofs with arcaded octagonal cupolae culminating in ogee-domed finials. The total length of the frontage, had they been built, would have been 100 m. and the forecourt depth 38 m., giving the house a very different appearance. Adam's plans in *Vitruvius Scoticus* show that the W pavilion would have contained stables and servants' rooms and the E pavilion the kitchen-quarters and a library. In the event, a cottage-like kitchen wing was built on the E side as an interim measure in 1759. In 1764, the year after James Duff succeeded his father as the 2nd Earl Fife, *John Woolfe* proposed an alternative scheme (*see Vitruvius Britannicus*, vol. V, 1771) in which five-bay galleries replicating the treatment of the main block's ground and first floors would have linked to three-storey five-bay pedimented pavilions with giant-order Ionic columns, but these too were left unbuilt. It was not until 1870 that *David Bryce Jun.* built a new pavilion on the site of the 1759 kitchen: it contained not only a new kitchen but a top-lit billiard room and seven bedrooms. It was linked by a corridor to the E side of the house, but was bombed in 1941 and afterwards demolished.

On PLAN the house is more or less symmetrical at first and principal floors. Adam's plans show the FIRST FLOOR containing the Entrance Vestibule and main family apartments. The Entrance Vestibule occupies the centre of the S front, and the Private Dining Room the centre of the N front, linked together by a small lobby or ante-room which opens into the tightly planned service stair between them; in the W bays are the Private Drawing Room with a 'cabinet' in the NW angle tower, the main stair and a bedchamber with closet in the SW tower;

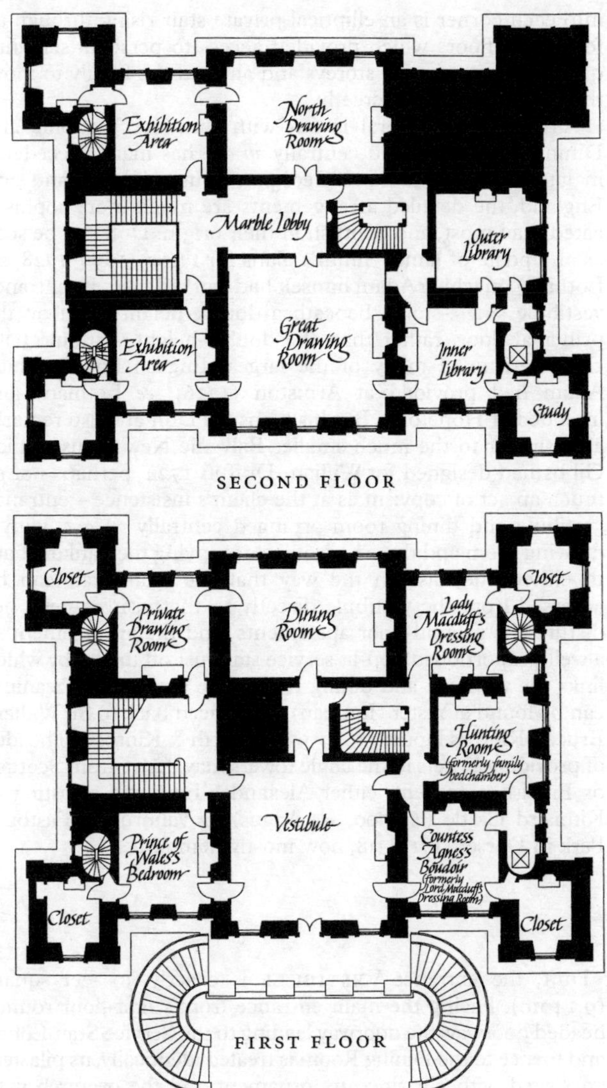

Banff, Duff House.
First-floor and second-floor plan

in the E bays are the Family Bedchamber with *en suite* twin dressing rooms, and small closets in the angle towers. Both in its formal and practical respects the planning of Duff is particularly neat: the Entrance Vestibule is a large square, the Drawing Room, bedrooms and dressing rooms are smaller squares, and the closets smaller squares again. Tucked neatly into each corner is an elliptical private stair rising through all four main floors which provided access to personal servants' quarters in mezzanine storeys and allowed the family to move through the house discreetly.

Although the general layout with Entrance Vestibule and Dining Room arranged centrally *en axe* has many precedents in later Stuart and Early Georgian houses in Scotland and England, the detailed arrangements are much more sophisticated than most, and Scottish in their origin. Duff can be seen as an update of James Smith's plans for Yester (1699–1728, *see* Lothian) on which Adam himself had worked, with its entrance vestibule single-storey beneath a double-height salon on the principal floor, rather than the double-height vestibule halls characteristic of many of the largest English houses which Adam had provided at Arniston (1726, *see* Lothian) and intended at Hopetoun. But his plans for Duff are also remarkably similar to the much smaller Balvenie New House which Gibbs had designed for William Duff in 1724, perhaps not so much an act of copyism as at the client's insistence – entrance vestibule and dining room arranged centrally *en axe*, with a drawing room and three bedrooms occupying the flanking bays to either side; also in the way that the main stair can be accessed from the vestibule directly so that visitors need not disturb the ground-floor apartments, and the arrangement of a well-proportioned, top-lit service stair just off the lobby which links the vestibule and dining room. The servants' mezzanines can be found at Yester (Lothian), and traced back to Sir William Bruce's Kinross House (1679–93, *see* Perth & Kinross). The idea of providing closets in the angle towers may derive from Scottish or English precedent, either Alexander Edward's recasting of Kinnaird Castle (*c.* 1700, *see* Angus) or Vanbrugh's Eastbury Park in Dorset (1713?–38, now mostly demolished).

Interior

At Duff, the entrance VESTIBULE is exactly 30 feet square (9.14 m.). Facing the main entrance front's first-floor round-headed doorway, the doorway leading to the Service Stair Lobby and thence to the Dining Room is treated identically, its pilasters encrusted with gilt rinceaux ornament and the overarch with Vitruvian scrolls; the doors to the apartments in the flanking bays are simpler, but still with pulvinated friezes and pediments, and the double-leaf doors are panelled, although the dado panelling is *trompe l'œil*. The fireplace is distinguished by elongated scrolls supporting its mantelshelf; the rococo plasterwork of the ceiling with ho-ho birds, vines and masks is probably by *David Crooks*, but the bas-relief rinceaux decoration around the walls, while similar to that of the round-arched doorways, is considerably later, by *John Jackson* of Edinburgh, 1814.

The SERVICE STAIR between the Vestibule and Dining Room was the principal means of communication between each storey

until the main stair was completed in the early 1790s. It is an interesting space in itself, rectangular, tightly planned around a central well, a simple almost skeletal structure not without a certain spare elegance: the inspiration may well be Continental, reflecting Adam's travels in France and the Low Countries before 1720.* In the PRIVATE DINING ROOM completed in 77
1761 (which Adam may originally have intended to be a bedchamber) the chimney-breast is framed by finely detailed Ionic pilasters supporting a pulvinated entablature and a mutuled cornice which extends round the ceiling, the decoration of which is not in stucco but in papier mâché giving a very refined effect. The doorway from the lobby is also Ionic pilastered,‡ the other doorways have pulvinated friezes and moulded cornices, and overall the quality of the woodwork is as high as the Vestibule's. The simple fireplace supplied by *John & James Adam* is in dark grey marble, framed by scrolls, and the walls are panelled with timber mouldings. In the NW corner the PRIVATE DRAWING ROOM, again completed by 1761, is finely finished with *goût-Grec* overdoor friezes and a fireplace carved by *Dott* with white marble slips supplied by the *Adams*: the *View of Loch Katrine* above this fireplace is set in a frame with a broken entablature designed, like the house itself, by *William Adam*.

In the SW corner what was the Countess Fife's bedroom in 1761 and since 1883 has been known as the PRINCE OF WALES'S BEDROOM has a particularly fine fireplace, richly treated doorways with console-cornices, a dado with Chinese fretwork decoration and a deeply coved ceiling again rising over a mutuled cornice; mirror-glass was inserted into the doors when the house was renovated by the 5th Earl Fife – or more accurately by Countess Agnes – shortly after his accession in 1857. On the E side of the house, the FAMILY BEDCHAMBER completed for James and Dorothea Duff on their marriage in 1759 and their *en suite* DRESSING ROOMS are simpler but still distinguished by dadoes with fretwork decoration and mutuled ceiling cornices; the marble chimneypiece in Lady Duff's dressing room is a later insertion. James Duff's dressing room, which opened directly off the Vestibule, could be used by him as an office for receiving visitors; if the quadrants and pavilions had been completed, it would also have connected to a large library in the E wing. The chimneypiece here is original, carved in wood with gilt ornament and red marble slips; the mirrored doors are again of *c.* 1860.

In the main STAIR HALL the plasterwork was executed by *James Lyon* in 1769 but the marble floor and indeed the stair itself were only put into effect by *James Robertson c.* 1791–2 as part of the 2nd Earl's fitting out of the principal apartments.

*In the early C20 when Duff House was used as a hotel this stairwell contained an elevator with its motor housed beneath the steps at ground level: tracks for the folding gates are still visible.

‡This has been identified by Ian Gow as deriving from an engraved drawing of the Chapel at Somerset House published in Isaac Ware's *Designs of Inigo Jones* (1731).

Although broad and supported by Ionic columns beneath its halfway landing, its relatively modest character with a moulded handrail supported on plain iron balusters is a sharp contrast to the first floor rooms of the late 1750s and 60s and a measure of how fashions had changed. Its chief purpose seems to have been the display of the 2nd Earl's pictures. Its enrichment with fictive mouldings and stencilled bands is of 1814 by *John Jackson*, who was also responsible for a *trompe l'œil* vase.

In Adam's plans the layout of the PRINCIPAL FLOOR corresponds closely to that of the first floor. The main stair rises to an ante-chamber – now opened out as the Marble Lobby – with a Saloon or Great Drawing Room above the Entrance Vestibule in the centre of the S front, and the North Drawing Room above the Dining Room on the N front. There are five bedrooms all corresponding to the smaller first-floor apartments, those in the corners again having closets within the towers. The MARBLE LOBBY appears to have been created from the ante-chamber by the 5th Earl and Countess *c.* 1860: the imitation Siena marbling (recreated during the C20 restoration) and inlaid geometric border are of that time, as are the doorcases to the apartments on either side and the consoles which frame the stairway opening, but the Neoclassical frieze and coved ceiling date from the original fitting-out by the 2nd Earl.

The GREAT DRAWING ROOM described in Adam's plans as a 'Sallon' (a Great Dining Room) was originally intended to be a 30 ft cube rising double-height into the attic storey behind the S front's pediment, but when the 2nd Earl came to fit it out in 1790 he decreed that it should be reduced in height, its ceiling rising to just 25 ft to allow for additional bedrooms upstairs. Adam had installed chimney-breasts for fireplaces at each end but that on the W was removed and the room very simply finished as a gallery for the 2nd Earl's pictures. A deep plain frieze supports the coved ceiling with its plaster fan, paterae, rinçeaux, eagles and husks by *John Paterson*, a simplified version of his initial design. The chimneypiece which was supplied from London is distinguished by its fluted Composite colonnettes, its mantelshelf with bas-relief depicting *The Triumph of Mars* with further low-relief figures at the ends, chaste ornament and a finely detailed cornice.

On the N side of the Marble Lobby is the NORTH DRAWING ROOM, which also seems to have been used as a dining room but was primarily a picture gallery. Here too Adam's W chimney-breast was removed in 1791, but even in the 2nd Earl's time this room was rather more richly treated than the Great Drawing Room, a swagged frieze supporting the coved ceiling with its Maltese Cross 'rose' surrounded by swags, vases and shields, and other elegant ornaments within the corners. The fireplace, again supplied from London, has Ionic columns, the central panel of its entablature representing 'A Boar-hunt in the Calydon Forest'. The splendid Baroque overmantel mirror with putti was part of the *c.* 1860 refitting. The BEDROOMS are also simple but those on the E side were adopted by the 5th Earl and

Countess for their own use and the Louis Quinze revival fireplace in the Countess's dressing room must date from their time.

In Adam's plans the ATTIC STOREY was to have contained a very grand Gallery for promenading on the W side, and bedchambers with closets on the E and N sides, the centre of the S front being occupied by the double-height Saloon rising up from the principal floor. The BEDROOMS AND CLOSETS were fitted out by James Duff *c.* 1760 and their style of decoration corresponds to the first floor. As a result of the colonnades and pavilions not being built, the Gallery was instead fitted out as a LIBRARY in 1774. It was divided up to provide more bedrooms during the house's conversion to hotel use in the C20, although some of the 'Chinese' bookcases by *Thomas Dott* still survive, and a Gothic revival fireplace in white marble seems to have come from the ground-floor Parlour.

An ARMOURY was provided in the NW angle tower. The GROUND FLOOR contained the NURSERY beneath the first-floor family apartments, together with the DOMESTIC OFFICES and a vaulted fireproof MUNIMENTS ROOM in the SW tower. The PARLOUR was used as a family dining room before the fit-out of the first floor was completed.

Policies

Although Lord Braco sought designs for the POLICIES from both *William Adam* and the Edinburgh nurseryman *William Boutcher* *c.* 1735, the landscape appears to be the work of *William Bowie* *c.* 1767, carried out by the 2nd Earl's gardener *Thomas Reid.* It is an early example of designing on Picturesque principles; further work seems to have been done by *Thomas White* in the 1780s. Not merely a delightful park but comprising a model farm, experimental woodland and a game preserve, the policies once extended for a considerable distance along the W bank of the Deveron, from Banff S to the Bridge of Alvah. *Bowie* devised a scenic route which starting from the open parklands around the house – since 1909, the Duff House Royal Golf Club (*see* Public Buildings) – passed through extensive woodlands to the romantic Crags of Alvah, the road then crossing over to the Duff estates on the E side of the river and returning N to Banff and Macduff (q.v.).

The entrance from the town was through Collie Lodge (*see* p. 87). However, the formation of the embanked approach from Banff Bridge to the High Street on what was once the route of the main driveway to the house (entered between twin pavilion gate lodges of which one only survives) has cut off the WALLED GARDEN. This appears late C18 in its present form, with a VINERY perhaps of the early C19; a small square tower at its NE angle is held to be a remnant of the House of Airlie built by the Lords Banff in the C17. On the other side of the embankment, on the N edge of the golf course, are the former STABLES.

The present route through the policies leads from Duff House along the W edge of the former parkland until it reaches the FIFE GATES at the entrance to Wrack Wood – late C18 with octagonal piers, the gates probably made by the *Banff Foundry*. The 2nd Earl was a prolific planter and the path winds through mature broadleaf trees for some 400 m. before passing a subterranean ICE HOUSE of *c.* 1800 (egg-shaped; its ante-chamber is later), then continues for another 500 m. before reaching the large MAUSOLEUM which the 2nd Earl built in 1790 to accommodate the remains of all his family, supposedly on the site of a Carmelite convent founded by Robert the Bruce. It is in a deliberately old-fashioned Rococo-Gothick style, three bays broad with a hipped roof. Its central doorway with fine cast- and wrought-iron gate was again probably by the Banff Foundry. The pointed-arch windows are mullioned and transomed in stone with basket-weave tracery, and clustered columns articulate the bay divisions. Against the rear elevation, the TOMB of Alexander Doune, Provost of Banff (†1663) is a round-arched recess with a recumbent effigy, which the 2nd Earl spuriously claimed to be that of Robert Bruce himself: he concealed the original inscription with one of his own devising which has now fallen away.

On the riverbank some 600 m. further on – though not part of the scenic route – is THE WRACK, a small mid-C18 industrial building, originally water-powered. Probably built for the flax and linen trade, it was later a sawmill. Then after skirting the trees for a further 1.5 km. the path reaches the S end of the
103 policies at Crow Wood and crosses the BRIDGE OF ALVAH. Built by the mason *James Robertson* in 1771–3, this is a Picturesque dream come true – a massive single arch, springing from rocky outcrops which occasionally generate a ferocious torrent between the steep and densely wooded banks of the usually placid Deveron. Admired from the water's edge, where it perfectly frames a bend in the river, the bridge is a spectacular intervention within its landscape, while from its ashlar-coped parapets at a height of 17 m. it commands views of the surrounding countryside which are in the truest sense Sublime. Towards its W end its approach abutment swings into the riverbank on a sharp curve, and within its structure beneath the road is a vaulted Gothick chamber with a fireplace, where the 2nd Earl reputedly held court amid the bonny local lasses.

The return journey along the E bank leads past two small vestiges of a designed landscape in the more formal taste proposed by *Adam* in the 1730s. On Hospital Island within the Deveron – fordable at low water – is a small circular FISHING TEMPLE of *c.* 1741, two-storey, with lugged doorpieces at both ground floor and first floor entered by a horseshoe stair and neat pedimental gable. It was originally domed with a gilded figure of Fame. Finally on the summit of the Hill of Doune above Macduff, the TEMPLE OF VENUS, an open rotunda of *c.* 1737 consisting of six keystoned arches rising from a continuous plinth to support a finialled dome – an eyecatcher in itself, and a splendid vantage point from which to view the Duff Estates, the town of Banff and the Moray Firth.

MONTCOFFER HOUSE. *See* Kirkton of Alvah.

BARRA CASTLE

7020

1.5 km. NW of Kirkton of Bourtie

A Scottish Renaissance castle on an open courtyard plan. Although described by MacGibbon and Ross as 'one of the most successful designs we have of this class of house', its three tall ranges, each of three storeys, are actually of several different dates of construction. The central range, set back on the W, is thought to be partly mid-C15, built by the Blackhalls but recast as part of an up-to-date stepped L-plan house when the S jamb was added for George Seton of Meldrum, Chancellor of Aberdeen, *c.* 1614–18; the more modest N wing is much later, built by John Ramsay of Melrose and Laithers *c.* 1760. The entrance front is enclosed by a low C17 screen-wall, the overall impression being one of picturesque semi-symmetry, but the castle has changed much in appearance during its 300 years' gestation from a late medieval fortified house to a mid-C18 gentleman's seat. It was restored by *George Bennett Mitchell* in 1909–11 and carefully repaired in the late C20 for Dr Nicholas Bogdan, preserving its remarkably authentic late C18 atmosphere.

The central (W) range is constructed in field rubble, 16.3 m. long, 8.5 m. wide and vaulted internally at ground floor. The ground floor is almost blind, its slit-windows with shot-holes; large first-floor windows in chamfered surrounds once lit the great hall; then smaller second-floor windows, one at a higher level breaking into a dormer gablet bearing George Seton of Meldrum's monogram and the three interlocking crescents from his heraldic arms. From the centre of the wall-head the immensely tall slim coped chimneystack of the hall fireplace rises as high as the steeply pitched roof: it has a square recess dated 1618 which must once have contained a heraldic panel.

The S wing is very ingeniously planned. It comprises a jamb 7.3 m. square on plan (cf. Esslemont (q.v.)), but with a circular drum tower at its SE angle. This jamb is hinged to the central range by a transverse half-lozenge plan tower containing the

Barra Castle.
Drawing of east front by David M. Walker

entrance vestibule and the stair, which begins as a straight flight, winding into a 3 m.-diameter turnpike on the S front. It has a simple straight-skewed gable above the entrance within the court, and forms the central feature of the remarkably picturesque S elevation, which steps back progressively from the SE jamb to the half-circle of the stair-tower in the re-entrant angle and thence to the gable of the W range, which has a circular drum tower at its SW angle, answering that of the jamb at the E. Whether this tower was part of the C15 work or part of the early C17 reconstruction is difficult to determine. Both corner towers are 4.3 m. in diameter and built with a pronounced batter, both have conical roofs and both have square rooms within. At the central stair tower the batter is slightly less marked and it is corbelled to a square attic caphouse (cf. Tolquhon). At the NW angle of the original block is the base of a further tower, indicating that it was intended in the early C17 that its W elevation should be balanced if not quite symmetrical. Its fenestration is irregular but as on the courtyard side the S end of the top floor has a pedimented dormerhead, here semicircular.

The N wing is a simple rectangular structure with a garret oculus in its E gable, at 6 m. wide rather narrower than the SE jamb. Although built *c.* 1760 of good coursed masonry with regular fenestration it probably stands on older foundations (it is unlikely to be coincidence that the court forms a perfect 9.75 m. square). Tusking at the NE angle of the SW jamb above the present screen wall shows that a two-storey forebuilding was planned, but there is no evidence of it having been built. It was to have replaced an earlier E range, the foundations of which can be seen in the court.

Inside at ground-floor level a right-angled corridor runs from the entrance vestibule to the kitchen at the N end of the W range, with two vaulted cellars opening off it. The kitchen still has its immensely wide fireplace – now occupied by a range at the N gable – and once had an oven in the base of the incomplete NW tower. Of the cellars, the S one has a turnpike stair very neatly contrived within the wall thickness on the E side of the SW tower. At first floor the great hall. This was divided *c.* 1750 or earlier to create dining and drawing rooms but the division was reversed in 2011. So the old fireplace is off-centre with a smaller fireplace set inside it. Sympathetic panelling in the drawing room is of 1909–11. The jamb contains a single square room directly accessible off the spiral stair both at ground floor and first floor, the SW corner tower providing en suite closets: the first-floor chamber was doubtless the bedroom, the panelling later C17 or early C18.

The castle gains significantly from the survival of its formal FORECOURT AND POLICIES. The forecourt is a large high-walled area about 22 m. wide, approached by an avenue running between matching mid-C18 pavilions, their original length curtailed by the present main road. The Castle's S elevation once overlooked a formal garden of which the N wall and one of the summerhouses remains, the latter pyramid-roofed and accessed by a forestair.

BARTHOL CHAPEL *see* TARVES

BELHELVIE 9010

A village near the Rocks of Balmedie quarry opened during the earlier C20, but its development was chiefly driven by the oil boom.

BELHELVIE NORTH CHURCH, 1.2 km. NE. A large, well-detailed Gothic design by *W. & J. Smith*, 1876, built by mason *Stewart* of Peterhead in 1877–8. Tall entrance gable facing SE has twin deeply splayed doorways and stepped triple gallery lancets with hoodmoulds and dripstones. Stepped buttresses, and pronounced skews with big kneelers which rise to a corbelled arch supporting a massive gablet bellcote. Six-bay flanks lit by individual lancets: a porch-stairhall giving access to the gallery abuts the entrance gable on its SW side. Chancel gable lit by cinquefoil roundel; prominent, asymmetrically placed chimneystack rising from boiler-house beneath the vestry outshot. Lofty wagon-vaulted ceiling of impressive span rests on arch-braces springing from corbels, the lateral thrust countered by iron ties. Original furnishings, SE gallery with arcaded front on slim iron columns.

In the churchyard, the WAR MEMORIAL *c.* 1921, a Celtic cross in Kemnay granite pierced and sculpted, tapered shaft rising from plinth and rock-faced base course: erected by *Taggarts Granite Works.*

Former BELHELVIE FREE CHURCH. *See* POTTERTON.

Former ANTIBURGHER CHURCH, Mains of Shiels, 2km. NNW. Dated 1791, in blue heathen stone. A modest structure altered with a wide opening slapped in its front elevation. Galleries added 1802; closed 1908. New Manse (now SHIELS HOUSE) by *George Marr* 1862, single-storeyed three-bay, harled with exposed margins and canted roof dormers. Completing the group, the SCHOOL now substantially altered. On the hilltop Mains of Shiels nearby, the OLD (ANTIBURGHER) MANSE of 1784, a much larger two-storey three-bay house built of granite rubble but with squared dressings and gabled roof with skew-putts, extended *c.* 2008.

BELHELVIE LODGE, 0.6 km. SSW. Classical country house for Harry Lumsden, advocate *c.* 1783, but with a later porch and wings stepped back on either side. Main block two-storey and three broad raised over a low basement, built in pinned squared golden granite with polished margins, hipped roof and simple gable chimneystacks. Robust earlier C19 classical porch. The wings are similar in proportion but different in dates and details: both two-storeyed, slightly lower than the main block with hipped roofs, and set back so that they project in a U-plan to the rear. Right wing *c.* 1800, left wing 1969.

0040 BERRYHILL HOUSE

3.5 km. W of Peterhead on the A950

Probably built for James Shirras of Old Deer who bought the Berryhill estate in 1825, or for Crawford Noble to whom he gave it in 1833. Vernacular classical of real sophistication. Single-storey centre with attic dormers framed between taller piend-roofed ends which extend back as wings. Unusual Doric portico, tetrastyle with slim columns paired to each side, reeded for two-thirds of their height, painted white; no pediment, but a low-pitched granite gablet rising from the wall-head behind effectively suggests one. Attractive pink harling, the astragalled windows in slim ashlar surrounds. Entrance hall with Doric columns, the rooms to each side with sliding doors to create a single large space. Curved stair; low first-floor bedrooms with coved ceilings. Simple office buildings at rear.

7030 BETHELNIE

5 km. NNW of Oldmeldrum

Former CHURCHYARD. No trace remains of the church, save those stones transferred to the new church at Oldmeldrum (q.v.). It was dedicated in the C7 to St Nathlan or Neachtan, and later associated with Arbroath Abbey. – MAUSOLEUM. Mid-C19. Rectangular enclosure in granite rubble, with a trabeated entrance, and three slit-lights just beneath the wall-head on each of the other sides. Panel above entrance with heraldic motif reads 'Beneath this Building Rest the Remains of Many Generations of Meldrums, Setons and Urquharts of Meldrum A.D. 1236 to A.D. 1863.'

BETHELNIE STEADING. By *James Duncan*, 1872. An exceptionally distinguished example. Principal elevation sixteen bays long, single-storey with gableted attic dormers, symmetrical. Built in dark squared granite rubble, coursed and pinned, with lighter grey dressings. Central six-bay cartshed arcade framed by astragalled sash-and-case windows linking to projecting gabled bays with broader arches and cottage-like bothies for labourers at each far end.

5060 BIRKENBOG HOUSE B

2.3 km. WSW of Sandend

A country house in the early vernacular classical style, with a heraldic panel dated 1693; built to supplement the accommodation of an older tower house burnt out in 1790, of which little now remains. The main block of the late C17 house, facing W, is semi-symmetrical, two-storey and five bays. Central architraved doorway and ground floor with windows in the outer bays only, five first-floor windows near-regular in arrangement (the astragalled sashes are recent replacements). Sand-coloured harl, some ashlar dressings over the doorway, the heraldic panel bearing the Abercromby arms. Tall gabled roof in Banffshire slate with stone ridge and coped ashlar end stacks. Abutting the S gable, a slightly lower two-storey stair-drum is a remnant of the burnt-out tower house; a single-storey kitchen outshot extending from the N gable is a later addition. Rear elevation has original ground-floor windows at each far end, and one formed more recently; four original windows at first floor, one now blocked, and a central wall-head chimneystack.

Almost detached from the main house, its derelict W wing, mostly rebuilt during the C18 although the tall single-storey section nearest the main block corresponds to the height of the original offices. Beyond this, the wing extends into two parts – a two-storey three-bay house, and two additional bays much more broadly spaced, which were evidently added shortly afterwards, and then subsequently altered with a segmental brick arch to accommodate a horse-gig. The W gable shows that these additional bays have been heightened slightly, the roof-lines being carried over from the older house with three stumpy chimneystacks all coped the same way, and only the central skewputt moulded. The W end gable also displays a roof-scar which shows that the wing once extended into a narrow single-storey building at its far W end. A simple wall encloses the S side of the forecourt; the railings are modern but the sturdy GATEPIERS are probably 1693. Behind the main house, a very large WALLED GARDEN, rubble walls lined with brick on the S aspect.

BLACKHILL HOUSE 0040

5 km. SW of Peterhead

Early C19. Single-storey three-bay villa with pilastered doorpiece over semi-sunk basement, approach stairs framed between podia, understated cornice and deep plain parapet. An interesting example of the familiar Aberdeen villa formula translated to a rustic context, very deep on plan with low-pitched roof and low end stacks, no dormers, the attic lit from gables and roof-lights. Fine granite ashlar construction, smooth at ground floor and rough beneath. Simply detailed interior. Circular front GARDEN enclosed by rubble walls with carriage gateway flanked by original turnstiles.

BODDAM 1040

A former fishing village. 128

TRINITY PARISH CHURCH, Manse Terrace. 'Erected 1865', perhaps by *William Clarke*. Georgian Gothic Survival, with

Y-traceried windows and small bellcote at apex of the entrance gable. Later C19 session house. Simple but intact interior with coved ceiling. W gallery supported on slim colonnettes. Octagonal PULPIT with stairs on each side. – COMMUNION TABLE and FONT in Stirling Hill granite. – MANSE, opposite. A two-storey villa, built 1878.

UNITED FREE CHURCH, Church Place. Built as the Free Church by *Duncan McMillan* (of *Mackenzie & McMillan*), 1881. Gothic front with hoodmoulded doorway, rose window and bellcote. Transeptal bays mask the five-bay aisles. Polygonally vaulted ceiling, the aisle arcades of slim cast-iron colonnettes. Original pitch-pine furnishings, including a very wide platform pulpit.

BODDAM HARBOUR. Plans for enlargement were furnished by Baillie Robertson of Fraserburgh in 1831. A second harbour was built for the fishermen *c.* 1845, largely at the expense of the 4th Earl of Aberdeen through whose influence Boddam became a registered port in that year. The harbour was substantially reconstructed by *William Aiton* in 1878 and deepened during the 1970s as the cool-water inlet for Peterhead Power Station (*see* p. 111).

BODDAM SCHOOL, Russell Street. Single-storey of 1840, substantially reconstructed and enlarged by *Andrew Kidd*, the Peterhead School Board Architect, in 1876, with further additions since. Projecting wing on the centre with bellcote and wide eaves.

DUNDONNIE MASONIC LODGE (No. 1087), Rocksley Drive. Vernacular classical *c.* 1830. Two-storey three bays, low ground floor and tall first, construction in rough red granite ashlar with centre door round-headed, plain eaves course and simple coped end stacks.

WAR MEMORIALS, Manse Terrace. Fine First World War memorial erected by *Hislop, Wilson & Co.*, a tall Neoclassical cenotaph with surmounting cross, constructed in grey granite ashlar. Second World War Memorial set behind it.

DESCRIPTION. Boddam has existed since at least the C16. The early settlement occupied the edge of coast opposite the rocky outcrop where Buchanness Lighthouse (*see* below) now stands, affording it some shelter. Expansion began in 1830 and in 1840 the 4th Earl of Aberdeen built Buchanness Lodge (*see* below) between the village and Boddam Castle. Perhaps his presence, together with the ready supply of granite from Stirling Hill, ensured that most of the cottages were of very good quality. They present an irregular, often picturesque appearance as they rise up the hillside in QUEEN'S ROAD, GORDON STREET and RUSSELL STREET; HARBOUR STREET is the principal thoroughfare, following the coast. The Great North of Scotland Railway arrived in 1897, also serving Stirling Village and its quarry. Although Boddam's harbour had been enlarged in 1878 it was not big enough to accommodate the steam trawlers of the early C20, which instead found berths in Peterhead (q.v.). The village went into prolonged decline, the railway closing to passengers in 1932 and freight in 1945. Its terminus was redeveloped as RAF Buchan in 1952, and partly in consequence of this BUCHANNESS DRIVE was formed in the late 1950s, still in a pre-war idiom. The most recent housing, in Seaview Road, Skerry Park and Laird's Walk was all spurred by the discovery of North Sea oil and the development of Peterhead Power Station (*see* below). The RAF base closed in 2005.

Boddam Castle. On a promontory site to the s of the village. Late C16–early C17, built by the Keiths of Lundquharn, occupied until 1700. The Rev. Dr George Moir, writing the first *Statistical Account* of Peterhead in 1795, recorded that the walls, although ruinous, were still standing, but only a solitary gable is recorded in James Giles's watercolour of 1840, and the castle is little changed now. This gable gives entry to an enclosure *c.* 30 m. square, of which only footings remain, there being evidence of building ranges on both the N and S sides.

Buchanness Lodge, by the coast off Inchmore Gardens. Built for the 4th Earl of Aberdeen who was later prime minister. Picturesque Italianate. The original two-storey villa in red granite ashlar with low-pitched roof was built by *John Smith I* in 1840; its large E wing with a new entrance and canted bay looking out to sea was added shortly afterwards, seemingly in two stages. A single-storey outshot is also later. Burnt 1984, only the original house has been restored. Terraced gardens stepping down the cliff edge from the main road to the sea are still discernible.

Buchanness Lighthouse. Designed by *Robert Stevenson*, 128
engineer to the Northern Lighthouse Board, and built by Aberdeen contractor *John Gibb* in 1825–7 following petitions from Peterhead Burgh and Harbour (qq.v.) in 1819 and 1822. Constructed in Stirling Hill granite, the tower shaft tapers gradually to a deep Gothic cavetto corbel course which is 36 m. above sea level; this supports a railed walkway and the domed lantern itself, square-paned and 40 m. above sea level. Around the tower's base on its landward side the plant-rooms are accommodated in a single-storey five-window bow, while two assistant keeper's cottages form symmetrical wings enclosing a court on the seaward side, the roofs being flat but the chimneystacks tall and octagonally shafted. Buchanness had the first ever revolving light, which floated in a mercury bath; this was replaced by refracting (dioptric) lenses in 1910, the lantern was enlarged in 1978 and it was automated in 1988. Columnar fluted sundial in lighthouse precincts. Concrete approach bridge of 1962 by *P. H. Hyslop*, engineer of the Northern Lighthouse Board, with *A.M. Robertson* of Helensburgh; contractor *H.M. Murray* of Glasgow.*

Peterhead Power Station. Built by the North of Scotland 128
Hydro-Electric Board, with architects *Robert Matthew Johnson-Marshall & Partners*, in anticipation of the increased demand resulting from the industrialization of the north-east with the discovery of oil. Construction began in 1973 and was completed in 1980, with additions since. The site was chosen for its exceptional ground strength, the availability of water for cooling and the proximity of Peterhead Harbour (q.v.) for

*The foghorn of 1904 was decommissioned in 2000 and is now demolished.

deliveries of oil. In architectural terms the power station is appropriately a rational technological composition in modern materials. The MAIN BLOCK'S massive glazed superstructure is supported by a large square podium, which results in a stepped appearance when seen from Boddam Harbour to the SE; the CHIMNEY is 170 m. high. The establishment of the St Fergus Gas Terminal (*see* p. 385) resulted in alteration of the main block's boilers, so allowing them to run on oil, gas or a combination of both as economics and supply made most prudent. Once fully operational in 1982 the power station's output of 1,320 MW doubled HydroElectric's total supply: since then the construction of additional gas turbines and improvements in efficiency have increased its contribution significantly.

SANDFORD LODGE, N of the Power Station. Built *c.* 1800 for James Skelton, Sheriff-substitute of Peterhead, and father of the author Sir John Skelton. Compact vernacular classical country house, two storeys and three bays with taller centre slightly stepped forward and rising into a pediment crowned by urn finials. Harled in white, with ashlar dressings and long-and-short quoins, the original architraved doorway concealed by a later porch built over the stair platt. Ground-floor Serlian windows, tripartites at first, tall hipped roof and very tall end stacks. Rear elevation with semi-elliptical stair bay, offices and later canted dormers. Large WALLED GARDEN with ball-finialled gatepiers and gates.

STIRLING VILLAGE, 0.5 km. SW on the A90. A line of mostly single-storey cottages built in the mid C19 for Stirling Hill quarrymen.

FLINT-WORKING SITE, Den of Boddam, 0.75 km. WSW. Above the slopes of Mill Dam hollows can be seen from flint-working in the Neolithic period. Flint was a very valuable resource in earlier prehistory that could be worked into tools for cutting, scraping and a range of other tasks. This is the only extensive inland deposit of flint in Scotland. Substantial pits over 2 m. deep were dug through the glacial till into the underlying gravel to obtain the flint. These hollows can be best seen in low sunlight. (GN)

BOURTIE *see* KIRKTON OF BOURTIE

6060

BOYNDIE B

A small kirkton since 1773, when worship transferred here from Inverboyndie (q.v.).

ST BRANDON (Parish Church). By *Alexander Duffus*, 1772–3; burnt out 2000. Four-bay preaching-box; the pulpit was once centred against the S flank, faced by galleries on all three sides. The ball-finialled birdcage bellcote still has the bell by *Hugh Gordon* of 1770. Porch 1922. Session house on N side, possibly 1903–4; E window lengthened by *John Fowlie*, 1909. A blocked

N opening at gallery level suggests the former existence of a laird's aisle before the session house was built.

St Brandon's House. Former manse built 1841–2, perhaps by *William Robertson*.* A handsome and unusual, almost cubical design. Three-storeys three-bays with principal entrance level raised over a basement. Neoclassical pedimented doorpiece with acroters, its approach stair enclosed by solid ashlar parapets. Astragalled sash-and-case windows in slim margin surrounds, first-floor windows lower beneath a hipped platform roof with central stairhall cupola and coped chimneystacks. Flanks three bays closer-spaced. – Steading 1841. – Two-storey former Beadle's House and Stables, late c19.

Ladysbridge Village, 0.8 km. e. A residential development around the former Banff District Lunatic Asylum (now Ladysbridge House), won in competition by *Alexander Reid* (of *A. & W. Reid*), 1861, opened 1865. Simple Tudor, a long symmetrical design handsomely proportioned and impressively situated on rising ground with a fine outlook towards the s. Central two-storey block three bays broad containing dining and recreation halls raised over a basement, with tall mullioned-and-transomed windows, those at first floor with attic gablets over the end bays. The long two-storey fifteen-bay ward blocks are set well back with gabled day-rooms projecting at regular intervals, slim truncated spirelet towers rising behind the wards towards each end, and roof-lines punctuated by tall chimneystacks. Main entrance on the n side in a central rear wing which also contained the kitchen and other ancillaries. Woodpark Succursal Asylum for females, plain two-storey and attic crowstepped, is also by the *Reids*, 1880, and Moor Newton Block is again by them, later c19. Mayfield Villa for male patients by *Kelly & Nicol*, 1903. The area to the n was developed after 1966 for Ladysbridge Hospital (closed 2003), now cleared for housing.

Former RAF Boyndie, 2.3 km. w. In use 1943–6. Comparable in scale to the airfields at Kinloss and Lossiemouth (Moray) but unique in being built on sloping ground. Three runways – two of 1 km. length, one of 1.8 km. – in the standard triangular layout, with circular hard-standings, most of which were formerly occupied by hangars. The control tower and operations block survive in derelict condition.

BOYNE CASTLE 6060

2.2 km. e of Portsoy

Probably begun by Sir Alexander Ogilvie who had married Mary Bethune, one of Queen Mary's personal attendants, in 1566, but reputedly completed by his cousin Sir George Ogilvie of Dunlugas who acquired the estate in 1575. Although now ruinous, the castle was once hugely impressive in size and scale, and as

*Its predecessor, by *Alexander Duffus* 1774–5, stood close by.

Boyne Castle, original C17 appearance from the SW.
Drawing by David M. Walker

much palatial as fortified in character although occupying a genuinely defensive site enclosed on three sides by the steep gorge of the Burn of Boyne. A courtyard plan, near-symmetrical, with ranges on three sides, it was 32 m. wide and 27 m. deep, clasped between drum towers 6.5 m. in diameter at all four corners; the construction was in harled rubble. The S entrance front was very formal, three storeys with an attic, approached by an elevated causeway between walled sunk gardens in a dry moat 38 m. wide: the entrance itself was flanked by drum towers about 4.2 m. in diameter. These were similar to the towers still extant at Rowallan (Ayrshire), Dudhope (Dundee) and Tolquhon (q.v.), and the forerunners of the arch-linked towers at Fyvie (q.v.). The angle towers had corbelled parapets and circular caphouses, reminiscent of those at Falkland (Fife) and Holyrood (Edinburgh), the overall effect rather like one of the simpler French châteaux. Originally the E and W ranges seem to have been two-storey and attic, their angle towers a storey lower than those on the S front but with the same corbelled parapets.

The principal accommodation was in the W range where the ground floor had four regular vaulted chambers, the generously planned staircase 3.4 m. in diameter being on the S front just to the W of the entrance transe. Above was the hall, with a bedchamber in the NW tower. All of this was very advanced for the 1560s, but by the later C16 or earliest C17 the W range appears to have been heightened a storey, an additional stair being inserted into the N re-entrant angle of the SW tower: the evidence for this is best seen at the N gable which has been raised high above the original corbelled parapet and at the NW tower where a two-storey drum was superimposed on its corbelled parapet. Only the walls of the W range stand relatively entire. The S front has largely fallen and the E range has almost completely disappeared. Sir Patrick Ogilvie was obliged to sell his estates in 1709 but his family were allowed to remain in the castle. After his son James's involvement in the 1715 rising, however, the castle was unroofed and its dressed stones reused for farmsteadings.

DOOCOT, 120 m. WSW. Late C16–early C17. Rectangular, rubble-built with tooled dressings; chamfered doorway and two rat courses, the second running across the crowstepped gables of the slated roof. About 750 nesting boxes.

BRUCKLAY CASTLE 9050

2.5 km. NNW of Maud

A large Baronial house by *Thomas Mackenzie*, 1848, for Capt. Alexander Dingwall-Fordyce, altered by *Matthews & Mackenzie* (presumably *James Matthews*) in 1881–94, but incorporating much older fabric at the SW, an original Crawford tower house of the C15–C16 extended in 1765 and again by *John Smith I* in 1814. All unroofed in 1953 but partial restoration of the house is proposed in 2012. The best surviving element is now Mackenzie's entrance front which is near-symmetrical. A central projecting three-storey tower with bowed angles rising into a crowstep-gabled attic caphouse, turret to one side, and fronted by a heavy round-arched porte cochère, also turreted, rising from steeply battered plinths. Two-storey and attic two-bay wings with corner turrets – l. first floor and attic, circular corbelled to caphouse; r. circular pepperpot at attic floor only. The dominant feature of Mackenzie's remodelling was once a tall tower with corbelled parapet and caphouse added to the S front.

STABLES, 180 m. NE, derelict. Hybrid Tudor-classical. W quad probably by *John Smith I c.* 1820. Two-storey Tudor tower flanked by classical three-bay wings with shallow oblong lights expressing the attic beneath the pitched roofs. Tower and end bays buttressed or pilastered, the tower originally with battlements and sculpture of a deer or hind, the ends with blocking courses. Squared granite construction with cherry-cocking.

KENNELS, 220 m. NNE, *c.* 1800. Roman castellated screen-wall. Battlemented centre with round-headed arch and battlemented ends with lower links between them. – WALLED GARDEN, 360 m. S. Rectangular, coped brick walls with bowed corners. It now contains a house. – NORTH LODGE, 0.6 km. NW. Perhaps by *John Smith I c.* 1830. Tudorish, single-storey L-plan, the small porch (later?) in the angle with decorative bargeboards. – EAST LODGE, 1.1 km. NE. Probably *James Matthews c.* 1860. Scottish Baronial, very grand for such a residence. Two storeys and three bays, l. bay broad and slightly projected under crowstepped gable with angle-turret, balanced by three-storey angle drum tower with conical roof to r. Segment-headed, moulded doorway flanked by ground-floor bay windows; upper windows have finialled dormer pediments; all astragalled sash-and-case. Harled masonry with granite dressings, coped stacks, the turret and drum spirelets with fish-scale slating. Large oriel in gable overlooking the road. Low quadrant walls with balustrades in ashlar extend out to square gatepiers with pyramidal tops on bracket-runs. – WEST LODGE, 1.3 km. SW. Probably by *James Matthews c.* 1860. Cottage-style, with open gabled porch, windows with half-moon pediments and thistle finials, crowstep-gabled roof. Basement exposed at rear. – SHEVADO STEADING, 0.8 km. SSW. A large single-storey courtyard plan, mainly early C19. Principal S front with the arched centrepiece and end bays rising into attic storeys beneath pedimental gables. Pinned granite rubble, partly residential and partly storage. E flank with projecting dairy annexe, W flank plain with segmental and trabeated openings, S side partly demolished. – LAUNDRY, 330 m. S. Two-storey. Restored from ruin by *Kenneth Thomson*, *c.* 2005–9, who added single-storey wings. – BRIDGE, 450 m. W. By *John Smith I*, *c.* 1830. Built in granite, a single segmental span with parapets, octagonal terminals with double-keyhole 'gunloops'.

BUCHANNESS *see* BODDAM

0060

CAIRNBULG CASTLE

2.7 km. WSW of Inverallochy & Cairnbulg

The story of Cairnbulg Castle extends from the early medieval period to the late C19. Its fabric reflects the development of Scottish military architecture from the original palisaded motte through the medieval great tower, the transition to more horizontal living in the mid C16, followed by lengthy abandonment, ruin and eventual reconstruction by the Victorians in their own interpretation of the Scottish Baronial style.

The oldest part of the castle is the MOTTE on which it stands. It must have been raised by the Celtic mormaers or their successors, the Comyn Earls of Buchan, and was seemingly part of a chain of defences guarding the N coast against Viking raids. The castle at Cairnbulg, which was closer to the shore then than now, defended the Water of Philorth, itself once much freer-flowing, and the E end of Fraserburgh Bay. The Water of Philorth partly encircled the mound, flooded its moat and resulted in the boglands defending it on its landward side.

As it stands today the castle comprises three main elements – the late medieval Great Tower at the NW, a much longer and lower block running W–E which is essentially Victorian on C16 foundations, and a C16 round tower at the SE, together forming a Z-plan. The mound was perhaps re-profiled when the GREAT TOWER was first built. This is rectangular on plan, 12.5 m. by

9 m.; its massive walls some 2 m. thick rise with a very slight taper through four storeys' height to merlons 17.5 m. above ground, but photographs taken before its Victorian reconstruction and harling show that it is of more than one build. The ground floor constructed in medium-sized boulder rubble laid in neat courses may have been built as early as the C13 or – as Dr Douglas Simpson has suggested – by Sir Alexander Fraser, who acquired Cairnbulg when he married the Earl of Ross's daughter Joanna in 1375, but the first-floor Great Hall and the second and third floors above have been subsequently reconstructed in large boulders with greater use of packing material at some point during the C15. The original entrance was at ground floor in the long S flank, near the SE corner, and for reasons of defence most of the windows were small. The door and window dressings are all worked in dark red sandstone and green or purple schist, moulded or chamfered. Around the wall-head, corbelling supports a high crenellated parapet with circular bartizans at three corners which rest on deeper corbelling: this is Victorian, reinstating what had formerly existed, although at the SE corner there was once a square turret to protect the doorway, the corbelling of which is still visible on the E side.

Internally both the ground-floor cellar and the much taller great hall which occupied the whole of the first floor are vaulted. The Great Hall is 7.75 m. long by 5 m. wide, and 5.5 m. to the crown of its vault. Its C16 fireplace at the W end is of 2.5 m. span. The hall was originally reached by means of a straight stair rising within the thickness of the E wall to the ingo of the large first-floor window on this side: the foot of the stair was apparently guarded by a large *meurtrière* or murder hole, now blocked. The original position of the stairs to the second and third floors is not clear. These floors were each partitioned to form two rooms, accessed by passages within the thickness of the wall, and again with intramural closets: one such on the second floor opened into a prison formed within the hollow above the Great Hall's vault. The old fireplaces are simple, some of them evidently C16.

Probably during the 1540s Sir Alexander Fraser, 7th of Philorth, built the 'LOW WARK', a lower block 23.5 m. by 8.75 m. providing more comfortable accommodation immediately SE of the Great Tower. This formed the S side of a very large walled court entered from the E, part of which survived into the C19. A turnpike stair bay was built in the angle between the original tower and the Low Wark, concealing the Great Tower's original doorway, and a new entrance formed.

It is not clear whether the ROUND TOWER standing at the SE corner of the Low Wark diagonally opposite the Great Tower and so forming the third 'arm' of the Z-plan is of the same date as the Low Wark, or whether it once formed part of a barmkin surrounding the Great Tower. It is 8.25 m. in diameter and rises through four full storeys into a battlemented parapet and circular caphouse some 12 m. above ground, both of which were reinstatements of 1896–7. Supported by a bracket-run, the parapet extended across the external walls of the Low Wark on its E, S and probably W sides. The Round Tower's ground floor was originally vaulted and there are still three shot-holes commanding each flank of the Low Wark and the wider field. Its polygonal first-floor chamber was quite a distinguished apartment with three windows, and even in 1881 when the castle was surveyed by Thomas Ross it retained traces of painted plasterwork decoration.

The Frasers of Philorth were obliged to sell the castle and much of their lands *c.* 1615 after incurring debts promoting Fraserburgh (q.v.) as a seaport and a university town. Attempts to annul the sale proved unsuccessful and after the Restoration the Frasers, ennobled in 1669 as Lords Saltoun, built the Philorth House (q.v.) just 1.5 km. away and in full view of their ancestral home. From here they could only watch as the castle passed from the Durris branch of the Clan Fraser to Lord Fraser, then out of the clan altogether to the Buchans of Auchmacoy, to Alexander Aberdein and finally to the 3rd Earl of Aberdeen. The earl stripped it to a shell in 1782, its timber, slates and window-glass all being sold for hard cash. During a great gale on Christmas Day 1806 the greater part of the Low Wark collapsed.

James Giles's watercolours of 1839 show much of the Low Wark reduced to its foundations, although both the Great Tower and the Round Tower had survived comparatively intact, as had the main gate on the E side of the walled court. Thomas Ross's drawings of 1881, however, show how perilous the castle's condition had by then become, the Great Tower shattered with extensive cracks running up its walls. But, implausible as it seemed, salvation was at hand. In 1862 Cairnbulg had been bought by the trustees of the Aberdeen shipbuilder John Duthie, who had designed and operated the famous tea-clippers and established the first regular service between Britain and Australia. His nephew and heir Sir John Duthie married the daughter of a stone-merchant who provided a fine supply of Corennie granite to rebuild the castle as a dowry. The Duthies then engaged *Jenkins & Marr* to undertake an ambitious RESTORATION AND RECONSTRUCTION carried out in 1896–7. As far as practicable the original appearance of the Great Tower and the Round Tower was preserved, but so little remained of the Low Wark that it was rebuilt in a C19 Baronial idiom, its symmetrical S front of two storeys and attic with central pedimented dormers and square-plan crow-step-gabled turrets at each end. During the reconstruction the stair bay linking the Great Tower with this new 'Low Wark' collapsed but it was rebuilt as near as possible to its previous profile, with a gabled caphouse at its head. The caphouse of the Round Tower was also reinstated with a crenellated parapet, Jenkins & Marr guesswork which Douglas Simpson believed to be correct. The resultant composition fusing together two if not three generations of the Baronial in Scotland is a remarkably happy one, picturesque and romantic as might be expected from the Victorians, but also honouring and preserving what is genuinely old.

INTERIOR. In the restored castle, the principal apartments comprise the dining and drawing rooms on the first floor of the rebuilt Low Wark, with the billiard room (which doubled as a more formal dining room) occupying the old hall of the Great Tower, and a business room on the first floor of the Round Tower. The DINING AND DRAWING ROOMS are very similar, but whereas the former is lined in dark oak with a Doric fireplace, the woodwork of the latter is painted white, its fireplace ornamented with flowers. The upper sashes of their windows contain small-paned leaded lights, some of which are painted with ships. The octagonal BUSINESS ROOM is lit by round-headed windows, with round-headed bookshelf recesses in alternate sides, also in dark oak. Over its fireplace is an inscription, 'Remove Not the Old Landmark'. The undersides of the ceiling beams are exposed, the interstices between them plastered and painted in black and gold with heraldic arms. At the top of the Round Tower, the third floor and fourth-floor caphouse have been combined to form a double-height octagonal LIBRARY, with an oak balustraded stair ascending to a continuous gallery. The lower ceiling has exposed beams like the business room but the caphouse ceiling is lined with moulded cypress panels.

Sir John Duthie's son sold the castle back to the Saltouns in 1934. Since then a number of changes have been made, including the insertion of fireplaces from Tarbat House (Highland) in 1966.

The WALLED GARDEN, 50 m. S, is rectangular on plan. On one side it incorporates a GATEWAY, round-arched with a panel above for heraldic arms. Prior to the restoration this gave access to the court, which was then still partly cobbled. The LODGE is by *Jenkins & Marr*, 1897.

CAIRNESS HOUSE 0060

2.8 km. NE of Lonmay

Cairness House, by *James Playfair* 1791–7, is of international 81
importance as the only house in Britain the design and construction of which reflected and evolved with the rapid advances in French Neoclassicism towards the end of the C18. Together with the equally advanced Townley, County Louth, built after Playfair's premature death on the basis of his sketches, it represents the climax of a brief but extraordinary career assisted by Henry Dundas (later Viscount Melville) who was Pitt the Younger's right-hand man in Scotland, and its survival is the more precious as so many of Playfair's other designs were either not built or have been lost or altered.

In its time, Cairness must have made a statement as a daringly unconventional, conspicuously modern house. The client, Charles Gordon of Buthlaw, had become rich through inheritance. He had received the estate from his mother and aunts, and proceeded to build an attractive vernacular classical house, seemingly to designs by *Robert Burn* and *Adam Porter*, in the early 1780s. But the real root of his wealth was the sugar plantation of Georgia in Jamaica, which he received in settlement of debts owed to his uncles. Such was his meteoric rise to riches and social standing that Burn and Porter's house was almost immediately inadequate for his requirements. It was Gordon's intention that his new house should double as a very grand Masonic temple, and its distinctive motifs are often not so much expressive of new developments in architectural style as laden with an age-old significance.

Playfair's first personal experience of developments in France came as the result of a visit to Paris in 1787. Gordon invited him to Cairness in summer 1789, and the first drawings of a beautiful folio now preserved in King's College, Aberdeen, were prepared during the winter of 1789–90. As built the house's main block, begun 1791, corresponds to these drawings quite closely, its unusual compositional massing representing a new development in Neoclassical architecture in Britain. But by that point Playfair had made a second visit to Paris – now in the throes of political as well as architectural revolution – and on his return redesigned the rear service court as a hemicycle, reflecting the latest French thinking. The Primitivist details were, however, something else, even by French standards, and put Playfair in the *avant-garde* in Europe. He made two Italian study-tours in 1791–2 and 1793, following which he produced a series of mesmerizing sketches for the principal interiors. He died in 1794 but an efficient site-agent ensured that construction was not delayed and most of the work was completed by the end of the following year; the original drawings for the portico having been lost, replacements were furnished by *John Soane*, whom Playfair almost certainly knew. In 1796 Charles Gordon himself died; the house was finished in July 1797.

For a design which appears so perfectly resolved, so canonical, it is perhaps surprising that there are few if any obvious precedents. The MAIN BLOCK's distinction lies not only in its originality of massing but its subtlety of proportions, complemented by its excellent construction mostly in granite ashlar masonry. Like all Playfair's houses, it is primarily a composition of simple unornamented planes, its detailing intentionally restrained to accentuate an intrinsically monumental character.

The ENTRANCE FRONT facing SW comprises a two-storey five-bay centre block framed by taller three-storey end bays, all raised over a semi-sunk basement forming a plinth. When seen in elevation the tall end bays appear like Palladian corner pavilions, but they are three-storey for the full depth of the house and clamp the centre block between them like bookends: perhaps Soane's remodelling of Chillington Hall, Staffordshire, in 1785 provided some inspiration. The main block's construction is in pale granite ashlar from Cairngall. The entrance is approached by a broad flight of stairs leading to a Roman Doric pedimented portico, the column spacing reflecting the doorway with its slim round-headed triple sidelights. The columns themselves are reputedly carved from standing stones which once formed a circle at Rora; the entablature is decorated with triglyphs and the pediment conceals behind it an elegant segmental fanlight. Flanking the portico on the upper stair parapets are the most overt symbols of the house's Masonic status: two broken-shafted columnar pedestals representing Joachim and Boaz guarding the entrance.

The windows in the centre block are broadly spaced, emphasizing the horizontal. The ground-floor windows rest upon a string course, the first-floor windows on a plain frieze-like belt course, and all of them are set in simple architraves. At the wall-head, a low parapet is jettied out above the mutuled cornice and incised with repeating swastika motifs. From ground level the platform roof is hidden but the skyline is punctuated in very precise and regular fashion by chimneystacks with tall cast-iron cans in the form of fluted Doric columns. In the end bays, by contrast, the emphasis is on the vertical. They are slightly set forward, with long-and-short quoins. Above segmental fanlights in the basement, the ground-floor Dining Room and Drawing Room are lit by very tall tripartite windows, low-relief consoles with carved-leaf decoration supporting refined pediments of very shallow projection. The first-floor windows and second-floor square windows have simple architraves like those of the centre block, and the oversailing eaves are supported on mutuled cornices without blocking courses.

The treatment of the FLANK ELEVATIONS represents a sharp contrast with the main front. The ground-, first- and second-floor windows are all set in plain architraves, but the five bays are tightly spaced. The emphasis is again on the vertical, to such an extent that even the first-floor window-sills are contained within their dropped architraves. At the REAR ELEVATION of the house, arched tripartite windows express the twin stair halls. The end bays are windowless, with tall blind arches.

Extending out behind the flank elevations are two PAVILIONS built predominantly in channelled ashlar with hipped roofs and deeply overshadowed eaves, which form the links to the service court. The front elevations of these pavilions, while windowless, are powerfully modelled. In each case the projecting base course supports a large semicircular recess which resembles a blind Diocletian window, but with very unusual Primitivist detailing. In fact it is a combination of two Masonic symbols, an altar within a royal arch, together representing the

Temple of Solomon. Above the arch on a low first floor is a row of three blind panels.

The great HEMICYCLE COURT is 50 m. in diameter, built in ashlar granite obtained from a local quarry at Cairness. This too comprises ground and low first floors, and is entered at the rear through a semicircular archway, hence a half-cylinder cutting through an arc. The arch-ring, which projects boldly but diminishes in thickness towards the top, is raised on square plinths and replicates vertically the horizontal plan of the pavilions and the hemicycle. The roofs are kept very low, with a few carefully placed stacks, but above the arch is a platform supporting a neatly detailed circular bellcote crowned with a small dome.

Within the hemicycle are inner and outer concentric courts. The hemicycle revolves around a circular building constructed in sandstone immediately behind the main block. Based on the Temple of Vesta in Rome, this contains the ICE HOUSE AND LARDER arranged one inside the other: the ice house rises above the low broad-eaved roof of the larder into a telescopic channelled drum with broad-eaved roofs of its own. The doorways are square-headed but the windows are round-arched and mostly blocked, with central slits to admit the light and air. This Round Temple has a curiously powerful aura. Inside the ice house, which is very tall since its floor is well below ground level, the brickwork is remarkable, in rich reds and cream and of at least three different types. In the semi-gloom it does not resemble British brickwork so much as an ancient Roman or Byzantine wall built up over several centuries, and perhaps excavated in an archaeological dig.

INTERIOR. Within the main house the ground-floor plan is symmetrical. The principal interiors are distinguished by the interplay of their strongly architectonic qualities, a blurred distinction between indoors and outdoors, their bold and often geometric decorative features brought out – then and now – by deep rich colours and a meticulous attention to fine detail. The original décor was overseen after Playfair's death by his client's wife, Christian Forbes of Ballogie, who appears mostly to have followed his intentions. The chimneypieces and plasterwork moulds were made by *Richard Rathbone* in London and all the furnishings supplied by the London cabinet-maker *Thomas Seddon*.

In Playfair's drawings the ENTRANCE HALL is marbled in yellow and articulated into three bays by pilasters which are painted in imitation of blue-grey granite. Its chimneypiece in channelled masonry has a round-arched opening with a pediment and acroters rather than a mantelshelf, echoing Playfair's Lynedoch Mausoleum at Methven (*see Buildings of Scotland: Perth and Kinross*) but miniaturized, and again of Masonic significance. In the side bays within either flank, and at the far end, rich friezes, white against a red background, pass across the lintels of five doorways, each with a round-headed fanlight formed in metal to produce exceptionally slim veins. Above is the entablature with another enriched frieze supporting the compartmented ceiling.

Across the main front of the house, the BREAKFAST ROOM is finished in lapis lazuli glistening above a dado painted to simulate fine stone or marble; the walls are niched for full-length figurative sculptures, the ceiling a flat roundel. The LIBRARY in pale green has a Soanean pendentived ceiling, again with a roundel. Its bookcases have lozenge panels in their lower sections, while the upper doors are intricately glazed, and a Greek-key frieze runs around the room across their entablatures: the sense of life and movement in this room is particularly strong. In the end bays, the DINING ROOM is painted pale blue. Its tripartite window, which reaches down to floor level, is framed by Cora Doric fluted columns *in antis* with finely moulded bases and capitals; the fireplace is distinguished by paired columns of the same order, the ceiling is plain over an enriched frieze. The DRAWING ROOM is in yellow, its tripartite window framed by Ionic columns *in antis* 'as in the Temple of Apollo Dydimaeus in Ionia'. At the opposite end of the Drawing Room the columns are answered by four pilasters, and the ceiling again features a central roundel flanked by panels of small circles. Both the Dining and Drawing Rooms are lit by three windows in the flanks, the latter with pier-glasses between them.

All of these front rooms are entered through richly detailed doorcases which, when the doors are opened, result in a magnificent enfilade – four successive doorcases seen one inside the other as they diminish into the distance, yet their bold detailing remains clearly discerned. The Dining Room and Drawing Room are entered through outer and inner doorways, for insulation and privacy, and to protect the inner doors' polish. Although they are panelled and jointed so as to appear double-leaf, they are single-leaf, and unusually wide. The doors' circular panels are a contemporary French detail.

On the rear side of the house, at either end, are a bedroom and business room. The BUSINESS ROOM is fitted out with simple glazed bookcases. The BEDROOM has a cornice with scallop shells symbolizing Venus and antefixae depicting the face of Isis, respectively the Roman and Egyptian goddesses of love. The two dog-leg STAIRWAYS, one towards each end of the house, are rather different in character. Both are distinguished but the W stair is notably grand, its balusters decorated with palmettes. From the mezzanine of this stair the upper landing presents a remarkable appearance: seen within the frame of an archway, it has a pendentive domed ceiling and a round-arched wall recess, resulting in a most attractive play of forms. The length of the FIRST-FLOOR CORRIDOR is also divided by a sequence of arches.

Modifications to the plans of 1789–90 resulted in the Entrance Hall opening straight ahead into what has become known as the billiard room but was originally the MASONIC 82
CHAMBER in the centre of the rear elevation. This apartment

was almost certainly the first anywhere in Britain to be completely finished in the Egyptian style. Like the Entrance Hall it has door and window architraves in simulated granite against a pale background. The ceiling is segmentally vaulted, and coffered at each end. The door architraves and frieze have been carved with Egyptic symbols including high priests, the Ankh, Compasses of God the Architect, masons' tools, animals and birds; some appear to reflect the influence of Athanasius Kircher and Piranesi's Caffè degli Inglesi. Astonishingly within such a stratified society, two identical panels facing directly opposite each other above the doorway and the windows give equal prominence to Charles Gordon the client and James Playfair the architect who were jointly responsible for the creation of the house, one of them already dead, the other soon to die. The panels commemorate the start of construction on 4 April 1791 and completion in 1797; according to the Bible, Solomon's Temple was begun in early April. Appropriately enough, the windows of the Masonic Chamber look out to the Round Temple in the courtyard beyond.

GROUNDS. Playfair produced two designs for LODGE HOUSES AND GATES which in themselves represent the development of his architectural style after his first and second trips to France: his original proposals of 1790 were Neoclassical, but he produced another scheme in 1793 which was Early Christian-Byzantine. Neither was carried out for a hundred years, until Charles Thomas Gordon, 'the zealous preserver and improver of Cairness', decided to construct the first set of proposals in 1891. These comprise two single-storey square pavilions linked by dwarf walls with railings to gatepiers on each side of the driveway. Towards the main road, the centre of each pavilion is slightly stepped out with a round-headed window in an arched recess and a pediment beneath a low pyramid roof with central cylindrical chimney. The gatepiers are massive in proportion, of channelled masonry, crowned with sphinxes; the gates and flanking railings themselves incorporate the hemicycle motif. In building these gates Charles Thomas Gordon completed the Masonic entrance sequence. The sphinxes ask visitors the riddle which – if they 'answer correctly' – admits them to the parkland Arcadia. Joachim and Boaz as represented by the broken columns guard the entrance to the Masonic Chamber and the Round Temple beyond.

The PARKLAND itself was designed in 1791 by *Thomas White*, whose watercolours are still preserved at Cairness. Whether they were acted upon at the time is unclear, but much of White's plan has recently been carried into effect by the Forestry Commission in conjunction with the Garden History Society. Seen from the slightly raised eminence of the house, the lie of the land extends absolutely flat for many miles with the sole exception of Mormond Hill some distance to the SW. The horizon is therefore very low and the sky appears overwhelmingly awesome, broad and vast. Whatever the changing climactic conditions, the sense of Cairness House and Mormond Hill as two focal points within this cosmos is profound.

WALLED GARDEN, 350 m. S. Originally laid out by *Robert Burn*, probably in the 1780s, then extended into its present irregular form by 1870. Walls of coursed and random snecked rubble with large roughly shaped quoins. Voussoired segmentally arched gateways to S and E, further pedestrian gateway to S. – C18 baluster SUNDIAL by *G. Adams* of London. The 1st Ordnance Survey shows another walled garden immediately S.

HOME FARM (BARNYARDS OF CAIRNESS), 330 m. N. Quadrangular steading of the Improvement era, probably part of the *Adam Porter* works of *c.* 1780. Principal front comprising ground and low first floors, built in pinned rubble cherry-cocked with a hipped roof, framed by gables of the flanking ranges. Some additions and alterations.

CARNOUSIE *see* OLD HOUSE OF CARNOUSIE

CASTLE OF PARK B 5050

1.1 km. SSE of Cornhill

A large three-storey-and-attic house of predominantly mid-Georgian appearance with harled walls and big three-window bows, rather like the Old House of Forglen before its 1830s rebuilding, and with an equally complex history.

A house existed here by 1292 but the core of the present building is probably the tower house built by the Lords Saltoun in the 1530s, and subsequently extended either by the Saltouns or by the Gordons, who bought the estate in 1605. By the early C17 it was a T-plan building, its main block orientated NW by SE with a single long jamb at its SE end. Its straight-skewed rooflines and Georgian sash windows date from a major remodelling for Sir James Gordon in 1717 and 1723 when the NE elevation was made near-symmetrical by grafting a short gabled outshot onto the N end of the main block, the footprint of the house now becoming H-plan; the bow on the SE front of the jamb also seems to have been added at that time, that on the SW front of the main block probably being added *c.* 1785 when Sir Ernest Gordon inserted a pedimented entrance façade into the recessed centre of the NE front. Finally in 1829 Col. Thomas Gordon extended the main block NW into a castellated tower, further small additions being made in 1876–8. By the mid 1960s Park was in poor condition and in the restoration by *Jack Meldrum* in the 1970s the pedimented entrance front and the 1870s additions were removed.

The C16 origins of the house are most in evidence on the SW FRONT where the original entrance – still in use – is the arched and roll-moulded doorway in the main block adjacent to the SE jamb; and within the re-entrant angle there are a quarter-circle stair-turret, an armorial and a monogram panel of boars' heads (Gordons), strawberry flowers or *fraises* (Frasers) and crescents (Setons). The lettering suggests however that it may be as late as the C19. But this familiar arrangement belies a complex building history. The JAMB is of exceptional size, 15.25 m. long, 8.25 m. wide at its SW gable and originally 5.5 m. wide at the NE, its walls 1.5 m. thick at its NE gable and 1.25 m. on the other three sides; although unvaulted it probably represents the 1530s house and seems to have been a slim L-plan structure similar to Inchdrewer as first built but 4.5 m. longer. At what is now the MAIN BLOCK the walls are only 1 m. thick, suggesting a date closer to 1600 when more generous domestic accommodation was required, but it too incorporates an earlier building: the cross walls of its vaulted ground floor are neither at right angles to the external walls nor even parallel to one another and are up to 1.5 m. thick. Its early slit-windows are still in evidence on the NE front, re-exposed in the 1970s works.

As restored Sir James Gordon's NE FRONT is essentially the same as the one he knew, a shallow U-plan achieved by balancing the gable of the SE jamb with a very short jamb on the NE. These two jambs are of almost mirror-image fenestration, each with a single central window on ground, first, second and attic floors set in simple surrounds, with a smaller file of windows close into the corners nearest the re-exposed back wall of the main block. This has a tall wall-head chimneystack as its central feature, matching those of the jambs to either side. At the gable of the SE jamb, a single garret window with a chamfer survives from the C16. The small windows at the SE jamb light closets, those at the NE jamb light a turnpike stair.

The SE FRONT is the long flank elevation of the jamb, built out into a big three-storey bow, its surprisingly early date of 1723 seemingly confirmed by its roll-moulded doorway, thick-walled construction and carved datestones; the 1780s bow on the SW front is much thinner-walled and ashlar-faced at its upper levels.

At the NW end of the house, the BATTLEMENTED TOWER of 1829 is a large oblong on plan. It is slightly intaken above ground floor and rises through three further storeys, each with two windows on the SW side, to the height of the main block's roof ridge: the first-floor windows retain their shutter-boxes. The battlements are carried on a bracket corbel course, with small round bartizans corbelled out at the corners and decorative blind crosslets. A lower quadrant STAIR-TOWER was formed in the angle between the battlemented tower and the NW jamb. It was raised to its present height in 1918. Since the late 1970s renovation the main entrance has been in this stair-tower, approached by the external double stair of the former pedimented front in a reconstructed form.

The unusual building history at Park has resulted in a plan which has no close parallel anywhere else. The generously proportioned main stair to first-floor level usual at the entrance jamb in houses of this vintage is absent, the 1.8-m. diameter turnpike in the re-entrant angle seemingly the only stair until a second 2-m. diameter turnpike was provided in the NE jamb in the 1717–23 works. The original plan has been significantly altered during the several phases of reconstruction and refurbishment. Inside, the present rectangular main stair between the main block and the jamb was formed during Meldrum's renovation to replace one accommodated within the pedimented frontage: at first and second floor it opens into the spacious bow-windowed rooms in the main block and SW jamb. The surviving historic plasterwork is very simple, late C18–early C19, and some Neoclassical fireplaces and door-pieces of that date remain.

In one of the rooms a minstrels' gallery has been formed recently, and both this and the beamed ceiling have been painted with delightful figures and patterns in a Scots Renaissance style by *Jennifer Merredew*.

The ESTATE of Park is first mentioned in a charter of Alexander II dated 1242 which defines its boundaries. WALLED GARDEN (200 m. WSW), a large trapezoid on plan. Adjacent Home Farm COURTYARD STEADING, dated 1867, quite plain. Single-storey COTTAGES were built at the same date. GATE LODGE (380 m. N), C19, single-storey two-bay block harled with entrance to rear; the ashlar GATEPIERS with ball finials are mid-C18.

CLOLA 9040

Former Clola Free Church. By *Campbell Douglas & Stevenson*, 1863–4, on the site of an Antiburgher church of 1784. Closed 1974, now a house. Gothic. Nave with short transepts, chancel and a sturdy square NW tower crowned by a bellcast pyramidal spire. – STAINED GLASS. E window, 'I am the Good Shepherd', installed in 1909.

Former MANSE by *Davidson & Son* of Ellon, 1832. Much altered.

Brae of Coynach, 1.2 km. WNW. Picturesque villa style by *Mackenzie & Matthews*, 1851. A two-storey three-bay house with its gabled ends slightly projecting, built into sloping ground so that the entrance is in the three-bay flank at first floor. Harled masonry with granite margins, the doorway itself sheltered under a hoodmould, windows astragalled sash-and-case. Bracketed overhanging eaves, gables with decorative bargeboards and slate-hung gableted dormers. Internally, a smart columnar stair hall.

Skelmuir House, 2.2 km. WSW. Probably late C18. A large two-storey three-bay house built in granite and whinstone rubble. Gabled roof with coped end stacks. Low single-storey service wing with very tall hipped roof and extremely tall chimneystack. Gig-house outshot at back. Simple transom-lit doorway, replacement sash-and-case windows. Restored late C20–early C21 and much enriched internally. Of the original features a simple but fine curved timber stair and the original kitchen hearths and bread oven. Separate steading at rear.

6050 ## CLUNIE HOUSE B

2.5 km. SSE of Aberchirder

Built *c.* 1825–30 for the merchant and shipowner Alexander Chalmers who founded Chalmers' Hospital in Banff (q.v.). A design of real sophistication, square on plan, perhaps by *William Robertson*. Entrance front single-storey five bays broad in smooth granite ashlar over a rock-faced basement plinth, semicircular Greek Doric portico approached by steps; tall ground-floor windows with apron panels, strip-pilasters at the angles, and a low hipped roof with oversailing eaves and coped ashlar chimneystacks. Within the portico, the entrance door is glazed above and panelled beneath, and its transom-light is decorated with an arc of roundels. The flank elevations are expressed as three broad bays; the rear elevation is of four bays, in rock-faced masonry at basement and ground floor. Beautiful interior: vaulted vestibule leads onto a kidney-plan stair hall lit by a cupola, with the elegant balustraded stairway curving *down* into the basement; the doors are finely crafted and the front rooms at ground floor distinguished by their moulded dadoes and ceiling plasterwork.

COACHHOUSE AND STABLE COURT, 100 m. ENE. Probably *c.* 1800. Long near-symmetrical entrance front, its ground floor with semi-elliptical carriage and cartshed openings and low attic-level hay loft, near-central gable rising into an elegant round-arched bellcote which is probably contemporary with the house. – WALLED GARDEN, 100 m. E. Long rectangle, with central columnar SUNDIAL and small rubble-built octagonal PAVILION in its SE corner. DOOCOT, 0.25 km. E. Square, two stages rubble-built, the lower vaulted chamber perhaps an ice house, the upper the doocot itself, still with nesting boxes but now roofless.

COLLIESTON *see* KIRKTON OF SLAINS

5050 ## CORNHILL B

Formerly Corncairn, a burgh of barony, later Old Cornhill: the estate village of Castle of Park (q.v.). Perhaps an improvement village of *c.* 1800, with an inn near its W end, it was little more than a single street until the later C20.

ORDIQUHILL & CORNHILL PARISH CHURCH, Mid Street. Built as a Free Church in 1844, interior remodelled by *Duncan McMillan* *c.* 1890, then 'practically rebuilt', probably by *D. & J.R. McMillan* in 1903–5: its sturdy low profile is similar in spirit to J.J. Burnet's churches of the same vintage. Early Gothic, modest in scale and character, a broad gable-fronted church with a square crenellated tower and pyramidal spire. Three-bay flanks with triple lights; rear elevation with two tall round-headed windows; vestry a modest gabled outshot with round-headed doorway, still as built in 1844. The interior is correspondingly simple but remains much as it was in 1905, gently raked seating, the ceiling carried on polygonal trusses. Stencilled decoration and attractive stained glass similar to that in the Hay Memorial Hall (*see* below).

The former MANSE nearby is early C19, its windows in slim margins very widely spaced, with projecting hip-roofed wing on the r. added later, all now finished in salmon-pink harl. Original doorway converted to window and porch formed in the angle. Outbuildings contain carriage house and stables.

Near the W end of MID STREET, the HAY MEMORIAL HALL by *Duncan McMillan*, 1893, gifted by William Hay who had made a fortune mining gold in Australia. Free Jacobean of substantial scale for so small a village, built in stugged ashlar with polished dressings. The broad entrance front extends into short transept-like wings ending in crowstepped gables and its central gable is also steeply crowstepped, rising into a clock aedicule with a broken pediment at its apex. Large semi-elliptically arched gallery window over the entrance, mullioned and transomed. Committee rooms occupy a lower block to the rear, again projecting out like transepts. The hall contains an attractive and extensive sequence of stained glass representing abstract patterns, flowers and birds; the gallery window contains a naïve portrait of William Hay, the epitome of a Victorian self-made man. WARDEN'S COTTAGE to the S, mid- to later C19, given minor details to correspond to the Hall. TORMORE HOUSE, E of the hall, was built in 1906 for workers on the Castle of Park estate (q.v.). Loosely Arts and Crafts, two-storey, its recessed centre rises into triple wall-head gables, the roofs of the flanking wings swept down over porches; there has been some loss of mock half-timber and original glazing but the centre door still has its gold mosaic threshold. S of Mid Street on the Aberchirder Road, two early villas in squared snecked whinstone with ashlar dressings. One was the POLICEMAN'S HOUSE with the Police Station itself an annexe beside it.

ORDIQUHILL SCHOOL, 2.5 km. SW. Dated 1850. Single-storey, built in coursed whinstone rubble with droved ashlar dressings. Former SCHOOL HOUSE slightly later, mid- to later C19, perhaps by *A. & W. Reid*. Single-storey with central porch and dormered attic gables, gabled roof with paired diamond-plan chimneystacks.

Former ORDIQUHILL PARISH CHURCH, 3.3 km. SSW. Designed by *Charles Disson* (*Dawson*?) of Banff in 1805. A tall hip-roofed rectangle. The centre of its S flank is slightly projected containing two round-arched Y-traceried windows still with square leaded glazing and shutter-pins, and rising into a low gable with reused birdcage bellcote once crowned by a ball finial. Round-arched doorways with original fanlights in E and W ends and bipartite gallery windows above, the N elevation with astragalled windows and vestry a later addition; walls harled with ashlar dressings.* Probably remodelled inside in 1862. Panelled U-plan gallery. – PULPIT. Probably *c.* 1805. Supported on a pedestal with acanthus brackets; has tall back with fluted pilasters framing a round-arched recess beneath a cornice and pediment. The odd location in one corner of the parish is explained perhaps by the suggestion that the church stands on the site of St Mary's Chapel, in existence by 1272 when it belonged to the common fund of the canons of Aberdeen; this chapel was associated with the miraculous St Mary's Well which survives nearby at Auldtown. Ordiquhill was not split from Fordyce until 1622 when a new church was built.

BURIAL ENCLOSURE for the Gordon Duffs of Castle of Park (q.v.), in use 1665–1923, with an armorial and a memorial panel. – WAR MEMORIAL. A smooth Celtic cross and shaft on a hammer-dressed pedestal and plinth, erected 1921.

Former PARISH MANSE (Wetherhill House), 0.5 km. S, by *A. & W. Reid*, 1865. Late Georgian vernacular survival. Two-storey three-bay entrance front in dark whinstone coursed squared and pinned, raised over a railed semi-sunk basement. Roman Doric pilastered doorway with forestair, long-and-short window surrounds and margins in pale golden ashlar sandstone. Gabled roof with coped end stacks. The basement, gable ends and tall rear elevation in which the basement is fully exposed are all harled in white.

CASTLE OF PARK. *See* p. 125.

9050

CORTES HOUSE

1.3 km. S of Rathen

A classical country house built *c.* 1810 for John Gordon of Cairnbulg (q.v.), an illegitimate son of the 3rd Earl of Aberdeen; it bears some resemblance to Rattray (q.v.) and Manar (1811; S), perhaps suggesting that *John Smith I* was the architect. A handsome two-storey entrance front, raised over a semi-sunk basement, six windows wide with the broadly spaced central pair slightly projected. Tall principal floor with Roman Doric

*The bell, now removed, was cast by *John Mowat* of Old Aberdeen in 1754.

portico with coupled columns, approached on each side by curved stairs with simple cast-iron railings and flanked by round-headed niches. Doorway with elegant segmental fanlight, the glazing of its sidelights slightly Gothic. All windows astragalled sash-and-case, walls harled but with ashlar granite dressings and margins. First-floor windows rise from a band course; very shallow wall-head cornice, and low parapet stepped up over the centre. Hipped roofs with coped chimneystacks. Deep three-bay flank elevations. Rear elevation four bays; the principal-floor doorway in the second bay from l. and its stairway are later alterations. Classical interior, planned around a handsome square-plan scale-and-platt staircase lit from a domical cupola. Some new plasterwork, fireplaces and other alterations as a result of restoration after sub-division into flats; some old plasterwork surviving, the first-floor bedroom cornices all different, charming modest scale in the attic bedrooms.

CRAIGDAM *see* TARVES

CRAIGELLIE HOUSE 0060

1.5 km. NNE of Lonmay

Picturesque Italianate by *John Smith I* for William Shand, 1840–1. A two-storey villa approximately square on plan, harled with granite dressings, console-cornices over the ground-floor windows and low broad-eaved roofs. W front of four bays with advanced pedimental gables at each end, and a neat Roman Doric tetrastyle portico projecting from the r. re-entrant angle. The three principal apartments are arranged across the five-bay symmetrical S front which has a shallow central bow with tripartite windows. The house is very efficiently planned, reflecting lessons learned from William Burn at Auchmacoy (q.v.). Entrance vestibule leads into a hall-corridor which opens into the principal apartments on one side and into the main stair with elegant cast-iron balusters on the other. Running behind and parallel to this, a secondary corridor to the N links the kitchen to three family rooms, one on the E side of the main house and two in its NE wing: these family rooms were designed to function separately from the principal apartments if required, connecting to the first-floor bedrooms by the square stair-tower in the E re-entrant angle. From the beginning the house had the luxury of a bath with running water supply. On the N side of the house is an enclosed kitchen court. The kitchen itself is on the E side, very much as at Auchmacoy, if smaller in scale.

Immediately NNW, the WALLED GARDEN *c.* 1840, but probably incorporating older walls; within the garden, the remains of the previous House of Craigellie, two-storey U-plan of the mid C18. – WEST LODGE, 0.6 km. WNW. Presumably by *Smith*. Harled with granite margins and broad-eaved roof.

7050

CRAIGSTON CASTLE

6 km. NE of Turriff

67 Craigston is one of a group of exceptional tower houses attributed to the *Bell* family of master-masons who worked in Aberdeenshire during the late C16 and early C17. Its flanking courtyard wings are mid-C18, and further alterations were made by *John Smith I* in the 1830s.

The TOWER HOUSE was built for John Urquhart, who through considerable acumen acquired substantial wealth and estates both on his own account and on behalf of his great-nephew and ward, Thomas Urquhart, Laird of Cromarty. It seems quite possible that he engaged closely with his master-mason, perhaps *John Bell*, in the conception of such a distinctive and unusual design, which may owe something to older U-plan castles – particularly Borthwick, although that was far away in Lothian, as well as Fyvie (q.v.), the remodelling of which in 1598–1603 has also been attributed to the Bell family. But Craigston was apparently built anew, an inscription panel recording its construction in 1604–7.

In this late flowering of the Scottish tower house the centuries-old conventions of defensive structures were brilliantly reinvented through a romantic imitation of the noblest examples of the past, fused with early Renaissance classicism to produce a country seat which, while conforming to accepted norms with their associations of heredity, land and power, also conveyed a new sense of splendour, sophistication and comfort. Craigston is convincingly massive, rising from a footprint 17 m. square, and impressively tall. But its ENTRANCE FRONT – which at first glance appears symmetrical – consists of two broad jambs framing a central recess bridged over by an arch at attic level. These jambs have a single window on each floor and rise through five storeys into wall-head gables and chimneystacks, that on the N being rather wider than that on the S for purely functional reasons. Immediately above the arch these two jambs are linked by a boldly corbelled and finely sculpted parapet, and the roof between them breaks into a low square tower, rising 20 m. above the ground, which is accessed by a stair-turret. At the outer corners between the third- and fourth-floor windows are deep corbel courses, clearly intended to carry square corner turrets which seemingly were never carried out. Construction is in Old Red Sandstone, lightly harled in white, but with massive, rough and irregular long-and-short dressings and quoins which make a striking contribution to the overall visual effect. The moulded arch however,

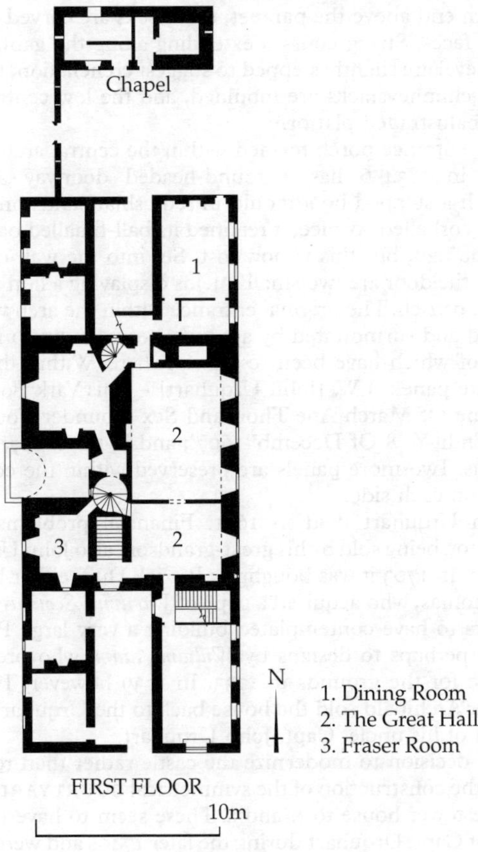

Craigston Castle.
Plan

of 3.4 m. span and 11.5 m. above the ground – almost exactly the same as that at Fyvie – is carried out in ashlar and, most unusually, traces of paint show that it was once decorated with *trompe l'œil* rib-vaulting springing from real corbels and perhaps meeting in a boss forming the plug of the *meurtrière* (murder hole) in its centre. The parapet above is jettied out on an elaborate sequence of corbel courses and mouldings, one of which is a dogtooth pattern which in England had died out in the C14. It is drained by four animal-head gargoyles, and its front is divided by *alto-relievo* Renaissance balusters into five panels, each of which contains a roundel: on the l. a young King David with his sling and a crown near at hand, in the centre a piper, and in the other three knights with swords and a spear, all sculpted with real vigour so that they can be appreciated from the ground far below; in character they are somewhat similar to panels at Huntly Castle (S) and Edzell (Angus).

At each end above the parapet, die-blocks are carved with old men's faces. String courses extending along the gables at the same level are slightly stepped to suggest crenellation, the short ashlar chimneystacks are moulded, and the low central tower has a balustraded platform.

The entrance porch formed within the central arch by *John Smith* in 1834–6 has a round-headed doorway sheltered beneath a stepped hoodmould in red ashlar sandstone, and a boldly corbelled cornice; it retained its ball-finialled balustrade into the C20, but this is now lost. Set into the wall on either side of the door are two small shields displaying a lion rampant and an ostrich. The original entrance within the arch was once flanked and surmounted by a number of SCULPTED PANELS, some of which have been re-set elsewhere. Within the r. bay the date panel: 'I.W. [John Urquhart] – This Vark Foundit Ye Fovrtine Of March Ane Thousand Sex Hounder Four Zeiris And Endit Ye 8 Of Decemb[r] 1607'; and in the l. bay, his coat of arms. Two more panels are preserved within the courtyard wings on each side.

John Urquhart died in 1631. Financial problems led to Craigston being sold by his great-grandson, also John Urquhart, in 1657. In 1703 it was bought by Patrick Duff: either he or his son Thomas, who acquired a copy of *Vitruvius Scoticus* in 1732, appears to have contemplated building a very large Palladian house, perhaps to designs by *William Adam*, who prepared a scheme for the grounds in 1733. In 1739 however, Thomas's brother Archibald sold the house back to the Urquharts in the person of his uncle, Capt. John Urquhart.

The decision to modernize the castle rather than rebuild it led to the construction of the symmetrical COURTYARDS flanking the tower house to N and S. These seem to have been the work of Capt. Urquhart during the later 1740s and were altered by his son William Urquhart *c.* 1770. On the entrance front, their western blocks present a modest two-storey four-bay appearance, with pairs of windows grouped together, but they are in fact single-storey only: they were raised slightly in height during William Urquhart's remodelling, and the second tier of windows formed, to give the façade greater dignity. The windows are set in slim sandstone dressings, and the mono-pitch roofs concealed. During the same remodelling the courtyards' eastern (rear-side) wings were deepened and raised to full two-storey height to provide new apartments at first-floor level, and their roofs can be seen rising behind the western wings. Just beyond the N courtyard is the small gable-fronted building with a ball-finialled bellcote known as the 'CHAPEL' which was also built during this phase of works.

The REAR ELEVATION is comparatively plain but equally impressive in scale. On this side the tower house rises through four storeys, with the double-height principal apartments expressed by four very large windows at first floor, and those on the ground and top floors contrastingly small. Those in the third bay from the l. are C18 insertions. Again there are corbel courses for turrets, and above is the big main roof with crow-stepped gables leading up to low but sturdy chimneystacks. The N courtyard range is two-storey, the S range two storeys and basement because of a fall in the ground. Within the walls of one courtyard, the royal arms – an indication that John Urquhart held his lands directly from the Crown – and the arms of Elizabeth Seton of Meldrum, his third wife, must once have framed or surmounted the main entrance. A small dormer gablet with scroll and finial decoration, carved with the face of a bearded man, clearly derives from elsewhere, perhaps from the vanished forecourt.

The Urquharts were well funded from their estates in Carriacou in the West Indies and the castle only narrowly survived in its present form. In the 1830s *Smith* proposed the demolition of the N and S courtyard wings and their replacement by a single larger S wing with Tudoresque details. Fortunately this did not take place, although his porch was a happy enough addition, perhaps replacing the classical one shown in the 1750 elevation. His hand is, however, much in evidence in the interior.

Notwithstanding Craigston's remarkable appearance, the planning of the INTERIOR was relatively conventional, an L-plan extended into a U-plan rather than a Z. The ground floor is all vaulted and devoted to services, with a cranked spinal corridor running from the S court to a turnpike service stair in the centre of the W front, the kitchen being in the NE corner. Immediately beyond Smith's entrance porch, a lobby opens on its r. (S) side to a single broad flight of steps rising directly to the first floor, an unusual arrangement, but one also to be found at Craigievar and Drum (S). The first floor originally contained a single tall great hall within the main block and smaller rooms in the jambs. Turnpike stairs – the main stair within the entrance front's recessed central bay and the service stair in the centre of the N flank – are contained within the thickness of the walls where the jambs meet the main block and rise through the jambs' mezzanine levels to the bedrooms on the second floor and third floor, the latter with a long gallery on the W side for promenading in bad weather. The laird's apartments presumably occupied the first floor and mezzanine of the larger N arm. Evidence has survived of the early décor at Craigston, some of the panelled walls and beamed-and-boarded ceilings having once been painted with floral patterns. None of this has survived intact however: the earliest complete interiors are the panelling in the third-floor gallery of *c.* 1730, installed by the Duffs, while that in the Fraser Room – the first floor of the S jamb – is *c.* 1750, and dates from the remodelling of the house after Capt. Urquhart bought it back.

During the Captain's remodelling the great hall was divided into two apartments, which became the drawing room to the N and a smaller ante-room to the S; an additional window was formed for the drawing room within the E wall at that time. Then *c.* 1770 the principal apartment suite was extended for

William Urquhart into the courtyard wings, the rear ranges of which had been heightened and deepened for that purpose. The N wing contained a dining room while the S wing held a saloon; the second floor was also remodelled at this time to provide more bedrooms, the Red Room's fireplace in pink and white Islay marble dating from this period.

The present appearance of the principal apartments owes much to *Smith* who remodelled them in 1834–6, the proportions of the two rooms in the courtyard wings being much altered internally, although the dining room's mid-C18 fireplace and cornice have survived. The drawing room and anteroom were transformed with new chimneypieces, doorcases, carved skirtings and deep coffered ceilings; and into their doors and shutters and those of the stair lobby outside Smith
69 re-set a remarkable series of CARVED WOODEN PANELS seemingly dating from the early C17. In the stair lobby, portraits of the more recent members of the House of Stuart: Queen Marie – King James VI and Anne of Denmark, both full-length – Hendrie Prence and James Prence, the latter no doubt in error for Prince Charles. The ante-room has all six King Jameses, and also the Four Evangelists, the Cardinal Virtues of Faith, Hope and Charity, two of the Theological Virtues, Justice and Prudence, Chastitie, Knowledge and two grotesque faces. The drawing room is devoted to the Nine Worthies, Hector, Alexander, Julius Caesar, Joshua, David, Judesma (Judas Maccabeus), Arthur, Charles (Charlemagne) and Gottfried (Godfrey de Bouillon), to whom are added Samson, Scandebeg (Skanderbeg) and King Robert the Bruce. Some at least of these panels may form part of the early decoration of the house, although they may also have come from Cromarty Castle, which the Urquharts held until 1763, while the religious subjects may derive from one of their laird's aisles: variations in quality suggest at least two different carvers, the more sophisticated examples perhaps being the work of a craftsman from the Low Countries or Germany. On the upper floors most of Smith's alterations were minor, but he reduced the gallery's length at its N end by forming the Feather Room, and redecorated the bedrooms in a simple but attractive Late Georgian manner.

POLICIES. The archives at Craigston preserve proposals for improvement by *William Adam* for James Duff (1733), *James May* for Capt. John Urquhart (1747–53), *William Urquhart* for William Urquhart (1777), and *J. Johnstone* for John Urquhart (1799), with further alterations during the C19. – DOOCOT, probably C17. Square, white-harled, with E doorway, slated roof with crowstepped and finialled end gables: that on the S contains the flight-holes. Red sandstone string course, eaves course and dressed margins. Inside, 512 stone nesting boxes; a window formed later. – COURTYARD STEADING, 140 m. WNW. Rectangular, loosely enclosed by detached single-storey ranges on all four sides, red rubble cherry-cocked with later cream harling, dressed surrounds, some crowstepped gables and ball finials. W range dated 1766 on its skewputts, altered; other ranges 1777. – 'PONS CASTELLORUM' over Craigston Burn. Dated 1885. Hump-backed single segmental span. Red ashlar sandstone with rock-faced key-blocks and voussoirs, playful castellated parapets framed by bartizans with seat recesses, short splayed approaches ending in coped drum terminals. Monogrammed initials P.U. (Pollard Urquhart) on E face. – LODGE. Also 1885. Baronial, small square turrets with spirelets, heraldic motifs and lion rampant finial over one gable. GATEPIERS square, banded with corbels supporting pyramidal ball-finialled tops; decorative iron coach and side gates.

CRIMOND 0050

A small village on the road between Peterhead and Fraserburgh, significantly developed to the S with a new school during the 1960s.

PARISH CHURCH, Logie Avenue. A delightful rural church, perhaps by *Robert Mitchell*, doing its best to follow the latest fashions of 1811–12. It combines the classical tower of Fraserburgh Parish Church with the latest Gothic preaching-box at Fyvie to surprisingly good effect. Tower slim and square, slightly projecting from the centre of the W gable, has a clock-dial panel and a small pointed window with basket tracery; it rises into an octagonal belfry which is arcaded with louvred belfry openings on alternate sides, and a stone spire moulded around its base with a fish-type weathervane. Flanking the tower, twin entrances with lozenge-pattern transom-lights, and above, pointed sash windows again with basket tracery lighting the gallery. Two-bay flank elevations and jerkin-headed roof. Cream-harled, with granite dressings and margins. Chancel added by *J. W. Reid* of Fraserburgh in 1904–5 between the E end and the session house, dated 1854. Fine original wrought-iron GATES, scarce survivors from the Second World War. The interior retains its original U-plan gallery with superimposed Roman Doric columns supporting the ceiling on segmental arcades, a scheme similar to that at Mitchell's more Gothic St Peter's Episcopal Church, Peterhead (q.v.), but it has been remodelled twice – in 1895 and 1904–5 – the round-headed chancel arch being Reid's work. – Raised octagonal PULPIT, with boldly carved side-panels representing the Holy Grail (twice), the Holy Monogram and a Cross and Crown. – ORGAN by *Conacher & Co.*, 1905. – STAINED GLASS. In the chancel. Faith and Hope.

WAR MEMORIAL (opposite the church), *c.* 1920. A simple tapered shaft of granite with the lion rampant at the top, on a rock-faced plinth.

CHURCHYARD, 0.8 km. N, contains the remains of the OLD PARISH CHURCH, reputedly early C15, repaired 1576. Only a length of the S wall is left: pinned random rubble with a rough round-arched opening, perhaps where the original door was torn out; square window with rope mouldings, carved tablets and moulded stones. One tablet with a five-armed candlestick, set within what may once have been a window for the rood screen; in the window splays, two heraldic panels; two more tablets on the 'inside' face of the wall, one dated 1697. Churchyard GATEPIER surmounted by two stone balusters and a triangular panel, together supporting a spike finial possibly from a former belfry; inset within the gatepier another heraldic panel of 1617. C18 GRAVE-SLABS, and an OBELISK to the Bannerman family, perhaps 1838, similar to that at Crimonmogate (q.v.).

Former MANSE. By *James Henderson*, 1845. Handsome two-storey three-bay house, rubble-built with ashlar dressings and margins, its centre slightly projected with the doorway in a pedimented surround approached by stairs with cast-iron balusters; low-pitched hipped roof with oversailing eaves. Ground-floor tripartite bay and other additions by *J.B. Dickie* of Peterhead, 1901–2, with amendments by *A. Marshall Mackenzie*. Twin flanking archways to rear court with office range of 1789.

Former SCHOOL HOUSE, Logie Avenue, W of the parish church and set back in its own garden, built 1791. Two storeys and four windows broad, its doorway off-centre under a tall fanlight. Granite and whinstone rubble roughly squared and pinned, small windows with original sashes. The adjoining single-storey L-plan school is *c*. 1870.

CRIMOND (or RATTRAY) AIRFIELD, 2 km. NE. Established by the Admiralty in 1944 for wartime training but disused from September 1946. In 1978 the Royal Navy set up a major wireless telegraphy station to facilitate communications in the North Atlantic and North Sea. The present MASTS, each nearly 300 m. tall, were erected *c*. 2003.

DIPPLEBRAE FARMHOUSE, 1.8 km. E. Dated 1735/55, an early example of a common type. Simple regular frontage, two storeys and three bays, rubble-built with gabled roof and coped stacks. Initials I.D. I.G. with faded date carved into one skewputt. Modern door and window-glazing. Interior *c*. 1820.

MILL OF CRIMOND, 1.6 km. NW. Mid- to late C19 in present form. Built into sloping ground, L-plan, tall two-storey basement and attic, with kiln in the wing. Pinned rubble construction, door and window openings with granite dressings and red brick internal splays. Floor-structure supported on cast-iron columns. Derelict and water wheel lost but most other machinery surviving.

LOGIE HOUSE, 1.7 km. NW, was demolished by 1852. The LODGES (on the A90) are late C18 (after 1781). Single-storey, square-plan, built in whitewashed rubble with rustic porches framing their entrances and relatively tall hipped roofs.

COACHHOUSE, 600 m. S of the lodges. Probably *c.* 1760. A very early example from a time before good roads when horse-drawn carriages were themselves rare; once part of a U-plan court. Gable-fronted with round-headed, finely moulded archway, the walls in pinned rubble, cherry-cocked.

WINDPUMP, Savock, 1.8 km. NNE. Built *c.* 1795 or 1840. Part of an elaborate and unsuccessful enterprise to drain Loch Strathbeg. A circular tower with slightly tapering sides, about 5.5 m. tall, built in boulder rubble with an ashlar top course, and formerly with sails to drive the mechanism.

HADDO HOUSE. *See* p. 237.

CRIMONMOGATE HOUSE 0050

2 km. E of Lonmay

Greek Revival by *Archibald Simpson c.* 1825, with mansard roofs 84
and other alterations of 1864. Simpson was first asked to design the house by Patrick Milne, who had made his fortune trading in China and the West Indies, in 1820, as a replacement for a house built sixty years earlier. Milne died almost immediately thereafter, but Simpson's commission was confirmed by Charles Bannerman who succeeded to the estate.

The entrance front, facing S, comprises a Greek Doric hexastyle portico *in antis*, projecting forward between two-storey end bays in Kemnay granite ashlar. The great dignity of the design is all in its concept and proportions; its detailing is very simple. The columns are unfluted, the entablature is without ornament or inscription, and the tympanum of the pediment is plain without sculpture. In the end bays, the tall ground-floor windows with architraves rising from the base course are sheltered by low-profile console-cornices; the smaller first-floor windows without surrounds brush an eaves course just beneath the cornice and wall-head parapet. Within the portico, the central entrance and flanking windows are frameless: the only ornament is in the soffit, painted banded decoration with rosette borders, appropriately Greek in character. The most likely precedent for the portico is that of Sir Robert Smirke's County Buildings, Perth, built 1815–19, which Simpson would have seen while travelling to Edinburgh: it had originally been cut for the Earl of Elgin's house at Broomhall (Fife).

Like the entrance front, the six-bay flanks are very simple. The E flank, with a central bow, expresses the principal apartments, and the W flank, with a two-bay projecting centre, the private rooms, with the entrance hall forming the link between them. On the rear side of the house – perhaps incorporating the remains of the previous house of *c.* 1760? – the flanks embrace an open service court. The roofs were originally shallow-pitched with low coped chimneystacks, emphasizing the naturally horizontal, very stable qualities of the design. The later mansard roofs with their richly detailed, round-headed dormers give the house a rather different character, taller and weightier.

Both flanks were extended to the rear in 1864, on the E side with a single-storey, basement and attic wing which contained a new dining room-*cum*-ballroom, and on the W an extension to the basement services.*

The most distinguished INTERIOR is the entrance hall. This is double-height and cubical in proportion, articulated into four bays on each side by fluted anta-pilasters with Miletus capitals. The pilasters support a plain architrave and a frieze decorated with anthemion beneath a coffered ceiling with shallow central cupola; the floor is a black-and-white chequer pattern. The glazed double-leaf doors with interlocking lozenge astragals which open from the outer vestibule reputedly came from Cairness House (q.v.).

The entrance hall opens on its E and W sides into corridors which give access to the principal and private rooms, all of which are simple but distinguished in treatment. From front to rear the principal apartments originally comprised the drawing room, morning room (with bow) and dining room: after the 1864 additions the old dining room was refurnished as a library. A further large apartment, a billiard room, lay immediately behind the hall. The main stair, which is tightly planned for so large a house, has very fine cast-iron balusters.

SUNDIAL, *c.* 1800, 50 m. S. Circular baluster with Prince of Wales feathers-type capital and a metal dial, by *Charles Lunan* of Aberdeen. – GAME LARDER, 30 m. NW. *c.* 1825. Single-storey with consoled openings, cornice and blocking course. – OBELISK, 190 m. E. By *Archibald Simpson*, *c.* 1821, erected by Charles Bannerman in memory of Patrick Milne. Granite ashlar, supported on a pedestal with inscription panels, base plinth and triple base-course. There is a closely similar monument in the churchyard at Crimond (q.v.). – WALLED GARDEN, 120 m. WSW. Formed *c.* 1840. Rubble walls, approximately rectangular, but with the long N wall slightly bowed.

STABLES, 130 m. W. Single-storey and attic, square on plan. Principal (S) front seven long bays with central segment-headed archway, small attic openings beneath gabled roof. Mostly mid-C18 in squared granite rubble, cherry-cocked, but remodelled and extended to E by *Simpson c.* 1825. Flanks probably also mid-C18, but lower, the W flank raised by Simpson into an attic with a rustic cartshed arcade at ground floor. N elevation plain single-storey with projecting gabled centre crowned by an elegant ventilator.

The following are probably all by *Simpson*, *c.* 1825: LAUNDRY, 170 m. W. Two storeys and four bays, rubble-built with long-and-short quoins. Continuous first-floor band of square

*A conservatory on the E side has been demolished for a further small extension.

louvred openings. – DAIRY, 170 m. WNW. Single-storey, octagonal, pinned rubble with granite dressings. Console-corniced doorway. Low-pitched slate roof with oversailing eaves. – CORN MILL, 350 m. SSE. Incorporating earlier work. Two-storey three bays. Centre with segmental cartshed arch and gable with blind oculus slightly stepped forward. Built in rubble. The MILL HOUSE is *c.* 1830, perhaps incorporating earlier work. Single-storey U-plan, with wings projecting rearwards. Entrance (S) front three-bay symmetrical, centre slightly stepped forward under a gable. Low-pitched roofs with oversailing eaves on simple brackets. – LODGE, 300 m. SE. Also *c.* 1825, subsequently extended. Single-storey three-bay house with centre projecting under low-pitched gable, whitewashed rubble with splayed door and window openings in granite margins. Console-cornice over doorway, casement windows with lying-pane glazing, oversailing eaves with simple bracketing, small square coped chimneystack. BRIDGE. Single hump-backed arch over Logie Burn, rubble-built with ashlar voussoirs, coped parapets splayed into wing walls on lodge side. – WEST LODGE, 0.85 km. W. Probably by *Simpson* *c.* 1825. Rustic classicism. Single-storey four bays, with the second bay projecting forward as a miniature pedimented portico and the fourth also projecting as a gabled bay of matching proportions. Whitewashed, simple attractive details with lying-pane windows, low-pitched roofs with oversailing bracketed eaves, and paired diamond-plan coped chimneystacks. Channelled masonry GATEPIERS with bold cornices and finials.

NORTH LODGE, 0.6 km. WNW. Mid-C19. A two-storey three-bay house, harled with granite margins and a tall hipped roof.

Former KENNEL-MASTER'S HOUSE (now The Lythe), 0.75 km. WSW. *c.* 1850. Single-storey and dormered attic, three bays broad, rubble-built with granite dressed work. Central entrance with double-leaf doors; the casement windows with lying-pane glazing are distinguished by blocky cills and console-cornices. Oversailing bracketed eaves with nicely detailed dormers (probably later) framed by pilasters with pedimental gablets. KENNELS are older but have been given a distinctly rustic character with a simple open porch and again oversailing bracketed eaves.

DOOCOT, 300 m. W. Mid-C18. Octagonal, two stages, rubble-built with slate roof. Round-arched doorway well above ground level, upper round-arched opening supported on rat course. Inside, brick and tile nesting boxes with potence.

CROMBIE CASTLE B *5050*

3.4 km. W of Aberchirder

A C16 tower house built in two phases, with C19 and C20 additions and alterations. The tower house was possibly begun by

James Innes who acquired the lands in 1543 but was killed at Pinkie in 1547, then completed by his son Alexander after he reached his majority. It is of three storeys, its main block 11 m. by 6.7 m. orientated N–S with a big NE jamb almost square at 6.3 m. by 6.5 m. The rubble walls, nearly all 1 m. thick, were harled with ashlar dressings. A simple round-arched doorway at ground floor in the jamb's S flank, close into the re-entrant, was protected by wide-mouthed shot-holes and by a wall-head bartizan, only the corbels of which remain. Above the doorway is a field-panel for an armorial and to the r. of it a recess with a cill, possibly for a lamp. The other openings have a simple chamfer and some of the windows once had iron grilles. The jamb had an attic storey and the main block had angle-turrets but these were removed in 1678 when the Rev. George Meldrum re-roofed Crombie with pedimented dormers; these dormers were themselves removed in the C19. In 1933 *J. Wilson Paterson* of *H.M. Office of Works* prepared drawings reinstating the dormerheads and turrets for Sir Thomas Innes of Learney who had bought Crombie and Kinnairdy (q.v.) back for the family. The partial restoration which subsequently took place, apparently by another architect, reduced the turrets to dummy bartizans in concrete, the W front's catslide dormers in the same positions as the C17 originals being also of that time.

The tower house was re-roofed by *John Bruce* in 1986; further work was carried out in the mid-1990s by *Leslie F. Hunter*. The single-storey S wing was added *c.* 1820 but has a later C19 E addition set parallel to the tower house's jamb and in a style and scale which reasonably complement it; a reset dormer pediment within the E end-gable bears George Meldrum's initials. Between this E addition and the jamb is a 1930s concrete arch with the Innes arms. The uncomfortably large W wing is early C19.

The plan of the C16 tower house relates to houses associated with the *Conn* family of master-masons based at Auchry (Cuminestown). Like the Conn houses it has a turnpike stair in its N wall at the junction of the main block and the jamb, and the kitchen occupies the jamb's ground floor. However, the main stair to first floor is a single-flight scale-and-platt almost 1 m. wide, perhaps suggesting a change in internal layout during the second phase of construction.

The kitchen has had a wide hearth in its E gable. Its arch has been lost but other details of interest remain, including a roughly formed bread-oven in its NE angle, a slop-sink in the N wall, and a serving hatch to the stair. The main block has two cellars, the N with an intramural service stair leading up to the hall. At first floor the hall has been entered by two lobbies at its N end, one from the main stair which has been partly lost, and one from the service stair. Above the latter is a mezzanine chamber with two diamond-shaped 'laird's lugs', access being through its ceiling from the second floor above. The hall fireplace near the W wall's S end – the 'high' end – was consolidated in the 1930s, the Innes arms being cast in concrete. The jamb is large enough to accommodate not just the laird's chamber with its own fireplace, wall recess, two aumbries and a probable garderobe, but also a private closet directly above the ground-floor entrance, again with its own small hearth. The first floor thus contains, albeit in somewhat unusual fashion, the hierarchical sequence of hall, outer chamber and inner chamber fashionable in the C16. The upper floors have been much altered and gutted, the turnpike stair being curtailed at the top during the 1678 works.

To the S and E are traces of STONE DYKES which once enclosed a formal garden corresponding to the old tower's forecourt. Early Ordnance Survey maps show a frontal range on its E side with a pend at its N end. This has gone but the OUTBUILDING which stands to the SE is of comparatively early origin.

CROSS OF JACKSTON *see* FYVIE

CROVIE B *8060*

Intimate in its traditional construction, organic layout and 5
modest scale, this little fishing village is the perfect human intervention within the rugged natural surroundings of the Banffshire coast. Stretched along the shoreline beneath the cliffs of Gamrie Bay, Crovie was reputedly founded with Gardenstown (q.v.) *c.* 1720 after the first wave of Highland clearances. By *c.* 1880 it possessed some sixty boats but its shallow waters were unsuitable for the larger fishing vessels of the C20. Although the fleet transferred to Gardenstown, the fishing community survived intact until the great storm of 31 January 1953 washed away a number of the houses. In 1962 a decision was taken to abandon the village but some twenty residents determined to stay and widespread objections to the demolition of the old fisher-cottages led to the establishment of a conservation society. Although only a handful of houses are occupied year-round today, the others have been preserved as holiday lets.

The COTTAGES date mainly from the late C18 to the mid C19. They stand on an embanked rubble shelf above the beach and for the most part are closely spaced together with their gables to the sea, their flanks facing in towards each other for mutual shelter; only at the N end of the village where the shelf is at its narrowest do they face the sea directly. They are mostly single-storey, some showing their rubble construction, others in traditional harl either white or sandy brown; a handful are two-storey, taking advantage of the rising ground to have an entrance on each level, the roofs in grey slate or red pantile. The PIER is *c.* 1900, rubble-built with concrete dressings. It stands opposite the point where the Crovie Den, the valley of a small burn trickling to the sea, forms a rupture in the cliffs and a natural division in the village, the nearest Crovie has to a public square. Towards the N end of the village rising above the cottages is the mid- to late C19 MISSION HALL, now converted to domestic use.

WINDMILL, Northfield Farm, 1.6 km. ENE. Early C19 tower mill. Square base, rubble-built, slightly tapered; the circular tower is also tapered towards the top, its sails lost. The base is incorporated into a much larger farmsteading with arched openings on two sides, cf. the windmill at Montbletton Farm near Macduff (q.v.).

0030 CRUDEN BAY

Cruden Bay is a former fishing village which even in the late C18 had begun to exploit the tourist potential of its attractive situation, with 3 km. of sandy beaches and the Bullers o' Buchan, a spectacular cliff formation, near at hand. In the later C19, responding to the epidemics which had swept through so many north-east coastal settlements, the 19th Earl of Erroll practically rebuilt the village as Port Erroll but it appears not to have developed as he had expected, perhaps because the harbour was too shallow to accommodate the fishing vessels of the time which were growing ever-larger. Instead BRIDGE STREET, following the main road N on gently rising ground, was progressively built up with smarter villas. Facing the S approach from Aberdeen, by 1900 the KILMARNOCK ARMS HOTEL had been formed from a two-storey L-plan of terraced houses built *c.* 1885, its main front with bay windows decorated in black-and-white diaper patterns and its Bridge Street flank in brown masonry also with canted bays and equally genteel.

PORT ERROLL was laid out on a grid-plan with three streets running from W to E linked by smaller side streets running N–S. Only the most southerly of the three long streets, MAIN STREET which overlooked a small burn, was developed quickly, its simple CONGREGATIONAL CHURCH built in 1884 with a small bellcote rising from one side of the gable. Main Street extends E beyond the grid into HARBOUR STREET following the burn towards the bay. The Port Erroll FISHERY is C19, single-storey in pinned red granite with an ice house concealed beneath its tarred wooden shed. At the far end, overlooked by Ward Hill where the fishing community had been first established, the present HARBOUR with its concrete pier was built by *John Willet, C.E.* in 1875–80 as part of the 19th Earl's improvements.

From 1899 the Great North of Scotland Railway attempted to exploit the potential of this 'Brighton of Aberdeenshire' by building the enormous Cruden Bay Hotel, but after a promising start it incurred substantial losses and was demolished in 1952.

CRUDEN OLD PARISH CHURCH (ST OLAF), 2 km. WNW. A picturesque composition. Originally a simple rectangular preaching-box of 1776. – Principal flank elevation facing S, round-arched door and window openings, its coursed squared golden granite cut from a single enormous stone; the birdcage bellcote over its W end is earlier, from a predecessor church. In 1833–4 it was enlarged by *John Smith I*, who deepened it on its N side to accommodate a new gallery, accessed by twin circular stair-towers with conical spires at the angles. In the new N wall he formed a single large round-arched and timber-traceried window, and framing it on either side he seemingly formed two porches, that on the l. surviving unaltered but that on the r. extended as a session house in 1840; the wall-head gable and oculus are however much later, by *George Bennett Mitchell c.* 1913. The S flank is of six bays, with the centre built out by Mitchell as a gabled organ chamber, again with an oculus, to accommodate an instrument purchased ten years earlier. All the S flank's windows are round-arched in the style of the original preaching-box, although those at the ends were formed from doorways by *William Davidson* during renovation in 1886. A quiet, rich atmosphere inside, Smith's U-plan gallery on circular cast-iron columns with simple gilt capitals; a second tier of columns rising from the gallery fronts supports the panelled ceiling. – FONT. C12, roughly carved. – PULPIT. 1834. Unusually high sounding-board. – PEWS have handwritten labels identifying their former occupants (mostly farm-workers). – ORGAN by *Wadsworth & Brother*, 1902–4, with decorated pipes.

CHURCHYARD with interesting C17–C18 stones, the GATES probably 1834. One large stone reputedly covered a royal Dane, killed at Battlefield of Cruden (1012). Extension with war memorial GATEWAY by *Mitchell*, 1922.

Opposite the church, the former MANSE. The original house was built in 1794. – Two storeys, three windows wide over a raised basement, harled with ashlar margins and later dormer gablets over the outer bays; extended E in 1907 by a gable-fronted wing with its canted bay rising through the ground and first floors, the work of *George Bennett Mitchell*. Former SCHOOL HOUSE to E of church, dated 1881, but probably only remodelled that year: the windows look *c.* 1840. Tall single-storey under tall roof with gable skewputts, central porch with round-headed entrance and steeply raked gablet, flanked by two-light window each side; harled, ashlar margins. The interior survives unaltered.

CRUDEN WEST PARISH CHURCH. *See* Hatton (q.v.).

ST JAMES (Episcopal), Chapel Hill, 2.3 km. WSW. Built through the efforts of the Rev. J. B. Pratt, author of *Buchan* (1858), and visible for miles around. A slim square W entrance tower and spire, standing against the gable of a tall six-bay nave. Austere Early English, designed by *William Hay* – his first commission

– and built in pale pinkish-gold granite by the mason *William McKay* in 1842–3; Hay returned to add a larger chancel, vestry and organ chamber in 1875–6. Tower has three stages with a large pointed front doorway and smaller doorways in its flanks, all in dressed surrounds; it is lit by lancet windows and supported by stepped angle-buttresses which culminate in pinnacles and gablets at the base of its stone-built spire, rising to a fleur-de-lys finial 27.5 m. above ground. The W gable behind the tower is stepped to suggest a nave-and-aisles arrangement, its flanks again buttressed with lancet windows. The walls of the chancel framed between the vestry (S) and organ chamber (N) are rather lower, but its roof is much more steeply pitched. The impressive scale continues inside with a hammerbeam roof; the nave is now rather plain but was formerly stencilled and decorated with illuminated texts (two survive in the vestibule). The later chancel is wagon-roofed in stained oak: a darker richer space. – FONT. Transferred here in 1982. Medieval, with later IHS vesica, it reputedly once stood in the chantry chapel at Battlefield of Cruden. – Gothic REREDOS and COMMANDMENT TABLETS designed and executed by *Rev. W. L. Low*, the incumbent, 1876. – ALTAR. Peterhead granite, by *William Kelly* (of *Kelly & Nicol*), 1922: 'The style is that of the old altars, consisting of twelve stones, one for each Apostle.' – ORGAN. Now reinstated to the W gallery, its original location. – STAINED GLASS. In the three E lancets, by *William Wailes*, 1840s, re-set from the original E gable.

RECTORY, 400 m. E, by *William Henderson* 1857–8, much altered. Former EPISCOPAL SCHOOL, 700 m. ENE, built by 'Subscription from The Right Honourable The Earl and Countess of Erroll . . . 1834', perhaps to designs by *John Smith I*. A two-storey school house, three windows wide in pinned rough red granite ashlar, its ground floor much taller than first; given a Tudor twist with diagonally shafted chimneystacks over the end gables. Its rear wing is presumably of the same date but its masonry is faced differently; it was originally accessed through a circular tower in the re-entrant angle (its conical roof now lost) with boys' and girls' classrooms on different levels. Altered *c.* 1899–1900 when *Arthur Clyne* added a new double-height classroom at the rear.

PORT ERROLL PUBLIC HALL, Serald Street. The former Free Church of 1850, converted to its present use in 1873.

GOLF CLUB. Aulton Road. The course was established in conjunction with the Cruden Bay Hotel. The wooden STARTER'S BOX with a log-column veranda is a rare survival from Cruden's tourist heyday before the First World War.

BISHOP'S BRIDGE, over Cruden Water, near the Old Parish Church. Dated 1697, built by Dr James Drummond, Bishop of Brechin. A single segmental arch reconstructed and widened by the 15th Earl of Erroll, 1763; the Bishop's and Earl's heraldic panels (much eroded) are on the S parapet.

SLAINS CASTLE, 1.2 km. E. A spine-tingling composition of broken gables, towers and walls on a cliff-top site, traditionally held to have inspired Bram Stoker's *Dracula*, although when the author dined with the 20th Earl of Erroll in 1904 the castle stood entire. The earliest fabric, the lower levels of a four-storey tower house, was built by the 9th Earl *c.* 1597; it was extended in the C17 and C18. In 1836–7 it was completely remodelled by *John Smith I* as a two-storey Tudor house in coursed granite, square on plan. Facing S, Smith's entrance front was five bays and near-symmetrical. The gabled centre with its first-floor doorway was approached by a broad flight of balustraded stairs and flanked by octagonal buttresses rising into pinnacles; the gabled end bays also projected with round towers rising into conical roofs built into their re-entrant angles. The first-floor windows were all mullioned and transomed. A large court at the rear was added by *Dan Gibson* in 1900. Unroofed *c.* 1930, all the fittings were removed, and much of the stonework robbed. The house's interior is arranged round a central octagonal hall of dramatic character but now hazardous to enter, with stairways to nowhere and unexpected openings leading to sheer and sudden falls. The gardens by Gibson's partner *Thomas Mawson* are lost. BRIDGE HOUSE on the lane to Slains Castle (*see* above) is a relic of the *Mawson & Gibson* works of 1900. Picturesque Old English remodelling of a row of early C19 cottages. It comprises a two-storey centre block framed by asymmetric single-storey wings, the principal fronts to N and S overlooking large walled gardens. Ground floor rubble-built across its length, irregular arrangement of casement windows, doorway in S front sheltered by pentice canopy on brackets; unevenly spaced rendered pilaster-buttreses, a later modification, support the centre block's half-timbered upper storey with leaded lights, hipped roof and red brick chimneystacks. The adjacent BRIDGE itself is C18 or possibly earlier. Nearby, SLAINS COTTAGE, built into the riverbank with diagonally shafted chimneystacks, was formerly a lodge.

NETHERMILL, 0.5 km. NW. Former GRAIN MILL, coursed squared granite, stepping down the riverbank; upper section dated 1820 with tusked masonry to allow the older, lower section to be heightened later. Double-framed start-and-awe wheel still substantially intact, though lade infilled, mechanism and kiln preserved inside; now residential. Former MILLER'S HOUSE next door, dated 1828, much extended. OLD BRIDGE (1818), a semicircular arch in coursed squared rubble, widened on the mill side. NEW BRIDGE by *William Davidson* 1895.

Former SCHOOL, Auchiries, 1.8 km. NW. By *J. & W. Smith*, 1847–9 (cf. Bogbrae School, Hatton, q.v.). Single-storey school house in red coursed granite with central porch, the door itself with a reeded consoled surround and neatly detailed fanlight. Grey dressings and raised margins, tall stacks on the gable ends. Rear schoolroom wing extended by *Alexander Cowie* *c.* 1893, then again in the mid C20.

LONGHAVEN HOUSE, 2.4 km. NNE. Originally Tillymaud, an Italianate villa by *James Souttar* and his son *J. A. Souttar* for the

Rev. G. Brown, *c.* 1885. Entrance front two-storey three bays in red stugged granite with bands of silver ashlar. Segment-headed transom-lit doorway framed by token pilasters, with consoles supporting a balcony in front of the paired first-floor windows; canted bays flanking the entrance on either side. Fine interior with hunting scenes by *C. S. Bull*.

8050 CUMINESTOWN

A planned village established in 1762–3 by Joseph Cumine of Auchry, a leading improver, to promote flax-spinning and stocking-weaving. With some neighbouring gentlemen Cumine established a linen manufactory which attracted a number of weavers and other skilled tradesmen. Although business was severely affected by the Continental wars and the enterprise folded, the village acquired a flourishing appearance with well-built cottages in the local red freestone. However, because it was not on a postal road it never joined the turnpike system. After the Cumines sold Auchry to the Lumsdens in 1830 the village was not maintained, although a small woollen mill at Asleid remained open until the early C20. The High Street extends almost 1 km. E to W. Several early cottages survive, some very simple – two windows wide with central doorway – others with an extra room perhaps built for the weavers' looms.

MONQUHITTER PARISH CHURCH, on the N edge of the village. By *James Matthews*, 1866–8. Classical, the N front with its centre slightly stepped forward under a gable and an arched, pilastered and pedimented bellcote. All the windows have Quattrocento tracery, those on the flanks with distinctive parabolic voussoirs, a motif more usually associated with Matthews' former pupil James Souttar. Vestry at rear. Re-set inscription stone above the back door, from the first stone church of 1684 (bell by *Patrick Kilgour* of Aberdeen, 1689). Spacious interior of quiet dignity. Single-span ceiling, the GALLERY a U-plan with panelled fronts supported on slim Doric columns of cast iron, facing the raised PULPIT with tall pedimented back. – Fine ORGAN with its richly decorated pipes, introduced in 1954, said to have come from Glasgow; part of the gallery has been removed to accommodate it – STAINED GLASS. Either side of the pulpit. 1915. Brightly coloured to take advantage of the S aspect: on the r. the Nativity, Christ as a boy, with beneath shepherds and wise men in praise and amazement, and above a heavenly choir – 'Glory to God in the Highest and on Earth Peace, Goodwill Toward Men'; – l. the Ascension, with mourners whose sorrow is giving way to scarce-comprehending joy, and another choir singing 'He is Not Here He is Risen.'

In the OLD CHURCHYARD, the MONUMENT to William Cumine, fragments of 1707 reconstructed in an early C19 ashlar surround. Original components include three low-relief columns with foliate capitals, two of which frame a Latin inscription; above, three carved panels including the Cumine arms, and beneath a characteristically gruesome skeleton laid out flat and other *memento mori*. GATEPIERS and WALLS with RAILINGS also by *Matthews*, 1868.

ST LUKE (Episcopal), Main Street. Originally a small gabled church in E.E. style by *John Henderson*, 1844, with a W door. In 1903 *Arthur Clyne* added the E-end chancel with its N organ chamber, the small gabled W baptistery and the S vestry without compromising its natural modesty. The entrance is now in the gabled S bay facing the road. Likewise simple interior with arches to the baptistery, chancel and organ chamber of 1903 when the gallery was removed. – FONT. 1894. A carved octagonal basin supported by a central shaft in Caen stone, flanked by four slim colonnettes in green marble. – ALTAR PAINTING. A triptych representing the Crucifixion, in an early Italian style by *Rachel (Edith) Ainslie Grant-Duff* of Delgatie Castle (q.v.) *c*. 1900. – Also by her the SCULPTURE of a Dove over the baptistery arch, carved by *Edward McKenzie* in red Delgatie stone. – STAINED GLASS. One of 1939 representing St Luke the Physician.

MONQUHITTER HOUSE, W of the parish church. The former manse built 1778 and enlarged to its present stylish form in 1830. Entrance front symmetrical, two-storey, its central doorway framed between taller and broader gabled end bays. White-harled, with dark red dressings and margins. Carved dates in the window lintels identify the W gable as the later C18 house. Further alterations and interior remodelled by *James Duncan* of Turriff, 1875 and 1889. The decision to build houses immediately in front of this fine manse when there was ample space to the E appears inexplicable.

PARISH CHURCH HALL, Main Street. By *W. L. Duncan* (of *Duncan & Munro*). Dated 1924.

AUCHRY ESTATE, 0.7 km. N. Once the seat of the Conn family of master-masons, who acquired Little Auchry in 1540 and Meikle Auchry in 1553–4; of the Red Tower built by them as a defence against their neighbours, the Mowats of Balquholly, no trace survives. Some fragments were preserved in its successor, Auchry House, built for Joseph Cumine in 1767 (*see* Introduction, p. 39) but this was demolished in 1969. Its walled garden has been developed with new houses, but in their time the Cumines and Lumsdens were fine foresters and plantsmen. – LODGE, *c*. 1850. Single-storey, with central porch supported on two fluted wooden columns, construction otherwise in red ashlar freestone with grey granite dressings, low-pitched roofs with overhanging eaves. – DOOCOT. Probably C16. A tall tapered telescopic drum with simple square-headed doorway, two rat courses and slab roof lit by an oculus, built in rubble with dressings in red freestone: apparently a *Conn* variation on the 'beehive' type, also to be found at Delgatie (q.v.).

The Garmond, 1.6 km. NNE. A single-street planned village established shortly after Cuminestown to encourage flax-growing, spinning and stocking-knitting, although curiously not mentioned in the *Statistical Account* in the 1790s. On the E side, a simple two-storey structure in red freestone rubble, *c.* 1800 – perhaps industrial when first built, with a single chimneystack at one end, latterly used as a hall.

Millfield Farmhouse, 0.6 km. E of The Garmond. A superior example of the breed. Two-storey three-bay house, red ashlar freestone, late C18. Ground floor with early C19 porch, tall first-floor windows, skewputts moulded, gabled roof with coped end stacks. Service court to rear.

7020 DAVIOT

St Colm. A small preaching-box of 1798 in dark pinned granite, built by *William Robb*, mason, and *James Melvin* and *Alexander Morice*, wrights, plasterers and slaters.* W gable with low square-headed doorway, small gallery roundel and ball-finialled birdcage bellcote. Three-bay S flank with tall round-arched windows brushing the eaves. The old W entrance – dated at its lintel – was blocked when the gallery was dismantled and the church reorientated by *George Bennett Mitchell & Son* in 1958. Its double-leaf doors were reused for the new entrance in the vestry against the E gable, which was altered and extended to provide a vestibule and choir room. The interior reordered *c.* 1958–62 is a real surprise. – PULPIT and FONT have a 'Festival of Britain' character, the pulpit octagonal, with sounding-board suspended from the ceiling. The font, by *D. Fleming*, is a circular wooden platform suspended from the ceiling and anchored to the floor by three wires representing the Trinity; its porcelain bowl is signed *Seviers* 1962. – COMMUNION TABLE, 1934, but bleached to match the later furnishings. – Light oak PEWS of simple design. – ORGAN by *E.H. Lawton* of Aberdeen, 1912–13. – STAINED GLASS. Gable roundel, by *Sadie McLellan*, 1973, depicting 'The World in God's Hands' with motifs of fruit and cereals and a bee for industry.

The CHURCHYARD reputedly contained a stone circle as late as the C19. Two family burial aisles arranged almost back-to-back: the Mackenzie Aisle *c.* 1828, square-plan, rubble-built with excellent iron gate set in lugged ashlar architrave, and a low pedimented gable with acanthus finials at the lower apices; behind it the Seton Aisle, *c.* 1812, on a slightly

*Morice may have been the lead designer; he was responsible for the Saltoun Arms in Fraserburgh (q.v.).

smaller plan but with walls rising equally high, iron gate set in a simple moulded surround, and Roman Doric pilasters framing the angles. Memorial to Lt-Col. Alexander Seton of Mounie (q.v.) drowned with 400 troops when HMS *Birkenhead* sank near Cape Town in 1852. Their valour and sacrifice established the principle of 'women and children first' and left the world profoundly moved.

Former MANSE. Built in two main phases. The original house erected by *William Robb* and *William Sangster* in 1800 was so substantially extended by a rear wing of 1830 as to effectively reorientate the plan. Principal elevation now faces W rather than S, with the gable of the old house projecting forward at one end to create an attractive L-plan frontage, and the windows in the angle identifying the stair which ties the two parts together. Two red sandstone canted bays were added to the original house by *James Duncan* in 1877. Recent single-storey extension against N gable. STEADING 1830.

GLACK ESTATE, 1 km. E. A seat of the Elphinstones until 1783, after which it was purchased by the Rev. Colin Mackenzie.* His grandson's cousin John Mackenzie sold Glack in 1887 to the Royal Mental Hospital, Aberdeen, for conversion to an outstation. The House of Daviot Hospital once operated a small farm supplying all the foodstuffs, including butcher's meat, required not only for its own inmates but for those of the Aberdeen Asylum as well. The Hospital closed in 1994, after which its principal buildings were adapted for residential use.

OLD HOUSE OF GLACK. Built for John Elphinstone *c.* 1723, but significantly altered. Entrance front is three-storey, five bays broad with central ground-floor doorway, harled in white with a gabled roof, moulded skewputts and end stacks. The relatively tall but narrow windows are consistent with the original date of construction, but that its three storeys are all equal in height is unusual in this or indeed any other period. It was probably originally two storeys, similar to Birkenbog or Hatton Manor (qq.v.) with a range of offices on its l. side forming a forecourt; its membership of that family of early houses is borne out by the half-moon stair which evidently once projected from its rear elevation but was incorporated within the walls when it was modernized in the later C18 by being deepened on plan. Altered in 1889 by *Matthews & Mackenzie* as a nursing home, and again in 1934–5 by *George Bennett Mitchell & Son*, who were presumably responsible for the attic dormers. Their two-storey-and-attic five-bay REAR WING, although clearly of its time with metal-framed, hinged horizontal lights, is nevertheless a surprisingly sympathetic addition. Restored as private dwelling-house by *Leslie F. Hunter* *c.* 2000, the entrance porch replaces one probably of the Victorian or Edwardian era.

*Minister at Fodderty in the Highlands, he established the spa at Strathpeffer.

The NEW HOUSE OF GLACK, 1875–6, is in the free Scottish Baronial which was characteristic of *James Matthews*'s middle years. Principal (W) front is predominantly three-storey and five bays broad with a central entrance tower: the far l. bay rises only two storeys to introduce an element of asymmetry and to ensure that the tall square stair-tower rising up from within the court behind is not concealed from view. Construction is in dark whinstone rubble, with some silver granite for dressings and margins. The entrance tower's ashlar moulded doorpiece supports an oriel at first floor where the angles are widely splayed, corbelling back to the square beneath the second-floor caphouse with its crowstepped gable. The second-floor windows break through the wall-head into dormerheads with pedimental gablets. At the r. end, the windows form a shallow rectangular bay in ashlar which tapers slightly at each level, and rises just above the wall-head into a larger gablet with stylized thistle finials; the r. corner turret with its conical spirelet appears to have once been answered by a similar turret on the two-storey l. bay, removed for the later N wing. A notable detail is the fine treatment of the large carved brackets fitted to the first-floor windows' upper sashes.

The New House of Glack's S front is symmetrical: a recessed three-bay centre flanked by broad two-bay ends which rise into crowstepped gables with corner turrets and chimneystacks, the stair-tower in the rear court again rising up prominently behind the roof ridge. The gabled ends have stone-roofed bay windows at ground floor; the tripartite doorpiece in the recessed centre is concealed by a 1930s colonnaded veranda. The 1889 EXTENSION on the r., although the same height as the main house, is four storeys, with much smaller windows more widely spaced and more evidently institutional. Again it has a veranda and gabled bay of slight projection, but at the far E end its turret corresponds quite closely to those of the original house. Inside, the New House's entrance hall is floored with encaustic tiles. The timber panelling and glazed doors which lead to the large inner hall may be by Mitchell. This inner hall and certain other apartments have fine Elizabethan ceilings.

COURTYARD STEADING, 150 m. W. *c.* 1840–50, converted for alternative use by *George Bennett Mitchell & Son* in 1935. A very long deep rectangle built on gently rising ground. External elevations in golden granite finely coursed and squared. Two-storey principal front, the central gabled bay with its semi-elliptically arched pend rising into a small square crenellated tower. Double-height round-headed windows with Georgian-style glazing to the l.; to the r., first-floor windows inserted in 1935. The flank ranges reduce to a single storey in the rise of the ground behind.

Former MALE HOSPITAL, 300 m. SW. By *George Bennett Mitchell & Son*, 1935. A striking Art Deco design which seems particularly appropriate for the architecture of health, rational yet genuinely welcoming with little sense of the institutional.

Two storeys on a shallow V-plan, essentially symmetrical on each side: its walls in sparkling white harl, contrasting slate roofs with overhanging eaves, and slim chimneystacks providing some vertical accents. External elevations facing SW. At ground floor the wings open into conservatories (which, like the windows, are modern replacements) extending across their full length until they meet with projecting bays which form large open terraces for the first-floor rooms at each far end. The NE elevation pivots around a neat bow-fronted centre, the entrances here and in each wing near the stair bays being set in heavy surrounds.

RECUMBENT STONE CIRCLE AND ENCLOSED CREMATION 8
CEMETERY, Loanhead of Daviot. A stone circle dating to the Later Neolithic or Early Bronze Age (*c.* 2600–2000 B.C.). Ten stones and a massive recumbent stone surround a central ring cairn that was found during excavation to cover a cremation pyre. Further burials were found deposited around the stones. Adjacent to the circle, two curving stone banks were built in the Later Bronze Age to enclose another area used to cremate the dead. (GN)

MOUNIE CASTLE. *See* p. 294.

DELGATIE CASTLE 7050

3 km. ENE of Turriff

Delgatie Castle stands on a defensive ridge high above the Idoch Water. There must have been some stronghold when a charter was sealed here in 1549, and perhaps remnants of it still survive within the present structure, but the great tower house which is the dominant feature of Delgatie today was built during the 1570s for William Hay of Dronlaw who married Lady Beatrice, daughter of George, 7th Earl of Erroll, the Hay clan chief. It is one of a group of strongly defensive tower houses, including Fedderate, Knockhall, Gight and Towie Barclay (qq.v.), as well as Colquhonnie and Craig in south Aberdeenshire, which were built for prominent Roman Catholic landowners during the difficult period of the Reformation and which through close similarities of plan and detail have been attributed by Dr Douglas Simpson to a single master-mason. Tradition – although not, as yet, documentary evidence – identifies this master-mason as *Alexander Conn*, 1st of Auchry. 62

If Delgatie had simply survived unaltered like Craig had done, its importance would be clear, but the unique and magical character of the house owes much to alterations since: its history has been, almost from the beginning, one of radical reconstruction and restoration in the face of sometimes desperate circumstances and its occupants' changing needs. Delgatie passed from the Hays of Dronlaw to the Earls of Erroll in the early C17, to Peter Garden of Troup in 1762, thence to the 2nd Earl Fife in 1798.

Subsequent additions, doubtless intended to be sympathetic, give the old tower a sense of whimsy – long low Gothick wings of *c.* 1768, further remodelling including a Tudor porch *c.* 1835, then a bay window by *A. & W. Reid* *c.* 1854. In 1866 Delgatie was inherited by Ainslie Grant-Duff, a career diplomat based in St Petersburg, who had married Fanny Morgan, the heiress to a Russian banking house. The Grant-Duffs' fortunes collapsed after the Russian Revolution in 1917 and they seem to have sold Delgatie in 1925–6. After that the castle gradually deteriorated until eventually part of its roof collapsed and all seemed lost. But shortly after the Second World War it was bought back for the Clan Hay by Diana, 23rd Countess of Erroll, who quickly sold it to her kinsman *Capt. John Hay* of Hayfield, Shetland, late of the Indian Army, and his wife, Everild Nicholls. Immense both in height and build, Jock Hay described himself as 'soldier, farmer, engineer, sculptor and Scottish patriot'; he was a prominent Freemason, being a member of the Royal Order of Scotland and Grand Master of the Guild of Masons. Restoration began in 1951, most of the structural repairs being carried out with the Aberdeen architect *Leo Durnin* in 1957–9, while the painted ceilings were restored by *V. Sovanov*. Capt. Hay understood Delgatie both in its age-old solidity and its whimsy, and added something of his own: indeed, the work of his hands is everywhere, and its survival stands testimony to his memory.

The recasting and enlargement of the TOWER HOUSE's main block make it difficult to understand the original appearance of that part of the structure clearly. Like the other members of Simpson's group, Delgatie was constructed as an L-plan, its internal layout much influenced by the fall in the site from W to E. Its main block orientated N–S was 12.5 m. long and 10 m. wide, dimensions closely similar to those at Craig and Towie, although smaller than that at Gight. It rises through five storeys, with vaulted ground floor and mezzanine, then principal apartments on the tall first floor, and second and rather lower third floors. The jamb extending from the S end of its E flank is relatively unaltered and is 11.5 m. long by 8.3 m. wide, much longer than any other of Simpson's group, including Gight. It is also five storeys, with vaulted ground and first floors, but with floor levels different from the main block. Inside, centred in the long S front between the main block and the jamb, is a spacious turnpike stair. The original entrance was on the N at ground floor on the E side of the main block, close into the re-entrant angle; it still survives but was concealed when the angle was infilled in the late C18 or early C19. As in the other Simpson castles, it opened into a vestibule with a groined rib-vault, in turn opening into a vaulted corridor leading to the turnpike stair.

EXTERIOR. The L-plan tower's main entrance was transferred to its present position on the long S front when the original entrance in the angle was concealed. On this S front the gable of the main block and the flank of its jamb stand together massive and tall between the low Gothick wings. The S

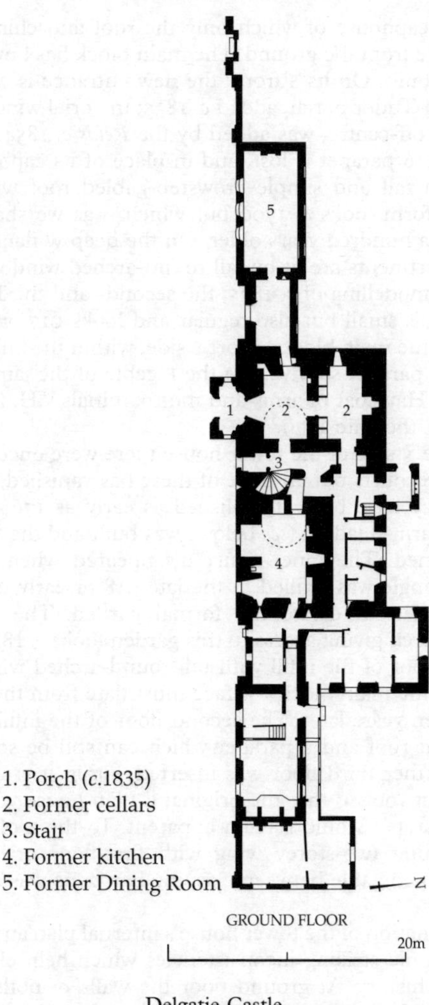

Delgatie Castle.
Plan

elevation of the jamb has survived more or less as built in the C16, with a slight set-off in its walls at third floor, as at Fedderate.* Just beneath its wall-head is a large square sundial, then a corbel course with rope moulding at the top supports a deep parapet with water cannon and bartizans; this conceals

*At Delgatie the position of the set-off has been determined by the crown of the main block's lost hall vault, as at Fedderate and Udny (q.v.). This has led Professor Charles McKean to suggest that the jamb is older than the main block: that it was a simple rectangle like Udny, and that it was in this stronghold that the charter was sealed in 1549. It is quite probable that some earlier fabric still survives incorporated within the existing structure. But the close similarity in planning with the other towers of this group suggests that it is much more likely that the main block and jamb are of one build.

an attic caphouse of which only the roof and chimneystacks are visible from the ground. The main block has however been much rebuilt. On its S front, the new entrance is emphasized by a Neo-Tudor porch, added *c.* 1835; the oriel window above, which is off-centre, was added by the *Reids c.* 1854. The main block's C16 parapet is lost, and in place of its caphouse there is now a tall and simple crowstep-gabled roof which in its present form looks *c.* 1700 but which – as we shall see – is perhaps a hundred years older. On the deep W flank the principal apartments are lit by tall round-arched windows formed in the remodelling of *c.* 1835; the second- and third-floor fenestration is small but also regular and looks C17 or early C18. Only on the main block's short E side, within the infilled angle, does the parapet survive. On the E gable of the jamb is a dial with the Hay coat of arms and motto, initials V.H. for William Hay, and the date 1579.

On the N side of the tower house there were once inner and outer forecourts but all trace of these has vanished. The outer court may have been demolished as early as 1768 when the Home Farm steading (*see* below) was built and the S approach was formed. The inner court disappeared when the tower house's angle was infilled in the late C18 or early C19: its site was levelled to create the formal garden. The two-storey Tudor porch giving access to this garden looks *c.* 1825, but the second floor of the infill with tall round-arched windows like those of the main block's W face must date from the remodelling of ten years later. The second floor of the infill originally had a flat roof and a parapet which can still be seen clearly, but a further third floor was inserted within it *c.* 1854, again with a flat roof so that the original L-plan house with its corbelled parapet would remain apparent. To the E of this infill, a projecting two-storey wing with first-floor oriel and low crowstepped gable between clasping bartizans was also added *c.* 1854.

Examination of the tower house's internal plan and structure reveals some striking inconsistencies which help elucidate its building history. At ground floor the walls of both the main block and the jamb are, like those of the other Simpson castles, immensely solid – 2 m. thick – clearly built to withstand a siege. Within the jamb the walls remain 2 m. for their entire height, and this together with the remarkable size of the turnpike stair results in rooms which are comparatively small. But in the main block the walls above the ground floor and mezzanine are much slimmer, 1 m. thick on the N and S and still less on the W, with the result that its rooms are larger but the tower house as a whole is much less defensible. Family tradition relates that, after the Catholic Earls of Erroll and Huntly rose in rebellion and defeated the Protestant Earl of Argyll at Glenlivet in 1594, they and their followers judged it prudent to flee before King James VI himself came north, and Argyll laid siege to Delgatie which was defended by the nineteen-year-old daughter (or mistress) of Alexander Hay, the formidably tall and red-headed Rohaise. She and her garrison held out for six weeks until Argyll shattered the main block's walls with heavy cannon shipped up from Leith. The king made his peace with the rebels in 1597 and Alexander was allowed to rebuild his tower, on condition that the new walls were only 'an arrow-shaft thick', to discourage such resistance in future.

The long E and W WINGS flanking the tower house were seemingly begun for Peter Garden *c.* 1768 with the construction of twin semi-elliptical arches with single-storey three-bay blocks beyond in a classical style. The arches, which formed 'in-and-out' entrances to the vanished forecourts, are built of ashlar, their channelled piers rising into voussoirs and central keyblocks with balustraded parapets above.* Then, probably *c.* 1814–15, the arches were enclosed by Gothick windows and the windows of the single-storey blocks were also Gothicized. The W block was built out with a shallow bow *c.* 1835, but a straight frontage was reinstated during the mid-C20 restoration. The E block, which had been increased to two storeys with a crenellated parapet, is virtually unaltered: its ogee-headed ground-floor windows rise into Gothic cross finials which stand out against the harl. Then at the outer ends each wing extends into a large gabled bay containing an infilled Gothic arch, framed by buttresses which are fluted at their upper levels before rising into crocketed pinnacles. The W arch has been pierced with pigeon-holes to form a doocot, and to make the point Capt. Hay has carved a dove. Then at the far end of the W wing is a sculpted round-headed arch of mid-C14 date‡ set beneath a concave gable with flanking urns and a surmounting cross. It is a pleasant place to sit, but this was reputedly the site of a former chapel, and the arch was once a tomb-recess: its effigy has vanished. Curiously amid these calm surroundings, the variety of arches, buttressed pinnacles, gables, urns and cross combine to give this W end of the house a distinctly Baroque, almost Spanish air.

In front of the tower house Capt. Hay laid out a semicircular FORECOURT with low stone walls: the masonry and gatepiers have been reused from several different sources to create a variety of colour and surface texture and an instant patina of age. On the l. side of the entrance gates a seated hound (?) bears a shield emblazoned with the arms of Hay, while to the right a 'Mannie' bears a scroll. The arms of Hay – three red escutcheons against a silver background – represent three mythical ancestors, 'Hoch' Hay and his two sons, who, armed only with their ox-bows, turned a Scottish rout into victory against the pagan Danes. Leaning against the forecourt walls close by the gates is an old grave-slab, shattered and broken.

*The wings closely resemble those added to Innes House (Moray) in 1768–9 by *James Robertson*.

‡The date given is Dr Matthew Woodworth's.

The GATES themselves are of a delicate wrought-iron design typical of the post-war period. The forecourt pavement is a skilful pattern of cobbles, expressing a Mason's interest in geometry, and is charged with potent signs and symbols. Near the castle's entrance is a triceps – three diamonds arranged in a geometric pattern – pointing to the three gateways of the forecourt. It is set into the centre of smaller and larger eight-pointed stars, which suggest the sixteen points of a compass; and between these points are four signs of the Zodiac (Libra, Gemini, Taurus and Virgo). Beyond the stars the forecourt is paved as twelve segments, almost like lines of longitude, but not all of equal size: most are laid out with squares and circles representing the Body and Soul, but the large central segment and the end segments are more personal and eccentric, among them a large r. foot possibly representing Capt. Hay himself. Further symbols around the edge of the forecourt include a heart and a sheaf of corn – a Masonic symbol of charity – laid out not in cobbles but in the lustrous bottoms of green glass bottles. From the forecourt the E gate opens onto a series of small, almost confined courts (the first with an excellent baluster sundial), past derelict glasshouses, prickly weeds and the stony heads of lions, stepping down the slope of ground, out of sight to Nowhere; but directly in front of the tower house the S gateway which opens onto a boundless expanse of Arcadian landscape is decorated with gilt cornucopiae and thistles, and proclaims the names of John and Everild in fancy scrolling letters. On the N side, framing the castle's entrance porch, are two unicorns, symbols of Scotland in heraldic terms, and of the realms of myth and imagination.

The INTERIOR has been substantially rearranged as a result of the many additions and alterations. The entrance hall and what is now the shop beyond it were originally cellars within the ground-floor vaults of the tower house's main block. On the other side of the stair, the old kitchen (now appropriately a café) occupies the whole ground-floor vault of the jamb. The turnpike stair is quite exceptional: at 3.5 m. diameter it is one of the widest in Scotland, and very unusually – though like those in all the other Simpson castles – it rises through the tower's full height, ninety-seven steps in all. Its carved decoration and some of the masons' marks were added by Capt. Hay during his restoration, but other marks are genuinely old: of the older marks, those near the top of the stair are different from those at the foot, perhaps suggesting its reconstruction after the siege of 1594. The stair first passes two small rooms on the mezzanine level within the main block, then reaches the solar on the first floor of the jamb. The solar is vaulted – as are the corresponding apartments at Gight and Craig – but at Delgatie the vault is ribbed with carved bosses and has corbels carved with portrait heads and arms of the family. In the N wall is a stone fireplace with the inscription 'I.H.S. My Hoyp Is In Ye Lord', the initials V.H. and B.H. for William and

Beatrice Hay intertwined, and the date 1570; during his restoration, Capt. Hay exposed the relieving arch over this fireplace, and carved it with his and his wife's initials and date, 1964. Again as at Gight and Craig, there are mural closets to each side of the kitchen chimney flue on the E gable.

The main block's first floor once accommodated the great hall. If tradition is correct and the main block was rebuilt after 1594, this probably had an expensive two-bay rib-vault as at Towie Barclay (q.v.). The ballroom which occupies the first floor now, and the drawing room built into the tower's re-entrant angle during the renovations of *c.* 1835, are in their majestic Neoclassical scale and character a most striking contrast with the C16 apartments of the jamb. Their great height is emphasized by the very tall windows formed during the C19, the ballroom's bay window over the entrance porch and the round-headed windows on the W and N flanks all with lying-pane glazing typical of the period, and pretty wrought-iron balconies. The ballroom has an Adam-school fireplace with Gothic triptych overmantel mirror, an apsidal recess framed by pilasters in the centre of the E wall, and a coffered ceiling. It connects with the drawing room through a rib-vaulted ante-chamber, and all three apartments can be thrown together for the largest social gatherings.

Continuing up the turnpike stair, a doorway and passage give access to smaller rooms at mezzanine level. A cupboard has been formed from what was evidently a small oratory with carved corbels supporting finely moulded rib-vaulting and a central boss, boldly sculpted with the arms of Hay: it must originally have opened into the great hall in similar fashion to the oratory at Towie Barclay. There is a window embrasure, now blocked up, on its E side.*

Then on the second floor of the jamb the INSCRIBED CHAMBER is the first of two rooms known to have had later C16 painted ceilings, although the naked female figures here were destroyed during the C19, leaving only rhyming proverbs on the beams, the dates 1592 and 1593, and the initials J.M. which may stand for the painter *John Melville* or *Mellin*. The rooms on the next floor of the main block are comparatively simple but N of the stair are the remains of a chamfered door which opens into a passage behind these rooms. It may have contained a small stair lit by the arrowslit window in the E wall.

The PAINTED CHAMBER on the third floor of the jamb is named after its celebrated ceiling which, after being hidden for 61
at least fifty years under lath and plaster, was rediscovered in 1885. The colouring was described in 1909 as being 'remarkably fresh' although it was touched up by *V. Sovanov* during the mid-C20 restoration. Divided by beams into nine compartments, the centre of this ceiling features the Hay coat of arms

*This oratory has been partly infilled: its entrance level is now roughly at the height of the springing of the vault. I am most grateful to Professor Charles McKean for pointing out its existence to me.

with initials A.H. for Alexander Hay and a victory wreath, supported by an old man and a young man representing Hoch Hay and his sons. Within the same compartment the arms of Hay are also shown impaled with those of Forbes between their respective heraldic supporters, a bearded mail nude – 'Grace Me Guide' – and a white hound with a red collar, signifying Alexander's second (bigamous) marriage to Barbara Forbes: the colours of the arms of Hay and Forbes are carried through the decoration of the ceiling as a whole. The stag's head stands for the Forbes family and it has been suggested that the sturdy, slightly monstrous elephants represent the Hays' ancestral link with the Oliphants, but the intense composition also displays a mixture of classical and Christian iconography: a merman with his viol, some buxom sphinxes, vases with floriate and verdant decoration, serpents, three intertwined fishes and conjoined triple heads, the last perhaps further references to the importance of the number three within Clan Hay's mythology. The beams are all inscribed with sound moral advice, taken from Thomas Paulfreyman's *Treatise of Moral Philosophie contayning the Sayings of the Wyse* which was first published in 1547, the lettering being in black Gothic script with red capitals against a white background. On its second beam the ceiling is dated 1597, the year in which the Catholic Hays and Gordons were received back into favour by King James VI, and Alexander's reconstruction of his tower house could begin. One of the compartments has lost much of its decoration, and this has been replaced by timber panelling painted with geometric patterns which formerly lined the walls. No doubt the painted decoration of the tower was once much more extensive than that surviving now.

Within the main block, Queen Mary's Boudoir still retains a small stone recess with an ogee opening framed by carved drapes which imply an early Renaissance date, probably the sacrament house from the oratory downstairs. The room at the top of the jamb, known as Attock Fort, has corbels carved by Capt. Hay, most with low-relief sculptures to imitate old Scots work, although two particularly fine examples represent the head of an elephant and the head of a dervish.

From the battlements the POLICIES were thus described by the Rev. James Cruikshank, writing for *The New Statistical Account* in 1842: 'The view from the top of the castle is commanding, the grounds tastefully laid out, the gardens extensive, and the green-house rich with choice flowers and plants. There is a lake well-stocked with fish, and a small island in its centre, approached by a rustic bridge, all in such excellent keeping as to render Delgaty one of the most beautiful seats in Aberdeenshire.' The LAKE is artificial, formed by *Mr Johnstone*, land surveyor of Hope Park, Edinburgh *c.* 1814. The BRIDGE over the Delgatie Burn (120 m. NE) is dated 1815, a single segmental span.* Its S flank is constructed in grey

*Perhaps the *J. Johnstone* who produced plans for the Craigston (q.v.) policies in 1799.

sandstone ashlar richly treated, with a triple key block and fluted and filleted pilasters (cf. the castle wings) rising to a low coped parapet; its N flank is in plain rubble with dressed voussoirs.

LAUNDRY, 90 m. NNE. *c.* 1815. Similar in detail to the wings of the castle. Two storeys, three windows wide, with gabled roof and end stacks, very unusual in its appearance. Broad doorpiece with flattened ogee top, and flanking ground-floor windows with ogee arches, supporting first-floor windows which are almost square; centre first-floor window flanked by small Gothick lights, all blocked; walls harled in white with dark red dressings and margins, the skewputts rising into crocketed pinnacles. The circular GARDEN ENCLOSURE and little Hansel-and-Gretel 'MILL' nearby are playful additions by *Capt. Hay* of the mid C20, but the Neoclassical pedimented tail-race arch bears the date 1863.

HOME FARM STEADING, 300 m. WNW. Vernacular classical entrance (S) front, 1768. Tall pedimented centre with round-headed double-height archway, attic windows framing niche and birdcage bellcote; two-storey four-bay flanking wings, end blocks with segmental archways which have now been glazed. Construction in local red ashlar sandstone with pronounced long-and-short quoins; within the niche, a statue of Artemis. Courtyard square, E range probably by *James Stuart* 1864, W range repaired by *James Duncan & Son* 1902, N range modern.

THOMSON MEMORIAL FOUNTAIN, 50 m. SW. By *William Liddle Duncan*, 1910.* Like a miniature temple it reinforces the arcadian theme. Square plinth with corner scrolls and seated lions supporting heraldic shields; columns and arches bear a low ogee dome formerly crowned with a lantern.

DOOCOT, 110 m. E of N. Perhaps late C16. Circular, telescopic in form, three battered stages each intaken, constructed in harled rubble with a square-headed doorway: 708 stone nesting boxes inside. Similar to that at Auchry (*see* Cuminestown), thus appearing to confirm that Delgatie's traditional association with the *Conns* is accurate.

GREENGATE LODGE, 2.2 km. W. By *A. & W. Reid*, 1854. A Baronial country house in miniature. Two-storey L-plan frontage with three-storey tower in the angle rising into a tall bell-cast pyramidal spire with fish-scale slates. Coped crowstep gables rising into diagonally shafted moulded chimneystacks; bay windows at ground floor with lying-pane glazing; scalloped angle-quoins and other Scots Renaissance detail standing out against cream harl. Similar to Eastside Lodge, Forglen (*see* p. 186). Banded square GATEPIERS with replica urn finials. (The original wrought-iron gates are currently in store.)

LODGE, 550 m. WSW. *c.* 1830. Single-storey rectangular building in squared rubble with ashlar quoins, hipped roof with central chimney rising into tall paired stacks.

*Transferred from the Square, Turriff (q.v.) after persistent vandalism.

NORTH LODGE, 750 m. WNW. *c.* 1830. Single-storey, central bay window flanked by twin angle porches with proto-Doric columns; painted ashlar dressings and margins. Pyramid roof with later swept attic dormers rising into a short square chimneystack.

DUFF HOUSE *see* BANFF

9060 DUNDARG

The defensive possibilities of a long slim peninsula which extends from a promontory of rock some 80 m. into the Moray Firth, yet is only 3.5 m. wide across its narrowest point, have been recognized since the C2–C3. The Gaelic *dùn darg* means 'the red fort', referring to the red sandstone which is an exceptional feature of this part of the coast.

DUNDARG CASTLE came to prominence during the Second War of Independence in 1334 when the English Sir Henry Beaumont was besieged by Sir Andrew Moray, Warden of Scotland, and Alexander Mowbray, who was Beaumont's wife's uncle. Beaumont was obliged to surrender only after his supplies ran low and his oppressors had seemingly resorted to cannon-fire for the first time in Scottish history. The site was again fortified in the C16.

Little survives, but two excavations directed by Marshall Keith in 1911–12 and Douglas Simpson and Frederick Wainwright in 1950–1 established that the promontory had been protected across its breadth by FOREWORKS, three ditches with two ramparts raised between them from the spoil. Immediately behind the innermost ditch a CURTAIN WALL 3 m. thick had extended across the promontory, linking a square TOWER, of which foundations survive at the W end on the cliff's edge, to an OUTER GATEHOUSE near the centre where Dundarg House now stands. The area of the promontory thus enclosed formed the chief accommodation. A square INNER GATEHOUSE guarded the peninsula itself as the ultimate defensive retreat, although within such limited confines the buildings which occupied it were obviously small: only their footings remain. Simpson believed he had found an early Celtic chapel here, and he considered it quite possible that this was the *cathair*, or fortified place, which the Book of Deer records Bédé the Pict as having granted to St Drostan in the late C6. Ascribing the later fortification of the site to the C16, Simpson suggested that it might have been reinforced by James, 6th Lord Borthwick, during the Rough Wooings, against English invasion from the sea. Geoffrey Stell, following his own investigation of the site in 1979, has challenged some of Simpson's findings, and sought to lay more emphasis on this later period, pointing to what appears to be a gun-platform raised behind the inner rampart, and suggesting that the castle remained equally defensible against attacks by land.

DUNDARG HOUSE stands at the neck of the promontory. Built 1937–8, reputedly designed by its first owner, Wing Commander *David Vaughan Carnegie*. Late Baronial, built in dark whinstone rubble with tooled granite dressings and margins, mostly retrieved from the demolished Aberdour Free Church (by *James Matthews* 1866–7).

The house is a two-storey three-bay asymmetrical composition. Landward front, facing S, consists of a central entrance bay flanked between a square tower (l.) and a gable (r.). Tudor-arched doorway with heraldic panel over, the windows variously square-headed, pointed or shouldered, replacement sash-and-case windows with timber astragals. Central bay and tower with blocky crenellation, the latter with a small bartizan concealing chimney flues; the distinctive chimneypots were salvaged from St Pancras Station during its restoration. Abutting the tower, a wide segmental archway with heraldic panel and bellcote leads through to the main entrance in the W flank – a pointed-arch doorway set in a gabled surround, reconstructed from the Free Church. Rear elevation facing the sea more villa-like, a stepped composition with the gabled section advanced forward of the main block and the tower recessed back, all the details mid-Victorian Gothic.

Interior of finely carved dark timber and exposed rubble masonry again incorporates much salvaged material from Aberdour Free Church and elsewhere. Entrance hall fireplace surmounted by RAF crest, the stairway with reused glass of RAF provenance. Ground-floor hall-corridor and drawing room panelled, the doors with fine fluted panels and good-quality brasswork of C19 date. The decorative cresting on the stair and two overmantels in the upstairs rooms appear to be genuine early Renaissance work.

DUNLUGAS HOUSE B 7050

3 km. SW of King Edward

Handsome vernacular classical house built for Hans George Leslie, dated 1793, retaining an earlier house of 1680 as its rear wing. Both in plan and elevation it is an updated version of the main block of Straloch (*c.* 1780, S).

The ENTRANCE FRONT facing W is two storeys over a raised basement, and five windows wide. Its slightly projecting centre is pedimented, and has a railed horseshoe stair leading up to a tripartite doorpiece with finely fluted Roman Doric pilasters supporting an entablature. The masonry is coursed squared whinstone with decorative cherry-cocking and long-and-short quoins. Astragalled sash-and-case windows are set in simple surrounds, and the low moulded pediment has coped die-blocks and an ovoid attic oculus. The house is laid out on a very deep double-pile plan with a pitch-and-platform roof; a small hip-roofed basement outshot on the N is perhaps by *John Smith I c.* 1820. There are round-arched attic lights in both end gables between tall twin ashlar chimneystacks, panelled with coped heads; the blocked doorways within the gables (replicated at basement level) suggest that the house was intended to have set-back flanking wings as at Straloch.

The REAR ELEVATION is five windows wide and its centre is slightly projected, with a round-arched window lighting the stair. A short link section connects to the EARLIER HOUSE built for George Ogilvie 1680 (datestone now lost), which extends back as a rear wing at a slight angle. Its entrance front faces S, two long low storeys harled with margins, the ground floor taller than first; fenestration is semi-regular with doorway and windows set in dressed chamfered surrounds, some original, some slightly enlarged in the C18. The tall gabled roof has simple coped chimneystacks, the E end bay with its hipped roof being a later addition.

The INTERIOR of the main house comprises three principal apartments at ground floor, with Dining and Drawing Rooms flanking the Entrance Hall to N and S, the Library behind the Drawing Room, and a simple broad stair. The Entrance Hall has distyle-*in-antis* Ionic columns and pilasters and a glazed screen with fanlight inserted *c.* 1940 which is of convincing classical appearance. The Dining Room retains its *trompe l'œil* ceiling – plaster painted to look like timber – of *c.* 1820; its fireplace is grey marble, with the Drawing Room's in white. The Library fireplace is remarkable in that a window above it reaches down to its deep mantelshelf seemingly with no room for a flue.

THE POLICIES are extensively planted with fine trees although the house enjoys an open outlook over gently falling ground towards the River Deveron. Immediately behind the house a BRIDGE – C18, rubble-built, with a single small key-block arch in ashlar and ashlar-coped parapets – spans the Dunlugas Den; two GATEPIERS with stepped caps survive to the NE. Nearby, semi-detached COTTAGES were formerly the stables; further ancillary buildings enclose a small court. Early C19 WALLED GARDEN.

EDEN CASTLE *see* KING EDWARD

6050

EDEN HOUSE

2.5 km. NW of King Edward

This complex house developed in three stages. A vernacular classical fishing lodge was probably built for the Duffs in 1724 on a rise of ground with its S front overlooking the Deveron. In 1828 this lodge was largely concealed by a new Greek Revival entrance front facing E designed by *William Robertson* for the soldier and statesman William Cunningham Grant Duff, late of the East India Company. Robertson also enlarged the original house with a gabled bay to the W; in 1903 it was again extended W and its riverside flank to the S remodelled for Sir Richard Nicholson, the Clerk of Middlesex County Council.

Robertson's Greek Revival entrance (E) front is single-storey, with its tetrastyle pedimented portico in polished Moray ashlar sandstone flanked by single bays with anta-pilasters. Its Doric columns are fluted with a slight entasis, the doorway set in an architraved lugged surround with tall geometric transom-light and flanking statuary niches. The windows also have lugged architraves, the pale grey sandstone a sophisticated contrast against the bright white harl. The end elevations are bowed; the low-pitched roof has a single central chimneystack.

The river front facing S is a long four-bay composition of picturesque variety. At the E end, Robertson's tall single-storey segmental bow with its lying-pane glazing is complemented by the smaller two-storey bows of 1903 which flank the gabled bay on either side, the bow near the centre largely concealing the old fishing lodge. The N elevation shows the house's development much more clearly. On this side the ground falls sharply and the original fishing lodge can be seen virtually unaltered. It rises through three storeys and is three windows wide with its doorway slightly off-centre; the carved panel bearing the Duff arms with initials I.D. M.D. and date 1724 has presumably been re-set. The segmental bow of Robertson's entrance front rises from a low basement, while his gable bay on the W is set back and partially concealed by a plain outshot with a hipped roof. The rear elevation is comparatively plain, and enclosed by trees.

The INTERIOR is mainly of 1828 and 1903. Within Robertson's Greek Revival entrance front, the hall is flanked to the N by the Dining Room with a black marble chimneypiece and to the S by the Drawing Room with its fireplace in white marble, the latter still with a deep blue Chinoiserie wallpaper featuring ho-ho birds and flowers which is either original or early. Behind the Drawing Room the N front constitutes a series of bright bow-windowed saloons leading to the Billiard Room of 1903 at the rear. The stair is still mid-C18 with balustrade of 1903, extended *c.* 1990.

The POLICIES were substantially improved by James Cunningham Grant Duff from the late 1820s until his death in 1858, but the estate was progressively sold off after the First World War. – WALLED GARDEN, 200 m. SSE, *c.* 1830. Rubble-walled, doorway in ashlar on the E. Against the N wall, excellent C19 cast-iron glasshouses but in derelict condition.

In the outside face of the N wall a re-set C16 lintel, 'My Hovp is in the Lord'.

Most of the ESTATE BUILDINGS are by *Alexander Reid* (of *A. & W. Reid* of Elgin). Former STABLES AND COACHHOUSE, 180 m. E of S, 1850. Gable-fronted central coachhouse, low single-storey linking bays with dormers, and cottages in the end bays. All harled in white with granite ashlar dressings and tall diamond-plan chimneystacks. – BELL COTTAGE, 130 m. SSE. The former estate school. Single-storey, harled in white with granite ashlar dressings, attic with pedimented stone dormers. S gable with railed right-angled forestair and bellcote; N end with crowstep gables subsequently extended. The bell is that of the *Terra Nova*, in which Capt. Robert Scott sailed to the Antarctic in 1910: it was brought to Eden by Surgeon-Commander Edward Atkinson. – HOME FARMHOUSE, 0.4 km. SE. Probably also by *Reid*, with alterations of the later C19. Long single-storey-and-attic entrance front, asymmetrical, harled in white, with tripartite doorpiece and bay windows at ground floor, first-floor dormers with stone gablets. Unusual DOOCOT, 0.45 km. SE, by *Alexander Reid*, 1852, very simple but stylish Italianate. Small square tower with bracketed pyramidal roof crowned by a pigeon cupola; short flanking wings contain the poultry houses; together with a small rear outshot these form a T-plan. Harled with grey granite quoins, overhanging eaves with timber bargeboards. – MILL HOUSE, 0.5 km. SE – L-plan, single storey with basement built into sloping ground, now derelict and gutted. – Twin N and S GATE LODGES. Simple Tudor *c.* 1840, L-plan single storey and attic with gabled porch in the angle, harled with granite ashlar margins, spike finials and diamond-plan chimneystacks.

9030

ELLON

An important settlement from very early times, and during the rule of the Celtic Mormaers and the Comyn Earls the capital of Buchan, Ellon was the lowest fordable point on the River Ythan. Sold by Forbes of Waterton to the merchant James Gordon in 1706, in the later C18 the town was chiefly noted for its prolific textile production – it briefly had a linen and woollen manufactory – and its excellent salmon and trout. Its growth was spurred by the construction of a bridge over the river in 1793, and the turnpike from Aberdeen to Peterhead (q.v.) which, reaching Ellon in 1799, flattened the Motte Hill which had protected the town since time immemorial. William Gordon feued out land in Ythan Terrace in 1815, further development being encouraged from 1845 by Alexander Gordon who feued out Bridge Street, Longley Road and the New Deer Road; Longley Road was renamed Station Road after the railway arrived in 1861. The town witnessed further substantial growth in the later C19, particularly during the 1890s,

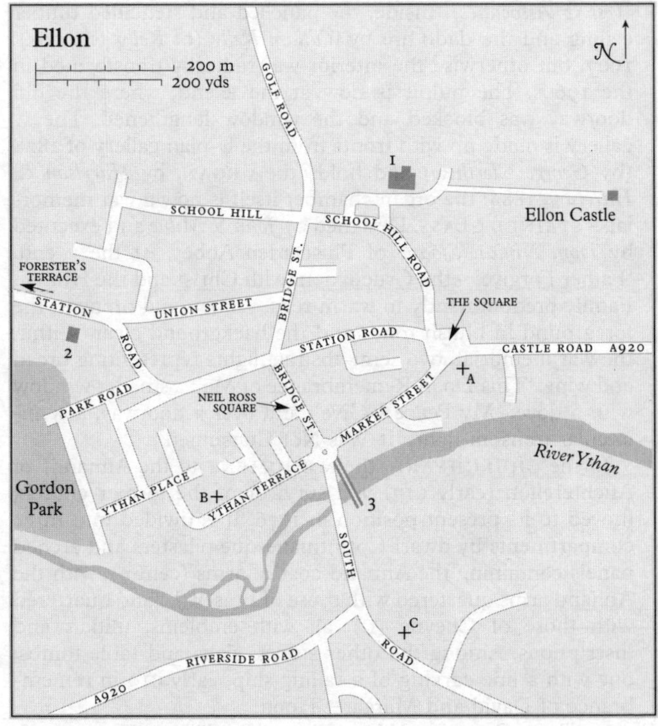

A Ellon Parish Church
B Free Church (former)
C St Mary on the Rock (Episcopal)

1 Ellon Academy
2 Victoria Hall
3 Old Bridge

and then again in the C20, with what is in effect a new town having sprung up on the Ythan's S bank in response to the oil boom.

CHURCHES

ELLON PARISH CHURCH, SE of The Square. A 'Muckle Kirk' – a big simple burgh church with a small birdcage bellcote built by *William Littlejohn*, 1777, in coursed granite masonry, some of it reused from the medieval church which had previously occupied the site. Originally entered through round-headed, key-blocked doorways in the W and E gables, and with further doorways at either end of the long S wall, flanking the pulpit which was centred on that side. N vestry 1872–3; canted organ chamber in the centre of the S wall by *George Marr* and *William Davidson* 1884. S doors formed into windows in 1888–9; a Pictish symbol stone is reputedly incorporated in the E end. Concrete W porch of 1967–8 by *David Kinghorn* (of *Herbert G.*

West & Associates). Inside, the panelled and stencilled timber ceiling and the dado are by *William Kelly* (of *Kelly & Nicol*), 1907, but otherwise the interior was radically transformed in the 1960s. The pulpit is now at the E end, where the old doorway was blocked and the window lengthened. The W gallery is made up with fronts from the U-plan gallery of 1828 (by *George Clerihew*) and holds the ORGAN, by *Harrison & Harrison*, 1884; the organ chamber itself is now a war memorial. – STAINED GLASS. Designed by *John S. Milne* and executed by *Dom Ninian Sloane* of Pluscarden Abbey. At the E end, 'Father Forgive' – the Crucifixion, with Christ and the Human Family predominantly in warm reds, yellows and oranges, the foreground in bluish tones and the background clear. Within the war memorial, two semi-abstract lights representing bread and wine, 'This Do in Remembrance of Me'; a smaller window with a dove, 'My Peace I Give'; and over a doorway, a semicircular transom-light, 'It Was Not Consumed'.

In the CHURCHYARD, the MONUMENT to the Annands of Auchterellon (early C17) is a survivor of the former church, moved to its present position in 1776. It is divided into three compartments by dwarf Corinthianesque pilasters and arched panels containing the Annand coat of arms (centre), with the Annand arms quartered with those of Fraser (l.) and quartered with those of Cheyne (r.), all with emblems, initials and inscriptions. Among the other stones, slabs and table-tombs, one with a fine carving of a sailing ship, early C19 in remembrance of David and Margaret Hood.

Former FREE CHURCH, Ythan Terrace. By *William Henderson & Son*, 1855–6. Closed 1905. Entrance gable in golden granite rubble and black whinstone, coursed and pinned, its centre slightly advanced with pointed-arch doorway and gallery window, rising up into an ashlar bellcote.

42 ST MARY ON THE ROCK (Episcopal), South Road. Early Middle Pointed by *G.E. Street*, built 1870–1. Powerful, assured modelling of the basic forms, together with bold yet delicate detailing and characterful use of robust materials, endow this building with great presence and reveal the hand of a master. Four-bay nave with tall roof entered through a narthex but without aisles, extending E into chancel and apse which are only slightly lower and narrower. Small organ chamber on the S side, and vestry on the chancel's N flank, with a slender bell-tower in the re-entrant angle. Granite masonry, roughly squared and pinned, with lighter dressings, the windows and string courses in freestone. W doorway simply moulded and framed by buttresses, the doors themselves on sinuous foliate bar-hinges, with paired trefoil-headed lights to either side. Above the narthex's hipped lean-to roof, a depressed-arch window with five lights ('distinguished by Mr Ruskin's approval') in the steeply raked nave gable, its apex crowned with a cruciform finial. The nave flanks are treated differently, the N as four identical bays with two-light windows, the S with a plate-traceried four-light

window at the W and two-light windows at the E. The organ chamber is very simple, with a low gable, and beyond it the wall-plane is canted in towards the chancel. The church's E end is also a strong composition: the apse has three cusp-headed lights high up, and the elegant flow of the roof is supported on timber brackets half-hidden by the eaves. On the N flank the vestry, low-walled under its own tall roof, partly conceals the rise of the bell-tower which, starting square, is broached to octagonal and thence to circular with a stone spirelet.

From within the narthex, which contains the baptistery, the view is framed by three archways supporting the W gable of the nave. The nave itself is by contrast a tall wagon-roofed space, its colours and textures carefully modulated to create a fine atmosphere: *Minton* TILES in a red, black and cream pattern, and the pews and dadoes stained dark to look like mahogany. The walls were decorated in 1883 to designs by *A.E. Street*, based on his father's sketches,* but are now plain. Chancel arch, supported on corbels and colonnettes, with a low SCREEN in Elgin stone, its arcaded treatment extending round the drum of the PULPIT near the organ chamber on the S side. Arcaded CHOIR STALLS and simple ALTAR RAILS, beyond which attention focuses on the ALTAR itself and the REREDOS – the latter carved by *Thomas Earp* and erected in 1877, polished alabaster divided into five panels with a central cross and marble insets, its carved canopy based on an early English model, and the outer wings in pale Caen stone. On one side of the altar is the SACRARIUM with brass door by *Hardman & Co.*, and on the other a PISCINA and two-seat SEDILIA, all trefoil-headed. – ORGAN by *Bryceson Bros & Morton*, 1876. – STAINED GLASS. In the nave, the four-light window is by *Jennifer-Jayne Bayliss*, 1996. The two-light windows representing the Sermon on the Mount, Our Lord Blessing the Little Children and (together) the Nativity and the Light of the World are all by *Lavers & Barraud*, 1871. Jesus Among the Doctors in the Temple is by *Clayton & Bell*, 1902; two others (the Wedding at Cana and Jesus and the Woman at the Well) by the same firm, 1880s. – Behind the pulpit, the Light of the World, with beneath the Shepherd rescuing a Lamb. – In the chancel, S side, another two-light window representing Jesus' Appearance to His Disciples after the Crucifixion, by *Clayton & Bell*, 1876. At the E end, Jesus in the Garden of Gethsemane, the Crucifixion and Christ in Majesty. – MEMORIAL TABLETS AND BRASSES. Neo-Jacobean cartouche and small aedicule, both dedicated to members of the Wolrige-Gordon family.

A good Madonna and Child in the CHURCHYARD. The former RECTORY is by *William Butterfield*, 1872, but significantly altered in 1887 and later.

*The decorator was *Hill*, who also carried out the scheme for *Street*'s Law Courts (now Royal Courts of Justice) in London.

PUBLIC BUILDINGS

ELLON ACADEMY, Bridge Street/Schoolhill Road. Split campus, with buildings chiefly of the 1930s and by *Grampian Regional Architects' Department*, 1979. To be replaced in 2015 by a new building in Aberdeen Road.

VICTORIA HALL, Station Road. By *Jenkins & Marr* with *William Davidson*, the Burgh Surveyor, begun 1897 for the Diamond Jubilee, opened 1901; much of the cost was met by Andrew Carnegie. A multi-purpose building with Volunteers' armoury, library and reading room, committee room, ladies' room and keeper's apartment all on the ground floor, with entresol retiring rooms, and the hall itself on the first floor. The tall Tudor Gothic gable front facing the street has a shallow four-light mullioned window bay, transomed at first floor and with a stepped crenellated parapet and plain escutcheon. Slender octagonal clock tower. Plainer flanks, all in red granite from Stirling Hill.

OLD BRIDGE, over the Ythan. By *James Robertson*, 1793. Three segmental arches rising from low cutwater piers, the centre span 14 m. and those at the ends 13 m.; construction in coursed pinned rubble with granite ashlar dressings. NEW BRIDGE of 1939–40 by *Tawse & Allan*. Three segmental spans springing from cutwater piers, but in reinforced concrete, and angled to meet its forebear on the N bank in dramatic juxtaposition.

ELLON CASTLE

Ellon Castle takes its name from the Fortalice of Ardgirth (late C16). This fortalice was incorporated in a massive classical mansion begun by James Gordon *c.* 1706–15 and then enlarged for the 3rd Earl of Aberdeen by the Edinburgh architect *John Baxter* in 1781–5: only the S front's E section with a pre-C16 round tower now survives. It has triple gunloops of the *Leiper* type. Baxter's W entrance front was a symmetrical tripartite design, four storeys high and seven windows wide, with the centre bay slightly recessed and the doorway at first-floor *piano nobile*. Two long wings extended back so that the E (rear) elevation was also symmetrical but open at its centre, resulting in an extended U-plan. The house was approached from the W through GATEPIERS (*c.* 1715) alternately faceted and pulvinated with globular finials. Ellon Castle was almost entirely blown up in 1851 to extend the driveway towards a later house by *James Matthews*, itself demolished in 1929. At that date the OFFICES, *c.* 1725 but altered by *Baxter*, were adapted to create the present attractive Neo-Georgian house on an L-plan, two storeys in white harl with crowstepped gables and the main entrance set in the angle, looking out over a large open court. At one end it incorporates the doorway of Baxter's house, distinguished by a segmental pediment inscribed 'George Earl of Aberdeen', and there is also a heraldic panel bearing the

Gordon arms. The very large WALLED GARDEN below the castle was formed in 1715 with a finely detailed two-storey garden house,* the N terrace with a sundial (cf. Pitmedden, q.v.), and another sundial in the central avenue, both early C18. The CASTLE PARK – gifted to Ellon 1907, renamed GORDON PARK – is surrounded by the 'DEER DYKES', 350 m. in length, up to 3.5 m. in height, also early C18 but much repaired, with gateways to the S and E. The WEST LODGE (1889) was recently removed stone by stone and rebuilt on the Ythan's S bank just downstream from the Old Bridge.

DESCRIPTION

THE SQUARE is the heart of the town. It is more of a triangle, formed by the convergence of Market Street and Station Road, and open at its E end where Castle Road extends dead straight as far as the eye can see. In its centre the WAR MEMORIAL is a kilted soldier in pale granite, reputedly by *James Cobban*, 1923. The early C18 tolbooth which stood in The Square's NW corner was demolished in 1842; what is thought to be its pediment, with James Gordon's coat of arms, has been preserved in the gable of the replacement building on the site, itself now sadly altered. The most sophisticated architecture in The Square belongs to the BANK OF SCOTLAND, formerly the Aberdeen Town & County Bank, built 1845–7 in the centre of the W side – a good example of the classic two-storey villa-type, with its broad l. bay advanced under a gable. Its consoled main entrance and triple-light telling-hall window both have chamfered surrounds and console-cornices which support first-floor balconies with cast-iron railings, all the other windows and angles having long-and-short quoins. Pity the former DAME SCHOOL at the E end 1848–9, pretty once-Picturesque villa-style, its stepped two-bay entrance front with curvaceous bargeboarded gables, and octagonal shafted chimneystacks. Just out of sight from the Square's NW side, in Station Road, the CHURCH HALL (now Ellon Kirk Centre) is early C20, single-storey three bays, with its centre rising into a gable, and tall coped end stacks; its crenellated canted bay is a later addition in paler granite.

MARKET STREET leads down from The Square to the bridges over the river. The NEW INN HOTEL incorporates fabric of a late C18 predecessor which once accommodated Ellon's assembly room and council chamber, but in its present form it is substantially the work of *James Matthews*, completed 1853. It is arranged on an extended Z-plan, two large blocks of roughly similar size being set at right angles to each other with their gables facing an open forecourt, and with a lower range of buildings with twin attic gablets linking them together. Matthews' W block, its gable set back from the road within the

*This was originally three storeys, being reduced to two storeys with stairs and a Tudor Gothic parapet by *James Matthews* in 1861.

forecourt, has a ground-floor canted bay, a tall first-floor window with console-cornice, and a crowstep-gabled attic, while the E block – the late C18 wing, remodelled by Matthews, with four-bay flank to the road – retains a tripartite sash-and-case window for the council chamber, and the Gordon coat of arms under the straight skews of its gable. Both blocks have tall chimneystacks rising from the wall-heads to punctuate the roof-lines. The link block, remodelled by Matthews, likewise has C18 origins, having once been entered by a round-headed doorway of *c.* 1770. Despite recent unsympathetic alterations, the New Inn is still a pleasing exercise in picturesque historicism. Beyond the Inn is the CLYDESDALE BANK (formerly North of Scotland Bank) by *Matthews & Mackenzie*, 1877, in the manner of an Italianate villa, the l. side boldly advanced as a broad canted bay to identify the telling room.

At the foot of the slope, on Ythan Terrace's junction with Bridge Street, the BUCHAN HOTEL was reconstructed in 1880, two storeys harled in white with a later pedimented doorpiece. BRIDGE STREET was laid out during the mid C19. On its E side, modest two-storey buildings, ground-floor shops with flats above, and a bakery on the Station Road junction with a red brick chimney. Much of Bridge Street's W side, where there formerly stood a BREWERY, has been redeveloped as NEIL ROSS SQUARE by *Michael Taylor*, 1989. On the junction with Station Road is an exercise in civic improvement, a handsome commercial block dated 1902 with large shop windows; its first-floor windows have Tudor hoodmoulds, and gableted attic dormers with regularly spaced wall-head stacks animating the roof-line.

STATION ROAD itself is lined with substantial two-storey granite VILLAS along its N side. They vary in quality and most are rather conservative for their date, looking perhaps twenty years older than they really are. Among these, OLRIG (the former Free Church manse) is stylish in a Simpsonesque manner: it is either by *Daniel Macandrew Sen.*, 1847 (and if so, his earliest known work) or *William Henderson & Son*, who built the Free Church (*see* Churches above). It is a two-storey stepped L-plan, harled with slim margins and low-pitched broad-eaved roofs. Its three-bay entrance front faces E, with its l. end slightly projected under a pedimental gable, and a round-arched porch in the angle; the garden front facing S is also three bays but symmetrical, the centre projected under a gable, with a canted bay at ground floor. FORESTERS TERRACE further W and S of Craigs Road looks like a long row of cottages, single-storey over tall raised basements, but is actually working-class flats on the Edinburgh Colony principle with entrances on both sides: built *c.* 1865–70 in coursed golden granite rubble, pinned and squared, they are surprisingly impressive in architectural terms. In clear sight is the four-arched former RAILWAY VIADUCT crossing the Ythan, designed by *Alexander Gibb* and built in 1860 for the Formartine &

Buchan Railway. The station has gone but in Station Brae the STATION HOTEL *c.* 1891–4 is Late Victorian villa-style, its large set-back wing added in 1925 for the exclusive use of Sir James McDonald, Governor of Rhodesia, who gifted MCDONALD PARK to his native town in 1928.

Further out, some houses of note:

Former PARISH MANSE (now Riversfield), Castle Road. Built 1790 (?), altered 1826 and again by *Daniel Macandrew Sen.* 1860. Two-storey, originally three bays, but with the entire frontage l. of the central porch swelling out as a segmental three-light bow, probably 1826. The porch itself has an inset Greek Doric doorpiece with large transom-light and modern dentilated cornice. The r. bay has a glazed fan-lit doorway, converted from a window, and opening onto a glazed veranda. Offices now converted into a separate residence.

AUCHTERCRAG, set back on the W side of Commercial Road, is dated 1894, but in the Scottish Baronial style of thirty years earlier. Built for William Smith, whose boot factory once stood nearby. Principal elevation is focused on a three-storey square entrance tower linking to a crowstepped gable over a canted bay, with short two-storey-and-attic wings set back on each side. Squared granite, the windows astragalled in the upper sashes only. Ball-finialled doorpiece, the tower's crenellated parapet supported on corbels, and turret with fish-scale slated spirelet at one rear corner. Wing to l. with angle-turret, and r. wing with gableted caphouse dormer over end window. Rear elevation has large round-headed stair window filled with coloured glass. Subdivided into flats.

RAMORNIE, Craigs Road. The only known work of *J. Girtrig Young*, dated 1914: Scots style of the C16–C17, akin to the work of Robert Lorimer. A long two-storey L-plan in pinned boulder rubble with granite dressings: roll-moulded, deep entrance architrave at the far end of the long wing beneath a tall crowstepped gable, the door itself of stout oak and studded; immediately next to it, a large canted bay with crenellated parapet expresses the stair hall. Irregular fenestration, windows of various sizes all astragalled sash-and-case, those on the first floor usually breaking through the eaves-line under gables, or as gableted stone dormers. Roof punctuated by tall chimneystacks with simple copings. The house reportedly once had an estate large enough for shooting.

HILTON OF TURNERHALL, 3.9 km. NNW. 'Lately built' in 1800. Simple three-storey three-bay house in coursed squared granite. Ground- and first-floor windows relatively tall, the second-floor windows small and square beneath the eaves of a gabled roof. Shallow plan, a single-storey rear wing with a very tall roof. Nearby its U-plan STEADING, built by *John Connon*, mason, in 1837, near-symmetrical with its central range predominantly two-storey: one wing clearly deepened on plan. Centred behind this steading a WINDMILL designed by

James Henderson and built by *George Donaldson*, 1849. Four storeys, approximately 9 m. high, slim and tapering with a small domical roof; sails blown off 1879, and all surviving machinery removed in 1956.

NETHER ARDGRAIN, 3 km. N. Mid-C18 vernacular classical, but reconstructed from an earlier house. Entrance (S) front is two storeys and five windows wide, the broad centre bay being slightly projected and rising well above the wall-head into an attic chimney-gable. The walls are harled, the fine roll-moulded door surround, chamfered ground-floor window dressings and first-floor dressings up to half their height are predominantly in pink stone; however, the door lintel in silver granite is a subsequent insertion, with initials of John Edward Bean dated (?) 1757. Use of the same silver granite for the upper halves of the first-floor windows shows that Bean heightened the walls at this time: Nether Ardgrain has been a member of the oldest family of country houses built in Banff, Buchan and Formartine including among others Birkenbog and Hatton Manor (qq.v.) and must therefore date from the late C17 or earlier C18. The ground-floor windows were once barred; the upper floor's originally broke through the eaves as dormers. The central and end gables' chimneystacks are coped and they have distinctive cavetto skewputts. Above the doorway a sundial is perhaps re-set from another house on this site or elsewhere; within the attic gable with its small triangular light a panel bearing the royal arms has also been re-set, neither of its two dates – 1626 and 1664 – appearing to bear on the history of Ardgrain. The tablet with a translation from Vergil's *Georgics* dates from *c.* 1800 and is a reference to the difficulties of agricultural, social and political change: 'How Happy would the Husbandman be if he Knew his own Good. Let Improvements and Liberty Flow.' The house retains its original single-pile plan, its rear (N) elevation almost blind except for two small windows lighting the stair. The OFFICE RANGE projecting from the l. side of the entrance front and so enclosing a two-sided forecourt is a survival from the original house, and comparatively little altered.

BOAT OF ARDLETHEN BRIDGE, 3.3 km. W, over the River Ythan. Dated 1893. Probably designed by *John Willet, C.E.*, and built after his death by *William Davidson*, Ellon's Burgh Surveyor. Three shallow segmental arches in rough red granite ashlar, dressed masonry for the voussoirs and cutwaters which rise into plain pilasters, the spandrels in pinned grey granite with simply moulded parapets.

Former GRAIN MILL, Nethermill, 5 km. NW. Low two-storey L-plan in pinned boulder-rubble, built into a slope. The basement rises only slightly above ground, the loft breaks up into the tall roof, with a crude forestair leading to the entrance within a dormered opening. Shorter piended wing at the foot of the slope still contains a brick-built kiln, its vent now removed. Metal frame of start-and-awe wheel and most internal machinery remains.

ESSLEMONT HOUSE 9020

2.5 km. W of Ellon

A Scottish Baronial country house built for Col. Henry Perkins 90
Wolrige-Gordon by *J. R. Mackenzie*, 1865–6, incorporating fabric from a house built for Robert Gordon in 1769. Impressively composed, especially from the approach drive where the entrance front facing E and the long S flank are seen together: both built in polychrome coursed squared granite, an attractive variety of pale silver, dark grey and gold with extensive finely dressed work.

The ENTRANCE FRONT is a lively stepped design with a tall square four-storey tower marking the SE corner, the entrance itself in a central three-storey drum tower which rises into a crowstep-gabled caphouse, and a lower three-storey block with a steeply pitched roof at the NE end. In the drum tower, the doorway and first-floor window above it are framed in a moulded surround, with the arms of the Wolrige-Gordons in a semicircular tympanum with monogrammed initials and the date of reconstruction; the caphouse gable rises into a chimneystack. The corner tower has rounded angles, a crenellated parapet resting on a deep corbel course and diagonal bartizans with dummy crosslets at three of its four corners, the fourth corner having a small bell-turret with an ogee dome. At the r. bays the second-floor windows rise into dormer gablets; and within the re-entrant angle formed by the entrance tower a turret rises into a slender slated spirelet.

The SOUTH FRONT echoes David Bryce's compositions, but with details kept simple for execution in granite. It comprises a two-storey, attic and basement block three windows wide, flanked on the E by the four-storey corner tower and on the W by a slightly projecting bay rising three storeys through the main wall-head into a tall crowstepped gable. This links through a re-entrant tourelle to a broader and more boldly projected gable with a canted bay at the far W end. The three-windows-wide block is the r. side of the 1769 house re-windowed and heightened; its l. bays have been rebuilt as the tall gabled bay, and the dormer gablets of the new attic-floor windows are carved with monogrammed initials and the date of the old house. In general, the string and corbel courses give depth and profile to the elevations, and the roof-lines are picturesquely varied. The W and N elevations are more simply composed and constructed in squared rubble with decorative cherry-cocking to match the retained N frontage of the house of 1769. The basement area is enclosed by fine cast-iron railings of a mid-Victorian pattern.

The INTERIOR is laid out on a corridor plan with most of the principal apartments ranged across the ground floor of the S front. From the entrance hall with its encaustic tile floor, doorways lead on the l. into the master's study within the four-storey tower, and r. into what was once the billiard room, separate from the other apartments and very much a male preserve. Across the S front, the master's study opens first onto the library with its three-window frontage, then into the small drawing room and the main drawing room itself in the SW corner; the dining room is on the NW. All these rooms are well finished, with notably good ceiling plasterwork. Alterations carried out by *A. G. R. Mackenzie* c. 1958 resulted in the library being opened into the corridor, and the stair which faced it on the N being replanned in more compact fashion to create a ground-floor kitchen; the billiard room has also been partitioned into smaller spaces. The principal bedrooms on the first floor are again laid out along a corridor, with the main bedroom rising into the second floor. A curious feature of the plan is that it never had a separate service stair.

The picturesque POLICIES above the banks of the River Ythan and Bronie Burn pre-date Mackenzie's reconstruction of the house. They are already shown as densely wooded in the 1st Ordnance Survey of 1869, and remain so today. The WALLED GARDEN, 100 m. E, is shown as rectangular, and probably adopted its present square-plan form with a gently bowed S end very shortly afterwards. The celebrated yew hedges are reputed to date from the C17 and C18; the rest of the garden was beautifully replanted with shrubs and roses after the Second World War. A small rubble building on the W side was originally a DOOCOT; hothouses once occupied the centre of the N side. The most important estate buildings are the STABLES (200 m. SW), probably by *J. R. Mackenzie* c. 1870 – near-symmetrical, two-storey gabled centre and single-storey wings with hay-loft attics; a small round clock tower with belfry and spirelet rising from the centre gable on one side, construction in coursed rubble with dressed quoins.

ESSLEMONT CASTLE, 0.8 km. S. Ruins of a three-storey L-plan tower house attributed to *Thomas Leiper* c. 1575–90. It stands in the easternmost angle of an older pentagonal enceinte built by the Keith Earls Marischal from whom the estate passed by marriage to the Cheynes of Straloch and, later, to the painter George Jameson, who held it until his death in 1644.

The ENCEINTE was excavated by Dr Douglas Simpson in 1938. The main western area of the pentagon was roughly 36 m. square, with semicircular angle towers 5.75 m. in diameter, the V of the eastern area taking the overall length to about 54 m. The curtain walls were 1.25 m. thick on a 2.5 m. base, the whole being surrounded by a fosse which may have been of still earlier date. Within the enceinte Simpson found the stump of a sizeable L-plan tower house, its main block 12.75 m. long by 11 m. wide orientated N–S and the jamb at the NE 8.25 m. wide and 6.75 m. in projection. Although only a fragment, it is of some interest as a precursor of the group of houses which includes Gight, Delgatie, Towie Barclay (qq.v.) and Craig (S), differing only in the position of its stair, which is in the SE angle of the main block, adjacent to the entrance, rather than in the centre of the longest wall. Simpson identified the granite ashlar weathering at its base course as early to mid-C15 on the analogy of similar work in the nave of St Machar's Cathedral, Aberdeen, while extensive traces of fire appeared to confirm that it was the Cheyne castle burnt by the Hays of Ardendracht in June 1493. The castle's reconstruction was licensed in 1500, the Cheynes being awarded 'XX pundis' for its repair.

The present CASTLE was built from the material of the old some eighty years later. Its plan is unusual for Aberdeenshire and appears to have been determined by the incorporation of the E angle of the enceinte into the new structure, the nearest parallel being the much larger Dunderave, far to the west in Argyll. The main block is approximately 10.5 m. by 7 m., orientated NW and SE with the curtain wall and incorporating its drum tower at the E angle; the jamb at the SW is 5.5 m. square, again raised from the ancient curtain on its SE side. The doorway is in the SW face of a stair-tower built into the re-entrant angle, the stair itself being a fairly generous 3 m. in diameter. Most of the main block and the drum tower still stand, although the jamb is almost completely lost and the windows are robbed of their dressings; the drum, which contained the main bedchamber, once had a square attic cap-house of which only the corbelling and part of the gable remains. Inside the main block, the stair and the floors have gone, although the vault of the square cellar in the drum still survives. In the N gable the outlines of a broad flue for the ground-floor kitchen and first-floor hall are clearly visible.

FEDDERATE *see* MAUD

FETTERANGUS 9050

The first Improvement village in northern Aberdeenshire, Fetterangus was laid out in 1752–3 for James Ferguson of Pitfour (q.v.) on a crossroads plan, with its central Square actually a circle. Houses in the main street are a mixture of old and new, almost exclusively single-storey.

FETTERANGUS (MISSION) CHURCH, Ferguson Street. By *James Laing* of Old Deer, 1880. Gable-fronted, with modestly projecting centre and bellcote over the roof ridge. Cusped-headed windows.

FETTERANGUS CHURCHYARD. The site of a chapel reputedly founded by St Fergus in the C6–C7. The OLD PARISH CHURCH, although much rebuilt, is thought to date from *c.* 1120. Rectangular, 10 m. by 3.5 m. internally, with rubble walls standing 1 m. high: doorway in the S flank. Used as a burial enclosure, with holy water stoop in the floor. Nearby, a

Pictish SYMBOL STONE with markings – scroll, mirror-case and triple-disc with cross-bar – now almost completely eroded. The GATEWAY is the First World War memorial, 1921.

PUBLIC HALL AND CHALMERS INSTITUTE, Ferguson Street. Jacobean, 1895. Two-storey gable front with projecting side bay on the r. flank. Central doorway sheltered by balcony of semi-elliptical first-floor window; name-panel beneath ogee pediment at the gable apex. Harled masonry with dressings and margins, arched windows with pronounced voussoirs. Much cheapened by replacement glazing and loss of balconies and balustrades.

OLD BRIDGE OF GAVAL, 1.1 km. NE, over the North Ugie Water. Late C18. Three arches, the centre slightly taller and wider. Squared rubble with distinctive cutwaters and ashlar voussoirs on both sides, the parapets stepped up towards the E in the mid C20. Wider approaches with wing walls at each end.

NEW BRIDGE, 1.3 km. ENE. Formerly carried the A952 over the North Ugie Water. Later C19. A single broad segmental span, squared rubble with rock-faced voussoirs, curving out slightly at each end towards terminal piers with truncated pyramid caps.

FINDLATER CASTLE *see* SANDEND

7020

FINGASK HOUSE

2.8 km. W of Oldmeldrum

A small country house built for the woollen manufacturer Thomas Elmslie in 1834, incorporating a house of 1821 as its rear wing.

Two-storey entrance front, three bays broadly spaced, the ground-floor windows much taller than those at first. The central bay is very slightly projected under a low pediment, its distyle Ionic portico with fluted timber columns, anta-pilasters and moulded entablature contrasting with the creamy-grey harl. It shelters a six-panelled door with elegantly detailed side- and transom-lights. Although the elevation gives an impression of symmetry the l. bay is slightly longer than those centre and r. as a result of the incorporation of older fabric. It connects through a set-back single-storey link block to the earlier house of 1821, a much smaller two-storey three-bay block in pinned squared masonry projecting to the rear, substantially rebuilt in 1923. On its rear face the main block is almost blind, but still articulated into three bays with a pedimented centre and large window lighting the stair. A long five-bay steading in coursed pinned rubble, single-storey and attic with oblong lights hard under the eaves, encloses the rear court, and behind this is a further farm court.

The GARDEN was laid out towards the end of the C18 and modified slightly later; there is a second relatively long and narrow garden extending across its SE flank, and two SUNDIALS, one dated 1851. The approach to the house is through a semi-elliptical archway flanked on its garden elevation only by empty niches formed within the boundary walls. On the main road are carriage and twin side gates: the four square piers of channelled masonry are all identical but the inner pair are crowned with urns (dated T.E. 1824 and 1827), while the outer pair have ball finials. The pretty LODGE HOUSE has a Gothic-arched doorway, tall hipped roof and tall chimneystacks.

FOLLA RULE 7030

The Rev. Alexander Lunan walked out of Daviot Parish Church in 1717 and established an Episcopal church at Folla Rule, doubtless because of its associations with the pre-Reformation church of St Regulus or Rule.

Former ST GEORGE (Episcopal). Sensitively converted to domestic use. A four-bay preaching-box, harled with round-arched windows, a tall gabled roof and small square panel dated 1796 in the centre of its S wall. Some of its masonry is reputedly medieval; a N transept (1811) has been removed. Two-bay chancel, first built in 1848–50 by *James Ross*, then extended to its present length in 1897–8 by *Arthur Clyne* (of *Pirie & Clyne*) who also built the square SW tower with pyramidal spire, and a four-bay aisle against the N flank. The tower is unbuttressed in the Scots Romanesque tradition and some 20 m. high, predominantly in silver squared masonry with red sandstone dressings. Its doorway, which is characteristic of Clyne's work, has slim polished granite columns supporting a boldly profiled arch with hoodmould, and its timber-boarded double-leaf doors are hung on decorative iron bar hinges. The N aisle is swept low down and lit by single and paired lights, all round-headed; the vestry on the N side of the chancel is accessed through a shouldered doorway. Internally the Romanesque arcade separating nave from N aisle still survives. The chancel retains its panelled barrel-vaulted ceiling, painted pale blue and gold with divine symbols – Chi Rho, Alpha and Omega, Lamb of God, Cross of Sacrifice, Star of David, S for Salvator – and an attractive frieze. The furnishings of 1898 have been removed. – STAINED GLASS. E window, the Crucifixion, by *Clayton & Bell*, 1898. W window, The Adoration of the Magi, 1899. Other windows (now in storage) are *c.* 1865 (by *John Hardman & Co.*), 1869 and 1907.

CHURCHYARD. Gifted and consecrated 1863. A very large Celtic cross in its centre, dedicated to members of the Crawford family.

Former RECTORY, 70 m. N. Built 1813. Two-storey, three bays in roughly squared granite and whinstone, the pinnings mortared over and cherry-cocked. The entrance door has the original transom-light with curvilinear lozenge glazing bars. Gabled roof with simply moulded chimneystacks. Large rear wing, also two-storey, forms an L-plan.

VILLAGE HALL, 80 m. NW. By *A. & W. Hendry* of nearby Wartle, 1904. Former church hall, single-storey and five bays, with walls and roof in corrugated iron. Gabled porch projecting at l. end; the r. bay rises rather taller into an attic gable. Idiosyncratic timber detailing with date in mock tie-beam over the doorway. Some features lost, but the gables retain their simple bargeboards.

Former EPISCOPAL SCHOOL HOUSE, 170 m. WNW. Built *c.* 1856–63, enlarged 1915. Stands with its back to the road on steeply sloping ground. Entrance front two-storey over raised basement, with projecting gabled ends framing a recessed centre and a railed forestair leading up to the doorway. Rear elevation four bays, the centre pair projected under gables; all harled with exposed red sandstone dressings and margins, simply profiled skewputts and moulded end stacks.

5060 FORDYCE B

A peaceful Banffshire village of irresistible charm, Fordyce was erected a burgh of barony for Bishop William Elphinstone in 1499, its charter being renewed in 1592. Until *c.* 1618 it was the centre of a very large parish comprising Ordiquhill (*see* Cornhill), Cullen and Deskford (Moray).

OLD CHURCH.* The church dedicated to St Talorgan or Talarican, along with its dependent chapels of Cullen, Deskford and Ordiquhill, was a possession of the canons of Aberdeen Cathedral by 1272. Following construction of a new church in 1804 (*see* below), much of the medieval building was demolished, apart from a number of structures that were either formed within its walls or that had been added around its periphery, as these continued to be used for burials. The plan of the medieval core was evidently a simple rectangle, and the chancel, which had served as the burial place of a branch of the Ogilvy family since at least the early C16, survived in modified form through its adaptation as two roofless burial enclosures for later branches of that same family. A CHAPEL dedicated to the Virgin that was added against the S flank of the nave in 1516 by Thomas Menzies, the builder of the adjacent castle (*see* below), has also survived as a roofless burial enclosure. There is a blocked rectangular window in its S wall and a smaller blocked window in the W wall. To the W of that

*This entry is by Richard Fawcett.

chapel is a structure which may have been first built (at an uncertain date) as a vaulted S porch, but which was heightened as a bell-tower in 1661, with a prison formed within it *c.* 1682. The handsome double-arched bellcote above its S gable, with gablets above corbel tables to the four faces, is dated 1661; the stair to the first floor against the tower's E face is said to be of 1721. In 1679 a two-storey family aisle was built against the N side of the nave for the Abercromby of Glasshaugh family, with a burial chamber at the lower level and a loft looking into the church above; there is a panel with the arms of Abercromby on the N wall and a small bellcote over the N gable. The openings towards the church were built up after 1804.

FURNISHINGS. St Mary's Aisle, an aumbry with a rebate for a door is reset in the blocked window rere-arch in the S wall. – MONUMENTS. Chancel. The E portion contains the canopied tomb of James Ogilvy of Deskford (†1509) and his 23
son (†1505). Its design demonstrates the continuing impact of tomb design of the type seen earlier in the monument of Bishop John Winchester (†1460) at Elgin (q.v.), albeit some of the forms at Fordyce are more loosely organized. The tomb-chest has a blind arcade of seven ogee arches with cusped cusping and cusped spandrels; the ogee-arched canopy has cusped cusping with foliate terminals and lavish crocketing. At mid height of the flanking buttresses and below the finial at the apex of the canopy are shields with the arms of Ogilvy of Deskford and their connections. The single effigy in plate armour rests its feet on a lion. – The W portion of the chancel, adapted as a burial enclosure for the Ogilvy of Birkenbog family, retains a medieval canopied tomb for a member of the Ogilvy of Findlater family that is a simpler variant on that in the E portion. There is no effigy, the tomb-chest is undecorated and the ogee-arched canopy has crockets along its extrados but no cusping to the soffit; there are the usual miniature buttresses with shields at mid height on either side. – Abercromby Aisle. A large and scholarly Ionic aedicular monument with a military trophy at the apex for Gen. James Abercromby of Glasshaugh (†1781), described as 'a strict but genteel economist'.

Former PARISH CHURCH, Church Street. Built in 1804; closed in 2011. Simple rectangular plan. Entrance gables with round-arched, fanlit, key-blocked doorways and gallery windows set in blocked surrounds. Distinguishing the E gable is a pedimented and finialled bellcote with acroteria at the corners added *c.* 1830 to house a bell cast by the Frenchman *Albert Gely* of Aberdeen in 1702. Four-bay S flank, N flank blind with a small outshot, all harled with dressed quoins, moulded skewputts, roof steeply pitched with Banffshire slates. The INTERIOR originally had the pulpit centred in the S wall, surrounded by a U-plan gallery: it was recast in 1894 when the introduction of a large organ required the W gallery to be partitioned off, with a session house below the organ chamber. (In 2011 the following were *in situ*: ORGAN by *J.J. Binns* of Leeds. A handsome array of pipes above the central console.

Octagonal pedestal PULPIT, seemingly 1894, panelled with Gothic arcading. It stood near the centre of the S wall, but facing E towards the majority of the congregation. COMMUNION TABLE probably also 1894, of exceptional length, panel-fronted. PEWS still in place.

VILLAGE HALL, East Church Street. Former Free Church, opened 1844, repaired and altered by *A. & W. Reid* 1880–1. Gable-fronted with modern porch, two tall square-headed windows and blocked round-arched window immediately beneath the bellcote, replaced in 1894. Three-bay flank elevations, all rubble-built with ashlar dressed work, tall roof with boldly moulded skewputts.

SCHOOL. *See* Description, below.

PUBLIC GARDENS, West Church Street. Remains of two C19 LIME KILNS near their entrance.

64 FORDYCE CASTLE. Probably built by *Thomas Leiper* for Sir Thomas Menzies of Durn in 1592, the year Menzies was elected Provost of Aberdeen and renewed Fordyce's status as a burgh of barony. This classic small tower house comprises a three-storey main block almost square on plan with angle turrets at diagonally opposite corners, and a slightly taller four-storey jamb containing a wheel stair to first floor, the upper storeys being accessed by a turnpike stair corbelled out from the re-entrant angle. The main block is probably on the same site as the tower house recorded in January 1493 and may incorporate some of its masonry.

The design is particularly refined in its details. There are doorways at ground floor in both the main block and the jamb, the latter being the main entrance, more finely treated with roll moulding and an empty field-panel above which is framed by balusters and dated: it must once have contained Menzies's coat of arms. The main block's doorway, which accessed the vaulted ground-floor services, is chamfered. Its rubble masonry, predominantly in long thin stones either golden or grey in colour, was originally harled. The stair-turret's magnificent deep corbelling is carved with variations of cable moulding rising from a foliate base-corbel; it has Leiper's distinctive triple and quintuple shot-holes, and it is simply capped by an C18 swept roof. Most of the castle's windows are small but that of the great hall on the main block's first floor is much larger, there being another such window, now blocked, in the end gable, and two more in the rear. The second-floor window breaks up through the eaves into a swept dormerhead, while in the jamb a chimney-breast is corbelled out above its third storey and rises up through its gable. The main block's second-floor angle turrets are corbelled out, the rubble masonry of the frontal one giving way to fine ashlar at window-sill level with a monogrammed roundel. The roofs are crowstepped and still clad in Banffshire slates; the coped chimneystacks are low but very sturdy.

The large three-storey harled wing known as 'GLASSAUGH'S HOUSE' built on the other side of the jamb, and set back from it to align with the tower house's main block although it is rather lower in height, was added *c.* 1700. Built into falling ground, its principal apartments are like those of the tower house at first floor, to which a long straight forestair built against the flank of the jamb provides direct access: a scar in the jamb's masonry suggests that the present wing replaced a much smaller predecessor. The windows are very small and semi-regular in layout, and the details are kept simple in deference to the older house, with the second floor expressed as timber dormers beneath a tall crowstepped roof. Between 1716 and 1789 the wing was used as the parish school.

DESCRIPTION. Most of the cottages and houses in Fordyce date from the early to mid C19. In Church Street many stand with their gables to the road, not so much for protection against the wind – as in local fishing villages – but so that they are angled S towards the sun. The cottages are low, single-storeyed and rubble-built, often with tall roofs and attic dormers, and set in attractive gardens, two small cottages sometimes linked together to form one. In East Church Street, a fluted cast-iron STAND-PUMP with lion's-mouth spout, a familiar later C19 type by *Glenfield & Kennedy* (there is another one outside the castle). Then at the junction with School Road stands the former HOTEL, mid-Victorian, a bowed corner block two storeys with tall ground floor and first floor breaking through the wall-head into gableted stone dormers. S of this in School Road, the former FREE CHURCH MANSE, a handsome two-storey three-bay villa of 1846, harled in white, with pedimented doorpiece in its slightly projecting centre, and a low hipped roof; its style suggests *A. & W. Reid* of Elgin.

Further down on the W side of School Road is the former FORDYCE ACADEMY (now Academy House), founded in 1801 as the result of a bequest granted by George Smith of Bombay to educate as many boys of the name of Smith as funds permitted. The original part was built *c.* 1801–2, and faces S over a large garden, presumably once a playground. It is two-storey and three bays with a later porch: its ground-floor windows have been converted to bipartites, and there are gableted dormers in the hipped roof. The later E wing of *c.* 1845 faces School Road directly: two storeys with a broad gabled bay at the S end, an off-centre porch and first-floor windows breaking up into gableted dormers. Across School Road, the present SCHOOL with two separate blocks – the N one of 1882 single-storey with broad gabled wings slightly projecting at each end, its S gable crowned by a Gothic bellcote with spirelet; astragalled windows, and separate porches for boys and girls. The later S block is by *James Wood*, Banffshire Education Department. Architect, 1923–4.* In

*Fordyce was celebrated for its schools, which have produced a distinguished roll-call of alumni, notably in medicine. The first parochial school in the village was built and endowed by Thomas Menzies of Durn towards the end of the C16. A hundred years later, Walter Ogilvie of Reidhyth built and endowed a new school, and in 1678 he endowed bursaries both at the school and at King's College, Aberdeen.

ST TARQUIN'S PLACE, the OLD SCHOOL-HOUSE is a single-storey three-bay cottage built *c.* 1830–40.

GLASSAUGH HOUSE. *See* p. 235.

6050

FORGLEN HOUSE B

1.8 km. N of Kirkton of Forglen

87 A splendid Neo-Elizabethan courtyard palace built for Sir Robert Abercromby *c.* 1839–40 to designs by *John Smith I*, perhaps with his son *William Smith* who returned from his apprenticeship with T. L. Donaldson in London at about that time. In certain respects, particularly its principal floor plan, Forglen is the antecedent for Balmoral (S), designed by Prince Albert with William Smith's assistance. Forglen is more economically built in golden-harled rubble but taken together these two houses illustrate the different approaches architects had to take when designing for granite and for sandstone. At Balmoral the detail is more hard-edged with predominantly timber mullions and transoms; at Forglen these are in stone and the details are generally rather more elaborate.

The ENTRANCE FRONT facing SE is skilfully balanced rather than symmetrical, three storeys high and eight generously proportioned bays in length. It has a large central canted bay window rising into a curvilinear gable, projecting bays with straight-skewed gables towards each far end, and a tall square stair-tower which rises up from within the courtyard behind. As in other Smith houses of this vintage however there are a number of asymmetric elements including the entrance porch, off-centre to the l., and a very slim octagonal four-storey tower at the S corner, both of which add interest to the entrance front's exceptional length. The single-storey porch is framed between octagonal buttresses which rise above a battlemented parapet into spike-finialled domelets; it has a round-arched moulded doorway sheltered by a stepped hood-mould, and above its parapet is Sir Robert Abercromby's coat of arms. The windows are mullioned and transomed in stone, those of the first-floor principal apartments being very tall and those at second floor rising into dormer gablets. The N-end gabled bay projects more boldly forward than that to the S, and its bay window is carried up a storey higher to second floor. The big three-light windows in the northern half of the elevation are projected into shallow rectangular bays with ball-finialled parapets and mark the position of the first-floor drawing room. Pinnacles rise from both the central canted bay and the S corner tower, and the steeply pitched roofs are punctuated by clusters of tall diagonally-shafted chimneystacks resulting in a lively and picturesque yet dignified profile, particularly striking when seen in perspective. The three superimposed coats of arms on the S tower, crowned by a carved gable, dated 1578 and with an inscription tablet beneath, have been reused from the previous house: the arms at the top are the Royal Arms of Scotland, and the others represent the Abercrombys, whose emblem is the oak tree.

The FLANK ELEVATIONS each have a slightly projecting gabled bay towards the far E end balanced by a square tower with a pyramidal spirelet towards the far W, but they are non-identical, the SW elevation being of five bays and the NE of six, its tower rather larger. Plain irregular REAR AND COURTYARD ELEVATIONS. Rising high above the roofs is the GREAT TOWER, lit by slim round-arched triple-light windows, its crowning balustrade with ball finials at each corner.

Internally Forglen is grandly Neoclassical rather than Elizabethan. While the principal apartments may be in the usual well-tried sequence the general arrangement of the PLAN has been determined by the falling site and has no obvious precedent. It is basically a courtyard rectangle, the entrance front 48 m. in length, the SW flank 24 m. broad and the NE flank 27.5 m. broad. The porch opens into a spacious double-height hall-staircase leading to the principal floor, its landing cantilevered out on long console brackets with acanthus leaves. The ground floor is devoted to billiards, guns and service accommodation; at principal-floor level the hall-staircase opens into a spacious corridor with a distyle-*in-antis* screen of Corinthian columns to the main stair. These have richly scrolled acanthus friezes and compartmented ceilings with late classical plasterwork. The principal apartments form a right-angled suite at the NE corner of the house, the library within the central canted bay, and two drawing rooms and an ante-room leading to the dining room with a sideboard recess framed by fluted Corinthian columns at its far N end and a coffered ceiling. The family rooms occupy the SW flank, with Sir Robert and Lady Abercromby's rooms on either side of the principal bedroom, and two small rooms for children or important visitors, one opening into a closet in the S tower. Service rooms are arranged on the NW side, with the double-height kitchen rising from the ground floor beneath. Two spiral stair-turrets in the angles of the courtyard give discreet service access to all three floors.

The house stands in the centre of a designed LANDSCAPE, partly laid out as pleasure grounds, partly as woodland and partly as tillage. It extends over some 960 hectares, mostly on the W bank of the River Deveron, being approached from Turriff across the handsome Eastside Bridge (*see* p. 413) completed in 1826. Some tree plantations already existed by 1723, and the grounds are shown richly wooded in Gen. Roy's maps published between 1747 and 1755. The origins of the present landscape however are attributed to Sir Alexander Ogilvie, 7th

Lord Banff, who succeeded in 1746 and over the next twenty-five years engaged in substantial improvements. Forglen was further developed by his son William who succeeded in 1771. 'His Lordship has done much of late to beautify his seat', the Rev. Robert Ballingall recorded in the *Statistical Account* in the 1790s. 'The workmen were sorry to put the first hand to change some of the improvements of his father, which they thought well enough, and to undo their own workmanship; but the execution pleased their eye so much, that they forgot their sympathy.' The Abercrombys continued the improvements, acquiring additional lands on the E bank of the Deveron. Sir Robert Abercromby, his son George Samuel and grandson Robert John developed Forglen into one of the grandest estates of the Victorian era.

The INNER PARK was planted both on the Deveron's W bank above the house and facing it on the E bank with limes, larches, sycamores and Douglas firs which still survive, although the elms have been lost to disease. To the N of the house, the inner park gives way to a WOODLAND GARDEN planted with exotic specimen trees and shrubs, a path lined with conifers leading to the WALLED GARDEN (0.3 km. NW) which was constructed in coped whinstone rubble during the mid C19. The garden is divided into two compartments, and still retains much of its historic structure of central and perimeter paths, as well as the fine original glasshouses against its N wall.

The GLEN BURN WATER GARDEN, N of the walled garden, seems to have been begun in the later C19, although the water pools were not formed until the early C20, the paths being lined with rhododendrons and azaleas, and the slopes, *inter alia*, with dawn redwoods, deodars, grand firs, spruces, beeches, copper beeches and western red cedars. Beyond the immediate policies of the house, the wider WOODLANDS are planted with a mix of deciduous trees and conifers to provide a rich setting for the drives and paths, and to line the estate boundaries.

NORTH LODGE, 0.6 km. N. Picturesque villa-style, possibly by *A. & W. Reid* of Elgin, *c.* 1865.* Single-storey and gabled attic, harled with ashlar dressings. Ground-floor canted bay forms balcony for attic windows, porch facing the main road. Steeply raked roofs with decorative bargeboards, tall coped chimneystack.

EASTSIDE LODGE, 2 km. SSE. A delightful composition, probably by the *Reids*, *c.* 1865.‡ Small L-plan, single-storey and gabled attic, with a slim two-stage tower and spirelet projecting forward in the angle. Light golden harl with ashlar dressings. Within the tower, a finely carved round-arched entrance opening, its hoodmould with mask label stops, and arms of the Abercrombys set above. Gargoyles announce the tower's

*‡ Shown in the 1st Ordnance Survey published 1867.

second stage with slim lights in each side rising into dormer gablets, the spirelet with fish-scale slates and a weathervane finial. Closely similar to Greengate Lodge, Delgatie (q.v.). Gatepiers channelled with Neoclassical spike-finialled urns, elaborate carriage and side gates.

COACHHOUSE AND STABLES, 0.3 km. SSE, *c.* 1840. Square courtyard plan, presumably by *J. & W. Smith.* Principal NW elevation with central two-stage tower containing segmental pend, window with hoodmould at first floor, and gable pediment with armorial and die-finial; in the side bays, ground-floor windows with smaller hay-loft openings above.

HOME FARM, 0.4 km. WSW. Early C19, square courtyard plan. Principal NE elevation with central two-stage tower containing segmental pend and first-floor loft opening, gable pediment with clock-dial; two-storey side bays with the upper windows breaking through the eaves as dormers.

KENNELS, 0.6 km. SSW. Mid-C19, possibly by *A. & W. Reid.* Two-storey three bays, harled with Turriff sandstone margins, the upper-floor windows breaking through the eaves as gableted dormers with trefoil finials; later rustic gabled porch with four tree-trunk columns. WALLED GARDEN COTTAGE, 0.4 km. NW. Mid-C19, single storey, three bays with bipartite windows framing central door, diagonally shafted chimneystacks, the broad bay to the r. added later; harled with Turriff sandstone margins. GARDEN COTTAGE, 0.4 km. NW, CROSSBRAE, 0.7 km. NW, and WESTWOOD, 1.3 km. W. Mid-C19 estate cottages, each single-storey three-bay with later rustic gabled porch, again harled with sandstone margins; both Garden Cottage and Crossbrae have attic dormers.

DOOCOT, 320 m. SW. Early C19 square-plan, two stages brick-built and harled, with doorway in S flank; alighting ledge and flight-holes in Turriff sandstone, brick frieze at eaves, truncated pyramid slate roof. ICE HOUSE (460 m. WNW). Early C19, rectangular plan, built into a steep bank with its opening at the top.

MONUMENT, 250 m. N, presumably by *A. & W. Reid*, *c.* 1868. A variant of the English Eleanor Cross type. Small octagonal Early Dec with spirelet, trefoil-arcading with colonnettes and gablets running round its shaft.

MAUSOLEUM, 780 m. S by *A. & W. Reid*, consecrated 1868. Gothic cruciform with each arm rising into a steeply raked gable, construction in coursed dark whinstone with golden ashlar dressings. Pointed doorway in NE arm with nook-shaft colonnettes and quatrefoil spandrels; superimposed Abercromby coat of arms under a stepped hoodmould with finely sculpted portrait heads for label stops. Flanking buttresses with tall crocketed pinnacles; within the gable-head a trefoil roundel, monstrous gargoyles, a decorative quatrefoil frieze and a floriate cross finial. SW arm has a large rose window, NW and SE arms small round-headed niches to contain statues of Faith and Hope. Fine gableted gatepiers and gates.

FORMARTINE CASTLE *see* GIGHT CASTLE

9020 FOVERAN

A small village close to Newburgh.

Former FOVERAN PARISH CHURCH. Built in 1794. Rectangular plan in coursed squared granite with round-headed doorways at each end and four round-headed windows in the S flank in ashlar surrounds. W gable with two gallery-level windows and ball-finialled birdcage bellcote. E gable with single gallery window and old-fashioned skewputts, that on the SE dated. Polygonal S organ chamber added in 1900, perhaps by *Jenkins & Marr*. Interior repaired 1852 by *William Buyers*, re-seated *c.* 1871–3. U-plan gallery with arcaded fronts renewed by *William Christie*, 1877: its cast-iron columns rise into broad segmental arches which support the ceiling. Further minor alterations to interior by *William Ruxton*, 1893–4; last re-seating mid-C20. – Raised PULPIT (with hourglass), the handsome ORGAN by *Wadsworth & Brother* rising up behind it within a depressed-arch recess framed by slim Corinthianesque pilasters. – FONT 1885 stone, with stiff-leaf carving. – MONUMENTS. – GRAVE-SLAB. *c.* 1400, in memory of two unknown knights. It probably lay in the Turing Aisle of the church's medieval predecessor. Grey sandstone, formerly painted, similar to Gilbert de Greenlaw's stone at Kinkell (S), and perhaps by the same mason; cracked across the centre but otherwise well preserved. – George and Alexander Udny, †1788. Marble portrait monument by *John Bacon R.A.*, erected 1794. – Among the C19 and C20 memorial plaques, one to the painter and etcher James McBey (†1959).

WAR MEMORIAL GATEWAY, to the churchyard extension. By *W. L. Duncan*, 1922, a round-headed arch framed by buttresses, and a stepped parapet rising into a gable; cast-iron gates by *J. & A. McFarlane & Co.*, Glasgow.

FOVERAN PARISH CHURCH. See Holyrood Chapel, Newburgh (q.v.).

FOVERAN HOUSE. Built near the site of the Turing Tower, which collapsed in 1720. A vernacular classical country house which has acquired much character through a series of alterations. Its main block facing SW is two storeys and five windows wide above a semi-sunk basement, the central entrance bay continuing up into an attic wall-head gable with a chimneystack; constructed in coursed, squared silver granite, it has simple window surrounds and long-and-short quoins. Reputedly built in 1771 for John Robertson, stocking-merchant and Provost of Aberdeen, the client may in fact have been Alexander Robertson whose initials are incised in the key-block of the attic's round-headed window. Its original appearance is recorded in 1821, but shortly afterwards the central porch was added. The porch's upper storey is however later C19 or early C20 and of the same period are the two single-storey side wings somewhat set back, seemingly for a billiard room (l.) and ballroom (r.). Rising up behind the main block, slightly off-centre to the l., is a large square tower with ogee-domed pepperpot turrets modelled on those at Pinkie House (Lothian) at each corner. This was built in the rear service court by *Matthews & Mackenzie c.* 1880 and is exceptional for such a date as it is of unreinforced shuttered concrete.* The oldest part of the house, in all probability, is not the main block but the single-storey S range of the rear court. Its chamfered door and window openings suggest it is C18, and it appears in the 1821 perspective.

Internally, the main block's ground-floor rooms have simple cornices and their panelling has been reset, but the dining room on the l. of the entrance hall has Ionic columns to frame a sideboard, these probably being later insertions of *c.* 1840. The corresponding room on the first floor and both the wings have much richer cornices, while the early courtyard range has been completely remodelled internally with deep coved ceilings.

ENE of the main house, the HOME FARM STEADING. A two-storey house in coursed granite with irregular fenestration, upper-floor windows relatively small and square, and lower asymmetric ranges extending from each flank to form a three-sided open court. Rubble-walled garden and two-storey building (perhaps the LAUNDRY?) on lower ground nearby probably the same age as the steading. – LODGE by *Matthews & Mackenzie*, with pedimented central entrance and canted bays in the gables; gatepiers themselves square with ball finials.

MILL OF FOVERAN FARMHOUSE, 1 km. W. Remodelled mid C19. Two-storey-and-basement former girnal in coursed rubble. Chamfered openings with sandstone dressings; gable skewputts with St Andrew's crosses, one dated 1609 (?). Balustraded stair to near-central doorway on main E front. Battlemented porch on W elevation, and consoled block cornice (perhaps originally a ratcourse?) which serves as guttering at the level of the first floor; the upstairs windows break into dormerheads. MILL of 1720, now raised in height and emptied of its workings.

FRASERBURGH 9060

Fraserburgh has its origins in the fishing village of Faithlie which was established near the Braeheads by the mid C14. *Circa* 1535–40 Alexander Fraser, 7th of Philorth, built a primitive harbour, and

*Matthews used the same material in the Tivoli Theatre, Aberdeen, in 1872.

in 1546 Faithlie was erected as a burgh of barony and a free port, contravening the exclusive rights which Aberdeen had hitherto possessed throughout the county.

Alexander was succeeded by his grandson, also Alexander, 8th of Philorth, a friend and adviser of King James VI – 'a man of great force of character, able, and of most progressive views . . . That he aimed high and destined Fraserburgh to be a place of great importance there can be no doubt.' Alexander seemingly built a simple tower house at Kinnaird Head in 1570–2 so that he could personally oversee his town's development, starting with a new parish church *c.* 1571–4, and in 1576 he either began to improve his grandfather's harbour or to build a new one. The town prospered, but Alexander's extensive works were funded by borrowing, mostly from his kinsmen. To secure his town's future, Alexander obtained a new charter in 1588 reaffirming its status as a burgh of barony and a free port, and received a licence to sell substantial land-holdings to fund further development. In 1592 he was granted permission to found a university, but it subsequently incurred royal displeasure and was not successful. In 1601 Alexander received another charter which authorized the election of town baillies, a treasurer, dean of guild councillors and free burgesses, and in 1613 as his creditors finally closed in, he received a charter erecting the town into a burgh of regality, entering that year into a feu-contract with thirty-two burgesses, and building a tolbooth and market cross where the Burgh Chambers now stand as the focus of local government and trade.

In contrast to other towns established at this time, Fraserburgh developed on what might be roughly termed a grid-pattern, enclosed on the E side by Eastgait – now Broad Street – leading up from the Kirkton of Philorth, and on the N by Backgait – later North Street, now High Street – on the road to Rosehearty (q.v.). After four centuries the grid is rather less obvious, but it can be traced in the three long streets High Street, Mid Street and Frithside Street winding E–W through the Old Town, and gently fanning out as they progress away from the seashore, while Broad Street, Cross Street, Manse Street and School Street correspond to the streets running S to N. The grid-like plan produced a different feuing pattern from the more conventional cruciform plan, with square feus (rather than narrow rigs) which encouraged the development of large courtyard houses particularly on North Street near the Castle Parks.

By the mid C17 Fraserburgh was the second-largest port in north-east Scotland. In 1705 it became a member of the Convention of Royal Burghs, with additional trading privileges. During the Jacobite Uprisings the Frasers of Philorth, by then Lords Saltoun, managed to maintain a relatively low profile but from the end of the 'Forty-five until the end of the French wars Fraserburgh was, however reluctantly, a garrison town, with consequences both for its society and its economic development.

Important developments took place from the late C18. The Kirk Green was recast as Saltoun Square in 1801, with the

Saltoun Arms completed in 1802 and the new parish church close by in 1803. In the Castle Parks a chalybeate spring was developed as a spa with recreation rooms following Peterhead's example and extended with baths in 1807. In 1810 Fraserburgh was linked by turnpikes to Aberdeen and Peterhead, then in 1816 the turnpike system was extended W to Banff (q.v.). After the French wars the baths seemingly encouraged proposals for the development of the Castle Parks on the N edge of town and the turnpikes led to further development in Saltoun Place to the S. Commerce moved gradually from the harbour area into Saltoun Square, Broad Street and Commerce Street but the busy port remained the engine of prosperity. From the early C19 the herring industry began to grow dramatically, and in 1832 the Harbour Commissioners allowed fishing vessels – hitherto consigned to Broadsea Bay – to use the enhanced harbour facilities for the first time.

During the mid C19 the port further prospered through whale and seal fishing and associated industries such as shipbuilding. In 1865 the Formartine & Buchan Railway established a terminus in South Harbour Road, opening up rapid access to fish-markets in the south; from 1870 the town participated fully in the herring boom, its wealth reflected in fine churches and public buildings as the streets expanded W with modest houses for solid tradesmen, S with comfortable villas for the well-to-do, and N over the Castle Parks where the poorest fish-workers were crammed into appalling slum conditions.

Fraserburgh prospered further when the Consolidated Pneumatic Tool Works was built in Aberdeen Road in 1904, but after the First World War and the Russian Revolution the export market for herring collapsed and the town went into severe decline until a revival of the herring industry took place during the 1930s. Notwithstanding its problems the town experienced a second remarkable expansion during the interwar years, with high-quality social housing to the W by *W.F. Hamilton*, Burgh Surveyor, then in the post-war period SW as far as Strichen Road. Recent times have not been kind to Fraserburgh, but it remains the largest shellfish port in Europe, and a major port for whitefish, while Macduff Shipyards retain a significant presence near the harbour.

CHURCHES

BAPTIST CHURCH, Victoria Street. By *James Souttar c.* 1877–80. A small gable-fronted church, large pointed-arch window with intersecting Y-tracery of the Aberdeen Greyfriars type. Steeply raked roof swept over a porch set back on one flank; on the other flank, three pairs of pointed lights. Granite ashlar with lighter-coloured ashlar for banded decoration, buttresses, quoins, margins and other details. – Interior. Arched hammerbeam roof on moulded corbels; small rose window at E end. Pitch-pine platform PULPIT arcaded with tall back rising into triple gables. The original PEWS have been preserved.

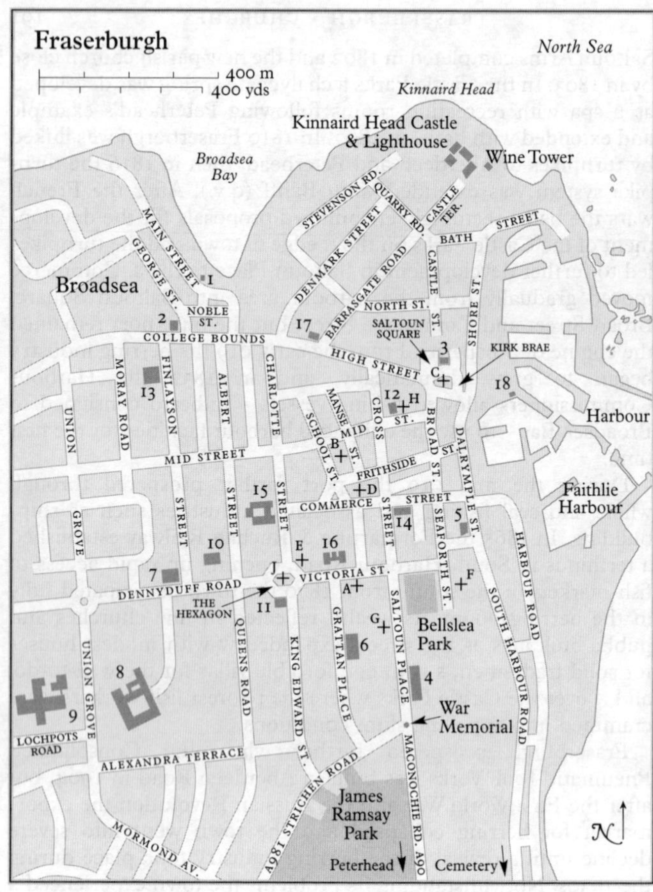

A Baptist Church
B Bethesda Evangelical Church
C Old Parish Church
D Our Lady Star of the Sea and St Drostan (R.C.)
E St. Peter (Episcopal)
F Fraserburgh South Church
G United Presbyterian Church (former)
H United Reformed Church
J West Parish Church

1 Broadsea General Assembly School (former)
2 Broadsea Village Hall
3 Burgh Chambers
4 Coastguard Station (former)
5 Dalrymple Hall
6 Drill Hall (former)
7 Fraserburgh Academy (Finlayson Street)
8 Fraserburgh Academy with swimming pool and community centre (Dennyduff Road)
9 Fraserburgh Hospital
10 Infant School (former)
11 Library
12 Macaulay Memorial Hall
13 North School
14 Post Office (former)
15 St Andrew's Primary School
16 St Peter's Episcopal School (former)
17 Strachan's Industrial School for Girls (former)
18 Lifeboatmen Memorial

Early GLASS with red margins, flank windows etched with fleur-de-lys.

BETHESDA EVANGELICAL CHURCH, Manse Street. Built as a United Presbyterian church in 1854. A simple five-bay preaching-box, flank-on to the road with central gabled porch and tall slim round-headed windows with diamond-pane glazing; harled with ashlar dressings and heathen rubble gables; church hall added to rear. – Wide-span canted and timber-boarded ceiling held together by tension rods and supported on corbels and a mutuled cornice.

OLD PARISH CHURCH, Kirk Brae, on or near the site of the church built by Alexander Fraser in the later C16. According to a 'Report of Inspection of the New Church', the plans were by *James Littlejohn* of Aberdeen, 1802, and its construction completed by *William Dauney* in 1803. A simple classical design, with a handsome entrance tower and spire centred in the W gable front of a four-bay preaching-box facing up the High Street. The tower built in ashlar masonry contrasting with the harled rubble gable is of very shallow projection, with a tall round-headed doorway sheltered under a console-cornice, and a round-arched window at first floor. It rises into a solid square plinth with shallow pediment and datestone, octagonal belfry with blocked arcaded openings and clock dials in alternate faces; the stone spire with bull's-eye openings culminates in a fish-style weathervane. The church gable has blocked doorways either side of the tower which once led up to the gallery; the first-floor windows are round-arched like the tower's but broader. Four-bay flanks. Rear elevation rising from lower ground is plain with a tall Serlian window; slim margins and eaves cornice throughout. Hipped roof with later ventilators. In the E gable a reused dormerhead with strapwork, a crescent and three shields, and a carved datestone with initials B.V.M./G.L. 1817. Vestry added by *James Matthews* during renovations of 1873–4.

The charming modesty of the Old Parish Church gives no clue as to its altogether grander INTERIOR, remodelled by *A. Marshall Mackenzie* (of *Matthews & Mackenzie*) in 1898–9 to challenge the Free (now South) Church (*see* below) for the devotions of the burgeoning N end of the town. Neoclassical rather than simply classical, its sheer scale comes as a surprise. It is a very large rectangle with a deep U-plan gallery containing the organ (1892) with its splendid display of pipes at the W end, the ceiling being carried on heavy beams – presumably steel – with arches supporting a barrel-vault above the central area. The gallery is supported on Doric columns, apparently those of 1803, and its fronts are balustraded. The octagonal platform PULPIT is immensely tall: it is the parish war memorial, its sides and base faced with brass plaques bearing names of the Fallen. The COMMUNION TABLE is panelled with a foliate cornice supporting its top. Generally, the interior still feels all of a piece, the original PEWS remaining *in situ*. The inevitable focus is the enormous Serlian window in the E gable

49 with its magnificent STAINED GLASS by *Douglas Strachan*, 1906 – the subjects Our Lord in Glory, Adoration and Praise (Psalm 148), with in the l. light, Miriam, and in the r. light, Deborah; above the window, simple stencilling at the cornice. A small but doughty CARVED SOLDIER in C16 garb is the unlikely survivor of a local shipwreck and has found sanctuary here to remember fellow travellers lost.

SALTOUN MAUSOLEUM, S of the Old Parish Church. Probably 1803 replacing the S aisle with burial chamber which had been built on the death of Alexander Fraser (†1623) against the church he had erected *c.* 1571–4. The present mausoleum is square on plan, its harled walls with stepped pyramidal roof crowned by an obelisk finial. Blocked pointed-arch doorway inset with older heraldic arms, further arms on the other flanks.

OUR LADY STAR OF THE SEA & ST DROSTAN (R.C.), Commerce Street. By *Ellis & Wilson*, 1895–6. Simple early Gothic in rough granite ashlar, neatly angled into its junction site. Entrance gable facing S, pointed-arch doorway set in gabled surround with vestigial pilaster-buttresses. Stepped triple-light above with centre light trefoiled, pinnacles at the angles and three blind lights beneath the roof ridge with cruciform metal finial. Broadly spaced four-bay flank facing W onto Lodge Walk, jerkin-headed N gable and polygonal apse. The PRESBYTERY is a simple two-storey villa set back on the E side, the whole forming an L-plan group. A long rectangular nave with gallery at its entrance end and scissor-beam roof reinforced by collar trusses; it opens into a polygonal apse, vaulted with slim gold ribs meeting in a circular boss. – Gothic HIGH ALTAR by *Beyaert* of Bruges, made in wood, the altar itself panelled with central Holy Monogram (IHS) and attached colonnettes; the REREDOS above, its ciborium with small crucified Christ in an arched canopy, flanked by paintings of SS Drostan (?), Andrew, Peter and Mary, finely carved decoration with much use of gold leaf. Two elaborately carved SIDE ALTARS containing sculptures of Our Lord and the Virgin and Child; arcaded ALTAR RAILS. Between the cast-iron columns supporting the gallery, the FONT, a very large octagonal basin supported on a foliate capital and short shaft of polished marble. – STATIONS OF THE CROSS, 1906. – Original PEWS. – Small ORGAN in the gallery.

ST PETER (Episcopal), Charlotte Street. Designed 1891 by *John*
45 *Kinross* with his apprentice *H. M. Nisbett*, the nave and chancel completed in 1893 (*James Rollo* of Fraserburgh, mason) but the entrance tower, although always intended, not added until 1909. Vestry also later. Scottish Romanesque, built in pink Corennie granite in shallow brick-like courses with pale ashlar dressings. Large square tower standing in front of the nave is buttressed with round-arched doorways in its flanks: above the N door a panel displaying St Peter's mitre and keys. At the tower's SW corner a gabled stair-turret rises to the Gothic belfry stage, which has traceried roundel openings. The deep parapet is jettied out on corbels with water cannon and shallow

crenellation, the low octagonal spire is slated with a dormer in its S face and cruciform finial. Five-bay nave with side aisles and clearstorey, the roof-lines continuing without interruption over the chancel; in both the aisles and clearstorey, each bay is expressed by a small round-headed window. Inside the church, the nave columns are red Dumfries-shire freestone with stylized scallop capitals, the walls above are whitewashed, and the ceiling barrel-vaulted in redwood timber with modillions at the cornices. An organ chamber opens off the chancel through a Norman arch, and also has a pointed arch facing into the S aisle.

All the FURNISHINGS appear to have been designed by *Kinross*, notably the elegant wrought-iron chancel SCREEN with fleur-de-lys finials, made by *Houston & Stewart* of Edinburgh, 1895. – PULPIT. Made by the *Albert Carving Works* of Edinburgh in 1899. Late Scots Gothic, octagonal, in dark oak, its five side-panels display shields tinctured and gilded with the Agnus Dei and emblems of the Evangelists, while the edges are elaborately carved with thistles, roses and vines. – HIGH ALTAR. Very simple with an elaborate metal crucifix set against a tapestry which reaches up to the sill of the three-light E window at clearstorey level. – SIDE ALTAR, S aisle. With an arcaded reredos and altar rail, modelled on the original choir stalls at Dunblane (*see Buildings of Scotland: Stirling and Central Scotland*). – LECTERN. Made by the *Albert Carving Works*, 1894, again oak – 'of an ancient pattern, somewhat after the style of that in the London Charterhouse' – it is designed to hold the Old Testament on one side and the New Testament on the other; decorated with coats of arms around its octagonal base. – FONT. An octagonal stone basin carved on alternate sides with Christian symbols and quatrefoils, and supported on clustered columns with moulded bases and capitals. – CREDENCE TABLE and BISHOP'S THRONE. Made by *Scott Morton & Co.* in 1906. Both finely carved in fumed oak. – ORGAN. From the previous Episcopal church in Mid Street. By *William Hill & Son c.* 1875, reconstructed and doubled in size in 1892 by *Wadsworth & Brother*. – YAWL. In the tower vestibule. Constructed on the River Dee in 1902, and originally hung in St Peter's Church, Torry, Aberdeen. Given in 1983.* – STAINED GLASS. E window by *Heaton, Butler & Bayne*, 1884. Our Lord flanked by the fishermen brothers SS Peter and Andrew. Originally for the church in Mid Street, re-erected here in 1892. – S aisle window, Judas Maccabeus, *c.* 1900. – WALL MONUMENT to Bishop Alexander Jolly (†1838). Scottish Renaissance in style with the inscription surmounted by an angel's head and spread-out wings, flanked by croziers and with mitre beneath, all finely carved.

FRASERBURGH SOUTH CHURCH, Seaforth Street. Built as a 44
Free church in 1878–80: *J. B. Pirie*'s first major ecclesiastical

*The registration A153 alludes to the second miraculous draught of fishes in which St Peter and others caught 153 fish (*see* John 21:11).

commission and a magnificent example of his uniquely personal Gothic style. Very tall nave with the main entrance set under a gablet and large mincer-plate wheel window lighting the gallery. Flanking N tower soars up and bursts into pinnacles framing its clock stage, belfry and spire, balanced by a smaller stair bay standing S of the nave. Construction of the entrance front in rough granite ashlar, monumental cold grey changing by magic into weightless pale gold in good sunlight with subtle touches of polychromy, the mason *George Simpson* and wrights *Brebner & Jenkins*.

Abundant inventive and idiosyncratic detail, witness the dwarf colonnettes with foliate capitals which support the arch over the main entrance, the horseshoe hoodmoulds encompassing small round lights immediately above, and the larger, bolder hoodmould which oversails the arched recess containing the big wheel window. The tower is a highly original concept – rising square from a battered base into long lancets lighting the stair inside and with angle pilaster-buttresses which emphasize the relentless ascent, these broaching to octagonal beneath a parapet which is jettied out on brackets on every side. In certain respects the distinctive treatment of the tower's upper stages is similar to Alexander 'Greek' Thomson's St Vincent Street and Queen's Park Church towers in Glasgow. Above the parapet, the buttresses culminate in pinnacles framing the clock stage; within the clock stage itself, very simple square openings set between blocky columns lead onto the parapet walkway. These columns bear gablets enclosing the clock dials, and above the gablets the belfry rises octagonal, with its own openings between short pilasters which are seemingly crushed by the weight of the spire. The spire is tall, slim and conical, built in granite like the rest of the church, and decorated near its summit by simple annulet mouldings. Both the tower and the S stair bay contain secondary entrances, that of the tower being set under a gabled surround. The flanks are comparatively simple, rubble-built with broad transepts of token projection, small square-headed ground-floor lights and pointed lights in the gallery; the wheel window is similar to that in the main front. Low vestry annexe with canted S end.

The INTERIOR is every bit as remarkable, a large open space with a gallery on three sides facing the pulpit, even if the splendid organ above it is later, Pirie's richly carved pews have been cleared from the nave, and the late Victorian décor of orange, blue and pink by *James Garvie & Sons* is long gone. Slim cast-iron columns support the gallery fronts on brackets, then rise into gilt foliate capitals which bear Gothic arcades, the ceiling being of depressed-arch profile, compartmented and lined in dark timber. The gallery fronts are themselves extremely unusual with decorative fretwork against a pale fabric background with large stylized gilt flowers. The interior was once lit by 'corona lights' designed by *Pirie* and made by *Fyfe & Co.* of Aberdeen. Circular platform PULPIT with open arcaded front and stairs on each side, its triple-arched back with a gablet behind; above is the ORGAN GALLERY with a majestic array of pipes in light gold, installed *c.* 1906–13. The original PEWS preserved in the gallery have curved bench-ends of very original design. – SCULPTURE. Moses holding the Ten Commandments. Said to have belonged to the University of Fraserburgh in the C16 and brought here in 1968 with two smaller fragments. – In the VESTRY a simple but excellent timber fireplace of Thomsonesque design. – CHURCH HALL by *George Bennett Mitchell & Son* 1935, annexe 1954.

Former UNITED PRESBYTERIAN CHURCH, No. 49 Saltoun Place. By *Alexander Ellis* (of *Ellis & Wilson*) opened 1875, closed *c.* 1918. Now a house. Modest gable front in pale granite ashlar. Very simple detailing, doorpiece with gablet and buttress-like pilasters in contrasting golden granite masonry, stepped triple lancets. Former MANSE by *Ellis* 1877 immediately to N.

UNITED REFORMED CHURCH, Mid Street. By *Jeffrey Smith* of *Davidson & Smith*, 2003. On the site of the Congregational church (1853) destroyed by arsonists. A modern take on traditional Gothic. Entrance gable expressed as a buttressed nave with splayed doorway and flamboyant gallery window flanked by side aisles which are canted back sharply and almost completely glazed with large mullioned-and-transomed windows. Construction in pale polished granite. Dwarf walls and low railings enclose a small forecourt. Beyond the vestibule and first-floor prayer room, the double-height nave and chancel are articulated into five bays by portal frames supporting a canted polygonal ceiling; on the W the frames open into an aisle as the exterior suggests but on the E they are embedded in the flank elevation, the nave floor being left clear with no 'true' aisle on this side. The walls are mostly painted white; there is however subtle symbolism, the dado painted pale brown for bread and the ceiling dark red for wine. CHANCEL FURNISHINGS in a contemporary idiom, made in beech by local craftsmen; triple-light STAINED GLASS of the Risen Christ by *Jennifer-Jayne Bayliss* of Fintray.

WEST PARISH CHURCH, The Hexagon. By *MacGibbon & Ross* of Edinburgh, with *Henderson* of Aberdeen as their mason and *Brebner & Jenkins* as wrights, built 1874–6. Gothic, very impressive if austere on its island site. E tower and spire with flanking transeptal bays and the church gable rising behind. Snecked squared sandstone rubble with smooth ashlar for contrast. Large pointed-arch doorway, supported by angle buttresses progressively intaken; above, twin gallery lancets with leaded lights and clock dial sheltered by a hoodmould; then the octagonal belfry with gableted openings and stone spire with lucarnes in alternate faces, all clasped by the buttresses' octagonal pinnacles. The transepts are lit by stepped lancets expressing the rise of the twin gallery stairs. Four-bay rubble flanks with sandstone dressings, the gallery's substantial depth expressed by the windows which break up through the eaves under gables on each side. Wheel window in rear gable, with beneath a low vestry annexe seemingly added by *A. Marshall Mackenzie* in 1899. Very simple interior, E-end gallery with panelled front supported on slim iron columns, roof carried on canted trusses reinforced by perforated iron plates and tie-rods. – WAR MEMORIALS. One a finely worked bronze panel representing a Celtic cross, reflecting the early C20 vogue for that style.

FRASERBURGH CEMETERY, Cemetery Road. The former Kirkton of Philorth, reputedly the site of a C6 chapel founded by St Meddan. The OLD CHURCHYARD, enclosed by C16–C17 walls with a moulded segmentally arched GATEWAY of that date, has been encompassed by substantial later extensions. Within this graveyard, C17–C18 lying slabs and wall monuments, and the BURIAL VAULT of the Frasers of Park, little different from an ice house for fish. During the course of extension works, remains of St Meddan's church, first recorded in 1274 and closed *c.* 1574, were discovered under the old graveyard's E wall. In the SOUTH EXTENSION the SALTOUN MAUSOLEUM is early C20, based on that near the Old Parish Church (*see* above), but with walls in rough granite ashlar. LODGE HOUSE dated 1884. The three sets of GATES with RAILINGS on Cemetery Road were designed by *W.F. Hamilton*, Burgh Surveyor, and made by *Walter Macfarlane & Co.* of Glasgow in 1936; the W set bear roundels displaying the Fraserburgh arms.

WINE TOWER
Kinnaird Head

A small tower probably built *c.* 1535–40 by Alexander Fraser, 7th of Philorth, to watch over the primitive harbour he formed at that time. It is 8 m. long by 6.5 m. wide, its rubble walls with grey sandstone dressings 1.5 m. thick at ground floor, and all three surviving storeys are barrel-vaulted. Converted *c.* 1803 into a magazine for local militia companies; William Daniell in 1822 shows it with a low pyramidal roof, but it may once have had a caphouse. The ground floor once had an access in the S flank, now blocked; the only other opening at this level is a narrow slit in the N flank, its embrasure widening with the depth of the wall. At first floor a large S-side opening may have been a loading door. On the second floor there is an entrance on the W, with corbels projecting which seemingly supported the landing of a forestair. This second-floor apartment has a fireplace and a chamfered window in each flank, the windows formerly barred with gunloops in their sills. Most remarkable are the freestone CORBELS over the windows and the roof PENDANTS in this apartment, some of which were probably carved after the tower's construction. They are charged with the Royal Arms, the arms of the 5th Earl of Huntly (Chancellor of Scotland 1566–7) and the 17th Earl of Mar (Regent 1571–2), as well as those of Fraser family members.

Although relief carving is not in itself unusual, such wrap-around heraldic decoration is extremely rare in Scotland. One corbel carved with two angels bearing a shield which displays the Arma Christi has led to speculation that the tower may have served as a chapel for Alexander the 8th laird's wife, Magdalen Ogilvie, who supposedly remained Catholic after the Reformation although Alexander himself was strongly Protestant.* Evidence was found, *c.* 1900, of an underground passage which appeared to link the Wine Tower and Kinnaird Head Castle, and tradition holds that the Wine Tower basement opens into the large sea-cave in the rocks immediately beneath. A DOOCOT which stood on neighbouring rocks was of three stages with a crowstep-gabled roof but was demolished during the formation of Balaclava Harbour (*see* Harbours). The CASTLE PARKS extended as far S as the Kirk Green but were developed in the C19. Remnants of the STABLES survive in the rear court of the Saltoun Arms Hotel (*see* Description), which stands on the site of Fraser's town lodging.

KINNAIRD HEAD CASTLE AND LIGHTHOUSE

70 m. W of Wine Tower

In more senses than one, the oldest light in northern Scotland. 96
Originally a four-storey tower house, it was reputedly founded on 6 March 1570 and completed in 1572 by Alexander Fraser, 8th of Philorth to protect his new burgh and harbour, and to provide a base closer than his main seat at Cairnbulg (q.v.) from which to oversee development. It was acquired by the newly established Northern Lighthouse Board in 1786, converted as its first lighthouse by *Thomas Smith*, and lit with twenty candles and reflectors on 1 December 1787. The present lantern was erected by Smith's son-in-law *Robert Stevenson*, progenitor of the celebrated family of lighthouse engineers, *c.* 1830 during a modernization programme of the older lights.

The TOWER is a plain rectangle 12 m. by 9 m., its rubble walls rising through four storeys and 18 m. height into a wall-head parapet supported on moulded brackets with square bartizans in the centre of each long face and circular ones corbelled out at the angles with simple water cannon. Large doors and windows were formed in Smith's conversion although some older windows and gunloops are still evident; the interior was altered, and the forecourt and its outbuildings, if still surviving in the late C18, were cleared away, but Stevenson's octagonally shafted chimneystacks at the W end are a playful nod to the historic past. The lantern is supported above the tower on a low ashlar plinth, offset asymmetrically to the E; there are two

*Those carved after *c.* 1540 have quite possibly been transferred from Kinnaird Head Castle (*see* below). The survival of the corbel charged with the Arma Christi is certainly surprising given Alexander's Presbyterian beliefs, which he seems to have inherited from his father.

walkways, one round the plinth and one round the lantern, which is triangular-paned with a low dome and weathervane. The LANTERN MECHANISM of 1851 is one of the very first – perhaps *the* first – of a kind which became standard everywhere. It comprises a large circular brass frame invented by *J. T. Chance*, supporting Fresnel lenses which greatly magnify a central light source. These lenses were supplied by *Chance Bros & Co.* of Birmingham, who made the glass for Paxton's Crystal Palace and afterwards became major manufacturers of lighthouse equipment. The frame and lenses are the second-heaviest in the world, at some 4.5 tonnes, yet so finely balanced on their rollers that they can be turned by a clockwork mechanism supplied by *James Dove & Co.* of Edinburgh. They remained in use until the NEW LIGHTHOUSE was built in 1990–1.

Stevenson's single-storey ENGINE HOUSE (N), ASSISTANT KEEPERS' COTTAGES (E) and PRINCIPAL KEEPER'S COTTAGE (S) built *c.* 1830, replaced a keeper's house illustrated by William Daniell in 1822. – FOGHORN. 1902–3. One of only two in Britain in which the horn itself can be rotated (the other, at Aberdeen, was built at the same time) so allowing it to transmit over the Moray Firth or the North Sea. The excellent
129 MUSEUM OF SCOTTISH LIGHTHOUSES designed by *Morris & Steedman* was opened in 1995.

PUBLIC BUILDINGS

Former BROADSEA GENERAL ASSEMBLY SCHOOL, Main Street. Dated 1883. Gable-fronted, rubble with stepped triple light beneath a hoodmould; entrance porch in flank.

BROADSEA VILLAGE HALL, College Bounds. 1894. Simple Gothic.

BURGH CHAMBERS, Saltoun Square. Stylish Quattrocento Renaissance by *Thomas Mackenzie* (of *Mackenzie & Matthews*, Aberdeen) 1852–5, built on the site of the early C17 tolbooth. Construction mostly in pale golden ashlar sandstone. Two storeys, with bowed corner rising into a domed rotunda, flank elevations of uneven length: three windows wide to Saltoun Square with Kirk Brae rather longer. Within the bow, the main entrance is framed in a peristyle of attached Doric columns; at first floor a pedimented aedicule contains a statue of Alexander George Fraser, 'the Waterloo Saltoun', by the London sculptor *Edward Stephens*, unveiled in 1859. Above the cornice, a low drum in granite ashlar supports the tall rotunda of six Corinthian columns with louvred openings between them, then the entablature bearing a lead dome with cupola. The flanks on each side are arcaded at ground floor, which was originally open for market traders, with pedimented aedicule windows at first; pronounced long-and-short angle quoins, bold bracket cornice and low hipped roofs. On the Kirk Brae elevation, seven bays at ground floor, but only five windows at first, their broader spacing an acknowledgement of the council chamber. Later four-bay extension at the foot of Kirk Brae by *Reid & McRobbie* provided POLICE CHAMBERS, 1906–7,

Fraserburgh, Burgh Chambers.
Drawing by David M. Walker

in pale granite ashlar but otherwise faithful to Mackenzie's design.

Former COASTGUARD STATION, Saltoun Place. Built *c.* 1860. Long two-storey block, with raised end bays slightly advanced under hipped roofs, sturdy coped chimneystacks. Golden granite ashlar with very simple detailing.

DALRYMPLE HALL, Dalrymple Street on its junction with Station Brae. Scottish Baronial by *Jenkins & Marr*, built 1881–3, and named after Capt. John Dalrymple who gifted over half the money required for construction. Towards the junction the Hall presents a bowed three-storey frontage flanked by slim gabled bays, and with a crenellated square tower rising up behind; the longer symmetrical front to Dalrymple Street is itself three storeys and five bays with the centre slightly projected under a gable. Granite ashlar with simple detail, the ground floor with stilted segmentally arched window heads; what survives of the original small-plane glazing endows the design with a more precise and intricate character. The ultimate multi-purpose building, the Dalrymple Hall provided a café and dining room; a public hall with 1,100 seats; recreation room, newsroom, library, museum and art school; public baths; and sheriff court.

Former DRILL HALL (now Community Church), Grattan Place. By *George Sutherland* of Elgin, dated 1901. Genteel rather than bombastic within its prosperous surroundings, a reflection of the social aspects of Volunteering – the military in mufti. Villa-like scale and decorum, but symmetrical with central crowstep gable flanked by token turrets and double-keyhole gunloops identifying its actual purpose.

FRASERBURGH ACADEMY, Finlayson Street. Competition win by *D. & J.R. McMillan* 1903, opened 1909. Simple Scots with Baronial elements. Big two-storey symmetrical block in brown granite, large windows mullioned and transomed, with central wall-head gablets and much bigger crowstepped gables at the ends. Neo-Baroque entrances in the flanks, detailing very robust. Economical mass-education establishment (ratepayer-funded, delivered under budget) and conspicuously designed to last.

FRASERBURGH ACADEMY, Dennyduff Road. Interwar Modern in style with Neoclassical elements, but begun by *Alexander McGall*, County Architect, in 1951 and completed in 1962. A tall square clock tower in dark red granite serves as the focus for blocks of various sizes containing the assembly hall, dining room, library and classrooms, all arranged on an asymmetric but functional plan within extensive grounds. The quality and character of the scheme have suffered much through loss of its original small-pane glazing, but it retains a fully glazed semi-circular staircase at its S end; on the W, a second-floor conservatory used for teaching botany. EXTENSIONS to S link to Swimming Pool and Community Centre; large W wing added *c.* 1980.

FRASERBURGH HOSPITAL, Lochpots Road. By *Moira & Moira*, 1961–8, on the site of the Infectious Diseases Hospital (*William Reid*, *c.* 1904–6). Low spreading plan, two-storey, concrete walls with flat roofs.

Former INFANT SCHOOL, Dennyduff Road. By *A. Marshall Mackenzie*, opened 1901. Scots Gothic. Long single storey with central range rising into stone dormers and the projecting wings with much larger crowstepped gables. A hall and ten classrooms for boys and girls segregated with separate porches. Pale Peathill granite: entrance front in dressed masonry with darker pinnings, rear elevation in ashlar.

LIBRARY, King Edward Street on its junction with The Hexagon. By *William Wilson*, 1904–5, built with funding from Andrew Carnegie. Edwardian Baroque, two storeys, with an octagonal corner bay rising into a slated spirelet and a cupola. The corner bay's entrance is framed between pedestals supporting blocked Doric columns and an open pediment. Symmetrical frontage to King Edward Street, gables at each end with ground-floor canted bays, first-floor windows with key-blocked arches. Silver and dark grey granite with bold detailing; single-storey reading room to rear.

MACAULAY MEMORIAL HALL, Mid Street. By *James Souttar*, 1870, with additions by him *c.* 1895. Built as the first

Fraserburgh Academy for John Park, a philanthropic local merchant, more like a church than a school. Two-storey Gothic gable front, flanked (r.) by slim spired entrance tower and (l.) by a smaller porch. Dark granite with some use of lighter grey for contrast, triple lights shouldered on ground floor and trefoiled at first, attic vesica and Maltese cross finial. Pointed-arch doorways, with voussoirs increasing in size towards the apex of the arch, a characteristic Souttar motif. Tower is three stages with octagonal belfry and slated spirelet.

NORTH SCHOOL, Finlayson Street. The school for Broadsea, by *D. & J.R. McMillan*, 1908–9, with additions *c.* 1912. Simple Scots idiom, a smaller sibling of Fraserburgh Academy (*see* above) opened in the same street on the same day. Big two-storey three-bay frontage, roughly symmetrical, with crowstep-gabled ends, the centre recessed between them under its own small gablet but with a projecting porch. Aberdeen Bond construction, brown granite with darker pinnings.

Former POST OFFICE, Commerce Street. By *Reid & McRobbie*, 1907. Neo-Baroque: two-storey four-bay block in puncheoned New Pitsligo granite, with the centre rising tall into a third storey framed by chimney-breasts and crowned by a dated blocking course and pediment. Simple bold detailing, the entrance with a low-relief open scroll pediment and obelisk finial, blocky ground-floor windows, and pronounced long-and-short quoins.

ST ANDREW'S PRIMARY SCHOOL, Charlotte Street, originally Fraserburgh Public School. Scottish Baronial by *Matthews & Mackenzie*, 1880–2. Two-storey main front in granite ashlar with tall four-stage clock tower at its r. corner, facing down the Commerce Street axis. Within the angle between the tower and main front, a slim circular stair-turret rises into an arcaded belfry with a conical spirelet. Overall a simple strong composition impressive in scale and constructed in good materials; U-plan court at the rear. The former HEADMASTER'S HOUSE to immediate S is probably by *Pirie & Clyne*, 1881.

Former ST PETER'S EPISCOPAL SCHOOL, Victoria Street. By *William Ramage*, 1854. Neo-Jacobean. A symmetrical composition with central gable-fronted classroom – low and broad with two-light pointed windows under a tall roof – and flanking mirror-image houses for the teachers, each two storeys rising into wall-head gables and dormer gablets. Construction in heathen rubble with granite dressings, and characteristically idiosyncratic Ramage details.

Former STRACHAN'S INDUSTRIAL SCHOOL FOR GIRLS, High Street. 1863. Single-storey four-bay block with centre windows below a gable and outer windows rising into dormers, master's house adjacent. Rough rubble with granite dressings, inscription panel now concealed.

TEMPERANCE JUBILEE FOUNTAIN, Broad Street. 1889. Alas now dry in every sense. A slim elaborate cast-iron column supported by wyvern scrolls which once spouted water into granite basins directly beneath.

WAR MEMORIAL, Saltoun Place on its junction with Strichen Road. Unveiled 1923. A Neoclassical bronze statue portraying Valour as a boy with sword and helmet guided by a seated female representing Justice; large granite base bearing bronze plaques with names of the Fallen. *Alexander Carrick*, sculptor, cast by *J. W. Singer & Sons*, with *Leadbetter, Fairley & Reid* as architects.

PARKS

BELLSEA PARK. Known as such since the C18, much extended 1904 over the grounds of a former rope and sail works, a gutting-shed and bothies; the home of Fraserburgh Football Club, established 1910. The cast-iron FOUNTAIN sheltered under its splendid domed canopy was designed by *James Boucher* and made by *McFarlane & Co.* of Glasgow, 1904, the crowning ostrich which holds a key in its beak a borrowing from Fraserburgh's coat of arms. The present silver colour dates from the Silver Jubilee of Queen Elizabeth II in 1977.

JAMES RAMSAY PARK. Named after the Fraserburgh-born Rev. James Ramsay (1733–89), Church of England chaplain, Royal Navy surgeon, essayist and propagandist, the key instigator of the anti-slavery movement, which culminated in the abolition of slavery through Acts of 1807 and 1833.

HARBOURS

The earliest manmade harbours are thought to have been constructed by Alexander Fraser, 7th of Philorth, shortly after 1534 and by Alexander, 8th of Philorth, in the years after 1576. There appears some doubt whether these harbours were formed in the creek on the N coast immediately beneath the Wine Tower – probably built by the elder Alexander as a look-out post, *see* Public Buildings – or on the E coast in the corner of the present-day Balaclava Harbour. Perhaps the younger Alexander first established the harbour in the E bay as he planned his new town of Fraserburgh immediately S of Faithlie. Its importance may be judged by its status, granted by King James VI, as a free port, thereby gaining rights hitherto exclusively held by Aberdeen throughout the county.

The earliest records of the harbour in its present form, however, relate to construction of a predecessor of the North Pier *c.* 1740. This with a stump of the Middle Pier of unknown origin provided a shelter, albeit badly exposed to the prevailing winds. During the C18 the harbour was able to accept vessels of 200 tonnes' burden, and the town's economy increased in consequence.

During the Napoleonic wars in 1802 *John Rennie* put forward a report suggesting that a very large harbour for some 400 ships

– effectively a National Harbour of Refuge (*see* Peterhead) – might be formed in the E bay at Government expense since it was easy of access for vessels in distress, and the Inch Rock and Boich Head Rock offered extensive natural protection. He recognized, however, that such a scheme would be too ambitious to be accepted and instead recommended a still substantial harbour with low-water piers and better shelter for 150 vessels.

The driving forces behind the pursuit of this intention were Lord Saltoun's Baron-Baillie, William Kelman, and Kelman's legal clerk, Lewis Chalmers (Sen.), who led the attempts to raise the funds. At their instigation the NORTH PIER was reconstructed in enlarged form under the superintendence of *William Stewart* between 1807 and *c.* 1812. Harbour Commissioners were first appointed in 1818, and between that date and *c.* 1822 the SOUTH PIER was constructed by Act of Parliament to designs of *Robert Stevenson*, with *William Minto* as contractor and *Mr Selkirk* as overseer of works. This, with the improvement of the MIDDLE JETTY by the early 1830s under *Mr Wallace*, created a good harbour with two basins, capable of receiving vessels of 300 tonnes.

The doubling of harbour revenues between 1840 and 1850 encouraged Baron-Baillie Lewis Chalmers Jun. to agitate, against considerable opposition, for a second North Pier to create another very large new basin, and to this end he secured a government loan of £20,000. Plans were prepared by *Alexander Gibb* of Aberdeen and the local contractor *Brebner* was engaged in 1850 but during a disastrous storm in 1852 their work was largely washed away. Construction of what became known as the BALACLAVA PIER was recommenced under the direction of *Robert Stevenson* in 1855 with *Thomas Davidson* as superintendent of works and completed in 1856–7, the Balaclava Harbour extending over much of what had once been Faithlie.

With the onset of the herring boom in the 1860s and the increasing size of steam-powered ships it became imperative that the harbours be developed further, and Sir Alexander Anderson, Commissioner of the Harbour Board and 'practically the maker of modern Fraserburgh', asked *James Abernethy* to prepare a scheme of improvements. The Balaclava Pier was widened and the BALACLAVA BREAKWATER, LIGHTHOUSE and LIFEBOAT JETTY were constructed to his designs between 1875 and *c.* 1883 under the supervision of *J.H. Bostock*, the resident engineer. Meantime Anderson secured a further £60,000 from the Public Works Loan Commissioners to deepen the North and South Harbours for large steamships and form the QUAYSIDE, BRUCE'S JETTY and SALTOUN JETTY in 1879–87, the superintendents being first *Bostock* and later *Alexander Buchan*. The works could not be completed however until Lord Saltoun, Sir Alexander and the other Harbour Commissioners had personally underwritten a further £7,500 in a remarkable display of public spirit.

The South Breakwater was built to designs of *Abernethy & Son*, with *Price & Wills* as contractor and *Gerald Fitzgibbon* as resident engineer, and the Balaclava Harbour was deepened with a new dry dock formed between 1893 and 1898, the jetties being improved at the same time. The North Pier was extended in 1905–6 and a spur added to the Balaclava Breakwater in 1906–8.

The advent of ever-bigger fishing vessels – specifically the steam drifter – ultimately prompted the construction of the largest of all Fraserburgh's harbours, the Station or Faithlie Harbour by the formation of the West Pier extending from the South Pier and the Burnett Pier extending from the South Breakwater to enclose 4.5 hectares of water, the Station Jetty providing additional berthing facilities for loading and discharging. The enormous sum of £95,000 was borrowed from the Public Works Commissioners, construction to the designs of *G.N. Abernethy* being begun in 1908 with *Mr Davies* as resident engineer, and completed in 1914, the final cost being approximately double the original loan.

The ship lift completed in 2000 by *Posford Duvivier* is one of the most modern facilities of its kind, and provides berths for six vessels of up to 38 m. in length and 850 tonnes in weight.

Lifeboatmen Memorial. By *Ian Scott*, 2010. A rugged lifeboatman in bronze, standing head bared and sou'wester in his hand; plinth bears the names of thirteen men lost at sea.

DESCRIPTION

Saltoun Square was formed in 1801 from the Kirk Green, the
98 market cross a reminder of a time when it first became a centre of trade. The cross comprises a carved head and shaft which originally stood over the early C17 tolbooth; after the tolbooth was demolished the cross was re-erected on a classical pedestal in its present situation. The head displays, N side, the Royal Arms of Scotland with a surrounding collar representing the Order of St Andrew, and S side, the Arms of the United Kingdom as used in Scotland, with collar representing the Order of the Garter, both arms being framed by a unicorn and crowned lion. Beneath the arms the round shaft is decorated, N side, by the Arms of Faithlie facing the old village, and S side, by the Arms of Fraserburgh facing the new town. The initials A.L.S. stand for Alexander Lord Saltoun, the date 1736 seemingly refers to the shaft, and perhaps the head itself; the cruciform granite pedestal is *c.* 1853–5, the head a replica of 1988; the original is now in the care of the Aberdeenshire Museums Service.

On the W side of the Square the Saltoun Arms Hotel, also of 1801, stands on the site once occupied by the Fraser family's town lodging. It was built for the Gardeners' Friendly Society of Fraserburgh to the designs of *Alexander Morice*. Provincial grandeur for this far-flung town – vernacular classical, three-storey five windows wide, with a broad distyle Doric portico welcoming to travellers: its ground- and first-floor windows are relatively small but the grander second floor is much taller. Construction is in squared heathen stone, with dressings in light granite ashlar. During mid-Victorian times the Saltoun Arms acquired a fashionable French pavilion roof over the centre bay, the flanking sections being altered to a mansard form with elaborate timber dormers. Originally the hotel contained a large hall, dining room, drawing room and two parlours, but only six bedrooms: it was as much a social venue as a hostelry. Within its rear court are the remains of the Frasers' STABLES which the hotel reused. Standing on the corner next to the hotel, a three-storey block is mid-C19, with street-level shops, upper floors in golden granite ashlar with darker pinnings, and a canted angle rising into a crowstepped attic dormer.

On the N side No. 14, the REGISTRAR'S OFFICE, is like the Saltoun Arms vernacular classical of *c.* 1800, two-storey and five bays wide, its slightly projected centre with block-pedimented doorway and a pedimental gable above the wall-head. Its ground-floor windows have evidently once been open to the pavement, suggesting a covered market place. Construction is in pinned rubble, with first-floor windows in the centre and end bays only. Moulded skewputts, gabled roof with modern dormers, coped chimneystacks. Carved stone in one gable with initials W.E. E.K.

At the NE corner, the BRAEHEADS DEVELOPMENT by *Baxter, Clark & Paul*, 1971–8, is much larger than it appears, occupying a substantial site between Castle Street and Shore Street. It attempts to infuse modern architecture with traditional characteristics. The simple bold blocks with steep monopitch roofs are arranged in picturesque fashion around open courts which, while making allowance for the car, remain primarily a pedestrian environment.

On the E side of the Square, Nos. 5–7, later C19, a hefty three-storey block with curvilinear attic gable and mansard roof. On the SE corner, the Burgh Chambers, 1852–5 (*see* Public Buildings) replacing the tolbooth, and nearby, the Old Parish Church (*see* Churches).

South and west of Saltoun Square

BROAD STREET was laid out *c.* 1600 between the previous parish church and Frithside Street (*see* below). Until the late C18 it was chiefly lined with buildings facing with their gables to the road, but none survives, the oldest buildings now Late Georgian and Victorian houses, all much altered with ground-floor shops. On its junction with High Street, Broad Street begins with Nos. 2–8, a large three-storey block of shops and flats built *c.* 1900 with a canted angle rising into a polygonal tower and slated spirelet. It is constructed in granite ashlar with a smattering of classical detail, and chimney-breasts corbelled out on each flank bursting through the wall-head. Nearby, *David Annand*'s remarkable SCULPTURE of a swirling shoal of fish, erected 1997, casts striking shadows in the sunshine, while within the gloom of a narrow close leading to No. 10 a much older monogrammed INSCRIPTION PANEL reads 'Ever will good pro[sper].' Further along on the Mid Street junction stands Nos. 28–32, another three-storey block of shops and flats *c.* 1900, again with a canted angle rising into a polygonal slated spirelet.

Both these blocks are builders' speculations, or perhaps concerted civic improvement making a worthwhile contribution to the townscape, but across the junction the CLYDESDALE BANK (formerly Town & County Bank) by *J. R. Mackenzie*, 1875, is architecture of a higher order. Neoclassical, three storeys in granite ashlar: its giant-order pilastrade rises from a heavy base course through ground floor – round-arched – and first floor to support a shallow entablature; second floor is lower. Its splayed angle corner contains the bank entrance sheltered beneath a balustraded balcony, with token pediment at the wall-head. Further along are Nos. 44–48, another big simple three-storey block of shops and flats dated 1906; then Nos. 50–54, *c.* 1840, two storeys and three bays with central moulded doorway flanked by ground-floor shops, and simple Neo-Greek scrolls above the blocking course concealing the roof. Across the road, Nos. 45–49 and Nos. 51–55 make a charming contrast: two adjoining buildings each two storeys with bowed corners and dormers, but very different in their character. Nos. 45–49 are later C19 with purpose-built shops, first floor ashlar-built with tripartite windows, and pedimented dormers in the gambrel roof; Nos. 51–55 early C19, a rubble-built two-storey house converted, and still retaining its old shopfronts.

On the junction something special: the former BANK OF SCOTLAND originally built *c.* 1820–35 as Lewis Chalmers' house and office and probably the work of *Archibald Simpson*. A broad two-storey bow set back behind an Ionic colonnade at ground floor, with two-storey flanks on either side; construction in sandstone ashlar. The main entrance in the bow is approached by stairs concealed by a low screen, the colonnade forming a large balcony for the first-floor windows with elegant cast-iron railings. Broad eaves and a low hipped roof; the Grecian urn finial over the bow is actually a chimneystack.

Diagonally across the junction is the ROYAL HOTEL, in its present form by *William Wilson*, 1909–11, three storeys mostly in rock-faced granite with a curved corner corbelling into a turret and spirelet. On the junction's fourth side a simple two-storey block with segment-headed ground-floor windows and quadrant corner, now ROYAL BANK OF SCOTLAND, built shortly after 1870. Then further along on the E side the former NATIONAL BANK OF SCOTLAND, a large Neo-Baroque block of two tall storeys with large attic gable flanked by scrolls, dated 1904 at a cartouche on its chimney-breast. Nos. 81–83, the former SAVINGS BANK built perhaps *c.* 1830, looks like a pretty two-storey house but has a second doorway in its bowed corner to the Commerce Street junction. The Broad Street front is in bright white stucco lined out as ashlar with only the margins showing, its dormers added later.

Turning down COMMERCE STREET (E) we find No. 5 and Nos. 7–9, early C19, simple three-storey blocks perhaps built to take in boarders or converted from a one-time warehouse. Of the same date, No. 10 a smart two-storey house in granite ashlar has a Roman Doric pilastered doorpiece. At the foot of the slope an attractive pair of two-storey blocks with bowed corners, again *c.* 1800, face each other across the junction.

SHORE STREET presents a ragged appearance but late C18 and C19 buildings near the Frithside Street junction suggest that improvements might be made. SHORE HOUSE, three storeys in granite rubble with its large attic gable at one end and smaller central dormer, was built by the Burgh in 1776–7 as Assembly Rooms above a ground-floor warehouse.

DALRYMPLE STREET was laid out in the early C19 in the grounds of THE WORLD'S END, one of the finest 102
Aberdeenshire houses of its date, perhaps built *c.* 1767. Two storeys and three windows wide over a low basement, its central attic rises into a shapely ball-finialled gable and tall chimneystack; its doorway approached by an elegant railed stair is set in a lugged surround with pediment. Construction is in squared heathen rubble with freestone dressings; it has pronounced long-and-short quoins, an eaves course, and coped end stacks. It was restored by *Herbert West* *c.* 1980. On the next corner is the Dalrymple Hall (*see* Public Buildings), convenient for train travellers whose terminus stood in South Harbour Street, and for those frequenting the harbour.

Returning up Station Brae, SEAFORTH STREET was laid out as an extension to Broad Street from 1857, although the stretch beyond Victoria Road was not formed until 1911. SALTOUN CHAMBERS, *c.* 1895, is a smart Italianate villa, two-storey three bays with round-headed door framed by pilasters and pediment. At the end of the street is the magnificent South – former Free – Church with its tall tower and spire (*see* Churches), built 1878–80 by *J. B. Pirie*.

VICTORIA STREET running E–W at right angles to Seaforth Street was also laid out from 1857 and forms a boundary between the Old Town and the Southern and Western New Towns developed during late Victorian and Edwardian times. At the crossroads SALTOUN PLACE, following the old turnpike, is lined by early to mid-C19 granite houses: No. 23 preserves its original elegant doorpiece. The former PARISH MANSE set back in its garden is by *William Robertson*, designed 1817 and built with its offices in 1818–19.

But looking S from the crossroads the houses which line Saltoun Place on the W side only with views over Bellsea Park are much later. The SOUTHERN NEW TOWN comprises four long streets running in parallel N–S: beyond Saltoun Place, GRATTAN PLACE, laid out 1893, and then KING EDWARD STREET, laid out 1902, with Alexandra Terrace and Strichen Road forming a boundary at the S end. Standing in long orderly rows, the big villas – many of them the work of local architects *William Wilson* and *Reid & McRobbie* – are all immensely solid and comfortable, and if none stands out in individual terms, nevertheless their variety of bay windows, dormers and tall wall-head gables, their bold period detailing and dark coloured glass – often with Art Nouveau characteristics – contribute to an environment of high quality. One of the earliest and best houses is the Church of Scotland MANSE at the Saltoun Place–Strichen Road junction, built by *James Matthews c.* 1862–5.

Within little more than a decade the Southern New Town had doubled Fraserburgh in size, and doubtless it would have developed further W had the First World War not intervened: but in the event, ALEXANDRA TERRACE (formed in the late C19) beyond its junction with Queen's Road, and QUEEN'S ROAD itself (*c.* 1905–9) were only developed after the War, with single-storey villas and bungalows still in granite but much more modest in character.

The abrupt curtailment of the Southern New Town's development explains why THE HEXAGON lies as far W as it does: a prominent six-sided junction between the Old Town and Southern and Western New Towns, and therefore a natural place for the Church of Scotland to build its West Church 1874–6 – its tall tower and spire looking down Victoria Street to face *Pirie's* Free Church in Seaforth Street (*see* Churches). Undaunted by its shadow, the Episcopalians established their presence in The Hexagon in such a way as would not be overawed with the Scots Romanesque St Peter (*John Kinross* 1891–3, *see* Churches); ST PETER'S RECTORY (by *J. Kinross*, 1889–90) is however late Scots Gothic, picturesquely composed. Some of its original Arts and Crafts fittings survive.

The WESTERN NEW TOWN was developed on a grid for solid tradesmen, encouraged by the Rev. Peter McLaren, who established the Fraserburgh Building Society. CHARLOTTE STREET was laid out in 1870 and quickly built up with smart cottages but the streets further W were less successful, probably because they were too far from the harbours. ALBERT STREET N from The Hexagon (originally Windmill Street), formed 1896, never took off: its WINDMILL TOWER is C18 with crenellated top added in the early C19, its cap and sails now lost. Likewise FINLAYSON STREET, also 1896, was only developed near Fraserburgh Academy and the North School which opened at its opposite far ends in 1909.

Charlotte Street leads directly to High Street and Broadsea. But turning down COMMERCE STREET (W) we pass the FREEMASONS' LODGE, built 1934, before reaching Our Lady of the Sea & St Drostan (*see* Churches). Further along is the old Post Office (*see* Public Buildings), but turning instead into

LODGE WALK beside the church are two rubble cottages, empty now but perhaps the oldest – C18 – still standing within the Old Town.

The OLD TOWN's historic core with its winding streets has been reconstructed in such piecemeal fashion that it feels fragmented, SCHOOL STREET with modest mid- to late C19 houses at various intervals facing flats of the mid and late C20, and partly cleared away at its N end to create a wasteland for buses and car parking. The name refers to an early parish school, not the former FREE CHURCH SCHOOL – contractor *Brebner*, *c.* 1858 – near the Mid Street junction which has itself been flatted. FRITHSIDE STREET is also a jumble, but of more interest, Nos. 62 and 64 both two-storey three-bay houses of the early C19, the latter retaining its elegant doorpiece. In MANSE STREET stands the old United Presbyterian church (*see* Bethesda Evangelical, Churches).

But turning into CROSS STREET – once Fishcross Street – and past Aberdeenshire Council's NORTHERN COURT completed in 1983, the Mid Street junction is marked by Nos. 12–14, a very large three-storey Baronial block with corbelled turret guarding the corner, this being built for A. MacDonald & Sons, merchants, to designs of *D. & J. R. McMillan* in 1902; another big three-storey block, Nos. 69–75 on the Commerce Street junction, is probably also by the *McMillans* and built just a couple of years later. Then turning E into MID STREET, the old PICTURE THEATRE by *Sutherland & George*, 1920–1, a three-storey asymmetrical granite front with curious Ionic columns framing the entrance, an oriel and large thermal window. Next to it, the Macaulay Memorial Hall (*see* Public Buildings); and next again the United Reformed church (*see* Churches). At the end of the road is Broad Street near its junction with Saltoun Square and High Street.

North of Saltoun Square, High Street and Broadsea

The Braeheads shopping arcade leads N of Saltoun Square to KINNAIRD HEAD, the oldest part of town, where Faithlie once stood overlooked by Alexander Fraser's tower house (*see* Kinnaird Head Castle). The tower house was converted to a lighthouse in 1787, and in 1791 Recreation Rooms were opened in the Castle Parks in association with a chalybeate spring. Fresh-air baths, carved from the rocks, opened in 1807. As a result of these developments a NORTHERN NEW TOWN was proposed on a cruciform plan, Castle Street running N–S from the Square being bisected by North Street extending W and Duke Street running E towards the shore. In the short term only CASTLE STREET was developed to any extent, its earliest houses good two-storey pinned rubble with segmental pends leading into rear courts, but from the mid C19 development increased, NORTH STREET being laid out from the mid 1840s with single-storey cottages, then BARRASGATE ROAD outwith the cruciform plan from 1858, and QUARRY ROAD and DENMARK STREET driven by the herring boom in 1870 and 1875. By then the Northern New Town had lost all pretension: it was home to the vast army of migrant workers employed by the herring industry who lived in appallingly overcrowded and insanitary conditions. BATH STREET was home to the Kinnaird Head Preserving Works established by the Maconochie Brothers in 1883 which provided army rations during the Boer and two World Wars. The Western New Town's failure to develop resulted in a polar division, with the very poor in the Northern New Town at one end of Broad Street and the very well-heeled in the Southern New Town at the other.

HIGH STREET – originally North, later Back Street – existed by the 1590s. From the early C17 many of the grandest houses had been built on spacious feus here, near the Castle Parks and Alexander Fraser's short-lived university, and at just a little distance from the markets and harbour, but during the C19 they were progressively replaced. Near the junction with Saltoun Square, on the N side, a three-storey block in heathen stone of *c.* 1800, then taller three-storey blocks with central attic gables built by *Ellis & Wilson* in 1889–90. The S side is a mixed bag: some small blocks with street-level shops and flats above, *c.* 1850, then near Cross Street bigger blocks *c.* 1875 in pinned granite ashlar. Beyond the junction the N side is mostly low two-storey houses in squared granite with their first floors breaking into gableted dormers; the S side is taller, two full storeys with attics.

COLLEGE BOUNDS is named after the university which Alexander Fraser founded here in the late C16. The College – including 'the Tower of Braidsea' – was ruinous in 1795 and is long gone, as now is the Alexandra Hotel (by *D. & J.R. McMillan*, *c.* 1898) which replaced it. On the N side the street is lined by early C19 cottages, each with a central door and two windows in pinned heathen masonry with lighter granite dressings; the S side is more varied but less orderly. Towards the W however both sides are lined with long rows of two-storey houses constructed in the earlier C20 with first-floor windows breaking into gableted dormers.

Turning down Broadsea Road leads to BROADSEA village, first recorded in 1612 and probably in existence earlier. From the mid C18 until 1832 the local fishing fleet was confined to Broadsea Bay, while Fraserburgh's harbour was exclusively concerned with trade: Broadsea remained administratively separate from Fraserburgh until 1872. MAIN STREET following the coast is lined on each side by low single-storey cottages, all built in heathen rubble, but all different. Although faultlessly picturesque they were once the setting for deprivation, squalor and terrible disease. The occasional taller houses were built in the late C19 by tenants encouraged by Lord Saltoun with greatly extended leases; the General Assembly School (*see* Public Buildings) is of 1883. NOBLE STREET laid out 1890 forms a link to GEORGE STREET laid out in 1893 running roughly parallel with Main Street. Both are lined with rows of single-storey cottages built in pale gold granite ashlar, with canted dormers in their roofs; Broadsea Village Hall, 1894, is simple Gothic. Although more regimented, the modest scale and sense of quietude in Noble Street and George Street is similar to that in Main Street and allows Broadsea to retain its special character.

FYVIE 7030

By repute a royal burgh, Fyvie is first recorded in 1264; its castle (q.v.) was the *capital messuage* of the Thanage of Formartine. A church may have been founded on the River Ythan by St Boniface in the early C8, and a Tironesian priory associated with Arbroath Abbey either by Fergus, Mormaer of Buchan, *c.* 1178 or by Sir Reginald de Cheyne, Lord Chamberlain of Scotland, *c.* 1285; substantial ruins of this priory survived well into the C18, if not the C19. From 1596 Alexander Seton, afterwards 1st Earl of Dunfermline and another Lord Chancellor, remodelled the castle as a spectacular Renaissance palace. Fyvie was re-erected a burgh of barony for the 3rd Earl in either 1671 or 1673, but although its fairs were popular it seems always to have been hampered by its poor communications. The N part of the village, laid out on a sloping site on a semi-regular half-moon plan, strongly suggests an attempt at a picturesque improvement settlement, probably by Gen. William Gordon or his son William Gordon Jun. in the early C19, aiming to take advantage of its situation close to the Aberdeen–Banff turnpike (now A947) where it meets the road from Ellon (B9005). However, not until the late C19 did Fyvie village become a place of any consequence, the half-moon plan only being built up in earnest from *c.* 1960.

PARISH CHURCH. Built in 1806–8, one of the first Gothic Revival churches in Aberdeenshire, and much larger and more sophisticated than any of the earlier examples: the choice of style no doubt owed to the tastes of the principal heritor, Gen. William Gordon, who had reconstructed Fyvie Castle (q.v.).* Its W gable, tall and broad, is built of large blocks of squared heathen stone cherry-cocked with ashlar granite dressings and margins. Its centre is slightly projected, corresponding to the internal arrangement of nave and aisles, and frames two identical pointed-arch doorways, their transom-lights filled with later coloured glass, and two Y-traceried gallery windows; larger windows of the same design in the aisle-fronts light the gallery stairs. Over the central clock face the gable rises into concave skews supporting a twin-arched double bellcote; the red sandstone spirelet is a replacement added by *James*

*In certain respects it is closely similar to St Peter's Episcopal Church, Peterhead (q.v.), by *Robert Mitchell*, 1813–14.

Henderson, 1863, and one of the bells is by *John Burgerhuys*, 1609. The flanks are four-bay, with rubble masonry roughly coursed and squared in an attractive variety of colours, the tall windows with dressed granite margins and Y-traceried late Victorian glazing. The roof changes plane at the top to reduce the height of its ridge, and over the E gable are three small pinnacles. The chancel and apse, with organ chamber, vestry and session house on the N, and Laird's Aisle on the S, were added by *A. Marshall Mackenzie* for Sir Alexander Forbes-Leith in 1901–2 – the Laird's Aisle is C16 in character, with a round-headed doorway in the S gable. The E end is clasped by buttresses at the angles, with a large triple-light set in an arched surround.

The plan was originally more like an early C19 burgh church than a country church, with the pulpit at its E end rather than centred in the S wall, perhaps to maximize the seating capacity. In contrast to the exterior, the interior was classical: the gallery of 1808 is retained, its simple panelled fronts resting on square columns, with an upper tier of Doric columns carrying the ceiling on segmental arches. Marshall Mackenzie's chancel is designed and fitted out in accordance with the principles of the Aberdeen Ecclesiological Society: his chancel arch, broad and round-headed in plain early C16 style, frames the chancel itself built in fine-dressed Corennie granite with a panelled oak dado; the chancel floor is raised to form a daïs approached by marble steps and its roof trusses are left exposed. The FURNISHINGS are mostly Mackenzie's – his the COMMUNION TABLE, the octagonal wine-glass PULPIT, and possibly the FONT. His also, on the S, the magnificent LAIRD'S PEW, predictably modelled on the Forbes Loft (1634) at Old Pitsligo Parish Church (*see* Peathill). Its sides are distinguished by richly carved panels and bold consoles; slim Corinthian fluted colonnettes carry the canopy with elegant cartouches, and the ceiling is panelled and painted pale blue with heads of putti and gilt initials of Alexander John Forbes-Leith and Mary Louise January, his American heiress wife. A central heraldic shield incorporates the arms not only of Forbes-Leith's own family but also of those who were lairds before him, with whom he claimed familial ties – hard not to imagine that one of the wealthiest and most powerful men in all the world did not feel more than kinship with Alexander Seton, Lord Fyvie, Earl of Dunfermline and Chancellor of Scotland following the Union of the Crowns. – LANTERNS. Fantastical Gothic, on brackets, by *Alexander Ironside* of Tifty *c.* 1906 (presumably the man of that name buried in Millbrex Churchyard, q.v.). – ORGAN. By *Wadsworth & Brother*, installed 1899, rebuilt and enlarged in 1902 by *E.H. Lawton*.

52 STAINED GLASS. Within the chancel, the great E window is by *Louis Comfort Tiffany*, and was donated by the American friends and business associates of Sir Alexander and Lady Forbes-Leith after the death in the Boer War of their son Percy. It represents the Archangel Michael, patron saint of soldiers,

standing over Time's Wheel, with a flaming sword and a banner of the Cross – an example of Tiffany's favrile technique, using different types of coloured glass mounted in two bronze saddles set one behind the other to produce a three-dimensional effect. If St Michael's face is stern and determined as befits God's field commander, then the window of a young St George in the Laird's Pew, donated by Ethel Forbes-Leith, is a portrait of her brother. – In the gallery stairs, the two former E windows: St Paul Preaching at Philippi commemorates Charles and Eliza Gordon †1851 and 1853; Moses Lifting Up the Brazen Serpent is dedicated to Capt. Charles William Gordon †1863. – In the narthex, a smaller window from St Mary, Cross of Jackston (*see* p. 217). – MONUMENTS. In the nave mostly Neoclassical memorials, but one to the Chalmers family is in champlevé enamel and by *Pittendrigh MacGillivray*, erected 1898. A panel on the S side of the gallery displays the arms and initials of Gen. William Gordon. Two others bear the arms of 'Alexander Seton, Lord Fyvie 1603' and the initials 'R.D., M.L. [Robert Dunbar of Monkshill and Marjorie Leslie] 1671.' - SCULPTURAL FRAGMENTS. In the E wall. A fleur-de-lys finial, thought to have come from St Mary's Priory, which stood nearby. – Also four other stones, of which three are PICTISH SYMBOL STONES, the fourth a fragment of a granite CROSS-SHAFT. They were arranged in the form of a crucifix at the instigation of the minister, the Rev. Dr A. J. Milne. One stone has a crescent and V-rod above a mirror and 'Pictish beast'; a second has an eagle with double disc and Z-rod. The third stone, found at Rothiebrisbane, is carved with a curious horseshoe and a disc enclosing three smaller circles. (GN)

The CHURCHYARD provides a magnificent setting – the church itself raised prominently on high ground, approached only gradually by three long flights of steps with intricate GATES AND RAILINGS between tall masonry piers set on the diagonal, probably by *Mackenzie & McMillan c.* 1883. To the S the churchyard is stepped down in broad terraces with the extensions of *c.* 1883 and 1924, the LOWER GATES seemingly designed by *W. L. Duncan* and made by *Walter Macfarlane & Co.*

In front of the church, the BURIAL ENCLOSURE for the Forbes-Leiths – a simple Scots Renaissance-style catacomb with six vaults flanked by columns at each end, forming a base-plinth for the composition as a whole; in the background a short diagonal bay with arched recess, flanking columns and pediment dated 1901–2 with heraldry, and asymmetric wing-walls, one with beautifully carved inscription panels, the other longer with five more vaults. – Percy Forbes-Leith †1901. A mournful pale white angel stands on a plinth in front of a simple cross, head bowed, wrists crossed with a wreath in one hand, watching over the helmet, sword and other accoutrements of the late young officer. By *A. Marshall Mackenzie*, the sculptor *Gaffin & Co.* of London. – Rear Admiral John Leith and Margaret Forbes, †1854 and †1899, a Maltese cross intricately carved with strapwork. – Elsewhere in the churchyard, an OBELISK to Agnes Smith †1673. She was immortalized in verse as 'The Mill o' Tifty's Bonnie Annie', who much to her family's disappointment loved the laird's trumpeter, not the laird. Her original gravestone was renewed by a later laird, William Gordon Jun., in the 1830s, the obelisk raised by public subscription in 1869. – A row of memorials lines the S side of the church, the railed enclosures as interesting as the stones themselves: one particularly large and fine Gothic wall monument, in memory of Col. William Gordon †1816, with bas relief of a phoenix rising triumphantly from the flames under a cusped arch. – Nearby, though not on the S wall, Alexander Henry Gordon, †1884. Tall Celtic cross with interlace, again within its own enclosure. – Among the other stones dating from the C17 onwards, the monument to Sir George Gordon of Gight and his wife, Dame Elizabeth Urquhart, whose initials and coat of arms are flanked by the date 1685, with mottoes (above) 'Bydand' (and below) 'By Sea and Land'.

Former PARISH MANSE (Ardlogie House). Built 1830–1. Entrance elevation two-storey, three windows wide in squared heathen rubble with pinnings and red sandstone dressings, the doorpiece with a console-cornice; later ground-floor canted bays; a broad-eaved roof. The wing is a remnant of the previous C18 manse, remodelled with a gable front and canted bay by *James Duncan*, 1906. White-harled rear elevation with taller bow stair. – CHURCH HALL. By *J. R. Mackenzie*, 1885. A broad rectangle with projecting entrance bay of the same height in pinned squared masonry; depressed-arch windows with red sandstone dressings in a plain but distinctive style.

WAR MEMORIAL, at the junction of Main Street and B9005. Erected 1921. A Celtic cross, the front of the shaft with sword and shield in low relief. In Main Street proper the former ABERDEEN TOWN & COUNTY BANK of 1866 by *James Matthews* is Georgian Survival, two storeys and three bays, its real date hinted at only by its skewputts and plate-glass windows; it stands with quiet country pride on its riverbank. The VALE HOTEL is the former Fyvie Institution by *A. Marshall Mackenzie*, *c.* 1900. Single-storey with an attic, in stugged red ashlar, symmetrical, but stepping up from a low centre into tall two-storey ends, the gables and dormers with bargeboards.

MONUMENT. In a field SW of the village, a Celtic CROSS in Corennie granite, 'Erected by W[illiam] Cosmo and Mary Grace Gordon of Fyvie . . . to mark the site of the Ancient Priory of Saint Mary . . . and In memory of J[ames] Hay Chalmers who died 1867.'

Former COTTAGE HOSPITAL, Cuminestown Road/Peterwell Road. Now a hostel. By *James Duncan*, 1879; the gift of William Cosmo Gordon and his wife, Mary Grace Abercromby. Improved by *W.L. Duncan* 1907, closed 1964. Single-storey and attic, seven bays broad, with the centre projected as a gabled porch and bays at the far ends canted. Built in pinned rubble with red sandstone dressings and margins. Tripartite doorpiece, the quoins angled beneath the gable. Roof ridge brattished, small triangular lucarnes with trefoil windows lighting the attic. Moulded chimneystacks with square shafts, and pyramid-roofed ventilators.

Former ST MARY, Cross of Jackston, 5.5 km. SSW. Built 1868 'by William Cosmo Gordon of Fyvie as a thank offering . . . for the preservation of Mary Grace Abercromby his beloved wife during a dangerous illness'. Gothic preaching-box, now distinctively altered for residential use by *Michael Rasmussen Associates*.

HOUSE OF TIFTY, 2.5 km. NNE, on the castle estate. By *Law & Dunbar-Nasmith*, *c.* 2008. On a graceful semicircular plan, two-storey, brick-built and harled with single-storey wings at each extremity; steeply raked slate roofs with box dormers and simply moulded chimneystacks. Convex elevation faces S over open falling ground: a curved and glazed projecting bay off-centre to the l. forms a terrace for the first-floor room above, with slim double-height windows towards the ends. Concave elevation enclosing a courtyard shelters the main entrance within a colonnade: the entrance is orientated on an avenue formed through trees which protect the house on its N side. Finely detailed interior with interesting spaces on account of the curve. Square WALLED GARDEN on the W.

FYVIE CASTLE 7030

1.3 km. N of Fyvie

Fyvie Castle seems to have been established by William the Lion 66
in the late C12, and is first mentioned as the *capital messuage* of the Thanage of Formartine in 1211–14 when he addressed a charter there. It remained a royal castle until 1370 when it passed from Robert II's son, also Robert, to his cousin Sir James Lindsay, who in turn granted it to his wealthy brother-in-law, Sir Robert Preston. At that time a rectangular castle of enclosure, a palace-block was added on its W side, probably in the C15. However Fyvie's most celebrated – and much imitated – aspect is its Scottish Renaissance S front, reconstructed *c.* 1599 for Alexander Seton, godson of Mary Queen of Scots and the finest lawyer of his day. He was appointed a Privy Councillor in 1585, an Extraordinary Lord of Session in 1586 and President of the College of Justice in 1593. He assumed the title of Lord Fyvie shortly after his purchase of the estate in 1596, and had probably completed most of his building work at the castle by 1603, the year before he was appointed Lord Chancellor of Scotland as the 1st Earl of Dunfermline. Seton had travelled in Italy and France and was a cultured man deeply interested in architecture – 'a great humanist in prose and poecie, Greek and

Latine; well versed in the mathematicks, and had great skill in architecture and herauldrie' – and it has been suggested that he planned the works himself. Certainly his influence is likely to have been considerable, but the stylistic similarities of Fyvie's S front to Craigston (q.v.) and in smaller details to Midmar (S) led Douglas Simpson and Harry Gordon Slade to contemplate the involvement of the *Bell family* as his master-masons, while John Gifford and Deborah Howard have proposed the involvement of James VI's own master of works, *William Schaw*, in the overall concept: after Schaw died in 1602, the epitaph on his tomb at Dunfermline Abbey (Fife) was composed by none other than Alexander Seton.*

By 1642 Seton's son Charles, 2nd Earl of Dunfermline, had incurred substantial debts supporting the king's cause during the Civil Wars, and was obliged to surrender his lands and baronies of Urquhart and Fyvie to James Earl of Callender and John Lord Hay of Yester, who had acted as his cautioners. But in that same year the castle was occupied first by Covenanting forces under the Earl of Montrose, then in 1644 by Royalist forces under the Earl of Aboyne: 'the house and planting of Fyvie was defaced and destroyed . . . and for a long time [it] was kept as a garrison'. The 2nd Earl was debarred from all public office in 1648, and fled abroad in 1649. During the Commonwealth in 1653 the Keepers of the Liberties of England confirmed Callander and Yester, together with Hew Lord Montgomerie, in possession of the 2nd Earl's lands, including Fyvie. By 1662, however, the castle had been repaired, Sir Robert Gordon describing it as 'Fyvie pulchrae et nobilis aedes Comitis Fermelinoduni'. 'Fyvie, the beautiful and noble house of the Earl of Dunfermline' – Two years later the 2nd Earl was able to redeem the estate from his creditors.

James, 4th Earl of Dunfermline, inherited Fyvie in 1677 and refurbished it but forfeited his lands after the Revolution of 1689. The castle seems to have remained unoccupied and inevitably deteriorated over the next forty years. In 1733 the estate was bought by William, 2nd Earl of Aberdeen, for the children of his third marriage, to Anne, daughter of the 2nd Duke of Gordon, and the castle was partly refitted as a temporary residence while their new house at Haddo (q.v.) was being completed: the work may have been undertaken by the architect of Haddo, *William Adam*. During the late C18 Col. William Gordon, later Gen. Gordon, made more substantial changes, deepening the plan of the S range in 1777 and building the Gordon Tower on the site of the medieval castle's NW tower in 1793. Whether it was the general or his son William who demolished the N and E ranges to create the L-plan courtyard which exists today is unclear, but by 1816 when William inherited the

*Although of strongly Catholic sympathies, Seton remained aloof from the Counter-Reformation rising of 1594, enabling him to broker peace between James VI and the Hay and Gordon families in 1597 (cf. Slains and Delgatie Castles; and Huntly Castle (S)).

castle it was again in disrepair. On the W side of the now-reduced courtyard William added an entrance corridor with a projecting porch somewhat smaller than that existing now, flanked by drum towers with conical roofs; his architect may have been *Archibald Simpson*, then recently returned from London, since these drum towers anticipated Simpson's additions to Meldrum House (*see* p. 330). Further repairs were carried out by *Mackenzie & McMillan* in 1881, but four years later Sir Maurice Duff-Gordon put Fyvie up for sale, and in 1889 it was bought with most of its contents by Alexander Forbes-Leith, a younger son of Leith Hall (S) and an indirect descendant of Sir Henry Preston.

Forbes-Leith had settled in the United States in 1871 and had made an immense fortune in the steel industry. He was president-elect and principal shareholder of the Illinois Steel Company, the largest industrial concern in the world at that time, with a capital of £10 million; in 1901, with John Pierpont Morgan and Nathaniel Thayer, he formed the United States Steel Corporation. It was under Forbes-Leith's ownership that the final alterations to Fyvie took place. He immediately commissioned *John Bryce* to design the Leith Tower on the W front but work came to a halt in 1896 after the Illinois Steel Company incurred heavy losses and by the time operations resumed in 1898–9 *Alexander Marshall Mackenzie* had taken charge, bringing the courtyard's many phases of construction to a more consistent appearance. From the Forbes-Leith family the castle passed to the National Trust for Scotland in 1984.

EARLY BUILDING HISTORY

It is only very recently that the full story of the castle's development has begun to emerge. Much was learned when it was restored in 1969, when its masonry was exposed for reharling in the mid 1980s, and as a result of Thomas Addyman's investigations of the structure *c.* 2000. Our understanding has been transformed, however, by excavation, geophysical survey and documentary research by Dr Shannon Fraser, Alison Cameron and Dr Susan Ovenden between 2010 and 2012.

The castle's site has been naturally defensive, a gravel mound enclosed by a bend in the River Ythan on the N and W and a marsh on the E, and only approachable from the S across a narrow isthmus of dry ground. The medieval castle of enclosure was almost square, 38 m. N–S by 40 m. E–W; it had angle towers just over 7 m. square at the SE and SW corners, and almost certainly at the NE and NW corners as well since their bases survived at least into the early C18. Its curtain walls rose from a battered base to a height some 5.5 m. above the ground in split boulder-rubble with small pinnings, and its towers had rounded corners, characteristics which suggested to Douglas Simpson and Harry Gordon Slade that it might date as far back as the C13. Roughly central in the S front was a modestly projecting gatehouse, perhaps of slighter later date than the rest, in the same position as the gatehouse is today.

In the late C14 Sir Robert Preston appears to have initiated a substantial strengthening of Fyvie even while his brother-in-law Sir James Lindsay was still living there. Masons were at work *c.* 1395 when Lindsay's wife was besieged by his nephew, Robert Keith. It may have been these masons who increased the castle walls to a height of 8 m. above the ground in red rubble freestone, and who built the drum towers – not quite in their present form – which stand boldly forward of the gatehouse, rising at that time to a height of 11 m.; certainly their (restored) double-keyhole gunloops are characteristic of that period. Keith may have thought that the castle would be a relatively easy target while such works were in progress, but in the event he was 'quyte discumfyted'.

Preston had evidently obtained full possession of the castle in 1397, and certainly by 1402. Perhaps during his tenure, although more probably during that of his son-in-law Alexander Meldrum who succeeded him in 1433, a palace-block was built within the W flank wall. This was of three storeys and contained on the first floor a sequential layout of hall, outer chamber and (within the SW tower) inner chamber, which corresponds to similar arrangements in the palace-blocks of Druminnor (S, *c.* 1430s) and Huntly (S, 1450s). The fabric of the castle walls and towers shows that they were raised once again in smaller freestone rubble probably in the late C15 or early C16: *Robert Mason* is recorded on site in 1500 and *George Mason* in 1508. Whether there were any buildings on the site of the now-demolished N and E ranges at that time is unclear.

EXTERIOR

Fyvie's greatest glory is its SOUTH FRONT, increased in height and completely remodelled by Alexander Seton in 1599 – a rich and relatively late Scottish Renaissance expression of the indigenous martial style, but married with the classical ideal of symmetry only recently brought over from the Continent. Symmetry was very exceptional at that date: the near-symmetry of the rather earlier Inverugie and Boyne, and the forework at Tolquhon (qq.v.) were the only precedents in the north-east. Inverugie, Boyne and Tolquhon had been built virtually anew, but at Fyvie the symmetry was to a considerable degree predetermined by the existing central gatehouse and the SE and SW angle towers. The S front of Fyvie thus owes as much to the simplicity and solidity arising from its defensive past as it does to the rich architectural display with which Seton crowned it.

Its focal point is its central gatehouse. 'In grandness and boldness of design,' Douglas Simpson tells us, 'as well as in the scale and rigour of its execution' this gatehouse – the Seton Tower, twice dated 1599– 'may rank as the crowning triumph of Scottish Baronial architecture.' Its massive drums flanking

Fyvie Castle, south front prior to 1777.
Drawing by David M. Walker

the entrance rise up through three storeys, then corbel to the square beneath the fourth, before being linked together by a splendid flying arch which supports a gabled attic caphouse flanked by pedimented dormers and small conical-roofed turrets. Its gables have chimneystacks with simple copings and at the intersection of its roofs there is a neat octagonal bellcote added in the late C18, removed during the mid C20, but reinstated in the 1980s by *Alexander Mennie*. Its bell is Dutch, perhaps earlier C18.*

Within the curtain walls linking the gatehouse to the angle towers Seton built a new S range, probably superimposed on a substructure of earlier buildings. A sketch by the Rev. Charles Cordiner shows that originally these walls rose through three storeys and an attic: at ground-floor level they were blind, the first and second floors had the windows existing now, and the attic floor windows had dormerheads. The S range was only 5.75 m. deep from front to back, the first floor containing a long gallery 3.5 m. wide linking up the domestic accommodation within the pre-existing towers. In 1777 the attic was removed by Gen. Gordon; it was reinstated in its present form by *Marshall Mackenzie* in 1898–9, when the crenellated parapets were redesigned to screen it.

At the SE and SW angles the pre-existing Preston (E) and Meldrum (W) Towers were remodelled to complement the Seton Tower in the 1599 works, rising through four storeys before being corbelled out slightly at attic level where in each case a single pedimented dormer is flanked by large conical-roofed angle turrets with boldly detailed corbel courses. Although these towers appear closely similar their different floor levels suggest that they were built at different dates as tradition suggests, or perhaps for slightly different functional requirements.

There is much of interest in the S front's details. The bay between the gatehouse drum towers is of red ashlar for its full height beneath the arch and contains an Early Renaissance round-arched doorway which once gave access to a pend with

*It may originally have hung in the belfry of the chapel demolished at that time (*see* below).

a studded timber door and an inner iron yett. This is guarded not only by shot-holes in the drums but by a *meurtrière* – a murder hole – in the flying arch above. The doorway's moulded and key-blocked surround is framed between idiosyncratic half-colonnettes which support an entablature, and above this is the first of three heraldic panels set between the windows, displaying Alexander Seton's coat of arms. At this level the drums are encompassed by simple string courses, and at attic level another string course steps up from the turret corbels, over the flying arch and across the head of a sculpted thistle with a crown. The caphouse window has a lion rampant in its pediment, and the caphouse gable itself a crown finial surmounted by a life-size figurine. Indeed, all the conical roofs have figurines engaged in courtly pursuits, including hunting, swordsmanship, musicianship and playing bowls: they may once have stood in positions relating to activities pursued in the policies beneath. Set into the fronts of the Preston and Meldrum Towers a little above ground level are two bas-relief portrait panels of PETRUS LA DUS DUX VENETIE and ARIADENVS BARBARVS, perhaps reset here from the formal garden (*see* below) which was cleared away by the mid C18.

Whether Seton's ambitions for Fyvie were fully realized is not known. That the S range was the same depth as the N range – 5.8 m. – and the E and W ranges were both 8.3 m. wide has been taken to suggest that Seton planned buildings of the same height on all four sides, but it is not easy to visualize what purpose such extensive accommodation might have served. Nevertheless it is obvious that he intended Fyvie to compare with the Scottish royal palaces and the great houses of Elizabethan England: the magnificence of the S front was far more than simply the ultimate expression of personal power, but of wisdom and scholarship.

Although the S front was clearly the castle's great showpiece in Seton's time, it was not actually the entrance front, which was on the E side. This was part of the original curtain, ashlar-faced by Seton (of which evidence was found in excavation by Ian Shepherd, 1985), with an entrance vestibule inserted at its S end during the 1730s and Seton's main gate at its N end. It had a crenellated parapet punctuated by niches, probably for statuary: a parallel is to be seen at Tolquhon (q.v.) where again a relatively low entrance front distinguished by statues of William Forbes and his family stands in a similar arrangement to the principal apartments. On the N side the terracing of the ravine suggests tiered gardens as at Arbuthnot (S) and Barncluith (Lanarkshire).

The date at which the N and E ranges of the quadrangle were demolished and the COURTYARD assumed its present L-plan form is not clear but it appears to have been some time after 1793 when Gen. William Gordon built the Gordon Tower (*see* below) on the site of the medieval castle's NW tower. His alterations to the castle had however begun much earlier, in

1777, when he increased the living accommodation in Seton's shallow S range by taking down its N (courtyard) front and rebuilding it 2.5 m. further forward, even paring back the inside face of the medieval curtain incorporated into the S front itself to provide additional space for corridors. He blocked the pend in the Seton Tower and instead formed a round-arched doorway in the centre of his new courtyard front, with his coat of arms above; this doorway was subsequently converted into the window we see now, and the coat of arms removed to a secondary entrance on the N side of the Preston Tower.

On the courtyard's W SIDE, the old palace-block remains substantially of the C15–C16 at its upper floors, the taller windows on the l. lighting the principal apartments and the small windows on stepped levels on the r. lighting the great stair. Above the corbelled wall-head are four evenly spaced pedimented dormers, two of which are dated 1598 and 1599, but they are not quite in their original relationship, the wall-head having been altered *c.* 1816 when the hall chimneystack was taken down and its flue diverted into the ridge-stack. At ground-floor level is the crenellated entrance hall and corridor added by William Gordon Jun. at that date. The projecting porch originally had conical roofs at its drum-towered angles, but these were omitted when *A. Marshall Mackenzie* enlarged it in 1898. Its enormous Gothic lanterns were part of the Marshall Mackenzie works and were made by the local blacksmith, *Alexander Ironside* of Tifty; they are similar to those at Fyvie Parish Church (*see* p. 213).

Marshall Mackenzie also remodelled the plain 1777 frontage on the courtyard's S side to bring it into a better relationship both with the W side and with Seton's S front. He formed an oriel at first floor and raised the wall-head, with dormers answering those of the W range. In the centre, twin spirelet turrets with Forbes bear finials are slightly corbelled out from the wall-plane and flank a round clock face set into a square surround. Beneath it is a panel displaying the arms of the five families associated with the house – Preston, Meldrum, Seton, Gordon and Leith; the dates 1390–1890 commemorate the quincentenary of what was then held to be the date of construction of the Preston Tower. Set above the clock face is a triangular pediment bearing the royal arms, from before the Union of the Crowns in 1603, which may formerly have graced Seton's main gate in the E range. In 1905 King Edward VII raised Forbes-Leith to the peerage, an event commemorated by a further large cartouche displaying the revision of his arms between the oriel and the clock ensemble. In the angle between the S and W sides the turret corbelled out from a squinch arch is actually a bathroom in the guise of a garderobe, the castle being civilized by modern plumbing.

At the NW corner of the courtyard is the GORDON TOWER, built by Gen. Gordon in 1793 to provide a new kitchen (now the Billiard Room), first-floor Dining Room and second-floor morning room (now the Drawing Room). In adopting a

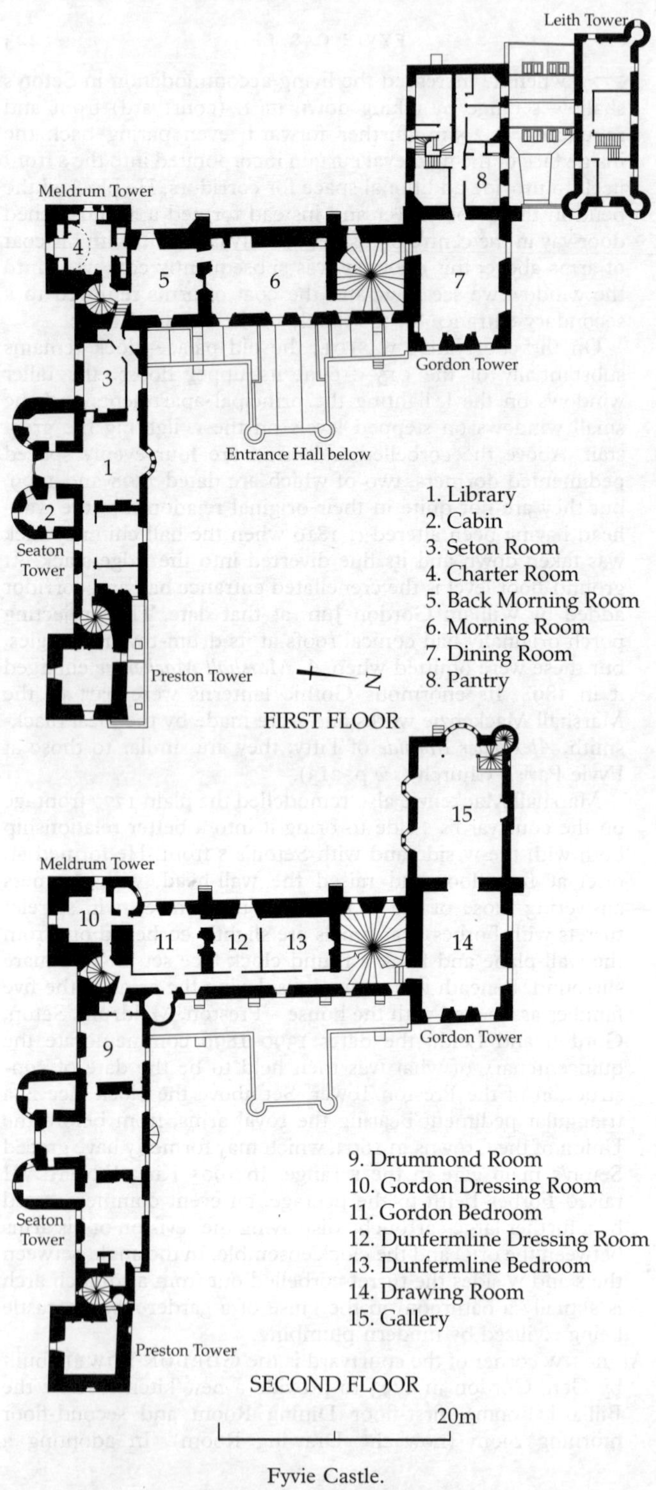

Leith Tower
Meldrum Tower
4
5
6
7
8
3
Gordon Tower
Entrance Hall below
1
2
Seaton Tower
Preston Tower
1. Library
2. Cabin
3. Seton Room
4. Charter Room
5. Back Morning Room
6. Morning Room
7. Dining Room
8. Pantry
N
FIRST FLOOR
15
Meldrum Tower
10
11
12
13
14
Gordon Tower
9
Seaton Tower
Preston Tower
9. Drummond Room
10. Gordon Dressing Room
11. Gordon Bedroom
12. Dunfermline Dressing Room
13. Dunfermline Bedroom
14. Drawing Room
15. Gallery
SECOND FLOOR
20m

Fyvie Castle.
First- and second-floor plans

Baronial revival style so well matched to Seton's work it is quite remarkable for its date. Its turret figurines take the form of Highland soldiers, their kilts flowing into the lines of the conical roofs. Its architect has still to be identified, as has the architect of a very similar addition to Leith Hall (S) built four years earlier. Although originally intended to be seen rising over the N and E ranges it now neatly balances the Preston Tower at the SE end of the entrance front.

On the WEST FRONT the Gordon Tower answered the Meldrum Tower, making that front near-symmetrical. The central section with stepped buttresses, corbelled parapet and pedimented dormers had achieved its present appearance by 1840 when it was drawn by James Giles, but an earlier perspective from Robert Adam's office shows an uninterrupted four-storey frontage with a central gablet and massive wall-head chimneystack which served the original kitchen. Whether the present wall-head and dormers are part of the remarkably precocious Baronial Revival works of *c.* 1793 or the almost equally precocious works of *c.* 1816–19 has still to be established. The near-symmetry was lost when Forbes-Leith commissioned *John Bryce* to design the LEITH TOWER which is built out from the W flank of the Gordon Tower but rather lower, three storeys and dormered attic under a crowstep-gabled roof – 'A thoroughly sensible piece of work, dignified, and in harmony with the original building', *The Builder* declared. Like the Gordon Tower it honours Seton's work in the detail of its turrets (the figurines are C20), but its chief inspiration was the Gordons' castle at Huntly from which it borrowed its second-floor oriels, the pair on the S front lettered with the appropriate Victorian homily, 'Gang East & Wast But Hames Best'. Huntly was, as Richard Emerson has pointed out, a most appropriate source, close to Fyvie not only geographically but also in historical chronology. The Leith Tower provided for the formation of a particularly grand apartment – the Music Room or Gallery – next to the existing Drawing Room on the second floor. At the back of the Leith Tower is a small annexe, its round towers with conical spirelets, which contained the BUTLER'S HOUSE. It may have been part of the 1793 works but was remodelled by Bryce.

INTERIOR

Fyvie's interior survives much as it was remodelled by *A. Marshall Mackenzie c.* 1900 as a magnificent American-inspired setting for Forbes-Leith's collection of paintings and sculpture, his fine furniture and twenty-five tapestries, his militaria and nautical artefacts. The focus of the ENTRANCE HALL is its oak fireplace, carved with putti and incorporating side-seats with dragons for their arms, above which a plaster relief by *Mark Feetham & Co.* represents the Battle of Otterburn (1388) in which Sir Henry Preston captured the English knight Ralph de Percy. The Entrance Hall is otherwise quite simple, with

Fyvie Castle, the Great Staircase.
Engraving by R.W. Billings, 1852

large segmentally arched openings on either side and an oak-grained compartmented ceiling with foliate details and heraldic shields which act as bosses. Its design and detail are very similar to the gallery at *Archibald Simpson*'s now-demolished Castle Newe (S) and it is probably his work of the 1830s, augmented by Mackenzie.* It opens, at its N end, into the BILLIARD ROOM which *John Bryce* formed for Forbes-Leith from the kitchen in the Gordon Tower: little altered from that time, its Baronial chimneypiece is again by *Feetham & Co.*, supplied in 1901.

The Entrance Hall corridor leads to the most celebrated of all the interiors at Fyvie, the GREAT STAIR. Before the N and E ranges were demolished and the Gordon and Leith Towers were added it stood in much the same relationship to the principal apartments as does the main stair at Tolquhon (q.v.). A turnpike almost 6 m. across, it was almost unprecedented in Scotland for its time, exceeded only by the 6.8 m. diameter of the NE stair within the Old Palace of Holyrood; and quite apart from its sheer scale, it is unusual in that it is contained within the main block rather than within any entrance jamb,

*Prior to 1889 this had mirror walls at both ends and seemed to stretch to infinity.

and that it continues through the full height of the building rather than terminating at first floor. Its remarkable construction implies a knowledge of staircases on the Continent, and is perhaps the strongest argument for assuming Schaw's – or Seton's? – involvement in developing the design. Its steps are supported from beneath by a series of ashlar vaults: these are formed between shallow segmental arches which extend out from the newel to corbels in the walls of the nearly square stairwell. The construction is exceptionally strong if the old legend is true that the Gordons rode their horses up the stair for a wager. Near its foot is a shield charged with Seton's arms and those of his first and second wives, Lilias Drummond and Grizel Leslie; further arms are set into the heads of the segmental arches, and at the top of the stair an oak panel – probably not *in situ* but originally at the high end of the great hall – displays the names of Seton and Leslie with the date 1603, suggesting a year for the house's fit-out and furnishing. Between the ground and first floors the newel is carved with a decorative frieze, and the window incorporates a roundel displaying Seton's coat of arms and date 1599 (re-set here *c.* 1900, it may once have been part of the glazing of the demolished castle chapel; *see* Parkland and Policies, below). An interesting feature is the manner in which, close by the newel, the risers of the stair are vertically moulded. The walls are plastered, but were once lined as ashlar.

On the FIRST FLOOR, the great stair gives access to the DINING ROOM in the Gordon Tower. This was enriched for Forbes-Leith by *John Bryce* with oak panelling and finely carved doors with portraits in their upper panels, and by a magnificent strapwork plaster ceiling in early C17 style with pendant bosses and coats of arms of the families associated with the castle. The chimneypiece, again with the various family arms, and the tall overmantel, framing a portrait of Marie Louise January, Forbes-Leith's American heiress wife, incorporates C17 twisted columns and figurative woodcarving which were salvaged from a church in the Netherlands.*

On the opposite side of the great stair, the MORNING ROOM – the drawing room in Gordon times – was formerly the hall of the old palace-block and still retains one of the eleven plaster ceilings executed for the 4th Earl of Dunfermline by *Robert Whyte* in 1683, simply compartmented with a circular centre and foliate decoration. However the panelling with fluted Composite pilasters and the fireplace inset with Delft tiles, although of convincing Caroline appearance, are actually of the Forbes-Leith era, either reusing or copying 1680s elements: the original chimneypiece was asymmetrically placed in the S wall. Beyond the morning room, the RAEBURN ROOM – formerly the small drawing room, originally the outer chamber – is distinguished by high-quality Regency joinery of the

*The previous ceiling, which also featured heraldic shields in the corners, described as 'light French', was probably a redecoration of the 1830s.

Aberdeenshire school and by its contemporary fireplace and ceiling, all part of William Gordon's work of *c.* 1816–19.* The CHARTER ROOM in the Meldrum Tower – the old inner chamber – has several safes in its walls and is panelled with antique fragments brought from other parts of the castle in the mid C19 by Capt. Cosmo Gordon, with the family arms again in plaster, but its basket-arched chimneypiece dates from the refitting of the 1730s.

Within the S range the SETON ROOM, latterly used as a boudoir, has the same Regency woodwork but the simple Tudor fireplace is a mid-C20 insertion. In the Seton Tower itself Lord Leith formed his LIBRARY, reusing William Gordon's bookcases of *c.* 1819. It is a bicameral apartment divided by a segmental arch with further small rooms in the gatehouse drums – a small library and Lord Leith's 'cabin', or private office. They were all redecorated in 1900. They have strapwork plaster ceilings and the windows incorporate the family arms and stained-glass roundels in antique styles. The arrises of the arch and some of the doorways have carved gilt decoration by *Marshall Mackenzie*, the mid-Georgian chimneypiece in the Library being supplied by *Feetham*.

The SECOND FLOOR probably consisted of the Countess's apartments in Seton times. It was replanned *c.* 1816–19 when the DUNFERMLINE PASSAGE was cut through what had probably been bed recesses and closets. The GORDON AND DUNFERMLINE BEDROOM SUITES have retained their Regency window woodwork, but the bold doorcases appear to be part of the refitting of the 1730s, and two of the ceilings are either survivors from the 1683 *Robert Whyte* programme or skilful *Marshall Mackenzie* Neo-Caroline.

Like the first-floor Dining Room beneath, the DRAWING ROOM in the Gordon Tower has a richly detailed Neo-Jacobean plaster ceiling with heraldic motifs for Forbes-Leith by Bryce. Its Neoclassical fireplace in grey and white marble with Corinthian columns and a fluted frieze is of Gen. Gordon's time, the survivor of one of two made in Rome to designs by *James Byres* of Tonley in 1773 but apparently not fitted up until 1794.‡ Then opening off the drawing room, the
93 GALLERY in the Leith Tower has a vaulted plaster ceiling rising up into the roof-space, modelled on that at Glamis Castle (Angus) but with ribs of much bolder profile: the effect of such a span at close quarters is quite striking, and still more particularly for the way it envelops the pipes of a self-playing organ by *Norman & Beard* which was erected in 1906 above the former minstrels' gallery as a focus at the W end of the room. The walls were panelled by *Joseph Duveen* to accommodate rich C17 Brussels tapestries based on cartoons by Rubens, with portraits of King Charles I and Queen Henrietta

*Behind the present chimneypiece there survives an earlier bolection-moulded chimneypiece.

‡He also supplied a fireplace for the Dining Room, now removed.

Maria above the chimneypiece: Charles had stayed at Fyvie under the care of Lord Seton from the age of three. The chimneypiece supplied by Duveen is a very exceptional import from France, of marble and dated 1521, magnificently carved with caryatid figures supporting a deep Corinthian-pilastered overmantel and inset with beautiful tiles; its original provenance has yet to be established.

Although modest in scale compared with the grandeur of the Forbes-Leith apartments, the THIRD-FLOOR ATTICS are not without interest and provide a glimpse of the interior as it was before Marshall Mackenzie's refurbishment *c.* 1900. At the head of the great stair is the DOUGLAS ROOM, which still retains its *Robert Whyte* ceiling. Since its chimneypiece has no flue, the panelling appears to have been refitted here from elsewhere in the house, probably during the time of William Gordon Jun. or Cosmo Gordon. At the S end of the W range is the PANELLED ROOM, completely unaltered since it was fitted up in the 1680s. Here as nowhere else it is possible to experience the atmosphere of the castle as it was in late Seton times.

PARKLAND AND POLICIES

Although the gardens and pleasure grounds known to Alexander Seton and his descendants have long since been swept away, evidence of their layout emerged during the archaeological investigation carried out by the National Trust for Scotland in 2011. The S front overlooked a walled formal garden which had a chapel on its E side just beneath the Preston Tower. The W range overlooked a large bowling green, and there was a kitchen garden to the SW; the formal garden was quite probably of considerable architectural and sculptural pretension, like that at Edzell Castle in Angus.

Although some of the trees may be much older, the parkland and policies were laid out in their current picturesque form by Gen. Gordon in the late C18 or very early C19, the marshland being transformed into an ARTIFICIAL LOCH perhaps by *Robert Robinson.* The grounds were extended *c.* 1816–19 by the younger William Gordon with the assistance of *James Giles R.S.A.*, who reputedly improved the loch *c.* 1830, some further horticultural contributions being made by Lord Leith. The disastrous hurricane of January 1953 resulted in the loss of some 160 hectares of old trees and considerable replanting. The BOATHOUSE or 'SWAN'S HOUSE' (600 m. SSE) is late C18 or early C19, perhaps *c.* 1816–20 – gable-fronted in pinned rubble, framed by square buttresses with pinnacles, its segment-headed archway with a slit attic light.

'PLAYHOUSE', 60 m. W of the castle. Presumably by *A. Marshall Mackenzie & Son*, dated 1903. A double-height recreation hall harled with red sandstone dressings, and with battlements and bartizans, its crowstep-gabled side-aisle contains a BOWLING

ALLEY supplied by the *Union Company* of the United States.* Entrance in N gable; in the S gable, a FOUNTAIN composed of fragments including an Italianate marble basin reportedly C16 or C17, set within a sculpted C12 or C13 arch surround; also three Italian Baroque cartouches and a Venetian Renaissance panel representing the winged lion of St Mark, presumably from Duveen.

EARTH CLOSET, 100 m. W. Late C18. Square, harled with sandstone dressings and margins, pyramidal slate roof with spike finial.

LAUNDRY HOUSE, 300 m. ESE. Late C18. Two storeys, four windows wide, harled with exposed dressings and margins beneath a bellcast hipped roof. Recent porch.

WALLED GARDEN, 300 m. E. Built *c.* 1816–19, replacing that immediately SW of the castle. Once more than twice its present size, embracing the area now occupied by the car park and beyond. The surviving garden is approximately a rectangle on plan, three gateways with modern pierced-metal gates in the S wall. Until the mid C20 it had a symmetrical range of greenhouses with a twin-towered central pavilion and twin octagons.

In the N wall, the HOME FARMHOUSE and STEADING, still part of the Fyvie Estate. Very extensive: one large courtyard with a pyramid-roofed doocot forming an eyecatcher, *c.* 1777, and three smaller courts of *c.* 1816–19, the latter with seven bays of semi-elliptical cartshed openings. Modernized 1895, further alterations since.

IVY BRIDGE, 150 m. WNW, over the River Ythan. Late C18–early C19 (perhaps *c.* 1816–19). A single segmental span, rubble-built with ashlar voussoirs and flanking pilasters on each side; belt course at road level, slightly curving wing walls and coped parapets.

COTTAGES, 300 m. ENE. Now Estate Office. Four in a terrace, single-storey and dormered attic, with projecting gabled porches; the inner pair dated 1892 and the outer pair to the same design dated 1901. Harled, with exposed dressings and margins. Shouldered doorways, bracketed oversailing eaves, dormers with bargeboards and spike finials, chimneystacks with moulded copings.

OLDWOOD COTTAGE, 600 m. ESE. Built or remodelled in the early C19 (*c.* 1824?) for Belle Black, widow of Gen. William Gordon. Two-storey three-bay symmetrical, harled with exposed dressings and margins, charming in its Gothick detail and its tall front coupled to a shallow plan. Central doorway with an elegant traceried and glazed door underneath a stepped hoodmould, ground-floor windows with lying-pane glazing; first-floor casement windows almost square, again with

*Recreation halls were clearly in vogue among the very affluent at this time: the Canadian Hall at Haddo House (q.v.) was conceived as an internal tennis court. The bowling alley is a very rare survival, as that installed at Sandringham (Norfolk) is now gone and that at Lochinch (Dumfries & Galloway) is in ruins.

hoodmoulds. Battlemented parapet and crowstepped gables with very tall diagonally shafted chimneystacks.

North Lodge (off A947), 600 m. nnw. Dated 1819 at its heraldic panel. Fine gatehouse with large round-headed carriage arch, three windows above lighting the keeper's flat, and a battlemented wall-head parapet, all clasped between twin drum towers with conical roofs. Pinned red rubble with red sandstone dressings. Low crenellated side walls extend out to circular piers. Within the pend, a heraldic plaster ceiling.

East Lodge and gates, 650 m. ese, *c.* 1816–19. Long and tall battlemented screen wall, rubble-built, with round-headed archway and empty field-panel overhead, a pinnacle at one far end; corbel course running beneath the crenels on inside face, where the lodge house is single-storey three bays, a central entrance and windows with paired lights.

entrance gates, 1 km. s, near the village. In their present form and location perhaps by *John Bryce* in 1890 when the route of the drive was changed. Square banded gatepiers in ashlar masonry with pulvinated friezes, heavy cornices and ball finials which look late c17 or early c18; fine wrought-iron carriage gates; round-headed side gate in the wing wall.

GAMRIE B *7060*

Former parish church. Built 1829–30, replacing the medieval St John the Evangelist near Gardenstown (q.v.). Probably based on designs requested by the heritors from *William Robertson*, although the final scheme was the work of *Alexander Cruikshank*, carpenter of Turriff, and *James Shand*, mason in Macduff. Simple rectangular plan, brown-tinted harl with ashlar dressings, four tall Y-traceried Tudor windows in the s flank with timber mullions and transoms and small-pane glazing. End gables with porches and small gallery windows, the w gable with a distinctive pointed-arch bellcote. Closed 1932, it became a workshop for the Troup Estate (*see* Gardenstown); now restored and sensitively converted to domestic use with an interesting galleried interior.

Large square churchyard with w carriage gates of *c.* 1900. – war memorial, 1920 by *D. & J. R. McMillan*. Short obelisk rising from sturdy scrolled pedestal.

Former parish manse (now Gamrie Lodge). Built 1830–1. Sophisticated Late Georgian in style, very similar to the parish manse at Aberdour (*see* New Aberdour), so perhaps by *William Robertson* (cf. Gamrie Parish Church). Entrance front two-storey, three windows wide, the tall ground floor with a console-corniced doorway and railed forestair. Big twelve-pane sash-and-case windows set in slim margins, a deep ashlar belt course implying the sunk basement beneath. First-floor windows are smaller twelve-pane sashes, gabled roof oversailing the eaves with coped chimneystacks. Simple dignified interior. Curved staircase within a bow on the rear elevation which rises to attic level with later dormers. Rear wing by *George Morrison*, 1915. U-plan STEADING and large rectangular WALLED GARDEN 1830–1.

7060 GARDENSTOWN B

A former fishing village in Gamrie Bay. The oldest part, the Seatown near the beach, was founded by Alexander Garden of Troup *c.* 1720 after the first wave of Highland clearances. The earliest herring station on the Moray Firth from 1812, Gardenstown prospered handsomely. During the mid C19 it expanded the only way it could, building into the perches and ledges of a sheer cliff-face immediately to the W. At one time Gardenstown was said to be the wealthiest fishing village in Britain.

PARISH CHURCH, The Green. 1898–9 by *R. G. Wilson* (of *Ellis & Wilson*). Dramatically perched on a precipice high above the village and the harbour, a landmark for mariners; built for a United Presbyterian congregation on the site of its predecessor of *c.* 1849. Simple Romanesque with a massive belfry at the salient W gable. Entrance (S) flank with broad buttressed gable bay towards the W end containing a round-headed doorway and gallery-level window; four round-headed nave windows with battered buttresses between them, tall slate roof. The SESSION HALL against the W gable by *Meldrum & Mantell*, 1987, is a substantial alteration, but sympathetic in design: Early Italian Renaissance in inspiration, simply detailed with a pedimental gable pierced by an oculus. – WAR MEMORIAL, in the vestibule. Brass plaque, *c.* 1920 signed by *F. Osborne & Co.*, London, and *Herbert Wauthier.*

REHOBOTH FREE PRESBYTERIAN CHURCH, 2 km. SSW. One of a very few churches built in Banff, Buchan and Formartine since the Second World War, and the only one within a rural context. Designed by its first minister, *Rev. Noël Hughes*, and opened 2004. Avowedly modern, practical and quite unpretentious, but with a few nods to tradition. Church, narthex and session house, in harled brick and pale gold stonework, with round-arched openings. Over the doorway a low-relief roundel of the Burning Bush. Good-quality interior.

ST JOHN THE EVANGELIST, 0.8 km. W. On a cliff-edge above the sea, reputedly founded in 1004 in gratitude for a Scottish victory against the Danes. The church was granted to Arbroath Abbey by King William the Lion in the late C12. Present structure probably built in two phases during the C16, but may incorporate earlier material. Repaired 1730, in good condition in the 1790s but a ruin since *c.* 1820–30, and now consolidated. Very long and narrow rectangular plan, walls constructed in loose grey rubble with some golden dressings; E and W end gables with simply moulded skewputts once rising into a tall roof. The walls at the E end are thicker and may date from *c.* 1513 when the church was granted to Henry Preston: when it was extended to the W later in the C16 the walls seem to have been raised, as suggested by the set-off in the E gable. In the S flank, two moulded doorways, one round-arched and one trabeated, and window openings at different levels and of different sizes; another round-arched doorway and a window, both blocked, on the N side. In the W gable a blocked doorway partly buried by the build-up of ground over the centuries, and a small window above in a chamfered surround with date inscription, the flattened apex indicating a former bellcote; E gable is blind but has a doorway (presumably C17) also blocked. Internally, various wall recesses including what appear to be an aumbry (E) and a credence (N); three others held skulls said to be those of the Danish chiefs. In the N wall a much-eroded later C18 MONUMENT of the Batty Langley school framed by clustered colonnettes supporting an entablature with a triglyph and quatrefoil frieze and curvilinear gabled top. – Set in the E gable, a fine INSCRIPTION PANEL to Patrick Barclay of Tolly (†1547) and his wife, Joneta Ogilvy, with foliate decoration around its margins. In the CHURCHYARD an excellent collection of well-preserved lying slabs and upright stones from the late C17 onwards, one of the earliest slabs clearly dated 1683 in the NW corner.

Former INFANTS' SCHOOL (Meeting Room), High Street. By *Sutherland & George*, 1910. Long single-storey with a gabled porch, set back from the road in a playground banked up by a retaining wall. Next to it a smart villa, perhaps for the master. BRACODEN SCHOOL SE of the village is also of 1910 by *Sutherland & George*.

DESCRIPTION. The fishing village of Gardenstown reveals itself only gradually to visitors descending from the plateau above the cliff, from the High Green spiralling through the hairpin loop that is The Green itself and past the parish church, then into steeply sloping Church Road cut into the face of the living rock. From here the village roofscape makes its first appearance, stepping down towards the harbour with the old Seatown stretching into the distance along the curve of shore. Seen from the quayside, looking up, the village appears amid an amphitheatre of grassy folds of cliff: then along the beach towards the W stands the Seatown, its short rows of houses perched on ledges gradually merging into a single entity, the greys, browns and whites splashed with pastel colour.

In such a place as this the narrow roads like Main Street which link the village from E to W across the breadth of bay seem scarcely more important than an underlying labyrinth of paths, alleyways and stairs. Although the village feels traditional, it was much rebuilt during the mid to later C19: its houses have good proportions but few are architectural even if many sites called for remarkable resourcefulness in planning and construction on the part of those who built them. Particularly within the Seatown the space is so restricted and the situation so exposed that the houses are mostly arranged in the old tradition, their gable ends facing towards the sea, each advancing very slightly forward of its neighbour as the coast curves gently round. Near the harbour end, where the cliffs allow, the alleyways between the houses extend further back to a second, third, even fourth house, each of these on higher ground stepping a little above its neighbour. At the far W end the houses on the shore gradually peter out between massive rubble retaining walls, robust like fortifications against the sea.

The HARBOUR was formed in the 1880s. Two concrete piers converge like the thumb and forefinger of a hand to enclose a polygonal basin with capacity for a hundred little boats. On the waterfront is a tall WAREHOUSE, three-storey five bays broad, probably mid-C19 and built in coursed rubble, its ground floor very tall but almost blind save for a doorway and broad segmental pend. At the rear the access is at second floor, made directly from Harbour Road which runs behind. To the l. another tall warehouse, converted piecemeal to a tenement.

Beyond the warehouses are two short thoroughfares in parallel. HARBOUR LANE, nearest the sea, has a former JOINER'S WORKSHOP which served the boatyard in the 'New Ground' – the post-industrial landscape of a fisher-village, with its own quietly ragged character. HARBOUR STREET has great variety on the N or seaward side, with a pair of former BOATSHEDS facing with gables to the street; the landward side is more regular, a terrace of small two-storey two-bay houses, some with slightly arched door- and window heads, and harl as refreshing and colourful as any street in Italy.

(TROUP HOUSE (now a Special School), 3 km. ENE. Three-storey asymmetrical design in pink harl with granite dressings, built for Francis Garden by *R. G. Wilson* (of *Ellis & Wilson*), dated 1897. English style with mullioned-and-transomed windows, castellated bays and half-timbered gables.)

GREENSKARES COTTAGE FARM, 1.8 km. SW. By *Alexander Reid* (of *A. & W. Reid* of Elgin), 1846, probably making use of designs by his late uncle, *William Robertson*. A delightful cottage villa. Single-storey three-bay entrance front, its centre with a shallow portico rising into a low gabled first floor and the end bays with lower hipped and platform roofs. Pale harl with slim ashlar dressings and margins. Portico Greek Doric distyle-*in-antis* sheltering the central transom-lit door and flanking windows with lying-pane glazing; the portico forms a balcony for the first-floor window. Rear elevation with its gabled centre boldly projected, the falling site exposing a basement; tripartite windows at ground floor.

MAINS OF MELROSE, 5.5 km. W. Earlier C18 farmhouse. Two storey, three bays, centre slightly projecting under a chimney gable. Its moulded round-arched key-blocked doorway has low-relief acanthus decoration. C19 extension and projecting wings, but all sadly spoiled by recent alterations.

GARMOND *see* CUMINESTOWN

GIGHT CASTLE 8030

Ruinous tower house on the precipitous summit of the Braes of Gight above the Ythan Water, formerly a Gordon stronghold. Also known as Formartine Castle, it is the largest of a group of closely related structures built for prominent Roman Catholic landowners during the Reformation period, the others including Colquhonnie and Craig (S), Fedderate, Knockhall, Delgatie and Towie Barclay (qq.v.): the plans of Gight and Craig are notably similar. Tradition suggests these castles were the work of the *Conn family* of master-masons based at Auchry. In 1564 Gordon of Schivas (*see* p. 250) and Gight was charged with 'hurting and wounding' Master William Conn of Auchry, perhaps a territorial dispute (the Conns held land at Rothiebrisbane) or a bust-up over costs or delays.

Like all the others in the group the tower at Gight is an L-plan with thick walls built in rubble, of which only the ground and first floors still survive. The main block is 16.25 m. by 11.5 m. orientated E–W, with a jamb 8.25 m. square at the SW. The entrance is in the angle, within the main block. It opens onto a ribbed- and groin-vaulted corridor, with a central boss displaying the Symbols of the Passion: this corridor extends past the main block's three vaulted cellars (the easternmost is the bakehouse) to connect with the kitchen, which occupies the whole of the jamb. At the end of the corridor between the main block and the jamb is a generous turnpike stair.

A straight flight of steps extending from the turnpike at mezzanine level rises up to enter the first-floor great hall through a window reveal; a service stair from one of the cellars likewise enters the hall through the reveal on the opposite side. An antechamber connects the great hall to the laird's chamber in the jamb, which has two mural chambers. A dormer gablet illustrated by *MacGibbon & Ross* with initials M.A.R. has now been removed to Tifty.

GLACK ESTATE *see* DAVIOT

GLASSAUGH HOUSE B 5060

1 km. N of Fordyce

Now ruinous. Italianate, built for Arthur Duff Abercromby *c.* 1835–40 to designs by *Archibald Simpson*, incorporating a Palladian house built for Gen. James Abercromby in 1770, and perhaps remnants of the Place of Glassaugh built by the

Ogilvies in the later C16 and much enlarged by the Abercrombys in 1675.

Simpson's entrance front, facing S, three storeys and seven windows wide with slightly advanced ends, originally had a broad portico across the three central bays at ground floor which has now been lost. The first floor is very tall, expressing the principal apartments with pedimented windows at the centre and end bays; the second-floor windows are almost square. A deep plain parapet conceals the roof and rises into three slim square chimneystacks with segmentally pedimented copes at the ends. Construction is in golden sandstone, mostly tooled ashlar with smooth ashlar dressings, and French casement windows with lying-pane glazing, all extremely elegant although in decay. The lost portico was unfluted Doric hexastyle with its intermediate columns paired together. It was afterwards transferred to Mulben (Moray) as a summerhouse.

The W elevation is the earlier Palladian house built for Gen. Abercromby in 1770. Five broad ashlar-faced bays, the central entrance and ground-floor windows in the slightly projecting ends set in Gibbsian surrounds, and the corresponding windows at first floor with architraves and window pediments, all with original sashes where surviving; the ends once rose into low Palladian corner towers removed during the Simpson remodelling. The E elevation is predominantly two-storey with a big three-window bow near the NE corner. A small SERVICE COURT at the rear is enclosed by a single-storey N range.

INTERIOR gutted. – Entrance vestibule occupying the centre and r. bays at ground floor, giving onto a large central staircase of 1840 directly ahead, and the bow-windowed saloon on the E side; the stair of the 1770 house is retained on the W.

A view of the house before Simpson's remodelling shows that it was flanked by a pair of pavilions, each of two storeys and five bays with very tall hipped and platformed roofs of late C17 or earliest C18 date. The N pavilion apparently survives, remodelled by *Simpson* *c.* 1840 as GLASSAUGH LODGE. Extending beyond the Lodge on its N side the early to mid-C19 former STABLES.

WALLED GARDEN. Probably C18. In the S side, four bee-bolls and a corridor linking the House and Lodge directly. In the NE corner a DOOCOT of *c.* 1600, circular, rough rubble formerly harled, with simple doorway and tapering sides rising through four stages with rat courses into a domical top. Inside, the old stone nesting boxes have been concealed by newer brick nesting boxes (184 in all) built in the late C18.

The BRIDGE over the Fordyce Burn was probably built by *Simpson* *c.* 1840 when the carriage drive was reorientated to approach his new E entrance front. A single segmental span rising above square end piers, coped parapets and curved abutments, construction mostly in tooled ashlar.

HADDO HOUSE 0050

2.6 km. ENE of Crimond

Vernacular classical, probably built by Robert Arbuthnott, 1st of 78
Haddo-Rattray, after his marriage in 1719; the proportions and details are characteristic of the earlier C18. A broad two-storey frontage, symmetrical with central doorway under a segmental pediment, and circular panel above. Six windows each floor, astragalled sashes-and-cases set in red sandstone surrounds, first floor slightly taller than ground. Construction mostly in granite rubble, tall gabled roof with single swept dormer, raised skews with moulded skewputts and coped gable chimneystacks. Fine detailing: the entrance pediment and circular panel are moulded; within the pediment, five incised keys. Window surrounds chamfered at ground floor and rounded at first; there is an eaves course and the skewputts are carved, one with initials B.M.C. Rear elevation overlooking the offices is mostly blind, but with two-window centre slightly projected under a gable, so forming a shallow T-plan; further windows in the ends. The offices are single-storey, forming inner and outer courts behind the main house: wings of the outer (rear) court are slightly taller and of different masonry, hence evidently later. Large WALLED GARDEN.

The interior is notably fine. All the principal apartments – ground-floor dining room and parlour, first-floor drawing room and principal bedroom, even the housekeeper's room at attic level – retain original C18 panelled woodwork. The dining-room and drawing-room fireplaces with their round-headed or shouldered panelled overmantels are framed by giant-order pilasters, fluted in the case of the latter. The brass box-locks are still in place, the front door secured by a heavy sliding wooden bar. The stair, closely similar to that at Kininmonth near New Leeds (q.v.), is particularly unusual: U-plan with turned balusters, its flights supported by slender reeded columns which stop some way short of the ceiling; the sides of the stair treads are carved with delicate foliate scrolls. The house has recently been restored by *Michael Ritchie* of *Mantell Ritchie*.

HADDO HOUSE 8030

3 km. SSE of Methlick

A classical country house designed for the 2nd Earl of Aberdeen 75
by *William Adam* in 1728 and built with minor revisions by *John Baxter Sen.* in 1732–6, both appointments having been made on the recommendation of Sir John Clerk of Penicuik, Scotland's

foremost arbiter on matters of good taste.* If later alterations and additions, including a Gothic chapel by *G.E. Street*, have modified the house's original character, Palladian on plan with details influenced by James Gibbs, then none has denied its intrinsic elegance.

The rectangular MAIN BLOCK is three full storeys high and seven windows (23.5 m.) wide across its principal fronts, but only five windows (19 m.) deep. Its entrance front, facing W, is set back between flanking wings with linking quadrants. Its three central bays are slightly advanced and pedimented, its whole frontage being constructed in pale granite ashlar with long-and-short quoins. The main entrance was once at first-floor *piano nobile*, crowned by its own segmental pediment with sculpted tympanum, and approached by a horseshoe stair rising at each end of a three-bay arcade to a balustraded terrace: the arcade was an alteration of 1822 by *Archibald Simpson*, overlaying Adam's simpler treatment and giving the house a more English Palladian look. The present ground-floor entrance dates from 1878–80, after the marriage of the 7th Earl (later 1st Marquess of Aberdeen and Temair) to Ishbel Marjoribanks. He commissioned *Wardrop & Reid* to form a new entrance hall at that level and remodel the interior. Their entrance, with its shouldered and key-blocked doorway flanked by niches, is in fact closer to Adam's original ground-floor elevation as published in *Vitruvius Scoticus*. They replaced the old stairs with a balustraded terrace on coupled Roman Doric columns and pilasters which extends across the full length of the front into their new curving stairways at each far end. The shafts are of red Peterhead granite, making the new work look unmistakably Victorian. At the upper levels the elevation was left unchanged. Adam's tall first-floor windows have simple lugged architraves; the second-floor band course is one of the changes which Baxter made to Adam's design and is incised with the names of William, Earl of Aberdeen, and Anne Gordon, his third wife, together with the date 1732. Above this is the Gordon coat of arms with scrolls forming the apron of the centre window, all the other top-floor windows having similar surrounds but resting on consoled sills. The octagonal pediment light is another Baxter amendment, but early illustrations of the house indicate the low wall-head parapets are later. They were in existence by 1834 and presumably part of *Simpson*'s works of 1822. There are urns at each corner of the pediment, the roof is piended with a central cupola, and a pair of broad panelled chimneystacks rise parallel to the main front, an unusual arrangement which gives the roof-line a tall and monumental profile.

*Haddo stands on the site of the Place of Kelly, which Baxter was paid to dismantle in 1732. It was originally built *c.* 1580, reconstructed from 1640 and left incomplete after the Covenanters' siege of 1644. The materials of the old house were used to build the new, a stone dated 1598 being found during alterations in 1883.

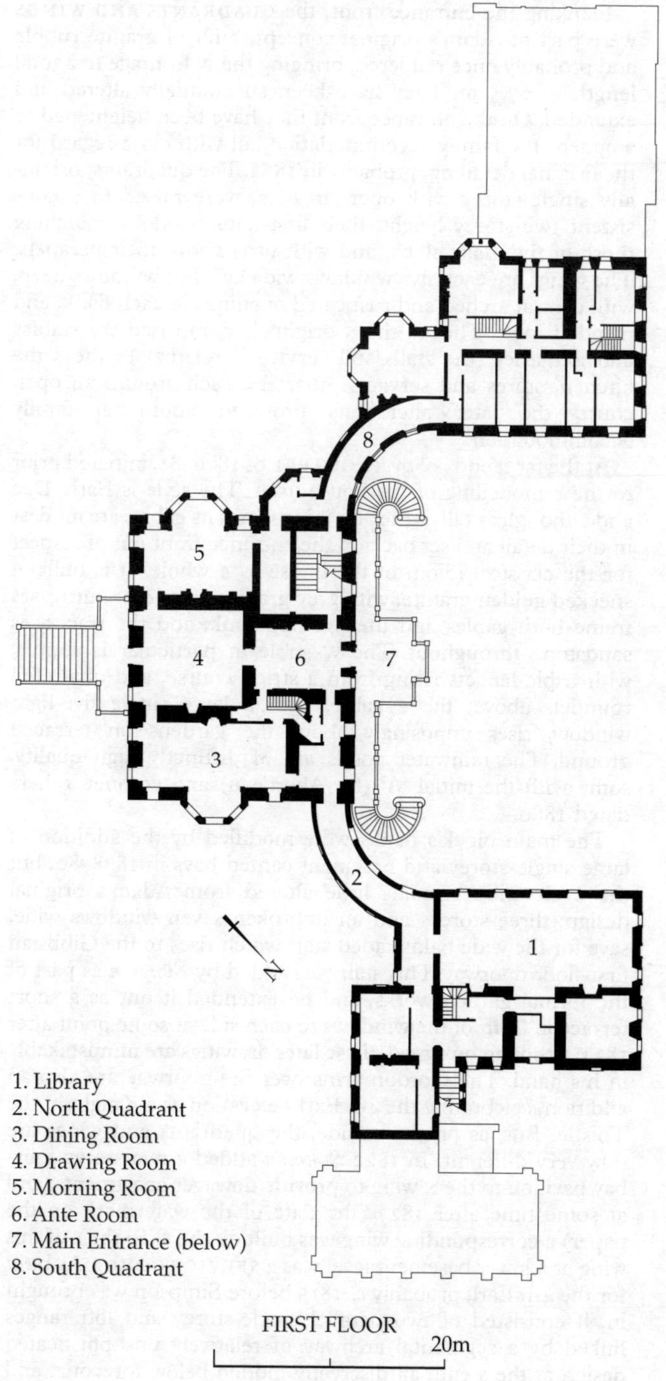

Haddo House.
First-floor plan

Flanking the entrance front, the QUADRANTS AND WINGS were part of Adam's original concept, built of granite rubble and probably once rendered, bringing the W frontage to a total length of 67.5 m. They have been substantially altered and extended. On the entrance front they have been heightened to augment the family accommodation, all with close regard for the original detailing, probably in 1822. The quadrants, originally single-storey with open arcades, were raised to a consistent two-storey height, their first-floor windows matching those of the main block, and with urns above their parapets. The wings are each five windows wide and five windows deep, with central arched and rusticated openings in each flank, and piended roofs. That to the N originally comprised the stables and granaries (the stalls still survive), and that to the S the kitchen, stores and servants' quarters, each around an open court; the later alterations provided additional family accommodation.

At the far N end is *Street*'s CHAPEL of 1876–81, initiated prior to the remodelling of the house itself. The style is Early Dec and although as tall as the adjoining wings its gables are modest in their detail and set back on the entrance front out of respect for the classical idiom of the house as a whole. It is built of snecked golden granite, with grey granite dressings; buttresses frame both gables and the five-bay flank, and the tracery is sandstone throughout. The W gable in particular is simple, with triple lancets rising from a string course, and quatrefoil roundels above; the E gable, with a large single five-light window, rises imposingly above the gardens on terraced ground. The rainwater goods are of distinctly high quality, some with the initial 'A' (for Aberdeen) and coronet, others dated 1880.

The main block's flanks were modified by the addition of large single-storey and basement canted bays in 1878–80, but the E elevation remains little altered from Adam's original design: three storeys and an unbroken seven windows wide, save for the wide balustraded stair which rises to the Gibbsian first-floor doorway. This stair was added by *Simpson* as part of the formal garden works, and he extended it out as a short terrace in front of the windows to each side at some point after 1834; although unsigned, these later drawings are unmistakably in his hand. The Gordon arms over the doorway are also an addition, celebrating the 4th Earl's elevation as a Knight of the Thistle. But, as on the W side, the quadrants and wings are now very different. In 1822 *Simpson* added a two-storey four-bay pavilion to the N wing to provide dowager apartments, and at some time after 1827 (the date of the watermark on the paper) a corresponding wing was built on the S. To the S of this wing at a lower basement level was a SERVICE COURT. As built for the 4th Earl, probably *c.* 1815 before Simpson was brought in, it consisted of two parallel single-storey and loft ranges linked by a segmental archway of relatively unsophisticated design at the S end, all discreetly hidden below forecourt and garden level. To this archway *Simpson* added a clock stage and peristyled cupola, sometime before 1834: his unsigned and undated drawing survives. This in turn was reconstructed by *Wardrop & Reid* in 1879–80, the W range being raised to two storeys, the E range completely rebuilt as a family wing extension to Simpson's 1827 block, and the archway being correspondingly heightened with Simpson's cupola re-erected at the new level. This wing was gutted by fire in 1930 and drastically curtailed by *George Bennett Mitchell & Son*, leaving the service court enclosed only by a screen wall.

INTERIOR. Wardrop & Reid's ENTRANCE HALL at ground floor is lined with red granite pilasters similar to those supporting their terrace outside, and panelled in oak with scenes from Aesop's fables by the Aberdonian artist *John Russell*; the ceiling is compartmented with painted decoration. The fireplace in bog oak, with unlikely carved date of 1652, was installed in 1878–80; it is framed by balusters from a dresser and incorporates a bedhead as its overmantel, the hearth being inset with English 'Delft' tiles. The new STAIRCASE from ground floor to first, still with its original carpet, is also by Wardrop & Reid, with superb Neo-Georgian balusters which may have been modelled on Baxter's originals.

At FIRST FLOOR, the ANTE-ROOM – the old entrance vestibule – is the only apartment to retain its original Adam panelling and doorcases with finely carved broken pediments. Its Neo-Adam ceiling with Aesthetic Movement leaf motifs at the coves dates from the 1880s remodelling. The Baroque white marble chimneypiece looks 1730s, but is more probably high-quality early Victorian Louis XIV Revival. It complements the white and grey marble overmantel which forms the setting for a bust, again of white marble, of the young Queen Victoria, sculpted by *Baron Carlo Marochetti* in 1845; it was gifted to the 4th Earl, Prime Minister 1852–5, in the last year of his premiership. The Queen visited him at Haddo with the Prince Consort in 1857. When she entered this room she found her bust presiding over a Valhalla of white marble busts of her ministers and courtiers, all by *Sir Francis Chantrey* and placed on yellow scagliola plinths: these included the earl himself, and are now to be seen in the central Square on the second floor.

The only other large room in Adam's first-floor plan was the square saloon lying directly beyond the vestibule in the centre of the E front. The remainder comprised a withdrawing room in the NE corner and bedchamber and closet suites. The replanning of the first floor was begun by the 4th Earl in the 1820s when he gutted the bedroom accommodation to create a main dining room, a drawing room and an informal library. He also remodelled Adam's FAMILY STAIR from first to second floor with an up-to-date rail and a splendid coffered ceiling with rosettes, the designs for which were by *Simpson*.

The changes made from 1878 were much more radical. The house was completely refitted and refurnished under Marjoribanks's direction by the London decorators *Wright &*

Mansfield, who had worked for him at Brook House, London, and at Guisachan near Fort William (Highland), Ishbel's childhood home. They were pioneers of the Adam Revival – the style of William Adam's sons, Robert and James – and their expertise, or perhaps more particularly *Alfred Thomas Wright*'s, was based on 'the real work of the best makers', of which they had a very large reference collection as well as all the relevant C18 publications. Haddo was their largest and most complete scheme of interior decoration and furnishing, achieving a splendour which challenged comparison with London's finest private palaces of the 1880s. Although not within the remit of *The Buildings of Scotland*, it has to be said that the magnificence of the rooms derives as much from their superb upholstery and furniture, supplemented by some imported French pieces, as from the decoration. The majority of the carpets are to their designs and are believed to have been made by *Templeton's*. Not surprisingly, Ishbel found the cost 'scandalously high' when the bills came in – maybe not high enough, for Wright & Mansfield's collection had to be sold after the partnership was dissolved in 1884, and when Wright died in 1890 he was comparatively poor. But with the loss of Brook House and the gutting of Guisachan, the survival of their interiors at Haddo is all the more important.

In their remodelling, the 4th Earl's library became the MORNING ROOM, enlarged by the big canted bay on the S front. It was fitted out with a white marble chimneypiece and gilt overmantel mirror, slim pilasters with grotesque stucco enrichments of the Syon House type, new doorcases and a very accomplished Neo-Adam ceiling. The 4th Earl's DRAWING ROOM, originally Adam's saloon in the centre of the E front, was redecorated with another Neo-Adam ceiling with stylized Aesthetic Movement leaf patterns, as in the ante-room: both ceilings were probably executed to Wright & Mansfield's designs by the Edinburgh decorator *Thomas Bonnar*. The origin of the chimneypiece, with its unusual Ionic columns of Italian rather than British character, is hard to determine. It is not that shown in a painting by James Giles, and must either have been retrieved from Ellon Castle (q.v.) or acquired on the London market as part of the 1880s refurbishment. The new DINING ROOM on the N front, enlarged into a canted bay like the Morning Room, has another Baroque white marble mantelpiece, again too big in scale to have been in William Adam's house as first built. The ceiling design, as Eileen Harris has noted, is taken from a design in *The Book of Ceilings* by Robert and James Adam's draughtsman, *George Richardson*.

Wright & Mansfield's most ambitious interior was the
91 LIBRARY in the N wing, an 18-m. double cube lined with bookcases, Neo-Adam in detail but executed in cedar of Lebanon with ebony enrichments, and with a much darker atmosphere than anything the Adam brothers would have contemplated. The twin chimneypieces under the portrait overmantels are of white marble with green and white jasperware plaques to

designs by *John Flaxman* and manufactured by *Wedgwood*, which had rediscovered the process in 1860.

At SECOND FLOOR fewer changes were made to William Adam's plan, although most of the bedrooms received new white marble chimneypieces to Wright & Mansfield's designs. Adam's library, over the saloon as at House of Dun in Angus, has long gone and the principal interior is now the top-lit central SQUARE, its deep cove enriched by Wright & Mansfield with Adamesque ornaments, and now the setting for Chantrey's busts.

Street's chapel is approached by a stencilled stair and a magnificent rib-vaulted ANTE-CHAPEL. The CHAPEL itself has a compartmented wagon roof and a vaulted two-bay S aisle; its fittings, including the ALTAR and CANDELABRA, are *Street* designs, but the fine CHOIR STALLS which occupied the central area of the chapel seem to have been removed as early as 1886. Where are they now? – ORGAN (originally water-powered). Personally built by *Father Henry Willis* and restored in 1976 by *Noël Mander*. – STAINED GLASS. E window, the Ascension, with angel minstrels in the upper tracery, almost certainly by *James Ballantine & Son*, mid 1870s.

GARDENS, PARKLAND AND POLICIES. Thanks to the public spirit of David Gordon, the 4th Marquess, the house, its contents and the gardens immediately surrounding it passed to the National Trust for Scotland in 1979, while 70 hectares of additional policies were also given to Grampian Regional Council for use as a country park.

Both the open lawn on the entrance W front, with its gravel approach drives bordered with urns, and the terrace on the E front were created by *William Adam* for the 2nd Earl and required substantial earthworks. The E terrace was replanted by the 4th Earl, himself a talented botanist and artist, to designs by *James Giles c.* 1830 as a geometric FORMAL GARDEN laid out around a circular pool with a scalloped FOUNTAIN BASIN: no doubt the earl had admired Giles's work at Fyvie Castle (q.v.) for his cousin and near neighbour, William Gordon the younger. In one corner, beneath the chapel's E gable, is a bronze MONUMENT to Monarch and Feuriach, two Skye terriers who exemplified the most noble qualities of the canine race, designed and executed by *Harold du Chêne du Vere* and dated 1909. The cubical SUNDIAL, with horizontal and vertical faces, is C17 or early C18, although its base is presumably later. On the lawn immediately beneath the S wing there is an ARMILLARY SPHERE in copper, mounted on a circular marble shaft with naked female figures (their backs to the viewer) carved in bas-relief, and with lions' heads at the base. The ash trees nearby were planted to form an avenue by George Gordon, who was created 1st Earl of Aberdeen and Lord Chancellor of Scotland in 1682. The Wellingtonias on the N side of the terrace were planted by Queen Victoria and the Prince Consort during their visit in 1857.

Two AVENUES extending dead straight to the E and W of the house, with their axis passing through its central entrances on either side, together constitute THE SCOTTISH MILE (longer than an English mile at 1,976 yards, or approximately 1.8 km.). The West Avenue – the Victoria Avenue, planted in honour of her arrival – is closed to the public, but from the formal garden visitors may pass down the stairs and walk the full length of the East Avenue. The East Avenue was laid out by *William Adam* for the 2nd Earl as part of his formal landscape of 1730–40, but the limes which border it on either side were planted in memory of Queen Victoria after her death in 1901. Little of Adam's planting now survives, for it deteriorated through neglect after the 3rd Earl moved to Ellon Castle (q.v.) and by the end of the C18 had become 'a bleak wilderness'. The fine appearance of the estate today is due to the 4th Earl and Catherine, his first wife. After he came into his inheritance in 1805 they threw prodigious efforts into a programme of land improvement and the planting of 14 million trees (mainly Scots Pine and larch) over 600 hectares for the benefit of their family and tenants; although Catherine died in 1812 and the earl's second wife, Harriet, found Haddo less congenial, the works continued even while his responsibilities in public life grew ever greater. Beyond the balustrade and the Animals' Graveyard, the East Avenue climbs for a considerable distance before reaching a BRIDGE, 0.8 km. from the house, a simple flat span with cast-iron railings set between pedestals, which crosses the Upper and Lower Lakes formed by the earl and *Giles* in 1836 and the duck-pond formed to the S in 1984. The bridge acts as an approach to 'THE GOLDEN GATES' by *J. & W. Smith*, 1847, four identical square piers of channelled ashlar framing a carriage entrance and two side gates; the central piers are crowned with urns, and the metalwork displaying arms and emblems of the Gordons over each opening is particularly fine. The central opening frames the final rise to the end of the Avenue, marked by an enormous urn. On the way up, one on each side, two STAGS – now minus their gilt antlers – standing on pedestals; then finally the URN itself, on a tall plinth, inscribed '*Futuri Haud Immemor Aevi*' – I Did This Not Unmindful of Future Times.

CANADIAN HALL, 100 m. SW of the main house. By *Daniel Macandrew Jun.* Conceived as an indoor tennis and racquets court but quickly adapted by the 7th Earl and Countess for community use, and opened by the American evangelists Moody and Sankey in 1891. Based on examples they had seen when the earl was governor-general of Canada, it is rectangular in plan, with tall double-height timber walls and a shingle roof with central ventilator. It included a lending library and was for many years the meeting place of the Onwards & Upwards Association (*see* Methlick Institute, p. 292). The Hall was subsequently remodelled by David Gordon, later 4th Marquess, and his wife, June Boissier, the pianist and conductor, with a performance stage for use of the Haddo House Choral & Operatic Society and for visiting musical and dramatic performers.

COACHHOUSE AND STABLEBLOCK, 150 m. SSW. Plain but sophisticated astylar Greek, mostly in coursed rubble, probably a clever remodelling by *Archibald Simpson c.* 1822 of a Baxter building of *c.* 1740. Main front symmetrical, a long two-storey range with central courtyard entrance, projecting coachhouse bays at each far end. All entrances trabeated in simple ashlar surrounds, those of the coachhouses exceptional in size. Upper-floor windows in central range relatively modest, sheltered by overhanging eaves of the roof; slim square wall-head chimneystacks and hipped roofs at the end bays.

HADDO HOUSE HALL, 150 m. SW. A walled enclosure in squared rubble, originally for storing peat, elegantly converted by the addition of a metal and glass superstructure into rehearsal rooms, bar, workshop and store by *Douglas Forrest Architects*, 1993. It incorporates a large heraldic sculpture re-erected from another Gordon seat, the House of Cromar (later Alastrean, S), built by *A. G. Sydney Mitchell* in 1902–5 for the 7th Earl.

MEATHOUSE, 130 m. SW. *c.* 1884, presumably by the Haddo Estate Office. Octagonal, bright red brick with yellow brick dressings, round-headed doorway and windows, low prismatic roof with apex ventilator.

OLD PHEASANTRY, 600 m. SE. Built 1884 in the same brick idiom as the meathouse, presumably also by the Estate Office. Long single-storey symmetrical range in bright red brick with yellow dressings, twenty-nine bays of round-arched openings with centre bay slightly projected under a gable. Slated pitched roof with tallish timber-boarded doocot crowned by bellcast spirelet, and smaller versions towards each end. Simple but attractive detailing. Converted into houses, more recently used for educational purposes.

OBELISK, 450 m. S. Built by *James Milne*, mason, 1815. Immensely tall, granite on a square base. Commemorates Lt-Col. Sir Alexander Gordon, killed while serving as the Duke of Wellington's aide-de-camp at Waterloo in June that year. Erected by his brothers and sisters, including the 4th Earl. There is a similar memorial to him on the battlefield itself.

LODGES. Four variations on a basic theme: single-storey three-bay with central porches and low-pitched broad-eaved roofs, perhaps by *J. & W. Smith c.* 1845. That at the S entrance, 2.4 km. SSE, is distinctly rustic, with an open log-columned porch and bargeboards, harled walls with dressed margins, and simple square chimneys. Further up the drive, SOUTH LODGE, 2 km. SSE, is Tudor with deeply chamfered door and window openings, often with hoodmoulds, the windows themselves mullioned and transomed; overhanging bracketed eaves and chimneystacks diagonally shafted. NORTH LODGE, 1.3 km. NNE on B9005, is closely related but its windows are astragalled sash-and-case and its chimneys octagonal. TANGLAND LODGE, 2 km. ENE on B9005, is plainer with short square chimneys, spoiled by replacement windows.

KEITHFIELD LODGE, 2.3 km. SW. Free Renaissance, dated 1878. A single-storey L-plan, snecked granite with crowstepped ball-finialled gables, but with round-arched porch and projecting bay window set diagonally within the re-entrant angle, both in ashlar. Key-blocked attic roundels in the gables and central chimneystack with an appropriately weighty character. Initialled 'A' for Aberdeen with Gordon heraldic crest. Hoodmoulded windows originally two-light, now with replacement glazing, modern box-dormer. Dwarf gatepiers with ball finials, the gates now gone.*

GARDENER'S COTTAGE, 600 m. WSW. Probably by *J. & W. Smith*, *c.* 1843 or earlier. Single-storey three-bay block with central Tudor porch, windows mullioned and transomed, low pitched roof, diagonally shafted chimneystacks.

BUTLER'S COTTAGE, 700 m. WSW. *c.* 1860. Single-storey three-bay block with log-column porch, attic lit by V-plan dormers with perforated bargeboards, palm-leaf chimneypots, taller rear wing.

LAUNDRY, 1.3 km. NNE, on B9005. Perhaps by *J. & W. Smith*, *c.* 1845. Like a pretty villa: single-storey, four bays, with the r. bay slightly projected under a gable; rubble-built, low-pitched roof with overhanging bracketed eaves and small square chimneystacks. Basement built into riverbank at rear.

MAINS OF HADDO, 1.4 km. W of S. Farmstead built *c.* 1809, perhaps altered by *Archibald Simpson* *c.* 1822 or *J. & W. Smith* *c.* 1845, then again in 1890. N range two storeys and thirteen bays, central segment-headed courtyard pend framed by small porches at the fifth and ninth bays, and with blind openings in the three bays at each far end suggesting mezzanines. Rock-faced masonry, harled with margins; roof hipped with overhanging eaves, the chimneystacks with simple copings. FARMHOUSE close by perhaps also *c.* 1800, but remodelled with a broad-eaved roof *c.* 1830: two storeys and three bays with central porch, entrance hoodmoulded, harled with exposed dressings and margins.

BURIAL ENCLOSURE, 0.5 km. E by Knockorthie Wood. By *Alfred Waterhouse*, 1884. Gothic. Freestone enclosing walls on bull-faced granite plinth with granite archway. Near to this, carved in the rock, is KEMBLE'S SEAT where the actor John Philip Kemble, a friend of the 4th Earl, used to memorize his lines.

0030

HATTON

A village of surprising distinction given its small size.

Former CRUDEN WEST PARISH CHURCH, Main Street. Built as the Free Church in 1884–5 by *William Davidson*, replacing

*The name 'Mains of Keithfield' (changed from Tillygonnie *c.* 1700), and the remains of a doocot are evidence that this was once a place of some importance.

a church of 1843. Tall broad gable front with stepped triple lancets, flanked by slim square belfry tower and spire. Six-bay flanks, also with lancets, rose window in rear gable, vestry annexe. Granite, pale grey harl, exposed dressings and margins. Closed *c.* 2007, future uncertain.

PUBLIC HALL, Station Road. By *William Davidson*, 1904–5. Tall two-storey Tudor-Jacobean gable front, its centre broken slightly forward. Main auditorium on first floor, windows with astragals in their upper sashes only.

HATTON MILL, Main Street. Dated 1849. Now a pub. Essentially L-plan in harled rubble, with a three-storey gable front and two-storey wing facing down Station Road; the pyramid-roofed kiln rising behind creates a focal point in the village centre.

Former SCHOOL, Bogbrae, 2.3 km. SW. By *J. & W. Smith*, 1848–9, similar to Auchiries (Cruden Bay, q.v.). Single-storey with central gabled porch, grey-harled with exposed dressings and margins, its fanlit doorway round-arched and key-blocked. Raised end gables beneath tall coped chimneystacks. Rear schoolroom wing rebuilt by *William Davidson*, 1885.

ALDIE HOUSE, 3.3 km. NE. An important mid-C18 house, badly altered *c.* 1970. Three-storey ashlar front, three windows wide, with gabled centre bay slightly projected. The whole ground-floor frontage has been removed to open into an ugly porch with flanking outshots.

AUQUHARNEY HOUSE. *See* p. 74.

HATTON CASTLE 7040

4.4 km. SE of Turriff

Castellated country house of 1814, remodelled by Garden Duff, 8th of Hatton, perhaps to designs of *John Paterson*. The previous house was of 1745, but incorporated fabric from the C16 Place of Balquholly, the aptly-named 'House in the Wood' which was held by the Mowats until 1709, and residence, when not imprisoned or exiled, of Sir Thomas Urquhart of Cromarty (1611–60), Royalist, free-thinker, polymath and the brilliant translator of Rabelais. A handsome entrance front facing W, three-storey and five bays, symmetrical with big drum towers at the corners, central Gothick entrance porch with shafted columns in dark red Hatton sandstone contrasting against the bright white harl. Windows astragalled sash-and-case, those on first floor very tall, all set within slim margins and crowned with stepped Gothick hoodmoulds. Battlemented ashlar parapets on bracket-runs, the drum towers rising slightly above the main wall-head to frame a platformed roof; above this a broad low central tower, also battlemented, rises over the principal stair inside. Almost square on plan, the three other elevations are each four windows wide between the drum towers, with attic dormers in the roof. The E elevation including its two towers and some internal partitions is partly reused.

The interior is simply detailed but very elegant. The four principal apartments are arranged on the S and W sides, at ground and first floor. The entrance hall extends across the W side, and opens through a triple archway into a very large stair hall, square on plan, top-lit by an oval cupola; at first floor, the drawing room, which is bowed at one end, extends across the full length of the S side, and the dining room, bowed at both ends, across the full length of the W, both with fireplaces in the Adam style; there is a service stair on the N side. Of the house's C16 origins the most obvious evidence is the survival of vaulting in the ground-floor SE and SW tower rooms, although in only one tower is this actually exposed.

The POLICIES were described in 1842 in the *New Statistical Account* by the Rev. Thomas Cruikshank: 'The grounds, shrubberies, and garden are well laid out, and contain a variety of such plants and shrubs, native and exotic, as are hardy enough to withstand the severity of the winter. Two approaches, which meet at a well chosen point, with two neatly constructed lodges and artificial lakes . . . happily unite in giving to this domain much to please the eye and gratify the taste.' E of the house, a SUNDIAL – a baluster bearing a cube with hollow dials, surmounted by a truncated pyramid of dials and sphere finial, dated '*Jean Meldrum* 1703'. The polygonal WALLED GARDEN enclosed by red rubble walls is exceptional, partly laid out over level ground but also taking in the dell of the Balquholly Burn, the winding paths leading between old trees and fine planting of much more recent times. GARDENER'S COTTAGE on the S side.

COACHHOUSE, 130 m. SW, probably late C18. Rectangular with two archways, hipped roof.

COACHHOUSE, 50 m. A second further SW is *c.* 1860. Single-storey centre block between taller two-storey end blocks with dormer gablets, built in red Turriff sandstone, the coach-shed arches now blocked up.

HOME FARM STEADING, 0.3 km. S, *c.* 1800. Principal front facing W, tall ground and lower first floors. Central double-height segmental arch in red Turriff ashlar sandstone supports the plinth of an octagonal upper stage, once crowned by a leaded dome.

MAUSOLEUM, 0.9 km. WNW. Perhaps by *A. & W. Reid & Mackenzie*, plans dated Elgin 1861. Small Gothic T-plan with pointed-arch doorway and wheel window in the wing, coursed red rubble buttressed with steeply raked roofs. Additional slit and wheel window in each end gable, cruciform finials.

GATEWAY, 1.2 km. WNW. By *William Leslie*, 1828. Tall round-headed arch crowned by battlements: it has short screen walls linking to a very slim round tower and a two-storey lozenge-plan Tudor lodge house. The lodge house is also battlemented, its entrance in a spiral stair-drum attached to its rear angle. Construction is chiefly in pinned red rubble formerly harled, although the battlements are ashlar; carved panels on both sides display the arms of the Duffs of Hatton. Main gates removed, side gate next to the lodge house survives.

HOUSE OF AUCHIRIES *see* RATHEN

HOUSE OF FORMARTINE 8030

2.5 km. SSE of Methlick

On the Haddo Estate. A classical country house of our own 95
times, designed by *Robert Steedman* (of *Morris & Steedman*) and built by the main contractor, *Hall & Tawse*, in 1994–5, within the walled garden of Haddo House (q.v.).

Two-storey symmetrical entrance front (facing NNW) with a central segmental archway rising double-height through ground floor and first floor, and end bays which project forward as short wings beneath piended slate roofs. The entrance itself is set well back within the archway which thus forms a recessed porch: above the panelled double-leaf doors a very deep transom-light echoes the form of the arch and is divided into small glass panes by astragals, a recurring theme throughout the design. All of the windows are astragalled, and the sense of light and elegance is reinforced by the walls in cream plaster. The centre block is lit on either side of the arch by small windows – roundels at ground floor, with slim segmental lights above; in the wings, the windows are larger, twelve-pane astragalled sashes-and-cases. The elevation is tied together across its length by its base course and band courses in rich red sandstone: the ground-floor windows are set in slim sandstone surrounds, the first-floor windows, although without surrounds, are framed by the band courses which run above and beneath them. Inset within the centre of the roof above the main archway is a shallow segmental dormer; the roof is punctuated by tall chimneystacks and its eaves oversail the wall-heads. Flanking the house on either side are low ranges of older single-storey outbuildings in coursed squared rubble masonry.

Slightly raised on a terrace of ground, the garden front facing SSE is also two-storey, symmetrical with a central double-height archway which is fully glazed to flood the vestibule with light, but the end bays are opened out as double-height round-arched recesses to enjoy the sun in shelter, so giving an additional sense of depth to the design. Between the central and end-bay arches, the ground and first floors are lit by twelve-paned windows; there is again a slim segmental dormer in the roof.

The interior is characterized by a sense of quiet elegance and clarity in keeping with the exterior. The principal apartments are naturally arranged on the S front overlooking the walled garden. The double-height VESTIBULE is, in every sense, the centre of the house, and through its glazed archway the distinction between the magnificent gardens outside and the naturally lit interior seems to vanish almost completely. A landing which, running across the N side of the vestibule, links the first-floor rooms on either side together, also forms a more elevated viewing platform, its metal balustrade of interwoven leaves the work – like that of the MAIN STAIR – of the architectural blacksmith *Adam Booth* of Castle Douglas. Flanking the vestibule, the DINING ROOM and DRAWING ROOM are on a more modest, familial scale than those of historic country houses but notably well finished: these and two other rooms have fireplaces.

The WALLED GARDEN itself, which is ensconced within Lady Mary's Wood, extends over 2 hectares and is the work of *James Giles c.* 1830, but with C18 gates. It has been beautifully replanted on the basis of designs provided by *Steedman*, the N half being laid out as a hemicycle lawn with a circular pond enclosed round its edges by trees, and the S half with an avenue of hornbeams terminating in two cypresses which frame the view of the house.

HOUSE OF GLENNIE *see* MARNOCH

8030

HOUSE OF SCHIVAS

4 km. E of Methlick

An L-plan tower house which through certain similarities with Tolquhon Castle (q.v.) can be firmly attributed to *Thomas Leiper*; it was probably built shortly after 1582 when George Gordon purchased Schivas from his uncle, John Gordon of Gight (q.v.). It has been much added to and altered since, burnt out in 1900, rebuilt for the 7th Earl of Aberdeen by *Sydney Mitchell* with *James Cobban* in 1902, then remodelled in an Arts and Crafts manner in 1934–7 for the 1st Baron Catto by *Fenton Wyness*, who had made a detailed study of the house in 1929. 'Perhaps the most sympathetic and attractive instance of restoration since the great undertakings of Sir Robert Lorimer . . . a triumph of Scottish craftsmanship', *Country Life* remarked at the time, and indeed an atmosphere akin to Lorimer's Earlshall (Fife) would appear to have been the intention.

The original tower house comprises a three-storey main block orientated E–W with a square-plan entrance jamb hinged to its NW corner, almost identical in height but containing four storeys. Above the doorway a stair-turret is corbelled out from the angle, while a much larger circular stair-tower projects from near the centre of the main block's N front. As first built Schivas may have been somewhat different: its wall-head was probably slightly lower, with the second-floor windows rising through the eaves into dormerheads. The wall-heads were certainly altered in the late C17 or early C18 when the house was given straight skews, a condition in which it was recorded by James Giles *c.* 1830–40. The present treatment of the upperworks with their crowsteps, angle turret with a conical spirelet, and the stair-tower rising above the wall-head into a larger conical spire, is all the result of Wyness' work. The square-headed doorway in the jamb is surmounted by an empty field-panel which presumably once contained George Gordon's coat of arms; the house is well defended by Leiper's distinctive triple and quadruple shot-holes, here notably varied, some of them circular while others are diamond-shaped. The granite rubble masonry, now exposed, would originally have been harled.

The two-storey block with straight skews which extends from the jamb's N gable is an early addition, altered by Wyness with its first-floor window rising tall through the eaves into a Gothic-arched dormerhead; he answered it with a new two-storey wing projecting from the E end of the main block, again with a tall dormer-headed window at first floor, which could be accessed directly from the gardens at the rear by its forestair. Another C18 addition projects from the main block's W end, altered by Wyness with a tower. The entrance forecourt approached through a miniature gatehouse, and with a very small round tower at the NE corner, is also a conjectural Wyness addition. The craftsmanship is excellent, the gatehouse's round-arched pend roll-moulded in imitation of old work, while its attic dormer is finely carved with Lord Catto's crest – a wildcat sejant proper – and his initials with those of his wife, Gladys Forbes; one of the main house's dormers is similarly sculpted with a charging wild boar. The forecourt's well-head is a particularly fine example of interwar ironwork.

On PLAN the main block of the tower house is 14.5 m. long by 7 m. deep, and the jamb is 5 m. square. The main block's ground floor was formerly almost blind, and within the forecourt its original narrow windows still survive, lighting the passage which connects two vaulted cellars with the kitchen at the far E end. The jamb contains the main stair up to first floor, in timber replacing the original stone winder, then a turnpike within the angle turret continues up to the second floor, mezzanine and modern attic floor. The first-floor landing opens directly into the great hall within the main block, entering at its 'low' end. The great hall once rose taller, its height reduced during the late C17 or C18 alterations to benefit the second-floor bedrooms. Its ceiling thus trims the top of a round-headed recess, with Holy Monogram I.H.S., from which sacraments were administered to the recusant Gordons long after the Reformation. Beyond the 'high' end where the laird sat is a broad fireplace and a doorway opening into his private chamber, heated by the warmth of the kitchen beneath. If the jamb's entrance and stair arrangements particularly recall Arnage (q.v.) as first built, albeit in reverse, the large turnpike stair within the stair-tower which links both the great hall and laird's chamber with the three other storeys bears close relationship with the S range at Tolquhon (1584–9) only 8.5 km. away.* The panelling of the hall in crimson sequoia, and the laird's chamber in waxed pine, with fine plastering in early C17 style, dates from *Sydney Mitchell*'s restoration in 1902; the aumbry door in oak with heraldic arms dated 1596 is however genuine, having fortunately been elsewhere when Schivas was burned in 1900.

The SUNDIAL standing in front of the gatehouse was brought to Schivas by Lord Catto. It comprises two hollow dial-blocks of C17 date with a surmounting ball finial, raised up on a platform of nine balusters arranged in square formation. Both the dial-blocks and the balusters are thought to have come from the Earl Marischal's house in Aberdeen via the old House of Rubislaw and thereafter Rubislaw Den, but the balusters were not originally part of the sundial.

WALLED GARDEN, 100 m. SW. Probably C18. Near-square, with rubble walls.

HOWFF OF SCHIVAS, 100 m. S. A small cemetery, enclosed by walls of squared rubble with copings. Entered through a segmental archway with surmounting urn, and with obelisks at the angles. Initials H.F. (Hugh Forbes) and C.G. (Christian Garden) on the archway imply a date *c.* 1783–90. The disastrous famine of 1782–3 prompted the Laird of Schivas to pay his tenants to clear their land of boulders as a first step towards agricultural improvement, the stone being used to enclose the fields with 'consumption dykes'.

INCHDREWER CASTLE *see* KIRKTON OF ALVAH

0060 INVERALLOCHY & CAIRNBULG

Formerly two fishing villages, one on each side of the Rathen road, rebuilt as a single planned settlement after a disastrous cholera outbreak during the 1860s. In the older streets the simple houses stand with their gables to the road and their flank elevations facing into one another to maximize the use of space and

*The jamb arrangements are also closely related to those at the Angus tower houses of Braikie, Forter and Flemington.

limit the occupants' exposure to stormy weather. In some streets the gables present a uniform appearance, but where they vary, the road is angled or two roads join together they present a picturesque appearance.

INVERALLOCHY PARISH CHURCH, Rathen Road. Originally *quoad sacra*. Built by *William Henderson*, mason, and *Brebner*, wright, opened 1842. A T-plan in granite rubble, coursed, squared and pinned, but with the buttressed gable of its S aisle rather more finely executed. The slim square tower in the SW angle is evidently later, broached above the level of the main roof into an octagonal belfry with a spire. Large pointed windows with simple Y-tracery. Very plain interior: a panelled U-plan gallery supported on fluted Roman Doric columns, facing the raised PULPIT centred in the four-bay N wall which appears of later date than the church itself: approached by a side stair, it has a balustraded front with finial at each corner, and its tall back is pilastered, rising into an entablature and hemicycle pediment.

MAGGIE'S HOOSIE, No. 26 Shore Street. A rare survivor of a fisher-cottage of probable mid-C18 date, preserved as a museum. Its interior with earthen floors, hanging lum and box-beds, no water, gas or electricity, is a stark reminder of the common life before the First World War.

INVERALLOCHY CASTLE. Begun by Sir William Cumyng *c.* 1504, after he was granted the lands by King James IV, and described as '*turre et castre*' in 1507; the castle was ruinous when visited by James Giles and MacGibbon and Ross in the C19, and has deteriorated much further since. Compact but impressive courtyard castle, a truncated wedge-shape on plan, 27 m. long, 14.5 m. at its W end and 23.8 m. at its E. A four-storey tower house with attics stood in the right-angled NE corner. This tower had a vaulted ground-floor kitchen, a hall with a large fireplace on the first floor, and a spiral-stair tower projecting at the SW. A two-storey range of private accommodation extended across the long E wall, and vaulted offices along the short wall on the W. The main entrance to the courtyard was through an arched passage in the narrow N range; the castle was raised on an artificial mound 1.5 m. high, partly for reasons of defence, partly because the surroundings were once marshy. A heraldic panel rescued from the ruins was incorporated into a nearby cottage.*

Former RATHEN FREE CHURCH, Bruxie Hill, 2.9 km. SSW. By *William Henderson*, architect,‡ 1843–4, altered by *Ellis & Wilson* *c.* 1896. Built after the minister of Inverallochy & Cairnbulg walked out of his new *quoad sacra* church during the Disruption, taking most of his congregation with him, and attracting

*The *Old Statistical Account* (1792) recorded a panel which had been mounted over the main doorway: 'I Jordan Cuming gat this house and land for bigging the abbey of Deer.'

‡This is a different William Henderson from the builder of Inverallochy Parish Church.

further members from Lonmay and Rathen. A broad Jacobean entrance front, its centre slightly projected to suggest a nave and side aisles, rising into a curvilinear gable with an apex bellcote. Token 'turrets' with finials corbelled out from the angles of the nave and at each corner. Simple three-bay flanks and rear outshots. Immediately E, *Henderson*'s MANSE, also 1843–4, reconstructed in the late C19 or early C20.

CAIRNBULG CASTLE. *See* p. 116.

6060 INVERBOYNDIE B

A tiny village, once the kirkton of a parish which included Banff (q.v.) until 1634.

ST BRANDON'S OLD CHURCHYARD. A site of religious significance since at least the late C12, a charge of Arbroath Abbey probably granted by William the Lion, but abandoned for worship in 1773. – CHURCH. W gable only survives, harled in a sandy golden colour: a round-arched doorway and small square gallery window dated 1723 set within chamfered ashlar surrounds, prominent corbelling on both the outside and inside faces for a C15–C16 octagonal bellcote, replaced by the present smaller bellcote perhaps of 1740 with a ball-finialled spirelet. Rectangular plan, with a mural burial recess on the N side. Ruinous by 1842. – GRAVESTONES. An excellent collection of table tombs and upright slabs from the C17 onwards: *inter alia*, an early upright slab with ogee top to George Anderson, †1694. Several other C18 stones are skilfully carved with angels or *memento mori*, two particularly fine ones representing full-length angels, one sounding a trumpet and the other raising an arm aloft in celebration of the final calling to the souls. Within the church itself, three Neoclassical WALL MONUMENTS to the Milne family, later C18 to later C19, and a slab commemorating Field-Marshal George Milne, †1948. Pyramidal coped GATEPIERS on churchyard's W side, and coped rubble walls, buttressed on the E to give an almost fortified appearance. Former MANSE, two storeys, three bays, early to mid C18, now incorporated within farmsteading and much rebuilt.

INVERBOYNDIE BRIDGE, 200 m. SE. Mid- to later C18, over Boyndie Burn. Small twin arches, keyblocked in tooled masonry with central cutwater pier, slightly humpbacked with long approach parapets curved out at the ends.

6040 INVERKEITHNY B

A small kirkton within the confluence of the Keithny Burn and the Deveron.

PARISH CHURCH. Plans submitted by *Alexander Reid* (of *A. & W. Reid*) in 1880, and built by *P. Christie*, mason (of *Fordyce & Sons*, Turriff), dated 1881, and opened the following year. A simple rectangular First Pointed church, beautifully constructed in squared stugged whinstone with Auchindoir dressings, and with excellent carved details perhaps by the Elgin sculptor *Thomas Goodwillie*. Entrance (E) gable has pointed-arch doorway framed by colonnettes, with its hoodmould resting on the sculpted headstops of a king and a queen. Flanking the doorway, two small vestibule lights, their hoodmoulds carved with floriate and foliate stops, and at the corners angle buttresses which are progressively intaken. Paired lancets at gallery level, again with hoodmoulds, and a trefoil roundel. The gable rises to a simple ashlar bellcote corbelled out over a roundel with date and initials J.S.M. (Rev. John Souter, minister 1859–1915). Four-bay flanks with vestibule and stairs lit by small pointed lights and quatrefoil roundel, and the church itself by three pairs of lancets on each side. W end pinned rubble with two tall lancets and wheel window. Small session house at NW corner with elaborate pedimented and finialled birdcage bellcote bearing arms and initials of Sir James Creighton of Frendraught and date 1638 retained from predecessor church. – Combed ceiling on trefoiled collar braces. E-end gallery mounted on cast-iron columns with panelled arcaded front. Organ *c.* 1914. – CHURCHYARD. A fine collection of C17–C18 table tombs.

MANSE, 130 m. SSE. By *W.L. Duncan*, built *c.* 1923. Its walled garden is shown in the 1st Ordnance Survey of 1868.

Former SCHOOL, on the road S of the church. The original two-storey three-bay school house is late C18, perhaps 1787. Facing the road, the new school of 1910 by *James Duncan & Son*, now derelict.

AULDTOWN OF NETHERDALE. *See* p. 74.

INVERUGIE 1040

A small village strung out along a minor road, with a BRIDGE spanning the River Ugie dated 1862 on its upstream side: a broad shallow segmental arch flanked by two smaller arches, rising from cutwater piers and with wing-walls built into the riverbanks at each end. A MOTTE known as Castle Hill some 300 m. N is the predecessor of Inverugie Castle.

INVERUGIE CASTLE. Protected within a loop of the Ugie, this site has reputedly been fortified since the Cheynes' tenure in the C13–C14. The date of the tower house, of which only haggard remains survive, has been the subject of some debate. Dr Douglas Simpson believed its relatively slender construction indicated that it was built by George Keith, 4th Earl

Marischal, in the late C16 or early C17. More recently, Dr Joachim Zeune has convincingly argued that it was built by William, 3rd Earl Marischal, in the 1530s and is the '*castro fortalicio*' referred to in 1538, citing the early C16 mouldings of its now lost hall chimneypiece and its crosslet keyhole gun-loops; he believes that it was only modernized in the C17. By the time James Bailey came to sketch the castle for his *Tour in the East of Scotland* in 1787 it had fallen into ruin, although its courtyards were used as a granary and brewery. It was restored by James Ferguson of Pitfour (*see also* Deer Abbey, p. 312) in the early C19, but his nephew George Ferguson had stripped it back to a shell by 1837. High winds brought down first the West Tower in 1890 and then the Cheyne Tower in 1899, George Ferguson Jun. blowing up the remainder in 1907, presumably in an attempt to prevent any further unexpected collapse.

As at Glenbervie (S) also of the 1530s, the TOWER HOUSE is unusual in that it did not follow the L-plan arrangement generally adopted for a house of this size and date. It was a rectangle orientated N–S, four storeys high and with big round towers at its NE and SE corners, the bases of which (facing the road) identify its position among the present ruins; on the W elevation near the SW corner there was a slimmer circular stair-tower entered by a vaulted forestair, but this is overgrown. A large hall occupied the whole first floor, and there was a private stair at the N gable at its junction with the NE tower. Construction is in pinned boulder rubble. Within what survives of the wall between the NE and SE towers, the sills of the great hall windows at first floor may still just be seen; there are ground-floor shot-holes, the crosslets similar to those at Ravenscraig Castle (*see* below) nearby.

To the N of the tower house stand the remains of a lower and shorter NORTH WING built by William the 7th Earl in the mid C17. From the tower house and wing three ranges extend westward at right angles to form a double courtyard or reversed E-plan. The NORTH RANGE has been reduced and converted into a two-storey cottage; the MIDDLE RANGE between the courtyards is ruined and overgrown. The shell of the two-storey SOUTH RANGE – perhaps substantially rebuilt by James Ferguson from reused stonework – survives more or less intact, its doorways and windows with chamfered surrounds. It is linked to the tower house by a GATEWAY, segmentally arched and moulded. A more magnificent outer gateway with armorial panel and the date 1670 which was illustrated both by James Giles and MacGibbon and Ross was afterwards incorporated with other fragments at Keith Hall (S).

In Ferguson's time both courtyards were laid out as splendid formal gardens distinguished by works of sculpture. It is probable that the large square of ground to the S and W of the castle, now occupied by Castlebrae Cottage, was formerly the Pleasance, entered through the lost outer gateway and surviving inner gateway. The main approach was probably through the outer (N) court, as would have been usual. Inverugie had an early ICE HOUSE, 30 m. N of the castle, and a DOOCOT 140 m. N; an OUTBUILDING survives in the grounds of Castlebrae House, 50 m. S.

RAVENSCRAIG CASTLE. Built by the Keiths of Inverugie Castle (*see* above) from which it stands only 800 m. away to the NW, although on the opposite bank of the Ugie Water. Now shattered and stripped of its dressings, its sheer size and strength nevertheless continue to impress. Suspended on a rocky outcrop above the rushing river and protected by earthworks on its landward side, it was the largest L-plan tower house ever raised in Aberdeenshire, although possibly constructed in two phases. The main block orientated E–W may be the oldest part, built pursuant to a royal licence granted in 1491. This is a substantial rectangle 17.3 m. broad by 14 m. deep, rising through three storeys, attic and garret with a straight intramural stair from ground floor to first within its N flank protected by the river and a turnpike main stair formed within its SW angle, its position suggesting that it was inserted later. The wing built onto the main block's W gable, 11.3 m. broad by 22.5 m. deep, and thus projecting 8.5 m. forward of the main block's S front, is four storeys and attic, the juncture ingeniously achieved by means of stepped floor-levels accessed from the turnpike stair which rises right up to the attics (just as in the later L-plan tower houses associated with the Conn family). If not original, both the wing and the stair must have been added relatively shortly afterwards, perhaps when the Keiths extended Inverugie in the 1530s or after John Keith received Ravenscraig from his niece, Margaret Keith of Inverugie, who had married the 3rd Earl Marischal. The walls of both the main block and the wing are exceptionally solid, mostly 2.8 m. thick increasing to 3.5 m. in the wing's S gable and W flank which were presumably deemed more exposed; the ground floors were vaulted although only that in the main block survives. The ground-floor windows were originally very small with crosslet gunloops similar to Inverugie's, and whether the wing was built in the late C15 or early C16 it was still thought necessary to have its main entrance at first floor, that at ground floor within the main block presumably being later. If Ravenscraig is really of one build its planning as well as its scale are exceptional and must imply a master-mason from outwith north-east Scotland, presumably associated with the royal court. Internally some evidence remains of fireplaces and their flues, together with a finely dressed corbel. There are traces of a BARMKIN to the S and the E.

BALMOOR BRIDGE, 0.9 km. E, crossing the Ugie. Two big semicircular arches with a broad central pier and long approaches, built 1686–8, widened in rock-faced granite by *John Willet*, engineer, in 1884 (contractor, *William Stuart*). Beneath the arches the old rubble bridge can clearly be seen, as also the rubble retaining wall and buttress of the N approach on its downstream side.

7050 KING EDWARD

A very disparate settlement which straggles along the A947: the name is an Anglicization of the Gaelic *Kin-Edar*, 'the head of the valley'.

PARISH CHURCH, on the A947. By *A. & W. Reid*, 1848. First Pointed, harled with ashlar dressings. Gable front has a doorway with a single order of shafts set into a gabled surround, tall flanking lancets on either side and angle buttresses at the corners; its square bellcote is supported on a corbelled plinth with arcaded panelling and has twin louvred openings on each side and a pyramidal spirelet with small lucarnes and a cruciform finial. Four-bay flanks, two-light windows with circled timber tracery; rear gable with large centre window and two smaller lancets, small vestry outshot. Inside, the original panelled U-plan gallery supported on slim cast-iron columns; the polygonal ceiling with iron ties is by *W.L. Duncan*, 1920. – MONUMENT. Fine brass plaque to Lt Thomas Henderson and Capt. Bertrand Henderson, both killed in the First World War.

OLD PARISH CHURCH, 0.6 km. W, on a rise of ground above the King Edward Burn. Abandoned for worship in 1848. Entrance (W) gable with round-arched doorway and the surviving W end of the nave may be C12; the finely carved two-stage bellcote is a replica of the original of 1619, the same date as the Craigston (S) Aisle added by John Urquhart, the builder of Craigston Castle (q.v.). The nave was extended E by Robert Keith, Commendator of Deer, in 1570, but his additions were removed in the 1870s.

A panel carved with a stag's head, dated 1570, which represents the arms of Keith was reset in the nave's S wall. The E gable's skewputts were reset in the W gable: they bear Keith's arms, initials and the date. Above the W door, an inscribed stone with initials M.W.G. stands for Master William Guild, minister 1608–31; beneath are the arms of Arthur, Lord Forbes, who was Laird of Blackton and Balchers in the early C17. Filling the church's E end is the GRANT DUFF MAUSOLEUM, Gothic by *Alexander Reid*, 1850.

Fine GATEWAY to the graveyard, erected by John Urquhart in 1621. Tall and square-headed with a moulded, round-arched opening and a superimposed ball-finialled gable with armorial panels on both sides. Cast-iron gates with carved stones in the reveals. Excellent collection of table tombs and gravestones. In the graveyard wall a round-arched tomb-recess, filleted and carved with thistles. It contained an effigy of Beatrice Innes of Auchintoul (q.v.), †1590, removed from the E end of the church in the 1870s.

Former PARISH MANSE. Originally a two-storey three-bay house dated 1767 but heightened with an attic storey in 1833, perhaps by *William Robertson*, and then progressively extended during the later C19 with large wings built out from both the front and the rear. Principal elevation faces SW towards the garden. The long front wing with a two-storey bay window was added in 1870, probably by Robertson's nephews *A. & W. Reid*, to provide a new dining room and drawing room; the attic dormers of the main house were added and the off-centre N wing would seem to have been begun then. The latter was completed in 1882–3 with a new stairway, kitchen and service bedrooms. A small two-storey outbuilding is early C19, perhaps a stable. To the E is an L-plan single-storey STEADING with walls on two other sides to enclose a court.

BALCHERS FARMHOUSE, 150 m. N of the parish church. Later C18, with additions. Original house two-storey, three windows wide. Ground floor with nicely detailed doorway and small windows generously spaced, ashlar dressings and margins; the first-floor windows are rather lower, brushing the eaves of a gabled roof, which is of graded slates with a stone ridge and moulded end stacks. Single-storey three-bay r. wing dated 1802; behind the house, a two-storey extension dated 1881.

CASTLETON OLD BRIDGE, 2 km. E of S of the parish church, across the King Edward Burn, built 1771. A simple rubble arch, its parapets lost. – NEW BRIDGE 1802–5. A single elliptical arch raised high above the water, its rubble now harled. Splayed ends, buttresses E side, flying buttresses on W. – KING EDWARD CASTLE, between the bridges on a prominence above the N bank of the King Edward Burn. Fragmentary ruins of a courtyard castle licensed in 1509, occupying a site fortified by the C13. Charles Cordiner's engraving of *c.* 1780 shows a tall tower house, collapsed by the early C19. A few carved stones were preserved in the steading of Castleton Farm.

EDEN CASTLE, 2 km. WNW of the parish church. Ruinous tower house on the Deveron, begun by William Meldrum who acquired the estate in 1546, and enlarged by George Leslie in 1676–7. Formerly three storeys on a Z-plan, the rectangular main block orientated N–S survives partly intact with the square entrance jamb attached at the SW corner, but the NE jamb was lost by the late C19. A circular angle tower was added to the NW during the 1676 works, but in the later C20 the N end of the main block collapsed altogether. The main block's ground floor comprised two vaulted cellars, with a corridor on the W; at first floor, the great hall with a fireplace at the N end and a service stair in the SE corner. The SW jamb contained a scale-and-platt stair of Leslie's time rising to first floor, the entrance doorway once being dated 1676.

The construction is somewhat coarse, in field rubble with rough quoins at ground and first floors, and a very loose use of packing stones: the walls are 1.5 m. thick. Small windows at ground floor, with crosslet keyhole gunloops mostly on the E side which was the most vulnerable; larger windows at first and second floors, their dressings removed, but the sills of the attic dormers survive. In one of the second-floor bedrooms a lintel dated 1677 bore the initials of George Leslie and his wife Margaret Gordon of Park.

MacGibbon and Ross's drawing shows the roof-scar of a two-storey N wing. A chapel is said to have stood on the W side of the tower, and the W front must once have been enclosed by a forecourt. This had been removed by 1828 when the Keilhall Road was laid; surviving drystone dykes are said to have enclosed the gardens. In the early C19 the tower was still habitable, used by tenant farmers for social gatherings.

STROCHERIE FARMHOUSE, 2.3 km SSE of the parish church, sheltered from the road within a dense belt of trees. Two storeys and three bays, *c.* 1800, harled in white with red sandstone ashlar dressings and margins; enlarged *c.* 1860 for James Duff, 5th Earl Fife, to facilitate visits to his estates in the area. Two wings form a Z-plan arrangement. The earl's apartments were in the N wing, which is like a smart single-storey villa. Central entrance under a small gable flanked by bay windows in red ashlar, gabled roof slightly lower than that of the old farmhouse, and coped end stacks. Internally the earl's meeting room and private sitting room both have high coved ceilings distinguished by fine plasterwork: the outlook is onto an attractive square garden.

DUNLUGAS HOUSE. *See* p. 163.
EDEN HOUSE. *See* p. 164.

KININMONTH *see* NEW LEEDS

6040

KINNAIRDY CASTLE B

1.25 km. ESE of Marnoch

Kinnairdy Castle occupies a naturally defensive site, a crag rising above the Kinnairdy Burn where it meets the larger Burn of Auchintoul and close to the latter's confluence with the Deveron, the ground thus being enclosed by water on the N, W and S. The crag may have been scarped to form the motte of a motte-and-bailey, and there appears to be some evidence of a very early tower or ha'-hoose within the present structure. The basic form of Kinnairdy, however, originated from a square tower house reputedly five storeys high built by Sir Walter Innes, 10th of that ilk, *c.* 1420, and a two-storey palace-block probably begun in the C16. These have been altered and remodelled by successive generations, starting perhaps as early as *c.* 1500 when the stair at the SW angle of the tower house was rebuilt in an enlarged form; the most drastic change took place in 1725 when the tower house was reduced to just three storeys with a very tall roof. Further changes were made in 1857. The house now owes much of its very crisp, cream-harled appearance to the restoration carried out by *George Bennett Mitchell* with *H.M. Office of Works* in 1927–35, which sought to recreate a house of the C16–C17. The restoration was commissioned by Sir Thomas Innes of Learney, whose family had held Kinnairdy until its sale in 1627.

The ENTRANCE (S) FRONT consists of the three-storey crow-stepped tower house, its stair bay at the SW corner stepped out on the W and now rising into a very convincing caphouse added in the 1930s, and the palace-block, also much altered, forming a low two-storey-and-attic wing extending to the E. The original TOWER HOUSE is 8.5 m. square on plan, its walls in loose rubble, and it seems once to have had a corbelled parapet. The original entrance is not clear, although doorways have existed both in the W gable, where the approach is steepest, and at the NE corner. The walls are 1.2–1.8 m. thick, with the ground floor vaulted, and the former great hall at first floor. The later entrance was at the foot of the turnpike stair with a doorway 1 m. above the ground, perhaps *c.* 1500 for Alexander Innes whose improvements to the house proved so expensive that his relatives had him committed. The great hall's fine E fireplace may be of his time, replacing an earlier fireplace on the N which became an aumbry, its carved oak panelling of 1493 perhaps a representation of Alexander and his wife. 60 The original small windows were enlarged in the later C16, possibly by Robert Innes *c.* 1585–90. The E wing PALACE-BLOCK has a very irregular arrangement of windows and was enlarged in the C17. It once extended further E than it does now.

Until at least the first half of the C17 the house was surrounded by a BARMKIN. This may have extended from the Baron Officer's Cottage on the E, and skirted round to take in the steading on the S (which incorporates fabric of a gatehouse), before its remains and the foundations of a laigh-bigging can be picked up on the W, and its course follows that of a garden wall to the N. Kinnairdy was still defensible in 1630 when Lady Crichton and her daughters took refuge from the Gordons after the 'Burning of Frendraught' (*see Buildings of Scotland: Aberdeenshire: South and Aberdeen*), the Crichtons having purchased it three years previously; but during the later C17 tenure of the Gregorys – the celebrated scientific family – it fell into disrepair. In 1704 it was bought by Thomas Donaldson, an Elgin merchant, and in 1725 was reduced to its present three storeys, the corbels of the wall-head parapet being reused as the gable crowsteps.

The house suffered further alterations in 1857 when the ground floor of the palace-block was rebuilt. This was undone in 1927–35 when a new doorway was provided, its fine moulding copied from that of the blocked doorway in the tower house's W gable. This new doorway, the palace-block's ground-floor windows, and the window surround of the stair-bay caphouse are all charged with Innes heraldic motifs, and the caphouse gable is crowned by an Innes Star.

6060 KIRKTON OF ALVAH B

The Hill of Alvah – a landmark to mariners – has been a place of religious significance since early Christian times, with holy wells associated with St Colman, St Breandan and St Katherine. Patronage of the Church of St Colman was granted by Marjory, dowager Countess of Atholl, to the Abbey of Coupar Angus in 1314. Until the mid C16 Alvah and Forglen (*see* p. 267) were conjoined as a single parish.

Former PARISH CHURCH. Built 1792, but reusing a birdcage bellcote, dated 1645,* over its W gable. A simple rectangular church with doorway and gallery window in each gable; four-bay S flank with two large central windows and smaller windows at the ends. The W porch and NE vestry are by *James Duncan*, 1882–3. Interior with panelled U-plan gallery resting on cast-iron columns and facing towards the pulpit in the centre of the S side. Approached by a balustraded stair, the raised PULPIT is octagonal, its sides carved with trefoil-headed panelling and with a tall back; the PEWS are still in place. – MONUMENTS. S wall. Elizabeth Campbell †1728, with composite half-columns framing an ashlar panel, concave pediment with putto's head and surmounting urn finial. – Vestry E wall. C16 once with initials I.M. G.M. – In the churchyard the Graeco-Egyptian OGILVY ENCLOSURE, early C19, now derelict inside. – John Findlater, †1907, near the S wall. Notable for its low-relief portrait. – Neo-Baroque WAR MEMORIAL in grey granite by *Geddes & Walker*, sculptors in Banff, unveiled 1921.

Former MANSE, S of the church. Built 1870, but incorporating a predecessor of 1764 as a rear wing. Two-storey entrance front, three windows wide, with central entrance bay slightly projected and rising through the wall-head into a short castellated parapet and gablet. Bay windows to either side at ground floor also crenellated, with first-floor windows rising into dormer gablets with spire finials. Harled in white, with ashlar dressings and margins, simple bold detailing.

INCHDREWER CASTLE, 2.3 km. WNW. On high ground, ruinous by the late C19 and still so despite a partial restoration in 1966–71 by *Jock Lamb* (of *George Bennett Mitchell & Son*) for Count Robin de la Lanne Mirrlees, Prince of Incoronata, a descendant of the Lords Banff.‡ The main tower house is of three storeys and attics and basically an L-plan, but its building history is unusually complex. The main block is orientated N–S, 10.3 m. long and surprisingly narrow at only 6 m. wide, with walls 1–1.5 m. thick; the jamb is at the SW and is 6 m. long with a projection of only 3.5 m. The walls of the jamb are relatively thin at less than 1 m., leading some to suppose that

*The bell by *Peter Jansen*, 1643, is preserved in St Mary, Banff (q.v.).

‡The Count, Richmond Herald of Arms in Ordinary at the College of Arms, was quite literally a figure out of a James Bond novel, providing Ian Fleming with the inspiration for Sir Hilary Bray in *On Her Majesty's Secret Service* (1963).

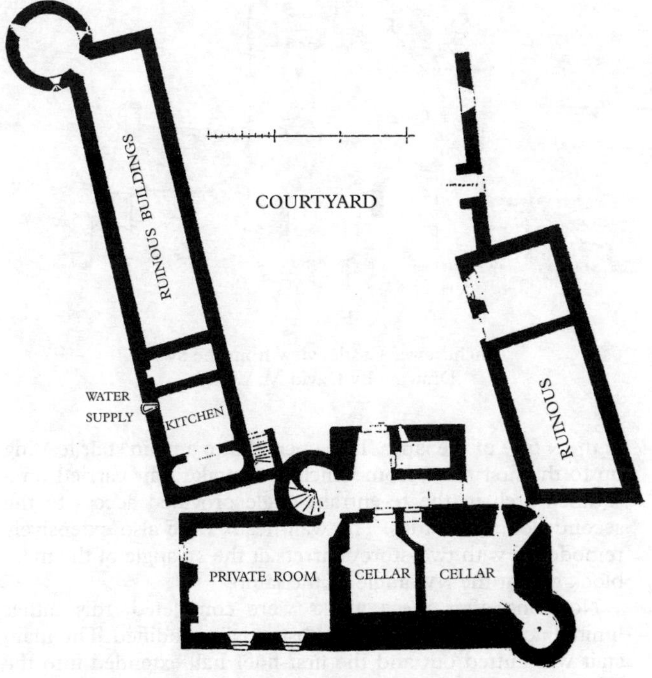

Inchdrewer Castle.
Ground floor plan, 1887

at first the main block was a simple rectangular tower. What appears to be the original square-headed doorway is, however, still clearly visible in built-up form at first-floor level on the N face of the jamb, a medieval arrangement which had almost completely died out in Aberdeenshire and Banffshire by the mid C15.* It must have led to an entrance passage subsequently gutted out to provide a more commodious but still rather small private apartment.

The house was acquired by the Ogilvies *c.* 1557 and reconstructed *c.* 1570–80 as a conventional L-plan, the only unusual features being that the jamb had a lower wall-head and roof-line than the main block, the NW angle of the main block was splayed and at the NE angle there was a circular tower, probably containing a private stair and evidently similar to that once existing at Eden (q.v.).‡ As remodelled the tower house now had a well-protected arched and moulded ground-floor door

*It is just possible that this was the original stair window but it is larger than one would expect, and there is no sign of sockets for the iron security grille one would expect at this level.

‡MacGibbon and Ross's plans are incorrect in assuming that the NE angle was square, probably because the main jamb appeared to be of early date. At the time of their visit the N end of the tower house was a great mound of fallen debris. The NE tower is shown in Francis Grose's view and its stump was found when the site was cleared in 1964–5.

Inchdrewer Castle, view from the SW.
Drawing by David M. Walker

in the N face of the jamb. This opened into a main stair leading up to the first floor, from which a turnpike stair carried on a squinch arch in the re-entrant angle provided access to the second floor and attics. The wall-heads were also extensively remodelled with two-storey turrets at the SE angle of the main block and at the NW angle of the jamb.

Not long after these works were completed, this rather limited accommodation was substantially modified. The main stair was gutted out and the first-floor hall extended into the jamb resulting in its unique L-plan arrangement, the wall above being carried on a very wide segmental arch. A new and much larger frontal doorway, similarly arched and moulded to that in the re-entrant angle, was slapped through the W gable of the jamb, opening into the area previously occupied by the main stair. A new circular stair-tower about 3.5 m. in diameter was added to the S face of the jamb, rising into a deep crenellated parapet which, together with its corbel table, returned onto the jamb's W front; this new stair ascended to second-floor level where a narrower stair-turret in its E re-entrant angle provided access to the attic and garret. The turret rests on a squinch arch similar to that in the W re-entrant angle, suggesting that the same master-mason was re-employed. The N gable, the NE tower and the greater part of the E wall are an intelligent guess of the 1960s at what previously existed from the first floor upwards; the pair of segment-headed windows on the rebuilt E elevation are however *Jock Lamb*'s, probably instructed by his client.

Because of the castle's situation on a hillside the FORECOURT RANGES are slightly skewed towards the S so that the forecourt itself is a parallelogram rather than a rectangle on plan. These ranges are C17. The S range was two-storey and no less than 20 m. long; it contained the kitchen with its fireplace next to the tower house, and had a circular angle tower at the SW. An external stair gave access to the upper floor and when complete it must have been rather like the wings at

Castle Fraser (S). Two surviving triple shot-holes in its angle tower suggests that the *Leiper family* were involved in its building and possibly other works at Inchdrewer. The forecourt's N range was shorter than its S range and may have had an angle turret; a doorway within the N range's flank and a moulded round-arched gateway in a surviving section of the N forecourt wall may have led into the gardens.* The forecourt's W wall has vanished entirely.

The tower's two-storey S WING was added after a fire in 1713, providing a second principal apartment, probably a drawing room.

Lamb's restoration respected the changes made to the roofline after the 1713 fire. It made much use internally of cast concrete and brise-block which was to have been plastered, but the external stonework is exemplary and has ensured the castle's survival: most of the original structure remains, together with some carved stones from elsewhere on the site reset into the walls. Work halted when an earthquake struck Robin de la Lanne Mirrlees' house at La Vanaria in Sicily: the interior of Inchdrewer, in its essentials completed, was never fitted out although the Count occasionally picnicked there while staying at the Fife Arms Hotel in Banff (q.v.). Whether it will now be finished remains to be seen.

LOWER INCHDREWER FARMHOUSE, 450 m. NNE of the castle. Early to mid-C18, large, simple but very handsome. Entrance front two-storey and asymmetrical, its two middle bays off-centre, with the doorway concealed behind a later timber porch. Built in field rubble, formerly harled, with slim ashlar dressings and margins, those at the angles rising into capitals which once reflected the profile of a wallhead cornice. Gables only one bay deep. Tall hipped roof, slightly bellcast, its ridge crowned by twin coped chimneystacks. Internally, two large rooms and one smaller on each floor, with a staircase near the main entrance.

MONTCOFFER HOUSE, 1.3 km. NNE of Kirkton of Alvah. Early C18, renovated by *James Robertson*, mason, *c.* 1774–5 to provide a residence for William Rose, Lord Braco's factor, then enlarged and remodelled *c.* 1880 for G. Skene Duff. The original house is simple: two storeys, three bays, rubble-built and harled; it has moulded skewputts and a tall gabled roof with coped end stacks. Its pilastered doorpiece and semi-elliptical bow windows with curved plate glass, their grey granite ashlar contrasting against white harl, were added *c.* 1880 when the taller and similarly detailed two-storey wing at the l. end was also built. The double-pile rear wing is partly early C18, and partly 1774–5; within the angle are the remains of a service complex. From 1906 Montcoffer was furnished from Duff House (Banff q.v.) as a residence for the Duke and Duchess of Fife when visiting their Banffshire estates.

*It is quite possible that the raspberries and gooseberries growing here are remnants of the kitchen garden.

The house overlooks a WALLED GARDEN, with ashlar gatepiers in its E end. At the rear is a very unusual and picturesque composition of three small octagonal GAME LARDERS built during the mid to late C19: one Neo-Tudor, one classical, one timber.* Cylindrical DOOCOT (220 m. E), built by 1790, Gothick with pointed doorway, flight-hole openings and small 'arrow slits', harled rubble, now roofless but its stone nesting boxes remain.

MAINS OF AUCHINBADIE, 2.5 km. SSE. Later C18 farmhouse. Two-storey, three bays very widely spaced, the doorpiece with roll-moulded jambs, perhaps reused; ground-floor windows enlarged, first-floor windows in slim surrounds all harled over, gabled roof with renewed end stacks. Demi-lune stair in otherwise blind rear elevation, long single-storey back wing.

BRIDGE OF ALVAH. *See* Banff, Duff House Policies, p. 104.

8020

KIRKTON OF BOURTIE

PARISH CHURCH. By *James Walker*, mason, and *William Sangster*, wright, 1807. Gothick (cf. Kildrummy Parish Church, S) of 1805. Small square plan, tall hipped roof. Two large pointed S windows with basket-tracery sashes. Two pointed N doorways. E and W elevations blind with small central gables lighting the gallery stairs; the W elevation alone is built in coursed rather than random rubble and its gable supports a small birdcage bellcote of 1728 from the previous church. Inside, the only Georgian church interior in north Aberdeenshire to survive completely intact – very chaste (no organ), boarded rather than plastered, intimate yet imposing on account of its height. Coved ceiling once frescoed with angels and apostles around a central geometric lattice of sky and stars. Original triple-decker PULPIT with ogee-capped sounding-board facing the N gallery in very close proximity. – From the old church a pew-panel with initials R.S. (Robert Symsone of Thornton), dated 1669. – MONUMENTS. In the foyer (formed 1933), medieval stone EFFIGIES of a knight and his lady, removed from the churchyard in 1955. – CHURCHYARD approached by an avenue of trees 'improved' in 1904 but still beautiful, with C19 square gatepiers and railings. Finely lettered stone for the architect A.G.R. Mackenzie †1963 (*see* Bourtie House, below).

PARISH MANSE. Essentially of 1780 but its centre and l. bays obscured by a boldly projecting gabled frontage of 1829, with a new doorway in the re-entrant angle. The small single-storey wing on the far l. may be a remnant of the previous manse of 1724. Large walled garden.

MAINS OF THORNTON, 1.5 km. ESE. Vernacular classical country house for Robert Simpson, 1754. Entrance front two storeys and five windows wide with a central doorway, the

*Cf. the doocots at Inverquhomery (Longside, q.v.).

walls battered and white-harled with exposed chamfered margins, a tall wall-head acknowledging additional accommodation in the attic. Gabled roof with ashlar chimneystacks, their pattern repeated in the later single-storey rear wing. Interior: the ground floor N room's fine panelling survives concealed under plaster.

BOURTIE HOUSE, 2 km. WSW. A vernacular classical country house built for Patrick Anderson and Elizabeth Ogilvie, dated 1754, and reflecting within the scope of lesser landowners something of the much grander houses built by the nobility. Entrance (S) front is three-storey and five windows wide with a very broad central bay rising into a low pediment beneath a much taller gabled roof. The windows of the lowest storey (devoted to services) are small square or oblong openings, set relatively high in the wall and barred; however the windows lighting the principal apartments are tall twelve-pane astragalled sashes, with those of the bedroom floor only slightly smaller, their lintels brushing the eaves. The pediment has an attic oculus, and is incised with the initials of the original owners; the end gables have moulded skewputts and low coped chimneystacks. Overall the proportions are tall and handsome, built for the most part in coursed golden granite masonry with roughly dressed quoins. It is evident however that the house was designed to be entered at the principal floor: the quoins of the central window extend down beneath its cill, implying that a platt for a stair was intended. Considerable earth-moving was evidently required to form the entrance at the lower level and the very lowest stone courses in random rubble are now revealed. Originally the house was T-plan but sympathetically extended to H-plan in 1882; the date-panel bears the monogrammed letters ΠΔ, which also appear at Ardoe House (S). Bourtie House was formerly the home of the architect A.G.R. Mackenzie. Inside, a pine stair leads from the entrance hall to the first-floor dining and drawing rooms, which retain their panelling, fireplaces with scroll pediments, and concealed cupboards; the drawing room has a built-in alcove with display shelves over drawers and a writing desk. The second-floor bedrooms are also simply panelled.

HILL-FORT, Barra Hill, 1 km. N. The hill is enclosed by a series 7
of banks and ditches. The interior measures some 122 m. by 95 m. and there were at least two entrances. Recent dating has shown that the fort was first constructed in the Iron Age and was refortified in the early medieval period. (GN)

BARRA CASTLE. *See* p. 105.

KIRKTON OF FORGLEN B 6050

2.5 km. W of Turriff

OLD PARISH CHURCH, on the Deveron's N bank. Built by George Ogilvie, Master of Banff, in 1652 when Forglen was divided from Alvah as a separate parish and annexed part of

Marnoch.* Rectangular, loosely pinned field rubble formerly harled, relatively small on plan. Walls coped when roof removed, windows blocked but E door remains. Inside, remains of a gallery stair in NE corner; piscina in N wall near W end. – NEW PARISH CHURCH, 500 m. N. Built 1806, reconstructed by *Mr Lawson* 1894–6. Now in private use, much altered. – MONUMENT. James George of Crovie (†1826) against the church's S wall: an inscription tablet framed by engaged columns with Composite capitals which support a frieze and entablature, idiosyncratic provincial details. Coped square GATEPIERS, early C19 partly composed of C17 fragments.‡

Former MANSE, N of the graveyard. Predominantly mid- to later C18, altered or perhaps reconstructed in 1796. Two-storey, three broad bays, cream-harled with red sandstone dressings and gabled roof with end stacks; single-storey hip-roofed flanking pavilions to either side enclose the forecourt. Rear wing 1828. Large trapezoidal walled garden.

FORMER FREE CHURCH, 3.3 km WNW, beyond Bogton. Built 1846. Gothic of the type associated with *William* and *James Henderson*, and better detailed than most. Simple gable-fronted design with its central entrance bay slightly advanced rising into a square-plan belfry with a stone roof; splayed pointed-arch doorway with small wheel window and clock oculus above. Three-bay flanks with hoodmoulded Y-traceried windows. Pale golden harl with cream sandstone dressings. Renovated 1878; now used as stables but retains some internal features including patterned glass. MANSE also 1846, renovated with new rear wing in 1878.

MEMORIAL HALL, 2.3 km. NNW on the B9025. By *W. L. Duncan*, dated 1924. Single-storey with steep hipped roof, Lorimerian gablet and belfry-like roof ventilator; two smaller wings. Outside, the WAR MEMORIAL, also by *Duncan*. Cenotaph, with pyramidal top and antefixae at the angles, 1921.

MILL OF RIBRAE, 2.1 km. NW. Dated with initials W.L.B. 1778. Two storeys, pinned rubble with gabled roof, built into a bank of ground; off-centre segment-headed opening, irregular fenestration and kiln chamber with ventilator at its l. end, formerly with a water wheel against its r. gable; some machinery survives inside.

FORGLEN HOUSE. *See* p. 184.

MOUNTBLAIRY. *See* p. 295.

OLD HOUSE OF CARNOUSIE. *See* p. 322.

9020

KIRKTON OF LOGIE-BUCHAN

ST ANDREW (now a private chapel). Small preaching-box of 1787 on a much older site. Two small square-headed windows in the S flank, harled with ashlar margins and a relatively tall

*The Rev. Robert Ballingall who wrote the *Old Statistical Account* of Forglen read the date as 1692, but 1652 appears correct.

‡It is the resting place of George Findlater, V.C. (see *Oxford DNB*).

roof, hipped at E. W gable's original doorway concealed by a vestry of 1891; birdcage bellcote reused from a predecessor church (bell by *Robert Maxwell*, 1728). E gable's exposed masonry reveals two blocked doorways at ground and gallery level; the E and N windows were formed during *William Ruxton*'s remodelling *c.* 1909–12, when paired timber Gothic lights were fitted on all sides. Inside Ruxton removed the E and S galleries; the W gallery displays the Buchan coat of arms carved by *George Reid* of Peterhead, the ceiling with its Adamesque centrepiece is original. – MEMORIAL TABLETS include Thomas and Robert Buchan, †1819 and 1825, and Albert and Alexander Guthrie, †1916 and 1917, by *Ruxton*.

Former PARISH MANSE. Dated 1775. By *George Jaffray* of Old Aberdeen, wright, and *James Bowman* of Fechil, mason. Two-storey, three windows wide, harled with exposed margins; gable skewputts and Victorian canted dormers. Large rear wing.

AUCHMACOY MEMORIAL FOOTBRIDGE, crossing the River Ythan to Denhead of Auchmacoy. Unusually ambitious reinforced concrete structure for small rural parish, built 1935. Nine spans supported on battered piers ramped in a gentle rise, the walkway guarded by balustraded parapets with square balusters. Central span with blind panels and bronze plaques commemorating the Fallen of two world wars.

MISSION HALL, Denhead, 1 km. NE. Accomplished late Gothic by *Kinnear & Peddie*, dated 1879 and 1891. A four-bay hall with gabled porch, harled in white with red sandstone details and margins, trefoil-headed lights and bracketed eaves; crow-stepped end gables with large W window. Two-storey keeper's house angled out slightly behind it, with jettied half-timbered upper storey of paired gables.

OLDYARD, 2.2 km. N. Built *c.* 1780–1800. Simple two-storey three-bay house, pinned split boulder-rubble formerly harled, with skewputts and coped chimneystacks. Rear elevation nearly blind.

SOUTH ARTROCHIE HOUSE, 2 km. ENE. Simple vernacular *c.* 1800. Two storeys, three bays, with lower wing at the back. Hints of sophistication in droved ashlar margins and pronounced skewputts, a small annexe projecting from the r. gable. Nearby farm offices by *William Christie*, 1870.

MAINS OF RANNIESTON, 7 km. SW. Handsome vernacular classical, described as 'entirely new' in 1800, but with some curious features for that date. Entrance is from the rear, through the projecting stair bay, and at mezzanine level; the house is partly sunk below ground. Its principal elevation – originally without any entrance – faces S onto the gardens: three storeys, three bays broad, with its centre windows paired: the ground-floor windows are relatively small and checked for shutters, the first-floor and second-floor windows are much taller. Construction is in granite ashlar, cherry-cocked, under a tall hipped roof with coped chimneystacks; the French doorway in the S front and the attic dormers are modern interventions. The interior is generally simple but the stair has distinctive details. Rannieston bears a familial resemblance to the Roman Catholic seminary of 1798 at Auquhorthies (1798, S).

AUCHMACOY HOUSE. *See* p. 70.

0020 KIRKTON OF SLAINS

PARISH CHURCH. Built 1806–7. A simple rectangular preaching-box in coursed granite rubble formerly harled, the four windows in its S flank and the W-end fanlit doorway set in ashlar surrounds, and the C18 bellcote probably from St Ternan's church (built *c.* 1599) previously on the site. Session house and vestry perhaps date from 1882 when the church was 'thoroughly repaired and renovated'. The E gable's doorway was blocked *c.* 1927–30 when *George Bennett Mitchell & Son* reorientated the interior: they removed the N and E galleries, opened two windows in the N flank, and transferred the pulpit and choir from the centre of the S wall to the E end. Octagonal PULPIT's sounding-board is suspended from the ceiling. – FONT in polished grey granite on a red granite column, *c.* 1875. – STAINED GLASS. In the former E gallery window, the Ascension, brilliantly coloured late Pre-Raphaelitism of 1931–2 by *A.N.M. Lundie* of *The Abbey Studio*, Glasgow; the Virgin, Child and St John the Baptist, 1938, on the S side.

ERROL AISLE, near the church's S flank, possibly the former St Ternan's Church, used for interments 1585–1758; N wall probably 1806. – MONUMENT (S extension). Cuthbert Graham †1987, journalist, historian and poet. His epitaph – 'This is my land, the land that begat me, these windy places are surely my own' – is a favourite quotation from Sir Alexander Gray.

Former PARISH MANSE (Slains House) by *William Smith* (of *J. & W. Smith*), *c.* 1877. Two storeys, three windows wide, centre bay slightly projected with large porch and steeply raked gablet; harled with margins. Porch with Tudor doorway and angles chamfered, its parapet with ball-finials. Ground-floor windows formerly tripartite. COURTYARD STEADING (now separate residence), its rubble-built circular doocot with reinstated conical roof and outer walls perhaps mid-C18, the single-storey ranges on the S and W early C19 in squared rubble. Late C19 former gig-house on E side; duck-ramp on N leading to a stream.

COLLIESTON, 250 m. S, is a former fishing village. Its cottages are arranged around the shore, in ledges within the bay and along the main street which climbs sharply with the ridge from N to S, overlooking a natural harbour enclosed by a PIER by *Alexander Melville, C.E.*, of 1894: a splendid aspect for so small a place. The former MARINE HOTEL (now flats) was built by *D. & J.R. McMillan*, 1898. Simplest Baronial, with gabled bay off-centre to the l. between wings of different lengths, a modest shouldered doorway, and first-floor windows crowned with dormer gablets; spired corner tower near to the cliff.

Coastguard Station (Cluny Cottages). Originally built for customs officers in the 1830s. Two-storey block at one end comprised the main living quarters, with workshops in a long single-storey range. Separate rocket-house nearby.

Old Slains Castle, 1.5 km. NE on the coast. Corner fragment of a massive tower house built by the Hays in the early C14. Four storeys, its stone walls approximately 2 m. thick with mural chambers; originally defended by a ditch and barmkin. After the 9th Earl of Erroll rebelled it was blown up by James VI in 1594. Half-hiding behind it, a contrastingly modern A-framed house, faced in timber with roof swept down to the ground: by *Stanley Ross-Smith*, mid 1960s.

KNOCKHALL CASTLE *see* NEWBURGH

LEASK 0030

St Fidamnan (or St Adamnan). Reputed parish church of Forvie before its union with Slains in 1573. Probably C15, roofless rubble-built rectangle with entrance in S wall, mostly ruined. E gable relatively complete with pointed-arch window, its tracery long gone. Remains of a piscina (?). Stump of W gable with window-sill surviving.

House of Leask. By *Archibald Simpson*, 1825–7, for Gen. William Cumming Skene Gordon. Italianate. Entrance front two-storey, five windows wide in coursed squared granite rubble, simply but neatly detailed and of beautiful proportions. Central doorway flanked by very tall ground-floor windows, their apron panels resting directly on the base-plinth, first-floor windows much smaller. Canted corners, wall-head band course and low hipped roof with overhanging eaves. Very deep flanks, W with a bow, E blind with lower two-storey rubble-built service wing. Burnt 1927, the main block restored *c.* 1987–2002. The exposed masonry (formerly harled), unpainted woodwork and reflective glass (which adopts correct lying-pane proportions) result in a surprisingly contemporary appearance.* – Doocot. Mid C18. Unusual of its kind. Square-plan, tall in snecked squared pink rubble, with segment-headed opening, and ledge with flight-holes just beneath the wall-head; pyramid roof with ball finial. Reportedly transferred from Pitlurg (Moray q.v.), *c.* 1981.

*Although the original drawings were lost, the owners recreated the plan on the basis of what little had survived of the interior, and through comparison with Simpson's similar house at Linton (S).

LONGHAVEN HOUSE *see* CRUDEN BAY

0040

LONGSIDE

During the late C18 the Kilgour family established a successful woollen mill at Auchlee close to Kirkton of Longside. In response to this James Ferguson of Pitfour (q.v.) set aside 40 hectares on the hill-slopes surrounding the early C17 church, and *c.* 1801 he engaged the services of *William Whyte*, land surveyor of Bridgend, who laid out a new village on Picturesque principles, the feus being offered on fifty-seven-year leases.

CHURCHES AND PUBLIC BUILDINGS

OLD PARISH CHURCH, Inn Brae. Built 1619–20. Rectangular plan, granite rubble, roofless from late C19, now a burial enclosure. W doorway chamfered with round-headed arch in soft red sandstone badly eroded, iron hinge-pins still evident. Two pointed-arch lights for gallery or loft now infilled. Fine sandstone bellcote with uprights moulded as very slim clustered colonnettes, inscribed frieze, dentilated cornice, and gableted top; displays Sibbald arms and initials A.S. for Abraham Sibbald, minister at Old Deer who provided much of the funding, as well as Bruce family arms, initials G.B., and 'Mr Meason', who was presumably the first preacher. S flank with archway now closed by large wall monument (its inscription lost), irregular fenestration, some windows open with chamfered edges and hinge-pins for shutters, others blocked. Moulded skewputts, one initialled G.B. E.M., referring to a marriage of the Keiths Marischal with the Cheynes, the other with Keith and Cheyne arms, dated 1620. Near the wall-head, an inscription panel 'Heare My Pryer O God PS.' N flank blind, two blocked doorways and one blocked window. E gable with chamfered trabeated entrance and two blocked windows above (one perhaps originally a doorway to a loft). Windows possibly altered for Lady Kinmundy's loft *c.* 1697, certainly for Laird of Faichfield's loft *c.* 1703, but all interior now lost. Next to the W door a Neoclassical wall monument designed by *William Davidson* in memory of Lt Vincent Connell Bruce, †1916. On the S flank a double-arch panel monument with initials W.A.R., date 1726, and full complement of *memento mori*: skull, coffin, hourglass, grave-digger's tools and crossbones. – LYCHGATE, dated 1705 but probably earlier, perhaps *c.* 1620 – a rare example in Scotland. A moulded, barrel-vaulted arch once gabled or pedimented, now with surmounting ball finial and sundial. Recesses within the vault on either side. Concave wing-walls and slim cornice.

PARISH MANSE, Glebefield. Built 1825. Two-storey three bays, harled with margins, doorway with elegant fanlight, gabled roof.

PARISH CHURCH, beside the old Church. By *John Smith I*, 1835–6, superseding the C17 church which stands parallel to the S (*see* above). Tall gable-fronted structure with four-bay flanks, attractively built in local gold and grey granite, coursed squared and pinned. W gable stepped forward at centre suggesting a nave-and-aisles design, round-arched doorway and windows retaining original woodwork, some Tudor details for dignity. The doorway is set in a shallow rectangular projection with blind parapet, its transom-light has patterned glass. Three long slim stepped lights, astragalled sash-and-case, beneath a hoodmould at gallery level, with larger windows each side lighting the stairs. Clock face also with hoodmould beneath bellcote and spike finial. E gable stepped out at centre with two tall windows. Vestry added 1889. U-plan gallery with panelled fronts on Doric columns. – COMMUNION TABLE. 1935, panelled and buttressed with Gothick detailing, foliate decoration around a bolection-moulded top. Octagonal FONT, 1955. – Fine BRASS PLAQUE to George Falconer Henderson, †1918, son of the minister; Art Nouveau, the angels particularly appropriate for an airman. Vestibule formed *c.* 1980.

WAR MEMORIAL. By *William Kelly* (of *Kelly & Nicol*), 1922. A tall granite pedestal with canted, slightly tapered corners supporting a die-block and octagonally shafted floriate cross. – OBELISK, erected 1869, for Jamie Fleeman, †1778, the Laird of Udny's fool (*see* Knockhall Castle, p. 311). Nearby, a memorial to the Episcopalian minister John Skinner, †1807, author of *The Ecclesiastical History of Scotland* and poet in Scots and Latin verse: a white marble slab framed by pilasters and entablature, crowned with an urn finial. In the churchyard's E wall, a roughly built aedicule or recess sheltering a coat of arms.

ST JOHN (Episcopal), on the A950 immediately ESE of Longside. Built 1853–4 to plans drafted in 1847 by *William Hay*. E.E., ecclesiologically correct and powerfully composed: the variety of wall-heights and roof-pitches and the lively detailing endow the design with real energy. A four-bay nave with broad aisles which passing through the flying buttresses of the crossing tower form token transepts. The tower itself rises strong and square through three stages to a saddleback roof with crow-stepped gables 25 m. above the ground; shorter stair-turret, a square broached to an octagonal with a stone spirelet. Single-bay chancel with E window of three stepped lancets, Celtic cross finial over the apex. Choir vestry (N) added *c.* 1896. Nave arcades with square piers, stop-chamfered, with simple pointed arches all in grey granite. Plastered walls above, once finely decorated. Compartmented polygonal ceilings in the tower and chancel. – PULPIT. Octagonal, in dark stained wood with open arcaded sides, raised on a sturdy granite column against the chancel-arch. – HIGH ALTAR, REREDOS and PISCINA all by *Hay*, sculpted by *Walker, Emley & Beall* of the *Neville Marble Works*, Gateshead, 1875. The altar is a slab of white Sicilian marble resting on three columns with shafts of red

Peterhead granite, their moulded bases and exuberant foliate capitals in alabaster. Superb reredos, chiefly of pure white Caen stone, but the individual bays are articulated by squat colonnettes of green Genoese marble, carrying trefoil arches within gablets. Within the bays, relief sculptures of the Annunciation to the Shepherds, the Adoration of the Magi, the Crucifixion, Resurrection and Ascension. Little aedicules above with crocketed spirelets containing the Evangelists, kneeling angels at each far end. – Piscina with pointed arch again in Caen stone. – Trefoil AUMBRY, plain triple SEDILIA. – TILES (chancel floor) by *Minton*. – CHOIR STALLS. 1930s. – EAGLE LECTERN, 1909. – FONT. Simple, but with a smart timber canopy surmounted by a cross finial. – SIDE ALTAR (nave). Possibly brought from St Fergus Chapel after it closed in 1960. – ORGAN. Originally built by *William Hill* of London, 1872. – MODEL of the church, *c.* 1853. – PROPELLER. Over the choir vestry doorway. A relic of H.M. Airship C25 from Lenabo Air-station, shot down in 1918.

STAINED GLASS. E windows by *Chance* of Birmingham, 1853–4: Crucifixion; Adoration, Our Lord Baptized in the Jordan, Our Lord Preaching, and the Garden of Gethsemane. Chancel S, St John, also by *Chance*. – Chancel N, St Andrew by *Ward & Hughes*, later C19. N window with paired lights and roundel all dated 1853 represents further scenes from Our Lord's Ministry including the Wedding at Cana. – In the N aisle, two more windows by *Chance* – the Good Samaritan, early C20, then paired lights 'Suffer the Little Children to Come unto Me' and 'Thy Kingdom Come, Thy Will be Done'. Behind the organ, St Margaret of Scotland by *J. Hamilton* 1935; at the W end, 'Though He Slay Me Yet Will I Trust in Him' – Job by *T. F. Curtis, Ward & Hughes*, *c.* 1895–8. – In the S aisle, St John by *John Aiken*, 1951; then, Joshua by *Ward & Hughes* dated 1897, in memory of Lawrence Cheves, who had been killed in Rhodesia a year earlier – an interesting contrast with the St George window at Fyvie Parish Church (q.v.), and probably also a portrait. Next again, paired lights with further scenes from Our Lord's Ministry, by *Hughes* and dated 1870 or 1876.

Former PARSONAGE, *c.* 1855, presumably by *Hay*, altered 1897. Granite, two-storey, three windows wide, recessed entrance flanked by canted bays rising into gabled roof. – CHURCH HALL, 1888. Long single-storey, four bays in rock-faced gold and grey granite with entrance doors set back at each far end. Widely spaced paired-light windows break through overhanging eaves into dormer gablets under a relatively tall roof; small ventilator with spirelet. Improvements 1911 including a balcony.

Former INFANTS' SCHOOL, 200 m. SE of the parish church. *c.* 1880, with short Germanic tower and slated spire in the angle of its L-plan (rather like that of North School, Peterhead, by *Clyne* (q.v.)). Relatively tall roof with oversailing bracketed eaves, tall chimneystack.

PRIMARY SCHOOL, Glebefield. Built 2005 by *M.R.T. Architects* and the *Holmes Partnership*, with *Ramsay & Chalmers* consulting engineers, for Robertson Capital Projects.

DESCRIPTION

The early growth of Longside was spurred by the opening of the first stretch of turnpike between Peterhead and Banff (qq.v.) in 1807 which ran through MAIN STREET. The TOLL HOUSE survives at the W end, an unusual two-storey vernacular building with a central drum stair-tower, built in golden granite rubble with a tall gabled roof. More characteristically Late Georgian are the former BRUCE ARMS (or Commercial Hotel, now a private house) on the junction with Inn Brae, two storeys, three bays with its porch, lying-pane glazing and canted dormers all later, and on the opposite side of the junction, FERNIELEA, another two-storey three-bay house of the early C19, its door and windows in simple surrounds.

The closure of a mill at Auchlee in 1828 caused the village's development to falter, although several houses at this end of Main Street are later. HADDO COTTAGE is particularly smart, a two-storey three-bay Late Georgian survival in granite with tripartite doorpiece, mid-C19, while the former NORTH OF SCOTLAND BANK is later still, *c.* 1900.

The railway arrived on the far side of the Ugie in 1862. This encouraged the development of STATION TERRACE on a ridge of ground with a fine S aspect overlooking the Haugh.* The villas are all different, detached or in pairs, and set back from the road in their gardens. UGIELEA, *c.* 1875–80, is among the most distinctive – two-storey, its entrance recessed between canted bays rising into bellcast spirelets. Similar in date but very different in style, GOWANLEA and THE ELMS are semi-detached, single-storey and attic, with entrances paired together beneath a veranda; the attic rooms are lit by half-timbered dormers in the lower pitches of the gambrel roof. Towards the E end where the road swings round sharply, ROBINHILL is two-storey on a butterfly plan with central porch. Slightly further on, AIRLIE LODGE, *c.* 1914, is two-storey with its entrance between canted bays to each side; the entrance itself is nicely detailed, with a balcony guarded by an intricate low railing.

CAIRNGALL HOUSE, 0.9 km. E. Perhaps of *c.* 1803, dating from the sale of the estate by Duncan Forbes to John Hutchison, but much altered since. Two-storey W front, five windows wide, very simple in appearance, grey-harled with long-and-short quoins under a hipped roof. The S front, remodelled *c.* 1900, is far richer, a four-bay centre-and-ends composition built in golden granite with silver dressed work, the windows

*Although by this date the Fergusons of Pitfour had sold the village of Longside to the Bruces, they still owned the land on this side of the river.

mainly tripartite; a slim cornice supports the wall-head parapet, the roof is punctuated by chimneystacks. Recent porch formed across the recessed centre in different masonry and with a different glazing pattern. – DOOCOT. 1811. – LODGE. Hip-roofed with tall end stacks.

INVERQUHOMERY, 2 km. SW. Occupied by the Bruce family in the C18. Purchased by James Bruce, merchant and shipowner in Peterhead, from George Ferguson of Pitfour (q.v.) *c.* 1825–7. DOOCOTS. Probably early C19, a rare group of three (cf. the game larders at Montcoffer House, p. 266). Largest in the centre is flanked by smaller siblings in a charming symmetrical grouping. They are circular, in pinned ashlar, with eaves courses supporting conical roofs, and crowned by spired cupolae with flight-holes. The centre doocot's cupola with Gothick finials is later. – Large courtyard STEADING (early C19, perhaps remodelled for James Bruce Jun. *c.* 1862) very irregular in pinned squared golden granite, but nevertheless of some distinction. Principal front facing N is balanced about a rustic pedimented centre, the bays on the r. are single-storey with small square loft openings above, but those on the l. are two-storey as a result of a fall in the ground. FARMHOUSE much altered – two-storey three bays, gable-roofed, but with its r. bay built out in a half-octagonal form, a crowstepped porch over the entrance, and canted bay l. at ground floor.

BRIDGE OF RORA, 2 km. N over the North Ugie Water. Rebuilt and widened 1860, but incorporating much older fabric, perhaps constructed after the late C17 Acts for improvement of roads. In its present state, two broad spans with central cutwater, and two smaller relieving arches, built in squared rubble with low parapets. The SE arches constitute what remains of the original bridge.

MILLBANK HOUSE, 250 m. SE of the bridge. Named after the mill at Auchlee which closed in 1828 and of which no trace remains; presumably the manager's house. Two-storey three-bay main block, white-harled, tall gabled roof with coped chimneystacks. Simple but distinctive with deeply recessed door and very slim margins. Low two-storey rear wing (perhaps earlier in date) forms an L-plan.

MILL OF RORA, 450 m. N of the bridge. Early C19. Two-storey three-bay mill house in coursed squared granite, gabled roof with coped end stacks. Tripartite doorway with slim wooden pilasters rising to elegant fanlight. Picturesque setting behind curved rubble walls of small front garden. Single-storey rear wing with attic dormers. Former grain mill built into steeply sloping ground in pinned rubble masonry, its kiln ventilator and water wheel lost.

LONG CAIRN, Cairn Catto, 5 km. SE. This cairn is among the few upstanding earlier Neolithic sites in Aberdeenshire. It consists of a large trapezoidal cairn of stones almost 50 m. long. It tapers from 22 m. wide at the SE end to only 7 m. wide at the NW and is around 1.8 m. high. The cairn is likely to overlie wooden structures and mortuary deposits, as has been found at other excavated examples. Two stone axes were found at the cairn in the C19. (GN)

LONMAY

0050

A straggle of houses with churches, school and hall all at some distance.

PARISH CHURCH, 2.3 km. NE. T-plan preaching-box with N aisle, built 1787. W gable in coursed squared granite with square-headed doorway and gallery window, dated at the simply moulded skewputts. Just beneath the gable apex, a recessed panel with a blind field; then a plinth with a deep cornice supporting a boldly detailed birdcage bellcote, its columns banded, crowned with a ball finial. Four-bay S flank also in coursed granite, all windows with shutter-pins. Present glazing is Victorian, each window with paired segment-headed lights. N flank with aisle lit by very large window, harled with margins; two low outshots in the re-entrant angles. E gable also harled, with square-headed doorway, gallery window, skewputts and ball finial; another small annexe added later. Interior partly refurbished by *George Marr* in 1872. – Fine PULPIT of 1787 in the centre of its S wall, raised on a platform, with a tall back and ogee-domed sounding-board. The back is carved with an arched panel framed between taller pilasters, its later carved clock face made by *Bulova* of Canada; the heavy sounding-board elegantly moulded with a blind fretwork frieze. – U-plan GALLERY supported on a lower tier of Doric columns; the upper tier rises to support the ceiling cove directly on the N side, or on semi-elliptical arcades on the E and W, with nicely detailed brackets of 1872 at the ends.

WAR MEMORIAL, in front of the church, signed by *William Boddie*, 1920. An adaptation of Blomfield's Cross of Sacrifice. – CAIRNESS ENCLOSURE. Low channelled walls with iron gates and railings, perhaps by *James Playfair*, containing inside a table tomb commemorating Charles Gordon †1796 who built Cairness House (q.v.), his wife Christina Forbes who oversaw its furnishing and decoration, and their children.

OLD CHURCHYARD, 200 m. NNE of parish church. It contains part of the OLD PARISH CHURCH, with inscription dated 1607, reused as the burial vault of William Abernethy of Crimonmogate, †1744. Large pedimented CRUDEN MONUMENT incorporates three memorial slabs, that on the l. dated 1733 being notably fine – splendid fluted pilasters with ornate capitals supporting a round-arched top with trumpeting cherubim sounding the Day of Judgment and resurrection of the souls, a cartouche, skull and winged hourglasses. C18 GATEPIERS in ashlar masonry with moulded cornices and surmounting ball finials, each inset with a heraldic panel.

Former ST COLUMBA (Episcopal), 2.1 km. NE of the village centre. Now in domestic use. Originally built 1797, substantially remodelled by *James Matthews* 1862. E.E. Nave four bays, lit by tall slim cusp-headed windows, long tall chancel with stepped triple light at E end. Transeptal N organ chamber with gableted bellcote. Small W porch (now garage).* Sparkling white harl with granite dressings, boldly moulded skewputts, graded slate roofs. Reglazed, the dormers and conservatory hidden on the S side. Chancel has a hammerbeam roof. – LYCHGATE with scissor roof trusses.

KNOWSIE HOUSE, 0.4 km. SW. Derelict Baronial villa, by *William Reid*, *c.* 1902 for William Maconnachie of Maconnachie Bros, Fraserburgh.

LONMAY HOUSE, 4 km. NE at Quarryhill. Begun *c.* 1720 by *William Adam* for James Fraser, a younger son of Lord Saltoun who had bought the estate in 1718. It is illustrated in *Vitruvius Scoticus* (pl. 95). Fraser died in 1729 and his widow sold it to William Moir of Whitehill in 1731. Only the pavilion wings were built, one of which remains. Two-storey four bays, of whitewashed rubble masonry with windows in red sandstone margins, tall hipped roof with central chimneystack. The first-floor windows have been lengthened: they were originally small and square. Modern glazing. Alterations at rear, no original features inside.

RECUMBENT STONE CIRCLE, Berrybrae, 1.5 km. SSE. A small circle of which only five stones remain. The stones are set in an oval bank enclosing a central area that may once have had a cairn within. Excavation in the 1970s found cremation burials in the centre and Beaker pottery in the oval bank. (GN)

CAIRNESS HOUSE. *See* p. 119.
CRAIGELLIE HOUSE. *See* p. 131.
CRIMONMOGATE HOUSE. *See* p. 139.

7060 MACDUFF B

Macduff began as the fishing village of Doune, in existence by 1369, and erected into a burgh of barony in 1528. Doune was purchased by William Duff, afterwards 1st Earl Fife, in 1733 but its development owes chiefly to his son James, Lord Macduff, who moved into Duff House (*see* p. 94) in 1759. The harbour's construction (*see* below) was 'well advanced' when he became 2nd Earl in 1763 and offered feus to 'artificers, traders and manufacturers'; by 1770 Doune was a chalybeate spa, its simple well-house still surviving in Tarlair Road. Doune became Macduff in 1781 when the earl wrote good-humouredly to his factor, William Rose, 'if any change is to be made it ought to be Macduff, for

*The organ is now at St Mary's Episcopal Church, Aberdeen.

Macduff, drawn by W. H. Bartlett.
Engraving, 1842

when I held that title, I worked more on the harbour with my own hands than ever you did in your whole life'.*

It proved unexpectedly difficult to attract tradesmen or establish industries and several ventures promoted by the earl collapsed, yet Macduff prospered as a fishing port through his support and that of his successors, who doubtless always intended that their burgh should challenge Banff (q.v.) with its inconvenient harbour facing across the Deveron where it meets the Moray Firth. Development was encouraged by Banff Bridge (*see* p. 86) between the towns in 1779, and turnpikes shortly after 1800; during the mid C19 High Street and Fife Street were formed on rising ground above the shore, the Banff, Macduff & Turriff Railway arriving in 1860. In the later C19 Macduff had a clubhouse, a riposte to Banff's Town & County Club (*see* p. 88).

Between the Wars Macduff's attractions as a holiday resort were enhanced by the Royal Tarlair Golf Club (1926) and Tarlair Open-Air Swimming Pool (1929–31, *see* Public Buildings), and it remained popular especially among Glaswegians in the days before cheap air travel. However, the perennial difficulty of attracting industries other than fishing and shipbuilding led to a loss of skilled workers which started after the First World War and reached its nadir during the Depression, being gradually reversed by social house-building which continued after the Second World War. The opening of Macduff Distilleries in 1961 was a major boost, but the earls' and later the town council's continuous investment in the harbour has been vital to the town's

*Rose was the earl's right-hand man for many years and became the first provost when the town was erected a burgh of barony in 1783, although he and the earl fell to arguing afterwards.

survival. Today the harbour is home to Macduff Shipyards, the last surviving in the north-east, and the only ones in Britain still constructing large trawlers both in steel and in timber.

CHURCHES

Former CONGREGATIONAL CHAPEL, Duff Street. By *T. Farquharson* of Macduff, dated 1881. Big simple Gothic gable front in coursed whinstone, pale golden freestone dressings. Splayed doorway and paired gallery lancets beneath an over-sailing arch which springs from buttresses, expressing the church's division into nave and aisles. SE flank to High Street lit by four tall windows, round-arched with horseshoe voussoirs and key-blocks, and mullioned-and-transomed glazing, the Italianate treatment at odds with the gable front; simply moulded eaves course and steeply pitched roof.

Former GARDNER MEMORIAL CHURCH, Duff Street. By *A. Marshall Mackenzie* (of *Matthews & Mackenzie*) 1897; dated 1899. Built as a Free Church. Big simple C15 Scots-Gothic gable front in coursed rubble with golden ashlar dressings, five-light window with basket tracery of the Aberdeen Greyfriars type. Four-stage corner tower rising with a pronounced batter, its deeply recessed entrance with mouldings dying into splays, the uppermost stage with Y-traceried windows beneath a wall-head parapet and gargoyles: its slated spire rises to a weather-vane. Five-bay flank with porch to Clergy Street and polygonal organ chamber at E end. Converted into Arts Centre by *Meldrum & Mantell*, 1992.

MACDUFF PARISH CHURCH, Church Street, standing on the Hill of Doune. By *James Matthews* 1865–7, 'practically rebuilt' from a chapel of ease of 1805. Big rectangular box, harled in white, with Franco-Italianate bell-tower centred on its seaward flank. Tower of three stages: first with slight batter and side porch tucked into its angle, second with angle pilasters and entablature, third stage an ashlar belfry with coupled pilasters framing louvred openings on each side; bold bracket cornice and square leaded dome with cupola and clock faces. Simple Italianate windows, each two lights with circled tracery in timber, and parabolic voussoirs, a motif more usually associated with James Souttar; they are replicated in the later porch but not the session hall. Simple interior, dark timber fittings contrasting against pale cream walls. – PULPIT. 1867 with blind arcaded front. Reduced in size, probably when the ORGAN (1905 by *E.H. Lawton* of Aberdeen) was installed behind it. – FONT. 1897. Alabaster basin on an octagonal stand. – COMMUNION TABLE. Also 1897, distinctly architectonic with dwarf arcading under a heavy ovolo frieze. – PEWS are mostly still in place on the nave floor and gallery. – STAINED GLASS. Two complex and colourful windows flanking the organ by the *City Glass Window Co.* of Glasgow, erected 1922: (l.) 'Suffer the Little Children to Come unto Me', (r.) 'Be Thou Faithful unto Death and I Will Give Thee a Crown of

Life,' the latter a poignant First World War memorial. – In the vestibule, Elizabeth Mantell windows by *Jennifer-Jayne Bayliss*, 2000.

The CHURCHYARD is particularly notable for two monuments commemorating the extended family of Dr Walford Bodie, a popular magician in the early C20, the larger with a mourning angel beneath a cross; there are also sculptural portraits, one a bas-relief and one a bust, of Mystic Marie (†1906) and La Belle Electra (†1919). In the centre of the churchyard, the headstone of Rev. Andrew Wilson (†1881) with his portrait.

Near the churchyard, an ANCHOR: French, mid-C18, salvaged by fishermen following François Thurot's attempted invasion of Banff (q.v.) in 1757. Placed here in 1972. – CROSS. Erected 1783, incorporating a stone from the old Macduff Cross in Fife. Inset, a two-sided panel with bas-reliefs of a medieval knight on horseback to represent the Duffs.

MYRUS CEMETERY on B9026 at the S edge of town, opened 1920. Neoclassical entrance gateway with decorative wrought-iron gates set between banded masonry gatepiers with torchères.

PUBLIC BUILDINGS

BODIE FOUNTAIN, Duff Street, 1910. With good bas-relief portrait of Miss Jeannie Bodie, daughter of Walford Bodie (*see* churchyard, above).

LIBRARY, High Street. Opened 1981; the cast-iron royal arms transferred from the former soup kitchen behind the Gardner Memorial Church are by *Macfarlane & Co.* of Glasgow, 1887.

MACDUFF ARTS CENTRE. *See* former Gardner Memorial Church, above.

MACDUFF MARINE AQUARIUM, High Shore. *See* Description.

MASONIC LODGE ST JAMES (No. 653), Gellymill Street. Single storey, five bays, tall windows with Tudor hoodmoulds, dated 1914 over entrance; converted from mid-C19 house with funding from Dr Walford Bodie.

Former MURRAY'S INSTITUTION, Market Street. Built 1879, originally founded for the education of poor children by John Murray in 1848–9. Two-storey five-bay block with slightly raised pedimented centre; ground floor now concealed behind sunrooms as the Knowes Hotel.

Former POLICE STATION, Gellymill Street. One of several in Banffshire designed by *F. D. Robertson* of Keith, 1893. Simple two-storey five-bay building with central semi-elliptical pend framed by 'minaret' buttresses, paired segmental windows at ground floor, paired first-floor windows rising into three broad dormer gablets.

Former BOARD SCHOOL, Shand Street. 1872, a quick response to the Education (Scotland) Act passed that year. Plain repetitive single-storey six-gabled frontage with triplet windows. Now domestic.

125 TARLAIR SWIMMING POOL, Tarlair Road. By *John C. Miller*, Burgh Surveyor, 1929–31. Set in a dramatic situation within a bay on the Moray Firth, an open-air swimming pool of a type which became popular during the interwar years; semi-derelict now, yet easy to imagine as it once was, a place of bracing good cheer for the masses. Two large basins – an inner boating pool and outer swimming pool – enclosed by walkways, the boating pool with small rock-pool and paddling pool closest to the Art Deco tea pavilion under the cliffs, and the swimming pool flanked by changing rooms to one side. Now a rare survivor, and the closest to its original condition in Scotland: it is the only example of a tidal pool left, being completely submerged at high tide.

TOWN HALL, Shore Street. Competition win by *Pirie & Clyne*, dated 1884, opened 1885. A curiously detailed confection. Tall two-storey and attic three-bay frontage, its slightly advanced centre rising into a clock stage framed by turrets with stone spirelets, and its gablet carved with a medieval knight on horseback to represent the Duffs. Round-arched doorway beneath a proto-Art Nouveau horseshoe hoodmould; banded pilaster-buttresses between the ground-floor windows supporting the corbelling of bulbous first-floor oriels, gableted attic dormers with Thomsonesque Graeco-Egyptian details set into the steeply pitched roof. All built in coursed hammer-dressed whinstone with smooth and rock-faced dressings in golden freestone. Thomsonesque T-plan glazing.

WAR MEMORIAL, Canker's Knowe. 1921–2. By *John Fowlie* (of *Henderson & Fowlie*), built by *Alexander Brown* and *Magnus Johnstone*, masons in Macduff. An octagonal tower 5.5 m. in diameter and 21 m. high, constructed in Kemnay granite, perhaps influenced by the Prop of Ythsie (*see* Tarves), its scale justified as a landmark to mariners. Raised on a stepped plinth, its rock-faced classical entrance stage has a deeply recessed square-headed doorway and panels commemorating the Fallen, with blind key-blocked roundels above; mutuled cornice, then the long rough ashlar shaft with small windows lighting the stair, a deeply shadowed bracket cornice and crenellated parapet with blind crosslets. Its siting seems significant, clearly visible from Banff, and perfectly aligned behind Banff's own memorial at the foot of Seafield Street (*see* p. 85).

HARBOUR

4 From the outset one of the safest refuges on the Moray Firth, the harbour's development was key to the Duffs' ambitions for their town. The original harbour, of which the WEST BASIN survives, was initiated by the 1st Earl Fife and Lord Macduff and completed by 1770. The CENTRAL BASIN comprises the original East Basin, constructed by the 1st Earl and his son, and the North Basin which began as a breakwater constructed by the 4th Earl to designs of *Thomas Telford c.* 1821. This breakwater was subsequently enclosed for the 5th Earl by

D. & T. Stevenson in 1876–7, but further investment was beyond the Duffs' resources. In 1898 the 1st Duke sold the harbour to the town for a nominal sum to enable state grants and loans for its improvement. This led to the harbour being deepened by *James Barron, C.E.* in 1902–3, and the LIGHTHOUSE and LIGHTHOUSE PIER also by *Barron* being built a few years later. The PRINCESS ROYAL BASIN was begun just before the First World War, work proceeding slowly under *Archibald Henderson, C.E.* until completion in 1920.*

Major foreshore repairs and strengthening took place in 1930, and the West Pier was repaired in mass concrete after storm damage in 1932; the present retaining wall and breakwater in reinforced concrete dates from 1938. The Princess Royal Basin was deepened and the jetty separating it from the North Basin was removed during works of 1949–52, when the Shore Street quay was extended. Further improvements were carried out following recommendations by *C. R. Wallace*, engineer-in-charge of fishing harbours at the Department of Agriculture & Fisheries for Scotland. In consequence the quay separating the old East and North Basins was removed to form the present Central Basin, all the works being carried out by *Archibald Henderson & Partners* under the direction of his sons *Ian and Gordon Henderson* in 1965, the new FISHMARKET opening in 1966.

The SHIP LIFT by *M. G. Bennett* of Rotherham (contractor *R. J. MacLeod*), completed in 2009, can accommodate vessels up to 25 m. length, 10 m. beam and 350 tonnes.

DESCRIPTION

Although Macduff feels battered the bones of a good town are clearly there. Crook O'Ness Street extends into Shore Street and then Union Road as they wend along the coast with the harbour on one side and later C18 and C19 buildings on the other. Behind them, Macduff's hinterland rises up on steeply sloping ground, the parish church on Hill of Doune with its distinctive tower (*see* Churches) conspicuous as a landmark. Shore Street's most important building is its Town House: like the parish church it has a curiously weighty, intentionally rogue quality (*see* Public Buildings), its erection celebrating the high-water mark of Macduff's fortunes. But some less obvious buildings attest to the town's early history. In CROOK O'NESS STREET, No. 2 dated 1763 and No. 4 (both altered) were once good vernacular houses perhaps built by Lord Macduff to encourage further feuing near the harbour. Such houses were often richly decorated, the tradition of beautifully painted
ships extending naturally to the land. SHORE STREET makes 4

*Its original slipway designed by *Henderson* with cradle, traverser carriages and haulage machinery – replaced by the new ship lift (*see* below) – was completed in 1922. Henderson patented his design, which was subsequently used around the world.

an impression through its variety of buildings, the different construction materials and roof-lines giving a narrative to the harbourside. Further along, late C19 buildings survive rather better, their central crowstepped attic gables paying homage to earlier traditions. Just before the Town Hall (*see* above), the T-plan frontage of the former North of Scotland (later CLYDESDALE) Bank, three-storey Baronial with crowstepped gable and corner turret, is by *James Matthews* 1868.

UNION ROAD begins with the early C19 SALMON HOUSE, derelict now but once fine: built into steeply sloping ground, it comprises a tall central range with a gabled roof, and lower wings projecting forward to enclose a court. The central range contains a vaulted ice house within its substructure, the upper floor with fireplaces at each end and its rafters blackened by smoking and boiling. The houses beyond in harl or whinstone are mostly early C19, the two-storey block Nos. 7–11 with central pend particularly appealing.

The town's hinterland is laid out on a rough grid of narrow streets, often lined in quite random fashion with buildings of different periods: the earliest houses near the harbour of the late C18 and early C19, very simple in their character, then buildings of the early to mid C19 in coursed whinstone with golden freestone dressings. The strength of the streetscapes lies chiefly in the town's topography, Skene Street and Duff Street falling steeply downhill W towards the harbour, and other longer thoroughfares, Gellymill Street, Market Street and High Street, crossing them as they decline in more gently undulating fashion N towards the Moray Firth. The town is best appreciated from the cross and anchor near the parish church or from the war memorial on Canker's Knowe.

A few buildings stand out. Between Crook O'Ness and West Skene Streets is a three-storey WAREHOUSE of the mid C18. In SKENE STREET, E side, the former NORTHERN AGRICULTURAL COMPANY WAREHOUSE is by *George Coutts* of 1903, while on the W the ABERDEEN LIME COMPANY WAREHOUSE was designed in 1909.* Further up, THE MANOR HOUSE, a near-symmetrical half-timbered villa with a veranda, was built by *A. Marshall Mackenzie & Son c.* 1905–7 for the magician Dr Walford Bodie: it has a fine interior, its music room reputedly once doubling as a Masonic chamber.

In DUFF STREET besides the Congregational and Gardner Memorial churches (*see* Churches), No. 31 is later C18, a two-storey three-bay frontage with round-arched key-blocked doorway and basket-traceried fanlight; then No. 41 set back from the road is a two-storey three-bay classical villa in golden freestone with Roman Doric portico and bold refined detailing, designed by *A. & W. Reid* and built in 1851.‡ On the hilltop the former PARISH MANSE, a plain two-storey house *c.* 1805, was enlarged to L-plan in the mid C19.

*The drawings for this warehouse are unsigned.

‡The datestone has been re-cut 1841 in error.

OSBORNE TERRACE in Clergy Street is a symmetrical row of houses enlivened at ground floor by round-arched key-blocked doorways and bay windows with miniaturized crenellation, dated 1901 with its name displayed on a wall-head plaque. In CHURCH STREET, DOUNE COURT is by *G.R.M. Kennedy & Partners*, *c.* 1984–5. Although depressingly neglected, attention should be drawn to the small temple-fronted building in HIGH SHORE – dated 1837, in the style of *William Robertson*, perhaps built as a school. Close by is the town's showpiece, the MACDUFF MARINE AQUARIUM opened in 1996: a broad single-storey circular building with a recessed glazed entrance front framed between two radial façades of rock, its conical roof rising into a corona of cliff-like stonework.

GAVENWOOD (originally Corskiebank), 1.4 km. SSW. Solid, handsome whinstone villa of 1859, built for the factor of the Fife Estates, probably by *A. & W. Reid*. Entrance (S) front two storeys and three bays with centre slightly projected under a shallow gable, and the doorway deeply recessed within a round-arched pilastered and key-blocked porch. W elevation with central bipartite lights and twin canted bays at the ends, pale golden ashlar with dressings; low hipped roof with coped chimneystacks. The E elevation once overlooked formal gardens but the house is now closely ensconced by trees. Fully sunk basement.

WINDMILL, Montbletton Farm, 3.4 km. SSE. Early to mid-C19. A square base, rubble-built, slightly tapered, within a much larger steading supports the tapered windmill tower in harl; the windmill sails are lost, but the ring for securing them survives. Cf. Northfield Farm, Crovie (q.v.).

FORT, Cleaved Head. The thirteenth green of the Royal Tarlair golf club sits on a headland cut off by a series of banks and ditches that represent a later prehistoric promontory fort. (GN)

LONG MOUND, Longman Hill, 4 km. SE. Located on a prominent eminence, the monument is likely to date to the Earlier Neolithic period *c.* 3700 B.C. and is a prominent skyline feature in this area. It is around 67 m. long with a pronounced mound at the northern end and a 'tail' projecting to the SW. The mound is likely to overlie wooden structures and mortuary deposits as has been found at other excavated examples. Two urns were found in the mound in the C19; these are likely to represent use of the mound in the Bronze Age for further burials. (GN)

MARNOCH B 5050

Near a ford of the Deveron, a site of significance since early times.

St Marnoch's Old Church. Marnoch (or Marnan) reputedly established a church and was buried here in the mid C7. The surviving church gable is medieval: a benefice of Arbroath Abbey, it remained a site of pilgrimage until the C16. In the churchyard, the Meldrum Enclosure is altogether exceptional in its ambitious design, quality of carving and fine state
31 of preservation. Within a balustrade, a large Baroque aedicule of 1699 in Moray sandstone, possibly carved by *John Faid*, contains a convincing half-length portrait-bust of Bishop George Meldrum of Crombie in his sacerdotal robes in an oval cartouche recess. It has an angel in the soffit and black marble inscription scroll beneath; a heavy entablature carries a segmental pediment bearing the Meldrum arms, with putti sounding the Last Judgment and a surmounting urn. Excellent detail, notably in the surround of the cartouche which unfolds top and bottom into ghoulish faces, the carver's understanding of anatomy, architecture and abstract design all outstandingly advanced. – Chalmers Memorial, 1707, leaning against the church gable. Another aedicule containing a large inscription panel, and with a broken triangulated pediment containing heraldic arms, again well sculpted. – Innes of Murrayfold Enclosure, 1780, has a pilastered and pedimented aedicule leaning back into a taller pedimented rear wall. watchman's shelter, *c.* 1831–2. Two churchyard extensions, in 1877 and by *Charles Cosser*, architect, in 1902.

Marnoch Parish Church, Cairnhill, 0.3 km. NE of Old St Marnoch. Built *c.* 1800, though a church appears to have been first erected here during the late C18 – 'from insufficiency [it was] rebuilt within a few years'. A simple four-bay rectangle with a round-arched W door and gallery window; the reused birdcage bellcote is dated 1690 and 1880. E gable also with doorway, now blocked, and a window at gallery level. Lying-pane glazing *c.* 1845; the N vestry by *James Duncan & Son*, 1884–5, when the church was restored and reordered. The bell, cast by *Thomas Lester* of Whitechapel in 1747, is one of the earliest English bells in Scotland. Inside, panelled and stencilled U-plan gallery on marbled columns. – Platform pulpit with a canted front and cast-iron railings at the E end. Behind the pulpit, the organ by *Wadsworth & Brother*, 1913.

The church stands in a circular walled enclosure which reputedly corresponds to the circle of standing stones within which the late C18 church was built. By the mid C19 only the present two remained: the larger stone to the S, 'St Marnan's Chair', is 2.5 m. tall. The stone on the N has evidently been moved.

Former manse, NW of the old church. Built 1805. A two-storey three-bay house over a raised basement, ground floor taller than first; railed forestair to central doorway. Coursed squared sandstone rubble, cherry-cocked, with stugged ashlar dressings, gabled roof with moulded skewputts and coped chimneystacks. The entrance front was extended by one bay to the r. by *William Kelly* (of *Kelly & Nicol*) in 1919–22; he enlarged the doorway to its present tripartite, transom-lit form, and formed the ground-floor windows into two-lights. Rear wing by *A. & W. Reid*, 1867.

BRIDGE OF MARNOCH, 1 km. SSE. Probably built by *William Smith* of Montrose to carry the Huntly–Banff turnpike (now A97) across the Deveron; crudely dated 1806 at one of its termini. A large segmental arch and smaller semicircular arch springing from a cutwater pier founded on rock near one bank of the river. TOLL HOUSE on SW bank.

MILL OF KINNAIRDY BRIDGE, 1.5 km. E. Carrying a minor road over the Burn of Auchintoul. Early to mid-C19, a single semicircular arch with parapets splayed out at the ends, built in coursed red rubble with dressed voussoirs.

HOUSE OF GLENNIE, 1.7 km. WSW. Beautifully situated fishing lodge by the Deveron, built for Major N.W. Aitken of Mayen (*see* p. 701) in 1936. Late Scottish Arts and Crafts style, freely inspired by the traditions of the C17. Courtyard L-plan, its long main block two storeys and attic beneath a tall roof, with a two-storey gabled porch; the short wing returns briefly as three storeys before continuing as a single-storey and attic range. A strong and subtle composition of considerable variety with distinctive details such as the bolection-moulded doorway, broad canted bays, dormer pediments and tall slim chimneystacks.

ARDMEALLIE. *See* p. 66.
KINNAIRDY CASTLE. *See* p. 260.

MAUD 9040

Maud came into being in 1861 when, through the perseverance and financial commitment of William Dingwall-Fordyce of Brucklay (q.v.), the Formartine & Buchan Railway opened a station (now a museum) in 1861 on its main line, which reached Peterhead in 1862. The railway then chose Maud as the junction of a branch to Fraserburgh, which it completed in 1865. Maud became a centre of the meat trade with 500 cattle sold each week in three large marts at the beginning of the C20. The railway closed in the 1960s, and the last of the marts in 2001.

PARISH CHURCH. Built 1874–6 by *James Laing* of Old Deer. W end lit by stepped triple lancets with hoodmould, the gable with quatrefoil rising steeply into a bellcote. Four-bay flanks with low N porch and paired cusp-headed lights. Patterned slate roof. Twin windows and low vestry annexe at rear. – STAINED GLASS. E windows by *Pluscarden Abbey*, 'Let the Children Come to Me' and the Good Shepherd, both 1977.

Former MAUD HOSPITAL, 0.4 km. SSW. Built 1866–8 as the Buchan Combination Poorhouse, the design won in competition by *Alexander Ellis*. Closed 2008. Two-storey T-plan designed to accommodate 125 inmates, set in its own enclosed grounds. Impressively broad symmetrical entrance front, three-bay central block under a tall gable, flanking seven-bay wings with occasional wall-head gablets and three-storey towers with spired roofs at the ends. Built in squared pinned whinstone with granite dressings. Eclectic detail – centre block's entrance bay slightly protruding with round-arched Italianate triple lights on first floor, attic gable lit by mincer-plate roundel, solid square angle buttresses, and flèche over roof. Wings with regular astragalled sash-and-case windows, the wall-head gablets and end towers with small openings to ventilate the attic. – The LODGE, with central entrance framed by gabled ends, was originally two houses, one entered from the road.

MAUD SCHOOL, School Road. By *George Sutherland* of *Harper & Sutherland*, 1895–6, for the Old Deer and New Deer School Boards.* Like half of a symmetrical composition, with centrepiece and one wing only, perhaps intended to be extended later. Single-storey, eight-bay asymmetric frontage, with first, sixth and eighth bays projecting under tall gables, and windows of the intermediate bays rising into smaller gablets or gableted dormers. Built of local masonry from a railway cutting with dressings in Pitsligo granite.

Maud village was laid out by *John Davidson*, ground officer of the Clackriach & Old Maud Estate, on a triangular plan formed by Victoria Street and Deer Road to the W, Station Road at the E end and Castle Street running WNW–ESE; the tip of the triangle was reserved for a market place. On the corner of Deer Road and Station Road, the STATION HOTEL, opened in 1862 and extended *c.* 1895 with a large new dining room to accommodate additional visitors: 'Political meetings held here decide the position to be taken by the constituency of Aberdeenshire; ministers find it a convenient centre for Presbytery meetings; school teachers repair to Maud for the discussion of questions affecting them.' The hotel continued to lay out dinner places for an army of ravenous travellers long after the lines had been lifted. By the late C19 the streets were lined with some fifty houses, many of them quite well-to-do, with the best WESTPARK in its own grounds at the W end of town.

OLD BRIDGE OF MAUD, 0.5 km. NE, carrying the B9106 over the South Ugie Water. Built 1784, widened *c.* 1932–6 on the upstream side but retaining its original appearance. A broad central span with a smaller span beneath the W approach, built in squared rubble, stone parapets. Upstream cutwater, crudely incised date between arches on the downstream side.

FEDDERATE CASTLE, 3.2 km. NW. Ruined L-plan tower house, four storeys high, standing on a mound; it was once surrounded by a fosse and morass, and approached by a causeway and a drawbridge. Built in 1557 it is one of a group of castles

*Replacing the boys' school at Bank and girls' school (Mitchell Trust) at Honeyneuk.

also including Colquhonnie and Craig (S), and Gight, Knockhall, Delgatie and Towie Barclay (qq.v.) which if tradition is a guide were the work of the *Conn family* of master-masons based at Auchry.

Of Fedderate itself, only two tall fragments of the stepped E elevation now survive, although both still rise full height. The plan was partially recorded by MacGibbon and Ross. – Main block approximately 13.8 m. by 9.8 m., orientated NE–SW; the square-plan jamb at the SE was approximately 8.5 m. wide as in the Auld Wark at Huntly (S). The overall length of the long SW wall, as in most later houses of this type, was recorded as 18 m. The main block contained the cellars with the hall above, and the jamb the kitchen with the solar above for warmth, all with barrel-vaults. But the entrance arrangements were unusual: not in the re-entrant, but directly under the solar window in the long SW wall, close to the 2.5-m. diameter main stair, which as in other houses of this group was at the junction of the main block and the jamb. The construction was in pinned boulder-rubble, the walls 2 m. thick with a marked batter; at second floor they are intaken slightly as at Udny and Delgatie (qq.v.), and as at Udny the angles are rounded; evidence still remains of intramural compartments and garderobes.

Fedderate was held by the Jacobites after Killiecrankie and damaged by Government siege in 1690. Ruinous in 1733, the vaulting collapsed in 1826, and in 1840 it was reputedly blown up to loosen its masonry for reuse elsewhere: fortunately James Giles recorded its appearance before that event. Much more fell in the 1930s and it has deteriorated significantly since then.

MAINS OF FEDDERATE, 0.3 km. NW of the castle, *c.* 1830. A two-storey three-bay farmhouse with an additional single bay slightly stepped forward to create a frontage four windows wide: the wing is so similar in design and detail that it must be original or very shortly afterwards. Harled over an exposed granite base, with dressings and margins. Simple doorway fanlight, squared-off skewputts, canted dormers in gabled roof, and coped end stacks.

BRUCKLAY CASTLE. *See* p. 115.

MEMSIE *9060*

A small village on a crossroads plan, most of the houses modern.

MEMSIE HOUSE, 1.2 km. S. An attractive composition of *c.* 1760, built for a branch of the Fraser family.* Symmetrical

*The Frasers of Memsie were a cadet branch of the Frasers of Philorth, Lords Saltoun (*see* Cairnbulg Castle and Philorth House, pp. 116 and 355). They sold Memsie back to the Saltouns in the earlier C19.

two-storey main block, five windows wide, with its central entrance bay slightly projected rising through the wall-head into a third attic storey and culminating in a curvilinear gable with chimneystack. Construction is in pinned rubble with granite dressings, moulded eaves course and skewputts, the roof steeply pitched with gableted dormers and coped stacks at each end. Single-storey quadrants link to flanking pavilions so creating a forecourt – the l. pavilion which contains the laundry is single-storey under a tall hipped roof; r. pavilion containing the stables and coachhouse is single-storey with small swept attic dormers and loupin' steps, its roof hipped at one end only. Forecourt central gateway with ball-finialled gatepiers. Interior woodwork replaced *c.* 1900.

OLD BRIDGE OF MEMSIE, carrying the A981 over the Water of Philorth, with datestones of 1792 (upstream) and 1907 (downstream), when it was widened. Rubble masonry, two segmental spans with ashlar voussoirs rising from a central pier with cutwaters on both sides, low parapets with rock-faced copings.

CAIRN, 600 m. SE of crossroads. This impressive cairn of stones, 24 m. in diameter and 4.4 m. high, was excavated in the C19 and found to contain a Beaker vessel and fragments of a bronze sword. Two other cairns once stood on the same ridge. (GN)

9020 MENIE HOUSE

1 km. NE of Pettens

Neo-Jacobean country house for Col. Sir George Turner, designed by *John Smith I c.* 1836 but based on William Burn's Auchmacoy (q.v.). Entrance elevation facing NW is a balanced composition of symmetrical and asymmetrical elements, essentially four bays with the centre recessed between gable-fronted wings; there is a porch in the angle of the r. wing, while the l. wing has a pencil tower. The porch has splayed angles, its arched doorway with a stepped hoodmould, and an ogee panel with spike finials in the parapet. The principal apartments are arranged across the symmetrical SW elevation, five windows wide, its centre bay with a broad curvilinear gable advanced between octagonal buttresses with spike finials, and with a canted bay at ground floor. Construction is in golden granite and black whinstone, pinned and squared, with freestone dressings, the windows mullioned and transomed. The SE elevation, although similar in style, was reworked from a house of 1782–3: it is stepped back towards the plain NE elevation with a bowed addition of 1978.

GOLF CLUB-HOUSE by *Douglas Forrest* of *Acanthus Architects df*, *c.* 2012.

METHLICK 8030

A small village on the River Ythan, first mentioned in 1275.

ST DEAVANACH. Ruinous preaching-box, dated 1780 at its Neoclassical W bellcote, now used as a burial enclosure. The doors and windows are all round-headed and mostly key-blocked. Gables each with an entrance and a tall gallery window. S elevation with two large windows set high in the wall, flanking the pulpit which was placed centrally on that side; smaller windows beneath each far end of the former gallery. At the E end of the S elevation a forestair to the Earl of Aberdeen's family pew. – MONUMENTS. Memorial slab with winged cherub dedicated to Patrick Maitland and Jean Robertson of Little Ardo set against inside face of E gable, on the N side. The BURIAL ENCLOSURE for the Earls of Aberdeen is immediately outside the E entrance. Large Celtic CROSS for the 5th Earl (†1864); the low surrounding walls display shields with the Gordon arms in high relief at each corner.

PARISH CHURCH. Accomplished First Pointed by *Brown & Wardrop*, 1865–7. A large T-plan, its nave conventionally orientated, with a S aisle for the Earl of Aberdeen. Set back from the W gable, a tall square-plan saddleback tower linked to the aisle by the S porch. W gable with stepped triple lights and plate-tracery roundels under a hoodmould. Polygonal E end, suggesting an apsidal chancel but originally containing a gallery. Low vestry and session house on the N side, picturesquely composed and well detailed with tall wall-head chimneystack and pointed relieving arch, shouldered and roundel openings. Prayer room formed below the W gallery, 1976, the rest of the interior reorientated in 1980, forming a chancel in the E end. – The PULPIT is the original one. It stood against the N wall, facing the earl's gallery which rests on cast-iron columns and has an arcaded upper tier. – PEWS, and perhaps the BENCHES, of similar date. – Although the organ recess was a feature of the original design, the ORGAN by *Henry Willis* was only introduced in 1877. – STAINED GLASS. In the chancel only, designed and executed by *Brother Martin Farrelly* of Pluscarden Abbey, 1982, in memory of David, 4th Marquess (1908–74): the centre light is based on Holman Hunt's *The Light of the World*, his favourite painting. – MEMORIALS to John Campbell Gordon, 7th Earl (1st Marquess) and Countess Ishbel, and immediately beneath to their son George, 2nd Marquess.

Former FREE CHURCH, 0.8 km. NE. By *James Henderson*, 1847–8. A tall gabled front with a narrow central entrance bay slightly projected between stepped buttresses, and rising above the apex into a belfry. The congregation merged with Methlick Parish Church in 1933. The FREE CHURCH MANSE is just to the N on the opposite of the road.

WAR MEMORIAL, between the old and new parish churches. By *George Watt*, architect, 1921. A broad tapering cenotaph with

Neoclassical and Baroque details. Names of the Fallen crowned by segmental pediments on each side, upper stage plain with slender cross or sword motif, and crowned by a recessed cornice influenced by Lutyens' Cenotaph.

Former PARISH MANSE, Main Street, 150 m. S of the parish church. 1860–1. Another example of *J. & W. Smith*'s versatile and long-lived English parsonage design for ministers' houses (cf. Tarves). Plain Tudor, two-storey front, three bays broad, the l. bay a projecting gable with bay window at ground floor. Boldly projecting centre porch also gabled, dormerhead gablet above r. bay. Pinned rock-faced granite; all windows with mullioned and transomed glazing.

BEATON PUBLIC HALL, Main Street. By *James Cobban*, 1908–9, the gift of James Beaton of Middlethird. A simple late Baronial front in pale granite, two storeys and four bays, with the crow-stepped entrance bay slightly offset to the r., and a low crenellated square tower projecting boldly on the l. Windows tall but relatively narrow, with shouldered lintels.

Former METHLICK INSTITUTE, Main Street. Built by the 7th Earl of Aberdeen and Countess Ishbel in 1880. Engagingly old-fashioned for its date, in the 'cottage style' of *c.* 1850. Single-storey and attic five-bay front, with broad centre and projecting end bays under tall spike-finialled gables, broad eaves on simple brackets. Harled and whitewashed, lined out in black at the windows and angle margins. Later the Ythanview Temperance Hotel.

Former NORTH OF SCOTLAND BANK, Main Street. By *James Matthews*, 1875. Designed as if it were a double villa, two-storey with paired central doorways under a canopy for the bank itself and the agent's house, between canted and projecting end bays.

IVY COTTAGE. Former residence for the mistress of the girls' school, by *William Clarke c.* 1876. Identical to that at Tarves (q.v.). Two-storey three-bay frontage, with centre slightly projected under a chimney gable; doorpiece with console-cornice, paired ground-floor windows, and first-floor windows breaking up into gableted dormerheads. Harled masonry with exposed ashlar margins, the end gables slightly raised with tall chimney-stacks diagonally shafted. Purchased by the 7th Earl of Aberdeen when the boys' and girls' schools amalgamated, re-opened as a training home for girls in 1884.

METHLICK BRIDGE over the River Ythan, 350 m. N of the parish church. By *J. & W. Smith*, 1844. The modesty and gracefulness of the arched central cast-iron span, 12 m. wide, with simple lattice guardrails all painted white, is in perfect harmony with the rural surroundings. The cutwater piers, floodwater spans and curved approaches are in squared granite. Sensitively widened in 2003, the six original under-arches which supported the deck being supplemented by four new arches in steel.

TANGLANDFORD BRIDGE, 3.5 km. ESE, over the Ythan. Unusual two-span cast-iron girder bridge of 1864 by *James*

Abernethy & Co. of Aberdeen supported by pair of cross-braced Roman Doric columns rising from the riverbed. Widened and re-surfaced 2005.

AUCHEDLY BRIDGE, 5.5 km. SE, over the Ythan. By *William Davidson*, 1901. Twin segmental arches with central V-plan cutwater piers, framed by token pilasters and parapet copings. Smaller flood and footpath arch on the W bank and splayed wing-walls at each end containing the embankments which carry the road. Squared rough granite with pinnings, main arches key-blocked with ashlar dressings, intrados of flood arch partly brick.

HADDO HOUSE. *See* p. 237.

HOUSE OF FORMARTINE. *See* p. 249.

HOUSE OF SCHIVAS. *See* p. 250.

MILLBREX 8040

Former MILLBREX PARISH CHURCH. By *Arthur Clyne* of *Pirie & Clyne*, 1882–3, replacing a primitive chapel of ease built fifty years earlier. Idiosyncratic Gothic, a tall rectangular structure rising from a deeply battered base in red stugged ashlar up into a steeply pitched roof. W gable with central doorway framed by broad shallow buttresses which rise into an overarch and form a recess; the N buttress is overlaid by a secondary buttress which is corbelled out to support a slim circular belfry with stone spirelet. Above the doorway, three windows and an octofoil roundel within the overarch; a square pinnacle answers the N turret on the S. Five-bay flanks in pinned rubble, with twin stairways expressed by three small lights at gallery level. Wheel window in rear gable, above a single-storey vestry with basement boiler-house.

MINTLAW 9040

Reputedly founded in 1813, its central square at the junction where the Aberdeen–Fraserburgh road crosses that from Peterhead to Banff. Its early development is represented by the simple Late Georgian cottages, originally thatched, lining South Street; the period after the railway arrived in 1861, by villas built in Station Road running W from The Square to meet it; and the post-war era by a series of residential developments, some council and some private housing, as a result of which Mintlaw grew into a small town. In The Square itself the PITFOUR ARMS, earlier C19, a two-storey three-bay frontage, its roof re-profiled into a tall gambrel to provide larger attic bedrooms. Nearby, the PUBLIC HALL of 1893, a low broad gable-fronted building like a Secession church, plain with round-arched entrance and pointed windows, its clock and belfry added 1897. The WAR MEMORIAL is a grey granite octagonal plinth with tapering shaft rising into a finialled Celtic cross.

7020 MOUNIE CASTLE

1.8 km. ENE of Daviot

A charming ensemble of mid-C17 laird's house – perhaps incorporating a diminutive tower house of the late C16 – with a much smaller Georgian cottage standing to one side at an angle. In its present form the 'castle' was built for Robert Farquhar, Provost of Aberdeen, who acquired the estate from the Setons of Meldrum (*see* Oldmeldrum) and was confirmed in possession by royal charter in 1643; it is a relatively unaltered example of the T-plan form usual at that date. Its entrance front, facing E, is a long two-storey and attic block built of harled rubble, with a few small doors and windows regularly arranged, steep crowstepped gables and a central drum stair-tower. At attic level this tower is richly corbelled out as a caphouse, its gables with straight skews; the caphouse is accessed by means of a stair-turret in the N re-entrant angle, the date 1641 being carved on its rear S skewputt. The original doorway is at the foot of the tower, close in on the r. near the main wall. It has the rounded arrises favoured in the late C16 and early C17, and was protected by a slit-window. The other windows were formerly barred, but are now simple sashes-and-cases. Two chamfered doorways have been formed in the late C17 or early C18, one to each side of the tower.

The Seton family repurchased Mounie in 1714. Either David Seton, 6th Baron Mounie, or his nephew Alexander, who succeeded him in 1894, engaged *Robert S. Lorimer* to design a

Mounie Castle.
Drawing by David M. Walker

much larger house in a similar idiom which would have incorporated the old castle as an autonomous wing, but this was never built. Lorimer did however restore the castle *c.* 1897–8, renewing its chimneyheads and crowsteps in granite. Its rear elevation appears plain, but as recently as the early 1970s there was a round-headed doorway, possibly C16, at its S end, with a heraldic panel above, and a blocked segment-headed opening in the S gable.

The ground floor is a single continuous vault throughout its length with the kitchen fireplace in the N gable, while the upper-floor rooms are very simple, owing their appearance to Lorimer, who heightened the first floor at the expense of the attic.

The COTTAGE is two-storey with a central entrance flanked by large ground-floor windows, but the first-floor windows are small and square, their rooms rising into the roof-space.

DOOCOT, 70 m. W. Dated 1694, restored by *Lorimer* in 1898 as a two-storey pavilion with small-paned casement and sash-and-case windows, and simply coped chimneystacks for his fireplaces. The ball-finialled GATEPIERS, 350 m. ESE, are late C17, fluted with banded rustication. They were re-sited by *Lorimer*, who provided the handsome armorial wrought-iron gates.

Near the house is a PICTISH SYMBOL STONE: a whinstone slab incised on one side only, with crescent and V-rod, a second crescent by itself, a mirror and a comb. It was cracked across its middle when it was transferred here from Newton of Mounie in 1866.

MOUNTBLAIRY B *6050*

4.2 km. N of Kirkton of Forglen

MOUNTBLAIRY HOUSE of 1791 for Major-Gen. Andrew Hay, with enlargements of 1825, was demolished in 1946.

HOME FARM STEADING. A quadrangular courtyard plan of 1791–1800. Simple two-storey W elevation in whinstone rubble with sandstone dressings, its centre with a segmental pend under a gabled tower with doocot and birdcage bellcote. Fine Greek Revival STABLES added on the E side by *John Smith I*, 1835. Doric distyle-*in-antis* portico with heavy entablature and pediment constructed in grey and cream granite ashlar. Harled wings with low attics have transom-lit doorways and paired pilasters at the ends.

MAUSOLEUM, 850 m. N of Home Farm. Built *c.* 1860. Like a small Gothic chapel in a peaceful situation overlooking the Deveron, the approach by a tree-lined avenue some 400 m. long. On lower ground beneath the mausoleum, the tomb of Lt-Col. Frederick Morison, †1911, with low-relief carving of St Andrew and his cross.

Mountblairy Bridge, 250 m. s. By *John Smith I*, 1836. All the grandeur of a great viaduct, but on the most modest scale. Three round-headed arches in coursed stugged granite, with ashlar voussoirs and coped parapets splayed out on a curve at either end, carry a minor road over an unnamed burn in Lilliputian majesty.

Gatepiers and gates near West Lodge, 500 m. nnw. Early to mid-c19. Fine cast-iron Neo-Jacobean carriage gates supported on tall square ashlar piers with flanking side gates and dwarf quadrant walls with railings.

6040 MUIRESK HOUSE

2.2 km. w of Turriff

A country house described as 'lately built' in 1794 (*Edinburgh Evening Courant*), probably for Alexander Dirom, son of the Provost of Banff, who had married Magdalen Pasley in the previous year: its vernacular classical style is, however, similar to houses built fifty years earlier. Two-storey entrance front facing w, five windows wide with central attic gable rising into a coped chimneystack, the doorway sheltered under a distyle Roman Doric portico added *c.* 1840. White harl, astragalled sashes-and-cases set in dressed margins, the gable with a round-arched window; moulded skewputts, small square attic windows within the ends. Slightly lower two-storey rear wings form a U-plan: s flank with regular fenestration has a c17 armorial panel reset, n flank is simpler. Courtyard largely infilled *c.* 1840 when the interior was remodelled, only the c18 drawing room on first floor and minor stair now remain, new stair in the s wing. Closely surrounded by trees but with an open outlook to broad lawns on the principal front. Very large walled garden, near-rectangular, at the rear.

Home Farm, 80 m. se. Square courtyard steading, *c.* 1785. Principal elevation has a pedimented centre with segmental arch and bellcote; flanking two-storey ranges with tall ground- and smaller first-floor windows set in slim margins, coped end stacks, and a doocot in one gable. Poor condition. The w and e lodges are both *c.* 1840 but altered.

6040 NETHERDALE HOUSE

4.8 km. sse of Aberchirder

Handsome classical house, possibly by *William Robertson* of Elgin *c.* 1825, built for the Rose-Innes family; enlarged by Robertson's nephews *A. & W. Reid* in 1856–7, then remodelled by *James Duncan & Son* *c.* 1900.

Three-storey entrance elevation, facing S, five windows wide with fully raised basement, tall principal floor. Central bay slightly projected, its Roman Doric portico with paired columns set beneath a Diocletian window rising as high as the principal apartment windows: both the portico and the window are additions by the *Duncans*, replacing the original entrance and its forestair. Above the Diocletian, bold cantilever brackets and a voussoir support a balustraded balcony in front of the tripartite first-floor window with crowning cartouche and scrolls. Excellent masonry in pale golden ashlar sandstone, the centre bay and ends articulated by long-and-short quoins. Restrained and refined detail, the portico entablature with triglyphs, guttae and a mutuled cornice, and the doorway lintel carved with interlocking scrolls. Principal-floor windows set in moulded surrounds with cornices, and above the first-floor windows a slim cornice and blocking course; the centre bay has a plain parapet and urns; low chimneystacks over a low hipped roof.

The original square plan results in deep three-bay side elevations, again in ashlar sandstone. Short wing blocks set well back are *Reid* additions, built in ashlar, their centres slightly projected with tripartite windows at principal and first floors with low pediments. The wings once formed part of a large enclosed court on the N side of the house, demolished after a fire in 1946. The rear elevation is now irregular, harled in grey with ashlar sandstone quoins. Entrance hall remodelled by the *Duncans* – elegant Neoclassical stairway with slim cast-iron balusters and handrails, its central flight separating above the mezzanine landing into two flights which return back to the principal floor. Within the principal apartment on the E side, fine wood panelling reused from a house in Edinburgh's Randolph Crescent. At the rear, a much older stair with cast-iron balusters, perhaps originally the main stair of the house.

COACHHOUSE, early C19. A pedimented centre with semi-elliptical arch and three-bay wings, built in squared rubble with ashlar dressings, almost symmetrical.

WALLED GARDEN. A large square enclosure, finely planted, on rising ground. Entered between square gatepiers with cornices and pyramidal caps, the central avenue leads past a SUNDIAL inscribed with the name of James Rose-Innes and an elegant gnomen, to a two-storey red brick PAVILION with its tall centre boldly canted out, a Gothick window above its doorway, prismatic roof and lower side-wings with their own doors.

NETHERMUIR HOUSE 9040

4 km. SE of New Deer

Perhaps incorporating fabric of a Gordon manor house built in 1721, but if so substantially rebuilt *c.* 1803 as a classical house by William Gordon 3rd Earl of Aberdeen for one of his mistresses, then remodelled to its present Baronial form by *William Leslie c.* 1875.

Symmetrical granite ashlar entrance front, two storeys and five bays over a low raised basement, the central entrance bay with canted angles corbelling to a square caphouse and steep crowstepped gable. Moulded doorpiece with field-panel which formerly carried Leslie's arms; the date May 1924 refers to its acquisition by James Mays of Auchnagatt (q.v.). Flank and rear elevations built in harled squared granite, all windows now replaced. Latterly used as a barn, vandalized, but restored to domestic use: one fireplace survives from Leslie's remodelling, together with the entrance hall's tiled floor, and some good plasterwork and stencilled decoration characteristic of the 1870s. Square stair bay projects from rear elevation with two patterns of railings.

STEADING. Courtyard plan. Main front single-storey and low attic built in roughly squared whinstone, pinned with lighter grey granite dressings, carriage arch off-centre to r. Dated 1803 over one doorway, extended by *John Smith I* 1838. Now converted as a house, modern glazing.

GARDENER'S COTTAGE. Much altered. Perhaps originally a low two-storey structure, now single-storey, extended at each end and with a conservatory built in front of the original doorway. Skewputts, badly eroded, with grotesque face and coat of arms, doubtless from earlier house at Nethermuir. Datestone removed and set in garden wall – initials and date refer to marriage of David Gordon to Janet Maitland in 1595.

8060

NEW ABERDOUR

A planned village laid out for William Gordon of Aberdour in 1798 comprising the High Street running N–S for almost 600 m., and two side-streets running in parallel which were never built up, with cross-lanes between them at regular intervals. Elphin Road runs across the top of High Street E–W, the parish church standing on the junction with the village hall (*see* below) and (once) the parish school next to it; markets were formerly held on the green, beneath the tall white pedestal fountain which flowed as if to symbolize flourishing prosperity, its basin now planted with flowers. At the opposite end of the village, Low Street loops across the bottom of the High Street, swinging round sharply in front of the former Free Church manse (*c.* 1870).

ST DROSTAN, High Street. A tall Tudor-Gothic four-bay preaching-box, 1818,* very similar in character to Telford's

*The design was virtually repeated at Gamrie (q.v.) in 1829, for which *William Robertson* prepared a design.

parliamentary churches of seven years later. Altered by *Ellis & Wilson* in 1885. Grey harl, with slim dressings and margins, original leaded Y-tracery glazing *in situ*. Sundial in S wall formerly with an inscription commemorating the church's erection by John Dingwall of Brucklay (q.v.) and Charles Forbes of Auchmedden, the sole heritors of Aberdour. Plain birdcage bellcote over W gable, 1771, reused from the old church (*see* below). Entrances at each end, with W doorway sheltered by a porch of 1885; the double-leaf doors with decorative bar-hinges are of this period, as are the finely patterned cast-iron down-pipes.

An engagingly robust character to the interior, still very much in the spirit of 1885. *Ellis & Wilson*'s alterations include the wide platform PULPIT centred in the S wall as its predecessor had been and responding to Smith's Gothick with Gothic of its own – its tall back with bold arcaded detailing, crowned by a turreted entablature with crowstep-gabled pediment. Facing the pulpit on three sides, the gallery deepened in 1885, but evidently reusing Smith's panelled fronts and slim cast-iron columns. The rafters of the kingpost open roof are strengthened by wrought-iron tension-rod trusses.

WAR MEMORIAL, in front of the church, 1921. Pale granite, a long-shafted Celtic cross on a plinth and pedestal.

OLD PARISH CHURCH, 1.3 km. N. St Drostan reputedly established the first chapel here *c.* 590; the present structure appears early C16, incorporating some remains of a Norman predecessor.* Ruinous T-plan in red rubble, with tooled sandstone and granite dressings. The old nave is 21 m. long by 6.5 m. broad, but with the E end partitioned off as two burial enclosures in 1819 by Charles Leslie, M.P. A blocked round-headed arch once opened into the long S aisle, rebuilt 1764, which is still roofed with straight skews and skewputts of that date. – FONT reputedly from an earlier religious cell at Chapelden. – MONUMENTS. Two round-arched and moulded recess monuments in the N wall, eastern illegible with two shields, western to James Baird of Auchmedden dated 1559. Weathered slab to George Baird, mathematician, †1593. Within the aisle, a white marble armorial wall monument to the Gordons of Aberdour, 1839.

Former PARISH MANSE, next to the old church. Plans by *William Robertson* in 1814–15 were rejected by John Dingwall of Brucklay (q.v.), the principal heritor, on the grounds that under an Act of 1663 he need contribute only £83 to the construction costs.‡ Robertson's plans were simplified by *Alexander Laing* before being built in 1821–3. A two-storey three-bay house, white-harled, with tooled ashlar door and window surrounds outlined in black – the nicely detailed doorcase has lost

*See W. Douglas Simpson, *Dundarg Castle* (1954), p. 4, n. 1.

‡The Rev. George Gardiner, with the Church's backing, took his case to the Court of Session and ultimately the House of Lords, with successful results, but in the meantime the Church had accepted Dingwall's increased offer of £600, leaving Gardiner to pay a substantial balance to obtain a manse of reasonable size.

its original transom-light, but the astragalled sash-and-case windows survive. Plain eaves course, with two canted hip-roofed dormers of the later C19, coped gable chimneystacks. In the centre of the rear elevation, a tall bow containing the stair. Low E wing built shortly afterwards, reducing from two storeys to one, forms a back court together with the L-plan stable and outhouses. DOOCOT, square-plan, prismatic stone spire with annulus, probably C17; its stone flight-boxes survive inside.

VILLAGE HALL, Elphin Street. Opened by the 7th Earl of Aberdeen in 1892. A gable-fronted structure with later square corner tower which rises three stages into a pyramidal spire; construction mostly in pinned squared granite or whinstone with pale dressings, but with the tower's battered base and clock stage in contrasting rock-faced masonry. Extended in the mid C20.

The High Street's most important building was the former COMMERCIAL (later DOWER) HOTEL, the street-front of which divides into two clear parts. The older part is two-storey, five-bay asymmetrical, rubble-built with small bedroom windows on the first floor, and a deep double-pile plan – probably as old as the village itself. The later block, also two-storey and five-bays, is slightly higher, with much taller first-floor windows, and is presently whitewashed; built in the early to mid C19. A two-storey stable court with doocot loft at the rear.

OLD MILL FARMHOUSE, 1.2 km. N. *c.* 1820–30. Two-storey, three bays broad beneath a gabled roof with end stacks. Lower single-storey wing built against r. gable slightly later. Grey-harled, entrance door with transom-light and astragalled sash-and-case windows set in slim ashlar surrounds. The CORN MILL itself is a roofless ruin, now much overgrown.

LADYSFORD HOUSE, 2.5 km. SSE. A simple, generously broad two-storey three-bay house of *c.* 1750–60, built in granite ashlar with moulded doorpiece, relatively small windows, skewputts and gabled roof with coped chimneystacks. Late C18 or early C19 single-storey hip-roofed wings project from each corner to form a forecourt. Conservatory built across the entrance front.

GLASSLAW BRIDGE, 5 km. SW, over the Burn of Gonar. Early C19. A single tall round-headed arch, built in roughly tooled ashlar, with low parapets and short wing-walls splayed down the steep approaches on each side.

8050

NEW BYTH

A planned village established by James Urquhart of Byth in 1764. It consists of two principal thoroughfares – Bridge Street and Main Street – laid out more or less at right angles in similar fashion to Cuminestown (q.v.), founded the year before. The earliest house (Nos. 11–13 Bridge Street) is dated 1765. There was a linen manufactory until 1792, when it became a chapel of ease.

Former PARISH CHURCH, Main Street. First Pointed by *A. & W. Reid*, 1851–2, similar to that at King Edward (q.v.). Entrance gable in squared red sandstone rubble with ashlar dressings and chamfered margins. Deeply moulded pointed-arch doorway, flanked by very tall trefoil-headed lights with square-paned leaded glass and hoodmoulds; bold intaken diagonal buttresses, a small spheric triangle light beneath the dated bellcote. Four-bay flanks in sandstone rubble. Vestry added *c.* 1900. Inside, a U-plan gallery with painted front. – MONUMENTS. Capt. Beauchamp Colclough Urquhart †1898, erected 1900 in Derbyshire alabaster, richly inlaid with gold mosaic, *verde antique* marble and *opus sectile* (cf. the Episcopal Church, Oldmeldrum). – In the vestibule, a memorial to the Rev. John Falconer, †1895.

The adjacent two-storey MANSE was built for the predecessor church in 1829, its bay windows added by *James Duncan* in the 1890s.

Former FREE CHURCH, Main Street, now the church hall. A simplified version of the parish church, built 1894.

NEW DEER 8040

New Deer owes its existence to two factors – first, the establishment of Auchreddie Chapel which with the Abbey of Deer (*see* p. 312) remained the only place of worship in an unusually large parish until the C18; second, its proximity to the junction where the road from Inverurie (S) to Fraserburgh meets the road from Turriff, which then divides in two directions towards Peterhead and Ellon (qq.v.). The advent of turnpikes encouraged James Ferguson of Pitfour (q.v.) and the Gordons of Cairnbanno (*see* below) to develop New Deer as a planned village from *c.* 1805.

CHURCHES AND PUBLIC BUILDINGS

NEW DEER PARISH CHURCH (ST KANE), Church Crescent. Neo-Perp by *John Smith I* – a proper whiff of Tudor England, and all the more striking in this context, rising high above the village. Tall square entrance tower centred against the gable of a four-bay nave: the nave itself built in 1839–41 but the tower not added until 1864–5, slightly modified from Smith's design. Squared granite masonry, the tower with diagonal buttresses rising into pinnacles above its crenellated parapet. It has pointed-arch doorways on all three sides, that on the front face taller with a hoodmould; high second stage with a timber-mullioned two-light window and clock dials, third stage belfry with two-light openings with louvres. Four-bay nave flanks with tall two-light windows and pinnacled angle buttresses at each corner. Figurative datestone from Auchreddie Chapel (1622) set in liturgical E gable. Large open space inside, its U-plan gallery on slim cast-iron columns with arcaded fronts, W wall lined out as if in ashlar. Octagonal pedestal PULPIT, 1936, from former Free Church (*see* School Hall). – ORGAN. 1887 by *Henry Willis & Sons*. – Neoclassical memorial TABLET to James Reid *c.* 1850.

CHURCHYARD, opposite. Site of Auchreddie Chapel (1622 or perhaps earlier), foundations of one transept supporting the NETHERMUIR TOMB. – WAR MEMORIAL by *Messrs John Fyfe*, 1921, a Celtic cross in Kemnay granite, its head with strapwork, plain shaft; raised on a rock-faced base-plinth.

Former FREE CHURCH (now SCHOOL HALL), Main Street. Competition win by *Ellis & Wilson*, 1883, built 1884–5 in their distinctively rugged Gothic style, the mason being *William Davidson* of New Pitsligo. Tall nave gable flanked by N tower slightly stepped forward, and S stair bay with slim buttresses rising into an open spirelet. Pointed-arch entrance framed by crocketed pilasters under a gablet, the doorway itself shouldered with three small lights above. Stepped lancets at gallery level, blind openings beneath the gable apex. N tower rises square with angle buttresses; its belfry is octagonal with colonnettes under a stone spire and spiky iron finial.

Former CONGREGATIONAL CHURCH, Main Street. By *Matthews & Mackenzie*, 1880. Entrance gable with pointed-arch doorway framed by vestibule lights and simple buttresses, five stepped lancets at gallery level within a pointed-arch surround. Built in pinkish granite, five-bay flanks, wheel window in E end above low rear vestry. Converted into flats.

CEMETERY, on N outskirts. Laid out in 1891, with a dated lodge house. Close by, the CULSH MONUMENT to William Dingwall Fordyce of Brucklay (q.v.), designed by *James Matthews* 1876, and built in 1877. Like a steeple by James Gibbs, approached by a ceremonial stair – tall first stage with round-headed, key-blocked arch built in pinned granite, second stage in ashlar with inscription panel and canted corners, third stage octagonal, arcaded like a belfry, slender stone spire rises to an urn finial 24 m. above ground.

SCHOOL, behind the parish church. By *John Smith I*, 1844, with substantial extensions by *James Matthews*, 1874. Worthless post-war additions have caused it to lose its shape and character.

DESCRIPTION. New Deer is really two settlements linked by a bridge across the Auchreddie Burn. That on the S bank is formed around a crossroads, with the EARL OF ABERDEEN ARMS a Late Georgian hostelry, two-storeyed, harled in white with a gabled roof. The settlement on the opposite bank of the river comprises two long streets on rather higher ground, Main Street running NW and Church Crescent NE with a C19 bank house (now the ROYAL BANK OF SCOTLAND) standing on the junction between them. MAIN STREET is a 700 m.-long vista lined on each side with single-storey cottages stepping up with the gentle rise of terrain. Most of the planned village's original thatched cottages were replaced in late Victorian times, but at the far end of Main Street, No. 7 HIGH STREET is seemingly the earliest survivor, the only one where the gable skewputts are moulded rather than square-cut.

Beyond St Kane (*see* above), CHURCH CRESCENT passes by the VILLAGE HALL (*John Sleigh*, 1863–4) and MANSE (*John Smith I*, 1832, reconstructed 1926), then descends into FORDYCE TERRACE with villas on one side only, the first of these the most distinguished – No. 2, built *c.* 1905, two storeys in granite ashlar, symmetrical with its central entrance flanked by bows which rise into stylized castellated parapets. In KIRKBRAE TERRACE, No. 8 (mid C19) is a pretty two-storey three-bay house with canted dormers in a faultlessly picturesque situation.

CAIRNBANNO HOUSE, 4.8 km. SW. *c.* 1770. Perhaps the result of reconstruction. Entrance front facing S, two-storey three bays broadly spaced with a central bow containing the replacement door and transom-light. Rear elevation with projecting centre rising into a gabled chimneystack faces N into a small walled garden. Rubble construction formerly harled, with dressed surrounds and moulded skewputts. Low two-storey W wing evidently rebuilt. Possibly a derivative of the Birkenbog/Hatton Manor (qq.v.) group.

NETHERMUIR HOUSE. *See* p. 297.

NEW LEEDS 9050

A planned village laid out on a crossroads plan by Alexander Fraser (son of Lord Strichen) in 1798, the name bespeaks the former ambitions of the place, but progress has been glacial with only a few houses to represent the generations since.

Former UNITED SECESSION CHURCH. Built 1853; altered by *Alexander Wright*, 1876. Neo-Jacobean gable front and bell-cote, central splayed doorway with depressed arch under a hoodmould, and round-headed ground-floor and gallery windows; three-bay flanks with manse at the rear, all in domestic use. – WAR MEMORIAL, 50 m. N. Small Maltese cross of polished granite on top of a rubble cairn.

The STAG formed in white quartz stones on the flank of Mormond Hill overlooking the village – inspired by the White Horse overlooking the Strichen side – was laid out to commemorate the marriage of F.W. Cordiner of Cortes (q.v.) in 1870.

Former KININMONTH CHAPEL OF EASE, 2.5 km. SE. By *John Smith I* 1836–8, 'repaired and improved' in 1893, now in domestic use. Tall T-plan mostly built in dark whinstone rubble coursed squared and pinned with paler granite dressings and margins, its projecting S aisle rising into a gable with clock dial and corbelled bellcote. In the re-entrant angles, l., a small ground-floor porch, and r., porches at ground and gallery levels, the latter approached by a forestair. Four-bay N flank; round-arched windows in E and W ends. Session-house annexe.

KININMONTH HOME FARMHOUSE, 1.8 km. S of E of the chapel. Set within pleasant wooded grounds, built by Charles Cumine, dated 1740. Entrance front is two-storey five-bay symmetrical; central doorway framed between token pilasters, tall slim windows broadly spaced in chamfered granite surrounds, walls otherwise harled in grey. Moulded eaves course and skewputts, tall roof with coped chimneystacks at each end. A bow window has been built out, *c.* 1980, from the ground floor to one side of the door. Modern conservatory built out from flank. Gabled central projection at back as at Haddo House, Crimond (q.v.), but slimmer. Two rear wings, one of them an earlier farmhouse, probably C17. Internally the stair is similar to Haddo's, U-plan with elegant turned balusters, the flights supported by slender reeded columns which stop some way short of the ceiling. Until *c.* 1960 the house had panelling, again similar to Haddo. Quadrangular STEADING and square DOOCOT formerly with pyramidal roof.

8050

NEW PITSLIGO

New Pitsligo was established on Turlundie Hill by the banker Sir William Forbes in 1787. Forbes was a great-nephew of the 4th Lord Pitsligo, who had forfeited his estates during the 'Forty-five. Afterwards his son, the Master of Pitsligo, bought some of these lands back, and when he died they passed to Sir William.

The village's hillside situation contributes much to its character, and when it was founded in the late C18 endowed it with many advantages: a bright aspect, good stone for building and heather for thatching, clear spring water and abundant peat mosses for fuel. But although Forbes offered perpetual leases on the most generous terms, and farmland rent-free if his tenants were willing to clear and enclose it, the natural state of the land was of little use for arable farming, and there were no transport links. In its early years the village attracted not honest citizens but illicit distillers, and in consequence presented a most miserable appearance. The turnpike system did not arrive until 1820 and even then it did not run the full course of the High Street but joined one-third of the way up its length, and afterwards ran out of money 5 km. further NW at Auchnagorth, with progress stalled for several years.

The village's development – the laying-out of streets, the take-up of feus and the construction of better houses – was thus a gradual process. When Forbes's grandson proposed to offer new feus in 1830, he met resistance from existing tenants, who objected to incomers sharing the land they had cleared. Nevertheless the village continued to grow. It diversified from weaving into cobbling and lace-making – New Pitsligo lace was of excellent quality, with an international reputation in the most rarefied circles – and the local granite which Sir William Forbes had identified as suitable for building proved so hard as to take an exceptionally fine polish, and was soon much in demand elsewhere. By 1870 New Pitsligo had reached a population of nearly 2,100, making it the largest planned village in Scotland.

CHURCHES

Former CONGREGATIONAL CHURCH, High Street. Now Royal British Legion Hall. First Pointed by *Alexander W. Bisset*, 1862–3, built in pale granite ashlar. Entrance gable originally with fine moulded doorway, gallery with three tall lancets of equal height, their hoodmoulds linked by blind arches; vesica opening for roof-space, datestone and octagonal stone finial over apex; four-bay flanks. Doorway now concealed by plain lean-to porch, boxy rear extension.

ST JOHN THE EVANGELIST (Episcopal), High Street. The 'Cathedral of Buchan', built 1870–1 on the site of a previous church of 1835. Commissioned by the Rev. William Webster (later Dean of Aberdeen & Orkney) to designs by *G.E. Street*, the mason *A. Findlater* and the sculptors *D. & A. Davidson*; an exact contemporary of Street's St Mary on the Rock, Ellon (q.v.). E.E., correctly composed in ecclesiological terms with nave, aisles and transepts, a bell-towerlet next to the S doorway, and large apsidal chancel: it is striking in its scale and its excellent construction, built in New Pitsligo granite laid in slim courses with some use of freestone for dressings. Tall W gable, facing the street, is lit by a geometric window of four stepped lancets and a small plate-traceried quatrefoil, steeply pitched roof with floriate cross at the apex; the aisles are set back, each with a two-light window and trefoil plate tracery. Bell-towerlet near SW corner with open belfry is slim and square on plan, its pyramidal stone spire closely similar to the main roof in height. In the S aisle's flank, the double-chamfered arch of a recessed porch with two doors opening into the nave and the towerlet; the nave itself is three bays, lit by cusped triple lights under deeply shadowed bracketed eaves. The transepts are flush with the aisles and lit by large three-light windows: as the ground falls away sharply, they are buttressed at the undercroft. The apse-ended chancel, fully double-height, is intaken twice and lit by four two-light windows; it is flanked on the S by an aisle with a double-pitched roof containing the organ.

Four-bay nave arcades in Elgin freestone rise from quatrefoil piers and support a kingpost roof; both the nave and the aisle roofs are lined internally with diagonally boarded stained pine. The floor is a diaper pattern of red, black and yellow encaustic tiles. Raised chancel with a richer floor pattern, its arch partly supported on corbels, and a wagon roof with diagonal ribs in stained pine, once intended to be decorated. The arch to the S organ chamber is divided by a centre shaft on the model of Boxgrove Priory, Sussex (cf. the N arcade of Street's St Mary Magdalene, Paddington, 1867–73). A screen was installed in the chancel arch in 1931 but has since been removed. In the basement, the SACRISTY has a granite vault resting on a single central column with moulded cap. Separate entrance from outside. – PULPIT. 1872, by *Street*, carved by the *Davidsons* in Caen stone – it is circular, with blind two-light arched panels and other decoration, but the base is octagonal, a central pedestal surrounded by a ring of five smaller columns, all with moulded capitals and bases. – Raised ALTAR in the apse; it has no reredos. On the N side of the chancel an AUMBRY; on the S a SEDILIA and a PISCINA, all in Elgin freestone. – FONT, at the W end. Grey granite, a fluted bowl resting on a thick round column and octagonal base, simply detailed, and looking rather later than the church itself. – Nicely detailed Gothic CHOIR STALLS and fine brass ALTAR RAILS and CANDLESTICKS. – ORGAN by *Blackett & Howden*, dedicated 1898, renovated by *Hill, Norman & Beard* c. 1946. – STAINED GLASS. The earliest examples are the six two-light windows in the chancel, by *Clayton & Bell*, 1898, executed in C14 style – the three centre windows represent The Annunciation, Our Lord as Man of Sorrows (Ecce Homo) and King of Kings (Ecce Deus) and Noli Me Tangere; the three other windows represent SS Matthew and Mark, Luke and John, and Peter and Paul.

CHURCHYARD. The dwarf walls to the street have retained their original gatepiers and gates, lamp-standards and cinquefoil-patterned railings. The churchyard itself contains a fine collection of stones amid a beautiful woodland setting; the tombs of Dean Webster (†1896), who commissioned the church, and his widow, Mary Hutchison, are at the E end, with close by that of his first wife, Catherine.

PARISH CHURCH, Church Street. Built as a rectangular preaching-box, orientated N–S, in 1799; substantially remodelled in a simple lancet style with new W transept and vestry by *John Henderson* 1853; vestry enlarged *c.* 1896 by *D. & J. R. McMillan*, who also added an organ chamber on the E side in 1903–4. Entrance gable facing S in granite ashlar, doorway set in gablet with flanking buttresses; stepped triple lancets with diamond-pane glazing under hoodmoulds at gallery level, finely detailed square bellcote with shaft-rings and spirelet. W transept with shouldered ground-floor triple lights and stepped gallery lancets. On the E flank the McMillans' organ chamber repeats Henderson's lancets in its canted sides; the stepped buttresses and battlemented parapet are however very much their own. The N gable has a relatively modest doorway with stepped gallery lancets, but a Celtic cross finial over its apex. U-plan gallery with stained panelled fronts, supported on cast-iron columns; it faces towards the pulpit, communion table and organ on the E side. Scissor-beam timber roof ceiled at the apex. Platform PULPIT also with a stained panelled front raised above the organ console, balustraded stairs on each side. – COMMUNION TABLE and FONT in oak. – ORGAN by *E.H. Lawton*, *c.* 1904. – PEWS. From the former Free Church, Banff (q.v.), transferred *c.* 1995; some original pews in the gallery. Vestry converted to session room in 1985.

PUBLIC BUILDINGS

NEW PITSLIGO & ST JOHN'S SCHOOL, School Street, by *Ellis & Wilson*, 1875. Simple Gothic. Long single-storey main block, near-symmetrical, constructed in pale granite ashlar. Centre pair of pointed windows rising beneath a gablet with roundel and belfry; projecting three-bay gable-fronted wings at each end, their centre windows again pointed. Doorway off-centre. TEACHER'S HOUSE, also by *Ellis & Wilson*, 1873. CLASSROOM EXTENSION by *George M. Hay*, 1936; CANTEEN AND KITCHEN BLOCK, 1947.

POLICE HOUSE, Low Street. Picturesque Late Victorian villa, two-storey three-bay symmetrical front, built in pinned masonry; round-headed doorway, astragalled sash-and-case windows with long-and-short dressings, first floor breaking up into gableted dormers under a hipped roof with tall gable chimneystacks.

PUBLIC HALL, High Street. By *D. & J.R. McMillan*, 1894–5. Miniaturized Free Baroque in local granite. Two-storey three-bay symmetrical frontage. Semi-elliptically arched doorway framed by boldly detailed pilasters and open scroll pediment; deep rough-hewn plinth and oblong ground-floor windows; the first-floor windows are segmentally arched with concave gablets bearing pediments.

PUBLIC LIBRARY, High Street. Dated 1803 but looks *c.* 1880 in its present form. Converted from a single-storey and attic cottage with a longer wing: once presumably the librarian's house and library itself, all built in granite ashlar with coped chimneystacks.

ROYAL BRITISH LEGION HALL, High Street. *See* former Congregational church.

ST JOHN'S CENTRE, High Street. Former Episcopal Church school, built by *James Campbell Walker* before 1865 for the Rev. William Webster. E.E. double-gable front in squared granite: the l. gable is distinguished by an apex bellcote, a small doorway and paired and triple-light windows all with slightly depressed arches. Master's house added to one side later, a two-storey three-bay L-plan villa with a projecting porch.

WAR MEMORIAL, High Street, 1922 by *J. A. Ogg Allan*. Modelled on Lutyens's Cenotaph in Whitehall.

DESCRIPTION

About halfway up its length New Pitsligo is bisected by a dense belt of trees on either bank of a small burn, crossed by a plain but substantial bridge. The S half of the village consists of three streets running broadly in parallel, with High Street flanked by School Street to the W, and Low Street to the E. Because of the steeply sloping site, a notable characteristic of the village is that, for parts of its length, the houses on High Street's W side stand well above the road, and those on the E well beneath it, so that the former can see clearly over the roofs of the latter. Most houses are single-storeyed: the feus were laid out 45 ft (13.7 m.) wide to accommodate traditional weavers' cottages, four or five bays in length, each with a living room and a room for the loom. Beyond the burn the High Street is crossed at right angles by Church Street, with the junction forming the nearest New Pitsligo has to a square.

In HIGH STREET there are two plain Late Georgian inns for travellers on the turnpike, the COMMERCIAL HOTEL and the PITSLIGO ARMS HOTEL, the latter of *c.* 1790 with later additions and good ball-finialled gatepiers to the rear court. Only slightly grander is the mid-C19 BANK OF SCOTLAND to the N with taller and later bank agent's house at one end. Among the houses No. 66 of *c.* 1800 is two-storey and five bays in granite ashlar, with a central tripartite doorpiece, long-and-short quoins and a gabled roof with moulded skewputts and deeply coped end stacks; its basement is exposed at the rear. Near the High Street's S end, the former FREE CHURCH MANSE of 1861 was probably altered *c.* 1890. Two-storey L-plan in squared granite, its projecting bay with a tall crowstepped gable; the porch in the angle, also gabled, contains a moulded round-headed doorway. Simple hoodmoulds and gableted dormers; fireclay shafted chimney-cans.* In LOW STREET, No. 92 is early C19. A two-storey three-bay front, granite ashlar under a gabled roof. Deeply recessed architraved doorway, with first-floor window-sill dropped to rest on its lintel; moulded skewputts, eaves course, coped chimneystacks. Intended as one end of a terrace, S gable tusked.

Former MANSE. 1799, presently derelict. Two-storey three-bay entrance front in granite ashlar, moulded skewputts and coped chimneystacks; end gables and slightly later rear wing are built in squared rubble. Gutted interior.

*The Free Church itself, on the junction of the High Street with the turnpike, was built in 1847 but demolished after the Second World War.

NEWBURGH 9020

In the mouth of the Ythan, Newburgh is first recorded in 1261 when a hospital was founded here by Alexander Comyn, Earl of Buchan; it also had a Chapel of the Holy Rood and a monks' home associated with Deer Abbey (*see* p. 312). It was established as a seaport for Ellon (q.v.) in 1276. Erected a burgh of barony for Henry Sinclair in 1509, Newburgh was once protected by the Turing Tower which collapsed in 1720. Its waters were relatively shallow, however, and remarkably there seems to have been no pier until 1841, vessels being loaded and unloaded at low tide. A prosperous village in the later C19, with its own schooners and steamships, it milled grain and imported coal, timber, lime and bones. The dominant features were once the tall grain mill and granary built in 1897 on Culterty Quay but these have been demolished.

HOLYROOD CHAPEL (Foveran Parish Church), Main Street. Formerly a school founded by John Mather, built 1838, and converted to an Established Church *c.* 1882. Gothic L-plan on a corner site, with nave orientated N–S, and transeptal aisle facing E, built in squared golden granite with two tiers of voussoirs over the windows. The SE entrance tower by *William Ruxton* is dated 1892 and has a tall belfry stage with twin louvred openings, dummy corbelled parapets and octagonal angle pinnacles clasping clock gablets; short slated spire. Timber tracery, internal reconstruction and refurnishing by *John Robertson* 1906–9: perhaps the church was reorientated then, the pulpit with its early C19 canopy moving from the N end to the S, the blind gable being occupied by an organ and the E aisle made redundant. Fine open roof with semi-elliptical collar braces, enclosed at the sides by timber groin-vaults: curious inasmuch as the springers hang in mid-air as pendants within the arches of the W side.

GRAVEYARD, New Street. Site of the Chapel of the Holy Rood, probably C13, the ruins of which were cleared *c.* 1890; it once belonged to Deer Abbey (*see* p. 312). – UDNY BURIAL VAULT. Early C18 square-plan with low rubble walls and moulded entrance just breaking into a very tall roof; railed enclosure.

OCEANLAB, N on the A975, for the University of Aberdeen. By *George Watt & Stewart*, with *Cameron & Ross*, Consulting Engineers, *c.* 2008.

GOLF CLUBHOUSE, Beach Road. By *David Warrender*, 2000. Two-storey with glazed central entrance bay and long wings folded back as a shallow V, reputedly inspired by an arctic tern. Ground floor faced in squared rubble with recessed window band; upper floor fully glazed across the main front, with continuous cantilevered balcony overlooking the links, and gently pitched corrugated roofs developing the angular theme.

FORVIE HOUSE, Main Street. Built for Capt. Thomson, a clipper-master, *c.* 1845. Two-storey, three windows wide in granite rubble, with dressed margins and apron panels beneath the ground-floor windows. Doorpiece unusually broad, with simply profiled architrave and cornice, the doorway set back between blind ashlar panels and pilasters with transom-light. Canted attic dormers and late Victorian fireclay ridge brattishing.

NEWBURGH HOUSE, facing down Main Street from its N end. Built 1775. Two-storey, three windows wide over a tall raised basement, squared granite rubble with ashlar details. Doorway with long-and-short quoins, and triple key-block voussoirs; windows of late C19 pattern with small-pane astragals in upper sashes only. Ashlar blocking course and later canted dormers. Inside, the main stair with early replacement cast-iron balusters of attractive design.

WAREHOUSE, Inch Road. Squared granite rubble, perhaps late C18; rendered ordinary in modern times on the waterfront side, with sheet metal roof, but retains its original appearance towards the churchyard.

CULTERTY QUAY. Residential development by *CHAP Homes*, *c.* 2008. A very large square open to Main Street, with stepped terraces of tall gable-fronted houses overlooking the water on the three other sides, and apartment blocks in the outer corners. Good sense of movement, well proportioned and detailed with a carefully chosen variety of materials and colours including steel, timber and glass.

KNOCKHALL CASTLE, 1.2 km. NNW. Built by the Lairds of Udny (q.v.) to defend the mouth of the Ythan. Accidentally burnt 1734, ruinous yet still dominant amid its low-lying surroundings. An L-plan tower house, three storeys with attics rising into gables with big chimneystacks. It consists of a main block orientated N–S and a NW jamb, both vaulted at ground-floor level, and a square stair-tower projecting from the middle of the N front masking a slight step N at the jamb. The entrance is in the jamb's S face close to the re-entrant angle, square-headed with an edge roll-moulding and two empty armorial panels above the lintel which is dated 1565.*

Although the relationship might not now be immediately obvious, Knockhall appears to have been a reduced version of the big tower houses at Craig and Colquhonnie (S) and Gight, Delgatie and Towie Barclay (qq.v.), all of which are probably associated with the *Conn family* of master-masons based at Auchry. As in all these houses the kitchen occupies the ground floor of the jamb and its solar the first floor, similar in particular to Craig albeit that the plan is reversed. The jamb itself is identical in width – 6.75 m. – to that at Craig, but 1.5 m. longer at 8.25 m.; in each case their walls are 1.3 m. thick, except at the fireplace gable, which is 2.5 m. thick at Craig but

*Knockhall and Udny Castles are more or less contemporary and the cost of building both together probably explains the old story of three generations of Udny lairds living in impecunious circumstances during the C16.

1.8 m. at Knockhall. Knockhall's main block is much smaller, only 11 m. by 7.5 m. (as against Craig's 13 m. by 10.5 m.), the significant reduction in width requiring the entrance and corridor to be accommodated within the jamb rather than in the main block, and for the main stair to be extruded to the N rather than contained within the junction of the main block and the jamb. As at Craig the diameter of the stair is 3 m.

As first built Knockhall probably had corbelled parapets. Its present appearance dates from the mid to later C17, perhaps as a result of the depredations of 1639 and 1640. At first floor a blocked original window survives at the re-entrant angle but the upper floors are now lit from the S and E by generously proportioned and regularly spaced windows with raised margins and finely moulded arrises. Above the entrance at attic level is a shelf resting on a corbel, its purpose uncertain; there are smaller lights of original vintage on the W and N. The S front once overlooked a court, of which the circular doocot at the SE corner survived to be recorded by James Giles and MacGibbon and Ross, but only its stump remains. Knockhall is closely associated with Jamie Fleeman (1713–78), 'the Laird of Udny's fool', who in the midst of the fire of 1734 rescued his master's heavy charter-chest by hurling it from a top-floor window.

YTHAN LODGE, close to Knockhall. Vernacular classical country house, dated 1775. Entrance elevation two-storey three windows wide over a raised basement, with a railed forestair leading up to the fanlit main door. Harled, with dressed margins, moulded skewputts and gabled roof with tall coped end stacks. The rear elevation's stair bay is enveloped in later additions by *D. Turnbull*, 1965. Remains of circular DOOCOT nearby; unusual GATEPIERS with serrated tops at entrance to the drive.

OLD DEER

9040

A small village in an attractive situation on the South Ugie Water, traditionally associated with the very first church in Buchan in the later C6, then with a Cistercian abbey (*see* below) from the early C13. Robert the Bruce granted the village, as part of the Barony of Aden, to Sir Robert Keith, Marischal of Scotland, in 1324. Following the Reformation Deer parish was conjoined with Foveran, Peterugie and Langley, and became a Presbytery seat in 1581. In 1689 the 8th Earl Marischal was authorized to hold markets near the village at Aikey Brae, but his son forfeited his estates after the 'Fifteen. From 1758 the Aden estate belonged to the Russells. Although they were noted improvers, Old Deer declined in the early C19 in relation to the surrounding planned villages as it was not on the turnpike system.

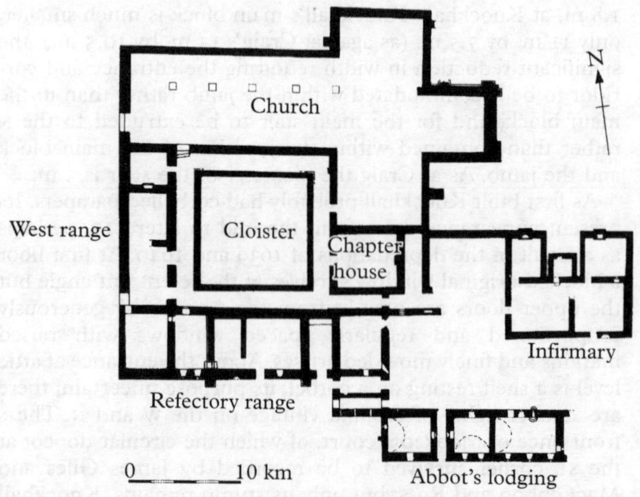

Old Deer Abbey.
Plan

DEER ABBEY*

18 Deer was the location of an early community traditionally associated with St Drostan, the most important relic of which is the late C9–early C10 Book of Deer. But it is unlikely that community was on the same site as the Cistercian abbey. The latter was established by William Comyn, Earl of Buchan, as a daughter house of Kinloss. As such it was one of a small group of early C13 Cistercian houses of modest scale and of comparable architectural form, the others being in Fife, at Culross of *c.* 1217 (also a daughter of Kinloss) and at Balmerino of *c.* 1227. Buchan's petition to establish Deer was remitted to the order's General Chapter in 1214, and the house was formally established in 1219.

As late as 1789 enough survived of the layout of the church, claustral complex and wider precinct for a plan to be drawn (now in the Hutton Collection in the National Library of Scotland), with some of the buildings evidently being still in domestic or agricultural use. In 1809 the precinct was enclosed for James Ferguson of Pitfour, when there was some excavation and conservation of the buildings.‡ Regrettably, his nephew Admiral George Ferguson caused considerable damage when in 1854 he built a Doric prostyle tetrastyle temple as a family mausoleum within the area of the S transept, possibly to the designs of *John Smith I*, who had died two years earlier but who had designed a number of Greek Revival buildings for the estate. The site is now marked by a memorial stone for Eliza Anne Ferguson.

*This entry is by Richard Fawcett.

‡James Ferguson also restored Inverugie Castle (*see* Inverugie).

Following the dissolution of the Pitfour estate, in 1926 the abbey was acquired by the Catholic diocese of Aberdeen, and clearance excavations were started under the direction of Dr Douglas Simpson. In 1933 the remains were placed in state care, and further excavation and conservation was carried out.

The most extensive remains are of the SOUTH CLAUSTRAL RANGE, where the fall of the land meant that a lower storey was required below the level of the cloister. There are also upstanding remains of a range to its E. The other buildings are largely reduced to reconstructed or consolidated footings, parts of which must be viewed with some suspicion.

No more than footings of the outline of the CHURCH are set out, with nothing of the internal arcades. Except where there is some ashlar facing along the N side of the presbytery and the S nave wall, or a bottom chamfer to the presbytery buttresses, much of what is now seen is likely to be modern reconstruction, and the location of door openings may not be reliable. Nevertheless, the plan is plausible, evidently having consisted of a short rectangular presbytery, transepts with two chapel bays on their E side, and a nave with a single N aisle. At Balmerino the lack of correspondence between wall-shafts and arcade piers suggests that the single aisle was an addition, with its placement on the side opposite the cloister representing the least disruptive option for expansion. It is equally possible that the single aisle was an addition at Deer, particularly in view of the slightly awkward relationship between the buttress on the W side of the N transept and the outer N aisle wall. Thus, as at Culross where the nave remained aisleless throughout its history, both Deer and Balmerino were probably initially aisleless.

The part of the EAST CLAUSTRAL RANGE towards the cloister was occupied by the square chapter house and a slype, while the S end of the range has what may have been a warming house at the lower level, with the undercroft of the latrine, through which the drain runs, beyond. The WEST RANGE was divided into three chambers, with a fourth at the junction with the S range. The SOUTH RANGE would have had the refectory at the principal level, and the undercroft that was required to raise that room to the level of the cloister is subdivided into a number of chambers. It might have been expected that the refectory would have been supported on vaulting over those lower chambers, but nothing of any such vaulting is now visible. Most of the door and window openings in this range are bridged by arches of evidently post-medieval construction, which perhaps date from the works carried out for James Ferguson in 1809 (they figure prominently in Keith's *View of the Agriculture of Aberdeenshire* of 1811).

SE of the claustral complex, and adjoining the SE angle of the latrine, is a rectangular range now consisting of a series of three barrel-vaulted chambers and a passage. In this location it is most likely to have been the ABBOT'S HOUSE, the hall and chamber of which would presumably have been supported on the vaulted basement. In this location the letter – if not the spirit – of the monastic rule that the abbot should live together with his monks could be observed. The atypically good state of preservation of this range and of the range on the S side of the cloister may be because these parts were adapted by the abbey's post-Reformation commendators as their residence, and that they had then remained in domestic occupation. Some support for this may be found in the fact that on the plan of 1789 the S range is referred to as 'the family's lodging', suggesting that it had been occupied within living memory.

NE of the Abbot's House are the footings of a U-shaped complex of four rooms, with a fifth room within the hollow of the U; this is probably identifiable as the INFIRMARY. It is linked to the E range by a cross wall, and there are slight indications that it may have been connected to the slype in that range by a pentice. At least one of the fireplaces in this complex is a late medieval insertion, suggesting that it had been adapted for the more comfortable accommodation of a group of the monks at a time when monastic life was pursued with a reduced drive for austerity. – FRAGMENTS* in a shelter to the NW of the church include the following: a C13 PISCINA basin that has evidently been damaged and then reversed, with a second basin carved on what had been the embedded tail; a pair of C13 moulded ARCHES, possibly from some liturgical fixture; a fragment of an effigy with a chain-mail coif and an angel holding the pillow head-rest.

The ORCHARD WALLS are the enclosures formed by James Ferguson M.P. in 1809 around the precinct which he made into his kitchen garden. The entrance has a tetrastyle Greek Doric portico that derives from the mausoleum erected by George Ferguson in the S transept of the abbey in 1854–5 and certainly reusing old stones. The mausoleum was dismantled after 1926 and the portico re-erected here.

CHURCHES

OLD CHURCH.‡ There was a parish church at Deer from before the time it was granted to the newly founded Cistercian abbey, *c.* 1219. What is now seen, in the churchyard to the rear of the later church, is the grey rubble shell of the roofless, truncated and much remodelled two-cell medieval church. The chancel had evidently been abandoned and adapted as a burial enclosure for the Fergusons of Pitfour by the C18. The nave was shortened in 1789, when the replacement church encroached on its W part, at which time it was adapted as a burial enclosure for the Fergusons of Balmakelly. The CHANCEL survives as an

*In the National Museum in Edinburgh is a fragment of finely carved timber FOLIATE CRESTING found in excavations of 1939.

‡This entry is by Richard Fawcett.

extensively rebuilt rectangle of about 11.45 m. by 5.1 m., with the only indications of the original wall thickness being the externally exposed footings below the E and N walls, together with a length of more substantial wall behind a mural monument to the wife of James Ferguson, who died in 1731. Chancel and nave are separated by a round-arched opening with broadly chamfered arrises, and with beam slots, possibly for a partition, within the opening. High in the wall on the S side of the arch, and more visible on the E side, is a blocked door, which appears to have been approached by a stair, the lower courses of which remain against the internal S chancel wall. It has been suggested that these were associated with a rood loft; but, since the presumed masonry support for the stair is associated with the wall in its pared-down state, it is perhaps more likely that they were provided as access to a post-Reformation E loft in the nave. When the walls of the chancel were rebuilt, a number of features were relocated: one heraldic stone has been reset in the E wall, but most features were reset in the nave walls.

The NAVE is now 8.28 m. from N to S and 7.4 m. from E to W, but was clearly originally longer, and the present W wall is of a similar reduced thickness as the rebuilt chancel walls. There is a length of medieval chamfered base course along the E wall on the N side of its junction with the chancel. Traces of a number of blocked openings with chamfers to the external reveals are to be seen in both the N and S walls, most of which are likely to be of post-Reformation date. The easternmost of those on the S side is smaller than the others, and presumably lit the area under either a rood loft or (perhaps more likely) a post-Reformation E gallery. – PISCINA, at the E end of the nave's S wall, with a trifoliate arch, and a cut-back basin, which possibly served an altar in front of the chancel arch. PISCINA BASIN, probably reset, in the E nave wall, on the N side of the chancel arch, below a roughly formed arch. AUMBRY (possibly a SACRAMENT HOUSE), reset at the centre of the N nave wall: a segmentally arched rebated recess below a super-arch containing a diagonally set cross in relief. – MONUMENTS. Reset CANOPIED TOMB-RECESS, at the W end of the external face of the S nave wall, a moulded equilateral arch within a hood-mould, now associated with a variety of other fragments, including an angel holding a shield and part of a tomb-chest(?) with two figures within an arcade. Several C18 and C19 WALL MONUMENTS, most notably that within the chancel for Anne Stuart (†1731), wife of James Ferguson of Pitfour, a framed inscribed tablet topped by a low-relief swan-necked pediment, with a winged angel holding scales and a sword; below the tablet is a skull suspended within a drapery swag.

PARISH CHURCH. A four-bay preaching-box built by contractor *Alexander Smith* in 1788–9 but subsequently altered in 1880–1 with a square SW tower and spire designed by *Sir George Reid*, a friend of the incumbent, and built by *Robert Raeburn*. Smith's church is in rough-faced granite, cherry-cocked, with Venetian windows in the front and rear gables lighting the gallery, and tall Y-traceried windows in the S flank, all with slightly dropped keystones. During the alterations the walls were raised in height slightly, and the porch added, with boldly profiled skew-putts, whereas the originals – still visible on the rear gable – are more modest; slight differences, too, in the ball finials over each end. Both the porch and tower are built in Aikey Brae granite. Slim tower in four undivided stages, third the clock stage and fourth the belfry with paired louvred openings; corbel table supports crenellated parapet and slated pyramid spire 31 m. high with cusped lucarnes, the weathercock by *Archibald Reid* now lost. S flank remains much as built by Smith, but the additional masonry courses below the eaves are clearly evident; cusped ventilators in roof. E gable with blocked round-headed doorway gives pattern for the original entrances at both ends, the gallery window lengthened during the alterations to take stained glass; to the r. of the doorway, the burial enclosure of the Russells of Aden (*see* below). N elevation with rubble session house, vestry and boiler room additions. Interior completely reconstructed 1880–1: new roof partly open with six pine couples exposed, new pews and Smith memorial window. Reordered 1897–8 by *A. Marshall Mackenzie*, the focus of worship transferring from the S wall to E: the half-octagonal platform PULPIT, COMMUNION TABLE, FONT and other furnishings are all by him, the ORGAN also against the E wall by *Henry Willis & Sons* installed shortly after.

The CHURCHYARD contains C18 lying slabs to early C20 stones: the most prominent is the Celtic cross of Dean Ranken (†1886) of St Drostan's Episcopal Church (*see* below), sculpted in red Peterhead granite by *J. Whitehead & Sons* of Aberdeen, and erected *c.* 1893.

ST DROSTAN (Episcopal), Abbey Street. Built on a site gifted by James Russell of Aden (*see* below) to house the Rev. Arthur Ranken's Scottish Episcopal congregation at Waulkmill, with whom his rival, Admiral Ferguson of Pitfour (q.v.), had fallen out. E.E. by *James Matthews* (of *Mackenzie & Matthews*), 1850–1, modelled on the same practice's Christ Church, Huntly (S) but omitting the spirelet; transeptal organ loft and larger chancel by *J. Ninian Comper*, 1896. Aisleless nave with gabled N porch and lancets with hoodmoulds between stepped buttresses. Walls harled with the dressings exposed. W gable lit by tall paired cusped lights and trefoil above; over the apex, a bellcote. Comper's organ loft and chancel are similar in detail but lower, with different skewputts. Loft gabled with single lancet and Celtic cross finial. Chancel with E-end triple light and lancets in its sides.

The nave roof has timber arches supported by moulded stone corbels. Polygonal trusses to the chancel roof. A smaller arch on the N side admits additional light to the organ loft. Most of the FURNISHINGS are by *Comper*, the raised oak PULPIT with panels carved by *Lt.-Col. George Arthur Ferguson* of Pitfour. His REREDOS consists of eight cusp-headed bays, but with the centre pair wider to take effigies of St Columba and St Drostan and the outer bays containing heraldic shields. – SCREEN. For the Children's Chapel at the W end, 1947 by *George Webster* of Stuartfield. – ORGAN by *Porrit* of Leicester. Originally installed in the Episcopal Chapel at Pitfour (q.v.) but gifted by Lt.-Col. Ferguson after its closure, and enlarged during the 1896 alterations. – STAINED GLASS. E window by *John Hardman & Co.*, installed in 1853, although Comper added stone tracery – the centre light represents the Crucifixion, with scenes of the Resurrection above and below; l., St Michael Slaying the Dragon, with beneath Moses and the Parting of the Red Sea; r., the Raising of Jairus's Daughter, and St Catherine Feeding the Hungry and Clothing the Naked. Chancel N, St Margaret of Scotland, 1907; chancel S St Michael Slaying the Dragon, also 1907, in memory of John Graham of Claverhouse, 'Bonnie Dundee'. Rev. Arthur Ranken, incumbent 1834–86, is supposed to have buried his bones under the chancel floor, hence the form of the crosses. – Nave S – Our Lord's Triumphal Entry into Jerusalem, with the Little Children, and with the Doctors in the Temple (1907); the Adoration of the Magi, Our Lord as the Good Shepherd, and with Simeon in the Temple (1907); Our Lord; Our Lord with the Cross, and the Martyrdom of St Stephen (1907); then the Passage of the Israelites through the Red Sea, St Drostan, and Our Lord and Nicodemus (1858). – N side – the Resurrection, Our Lord at the Door, and Joseph raised from the Well (1907); the Annunciation, the Virgin and Child, and Our Lady and St John (1907); the Ascension, the Last Supper and the Offering of Abraham to the Priest and King of Salem (by *Wailes & Strang*, 1888). – In the Children's Chapel (W end), S side, Our Lady and St Anne, and Our Lord during the Sermon on the Mount (1860); N, the Adoration of the Lamb, a Wise Virgin and the Ark Carried through the Red Sea (1865). – W window (1851). Originally in the S side of the chancel before re-erection here in 1907: medallions bearing emblems of the Evangelists, the Pelican in Piety and the Agnus Dei.

ABBEY BRIDGE, W of the Abbey, over the South Ugie Water. Its irregular appearance suggests a vernacular structure of great antiquity, but is in fact the result of a feud between the Fergusons of Pitfour (q.v.) and the Russells of Aden (*see* below) in the early C19. The original bridge was constructed in 1718 for James Keith of Bruxie, whose arms appear on the N flank. A century later it was to have been widened by the lairds of Pitfour and Aden, but Aden demurred to prevent Pitfour's carriage crossing into his lands. The bridge thus comprises three semicircular arches on cutwater piers which increase substantially in height from S bank to N; the carriageway has been widened at its N end only, and so the parapets are pinched in over the S arch before curving out again as wing-walls. Generally rubble construction, but with squared voussoirs and parapets which have been heightened with copings. Buttress at N end on E side.

BRIDGE OF DEER. A twin-arched structure, with smaller relieving arch, carrying the B9030 over the South Ugie Water. Probably *c.* 1800, widened *c.* 1900.

DESCRIPTION

The parish church with its impressive tower dominates the S end of ABBEY STREET, which is lined with short rows of late C19 single-storey and attic houses, their dormers corbelled out just below the wall-head. On the N side, the OLD BANK HOUSE (former North of Scotland Bank) is altogether grander in scale, and rather earlier, built *c.* 1850 probably by *Mackenzie & Matthews*. Two-storey three bays in pale ashlar granite with ground-floor console-cornices and long-and-short quoins, its gabled roof has triple-light pedimented dormers and coped end stacks. Roman Doric porch. Facing down Abbey Street on its junction with Russell Street, the ADEN ARMS HOTEL designed by *Alexander Hay* and opened 1891 is like a picturesque villa, two storeys, three windows wide with tripartite central entrance, slightly projecting ends rising into low gables, bracketed cornice and a hipped roof. Replacing an earlier hotel of the same name which once stood on the riverbank, it was built in local Tillypestle granite for Col. Francis Russell of Aden, who hoped to develop Old Deer as a tourist resort. Close by, the KEMP MEMORIAL HALL, by *George Watt & Stewart*, gifted by the Rev. Dr Robert Sangster Kemp, 1937.

Beyond the Aden Arms on the outskirts of the village are three former schools. Two are mid-Victorian villa types, the first the GIRLS' SCHOOL built by *William Clarke* in 1861 as a result of the Mitchell Bequest, and somewhat further on the PARISH SCHOOL for boys of similar date. Between these two schools stands their replacement (now MAIDSTONE HOUSE), a much larger building by *Sutherland & George*, 1909 – Neo-Baroque, tall single-storey front, a five-bay centre with round-arched lights set between gabled ends with Serlian windows.

THE COTTAGE in Russell Street was once the Aden Estate factor's house. Its entrance front, facing S, is plain Scots Jacobean of *c.* 1840, single-storey three-bay symmetrical with its narrow gabled centre stepped forward, and gableted attic dormers. However, the triple-gable frontage of the Russell Street flank shows that it has been built in two or more probably three stages, its crowstep-gabled bays perhaps of *c.* 1700 and *c.* 1740, although no C18 features survive inside. The former RECTORY, *c.* 1860, is a picturesque villa, its single-storey L-plan front with the r. bay rising into a tall attic gable. Pinned masonry, with paired and triple lights at ground floor. The porch was added and dormers replaced (?) *c.* 1900. Pronounced skewputts and gable fleur-de-lys; roof brattishing and end stacks with square terracotta cans.

Former MANSE, somewhat separate from the village on its E side, close to the Ugie. Plans by *John Smith I* were approved by Presbytery in 1822 although the *New Statistical Account* gives the construction date as 1832. Two-storey over a low raised basement, three windows wide with a gabled roof, it is harled in white with dressings and margins. Its eight-panelled door with nicely detailed fanlight is approached by a flyover stair with cast-iron lyre-type balusters. Astragalled sashes, twin canted dormers, and tall end stacks; rear elevation with a projecting central stairwell, the S bay neatly remodelled in the late C20. STEADING altered for domestic use. Single-storey and attic U-plan in pinned rubble, seemingly built in three stages: plans approved 1788 (contemporary with the church), 1798 and 1809. W range has curved gable end; E range has datestone (1810) above the doorway at the top of the external stair. Close by, a square DOOCOT with pyramid roof, stone nesting boxes inside.

Aden Country Park

The Barony of Aden was sold by the Fergusons of Kinmundy to Alexander Russell, formerly of Montcoffer (*see* Kirkton of Alvah) in 1758. The Russells were vigorous improvers who built a new house overlooking the Ugie, reorganized their tenant farms and planted shelter-belts. During the Victorian period their estate grew to 80 sq. km. encompassing Lundquharn and Kininmonth (*see* p. 304). The rivalry between them and their neighbours, the Fergusons of Pitfour (q.v.), was expressed in all sorts of ways, most conspicuously in the beauty of their estates. The policies of Aden House were transformed by the introduction of native and exotic trees and shrubs – 'The natural beauty of the winding valley has been strikingly brought out and greatly added to by the wealth of woodland' – Aden and Pitfour together becoming known as the Garden of Buchan. But in the C20 financial pressures led to drastic land disposals and the Russells left in 1937. The house was requisitioned as a billet for troops in the Second World War and afterwards the estate was used for sporting purposes, its buildings and parkland neglected. In 1975 Banff & Buchan District Council bought 90 hectares of parkland, including the most important buildings, to form the Country Park. Restoration has continued ever since.

ADEN HOUSE. Built after 1758, remodelled by *John Smith I* in 1832–3; now a roofless shell, but consolidated in 1983. Principal S front two-storey six-bay asymmetric, its pedimented centre and ends projecting; tetrastyle porte cochère with paired Roman Doric columns built out from W intermediate bay, detailing otherwise simple. The differences in construction hint strongly at the building's complicated background – centrepiece in golden granite with long-and-short quoins, Smith's porte cochère and W end bay in grey granite ashlar with tall ground-floor windows expressing the principal rooms on this side, E bays built in contrasting rubble. W elevation also by Smith, symmetrical with two bays on each side of a Roman Doric colonnaded bow formerly with a dome. A large top-lit atrium in the centre of the house accommodated a library and (latterly) billiards. Schoolroom and business room occupied the centre and E bays of the main front, with the kitchen and servants' hall on the rear side; the laundry annexe was a Smith addition. Most internal walls and partitions were lost when the remains of the fireclay balustraded parapets were removed.

Former STABLES AND STEADING, 130 m. NE. Built *c.* 1800, restored as ABERDEENSHIRE FARMING MUSEUM by *McAdam Partnership*, 1976–80. Rustic vernacular classical, harled, a very rare and exceptional steading on a semicircular plan. Bold four-stage tower framed by two-storey quadrant wings which enclose the N half of a circular forecourt. In the centre, six segmental cartshed arches in the tower and wings, absolutely plain. The tower's first and second floors have Serlian windows (second floor blind), the third is a doocot with thermal windows on each side; truncated pyramidal roof with Roman Doric peristyle. Quadrant wings with functional external stairs have simple windows, first floor relatively low, dramatic sweeping roofs. Some of the original interior remains, including the nesting boxes. Rear coachhouse probably added by *John Smith I* in the 1830s. A separate single-storey BYRE and DAIRY extends the buildings into a three-quarter circle around the S half of the forecourt. The COACHMAN'S HOUSE was built across the E–W axis of the forecourt *c.* 1830. Ground and low first floors extending across five broad bays, with slightly projecting pedimented centrepieces on each side, that to the S incorporating a carriage arch with slit-windows above. Rubble-built, generally plain, some interior features survive.

WALLED GARDEN, 200 m. E. Now sawmill and nursery. Random rubble walls with datestone 1766 but probably rebuilt early to mid C19. BOTHY at NW corner, single-storey three bay with lying-pane glazing, hip-roofed attic. HEAD GARDENER'S HOUSE at NE corner, single-storey three bays with attic, with narrow door and window openings, one of them blind; C19 skewputts.

LAUNDRY, 70 m. NNE. Perhaps late C18, converted into NORTH-EAST FOLKLORE ARCHIVE by *Leslie F. Hunter*, 1995. Two-storey three-bay frontage, with low first floor; harled with margins. Modern porch.

ICE HOUSE (30 m. SW). C18 or early C19. Subterranean stone chamber (egg-type) with brick approach stairs guarded by railings.

HARESHOWE WORKING FARM, 450 m. SE, is a typical C19 farm cottage with associated steading, railway carriage store and tractor shed, formerly at Ironside before reconstruction at Aden 1990–1, complete with contents of *c.* 1955. Nearby, the ruins of the former EPISCOPAL MEETING HOUSE of Rev. John Skinner ('Tullochgorum'), burnt by Hanoverian troops after the 'Forty-five.

FOOTBRIDGE, 250 m. SSW over the South Ugie Water, close to Old Deer, *c.* 1830. A single segmental arch in pinned rubble. Solid coped parapets guard the approaches; cast-iron lattice railings guard the span over the water, with central stone field-panels.

BRIDGE on S edge of Old Deer, carrying minor road over the South Ugie Water, *c.* 1830. Single segmental span in squared rubble, dressed voussoirs and coped parapets, framed between pilasters and curved wing-walls at ramped approaches. Panel on N side indicates reconstruction in 1908.

The GATEPIERS and NORTH LODGE on Station Road, and the WEST LODGE just N of Bridge of Deer, are presumably by *John Smith I*, *c.* 1832. The lodges, both ruinous, are Greek; the North Lodge with tetrastyle pedimented portico of monolithic antae. – TWIN LODGES. Shells only, no roofs. Single-storey, each with a lancet facing the road, trabeated doorway and window towards the drive.

CARTLEHAUGH, 0.7 km. N. Probably late C18, once known as the Dambrod (or Damboard) Inn. Two-storey four-bay frontage in black whinstone and rust-tinted granite forming a chequerboard pattern with grey granite dressings at the windows, all cherry-cocked. Gabled roof with moulded skewputts and coped end stacks. Later ground-floor bay window. Previous house to rear perhaps built *c.* 1760 to replace Saplinbrae (*see* below) as a coaching inn.

SAPLINBRAE HOUSE, 0.8 km. NW on the A950. The original house was two storey and three windows wide with a wall-head gable, dated 1756. It was perhaps built as a coaching inn, but by 1760 it was in use as the rectory of an Episcopal chapel at Waulkmill (now demolished). It was extended as Pitfour's dower-house in 1854, reputedly using stones from Deer Abbey (*see* above), and again by *Ellis & Wilson* in 1894, their SE wing resulting in a two-sided open court. Predominantly harled in white with plate-glazed windows, the doorway is blocked, the present entrance in a further modern extension.

NEWLANDS, 1 km. WNW on the A950. Standing on a slope overlooking Deer Abbey (*see* above), the former residence of the head gardener of Pitfour (q.v.). Built *c.* 1820, much altered. Two-storey three bays, with broad-eaved piended roof and tall blocky chimneystacks. Entrance framed by projecting bays with a continuous roof, added *c.* 1900; first-floor windows with stepped hoodmoulds. Harled in white with dressings and margins. Stepped wings with battlements single-storey at front, two-storey behind.

RECUMBENT STONE CIRCLE, Loudon Wood, 2.5 km. NW. Seven stones, four of which are still erect, standing on a bank of raised ground some 19 m. in diameter. (GN)

RECUMBENT STONE CIRCLE, 2 km. WSW, on the hillside of Aikey Brae. A fine circle dating to the Later Neolithic or Early Bronze Age (*c.* 2600–2000 B.C.). The recumbent stone and the stones of the circle are set on the edge of a large circular enclosure and linked by a narrow stone-kerbed bank. (GN)

LONG MOUND, Knapperty Hillock, 5 km. NW. This Neolithic long mound lies just below the crest of a hill near the Forest of Deer. It forms an impressive skyline feature when approached from the W, measures some 86 m. long and has enlarged projecting 'horns' at the W end, creating a defined area at this end of the cairn that may have been used for ceremonies at the monument. The mound is likely to overlie Neolithic mortuary deposits; a number of later cist burials dating from the Bronze Age have been found on top of the cairn. (GN)

PITFOUR. *See* p. 356.

6050

OLD HOUSE OF CARNOUSIE B

2.25 km. W of Kirkton of Forglen

A Z-plan tower house of *c.* 1577, remarkably the only one to survive in its original form in Banff, Buchan and Formartine, standing on a rise of ground enclosed by the Deveron on the S and by smaller burns on the E, N and W. Carnousie was probably built for Walter Ogilvie of Dunlugas, who sold it to his brother as early as 1583. A large wing added by *William Adam* as part of renovations *c.* 1740 was removed during the restoration begun in 1976, at which date the house had long been derelict.

The three-storey central block orientated E–W, 13 m. long and 8 m. deep, is linked by re-entrant angle turrets to a four-storey jamb 6 m. square with a gabled roof at its SE corner, and to a three-storey drum tower 7 m. in diameter with a conical spired roof to its NW. Construction is in loose pinned rubble, the walls for the most part 1 m. thick and harled in cream, with dressings in the local red sandstone. The entrance, a round-arched, roll-moulded doorway, is set into the SE jamb at ground level, facing along the flank of the central range and protected by wide-mouthed shot-holes. All the windows are chamfered; the ground-floor windows are very small for defensive reasons but at first floor the great hall in the centre block is identified by three large sash-and-case windows facing S which were formed *c.* 1740, while the second floor is lit by three windows breaking up through the wall-head into catslide dormers. The first- and second-floor windows in the NW drum tower were also formed *c.* 1740, but those in the SE jamb are much smaller, their openings unaltered since the late C16. Most of the windows face S, W or E; there are comparatively few windows facing N, to keep the cold out.

The slate roofs are very steep: that of the tall SE jamb is swept down over a moulded eaves cornice across the small stair-turret which is corbelled within the angle above the doorway, and into the roof of the central block. Within the angle between the central block and the NW drum tower, another small stair-turret has a semi-conical roof. The roof of the drum tower has a remarkable sculptured stone finial reinstated during the restoration.* Both the main block and the SE tower have crowstepped end gables; the chimneystacks are of different heights but all have a massive quality with very tall tapered copes. The date 1577 with thistle motif is carved into one of the SE tower's skewputts but this seems to have been added during the restoration. Three others are carved with fine portraits, the gentleman with beard and cap perhaps Walter Ogilvie himself.

Within the SE jamb, a scale-and-platt stair rises around a spine-wall from the entrance corridor to the first floor. The ground floor of the central block contains two vaulted chambers, the larger nearest the drum tower being the kitchen with its range in the N wall. The great hall occupies the whole of the central block's first floor, with an intramural chamber on the N side, and its fireplace bears the inscription 'My Hovp is in ye Lord God' with a frieze sculptured with dragons and unicorns in low relief. The circular and ovoid stair-turrets in the re-entrant angles provide access to the second floor which is partitioned, the stair-turrets continuing up to the fourth-storey bedroom in the SE tower and an attic-floor bedroom within the roof of the NW drum tower.

Just which of the Aberdeenshire mason families designed Carnousie is a matter of speculation. It has a familial resemblance to *Thomas Leiper*'s much earlier and much smaller Terpersie (S), and it has the square-plan entrance jamb characteristic of his later houses. The high-quality sculpture is also consistent with his work, and while his triple gunloops are absent, the wide-mouthed gunloops are of the same indented type as at Tolquhon (q.v.). The planning of the entrance corridor has however led Harry Gordon Slade to conclude that it is a less martial work of the *Conns* of Auchry.

MAINS OF CARNOUSIE STEADING, 180 m. WNW. Built for Gen. Duff (cf. Delgatie Home Farm Steading), dated 1797 but probably incorporating earlier fabric. Square courtyard plan. Neoclassical entrance tower in centre of S front, two-storey in granite ashlar, its round-arched pend and first-floor Serlian window with triple key blocks; pediment with oculus supporting the plinth of an ogee-domed, ball-finialled bellcote with date. The steading buildings consist of long low ranges, rubble-built with ashlar dressings and hipped roofs, the S elevation being blind externally. Within the courtyard, E side, a simple but handsome seven-bay cartshed arcade, and a further round-arched pend on the N side; condition now sadly derelict.

NEW HOUSE OF CARNOUSIE, 0.8 km. S. A magnificent Italianate palace built by *Archibald Simpson* during the late 1830s but seemingly never fully fitted out, and demolished *c.* 1929 when its masonry was reused for Aberdeen University's Elphinstone Hall (*see Buildings of Scotland: Aberdeenshire: South*

*A tapered rope finial formerly on the N gable of the SE jamb is still at Craigston (q.v.), removed there for safety when the future of Carnousie was uncertain.

and Aberdeen). Its NORTH LODGE, *c.* 1880, and RED LODGE, *c.* 1890, survive, along with their GATEPIERS.

AULDTOWN OF CARNOUSIE, 1.4 km. WSW of Old House of Carnousie. A sophisticated early C19 villa incorporating a much simpler C18 farmhouse as its rear wing. Entrance front of villa, facing S, single-storey three bays raised over a basement with a finely detailed railed approach stair leading to a tripartite pilastered doorpiece with a delicate radial fanlight. Coursed rubble construction with raised margins and classical details, canted attic dormers.

8020 OLDMELDRUM

Situated on the junction of the old drove roads linking Aberdeen to Banff and Newburgh to Huntly, Oldmeldrum has existed since at least the 1640s, rising to prominence as Inverurie (S) fell into decline, hampered by its poor communications. The Commonty (now Jubilee Park) was granted to the feuars by King Charles I, and Oldmeldrum's status was confirmed when it was erected a burgh of barony under Adam Urquhart in 1671, the parish church moving from Bethelnie (q.v.) to the present site *c.* 1684. Markets were held in The Square, the citizens building their first Town Hall in 1741. They dealt both in arable produce and in cattle, which became increasingly important as the century progressed; the town also diversified into the manufacture of textiles, leather goods, alcohol, pistols and snuff.

In 1804, as improved agricultural practices began to take hold, and population swelled with workers displaced from the farms, the town was connected with the turnpike under construction between Aberdeen and Banff, but only a year later its pre-eminence was challenged – and ultimately overtaken – by its old rival Inverurie, which was linked with Aberdeen by the Aberdeenshire Canal. The canal closed when the Great North of Scotland Railway, which largely followed its route, opened in 1854, but a branch was extended to Oldmeldrum in 1856 with its terminus W of the Square in Eavern Place, just off Commercial Road. The large board school erected here by *William Smith* in 1876 was much extended and spoiled in the mid C20. However, the town's substantial expansion as a consequence of the oil boom encouraged construction of a new secondary school, library and police station on its western outskirts in 2002.

CHURCHES AND PUBLIC BUILDINGS

MELDRUM PARISH CHURCH. A T-plan preaching-box of *c.* 1684 incorporating stones from the previous church at Bethelnie (q.v.); enlarged in 1767; S aisle rebuilt in present transeptal Gothic form by *William Smith* (of *J. & W. Smith*) in 1861; original church re-windowed by *Matthews & Mackenzie* in 1885–6; internally refitted by *George Bennett Mitchell & Son* in 1952–4 after a period of disuse. On its long N flank the nave is lit by three pointed-arch windows with the basket tracery characteristic of Mackenzie and dark granite voussoirs; on the S, Smith's aisle gable is buttressed on one side only to support an asymmetrical bellcote and has a tall plate-traceried two-light window with silver-grey and dark granite voussoirs over paired shouldered lights which have been blocked.* Mackenzie also built the narrow gabled E stair bay which replaced an earlier forestair, and within the angle thus formed Mitchell added a simple porch. The interior is as remodelled in 1952–4. The S aisle gallery has been closed off, the furnishings are modern. – STAINED GLASS. Two fine windows by *Gordon Webster*, 1957: in the chancel 'There Shall Be One Fold & One Shepherd'; in the S aisle 'And a Little Child Shall Lead Them'. Two other lights in the S aisle, 'I Shall Sing and Make Music to the Lord' (King David with his harp) and 'Well Done Good and Faithful Servant' (Christ receiving his flock) are later, by a different artist. Near the church, the WAR MEMORIAL by *D. Morren & Co.*, 1920. A kilted granite soldier on a very plain Neoclassical plinth, head bowed, hands resting on his rifle in a conventional pose of mourning (cf. Udny and Portsoy (qq.v.) and Rhynie and Tarland (S)).

CHURCH HALL, Albert Road. Converted 1908 by *James Cobban* from the former Secession (United Presbyterian) Church, built *c.* 1822–3 and closed 1905. A simple three-bay preaching-box with slim round-headed windows and tall roof inset with neat dormer ventilators. Small two-storey three-bay house (THE BEECHES) built to the S shortly afterwards was formerly the U.P. manse.

ST MATTHEW AND ST GEORGE (Episcopal), Urquhart Road. By *Ross & Joass*, 1862–3, on a site occupied by this congregation since the early C19. Early Dec, simple yet refined. Five-bay nave and chancel with a SW tower and spire, all built in dressed silver granite coursed and pinned. The nave and chancel walls are kept relatively low but buttressed at the corners to receive the thrust of tall, steeply pitched roofs. Large gable windows with freestone tracery and smaller windows in the flanks have polychrome voussoirs, the silver granite contrasting with black blocks; roofs clad in blue slate with moulded skewputts, bracketed eaves, dormer ventilators and decorative ironwork by *Francis Skidmore*. Square-based tower is deftly broached to octagonal with slim lights in alternate sides, and carried into a small belfry with louvred openings and stone spire with lucarnes and weathervane 24 m. above ground. Within the angle between tower and nave, a gabled porch, its entrance arch supported on inset columns of Stirling Hill granite. Chancel roof-line rather lower than nave, with organ chamber and vestry annexe lower still on the N side. Beneath the E gable

*The original aisle had a bellcote similar to that at Culsalmond (S) on its S gable. The stonework does not appear to have been kept.

window, a square panel contains a floriate cross and dedicatory inscription round its circumference to Leonora Sophia Ramsay, in whose memory the chancel was paid for by her husband, John Ramsay of Barra.*

Inside, white plastered walls, with open roofs supported on arched collar-braces which spring from stone corbels, those in the chancel finely carved. The chancel arch rises from four inset columns with shafts of Purbeck marble, and bases and foliate capitals in Caen stone. The chancel is raised; its floor in *Minton*'s encaustic tiles now covered over and the original choir stalls also removed. – SEDILIA and PISCINA in arched freestone surrounds. – FONT, from the previous church. Octagonal in Caen stone, richly sculpted and supported on four squat clustered columns. – PULPIT. Red pine with traceried panels. – STAINED GLASS. Three-light E window – the Agony in the Garden, Crucifixion and Resurrection – and W window – Scenes of Baptism – both by *John Hardman*, 1863. Of the same date, the Ascension Witnessed by the Disciples and Angels in the chancel's S flank. The nave windows are later: on the N side, Our Lord Driving the Moneylenders Out from the Temple, 'Hosanna to the Son of David' (Our Lord's entry into Jerusalem before the Passion) and two scenes from the Garden of Gethsemane, both early additions to the church with dates 1857 (evidently transferred) and 1865. Two windows in the S wall, 'Hail Highly Favoured' (the Annunciation) and the Magi, are both of *c.* 1887. Nearest the porch, the Presentation in the Temple, *c.* 1895. – MONUMENTS. Grandiloquent WALL TABLET by *Powells* to Capt. Beauchamp Colclough Urquhart of Meldrum, †1898, last of the Urquhart lairds. Cherubs surround an inscription which records a heroic death leading his troops into battle against the dervishes of Sudan (cf. his memorial at New Byth Parish Church (q.v.)).‡

In the CHURCHYARD, immediately S of the nave, twin low TOMB-CHESTS decorated with long-shafted foliate crosses mark the final resting place of John Ramsay (†1895) and his wife, Leonora Sophia (†1862). The powerful Ramsays vied for influence with the local lairds on their own territory: the Urquharts and the Duffs are buried in their railed ENCLOSURE at the E end of the churchyard, where a tall CELTIC CROSS with ornate strapwork commemorates Capt. Beauchamp Urquhart, Khedive Star, †1898 (*see* church interior). A smaller Celtic cross, with pierced head again with strapwork, is dedicated to his father (?) who died two years previously. – Lying slab for Robin Beauchamp Duff, †1990, the last hereditary laird of Meldrum and Byth, distinguished journalist and broadcaster, adviser to the Maharajah of Bundi, discerning *bon viveur* and chairman of Scottish Ballet.

*Although the nave and tower were paid for by public subscription, he was probably the driving force behind the rebuilding of the church as a whole.

‡Meldrum passed through his sister to the Duffs of Hatton (q.v.).

TOWN HALL, The Square. Built by *William Smith* (of *J. & W. Smith*) in 1877. A dignified classical edifice in grey granite, two storeys, five windows wide, with its entrance bay slightly stepped forward and rising through first floor with a tinctured Urquhart coat of arms (from the old Town Hall) up into the clock tower. The architraved doorpiece and flanking ground-floor windows are all round-headed, and the corners are bowed to protect them from traffic; they corbel to the square beneath the municipal apartments at first floor. A wall-head cornice and parapet enclose the tall hipped roof, with stylized scrolls and anta-pilasters flanking the clock stage; this, in turn, supports a square timber belfry, also pilastered, with leaded ogee dome and weathervane.

DESCRIPTION

THE SQUARE is the heart of Oldmeldrum – the focal point of its Old Town – but is itself of mid- to late C19 appearance, dominated on its W side by the Town Hall (*see* Public Buildings). It once extended rather further to the N until it was foreshortened in the late C19 by the modest row of two-storey shops and houses now standing on that side. On the E side, the former ABERDEEN TOWN & COUNTY BANK, built 1855, is similar to an Italianate villa, two storeys and three bays in pale granite, but with a Roman Doric porch built at an angle against its S flank. On the S, the former Free Church MANSE, built immediately after the Disruption of 1843 by *James Henderson*, follows familiar Georgian precedents, two storeys and basement, three windows wide, within a railed area; its pilastered doorpiece with simple consoles and shallow block-pediment and the wall-head's block cornice are the chief indicators of its late date.

Close to the Town Hall but just off the Square, the mildly Baroque CLYDESDALE BANK (originally North of Scotland Bank) was built by *R. G. Wilson* (of *Ellis & Wilson*) in 1903. Its principal front is two-storey five bays broad with a central entrance but is asymmetric, the r. bays occupied by the bank itself slightly advanced under a pedimental gable. The doorway and windows of the business premises rise into boldly key-blocked arches, while the windows of the bank agent's house are contrastingly simple and modest. Also nearby, MORRIS'S HOTEL was opened as a coffee-house in 1673 – Scots vernacular, two storeys and attic with irregular fenestration, harled with moulded skews at its gables. Integrated into the NATHALAN COURT SHELTERED HOUSING COMPLEX (*see also* Barnett Court and Wyverie Court below), an attractive Late Georgian house, its two-storey three-bay frontage built in rubble, and dated 1829 over its doorway.

The Old Town developed predominantly to the N of The Square within a triangle of ground formed by the gradual convergence of two long streets, Cowgate on the W and King

Street on the E. Within this area the relatively narrow feus encouraged the construction of buildings with their gables facing the road, hence, for example, the attractive parade of gables along MAJOR LANE to the NE of The Square. Then on the gentle curve where Major Lane merges into King Street, and King Street branches into Urquhart Road, a simple L-plan block, the old GORDON ARMS HOTEL initialled and dated IT♡CS 1727 on its S gable skewputt, and then the next short row of gables steps forward in line with the changed course of the street in the most natural way possible. In the tight junction site itself, there is a small building with a plain two-storey drum at the angle. Together with AIRD HOUSE of *c.* 1880, this forms a picturesque approach into King Street.

In KING STREET itself No. 1 is a pretty two-storey three-bay house of *c.* 1830 in the vernacular classical style, its doorway and windows in slim granite surrounds standing out against the harl; its transom-light has intersecting glazing bars. Further good houses in JAMES STREET, particularly No. 16 built in the late C18, two-storey three bays in squared rubble with lighter doorway and window surrounds, and set back within a railed garden. Just beyond the junction of James Street with King Street are BARNETT COURT and WYVERIE COURT, sheltered housing developments built by the local authority. They represent a good example of how modern housing can be grafted into a historic environment through well-considered design informed by sensitivity to the existing surroundings. The houses are mostly small single-storey, but with some two storeys for variety, and are consequently easy to manage; they are laid out in short rows on an irregular but intelligible street-plan which is dense but not claustrophobic, and with a single entrance for cars off Urquhart Road rather than being a through route. The houses are brick, but in light grey or occasionally golden-brown pebbledash, the roofs are slate, with square chimneystacks and cans at the gables, the doors panelled, with neatly detailed handrails, and the timber-framed windows look like (and in a few cases actually are) the traditional sash-and-case type. Small areas of grass are planted with trees, and hardstandings are broken up by a variety of different surfaces. Returning towards The Square, COWGATE and LOWER COWGATE extending off it are lined with more late C18 and C19 cottages, one house set back from the road being simple Gothic of *c.* 1875.

Crossing back over The Square, KIRK STREET leading to Kirk Brae was as its name suggests formed as the route to the new parish church and is therefore late C17; the charming open area just off The Square is a typical example of early town planning, the houses on the S and W sides being mostly two-storey Scots vernacular of the C18, while those on the N side are the same two-storey height but built in the C19. On the S, No. 10 faces gable-on to the road, with two doorways in its flank: the original one is set in a simple surround with its key block dated 1734.

SOUTH ROAD begins with the MELDRUM ARMS HOTEL, an attractive row of two-storey vernacular buildings in cream harl which steps down with a fall in the ground to the E. Reputedly established in the 1670s, the central range of buildings is rather later, presumably mid-C18, although extended at each end. Outside is a STATUE, early to mid-C19, of a sailor brought here by the hotel's erstwhile proprietor, Commander Kelly R.N., in 1938. Around the corner on the opposite side of the road, three good houses. First WILLOWBANK, a villa of *c.* 1870 with its central spired entrance tower added *c.* 1900. Then CROMLETBANK, two-storey three-bay with a gabled roof in the vernacular classical style, *c.* 1830, and small single-storey side wings; its ground-floor canted bays are later additions. CROMLETHILL also *c.* 1830 is in the same idiom, but of rather broader proportions, with a timber Roman Doric porch.

Former PARISH MANSE (Cromlet House), Mill Road. Probably *c.* 1790, enlarged 1813, 1829 and again by *William Smith* in 1878–80; further reconstruction in 1957–8 during which the 1829 wing was demolished. Entrance front is two storeys, three windows widely spaced, with a recent conservatory built over the doorway. Openings chamfered, with hinge-pins for shutters, moulded gable skewputts, later canted dormers. Rear elevation mostly blind except for the central gabled bay; modern glazed link to former coachhouse and byre enclosing a three-sided court.

KIRKHILL, Kirkhill Drive, off Albert Road. Neo-Jacobean by *William Smith* (of *J. & W. Smith*), *c.* 1850. Principal front tall two-storey, symmetrical over a semi-sunk basement. Central entrance framed between broad projecting ends rising into curvilinear gables, the ground-floor apartments lit by canted bays. Harled, with some exposed deep red stonework. Four-centred arched doorway, with the window above breaking into a large dormer gablet, all first-floor windows with timber mullions and transoms, steep roofs punctuated by tall simple chimneystacks. Left flank with lion (?) mask on corbelled chimney-breast, single-storey and attic side wing.

GLEN GARIOCH DISTILLERY, Distillery Road. A picturesque composition of several dates; reputedly founded *c.* 1790 by John Manson, a local merchant, although its origins may stretch back still further. It was substantially rebuilt throughout the C19. The MALTINGS erected *c.* 1830 for Ingram Lamb & Co. are the earliest surviving part of the complex, a simple but impressive block of squared grey granite rubble coursed and pinned, four storeys high and eleven bays – some 30 m. – in overall length. The structure is tied together at the second and low third floors with anchor-plates, and the floors themselves are supported internally on cast-iron columns. A second maltings, similar in its length and depth but only three storeys, was subsequently built to the rear of the first. It is linked across an alley by an enclosed bridge to the KILNS (in squared grey and gold granite, no pinnings) which are set back from the road within an enclosed court, but easily identifiable by the twin pyramidal roofs which are truncated to support their ventilators. The kiln floors are perforated iron plates, once fired with local peat. The STILL ROOM is the double-height gable-fronted structure standing immediately on the N side of the junction with King Street, which was built in grey and gold granite immediately following the acquisition of the distillery by J.F. Thomson & Co. of Leith in 1884; through its large (altered) window the copper stills themselves are clearly visible. The gables of the TUN ROOM and MASH HOUSE behind the Still Room can be seen in the lane which forms a continuation of King Street and passes between the distillery itself and an irregular row of single-storey buildings which constitute the FILLING STORE and three BONDED WAREHOUSES. Opposite the Still Room on the S side of the junction the WORKSHOPS, STORES and COOPERAGE occupy a long single-storey and attic range in its own walled forecourt; they were partially converted in 2005 to provide the present visitor centre. Behind these workshops, the twin gables visible from King Street represent an additional GRANARY, MALTINGS AND BONDED STORE dated 1901 on a drainpipe. A short distance (80 m.) to the E along Distillery Road, set within generous gardens, the single-storey and attic GLEN GARIOCH HOUSE is the manager's residence.

MELDRUM HOUSE

2 km. N

The Barony of Meldrum was reputedly granted by the Abbot of Arbroath to Philip de Fendarg, a Flemish soldier, in 1236, and the site of Meldrum House was occupied by his descendants until it passed to the Setons in the mid C15, thence to the Urquharts and finally the Duffs. Meldrum House itself claims origins – and a datestone – as early as 1625, and was extended in the C18. Its Jacobean style, however, reflects a major remodelling by *Archibald Simpson* for Beauchamp Urquhart *c.* 1836–40, when it was recast as a three-sided open courtyard plan with its central entrance range on the N side. Its current appearance is more recent still, the result of further reconstruction by *Duncan & Munro* for Doris Duff in 1934–7. During this last reconstruction Simpson's house was substantially reduced both in height and extent, and adopted its current L-plan form with the main entrance in the outer elevation of the short arm facing W.

The present ENTRANCE FRONT, although of consistent two-storey height, is thus composed of the main block's end gable in coursed brown granite to the N, balanced on the S by the wing in grey granite rubble clasped between circular angle towers with spirelet roofs. The main block's end gable has a canted bay which Duncan & Munro made into the new principal entrance by adding a doorpiece. A magnificent C17 balustraded stair with ball-finialled pedestals rises in two flights to French doors in the first floor of the wing, half-concealing two segmental archways at ground floor, but its original location is uncertain.* Over the N doorway are the tinctured arms of Urquhart, and over the S doorway, set in a recess, is another heraldic motif with monogrammed initials V.S.C.A. and date 1625, in reference to Walter Seton, Chancellor of Aberdeen.

On the SOUTH FRONT, Simpson's principal elevation was rather different from how it appears today. It was originally taller, three storeys and nine windows wide, with a central entrance sheltered under a very grand open porch. Its crowstep-gabled end bays were advanced forward to link up with the lower two-storey wings, and its third and seventh bays had curvilinear Dutch gables. The porch had a coat of arms set into its parapet, and octagonal piers which rose into bold pinnacles framing the semi-elliptical archways. The windows, although generally astragalled sash-and-case, were mullioned and transomed with hoodmoulds at the curvilinear-gabled bays and on the inner flanks of the advanced end bays: these had stepped hoodmoulds which were eliminated during the reconstruction. When Duncan & Munro reduced the house, they rebuilt the crowstepped and curvilinear gables above their lower wall-head, and reinstated the square-shafted chimneystacks so that the house retained its familiar roof-line. The porch has been removed but its coat of arms is perhaps that now above the W entrance.

Internally, the vaulted ground floor suggests the house's early origins. In the entrance hall the stair is by Duncan & Munro, Simpson's stair having been demolished, but many of his interiors (with fireplaces by *MacDonald & Leslie*, granite and marble cutters in Aberdeen) have survived. After the 1930s reconstruction, the principal apartments arranged across the S front became the dining room, billiard room and study, with a small flower room and drawing room at the far E end, and cellars and office in the W wing; the first floor contained eleven family and servants' bedrooms. After the Second World War the house was operated as an upmarket hotel and it has served that purpose ever since.

Opposite the S elevation are a pair of C17 GARDEN HOUSES, two-storey, circular with conical roofs. Built into sloping ground, their first floors are reached by wooden bridges.

The principal approach was formerly through the GATEHOUSE, STABLE AND COACHHOUSE, dated 1628, standing 80 m. NW of the main house. They are symmetrical in general outline – a tall central gatehouse with a round-headed archway and first-floor doocot with pinnacles at each corner, flanked by lower two-storey wings which return back at the ends to present a shallow U-plan towards Meldrum House itself; the walls are harled in white, the roofs steeply pitched. On the NW front – farthest from the house – the archway is richly rusticated, with

*The claim that these stairs derive from Castle Fraser (S) is incorrect. They were here by the 1770s.

the royal arms above; on its SE face to the court it is roll-moulded, while the vault has twin bosses with recesses in its sides. Carriage arches were formed in the wings in the late C18 (perhaps 1777), with further alterations by *Archibald Simpson* in 1836–9.

The SOUTH GATEWAY, 0.9 km. SSW, is Tudor-Jacobean, presumably 1851, the date of the adjacent lodge. A four-centred carriage arch set between tall slim octagonal piers with double-globule finials, and tinctured Urquhart arms, the design has been adapted from the porch which Simpson added to the main house. It has long gently curving flank walls with pedestrian gateways to each side, again terminating in octagonal piers with finials; these are harled in white with exposed granite dressed work. Just inside the gateway, the CHAIN LODGE matches it in style but is not harled. The central entrance is canted out beneath a tall bargeboarded gable which rises to the height of the roof.

KILBLEAN HOUSE, 3 km. ENE. Well-proportioned vernacular classical farmhouse of 1827 built for the Manson family (*see* Glen Garioch Distillery, above) who had purchased the estate in 1809. Two storeys, three bays and attic, built in coursed pinned whinstone rubble with light golden rubble for the window surrounds and quoins; finely detailed front door; gabled roof with simply moulded end stacks. An earlier cottage, formerly thatched, is retained as the rear wing. Large garden enclosed by good rubble walls incorporating a cheese press.

MILL OF FORESTERHILL, 3 km. NE. Now converted to domestic use. An L-plan grain mill, partly of early date, but raised in the early C19. Aberdeen kiln ventilator mounted on roof. The external overshot wheel 1.8 m. in diameter and mid-C19 internal gearing have been substantially preserved.

FINGASK HOUSE. *See* p. 178.

ORDIQUHILL *see* CORNHILL

ORROK HOUSE *see* PETTENS

9060 PEATHILL

A kirkton in the centre of Pitsligo parish, its focal point before Rosehearty and Sandhaven (qq.v.) developed on the coast.

OLD PITSLIGO PARISH CHURCH. Known as the 'Visible Kirk' since it was used as a landmark by sailors. It was built by Sir Alexander Forbes, 1st Lord Pitsligo, after the minister of Aberdour had railed from his pulpit against the three Pits of Hell – Pittendrum, Pittulie and Pitsligo (qq.v.) – an outburst doubtless prompted by religious differences with the heritors. T-plan, comprising a rectangular preaching-box of *c.* 1632, with Laird's Aisle on the S added in 1634. Pinned grey granite and red sandstone rubble formerly harled, with red sandstone dressings. Only the W gable and the S flank including the Laird's Aisle survive practically intact, the W gable crowned by a birdcage bellcote, the finest (with Old St Congan, Turriff, 27 q.v.) to be found anywhere in Scotland. Its triple clustered colonnettes frame traceried openings and support an entablature, with a pyramidal spirelet announced on each side by demi-lune pediments, and pinnacles at each corner. It is initialled A.L.P. (Alexander Lord Pitsligo) with date 1635 on the rear. Beneath this, between the small arched gallery windows in moulded surrounds, a panel displays Lord Pitsligo's arms, with the three boars' heads of the Forbes family, three *fraises* (strawberry flowers) for the Frasers of Philorth, a coronet and the initials A.F. One of the church's NW quoins is carved with arcading. The Laird's Aisle lit by a large pointed-arch window in its S gable has external stairs to the loft, which opens into the church through a broad sandstone archway. The magnificent pew which it contained was transferred to the new church (*see* below) in 1890. Immediately W of the Laird's Aisle, a blocked doorway, one moulded jamb still surviving, with above a panel representing death's-head, hourglass and gravedigger's tools with initials A.L.P. and date 1634. The E-end gable was formerly graced by a portrait of the church's first minister, 'Canting Andrew' – the Rev. Andrew Cant. Inside, in the NE and NW corners are the remains of neat spiral stairs added in 1793 which rose to the galleries at each far end.

Former PITSLIGO NEW PARISH CHURCH. By *A. Marshall Mackenzie* (of *Matthews & Mackenzie*), 1889–90, built for the Rev. Dr Walter Gregor to replace the Old Parish Church (*see* above), which had become inadequate.* Although only half the size that Gregor had demanded, despite a declining congregation, it is nevertheless a very substantial structure, robustly built in tooled ashlar granite from New Pitsligo (q.v.) with darker pinnings. Scots Gothic of the Aberdeen Greyfriars type on a cruciform plan. W gable is lit by two tall Y-traceried windows and a roundel beneath a relieving arch, moulded skewputts; its bellcote with trefoiled openings and finialled diagonal pinnacles is crowned by a spirelet with a weathervane. Entrance porch in the four-bay S elevation, a round-arched doorway framed by broad clasping buttresses with slim

*Attempts by the civil authorities to compel the Free Church and Presbyterian feuars of Rosehearty (q.v.) to meet their legal obligations to contribute to the church's construction resulted in a serious fish-fight and subsequent criminal charges. The townspeople struck an appropriate revenge against their parish minister – who was the leading expert on Scottish folklore – by burning him in effigy, after which he retreated to Lasswade in Midlothian, although he remained technically in post until 1895. In his defence it should be noted that (like Peter McLaren in Fraserburgh) he was also exceptionally brave, single-handedly nursing his flock during an outbreak of cholera.

oversailing hoodmould beneath its gablet, cross finial over the apex. Large three-light basket-traceried windows on each side of the porch and in the three bays of the N flank. The transepts are of different sizes, with roofs of different heights – that on the S relatively shallow on plan, designed to accommodate the Laird's Pew from the Old Church, with a Y-traceried window and side porch; the N transept much wider and deeper for additional seating capacity and lit by a larger window with basket tracery, both having small trefoiled lights in their flanks. Three-sided apsidal E end with Celtic cross finial stands very tall because of the falling ground, its long slim windows trefoiled.

Inside, a handsome wagon roof, boarded in pitch-pine, the bay divisions' timber arches supported on corbels. The
28 LAIRD'S PEW is perhaps the best in Scotland, a magnificent example of finely detailed woodcarving. Whether it was made by indigenous or foreign craftsman, or imported from England or abroad, is not known, but the details are Netherlandish in character. Raised a little above nave floor-level, and constructed in oak, it consists of a boldly panelled and consoled front, above which slim columns at each end support a decorated canopy over the front row of seats. This canopy has a compartmented and panelled ceiling and is fronted by an entablature divided into four bays by dosserets with Corinthian capital pendants; shouldered flat arches with fretted fringes at the soffits link these together. Above the entablature, spike finials flank rich cartouches, the central one spanning two bays. Behind the front seats the canopy is supported by a screen of six further columns, the second row occupied by lesser family members and important servants being open to the transept ceiling; its entrance is by an architrave frame at the rear, again finely detailed. The panels in the front of the Laird's Pew and the cartouches over its entablature are carved with initials and heraldic symbols representing Alexander, Lord Pitsligo, and his wife, Dame Isabella Keith. In the spandrels are the date, 1634, a woodcarver's tool, and the initials B.M.V. for Beata Maria Virgine – a stark indication of the laird's lack of sympathy for the Presbyterian régime.*

Other early WOODWORK from the old church includes the raised octagonal PULPIT in pitch-pine, inset with carved panels, that in the front displaying the arms and initials of Andrew Cant, first minister of Pitsligo, with heraldic arms and date 1634; further PANELS in the side of the choir seats and apse represent lions rampant for the Keiths (?) and *fraises* for the Frasers. – GASOLIERS, 1903. Brass with glass shades. A rare survival in an Aberdeenshire parish church. – ORGAN, in the apse. By *Conacher & Co.*, installed *c.* 1900.‡

*At some point, seemingly in an attack of Puritanism, the Laird's Pew was painted white; and it is said that it was restored to its former appearance in the mid C19 through the efforts of two fishermen, who painstakingly scraped off the paint over many years.

‡There were plans in 2012 to convert the church into a Jacobite Centre.

In the CHURCHYARD, around the old church, a fine collection of lying slabs and table tombs, C17 onwards, many well preserved: a slab for Ann Sims, †1724, is carved with a Resurrection scene, the angels dressed in kilts.

PITSLIGO PARISH CHURCH. *See* ROSEHEARTY.

MOUNTHOOLEY DOOCOT, 1 km. W. Dated 1800. Eye-catcher on a prominent site overlooking Rosehearty Bay. Stumpy tower, square with canted angles, built in massive rubble masonry. A hint of elegance in the large round oculi on each side, and a touch of fancy in its wall-head parapet, with tall crenels crowned by ball finials. Simple doorway. Nesting boxes with potence inside.

PENNAN 8060

A former fishing village in a beautiful situation, comprising a long row of houses following the gentle curve of Pennan Bay. Most are two-storey vernacular buildings with slate or pantiled roofs, probably built or reconstructed in the early to mid C19. Some face the street and look directly over the Moray Firth, but others are arranged with their end gables to the road as protection against the weather, and where two are arranged one behind another they form small alleyways or closes. All are rendered white, which gives the village a sparkling appearance; some are lined out as if built in ashlar, and some have painted doorways and window margins. At the foot of the steep hairpin bend which is the sole approach to the village stands the PENNAN INN, similar in style to the houses. The village had three small boatyards and a population of 300 at the beginning of the C20 but declined after the advent of larger steam-propelled vessels. The HARBOUR was important not only for fishing but also for the export of millstones from nearby Cummerton: its red ashlar E pier is of *c.* 1850; the concrete W pier by *James Barron, C.E.*, 1902–4, replaced one destroyed *c.* 1860 and both were extended by *D. & C. Stevenson*, 1909. Pennan was the setting for Bill Forsyth's film *Local Hero* (1983). Its success encouraged several local and national bodies to join together to assist the village's conservation in 1987–8, and those on whom the film made a lasting impression have continued to visit from all around the world.

AUCHMEDDEN CHURCH. A mission hall on the crossroads above Pennan, by *John Sleigh*, 1884. 'Muscular Gothic', strong and craggy like the old fisherfolk themselves. Tall entrance gable in rock-faced grey granite framed by slim intaken buttresses which rise into pyramidal pinnacles, transept-like stair halls on either side. The pointed-arch doorway is set within a buttressed and gabled surround; above it is a plate-traceried two-light window, and above that again is a simple bellcote. The flanks are harled over local Red Head sandstone with plain lancets. Impressively scaled interior, with a deep gallery at the entrance end, and the open roof supported on queenpost trusses. Distinctive pitch-pine woodwork including the strongly architectonic platform PULPIT and flanking doors to the vestry crowned by segmental pediments. – COMMUNION TABLE with Early Italian Renaissance baluster colonnettes, *c.* 1895, brought here in 1967. FONT. Gifted in 1968, from a Glasgow church. Carved stone, excellent lettering. – ELDERS' CHAIRS of *c.* 1860, perhaps from Aberdour Free Church.

NETHERMILL BRIDGE over Tore Burn, 0.7 km. WNW of Pennan. Later C18. A single hump-backed span with long approaches, rubble-built with tooled voussoirs and low coped parapets in tooled ashlar.

PROMONTORY FORT, 1 km. NW of Pennan, overlooking Cullykhan Bay. The site is reached by crossing a narrow spit of land which joins the promontory to the mainland. Excavations have uncovered evidence for timber palisades, earthen ramparts and timber and stone walling cutting off various portions of the promontory during the Later Bronze Age and Iron Age. Metalworking debris has also been found. Later, a medieval castle stood on the promontory. (GN)

1040

PETERHEAD

Peterhead has its origins in two early fishing villages, the Kirkton near Old St Peter's Church and the Roanheads where Almanythie Creek formed a natural haven: over the centuries incomers gradually occupied the shoreline between these two villages. In 1587 Robert Keith, Lord Altrie and brother of the 3rd Earl Marischal, received a charter erecting Peterhead into a burgh of barony and permitting him to build a harbour. Either he or the 4th Earl, who succeeded in 1593, built a tower house on Keith Inch, a small island accessible at low tide; its landing pier formed the basis of the South Harbour. Port Henry was also begun about this time, enlarged in 1616, then seemingly further improved in 1631. Associated with these changes was the growth of the burgh itself, with two broad thoroughfares branching from the E end of what is now Erroll Street: one towards the original harbour (now Marischal Street and Broad Street, the latter forming an elongated market square) and the other towards Port Henry along Commongate (now Back Street, Back Gate and Ellis Street), with Longate running N–S between them.

After the Jacobite Rebellion of 1715 the 9th Earl was attainted. Peterhead was forfeited to the Crown and eventually sold to the Governors of the Merchant Maiden Hospital in Edinburgh. The townspeople supported the Jacobite cause in 1745, but afterwards major improvements made to what is now the South Harbour led to much greater peace and prosperity. In the later C18

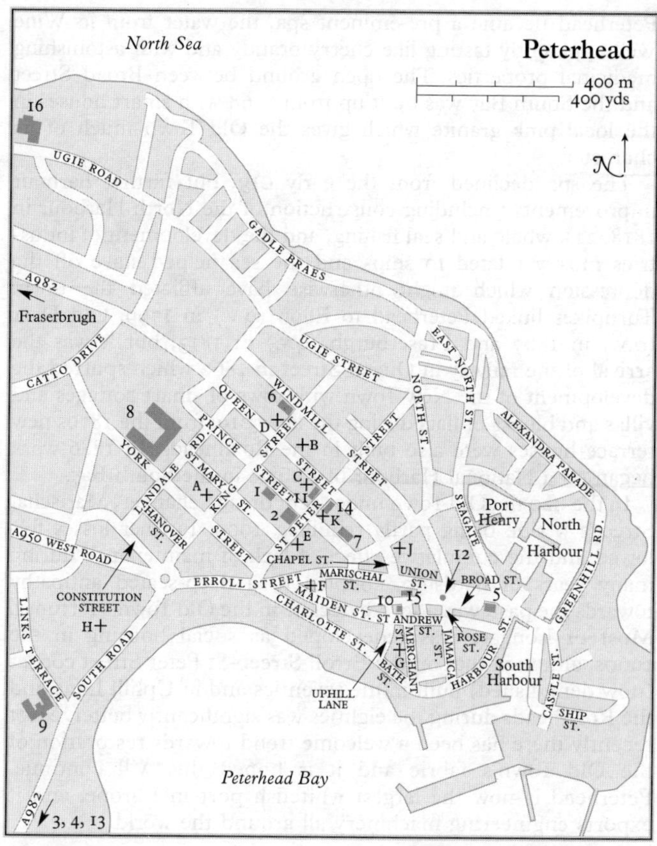

A	Baptist Church	1	Burgh Prison (former)
B	Congregational Church	2	Central School
C	Methodist Church	3	H.M. Prison Grampian
D	St Andrew	4	Meethill Tower
E	St Mary (R.C.)	5	Municipal Chambers (Arbuthnot House)
F	St Peter	6	North School (former)
G	St Peter (Episcopal)	7	Parish School (former)
H	St Peter's Old Church	8	Peterhead Academy
J	South Free Church	9	Peterhead Community Hospital
K	Trinity Parish Church	10	Police Station
		11	Public Library & Arbuthnot Museum
		12	Reform Monument
		13	Sailors' Memorial
		14	Sheriff Courthouse
		15	Town House (former)
		16	Ugie Hospital

Peterhead became a pre-eminent spa, the water from its Wine Well apparently tasting like cherry brandy and with astonishing medicinal properties. The open ground between Broad Street and the South Bay was built up from 1768 with smart houses in the local pink granite which gives the Old Town much of its character.

The spa declined from the early C19, but further harbour improvements (including construction of the North Harbour in 1818–22), whale and seal fishing, and the development of industries mostly related to ships and the sea helped stave off the depression which might otherwise have afflicted the town. Turnpikes linked Peterhead to Ellon (q.v.) in 1799, Old Deer (q.v.) in 1807 and Fraserburgh (q.v.) in 1813, but it was the arrival of the railway in Queen Street in 1862 which spurred the development of the New Town with rows of smart cottages and villas and blocks of flats during the later C19; from the 1870s new terrace houses were also built in the Roanheads. In 1886 work began on a National Harbour of Refuge in the South Bay.

In the C20 the Old Town underwent drastic changes, Marischal Street's N side being partly rebuilt *c.* 1909. Further losses followed and the cumulative effect of lack of maintenance during many years of hardship, coupled to a deep-seated antipathy towards the past, was a severe decline in the Old Town's fortunes. Most of Longate was redeveloped as social housing in the 1960s, although that on the Erroll Street–St Peter Street corner (now demolished) built in the seventies and in Uphill Lane and the Roanheads during the eighties was significantly better. Most recently there has been a welcome trend towards restoration of the Old Town's fabric and it is hoped this will continue. Peterhead is now the largest whitefish port in Europe, and it exports engineering machinery all around the world.

CHURCHES

BAPTIST CHURCH, King Street. By *James Anderson*, 1878. Broad gable front in Peterhead granite, splayed pointed doorway, stepped triple lancets above. Angle pilasters with pinnacles, squared rubble flanks.

CONGREGATIONAL CHURCH, Queen Street. By *James Matthews*, 1869–70. Gothic gable-front expressed as nave and aisles, built in Peterhead granite with gold and grey granite dressings. Paired pointed doorways, two-light plate-tracery window above. Intaken buttresses rise into small pinnacles; five-bay rubble flanks. Single-span interior, roof trusses partly exposed. Original central PULPIT; mid-C20 ORGAN CASE. – HALL by *James Watt C.E.* of Peterhead, 1909.

HARVEST COMMUNITY CHURCH, Chapel Street. *See* South Free Church.

METHODIST CHURCH, Queen Street. By *Ogilvie*, 1866. First Pointed gable front built in Peterhead granite with contrasting darker stone dressings. Cavetto-splayed pointed doorway, corner buttresses progressively intaken beneath finialled pinnacles;

stepped triple-light gallery window with the gable crowned by a blocky Maltese cross. Very low squared granite flanks, cherry-cocked. Interior single-span with roof trusses partly enclosed, central pendants. Original platform PULPIT with triple-arched back.

ST ANDREW, Queen Street. Former East Free Church. By *James Souttar*, 1868–70. Idiosyncratic Gothic. Gable front in Peterhead granite with golden granite dressings, framed between corner porches rising into low octagonal towers with stone spirelets. Three large windows, slightly pointed, and equal in size; their voussoirs increase in depth at the crown of the arch, a characteristic Souttar motif. Tracery displays proto-Art Nouveau features. Vestry added 1872, extended 1914. Plain single-span interior with canted ceiling. Central PULPIT, mid-C20. High-quality STAINED GLASS in W gable by *George Donald & Sons*, *c.* 1908.

ST MARY (R.C.), St Peter Street. First Pointed, 1850–1, probably designed by *Bishop James Kyle* (who presided at the opening) on the evidence of his typical L-plan arrangement of church and presbytery. Church's W gable with stepped triple lancets and a spheric triangle with tiny quatrefoil light, slim angle buttresses rising into finialled crocketed pinnacles. The angle is now filled by a C20 porch with bellcast gablet. Some original stonework reused at the doorway in its gabled and buttressed surround. Modernized interior. – FONT by *R.B. Leslie*, 1886.

ST PETER. The 'Muckle Kirk' on the Erroll Street–Maiden Street junction near the S entrance to town. Designed by *Alexander Laing* of Edinburgh, who had been recommended by the Governors of the Merchant Maiden Hospital, its substantial cost outraged the mostly Episcopalian feuars who went to the Court of Session to try to prevent it. Construction in 1804–6 was overseen by two local wrights, *Robert* and *John Mitchell*, with *Patrick Scott* of Aberdeen as their mason. A classical composition, the pedimented porch forming a frontispiece to the taller, broader block of the church behind, and supporting a tower with spire 36 m. high. Built in grey-brown granite ashlar, the three-bay porch has a central fanlit doorway. The tower rises square from a low plinth in three stages, its second clock stage pilastered with pediments, then the octagonal belfry with a plain frieze and cornice and a slim stone spire. Perhaps Laing was influenced by the tower of John Baxter's old Town House, Broad Street (*see* Public Buildings) which is noticeably similar. Behind the porch and tower, the church itself is a simple rectangle – the entrance front expressed as two storeys five windows wide, with a balustrade embracing the tower at the wall-head, and a hipped platform roof. Its Erroll Street flank is of five bays, lit by two tiers of windows with a large central doorway, but on Maiden Street it is lit by just four very tall round-arched windows, a reflection of the layout inside. The two-storey CHURCH HALL is by *Alexander Webster*, 1895–6. *p. 341*

Inside, a classic preaching-box with the pulpit centred in the E flank surrounded by original pews and a U-plan gallery carried on reeded Roman Doric columns. The insertion of cast-iron columns in 1830–1, following a report by *John Smith I*, was doubtless prompted – as at Laing's contemporary Huntly Parish Church (S) – by the collapse of the gallery at the parish church of Kirkcaldy in Fife; further remodelling took place in 1894. The oak PULPIT dates from a renovation of 1966–7 by *John Herdman Reid* of *Ian G. Lindsay & Partners*, and evokes much older examples: octagonal, raised well above the nave floor and with a sounding-board, its three carved emblems represent the Merchant Company of Edinburgh, the Church of Scotland and the Burgh of Peterhead. – The COMMUNION TABLE AND CHAIRS are more traditional Gothic revival, early to mid-C20. – FONT is in pink Peterhead granite, dated 1923. – ORGAN, in the W gallery, by *Rushworth & Dreaper*, 1967. – Fine STAINED GLASS on each side of the pulpit, by *Brother Gilbert Taylor* of Pluscarden Abbey, again from the 1960s: Christ in the Universe ('Nor May His Devices with the Heavens Be Guessed') and Christ and the Fishermen ('Come and I Will Make You Fishers of Men').

ST PETER (Episcopal), Merchant Street. By *Robert Mitchell* of Peterhead, 1813–14, on the site of an earlier Episcopal chapel. 'Churchwarden's Gothic', originally a modest rectangular structure built in squared rubble, with polygonal E apse added *c.* 1847 to the street, flanked by four-centred doorways and gallery stair windows. N porch 1884, further alterations by *A. Marshall Mackenzie* in 1904–5. The street-front was formerly enclosed by railings between granite Doric columns.* The interior, although Gothic rather than classical, is close in character to Crimond Parish Church (q.v.). Facing the apse, the original U-plan gallery with panelled fronts is carried on Roman Doric columns supported on very tall hexagonal bases; at the upper level, clustered colonnettes rise into three-bay Gothic arcades which carry the ceiling. Chancel arch opening into the apse likewise has clustered columns, and slim colonnettes in the angles support the vault. – Octagonal PULPIT with arcaded openings, probably dating from a remodelling of 1867. – Simple ALTAR with arcaded panelling and columns supporting its top. – Large bulbous FONT erected 1879, red Peterhead granite with twelve bosses of coloured spars, base in Rora granite and moulding in granite from Cairngall. – Apse PANELLING serves as a REREDOS incorporating a piscina and ciborium by *Robert Thompson*, *c.* 1926, with the usual mice as his signature. – Brass eagle LECTERN, introduced in 1902. – Simple Gothic pitch-pine PEWS. – ORGAN in pitch-pine stained as dark oak by *A. Marshall Mackenzie*, the instrument itself by *Wadsworth & Brother*, 1904, rebuilt in its present position by

*The columns were removed to separate addresses in Peterhead – one in Middle Grange, the other Grange House, Cairntrodlie.

Peterhead, St Peter.
Drawing, 1890

David Loosley in 1979. – STAINED GLASS. In the apse. Centre, dated 1853, St Andrew, with above St Margaret of Scotland holding a cross and her husband King David holding a church; below, St Kentigern and St Ninian; l. (dated 1847), St Peter with the Key of Heaven, flanked by scenes of sacrifice – a pelican feeding her young and the Agnus Dei; r. (1847), St Paul, flanked by scenes of martyrdom. – Under the N gallery, a small CHAPEL formed after the First World War. – MEMORIAL. Gothic tablet to William Bruce, M.D. †1879.

CHURCH HALL. A simple four-bay structure, its windows with coloured glass. Mid-C19, altered (rebuilt?) by *W. Stuart* in 1898, incorporating a late C18 house at the rear.

ST PETER'S OLD CHURCH,* South Road. The medieval church, which remained in use until 1803 (*see* St Peter's Parish Church, above), was a two-cell structure of which the pink granite

*This entry is by Richard Fawcett.

rubble side walls of the chancel and the chancel arch survive in fragmentary state, together with short return sections of the nave walls. A simple W tower of square plan with a pyramidal slated roof was added *c.* 1647; it possibly incorporated parts of the medieval W wall, though harling prevents certainty. Both the jambs and arch of the chancel arch are of unmoulded rectangular profile, and the simply blocked-out capitals point to a late C15 or early C16 date (rather than the C12 date commonly suggested); the abaci extend back as string courses along both the E and W faces of the wall. There is a blocked round headed window rear-arch in the S wall. – MONUMENTS. Inside the chancel area is a collapsed headstone with a skull, crossed bones and crossed sexton's tools flanked by pilasters supporting a swan-neck pediment, within which is a Baroque cartouche. Against the S flank of the chancel is the monument to Robert Kilgour, bishop of Aberdeen, †1790, framed by a pink granite architrave bereft of its pediment. To its E is a pink granite aedicular monument.

The CHURCHYARD contains a wide range of headstones, table tombs and obelisks, with a predominance of C19 polished pink granite. – WATCH-HOUSE of 1827. – WAR MEMORIAL. By *Messrs Charles MacDonald*, 1922. Square obelisk of Peterhead granite ashlar, 12 m. high, with acroteria; smaller SECOND WORLD WAR MEMORIAL behind.

SOUTH FREE CHURCH (now HARVEST COMMUNITY CHURCH), Chapel Street. By *William Hay*, 1878–9. An impressively tall and broad gable-fronted church in Peterhead granite ashlar. Pointed doorway with three-light plate-traceried Geometric window above; octagonal corner spirelet on the junction with Backgate cut down to a short crenellated parapet.

TRINITY PARISH CHURCH, St Peter Street. Built as the East Church, 1842, but became Free at the Disruption. Tudor-Gothic. Simple gable front with centre slightly stepped forward in grey granite ashlar to suggest a tall nave with its aisles in squared brown masonry for contrast. Three pointed-arch doorways, four-light gallery window, the gable rising into gablet pinnacles and a small peristyled cupola, classical in detail. After the restraint of the exterior, the interior comes as a surprise. The U-plan gallery with Gothic arcaded fronts rests on cast-iron columns with a second tier continuing up into shallow pointed arches which support the ceiling. It faces towards the E-end half-octagonal platform PULPIT approached by balustraded stairs on each side; this is raised up in front of a very handsome ORGAN with a fine display of painted pipes, probably installed in 1897 when *D. & J.R. McMillan* carried out alterations including the hall and vestry at the rear. Good bold COLOURED GLASS. The E end's excellent late Pre-Raphaelite MURAL DECORATION by *Ralph Hay*, 1912 – Christ flanking the organ on either side with, above, angels kneeling before a cross – is not only exceptional for a Free Church congregation but unique within the context of north Aberdeenshire.

PUBLIC BUILDINGS AND MONUMENTS

Former BURGH PRISON, No. 27 Prince Street. By *John Smith I* c. 1842–3, now residential. Robust two-storey three-bay front with recessed arches. Doorway with console-cornice and windows segment-headed at first floor.

CENTRAL SCHOOL, St Peter Street. Austere classical. Originally single-storey, built in 1838–40 as Peterhead Academy. Reconstructed to its present two-storey form by *Arthur Clyne*, c. 1905–6.

COMMUNITY CENTRE. *See* PETERHEAD ACADEMY.

H.M. PRISON GRAMPIAN, South Road. Designed by *Holmes Miller* and built by *Skanska Construction U.K.*, 2012–13. It replaces H.M. Prison Peterhead built in 1886–91 to provide convict labour for the National Harbour of Refuge (*see* Harbours).

MEETHILL TOWER. Built by the Liberals to celebrate the Great Reform Act of 1832, and originally fitted out as an observatory. A tall slim tower, square with canted angles, rising through five stages with a pronounced batter to a crenellated wall-head parapet added in 1907. Base stage with square-headed doorway, rusticated quoins, the shaft in squared granite.

MUNICIPAL CHAMBERS, Broad Street. Originally ARBUTHNOT HOUSE, built *c.* 1770 for James Arbuthnot and extended to the rear by his son George in 1805. The original house is a two-storey-and-basement block in pink granite ashlar with central pedimented attic gable, its symmetry and proportions compromised by the heightening of its S wing in 1960. Its Gibbsian doorway is approached between ball-finialled gatepiers supporting a wrought-iron lantern arch, all of *c.* 1770. Much more impressive is the N elevation of 1805 facing the harbour. Rising from lower ground this is three full storeys and three broad bays – an almost square frontage – with its central entrance framed between three-window bows, all in fine pink granite ashlar with low hipped roofs. The Union Street flank is in squared brown granite with central tripartite windows, long-and-short quoins and a wall-head pediment framed between panelled stacks. Magnificent interior, *c.* 1770 and 1805 with embellishments *c.* 1835, George Arbuthnot having become Provost of Peterhead in the previous year. Entrance hall leads into 1805 inner hall between eight slim reeded columns supporting an elegant segmental fanlight; the inner hall itself is double-height with oval first-floor landing. One room has raised and fielded panelling of *c.* 1770; the former dining room (?) remodelled *c.* 1835 has Greek Ionic columns and the interior generally is enriched by finely detailed doors and doorcases, wall panelling and plasterwork.

Former NORTH SCHOOL, King Street. Built 1877 by *Andrew Kidd*, Architect of the Peterhead School Board, with improvements in 1879, and further additions at the rear by *Arthur*

Clyne in 1903–4.* Gothic. A single-storey asymmetrical composition with gabled centre, porches and projecting wings, and a short Germanic tower with slated pyramid spire at the corner. A lively, modestly scaled building appropriate for young children with playful details including blocked Doric column chimneyshafts.

Former PARISH SCHOOL, Prince Street, now Aberdeenshire Council Offices. Built 1838, a temple to education. Single-storey symmetrical, central pedimented portico with three-bay wings to either side. Originally T-plan with a rear outshot but much extended. Portico Roman Doric distyle-*in-antis*, channelled masonry pilasters with the pediment crowned by a square bellcote, construction in good granite ashlar.

PETERHEAD ACADEMY. The original building in Prince Street by *Pirie & Clyne* was built in 1890–1, altered in 1896–7 but bomb-damaged in 1940 and reconstructed in simpler form by the Burgh Architect *c.* 1953. Much more impressive is the York Street extension by *J.A. Ogg Allan*, 1922–4, in stripped Neo-Georgian. Symmetrical, its two-storey entrance pavilion with minimal emphasis flanked by classroom blocks of equal height, constructed in good granite ashlar under a long hipped roof; the N wing was bomb-damaged and reconstructed in extended form. The St Mary Street extension is dated 1961. To the E is a much more substantial extension of 1978 which also incorporates the COMMUNITY LEISURE CENTRE on Queen Street, elaborately composed of dark red brick hexagons of mixed heights with copper mansards, limited fenestration and very spare bold modelling.

PETERHEAD COMMUNITY HOSPITAL, Links Terrace. Two-storey main block, partly in squared granite, built *c.* 1960–70, originally as an extension to the Cottage Hospital (1934, dem.). Enlarged to the rear *c.* 2000 as a three-sided court.

POLICE STATION, Merchant Street. By *William Henderson & Son*, 1898–9. Built in Peterhead granite, quietly dignified classical. Two tall storeys and attic, three bays broad with slightly advanced centre rising through the wall-head into an open pediment. Wide doorway with Doric columns, four-light segmentally pedimented window above.

PUBLIC LIBRARY AND ARBUTHNOT MUSEUM, St Peter Street. Won in competition by *D. & J. R. McMillan*, and built in 1891–3 with financial assistance from Andrew Carnegie. Free Renaissance two-storey corner block with tower at the angle, constructed in pink Peterhead granite. St Peter Street entrance framed by pilasters bearing stylized scrolls and surmounted by a gablet with a small pediment; first-floor windows rise into depressed key-blocked arches, the centre

*Note the similarity of the tower – shown in the 2nd Ordnance Survey of 1901 – with that of Longside Infants School (q.v.). The authorship of the Longside school is not confirmed, but Clyne had a connection with the Episcopal Congregation there, having redecorated St John's Church (q.v.) in 1893–4.

and end oriels break up into curvilinear gables. Tower rises into short ogee pinnacles, and broaches into a domed octagonal clock stage with pedimented dials; the dome is crowned by a tall cupola looking like a small minaret.

Reform Monument, Broad Street. *See* Description.

Sailors' Memorial, South Road. By *Peter Regent*, 2001. In the form of a cast bronze sail displaying scenes of fishing life in the early C20, mounted on a granite pedestal.

Sheriff Courthouse, Queen Street. By *John Smith II* (of *J. & W. Smith*), 1869–71, more ambitious designs by *Peddie & Kinnear* having been passed over. Modest two-storey with crowstepped gables, like a comfortable villa. Extension to St Peter Street, 1983 by *Property Services Agency* (*John Bull*, architect-in-charge), an uncompromisingly modern design in glass with stepped roof-line, but sensitive to its neighbour. Reconstructed late 1990s.

Former Town House, Broad Street. By *John Baxter*, 1788, on 105
the site of the old tolbooth. Dignified restrained classicism. Three storeys and five bays broad in pink granite ashlar with a slightly projecting centre rising into a plain pediment and hipped roof supporting a massive square plinth. Clock tower with pedimented faces, belfry and spire with bull's-eyes and ball finial 38 m. above ground, all in darker masonry than the rest. The ground floor was originally an open arcade for market traders, with a fine external stair to the upper floors; the present double-height porch, with giant-order square columns supporting a moulded pediment, was added when the ground floor was infilled by *William Stuart* in 1881.

Ugie Hospital, Ugie Road. The old Fever Hospital, built on the 'villa principle' by *T.H. Scott*, Burgh Surveyor, in 1905–7, subsequently altered and extended; two villas surviving. The coastal location in Buchanhaven allowed seafarers with infectious diseases to be brought ashore with minimal risk.

HARBOURS

There are three harbours – South Harbour, North Harbour and Port Henry – formed into a single complex between Keith Inch and the mainland, and the separate National Harbour of Refuge in the South Bay.

The South Harbour has its origins in a landing pier some 30 m. long which was built for the tower house (dem.) on Keith Inch *c.* 1590. This harbour was dry at low tide with treacherous rocks. During the 1730s the Governors of the Merchant Maiden Hospital in Edinburgh convinced the Convention of Royal Burghs that Peterhead's harbours were of national importance and funds were granted towards their improvement. In 1738–40 the South Harbour was deepened and piers constructed and extended, some of the spoil being used to form a causeway known as the Quinzie between Keith Inch and the mainland. Further improvements were carried out as burgh finances allowed and by 1768 what is now Bridge Street had been reclaimed from the sea.

During these years the growth in shipping and the size of ships was such as to encourage further application to be made to the Convention of Royal Burghs in 1771. This resulted in the appointment of *John Smeaton* who prepared a report on the South Harbour in 1772. Plans were drawn up and work began in 1773 under the supervision of *John Gwyn*, a new South Pier being completed in 1775–81, with the West Pier reconstructed from 1782.

However the South Harbour remained impossible to access in stormy weather and offered limited protection inside. Damage caused by a major storm in 1793 ultimately led to *John Rennie* being commissioned to recommend further improvements. His report of 1806 and plans of 1807, although not fully taken up at the time, resulted in an Act of the latter year, the establishment of Harbour Trustees and the appointment of *William Wallace* as resident engineer in 1808. The South Harbour was deepened by 1810 under Wallace's supervision, its West Pier extended by 1813 and its slipways enlarged. The Harbour Trustees also enlarged the South Harbour on its E side, forming a new quay. The excavated rubble was heaped up as an embankment between Keith Inch and the Greenhill – a large rock which, with the mainland, enclosed the North Bay – as a first step towards establishing a North Harbour. The South Harbour was further deepened in 1905–8.

The NORTH HARBOUR had first been proposed in Rennie's report of 1806, but not until work on the South Harbour had been completed were the Trustees ready to begin construction in earnest, the plans being prepared by *Thomas Telford* and carried out under the supervision of *John Gibb* in 1818–22. The East Wharf with graving dock and pier was completed in 1821, and the North Pier facing it in 1822; Birnie's Pier was built by 1824 and the cross-pier which splits the North Harbour into two basins was finished in 1825. The North Harbour was deepened with further alterations including a new graving dock near Union Street by *D. & T. Stevenson* in 1852–5. The entrance to the North Harbour was sealed off in the 1980s when Alexandra Parade was created. Entrance is now from the South Harbour via the JUNCTION CANAL which was planned in 1847 by *David Stevenson*, Engineer to the Convention of Royal Burghs, and cut in 1849–50 by contractors *William Walker* of Manchester and *Stuart & Pyper* of Peterhead (*Rennie*'s report had proposed such a link in 1806). At its N end, the passage into the North Harbour is spanned by a rolling-lift BASCULE BRIDGE by *Sir William Arrol & Co.*, 1953. This replaced *Stevenson*'s original cast-iron SWING BRIDGE made by *James Blaikie & Sons* of the Panmure Foundry, Edinburgh, and installed in 1850.

Thomas Stevenson designed the North and South Harbours' ENTRANCE BEACONS in the form of small octagonal lighthouses, built in ashlar masonry in 1849. They were the first to use holophotal lanterns (i.e., lanterns with reflectors to prevent loss of light), these seemingly being made by *James Milne & Son* of Edinburgh.

PORT HENRY, opposite Seagate, is a natural haven which has been much enlarged. Concurrently with his early development of the burgh in Longate, Back Street and Back Gate, the 4th Earl Marischal formed a harbour bulwark *c.* 1593. In 1616 this harbour was substantially enlarged, *Henry Middleton* of Clerkhill being at least partly responsible for the works; further improvements seem to have been made in 1631. Port Henry's present appearance is due to C19 and C20 improvements, the first *c.* 1878 to designs by *D. & T. Stevenson*, in conjunction with *Thomas Meik*, and with *Whately Eliot* as resident engineer. Then in 1895 *James Barron* of Aberdeen prepared further plans for its enlargement and deepening, and its division into two basins, the work being carried out by *William Shield* in 1896–7; the excavated rubble was used to form the SMITH EMBANKMENT in the South Bay. In 1905–8 the entrance was widened to designs by *Shield*, now with *Mr Wookey* as resident engineer, and the inner basin deepened. Port Henry was further modernized in 1931–2.

The SHIP LIFT by *Syncrolift*, completed 2001, can move vessels up to 2,685 tonnes. The SLIPWAY accommodates four vessels with a 24.7-m. keel and 7.2-m. beam; the DRY DOCK vessels up to 57.9 m. length, 10.6 m. width and 4.5 m. draft; and the REPAIR SHED vessels up to 47 m. long and 25.2 m. high.

The NATIONAL HARBOUR OF REFUGE was sanctioned by Parliamentary Act in 1886 after prolonged pressure from shipowners, sailors and insurers for a very large harbour for vessels in peril between the Firth of Forth and the Cromarty Firth. The South Bay's geographic location, its depth and the proximity of abundant supplies of granite for building were ideal for the purpose. In preparation for such a substantial undertaking, ADMIRALTY YARD was formed as a base for construction, and Peterhead Prison – Scotland's only penal institution – was established next to it so that convicts could supplement the contractors' labour and limit the overall cost; the British State Railway was laid by 1899 to transport the convicts from Admiralty Yard to the Stirling Village quarry. The Refuge consists of two bulwarks, each built with the assistance of a massive Titan crane which lifted the granite blocks into place. The SOUTH BREAKWATER extending from Admiralty Yard was designed by *Sir John Coode* in 1885, work beginning in the 1890s under the supervision of *William Shield*, the first resident engineer; although shorter than intended as a result of Treasury restrictions, it still stretches 750 m. into the North Sea, the beacon at its far end being completed in 1914. Construction then began on the NORTH BREAKWATER, which extends 400 m. out from Keith Inch. It initially made good progress but was stalled by the Great Depression and the Second World War. The Harbour of Refuge was finally completed in 1956.

DESCRIPTION

Broad Street and the Spa Town

BROAD STREET has been Peterhead's market square since the C17; like so many other Scottish squares, it is actually rectangular, and unusually long, reflecting the business generated by the harbour. It presents a varied streetscape, now mostly C18 and C19 and of two to three storeys with later shopfronts, dominated by the old Town House at its higher W end and closed downhill to the E by Arbuthnot House (*see* Public Buildings). In front of the Town House is a bronze STATUE of James Keith, brother of the 9th Earl Marischal and himself a Prussian Field-Marshal during the Seven Years War; this statue, a replica of one formerly in the Wilhelmplatz in Berlin, was gifted to Peterhead by Kaiser Wilhelm I in 1868. In the centre of the square is the REFORM MONUMENT of 1832–3, 'design produced by Baillie [Roderick] Gray', erected by the Peterhead Tories on the site of the old market cross to celebrate the Great Reform Act which enfranchised the town as a Parliamentary burgh. A Roman Doric column in pink granite, it bears a die-block displaying the arms of the Earls Marischal taken from Inverugie Castle (q.v.), with Latin inscriptions celebrating Peace and Union, and above all a gilt lion rampant.

The older surviving buildings in Broad Street are on the N side – a long three-storey block (Nos. 29–33) now rather battered but built as the townhouse of Robert Arbuthnot, 1st of Haddo-Rattray, and his wife Mary Petrie in 1730,* and Nos. 39–41 of *c.* 1780, two storeys in squared granite with club skewputts. Further downhill No. 59, mid-C18, reflecting the narrow feu-plots of earlier times, is the only building which still stands with its gable facing the road, two storeys in pinkish-brown granite rising into a big chimneystack. Nos. 61–65 are *c.* 1800, again two storeys in ashlar with a Gibbsian doorway – a motif of late C18 Peterhead – and moulded skewputts and coped stacks. Then a semi-formal two-storey composition created by No. 75, the old North of Scotland Bank, and its earlier neighbours which form asymmetric wings on either side. The two-storey bank, by *Archibald Simpson* 1835, has windows beneath console-cornices and a blocking course framed by Greek scrolls. N of this Nos. 67–73 of *c.* 1790 with two arched pends and tripartite windows at first floor; S No. 77, again with a Gibbsian doorway, all small-scale but still very elegant. At the far E end of the street stands ELLIS'S HOUSE, built for Alexander Ellis in 1768, three storeys, three windows wide with a central attic gable, in fine granite ashlar. Ellis was not only Peterhead's Baron-Baillie but reputedly its King of

*The Arbuthnot family, who continued to figure prominently in the affairs of Peterhead for over a hundred years after the 9th Earl Marischal had been attainted had a very early connection with the town, Sir Robert Arbuthnott of that ilk having married the 4th Earl's daughter Margaret, although they had no issue.

the Smugglers, and the house's flank elevation to Union Street allowed him to signal to ships approaching the harbour while its cellar was used for the storage of contraband. It was substantially enlarged in the early C19 across Union Street with a very grand four-bay elevation with gable pediment, and bowed corners turning into both Broad Street and Seagate.

Among the later insertions into Broad Street are a number of tall mid-C19 buildings, including the former ROYAL HOTEL of 1854 on the N side near the Town House, a big four-storey block with central rusticated archway supporting giant pilasters which rise into a gargantuan crenellated parapet. Its appearance would be much improved if the elegant balcony which once ran across its first-floor windows and the clock dormer in its roof were reinstated, but its shopfront at No. 27 is still distinguished. On the S side the principal buildings are two banks. The SCOTTISH BUILDING SOCIETY (formerly the Commercial Bank) is a tall three-storey five-bay Italianate palazzo with its end bays stepped well back behind twin entrance porches, and was designed by one of the great masters of the style, *David Rhind*, in 1863–5. Constructed in Morayshire sandstone ashlar laid in slim courses, it is tightly composed astylar, bold yet delicate in its detail. Next to it is the BANK OF SCOTLAND (formerly the Union Bank), probably by *William Smith*, 1858.* This is a simple Italianate corner block, three storeys in granite ashlar with a bowed quadrant angle to the Rose Street junction and matching additions to the W end by *William Low Henderson*, 1888. Otherwise of note, the MASONIC TEMPLE (although not built as such) by *William Hay*, 1872, a tall three-storey frontage with central attic gable, pilasters terminating in scrolls and ball finials. Hay also designed Nos. 22–24 for his mother, *c.* 1851–3 with attractive Germanic dormers.

Now to the SPA TOWN S of Broad Street, where the streets are relatively narrow, closely lined on each side mostly with simple handsome houses of the later C18 and earlier C19, and all built in local granite which varies in colour from pink to grey depending on the sun, infusing the fresh briny atmosphere with a rich dark tinge. ROSE STREET was formed in 1775 along with Jamaica Street to connect Broad Street with the S shore where the Wine Well, the Keith Masonic Lodge and the New Inn – all now lost – were the chief centres of society. At least some of the houses were purpose-built for taking in boarders. Even after the Spa Town's Georgian heyday, builders in the later C19 and even the early C20 remained surprisingly faithful to the traditions of *c.* 1800, with the result that it remains remarkably consistent in character.

Because JAMAICA STREET runs at a slight angle to Rose Street it opens up only gradually, with the picturesque row of two-storey houses on the W side which are first to show

*It was built in parallel with a similar one in Fraserburgh which was lost during the Second World War.

themselves enlivened by varied wall-heads and steeply pitched roofs rising into tall chimneystacks: like a line of guardsmen all a bit different in height but still very smart. Nos. 18 and 20 were originally two-storey detached houses (although No. 20 was later divided), their Gibbsian door surrounds a mark of superior rank. No 26 is slightly later, *c.* 1810, with a rock-faced semi-sunk basement. Steps lead up to a deeply recessed doorway, which is finely treated with sidelights framed by slim reeded pilasters, and a delicate fanlight with elliptical tracery. The twin band courses between its ground- and first-floor windows are a motif encountered throughout the Spa Town. On the Wallace Street junction, an attractive recessed convex corner, and on the other side of the road, at the junction with James Street, a monumental WAREHOUSE built for the Aberdeen Commercial Co. by *Jenkins & Marr* *c.* 1903, still very much in the Georgian tradition. Four storeys, sixteen bays, near-symmetrical in pink granite ashlar, and absolutely disciplined, it is an impressive show of uniformity within the generally varied, small-scale character of the Spa Town. It has a central round-arched and key-blocked portal, a shallow arched recess above enclosing paired first- and second-floor windows, then smaller third-floor windows above. At the back, loading bays, and at the roof's S end a low tower with a glazed top. Among the three-storey houses, No. 15 retains its original doorpiece; Nos. 17–21 have a jerkin-headed gable which we shall see again in the Spa Town, and which was clearly the hallmark of one of the builders of the period, perhaps *Robert Mitchell*.

In the streets E and W of Rose Street and Jamaica Street, more of the same good townscape of *c.* 1800. In ST ANDREW STREET Nos. 4–6 of *c.* 1790 combine Neoclassical sophistication with the traditional vernacular, having Venetian and round-headed windows on the first floor although they are quite asymmetrical with bold moulded skewputts. Further up a handsome three-storey WAREHOUSE (now flats): its ground and first floors are relatively low but the second floor is much taller, again with the jerkin-headed roof characteristic of Peterhead *c.* 1800. In MERCHANT STREET stands the WAVERLEY HOTEL, also *c.* 1800, three storeys over a basement plinth, with an impressively tall and deep round-arched portal sheltering the steps that lead up to its doorway (cf. Nos. 3–5 St Peter Street). The fine pink granite ashlar and the simple treatment of the windows, tall at ground and first floors, relatively low at second, only adds to its sense of monumental character. The doorway itself is finely treated, framed by Ionic pilasters. The flank elevation rises into a jerkin-headed gable with twin chimneystacks. Then beyond in MAIDEN STREET, one of the finest sights in the Spa Town – a picturesque, slightly bowed terrace of two-storey three-bay houses all built in squared granite *c.* 1800, each a little different from its neighbours. No. 7 retains its original elegant doorpiece, and at the far end are two original shopfronts, Nos.

15–19 and 21–23. On the opposite side Nos. 42–46, one of the most impressive late C18 blocks in Peterhead, three storeys high and seven windows broad with a big roof, jerkin-headed gables, and enormous paired chimneystacks. Much of the N side of Maiden Street, however, together with that of Tolbooth Wynd and half of Threadneedle Street, was destroyed to produce a car park, still a barren and deeply depressing sight. In UPHILL LANE, S of Maiden Street, in contrast, a development of 1989 by *Baxter, Clark & Paul* for the Scottish Special Housing Association has been imaginatively composed within the steeply sloping, winding street. Their scheme takes its cue not so much from Georgian houses of the Old Town as from traditions of the late C16 and C17 when the Burgh was founded, e.g. gabled frontages with jettied upper storeys. Some older buildings have been preserved and incorporated, and the overall character is engagingly lively, human and rugged.

Along the coastal road stand houses in gardens facing the shore, the best of which is BATH HOUSE in BATH STREET of *c.* 1815–20. Two storeys, three windows wide raised over a basement, it is mostly built in fine granite ashlar with set-back screen walls on each side, and a gabled roof with later canted dormers. Its splayed approach stair rises to a pilastered doorpiece, band courses run under the windows, and it has long-and-short quoins and modillions at its slim wall-head cornice. The continuation of this road is HARBOUR STREET, falling away in a gentle curve, within which the houses – again on one side only, looking out to the sea – represent a study in contrasts. No. 4 is a two-storey three-bay house with a broken frontage, one end only stepped back behind the main wall-plane, its railed area with steps to the doorway, and twin band courses: it looks like half of a pair which was never completed. Then Nos. 5 and 6, two houses built in the old tradition with their end gables facing seawards and their long flanks giving mutual protection against the storm and the wind: No. 5 harled, two storeys and attic, dated 1739, with later tripartite windows at ground and first floors; No. 6 BRAE COTTAGE with a bowed end to the street is much later, *c.* 1830 in its present form with lying-pane glazing characteristic of that time. Nos. 7–10, adjoining buildings of contrasting character, are set well back from the road within their own courtyard. First, a Late Victorian villa incorporating an C18 house at the rear – loosely Baronial, its two-storey end gable with bay window facing the road, and crenellated entrance bay on one flank; then, standing at an angle, a lower two-storey range, harled with playful wall-head gables. Following round the curve of the road, the old CUSTOM HOUSE (Nos. 12–14) is *c.* 1800; Nos. 18–19 of the same date still have their original doorpiece and twin band courses between ground and first floors, a common motif in Peterhead. The former HARBOUR OFFICE next to this is three storeys in squared granite with a broad central pend; the paired windows above were once loading doors. Nos. 23–25 are early, a three-storey five-bay block of 1740, with irregular first- and second-floor fenestration, harled with moulded skewputts.

Finally, by the harbour entrance, are two former WAREHOUSES: first an C18 three-storey five-bay block with bowed corner to James Street; then the huge four-storey Caledonian Warehouse totalling eleven bays, its W end *c.* 1800 and the remainder *c.* 1806. This is an outstanding example of the genre, with broad ground-floor pends, the centre bay formerly with loading doors at each level, and a bowed corner to Union Street corbelled to the square at first floor. The whole building is very deep on plan with jerkin-headed gables and moulded skewputts.

North of Broad Street: New Town and Roanheads

MARISCHAL STREET is Peterhead's principal shopping thoroughfare, and still retains the centuries-old pattern of narrow pends opening off its S side, their entrances enhanced by modern canopies and brass thresholds made by *Andy Scott* of Glasgow. Also by *Scott* is the statue of FISHER JESSIE, 2001; artworks within the pends were co-ordinated by *Wilma Eaton*. Marischal Street's N side, from Chapel Street to Thistle Street, was almost totally reconstructed in 1909 with a very large Free Renaissance block of shops and offices of the Brown & Watt school, designed by the unrelated *James Watt, C.E.* of Peterhead; there is a building in similar style at the far end of Thistle Street, dated 1888. On the opposite side of Marischal Street, No. 39 is Late Victorian Free Renaissance, with some details akin to *Pirie & Clyne* at its dormers. The CLYDESDALE BANK, formerly National Bank of Scotland, is interwar classical by *George Bennett Mitchell & Son*, *c.* 1938. At the S end DRUMMER'S CORNER is a parade of shops in alien brick and concrete by *Baxter, Clark & Paul* on the site of Albion Street, 1975–81.

CHAPEL STREET to the N off Marischal Street was named after the Episcopal chapel of 1767, now concealed behind the two-storey block on the corner with Back Street. It acquired new significance once Queen Street became the main route N and the New Town began to be built up in earnest during the 1860s and 1870s, leading the Burgh to promote major redevelopment, probably with *William Hay* as its architect. Chapel Street's E side was built up *c.* 1873 as a splendid three-storey and attic concave crescent with tall ground-floor shops, the first and second floors in pink granite ashlar with plain pilasters crowned by urn finials every four bays, and attic dormers lining the wall-heads. The earlier blocks have Hay's characteristic trapezoidal door- and window heads and at the far end is his South Free Church (*see* Churches). On the W side the three-storey crescent is answered by a lower two-storey and attic convex crescent built from *c.* 1890 which is more obviously Victorian in its style and proportions. Until 1936 the view S to Marischal Street was closed off by *Hay*'s magnificent Music Hall of 1872–3, regrettably destroyed by fire.

Chapel Street leads us N into the NEW TOWN. Although the parish school was opened in Prince Street in 1838 and the Central School in St Peter Street in 1840 (*see* Public Buildings), what really spurred the layout and development of its grid of streets was the arrival of the Formartine & Buchan Railway in 1862, its terminus at the N end of Queen Street where the Community and Leisure Centre now stands. The principal thoroughfares are ST PETER STREET, KING STREET and LANDALE ROAD running NE–SW, crossed by QUEEN STREET, PRINCE STREET, ST MARY STREET, YORK STREET, HANOVER STREET and CONSTITUTION STREET. The New Town's villas, cottages and blocks of mansion flats are testimony to the wealth of Peterhead at this time. Standing in orderly rows, they are immensely solid and comfortable, much bigger in scale than the houses in the Old Town. Their frontages are nearly all built in finest granite, machine-cut and machine-polished. Although there are no great masterpieces, the two-storey villas are endowed with real variety by their proliferation of bay windows, attic gables and dormers, and their granite is often hammer-dressed for texture with some bold decorative details. At the centre of this existence is the PETERHEAD BOWLING CLUB, established in 1901, its pavilion a pleasant place of ease with knarly log-column veranda and mock half-timbering.

In the late C18 and early C19 the old fishing village of the ROANHEADS NE of the town centre was built up with modest cottages and houses following the shore, and on each side of two short roads leading inland towards North Street. Much of the Roanheads' informal character remains in spite of alterations. The railway cut through in the 1860s, its course now represented by East North Street. In 1871 the Superiors, perhaps prompted by a cholera epidemic which ravaged the north-east fishing villages, feued five streets – Great Stuart Street to New Street – with simple but attractive two-storey terraced houses, built up from S to N between 1877 and 1905.

During the 1930s standard four-in-a-block municipal flats were built in BATTERY PARK, SKENE STREET and GADLE BRAES following the long sweep round the coast towards Buchanhaven. In contrast to this, at the junction of Roanheads with North Street, is the SOCIAL HOUSING of 1977–82 by *Baxter, Clark & Paul* for the Scottish Special Housing Association where avowedly modern design nevertheless maintains the small scale and varied form, colour and texture of the vernacular, the new fabric knitting in with the old. Different again is the housing by Tenants First such as COOPERAGE COURT, 2007, which is more classical in concept, with relatively large houses laid out around a formal square.

SALMON HOUSE, Golf Road. Built in 1585 as a coastal store for Inverugie Castle (q.v.) by the 4th Earl Marischal; his initials and the date on a skewputt. Rebuilt *c.* 1801.

DALES, off Damhead Way, 1.5 km. SW of Broad Street. Gothick *cottage orné*, *c.* 1800 with Regency, Early Victorian and more recent additions. Pretty three-bay symmetrical entrance front with Victorian bowed enclosed porch framed by four-centred basket-tracery sash windows, white harl with grey granite dressings; above the ground floor the dark slate roof is swept up in cavetto piends from the corners over low first-floor windows, that in the centre breaking through the eaves as an ogee-gabled dormer. Very deep flanks with canted bay additions and slate-hung box dormers, distinctive diamond-plan chimneystacks. Regency interior. Large WALLED GARDEN; single-storey LODGE HOUSE with log-column porch and decorative bargeboards.

BERRYHILL HOUSE. *See* p. 108.
BLACKHILL HOUSE. *See* p. 109.

9010 PETTENS

OLD PARISH CHURCH (ST COLUMBA). Ruinous, but nevertheless the earliest-known post-Reformation parish church of which any fabric survives in north Aberdeenshire. It was built in 1762 for Belhelvie parish and is the first of a long series of modest late C18 and early C19 preaching-boxes in the north-east. The W gable survives relatively entire, built in roughly squared rubble with a chamfered doorway and a gallery window; a second blocked doorway, on the r. some way above ground, presumably provided access by means of an external forestair to the gallery directly. The birdcage bellcote with ball finials is dated and initialled T.R. for the minister, Thomas Ragg.* The gable bears a close resemblance to that at Keithhall & Kinkell Parish Church (S, 1772–3 by *William Littlejohn* or *James Hector*). It is of further interest as a T-plan, an example not followed until Lonmay Parish Church (q.v.) twenty-five years later. The remains of the S transept are now overgrown. The E gable, of which no evidence survives, was supposedly pre-Reformation. The W gable's inside face has a broken marble WALL MONUMENT to John Orrok, †1823. Two MORT SAFES: a vaulted chamber forming a hump in the ground, with steps down to a chamfered arch entrance; and a gabled block at the churchyard's SW corner, 1835, its ashlar entrance gable with sturdy oak door, an inner door of iron and a stone vault concealed beneath the slated roof.

*Its English bell, a very early example in Scotland, was inscribed 'Henrick Ter Horst Me Fecit Daventriae 1633'. It was stolen in 1966.

Nearby, the former PARISH MANSE of 1768–9 by *Robert Smith*, mason, dated at the skews. Two storeys, three windows wide. Its transom-lit entrance door is framed by two-storey canted bays with prismatic roofs, added by *George Rae* in 1888, with hipped attic dormers above; chimneystacks with moulded copes. Large rear wing and separate piend-roofed offices.

ORROK HOUSE, 0.5 km. W. Vernacular classical country house built *c.* 1781–2 by John Orrok, a West Indies sea-captain.* Main block, facing S to the sea, three storeys, five windows wide in coursed squared granite, absolutely regular: it is not clear whether the central bay at ground floor was once a doorway. The first-floor windows expressing the principal apartments rise from a band course; second-floor windows support a plain eaves course beneath a very big gabled roof. Round-arched attic windows in the gable ends with letters O for Orrok and broad panelled chimneystacks. The single-storey single-bay wings with hipped roofs are early additions of *c.* 1800. The approach to the house is on the N side. The main block has windows in its centre and end bays only, the doorway at ground floor with sidelights, semi-elliptical fanlight of *c.* 1800, and the scar of a Victorian porch, now removed. Low-walled oval forecourt with axial ball-finialled gatepiers contemporary with the house but perhaps resited; the railed screen with foot-gates is mid-C19. Simple interior with original woodwork. Steadings converted to domestic use.

MENIE HOUSE. *See* p. 290.

PHILORTH 9060

PHILORTH HOUSE. Once a seat of the Lords Saltoun, mostly destroyed by fire in 1915. The house comprised three ranges forming an open courtyard plan, the W range dated 1666, the S range by *James Matthews* 1858–60 and the E range also by *Matthews* 1873–4; only the E range's front elevation and vaulted entrance hall survives, roofless but substantially intact. The present FARMHOUSE incorporates fragments from the ruins but its Grecian doorway is reportedly from Strichen House (*see* Strichen). In the garden, a SUNDIAL with three cherub's heads. Large quadrilateral WALLED GARDEN (200 m. E); STEADING (300 m. E) incorporates 1688 datestone; simple Gothic S LODGE (1.2 km. S).

BRIDGE OF PHILORTH, 1.8 km. ENE. Formerly carried B9033 over the Water of Philorth. C18, two segmental arches, not quite identical, pinned rubble harled on downstream side with chamfered voussoirs. Widened in rubble on the upstream side

*The name was transferred from the family's Fife estate, which had been sold.

with dressed voussoirs, central cutwaters and low coped parapets on both faces.

NORTH SCHOOL CROFT BRIDGE, 1.6 km. S, over Water of Philorth. C19. Single span, rubble-built with dressed voussoirs; low coped parapets slightly splayed out to terminal piers with pyramid caps and small wing walls.

KINBOG FARM DOOCOT, 1.4 km. S. Built *c.* 1800. Octagonal, two stages in squared rubble slightly battered with rusticated quoins, rat course and crenellated parapet. Square-headed doorway in lower stage and large circular openings in upper. Brick interior.

9040

PITFOUR

At their greatest extent, during the later C18 and C19, the lands owned by the Fergusons of Pitfour stretched across five parishes and 130 sq. km. of north-east Aberdeenshire. James Ferguson, Advocate and Writer to the Signet, bought Pitfour in 1700, then acquired the neighbouring Kinmundy on behalf of his cousin, for whom he acted as guardian, *c.* 1705; his brother-in-law, John Stuart, coincidentally acquired Dens and Crichie in 1709. After the 'Fifteen, the 9th Earl Marischal was attainted. His forfeited estates were purchased by the York Buildings Company, but its financial difficulties resulted in resale of its lands relatively cheaply to those untroubled by past or provenance, and Ferguson, although himself an Episcopalian and a Jacobite sympathizer, quietly built up holdings in Longside, Bruxie, New Deer and Old Deer (qq.v.), buying further land at Old Deer and Aden on behalf of his Kinmundy cousin. He died in 1734 and was succeeded by his son James, 'the ablest lawyer in the land', who after the 'Forty-five defended Jacobite prisoners at Carlisle, with surprising success; in 1764, the year he became a judge in the Court of Session, he purchased certain estates of the Earl Marischal, who had reacquired 30 sq. km. of St Fergus (including Inverugie Castle, q.v.) after his attainder was reversed in 1761, but soon returned to the Continent.

Lord Pitfour's son, another James, was also a lawyer before giving up practice to become M.P. for Aberdeenshire in 1790. His elevated station called for a grander residence than the modest seat then existing, and *c.* 1809 he retained *John Smith I* to build a Neoclassical house. It was three storeys high and seven bays broad across its S entrance front, the three-bay centrepiece slightly projected with a panelled parapet, and balustrades across the wall-head; the principal apartments were at first floor which was consequently taller, and all the windows had *persiennes* – slatted shutters – giving it a somewhat Continental appearance. The entrance itself was framed by a single-storey portico and the flank elevations were eleven bays deep. The estate passed to a nephew, George Ferguson, in 1820, and by 1828 the house had been altered by the addition of a first-floor glazed gallery raised up on an Ionic colonnade across the entrance front, subsequently deepened at the centre to form a large porte cochère. Unfortunately George and his son were extravagant even beyond their extensive means at a time when farm rents were in sharp decline. The family finances and the quality of the land itself deteriorated; piecemeal sale of property and other assets were of no avail and the results were bankruptcy, the wholesale break-up and disposal of the estates in 1926, and the house's demolition shortly after, its masonry reused for a council estate in Aberdeen.

Nevertheless enough survives of the POLICIES to give some idea of their former grandeur. To provide a suitable outlook for his new house, James Ferguson M.P. formed the artificial lake, and substantially augmented the planting begun by his father, Lord Pitfour, if not his grandfather. 'A wise and spirited landlord with many interests, he is to be credited with the first serious endeavour to restore the bygone beauty of Deir by clothing the heights with wood . . . it is to his taste that our countryside owes the wealth of pleasant hedge-rows, so rare in northern Scotland.' The hardwoods included oak, beech, sycamore, ash and larch. A flower garden lay to the E of the house, focused on a fountain with a chrysanthemum bowl of which only the pool now survives; there was another fountain on the W flank. The grounds' development may have benefited from the advice of *William Sawrey Gilpin* who was working at Strichen House (q.v.) *c.* 1820. In many respects the Fergusons were good landlords – although the wider family owned sugar plantations in Trinidad and Tobago – and in their fervent competition with their neighbours, particularly the Russells of Aden (*see* p. 319), they created what became known as the Garden of Buchan.

Behind Pitfour House were the STABLES (now derelict), also built by *John Smith I*. A Classical U-plan court, with tall ground and low first floors under a cornice and blocking course, and low-pitched roofs. The pilastered centrepiece with carriage arch supports a deep entablature and plain pediment. Rubble-built, formerly harled with grey ashlar dressings, the clock stage and domed peristyle which once rose above the pediment were in timber. There was originally a separate riding school.

Former CHAPEL (English Episcopal Continuing). Built 1850–1 as the result of a disagreement between George Ferguson and Arthur Ranken, the Episcopal incumbent at Old Deer. Simple E.E., with strong square tower fronting a five-bay church, rubble-built, cream-harled with dressed margins. Tower rises in four stages to 18 m. height – pointed-arch doorway, second stage with Y-traceried window beneath a low third clock stage; tall fourth stage again with Y-traceried window, then the parapet, very deep with small crenels. Octagonal stairwells between tower and nave.

OBSERVATORY, in Drinnie's Wood. *c.* 1840, probably by *John Smith I* for George Ferguson. An octagonal tower 15 m. high, standing on a hill as a vantage point overlooking a private racecourse and out to the sea. Constructed in brick but harled in white, it has three stages, the second arcaded and the third relatively low with square windows on all sides; stone dressings, cornice and crenellated parapet. Interior with circular brick stairwell now remodelled, contains two concentric stairs: one outside the well giving views from the second stage, the other inside rising directly to the top.

At the W end of the lake, the TEMPLE OF THESEUS, perhaps *c.* 1835, based on the original Athenian temple of 449–415 B.C., but miniaturized. A similar arrangement of thirty-four columns enclosing an inner sanctum and supporting a deep entablature and pedimental gable. Its Greek Doric columns are however unfluted and the entablature with triglyphs much simpler. Derelict, the roof collapsing. Sanctum contains a cold bath, fed by the lake.

Three bridges on the lake – the NE and SE bridges carried the driveway from the South Lodge to the House past a BOATHOUSE in the form of a Gothic ruin. NE BRIDGE, *c.* 1810–20. Three low segmental spans rising from cutwaters, but with no piers visible above the surface. Plain panels in squared granite spandrels; fluted cast-iron posts, originally with chains. SE BRIDGE, a single segmental span with slightly curved approaches, rubble-built, again guarded by posts and chains. NW BRIDGE probably contemporary, a single segmental span in granite ashlar.

Former GAME LARDER, 1826. Harled single-storey octagonal. Entrance door and astragalled sash-and-case windows set in granite surrounds. Broad-eaved prismatic roof with neat central chimney.

LAUNDRY *c.* 1820, derelict. Two storeys, five windows wide with centre bay boldly projecting, rubble-built with broad-eaved hipped roof. Twin doorways in the intermediate bays with lattice-pattern transom-lights, windows astragalled sash-and-case.

KENNEL-MASTER'S HOUSE, perhaps pre-1820. Cottage classicism. Single-storey three-bay with a pedimented portico Doric distyle-*in-antis*; recently extended to five bays with slightly lower side wings. Casement windows, distinctively glazed. Low-pitched roof with low chimneystacks.

EAST (or STATION) LODGE and BRUXIE LODGE, *c.* 1850. Similar but not quite identical to kennel-master's house (*see* above). Each single-storey, three bays with central portico distyle-*in-antis*, the pediment decorated with timber fretwork. Flanking windows with console cornices, low-pitched roofs and chimneystacks. East Lodge now harled with margins, Bruxie with pinned rubble exposed. WEST LODGE, probably *John Smith I*, *c.* 1820. Single-storey three-bay house, pinned rubble with margins, gabled roof with squared skewputts and central stack.

SOUTH LODGE *c.* 1850, altered *c.* 1910. Two-storey, three-bay ashlar granite S front, porch tucked in NE corner. Paired central lights, windows in outer bays square. Hipped slate roof with clay-tile ridge and bracketed overhanging eaves, chimneystack rising from rear wall-head. N and W elevations harled. Possibly once two houses. GATES, probably 1816. Outer piers only survive, circular Roman Doric standing on pedestals but with no bases, surmounted by abaci with low urns. Facing the Lodge, a Latin INSCRIPTION to Pitt the Younger and Viscount Melville, dated 1816, and framed between pilasters on a screen-wall.

BOUNDARY WALLS, rubble-built, 5.5 km. in length, varying height. Perhaps commissioned by the Fergusons to provide work for tenants in times of hardship, cf. the Deer Dykes at Ellon and Consumption Dykes at Schivas (qq.v.).

PITMEDDEN 8020

A small village on the junction of three main roads, the A920, B9000 and B999.

PITMEDDEN CHURCH, Main Street. Former Free Church. Idiosyncratic First Pointed by *William Knox,* 1864–5. Tall broad gable front with its centre slightly stepped forward to suggest a nave-and-aisles arrangement – the nave with a pointed-arch doorway under its own small gablet, and stepped triple lancets with robust plate tracery. A tower on the l. with angle buttresses and a shouldered doorway rises into a neat belfry with fish-scale slated spirelet and weathervane; the aisle on the r. is simply acknowledged by a quatrefoil panel. Golden granite rubble, the flanks of the aisles articulated into six bays by buttresses, with a polychromatic slate roof. Deep gallery supported on cast-iron Egyptic columns; originally U-plan but now extends across the S side only, its front stencilled; so, too, the pendant posts of the pitch-pine herringbone ceiling, erected during the earlier C20. Rear vestry demolished 1995 and new extension built.

LINSMOHR HOTEL, Oldmeldrum Road. The Free Church manse of 1844. A long asymmetrical two-storey villa, presumably by *James Henderson* who built the original Free Church at Udny Green (1843) and the essentially similar manse at Kinellar (S).

LOGIERIEVE HOUSE, 3.2 km. ESE. Smart Tudor, perhaps by *J. & W. Smith*, built *c.* 1850 for the Legertwood family. Symmetrical tripartite entrance front, its round-headed doorway set in a narrow single-storey bay flanked by broader two-storey ends rising into shallow-pitched gables. Timber mullioned and transomed windows, three-light on ground floor, two-light with hoodmoulds on first, pronounced skew-putts and spike finials; central bay with token crenellation and elaborate iron railing, roof punctuated by diagonally shafted chimneystacks. Deep plan with first-floor dormer gablets; rear elevation facing into steading court very plain, its masonry and different skewputts indicating an older building incorporated within the fabric. (WATERTON HOUSE, Ellon, has a near-identical entrance front and is presumably also the work of *J. & W. Smith.*)

PITMEDDEN HOUSE, 0.5 km. WNW. A complex building history. An early country house built by the Setons in the C17 was damaged by fire in 1807. It survived until *c.* 1855–65 when it was largely cleared away by *William Henderson* for Sir William Coote Seton. Its N and S wings, which had formed a forecourt to the W, were retained and Henderson inserted a two-storey five-bay block between their W ends, resulting in a U-plan open to the E. The rebuilt house's W front is stylistically inconsistent, with a pyramid-roofed tower partly obscuring the gable end of the N wing. The N wing itself retains recognizable C17 features but its jerkinheaded gable may be late C18. In what appears to have been a second phase the S wing was rebuilt in the crow-stepped manner of the C17 house. The tall crowstepped gable over the fourth bay of the W front is probably of the same date but the pend below is part of further work by *A. G. R. Mackenzie* in 1953–4, following the gift of Pitmedden to the National Trust for Scotland in 1952. The COURTYARD STEADING (Museum of Farming Life) is of late C17–early C18 origin; the stable also has half-hipped gables.

71 To the E the house overlooks the GREAT GARDEN, 'Fundat 2 May 1675' by *Sir Alexander Seton* and his wife *Dame Margaret Lauder*. It is approximately square, 175 m. by 145 m., with a retaining wall separating the W half on which the house stands from the lower E half. Between the two levels, banded pilaster GATEPIERS with giant acorn finials open onto a handsome DOUBLE STAIR incorporating a gargoyle font recess. At each end of the retaining wall stand two-storey ogee-roofed PAVILIONS, square-plan with vaulted ground floors. Their details correspond to the terraced garden of Hatton House (Lothian) and imply the same hand.* The N pavilion has late C17 panelling at first floor, reportedly from Woolmet House (Lothian, dem. *c.* 1953). The perimeter wall is in granite, the lower garden overlooked by viewing terraces on both the N and S. The ball-finialled GATEPIERS at the E end of the lower garden were seemingly reused from the forecourt of the old house; their GATES designed by *Walter Schomberg Scott* were erected in 1972.

From 1952 the National Trust for Scotland set about re-creating the Great Garden (the original plans had been lost) with the assistance of *Dr James Richardson*, the initial planting being carried out by *George Barron*. The LOWER GARDEN was laid out as four parterres, three based on those recorded at Holyroodhouse, Edinburgh, in the mid C17, and the fourth a new design incorporating Alexander Seton's coat of arms. The

*A sundial at Hatton, dated 1675, bears initials of Charles Maitland and Elisabeth Lauder (presumably Margaret's younger sister).

polyhedron SUNDIAL in the SE parterre, illustrated by MacGibbon and Ross, is apparently of Seton's time; the FOUNTAIN reuses sculptured stones of the Restoration period, seven from *John Ritchie*'s Cross Fountain at Linlithgow (1628), and three from Pitmedden itself, but all seemingly cut by one mason. In the UPPER GARDEN, the S parterre, formed 1993, and the N parterre, 1996, are based on a design from Heriot's Hospital, Edinburgh;* the older herb garden follows a *Richardson* design, and the fountain is of Seton's time.

Recent research by Peter McGowan Associates and Addyman Associates has revealed that the house and garden formed the centrepiece of a very early DESIGNED LANDSCAPE inspired by Continental examples: a rectangle of ground 1.1 km. E–W by 0.75 km. N–S has been enclosed by dykes of superlative quality built of sharp quarried stone, most of which still survive.

PITSLIGO *see* PEATHILL

PITSLIGO CASTLE *see* ROSEHEARTY

PITTRICHIE HOUSE *see* UDNY GREEN

PITTULIE 9060

Continuous with the W edge of Sandhaven (q.v.), but the earlier of the two settlements to develop. Its single-storey fishermen's cottages are built in the traditional manner with their end-gables facing the High Street and the sea, and closely spaced together, the need for mutual protection against the weather more important than the need to admit light through their windows.

PITTULIE CASTLE, 1.8 km. WSW. C16–C18, begun by the Frasers of Philorth (q.v.), extended by the Cumines. Ruinous. Formerly a small courtyard castle like a miniature Tolquhon (q.v.), the principal S and W ranges with a square-plan tower forming a hinge between them have survived relatively entire. Of the E range only one gable with a tall chimney is left standing, while the gateway which stood between the E and W ranges on the N side is altogether lost. From what remains, and from James Giles's perspectives of *c.* 1840 when the courtyard, although roofless, was still substantially complete, it is clear that Pittulie was once of some sophistication in both its plan and its detail.

The TOWER within the SW angle is four storeys, square on plan. Its ashlar doorway in the N face near the E corner is

*Although no archaeological evidence was found for these upper parterres, their former existence was implied by historical sources.

chamfered with a rope moulding, and two empty field-panels above its lintel are surmounted by a classical pediment, the carved tympanum of which has been severely eroded away.* Above the ground floor, which contained the main stair leading to first floor, the tower's N face rises blind to the third floor where angle turrets in ashlar look seawards both NE and NW, there being a moulded lozenge panel immediately next to the NW turret. From the tower windows on its W face it is clear that the first, second and third floors were lofty apartments; they were reached by a stair-turret corbelled out from the SE angle where the tower hinges with the S range. The height of this turret strongly implies that there was further accommodation in the attic but the gables have long since fallen in. It is possible that the tower is the earliest part of the castle, built as a look-out post protecting Pittulie and its haven like the 'Wine Tower' at Fraserburgh (p. 198). As at Cairnbulg (q.v.), the shoreline may once have been nearer the castle than it is now.

The layout of accommodation in the tower together with that in the SOUTH RANGE is developed from later C16 L-plan tower houses. The relatively long and low S range comprises an almost blind ground floor lit by slit-lights but without any vaulting, which provides a plinth for the first-floor principal apartments, the great hall to the W and laird's chamber to the E. The external front facing S was a fine symmetrical composition, with six large first-floor windows evenly spaced and with a central doorway once with a stair leading down into the formal gardens, presumably a result of remodelling in the C17 or early C18. At second floor the windows rose into dormers within the roof, while boldly detailed corbel tables supported pepperpot turrets at each far end, and there was a generous attic wholly within the roof-space, the high crowstepped end gables once rising into tall coped chimneystacks. Not much is left of the interiors, although the doorways have been formed in dressed stones and some of the fireplaces and an aumbry survive. Remnants of an intramural stair seemingly relate to the turret corbelled out from the first floor on the courtyard front; its position roughly corresponds to the stair-tower centred in the courtyard front of the S range at Tolquhon.

The WEST RANGE stands at a slightly obtuse angle to the S range: the courtyard was a quadrilateral rather than a simple rectangle on plan. It is much smaller and shorter, being only two storeys, the upper-floor windows having again risen through the eaves into dormers. The EAST RANGE's surviving gable with its enormously tall chimneystack evidently contained the kitchen's fireplace. The perspectives by James Giles and Thomas Ross show that the E range was dated 1651, and the W range 1674, another recorded datestone suggesting that

*Rev. J.B. Pratt's *Buchan* (1858) records that the Saltoun arms were still displayed on the SW tower. Two panels with monograms and coats of arms preserved at Mains of Pittulie have possibly been reset.

further works were undertaken in 1727. Giles's view of the entrance front shows that the end gables of the E and W ranges projected slightly forward of the gateway, flanking it in a semi-symmetrical composition. The gateway itself was two-storeyed with a tall chimneystack and a central round-headed archway, the pend framing the view into the courtyard looking directly towards the doorways in the S range and the SW angle tower. The gateway rose into a tall chimneystack, and it is clear that the castle must have possessed a picturesque and memorable roof-line.

A BARMKIN WALL once extended from the SW corner of the castle to a ruinous DOOCOT about 50 m. WSW, then continued SE for a further 85 m. where it meets a modern field dyke.

PORTSOY B *5060*

Once a Banffshire seaport of considerable importance, Portsoy was erected into a burgh of barony in 1550 for Sir Walter Ogilvie, 3rd of Boyne (q.v.). Permission for the harbour was obtained by Sir Patrick Ogilvie in 1679, but it was not completed until 1692–3. Sir Patrick built a lodging near his new harbour in 1696 and about that time began to quarry the serpentine 'Portsoy marble' which enjoyed an early vogue in France, doubtless because it was used for two chimneypieces in the Palace of Versailles.* However, tainted by association with his son's involvement in an abortive Jacobite rebellion of 1708, Sir Patrick sold his estates to his kinsman, James Ogilvie, the 1st Earl of Seafield. Meanwhile, merchants built houses around the Harbour, and in the High Street and Low Street, in the excellent local limestone and distinctive buff-coloured granite. Prominent among them during the early C18 was Alexander Bremner, 'Laird Bremner', who operated a mercantile fleet for both duty-paid and contraband goods; he ended his days in prison, but his place was soon taken by the Robertsons and others.

In the 1820s a modest 'new town' developed along the route of the turnpike road (1802) and in 1825–8 Col. Francis William Grant, the 5th Earl of Seafield's younger brother, instigated a New Harbour near Craig Duff, but this was destroyed by two ferocious storms in 1839; after the Colonel succeeded as 6th Earl, he rebuilt the Old Harbour in 1843. In 1859 the Banff, Portsoy & Strathisla Railway built a station on the banks of Loch Soy on the S edge of the town, then ruthlessly cut its way under Seafield Street and demolished the W side of Church Street to provide a

*It fell from fashion after the outbreak of the War of Spanish Succession and never recovered. At the end of the C18 an unwanted shipload was reported as still littering the banks of the Seine.

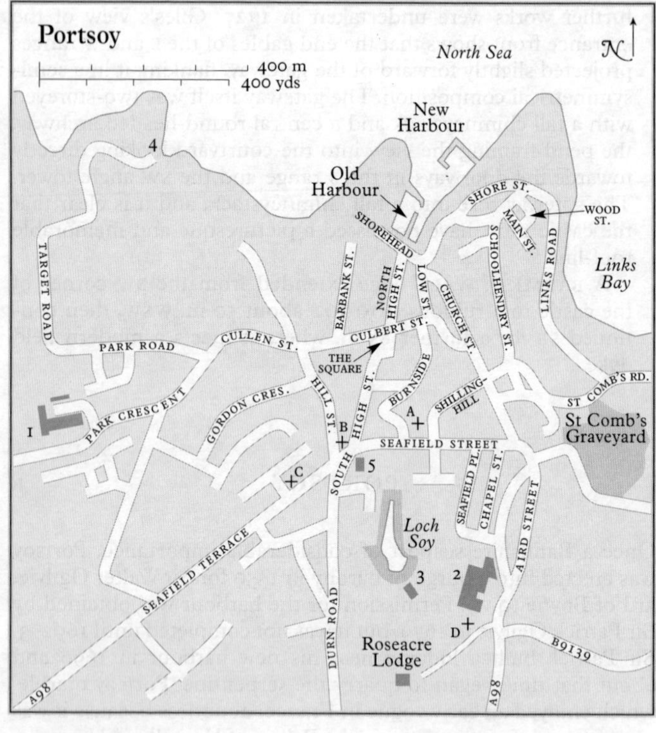

A Parish Church (former)
B St John the Baptist (Episcopal)
C Fordyce Parish Church (former Free Church)
D Church of the Annunciation (R.C.) (former)

1 Campbell Hospital (former)
2 Portsoy School
3 Railway Station (former)
4 Swimming Pool
5 Town Hall (former United Presbyterian Church)

direct (if steep) link to a terminus at the Harbour, which in the 1860s benefited from the boom in the herring industry. After the extension of the railway as far as Elgin Portsoy fell into a prolonged decline. But following the example of the National Trust for Scotland's restoration of the Fife burghs and the Historic Buildings Council's restoration of Inveraray (*see Buildings of Scotland: Argyll and Bute*), during the early 1960s the town council led by Provost George Wood with James McLeod its town clerk and *J. J. Meldrum* as architect began to restore the almost deserted historic burgh to provide social housing. It was the first town council to do so, the only parallel being Haddington where the initiative mostly came from the County Council's planning department. Today Portsoy survives as a picturesque C18 seaport, and an appropriate venue for the Scottish Traditional Boat Festival held here each year.

CHURCHES

Former PARISH CHURCH, Seafield Street. Built 1815, with tower added by *Charles Cosser* in 1876. Four bays with round-arched key-blocked windows. Centred against the W gable, the four-stage tower with angle buttresses progressively intaken is in slightly darker pinned rubble with pale golden dressed work. Its round-arched fanlit doorway with bold ashlar surround is a relic of the 1815 entrance porch; its belfry has louvred Venetian openings, the fourth clock stage crowned by a machicolated parapet with coped battlements. Two-storey E porch is 1815, with parapet perhaps 1876. Arch-braced timber roof corbelled out from the side-walls and diagonally boarded with small roof-lights and stencilled decoration, apparently dating from renovation in 1881.

In front of the church, the WAR MEMORIAL of 1923, by *D. Morren & Co.* of Aberdeen. A young soldier in granite, leaning on his rifle, head bowed in sorrowful reflection (cf. Oldmeldrum and Udny (qq.v.), and Rhynie and Tarland (S)).

ST JOHN THE BAPTIST (Episcopal), Hill Street/Seafield Terrace. By *James Ross*, 1840–1. Miniaturized Gothic. Entrance gable with slightly projecting centre rising into a belfry to suggest a tower and spire framed between flanking aisles, the three-bay side elevations with token central transepts. Pinned whinstone rubble with pale gold ashlar dressings (cf. St Mary's Episcopal Church, Inverurie (S), 1842). Simple interior. – FONT. Stone basin supported on short clustered columns with moulded bases and capitals. – HARMONIUM by *Dominion Organ & Piano Co.* of Bowmanville, Ontario. – STAINED GLASS representing Christ with His Disciples in the Garden of Gethsemane, *c.* 1875.

FORDYCE PARISH CHURCH, Seafield Terrace. Gothic, built as a Free Church by *J. R. Mackenzie*, 1869–70, with *W. K. Gray* as mason, possibly incorporating fabric of an earlier Free Church designed by *Hendry* and built by *Watt* in 1843–4.* Entrance gable has a pointed doorway and wheel window flanked on the l. by a slim square tower and spire, and with a crocketed pinnacled buttress on the r., reflecting the nave-and-aisles plan inside. Construction in dark hammer-dressed whinstone coursed and squared with substantial pale golden ashlar sandstone as a richly striking contrast. The doorway has twin shouldered openings framed between timber columns with stylized capitals and an oversailing arch and hoodmould with foliate carved bosses. Tower slightly advanced rises square with progressively splayed corners, then broaches to octagonal beneath a buttressed belfry; the sandstone spire is banded with lucarnes and has blind arcading running around its base and the apex beneath the weathervane.

*It was perhaps prompted by a split in the Free Church congregation which had resulted in the United Presbyterian church being built in Seafield Street in 1865–6 (this became the Town Hall: *see* Public Buildings).

Four-bay arcaded nave and aisles: cast-iron clustered shafts with stiff-leaf capitals support the arcades and the arched timber trusses of the open roof above the nave. Panelled gallery above the entrance vestibule now converted as an organ loft. – STAINED GLASS. In the aisles, two vibrant windows of 1938 signed by *Walter Pearce* of Manchester: on the l., 'The Name of One Whom God Hath Blessed', and r., 'Write Me as One That Loves His Fellow Men'.

MANSE, W of the church but linked to it, by *W. Stephen*, mason, 1846–7, the porch added in 1880 and the canted and projecting window bays probably in 1888. – VESTRY HALL by *William Donald*, builder, 1927. The CHURCHYARD WALLS of 1895–6 have rock-faced bluestone GATEPIERS (by *Matthews*, masons) and good cast-iron GATES AND RAILINGS (by *Macdonald Bros*).

Former CHURCH OF THE ANNUNCIATION (R.C.), off Aird Street. A broad harled rectangle designed by Bishop *James Kyle* and built by *Charles Dawson* of Banff in 1829, the year of Emancipation. Tripartite Gothick entrance gable divided by giant ashlar pilaster-buttresses rising through the crenellated wall-head into stepped and banded pinnacles. Central pointed doorway, ground-floor and gallery windows in dressed surrounds with basket-weave glazing bars, central gallery window blind. Three-bay flanks, apse added 1925. Interior gutted. PRESBYTERY adjoining on r. built mid 1830s, two storeys, three bays, gabled porch later.

ST COMB'S GRAVEYARD, St Comb's Road, in the dramatic setting of a very broad shallow valley. The N end is the original graveyard opened *c.* 1728, with a fine collection of memorials including lying and upright slabs, table tombs and burial enclosures; it was extended 1874, *c.* 1960 and *c.* 2000. Remains of an early CHAPEL stood within the SW extension until the early C19. ST COMB'S WELL reputedly possessed medicinal properties: in 1893 it was enclosed beneath a stone dome with a narrow entrance archway, and grassed over as a mound.

UNITED PRESBYTERIAN CHURCH, Seafield Street. *See* Town Hall (Public Buildings).

PUBLIC BUILDINGS

Former CAMPBELL HOSPITAL, Park Crescent. By *William Kelly* (of *Kelly & Nicol*), 1902–4. Built for treatment of infectious diseases at the instigation of Dr James Campbell, cashier of the Seafield Estates and convener of Banff County Council. He personally donated £4,000, the site being given by the Countess of Seafield. Villa-type – two-storey central block with single-storey wards at right angles for males and females. Extended by *Malcolm S. McCallum*, 1924–6. West Pavilion 1938–9.

OLD TOWN HALL, The Square. *See* Description.

PORTSOY SCHOOL, Aird Street. Opened *c.* 1876, much rebuilt *c.* 1936. Entrance front is C20 but the original playground elevation survives. Long single-storey built in pinned rubble with tall close-spaced windows in ashlar surrounds and big attic gables giving variety to the roof-line.

PUBLIC PARK. Laid out 1973. Its pavilion is the former RAILWAY STATION, a simple timber structure built in 1859 for the Banff, Portsoy & Strathisla Railway, and closed in 1968.

SWIMMING POOL, Target Road, N of the town on the seashore. Open-air, formed 1936 by enclosing two rock spurs with a concrete wall.

TOWN HALL, Seafield Street. Former United Presbyterian church of 1865–6. Closed 1913,* converted by the town council in 1923. Gable front with 1920s vestibule extending across its ground floor, all built in coursed squared whinstone with pale golden ashlar dressings. The original gable front is articulated into nave and aisles by pilaster-buttresses rising into pinnacles, the paired gallery windows inserted in the 1920s. Depressed-arch doorway and crenellated wall-head parapet over the vestibule. Four-bay flanks, session house set back on r. Rear gable with 1793 datestone, a relic of the failed Relief Church congregation.

DESCRIPTION

The Old Town

Portsoy's OLD HARBOUR was constructed in 1680–93 in the Bay of Portsoy by Sir Patrick Ogilvie of Boyne (q.v.). A roughly rectangular basin, a history of repair and alteration is recorded in its stones – some laid flat and others laid upright, a rich geolithic pattern of silvers and greys, yellow, green, gold and black, all washed and polished to a glittering shine by the sea. The Old Harbour is known to have been rebuilt in 1843 and again in 1884 but the many-layered sea wall is reputedly of the first build, looking like some primitive leviathan flexing and writhing as it basks in the dark water.

Around the Old Harbour, in SHOREHEAD, a variety of traditional buildings present the classic image of Portsoy. Two substantial buildings on the E side – one of them Sir Patrick Ogilvie's Lodging of 1696 – were demolished in the mid 1930s, but otherwise the early part of the burgh survives substantially intact. On the S side, the SHORE INN *c.* 1800 is harled in white, its windows with long-and-short quoins bracingly suggested in nautical blue. Following the curve of the quay, an enclosed courtyard is framed between two contrasting end gables of houses in Low Street and North High Street, the former with a case for the harbour's FitzRoy barometer (cf. Banff, p. 93).

Towards the W is LAIRD BREMNER'S HOUSE, built in 1726. It is a classic of its kind – three-storey five bays, harled in a pale sandy colour with steep crowstepped end gables

*As the result of a schism in the Free Church congregation (*see* Fordyce Parish Church).

which rise into coped chimneystacks. It has a broad pend with a semi-elliptical arch, and two doorways in red dressed surrounds; the first- and second-floor windows are near-regular in arrangement. The attic is lit from oval oculi at the ends, and one skewputt is dated. At the rear a large wing gives entrance to the attic from Barbank Street. Inside there were once secret stores for contraband goods; the attic certainly appears to have been used as a warehouse, the frontage to the shore having bowed out under the weight it has carried. Close by are WAREHOUSES, that on the l. with its end gable to the shore and a forestair against its flank being mid-C18, the small upper-floor windows hard under the eaves. That on the r. was rebuilt as a granary from 'Lord Findlater's Corfe House' by *John Adam* in 1765, and an architect's hand shows in the monumental character he bestowed on so simple a building. The ground floor is in pinned boulder rubble with five separate doorways, but the three upper storeys are in lighter cherry-cocked rubble; first floor is almost blind but at second and third floors the small square windows are precisely regular in their arrangement. The Corfe House is a shallow single-pile plan, with rear entrances at first floor on account of the rise in the hill. Behind it almost hidden from view is another mid-C18 warehouse with a canted first-floor window recessed in one corner overlooking the harbour. At the W end of the Bay is a much-altered three-storey warehouse, late C18.

Until the late C19 the Seatown which grew up between the Bay of Portsoy and the neighbouring Links Bay extended considerably W along the shore with scarcely a break, the SHORE STREET cottages originally facing with their end gables to the sea like those in Pennan, Crovie or Seatown of Gardenstown (qq.v.), but only No. 2 is now left. In 1825–8 the NEW HARBOUR was formed by Col. Francis Grant, the 5th Earl of Seafield's younger brother, to accommodate vessels of over 200 tonnes' burden, but it was destroyed by two disastrous storms in 1839. The present rectangular basin in stone and concrete, 1884, is only suitable for much smaller vessels. Some distance further on the Seatown survives in MAIN STREET, where the cottages stand with their gables to the road on the landward side, some early C19 and others rebuilt later, and WOOD STREET with terraced houses of *c.* 1860–70. At the end is the three-storey SALMON BOTHY, dated 1834, where fish catches were prepared prior to transport and cooled with ice from Loch Soy. It remained in use until 1990, and was restored in 2007–8 by *Mantell Ritchie* as a museum and community centre.

The streets S of the Old Harbour climb steeply uphill. NORTH HIGH STREET is (despite its name) narrow, gently winding and couthy. Near the harbour the OLD STAR INN was built in 1727, its sheer scale a measure of the number of passengers travelling by sea – three storeys and eight bays long, harled with a round-arched pend near-central in the ground floor and a railed forestair to the first floor. The doorway and windows are modest openings in red ashlar surrounds, the fenestration at first and second floors regular in arrangement; the skewputts once bore the builder's initials and date. The long rear wing is an extension of the later C18. Facing the Old Star, Nos. 23–27, a very handsome house with a round-arched pend and tall curvilinear 'Dutch' attic gable. At the top of North High Street, a late C18 house with an Ionic doorpiece, its finely fluted and filleted pilasters with angle-volute capitals beneath a moulded cornice. Opposite, THE BOYNE HOTEL just off The Square, provided competition for the Old Star from the mid C18. Two storeys and three bays, its centre projects under a tall gable restyled to its present polygonal profile when the roof was modified to mansard form during the early 1960s. It has a lugged entrance architrave moulded with cornice, the windows are set in dressed surrounds, but the harling has been stripped to leave the rubble exposed. Falling ground to the front and flank provides for the basement cellars.

In THE SQUARE, the buildings are plainer and later than those near the harbour – predominantly two-storey, loosely enclosing what is actually a rectangle where markets were held. The Square's civic importance is denied by some alterations to these buildings resulting in a poor appearance, and its use as a car park. The best buildings are on the N side, Nos. 13–14, early C19, a two-storey four-bay frontage in random rubble, and the OLD TOWN HALL tucked into a corner: tall single-storey with its gabled centre slightly projected, transomed windows and a doorway at the r. end, converted in 1892 from a Masonic hall of 1798.

In SOUTH HIGH STREET the buildings on both sides nearest The Square stand at an angle to the road producing a lively saw-toothed appearance. The NORTH OF SCOTLAND BANK is a two-storey Z-plan, its street-front just a single bay and ashlar bowed corner with finely detailed doorpiece enlarged in the early C20, but its long rubble flank is five bays deep with vestibule porch for the bank agent's house, and at the rear, a slightly taller two-storey block with a canted bay window. Then further up on the opposite side, smart houses set back in their gardens, No. 12 late C18, two storeys harled with a later gabled porch and a long single-storey wing at right angles, and No. 14, the former Episcopal rectory a two-storey L-plan. The wing was reputedly an Episcopal chapel during the late C18; the taller main front with corniced doorway and ground-floor windows is *c.* 1830, its first-floor windows altered as dormers *c.* 1900.

In CULLEN STREET W of The Square, TOWER HOUSE is curious and rather engaging with its end-gable bay window and spired corner tourelle facing the road, *c.* 1850 in its present form; then further along MARINE VILLA, an C18 house with later Regency oriel supported on slender columns.* E of The Square, CULBERT STREET, Nos. 1–3 altered as the rear wing

*This oriel has been reconstructed recently in new materials.

of The Boyne Hotel but still with a lugged and architraved doorpiece, then Nos. 9–11, a two-storey block *c.* 1830 which turns the foot of the hill into Low Street with an elegant bow.

In LOW STREET itself a very attractive group of mid-C18 houses either side of the close which leads up into the rear court of the Old Star: this is itself one of the most picturesque views of Portsoy. Best of the group are Nos. 21–23, refronted in an elegant vernacular classical style during the late C18 or very early C19. Three storeys in pale gold ashlar masonry, the ground floor with alternating doorways and windows, and the main entrance at No. 23 with an excellent radial fanlight; first floor with a central round-arched and key-blocked window and Serlian windows at either end, all with basket-weave tracery, then low oblong windows at second floor just under the eaves.

CHURCH STREET suffered severely when the railway cut through to the harbour in 1859, the whole W side being lost beyond the crossroads where it passes Shillinghill and Institute Street. SOYE HOUSE (Nos. 30–32) is the oldest surviving in Portsoy – three-bay semi-symmetrical, the end-bay gables (non-identical) framing a two-storey centre. It has been built in two distinct phases: on the l., the three-storey-and-attic harled and crowstepped gable is of 1694; the two-storey centre and the r. gable are a late C18 addition with much larger windows, and a Venetian in the flank.

In contrast with the Old Town's hilly winding thoroughfares SEAFIELD STREET, the former turnpike which bypasses just to the S, runs absolutely broad straight and level for some 300 m.: the former COMMERCIAL HOTEL at the E end – itself early C19 with a pend-arch to the stables – stands on the site of an inn which was one of Laird Bremner's ventures. The building of the parish church in 1815 suggests that Seafield Street was meant to become a new high street, and to some extent it succeeded. Nos. 22–24 in granite ashlar with a bowed corner slightly recessed is in the style of *William Robertson* *c.* 1820–5, and may have been intended to form part of a much longer row: the Station Hotel, although much altered, was probably similar, and Nos. 2–4 towards the far W end (*c.* 1830) was perhaps also part of the scheme. Predictably the Union Bank of *c.* 1870, now BANK OF SCOTLAND, is one of the best buildings – a late Neoclassical 'money-box', its two-storey three-bay front in deep golden ashlar, the canted corner containing a pilastered and pedimented bank entrance, while at the rear the bank agent's house is set back in its garden. Nos. 21–27 is a big three-storey block of the Aberdeen School but roguishly freestyle, its second floor breaking into gabled and finialled stone dormers.

Towards the E end of Seafield Street, AIRD STREET, CHAPEL STREET and SEAFIELD PLACE were laid out in parallel after the railway established a station nearby in 1859, but development at the time was patchy; MACRAE COURT is by *Baxter, Clark & Paul*, 1990. SEAFIELD TERRACE, which continues the route of the turnpike W, is chiefly notable for its churches (*see* above) but a few houses stand out, among them

HERMISTON of *c.* 1820, a beautifully proportioned two-storey three-bay front in cherry-cocked squared masonry with sandstone ashlar dressings, a smart pilastered doorpiece with paterae and a very tall gabled roof; it is set well back from the road and approached by fine ball-finialled gatepiers.

ROSEACRE LODGE, within extensive wooded grounds W of Aird Street. Mid-C19. Two storeys, three broad bays; central ashlar porch is later, otherwise harled. Tall ground-floor windows, astragalled sash-and-case; lower first-floor with windows paired, astragals in upper sashes only, hipped roof. Elegant cast-iron gatepiers and gates. Former STABLES, near Durn Road.

DURN HOUSE, Durn Road. Perhaps built for Sir James Dunbar, 4th of Durn, after he succeeded in 1786; it replaced a tower house. Two-storey classical entrance front in fine ashlar over a semi-sunk rubble basement, with three-bay pedimented centre slightly stepped forward. Later, well-detailed, pedimented porch built out over the stair-platt. In the single bays at the ends, key-blocked Serliana at ground floor and single windows at first floor, hipped platform roof with twin coped chimneystacks. Flanks in field rubble, roughly coursed and squared with cherry-cocking, the dressings and quoins in ashlar. Rear elevation also rubble with its elegant three-window bow ashlar-built at ground floor and first floor; pedimented attic dormer added *c.* 1900. Entrance hall with fine ceiling rose opens directly into large rear saloon with a bow; the other principal apartments with simple plasterwork. Staircase on E side with cast-iron balusters, 1605 datestone set into wall. CARRIAGE HOUSE AND STABLES, 60 m. NNE, also late C18. Two storeys, ground and low first floors with centre slightly projected under small bellcote gable. Forestair at S end. In the end bays the original carriage sheds, under segmental arches. 'Goose bay' in forestair flank; N-end gig house later. Next to it, the DOOCOT, probably C17. Two storeys with crowstep gables. Internally *c.* 500 stone nesting-boxes.

DURN BRIDGE over Burn of Durn, 90 m. ENE. Mid-C18. Single-span, slightly hump-backed; rubble construction with long approaches and low coped parapets.

SCOTSMILL, 2.2 km. ESE. Late C18 or early C19, perhaps incorporating earlier fabric. Two-storey main block in rubble, the later wing forming an L-plan accommodated the grain kiln. SCOTSMILL BRIDGE, late C18, carrying B9139 over Burn of Boyne. Single round arch in tooled rubble with tooled copes to parapets; slopes noticeably downwards from W to E.

POTTERTON 9010

Two very separate residential developments, both prompted by the oil boom in the later C20, linked by the length of Panmure Gardens, and with a much earlier Free Church.

Former Belhelvie Free Church. Now in domestic use. Built 1843, reconstructed 1883 by *Daniel Macandrew* with slightly higher walls, new roof and square-plan tower centred against the entrance W gable. Modest but engaging. Adjacent manse single-storey with canted attic dormers, by *William Henderson* 1852.

0060 RATHEN

Former Rathen Free Church. *See* Inverallochy.

Rathen West Parish Church. Designed by *William Smith* (of *J. & W. Smith*) 1867, built 1869–70. Impressive First Pointed. Entrance gable rising into steeply raked roof, flanked by three-stage tower with broach spire. Built predominantly in granite ashlar with bright red pinnings, both the gable and the tower are buttressed in contrasting brown masonry. W gable is expressed as a nave and aisles: twin Gothic doorways, their double-leaf doors mounted on decorative iron bar-hinges, with the wall-plane taken in by a deep weathering above them; stepped lancets at gallery level all under red and black polychrome voussoirs; the side aisles have trefoils in spheric triangle surrounds to light the gallery stairs. Tower framed by angle buttresses on all sides, which are taken in at the two lower stages: tall belfry stage with two-light openings and plate-tracery roundels under hoodmoulds. Bracket cornice supports the broached stone spire, with lucarnes in alternate sides. Six-bay flanks in mixed grey and red granite, with lancet windows and buttresses, small trefoiled dormer vents set in the roof. E end with vestry and mincer-plate window, small trefoil opening high up near the apex. Interior with open polygonal roof supported on arches rising from corbels; gallery at the W end. Simple handsome furnishings remain *in situ*. Bell from old church (*see* below) by *Peter Jansen*, 1643.

Old Parish Church. The first church here was reputedly founded by St Ethernan (or Eddran) in the late C6. The present structure comprises a nave begun in the C17 or earlier, and a S aisle erected by the Frasers of Memsie dated 1633. The nave is roofless and partly demolished. Its tall W gable in boulder rubble with free use of packing material has perhaps been built in two phases or substantially reconstructed. Shouldered sandstone doorway (now much eroded) with S jamb roll-moulded; round-arched moulded gallery window still with shutter-pins; carved skewputts and steeply raked skews; classical bellcote dated 1782 and initialled L.A.S. for Lord Abernethy & Saltoun or Alexander Lord Saltoun, its stepped top with a ball finial. S wall mostly in large square stones with cherry-cocking; two large chamfered windows towards the W end, that nearest the gable stepped up perhaps to light the gallery stair; between these windows, a lozenge-shaped sundial dated 1625. A broad round-headed chamfered archway (now partially blocked) opens into the long S aisle, also roofless. Of the N wall only a stump survives and the E gable has been entirely lost.

The S aisle's rubble walls rise slightly lower than the nave. Over the round-arched doorway in the W flank, three panels, one with raised letters 'Alexander Fraser of Philorth Patron', one with a coat of arms; these and the date-panel near the S end may be later insertions. S gable with large moulded window was formerly crowstepped, skewputts only survive with much-eroded faces; smaller windows in the flanks. Inside, within the E wall, an ogee-headed aumbry and small square opening (perhaps a piscina) now infilled with memorial tablet. – CHURCHYARD. Channelled red granite GATEPIERS with ball finials, C18.

Former PARISH MANSE. 1803, rebuilt by *William Smith* (of *J. & W. Smith*) in 1852. Originally a tall narrow house, two-storey and basement, two bays broad, golden granite rubble with tall hipped roof and central chimneystack. Smith deepened the house and formed the present entrance elevation on its flank – three bays broad, the l. one the original gable; the central doorway is approached by a splayed railed stair, and slightly projecting gable on the r. Canted bay windows were added to the original front at the same time.

THE HOUSE OF AUCHIRIES, 2.3 km. W, consists of two country houses both built in the early C18, their distinct identities reflecting the rapid increase in sophistication of Scottish domestic architecture at that time. Both are roofless, a slightly later and simpler service wing being still in residential use. The three buildings together form a Z-plan arrangement with a forecourt to the W. At the E end, the OLD HOUSE facing S is a two-storey and attic block with central entrance, its chamfered windows on ground and first floors all the same size but asymmetric in arrangement, with roughly dressed stones formerly a contrast against the harl. The entrance, which has been widened, is protected on each side by shot-holes, with above the monogrammed initials of its Ogilvy owners, and the date 1715; the ground-floor windows, at least, were formerly barred. Two small rear wings have been added later. Inside, a simple first-floor fireplace in the W gable. The NEW HOUSE constituting the Z-plan's central block presents an entrance front facing W, the same two-storey and attic height but five windows wide and symmetrical, effectively incorporating the Old House as its rear wing. The New House has moulded door jambs and chamfered window surrounds, walls in pinned rubble formerly harled, and bold skewputts at the gables which rise steeply into massive coped chimneystacks. Although much overgrown, this was presumably the block on which the Ordnance Survey recorded a datestone of 1726. Inside, a large arched recess within the S gable at ground level, and bolection-moulded fireplace in the N gable at first floor. The long NORTH-WEST WING is mid-C18, single-storey and attic lit by ground-floor windows only nearest the New House, with a two-storey three-windows-wide section at the far W end, all under one roof: a long modern dormer has been formed at the central section. The wing is built of granite ashlar with slate cherry-cocking, and has two shot-holes like those in the Old House; the gables have square-cut skewputts and sturdy coped chimneystacks.*

Just S of the house, a small single-storey rectangular building, rubble-built under a hipped bellcast roof, was originally a BARN. The tenants carried their sacks up to attic level before depositing the contents into storage bins which still line the walls on each side. Another simple OUTBUILDING, single-storey rubble with a gabled roof, on the N. The house was once enclosed within a WALLED GARDEN, of which parts of the walls still remain.

BRIDGE OF AUCHIRIES, 130 m. WNW. A small hump-backed bridge mostly in squared granite, with wider approaches in random rubble; initials G.O. and date 1790 (?) on inside face of S parapet.

CORTES HOUSE. *See* p. 130.

0050 RATTRAY

16 ST MARY'S CHAPEL.[‡] This isolated ruin, on a windswept site at the S end of Loch Strathbeg, is thought to have been built in the earlier decades of the C13 as a chapel for the Comyn Earls of Buchan; one of the earl's castles was nearby, where it is presumed to have overlooked an important harbour. The chapel is likely to have fallen out of use following the construction of a parish church at Crimond (q.v.) in the C15. It is a rectangular structure 15.5 m. by 7.5 m., built of grey whinstone rubble with red ashlar dressings, though most of those dressings have been robbed. The two gable walls stand to almost full height; parts of the N and S walls also survive, with gaps suggesting that there were opposed N and S nave doorways. The E gable is pierced by an echelon triplet of round-headed windows, and there is a single window in the W wall. The E part of the church is fenced in as a burial enclosure for the Cumine of Rattray family.

RATTRAY HOUSE, 2 km. S of St Mary's Chapel. A classical country house built for Capt. Adam Cumine, R.N., after he purchased the old Comyn estate of Broadlands in 1817; its familial resemblance to Cortes (q.v.) nearby and to Manar (1811, S) suggests *John Smith I* as the architect. It incorporates an older C18 house in its rear flank.

*The House of Auchiries is celebrated in Buchan folklore as the hiding place of the prominent Jacobite – and noted philosopher – Alexander Forbes, 4th and last Lord Pitsligo, who was still being hunted by Government soldiers in 1756, and was concealed in a closet during a surprise search, remaining afterwards in hiding at Auchiries until his death in 1762.

‡This entry has been contributed by Richard Fawcett.

Cumine's new entrance front is two storeys and seven windows wide over a raised basement plinth. The ground-floor windows are taller than first and the centre three bays which are relatively closely spaced together are slightly projected. It is stuccoed in white, against which the grey granite ashlar of an entrance porch stands out in striking contrast. This porch, added in 1890, replaced an original tetrastyle portico similar to that still existing at Cortes. Detail is kept to a minimum: only a very shallow cornice beneath the wall-head parapet which is raised and panelled over the centre, with a pair of tall chimneystacks in front of the hipped roof countering the horizontal emphasis of the design. Flanking the entrance front are two elongated concave wing-walls. A conservatory, probably added in 1890, opens off the principal apartments on the r. side.

On the rear elevation, the older C18 house presents a narrower three-bay frontage, but is of similar three-storey height to the later front block, harled with a gabled roof and end stacks. The windows are astragalled sash-and-case, the centre bay's stepped up to light the landings of the stair which continues into the attic lit by pedimented dormers. There are three outshots – two small single-storey ones under hipped roofs against the main front, and one extending from an end gable within the angle formed by the new block.

The interior of the new house is in a simple classical style, but the old house's is rather richer, its doorways with pulvinated friezes and finely detailed pediments with painted tympana; in the former drawing room, a Rococo fireplace with painted overmantel. WALLED GARDEN, 50 m. S, its triangular arched gateway with long-and-short quoins and voussoirs, initials J.C. H.H.C. and date 1842 probably a later insertion. A single-storey hip-roofed COTTAGE next to the garden is balanced on the N by a LAUNDRY, so that together they appear like pavilions flanking the main house. GATEPIERS in red granite, square, with slim cornices and ball finials: the S pair with convex wing-walls. COURTYARD STEADING, single-storey U-plan in cherry-cocked rubble, centre range with gable rising into a bellcote.

MIDDLETON OF RATTRAY FARMHOUSE, 4.3 km. S. Early C19, two-storey three-bay, harled with coped stacks; later porch and attic dormers; single-storey wings.

RATTRAY HEAD LIGHTHOUSE, The Ron, 2.5 km. E. Built by direct sanction of the Board of Trade in London, the Commissioners of Northern Lights having previously refused requests despite increasing pressure in 1875, 1887 and 1890. Plans were prepared by the brothers *D. A.* and *C. A. Stevenson* in 1891 and construction was carried out over three seasons by *David Porter* of Aberdeen in 1892–5. A major innovation in lighthouse design, the foghorn and engine room were accommodated within a tapered granite plinth; above this the lighthouse tower in white enamelled brick containing the keeper's room and the lantern rose off-centre to a total height of 36 m.

above sea level. The original oil light was an exceptional 44,000 candlepower and the siren the earliest use of a first-class fog signal on a rock-based lighthouse. Now electrically powered, fully automated since 1982. Associated SHORE STATION, a simple two-storey block, harled in white with red rock-faced dressings and margins.

RORA *see* LONGSIDE

9060 ROSEHEARTY

Tradition holds that this former seaport was established in the C14 after shipwrecked Danes settled among the local crofters and introduced new fishing techniques from their native land. In 1573 the Forbes of Pitsligo (*see* below) built town lodgings known as The Jam and in 1681 Rosehearty was erected a burgh of barony for Alexander, 3rd Lord Pitsligo. The Square – formerly Broad Street – was presumably laid out by him, a rectangular market space which like Peterhead's was of unusual length; it was sheltered from the seafront by a tolbooth (dem.) which was completed in 1683. Lord Pitsligo built the fishermen a new Seatown on the line now followed by North Street, improved the pier, and provided boats for every six men in exchange for a fifth-share of their catch. He encouraged trade with England, Scandinavia and the Continent; Rosehearty flourished and its population diversified into other trades including shipbuilding from at least the C18.

After the 'Forty-five Lord Pitsligo forfeited his lands and Rosehearty was acquired by Alexander Garden. By the late C18 the Seatown had become a stronghold of evangelism – 'the Rosehearty fishermen spoke more like the old apostles than any class I ever met', one minister remarked – so earning the village its soubriquet of Bethsaida. The Gardens built the Old Harbour in the 1790s, its smaller E pier in rubble dating from that time: the longer W pier in coursed masonry is probably earlier C19, with a C20 mass-concrete beacon. By 1840 the harbour could accommodate vessels of 70 tonnes' burden and Rosehearty grew rapidly with the development of the herring industry, its fishing fleet second only to Fraserburgh's on the Aberdeenshire coast, and well ahead of Peterhead's (qq.v.). In the 1860s more docking space was needed and a second harbour was established at Port Rae. This inaugurated the boom years when Rosehearty was largely rebuilt on a gridiron plan between the Seatown and The Square. By the 1880s some 120 boats operated from its harbours and up to 20,000 herring barrels were exported annually, but as a result of overfishing the herring trade went spectacularly bust in three disastrous seasons in 1884–6. This was a turning point: Rosehearty's tidal harbours could not compete with the deep-water harbours of Fraserburgh and Peterhead, and the crash dissuaded the Great North of

Scotland Railway from extending its line to the town. A comeback was subsequently staged through white-fishing.* Between and after the wars the area S of The Square was developed with social housing constructed in traditional granite with slate roofs, and today Rosehearty serves as a dormitory for Fraserburgh, with just a few pleasure boats berthed in its harbours.

Former FREE CHURCH, Kirk Street, facing down the Loch Street axis. Now a warehouse and thoroughly altered. Built shortly after the Disruption *c.* 1845. Plain with pointed doorway and windows, all blocked, bellcote removed. Vestry house at rear added *c.* 1900.

PITSLIGO PARISH CHURCH, Pitsligo Street. By *Ellis & Wilson* 1882–3. Built for the United Presbyterians as a replacement for the 'Fishers' Chapel' established in Union Street in 1787–8, a measure of the strength of Dissent in Rosehearty, and of its prosperity at the height of the Herring Boom. Very robust First Pointed in dark blue local stone with pinnings, the dressed work in pale granite from New Pitsligo. The church is orientated E–W with its gable front facing E, flanked by stair halls which mask its full width; the N stair hall contains the main entrance. Within the gable itself is a two-light plate-traceried window framed by buttresses which are progressively intaken, the l. buttress rising into a tall gablet belfry. Three-bay flank elevations, with gablets over the westernmost bays; a transverse schoolroom and vestry annexe projecting at the SW. Simple and dignified interior with a panelled gallery across the E end on cast-iron columns, and the ceiling carried on pitch-pine trusses with a bold columnar detail. To the S, the former MANSE, built 1896.

ROSEHEARTY SCHOOL, Pitsligo Street. Built 2004–7 by *M. R. T. Architects*. Large, steel-framed, with bright cladding and shallow curved roofs. It replaced the school of 1888 by *Ellis & Wilson*.

WAR MEMORIAL, Cairnhill, 0.5 km. S. By *Jenkins & Marr*, 1921. A short solid rubble-built tower of three stages on an elevated site above the village and the bay. A prominent landmark, isolated and windswept, a place set apart for pilgrimage and remembrance.

THE JAM, Union Street. The derelict remains of the lodgings built by the Forbes of Pitsligo in 1573. A long rubble frontage, formerly harled, with windows of modest size, some on the upper floor having broken through the eaves as dormers.‡

*The GNoSR had been at an advanced stage of planning the line, with Parliamentary powers already in hand.

‡The dormerhead with initials and date A.G. 1763 reset in its walls has often resulted in The Jam being confused with the Lodging (dem.) built by Alexander Garden in that year on the SE side of The Square; the dormerhead itself appears more mid-C16 than mid-C18. The very name 'Jam' – jamb – implies that the lodgings in Union Street were built as an adjunct of an earlier structure: very probably a small tower house like that at Kinnaird Head, Fraserburgh (q.v.) or formerly at Keith Inch at Peterhead.

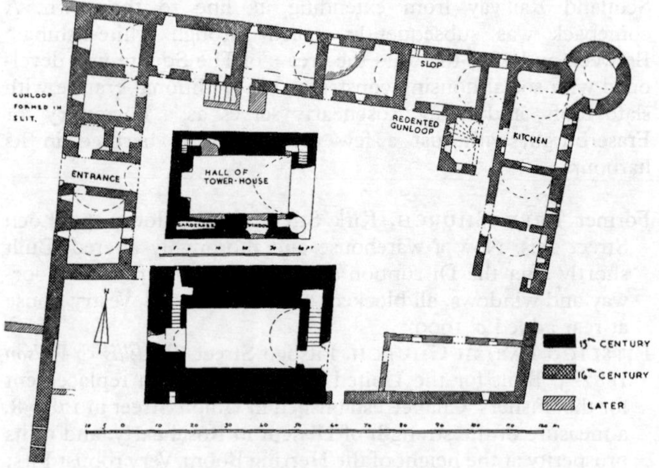

Rosehearty, Pitsligo Castle.
Plan of ground floor and first floor of tower

PITSLIGO CASTLE, 0.8 km. SE. A courtyard castle on a quadrilateral plan, incorporating an earlier tower house, and approached through a long walled forecourt on the W. C15 to early C17, now a consolidated ruin.

The TOWER HOUSE standing on the S side of the courtyard near its W end is approximately rectangular, 16 m. long by 11.3 m. deep. It was reputedly built by Sir William Forbes after he acquired the Kynnaldy estate through marriage in 1424, and its well-coursed boulder masonry with red freestone dressings appears to bear that out. Originally it rose rather taller, three storeys and an attic caphouse, but *c.* 1700 the top bedchamber storey and the caphouse were taken down, leaving only the ground floor and very tall first floor, both of which are vaulted, rising some 10 m. above ground. The round-arched ground-floor doorway was in the E gable. The walls of the tower are mostly 3 m. thick, though slightly less on the N side; within the NW and NE angles, intramural stairs lead up to the first-floor great hall, that on the NE being the main stair. Above ground floor the E wall had collapsed by the time John Claude Nattes came to draw the castle in 1801, leaving the first-floor vault – almost 7 m. high – clearly open to view from the courtyard outside. From the great hall a spiral stair in the SE angle once gave access to the bedchamber storey and caphouse; there was a garderobe in the SW corner. Both the arched entrance doorway and the great hall fireplace at the W end have long since been removed.

The COURTYARD COMPLEX was built during the second half of the C16 to provide more comfortable and convenient accommodation than the old tower house, but was seemingly never quite completed. It is entered by a vaulted transe on its

W side. It is 43.5 m. long on the N side, 41.8 m. on the S, 36 m. wide on the W and 30 m. on the E, with single-pile ranges enclosing an area approximately 30 m. by 16.5 m. These ranges were originally two storeys with an attic lit by dormers, but are now much dilapidated, with only the ground-floor rooms – mostly vaulted – surviving to any great extent. The palace-block occupied the E and S ranges, and a long gallery the N range. At the palace-block's outer NE corner is a circular tower of three storeys which formerly rose into a conical roof and coped chimneystack. Although it contained bedchambers this tower had gunloops for defence, one commanding the N flank, one the E flank, and one the open field. Then within the palace-block itself two of the first-floor rooms have fireplaces with Gothic jambs and capitals; the ground floor contained the services, the kitchen being at the N end of the E range. Within the NE angle is a square stair-tower of three (originally four) diminishing stages with a redented gunloop which Dr Douglas Simpson remarked upon as of an unusual kind. This stair-tower is dated 1603 and contains a stairwell 3.5 m. by 3.5 m. As Professor Charles McKean has observed, it is an interesting parallel to that at Fyvie (q.v.), the vaults carrying the risers being supported on radial segmental arches from a central newel, here octagonal rather than circular. Above the entrance to the stairway are three field-panels, two of which contain heraldic devices, the third now being empty. The panel in the S face represents the Royal Arms of Scotland, a lion rampant with double tressure; it is dated 1577 and the initials I.R. flanking the Scottish Crown stand for Jacobus Rex – James VI. The panel in the W face dated 1603 represents the Royal Arms of the United Kingdom in the year of the Union of the Crowns, both panels being very clear expressions of loyalty to the Sovereign. Above the entrance front's archway is another panel displaying the arms of Forbes and Fraser impaled with those of Buchan: the initials A.L.P. stand for Alexander, 2nd Lord Pitsligo and M.L.Æ. for Lady Mary Erskine, a daughter of James Erskine, 7th Earl of Buchan; the date 1663 refers to the year Lord Pitsligo was served heir to his father.

The surrounding layout is unusually well preserved. The WALLED FORECOURT, 71 m. by 23.8 m., is entered on the W side through a tall round-headed archway which is both moulded and chamfered. The wall, 2 m. high, rises over this archway to support a triangular gablet. Inset into this gable is an inscription now much weathered but which is recorded as having read *Haec Corpus Sydera Mentem* ('the body here, the mind in the stars') with the date 1656. To the N of this is an extensive WALLED GARDEN. Despite their exposed location, the Pitsligo gardens remained among the best in Aberdeenshire long after the castle fell into dilapidation.

After generations of neglect the ruins of the tower were consolidated by *Douglas Forrest* for Malcolm Forbes *c.* 1990; on Forbes' death the Pitsligo Castle Trust took over, the consolidation of the courtyard buildings being undertaken in 2010 by *Nicholas Groves-Raines*. It is hoped that the garden can be returned to something approaching its former condition.

DOOCOT, Braco Park, 1.3 km. SW. Perhaps C18. Small and square, built in boulder rubble, with low pyramidal roof. Simple doorway with rat course above. Inside, most of the nesting boxes survive.

7030 ROTHIENORMAN

The former estate village of Rothie House (*see* below) which developed into a small town with an auction mart after a railway station opened here *c.* 1860; both the station and the mart are now closed.

ROTHIENORMAN CHURCH. Late Arts and Crafts by *George Bennett Mitchell*, 1935–6. Relatively low walls harled in white, their sense of mass exaggerated by bold battered buttresses which articulate the flanks into five bays beneath a slated jerkin-headed roof with end gablets, pronounced oversailing eaves and a small bellcote with pyramidal spirelet. Entrance porch with hipped roof projecting from first bay of S flank. Windows mullioned and transomed. Interior very simple; within such a confined space the close proximity of the massive segmentally arched roof trusses has a striking impact. Gothic PEWS in stained pine perhaps transferred from Millbrex (q.v.). The former MANSE is also *Mitchell*'s.

CLYDEBANK HOUSE, Forgue Road/Main Street. The former Clydesdale Bank by *R. G. Wilson*, *c.* 1903. Simple classical design, two storeys, five windows wide, the hipped roof kicked up into pedimental gables bearing tall stacks at each end. Pedimented central doorway with deep transom-light set into a lugged architrave.

KINBROON HOUSE. Demolished 1937. Its LODGE, early C19, survives on Forgue Road. Originally a single-storey square with Gothick door and windows openings distinguished by red sandstone dressings, and a piended, bellcast roof with oversailing eaves.

ROTHIE HOUSE, 1 km. ENE. A roofless Baronial house in perilous condition. By *James Matthews*, 1862–4, incorporating a plain classical house built for James Leslie in the later C18. The original house was three storeys and three bays in coursed dark rubble with cherry-cocking. Matthews built out the centre of its S entrance front with bipartite and tripartite openings, and substantially enlarged the house by grafting a second block of similar height against the rear; this is stepped out on the W (left) so as to form an angle in which he built a three-storey entrance tower, circular but corbelled to the square under a crowstepped attic caphouse, with a slim cylindrical turret rising higher still. The original house was given small bartizans, crowstepped gables and a blocky arcaded wall-head parapet which once had dormers. The coat of arms over the tower entrance and muzzled bear with motto *Spe Expecto* above its first-floor window identify the owners as the Forbes family.

ST COMBS 0060

A fishing village replanned after a severe cholera outbreak during the 1860s, with most of the single-storey houses in granite or whinstone rubble standing side-on to the road with their gables facing the sea. There is sufficient variety in their appearance, and so many byways running between them, as to give the village a very traditional organic character.

OLD CHURCHYARD, near the coast. This contains the remains of the medieval church, abandoned in 1608. Rectangular on plan, only a fragment of the W gable and a few courses of the N flank survive. Most monuments are C19 or earlier C20, a few of them finely carved.

ST FERGUS 0050

St Fergus came into being in 1616 when worship transferred from Inverugie (*see* below), the KIRKTOWN being a long straight street extending W from the parish church. Lord Pitfour who acquired the 9th Earl Marischal's St Fergus estates in 1764 attempted to set up a fishing village, but without success; either he or his son then established NEWTON, a planned settlement of three concentric U-plan streets cut into the sunny aspect of a hillock with a central axial street rising to its summit. This venture was apparently unsuccessful: the *New Statistical Account* (1834–5) refers to it as 'an acquisition which it would have been no disadvantage to the parish never to have possessed'. The village remained more or less undeveloped until the Gas Terminal (*see* below) was begun in the mid 1970s.

PARISH CHURCH. By *James Matthews*, 1868–9. Simple Gothic T-plan. Entrance W gable with a very broad tall porch and small clock dial, the bellcote reused from the previous church of 1644. Pointed doorways, long slim lancet windows, harled walls with ashlar dressings and margins. S transept with side porch in the angle, N transept with lean-to outshot. Bellcote has pedimental gablets triangular to E and W, semicircular to N and S. It is carved with inscriptions and initials D.R. J.R. for David and John Robertson, ministers 1599–1678. E gable with two datestones from the old church, V.L.K. 1616 (William

Lord Keith) and M.R.G. 1763; a third commemorates the construction of the new church for M.J.M., Minister James Mitchell. The interior has a W gallery supported on cast-iron columns (the hall was formed beneath in the 1990s) and a coved ceiling with gilt bosses. Above the pulpit a SCREEN, painted by *Miss Mitchell*, daughter of the minister, in the later C19: Agnus Dei and finely lettered scrolls with the Lord's Prayer and Psalm 24. – STAINED GLASS. Either side of the pulpit, by *Douglas Strachan*, probably *c.* 1898: Faith, Love and Hope (l.), and Justice, Humility and Mercy (r.).

Former MANSE. By *William Smith* (of *J. & W. Smith*), built 1860. A big simple two-storey three-bay house, central doorway in splayed ashlar surround with stepped hoodmould; harled walls, slim window margins; gabled roof with skewputts and end stacks. At the rear older manses of 1839, 1804 and possibly 1766 forming back wings in parallel.

SCHOOL, School Road. By *David Fraser*, 1872; extended 1897 and again by *J. M. Dickie* of Peterhead in 1933.

ST FERGUS CHURCHYARD, 2.5 km. SE at Scotstown Head, contains remains of Inverugie Church. MAIN GATEWAY with round-arched chamfered opening: its eroded inscription panel once recorded that it was built by public subscription in 1751. It was repaired when the churchyard was enlarged in 1833, the N extension also enclosed by rubble walls being formed in 1929. In the old walls, hooks for tying horses. INVERUGIE CHURCH belonged to Arbroath Abbey before the Reformation and was abandoned in 1616. Its N wall forms part of the boundary between the old churchyard and the C20 extension, with the S wall running parallel to it, both gables lost; a small semi-circular recess in the N wall. The walls incorporate a fine collection of well-preserved gravestones from the C17 onwards, with further lying slabs throughout the grounds.

KINLOCH FARMHOUSE, 1.5 km. S. Two-storey, *c.* 1820–40 with later additions including the upper portion of a conservatory from Pitfour House (demolished 1927), although the cast-iron waterleaf columns at the far ends may derive from elsewhere. Other Pitfour relics are preserved in the farmhouse itself, and also nearby at Ednie Farm.

ST FERGUS GAS TERMINAL, 2 km. N. Initially developed by Shell and British Gas in the early to mid 1970s, and much expanded since. Three receiving terminals for Total, Shell and ExxonMobil and a fourth distribution terminal for British Gas (later Transco) supplying the National Grid. The Total and British Gas terminals are by *Architects Design Group*, 1977.

The receiving terminals beach approximately 20 per cent of UK gas supplies from fields in British and Norwegian waters – Total through the Frigg transport system (UK pipeline commissioned 1977, Norwegian Vesterled 1978) and Miller system (commissioned 1992, ceased 2007); Shell and ExxonMobil through Flags (1982) and Fulmar (1986). Liquid by-products are sent to plants at Mossmoran, Fife, and Grangemouth, Stirlingshire.

SANDEND B

5060

A picturesque former fishing village focused around a small creek which contains the harbour in the NW corner of Sandend Bay. The village was first recorded in 1624 and reputedly bolstered by Highland immigrants after the C18 Clearances. The FISHER-COTTAGES, mostly of the early to mid C19, are laid out in traditional fashion as a series of short rows with only their end gables facing the sea, their long elevations facing in towards each other for mutual protection against the elements. Some have exposed rubble stonework, others are harled or rendered different colours, a few are whitewashed and lined out as ashlar. A feature of the village is the survival of several FISHING STORES – one or two of them perhaps former cottages – and FISH-SMOKING KILNS, the latter vertical structures in timber weatherboarding with tarred felt roofs. The HARBOUR itself, built 1883, comprises two piers enclosing the basin and a breakwater extending from an outcrop, all rubble-built refaced in concrete.

FINDLATER CASTLE, 1.8 km. WNW. Reputedly a stronghold since the late C13, Findlater Castle was built pursuant to a licence granted by King James II to Sir Walter Ogilvie of Auchleven in 1455, with additions later. Only fragments now survive on this naturally defensive site, a rocky steep-sided peninsula in the Moray Firth approached from the mainland cliffs by a narrow path of perilous descent. Abandoned by the mid C17 ('*deserta arx*' in 1662) when the Ogilvies moved to Cullen House (*see* Moray), it had been reduced to its present state by *c.* 1800. What remains is the substructure of the palace-block, consisting of two basement storeys built into the W side of the peninsula, constructed in the local clay slate masonry which is chocolate brown or dark blue in colour: shorn of all dressed work it now presents a most haggard appearance. Projecting from its W elevation is a small garderobe tower, its window openings indicating entresol floor-levels between those of the main block: these were reached by a newel stair immediately behind the tower, the remains of which still survive. In both basement floors all the rooms are vaulted: at the N end of the sub-basement is a prison with a pit; the upper basement contained, in the centre of its five apartments, a kitchen with its hearth still surviving. Examination by James Buie in the later C19 recorded that its principal floor consisted of three apartments in the traditional arrangement of hall, great chamber and inner chamber, the newel stair which opened into the garderobe tower projecting into the hall. Buie's drawings also show a secondary stair in the SE angle of the tower adjoining the main newel stair which provided access to the apartments in the upper part of the tower. The entrance to the court from the cliffs was by a narrow transe from which provisions could be raised from boats in Castle Haven; directly in front of the entrance to the hall at its S gable was a pit normally bridged over by a board which could be removed as a last line of defence.

In the NE corner of the peninsula foundations of a long slim building have been identified as the STABLES with their own stable court. Footings of a rectangular building on the SE side have been identified as a CHAPEL. The very limited space on the peninsula, and its restricted access, resulted in the walled FORECOURT being formed on the mainland, a substantial enclosure protected by a fosse and approached by a central causeway with gatehouses: the remains of this forecourt can still just be traced. – DOOCOT, 120 m. S, probably C16, restored by Banff & Buchan District Council in 1992. Circular 'beehive' type, three tapering stages in harled rubble with rat courses; square-headed doorway, square flight-holes in the top stage and oculus opening in the top; 700 nesting boxes.

GLASSAUGH WINDMILL, 0.8 km. SE. Mid-C18, perhaps 1761. A low broad circular base with four wide segment-headed doorways, supporting a tapered rubble tower, its sails lost. A striking form in the landscape, known locally as the 'Cup and Saucer'.

PROMONTORY ENCLOSURE, Crathie Point, 1.2 km. NW. This enclosure is defined by two earthen banks and ditches cutting off the headland. The site is likely to date to the Iron Age or early medieval period. (GN)

BIRKENBOG HOUSE. *See* p. 108.

9060

SANDHAVEN

A fishing village closely associated with Pittulie (q.v.) to the immediate W.

SANDHAVEN PARISH CHURCH, High Street. Built as a Free Mission church by *Mr McKay* of Fraserburgh, 1881. Simple N gable front with entrance tower and spirelet at one corner. The gable, buttressed to suggest a nave and aisles, is lit by stepped triple lights with a roundel above. Five-bay rubble flanks with small shouldered lights. Simple, dignified interior with original pews. The partitioning of the S bay to create a church hall *c.* 1950 has not harmed its character: the distinctive Greek doorway which opens into the hall from the W side of the chancel has obviously been reused. PULPIT also in this style.

Former CHURCH OF SCOTLAND MISSION CHURCH, St Magnus Road. By *Brebner & Jenkins* of Fraserburgh, 1882–3, subsequently church hall. W front with crowstepped gable and uncompleted angle tower, built in squared granite, its doors and lancet windows now blocked up.

DESCRIPTION. Sandhaven's development was tied to that of its HARBOUR, which was improved with the growth in the fishing industry: the small W basin was formed *c.* 1840 and the much larger E basin seemingly by *John Willet c.* 1875 at the height of the Herring Boom.* Just inland, two former BOATSHEDS erected for Forbes' Boatyard, which opened here *c.* 1902, and closed ninety years later. In marked contrast to the earlier fisher-cottages of neighbouring Pitullie the single-storey houses are arranged in terraces facing the street. Feuing plans prepared by *James Beattie & Son* in 1873 indicate an intention that Sandhaven should develop considerably on its landward side, but given its proximity to Fraserburgh and Rosehearty (qq.v.) that may always have been impractical, certainly so after the collapse of the Herring Boom in 1884. From the end of the Second World War until the mid 1970s Sandhaven developed as a dormitory for Fraserburgh.

MEAL MILL, Stuart Street. Early C19, a conventional L-plan with two storeys and basement, built in pinned rubble; at its roof ridge the kiln ventilator has an attractive pig wind-vane. Overshot water wheel, 3 m. diameter, with cast-iron frame. Very completely preserved and restored as a working museum.

MAINS OF PITTENDRUM, 0.3 km. S. Small house in the vernacular classical style, built by the Cumines in 1734. Main block of very tall upright proportions, three storeys and three bays broad, with a lugged and moulded door architrave and segmental pediment containing the Cumine coat-of-arms, thistle, rose and date. Rubble construction, harl-pointed. Tall first-floor windows to express the principal apartments, second-floor windows break up into swept dormers within the steeply pitched roof, which has shaped skewputts and coped chimneystacks at its gables; these gables are now blind, with blocked window openings. Wings harled with ground and attic floor windows, and gable stacks above, their roofs returning into the main block. The rear elevation is similar in appearance to the front, but its entrance has been blocked; the wings are set back on this side, their steep roofs piended at the angles. Interior remodelled later C19.

SCHIVAS *see* HOUSE OF SCHIVAS

SHIELS *see* BELHELVIE

SKELMUIR HOUSE *see* CLOLA

*The claim made elsewhere that J.F. Beattie was responsible for the improvements of that time would appear to be in error as Willet's plans of 1872 survive.

6050 STRATHORD

A church built for those inconveniently placed for Alvah, Banff, Marnoch or Ordiquhill parish churches (qq.v.), with an associated manse.

Former ORD CHURCH OF SCOTLAND. Built 1835–6, but still in the style of *c.* 1780–1800. A simple rectangular preaching-box lit by four tall round-arched and key-blocked windows in its S flank and small square windows at gallery level in the end gables; it is harled with slim ashlar dressings and margins. The ball-finialled birdcage bellcote is set over the E gable, probably transferred from the W gable when a vestry porch was added to that end during the internal reordering by *James Duncan & Son* in 1899. Matching E porch added during conversion to domestic use *c.* 1975. WAR MEMORIAL *c.* 1920, a small tapering square shaft with Maltese cross in polished grey granite rising from a plinth and pedestal.

Former MANSE OF ORD, 160 m. NNW. Originally a simple two-storey three-bay house with a broad shallow rear wing, built 1835–6, but substantially enlarged by a much longer wing built out from the front elevation in the later C19 to create the present cruciform plan. Cream harl with slim ashlar dressings, with margins for the older house.

9050 STRICHEN

Strichen village (originally known as Mormond) was laid out in 1764 by Alexander Fraser, a judge of the Court of Session, as a planned settlement on the junction of two important roads linking Aberdeen to Fraserburgh and Peterhead to Banff (qq.v.), close to the Ugie Water and sheltered in the lee of Mormond Hill. It was intended to promote 'the Arts and Manufactures of this country, and for the accommodation of Tradesmen of all denominations, Manufacturers, and other industrious people'.

CHURCHES

ALL SAINTS (Episcopal), West Street. By *William Ramage*, 1861, substantially altered and extended by *Arthur Clyne* in 1891. W gable front in snecked squared granite, with belfry over the apex; the Early Geometric two-light window and the liturgical S aisle with splayed doorway both date from Clyne's remodelling. Chancel with stepped triple lancets also by Clyne, N flank lit by alternating paired and single lancets, the aisle by small pointed lights. Three-bay nave arcade, circular piers with moulded capitals. Wagon ceiling with moulded ribs. Chancel with polygonal compartmented ceiling with IHS monogram, Lamb of God, pelican and phoenix. Encaustic tiles. Furnishings mostly simple but the boldly detailed wooden LECTERN is probably by *Clyne*. – ORGAN by *Wadsworth & Brother*, 1893.

PARISH CHURCH. Built as the Free Church by *Duncan McMillan* (of *D. & J.R. McMillan*), 1893–4. A dramatic conclusion to this end of the High Street. Victorian Gothic – tall nave gable with corner tower and spire, built in grey granite ashlar with extensive use of brown stone for dressings and margins. The gable window is geometric, four lights with quatrefoil and sexfoil roundels; above, a trefoil and a finial at the apex. Tower of three stages: rock-faced battered base with splayed pointed doorway; shaft slightly intaken at second stage with lancet windows; then the tall belfry with narrow louvred openings, and gablets and engaged corner-shafts breaking into pinnacles which clasp the octagonal stone spire. Five-bay flanks lit by lancets with sexfoils above, stepped up at the chancel where two-light windows rise into gables. Simple rose window in rear gable, session house behind. Interior with gallery at S end; the focus is the large platform PULPIT at the centre of the N gable, half-octagonal and panel-fronted with steps on each side, and a panelled back rising into a finialled gablet. – ORGAN *c.* 1898.

Former R.C. CHURCH (now The Cloisters), Brewery Road, 1854. Very small chapel with curvilinear gable front lit by stepped triple lights, round-headed with decorative coloured glass. Two-storey bay-windowed presbytery attached to one flank.

Former ST ANDREW, 0.5 km. S. Closed, gutted and shuttered up. A very big four-bay preaching-box, by *John Adamson Jun.*, 1798–9. Gables with round-headed doorways and Serlian gallery windows; their square-cut skewputts must date from the 1890 remodelling by *Alexander Ellis* of *Ellis & Wilson*. S flank with four tall round-arched windows; N flank with smaller square-headed windows at ground and gallery level. Birdcage bellcote (dated) at W end. Vestry at SE corner by *George Bennett Mitchell*, 1919. Nearby, the LAIRD'S AISLE of the old church, built for Thomas Fraser of Strichen *c.* 1620. A square building in pinned rubble, two storeys with ground-floor burial vault and upper-floor laird's aisle approached by curved stone forestair on the W side, its doorway breaking up into the gabled roof; two windows at loft level in the S gable, moulded skewputts and coped stack, evidence of a nave opening on the N side. Field-panel probably once for a coat of arms. Restored by Banff & Buchan District Council, 1988.

PUBLIC BUILDINGS

TOWN HALL, on the junction of High Street and Bridge Street. 109
Probably built by *John Smith I* for Mrs Fraser of Strichen in 1816; in its modesty of scale and quality of detail it possesses a touching gentility which seems somehow appropriate to the village as a whole. Part Scots tolbooth, part Tudor, part classical, with a square tower on the corner which has a

battlemented parapet with corbels and bartizans, and an octagonal lantern stage bearing the elegant stone spire. Main block to Bridge Street has four-bay round-arched arcade on ground floor, now lit by astragalled sash-and-case windows but originally open for market stalls; first-floor council chamber with three square-headed windows, again sash-and-case with Tudor hoodmoulds, battlemented parapet, and crowstepped rear gable expressing a shallow-pitched roof.

SCHOOL, North Street. By *Edwin Williamson*, 1936. Stripped classicism. Two-storey main block in polished grey granite with piended roof, broad five-bay centrepiece slightly stepped forward with plain giant pilasters rising into vestigial entablature and pediment. Entrances in short single-storey wings with canted angles.

Former GOOD TEMPLARS' HALL, off High Street between Police Lane and White Ship Court. Built by *W.A. McRobbie*, 1909.

DESCRIPTION

Strichen has three long streets extending NW to SE: High Street, on the road between Peterhead and Banff (qq.v.), running broad and straight for over 50 m., with North Street in parallel, and Water Street which, starting at High Street's W end, angles S to follow the bank of the Ugie. Towards the E, Bridge Street crosses all three at right-angles, and Market Terrace runs parallel to it, looking out across open ground where fairs were once held.

To encourage development, Alexander Fraser charged only a nominal feu duty for the first nineteen years. The feus were a generous 45 feet (13.7 m.) broad to accommodate weavers' cottages, long low single-storey houses generally with four small windows and a doorway off-centre, marking the division between the living room and a room for the loom. The shell of such a house, walls and thatched roof, with an earthen floor, cost about £30. Nearly all the cottages have survived in WATER STREET to give a sense of Strichen's early character, even if they have been altered in their details. The best preserved is No. 18. Nos. 24–26 constitute an example of two houses built on a single feu, one longer than the other, with the short house, a door and a window, often occupied by a widow or spinster who scraped a living selling modest wares. At Water Street's N end are two MILLS. The ANDERSON & WOODMAN INSTITUTE was built as a thread mill in the late C18, a long three-storey six-bay block in squared granite rubble, its low top floor with oblong windows just beneath the eaves. It was powered by a rope drive connected to a water wheel in the River Ugie on the far side of the road. It closed in 1815 and was converted to a house – the glazing is late C19 – then became the Institute in 1923, its first and second floors combined as a single tall space. Next to the mill, the former MANAGER'S HOUSE is one of the most distinguished in the village, two storeys and three bays with granite ashlar frontage, moulded skewputts and coped chimneystacks. On the opposite bank of the Ugie, the MILL OF STRICHEN was built in 1791 to grind corn for tenant farmers but was subsequently reconstructed, a robust L-plan building in squared granite rubble, piend-roofed at one end and gabled at the other, with a smaller and lower block in the angle. It gains much from its group value with two smaller buildings, and, in particular, from its situation adjacent to a twin-arched bridge which is seemingly contemporary.

At Water Street's S end, on its junction with Bridge Street, the MORMOND INN was established in the early C19 to catch traffic passing between Aberdeen and Fraserburgh – vernacular, two storeys with a gabled roof, but with the doorway off-centre and the windows unevenly spaced, harled with granite margins now painted black against the white harl; eaves course, square-cut skewputts and moulded chimneystacks, its sash-and-case windows are modern replacements.

The BRIDGE itself is early C19, a broad segmental span over the North Ugie Water, with small flood arches each side: the arch-rings are dressed masonry although the construction is largely in rubble. It has been widened twice – once in masonry during the later C19, then more recently by jettying out its parapets.

Opposite the Mormond Inn, on BRIDGE STREET's E side, Nos. 1–3 look very early and are the only example of two-storey houses built two-to-a-feu, their modest doorways without thresholds; No 5, slightly later, is more typical of the two-storey houses built by wealthier feaurs in Bridge Street and High Street, its first-floor windows with long-and-short quoins beneath an eaves course.

In MARKET TERRACE, at its S end, the late C18 MART HOUSE has a two-storey four-bay frontage, ashlar granite cherry-cocked with moulded skewputts and coped gable end stacks, set back in its garden with dwarf walls and railings; its roof dormers and rear wing are later. The rest of the street is Victorian. HIGH STREET was largely rebuilt between the mid C19 and the early C20, no doubt as the original leases fell in. Beyond the parish church, HOLMWOOD built for Dr Alexander Gavin *c.* 1800 is one of Strichen's most sophisticated houses, a two-storey three-bay ashlar frontage with single-storey side wings, its virtues partly concealed by a modern porch and conservatory. Within High Street proper, Nos. 62 and 75 represent the original single-storey weavers' cottages with the latter particularly true to type as its roof has been kept clear of dormers and skylights. Nearby Nos. 52–54, also single-storey, have been badly cut about but are notable because they are early, dated 1765 with initials A.A. I.S. of their builders, Alexander Anderson and Janet Shearer.

Much of the most ambitious rebuilding naturally focused on High Street's crossroads with Bridge Street. Facing each other on the E side, a pair of two-storey blocks with bowed corners, ashlar-built with elegant roofs: that on the r. is dated 1877 but its character is generally Late Georgian vernacular. Then on the W side, another two-storey block with bowed corner corbelled to the square, and gables with scrolls, the High Street gable rising to ball finials and pediment; T-pattern glazing, with details suggestive of *Pirie & Clyne*, dated 1886. The WHITE HORSE HOTEL was built about the same period on the site of an earlier hostelry, with a distinctive two-storey three-bay front in grey squared granite and darker pinnings. It has a canted angle on its junction with the side lane, and in an arched and pedimented panel above its first-floor window are compasses, perhaps suggesting that it was used for Masonic meetings.

Towards the High Street's S end, the former NORTH OF SCOTLAND BANK, on the Market Terrace junction, is simple Italianate in the style of *James Matthews*, *c.* 1860 – two-storey, three bays on each side, with a quadrant bow at the angle – the bank itself entered from High Street, and the bank agent's house through the flank. Then at the far end, the former ABERDEEN TOWN & COUNTY BANK by *Pirie & Clyne* *c.* 1892, surprisingly restrained and classical for that practice. A two-storey five-bay ashlar front with a hipped roof, its doorway is sheltered under a console-cornice. The ground- and first-floor windows in simple architraves rest on band courses, and oversailing eaves rise into gablets beneath the tall chimneystacks at the ends.

NORTH STREET was reconstructed later than High Street, with COUNCIL HOUSING of the mid 1930s for much of its length. Although the flats conform to standard patterns, their two-storey height, granite construction and simple detailing allow them to fit in comfortably with the village's traditional character, only the occasional red-tile roofs being alien. At the S end, NORTHCOTE *c.* 1800 is as sophisticated as Holmwood albeit without a front garden, but is much better presented, a two-storey three-bay ashlar frontage, central doorway with pretty arcaded transom-light sheltered by a consoled and pedimented canopy.

BURNSHANGIE FARMHOUSE, 0.7 km. ENE. Built *c.* 1800 by Alexander Anderson and Janet Shearer who had been among the first feuars in High Street thirty-five years earlier. They had evidently prospered for the seat of their later years was a pretty rustic villa in an attractive walled garden. Single-storey, three bays in granite ashlar, originally with a Doric timber portico framing a tripartite doorpiece.

STRICHEN HOUSE, 1.5 km. SW, replacing the C17 Palace of Strichen. A very large classical mansion by *John Smith I*, built for Thomas Fraser 1818–21, derelict by 1949 but still retaining landscape value. Two-storey entrance front, nine bays broad, built in local granite ashlar. Pedimented centre slightly projecting once with a tetrastyle Doric portico, end bays with windows in recessed arch surrounds, a bow on the NW flank now demolished.

In the farmyard (250 m. SE), the remains of *Smith*'s once-impressive STABLE BLOCK, of which only the pedimented centrepiece and stump of one arcaded wing have survived. KENNEL-MASTER'S HOUSE (400 m. W) also by *Smith*, *c.* 1821, very similar to that at Pitfour (q.v.) with pedimented Doric portico distyle-*in-antis*; likewise *Smith*'s KENNELS, although small in scale, have a simple monumental character. Courtyard plan, central squat two-storey tower with low oversailing pyramid roof, flanked by single-storey wings, now partly lived in, partly a shell. – DOOCOT, 250 m. NE. Early C19, a low drum in pinned rubble, with square-headed doorway, belt courses and a triangular opening for the 'doos', its lead dome removed. – 'HERMITAGE', 150 m. NW, a small circular ruin of C19 date. – R.C. CHAPEL. Mid-C19. Simple Gothic, with pointed doorway, a roofless ruin: seemingly never completed.

Former PARISH MANSE, 1 km. S. An elegant Italianate villa by *Thomas Mackenzie* (of *Matthews & Mackenzie*), 1853. Two-storey three-bay frontage with boldly projecting gabled bay on the r. and porch in the angle. Harled, with dressings and margins. Gabled bay has triple lights with lying-pane glazing at ground floor, triple arcaded lights at first; porch framed by antae and crowned by ball finials, low-pitched roofs with pronounced overhanging eaves.* Simple but attractive interior. OUTBUILDINGS to rear are older, perhaps mid-C18.

ADZIEL HOUSE, 1.6 km. SSE. *c.* 1800. Two-storey three-bay frontage in granite ashlar, neatly proportioned under a tall gabled roof, coped chimneystacks. Nine-panelled door and astragalled sash-and-case windows. Single-storey L-plan wing built into falling ground at the rear.

HOWFORD FARMHOUSE, 0.8 km. ESE. Presently derelict but very unusual of its kind, like a picturesque *cottage orné*. Early C19, built for Louis Savan, a French émigré. Single-storey, three symmetrical bays: central entrance (originally tripartite) framed by small Gothic lights, with flanking bows. Two small wings to the rear, again with Gothic lights, and internally some good surviving woodwork. Close by, the 'ROMAN BRIDGE' over the North Ugie Water, dated 1777, restored *c.* 1995. A single segmental arch, rubble-built, with dressed masonry base courses and voussoirs. Broader approach ramps splayed into the arch.

TECHMUIRY FARMHOUSE, 5 km. NNE. Described as 'new' by the *Caledonian Mercury* in 1744. Two-storey, originally seven windows wide, harled with crowstepped gables. Mid-C19 porch with Gothic window; now with canted bays at each end, added during the late C19. Over one of the ground-floor windows, the triangular date-panel of an earlier house built 1600, with Latin inscription. Lunette stone with initials M.F. in rear elevation; the NE skewputt has a grotesque face now eroded of its features. Lower rear wing, one window framed

*Plans show that part of an earlier house was incorporated at the back, and that a kitchen wing which Mackenzie built against the r. gable has been demolished.

by baluster-type pilasters. Modern door and windows. Separate two-storey STEADING, probably also 1744, still with bothy at ground floor and external stair to first-floor loft.

ROB GIBB'S LODGE, on the summit of Mormond Hill, 1779. 'In this Hunter's Lodge Rob GIBB commands MDCCLXXIX'. Reputedly built by Capt. Alexander Fraser of the King's Dragoon Guards, the son of Lord Strichen. Two storeys, two bays, rubble-built, now ruinous, the entrance front with chamfered doorway and square windows checked for shutters; the ground-floor fireplace was large enough to roast a deer, the upper floor provided accommodation for a gamekeeper.*

WHITE HORSE on the slope of Mormond Hill overlooking the village. Formed in quartz stones, thought to be the memorial of Capt. Fraser to Sergeant John Hutcheon, who in giving up his own horse during the Battle of Gilze (1794) saved his captain's life but lost his own. It measures 49 m. nose-to-tail, and is 38 m. high.

RECUMBENT STONE CIRCLE, 1.25 km. SW. On a prominent rise, this stone circle gives fine views to the S. The circle was reconstructed in the 1980s after stones were removed in the C19 and C20. Quartz, flints and sherds of prehistoric pottery and a cremation deposit were found during the excavation of the original site. (GN)

9040

STUARTFIELD

Stuartfield was laid out by John Burnett-Stuart of Dens and Crichie *c.* 1772. It is centred on The Square, with Burnett Street extending N and Mill Street to the S together forming the High Street, while Windhill Street leads W and Knock Street E. THE SQUARE itself is a large pleasant rectangle surrounded on each side by modest one- or two-storey houses, all of different dates and styles. On the W, the CRICHIE MART, perhaps built as an inn, looks much the oldest, a long two-storey rubble block with simple chimneys. Most other houses are mid or late C19: the single-storey cottages were often occupied by weavers and thus asymmetrical, the windows and doors expressing a division between living quarters and a room for the loom. A two-storey house on the E side is distinguished by gableted dormers, while on the N the houses are single-storey with attic oriels. The houses in the side-streets are mostly similar in character.

PUBLIC HALL, Burnett Street. Built 1900 by *George Scott* of Dyce. Gable-fronted in squared granite masonry with darker

*Gibb himself was a court jester whose renowned loyalty to the House of Stuart made his name a byword for true friendship and, it is thought, Jacobite sympathies for many years afterwards.

pinnings, doorway with console-cornice and round-headed lights, clock dial beneath a bellcote at the gable's apex.

Former FREE CHURCH MANSE, Quartalehouse. By *James Henderson*, *c.* 1845. Mildly Jacobean.

Former EPISCOPAL RECTORY, 1.2 km. NNE. Built 1799 for the Scottish Episcopal church. Two-storey three-bay block, rubble-built with gabled roof and end stacks; the original entrance was a gabled porch.

The most remarkable buildings in Stuartfield are its mills. The former FLAX MILL (now The Dyesters) at Quartalehouse was established by John Burnett-Stuart in 1783, and converted to a woollen mill in the mid C19. It was closed in the 1970s and restored in 1980–1 – a single-storey and attic L-plan, rubble-built, with its short arm extended later. Its machinery, wheel and mill pond are fully operational. At the other end of the village, CRICHIE MILL was established in the early to mid C19 and closed in 1969. A meal mill, three storeys and attic in squared rubble, with segmental arch at ground level, and relatively small windows on each floor, the stump of a kiln ventilator remains on its roof. Next to it is the smaller gable-fronted thrashing mill, with a large iron wheel powering them both. The machinery in the meal mill remains, although not presently working.

CRICHIE HOUSE, 0.8 km. SE. Probably by *James Laing* of Old Deer, built 1875. Square plan, tripartite W doorway, canted bays on the S front.

MILLADEN (J. C. Rennie & Co.), 1.5 km. NE. Begun as a flax mill in 1789, converted to wool-carding 1798, and still in use today. The original mill is a single range built out from a sharply sloping hillside – nine bays long, progressively increasing to three storeys and double attic with the fall in the ground, the wheel-pit and lade at the bottom. Extended into an L-plan in the mid C19, with further alterations since. The wheel of 1868 (altered in 1912) is *in situ* but not presently working. The larger of the two associated houses is by *Arthur Clyne*, *c.* 1901.

CEMETERY, 0.5 km. N. Laid out by *James Beattie & Son* in 1872, with (dated) sexton's house. – WAR MEMORIAL. A Celtic cross in pale granite, its tapering shaft with strapwork rising from rock-faced steps and a double plinth.

TARVES 8030

PARISH CHURCH, Kirk Brae. Handsome four-bay preaching-box built in 1798 by *William Littlejohn*, wright in Old Aberdeen, and *James Walker*, mason in Denend; it replaced a cruciform medieval predecessor which had stood here since the C14 or earlier. W gable with finialled birdcage bellcote and principal S flank in golden brown ashlar granite with cherry-cocking, N flank and E gable in coursed rubble. Originally each gable had a round-arched central doorway, gallery window with diamond-pane basket tracery, and old-fashioned skewputts. The S flank windows are also round-arched but at the second bay from E an organ chamber was added by *James Cobban* in 1892; later in 1905 he added the crowstepped porch and vestry annexe at the W gable. A stone initialled M.R. 1613 is incorporated in the S flank towards the E end.

In 1825 the very wide roof pushed out the walls, which were fastened back with tie-rods. Internally, the ceiling has been altered, possibly about this time. The gallery supported on cast-iron columns extends round three sides, facing the PULPIT centred in the S wall, with the organ next to it. The pulpit has been modernized but its back is mid to late C18 with an arched and fielded panel between fluted pilasters, perhaps reused from the earlier church; the hexagonal ogee sounding-board is probably of 1825, discreetly suspended from the roof by an iron rod. Flanking the pulpit, two illuminated texts in gold on azure with mid-C19 Gothic lettering. ORGAN in oak with simple Gothic detailing. – COMMUNION TABLE with Lorimerian carving at its cornice. – Eagle LECTERN. – FONT with panels depicting a shepherd with a lamb, a dove and a burning bush, all earlier C20. – STAINED GLASS. Two excellent windows by *Marjorie Kemp*: S wall, r. of the pulpit, 'Behold I Am Alive for Evermore', the Risen Christ with (beneath) the Last Supper and (above) the Kingdom of Heaven with angels, erected 1954; in the N window, King David with his Harp and Sheep, 1965.

The only survival of the predecessor church is the
25 TOLQUHON AISLE commemorating William Forbes and Elizabeth Gordon and erected in 1589. Dr Douglas Simpson attributed it to *Thomas Leiper*, who was completing Tolquhon Castle (q.v.) at that time. Inspired by the Dunbar Tomb at St Machar's Cathedral, the monument is 2.3 m. high by 2.7 m. broad, under a later pediment probably of 1798. A segmentally arched recess, moulded and inset with roses, rests on a blind seven-bay dwarf arcade with baluster columns, and is framed by balusters which support a mutuled cornice. Within the recess, facing each other at opposite ends, statuettes of the laird and his lady, and springing from their heads pendant-cusped tracery. In the spandrels above the arch, on the laird's side, his initials and arms quartered with those of Preston (*see* Tolquhon Castle), a helmet, and motto *Salus per Christum*; on the lady's, her initials, arms impaled with his, a plumed hat and ancestry 'Dochter to Lesmor'. The complex balusters also incorporate their respective emblems, his a muzzled bear and hers a boar. Running round the outer edge of the arch, on his side a hound chasing a fox with a goose in its mouth, on her side a hound chasing a hare, and over the centre unicorns flanking a crown to signify Forbes's status as a tenant-in-chief.

Just outside the churchyard, the WAR MEMORIAL, a Celtic cross of 1920.

Former PARISH MANSE, Manse Brae. By *J. & W. Smith* 1847. Plain Tudor in coursed squared granite, their Aberdeenshire version of an English parsonage. Two storeys and three bays, with the l. bay stepped forward under a gable, and lozenge-plan stacks over the ends. Porch projecting from the re-entrant angle in grey granite ashlar has an arched doorway and chamfered angles. Original timber mullioned-and-transomed windows: those at first floor have dormerhead gablets with escutcheon panels. The former offices were converted into the CHURCH HALL in 1957.

DESCRIPTION. The centre of the village is THE SQUARE – actually a long rectangle – lined on each side by simple buildings designed by the *Haddo Estate Office*. They are mostly low single-storey and attic blocks in granite rubble, but with enough variety to maintain interest. The most important buildings are, on the S side, the two-storey ABERDEEN ARMS HOTEL of *c.* 1810–20, Duthie & Co.'s GENERAL STORE of *c.* 1880 to the W, and the former BOYS' SCHOOL (now TARVES HERITAGE CENTRE) on the N side, endowed by the 4th Earl of Aberdeen in 1837. Its master's house is single-storey and attic with a central porch and gablet dormer, the chimneys tall and diagonally shafted; the classrooms to the E were extended in 1881. Nearby, a curiosity – a bright red PETROL PUMP manufactured by *Theo & Co.* of Liverpool *c.* 1930. Capable of supplying six different brands without any cross-contamination, this is the basic model, with fuel once drawn up by a hand-operated crank. On the Square's E side, all the houses are single-storey and continue in delightful fashion down the fall of KIRK BRAE. In MANSE BRAE, at the W end, HOSPITAL HOUSE, built as the GIRLS' SCHOOL by *William Clarke* *c.* 1875, the twin of that at Methlick (q.v.); a bronze memorial plaque to Mary Jane Greenhalgh, village nurse 1883–90, by *Henry Bain-Smith* is set in one gable. Immediately to the S, THE COTTAGE, actually a large villa of *c.* 1900 with idiosyncratic timber and half-timber details and a veranda, was built for the Duthie Webster family who owned the famous Collynie shorthorn herd.

In DUTHIE ROAD, which extends W from The Square, the first building of note is the broad gable front of the MELVIN HALL (1875), named after George Melvin, M.A., a long-serving Tarves dominie who left funds for 'some public purpose'. It has a pointed-arch doorway between segment-headed windows and a sexfoil wheel window above. Flanking it, with stylized crowstep gables, the Library Room (l.) of 1892 gifted by Andrew Carnegie and the Queen's Room (r.) of 1897. Opposite the Hall, the former ABERDEEN TOWN & COUNTY BANK (now a house), a tall plain two-storey asymmetric villa in ashlar granite by *William Clarke*, 1881. Then the PUBLIC SCHOOL, built by *James Cobban* 1911 in New Pitsligo granite, a triple-gable frontage, tall single-storey with its central bay slightly set back, and a broad welcoming round-arched entrance, its radial transom-light filled with coloured glass.

BARTHOL CHAPEL CHURCH, 5.8 km. NW. By *William Smith* (of *J. & W. Smith*), 1875, replacing an earlier church which is now a house. It was built in memory of George Hamilton-Gordon, 6th Earl of Aberdeen, who went to sea under the assumed name of George Osborne but was washed overboard and drowned in 1870, hence the quotation from Psalm 93 in the red granite tympanum over the doorway: 'The Lord on High is Mightier than the Noise of Many Waters, Yea than the Mighty Waves of the Sea.' First Pointed, a simple rectangular plan, built in pinned squared granite with ashlar dressings and margins. W gable front with stepped triple lancets beneath a steeply pitched roof; a slim square towerlet on the N culminating in a spirelet belfry, and on the S a porch. Unbuttressed six-bay flanks, with vestry and session house outshot on the N. Rear gable with mincer-plate wheel window, and quatrefoil above. Inside, a polygonal wagon ceiling with chevron-pattern boarding, its ribs carried on corbels. – ORGAN. Small Gothic case, perhaps introduced in 1889. Most of the original PEWS remain in place, although the PULPIT which was formerly raised against the rear gable has been brought down to chancel floor-level. STAINED GLASS. Chancel S. Late Gothic style, 'I am the Good Shepherd', in memory of the Rev. William Wilson M.A. (†1906), who was schoolmaster at Barthol Chapel for fifty-one years. By *Atkinson Brothers* of Newcastle. – WAR MEMORIAL. By *J.A. Ogg Allan*, 1919.

CRAIGDAM, 2.1 km. WSW. A village originally focused on its United Presbyterian church (1805–6; dem. *c.* 1958), manse and school house. The Antiburgher congregation established in 1752 was for a long time the only one of its kind between the Dee and the Spey. CHURCH HALL by *James Cobban*, 1914 with Romanesque doorpiece. The MANSE was built in 1872 and the SCHOOL HOUSE evidently by the same architect, since it is closely similar in design and detailing.

SHETHIN FARMHOUSE, 2.3 km. NE. Built by the Haddo Estate *c.* 1830–40 for William Hay, a noted shorthorn breeder. He was reputedly the first to send cattle from Aberdeenshire to Smithfield by sea. Two-storey three-bay and basement, pinned rubble masonry with single-storey wings slightly set back. A railed stair leads to the door in a timber pilastered surround with astragalled transom-light sheltered beneath a console-cornice; wings also with consoled doorways, that on the r. a screen-wall only.

The contemporary STEADING, despite its corrugated iron roof, is still a magnificent example of its kind. A long low quadrangle, its symmetrical front has a tall central pend arch flanked on either side by lower segmental cartshed arches, and loft openings under the eaves. Shethin had an early fixed steam mill in the 1830s.

PROP OF YTHSIE, 1.5 km. E. Colloquial name for a slim square tower which stands like a gigantic chessman over a crazed chequerboard of fields. It was built in 1861–2 in memory of the 4th Earl of Aberdeen, Prime Minister 1852–5, perhaps to designs of his son and namesake *George Hamilton-Gordon*, the

5th Earl. £500 was subscribed by tenants of the Haddo Estate whose fortunes had been transformed by the improvements the earl had conceived. Constructed in rough-faced granite, with silver ashlar dressings and quoins; base steeply battered, a simple, almost sepulchral entrance with a heavy iron door, and above the lintel a dedication panel. Within the tower shaft, a spiral stair, ninety-three steps rising round a central brick newel, dimly lit by slit-windows. At the top, corbels support a parapet, with a single crenel on each face now guarded by railings.

NORTH YTHSIE FARMHOUSE, 0.8 km. S of the tower. T-plan, single-storey, early C19, framed by short wings with roundel windows added in 1957. At the back the ground falls away to reveal a basement, which links by a timber bay window to the original late C18 farmhouse, rubble-built with ashlar chimneystacks.

SOUTH YTHSIE FARMHOUSE nearby was built or remodelled *c.* 1810, although the heavily weathered skewputt of the l. gable seems incised with one half of a date '17'. The wings are mid-C18 in darker masonry with very tall hipped roofs and appear to survive from a previous house.

TOLQUHON CASTLE. *See* p. 398.

TILLERY HOUSE 9020

5 km. SE of Udny Green

Classical country house for John Chambers, a retired American planter, built 1788; remodelled in the Greek Revival style with a new service wing by *Archibald Simpson c.* 1826 for Mr Hunter. Gutted by fire in 1939, the main block is a shell, but the service wing remains occupied. Entrance front of main block facing W, two storeys, three windows wide, with ground floor much taller than first, built of pinned squared masonry formerly harled with raised parapet over the central bay; the tetrastyle Doric pedimented portico is Simpson's work. S flank has a central bow; internally hazardous, remains of an oval staircase. – STABLES AND COACHHOUSE, single-storey and attic on a courtyard plan, with separate doocot, the byre and sawmill with generating house, all now with tiled roofs. Subterranean ICE HOUSE, domical vault inside.

TILLYCORTHIE CASTLE 9020

4 km. SE of Udny Green

By *John Cameron*, 1911–12, for James Rollo Duncan, a Bolivian tin magnate. A mischievous mix of styles and disproportionate historical details. Described at the time as 'a Spanish villa', but more obviously a deeply idiosyncratic castle in reinforced Hennebique concrete (contractor *James Scott & Co.* of Aberdeen), lime-harled with exposed dressings. At first glance a rectangular courtyard, it is actually a U-plan with the SW entrance front just a playful wafer-thin screen for the Winter Garden which doubles as a great hall and entrance forecourt: its dimensions – and hence those of the house as a whole – were determined by the turning circle of James Duncan's Rolls Royce. The entrance front is five bays, symmetrical, its central Tudor tower connected by glazed colonnades with outsize crenellation to Franco-Scottish wings at either end. The tower itself is of three stages, with a triple light for its stair beneath a dated hoodmould, and a first-floor oriel beneath a corbelled, crenellated parapet; the flanking bays have Doric columns supporting the first-floor 'windows' with open air behind and the end bays have projected fronts, crowstepped gables, tourelles and bartizans.

The interiors were once richly varied, often panelled or decorated with murals and friezes. The drawing room was in the Neo-Adam style; there were chimneypieces by *George Bennett Mitchell* in the dining, smoking and billiard rooms, brought from Dunecht House (S) in 1912. All the contracts for the original fitting-out were overseen by *Vitali Behar* of the *Oriental Furnishing Co.*, Glasgow. In the centre of the WINTER GARDEN, its steel girders once draped with flowering creepers and its walls with virginia and Russian vine, there was a magnificent granite fountain brought from Aberdeen's New Market (dem.). Tillycorthie was restored in the early C21 after a long period of neglect followed by division into three separate residences.

Next to an artificial lake, a two-storey sparkling white haçienda, formerly the POWER HOUSE AND WORKSHOP with a rooftop ice rink, now a separate residence; its 7.3 m. diameter water wheel has gone, but its brick chimneystack survives nearby. Coachhouse, stables and lodge houses are all relatively conventional.

TILLYMAUD *see* LONGHAVEN HOUSE, p. 147

8020

TOLQUHON CASTLE

2.5 km. SSE of Tarves

63 A courtyard castle built by *Thomas Leiper* for William Forbes in 1584–9, with alterations of 1600, but incorporating an earlier tower house built either by Sir Henry Preston *c.* 1400 or more probably by his son-in-law Sir John Forbes *c.* 1420. Preston's Tower is shattered but the fabric of the courtyard, although

roofless, survives relatively entire: not so much a defensive structure as a small private palace, it still evokes Scottish courtly life in late Renaissance times.

PRESTON'S TOWER stands at the NE corner of the courtyard, its craggy ruins forming the l. element of Leiper's N entrance range. It was a simple rectangle on plan, four storeys high; orientated N–S, and thus presenting only its gable elevation on the entrance front, it is 13.5 m. deep by 9 m. broad. Its walls built in pinned boulder rubble with dressed quoins and window surrounds are massively thick – 3 m. – and the windows themselves are small. The entrance was on the S flank, giving access both to the vaulted ground-floor cellar and to an intramural stair leading directly up to the great hall on the first floor, where the jambs of a fireplace and remains of a flue can be seen in the N wall together with an aumbry in the NE corner. Evidence survives of a turnpike stair in the largely fallen W wall, but the main access to the upper floors appears to have been by another intramural stair, probably in the collapsed SW angle. The parapet has gone but the corbelling of the circular bartizan at the NW angle has survived, its details late C15 or C16.

The ENTRANCE RANGE or FOREWORK is a balanced if not symmetrical composition, a miniaturized version of that at Boyne (q.v.). At its centre is the gateway, its relatively modest roll-moulded and round-headed arch with two heraldic panels superimposed above. It is flanked by small drum towers with the distinctive triple gunloops which are synonymous with Leiper; these drum towers retained conical slated roofs until the 1840s. Balancing the great mass of Preston's Tower on the l. is the Round Tower, 8 m. in diameter, on the far r., which must once also have been crowned by a tall conical roof. Although the ground floor is almost blind, the first-floor windows, protected by iron grilles, are of substantial size. A string course which runs across the entrance front at first-floor level between Preston's Tower and the Round Tower supports five sculpted figures – there were originally six – the mature gentleman with long whiskers and a short flowing beard evidently William Forbes himself (cf. his effigy in the Tolquhon Aisle at Tarves) and the lady facing him his wife, Elizabeth Gordon of Lesmoir. The lower heraldic arms are those of Forbes; the arms above are those of King James VI, who visited Tolquhon just as the castle was nearing completion. An inscription between the gateway and the Round Tower records 'Al this Warke excep the Auld Tovr was begun be William Forbes 15 Aprile 1584 and endit be him 20 October 1589'.

On PLAN Forbes' castle is roughly rectangular, some 15 m. E–W by 20 m. N–S. The vaulted ground-floor rooms are almost windowless and were devoted to services and cellars. The kitchen and bakehouse are in the SE corner, two bread ovens being contained in a 6.5-m. Square Tower which projects from

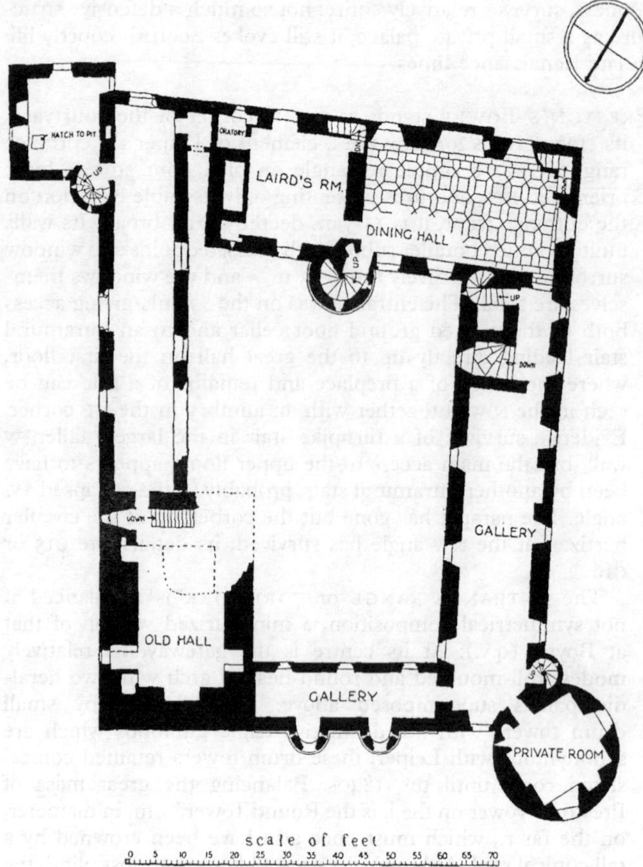

Tolquhon Castle.
First-floor plan, 1945–6

the angle. This tower also contained a pit-prison which must have been miserably cold until the ovens were fired, when it became stiflingly hot.

The principal apartments are at first floor, those of the family occupying the S, W and N ranges, and the chief steward probably occupying the E side. The planning of the three-storey S range, and the square-plan entrance jamb adjoining it at its NW, bears close resemblance to late C16 L-plan tower houses and particularly House of Schivas (q.v.) just 8.5 km. N, which has also been attributed to Leiper and is of similar date. At Tolquhon as at Schivas the broad winding main stair is entered through a doorway close into the SW angle and rises only to first floor. The second floor and attic are reached by a much smaller turnpike, accommodated within a turret at Schivas but within the thickness of the walls at Tolquhon. This and the layout within the S range – great hall (14.5 m. by 6 m.) with the laird's chamber beyond it placed over the kitchen for warmth – is all in accordance with Scots tower house planning; both the great hall and the laird's chamber have service stairs to the cellars for the ready provision of drink and comestibles. What is particularly distinctive at Tolquhon, however, is the round tower at the centre of the S range's courtyard elevation between the great hall and the laird's chamber. This contains a 2.5 m.-wide spiral stair rising the full height of the block, and is corbelled out into a tall gabled caphouse as the dominant feature of the court, its skewputts being carved with Leiper's initials. Both the great hall and the laird's chamber have good-sized fireplaces. The great hall is distinguished not only by its size but by its minstrels' gallery and its interlocking hexagonal paving (cf. that of the great hall at Udny, q.v.), while the more intimate laird's chamber has a small oratory and closet. The main stair also gives access to the long gallery (17.8 m. by 4.3 m.) which occupies the W range, for promenading in bad weather; the recess in its outer wall probably contained Forbes's books – some of which, signed by him, still survive – and other prized possessions. The S and W ranges looked out over formal gardens, traces of which remain, and the N entrance range over the castle's large pentagonal FORECOURT. It is 75 m. long and 45 m. wide and may once have been a formal events area like the Barras Green at Fyvie (q.v.). The W side of the forecourt's W wall contains twelve bee-bolls for the supply of honey, and near its iron yett are the remains of a DOOCOT with a few surviving nesting boxes.

While not unique, Tolquhon was remarkably sophisticated in plan for the late C16, having effectively been conceived and built in a single campaign. In its arrangement of dining room (i.e. great hall), library (i.e. W gallery) and drawing room (i.e. forework gallery) *en suite*, with a convenient set of private apartments for the laird and his family, and with a service wing and bakehouse in the ground floor on the E side, Tolquhon anticipates in its own fashion not just the Baronial idiom but also the sequential planning of country houses of the Burn-Bryce school by a quarter of a millennium. Robert William Billings, whom Burn sent to record Tolquhon for the *Baronial and Ecclesiastical Antiquities of Scotland*, arrived in the 1840s to find the last occupants, a farmer's family, not long gone, Preston's Tower only recently collapsed with its rubble strewn over the courtyard, and the forework roofs still partly in place although the painted roof timbers of the state apartments had by then fallen in. When MacGibbon and Ross surveyed Tolquhon in 1881 the large rectangular Pleasance immediately to the W of the castle was still formally laid out on a cruciform plan with holly and yew trees. The site was cleared up in 1929 when it was transferred to state care by Lord Haddo, son of the 1st Marquess of Aberdeen. Two of the forecourt outbuildings have since been reconstructed to provide a custodian's house and a shop.

7040 TOWIE BARCLAY

6.5 km. SSE of Turriff

65 Situated on the Ythan Water near to its confluence with the Kingsford Burn, and the setting for the first skirmish of the Civil Wars on 10 May 1639, Towie Barclay was originally a four-storey L-plan tower house built for the Barclays perhaps *c.* 1550–80, although on the basis of a recorded datestone it has traditionally been ascribed to 1593. It was identified by Dr Douglas Simpson as one of a group of four castles including Delgatie, Gight (qq.v.) and Craig (S) which were constructed for prominent Roman Catholics during the difficult Reformation period, and which through close similarities in plan and detail could all be attributed to a single master-mason. Other members of this group are Fedderate (Maud, q.v.), Knockhall (Newburgh, q.v.) and Colquhonnie (S), and if tradition is a guide they were all the work of the *Conn family* of master-masons based at Auchry. Further datestones suggest alteration works in 1604 and 1695. In 1792, however, Towie was substantially reduced; it was partially reconstructed by *James Duncan* in 1874, and after falling into neglect during the mid C20 was again reconstructed by Marc and Karen Ellington *c.* 1970, initially with the assistance of *Jack Meldrum* and later that of *William Cowie*. Their work received a Saltire Award in 1974.

The partial demolition of the late C18 reduced the tower to a relatively squat two-storey form, retaining only the main block's vaulted ground floor and first-floor great hall, and drastically curtailing the jamb. In his reconstruction *Duncan* did not attempt to recreate the tower's former four-storey height, but he rebuilt the jamb to two low storeys and by adding battlemented parapets did something to improve the appearance of the wall-heads. The Ellingtons' reconstruction accepted these historical changes but by adding a stylish new caphouse with very tall crowstepped attic, elegant swept dormers and a tall central lum, they managed to reintroduce to Towie much happier, more vertical proportions. Spirelets were added to the main block's corner bartizans to enhance the interest of the roof-line, and by covering over the red rubble masonry in traditional pinky-gold harl with only the quoins and margins left showing, they further set off the picturesque qualities of their remodelled house.

The main block orientated N–S measures 13 m. by 10.3 m. over walls some 2 m. thick. The jamb is 8.3 m. wide as at Delgatie, but as a result of the C18 demolitions its original length is uncertain. The doorway is set close into the angle within the main block: it is round-arched and moulded, and protected by a shot-hole. What survives of the original jamb provides space for a N–S corridor giving access to the main block's two ground-floor cellars and a spiral stair 2.5 m. in diameter within the thickness of the wall at the SE corner which

Towie Barclay Castle, Hall.
Engraving by R.W. Billings, 1852

rises up to the great hall at first floor. This arrangement of entrance vestibule, corridor and stair, with certain other details, is very similar to those at Delgatie, Gight and particularly Craig; like Gight and Craig it has a second service stair, opening off one of the ground-floor cellars in the SW corner. Above the doorway there was once an inscription: 'Sir Alexander Barclay of Tolly Foundator decessit Anno Domini 1136. In tim of valth al men sims friendly – an frind is not knawin but in adversity' and the date 1593, but this has now been eroded away.*

Inside the small vaulted vestibule characteristic of these castles, the ribs rise from corbels into a central boss with Patrick Barclay's coat of arms and initials. The spiral stair opens into the great hall beneath a gallery which runs across

*The Rev. J. B. Pratt's *Buchan* records that the Saltoun arms were still displayed on the SW tower in 1858. Two panels with monograms and coats of arms preserved at Mains of Pittulie have possibly been reset.

the 'low' S end in an arrangement similar to that at Craig, the fireplace being at the 'high' N end. The great hall is the finest surviving interior in Simpson's group of four related castles, groined and vaulted in two compartments: its ribs spring from foliate capitals and meet in octagonal bosses charged with the royal arms at the 'high' end and the Barclay arms at the 'low' end.* The gallery has its own small vault, its ribs springing from corbels decorated with emblems of the four Evangelists into a central boss which displays the Stigmata. Flanking the opening towards the hall are two niches clearly meant for statues, and there seems little doubt that this gallery was once used as an oratory: as MacGibbon and Ross observed, 'It is entered by a small stair from the floor above, so that the baron and his family might use it privately, or by drawing a curtain it might be opened to the Hall, when all assembled there might witness the service.' The present quatrefoil gallery front was added by *James Duncan* during his restoration in 1874. Within the C20 caphouse the rooms are simply finished, the attic with a timber-boarded ceiling carried on segmentally arched trusses.

COURTYARD STEADING, attributed to *John Smith I c.* 1840, reconstructed into its present form by *James Duncan c.* 1874. Single-storey and attic ranges rubble-built on three sides, with doocot and other fragments reused from the castle. Handsome meeting room with an open timber roof of the 1840 period. On the fourth side is the WALLED GARDEN, which has been laid out to recreate as far as possible that shown in William Roy's maps of the mid C18. A larger GARDEN enclosed by trees also survives to the S: it is shown formally laid out in the 1st Ordnance Survey of 1871.

7050

TURRIFF

Turriff spreads across a steep S-facing slope above the Idoch Water, near its confluence with the Deveron on the W. The town's name in Gaelic signifies rising ground or a defensive tower, the 'Tower of Torray' surviving into the C19. A monastery was reputedly founded by St Congan *c.* 732; the present St Congan's Church (*see* churches) was probably begun by the early C13, and St Congan's Hospital established by Alexander Comyn, Earl of Buchan, in 1272.[‡] In 1511–12 the town was erected a burgh of barony for William Hay, 4th Earl of Erroll. Under the Errolls' patronage Turriff, the only settlement of consequence in

*As Dr Matthew Woodworth has observed, the web of these vaults is constructed in the French manner, suggesting that the Conns were either French or had learned their craft under someone who was.

[‡]Alexander's Hospital stood on the site known afterwards as *Maison Dieu*, or Abbey Lands; the Knights Templar gave their name to Temple Brae.

north-west Aberdeenshire, and situated on the highway linking Aberdeen with Banff (q.v.), was assured of success. The Errolls sold Turriff to Peter Garden of Troup in 1762–3. He laid out a New Town on a crossroads plan, with Main Street starting from the E end of the old High Street and rising up the steeply sloping Idoch Valley towards a central Square before continuing further N as Market Street, while Duff Street and Fife Street ran across The Square W–E. The area enclosed by Main Street and Fife Street was developed on a grid-plan with Balmellie Street – a continuation of High Street – and Chapel Street running W–E, and smaller lanes N–S. Church Street and Church Terrace were formed between Market Street and Duff Street, taking their names from St Ninian's church (*see* Churches) of 1794–5. Although the turnpike (now the A947) ran through Turriff the town benefited less than expected, seemingly because of its route and its poor standard of construction, but in 1826 the Eastside

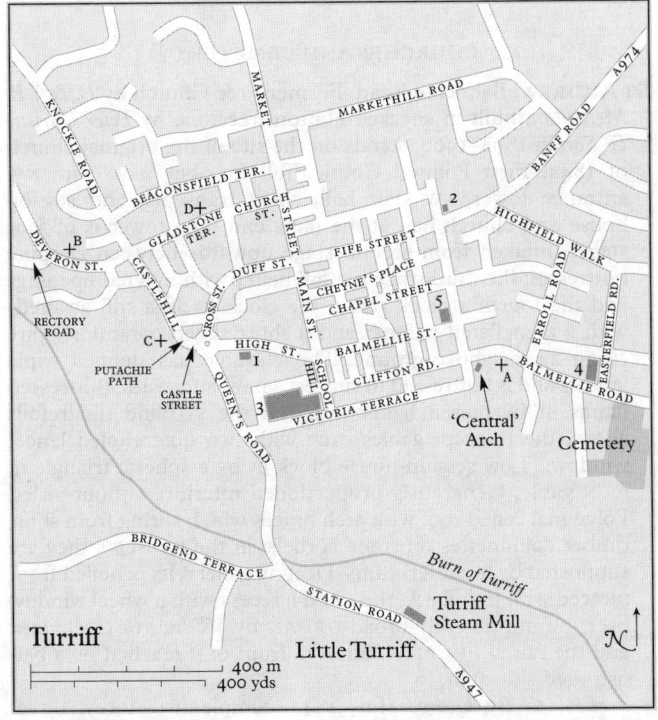

A St Andrew
B St Congan (Episcopal)
C St Congan's Old Church
D St Ninian & Forglen

1 Council Chambers
2 Chalmers Infants' School (former)
3 Turriff Academy
4 Turriff Cottage Hospital
5 Drill Hall (former)

Bridge across the Deveron opened a new route into Banffshire. The Banff, Macduff & Turriff Railway's arrival in the valley in 1857 encouraged development of Victoria Terrace from *c.* 1866 with prosperous villas overlooking The Haughs. The draining of The Haughs and their amalgamation with Brodie's Braes and Brodie's Den as public parks, together with sporting facilities and a new Free Church (now St Andrew), contributed to the completion of Victoria Terrace by the turn of the century, and development along Balmellie Road. An exclusive enclave also developed around Brodie's Braes and Brodie's Den from the 1890s, while on the valley's opposite slopes more villas were built at Little Turriff. *James Duncan & Son* exerted an iron grip on patronage throughout the town, continued by *W.L. Duncan* until the appointment *c.* 1934 of *Douglas Turnbull* as Burgh Surveyor. During the 1930s Turriff expanded E and N; notwithstanding the railway's closure to passengers (1951) and freight (1966), after the wars the town continued to prosper with development to E, N and W. It is now expanding W again, towards its natural boundary with the Deveron.

CHURCHES AND CEMETERY

ST ANDREW, Balmellie Road. Former Free Church by *D. & J.R. McMillan*, built in snecked Hatton freestone by *Peter Christie & Son* in 1898–1900, stands on the site of the original church of 1844. First Pointed Gothic. Tall four-bay nave with NW entrance tower, SW stair hall, short transepts, and session house and church hall at the far E end. The tower is of four stages, intaken from second stage upwards between clasping buttresses; the third stage is a tall belfry with louvred openings and the fourth a clock stage (the clock itself is still awaited) with a crenellated parapet and a short slated pyramidal spire rising 24 m. above ground. The W gable has stepped triple lancets and is buttressed to suggest a nave and aisles. Buttressed flanks lit by paired lights with (on the S) blind quatrefoils above, the transept gables each with two quatrefoiled lancet windows. Low session-house block lit by a spheric triangle in its N gable. Generously proportioned interior, without aisles. Polygonal ceiled roof with arch braces which spring from short timber colonnettes on stone corbels; in the transepts they are supported by hammerbeams. Deep W gallery, its panelled front pierced with trefoils. At the E end a recess with a wheel window over the impressively broad ORGAN by *Wadsworth & Brother*, and the raised PULPIT centred in front of it reached by a balustraded side-stair.

MANSE. By *George Hay*, 1847. Simple two-storey, three-windows-wide, with pilastered entrance and a gabled roof, the ground-floor bay windows added later. Rear addition 1869. Stable 1850, with later offices and dairy 1854.

ST CONGAN (Episcopal), Deveron Street. Externally and internally, one of the more idiosyncratic E.E. designs of *William Ramage*, built in 1862–3 in deep red Turriff sandstone. Five-bay nave with W porch and small SW corner tower with a steeply battered base broaching to octagonal and belfry of slim colonnettes under a spirelet. Long E chancel with organ chamber and vestry on its S side. Lancets in the flanks, triple light in the E gable and a W rose window. Inside, the nave rises into an unusual open timber roof of very slim construction, scissor beams cross-braced with pendants at the intersections. Delicate traceried SCREEN in the chancel arch. – FONT. 1862. Octagonal with angle colonnettes, mounted on a stumpy column and low broad base. Most of the other furnishings are later. – ROOD SCREEN. Three bays of Gothic arches with delicate open tracery. – Magnificent Gothic PULPIT of 1893, oak carved with groups and individual figures under tracery canopies, all high quality. – LECTERN by *Jones & Willis*, 1901. – STAINED GLASS. The chancel windows are by *W. Wailes* of Newcastle, 1867: in the E windows the Crucifixion, flanked l. by the Blessed Virgin and r. by St John; beneath, a portrait medallion of Alexander Jolly, Bishop of Moray (1756–1838). – In the W gable, the later C19 rose window is centred on the Lamb and Banner, with ten surrounding petals containing angels. In the nave, S side, memorial windows, one representing St Congan's first priest, the Rev. James Christie (†1888) being received by an angel bearing the Holy Grail, with above the Lamb of God and the Kingdom of Heaven; on the N, Christ with Children and Young People, by *Karl Parsons*, 1933. – Lancet (Agony in the Garden and Agnus Dei) by *Clayton & Bell*, 1926.

In the CHURCHYARD, extended by *G. G. Jenkins, C.E.* 1906, a tall Celtic cross of that year to Lt Garden Andrew Duff who died at Simla.

CHURCH HALL, Rectory Road. By *John Fowlie*, 1897. Red Delgatie sandstone.

ST CONGAN'S OLD CHURCH, Putachie Path. Still an impres- 22
sive monument at the W end of the High Street, although not used for worship since 1795, and now a burial enclosure. Reputedly founded by Malcolm Canmore in the late C11, but perhaps begun in the early C13 by Marjory, Countess of Buchan, when she endowed it with lands and granted the revenues to Arbroath Abbey in exchange for religious services.

A rubble-built rectangle, later extended W – 'the length being 120, and the breadth 18 feet' (36.5 m. by 5.5 m.) according to the *New Statistical Account* of 1842. The tall E gable facing the town is that of the CHOIR built by Alexander Lyon, Chanter, who was buried beneath it on his death in 1541; C16 wall paintings of two figures were discovered in the splays of the choir windows in 1861. The Chanter was a son of the 4th Lord Glamis who trained for the priesthood and was described as 'a singular scholar of these times'. The choir has a small moulded doorway off-centre to the r., with what appears to be a large socket for a drawbar. Above this, the wall is intaken slightly, with two small blocked windows. The skewputts are carved with heraldic arms, and the gable rises into a magnificent double BELLCOTE, dated 1635, the best (with that at Peathill, q.v.) of its type and date in Scotland in spite of weathering. It displays the Hay coat of arms, the initials of William Hay, 11th Earl of Errol, and those of the minister, Thomas Mitchell. Finely carved double pendant arches rise in two stages into a cornice crowned by small strapwork gablets and a pyramidal finial. The bell itself, initialled V.H. and dated 1556, was removed to St Ninian's (q.v.) in 1795 but reinstated in 1828 together with the clock (of 1797, from Carnousie).

The original flank elevations survive to their full height, but those of the extension have been reduced, and the W gable is now gone; within the S flank, a low moulded doorway sealed with a grave-slab. The windows are mostly blocked but their quoins are easily discerned. Set in the window at the far W end, which remains open, a large simple basin, possibly a font; the lintel of the window at the E end is carved with a heraldic device; and in the centre, a small window just beneath the wall-head may indicate the position of the pulpit. The N flank is absolutely blind, and probably once had a gallery. Only the E end is roofed: a cross wall immediately behind the choir gable and like it with heraldic devices at its skewputts encloses the private burial area of the Gardens of Delgatie (q.v.) and Troup and Glenlyon. – SCULPTURE. Above the doorway in the choir gable, a much-eroded arched panel carved in red freestone. It seems to come from St Congan's Hospital, the medieval almshouse. Ten portrait heads of which the centre three are said to represent King Alexander III, who was witness to the hospital's foundation, framed by Alexander Comyn, Earl of Buchan, and his wife, Elizabeth; the seven others are supposed to be the Master and the chaplains. (Or, perhaps, the three central heads represent the Magi). – WALL MONUMENTS. Mid-C16 to mid-C18. On the N side, one of 1636 erected by the Barclays of Towie Barclay (q.v.) – slim columns and bold strapwork scrolls framing a beautifully lettered Latin inscription, with a deep entablature and crowning ogee pediment carved with the Barclay arms. Another slightly simpler monument of the same period, also with a Latin inscription framed by columns with deep entablature and a heraldic device. Within the E-end enclosure, a large Gothic memorial erected to the extended Garden family, 1848, with a splendidly carved armorial tympanum.

Some early LYING SLABS, e.g. one next to the S wall clearly dated 1658. W of the church two good examples of this tradition for Everild and John Hay (†1975 and 1997), both designed by the sculptor *John Hay* of Hayfield and Delgatie (q.v.). – GATEWAY. C17 Renaissance – a segmental arch in red sandstone ashlar framed between slim fluted pilasters and surmounting cornice, the gates early C19.

ST NINIAN & FORGLEN, Gladstone Terrace. In its present form, largely as reconstructed in 1913–14 by *A. Marshall Mackenzie*

& Son. It began as a simple rectangular church of 1794–5 by *James Robertson*, mason in Gellymill, with *Massie*, wright, built to succeed St Congan's Old Church (*see* above). N aisle, creating a T-plan, added 1830. The chancel, with Serlian W window, and the additional N aisles date from the Mackenzies' reconstruction but their proposals for a low E tower with spire were unrealized. Construction is mostly in squared red sandstone, with pronounced long-and-short quoins, and moulded skewputts. S flank facing the street with four tall round-arched windows with voussoirs and key blocks (reconstructed after the removal of an organ chamber and session house by *James Duncan*, 1875–6). Above the E door, a Serlian gallery window and a fine Italian Renaissance-style bellcote of 1875, by *William Smith* (of *J. & W. Smith*), with pilasters and scrolls carrying a segmental pediment. Galleried interior almost wholly by the Mackenzies. Within the N aisles the galleries are articulated into bays by superimposed columns carrying very shallow segmental arches but the gallery is now enclosed on two levels. S windows in simple classical surrounds. Chancel furnishings by the Mackenzies, finely carved in oak. – Handsome PULPIT, octagonal, supported on bold scrolls over a low square base; panelled sides with fluted square columns, moulded top. – STAINED GLASS. Chancel window, 1914, 'Blessed Are the Pure in Heart'. Christ, flanked by Saints and with all the Faithful gathered at His feet, standing against a handsome colonnaded background. S windows: 'Thy Faith Hath Saved Thee Go in Peace', erected *c.* 1870, and St Ninian, erected about a century later. – FIRST WORLD WAR MEMORIAL. Oak panel with low-relief gilt cross and blue and green foliate background.

Former CHURCH HALL, also in Gladstone Terrace. By *James Duncan & Son*, 1893–4. First Pointed, seven bays in snecked Delgatie ashlar sandstone, tall slate roof with central ventilator flèche. W end with gabled porch and rose window; large gabled wing at E end perhaps a Sunday School.

CEMETERY, Balmellie Road. Good 'Old Scotch' lodge house, *c.* 1900, with Bryce-type canted bay and ball-finialled gatepiers with cast-iron gates, by *James Duncan & Son*. Excellent Gothic rib-vaulted LYCHGATE in red sandstone by *William Kelly* (of *Kelly & Nicol*) *c.* 1922–3, the names of those killed during the First World War finely lettered within its deep reveals, and a figure of St Congan set within an aedicule in the gable towards the cemetery. Outside the gateway, SECOND WORLD WAR MEMORIAL, bronze plaque signed by *Henshaw*, Edinburgh.

PUBLIC BUILDINGS

COUNCIL CHAMBERS, High Street. By *W.L. Duncan*, *c.* 1907–8. Edwardian Baroque in red Delgatie freestone. Symmetrical single-storey, its central entrance with balustraded parapet recessed between broad pedimented wings containing tripartite windows with columns carrying segmental pediments. The 'Mannie' sculpture perched on the r. gable is a real curiosity. Inside, council chamber and courtroom.

Former CHALMERS INFANTS' SCHOOL, Banff Road. A charming design by *James Matthews c.* 1862, like a suburban villa set back from the street in a small railed garden. Gable-fronted, two storeys with attic pierced by a quatrefoil. Shouldered central doorway and paired lights each side at ground floor, a deep platband at first floor. Square-shafted chimneystacks rising from the end gables. Closed *c.* 1900, Volunteers' Drill Hall until *c.* 1938.

Former DRILL HALL, Balmellie Street. By *David Polson Hall* (of *Rollo & Hall*) *c.* 1936–8. Cottage-style entrance front, harled single-storey with central round-arched key-blocked doorway, small-paned glazing and broad-eaved roof with swept dormers. It conceals the large hall at the rear. In use until *c.* 1970, fenestration now partly altered.

TURRIFF ACADEMY, Victoria Terrace. Designs by *Alexander Gill*, Aberdeen County Architect, from *c.* 1957, built in four stages 1961–71 on the site of the former Higher Grade School.

TURRIFF COTTAGE HOSPITAL, Balmellie Road. Originally the infectious diseases hospital of 1895–6 by *James Duncan & Son*. Symmetrical single-storey villa-type – central administration block with links to male and female wards on either side. Closed 1931–2; re-opened as Cottage Hospital 1935, with new NURSES' HOME by *W.L. Duncan c.* 1936–7. Further extension in Balmellie Place 1996–8.

'CENTRAL' ARCH, Balmellie Road, at entrance to the Den. Baroque semi-elliptical arch flanked by pilasters with surmounting scrolls and segmental pediment, constructed in red sandstone. Originally built 1899 as the entrance to the Central Auction Mart; the architects were probably *James Duncan & Son* who carried out further work at the Mart in 1902. Reassembled in its present position in 2000.

DESCRIPTION

Turriff's MARKET CROSS stands near the junction where Castle Street and High Street running W–E along the slopes of the Idoch Valley are bisected by Queen's Road approaching from the S, which continues N into Cross Street. The cross, designed by *James Duncan* with sculpture-work by *Thomas Goodwillie* of Elgin, 1865–6, replaced the original cross erected in 1512, and repaired in 1842. Its tall octagonal base with angle colonnettes and Gothic finialled gablets supports an octagonal shaft with a wheel cross-head, all constructed in red sandstone ashlar. CASTLE STREET and CASTLEHILL are named after two different buildings – the Tower of Torray, which stood to the W, and 'Castle Rainy', thought to have its origins in the Knights Templar and Hospitaller. Castle Rainy was replaced by the OLD TOWN HALL, early Victorian classical of 1845 although much altered. A two-storey three-bay building with its centre slightly projected under a low gable pediment, originally it contained a school at ground floor and municipal chambers lit by round-arched windows at first floor.

The Earls of Erroll established their town lodging at the top
of HIGH STREET in 1590 to succeed the 'Tower of Torray'. It 3
was destroyed in 1974 to ease traffic through Turriff, but at the cost of splitting High Street from Castle Street, the latter's atmosphere like a cathedral close dominated by St Congan's choir being lost forever. The Earls also gave off deep feus on both sides of the High Street which to a considerable extent dictated the town's future development. During the C19 and early C20 High Street was rebuilt in dark red sandstone from Delgatie, Hatton and Ardinn. Perhaps the earliest survivor is the modest Late Georgian house, No. 61 standing NE of the junction; also Late Georgian, at the other end of the street, are No. 10 smart classical and No. 16 vernacular, both altered with street-level shops. Most blocks are simple Victorian, two-storey ashlar or snecked rubble: a notable feature is how many ashlar buildings are constructed in masonry laid in slim courses. Within this streetscape, three blocks – Nos. 14 (White Heather Hotel), 17 and 20 (the last dated 1891) are distinguished by their broad pedimental gables. In their midst No. 18, a single-storey building with curvilinear gable, is a striking contrast, mid-C18, but remodelled *c.* 1905. The High Street's handsome provincial dignity, its generous width as it weaves along the hillside and the way in which, behind the smart frontages, the buildings often extend back at a sharp angle (the old higgledy-piggledy feus still asserting themselves 300 years after) create a sense of variety and movement, and lay the foundations of its essential character.

James Duncan built the Aberdeen Town & County Bank, now SCOTTISH BUILDING SOCIETY, on the N side *c.* 1873. It is a modestly scaled Cinquecento palazzo in stugged red ashlar with doorways at either end, one for the bank office and one for the agent's house. Key blocks finely carved with heads of kings and bacchantes and richly treated doorway consoles suggest an excellent craftsman working in the later C19. Across the road, the OLD POST OFFICE, 1899, and Council Chambers *c.* 1907–8 (*see* Public Buildings) are by the *Duncans*, as is the façade of Nos. 13–15, house, shop and Union Bank – all now BANK OF SCOTLAND – built in 1897–8 for Turriff's photographer, William Gammie. *James Duncan* had already remodelled the adjoining plain Neoclassical Commercial Bank (now ROYAL BANK OF SCOTLAND) in 1878, while the Commercial Hotel (now ROYAL BRITISH LEGION) was another reconstruction of a plain classical house in 1896–7, similarly detailed to the Post Office at its curved angle and gable. Close by a SCULPTURE, the 'Turra Coo' by *David Blyth*, *Ginny Hutchison* and *Charles Engebretsen*, 2010. A charming feature of the High Street is its collection of ENAMEL ADVERTISING SIGNS of the early C20. Over the crossroads in

BALMELLIE STREET, the former ABERDEEN SAVINGS BANK is Neoclassical by *W.L. Duncan*, *c.* 1910.

In contrast to High Street, the axis of Schoolhill, Main Street and Market Street rises up the valley dead straight for 500 m. Like High Street, however, MAIN STREET was substantially rebuilt during the later C19 and early C20. The North of Scotland (now CLYDESDALE) BANK of *c.* 1873–5 is a neat two-storey and attic frontage in stugged red ashlar sandstone, its corner tower rising into crowstepped clock gables with water cannon, and a French pavilion spirelet with a brattishing crown: all its details suggest *James Matthews*. Further up, the UNION HOTEL was built *c.* 1896 in rock-faced grey Clinterty granite, two storeys with gabled attic and dormers. Its Main Street frontage was extended in the same style when shops and flats were added in 1903. The Neoclassical British Linen Bank (TSB) is by *W.L. Duncan c.* 1926, who altered it ten years later. Much of the rest of Main Street is lined by simple two-storey and attic blocks with ground-floor shops, that on the Chapel Street junction dated 1875 with a fine sculpted lion looking down from the corner. In CHAPEL STREET the OLD POLICE STATION is a tall single-storey and attic block on the Angus Lane junction, extended by the two-storey gable-fronted block next door in 1904–5.

At the top of Main Street, THE SQUARE is a pleasant open space, loosely laid out with buildings of different styles and dates. On the W, short two-storey terraces, mostly early to mid-C19 in snecked rubble; the N terrace has been significantly altered over time. On the E side, Grange Villa (now the PUBLIC LIBRARY) *c.* 1875–80 presents a tall two-storey L-plan frontage, its projecting gable with a canted bay. Facing it across the Fife Street junction, a tall two-storey and attic block of *c.* 1880 makes clever use of its sloping site: it has plate-glazed ground-floor shopfronts to Fife Street and a first-floor and attic maisonette entered from a terrace off The Square. On the N side is the FIFE ARMS HOTEL, late C18 two-storey vernacular, and substantially extended in the same idiom; facing it across the Market Street junction is the POLICE STATION built *c.* 1960, but respecting the modest scale and domestic character of its surroundings.

E of The Square in FIFE STREET stands PANTON HOUSE of *c.* 1845 – Late Georgian classical Italianate in the manner of *A. & W. Reid*, two storeys and three windows wide with a platform roof; it is harled in white with a dark red entrance porch, long-and-short window dressings and raised angle quoins, and pairs of diagonally shafted chimneystacks rising up from the end gables. W of The Square, Church Street extends into GLADSTONE TERRACE with ST CONGAN'S LODGE No. 922 by *Brother Joseph Rae*, still Late Victorian classical although built in 1924–5; stained glass of St Congan in its transom-light.

Turning down Church Terrace leads to CROSS STREET, realigned in the late C20 to provide a more convenient link between The Square and the Market Cross junction. TOWIE

HOUSE, dated 1888, is two-storey and semi-symmetrical in the familiar red sandstone, its central doorway set in a Baroque surround, first-floor windows beneath a swept roof with fanciful gables, a small attic dormer and low coped chimneystacks at either end.

Then just off Cross Street, the former ST NINIAN'S MANSE (by *W. L. Duncan*, 1924–5) is two-storey symmetrical with its doorway flanked by ground-floor canted bays and a Serlian window on first, its beautifully crafted masonry looking like C18 work. It stands on a tall terrace: before the Manse Garden cottages were built underneath it possessed a real presence. Returning back *via* Castlehill, Woolmanhill Road climbs round St Congan's Churchyard as a private drive to HALLHILL HOUSE, bought by *James Duncan* and altered in 1897 both as his house and his office – a large villa, two tall storeys and attic, with drum tower and slated spirelet on its l. corner and projecting gabled bays on the r., a testimony to the man who made Turriff as it is now.

Finally on the other side of the valley, LITTLE TURRIFF. Later C19 suburban villas along the S side of STATION ROAD, most if not all by *James Duncan & Son*, with the former GEORGE TEMPERANCE HOTEL opened in 1906. The former TURRIFF STEAM MILL (later North of Scotland Milling Co.) was begun by 1870 and extended eastwards before 1900. Built into sloping ground, its full scale is only evident from the valley basin. Four storeys, seventeen bays in pinned rubble, internally its timber floors were supported on cast-iron columns. Recently converted into flats, its loading bays replaced by glazed oriels and its Aberdeenshire kiln ventilator cut down in size, it nevertheless remains eloquent testimony of the importance of grain in Scotland's north-east.

DEVERON (or EASTSIDE) BRIDGE carrying the B9025 over the Deveron. Probably designed by *William Minto*, 1824, completed by *William Smith*, builder, in 1826.* A broad central segmental span of 18 m. and two smaller spans of 12 m. with low coped parapets and wing-walls, all coursed squared red sandstone with ashlar voussoirs, rising from bull-nosed grey granite piers. Picturesque single-storey TOLL HOUSE, octagonal in red sandstone ashlar. Recessed doorway framed by Roman Doric columns, windows with lying-pane glazing and broad-eaved roof rising into a central chimneystack.

BRIDGEND FARMHOUSE, off Bridgend Terrace. Early C19. Simple vernacular classical. Two-storey three-bay frontage, the doorway and windows set in dressed surrounds, walls harled in cream. Long single-storey-and-attic rear wing. Recent restoration has added the small gabled porch and a bow-ended stair against the rear elevation.

BURNSIDE HOUSE, 3 km. NE. A country villa built *c.* 1889 for James Beaton but still mid-C19 classical in style. The rear wing

*Minto had been Telford's site engineer for the bridges at Potarch, Alford and Keig (all S).

is a slightly earlier house. Miniature designed landscape, the Burn of Kinminty running through a shallow valley lined with trees on both sides immediately to the W.

KNOCKIEMILL FARMHOUSE, off Deveron Road. Dated 1809, but following the traditions of the later C18. Two storeys and three bays, with ground floor taller than first. Doorway and windows set in red dressed surrounds against walls harled in light grey, gabled roof with moulded skewputts and coped end stacks.

FINTRY FARMHOUSE, 5.6 km. NE. Z-plan, built up in stages. Original house is later C18, seemingly built as an L-plan with ground floor taller than first, the doors and windows in dressed surrounds. What is now the central range of the Z-plan was extended slightly later, with a basement milk-room. Additional wing added in 1886, taller, two-storeyed in coursed squared red sandstone, entrance porch and square bay at ground floor, first-floor windows breaking through the eaves as gabled dormers (one dated). C18 house with new door and windows. Extensive outbuildings.

WOODHEAD FARMHOUSE, 4.8 km. S. Built 1831. Tall two-storey frontage, three windows wide, harled in white with very pronounced long-and-short dressings and margins in the local red sandstone, doorway concealed by modern glazed porch. Band course forms sill of first-floor windows; string course and slim moulded cornice suggest a heavy entablature, gabled roof with coped ashlar chimneystacks.

WRAE FARMHOUSE, 2.9 km. N. Built *c.* 1840. Two-storey, three windows wide. Richly textured red rubble construction with slim ashlar dressings and long-and-short quoins, gabled roof with coped end stacks. Replacement glazing. Small bay window in flank for paying staff wages, harled rear wing.

ARDMIDDLE OR SCOBBACH LODGE, on B9024, 4.1 km. WSW. Built *c.* 1840. Gothic, single-storeyed; the house it served was demolished *c.* 1960.

IDOCH DOOCOT, 4.5 km. E. Perhaps C17, built for Idoch Castle (reputedly C14, dem.). Cylindrical, with two rat courses, built in red sandstone rubble.

CRAIGSTON CASTLE. *See* p. 132.

DELGATIE CASTLE. *See* p. 153.

HATTON CASTLE. *See* p. 247.

MUIRESK HOUSE. *See* p. 296.

TOWIE BARCLAY. *See* p. 402.

9060

TYRIE

A hamlet with outlying church, manse and school.

ST ANDREW, 1 km. NE. A rectangular preaching-box, built in granite ashlar in 1800, reordered 1902–3 with sympathetic alterations and additions by *William Reid* of Fraserburgh, perhaps based on a scheme by *A. Marshall Mackenzie*. W gable with square-headed doorway, round-arched gallery window, moulded skewputts and dated bellcote with ball finial. The S flank was originally symmetrical, with just two tall windows in its centre and smaller windows at the ends, reflecting the internal arrangement with the pulpit once centred on this side, and galleries to both E and W. When worship was reordered in 1902–3 the E gallery was removed and an archway formed opening into the new chancel, with a session house on its N side: the small E-end window in the S flank was enlarged to admit more light. The diamond-pane glazing which now fills the windows must be of that time. Internally, the chancel arch is Neo-Romanesque. – Furnishings of 1902–3, the COMMUNION TABLE carved by *Cairnie*. – PICTISH STONE, a slab of rough mica, reputedly found beneath the previous church, although the exact find-spot is not clear. It represents a raven (or an eagle), wings folded, above a 'tuning fork' with double-discs, and divided by a Z-rod with scrolls.

CHURCHYARD. Striking memorial to Elizabeth Willox and Joseph Taylor, a well-sculpted angel floating before a cross, *c.* 1900. WAR MEMORIAL, *c.* 1920, a rough-hewn obelisk in granite, sculpted with the insignia of the Gordon Highlanders, and raised on a pedestal and base course.

CHURCH HALL (former parish school), 120 m. W of the church. Built 1858, subsequently extended. Harled rectangle like a Secession church, segment-headed mullioned and transomed windows with diamond-pane glazing.

Former PARISH MANSE, 0.4 km. WSW of the church. By *John Smith I*, 1843–4. Two storeys, three bays broad, golden granite rubble with grey granite dressings, gabled roof. Doorway sheltered under plain console-cornice, neatly detailed timber architrave enclosing an arcaded fanlight. Ground-floor windows taller than first, distinctive glazing with tall slim panes. Eaves course, square-cut skewputts and pronounced skews, low coped gable end stacks. Rear elevation with central bowed stair projection, and a single-storey L-plan wing which forms a small court. Gables non-identical, E with three windows at ground floor and first floor which are mostly dummies, W with single window at ground floor and blind at first, both with small round-headed lights for the attic. Simply detailed interior, original woodwork. Walled garden. Steading still with its horse stalls.

SCHOOL, 0.5 km. S. By *George Bennett Mitchell & Son*, *c.* 1932, with dining hall and kitchen added in 1948.

BOYNDLIE HOUSE, 0.9 km. SW. In a striking setting within the depths of a glen, perhaps the site of a mansion house as early as the C16. The present house was built for John Forbes, 5th of Boyndlie in 1814 (it is dated above the first-floor windows), restyled *c.* 1846 with a broad-eaved roof, and then extended to designs by *Ellis & Wilson* in 1894. Originally symmetrical, a two-storey five-bay centre-and-ends composition in heathen rubble with pronounced grey granite dressings, raised over a tall grey granite basement; central entrance flanked by relatively narrow windows in the intermediate bays, all astragalled sash-and-case. Eaves course beneath the oversailing platformed and piended roof. When the house was extended in 1894, the r. end was built out as a much broader and deeper pavilion wing in pinkish-grey granite squared with slim ashlar dressings, resulting in the present L-plan frontage. The porch and the low parapets guarding the stairs are also later, as are the slate-hung dormers, but the porch's Neo-Greek anta-pilasters and pediment have probably been reused from the doorpiece of *c.* 1846. Rear elevation in heathen stone with central three-window bow in grey granite ashlar, large conservatory built out from the stepped r. flank.

STEADING, 120 m. W. Large irregular quadrangle, single-storey and attic, progressively built and rebuilt in the C18 and C19; walls substantially intact although partly roofless. Segmental and semi-elliptical archways, windows with diamond-pane glazing, doocot and dial for wind direction linked to vane over the apex. LODGE, 350 m. SE, probably 1814. Single-storey T-plan, harled with margins, central porch supported on cast-iron columns; canted bay in gable facing main road, and a broad-eaved roof. The 2nd and 3rd Ordnance Surveys (1902 and 1926) indicate an R.C. CHAPEL 120 m. NE of the house within wooded grounds.

8020 UDNY GREEN

A delightful estate village laid out around a rectangle of sward.

PARISH CHURCH (CHRIST CHURCH). Tudor Gothic by *John Smith I*, 1821, and very early of its kind: quite different from a conventional Scottish preaching-box of the late C18 or early C19, even a contemporary Gothic example such as Smith's own Fintray Parish Church (S). Square-based entrance tower centred in front of a broad nave gable, all ashlar-built, four-bay rubble flanks with timber Y-tracery and original small-pane glazing. Tower doorway with a four-centred arch and hood-mould, two-light glazing at the second stage, louvred belfry openings at third; the fourth clock stage was added in 1895, with Smith's crenellated parapet reinstated at the higher level, the stepped angle buttresses rising into pinnacles. Some of the church's fabric was reputedly reused from Christ's Kirk of *c.* 1600 (*see* Graveyard). The interior is also Tudor Gothic and liturgically it too is very different from past Scottish precedents (although similar to James Gillespie Graham's larger churches built just a few years earlier), the congregation facing down the nave rather than towards the minister's pulpit against one flank wall. The U-plan gallery is supported on cast-iron columns, an early example of their use in Scotland. But if the basic structure is Smith's work, much of its character derives from the remodelling by *A. Marshall Mackenzie* (of *Matthews & Mackenzie*) in 1890–1. Mackenzie was responsible for the new panelled gallery fronts in oak, and the boarded ceiling on arched trusses. Most of the FURNISHINGS are to his designs – the raised PULPIT with its canted front centred immediately beneath the organ pipes in the chamber he built for them, the columnar COMMUNION TABLE with its carved trefoil and stylized floriate decoration, and the small square pedestal FONT, although the LECTERN carved with fleur-de-lys and leaves is later. – MEMORIALS. Several good examples, those to George Udny (†1915) and John Udny (†1934) in marble, the Second World War memorial in bronze, that of Robert Udny-Hamilton (†1950) carved in oak, painted and gilded. – STAINED GLASS. In the window above the organ, St Machar and Dorcas by *Clayton & Bell*, 1927.

GRAVEYARD, on the S side of the Green. With Pitmedden and Pittrichie enclosures on the site of the Chapel of the Holy Trinity ('Christ's Kirk' by *Thomas Leiper*, *c.* 1600) of which no trace remains. Unusual MORT HOUSE by *John Marr* of Cairnbrogie, 1832. Circular in rough granite ashlar with a truncated conical roof, outer oak and inner iron doors, revolving platform for coffins inside.*

DESCRIPTION. The Green falls gently from the parish church on the N towards SPENCE HALL (*George Watt & Stewart*, 1936–7), a row of small houses and a symmetrical late C18 INN (formerly a farmhouse) on the S side. Udny Academy, founded 1786, once stood on the W, flanked by its two-storey SCHOOLMASTER'S HOUSE (by *George Marr*, 1867) and the villa-like LIBRARY (1912). Near the church, the WAR MEMORIAL of 1921 by *D. Morren & Co.* of Aberdeen (sculptor, *Francis Coutts*) – a young infantryman in Creetown granite, head bowed, standing with rifle reversed on a Neoclassical plinth (cf. Oldmeldrum and Portsoy (qq.v) and Rhynie and Tarland (S)). The E side of the Green was left open until the SCHOOL was built *c.* 1970; Udny Castle (*see* below) is approached through gates discreetly set back on the NE corner.

Former PARISH MANSE, near Manse Road. By *J. & W. Smith*, 1851. Symmetrical Tudor, two-storey three windows wide in pinned granite rubble, centre bay slightly projected with steeply raked gable and ashlar-fronted porch; the windows were originally mullioned and transomed with lying-pane glazing. Altered internally by *J. R. Mackenzie*, 1885, rear wing heightened in 1897.

*Too late to be useful as the bodysnatching era had passed; it was subsequently used as an ammunition store.

Udny Castle.
Drawing by David M. Walker

UDNY CASTLE, 450 m. NE. A tower house built by the Udny lairds probably *c.* 1550–80, certain characteristics suggesting that it is the work of the *Conn family* of master-masons based at Auchry; its wall-head is however early C17. Abandoned *c.* 1775, it was modernized in 1801 with much larger windows.*

The tower is a simple large rectangle, 13 m. long E–W by 10.5 m. wide N–S, the same dimensions as the main block of Craig Castle (S), also attributed to the Conns. It rises through three main storeys, its walls harled and its angles rounded. In the long S flank the round-headed doorway at ground floor near the W corner is protected by wide-mouthed shot-holes. The first-floor great hall is clearly expressed by two very tall windows, there being a set-off in the walls above the level of its vault (cf. Fedderate and Delgatie, qq.v.); then above the two second-floor windows rope mouldings, a corbel course and water cannon announce a parapet walk which runs on this side only in front of a crowstep-gabled caphouse with end stacks which contains an attic and garret, there being circular turrets at all four corners crowned by spirelets with a weathervane and spike finials. The parapet walk results in the end gables being slightly off-centre, the W gable having a string course linking its turrets. For some reason the NE turret's corbelling is simpler than the others, while the N elevation is severely plain.

At ground and first floors the walls are as much as 2 m. thick. The doorway opens into an entrance corridor with a turnpike stair 1.8 m. in diameter in the SW corner which as in all Conn houses ascends not just to the first floor but all the

*Although the *New Statistical Account* notes that the modernization was not completed at that time.

way up to the attic. The position of the stair here suggests that the plan of Udny was conceived with the possibility of extension into an L-plan by the addition of a SW jamb at a future date. The ground floor consists of a kitchen and two cellars, the larger one of which has a right-angled intramural stair in the NW corner rising to the 'low' end of the first-floor great hall. This is an impressive chamber, its vault rising 6 m. above floor level, with its 'high' end warmed not only by the kitchen beneath but by a large fireplace in the E wall. 'It is neatly floored, or rather pavemented, with oblong hexagonal granites, very neatly jointed' (*New Statistical Account*), and it has windows not only on the S but one each on the W and the N (cf. Tolquhon). Also at the high end, in the SE corner, is a small spiral stair rising to the second floor, which was originally a single chamber.

In 1874–6 the tower house became the dominant element of a large Scots Baronial house designed by *J. M. Wardrop* (of *Wardrop & Reid*) but his additions were demolished in 1964–7 and the original structure was restored by *Jock Lamb* of *George Bennett Mitchell & Son*. *H. M. Wardrop*'s Neo-Jacobean plasterwork (1886–7) in the great hall was retained. The STATUE of a Highlander standing in the gardens once surmounted the castle.

POLICIES. The castle is still surrounded by a fine Victorian parkland. The SOUTH LODGE is by *J. M. Wardrop*, c. 1875. Single-storey, three bays in snecked granite, its central doorway and r. bay window are sheltered under paired asymmetric bargeboarded gables, finely traceried with spike finials, while the l. bay is slightly set back. Tall paired square-shafted chimneystacks. GATEPIERS late C17–early C18 with pulvinated rustication, their ball-capped console crowns c. 1875. NORTH LODGE, probably by *H.M. Wardrop* c. 1886. Single-storey near-square plan with sophisticated asymmetrical elevations, tall roof with oversailing eaves. Doorway sheltered by a bracketed, spike-finialled gablet, living room with bay window and grid-pattern timber gables overlooking the drive and the main road.

ATHOLHILL, 850 m. NNW. A vernacular equivalent of the classic small Aberdeen villa of c. 1840. Single-storey three bays broad over a raised basement, built in pinned golden granite ashlar with a central splayed stairway rising to a transom-lit doorway; astragalled sash-and-case windows on each side, dormers in roof.

PITTRICHIE HOUSE, 2.5 km. WSW. For J.W. Mackenzie, dated 1818. Small country house, two-storey, three bays over a low raised basement, the central entrance bay slightly recessed. Coursed squared pale granite, formerly harled, with ashlar margins and first-floor band course. Projecting rear stair bay with gable and date-panel. Unroofed c. 1950, but its shell consolidated. The derelict HOME FARM STEADING is a single-storey symmetrical courtyard plan, with two-storey bothy centred in its E range. Armorial panel with motto *Invidos Virtute Torquebo*, dated 1823(?). – DOOCOT. c. 1823. Square, dark granite, two storeys of pointed arches with red voussoirs. Restoration of the house and most of its outbuildings is proposed by the *Voigt Design Partnership* in 2012.

UDNY STATION, 3.5 km. SE, is a small village which began to develop after the Formartine & Buchan Railway opened a station in 1861; much of it was built by James Rollo Duncan of Tillycorthie (q.v.) in the early C20.

TILLERY HOUSE. *See* p. 397.

TILLYCORTHIE CASTLE. *See* p. 397.

6060 WHITEHILLS B

A Banffshire fishing village first recorded in 1624, but much extended with long straight streets during the C19 and with council housing in the mid C20.

Former METHODIST CHAPEL, Chapel Street. Dated 1840. Small preaching-box with round-arched windows and oculi in the end gables. E porch appears late C19, W porch mid-C20. Now domestic, good replacement glazing which replicates the original Y-tracery.

ST BRANDON'S CHURCH CENTRE, Seafield Street. A mission hall for Boyndie Parish Church (q.v.), 1900–1. Four round-arched key-blocked windows set in dressed surrounds. Smaller session-house wing against S gable.

WHITEHILLS PARISH CHURCH, Seafield Street. Originally built as Trinity United Presbyterian Church, Banff (by *Alexander Ross*, 1879–80) but taken down stone by stone and rebuilt here for the United Free Church in 1925–6. Gothic, a simple rectangular plan orientated N–S with steeply pitched roof, SE porch and an unusual pencil turret broached from an octagon to a cylindrical top with a conical spirelet. Boldly sculpted capitals to the moulded pointed-arch doorway; five lancets with quatrefoils in the heads along the E front. Large Geometric S window and smaller N one, a cusped spherical triangle. Broad, open, orderly interior, with a lofty kingpost roof supported on arch-braced pine trusses which spring from the side-walls above corbels and spandrels. Platform PULPIT at the N end with trefoil panelling and a canted front, side-stair with arcaded balustrading; the minister's seat is set against the pulpit back which rises into a cusped and canopied backboard. – FONT from Boyndie Parish Church (q.v.), an octagonal basin lettered around its top and quatrefoiled in alternate sides, rising from a buttressed stand. – STAINED GLASS. Two Pre-Raphaelite designs of 1939, the Good Samaritan and the Sower by *James Nicol* of *George Donald & Sons*. – Also, a semi-abstract Christ Saving a Drowning Sailor, *c.* 1970.

BLACKPOTS HARBOUR, Harbour Place. Late C18 rubble pier, sea-wall and quayside. Once associated with a substantial brick and tile works founded in 1766 of which only a house built for the proprietor, Dr Saunders, in 1788 still survives.

HARBOUR with LIGHTHOUSE, Harbour Place. Built in concrete by *D. & C. Stevenson* in 1900 to supplement the Old Harbour in Low Shore (now infilled) which had become too shallow for the new fishing vessels introduced at that time. Divided into two basins in 1952. LIFEBOAT-HOUSE, 1933; closed 1969.

PUBLIC HALL, Reidhaven Street. By *D. & J.R. McMillan*, 1910–11. Very simple Scots Renaissance. Crowstep-gabled front, built in snecked squared whinstone with five tall slim windows in lighter dressed surrounds, small porch in flank.

WAR MEMORIAL, Seafield Street. Granite obelisk by *Malcolm Sinclair McCallum*, architect to the Seafield Estate, with red sandstone reliefs of a soldier and sailor by *J. W. George*. Erected *c.* 1920.

DESCRIPTION. The fine sweep of Whitehills Bay endows the SEATOWN – the historic heart of the village – with considerable picturesque quality. The fisher-cottages of West End extending round into Low Shore mostly face with their gables to the sea in the traditional fashion, single-storey and attic occasionally rising to two storeys, and tightly packed with their three-bay entrance fronts facing close into each other for protection against the storm and the chill, though often they have small gardens. Nearly all of them were built during the early to mid C19, and many have been altered or enlarged since. Towards the E end of Low Shore in particular, where the curve of the coast allows, two houses are often arranged one behind the other.

A fish factory stands on the site of the Old Harbour, infilled *c.* 1960; directly opposite is the Seafield Estate's GRANARY AND WAREHOUSE, built during the late C18 or early C19, absolutely simple and yet nevertheless impressive. It is three-storey and attic, seven bays broad in pinned random rubble with a central doorway, its attic floor's oblong windows brushing the eaves of a piended roof. Very deep on plan, it is embedded into the slope with Seafield Street running behind it giving direct access to the first floor.

Between Low Shore and Seafield Street, the little cottages around THE BRAEHEADS and SEAFIELD PLACE are similar in character to those near the waterfront but are arranged in quite irregular fashion, forming a maze of alleyways and paths. Perhaps the prettiest house in Whitehills is No. 22 SEAFIELD STREET – a two-storey three-bay main block in random rubble formerly harled, doorway and windows in slim dressed surrounds and a gabled roof with end stacks. It was built in 1794 with its single-storey S wing probably once balanced by another wing on the N. Among the low stone cottages in Knock Street, KNOCK HOUSE is of 1825, two storeys, three bays, flanked by single-storey piend-roofed pavilion wings slightly projecting. It has been altered with asymmetric fenestration on the ground floor and entrances in the pavilions, that on the r. now blocked. Its principal elevation faces S to the rear.

MILL OF BOYNDIE, 1.6 km. SE. Former mill house. Broad two-storey three-bay frontage of 1809, built in rubble originally harled. Central doorway with elegant transom-light and console-cornice, astragalled windows in slim surrounds. Gabled roof with moulded skewputts (that on the W dated) and coped chimneystacks. The large wing projecting from the rear elevation was an C18 house, two storeys but much lower than the 1809 block with a tall hipped roof. Interior with a small stair hall containing a round-arched recess for a grandfather clock.

7030

WOODHEAD

Woodhead was erected into a burgh of barony *c.* 1671–3 for the 3rd Earl of Dunfermline, challenging the importance of Fyvie (q.v.) as a market town until *c.* 1860 when the railway established stations at Fyvie and Rothienorman (qq.v.). The site of its tolbooth is now occupied by a farmhouse which may reuse some of its masonry, or masonry from Gight Castle (q.v.); the market cross was rebuilt in 1846.

ALL SAINTS (Episcopal). The seat of a congregation formed shortly after the Revolution of 1688. Tractarian E.E. Four-bay nave with slightly lower chancel and S entrance porch, built to designs by *John Henderson* in 1848–9, the tower and spire a neat addition raised up from the vestry annexe on the N by *James Matthews* in 1870. The site was given by the 4th Earl of Aberdeen and Queen Adelaide was among the donors to the original building fund. Attractive masonry, thin blue rag rubble with red Dalgetie sandstone dressings and margins, roofs steeply pitched. Nave lit by paired lancets with hoodmoulds, its bays divided by stepped buttresses with those at the W end splayed. Early Dec two-light W window. The chancel is narrower than the nave, with only a slightly lower wall-head, but a rather lower roof ridge. Triple lancets at its E gable, with trefoil roundel over. Chancel flanks each with a single light; in the angle between the nave and chancel on the S is a quarter-drum which contains the pulpit stair, and on the N a lean-to porch giving entry to the tower. The tower has a single diagonal buttress and large louvred two-light openings with hoodmoulds at the belfry stage; it rises into a tall broach spire with bands of lighter-coloured slates and a crucifix finial. FRAGMENTS. E wall. Three consecration crosses believed to derive from St Mary's Priory, Fyvie; so too the stone set in the porch's gable, and the finial in a niche within the tower.

Inside, the nave is very simple but of great presence, its roof trusses left exposed. There is a single step to the chancel, which is floored with encaustic tiles and has a dark blue ceiling with gold stars. Fine Gothic ALTAR RAILS, ALTAR and REREDOS carved with Our Lord and the Evangelists which looks *c.* 1900.

– PULPIT. Polygonal, its deep corbelled base supported from beneath by a slim iron rod. – FONT. In Peterhead granite. A cylindrical basin supported on clustered columns, by *MacDonald & Leslie* of Aberdeen, presented with other gifts by the Hon. Archibald Gordon, the 4th Earl's son. – ORGAN. Pinnacled Gothic case by *David Hamilton* of Edinburgh, 1850. Removed from the N recess to the W end *c.* 2007. – STAINED GLASS. W window of 1851: 'I am the Good Shepherd' and 'Feed My Lambs, Feed My Sheep'. – In the S wall, also 1851, 'Feeding the Hungry', 'Clothing the Naked', 'Moses Collecting Gifts for the Tabernacle' and 'Solomon Dedicating the Temple'. – Nave's NW window, 1911 by *Douglas Strachan,* taking as its theme The Glory of Our Lord. – Chancel window of 1873–4 by *J. Powell & Sons.* In the centre the Crucifixion and Our Lord Appearing After the Resurrection; sidelights of the Holy Family and Our Lord Baptized by St John, and the Sermon on the Mount (?) and Our Lord Healing the Sick.

CHURCHYARD approached through a simple but distinctive GATEWAY, with round-headed arch on marble columns. It came from Kingsford House (S) in 1922.

CHURCH HALL by *William Clarke*, 1892. A long single-storey three-bay structure, thin rag rubble with red sandstone dressings like the church. Doorway (now altered) at the N end of the W flank, windows mullioned and transomed with leaded and coloured lights. Small bargeboarded lucarnes in roof, end stacks with simple copings.

Former RECTORY. Built 1876. Two-storey front with projecting gable on r. and porch within the angle, gableted dormers. Built of thin rag rubble and red sandstone dressings like the church and hall.

Former FREE CHURCH MANSE. By *James Henderson*, 1844–5. A well-detailed house, two storeys, three bays broad, doorway with console-cornice and windows with refined glazing with slim margin panes. The gabled stair bay which rises above the rear wall-head to give access to the attic is lit by a round-headed window and dated 1844. Internally, the walls were painted so as to suggest dadoes with marble panelling and construction in massive blocks of ashlar – this *trompe l'œil* is preserved under the present decoration.

YTHAN LODGE *see* NEWBURGH

YTHSIE *see* TARVES

MORAY

BY MATTHEW WOODWORTH

The landscape, geology and building stones of Moray are covered on pages 2–9. For the archaeological record see pages 9–21.

CHURCHES

The limited evidence of Early Christian monuments in the north-
east has been discussed on p. 20, and so this introduction begins
with the MEDIEVAL CHURCHES. In stark contrast to North
Aberdeenshire, Moray boasts an extraordinary collection of
ecclesiastical buildings dating from the late Middle Ages.
Although most are ruinous, the quality of the remains is unparal-
leled in north Scotland, and seldom found north of the Borders,
Edinburgh and Glasgow. The episcopal see of Moray was founded
c. 1107 and its first cathedral church (now a parish church) built
at Birnie *c.* 1120. It is the only extant Romanesque building in 12
the entire region covered by this volume. Although heavily
restored, much of the masonry is *in situ* from the early to mid
C12, including two original E windows and a fine double-order
chancel arch with engaged columns and scallop capitals. Of the
small cathedrals which succeeded Birnie at Kinneddar and
Spynie, there is now nothing to see above ground. When the see
was finally settled at Elgin in 1224, a new CATHEDRAL was built
on an exponentially greater scale – in terms of both size and
architectural splendour. Even in its ruined state, Elgin Cathedral 14, 15
is the most important ecclesiastical monument in the north-east
of Scotland. It was constructed in three principal campaigns
stretching well into the C15, serving as an unmistakable pronouncement of the diocese's ever-increasing power and wealth.

Of the first phase of building, little remains except the long N wall of the choir (now solid, but originally pierced with windows) and the S transept façade with its gabled doorway and two tiers of tall windows. The lower level of the latter is pointed while the upper ones are round – a good reminder that medieval architects continued to flout tidy taxonomies of 'Romanesque' and 'Gothic' well into the C13. The surviving arcade responds and clearstorey jambs in the W nave show that the building featured a two-storey elevation from the start, making it one of the earliest – and very possibly the first – major Scottish church to abandon the use of false galleries or triforia. Even more precocious was the building's original complement of three tall towers, one over the crossing (collapsed in 1711) and two framing its broad symmetrical W façade. Among competing cathedrals, only Aberdeen and Glasgow could match Elgin's prototypically 'Gothic' triple-towered silhouette, and neither one achieved it until much later.

A fire in 1270 caused extensive damage and the cathedral was greatly increased in size. Dating from this second campaign is the stately E front with its two tiers of five lancets, an austerely elegant solution to the perennial problem of designing E.E. cliff-like façades. The lower row of windows was originally pierced by a plain sub-arch and unfoiled circlet – a simple effect, but nevertheless one of the earliest documented uses in Scotland of BAR TRACERY, which appeared around the same time at Pluscarden and Sweetheart Abbey (Dumfries and Galloway). Even more remarkable was the addition of a second aisle to the nave, creating a five-aisled structure W of the crossing – a highly unusual arrangement in the British Isles, and the closest that Scotland ever came to the Constantinian ideal of the early Christian basilica. Also added after 1270 was the grand new doorway in the W façade, again the most ambitious church entrance built in Scotland during the C13. The jambs feature a profusion of shafts and the arch hollows are carved with dog-tooth and trails of stiff-leaf. Another campaign of building, much protracted, began after an attack by the notorious 'Wolf of Badenoch' in 1390, and at least two of the windows of the S nave aisle were remodelled and topped by lateral gables – nice bits of Rayonnant cosmopolitanism.

MONASTIC FOUNDATIONS in Moray were not large in number but their remains are significant. The earliest foundation, Urquhart Priory, was established by David I for the Benedictines *c.* 1124 and was a dependency of Dunfermline Abbey (now no trace above ground). The major monument of the Cistercian
19 Order is Kinloss Abbey, founded by David in 1150 but now represented only by fragmentary remains of the late C12 and early C13. The plan of the building is anomalous, its E end in the form of a squat two-bay outshot flanked by vaulted aisles. This makes Kinloss one of only two Cistercian buildings in Scotland that eschewed the classic 'Bernardine' layout exported from Cîteaux in the mid C12. The only real survival of the abbey church is the former E chapel off the S transept, its rib-vault carried on waterholding bases and attenuated, very French-looking bell capitals.

The typical form of Cistercian church – a cruciform plan with
13 aisle chapels to the transepts – is found at Pluscarden Abbey (formerly Priory), founded *c.* 1230 by Alexander II and occupied by the little-known Valliscaulian Order which followed

predominantly Cistercian (and some Carthusian) rules. The transepts were built first, the elevation again two-storeyed and the terminal N façade with two rows of long lancets below a colossal oculus for a rose window. It was likely built just after Elgin's S transept façade but before its new E end, and so the combination of the three nicely show the development of FAÇADE DESIGN in Moray throughout the C13. The E arm at Pluscarden dates from *c.* 1270 – roughly coeval with the second campaign at Elgin – and in its original state was extremely luminous, with vast, curtain-like walls of glass. These were disappointingly filled in in the late C15 after the Priory had been united with Urquhart and placed under Benedictine rule. Enough survives, however, to know that the original geometric TRACERY pattern had been of the type first produced at Westminster Abbey in the mid to late 1240s, and which can still be seen in one bay of the S choir aisle at Glasgow. The central vessel of the choir at Pluscarden was originally vaulted in stone, likely in tierceron pattern, although this was removed in the late C15. Not even Elgin could boast this kind of luxury, as the cathedral's choir and nave were covered by segmental wooden ceilings.*

The former Greyfriars convent at Elgin is yet another monument of national significance, and one of the most complete examples of MENDICANT ARCHITECTURE in Scotland. The building was constructed in the late C15 as an Observant Franciscan friary and much of the masonry is intact despite heavy restoration at the end of the C19. As was typical of late medieval mendicant buildings, the abbey church was a simple aisleless rectangle built of rubble, nave and chancel in one with only a single buttress to demarcate them externally. The N side had five Y-tracery windows and there was another on the S; the E and W gables had four lights of intersecting tracery. Of the Dominican Friary at Elgin (established by Alexander II in 1233–4 and dedicated to St James), nothing survives above ground.

The selection of CONVENTUAL BUILDINGS in Moray is nearly as fine, although again only fragments remain. In the S transept at Pluscarden, the stone flight of night stairs remains *in situ* from *c.* 1230, a very rare survival in Britain (see also Hexham Abbey, Northumberland). Just beyond them lies the former sacristy, now used as a Lady Chapel and screened off from the S transept chapel by a large arch looking like a mega-sized squint. The chapter house features an impressive entrance with a round-headed arch subdivided by a trumeau and flanking Y-tracery windows. The main chamber inside is a four-part square on the 17
usual Cistercian model with a free-standing pier in the centre, the capitals of the major shafts deleted so that they sweep out to form the ribs of cell vaults. It is an early (again *c.* 1230) example of uninterrupted vault springing. The former day room has six rib-vaulted compartments carried on octagonal piers, again

*Although the new aisles added to Elgin after 1270 likely had tierceron vaults of stone.

without capitals. At Kinloss, the former sacristy/library remains attached to the S transeptal chapel, while the former abbot's cell is stacked on top of it. It features an octopartite rib-vault carried on more bell capitals (one of them still partially scalloped). In the S arm of the cloister is the former refectory entrance, its decoration still a hybrid of the C12 and C13 – a wide, round-headed arch with deeply undercut, hyphenated half-chevron and dog-tooth hoodmould over spool-capitaled shafts. The finest precinct survival is the chapter house at Elgin, added to the N choir aisle after the fire of 1270. It is octagonal in plan, built on the centralized model of the English secular cathedrals (e.g. Lincoln, Salisbury, Wells, London, York and Hereford). The interior was
20 almost completely refaced by Bishop Andrew Stewart (1482–1501), who added the central pier with its sixteen sprouting ribs and fine tierceron vault with concentric ridge rib. The original tracery of *c.* 1270 was also replaced in the late C15, given a nice selection of inventive curvilinear Dec patterns.

The medieval PARISH CHURCHES of Moray were much more modest. The locations, dates and dedications of many are known, although only a handful have survived, along with minor wall fragments in some of the burial grounds. A good number of these churches were established in the mid C12, when the foundation of the cathedral at Birnie prompted the creation of recognizably modern parish boundaries, many of them still in use today. More churches date from the early to mid C13, their proceeds collated to fund the dignitaries and clergy of Elgin Cathedral. The late C13 former church at Altyre is a good example of the GOTHIC PERIOD – a small, unassuming gabled box with lancet windows (the E one formerly with elementary Y-tracery). Even in its roofless state, Altyre remains the best indication of what a typical rural church in Moray would have looked like during the Middle Ages. The church of Mortlach, just outside Dufftown, is more impressive, its core composed of an aisleless rectangle dating from the early to mid C13. A similar chapel was built at Cullen in the early C13 and given a new S aisle *c.* 1536, originally built as a chaplainry for St Anne and then reformed as a collegiate church in 1543. The ruined church at Kirktown of Deskford is another simple, gabled box, rebuilt
21 *c.* 1538 on the site of an earlier and smaller chapel. At St Peter's Church, just outside Duffus, the base of a medieval tower (likely early C14) and a S porch built in 1524 were retained when the church was rebuilt in 1730–2.

Because so many of the medieval churches are ruinous or destroyed, good medieval LITURGICAL FURNISHINGS in Moray are rare. The four-seat sedilia at Elgin date from the late C13 but are now missing their original arcaded screen and micro-architectural canopies. The lectern of the chapter house (still embedded in the central pier, again a rare survival) dates from the late C15 and is carved with worn, proto-Rubenesque angels. Moray also boasts two excellent SACRAMENT HOUSES of national importance, both provided by Alexander Ogilvy and Elizabeth Gordon (then of Findlater Castle; see also their tomb below) in the mid C16. The first is at Cullen and features an aumbry set within an ogee arch studded with stylized crockets. Above it, a levitating pair of angels display an elaborate monstrance with good Gothic micro-architectural detailing. The sacrament house at Kirktown of Deskford (a chapel to Cullen) is even finer, dated 1551 and certainly the work of the same team of sculptors. Trailing grapevines, inscriptions and heraldic shields are rendered with robust sensitivity, and all of the carving is in a remarkable state of preservation. The wings of the upper angels unfurl in sweeping hieratic curves, and their cinctures appear to flutter in the breeze as they make their earthly descent. A third (and reconstructed) sacrament house survives in the chancel at Pluscarden, again mid C16, but smaller and less impressive. Pluscarden also retains scant remains of WALL PAINTINGS, now very faded but still valuable as some of the only survival of architectural polychromy in north Scotland.

Elgin boasts the largest collection of MEDIEVAL MONUMENTS in any Scottish cathedral, and many of them are of excellent quality. The tomb-recess in the presbytery, likely made for Bishop Archibald (1253–98), consists of a gabled, cinquefoiled arch that probably also doubled as an Easter Sepulchre. The screen-like former tomb of Bishop Andrew Stewart (1482–1501) featured a passageway between aisle and main vessel, inserted between two piers in the usual Perp fashion. The memorial to Bishop John Winchester (1436–1460) is a crocketed ogee arch with delicate cusping and sub-cusping, and its intrados retains its original underpainting of angels tending to the bishop's soul. The design was soon adopted as an exemplar of high status, including the tomb in the S transept (likely made for Bishop David Stewart, 1462–76) and another at Fordyce (Aberdeenshire, p. 181), built for Sir James Ogilvy of Deskford (†1509). The final successor to the 'Winchester tradition' is the monument at Cullen to Alexander Ogilvy of Findlater (†1554) and his wife, 24
Elizabeth Gordon, which is once again a memorial of national quality. Its long ogee arch is cusped, sub-cusped and extravagantly crocketed; more precociously, the spandrels are filled with roundels containing full-length donor portraits, tell-tale signs of the approaching Renaissance. More unusual at Elgin is the monument to Bishop William Tulloch (1477–82), consisting of a four-centred arch (rare in Scotland) and spandrels nicely studded with trilobes set in spherical triangles. The headless figure of a kneeling bishop in the cathedral's S nave aisle may have come from the tomb of John de Innes (1407–14), and the two huge fragments flanking it (one of a bishop and the other a knight) probably come from the destroyed central tower which Innes had rebuilt. Their reverse foreshortening was meant to correct for perspective when seen from far below.

Most of the cathedral's tomb-recesses contain EFFIGIES, although some are unidentifiable or have been moved from their original locations. The finest is the wisp-waisted William de la Hay of Lochloy (†1422), his metal belt and buckle rendered with geometric precision. Another is Alexander Gordon, 1st Earl of

Huntly (†1470), raised up on a tomb-chest and shown, quite unusually, in civilian dress rather than armour. The fine mid- to late C16 effigy at Cullen, likely depicting John Duff of Muldavit, is similar; and the good effigy at Mortlach, likely depicting Alexander Leslie of Kininvie (†*c.* 1549), reverts to conventional armour. Also medieval is the stone effigy at Lhanbryde burial ground, a type rarely encountered outside of a cathedral or monastic context. It likely commemorates Robert Innes of Innermarkie (†1547), who is depicted in full armour with hands clasped in prayer and a sword by his side.

The N transept of Pluscarden features a good collection of incised medieval SLABS, and a few others are scattered around the county's churches. Mortlach contains a ledger slab for John Gordon of Broadland †1533, its enormous round cross-head decorated with big split petals. At Cullen, a slab for Alexander Innes dates from the early C15, finely carved but now very worn. The earliest memorials in GRAVEYARDS are the four COFFIN STONES at Spynie burial ground (likely C13), their blocky solidity enlivened by faded roundels of stiff-leaf foliage.* Nearby are two slabs decorated with a Jerusalem cross and sword, rare survivals from the late Middle Ages, and demonstrating the kind of unpretentious, lower-cost memorials that would have been ubiquitous before the Reformation. Also at Spynie is a CONSECRATION CROSS of *c.* 1208, the only evidence of the now-vanished church's short-lived elevation to cathedral status (rescinded in 1224). The sculpture likely owes its survival to reuse as the top of a mercat cross in the mid C15.

No medieval STAINED GLASS has survived in Moray except for isolated fragments. The only important ARCHITECTURAL SCULPTURES are the two Dec niches now on the flanks of the mausoleum at Inveravon, likely carved in the C15 and re-set here by *William Robertson* in 1829. They are a very late – and a very sensitive – appearance of medieval *spolia*.

Churches from the Reformation to the present

In August 1560, the Scottish Parliament officially rejected papal authority and outlawed the celebration of the mass, instead adopting the Calvinist confession of faith. The collegiate and monastic establishments were disbanded, and Elgin Cathedral, Kinloss Abbey and Pluscarden Priory gradually succumbed to ruin.‡ The medieval parish churches remained in use throughout the rest of Moray, although stripped of their 'Popish accoutrements' and adapted for profound liturgical and spiritual changes.

*Several of these burial grounds are of great antiquity. Those at Dipple (Mosstodloch) and Essil (Garmouth) are roughly circular in shape and St Andrews, Kirkhill (Lhanbryde), is polygonal – tell-tale indications of early Christian occupation in Pictland. The churchyard at Dundurcas (Rothes) is also raised and features a ditch to one side, indicating that it probably served as an Iron Age fortification.

‡Elgin's local congregation moved to St Giles on the High Street, and the former chapter house at Kinloss was fitted up for parochial use.

. Spey Valley (M), aerial view looking south (p. 1)

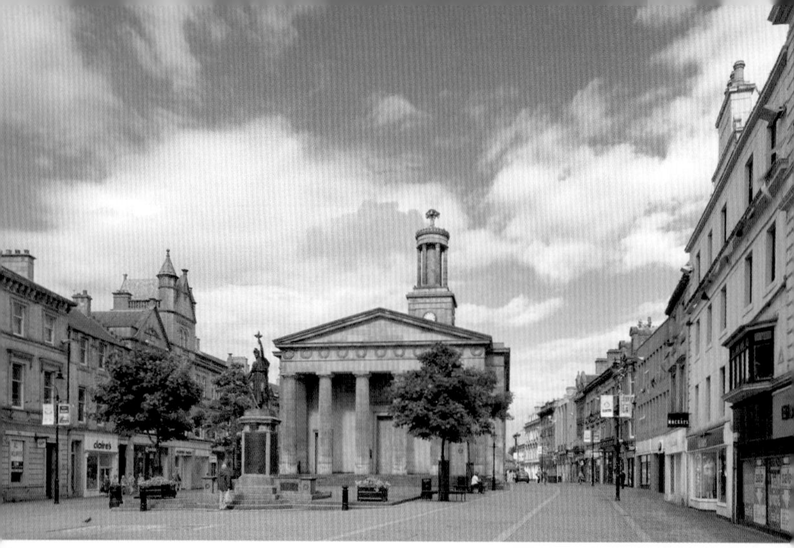

TURRIFF
McRAE

2. Elgin (M), High Street, view from W (p. 593)
3. Turriff (A), High Street, view from E (p. 411)
4. Macduff (A), Shore Street and harbour, view from W (pp. 283, 282)
5. Crovie (A), view from S (p. 143)
6. Chapeltown of Glenlivet (M), Scalan College, 1767 and 1788 (p. 502)

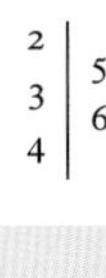

7. Kirkton of Bourtie (A), Barra Hill, hill-fort, Iron Age (p. 267)
8. Daviot (A), Loanhead of Daviot, stone circle, Later Neolithic or Early Bronze Age (*c.* 2600–2000 BC) (p. 153)
9. Brodie Castle (M), Rodney's Stone, Pictish (p. 486)
10. Burghead (M), well, probably Pictish (p. 494)
11. Burghead (M), incised carving of bull, Pictish (p. 494)

7	9 10
8	11

12. Birnie (M), parish church, chancel arch, *c.* 1120 (p. 477)
13. Pluscarden Abbey (M), E limb from SE, *c.* 1230 (p. 717)
14. Elgin (M), Cathedral, W front, *c.* 1230 and post-1270 (p. 575)
15. Elgin (M), Cathedral, E limb from SE, mostly post-1270 (p. 566)

12	14
13	15

16. Rattray (A), St Mary's Chapel, early C13 (p. 374)
17. Pluscarden Abbey (M), chapter house, interior, *c.* 1225–50 (p. 721)
18. Old Deer (A), Deer Abbey, aerial view from SW, C13 (p. 312)
19. Kinloss (M), Kinloss Abbey, view from SW, late C12 to early C13 (p. 672)

16	18
17	19

20. Elgin (M), Cathedral, chapter house, interior, late C15 (p. 569)
21. Duffus (M), former St Peter's Church, view from SW, tower base C14, porch 1524, nave 1730–2 (p. 551)
22. Turriff (A), St Congan's Old Church, view from SE, possibly begun in the C13, choir earlier C16, bellcote 1635 (p. 407)

20 | 21
22

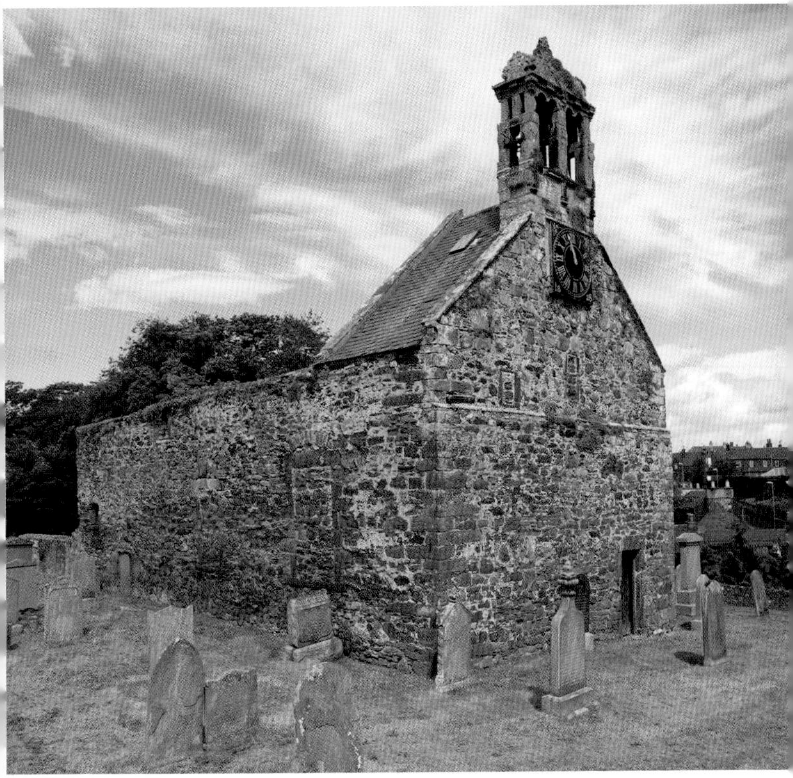

23. Fordyce (A), Old Church, effigy of James Ogilvy, †1509 (p. 181)
24. Cullen (M), Cullen Old Church, monument to Alexander Ogilvy of Findlater, †1554 (p. 518)
25. Tarves (A), parish church, Tolquhon Aisle, monument to William Forbes and Elizabeth Gordon, 1589 (p. 394)
26. Cullen (M), Cullen Old Church, Seafield Loft, *c.* 1602–8 (p. 517)

23 | 25
24 | 26

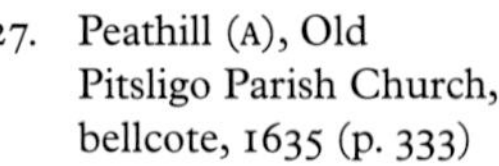

27. Peathill (A), Old Pitsligo Parish Church, bellcote, 1635 (p. 333)
28. Peathill (A), former Pitsligo New Parish Church, Laird's Pew, 1634 (p. 334)
29. Elgin (M), St Columba, pulpit, 1684 (p. 586)
30. Dufftown (M), Mortlach Parish Church, monument to Alexander Duff and Helen Grant, by John Faid, 1694 (p. 544)

27 | 29
28 | 30

31. Marnoch (A), St Marnoch's Old Church, Meldrum Enclosure, monument to Bishop George Meldrum of Crombie, 1699 (p. 286)
32. Gordonstoun (M), Michael Kirk, W window, 1705 (p. 652)
33. Fochabers (M), Bellie Parish Church, by John Baxter, 1795–8 (p. 616)

31 | 32 / 33

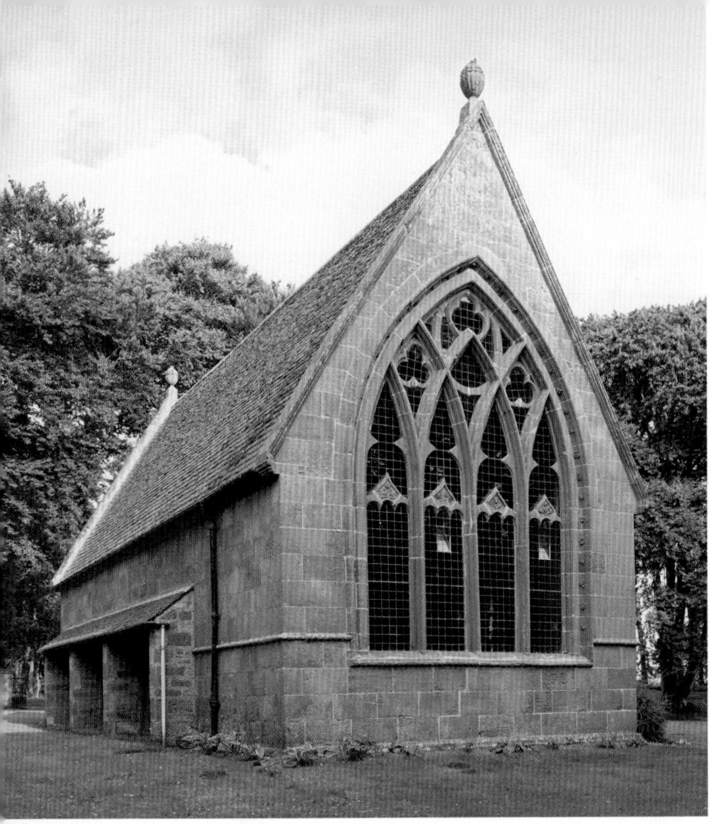

Banff (A), St Mary, W tower, 1789–90 and 1849 (p. 80)

Keith (M), St Thomas (R.C.), 1830–1 by William Robertson, dome by C. J. Ménart, 1916 (p. 665)

Elgin (M), St Giles, by Archibald Simpson, 1825–8 (p. 586)

Keith (M), St Rufus, by J. Gillespie Graham, 1816–19 (p. 665)

34 | 36
35 | 37

38. Forres (M), St John (Episcopal), by Thomas Mackenzie, 1842–4 (p. 631)

39. Aberchirder (A), Marnoch New Parish Church, by James Henderson, 1841–2 (p. 63)

40. Longside (A), St John (Episcopal), 1853–4, by William Hay (p. 273)

41. Elgin (M), former South Free Church, by A. & W. Reid, 1852–4 (p. 585)

38 | 40
39 | 41

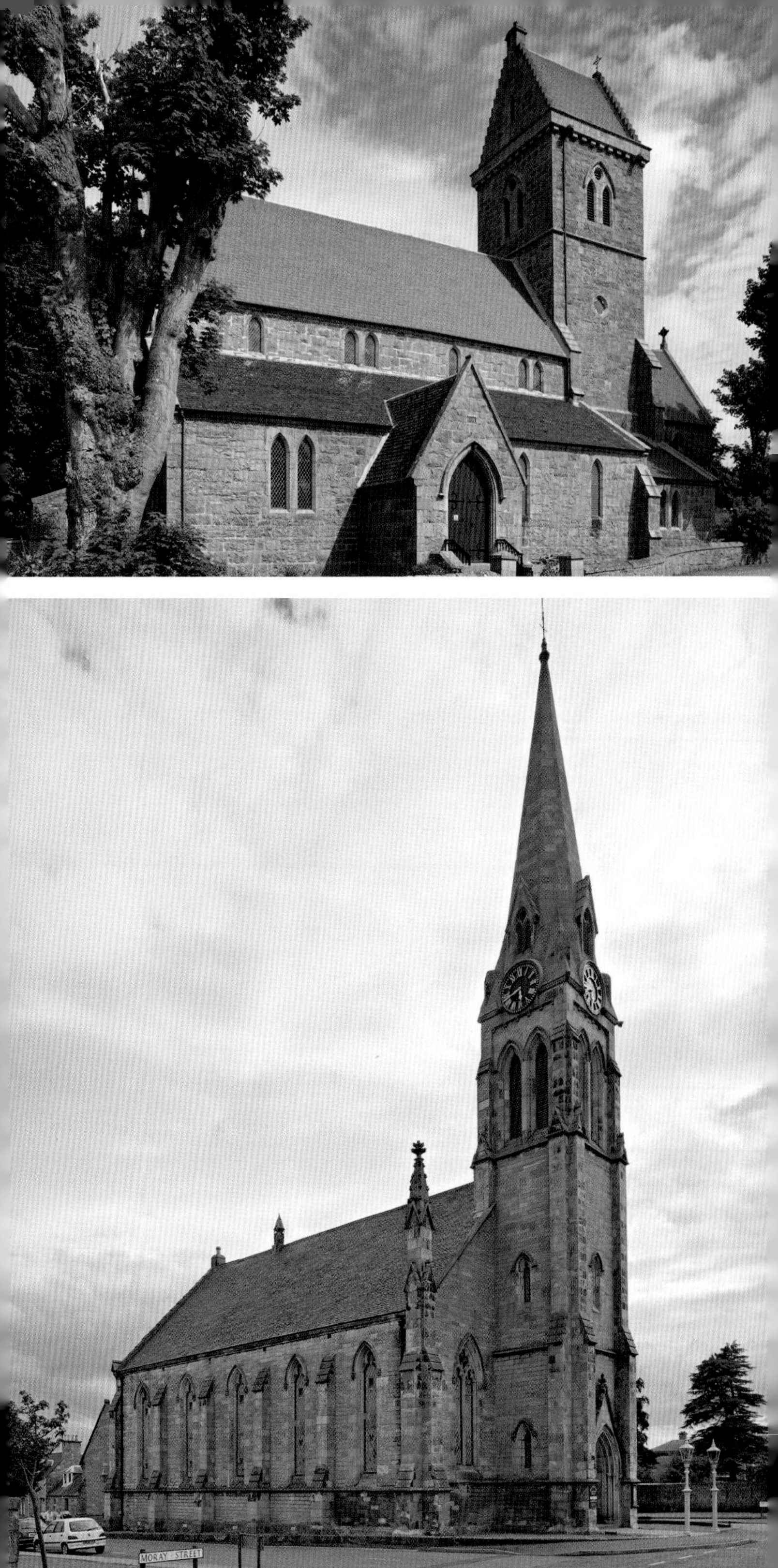
MORAY STREET

42. Ellon (A), St Mary on the Rock (Episcopal), by G. E. Street, 1870–1 (p. 168)
43. Charlestown of Aberlour (M), St Margaret (Episcopal), nave looking E, by Alexander Ross, 1874–9 (p. 503)
44. Fraserburgh (A), Fraserburgh South Church, by J. B. Pirie, 1878–80 (p. 195)

45. Fraserburgh (A), St Peter (Episcopal), by John Kinross and H. M. Nisbett, 1891–3, tower 1909 (p. 194)
46. Chapeltown of Glenlivet (M), Our Lady of Perpetual Succour (R.C.), interior, by John Kinross, 1896–7 (p. 501)
47. Forres (M), St Laurence, by John Robertson, 1902–6 (p. 631)
48. Lossiemouth (M), St Gerardine's High Church, by J. J. Burnet, 1899–1903 (p. 693)

45	47
46	48

49. Fraserburgh (A), Old Parish Church, E window, stained glass, by Douglas Strachan, 1906 (p. 194)
50. Fochabers (M), Gordon Chapel, stained glass, The Crucifixion, detail, by E. Burne-Jones of Morris & Co., 1876–7 (p. 619)
51. Pluscarden Abbey (M), N transept E chapel, stained glass, detail, The Visitation, by Br. Gilbert Taylor, 1965 (p. 723)
52. Fyvie (A), parish church, E window, stained glass, by Louis Comfort Tiffany, 1902 (p. 214)
53. Gordonstoun (M), St Christopher's Chapel, Murray, Ward & Partners, 1965–7 (p. 651)

49 | 52
50 51 | 53

54. Duffus Castle (M), aerial view, mid-C12 motte and early C14 keep (p. 553)
55. Darnaway Castle (M), Great Hall, roof, 1387–8 (p. 535)
56. Spynie (M), Spynie Palace, late C14–late C15 (p. 741)
57. Dufftown (M), Balvenie Castle, aerial view, C13 enclosure with mid-C16 additions (p. 545)

54	56
55	57

58. Auchindoun Castle (M), tower from SE (p. 468)
59. Ballindalloch Castle (M), view from SE, mid-C16 tower and S wing of 1718, altered by Mackenzie & Matthews, 1847–50 (p. 473)
60. Kinnairdy Castle (A), great hall, panelling, detail, 1493 (p. 261)
61. Delgatie Castle (A), Painted Chamber, ceiling, detail, late C16 (p. 159)

58 | 60
59 | 61

62. Delgatie Castle (A), tower house *c.* 1570, wings *c.* 1770 remodelled in early C19 (p. 153)
63. Tolquhon Castle (A), aerial view, by T. Leiper, 1584–9, tower house *c.* 1400 (p. 398)
64. Fordyce (A), Fordyce Castle, 1592, wing added *c.* 1700 (p. 182)
65. Towie Barclay Castle (A), view from E, late C16, reconstructed by James Duncan, 1874 and J. Meldrum and W. Cowie, *c.* 1970–4 (p. 402)

62	64
63	65

66. Fyvie Castle (A), view from SW, *c.* 1200–*c.* 1900 (p. 217)
67. Craigston Castle (A), view from W, attributed to the Bell family, 1604–7 (p. 132)
68. Innes House (M), view from S, remodelled by William Ayton, *c.* 1640–53 (p. 658)
69. Craigston Castle (A), drawing room, detail of carved panels, probably early C17 (p. 136)

66	
67	69
68	

70. Brodie Castle (M), Blue Sitting Room, *c.* 1635–40 (p. 484)
71. Pitmedden (A), Pitmedden House, Great Garden, begun 1675, restored since 1952 (p. 360)
72. Gordonstoun (M), Round Square, *c.* 1690 (p. 651)
73. Gordonstoun (M), S front 1728–30, wings late C16 and early C17 (p. 649)

70 | 72
71 | 73

74. Brodie Castle (M), Dining Room ceiling, probably early C18 (p. 484)
75. Haddo House near Methlick (A), designed by William Adam, 1728; built with alterations by John Baxter, 1732–6 (p. 237)
76. Banff (A), Duff House, S front, by William Adam, 1735–9, stair *c.* 1760 (p. 9
77. Banff (A), Duff House, Private Dining Room, 1760–1 (p. 101)

78. Haddo House near Crimond (A), early C18 (p. 237)
79. Letterfourie House (M), S front, by Robert Adam, 1772–3 (p. 686)
80. Darnaway Castle (M), N front, by Alexander Laing, 1802–12 (p. 533)
81. Cairness House (A), by James Playfair, 1791–7 (p. 119)
82. Cairness House (A), Masonic Chamber, *c.* 1794–7 (p. 123)

78 79 80	81 82

83. Invererne House (M), S front, 1818 (p. 662)
84. Crimonmogate House (A), by Archibald Simpson, *c.* 1825, roof remodelled 1864 (p. 139)
85. Auchmacoy House (A), by William Burn, 1831–3 (p. 70)
86. Brodie Castle (M), S front, late C16, remodelled and extended by William Burn, *c.* 1824, and James Wylson, *c.* 1845–50 (p. 480)
87. Forglen House (A), by John Smith I, *c.* 1839–40 (p. 184)

83 84 85	86 87

88. Drummuir (M), Drummuir Castle, Entrance Hall, by Mackenzie & Matthews, 1846–9 (p. 539)
89. Arndilly House (M), *c.* 1770 with additions and alterations by Mackenzie & Matthews, 1850–1 (p. 467)
90. Esslemont House (A), by J. R. Mackenzie, 1865–6 (p. 175)
91. Haddo House near Methlick (A), Library, by Wright & Mansfield, *c.* 1878 (p. 242)

88 | 90
89 | 91

92. Dalvey House (M), Entrance Hall, by Peter Fulton, 1897–8 (p. 531)
93. Fyvie Castle (A), Gallery, by John Bryce, 1890s (p. 228)
94. Kellas (M), Kellas House, by F.W. Deas, 1913–21 (p. 670)
95. House of Formartine (A), by Robert Steedman (of Morris & Steedman), 1994–5 (p. 249)

92 | 94
93 | 95

96. Fraserburgh (A), Kinnaird Head, Lighthouse, tower 1570, light added 1787; present lantern *c.* 1830 (p. 199)
97. Gordonstoun (M), Ogstoun market cross, late C16 (p. 653)
98. Fraserburgh (A), market cross-head, probably 1746; replica of 1988 (p. 206)
99. Elgin (M), High Street, Braco's Banking House, 1694 (p. 597)

96 | 97 98
99

100	102
101	103

100. Banff (A), High Shore, No. 1, 1675; No. 3, 1740; Market Arms, late C17–C18 (p. 91)

101. Banff (A), Low Street, Town House by James Reid, 1795–1800, and tolbooth steeple by John Adam, 1764–7 (p. 89)

102. Fraserburgh (A), Dalrymple Street, World's End, *c.* 1767 (p. 209)

103. Banff (A), Duff House, Bridge of Alvah, 1771–3 (p. 104)

104. Banff (A), Banff Bridge, by John Smeaton, engineer, and James Robertson, master-mason, completed 1779, widened 1881 (p. 86)
105. Peterhead (A), Town House, by John Baxter, 1788 (p. 345)
106. Forres (M), Nelson's Tower, by Charles Stewart, 1806–12 (p. 635)
107. Craigellachie (M), Bridge, by Thomas Telford, 1812–15 (p. 514)

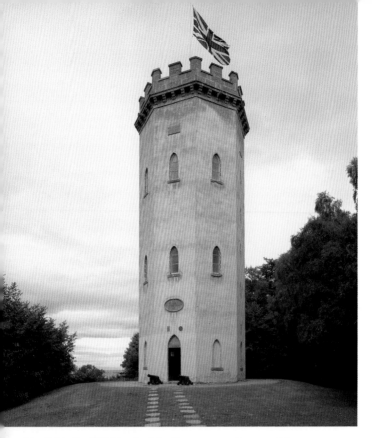

104 | 106
105 | 107

108. Elgin (M), Gray's Hospital, by J. Gillespie Graham, 1815–19 (p. 590)
109. Strichen (A), Town Hall, probably by John Smith I, 1816 (p. 387)
110. Cullen (M), Town Hall, by William Robertson, 1822, extension by J. Fowlie, 1899–1900 (p. 520)
111. Edinkillie (M), Edinkillie House, by John Paterson, 1822–3 (p. 561)

108 | 110
109 | 111

112. Elgin (M), Anderson's Institution, by Archibald Simpson, 1830–3 (p. 588)

113. Banff (A), Wilson's Institution, by William Robertson, 1836–8 (p. 85)

114. Banff (A), Low Street, Fife Arms, by Burn & Bryce, 1843–5 (p. 90)

115. Fochabers (M), Milne's Primary School, by Mackenzie & Matthews, 1845–6 (p. 620)

112 | 114
113 | 115

116. Lossiemouth (M), Covesea Skerries Lighthouse, by A. Stevenson, 1844–6 (p. 700)
117. Forres (M), Bank of Scotland, by Mackenzie & Matthews, 1852–3 (p. 638)
118. Banff (A), Chalmers' Hospital, by W. L. Moffat, *c.* 1860–6 (p. 83)
119. Banff (A), Sheriff Court, by J. Matthews and J. B. Pirie, 1868–71 (p. 84)

116 | 118
117 | 119

120. Forres (M), Falconer Museum, by A. & W. Reid, 1868–70 (p. 634)
121. Edinkillie (M), railway viaduct, by Joseph Mitchell, engineer, 1861–3 (p. 562)
122. Elgin (M), Mansion House Hotel, by A. & W. Reid, 1850–1, and William Kidner, 1882–3 (p. 607)
123. Elgin (M), Johnston's of Elgin, office and goods store, 1865 (p. 611)
124. Dallas Dhu Distillery (M), by Charles C. Doig, 1898–9 (p. 529)

120	122
121	123
	124

125. Macduff (A), Tarlair Swimming Pool, by John C. Miller, 1929–31 (p. 282)

126. Elgin (M), No. 31 Wittet Drive, by J. & W. Wittet, 1947 (p. 602)

127. Mulben (M), Auchroisk Distillery, by Westminster Design Associates, 1973–4 (p. 710)

128. Boddam (A), aerial view showing Buchanness Lighthouse, by R. Stevenson, 1825–7 and Peterhead Power Station, by Robert Matthew, Johnson-Marshall & Partners, 1973–80 (p. 111)

125 | 127
126 | 128

129. Fraserburgh (A), Museum of Scottish Lighthouses, by Morris & Steedman, 1995 (p. 200)

130. Alves (M), Roseisle Distillery, by Austin-Smith: Lord (ASL), 2007–9 (p. 466)

Stone altars were removed and replaced with wooden tables, while the new emphasis on preaching meant that the pulpit became the primary focus of the building, often placed in the centre of the long side. Surviving heritors' accounts show that the need to maintain these buildings was extremely onerous for local populations. Nearly every parish church underwent continual repair in the late C16 and C17, and a seemingly endless succession of falling walls, collapsed gables and un-thatched roofs shows that most of these buildings had outlived their usefulness several centuries before.

Nevertheless, owing to intense civic unrest and political and religious upheavals, few new churches were built in Moray in the SEVENTEENTH CENTURY. The only one to have survived is at Boharm burial ground (Craigellachie), built in 1618 and now in ruins. As elsewhere in Scotland, the most common survivals of the C17 are new aisles that were added to pre-existing medieval churches, usually at a ninety-degree angle to form the familiar capital T. These aisles were built either for increased accommodation or as combination lofts and burial vaults for the local scions of each parish. The later disappearance of the medieval section has often left the C17 aisles standing by themselves, their survival into the C21 guaranteed because they were used to display tombs and monuments (*see* below). The former S aisle in Rathven churchyard is *in situ* from 1612 (although heightened and vaulted in 1798), while the aisle at Botriphnie (built in 1617) is now much reduced in scale. Also of this date is the superb loft built for the Seafield family in 1602 at Cullen Old Church, its 26
square piers faced with reused pew-backs of the late C16 and early C17. Of similar quality is the pew-back now at Speymouth Parish Church (and originally from Dipple (Mosstodloch)), dated 1634 and in a wonderful state of preservation.

By the start of the C18, most of the medieval churches in Moray were beyond salvaging and had to be rebuilt completely. As a result, a surprisingly large number of churches date from the GEORGIAN PERIOD. Of the many that survive, seventeen were built in the form of a simple rubble rectangle, while three (Edinkillie, Rothes and Spynie) were laid out on a T-plan with projecting central aisle.* These buildings were stylistically austere but functionally elegant, the long elevations pierced with windows (usually round-headed but in four cases square or rectangular) and the short ends invariably gabled, one side often topped by a birdcage bellcote. Of the 'Georgian box' churches in Moray, the earliest are the ruinous St Peter outside Duffus (1730–2) and 21
Speymouth (1731–3); the finest are the church at Dyke (1781) and the disused one at Alves (1769–71). The old parish church at Kirkmichael (Tomintoul; originally 1804–7) and Rothiemay (1807) are also good examples. The latest one built was the church at Botriphnie (1816–20), showing that this intractable form survived well into the C19. The interiors of these churches

*Three others (Boharm, Kinloss and Speymouth) were originally rectangular but given aisles at a later date.

were originally laid out with the pulpit in the centre of the long side, an arrangement that has survived at six places: Botriphnie (Drummuir), Dyke, Edinkillie, Rothes, Speymouth (Mosstodloch) and Spynie. Fine furnishings of this period are rare, but the pulpit at Dyke (made 1780–1) is one of the very few triple-decker pulpits still remaining in Scotland.

A small number of Georgian churches were more creative and architecturally assertive, breaking free of standard parochial pat-
32 terns. The delightful Michael Kirk at Gordonstoun was originally built in 1705 as a mausoleum and despite much restoration is an extraordinarily early instance of the Gothic Revival – so very early, in fact, that it should probably be viewed instead as an extremely late seismic aftershock from the Middle Ages, i.e. a Gothic Survival. The E and W gables are filled with striking Dec tracery, and if the date were not documented no responsible scholar would ever assign them to the early C18. From the tail
33 end of the century is the grand Neoclassical Bellie Parish Church by *John Baxter* (1795–8), with its tall octagonal stone spire and tetrastyle, pedimented porch, all designed as the crowning jewel to the Duke of Gordon's planned town of Fochabers. As strange as it seems, this was very likely the largest, tallest church to have been built in Moray in the previous five centuries. In Elgin,
36 *Archibald Simpson*'s church of St Giles (1825–8) is the only large-scale example of the Greek Revival in the county, and is indeed a monument of national importance. Particularly inventive is Simpson's use of dual façades, the W with a mighty hexastyle Doric portico and the E topped by a copy of the Choragic monument of Lysicrates – a relatively common motif on British monuments but rarely seen on churches. The parish kirk at Tomintoul (1826–7) is far less grand, but notable as the only example in this volume of a Parliamentary church, the large Highland building programme executed under *Thomas Telford*.

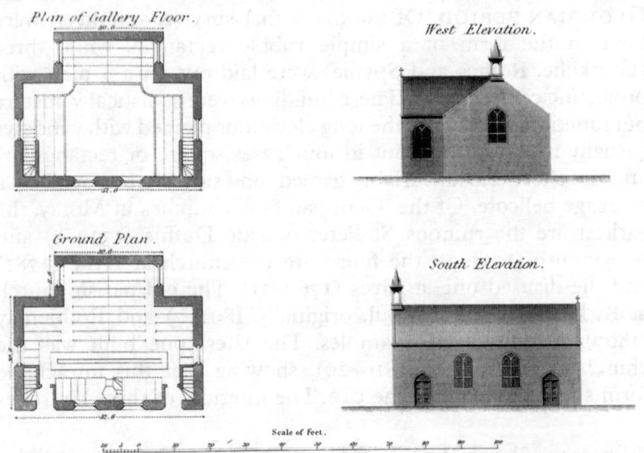

Highland church.
Model plans and elevations by G. Turnbull, 1838

In the early to mid C19, the coming GOTHIC REVIVAL is represented by three good churches in the Perpendicular style, two of them not surprisingly the work of *James Gillespie Graham*. The finest is St Rufus at Keith (1816–19), the proportions and 37 tracery convincing enough from a distance to appear genuinely medieval; his other church at Rafford (1824–6) is smaller but displays the same conviction. Another good stab at Perp is the old parish church at Urquhart (1842–3), a very early design by *Alexander Reid* of Elgin but much indebted to his famous uncle, *William Robertson*. The fine Episcopalian Gordon Chapel at Fochabers is again by *Archibald Simpson* (1832–4), and a very rare example of a church built as a two-storey structure – originally Romanesque on the bottom and E.E. on top.

The ROMAN CATHOLIC churches must be dealt with separately as they form a group of the highest national – and even international – importance. Moray can justly claim to be the staunchest 'hotbed' of Catholicism in Scotland, first in the turbulent decades after the Reformation and then again when the 'Popish scourge' was outlawed after the rebellions of 1715 and 1745. In contrast to the rest of the country, the Catholics of Moray were left in peace – partly owing to the county's relative insularity (both geographic and political) and partly owing to the tireless protection of the Gordon family. They were among the most steadfast Catholics in Great Britain, and none of the buildings described below could have been built without the Gordons' security. At Tynet, the little chapel of St Ninian was erected (or, more correctly, converted from a sheep barn) in 1755, making it the earliest surviving Catholic church built in Scotland after the Reformation. Its exterior is utterly plain and unassuming to avoid detection, while the interior remains one of the best-preserved clandestine churches in Britain. Of equal importance is the seminary tucked away at Scalan (*see* Chapeltown of Glenlivet), built 6 in 1767 to train priests and actively promulgate the outlawed faith. It succeeded a college founded by Bishop James Gordon as early as 1711.

The church of St Gregory, Preshome, then represents a giant leap forward, as it was the first post-Reformation building in Scotland that did not attempt to disguise its Catholic identity. The designer was Father *John Reid* and the church is very large – shockingly so, as it was built in 1788–9, four decades before Emancipation. Three more good churches were built in the 1820s, again preceding the Roman Catholic Relief Act of 1829. Their façades are to a similar design, first conceived by Rev. (and from 1828 Bishop) *James Kyle* and meant to signify a new, unified church for a more enlightened age. St Mary of the Assumption in Dufftown came first (1824–5 by Kyle). The design was adapted with minor changes at Tombae (near Tomnavoulin) in 1827–9, with assistance from Father *Walter Lovi*, its fine interior a rare example of fully articulated, arcaded Gothic with rib-vaults and aisles. A much more cosmopolitan iteration of the Kyle design appeared at St Mary's, Fochabers, in 1826–8, enlivened by *James Gillespie Graham* with good Perp tracery and fine, gleaming ashlar walls.

35 The first Catholic church built after Emancipation was St Thomas, Keith (1831, again by *Lovi*), its religious identity now insistent and overt: very prominent situation, cruciform plan and an extravagant façade lifted directly from Roman Baroque. A large, bulbous dome was added by *C.J. Ménart* in 1916, giving the church even more visibility. The church of St Sylvester at Elgin dates from 1843–4, with Dec tracery and fine Gothic detailing by *Thomas Mackenzie*. The twin-towered Gothic façade of St Peter's, Buckie (1850–7 by *Kyle*, with assistance from *A. & W. Reid*), is on a metropolitan scale, and likely the second largest church ever built in Moray. It was conceived as the C19 'reincarnation' of Elgin Cathedral, broadcasting a new Catholic world three centuries after the Reformation. After Keith and Buckie, little was erected by the Catholics until the end of the century,
46 when the church of Our Lady of Perpetual Succour (*see* Chapeltown of Glenlivet) was built by *John Kinross* in 1896–7. It features a ponderous mixture of Neo-Romanesque and Scots Renaissance, its plain exterior a strange reversion back to clandestine self-effacement. Here the moving influence was the 3rd Marquess of Bute, who converted to Catholicism in 1868 and employed Kinross on the restoration of Falkland Palace, the Greyfriars Convent in Elgin and the (unrealized) restoration of Pluscarden Abbey.

Most of the churches just mentioned have excellent interiors, the reredoses at St Mary Fochabers (by *Pugin & Pugin*, *c.* 1885), Preshome (1896 by *Peter Paul Pugin*, and of wood) and St Peter's, Buckie (1906–7 by *Ménart*) all opulent and profusely Dec. At Preshome the chancel is painted in full Puginesque brocades, while the ceiling of Chapeltown is a symphony of bright green and red. Pugin-inspired detail is also found on a smaller scale at the Sacred Heart church in Aberlour (also Catholic, 1909–10).

This has taken us beyond the DISRUPTION of 1843, when the usual 'building boom' of FREE CHURCHES was unleashed on Moray, just as everywhere else in Scotland. Most of them were broad, gabled boxes, hastily constructed and understandably short on architectural finesse. Some of them (as at Alves, 1877–8) were later given towers or ashlar veneers to smarten up their workaday façades. As expected, the Free Churches in the burghs offered a greater budget (and audience) for creativity and even opulence. At South Street, Elgin (1843), *Thomas Mackenzie*'s suave Romanesque detailing cut a distinctly finer figure than that of his parochial competitors. By contrast, the best Free Churches of the following decade returned to E.E., each one growing in size and confidence. Keith North (by *A. & W. Reid*, 1845–6) was already large by the standards of its day, but Buckie South and West (1849 by *A. & W. Reid*) and the former South Free Church
41 at Elgin (*A. & W. Reid*, 1852–4) are on a mammoth scale, boldly asserting themselves with tall towers and octagonal stone spires. The finest former Free Church in Moray is at Pluscarden (by *A. & W. Reid & Wittet*, 1898), built in a charming Gothic mode that complements the nearby Abbey. Five new churches also appeared in the burghs around this time, all hefty Gothic with

large corner towers and spire – Lossiemouth (now St James), 1887–8, and Rothes, Cullen, Fochabers and St Leonard, Forres from the turn of the century.[*] Three of their façades are craggily rock-faced and two of them (Cullen and Fochabers) have windows with big Dec tracery. St Leonard, Forres, is the most creative, a wild pastiche of French Gothic details as if lifted directly from the treatises of Viollet-le-Duc.

The UNITED PRESBYTERIANS also built three churches of real merit during this period. The converted former church on Moss Street, Elgin dates from 1856–8, vigorous Dec now shorn of its good original tower. The former South U.P. Church (now Elgin and Forres Free Church) is very well-studied E.E. by *Alexander W. Bisset*, 1862–4, even down to the style of its mouldings and label stops. The now-derelict Castlehill church at Forres (1870–1) has flanks with Dec lateral gables and a surprising rose window added in 1901–2, the only Victorian example in Moray of the Flamboyant style. By this date (1900), the United Presbyterians had joined with the Free Church to become the UNITED FREE CHURCH, by which point these large new churches were ideally suited to accommodating newly doubled-up congregations.

Apart from the Free Churches, the EPISCOPALIANS were the only denomination to build in earnest after the Disruption.
St John, Forres, is one of the earlier examples of new Episcopal 38
churches in the Aberdeen diocese, following the repeal of the penal laws in 1792. The original church is of *c.* 1834 but remodelled by *Thomas Mackenzie* in 1844. His style is a very early appearance of the Italianate style, otherwise quite rare in Moray, trumpeted by a Tuscan portico and an aggressively campanile-like tower. A decade later, Mackenzie added Gothic ostentation to Holy Trinity, Elgin, including a smart polygonal apse and a broad Perp porch encased in fine ashlar. Later in the C19, *Alexander Ross* of Inverness seems to have become the *de facto* architect for the Episcopalians, building three of its new burgh churches: the very large St Margaret, Aberlour (1874–9), and the smaller but prettily Anglicized All Saints, Buckie (1875–6), and its cousin, Holy Trinity at Keith (1882–4).[‡] Also Episcopal was the charming little wooden chapel built *c.* 1900 for Lady Florence Gordon Cumming in the grounds of Altyre House, and her mausoleum at Michael Kirk, Gordonstoun, by *John Kinross*, 1898–1900.

The CHURCH OF SCOTLAND built very little after the Disruption, as so many churches had been constructed in the previous century that there was little need for new construction. As a result, the 'Established Church' remained in creative stasis while other denominations scrambled to build around it. It was not until 1861 that a new parish church was erected in Moray;

[*]The original Free Church at Aberlour (now the Scout Hall) of 1847 was also refronted in a similar manner in 1899–1901.

[‡]Ross also oversaw the complete remodelling of Gordon Chapel, Fochabers, in 1874.

but even then, *George Petrie*'s muscular Neo-Romanesque nave at Aberlour was only rebuilt after its predecessor had burnt down. The next churches to go up from scratch reverted to Gothic with a resolutely – if occasionally bland – E.E. style, as at Duffus (1868–9), Deskford (1869–72) and the former Glenrinnes (1883). The most impressive new church of this period remains Buckie North (1878–9 by *Mackenzie & McMillan*), its diagonally buttressed tower topped by a pierced crown spire derived from the C16, and serving as a landmark for miles around.

The turn of the C20 finally brought two buildings of prestige, no doubt as a riposte to the recently unified Free and United
47 Presbyterian churches. St Laurence in Forres (by *John Robertson*, 1902–6) is an Edwardian crown jewel, its monumentality soft-
48 ened by a delicate silhouette of rippling spires. St Gerardine, Lossiemouth (by *J. J. Burnet*, 1899–1903), and St Columba in Elgin (by *P. Macgregor Chalmers*, 1905–6) both reverted to Romanesque, nicely invoking features that had been used at Birnie Church nearly eight centuries before. For the rest of the
53 C20 there are virtually no churches to report. St Christopher's Chapel at Gordonstoun (by *Murray, Ward & Partners* of London, 1965–7) is concrete Brutalism, its stark walls punctuated by vertiginous slit-windows. Of contemporary design, the only good example is Knockando Parish Church, rebuilt by *Law & Dunbar-Nasmith Partnership* after a fire in 1990.

As expected, the most attractive Victorian and Edwardian church INTERIORS are to be found in the burghs: Buckie North, St Laurence, Forres; St Columba, Elgin; and St Rufus, Keith. Even so, the palm for the most impressive interior in Moray must
43 go to St Margaret (Episcopal) in Charlestown of Aberlour, its polished marble columns and capitals carved with tremendous flowers and vegetation. It also features a dazzling array of furnishings. The galleries at St Giles, Elgin (1825–8), and Bellie Parish Church, Fochabers (1835–6), are both by *Archibald Simpson*, and panelled with his trademark Greek key ornament (the latter carried on fluted Doric supports). Elsewhere, as in the rest of Scotland, many church interiors underwent radical changes in the mid to late C19, after the foundation of the Church Service Society (1865) and the Aberdeen (later Scottish) Ecclesiological Society in 1886. Buildings were rearranged to accommodate new organs, often by blocking off chancels or adding shallow salients. Many of the Georgian oblongs were reorientated at this time and the pulpits relocated to one of the gable ends to achieve a 'correct' liturgical axis. These recastings often prompted a whole new complement of furnishings (e.g. pulpits, communion tables and fonts) in the Gothic style, rarely of great distinction and with varying degrees of historicism.

STAINED GLASS is not a prevalent feature in Moray, but among its figurative glass are some windows of high quality. The Gordon Chapel at Fochabers holds the largest collection of Pre-
50 Raphaelite glass in Scotland, with nine windows designed by *Edward Burne-Jones* and fabricated by *Morris & Co.* between 1876 and 1919. At St Laurence, Forres, the group of windows by

Douglas Strachan is again the largest in Scotland, with fourteen
excellent windows created from 1931 to 1939. As always with
Strachan, they look far more modern than they actually are,
with dramatic poses, swirling movement and a mesmerizing
interplay of powerfully saturated colours. Smaller Strachan
panels can be seen at St Columba, Elgin (*c.* 1910), and Mortlach
(*c.* 1917) as well. Moray is also home to the glass studio at
Pluscarden Abbey, the 'colossus' of Scottish window production
since its establishment in 1948 by the monks of the community.
The style of the studio is immediately recognizable, with luminous colours surrounded by sinuously abstracted contour lines.
The abbey itself features the largest number of windows (both
figural lights and *dalle-de-verre*), mostly installed 1958–98 and 51
predominantly by *Br Gilbert Taylor*, although some later windows
were added by *Sadie McLellan*. There are also Pluscarden
windows at Birnie (1965–79), Hopeman (1979–91), St Margaret,
Lossiemouth (1968) and Gordon Chapel (1990). Elsewhere,
good contemporary stained glass has been undertaken by *Charles
Florence* at St James, Lossiemouth (1971), and by *Shona McInnes*
at Bellie Parish Church (1997–8), Knockando (1999–2006) and
Rothes (2009).

The graveyards and burial grounds of Moray offer a fine selection of post-Reformation MONUMENTS. The finest memorial of
the C16 is at Rothes burial ground and commemorates James
Leslie †1576, with excellent, well-preserved heraldic carving.
Among other earlier works, that to Alexander Duff at Mortlach 30
Parish Church (1694, likely by *John Faid* of Elgin) is a boisterous
hodgepodge of Scots Renaissance and incipient classicism, the
base with two half-length busts of the deceased (a rare case of
early portraiture). Also attributed to Faid is the wall memorial
to Capt. John Grant †1715 inside the Elchies chamber at
Macallan burial ground (Easter Elchies), featuring long engaged
Corinthian columns under a ribbon-moulded entablature. The
fine double wall memorial at St Gerardine, Lossiemouth, to
the Gordon family (1700–41; *ex situ*) is again muscularly classical, with swirling helm trails and elliptical urn finials. The
Gordon family memorial in Michael Kirk, Gordonstoun, dated
1705, features little wildman caryatids and billowing ribbon
ornament.

Elsewhere, the best monuments are aedicular in form and proficiently classical in both pretension and vocabulary. At Botriphnie, the plaque to George Chalmers †1727 is decorated with putti heads under a swelling cornice and pulvinated architrave, while the upper pediment is ripped open by a massive cartouche. It shows just how cosmopolitan the sculptors and patrons of Moray could be. At Keith, the tablet to James Milne of Kinstair †1771 and family is flanked by tall Corinthian columns and a basal frieze with superbly carved recumbent skeleton. The memorial to Abraham Leslie †1793 at Spynie features two fluted Corinthian columns with suave entasis and leafy capitals of near-Mediterranean correctness. And at Rothiemay, the monument to Alexander Duff of Mayen †1816 features a Latin inscription and columned pediment that could easily be mistaken for a century earlier. Everything is self-consciously antiquated, as if the very act of memorialization could be achieved only through stylistic retrospection.

C17 and C18 HEADSTONES, LEDGER SLABS and TABLE TOMBS (or slabs raised on short legs) are often carved with angels' heads (winged souls) and emblems of mortality (skull and bones, shovel, bell and hourglass). As a whole, they are finished with great gusto and ingenuity; and if the sculptors' technique occasionally lapsed toward the primitive, the final products more than make up for it by evoking charm and terror in equal measure. Many display a thoroughly medieval sense of the macabre alongside nascent classical motifs. The best of the C17–C18 work in Moray are the table tombs at Cullen Old Church and at St Peter's Church, Duffus, although nearly every graveyard has several good examples. There are also several fine MAUSOLEA. The hall now attached to Dyke Parish Church was originally an aisle attached to the medieval church, converted into a mausoleum for the Brodie family in the late C17 and now much modified. Two of the others were commissioned from *William Robertson* in the early C19, each in a completely different style. The mausoleum for the Macpherson Grants at Inveravon (1829) is crow-stepped Gothic with a thick Tudor entrance arch, reusing medieval niches on the flanks; but at Bellie Burial Ground, the chamber for the Gordons (1825–6) is a serenely Neoclassical 'mini-temple' with Ionic peristyle. At Charlestown of Aberlour burial ground, *A. & W. Reid*'s work for the Macpherson Grants (1859–60) is one of their rare forays into Gothic, with a steeply pitched roof and excellent E.E. and Dec detailing. As elsewhere in Scotland, the fashion for mausolea had abated by the end of the C19, although a surprisingly late example appeared at St Ninian's Cemetery in Chapelford (Tynet), 1939 by *Reginald Fairlie*.

In addition to tombs, there are also half a dozen MORT HOUSES in Moray, all built in the early C19 before the Anatomy Act of 1832 put an end to rampant 'body-snatching'. They are simple and mostly rectangular, although the watch houses at Edinkillie and Mortlach have polygonal plans (the former hexagonal, the latter with a canted front).

CASTLES AND TOWER HOUSES

From the late C9, the province of 'Moray' occupied a far larger area than the present county, stretching all the way from modern-day Perthshire to the tip of the Highlands. It was ruled by a series of Mormaers (or kings) from the late C10, of which the most famous was Macbeth, who reigned from 1040 to 1057. King David defeated Ōengus in 1130, effectively destroying the kingdom of Moray, after which the region became of high strategic value to the Crown. By the mid C13, royal authority was concentrated in the four sherrifdoms of Inverness and Nairn (Highland and Islands) and Forres and Elgin. Of the latter two CASTLES, Forres is now represented only by its much-modified motte and the former stronghold at Elgin has nothing but short wall fragments. King David appears not to have built any large stone keeps in Moray as he did at Roxburgh (Borders) and Carlisle (Cumbria), and so castles remained very simple in the C12 and C13: low, wooden towers perched on top of mottes and encircled by timber palisades. The earliest castle at Darnaway was certainly of this type, built by the Comyn (later Cumming) family, who were once the most powerful clan in Scotland. They were eclipsed after 1306 but still retain their seat at Altyre. The other important family of the early medieval period were the Inneses, who claimed descent from Berowald, a Flemish knight who was given his land by King Malcolm IV in 1160.

Thanks to its relative isolation, Moray remained largely unmolested during the civil wars. Subjugation finally came in 1303 under Edward I, who visited (and destroyed) the castles at Cullen, Elgin and Rothes. Even so, this damage was minor compared to the rest of the country and the English only ever entered Moray three times (in 1296, 1303 and 1335). In 1312, Robert the Bruce created the first Earldom of Moray for his nephew Thomas Randolph, although it ended with the 3rd Earl's death in 1346. A second creation was initiated for his nephew John Dunbar, in 1372, after which power was split with the infamous Alexander Stewart (the 'Wolf of Badenoch' family, who were also Earls of Buchan and once the most powerful), who terrorized Elgin in 1390 and set fire to the burgh and cathedral. By the mid C15, most of the power rested with the Gordon family, who dominated the county for the rest of the Middle Ages.

Many of Moray's castles were rebuilt in stone in the C14 and given large forecourts (often with gatehouses) to one side. Any discussion of this process would be purely academic if it were not for the survival of Duffus Castle, one of the finest MOTTE 54
AND BAILEY CASTLES in Scotland. Around the year 1140, the site was given by David I to Freskin, a Flemish mercenary, whose extraordinary earthwork survives from the mid C12. It is a steep-sided cone with a truncated top, entirely manmade and one of the finest of its kind to have survived in Britain. The central keep at Duffus was rebuilt in stone in the early C14 for Sir Reginald de Cheyne and is ponderously impressive – excessively so, as the motte was only meant to support a timber building and the whole N side of the castle has sheared off under its own weight. Even so, the keep at Duffus is still the finest example in Moray of a hall house, comprising a vast two-storey rectangle, but now without its original roof and battlements. Of the latter part of that century is one of the county's crowning glories, the timber
roof of the GREAT HALL at Darnaway Castle, constructed in 55
1387–8 and disassembled and reconstructed in the first decade

of the C19.* Darnaway is one of the few monumental medieval roofs to have survived in the country, and none of the others comes close to its quality. Seven principal trusses form six (originally eight) bays, the lower horizontal elements fashioned as 'false' hammerbeams and carved with delightful sculptures of humans, animals and foliage. There are also faint traces of the original polychromy and heraldry.

As in the rest of Scotland, the other common type of fortification before the C15 was the CASTLE OF ENCLOSURE, consisting of a large courtyard surrounded by curtain walls, and with one or more of the corners taken up by towers. The only major
57 example to have survived in Moray is at Balvenie, but here again the remains are of national importance. It was originally built for the Comyns, Earls of Buchan in the late C13, and much of the vast quadrangular enceinte is *in situ* from that date, along with two sides of the stone-revetted fosse that ran around the perimeter. Balvenie Castle also marks a fundamental point of transition in interior design and the disposition of rooms. Whereas from the early C13 the domestic accommodation (hall, solar, chapel, kitchen, etc.) had been relegated to a corner *donjon* or keep, the architect of Balvenie provided a self-contained residence that straddles the main entrance and thereby forms a kind of 'keep-gatehouse'. Its form is confirmation, even at this early date, that domestic comfort was beginning to eclipse defensive function. Besides Balvenie, the only other important castle of enclosure in Moray was built at
58 Auchindoun, where the original curtain walls are intact from the early C14.

56 The Episcopal Palace at Spynie is also essentially a castle of enclosure, much of its sprawling quadrangular plan rebuilt in the C15 and C16, but occupying the dimensions of the original enceinte formed in the early C14. The finest features of early date are the C14 chapel on the first floor of the S range, its original lancets blocked or given ogee-headed lintels *c.* 1450. The imposing gatehouse in the E range dates from the early C15, features corbelled diamond turrets and is much indebted to northern English models.

By the C15 TOWER HOUSES had become the primary form of grand-scale domestic architecture. These consisted of a large rectangular or square main block, usually three or four storeys tall, with one or two side towers extending to form an L- or Z-plan. The ground floors were originally vaulted and contained the kitchen and cellar (as well as protection for animals in the event of attack); the hall was located on the first floor and domestic apartments were stacked above. The earliest surviving tower house in Moray is the thick and severe Drumin Castle (Glenlivet), built in the late C14 for the Wolf of Badenoch himself. It is in the form of a tall, simple rectangle and evidently never featured a jamb.

*The great hall in the N arm of Spynie Palace originally had a similar ceiling, built in the early to mid C15 but now represented only by stray corbels and the flash line of its gabled roof.

Another early specimen is the small L-plan built by the Dunbars at Dunphail, dating from the early to mid C15 (now ruinous). The first tower house on a national scale is the large central keep replacing the original one at Auchindoun, built *c.* 1470 for John Stewart, brother of King James III, and probably designed by the master-mason *Thomas Cochrane*. It is a giant, four-storey L-plan, the main entrance located directly on the S wall and not, as one would expect, in the re-entrant angle. The hall on the first floor was covered with two bays of quadripartite rib-vaulting, of which the ashlar springers are still *in situ*. David's (or Davy's) Tower, built in the mid to late C15 in the SW corner of Spynie Palace, was among the most colossal tower houses ever erected in Scotland. It overlies an earlier basement and is hulkingly austere, rising up an impressively tall five storeys. Its interior is now gutted, but enough remains to show that it had an unusual plan consisting of one large main chamber on each floor and a row of smaller mural chambers stacked on the E side, each vaulted in stone.

As elsewhere in Scotland, the majority of Moray's tower houses were built in the C16 and early C17. At Brodie, the nucleus of the current castle is an L-plan of *c.* 1540–60 with a large SW tower added in 1567 to form a Z-plan. The resulting structure is unusually tall, placing Brodie on a par with the very biggest L- and Z-plans, notably Inverugie (q.v.), Castle Fraser, Midmar and Harthill (S) and Inshoch (Highland and Islands). Even more importantly, the defining characteristics of Brodie's plan as first built in the mid C16 relate it to houses associated with the *Conn* family of masons (*see* p. 31). Of the same period is the very large tower house begun at Ballindalloch in 1546, now forming (as at 59
Brodie) the core of a much-expanded C19 country house. Ballindalloch is a strange variant of the Z-plan, featuring the usual diagonally aligned towers but also a large stair-tower in the centre of the hall block (now the rear of the castle). It is topped by a big square caphouse added in 1602. Also of the mid to late C16 are the L-plan tower houses at Findochty (for the Ogilvys, ruinous, and with an additional tower attached to the N side), Blairfindy (Glenlivet; for the Gordons, succeeding Drumin, dated 1564 and again ruinous but with a rare box machicolation), Milton Tower in Keith (original plan unknown, also built for the Ogilvys) and Kininvie (for the Leslies, its square main wing extended in the C19 and C20).

In 1547–57, Balvenie was given a new L-plan domestic range 57
by John Stewart, 4th Earl of Atholl, and its chic modernity announces the arrival of the Renaissance. It features two stair-towers, vaulted bedrooms on the ground floor and sumptuous bowed oriels to the exterior – everything ostentatious but also built for comfort in a new, modern age. Also significant in this respect is the Gordons' transformation of Bog o' Gight (now Gordon Castle, Fochabers), originally a late C15 hall house recast as a resplendent palazzo-cum-chateau. This was the first foray of construction in Moray by the Gordon Earls of Huntly, completed *c.* 1599 and among the most avant-garde works of its day. Most of the building succumbed to demolition by *John Baxter* in 1769,

and only the former SE tower now survives, made free-standing after substantial demolitions in 1952–3. It is six-storeyed and very tall, the upper corners with glazed tourelles in the manner of quasi-bowed oriels, and topped off by unusual squared, crenellated platforms. Elsewhere in the county, the ruinous towers at Blervie (Rafford) and Burgie (again mid to late C16) were once very fine specimens of their kind, and so similar in plan that they must surely have been designed by the same architect.

The delightfully small and charming Coxton Tower was begun *c.* 1587 by Alexander Innes, a simple square plan that is, very unusually, vaulted in stone on all four storeys. The clever architect rotated each vault ninety degrees so that each ridge lies perpendicular to its neighbour above or below, thereby forcing the lateral thrust of each floor to be counteracted. It is an ingenious solution and seems to have no parallel in Scotland. Much of the interior at Coxton remains unaltered, and the vault of the upper floor is pointed to support the gabled roof resting directly on top of it. At the other end of the spectrum is the very unassuming hall house at Kilnmaichlie, built in the early C17 and retaining its little projecting stair-tower with crowstepped caphouse.

Two major tower houses were built in Moray in the C17. The massive L-plan at the core of Cullen House was built 1600–3 by Sir Walter Ogilvy as the successor to his seat at Findlater Castle (*see* p. 381). It retains a fine original entrance with waisted Jacobean pilasters (crudely converted into a window *c.* 1711), and its former gallery once featured a striking painted Jacobean ceiling of *c.* 1605, tragically destroyed by fire in 1987. Of the same date (1602) is the large, blocky NW wing added to Brodie in the never-ending quest for more accommodation. And finally, the
68 magisterial Innes House shows a radical transformation of the tower house tradition just described. Innes is stripped of its defensive functions, conceived as a fully domestic (i.e. not castellated) house and designed for grandeur and comfort. It was remodelled from an earlier house by the Court architect *William Ayton*, who from *c.* 1640 to 1653 regularized its appearance and inserted a new, large six-storey stair-tower in the re-entrant angle. The latter features a splendid scale-and-platt staircase, a very avant-garde feature for its date. The remaining interiors at Innes are rather unassuming, and so the finest decoration of the period
70 is to be found at Brodie. There, the Blue Sitting Room (originally a laird's chamber) retains its original plasterwork of *c.* 1638,
74 featuring bold and vigorous strapwork. The ceiling in the dining room appears to date from the late C17 or early C18 and is ornately detailed, including four half-nude females (likely symbolizing the four elements), mythological scenes and a superabundance of flowers, foliage and vines.

MANSIONS AND COUNTRY HOUSES

The process of transition from tower house to mansion – already begun at Innes House in the mid C17, as just described – is more difficult to visualize for the more modest LAIRDS' HOUSES of Moray. At Edingight, a small laird's block of *c.* 1559 was given a taller extension in 1681. And at Mains of Mayen, an analogous house of *c.* 1608 was lengthened in 1680 to provide more domestic space. Other good examples of lairds' houses are Kilnmaichlie (early C17) and Mains of Drummuir (early to mid C17). The evolution to prototypical country house is probably best seen at Easter Elchies, dated 1700 and seeming to straddle the post-medieval and Georgian worlds. Its solid walls and crowstepped gables are those of a C16 hall house, but its stair wing has been relocated to the middle of the rear, forming a T-plan rather than the usual L or Z. With its flat frontage, central crowstepped gable and reshuffled interior, Easter Elchies is already a domestic ideal that was to dominate Scottish architecture for the next 120 years.

A very large number of country houses were built in Moray during the EIGHTEENTH AND EARLY NINETEENTH CENTURIES, and in order to make sense of them they are best divided into four sub-categories. The first group, dating from the period after the first Jacobite rebellion in 1715, took the form of a U-plan with central block flanked by wings. The earliest is Knockando House, built 1732 for Ludovic Grant of Grant and featuring pavilions linked up by mirrored quadrants (the r. one now covered up by late C19 additions). The original house at Milton Brodie was begun *c.* 1710 and its rear wings added in the mid to late C18, the corners strangely aligned so that they only just touched the angles of the main block. Newton House (Alves), built 1793, was a more conventional U-plan with a slightly advanced centre and rear courtyard.

A decisive turn in sophistication was made by Balvenie New p. 444
House (Dufftown), built by *James Gibbs* for William Duff in 1724–5. It was the first overtly Palladian mansion in Moray. Its seven bays were finely proportioned, the centre minimally advanced and channelled under a large pediment. Although mostly demolished in 1929, New Balvenie provided a clear exemplar that was immediately taken up elsewhere. Its most
impressive iteration was the new, very large central block at 73
Gordonstoun, begun 1730 by Sir Robert Gordon and straddled by the mirrored wings of an earlier tower.

The Adam style arrived in Moray at Moy House, built 1762–3 by *John Adam* for Sir Ludovic Grant of Grant. It is still an impressive building despite being gutted by fire in 1995. The house is two storeys over a raised basement, the slightly recessed centre decorated with a suave Venetian doorcase and window.
Arndilly (*c.* 1770, architect unknown) is much larger and severe, 89
its austerity softened by tall canted bay windows on the flanks and excellent Adamesque plasterwork in the drawing room. Dating from the end of the century is the solid Mayen House (begun 1788 and originally featuring a pair of detached, very recessed wings) and Cairnfield House (by *Robert Burn*, 1799–1804) with its inventive, geometrically determined interior. Burgie House (begun 1802) is the final example in Moray of the Georgian rectangle, and its façade is also the longest.

Balvenie, New House.
Drawing, 1724

The third category of the C18 is perhaps the greatest eccentricity in the county: large, extremely cube-like houses whose dimensions seem to flout the usual Georgian obsession with rectangular-based proportion. The earliest example is at
79 Letterfourie (by *Robert Adam*, 1772–3), whose tall and wide central block is almost manneristically distorted. Here, the Gordon patrons seem to have clung to the tower house ideal: this is Coxton Tower as reimagined for the genteel C18. The near-contemporary house at Pitgaveny (built 1776) is similarly treated, the unknown architect even accentuating its sheerness by increasing the height of the first-floor windows. Adam-style pavilions were later commissioned to soften the cubical effect, although unlike at Letterfourie they were never built. Pitgaveny marks a significant departure in other ways as well, as it was one of the earliest houses in Moray to be commissioned by clients who were newly rich from international trade, and not by branches of the old families. The trend was to continue in the early to mid C19 with 'nabobs' who made their fortune in either the West Indian colonies or the East India Co. Orton House, built 1786, was originally similar to Letterfourie and Pitgaveny but evidently found too severe, as single-storey wings and an advanced, pedimented centre were added in the early to mid C19.

The two grandest and most important country houses in Moray were both built in the CASTELLATED STYLE, their smoothly patrician and regularized appearance achieved by little more than multi-pane windows and crenellated parapets. The first was the utterly gigantic Gordon Castle by *John Baxter*, 1769–83, the longest country house ever built in Scotland (mostly demolished in 1952–3, leaving only the former E wing). The

original SW tower of its predecessor Bog o' Gight, completed *c.* 1599 (*see* above), was retained as the centrepiece of Baxter's sprawling new façade and served as a public totem of the Gordons' illustrious past. Similar antiquarian interests prevailed at Darnaway, where *Alexander Laing* retained the medieval great hall (*see* above) in the new castle built for the 9th Earl of Moray 80
in 1802–12. It was sensibly made smaller than Gordon Castle, but its interior (including plasterwork and mirrored, cantilevered staircases) is among the finest of its date in Moray.

The final category is three interrelated houses dating from the start of the C19, best studied as a group and all built for new property owners in Moray who had made their fortunes in trade. Grange Hall (1805, and attributed to *William Stark* of Edinburgh) is the earliest, establishing the pattern of a five-bay frontage over a raised basement with a pediment over paired giant pilasters. Dalvey House (built *c.* 1810 for Major Alexander Macleod) was clearly based upon it, but given a much wider centre with Venetian window slightly breaking into the pediment. The final house in the group, Invererne (begun 1818 by Gen. William 83
Grant) has a centre that is once again tightened up with an even higher Venetian window and a return to paired pilasters. All three houses are compact and share a common plan, with a hall running down the centre (ending in a staircase) and public rooms to either side. The interior at Grange Hall is uncommonly fine, remarkably unaltered since 1805.

After the frenzy of construction just described, only four completely new country houses were built in Moray in the NINETEENTH CENTURY. Substantial activity occurred elsewhere, but most of it was confined to additions and remodelling of pre-existing structures. There is no pure example of the GREEK REVIVAL style to compare with Cairness in Aberdeenshire (p. 119), but what there is belongs to *William Robertson*, the finest architect in Moray of the early to mid C19. Aberlour House dates from 1838–9 and is his masterpiece, sombre but brilliantly proportioned (at least originally) and featuring an excellent stair hall inside. Robertson's versatility is demonstrated by his remodellings at Auchlunkart (1825–8) and Aldroughty (1829–30) and his spry, rather fairytale-like façade at Milton Brodie (1835–41).

By contrast, Dunphail House is a superlative and precociously early example of the ITALIANATE style, built by *W. H. Playfair* in 1827–8 with round-headed windows, a campanile-like tower and deeply projecting eaves over boxy modillions. Even in its reduced state Dunphail is of national importance, as such finesse was usually not matched elsewhere in Scotland until *c.* 1840. The Italianate style was to become very influential in the work of others such as *Archibald Simpson* of Aberdeen, an architect who strangely never received a single commission for a country house in Moray. Leuchars House was built *c.* 1845 in the Italianate style, likely by *Mackenzie & Matthews* and stylistically closely aligned with their work at St John's church, Forres, and the Museum in Elgin. The same firm reached the TUDOR GOTHIC phase at Drummuir Castle, built on a new site between 1846 and 1849.

88 Its entrance hall is the finest in Moray, top-lit by a tall tower with Gothic balustrades and a Neo-Perp vault with radiating oculus, clearly derived from Taymouth Castle (Perth and Kinross).
89 Meanwhile Mackenzie's additions at Arndilly, 1850–1, are NEO-JACOBEAN in flavour, the shaped gables and square turrets with ogee domes indicative of the influence of e.g. Heriot's Hospital, Edinburgh. By this time, the spread of the BARONIAL STYLE had begun, and from *c.* 1840 there was a county-wide obsession with remodelling old buildings in this way. Ironically, a few of these buildings were already of ancient date but deemed insufficiently 'correct' in their details, and so were given a retrospective cachet that the originals had lacked. As elsewhere in Scotland, much of this interest was sparked by R.W. Billings's *The Baronial and Ecclesiastical Antiquities of Scotland*, which began publication in 1846 (see also p. 42).

One example of the new antiquarianism is *William Robertson*'s extension (one of his few commissions in that style) at Kininvie, nicely harmonizing with the original C16 tower house. But the undisputed master of Baronial in the north-east was *Thomas Mackenzie* of *Mackenzie & Matthews*, who vigorously showered old houses with tourelles, crowsteps and new doorpieces until his premature death in 1854.* His finest achievement was undoubtedly Ballindalloch Castle (1847–50), with its very fine, aggressively historicist C17-style doorpiece and dining room. Mackenzie carried out similar work on a smaller scale at Newton House (Alves) in 1850–2 – once quite fine, although the house was gutted by fire in 1992. Of the other major Baronial projects in Moray, among the most important is the E range at Brodie
86 Castle (originally built *c.* 1825–8 by *William Burn*, but remodelled by *James Wylson* of York *c.* 1845–50). At Cullen, *David Bryce*'s huge alterations of 1858–68 created a unified composition that belies its early C17 origins, while at Logie an early tower house was subsumed within additions by *A. & W. Reid* in 1861. The only completely new Baronial country house to be built in all of Moray was Rothes Glen (by *Ross & Macbeth*, 1892–4) – seemingly old-fashioned for that date but in fact replacing an earlier house designed by Ross in 1869–71.

The turn *c.* 1900 towards a style regarded as more 'authentic' – i.e. based on the early C17 Scottish Renaissance as typified by
68 Innes House – has no major representation in Moray. The remodelling of the interiors of Logie House in 1924–7 shows influence from the ARTS AND CRAFTS MOVEMENT in the early part of the TWENTIETH CENTURY; to the exterior, these additions are a final burst of Baronial, but they signal nothing more than a desire to harmonize with the original house. Kellas House
94 (by *F. W. Deas*, 1913–21) is the only country house in Moray to be built completely in the Arts and Crafts style. By this time, however, Blervie House (by *J. M. Dick Peddie*, 1906–11) shows the return to classicism, not of the monumental early C19 kind but towards the strain of Scottish Renaissance promoted by

*Mackenzie even rebuilt his private house (Ladyhill in Elgin) in the Baronial style, and it served as a repository for all of his antiquarian artefacts.

Lorimer. The alterations to Burgie House (by *W. H. Woodroffe* of London, 1912–14) are in the same tradition but more certainly Neo-Georgian.

Estate buildings

Most of the policies have at least one or two good ancillary buildings. As might be expected, their quality increases along with the size of the estate, and the largest (Altyre House, Cullen House, Darnaway Castle and Gordon Castle) have particularly fine examples. Altyre and Darnaway were so large that ESTATE VILLAGES had to be built to house the workforce and even school their children.

LODGES often echo the style of the main house, providing an *amuse-bouche* to what lies ahead or generally advertising the owners' aspirations. Among the best examples are the mammoth castellated W lodge at Gordon Castle (1791–2, by *John Baxter*) and its tidily octagonal counterpart to the E, 1826–40 by *Archibald Simpson*. The E and W lodges at Aberlour are a similar (and again very deliberate) contrast in styles, the former Grecian by *William Robertson* (*c.* 1838) and the latter Italianate by *A. & W. Reid* (1856). The S lodge at Ballindalloch (1850–3) is by *Mackenzie & Matthews*, exactly the self-assured, excellent Baronial that one would expect. At Darnaway, the E and W lodges (both 1868 by *James Maitland Wardrop*) are pumped-up Tudor *cottages ornés*, still miraculously flanked by their original GATES. They make very impressive entrances, one decorated with radiating spokes and the other topped by a suitably imperial-looking overthrow. Nearly as fine is the pedimented and elegantly tall Ionic ENTRANCE ARCH to Cullen House, designed by *James Adam*, 1767–8.

Four of the country houses in Moray have important DESIGNED LANDSCAPES. The earliest documented gardens in the county were those at Spynie Palace, long vanished but much admired in the early C16. Innes House had formal gardens in the early C17; these were extended in the mid to late C18 and much improved throughout the C19. The gardens now surrounding the house date from *c.* 1912, altered in 1918 by *Robert S. Lorimer*. Brodie Castle also had an 'ornamental plan' from the early C18, when the stately SW avenue was laid out. This was made more self-consciously picturesque in the early C19, when the original canal and its four lagoons (all of *c.* 1770) were converted into an elongated pond. At Gordon Castle, the removal of Old Fochabers and the establishment of the new town *c.* 1776 finally allowed a radical re-thinking of the policies. The C18 formal gardens were swept away to make the present parkland, likely designed by *Thomas White* in 1786–90. Of that period are the lake and two walled gardens, each with an interesting early C18 house attached to their N walls. A similar practice occured at Cullen, where the clearance of the old village in 1820 allowed partial implementation of a design made by *White* in 1789. The contemplation of this scheme in the late C18 proves that the desire for broad new landscapes was often the main impetus for the clearances, rather than the oft-cited need for privacy.

SCULPTURE and FOLLIES are rare on Moray's policies. The only real examples are the large column by *William Robertson* at Aberlour (1838–9; re-erected in 1888) and his colonnaded Temple of Fame at Cullen (1821–3, but heavily based on *James Playfair*'s designs of *c.* 1788–9). FOUNTAINS and WATER FEATURES are equally infrequent. One in the SE garden at Gordon Castle is a mid-C19 hodgepodge of fine heraldic plaques, and the
79 two Adam-styled ones at Letterfourie date from the early to mid C19. Aside from Gordon Castle, WALLED GARDENS are prevalent and occasionally gargantuan. Those at Aberlour and Darnaway feature good entrance arches by *Lorimer* and *Lorimer & Matthew* (1893 and 1927–8, respectively). GAZEBOS are surprisingly rare, although a good early example survives at Milton Brodie from the mid C18 (now very decayed).

Navigating the policies often required the construction of BRIDGES. The best are the hump-backed Ivy Bridge at Cullen House – a fine survival of the late C17 or early C18 – and the gigantic but graceful single arch over the Burn of Cullen by *William Adam*, 1744–5. His son *Robert* probably designed the equally impressive Craigmin Bridge at Letterfourie, an unusual and picturesque double-decker of *c.* 1773.

The former STEADING at Gordonstoun House (now the
72 Round Square) was begun *c.* 1690 and is again of national importance owing to its centralized plan, consisting of a huge circle surrounding a central courtyard. The delightful rear wing of Dallas Lodge was built as a homage to it in the late C17. HOME or MAINS FARMS are frequent, developing as part of the general pattern of agricultural improvement on large estates. Few houses in Scotland could boast the extraordinary Italianate complex at Altyre, built *c.* 1834 and likely designed by *Archibald Simpson*. His red-harled quadrangle for Gordon Castle dates from slightly earlier, 1828–9. DOOCOTS are also common, sometimes surviving as lone sentinels to houses that have long since been demolished. The cotes at Gordonstoun, Quarrywood and Pittendreich all date from the late C16, the last two with unusual stone slab roofs carried on internal arches.* Other early examples remain at Burgie (early C17), Dalvey (*c.* 1614), Findrassie House (1631), Leitcheston (Portgordon; early to mid C17), Ballindalloch (1696) and Knockando (late C17 or early C18). The doocot at Rothiemay (early C18) was by far the largest in the county, with *c.* 1300 nesting boxes lining its inner walls.

Surviving ICE HOUSES are generally unimpressive, but there are two good examples at Moy House and Cullen (both late C18). The former DEER KEEPER'S COTTAGE (now the Swiss Cottage) at Gordon Castle dates from 1833–5, a rare burst of timber painted bright red and studded with buoyant geometric patterns. A similar but tamer model was built at Ballindalloch Castle

*The doocot at Leuchars House was probably earlier (*c.* 1583, but mostly collapsed *c.* 1970).

c. 1860. More modern requirements are represented by the former GARAGE at Logie House, a good interwar design by *R. Neish & Forsyth* of Forres (1939, but never completed). The former ELECTRIC WORKS and GENERATOR HOUSE at Altyre (by *Kinross & Tarbolton*, *c.* 1902) show how surprisingly well Scots Renaissance could be adapted to industrial buildings.

Three castles, including Brodie, have their own dedicated
BURIAL GROUNDS on the policies. There are also purpose-built
MAUSOLEA at Gordonstoun (1705; converted into Michael Kirk, 32
1898–1900), Ballindalloch (1807) and Orton House (a fine
Gothic quasi-chapel by *Mackenzie & Matthews*, 1844).

BURGH, VILLAGE AND RURAL ARCHITECTURE

Of the five major BURGHS in Moray – Buckie, Forres, Elgin, Keith and Lossiemouth – three were occupied from a very early date, probably even in Pictish times. Forres already had a comparatively large population in the mid C12, when residents complained that the monks of Kinloss Abbey were encroaching on their land. In the early C13, the inchoate town of Elgin was already important enough to be chosen as the seat of the bishopric's new cathedral. Numerous survivals in Elgin show that there was rebuilding there on a massive scale in the C17, and minor survivals in Forres likely indicate the same. The C18 brought about a period of decline, eventually rectified in Elgin *c.* 1820–40, when the town was transformed into the stately Neoclassical version that survives today. Forres prospered a little later, its sumptuous villas and hotels built in the late C19, many of them by people who were newly rich from the whisky industry.

Keith, too, was an important community by at least the C12. The 'auld Keyth' was abandoned for a new town laid out by the Earl of Seafield *c.* 1750, and its regularized, gridiron plan is the largest in the county. The best buildings, like those at Forres, date from the later C19. In complete contrast, Buckie and Lossiemouth began as very modest coastal villages with rows of simple fishermen's cottages clinging to the shoreline against the windswept sea. Expansion began only in the mid C19, when new harbours brought huge influxes of cash from trade and shipbuilding. Both Buckie and Lossiemouth assumed their current forms in the late C19, and Lossiemouth enjoyed a brief period of fame (*c.* 1885–1905) as one of the premier holiday destinations in Britain.

As in North Aberdeenshire, Moray's VILLAGES are divided into three sub-categories – kirktouns, coastal villages and improvement villages of the mid C18 to early C19. Most of the kirktouns were founded in the early Middle Ages but have been destroyed or otherwise subsumed within later developments. Old

Duffus is the finest example, its church now ruinous but still conveying an idea of a how a rural kirktoun would have appeared at any time from the C13 to the C18. Elsewhere, the most important kirktouns (e.g. Dallas, old Fochabers and Kinneddar) are represented only by their former market crosses.

In the original, pre-1975 territory of Moray, the only real coastal village in the county was Findhorn, founded in the late C15 as the port to landlocked Forres. It was once among the most important ports in North Scotland, site of a thriving trade with Scandinavia and the Continent. The current sleepy beach-hamlet, founded at the start of the early C18 after two natural disasters, is in fact the third Findhorn. It was eclipsed in the mid to late C19 by the much larger harbour at Lossiemouth. In complete contrast, the coast of the former Banffshire saw the growth of a whole host of seaside communities, and its section of the Moray Firth is lined with a pleasant string of good maritime villages: Portgordon (founded *c.* 1794), Findochty (founded 1711 and reconfigured *c.* 1833) and Portknockie (developed in the mid C19).

Northern Scotland features more Improvement Villages than anywhere else in the country. There are a total of twelve in Moray, laid out to provide employment, suitable accommodation and improved agricultural productivity.* They took the form of a grid-plan, initially often with just a single straight road, and replaced the crumbling old kirktouns with brand new buildings and clean moral order. The two finest planned villages in Moray are Fochabers and Cullen, the former founded *c.* 1769 by the 4th Duke of Gordon and the latter by the 5th Earl of Seafield in 1820. Both had the distinct advantage of clearing the lairds' policies of unwanted tenants while giving their country houses much-needed privacy. Of the other improvement villages, Charlestown of Aberlour (founded in 1812 by Charles Grant) is the finest, with a good central square and well-designed public buildings. The others are smaller and relentlessly rectilinear, as seen at Archiestown (found 1758 by Archibald Grant of Monymusk), Dallas (1811), Dufftown (a big T-plan founded 1817 by the Earl Fife) and Tomintoul (founded *c.* 1777, again by the 4th Duke of Gordon).

Communications

The oldest official ROAD in the north of Scotland ran between Inverness and Aberdeen, a route now followed (with minor variations) by the modern A96. A well-used road between Elgin and Forres is documented in the early C13 but fell into disrepair after the Reformation; it must have been repaired by *c.* 1672, when the same route was used to deliver the post via horse. In the late C18, the road was recorded as being *c.* 6.1 m. wide and regularly

*They are Archiestown, Burghead, Charlestown of Aberlour, Cullen, Dufftown, Fife Keith, Fochabers, Hopeman, Keith, Kingston, Portgordon and Rothes.

Fochabers, Spey Bridge.
Watercolour by J. Giles, 1823

freed of obstructions. E of Elgin, the route ended at Boat o' Bog, where two ferry boats (also documented in the C13) carried travellers across the Spey. Despite all of these conveniences, conditions often made travel extremely slow. In 1680, James Brodie of Brodie recorded that his journey from Edinburgh to Brodie Castle took him a grand total of eight full days.

The great MILITARY ROAD was laid out from Coupar Angus (Perth and Kinross) to Fort George (Highland and Islands) by *Major William Caulfeild* between 1741 and 1757. The main section in Moray was completed in 1754 and crossed over the dangerous pass of The Lecht in the Cairngorms. Caulfeild's road is still followed for most of its course by the present-day A93 and A939. From 1761 to 1784, the old road between Fochabers and Huntly (via Keith) was also improved, and a new road from Keith to Cullen opened in 1836. It was not until 1805 that the Elgin–Forres route was made into a turnpike, and then completely resurfaced in 1812 when the first mail coach service began between Inverness and Aberdeen. More turnpikes followed and soon TOLL HOUSES began to appear throughout Moray. Most of these have now been badly converted into cottages, but two good ones by *William Robertson* survive at Boat o' Brig (Mulben; 1830, with a smart portico) and at Newton (Alves; 1822, a Grecian–Tudor hybrid that could only work on such a small scale).

The oldest surviving BRIDGE in Moray appears to be the hump-back 'auld brig' in Keith (built 1609), followed closely by the Bow Bridge in Elgin (*c.* 1633). Two good packhorse bridges also survive at Aberlour and Bridgend of Glenlivet (Glenlivet), both early C18, and the Ivy Bridge at Cullen House may have been built in the late C17. Then came disaster. In 1829, nearly

every bridge in Moray was destroyed by the near-apocalyptic
floods known as the Muckle Spate. *George Burn*'s beautiful
Bridge of Avon in Ballindalloch (1800–1) survived the catastro-
p. 451 phe, as did two of his original arches at the old Spey bridge
(1801–4). Also resplendently intact was the bridge at Craigellachie,
107 *Thomas Telford*'s masterpiece of 1812–15 – and now the oldest
surviving monumental cast-iron bridge in Scotland.* It is a work
of uncommon elegance, with a road deck carried on remarkably
lacy ironwork and a gracefully parabolic arch-ring. The bridge at
Carron (by *Alexander Gibb*, 1863) is a fine iteration of the same
theme, again one of the best preserved in Scotland. The Victoria
footbridge near Charlestown of Aberlour (by *James Abernethy &
Co.* of Aberdeen, 1902) is the only surviving SUSPENSION
BRIDGE in Moray.‡

Moray's enviable coastal position has long been studded with HARBOURS, likely from Pictish times and certainly by the early Middle Ages. A 'hanse' (or trading union resembling the Hanseatic League) was recognized by King David I in the mid C12, when it was composed of Aberdeen, Inverness, Elgin, Forres and Nairn. All of the goods were exchanged by sea, proving that harbours, however primitive, were the life-line of the northern Scottish economy. Findhorn once served as the harbour for Forres and is documented as a major port in the C17 (now completely vanished). Garmouth likewise carried on vigorous trade with the Continent from at least the C16, although its harbour was undone by the shifting shoals of the Spey. It was replaced by Lossiemouth, where the first river harbour had been built by Elgin burgh in 1703, and then by the present port at Branderburgh (1837–9, with various extensions throughout the C19).

Despite its long stretches of coastal territory, the former Banffshire strangely lagged behind Moray and had virtually no trade well into the mid C19. The activity along the Firth focused almost exclusively on fishing. The first 'real' harbour at Nether Buckie was constructed in 1855–7 (now infilled as a park), replaced in 1873–80 by the cavernous Cluny, the first harbour in Scotland to be built of concrete. The neighbouring villages soon followed suit with much smaller versions: Portgordon (1870–4), Findochty (1882–4) and Portknockie (1886–90).

116 Covesea Skerries near Lossiemouth is the only major LIGHT-
HOUSE in Moray, but it is an example of singular charm. Whitewashed and beautifully sited over the sea, it was designed by *Alan Stevenson* in 1844–6 with entrance portal and keepers' quarters rendered with unusual Neo-Egyptian detailing. Also of note is the tall LEADING LIGHT overlooking Buckie harbour, *c.* 1878. The promontory at Burghead retains a rare STORM SIGNAL (early to mid C19), with steps leading up to the viewing

*In 1803, Parliament appointed Telford as chief surveyor of the new Commission for Highland Roads and Bridges, which did so much work to improve communications in Scotland.

‡Important suspension bridges formerly crossed the Findhorn near Forres (1830–2 by *Capt. Sir Samuel Brown*; replaced 1936–8) and the Spey at Boat o' Brig (1829–30; replaced 1956).

platform; nearby is a COASTGUARD STATION dating from *c.* 1807.

Turnpikes survived until 1864, by which time RAILWAYS were the most popular and lucrative form of travel. The Morayshire Railway came first, offering services from Elgin to Lossiemouth (in 1852) and Craigellachie (from 1862; both closed 1968). In 1881, the Morayshire was amalgamated with the Great North of Scotland Railway, which had reached Keith from Huntly (S) via Rothiemay in 1856, and then invested in the Keith & Dufftown Railway, which opened in 1862. The GNoSR sponsored the Strathspey Railway from Dufftown and Ballindalloch (opened 1863, closed 1968) and also ran the Moray Coast Railway from Lossiemouth to Buckie from 1886 to 1968. The two other major companies were the Inverness & Aberdeen Junction Railway, laid out between Nairn and Keith in 1857–8, and the Inverness & Perth Junction Railway, which ran from Aviemore to Forres from 1863 (closed 1965). The two Junction railways merged to form the Highland Railway in 1865. Eight large VIADUCTS were built to carry them through Moray, all of high quality. The most impressive feat of engineering is the one at old Spey by *Blyth & Cunningham* (1883–6), a long behemoth with a titanic bowstring truss in its centre. Two others are now disused but have become indispensable picturesque features of the landscape: the Divie 121
(by *Joseph Mitchell*, 1861–3) strides poetically across the horizon at Edinkillie and the high arches at Cullen (1884–6, again by Blyth & Cunningham) nicely frame the vistas of the new town and sea. Many of the former RAILWAY STATIONS in rural areas have been converted for domestic use and retain their original platform shelters with cast-iron columns. In the burghs, the major survival is the former station of East Elgin (by *Patrick M. Barnett*, 1898–1902), its exterior Baronial but with an excellent coved ticket hall and waiting rooms inside.

Public and commercial buildings and housing

MARKET CROSSES are the earliest emblems of burgh architecture, and Moray has several good (albeit battered) survivals: old Duffus (mid C14), Dallas (early C16), Kinneddar (mid C16), Ogstoun (late C16; now Michael Kirk, Gordonstoun) and old 97
Fochabers (early C17, with original whipping chains still attached). The Georgian cross at Lossiemouth dates from 1764. Of similar type is the PRECINCT CROSS (now the Little Cross) at Elgin, erected in 1733 to replicate a monument of 1402 and incorporating its original finial. The market crosses at Forres, Cullen and Elgin are essentially Victorian but the latter two appear to at least follow the design of their C17 predecessors.

In contrast, of the CIVIC BUILDINGS associated with the burghs there is nothing before the early decades of the C19, at which time there was considerable activity. In 1836–40, *William Robertson* rebuilt the TOLBOOTH at Forres as an imposing two-stage battlemented tower with octagonal cupola and bellcast

roof, all in homage to the original of the C16. His adjacent block also served as the town's courthouse. The ground floor of his
110 present town hall in Cullen (1821) served the same function, and the upper floor (still with good original features inside, as at Forres) was used as the COUNCIL CHAMBERS. In 1836–9, the large clock tower in The Square at Dufftown was built as a GAOL, and then converted into burgh chambers in 1895. Surviving civic buildings from after the mid C19 are rare but the finest is the COURTHOUSE at Elgin (by *A. & W. Reid*, 1864–5), reassuringly Neoclassical with doubled-up Ionic engaged columns and pilasters. Straddling either side of Elgin are two of the finest public buildings in the county. On the W end is the massive but
108 supremely simple Gray's Hospital by *James Gillespie Graham* (1815–19), its tall tetrastyle portico and huge dome announcing a new era of institutional monumentality. Every visitor to Elgin would have immediately understood the town's wealth and importance at the start of the C19. Anchoring the E side is
112 *Archibald Simpson*'s Anderson's Institution, built in 1830–3 to provide care for the elderly and education for the young. It is prodigiously long, well-proportioned Greek Revival, the advanced ends flanking a centre with full-height *in antis* portico and saucer-domed rotunda.

Elsewhere, the only other important SCHOOL is at Forres (1823, again by *Robertson*), its trim Neoclassicism and Gibbsian spire indicating that only discipline and the highest learning lay
115 within. Milne's Institution (now Primary School) at Fochabers (*Mackenzie & Matthews*, 1845–6) is among the finest charity schools in Scotland – a spectacular, wildly Neo-Tudor palace, bursting with crenellated turrets and Perp canted oriels. From the period after the Elementary Education Act of 1870, the best schools are those at Alves (by *A. & W. Reid*, 1873–5) and at Aberlour and Craigellachie (by *Brown & Watt*, 1895–7 and 1900). Also of note is the former school at Garmouth (1874–6 by *A. & W. Reid*), an early instance in Scotland of construction in concrete. In addition, two other schools of distinction are both located in Elgin. The former Academy (1885–6, again by the *Reids*) is highbrow Neoclassical with a tetrastyle portico; just opposite is the Victoria School of Science and Art, a wildly different Romanesque hodgepodge by *George Sutherland* of 1889–90. Moray is also famous for its former ORPHANAGE at Aberlour, founded 1875 and once the largest in Scotland. Its gigantic complex of buildings (built by *Alexander Ross* between 1876 and 1913) was demolished in 1967, now represented only by its two lodges and the clock tower of its former school.

Of the few good PUBLIC HALLS remaining in the county, the finest is Charlestown of Aberlour's Fleming Hall, a Scots Renaissance bulwark with bold tower by *A. & W. Reid*, 1888–9. By contrast, the hall at Lossiemouth (1884–5 by *Duncan Cameron*) is rather boxy Italianate with a corner pyramidal spire. Many of the buildings now used as halls in Moray were originally built as MECHANICS' INSTITUTES. That at Elgin is robust Italianate by *Matthews & Petrie* (1859), while Keith's (by *Francis D. Robertson*,

1885–9) is by far the grandest piece of architecture in the new burgh – profusely Italianate with a domed octagonal tower. The fine, very regal Institute at Forres incorporates a substructure by *Archibald Simpson* of 1827–9, veneered with a new façade of polished Peterhead granite by *John Forrest* in 1899–1901. In addition to the above, Moray boasts two fine purpose-built MUSEUMS. Elgin's was built for the Elgin and Morayshire Literary and Scientific Association, with a bright, basilican Italianate design by *Thomas Mackenzie* (1841–2). The interior is extremely impressive, and the campanile tower originally served as the caretaker's house. The Falconer Museum (by *A. & W. Reid*, 120
1868–70) cuts a grand profile in Forres, a Renaissance palazzo with entrance front marked off by a Greek Doric portico, Vitruvian scroll and gigantic swagged finials. For LIBRARIES, the only important survival is at Lossiemouth (1901–4, by *A. & W. Reid & Wittet*), paid for by Andrew Carnegie and placed directly against the earlier hall.

As so often in the mid to late C19, HOSPITALS tend to be large and rather plain. Leanchoil at Forres (1889–92, to a design by *John Rhind*) is the best, a broad Neo-Jacobean U-plan with central tower and two tall Dutch gables. Only one section remains of what used to be Elgin's colossal LUNATIC ASYLUM (by *A. & W. Reid*, 1863–6, with multiple extensions) – now subsumed within Gray's Hospital. Almost as large is the sprawling former HYDROPATHIC ESTABLISHMENT at Forres, a harled concatenation of gables built in 1863–5 and extended at least two times.

All of the major TOWN HOUSES of the period before 1840 are in Elgin, and they are a very fine group indeed. Thunderton House was founded at the start of the C14 but the fabric is now mostly of the early C17, its entrance originally flanked by hulking caryatids (now in the Elgin Museum). High Street retains the early C17 stair-tower and caphouse, known as Tower House, built by Andrew Leslie and Jean Bonyman, and Ritchie's House features a superlative chimneypiece dated 1688. Braco's Banking 99
House (at the E end of High Street) is a fine survival of 1694, its ground floor recessed to form a triple-arcaded loggia – once a ubiquitous feature in the burgh, and allowing the town to be circumnavigated without exposure to the elements. Two more arcaded houses have survived across the street, dated 1688 and 1694. Nearby is a spare but very *chic* four-house block dating from the early C18, the r. pair dated 1728 and dignified with a Venetian window on the first floor.

Unsurprisingly, many of the important SUBURBAN VILLAS are also in Elgin. Grant Lodge began as an austere double pile by *Robert Adam* in 1766–8 – his earliest work in the county, and now disgracefully falling into ruin after a fire in 2003. South Villa (1830–1 by *William Robertson*) is country-style sophistication with a semicircular portico, anthemion window cornices and Doric entrance hall. Also of note is Robertson's fine collection of villas built *c.* 1829–40 on Seafield Place in Cullen. These are, however, on a much smaller scale than their Late Victorian successors which jam-pack the hinterlands of Elgin and Forres. Among the

highlights in Forres are Cluny (*c.* 1835, likely by *Robertson*), Ramnee (1907, with trussed gables and bellcast turret), Cluny Bank (*c.* 1885, fairytale Gothic with excellent bargeboarding) and the monumental Baronial splendour of Newbold House (1899–1901 by *Peter Fulton*) and Cathay House (by *George Simpson*, 1887–8). The latter two have fine glass conservatories. In Elgin, the best villas are Maryhill House (*A. & W. Reid*, 1866–7), with its balustraded parapets and phalanxes of chimneystacks; Braelossie (*A. & W. Reid*, 1862–3), an unusually creative Baronial design; and Connet Hill (by *A. Marshall Mackenzie & Son*, 1913, with a good apsidal extension of *c.* 1933). By *William Kidner* are the fine Baronial houses at Lesmurdie (1880–1) and the former
122 Blackfriarshaugh (1882–3; now the Mansion House Hotel), with their big asymmetrically turreted towers. Lossiemouth also had several good marine villas of the period *c.* 1900. Another house of significance is The Bield outside Elgin (by *J. B. Dunn*, 1927–32), its exterior Scots Renaissance with good Arts and Crafts
126 decoration inside. For the mid C20, No. 31 Wittet Drive in Elgin (by *J. & W. Wittet*, 1947) is a late but pure example of the 1930s Modern Movement.

At nearby Oakwood is one of the only early roadside MOTELS to have survived in Great Britain, built 1932–5 by *Dougal* and *Andrew Duncan*, and a riot of geometric, timber-clad, log-cabin-esque rusticity. Another interwar delight is the Playhouse CINEMA at Elgin (1932 by *Alister Gladstone MacDonald*), which retains much of its original Art Deco interior. Macdonald was the son of Ramsay Macdonald, Labour prime minister who came from Lossiemouth.

Like the villas, the HOTELS in the towns grew ever larger in this period, demonstrating the popularity of Moray as a Victorian tourist destination. The earliest after *c.* 1840 is the Laichmoray in Elgin, a big but spare Italianate box by *Mackenzie & Matthews*, 1853. The Longview at Forres (1881–2 by *John Rhind*) is thick Scots Revival with pierced, two-storey oriels on the ends; the 1888 extension to the Gordon Arms, Elgin added a two-storey canted bay window and segmental, shell-carved pediment. Very different is the hotel at Craigellachie (1892 by *Charles C. Doig*, with several extensions), its exceptionally long, picturesque rear frontage perfectly suited to its pastoral site overlooking the Spey. The masonry of the hotels of the turn of the century tends to be aggressively rock-faced: the Grand Hotel at Elgin is a three-storey juggernaut by *A. & W. Reid & Wittet* (1898), while the Carlton in Forres (by *Peter Fulton*, 1900–2) is Scots Renaissance with vast Dutch gables spanning the wall-head.

Among COMMERCIAL BUILDINGS, the most interesting are the BANKS. *William Robertson*'s British Linen Bank at Forres (1839, now Clydesdale) is the only major example of the early period, its calm ashlar front (with ends minimally advanced) exuding patrician confidence. Such restraint was to become unthinkable even a decade later, a change typified by the Bank
117 of Scotland in Forres, a three-storey, five-bay Renaissance palazzo of 1852–3. It is, very surprisingly, the work of *Thomas*

Mackenzie – usually associated with Gothic and Baronial work – but showing immense facility in this idiom as well. Two banks in Elgin also date from this decade. The former Royal Bank (by *A. & W. Reid*, 1856) has alternating triangular and segmental pediments on the first floor; the very ostentatious Union Bank (by *Matthews & Petrie*, 1857) is the finest building on its side of the High Street, with first-floor windows framed by balustraded aprons and fluted shell ornament. Opposite, the former Royal Bank (by *Peddie & Kinnear*, 1876–7) is a more subdued palazzo, its wild doorpiece carved with florid consoles and lintel. At Buckie, the former Caledonian Bank (by *Ross & Macbeth*, 1905–6) has key-blocked, giant-order Ionic pilasters and a big pediment with excellent carving in the tympanum.

Of the SHOPS, the best are the former St Giles' Buildings and the Manchester Drapery Warehouse on Elgin's High Street (both by *R.B. Pratt*, 1903–5), large Edwardian proto-shopping malls. Good Victorian MARKETS survive at Forres (the Agricultural Hall by *A. & W. Reid*, 1867, and their New Market building of two years later) and at Elgin. The C19 shopfronts on the High Street of Forres are pleasingly varied and uncommonly well preserved, many of the fascias escaping 'improvement' over the past half century.

PUBLIC MONUMENTS are rare in Moray but begin in quite
spectacular fashion with Nelson's Tower at Forres (by *Charles* 106
Stewart, 1806–12) and the York Tower near Newton, Alves, (1827–8, by *William Robertson*) before the huge column was erected at Ladyhill, Elgin, in 1838–9 by *William Burn*. It was initially topped by a strange lantern and then given its present statue of the 5th Duke of Gordon in 1854–5. The largest public memorial of the period is the obelisk to James Thomson at Castle Hill, Forres (1857). There are also good public FOUNTAINS at Elgin (by *Mackenzie*, 1845–6), Fochabers (1878) and Tomintoul (1915). Nearly every town and village commissioned WAR MEMORIALS after 1918, many of the smaller ones designed by *John Wittet* and dedicated in the summer of 1921. The finest memorials in the burghs (Buckie, Elgin, Forres, Keith and Lossiemouth) were topped by bronze figures, and the sculpture at Elgin and Lossiemouth (by *Percy Portsmouth*, 1920–2) is the best. The memorial at Fochabers (1920–1 by *A. Marshall Mackenzie & Son*) is the best architecturally, a simple, huge column set theatrically in front of the main entrance to Gordon Castle. The memorial at Newmill (by *Francis D. Robertson*, 1922–3) takes the form of a quasi-Baronial clock tower and serves as the main focus of the village.

Rural buildings

Beyond the towns the most distinctive buildings in many villages are the MANSES, the majority of which were built before *c.* 1840. The old manse at Duffus is the oldest in Moray and retains a core of *c.* 1736; also of the C18 is the manse in The Square at

Fochabers, built 1788 (likely by *John Baxter*). *William Robertson* designed nine of the others, the finest of which are Lhanbryde (1825–6), the S frontage at Inveraven (1834) and Rothes (1839–41). The manses at Rafford (1817–18) and Kinloss (1819–21) are surprisingly generic, un-Gothic rectangles by *James Gillespie Graham*. Far and away the best (former) manse in Moray is the
III superlative Edinkillie House, built 1822–3 by *John Paterson* – magically sited over the Divie with an elegant butterfly plan and good circular rooms in the interior. Aside from the Free Church, few manses were built after *c.* 1840. The best are the former Drainie manse (by *A. & W. Reid*, 1853–5; *see* Lossiemouth) and the jaunty Scots Revival manse at Dallas by *John Wittet*, 1904–5.

Several FARMHOUSES of quality were built in the C18 and earlier C19. Cots of Rhininver (Dallas) is a strange, pleasing survival of *c.* 1798, its rear section sweeping around in a large horseshoe shape – another centralized plan in the vein of the Round Square, Gordonstoun. Stynie Farmhouse (Mosstodloch; early C19) is to a very high standard of execution, while Fisherton (Charlestown of Aberlour) (1839) nicely demonstrates Robertson's talents for a less well-heeled clientele. Just as fine is the crowstepped Mary Park (Ballindalloch) by *Thomas Mackenzie*, 1844.

Much further afield, usually tucked away in the most remote parts of the south, are a variety of SHOOTING LODGES. Glenfiddich Lodge (Dufftown; by *John Plaw*, *c.* 1790) is an important early survival, as its surrounding deer forest was one of only about six that remained in operation during the sheep-farming clearances of *c.* 1730–1830. Also of interest are the lodges at Braemoray (Edinkillie; 1838–40), Inchrory (begun 1847), Strathavon (Tomintoul; late C19) and Delnabo (Tomintoul; the best part by *Charles C. Doig*, 1891–2). The best shooting lodge in Moray remains Kylnadrochit (by *George Mackie Watson*, 1898–1900), with a mightily Scots Renaissance exterior and good, original Arts and Crafts features on the inside. FISHING LODGES were also built to capitalize on the famous angling of Speyside. Best are the original sections of Carron House (mid C19).

Industrial buildings

Moray was primarily an agricultural region and its industrial enterprises were largely associated with its natural resources. *William Anderson*'s KILN BARN at Rothiemay (built 1742 and now roofless) is one of only a few surviving in Britain, with slit vents and hinged door to control the draught for winnowing. The two-storey CRUSHING PLANT in The Lecht (1842) is all that remains of what was once the largest and most active manganese mine in Scotland, established by the Duke of Gordon. The late C18 FISHING STATION at Tugnet (likely designed by *John Baxter* and again for the Duke of Gordon) allowed workers to catch the famous avalanches of salmon at the fast-moving mouth of the Spey. Its subterranean ICE HOUSE was built in 1830 and is among the largest in Britain; the ice houses at Findhorn and Gollachy (Portgordon) are smaller but roughly contemporary. That at Hopeman, built *c.* 1845, is unexpectedly grand, its U-frame entrance and mighty cavetto cornice another strange appearance of the Neo-Egyptian style.

Two of the MILLS in Moray are of national importance. The 'waulk mill' at Knockando is first documented in 1784 and has been in continuous operation for two centuries, longer than any other in Britain. Its simple but tidy complex of buildings mostly dates from the late C19 and early C20, nicely showing a mill's evolution over a century and a half of expansion and mechanization in the Industrial Age. Johnston's wool mill outside Elgin is 123
far larger, with a host of support buildings, a mid-C19 steading (now converted into a shop) and a surprisingly grand residence for its former owners. The WATER TOWER at Garmouth (by *Jenkins & Marr*, 1898–1901) is one of the first buildings in Scotland to have been built out of reinforced concrete.

And so to the DISTILLERIES, of which Moray has the highest concentration of anywhere in the world. They are encountered everywhere, often where one least expects it. The passage of the Excise Act in 1823 legalized whisky-making (for a fee) and the die was cast: with its clean, powerful rivers and burns, Moray was made for whisky-making, much of it nestled in the legendary and picturesque Speyside valley. The Glenlivet (founded 1824) was the first legal distillery in Scotland, but widespread building in Moray did not occur until *c.* 1880, when the railway infrastructure finally enabled reliable supply of materials and export of the heady, finished product.

Nearly forty new distilleries were built between *c.* 1885 and *c.* 1905, most of them by *Charles C. Doig*. Over time, he developed a standardized design that provided optimum performance. The classic 'Doigian' plan was in the form of a gigantic capital E, with malt barn on the lower arm, mash house in the middle and bottling plant on top.* Doig's other breakthrough also came *c.* 1885, when via trial and error he perfected the pagoda-roof ventilator, allowing for controlled heat when drying the germinated barley in the kiln. Even though few of them are still in use, the ubiquitous pagoda kiln will remain the most iconic architectural feature in Moray for at least the next few centuries. Most of the remaining architecture is plain and utilitarian, and many complexes were wrecked by bad additions in the 1960s and '70s. The most picturesque distilleries are Strathisla in Keith, with its graceful paired pagoda ventilators of *c.* 1872; Speyburn Distillery, Rothes (by *Doig*, 1896–7), picturesquely set in a narrow ravine; Benromach near Forres (1898–9, again by *Doig*) with its tall whitewashed malt barn and red chimney; and Dallas Dhu (also 124
1898–9), now run as a tourist attraction by Historic Scotland.

*The best way to understand the layout of distilleries – as well as the purpose and function of each individual building – is to visit the former Dallas Dhu Distillery near Forres, which is now operated as a museum. The entry in the gazetteer describes each part of the complex in full detail.

The most creative design is Dailuaine, Carron (1882–93), where Doig unveiled his first pagoda kiln and crowstepped gables line the phalanxes of warehouses. The post-Victorian era is reached
127 in resplendent fashion at Auchroisk Distillery, Mulben, a beautifully spare complex by *Westminster Design Associates*, 1973–4. The
130 distillery at Roseisle, Alves (by *Austin-Smith: Lord*, 2007–9) is a radical re-thinking of whisky-making architecture, propelling Moray's time-honoured elixir into the C21. At the time of writing, plans are also in hand for a major reconstruction of the Macallan Distillery (Easter Elchies) by *Rogers Stirk Harbour & Partners*.

A review of buildings since the early C20, other than those already mentioned, should note that Moray's strategic coastal position prompted construction of two large AIR FORCE BASES in 1938–9 – the new 'harbours' of the modern era. Lossiemouth is one of the RAF's largest, while Kinloss was decommissioned into an army barracks in 2012. The concrete SECOND WORLD WAR FORTIFICATIONS at Innes Links, built 1940–1, are among the most complete and unaltered in Great Britain, including engine houses, barracks and seemingly endless rows of anti-tank blocks. There is little to say about the character of POST-WAR HOUSING although there is a good deal of it in burghs such as Elgin, but since 1982 the simple but often inventive houses in the eco-village at Findhorn have provided models of green and sustainable architecture, allowing the Findhorn Foundation to have one of the lowest carbon footprints in the world.

GAZETTEER

Places with B against their name lie in the historic county of Banffshire.

ABERLOUR *see* CHARLESTOWN OF ABERLOUR

ALDROUGHTY HOUSE 1060

3 km. WSW of Elgin

The estate was owned by the Sutherland family from at least the mid C17, but was forfeited in 1715 when William Sutherland (son of James Sutherland, second Lord Duffus) participated in the Jacobite uprising. A Georgian mansion on the site was occupied by William Murdoch of the East India Company from *c.* 1800. Present house built for George Taylor in 1829–30, very likely designed by *William Robertson* and in his usual poised, rational style. Symmetrical five-bay S front, the centre a tall single storey with pedimented Greek Doric portico. It is oddly dated 1824, likely indicating a five-year delay in financing. Slightly taller end bays, minimally advanced and divided into two storeys with some original lying-pane glazing. Two single-storey extensions forming a U-plan to the rear, the E by *A. & W. Reid & Wittet*, 1899. The W is dated 1930 and is likely by *Charles C. Doig & Sons*, who designed the Lodge in the drive *c.* 1928.

ALTYRE HOUSE 0050

3.6 km. WSW of Rafford

The lands of Altyre were held from the early C14 by the Cumming family, descendants of Robert of Comyn who fought alongside the Conqueror. They became the Gordon Cumming family in 1795 and a new baronetcy was created in 1804. The house (dem. 1962) had a core of *c.* 1820 by *James McBride* but was altered in 1858 and extended by *A. & W. Reid* in 1892–3. The present house was built *c.* 1895 by *W.L. Carruthers* as the parsonage for the Episcopal chapel (*see* below) and doubled in size by *James Grant Shearer*, 1931–3, as the family's principal residence after the original house was abandoned.

In 1891, Sir William Gordon Cumming married the American cotton heiress Florence Josephine Garner, and they brought about many improvements to the house and policies. The EPISCOPAL CHAPEL (200 m. NW) was built for her (cf. Michael Kirk at Gordonstoun). Weatherboarding painted red with jerkin-gabled transepts and E bellcote. Furnishings are now at St Margaret, Lossiemouth (*see* p. 695) except for a CHAIR in the N vestry, *c.* 1900.

OLD CHURCH,* 1 km. NE, in woodland at the heart of the estate. A parish church existed at Altyre by no later than 1239, when it was granted to the canons of Elgin Cathedral. In 1657 the parish was annexed to Rafford (q.v.), and it is likely that the church passed out of use soon after then, other than for burials. Apart from the loss of its roof and the minor lowering of the N and S wall-heads, the only identifiable modifications are the addition of buttresses towards each end of the N wall and changes to the W window head. It is therefore of particular interest as a single-period medieval church, which is most likely to date from the later C13, and its value is enhanced by the modestly high quality of its detailing.

The church is of rectangular plan, with no structural differentiation between chancel and nave; the walls are of rubble with freestone dressings, and areas of harling survive. There are opposed pointed-arched doorways towards the W end of both the S and N walls with simply chamfered surrounds and round-headed rere-arches. Pairs of pointed windows with broadly chamfered reveals light the E end of the nave area through both S and N walls, and there is a third window on the S side in the chancel area. In the E wall is a wider window that had Y-tracery. All the windows are internally rebated for glazing frames. With the exception of the E window, all openings are without hoodmoulds. The upper part of the single window in the W wall has been modified by the insertion of an upper square window with reveal mouldings consisting of paired rolls separated by a spur, above which is a timber safe lintel. This modification was perhaps associated with the insertion of a post-medieval gallery. At the base of the E gable are skewputts carved with what appear to have been small masks; they were perhaps initially the ends of a wall-head cornice. Internally, a degree of finesse was introduced by the provision of a chamfered rib to the rere-arches of the windows in the S, E and N walls; the rib of the E window remains, though along the N and S walls only the supporting corbels survived the lowering of the wall-heads.

CROSS-SLAB, 300 m. E of church. A rare early Christian survival with rudimentary text, fabricated in the early C9 and

*This entry is by Richard Fawcett.

relocated here *c.* 1820 from near Burghead (q.v.), where it likely originated. Sandstone, *c.* 3.4 m. high and 17.8 cm. thick with a partially preserved cross on the front. On the back, half of the vertical beam of another cross. Defaced ogham inscription on the undressed l. side, one of two in Moray (cf. Rodney's Stone, Brodie Castle, p. 486).

BLAIRS HOME FARM, 200 m. NNE. Excellent, large complex built *c.* 1834. Its Italianate style strongly suggests that it was designed by *Archibald Simpson* and, if so, it is the greatest surviving testament to his long Italian 'pilgrimage' before setting up practice in Aberdeen in 1813. Late C19 alterations by *W. L. Carruthers*. Now disused and in poor condition, but there are plans to convert the farm into a learning centre and education complex.

Imposing tower of four stages with round-headed lights and a mighty quasi-battlement on top, of heavily corbelled ashlar with shallow pyramidal roof and ball finial. The E range (formerly farm offices) has a bizarre three-stage tower that looks like a C17 lectern doocot as re-imagined by a Tuscan mannerist. Lower E-facing tower beyond with an exaggerated band course of round arcades. SW, a tall former CARTSHED and GRANARY with round-headed cart bays and double-decker open bellcote.

Down the slope to the W, a CRICKET PAVILION with slightly taller advanced centre and recessed wing with four tall, arcaded CART BAYS.

There are many other late C19 and early C20 ESTATE BUILDINGS, e.g. the former estate SCHOOL (now Office Cottages), 0.5 km. NE, likely also by *Carruthers*. It has segmental-headed dormers and deep verandas on the ends, originally used as sheltered play areas. Other good examples by *Kinross & Tarbolton*, including the STABLES (0.9 km. SE), a crowstepped

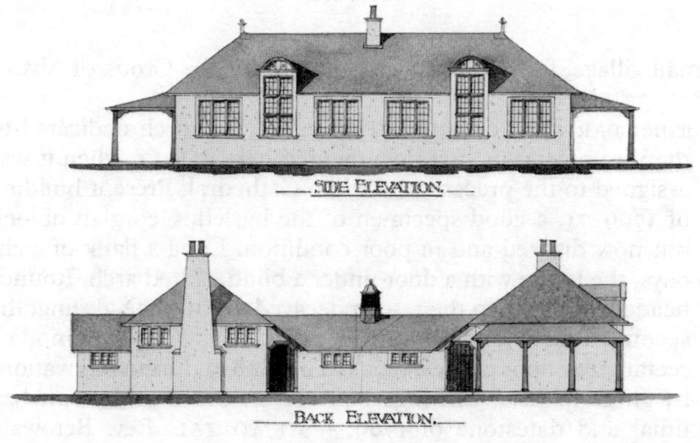

Altyre, school.
Elevations

Scots Renaissance quadrangle of 1901–2. Fine carving on the wall-head dormers, including monograms and Jacobean 'pinnacle' pilasters. The former carriage houses have joggled lintels and a segmental pediment. To the NW, the former ELECTRIC LIGHT WORKS and GENERATOR HOUSE, *c.* 1902, in a similar but more severe style. Steeply pitched crowstepped gables and louvred cupola with ball-finialled ogee dome. The GARDENERS' COTTAGES, 0.8 km. E of the house, were built 1901, a surprisingly grand pair, again Scots Renaissance style. The head gardener's cottage has a bolection-moulded doorpiece and overdoor with Neo-Jacobean obelisks and console brackets flanking monograms. COLTHALL COTTAGES (0.7 km. W) is of 1900–1, a tall continuous range to house the estate's foresters. W front facing the A940 with spiky door mouldings poking up like cats' ears.

MANACHY LODGE, 1.7 km. NNE. Originally the East Lodge by *A. & W. Reid*, *c.* 1866, with red eaves and big iron finials. Fine wrought-iron GATES of *c.* 1900 in C18 style, made for Gordonstoun House (q.v.) and resited here *c.* 1950. Virtuosic ballflower suspended from the top with wispy trails below; rinceau pattern on the bottom. – The WEST LODGE (0.7 km. SW of the house) has similar gates with nicely unfurling leaves in the upper centre. Lodge itself of the early C19 in the Tudor Gothic strain of William Robertson, with Y-glazed windows, lugged hoodmoulds and a bowed central porch.

SCURRYPOOL BRIDGE, 2.1 km. SE. High segmental rubble span over the Altyre Burn, early to mid-C19 with a narrower semicircular flood arch to the l. and r. Large elliptical-headed arch added to the E by *Joseph Mitchell* for the Inverness & Perth Junction Railway, 1862–3.

1060

ALVES

Small village, formerly known as Crook (or the Crook of Alves).

Former PARISH CHURCH, 0.9 km. NNE. A church dedicated to the Virgin Mary is first documented here *c.* 1213, when it was assigned to the precentor of Elgin Cathedral. Present building of 1769–71, a good specimen of the harled, Georgian oblong but now disused and in poor condition. Long S flank of eight bays, the l. side with a door under a blind, stilted arch. Round-headed windows to the r. with decayed multi-pane glazing; the second, fourth and fifth have raised sills to accommodate rectangular door frames, blocked in 1848–9 during renovations by *A. & W. Reid*. Birdcage bellcote on the E gable with ball finial and datestone of 1769. – MEMORIAL. Rev. Berowald Innes †1722 by the former E door, re-sited from the previous church. Long Latin inscription on a tablet; tall aedicule with engaged Corinthian columns and initials (including those of his wife, Jean Falconer). Thick entablature with a pair of winged souls under a ball-moulded, triangular pediment.

Former MANSE (The Anchorage) to the W. 1832–5 by *William Robertson*. Pilastered, corniced doorpiece surrounded by generous twelve-pane glazing. Piended roof with two longitudinal chimneystacks.

PARISH CHURCH, 0.9 km. SW. Built 'hurriedly' as a temporary Free Church by *John Urquhart* in 1845; exterior envelope retained but remodelled by *A. & W. Reid & Melven* in 1877–8. Broad, harled N front, its advanced three-stage tower veneered in ashlar in 1877–8. Round-headed entrance, louvred rectangle in a sunken panel, and very large open bellcote with panelled aprons, scrolled volutes and angle urn finials. Arched windows on the flanks and twelve-petal rosette in the S gable.

Bright interior as reorientated and remodelled by Reid & Melven. Elliptical barrel-vault running down the centre, the flat sections to the l. and r. carried on slender cast-iron columns. – GALLERY on the N, blocked in 2010. – Wide, rectangular PULPIT, 1878, with little twisted balusters on the parapet. – Two original GASOLIERS on it with flame-like shades. Six more on the ends of the PEWS. – Small ORGAN by *E. F. Walcker*, *c.* 1900. – Two BELLS by *Michael Burgerhuys*, dated 1637 and 1639. Made for the predecessor of the parish church. Former MANSE to the NE, 1845–6 and likely also by Urquhart. Bolection-moulded doorpiece and spiky central gable. Orange-ochre harling.

PRIMARY SCHOOL, Main Road. By *A. & W. Reid*, 1873–5. Double U-plan with trussed gables and paired apex chimneystacks on the ends. Projecting, apse-like W entrance. Small former infant school to E.

WAR MEMORIAL, E of the school. By *John Wittet*, 1921. C17 mercat-cross style. Octagonal, pilastered drum and Ionic column with a lion on top.

ARDGYE HOUSE, 2.4 km. ENE, off the A96. Big villa of rock-faced granite, built for George R. MacKessack by *John Wittet* in 1904–5. Pedimented r. end over a rectangular bay window and another full-height window on the far l. side. Well-preserved Edwardian interior with top-lit stair hall, including ceiling with ribbed panels and lozenges and cantilevered wood staircase with barley-twist balusters.

INCHSTELLY FARMHOUSE, 1.5 km. NNE. Built *c.* 1835, likely by *William Robertson*, for it is similar to his Fisherton House, Aberlour (*see* p. 509). Advanced, pedimented centre; canted bay windows to the l. and r. added *c.* 1860.

NEWTON HOUSE, 3.3 km. ENE on the B9013. Gutted by fire in 1992, but still retaining quite a bit of dignity. The core is a U-plan house built by George Forteath in 1793 after he made his fortune in the West Indies. From 1850–2 the house was 'Baronialized' into full-blown Neo-Jacobean grandeur by *Mackenzie & Matthews*, who seized on every last modern feature and rushed to include them all. Advanced centre with pilastered doorpiece under triglyph architrave. Lunette above flanked by fruit-spilling lions, then a canted bay window framed by banded obelisk finials. The original Georgian gable above was given crowsteps and diamond chimneystacks; Mackenzie's also the rope-moulded cornice with waterspouts and tourelles on the ends (the l. retaining its original candle-snuffer roof with fish-scale slates). The plan and severity of the original house are best seen from the rear, with its narrow former service courtyard.

Former ALVES STATION (closed 1965; now Station House), 0.4 km. SSE. By *Joseph Mitchell*, opened in 1863 for the Inverness & Aberdeen Junction Railway. Keystoned Italianate windows with T-bracketed sills. Good original platform shelter with five cast-iron columns supporting thick, bracketed eaves.

130 ROSEISLE DISTILLERY (Diageo), 3.4 km. NNW. By *Austin-Smith: Lord (ASL)*, 2007–9. The first major distillery built in Scotland in thirty years. Colossal, its three distinct sections echoing the main processes of whisky-making – fermentation, mashing and distilling. E flank with a huge curtain of glass to show off the fourteen stills inside.

TOLL COTTAGE, 3.5 km. ENE, junction of A96 and B9013. By *William Robertson*, 1822, built by Alexander Forteath of Newton for the new road to Burghead (q.v.). Lintelled porch with Roman Doric columns. Rope-moulded ogees over the windows added in the early to mid C20.

YORK TOWER, 3.1 km. ENE, on the Knock of Alves. Tall Gothic folly by *William Robertson*, 1827–8, in a commanding position on the summit of a Pictish fort. Built by Alexander Forteath of Newton in memory of Frederick, Duke of York. Three-storey octagon with pointed entrance studded with dogtooth. Huge dummy cruciform slits in the diagonals of the lower two floors. On the third storey, narrow slit-windows alternating with arched windows over sills with head corbels. Crenellated parapet.

To the NW is the MAUSOLEUM of Dr Alexander Forteath †1866. By *A. & W. Reid*. Subterranean vault accessed by a block-pedimented doorpiece (now blocked). Above, a stone SARCOPHAGUS in railed enclosure commemorating members of the Forteath family. Tester with stags' heads in low pediments and angle acroteria carved with thistle.

2040 ARCHIESTOWN

Founded 1758 by Sir Archibald Grant of Monymusk and laid out on a grid *c.* 1760. A fire in 1783 caused extensive damage.

At the W end is THE SQUARE, leafy and pleasantly long, with the mercat-cross-style WAR MEMORIAL of 1919–20 by *William Cummings*. Granite column with Ionic capital and a heraldic lion. Several handsome buildings line the perimeter, notably THE OLD MANSE (NW corner), built 1848 for the Free Church which formerly stood to the SW (built 1843–4 and dem. *c.* 1968). Doorcase with two Roman Doric columns and a pediment perched on the wall-head. To the r. (in the NE corner) is OLD ST ANDREWS, *c.* 1764, a small house of coursed Ben Rinnes granite (pink and yellow, with contrasting dark pinnings). In the SW corner is the harled CARLOWRIE, early C19, with renewed lying-pane glazing and a single-storey, three-bay wing to the r. In the centre of the E side is the ARCHIESTOWN HOTEL, *c.* 1881, with a pilastered, pedimented doorcase and gambrel attic added after a fire in 1967.

E of The Square is THE COTTAGE (No. 31 High Street), built 1790–3 – a miniature and extremely charming laird's house said to have been designed by *Robert Grant* of Wester Elchies (*see* below). Single-storey central block of three bays, looking as if a Georgian manor house had been shrunk to a fifth of its original size. Piended roof and tall gable-end chimneystacks. Central door with panelled fanlight; twelve-pane glazing in the windows. Lower, single-bay pavilions forming a shallow U-plan, each with a little pyramidal roof and chimneystack. Dwarf walls line the side of the street, with pint-sized gatepiers and arrowhead railings to complete the illusion.

Former ELCHIES CHURCH, 1.6 km. E. By *A. & W. Reid*, 1873–4; converted into a house, 1981–2. E.E. with narrow lancets and gableted SW entrance. W gable with a plate-tracery window, louvred cinquefoil and apex bellcote. Former E vestry, 1933.

WESTER ELCHIES, 2.8 km. SE. The house first built for the Grants of Carron in the early C17 and sold in 1783 to Robert Grant, whose business was in Canadian fur trading. Demolished, 1967–8. – Rectangular DOOCOT to the S of the site. Early C18, similar to the one at Ballindalloch Castle (q.v.).

CRAIGNEACH CASTLE, 1.9 km. SSE. Foundations of a substantial L-plan stronghold with additions to the N, likely plundered by the Covenanters in 1645.

ARNDILLY HOUSE 2040

2.1 km. N of Craigellachie

A mighty but refined house, built as the seat of the Grant (later 89
Macdowall-Grant) family. The core was constructed *c.* 1770 and is of mixed granite rubble with tooled margins and quoins. Symmetrical and imposing (S) front of three storeys with an attic, the first floor tallest, and of three broadly spaced bays. The predominantly Neo-Jacobean character, however, was established in 1850–1 by *Mackenzie & Matthews*, who remodelled the central entrance and added the large porte-cochère with round-headed arches, grand balustrade and four large

urns. Above in the centre they added a projecting canted window topped by a balustrade and over this a Dutch gable. Flanking the gable and at the angles are four square Tudor-ish turrets with nice bellcast-ogival slated roofs. The E and W flanks have mid-C18 full-height canted bays, also given big Dutch gables. Also mid C19 the very attractive circular, single-storey W wing (originally a cool store) with a shelter inside an arch on the S front. It supported a glass-domed conservatory, to which a staircase curls in a single sweep around the S wall. The rear retains its central stair-tower of *c.* 1770. Stretching out on either side, long, single-storey wings, C18 but much renewed, the W attached to the main block by a slightly lower quadrant. The E quadrant was replaced in 1829 by *William Robertson* with a three-storey service wing. The two long and straight wings beyond form a narrow service court, bounded on the N by a pair of two-storey stable blocks.

Inside the porte cochère, a ceiling with pendant finials (a copy of the original *c.* 2004). The interior proper has a circular STAIR HALL with a very fine C18 cantilevered spiral staircase to the second storey, the balustrade kept sensibly simple so as not to detract from the elegance. The principal rooms are at first floor, the DRAWING ROOM (W) still with C18 fittings and decoration, notably the ceiling with central fan set within an octagonal border and in the semicircle over the bay window a rose and foliage. Ornate urns in the angles of the main room. Intricately carved overdoors and patterned cornices. The SITTING ROOM is as remodelled in 1850. Carved white chimneypiece with two Ionic pilasters; rinceau and urn on the lintel. Panelled ceiling with husk ornament, all reflecting the original Georgian décor.

Arndilly stands on the former burial ground of an early medieval chapel, owned by a prebendary of Elgin Cathedral (q.v.) and already in ruins by *c.* 1560.* From the chapel is a PICTISH STONE, reset in the house's W flank, with notched rectangle, Z-rod and 'mirror-case'.

MACDOWALL BRIDGE, 1.4 km. SSE. Three granite spans over the Macdowall Burn, *c.* 1830.

AUCHBRECK *see* GLENLIVET

3030

AUCHINDOUN CASTLE B

3.6 km. SE of Dufftown

58 An impressive and deeply melancholic ruin, perched on a commanding hill that has been occupied since the C1 B.C. To S and E, the terrain declines sharply into the Fiddich valley, allowing

*About twenty skeletons were found below the kitchen floor of Arndilly House in 1965, all on an E–W orientation consistent with Christian burials.

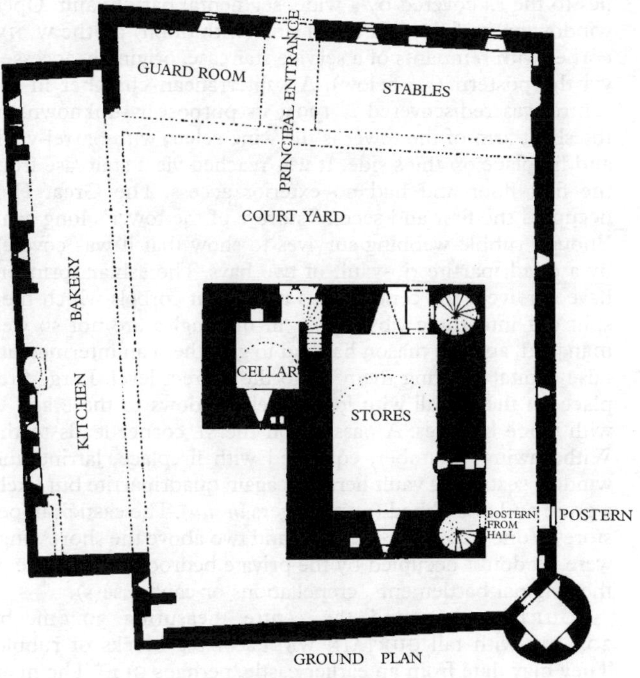

Auchindoun Castle.
Ground-floor plan

control over one of the most important routes from Speyside into Aberdeenshire. The S approach (on the A941) is the best, revealing the castle in all its imperious, windswept glory.

The present Auchindoun was built *c.* 1470 by John Stewart, Earl of Mar, younger brother of King James III, but he was murdered in 1479. It was probably designed by *Thomas Cochrane*, the king's favourite, to whom the earl's estates were passed. Cochrane was hanged from Lauder Bridge in 1482 following the king's imprisonment by Albany, and Auchindoun was acquired by the Ogilvy family in 1489 and by the Gordons in 1535. In 1592, it was sacked and burned by the Macintosh clan in retaliation for the murder of the Earl of Moray by Sir Patrick Gordon. The fabric was then restored but fell into disuse by the start of the C18; in 1724, William Duff of Braco removed some of its stone to build Balvenie New House (*see* Dufftown).

The CENTRAL KEEP is a four-storey L-plan tower – a substantial and nearly complete ruin, with thick rubble walls. The S wall has been lost, allowing a full 'cut-away' view of the interior. The main entrance was here – not in the re-entrant angle, as one would expect – and the curved rear wall of the spiral staircase that once connected to it remains. The main cellar lies to the r., covered by a wide, segmental barrel-vault. Open window on its far N end and a sink (with drain) on the W. NW corner with remnants of a service staircase, originally accessed via the postern (*see* below). A subterranean chamber in the centre was rediscovered *c.* 1993; its purpose is unknown. In the short arm of the tower is the wine cellar, with barrel-vault and fireplace on the S side. It was reached via a staircase from the first floor and had no exterior access. The Great Hall occupied the first and second storeys of the tower's long arm. Enough rubble webbing survives to show that it was covered by a quadripartite rib-vault of two bays. The ashlar springers have survived, the central ones resting on corbels which then split out into three ribs. Those in the angles are not so well managed, and the mason has had to give them an intermediate false capital to bring them up to the correct level. Large fireplace on the N wall with long lintel; windows to the E and W with stone benches. A passage off the SE corner leads to the Withdrawing Chamber, equipped with fireplace, latrine and window seats. The vault here was again quadripartite but likely a groin and not ribbed (no springers *in situ*). The castle's upper storeys (one over the Great Hall and two above the short wing) were no doubt occupied by the private bedrooms. No trace of the original battlements, crenellations or caphouse(s).

COURTYARD around the centre measuring 30.7 m. by 20.6 m., with tall CURTAIN WALLS of big blocks of rubble. They may date from an earlier castle, perhaps C14.* The main entrance was in the S wall and just inside were two ranges, both now destroyed (guard chamber on the r. and stable on the l.). The E wall protrudes beyond the original perimeter and was probably built after the late C16 sacking. Flash lines to the N and S and spurs of interior walls show that it once housed a range, likely the kitchen, bakehouse and brewhouse. Large former fireplace and chimney flue in the NE corner. In the far NW corner was a round tower (mostly destroyed) with postern gate to the r.

Surrounding the walls and occupying the hilltop are EARTHWORKS of an Iron Age fort complex. Large ring of deep, well-defined ditches, said to have been reoccupied by the Picts.

2050

AUCHINROATH HOUSE

2.4 km. NNW of Rothes

A late C18 shooting lodge recast in Baronial splendour by *A. & W. Reid & Wittet*, 1900–1. SW front dominated by a projecting central tower with rounded ground floor and off-centre

*The thick triangular buttresses to the exterior are modern.

entrance; faux caphouse corbelled out above with diamond oriel and crowstepped gable. Slender stair shooting up the r. re-entrant angle topped by a candlesnuffer roof. Fat, round tourelle added to the upper r. corner and an octagonal one to the l.

AUCHINROATH BRIDGE, 250 m. WSW. Tall, stilted segmental span over the Millstoneford Burn, *c.* 1830. Pilaster buttreses.

AUCHLUNKART HOUSE B 3040

1.7 km. SW of Mulben

Nestled in a secluded ring of trees. Until 1947 the seat of the Stewarts of Auchlunkart and Forres.

The house is large and of three main campaigns, all covered in faded harling. The centre of the E front is *c.* 1760, two storeys and eight bays, with taller bows added N and S *c.* 1790. Of the same date the lofty attic (see the original mid-C18 band course running below). Central entrance remodelled by *William Robertson*, 1824–5, with Greek key pilasters and tetrastyle porte cochère carried on Greek Doric columns. Five-bay S front also by Robertson, the centre with an ashlar niche topped by a large, strange chimneystack shaped like a spiralled urn. Robertson's CONSERVATORY stretches below with more fluted columns and anthemion-palmette brattishing. Rear additions and restorations by *Bruce & Sutherland*, 1886, including the walled SERVICE COURT to the N.

Remarkably untouched interior with distyle Greek Doric screen (later glazed) between entrance and inner halls. Full-height STAIR HALL, its open-well staircase cantilevered and bizarre. Its second quarter-pace landing has a door to the first storey of the mid-C18 house; the third leg in front of it starts out flat and begins to climb only halfway up, and is also canted out at the end. It is an expedient to reconcile the mismatched elevation of the same, but higher, floor in the late C18 wing. Later dado panelling and cast-iron balustrade of 1886.

The DRAWING ROOM as remodelled by Robertson has overdoors with triglyphs and cornices, and a plaster cornice with Greek decoration, some of it however late C19. Bright white marble chimneypiece with caryatids. DINING ROOM also early C19 with late C19 additions. Dark wooden dado with three tiers of panelling; overdoors with ogee-sided architraves and cornices. Reset in the conservatory wall, a large C17 ARMORIAL PANEL with names and five coats of arms. In excellent condition, so it was never outside.

WEST LODGE, on the A95. 1886, also by *Bruce & Sutherland*. Harled, the first floor enlivened by half-timbering.

1030 BALLINDALLOCH B

A loose collection of buildings skirting the policies of Ballindalloch Castle, near the confluence of the Avon and the Spey.

INVERAVON PARISH CHURCH. On a beautiful, secluded bluff overlooking the Spey. Built 1806, but the S wall incorporating part of the medieval church's N wall. Four round-arched windows; corniced birdcage bellcote on the W gable with ball finial on top. Timber Y-tracery inserted in 1876 during large-scale renovations by *A. Marshall Mackenzie*. His also the semi-circular entrance and sexfoil on the E gable, the lancets and Gothic porch on the N, and the low vestry to the W. Mackenzie reorientated the interior and gave it its present coomb ceiling with scissor-brace roof and pendant finials – Dec-Perp wooden BACKBOARD, 1876 – Similar PULPIT, *c.* 1901, from Wishart Memorial Church, Dundee. – ORGAN. By *Hill & Son*, London, 1876; case by *E.H. Lawton*, 1911. – PICTISH STONES. In the porch. Three were found in 1806 in the foundations of the medieval church, the fourth was discovered in the churchyard in 1964. – On the l., an incised crescent and V-rod over a complete 'beast'. – Above to the r., a small fragment with the head of a 'beast' in sinuous curves. – In the centre, an impressive, large eagle with mirror case. Smaller, worn mirror-and-comb to the r. – On the r., a crescent and V-rod with triple disc and mirror-and-comb – the finest (and oldest) of the four.

MAUSOLEUM to the E for the Macpherson Grants of Ballindalloch, built 1829 by *William Robertson* and succeeding one of 1586 that adjoined the medieval church. Angle buttresses and Tudor entrance arch; crowstepped gables with crosses on the apexes. The flanks have fine Gothic statue NICHES reset from the former church, probably C15. Trefoiled canopies with little rib-vaults.

INVERAVEN HOUSE, 50 m. SW. Formerly the manse. Original three-bay block of rubble running N–S, built 1775–6. Harled S front added by *William Robertson*, 1834, two storeys and three bays with piended roof. Minimally recessed centre with bracketed pediment; porch added by *A. Marshall Mackenzie*, 1876. – Small STEADING to the E by *Alexander McCondachy* (mason), 1769–70, and much altered in 1807.

INVERAVON PRIMARY SCHOOL, 300 m. SE. By *Mackenzie & Matthews*, *c.* 1850. Gables with wavy bargeboarding. The SCHOOL HOUSE of *c.* 1818 has a gently bowed stair-tower.

Former BLACKSBOAT STATION, 1.3 km. N. 1863, for the Strathspey Railway. Single-storeyed with fluted pilasters supporting signage (cf. Cragganmore). – Timber-clad GOODS SHED to the S, also 1863.

At the junction of the A95 and the B9008, 250 m. SE, a good former POLICE STATION (now GLEN A'AN) by *F. D. Robertson*, 1896–7, and Celtic cross WAR MEMORIAL by *John Wittet*, 1919–20. 0.5 km. NNW from here, the BRIDGE OF AVON, 1800–1 by *George Burn*. One beautiful high, wide segmental arch and a smaller flood arch to the r., crossing over the S lodge of the Castle. Two plaques on the S spandrel, the upper one a datestone and the lower one marking the height of the floods on August 4th, 1829 – an alarming demonstration of the power of the Muckle Spate. Nearby is LADY MACPHERSON-GRANT HALL, originally a school of *c.* 1872 and likely by *Matthews & Lawrie*. Scots Baronial with crow-stepped gables; drum tower in the re-entrant angle under a candlesnuffer roof.

PITCHROY LODGE, 2.5 km. NNW across the Spey. Shooting lodge of *c.* 1895, in gleaming harl. NW corner tower with fish-scale-slated conical roof. Similar one to the rear and a SW extension, 1930 by *Charles C. Doig & Sons*. – STONE CIRCLE, 275 m. NNE. Two stones from an early Bronze Age clava cairn, one standing and one fallen.

MARY PARK FARMHOUSE, 2 km. NNE. Good mixed pinned granite of 1844, likely by *Thomas Mackenzie*. Crowstepped gables and lying-pane glazing. Contemporary large, quadrangular STEADING to the N, converted into bonded warehouses by *ANTA Architecture* of Fearn, 2013. Diamond chimneystack over the central S tower.

BALLINDALLOCH CASTLE

1.2 km. SSW

One of the finest country houses of historic Banffshire, cutting a 59
mighty but elegant figure on a very strategic location, just SE of the junction of the Avon and the Spey. The medieval castle burned down in the late C15. Pont's map of *c.* 1590 shows the Z-plan tower built in 1546 by John Grant which forms the core of the present castle. There were small additions in the beginning of the C17 and two wings were built in the C18. From 1847 to 1850, there was a grand-scale remodelling and extension for Sir John Macpherson-Grant by *Mackenzie & Matthews*. It was they who covered the castle with its Baronial mantle.

The rear of the castle is its W front and here the C16 TOWER HOUSE is largely unchanged. Its plan is an unusual variation of the Z-configuration for in addition to the expected SE and NW corners there is also a large bowed stair-tower in the middle with slit-windows and a quatrefoil shot-hole near the top. On the bottom l. is a segmental, bolection-moulded door frame, formerly the main entrance until Mackenzie's recasting.* Little stair-turret corbelled up in the re-entrant angle above it. On top of the tower, a square caphouse added in 1602 by Patrick Grant (fourth Laird) and his wife, Helen Ogilvie. Corbelled base of striated mouldings and a bowed oriel in the centre (now glazed in the back), like those at Balvenie, Gordon Castle and the 'Bishop's House' in Elgin (qq.v.). Sculpted

*In the C16 and C17 the main entrance would have been via a forestair to the great hall on the opposite side.

plaques to the l. and r. with datestone and the patrons' initials. The original hall block extends one bay to the l. and r., three bays and four storeys with crowstepped gables on the ends. Four windows in the upper half, the top ones given wall-head gablets by *Alexander Ross* in 1869. Big initials for Sir George Macpherson-Grant and his wife, Frances Elizabeth Pocklington; thistle and rose finials as per C17 custom. To the l. is the NW tower of 1546, extending slightly beyond the main block and topped by a conical roof with chimneystack. Looming on the far r. is a tall transverse caphouse with two chimneystacks, looking deceptively C16 but actually added by Mackenzie.

Two wings form a U-plan with courtyard in the centre. The S WING was built in 1718 by Col. William Grant. Three storeys and two very wide bays with datestone in the middle of the l. side. Upper windows breaking the wall-head under gablets, the r. added *c.* 1965 by Sir Ewan Macpherson-Grant. It shows a primitive cat sitting on a band of rope moulding. In the r. corner, a three-stage drum tower added by Mackenzie with conical roof on top. The terminal (W) gable has a canted oriel with long, roll-moulded windows and a corbelled stone roof. The similar N WING was built *c.* 1770 for Gen. James Grant, former governor of Florida and notorious gourmand, as a kitchen and house for his favourite French chef.

The S FRONT of the castle is composed of the 1718 wing as refenestrated by Mackenzie with four voluptuously C17-style dormerheads. Tourelle at the E corner where it joins to the SE tower of the original tower house, to which Mackenzie gave the high, corbelled stair-turret with candlesnuffer roof, oriel window and caphouse. The tower was reconfigured as the grand new entrance and here Mackenzie unleashes his full arsenal of Baronial vocabulary in the mighty rectangular ashlar doorpiece with bolection moulding, the sides key-blocked with Neo-Jacobean strapwork. Plaque above it carved with helm, coat of arms and two rather racy heraldic Hercules. On the bottom is the Macpherson motto, 'Touch not the cat bot a glove' and on the top, the Grants', 'Ense et animo' ('With a sword and courage'). Rectangular window above flanked by square chain links; blind ogee arch over it topped by an angel with excellent, feathery wings. N of the tower on the E front is again the C16 hall block with mid-C19 short drum tower on the r. corner with tall candlesnuffer roof. A large bedroom wing built in front in 1875–8 by *Ross & Mackintosh* was wisely demolished 1965–7. N SERVICE WING added in 1847–50 in a style to match the rest, one and a half storeys. Its E arm ends in a tower set at an angle, with chamfered angles and crowstepped caphouse. N arch under a crowstepped gable with lion skewputts and bellcote.

The INTERIOR was thoroughly remodelled by Mackenzie in a consciously historicist style, invoking all of his antiquarian interests. Octagonal ENTRANCE LOBBY, converted from one of the original cellar storehouses. Windows with segmental rere-arches and deep embrasures covered by beaded panelling, preceded by a big band of nailhead. Complex plaster rib-vault springing from dragon corbels, the centre a round fan tapering into a consoled pendant finial. A passage leads to the quasi-octagonal ENTRANCE HALL, with depressed segmental ribs springing from corbels and a centre column, the ribs with excellent, very rich foliage. Off this is Mackenzie's cantilevered, open-well STAIRCASE, with thick, tapered balusters and ball-finialled newel posts. The DRAWING ROOM (originally the Billiard Room) is in the centre of the 1718 wing. White marble chimneypiece with engaged, fluted columns on the jambs. SMOKING ROOM beyond with an elliptical patera on the mantel. On the upper floor the LIBRARY, completely panelled in 1847–50, the bookcases with entablatures. The DINING ROOM on the first floor of the central block is the site of the Great Hall. Just outside on the stair landing is a fine rectangular TABLET dated 1601 with Patrick Grant and Helen Ogilvie's initials. The dining room itself is a feat of Neo-Jacobean verisimilitude – panelled in American pine and the overdoors with more big nailhead. The chimneypiece is bolection-moulded with substantial surround on caryatids of wild men with clubs. Enormous heraldic crest for the overmantel. Opulent ribbed plaster ceiling, designed from casts taken from Craigievar Castle (S). Each compartment is a large octagonal flower, the cardinal petals round and the diagonals ogival. Squares (and one circle) with foliate borders and pendants in the centre.

A few other relics are scattered around the original tower house. The original turnpike staircase winds up the central tower in the W side. Further stairs to the caphouse with machicolation over the original entrance, its lintel dated 1602 with the names Patrick Grant and Helen Gordon carved in good script. The so-called PINK TOWER is one of the original castle bedrooms, its chimneypiece incorporating a marriage lintel of 1546. Long inscription in capital letters to John Grant and Barbara Gordon, the original builders of the tower house.

Good collection of buildings in the POLICIES. The beautiful parkland was laid out with 'formal avenues' in the early to mid C18 but ravaged by the 1829 floods. 200 m. NNW of the castle a large piend-roofed DOOCOT built in 1696. At the former HOME FARM, 200 m. SSE a good STABLE of *c.* 1800. Single-storey-and-attic, nine bays in all, the middle three pedimented over elliptical arches. – Atop the hill to the NE is THE BOW, built as a kiln barn *c.* 1775 but a cottage from the early C19. Placed here to maximize the wind for winnowing. Two storeys and four bays, the kiln formerly in the S gable (upper brick dome still *in situ*). On a ridge 400 m. N of The Bow is the MAUSOLEUM for Gen. James Grant †1806. Granite square with rusticated quoins and crenellated wall-head. Each side has a minimally advanced centre with an elliptical arch. Vault below with a marble sarcophagus. Tall obelisk on top.

The SOUTH LODGE, 900 m. SE is the finest building on the policies. Impressive Baronial by *Mackenzie & Matthews*,

1850–3 – a fitting precursor to the splendour they unleashed upon the main house, incorporating a round-headed arch studded with nailhead. GATES like two gigantic hinged yetts. Close to this, on the A95, the delightful SWISS COTTAGE of *c.* 1860. Weatherboarded first storey with jettied balcony, silhouette balusters and deep bracketed eaves (cf. the Swiss Cottage, Gordon Castle, Fochabers).

CLAVA CAIRN, in the field W of Lady Macpherson-Grant Hall. Early Bronze Age, originally with an outer circle ringed by monoliths (diameter *c.* 30 m.). Five stones remain *in situ*, three standing and two fallen on the ground. – STONE CIRCLE, 0.5 km. WSW of the cairn on an exquisite site overlooking the Avon. It was once a clava-type passage grave, now with five stones upright and a longer one fallen to the SE. Fairly complete kerb of rectangular blocks, the S with a projecting entrance that is still partially lintelled. Remains of another cairn lie within the policies of the castle. Its outer circle originally comprising eleven orthostats, *c.* 14 m. in diameter. Five stones are now upright and four have fallen. One kerbstone remaining in the W part of the arc.

BALVENIE CASTLE *see* DUFFTOWN

1060

THE BIELD

2.4 km. W of Elgin

Scots Renaissance mega-villa by *J.B. Dunn*, built 1927–32 for Edward Stroud Harrison, woolmill magnate of Elgin. Rather amorphous N façade, the centre crowstepped with a bolection-moulded doorpiece under stepped hoodmould. Four flat-walled bays to the r., the first two with long rectangular stair windows. Two built-in garages beyond with joggled, keystoned lintels and thistle-finialled hinge plates. Service court on the far l. with arched entrance and Neo-Jacobean balustrade. S façade facing out over the Lossie, its centre with a double-arcaded loggia with round column and capitals carved with

The Bield.
Drawing of south elevation, 1928

exaggerated volutes – allusions to the C17 arcading of Elgin's High Street. Stilted segmental dormerheads above; crow-stepped gables minimally advanced to the l. and r., the former jettied out over a canted bay window. Nicely bizarre chimneystacks on the flanks.

Good original detailing inside, including an oak STAIRCASE, top-lit BILLIARD ROOM and former LIBRARY (over the garage) with bold modillioned chimneypiece and original intercom unit.

BIRNIE 2050

PARISH CHURCH, Paddockhaugh.* A most significant Romanesque church, set in rural isolation on a small hillock. Traditionally said to be dedicated to St Brendan. Although small it is a building of high quality, presumably because, together with Spynie and Kinneddar, it was one of the churches on which the earlier bishops of Moray based their see (Bishop Simon de Tosny is said to have been buried here in 1184). An episcopal residence probably stood on Castlehill, about 1.5 km. SE. After the see was fixed at Spynie *c.* 1207, Birnie was ineffectively granted to Kelso Tironensian Abbey; in 1239 it was instead granted to the canons of Elgin Cathedral.

The church probably dates from not long after the first record of a bishop of Moray, *c.* 1120. It is a two-cell structure built of fine ashlar; externally, a narrow chamfered base course remains visible below the E parts of the chancel where the ground is still at the medieval level. The only original openings are single small windows in the S and N chancel walls, their round-arched heads being cut into lintels; they have a narrow rebate externally. There is no E window. A larger window has been inserted in the W part of the S chancel wall; only the tracery stubs remain, but it may have had two cusped circlets at the head of a pair of lights. A rectangular doorway has been inserted below it. All openings in the nave are post-medieval. There are opposed round-headed doorways towards the W end of the S and N walls (the latter blocked) which perhaps date from 1817 in their present form. There are three windows in the S wall, two E of the doorway and one to the W; these had three-centred arches, possibly of 1817 when repairs were made, but they were reduced in size and given semicircular heads *c.* 1970 by *John Wright* of Elgin. The W gable has a bellcote capped by an ogee-profile rectangular dome with an urn finial; its W face is dated 1734, when the nave was slightly shortened.

The chancel arch is the finest feature, its square-profile inner 12
order carried on semicircular shafts, and on the W side a

*This entry is by Richard Fawcett.

hoodmould with a lower chamfer supported by extensions of the abaci of the respond capitals, which are scalloped with inverted stepped ornament cut into the lunettes. The C12 windows in the chancel flanks have widely splayed rere-arches. Until the restoration of 1891 by *A. Marshall Mackenzie* the E part of the chancel was partitioned off as a vestry, and there was a gallery for the poor of the parish in the nave. Mackenzie inserted the boarded ceiling of polygonal profile over the reopened chancel, and constructed the open-timber nave roof with arched braces below collars.

FURNISHINGS. – PULPIT, *c.* 1891, with linefold panels. – FONT, set on a spiralling shaft of 1885, the semi-hemispherical bowl has an octagonal rim, but no drain – was it a domestic mortar? – STAINED GLASS. Four windows by *Crear McCartney*, the three in the chancel with especially rich and luminous colouring. – S side, St Ninian, 1979, and Christ stilling the storm, 1965. – N side, St Brendan, undated. – W nave window, St Columba, 1998. – MONUMENT. Rev. William Sanders †1670. Tablet (reset) framed by pilasters capped with angel heads, below a tall pediment with arms and *memento mori*. – HAND BELL, behind a grille in the S chancel window rere-arch, *c.* 900, the largest of the Scottish bells of this type; tall and of tapering rectangular section, formed from two pieces of riveted iron, with a loop handle.

CHURCHYARD. Railed enclosure with monuments for George Leslie †1871 and his parents (†1857 and †1853). Inscription on an unfurled scroll, the bottom spilling diagonally over the base. Inverted trapezoidal finial with demi-urns to the l. and r. – PICTISH SYMBOL STONE, at the NW corner of the original churchyard. An irregular granite boulder incised with an eagle above a divided rectangle and Z-rod. The whereabouts of four other fragments, possibly all from a single cross-slab, is currently unknown. – WAR MEMORIAL (W wall), 1921. Gabled surround to a stepped round-headed arch with two scalloped capitals like the chancel arch.

THE GRANGE, 150 m. WSW. Formerly the manse. Much-altered rear section incorporating original building of *c.* 1753 and 1810–11 (by *David Baxter*, minister of Birnie, and *George Brown*, the Earl of Seafield's factor). E front by *Peter Brown*, the subsequent factor, 1839–40.

THE BENRIACH DISTILLERY, 2.3 km. E. Built as Ben Riach-Glenlivet Distillery by *Charles C. Doig*, 1897–8, but closed two years later. Production resumed 1965. Not to Doig's usual E-plan, but split in two long parallel lines straddling the former rail spur (now paved over). On the N side are the MILL ROOM, pagoda-roofed KILN and double-piended MALT BARN. – Long string of WAREHOUSES to the SE, the first two of 1897.

Former COLEBURN DISTILLERY, 4.9 km. SE, off the A941. Built as Coleburn-Glenlivet Distillery by *Doig*, 1895–7. Closed 1985; to be converted into a hotel and conference centre by *Colin Armstrong Associates*. Classic E-plan on a large scale and in an unusually well-hidden location. Long double-gabled malt barn flanked by a pagoda-roofed kiln (on the l.) and slightly lower barley drying mill with depressed segmental roof (on the r.). – Original EXCISE OFFICER'S HOUSE next to the main entrance. Gabled dormers.

GLENLOSSIE & MANNOCHMORE DISTILLERIES (Diageo), 1.2 km. SE, Thomshill. Glenlossie (originally Glenlossie-Glenlivet) was designed by *A. Marshall Mackenzie* in 1876–7 – an early example of concrete construction, fulsomely praised at its opening for looking 'beautifully white and clean'. Mackenzie's tall, pagoda-roofed KILN and long MALT BARN to the rear survive near the main entrance, the rest rebuilt after a fire in 1929 and later modernized. Drab Mannochmore Distillery laid out immediately to ENE in 1970–1. Along the whole N side of the complex runs a behemoth row of WAREHOUSES, the first three gables the originals and standing alone until *c.* 1913.

LONGMORN DISTILLERY (Chivas Brothers), 2.9 km. E, next to BenRiach. Built as Longmorn-Glenlivet Distillery by *Charles C. Doig*, 1893–7, on the site of an early C18 corn and sawmill. Of the original E-plan, the long MALT BARN and pyramidal, pagoda-roofed KILN attached to its NW corner. – Disused STATION to NW, opened 1862 for the Morayshire Railway. Closed 1968. Yellow and brown weatherboarding; piended roof with three square chimneystacks in the back. – Former MANAGER'S HOUSE (Culdeen) on the main drive. Gableted dormers and canted bay windows. Multi-pane glazing in the upper sashes. – LONGMORN HOUSE (0.2 km. ENE), built for William Ramsay and later used by the owners. Grand, charming single-storey villa by Doig, 1890–1, with rippling ridge-tiled gables and Tudor-style chimneypots.

BLAIRFINDY *see* GLENLIVET

BLERVIE CASTLE *see* RAFFORD

BLERVIE HOUSE 0050

0.9 km. SSE of Rafford

Large, and in the restrained Scots classical style of *c.* 1700, by *J.M. Dick Peddie*, 1906–11. The patron was Major Harold B. Galloway, killed in the Battle of Loos, whose memorial window is in Rafford church. Blervie is the last country house built in Moray before the First World War, and the dying pronouncement of Edwardian confidence. E façade of two storeys and twelve bays in snecked rubble, the ends slightly projecting with channelled angle pilaster strips. Generous multi-pane glazing, longer on the ground floor. Central porte cochère on two pairs of Roman Doric columns; windows above with key-blocked, quasi-Gibbsian architraves and then a large segmental pediment on the wall-head with helm, coat of arms and the motto 'Higher'. Broadly similar W front to the garden with central pediment flanked by three segmental-headed dormers to the l. and r. The ends here are given full-height shallow bows with tripartite windows, as at Lorimer's Wemyss Hall (Fife).

Spacious interior with simple detailing, as outside; it was gutted and carefully restored by *Michael Laird & Partners* in 1985. A transverse HALL spans the length of the building with groin-vaults springing from paired Roman Doric columns and pilasters. The latter form a screen to an open-well STAIRCASE with turned wooden balusters, all top-lit by a cupola. Long DRAWING ROOM on the garden front of two sections with retractable partitions to separate them. The S half has French doors to the hall with semicircular fanlights and Neo-Georgian radial glazing; simple chimneypieces at each end.

SSW of the house, a delightful TOPIARY MAZE designed by *Randall Coate*, *c.* 1988. Large and of four stages, arranged stepwise in 'ziggurat' fashion. – FOUNTAIN at the top, originally located in the E garden. – STABLE BLOCK flanking it, 1908 and also by *Peddie*. – The drive's GATEPIERS with swagged urns are of *c.* 1776 and were formerly at Blervie Mains House (*see* Rafford).

BLERVIE MAINS HOUSE *see* RAFFORD

BOAT O' BRIG *see* MULBEN

BOGMOOR *see* TUGNET

BOHARM *see* MULBEN

BOHARM BURIAL GROUND *see* CRAIGELLACHIE

BOTRIPHNIE *see* DRUMMUIR

BRIDGEND OF GLENLIVET *see* GLENLIVET

9050

BRODIE CASTLE*

1 km. SW of Dyke

86 A massive tower house built incrementally in the C16 and C17, then enlarged in the C19. It was probably begun *c.* 1540–60,

*This entry is by David W. Walker.

perhaps by Thomas, 11th Brodie of Brodie, who was killed at the Battle of Pinkie. Originally an L-plan, it was augmented to a Z-plan by the addition of a tall SW tower in 1567. Its NW wing was added or completed by Alexander the 15th Brodie *c.* 1635–40 and further renovations took place in 1714. In the 1730s and 40s the house was more radically remodelled with a new main stair by the Elgin master-mason *John Ross*. Immediately after his accession in 1824, William the 22nd Brodie commissioned *William Burn* to massively enlarge the house in the newly fashionable Jacobethan style – similar to Burn's Riccarton (Lothian; dem.) – but only the E half of the scheme was built, doubling the house in size. After William married Elizabeth Baillie of Redcastle, a wealthy heiress, he approached *James Wylson* of York, who partially remodelled Burn's work *c.* 1845–50 in a Baronial idiom more consistent with that of the tower house. Still a seat of the family, Brodie is now cared for by the National Trust for Scotland, which restored it *c.* 1979–80.

EXTERIOR. The original L-plan TOWER HOUSE forms the E part of the C16–C17 structure. It comprises the three-storey-and-attic main block (*c.* 12 m. by 8 m.) orientated E–W* in local pink sandstone with its small windows still surviving at ground and second floor, and a taller NE jamb which contained the entrance on its N face, now enveloped by later additions. As first built the main block had parapets and a caphouse but these were removed in the 1730s when *John Ross* gave it its present gabled roof, very conservative in style for that date. It had three pedimented dormers seemingly reused from the caphouse, but those now present are copies dating from the 1840s.

The original plan of the tower house was related to the group of tower houses associated with the *Conn* family of masons (*see* North Aberdeenshire) in having a turnpike stair (now an empty well) in its E wall, but the jamb was smaller than usual, resulting in a very small private apartment adjoining the hall on the first floor. To remedy this defect the tower house evolved into a Z-plan with the addition in 1567 of the SW TOWER. It is unusually large – 7 m. square – reflecting a requirement for a significant increase in accommodation on each floor, and four storeys high with a richly detailed corbel course, a wall-head parapet with square and circular bartizans and water cannon, and a crowstep-gabled caphouse. Unlike the NE jamb it is hinged at the angle to produce a stepped frontage on both the S and W, with a deeply corbelled turnpike stair in its E re-entrant angle. A datestone carved with mason's tools has been set into the caphouse walls. In the tower's flank are two wide-mouthed shot-holes; those on the N are blocked by the later additions.

*Strictly speaking, the main block lies NE–SW, but the orientation has been simplified here to aid understanding.

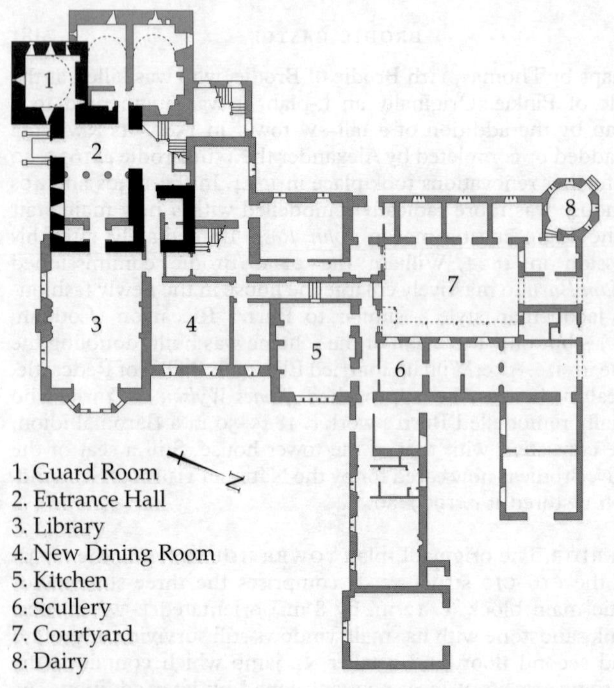

GROUND FLOOR

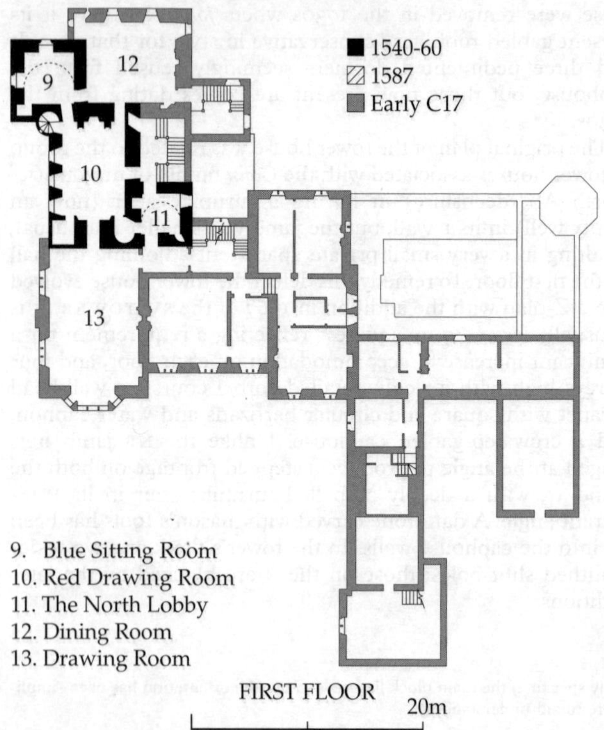

Brodie Castle.
Ground-floor and first-floor plans

Built into the angle between the main block and the SW tower is the early C17 NW wing. Like the main block it is three-storey-and-attic, is of comparable size (11 m. by 9 m.) and has a another wide-mouthed shot-hole in its end gable. Two offsets between the first and second floors suggest it has been completed to a modified design. Its renewed dormers bear the initials of David the 14th Brodie (†1632) and the monogram of his son Alexander and daughter-in-law Elizabeth Innes (married 1635–40). Its N gable and diagonally shafted chimneystacks look later C17 but may be part of the 1714 works. The addition of this wing resulted in a U-plan N front, infilled by a new stair in the 1730s which also enclosed the original entrance; the replacement entrance was a N porch (itself now long demolished) with an elliptical forecourt. In the NW wing and SW tower, three diptych SUNDIALS.

The E WING, dating from *c.* 1825–8, is the only executed part of *Burn*'s proposals, which had included reorientating the entrance to a new stair-hall porch on the S side of the original tower and adding a large W wing. The old tower house escaped largely unaltered, though with its entrance moved from N to S. The E range was built by Burn at right angles to the tower house, two-storey-and-attic with big mullioned-and-transomed windows under stepped hoodmoulds and projecting end bays which originally rose into curvilinear gables. Its S end was taller than the remainder to accommodate the Drawing Room, its flank on the main entrance front rising into twin gables. The S front owes its final form to *James Wylson*, who restored the SW tower's caphouse *c.* 1846 and raised its stair-turret into a spirelet while also remodelling Burn's E range so that the entire S front now presented a more consistently Baronial appearance – a reflection of the development of interest in Scottish styles over twenty years. The gables of the E range were reworked as as crowsteps with a buttressed chimney-breast between them (with a reset stone carved with David the 13th Brodie's arms impaled with his wife's, dated 1602), so answering the crowsteps of the SW tower's caphouse. He also formed the short stone balustrades leading to the entrance in the angle between the SW tower and the main block, their pyramid-capped, ball-finialled terminals carved with the monograms of the 22nd Brodie and his wife.

In the late C19 the single-storey-and-attic SERVICE WING, originally separate from the main house, was linked to the E range's N end, and the SERVICE COURTS begun by *Burn* *c.* 1825–8 were completed behind them. These have an octagonal dairy at their NW angle. Two small outshots built against the tower house's N elevation provided a butler's pantry and service stair.

INTERIOR. The original internal layout, in which the great hall occupied the whole of the main block's first floor, is characteristic of larger early to mid-C16 tower houses in the north-east. As a result, the principal accommodation is stacked vertically and the structure is unusually tall – cf. Inverugie

(North Aberdeenshire), Castle Fraser, Midmar and Harthill (South Aberdeenshire) and Inshoch (Highland), with which the Brodies had connections.

The crypt-like ENTRANCE HALL on the ground floor was formed by *Wylson* from the tower house's kitchen and cellar, their segmental vaults being supported on two massive squat columns and two half-columns with Neo-Romanesque capitals of scrolled waterleaf, carved by Mr *Square*, mason. The Hall opens onto the MAIN STAIR, which at this lowest level with twisted balusters is either *Burn*'s or *Wylson*'s work, although the cantilevered upper flights are by *Ross* working in the 1730s–40s. Behind the main stair is the late C19 DINING ROOM STAIRCASE, its stained-glass window displaying the Brodie arms, possibly by *William Wailes*. The vaulted GUARDROOM still survives in the SW tower. On the Entrance Hall's E side the original doorway in the NE jamb has also survived, a carved stone above it recording works in 1602 and 1714. It leads into a LIBRARY formed by *Wylson* from storerooms in the ground floor of Burn's E range. Its panelled island bookcases with egg-and-dart cornices support a compartmented ceiling. Floors and doors are American oak and the walls were once lined with imitation morocco. The fireplace between the S-side windows is of a reddish-pink marble.

The FIRST-FLOOR rooms are much taller with larger windows, and are correspondingly brighter. The RED DRAWING ROOM is the former great hall of the tower house. It was transformed by *Burn* into a picture gallery and has classical pedimented doorpieces on the N and E sides and a compartmented ceiling with egg-and-dart and waterleaf moulding. These clash with the remarkable Gothic fireplace at the W end by *John Carter Allan* and *Charles Manning Allan* (the eccentric brothers known also as the 'Sobieski Stuarts') and *Augustus C. Clarke*. Installed in 1831 it is designed like a reredos with tiers of niches for carved wooden figures, apparently C17, acquired by the 22nd Brodie in the Low Countries. The Red Drawing Room may once have been vaulted and plastered like the BLUE
70 SITTING ROOM adjoining in the SW tower. The vaulted ceiling here, centred on a hand clutching a fistful of arrows, is decorated with rough but vigorous strapwork dating from Alexander the 15th Brodie's marriage to Elizabeth Innes (1635–40): their arms appear over the fireplace and there is a loving token in the S window's soffit. It has a deep frieze of scrolls and fruit between moulded cornices, richly decorated ribs, geometric patterns, thistle and rose motifs, and foliage and cherubs' heads. The deep-blue flock wallpaper is mid-C19.

74 The plasterwork of the DINING ROOM (originally the laird's room) in the NW wing is quite different. This is compartmented and modelled in very deep relief. There are octagons on the sides and ends, and beams thickly decorated with foliage and garlands. At each corner are half-naked female figures interpreted as the Four Elements, but smaller motifs among the elaborate detail represent the Scottish thistle and

crown, a pelican in piety, a unicorn, and an angel with a sun and a crown. Although in form and decoration it is ostensibly similar to late C17 ceilings at Holyrood (Edinburgh) and Thirlestane (Borders) carried out by London plasterers, this is provincial work and very probably C18, perhaps even as late as the 1730s–40s. The room does indeed have a veined marble fireplace typical of that period and the fielded panelling is also of that date. During the late 1820s both the panelling and the plasterwork were grained to resemble oak (cf. Burn's grained rooms at Auchmacoy and Banff Castle in North Aberdeenshire).

In contrast to the dining room, the DRAWING ROOM in *Burn*'s E wing is relatively demure; like the Red Drawing Room it was intended as a picture gallery. Typical of Burn at this time, it has a Louis XV fireplace. The proto-Puginian ceiling may be *Burn* or *Wylson* but the painted Neoclassical decoration of the doorways, architraves and ceiling – once gilded – is of after 1868 (dated by the initials of Hugh Brodie and Elizabeth Moreton, who were married in that year). Accidentally overpainted in the earlier C20, it was restored by *Rab Snowden* in 1982. The Drawing Room opens, following usual Burn precedent, into the PRIVATE APARTMENTS, including the family bedroom, two dressing rooms, a bathroom and what was possibly a small breakfast room, accessible from the ground floor by means of their own grand stair.

On the SECOND FLOOR what is now the PICTURE ROOM in the tower house's main block would once have provided bedchamber accommodation. It may have been divided into two rooms when the SW tower was added to the original L-plan in 1567, each being accessed by one of the turnpike stairs. In the NW wing the BEST BEDCHAMBER retains a simple mid-C17 band of plasterwork around the ceiling edges with motifs at the corners. Its frieze is concealed by bolection-moulded panelling of *c.* 1680–90.

POLICIES. The process of draining and enclosing the marshy ground around the castle was begun after 1724. William Roy's survey of 1747–52 shows the results, but re-landscaping continued for decades and George Brown's estate survey of 1770 shows an ambitious – evidently ornamental – landscape in which the Pennick Road which once cut through the policies had been diverted along the S boundary. When William the 22nd Brodie inherited in 1824 he favoured a more picturesque approach. In 1868 he engaged *John Clerk* as head gardener, who was responsible for many improvements and was still in service in 1889. Five avenues radiate from the castle. The SW AVENUE is shown in Roy's survey and at that time extended for 1 km. from the NW wing. By 1770 a green had been formed nearest the castle and the avenue's far end curtailed by a formal canal ending in a *rond-point* with four lagoons beyond. The canal was de-formalized and amalgamated with the lagoons as an elongated pond during the C19 changes. The SE AVENUE was originally formed as a serpentine path in the 1750s or 60s but straightened out probably *c.* 1830 to run towards the castle's new S entrance; with the E AVENUE, formed in 1832 from a vista running through the 'Bush of Begarrack,' it enclosed a fruit orchard, now a woodland. To the NE lies an informal SHRUBBERY, also laid out by the 22nd Brodie, where in 1770 there had been a 'Wilderness'. The shrubbery contains two re-set SUNDIALS – one a carved stone polyhedron, perhaps C17, on a slim tapered shaft and base; the other a C19 baluster-type, with copper dial signed by *Adie* of Edinburgh. Beyond the shrubbery lies the WALLED GARDEN, its random rubble walls on its N and E sides probably dating from 1832 but on the site of a formal garden and nursery laid out between 1752 and 1770.

COACHHOUSE AND CARTSHED, 100 m. WNW. Probably after 1770; built as an addition to a structure (perhaps C16–C17) since demolished. Two-storeyed, rectangular on plan. On each long flank, three segment-headed carriage arches and oculi in raised ashlar surrounds. The roof was supported by posts rising from a central spinal wall but these were removed in 1846 during a disastrous attempt by *George Fowler Jones* to add a doocot tower. It was not proceeded with and the buttresses and partial infilling of the carriage arches date from his time.

The three LODGES are by *William Burn c.* 1825–8.

9 RODNEY'S STONE. By the driveway at the castle's entrance. A Pictish symbol stone found during excavations of the foundations for Dyke Church in 1781. It bears on one face an elaborately carved interlaced cross and on the back two fish monsters, a 'Pictish beast' and a double-disc and Z-rod. On the sides and back are the longest ogham inscription in Pictland, which includes the name EDDARRNONN. The inscription may be a dedication.

4060

BUCKIE

B

A fishing station from at least the mid C17. When Robert Burns visited in 1787, there were about 700 people and fourteen boats; by 1840, the herring boom had quadrupled the population. Cluny Harbour, begun 1873, was once the finest Scottish port N of Aberdeen. Until the early C19, the village was centred around the mouth of the Burn of Buckie (comprised of Seatown and Nether Buckie). The 'Newtown' was laid out to the E in the early to mid C19, consisting of two short streets set at right angles with the usual square in between. There was much expansion in the late C19 with many very windswept – and grim – streets lined with the usual cottages of the Moray coast.

CHURCHES

ALL SAINTS (Episcopal), Cluny Square. By *Alexander Ross*, 1875–6. A foil to the North Church, which it answers with subtle aplomb. Aisleless nave with three Geometric Dec S windows under gables and fine SW porch-tower with broach spire. Lower apsidal chancel with a ring of narrow cusped lancets. Simple but good interior, the chancel with a ribbed, panelled vault with light-blue sarking and roll-moulded chancel arch on chamfered responds. Kingpost roof over the nave. – FONT, 1877–8 by *Mr Leslie* of Inverness. Gothic – PULPIT and LECTERN by *A. Mardon Mowbray* of Oxford, 1892 – ORGAN. By *Bevington & Sons* of London *c.* 1872, for Cluny Castle (S). Here since 1877. Fine case with stencilled and gilded pipes. Angel on the W face with a scroll. – STAINED GLASS. Ten small panels of saints in the apse. In the centre, Peter, Madonna and Child, and John by *A.R. Mowbray & Co.*, 1925–6. Remainder by *St Enoch Studio*, 1928–31. – W windows by the same studio, 1930–1. – HALL, 1926 by *John Watt*. – RECTORY, 1877–8 and likely also by Ross.

BAPTIST CHURCH, Cluny Place. By *George Macpherson* of Buckie, 1909–10. E.E. with a W gable of coursed, rock-faced whinstone and buttresses with pinnacles. N entrance by *CM Design*, 2010–11.

GOSPEL HALL, West Church Street. 1905–6. Like a Scots Baronial villa.

METHODIST CHURCH, North Pringle Street. By *John Fowlie*, 1906–7. Wide front with a four-light, Tudor-arched window. Pairs of pointed rectangular windows in the flanks.

NORTH PARISH CHURCH, Cluny Square. Substantial, Dec style by *Mackenzie & McMillan*, 1878–9 following the creation of the new parish.* Its Scots crown spire is the landmark of the town. Gabled S door with trumeau and tympanum with thick Y-tracery. Five-light window above, the centre a tall lancet topped by two quatrefoils and a trefoil. Five lancets on the buttressed W flank. Impressively lofty interior with cast-iron columns supporting arched roof trusses across the centre and cusped straight braces in three directions for the roof over the U-plan gallery. – Classical rostrum PULPIT, 1879, in front of the ORGAN by *Brindley & Foster*, 1898 (brought from the Wesleyan Church, Keighley, Yorkshire, in 1953).

SOUTH AND WEST CHURCH, High Street/East Cathcart Street. The Free Church of 1849–50 by *A. & W. Reid*. W gable with three attenuated lancets under cusped heads and tall, three-stage tower to the l. with stepped angle buttresses and a ribbed broach spire. Lancets to the flanks. Inside, warmly coloured, with a GALLERY on three sides on cast-iron columns. Massive ORGAN against the N wall by *Wadsworth & Brother* of Manchester, 1900–1, behind the PULPIT. Octopartite rib-vault over the N entrance. – STAINED GLASS. W roundel, formerly in the West Church. Suffer the Little Children, *c.* 1930.

ST PETER (R.C.), St Andrew's Square. C13 Gothic on a metropolitan scale, visible from miles around as the Catholic 'cathedral' of Moray. Designed by Bishop *James Kyle*, 1851–7, with

*The chapel of ease to Rathven on the same site was by *William Robertson*, 1835–6.

much assistance from *A. & W. Reid*. The imposing W front is a version of Elgin Cathedral (q.v.), symbolic of newly emancipated Catholicism, with two towers flanking a gabled centre, each with plate tracery to the belfry and stone spires with pinnacles on the broaches and gabled lucarnes. In the centre the entrance has a pointed arch over cusped arches divided by a trumeau and blind quatrefoil in the tympanum. Four-light Dec window above, its cusped lights topped by sexfoils and a big, lobed sexfoil at the top with more fleur-de-lys spurs. Five bays to the flanks, with simple triple lancets in the clearstorey but completely windowless aisles. Slightly lower, rectangular chancel added by *C.J. Ménart*, 1906–7 (cf. Keith) and with the original E rose window re-set. Ménart's also the gableted NW porch and small SW baptistery (originally in the base of the SW tower). Nave arcades of five pointed arches, simply chamfered and hoodmoulded over lozenge piers. Open scissor-brace roof in the central vessel, the sides with herringbone panelling. Marble dado to the aisles, *c.* 1913. The pointed chancel arch was raised in 1906–7 and the semi-octagonal responds marbled in 1911. The one-bay SANCTUARY beyond was the original extent of the church; Ménart's is the arch to his extension.

Large and rich array of FURNISHINGS, mostly Gothic. Very ornate Dec REREDOS, 1906–7 by Ménart in Caen stone and polished Languedoc marble. Riot of pinnacles along the top divided by six angels with high wings. Diagonal square niches to the l. and r., linked to the back-board by crocketed arch braces. TABERNACLE in the centre with the Agnus Dei and pelican feeding her young. The ALTAR, also by Ménart (detached from the E wall, 1972) has cusped ogee arches with pierced Perp panelling above. Triple shafts of green marble. – LECTERN. Part of the original pulpit of 1911 by *George Scott* of Buckie (cut down in 2001). More Dec foliage and Languedoc marble; the rest of the PULPIT has a ribbed wooden canopy with dove in the centre and quatrefoil frieze with pinnacles and brattishing. – COMMUNION RAIL, 1906–7 with five different kinds of marble. Pierced quatrefoils and black cornice. – Bad WALL PAINTINGS on the inner bay of the sanctuary, whitewashed in 1947 and restored in 1990–1. Christ stilling the waters (on the r.) and walking on water (on the l.). – TILES (sanctuary) by *J. & R. Henderson* of Elgin, 2000–1. Crosses and crossed keys. – STATIONS OF THE CROSS, 1891–2, in gableted Dec frames. – FONT in the baptistery, *c.* 1906. Octagonal pillar and circular stone basin. Wooden cover with Christ kneeling before John the Baptist. – Wooden SCREEN behind it, 1922, originally in the entrance arch. Three elliptical arches under ogival hoodmoulds (formerly topped by a Crucifixion group). – ORGAN by *Bryceson Bros*, 1875. From the monastery of Fort Augustus (Highland and Islands), rebuilt here by *Rushworth & Dreaper*, 2000–1. W GALLERY rebuilt to support it at the same time.

STAINED GLASS. – E rose, *c.* 1880 and reset here in 1906. Brightly coloured foliage with Agnus Dei in the centre.

– Central window in the clearstorey triplets. N side (W to E): SS John, Andrew, James and Peter. S side (E to W): SS William, Mary Magdalene, Margaret, Stephen and Martin. – In the baptistery, a trefoil with descending dove, *c.* 1906. – WAR MEMORIAL. W wall. 1922, designed by *Cameron Macdonald*, carved by *Nicol Bros* of Buckie. Pietà of Carrera marble against an ogee arch with flanking niches with pierced octagonal canopies.

GATES by *Hendry Dyce*, 1957. Crosses, scrolls and trabeated overthrow with Papal tiara and crossed keys of St Peter. – PRESBYTERY attached to NE, *c.* 1858.

Former WEST CHURCH, Cluny Square/Cluny Place. Now flats. Built as the United Presbyterian church, 1869–70.

PUBLIC BUILDINGS

CLUNY PRIMARY SCHOOL, West Cathcart Street/South West Street. Long double-U plan, begun 1938, the design by *James Wood*, Banffshire County Architect; completed 1947. S front of twenty-one bays with piended roof, cupola in the centre.

COMMUNITY HIGH SCHOOL, West Cathcart Street. Long piended I-plan of 1924–6 by *James Wood*, then Banffshire County Education Dept Architect. Stripped classical style. Central pavilion wing with square cupola and leaded domelet. Large complex to the rear, built 1974 with extensions by *Moray Council*, 1989–90 and 2008–10.

FISHERMEN'S HALL, North Pringle Street. 1885–6. Classical façade, tripartite with pilasters (channelled on the ground floor) and central pediment.

LIBRARY, Cluny Place. Built as the MASONIC AND LITERARY INSTITUTE, 1889–90 (extended by *John Wittet*, 1910–11). Wide, gabled bay on the l. with a large corbelled, canted oriel; consoled wall-head pediment to the r.

HARBOURS

BUCKIE (or CLUNY) HARBOUR. The first large harbour complex in Scotland to be constructed of concrete, now in use as a shipyard. Original section is on the W, a rough triangle built 1873–80 by *William Dyce Cay* (engineer) with assistance from *David Cunningham* and *James Barron* (resident engineer). Two piers off the S shore, the l. canted and enclosing a basin (now mostly infilled). Canted arm to the NE with a concrete lighthouse of 1878. Slightly tapered circular tower with projecting balcony and metal domed cupola with light. Major extensions to the E by *Charles Brand & Sons* of Glasgow, 1910–32 (*W. T. Douglas*, engineer, *c.* 1911–18). Very long pier on the N running E–W (parallel to the shoreline); three jetties to the S forming four basins.

BUCKPOOL (or SEATOWN) HARBOUR, off Main Street. By *D. & T. Stevenson* (engineers), 1855–7, overseen by *William Middlemiss*. Two piers, the l. arm long and canted and the r.

one shorter and pointing NW. Excellent masonry towards the sea, some of the courses laid diagonally. Superseded by Buckie Harbour *c.* 1878; infilled in 1985–6 after years of disuse and now serving as a park. – Pair of late C19 fish-smoking KILNS to the WSW, a rare survival. Tall vertical weatherboarding; corrugated-iron roof with raised, louvred ridges.

DESCRIPTION

The centre is CLUNY SQUARE, originally very unassuming but given its current form in 1897, when gigantic amounts of earth were extracted to make it level. In the NE corner the North Church (*see* above) and in the NW quarter the WAR MEMORIAL of 1924–5 by *John Kinross*, a tall pedestal supporting heroic bronze figures of a sailor and Gordon Highlander with a banner by *W. Birnie Rhind*. Behind this STRUAN HOUSE (No. 15), completed *c.* 1885, with crowstepped dormerheads and an octagonal tower with faceted bellcast roof (original upper stage and finial now missing) and the Episcopal church (*see* above). In the SW quarter, the CLUNY HOTEL, 1880, three storeys with crowstepped dormerheads and thick chimneys.

HIGH STREET bisects the square N–S. The section S of the square was laid out *c.* 1825 to form the nucleus of the Newtown. On the E side VIRGINIA BUILDINGS, *c.* 1897, seven bays with a central canted oriel and flanking Ionic pilasters. Pyramidal roof on the far l. with cast-iron brattishing.

EAST CHURCH STREET was established in the early to mid C19 as the other main street of the Newtown. On the N side a house and shopfront of 1884 with a nicely strange, scrolled Dutch gable topped by a little pediment and chimneystack and just beyond it the BANK OF SCOTLAND (formerly Caledonian Bank) by *Ross & Macbeth*, 1905–6. Channelling on the ground floor with exaggerated keystones; three key-blocked Ionic pilasters supporting a block modillion cornice. Big pediment with tympanum carved by *A. Milne & Son*, Buckie. Much further on, on the other side, the former POST OFFICE by *Sutherland & George*, 1914–16, with an open eaves pediment. Opposite, the former FREE CHURCH MANSE, 1887–8, with a stout chimneystack corbelled up over its central crowstepped gable. 'Nec tamen' and burning bush over the bolection-moulded door; recycled datestone to the r. from the original manse of 1843.* This begins the residential part of the street. No. 51 however is the former GENERAL REGISTER OFFICE, built 1919–20 with a tall pierced balustrade flanked by ball finials. PRESTON VILLA, 1897, on the S side, is the best of the houses, with a full-height canted bay window, two trussed gables and a fine original cast-iron gate. However, beyond the end of the street is CLIFF TERRACE, laid out *c.* 1904 to

*Formerly located in Cluny Square and dem.

capitalize on views over the harbour. Long row of mini-villas of 1904–12, each varied enough to make it unique. In front, a LEADING LIGHT by *Munro & Co.* (engineers), *c.* 1878, a tall, white metal cylinder with a little red dome.

WEST CHURCH STREET, W of Cluny Square, was created *c.* 1883 to link the centre with Nether Buckie. There is less here than in East Church Street but Carlton Bingo (No. 29) is the former PLAYHOUSE CINEMA by *Alister G. Macdonald* (son of Ramsay), 1938, behind an 1880s shopfront. Its cavernous interior retains an original balcony and painted columns on the walls. Further W, PRINGLE COURT on the S side is the former Public School of 1875–6 but with a three-stage tower added to the centre by 1893, its entrance with a blind quatrefoil in the tympanum. Triplets of pointed arches on the top storey, good ashlar with a corniced blocking course on top. QUEEN STREET, at the street's end was laid out 1907–9 to overlook the Burn of Buckie. The villas date from 1908 to 1913, the corner (No. 1) a Baronial bulwark of *c.* 1910 with crowsteps and crenellated bay window. VICTORIA BRIDGE of 1901 by *Stewart & Sons* of Peterhead (*P. M. Barnett*, engineer) carries West Church Street on three arches over the Burn of Buckie. Their first attempt collapsed in February 1801.

ARRADOUL HOUSE, 2 km. SSW. Big, harled T-plan of two separate campaigns, formerly the rectory for an Episcopal church built on the site *c.* 1772. The N–S arm is of 1833–4 by *William Robertson*, incorporating a mid-C18 core. Two storeys and four bays with twelve-pane glazing on the first storey. Upper arm added *c.* 1915 to create a new N front. Wide E porch with channelled end pilasters; two bay windows on the W and full-height bay window on the S gable, all also early C20.

INCHGOWER DISTILLERY (Diageo), 1.5 km. S. A tidy, rational plan by *A. & W. Reid*, 1870–1, replacing the former Tochieneal Distillery founded 1830 near Cullen (q.v.). Main complex aligned E–W around a tight rectangular courtyard. Former T-plan maltings in the lower r. corner; two former kilns with pagoda ventilators to the NW (the N now a boiler house). – Housing lining the l. side of the drive, also 1870–1 by the Reids. Warehouses across from them, the triple gable on the N of 1870 and the rest added 1960–78.

To the SSW (across the A98), the disused entrance to the former Buckie RESERVOIR, built in 1882. Ball finial on a tapered base with barrel-vault running behind.

BURGHEAD 1060

An exposed sandstone promontory, jutting out like a huge ledge into the Moray Firth. The peninsula was ideally suited for defence and likely occupied by the Romans. From the C4, it became the site of the largest Iron Age fort in Scotland and the mighty capital of Pictish Moray. Most of the ancient earthworks were obliterated by a new planned village laid out in 1805–9 by a group of investors including William Young of Inverugie, the founder of Hopeman (q.v.).* Standard gridiron plan composed of five streets with a sheltered harbour to the SW. The NE corner is now dominated by the Diageo maltings complex, opened in 1966 and expanded in 1969–71.

PARISH CHURCH, corner of Grant Street and Park Street. Built as the United Presbyterian church by *A. W. Bisset*, 1861–2. Simple E.E., the S gable with stepped triple lancets below a blocked trefoil. Shallow gabled porch in the centre added during renovations by *Wilsons & Walker*, 1907–8, when this became the United Free Church. Original three-stage tower to the r. with angle buttresses and octagonal stone broach spire on top. Area behind the tower filled in as a hall, 1897. The W flank has three original bays with lancets and then a single-bay extension with wall-head gable and vesica.

Simple interior with flat ceiling, as renovated in 1907–8. Two arches on the far r. carried on a wooden octagonal column (formerly fronting a short aisle, blocked off *c.* 2006 to form a kitchen). – GALLERY in the S on two cast-iron piers with rolled capitals. – STAINED GLASS. Two *dalle-de-verre* windows by *Dom Ninian Sloane* of Pluscarden Abbey, 1969. Abstract faceted glass set with 'Nec tamen consumebatur', motto of the Church of Scotland, spanning both.

FREE CHURCH, Grant Street. Neo-Romanesque by *A. & W. Reid*, 1844. T-plan vestry and hall attached to the rear, the latter with a little pyramidal-roofed belfry on its W gable as it served as the school until *c.* 1893. Interior as restored by *Sutherland & Jamieson*, 1891–2, with U-plan GALLERY on cast-iron piers.

OLD BURIAL GROUND, NW end of Grant Street. Site of an early Christian chapel, likely founded in the mid C6 and dedicated to St Aethan (or Aidan), a follower of Columba. Medieval ruins were visible until the end of the C18, and foundations of a square building were revealed in 1809 when the new town was built. – Reset on the W wall, an ogival DORMERHEAD dated 1680 with thistle finial, two horses and the monogram TCMS. Lower base course with the worn inscription 'Those that have sinned should not sit in judgement over others'.

COMMUNITY HALL, corner of Grant Street and Sellar Street. The former parish church by *A. & W. Reid & Wittet*, 1901–2; closed 1929 and converted *c.* 1947. Richly moulded entrance with round arch dying into chamfers; three quatrefoils above with crocketed hoodmould. Sturdy octagonal buttresses with spirelets and similar bellcote on the gable. Good corbel below it of the burning bush.

HARBOUR. *See* Description, below.

*He became the sole proprietor in 1818.

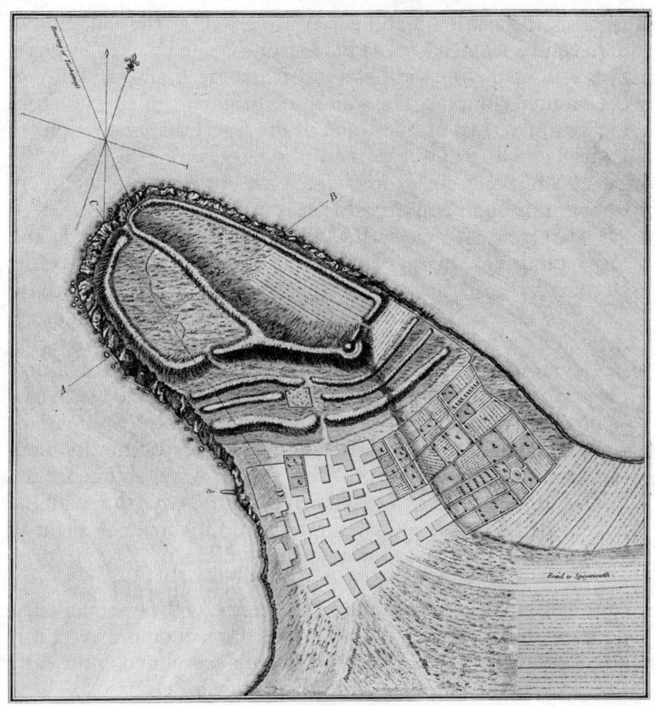

Burghead.
Plan, 1793

PRIMARY SCHOOL, Grant Street. By *A. & W. Reid*, 1886. Long, with two advanced porches (former boys' and girls' entrances) under fleur-de-lys finials. Cusped, circular belfry in the centre with good witch's hat spirelet and tiers of fish-scale slates.

WAR MEMORIAL, Grant Street/Granary Street. By *John Wittet*, 1920–1. Square pedestal with fluted angle pilasters and modillion cornice. Column on top with a lion seated on a composite capital.

DESCRIPTION. The W end of GRANT STREET gives way to grass-covered hillocks, all that now survive of what was once the largest PICTISH FORT in Scotland. Its original form is now difficult to make out, as most of the remains were destroyed to create the new planned village in 1805–9. Engravings from the mid C18 show a long ridge running down the centre of the promontory, demarcating one compound to the N and another to the S. These were protected from landward invasion by three ramparts in arrowhead formation, each *c.* 244 m. long. The walls were timber-laced and have been radiocarbon-dated to between 340 and 680 A.D. The original fortress is said to have been destroyed by fire *c.* 850 and rebuilt in 899 by Earl Sigurd of Orkney. The Danes refortified it in 1008 but were expelled from Moray by the Scots in 1010.

The central RIDGE still survives, as well as the tail ends of the N and S RAMPART WALLS. Despite being covered in grass, they still evoke the vastness and fearsome monumentality of the original complex. The walls were originally lined with strik-
11 ing SCULPTURES of bulls, one of the finest demonstrations of Pictish sculpture. Over thirty of the figures were discovered in the C19, but only six are known to have survived, a few of them now in the Elgin Museum (*see* p. 589).

DOORIE HILL sits at the junction of the central ridge and the S rampart. On top of it is the CLAVIE STONE, a short circular base of charred rock likely dating from the early to mid C19. Every 11 January (the 'Auld New Year'), villagers deposit a barrel of burning tar and wood here after processing with it around the town – a suitably pagan ritual for this bizarre
10 place. To the NE (at the end of King Street) is the BURGHEAD WELL, discovered in 1809 and misattributed by antiquarians to the Roman occupation. It is a unique survival but its function remains enigmatic – probably a fresh-water source for the Picts and later used as a baptismal pool in connection with the cult of St Aethan (*see* Old Burial Ground, above). A flight of steps leads down to a murky, spring-fed basin, *c.* 1.5 m. deep and hewed directly out of the rock. Square chamber with rounded corners surrounded by a ledge with a semicircular pedestal in the NE corner and a smaller basin on the SW. Little else is original – the pointed barrel-vault was added in the early C19, as was the entrance with its massive lintels.

The fortress's central ridge leads to the circular STORM SIGNAL, an unusual survival of the early to mid C19. Harled, whitewashed perimeter wall with stairs leading up to the top (formerly with a timber shelter used to guard the entrance to the Moray Firth in the Second World War). To the S is the harled former COASTGUARD STATION, two storeys and three bays of *c.* 1807 with a slightly lower piended wing to the l. Off the r. gable is a rescue equipment store, *c.* 1860, with sliding doors and a glazed oculus facing E. The HARBOUR stretches out below, originally designed by *Thomas Telford* in 1807–9. Thick quay on the S enclosing a long, rectangular basin. Long, canted W pier (extended in 1835 and 1839) with a pulvinated string course to the sea. Final canted angle of the late C19 beyond a whitewashed concrete beacon.

GRANARY STREET runs along the harbour's landward edge, its W end featuring two large former WAREHOUSES designed by Telford *c.* 1810 (now converted into flats). Four storeys and five bays each, originally served by their own siding on the Hopeman branch of the Inverness & Aberdeen Junction Railway (opened 1862; closed 1966). TORFNESS HOUSE, 1881, further down, is broadly similar, with two elliptical former cart bays on the ground floor. Continuous modern box dormer above.

BBC TRANSMISSION STATION, 1.3 km. ESE. Three tall lattice-girder masts secured by guy-wires, the first two 154.2 m. and 153.6 m. in height and the other one shorter. The mildly Art

Deco buildings by *Wimperis, Simpson & Guthrie*, 1934–6 (with *M. T. Tudsbury*, BBC engineer) were dem. 1984.

BURGIE HOUSE 0060

3.5 km. SE of Kinloss

The lands of Burgie were held by Kinloss Abbey (q.v.) from 1221 and then acquired by the Dunbar family in 1567. The present house is of 1802 for Lewis Dunbar Brodie, reusing stone from the earlier tower house (including a 1621 datestone on the E gable with the monograms of Robert Dunbar and his wife, Isobel Sharp). But its present character was established first by *Charles C. Doig* in 1903–4 and then by *W.H. Woodroffe* of London in 1912–14 during remodellings for Alexander Thomson, who had made his fortune in Ceylon. The result is handsome, substantial and well proportioned.

Long S entrance front of two storeys and seven bays over a raised basement, divided 1–1–3–1–1. Minimally advanced centre, the tall and steep piended roof – practically a mansard – and its three dormers added by Doig. Tall, narrow chimneystacks to the l. and r., greatly heightened in 1912–14 with sharply corniced bands of quatrefoils, a pattern also adopted for the parapets of the wings. Tetrastyle porch of paired Roman Doric columns added in 1914 with bowed windows on the flanks. Tripartite windows l. and r. with fasce and a Venetian window in the ground floor of the wings. Wide rear elevation, the advanced bay on the l. added by Woodroffe and topped by a piended roof. Five bays to the r. with four piended roofs and one box dormer; one more beyond it with another inserted Venetian window.

Good INTERIOR, remodelled in Arts and Crafts style by Doig and Woodroffe. The ENTRANCE HALL is set across the width of the centre block. Cantilevered, dog-leg staircase on the l. with knobby wooden balusters by Doig. It is screened off by three round arches carried on fluted Ionic columns. Similar elliptical arch in the centre of the hall and a timber chimneypiece with a reclining goddess and dog. In the former DINING ROOM, an Adamesque marble chimneypiece of 1802 with fluted pilasters and swagged urn in the centre. Beaded panelling on the dado, window shutters and doors, some original to 1802 and others early C20. Narrow cornice of acanthus from the original house; ceiling of geometric lincrusta added by Doig. The DRAWING ROOM has a fine original plaster frieze of 1802, the ground still painted yellow. Very thick with swagged urns, scrolls and paterae surrounded by concave lozenges.* In the OAK ROOM in the E wing a wide, recessed

*The ceiling originally matched but collapsed *c.* 1978.

Burgie Castle, before demolition.
Drawing, 1887

inglenook covered by panelling. Ceiling with thick, canted friezes of jumbo grapevine. The BILLIARD ROOM in the basement is 'textbook' Arts and Crafts with little glazed, pedimented cabinets on the overmantel. Panelled ceiling with ribs of bracket and egg-and-dart; copper light fixture with knobbed arms and six hanging lamps.

Former GARDENER'S LODGE on the drive, 1919–21 by *Charles C. Doig & Sons.** Two-stage tower in the re-entrant angle with bellcast pyramidal roof.

BURGIE TOWER, 0.3 km. SE. Of the Z-plan BURGIE CASTLE, first documented in 1589 and completed *c.* 1602 by Robert Dunbar, 1st Laird of Burgie, only the NW tower is intact, along with spur walls of the hall block to the E and S. A remarkably similar design to the tower of Blervie Castle (q.v.), it is of six storeys, impressively sheer with a fine crenellated parapet carried on triple corbels with long cannon waterspouts and three round, open tourelles. N face mostly plain, the base with two little elliptical gunloops and two rectangular windows above (the lower one grilled). The W and S sides have five windows running up the centre, the lowest with iron grilles and the upper ones narrower with chamfered margins. Circular stair-tower in the N re-entrant angle, corbelled out on the first floor as at Blervie.

The interior of the central block consists of a stack of single chambers, the top two (and basement) originally with segmental barrel-vaults. Door on the ground floor with an iron yett; fireplaces on the first, second and third, along with the usual collection of windows, aumbries and shot-holes. All that remains of the great hall in the central block is the large

*Replacing the original lodge just to the NNW by *John Urquhart*, *c.* 1835 (dem. *c.* 1920).

CHIMNEYPIECE with its mighty joggled lintel, thick segmental relieving arch and armorial plaque with the initials of Alexander Dunbar and Katherine Reid. Below them are Robert Dunbar's initials and the very faded date of 1602 and inscription 'MANET IMMUTABILE VIRTUS' (Truth Never Changes).* A drawing by Nattes of *c.* 1799 shows the hall block with a steep gabled roof and giant diamond bartizans with long faceted roofs – very unusual, picturesque features. To the S was the laird's extension by Ludovic Dunbar, *c.* 1702, five bays with a crowstepped gable and low pedimented dormerheads. Most of it was demolished a century later to construct Burgie House.

Just to the W, a tall lectern DOOCOT of the early C17, originally attached to the barmkin. Steep lean-to roof and chamfered central entrance. – Capacious former WALLED GARDEN to the S and E, laid out *c.* 1802. On the far E wall, the original portico of Burgie House with paired Roman Doric columns and a thick, corniced entablature.

THE CABRACH B 3020

Just a few buildings scattered amid dramatic scenery, beautiful and desolate in equal measure.

UPPER CABRACH CHURCH. Simple rubble rectangle, dated 1786 on its l. skewputt.[‡] S flank with four rectangular windows. E gable with a corniced birdcage bellcote and large ogival finial; vestry beyond it, *c.* 1900.– MONUMENT. Elizabeth Grant †1771 and her sons, George and John Gordon (S wall, reset from the previous church). Painted heraldic shield with a stag's head and the Gordon motto, 'Bydand'.

DEVERON HOUSE, 150 m. NNW. The manse of 1801–2. Two storeys and three bays with tall attic over raised basement. Similar rear block forming a double pile by *A. H. L. Mackinnon*, 1914. – BRIDGE, 100 m. WSW. Stilted segmental span over the Allt Deveron, 1820. Terminal pilasters with cushion finials.

Former LOWER CABRACH CHURCH, 4.6 km. NNW. Built as the United Presbyterian church by *Alexander Tod*, 1874–5; converted into a house by *Archid Architects*, 2012–13. Simple E.E. Former MANSE also by Tod, 1874, linked to the church by lower HALL and VESTRY added 1908.

BLACKWATER BRIDGE, 550 m. SSW. Single humpback span over the Blackwater Burn, late C18. Broad elliptical arch with gently peaked parapet.

BLACKWATER LODGE, 5.6 km. WNW of Upper Cabrach church. Used as a shooting lodge by the Dukes of Gordon and Richmond from the mid C19 (now greatly decayed). Two

*See also the datestone of 1621, now reset on the E gable of Burgie House.

[‡]Replacing a church of *c.* 1580 on the same site, itself a reconstruction of a late C12 chapel dedicated to the Virgin Mary.

storeys and three bays, the core built 1788–9 by *John McInnes*, mason, and enlarged twice in the C19. Similar rear block forming a double pile; service range beyond, partially laid out in the mid C18.

CABRACH HOUSE, 0.5 km. SE of Upper Cabrach church. Originally a simple T-plan shooting lodge of the late C18, augmented to an H-plan in the late C19. From 1980 to 1988, the entrance was reoriented to the N and extended to the NW. Exterior very plain and harled, mostly two-storeyed with ball finials on the gable ends. N porch with square piers and a big crenellated parapet. Rear front with two full-height, crenellated bay windows and single-storey loggia.

In complete contrast, interior remodelled on a lavish scale in the 1980s, with superb craftsmanship in hybrid Tudor/Jacobean style. Of special note the lofty and spacious L-plan GREAT HALL with a balcony at one end. Sumptuous half-panelling separated by pilasters with rinceau and lions' heads. Plaster ceiling with octagonal, compartmented rose in the centre. Large chimneypiece of Ham stone with Tudor arch and foliage spandrels. Another in the DINING ROOM, which has an open compartmented ceiling with cusped ogee beams and simple kingpost trusses. Edwardian-style BILLIARD ROOM with a chimneypiece from the former Eccentric Club, Ryder Street, London. Main STAIRCASE of the late C19 with trapezoidal balusters and Ionic-esque capitals.

LESMURDIE HOUSE, 350 m. ENE of Lower Cabrach church. L-plan of *c.* 1905, two storeys and three bays of pinned rubble with canted bay windows and gableted dormerheads. Observatory tower added by *Morrison & McCombie*, *c.* 1912; theirs also the former billiard room.

4060

CAIRNFIELD HOUSE B

3.4 km. SSW of Buckie

1799–1804 by *Robert Burn* (father of William) for Adam Gordon. Good, stately Georgian, nicely secluded in a pocket of trees. William Gordon, 1st Laird, had acquired the land *c.* 1615 but the C17 house was destroyed by fire in 1798. A re-set plaque (probably once a dormerhead) dated 1666 with helm, heraldry and the initials A.G. is all that remains. Seat of the Gordons of Cairnfield until *c.* 1972.

Built of pinned rubble with long-and-short ashlar dressings, two storeys over a raised basement with a platform-piended roof. Three wide bays on the N front, the centre minimally advanced with a Venetian window over a tripartite doorpiece approached by splayed steps. Pediment above. Plain S front, the centre again slightly advanced with a Venetian window on the ground floor. Tripartite window above it with a wide painted centre, both somewhat modified in the early to mid C20. This and the flanks are nicely harled in pink; the W has elliptical bullseyes in the centre of the basement and first floor.

E wing by *William Robertson*, 1825, a two-storey kitchen pavilion with a quadrant link to the house. On the N front a broad segmental arch containing baseless Doric columns under a trabeated lintel. Attached columns in the link. To the garden its centre is advanced as a semi-octagon. It became the garage and chauffeurs quarters *c.* 1926. A glazed vinery and peach house range was dem. in the early to mid C20. Behind the wing a detached outbuilding with a bellcote and reused C17 lintel with faded inscription of 'Gloria in . . .' and the initials NG. Robertson would have undoubtedly preferred a corresponding W pavilion, but the steep slope down to the Burn of Cairnfield rendered this impossible. Instead, added to the l. bay of the S front an extension of *c.* 1930 by *R.B. Pratt*.

Fine and inventive interior, using rectangular, circular and D-ended rooms, offering a pleasing interplay of differing spatial volumes. The ENTRANCE HALL is a compact ellipse. Good plaster ceiling and painted bucrania frieze with mutuled cornice. Good panelled doors and panelling also in the DRAWING ROOM, which has fine corniced overdoors with wispy foliage. The LIBRARY (former dining room) had especially fine overdoors carved with ferns and flowers. The library fittings and Adamesque chimneypiece are *c.* 2004. The small PARLOUR facing the garden has its Venetian window recessed in an elliptical arch and flanked by Corinthian pilasters. Modern cornice around the other walls with anthemion and palmette, deceptively good Georgian. Reassembled marble chimneypiece with a white Adamesque urn on the lintel. The whole centre of the house is taken up by a narrow STAIR HALL – and, with charming quirkiness, it can be accessed only via one door in the parlour or the SE door in the entrance hall. Full-height cantilevered staircase top-lit by an elliptical skylight. Delicate cast-iron balusters with pierced lozenges.

Former LODGE of *c.* 1840 for the factor. Early C20 timber trussing and rear extension by *Charles C. Doig & Sons*, 1939.

CARDHU *see* KNOCKANDO

CARRON 2040

Small Speyside hamlet, its main road running N from the distillery.

IMPERIAL DISTILLERY (Chivas Bros). Large Y-plan complex by *Archial*, 2013–14, one arm housing the mash tun and the other the still house. Tall chimney in between and long tun room running down the central spine. Its predecessor (by *Doig*,

1897–8; closed 2000) was the first fire-resistant distillery in Scotland, of Aberdeen red brick and featuring an enormous gilt crown over its kiln. Doig's range of stone WAREHOUSES and OFFICES is intact to the E, the latter with crowstepped gablets and crenelled parapets. – Five WORKMEN'S COTTAGES, 0.7 km. NW. Also by Doig, *c.* 1900, and inventively bizarre, with the sides of their lofty, piended roofs swept down into gableted entrances. – Former STATION by the main entrance, 1863 for the Strathspey Railway (closed 1968).

BRIDGE OF CARRON, 0.4 km. SE. By *Alexander Gibb* (engineer) and *William McKinnon & Co.* (ironfounders), 1863 for the Strathspey Railway. One of the best preserved, large-scale cast-iron bridges in Scotland – the last to be designed for railway traffic, and the final heir to the Telford tradition. Single segmental arch of 45.7 m. composed of three huge ribs, each cast in seven parts. Surprisingly graceful lattice work in the spandrels; wide, sturdy termini of rock-faced rubble with polygonal refuges. Large segmental flood arches below, one on each bank.

CARRON HOUSE, 1.1 km. E, in a secluded spot along the Spey. Originally a single-storey fishing lodge of *c.* 1840 with three sets of octagonal chimneys. Single-storey extensions to N, S and E (the kitchen block) *c.* 1860, thereby creating a broken quadrangular plan. NE corner filled *c.* 1890 by a conical-roofed turret with fish-scale slates. At the S end of the drive, a BRIDGE of *c.* 1862 over the former Strathspey Railway. Good ironwork on the parapet.

DAILUAINE DISTILLERY (Diageo), 1.7 km. ESE across the Spey. Opened by the farmer William Mackenzie in 1854; rebuilt and much expanded under his son, Thomas, from 1884–9. The architect was *Charles C. Doig*, and Dailuaine was the first distillery in Scotland to receive his now-iconic pagoda kiln ventilator. Doig finalized the design in 1889, allowing for optimal control of the peat smoke as it passed through the barley. The pagoda's inherent – and slightly exotic – aesthetic appeal were largely unintended. Doig's kiln was destroyed by fire in 1917 along with much of his complex, and there was then a major reconstruction in 1959–60. Still surviving from the late C19 are the continuous range of eight WAREHOUSES with unusual crowstepped gables, as well as the OFFICE with two glazed tourelles corbelled out under candlesnuffer roofs.

Former ENGINE SHED by the main entrance, *c.* 1902, now used as a store. Whitewashed brick with louvered spirelet. – Terrace of former WORKMEN'S COTTAGES along the ridge 250 m. to the NNE, also by Doig.

LAGGAN HOUSE, 1.3 km. ENE. In a tranquil position by the Spey. It was designed in 1860–1 by Major Gen. *Charles Simeon Thomason* while on sick leave from the Royal Bengal Engineers; he later oversaw the construction of many harbours, bridges and roads in India. Pleasant, asymmetrical Baronial with crowstepped gables and canted bay windows; two-stage drum tower in the re-entrant angle with big conical roof. The core was of red brick – a very rare material in N Scotland – but unfortunately now rendered. Additions – including the SW flank and rear service wing – by *A. & W. Reid*, 1879–83. The simple interior was remodelled by them and again in the early to mid C20.

TOMBRECK HOUSE, 0.4 km. NE. Large, asymmetric U-plan, built *c.* 1882 and incorporating a fishing lodge of *c.* 1870. Two storeys of rubble, the S gables with canted bay windows and the centre with gableted wall-head dormers. E arm of five bays.

CHAPELFORD *see* TYNET

CHAPELTOWN OF GLENLIVET B 2020

Small collection of buildings on a remote road in the Braes of Glenlivet.

OUR LADY OF PERPETUAL SUCCOUR (R.C.). By *John Kinross*, 1896–7, replacing a church of *c.* 1835. Much of the cost was met by the Marquess of Bute, a Catholic convert and regular patron of Kinross (cf. Pluscarden Abbey and Elgin Greyfriars, pp. 714 and 580). Harled, rather ponderous Romanesque but with a surprising tower over the entrance, with a statue of the Virgin, quatrefoil openings for the belfry and saddleback roof
with crowsteps. Late C19 N sacristy. Excellent interior with a 46
ceiled barrel-vault spanned by trusses. Over the chancel it is painted bright red with 'IHS' and paterae in gold; painted frieze below with calligraphic 'Sanctus'. White centre in the nave with flattened ogee coving painted green; long scroll with the Lord's Prayer (in Latin) in Gothic script. Row of fleurons below on blue ground; painted shields above with instruments of the Passion and sigils of the Trinity. Below, the walls are stencilled with extremely rich brocades of green. W gallery on basket-headed arches, its front also stencilled. – Tall REREDOS with excellent two-tier canopy and paintings on gilt backgrounds of the Virgin and Child flanked by SS Bernard and Alphonsus. The TABERNACLE has a brass door embossed with the Agnus Dei. – Semi-octagonal wooden PULPIT with vigorous grapevine.

Former PRESBYTERY to the rear of *c.* 1835 but altered. – BURIAL GROUND with a good collection of C19 Tomintoul slate headstones. Former SCHOOL and SCHOOL HOUSE, NW, of 1832 and 1860 with crowstepped gables.

BRAEVAL DISTILLERY (Chivas Brothers), S of the church. Formerly Braes of Glenlivet Distillery. By *William Nimmo & Partners*, 1972–3. Modern traditional, with harled walls and a mock pagoda ventilator placed anachronistically over the still house.

6 SCALAN COLLEGE (Scalan Association), 2 km. S. Set in an exceptionally and intentionally remote location. Scalan was founded by Bishop James Gordon in 1717 as a hidden Catholic seminary, and over eighty years over 100 youths were illegally trained here. The earliest building was a small cottage, raided by Hanoverian soldiers in 1726 and 1728 and burnt down by the Duke of Cumberland in 1746 (after Culloden).* In 1767, Bishop John Geddes oversaw construction of the present unassuming building. Harled W front with an off-centre entrance. It originally had only a single floor and low attic, but was given its second storey in 1788. The ground floor contained a living and study/dining room, the upper a dormitory and chapel (private oratory after 1788). Wings added in 1772–3 to create a U-plan, originally closed on the W by sheds and a gate. N wing now roofless and reduced to low rubble walls; it was the kitchen but turned into the chapel after 1788. The boarded rectangular vent on the l. of the main house served as a squint to see inside. Abandoned in 1799 for a larger complex near Inverurie (S) and subsequently turned into a farmhouse. S wing demolished in the mid C20.

2040 CHARLESTOWN OF ABERLOUR B

Founded in 1812 by Charles Grant of Wester Elchies (*see* Archiestown). A hundred feus were created and laid out on a grid-plan, and by the time Aberlour was raised to burgh status in 1814 the town had a population of 501. It has the usual layout of an early C19 planned village, with a High Street intersected by a square in the W (like Archiestown), but on a grand scale.

CHURCHES

Former FREE CHURCH, High Street. Now Scout Hall. 1847 by *Alexander Tod*. E.E. style. Extended by *D. & J.R. McMillan*, 1899–1901, with new rock-faced S façade and stepped lancets. SW tower with trefoiled entrance, crenellated parapet and pyramidal roof.

Former MANSE recessed to the W, 1859 and also by *Tod*. Pilastered, corniced doorpiece and raised, channelled quoins.

PARISH CHURCH. Theatrically sited at the N end of The Square. Originally a simple box of 1812, to which in 1839–40 *William Robertson* attached the Romanesque W tower with its crenelated parapet and dummy tourelles. This was all that survived a fire in 1861, after which *George Petrie* rebuilt the nave in its commanding Romanesque style. Five long arched windows, the second and fourth shafted with scallop capitals. Chevron, interlace and ball moulding around them; T-corbel table over

*Remains still visible to the W on the other bank of the Crombie Water.

the other windows. In 1933–5, *J. & W. Wittet* built the apsidal chancel, with three shafted, round-headed windows. The frieze of corbels is continued around it. The wide interior and furnishings mostly date from the Wittets' remodelling, their chancel arch with scallop capitals flanked by shorter round arches (blind on the r.). – W gallery on iron piers with scallop capitals. Its front has blind, round-headed arcading, reused from the gallery of 1861. – ORGAN by *Sandy Edmonstone*, 1992. – STAINED GLASS. Apse windows by *Gordon Webster*, 1933–4: St John, his eagle with fantastically coloured feathers and scales; Christ in a red robe over a staff of Asclepius; St Andrew. – NE vestry, 1933–5.

SACRED HEART (R.C.), Chapel Terrace. 1908–9 by *Archibald Macpherson*. Small and externally austere in rough granite but inside a Gothic Revival ideal, with much painted decoration of 1913, to Macpherson's design. The FURNISHINGS, designed by Macpherson and executed by *Hughes & Watt* of Edinburgh, 1909–10, also liberally painted and gilded, include a ROOD SCREEN with ogee-arched sidelights and statues on the rood, ALTAR and REREDOS with baldacchino. – STAINED GLASS. Chancel S, Christ, Mary and three angels with coloured wings, also *c.* 1913. Substantial L-plan former PRESBYTERY (also 1908–9) attached N.

ST MARGARET (Episcopal), off High Street. In a secluded wooded setting at the end of a long drive. By *Alexander Ross*, 1874–9, contemporary with his orphanage for the town (*see* below), which the church served as its chapel. Much of the cost was borne by Margaret Macpherson Grant of Aberlour House. The tall nave was built first, from 1875–7, and is of five bays. Triple cusped lancets in the clearstorey; paired versions of the same in the buttressed aisles. Four-light W window of Geometric Dec tracery high on the façade. Gabled SW porch with pointed entrance arch on shafts with huge foliate capitals – a mere hint of what is to come. Statue niche above with St Margaret; foliate corbel below. In the W re-entrant angle, a slender, three-storey octagonal spire.* Skinny louvred lancets in its top stage; faceted roof with four triangular lucarnes. The lower transepts and chancel were added 1877–9. Transept gables with two cusped lancets and a quatrefoil; E façade three stepped lancets under a continuous hoodmould.

The interior is sumptuous. Nave arcades on stout circular piers of polished red Peterhead granite on octagonal ashlar 43
bases with extraordinary monumental sandstone capitals, very richly carved with fruit, rose, grape, thistle, daffodil, oak and squirrel, etc. by *Dawson & Strachan*. The scale is far larger than life, and the capitals burst with a kind of tense vigour, a few of them so unrestrained as to verge on the grotesque. The tall, stilted chancel arch has its capitals on half-length granite shafts raised up on voluptuous corbels. Open nave roof carried

*Ross's original plan called for a massive square and battlemented tower, 18.3 m. high, with spire rising a further 7.6 m.

on six tall pointed-arch braces resting on stone corbels. Curved kingposts in the apices. Raised sanctuary, the lancets decorated with more Peterhead colonnettes (doubled in the centre) and shaft-rings. The transepts do not communicate with the main church, as the N is the VESTRY and the S is the ORGAN LOFT.

FURNISHINGS, mostly of 1879 and a dazzling array. – SEDILIA, ALTAR and REREDOS by *Dawson & Strachan*, the latter items of Caen stone. Altar frontal with trefoil-headed arches on stunted marble shafts. Three arches on the reredos, the heads moulded with ballflower and set in crocketed gablets. Pinnacles in between topped by musician angels. – TABERNACLE. Beaten brass by *J. W. Singer & Sons*, 1887, with crystals inserted into trails of foliage. Very rich and very Dec, convincingly medieval. Caen stone base with an excellent alabaster relief of the Entombment by *Hardman & Co*. Also by *Singer & Sons* the SANCTUARY LAMP. – CHANCEL SCREEN, metalwork by *Jones & Willis*, originally finished with gold. Tall, multi-cusped gable over the centre. Sides with trails of foliage surrounding four trefoil-headed arches. – TILES (choir and chancel) by *Minton & Co.* including Presentation in the Temple, Joseph and the Well, and Sacrifice of Isaac. Standard geometric patterns in nave. – PULPIT. By *D. & A. Davidson*, 1936. A Romanesque interloper. Big stone drum on a thick, shaft-encircled column. – STALLS (from the choir, now in the nave). Oak, with praying angels and poppyheads on the ends. – FONT. W end. Dec, quite overblown. The COVER with open, crocketed ogival dome, comes from Christ Church, Lancaster Gate, London (dem. 1977). – STAINED GLASS. The vast majority is by *G. J. Baguley*, 1887–1908, comprising all of the nave aisle windows, many with figures of saints, and the S porch. The choir and transept windows may also be his. Chancel E windows with scenes from the life of Christ. – In the lancets to the N and S, assembled fragments of heads and scrap glass of various colours and patterns. – Same in the gable of the N transept. – E lancet of the N transept, by *Martin Farrelly*, 1987.

BURIAL GROUND, W end of High Street. In a beautiful setting along the Spey. A church was founded here by St Drostan in the early C7, where his relics became a popular site of veneration. Of the church first documented *c.* 1226 there are scant, ivy-covered remains including part of the S transept gable and a window. – MAUSOLEUM by *A. & W. Reid*, 1859–60, for the Macpherson Grants of Aberlour House (*see* below). Good Dec with a steep-pitched roof and apex crosses. Shafted entrance with stylized stiff-leaf; Grant coat of arms above with 'Touch not the cat but a glove' and 'Stabit'. Two-light Dec window on the N gable.

Fine group of MEMORIALS. – In a gablet on the N wall, a PLAQUE for the Anderson family, its upper section dated 1761 with winged soul and the initials R.A. and D.C. – On the wall beyond the mausoleum, a PLAQUE with long dedication to William Innes and Elizabeth Barclay, dated 1664. Long inscription over a smaller plaque for Anna Innes †1663. – In front of the church fragment, a cratered basin of mica schist (0.6 m. wide), likely the FONT from the medieval church.

PUBLIC BUILDINGS

Former ABERLOUR ORPHANAGE, Conval Drive and Tower Place. Founded 1875 by Canon Charles Jupp; in its heyday, it housed more than 1,000 children. Between 1876 and 1913, *Alexander Ross* of Inverness (*Ross & Macbeth* after 1887) built a vast complex, including the orphanage itself with five connected houses (each with its own matron), school, hospital, gymnasium and myriad wings and extensions. These ran in a straight line directly W of St Margaret's church (*see* above). Closed in 1967 and demolished 1969–70 but in the midst of a housing development is the Romanesque-style CLOCK TOWER of 1888–9, and to the W (diagonally across from Speyside High School) the former S LODGE, *c.* 1886. The former E LODGE, at the bottom of the drive to St Margaret's church, is *c.* 1881.

BRIDGE OF SKIRDUSTAN, SSE of the burial ground, over the Lour Burn. A humpbacked packhorse bridge of *c.* 1700.

Former DRILL HALL, The Square. Single-storey Italianate on a T-plan, most of the E–W arm designed as a school by *Thomas Mackenzie* in 1850 but not built until 1856–8. Restored in 1897 (cf. the mural inside), when the long arm was added and the original gableted bellcote reset on the S gable.

FLEMING HALL, Queen's Road. By *A. & W. Reid*, 1888–9, paid for by James Fleming, banking agent and builder of Aberlour Distillery, Fleming Hospital and the Victoria footbridge (*see* below). Scots Renaissance style, with a big crowstepped gable to the street and a square three-stage tower with square bellcast roof with ogival dome, all very C17. The flanks have windows crowned by ball-finialed, triangular gablets.

FLEMING HOSPITAL, Queen's Road. Main block by *Dunn & Findlay*, 1897–1900. Domestic Arts and Crafts. Single-storeyed with a very tall attic in the centre. The lower half of the roof is piended and bellcast, the upper conventionally gabled and framed by flat chimneys. Shallow U-plan rear, each wing with a bellcast, piended roof and canted bay window on the W gable. Charmless later extensions.

LIBRARY, High Street. *See* Description.

MASONIC HALL, No. 29 High Street. 1927–8 by *J. Wittet*. Pilastered broken pediment.

Former PARISH HALL, High Street. By *J. Wittet*, 1926. Pilastered doorpiece with rectangular fanlight and big pyramidal-capped finials. Large glazed oculus in the E gable.

PRIMARY SCHOOL, Mary Avenue. By *Brown & Watt*, 1895–7. In the centre, two storeys with a piended roof. Lower entrance hall in front with datestone under a segmental pediment. To l. and r., tall, single-storey classroom wings with gabled ends.

Former STATION, N of The Square. Built 1863 on the Strathspey Railway. Closed in 1965. N front of eight harled bays; central entrance with weatherboarded pediment and clock. Attached to the W, the SPEYSIDE WAY VISITOR CENTRE, 2005, in a similar style.

VICTORIA BRIDGE, over the Spey, WNW of the park. By *James Abernethy & Co.*, ironfounders, 1902. Good iron suspension footbridge, long and gracefully parabolic. Lattice-truss span with suspender rods and main cables of wire ropes. Two tall lattice-girder pylons with ball and spike finials.

WAR MEMORIAL, The Square. Mercat-cross-style by *J. Wittet*, 1920–1 (cf. Alves). Hexagonal drum and Corinthian column with a lion.

DESCRIPTION

HIGH STREET is long and straggling, with good buildings scattered. The first house at the far E (or NE) end is RIVERSYDE, *c.* 1890, with a pedimented porch on Roman Doric columns with blocky bases. A little further W on the N side is MILFORD, the former signal post cottage. Its core is a single storey of *c.* 1740 arranged on a shallow U-plan; an early C20 pyramid-roofed addition fills the centre. Diagonally across, the two-part former RECTORY for St Margaret's church (*see* Churches, above). Three bays to the street of the early C19, and then a tall T-plan attached at an angle (*c.* 1860, with diagonal porch and canted bay windows). Past the former Free Church and manse (*see* Churches, above) is Nos. 70–7, a symmetrical two-storey, three-bay house of the late C19 with split entrances. Four giant-order pilasters, the lower half channelled and the upper half panelled. Broken central pediment with rope moulding and a ball finial; glazed bullseye in the tympanum. At Nos. 92–94, twin buildings of 1891 linked by a basket-headed arch (the l. one is now the Library). Each is of two storeys and three bays, with an original shopfront on the l. with slender cast-iron columns and foliate capitals. Canted oriel window corbelled up on the r. Just beyond, High Street cuts perpendicularly through THE SQUARE, giving a welcome sense of expansion. In the SE corner is CLYDESDALE BANK, *c.* 1880 by *James Matthews*. Two storeys and four bays, the l. three minimally advanced under a wide gable. Doorpiece with thick pilasters and cornice; contrasting long-and-short margins and quoins. VICTORIA TERRACE forms the W side of The Square, with three attached houses (subdivided into six) by *Ross & Macbeth*, 1896–7. Each is of one and a half storeys with a half-timbered centre gable and piended dormers to the l. and r.

THE MASH TUN, Elchies Road. Of 1896. Two storeys and three bays with a big, smoothly bowed E-facing storm gable. Later wall-head chimneystack.

TOWER VILLA, Mary Avenue. By *Alexander Ross*, 1874–5, originally built as the Episcopal girls' school; in 1889 it was superseded by *Ross & Macbeth*'s school at the Orphanage (*see* above) and converted into the headmaster's house. Large quasi-cruciform plan, the NW re-entrant angle taken up by a wildly French, Victor Hugo-esque tower (cf. St Leonard's church, Forres, also by Ross). Third stage with shafted window in plate tracery. Gargoyles below an attenuated pyramidal roof.

ABERLOUR DISTILLERY (Pernod Ricard), W end of High Street. Built as Aberlour-Glenlivet Distillery in 1879–80 by James Fleming, and on the site of a late C18 corn mill. This 'perfect model of a distillery' burnt in 1898 and was rebuilt by *Charles C. Doig*, although little of interest remains from his complex. Next to the main entrance, the former OFFICE (by Doig, 1897), converted into a SHOP and VISITORS' CENTRE in 2002. L-plan with drum tower in the re-entrant angle; candle-snuffer roof with fish-scale slates.

BENRINNES DISTILLERY (Diageo), 3.2 km. SSW. Established on this site, a splendid position on the N bank of Ben Rinnes, in 1835. It replaces the distillery founded by Peter McKenzie in 1826, and destroyed by the Muckle Spate in 1829. The PRODUCTION BLOCK was completely rebuilt in 1955–6 and expanded in 1966. Behind the BOILER HOUSE, the painted red-brick chimney stands tall and proud, its height and colour the perfect complement to the surrounding landscape.

GLENALLACHIE DISTILLERY (Pernod Ricard), 3.3 km. SSW. An incisive, clean design by *Lothian Barclay Jarvis & Boys*, 1966–7, with additions in 1975–9. Swept, asymmetric gables with corrugated roofs mounting to a square, pyramidal-roofed lantern.

DOWANS HOTEL, 0.6 km. SW, Dowans Road. Hybrid Scots Renaissance-Baronial villa, built *c.* 1892 for John Cumming, the owner of Cardhu Distillery (Knockando). It became the nursery school for Aberlour Orphanage (*see* above) in 1953 and was converted to a hotel in 1972–3. To the N, two broad shaped gables straddling the original main entrance. Drum tower in the l. corner under a tall conical roof; E elevation beyond with Dutch gablets and diagonal bay window. To the W, a tall extension by *Charles C. Doig*, 1907–8, with Venetian windows in the gables. Panelled entrance hall and staircase inside.

KEILLS HOUSE, 0.4 km. SW. The former parish manse by *William Robertson*, 1837–8. Two storeys and three bays, harled, with platform-piended roof and two long rows of chimneystacks. Cast-iron anthemion balustrade leading to the raised entrance. One reused door lintel dated 1672 with initials for Robert Stephen, minister from 1669 to 1706.

ABERLOUR HOUSE, 1.5 km. NE. Situated on a high bluff over the Spey, and exuding a palpable sense of patrician coolness. Built in 1838–9 for Alexander Grant, a native of Glenrinnes (*see* Dufftown) who made his fortune as a planter and slave-owner in Jamaica. This is the only country house built from scratch by *William Robertson* and undoubtedly his masterpiece. Aberlour passed to Grant's niece Margaret Macpherson Grant in 1854 and she carried out extensive additions under Robertson's nephews, *A. & W. Reid*, 1854–7. Further changes were made after her death by *Kinnear & Peddie* (1885–7) and by *Robert S. Lorimer* (1890–3) after the house had been purchased by John Ritchie Findlay, proprietor of *The Scotsman*. In 1947, Aberlour was taken over by Gordonstoun Preparatory School but after they returned to the main campus (*see* p. 648), the house was beautifully restored by the *Ashley Bartlam Partnership*, 2006–10, for Walkers Shortbread as their corporate headquarters.

N-facing main block of two storeys and five bays, all in polished grey ashlar and Grecian in style. Robertson's original centre is now gone, as the Reids replaced it in 1857 with a two-storey tetrastyle portico. The lower storey projects forward as a porte cochère, its fluted Greek Doric columns supporting an entablature with Empire garland frieze. Four square piers above it – not a choice that Robertson would have made – below a plain pediment with angle acroteria. The ends are minimally advanced, the ground-floor windows marked by lugged, corniced architraves and panelled aprons. On the W flank, an 1850s bay window. Set back from this range is a large wing added by the Reids, a tall single storey with a blind arch of Grecian columns distyle *in antis* below an over-tall fragment of blocking course. On the wing's W front, more typical of the Reids, arched recesses in the outer bays with Empire garlands. There was a corresponding wing to the E but the re-entrant angle between it and the main house was completely filled by Lorimer with a two-storey addition (the ground floor for a new drawing room) that nicely copies Robertson's style for three more bays, but nevertheless renders his work asymmetrical – a solecism that he would never have tolerated.

Good interior, the low entrance hall leading into a dramatically spacious, full-height STAIR HALL. It is one of the most thrilling effects that Robertson ever achieved. Cantilevered imperial staircase with good S-scroll balusters and Ionic newel posts of cast iron. Impressive coffered ceiling with gilded, foliate paterae, the petals swept boldly forward. The dining room to the NW was made into the LIBRARY by Lorimer in 1892–3. Lozenge-coffered ceiling, wooden panelling and bookcases with glazed doors. Marble chimneypiece with bolection moulding and (re-set?) medallions of scenes from the lives of Christ and the Virgin. Original DRAWING ROOM opposite the entrance hall, its red marble chimneypiece of 1838–9 carved with inventive foliage. Large former BALLROOM in the W wing (later the billiard room and now a cafeteria). Coved, panelled ceiling with open-well centre, *c.* 1864. Lorimer's decoration (1892–3) for his drawing room in the NE corner has not survived.

In front of the house is a TERRACE by *Peddie & Kinnear*, 1885, from which steps in line with the portico descend to a lower lawn. Further N (but slightly off-axis to the main house) is a Roman Doric COLUMN by *Robertson*, *c.* 19.2 m. high on a big cubical plinth. The top supported a massive granite ball finial, destroyed when the column collapsed in 1874.* When re-erected in 1888, it was given a heraldic unicorn with the letter 'F' (for Findlay) on its iron pennant.

The rear of the house is flanked by pedimented arches by Robertson, each with paired pilasters, acroteria and anthemion. His severe STABLE BLOCK lies beyond (the quadrangle mostly by the Reids). Nine-bay N front, central basket-headed arch flanked by paired pilasters. Tall blocking course and pedimented bellcote, both 1854. Wide, minimally advanced outer bays with pediments propped up on very thick pilaster margins. In the links nothing but strangely large blank panels.– Mid-C19 former GAME LARDER, octagonal with a faceted roof.

Robertson's WALLED GARDEN (250 m. SE, now a caravan park) is a huge D-plan, its N gate by the *Reids*, *c.* 1858, with a pediment and round arch with a keystone monogrammed 'MG'. – Cast-iron trellis gatepiers and gates. – S gate by *Lorimer*, 1893, simply delightful with tall piers with pineapple finials framing a strainer arch inscribed over the entrance with 'HERE SHALL YE SEE NO ENEMY | BUT WINTER AND ROUGH WEATHER' and 'BE YE WISE AS SERPENTS | AND HARMLESS AS DOVES'. Handsome scroll consoles to the sides of the piers and capitals with shell ornament. Beautiful wrought-iron gates with cusped quatrefoils.

The LODGES are excellent too. The E one (350 m. NE) by Robertson, 1838, is now greatly decayed. Single-storey cruciform plan with pediments, the W with a tetrastyle portico of unfluted Greek Doric columns. S side with double pilasters and two columns *in antis*. Channelled GATEPIERS with big, swagged urn finials. – The W LODGE (400 m. WSW) is a deliberate contrast of showy Italianate by *A. & W. Reid*, 1875, sporting a three-stage *campanile* with streamlined angle pilaster strips and bracketed pyramidal roof. Very grand GATEPIERS with swagged obelisks over square urn bases.

FISHERTON HOUSE, 0.6 km. WSW of Aberlour House, is by *William Robertson*, 1839, and stood originally in Aberlour House's policies. Two storeys and three bays of unharled granite; central pediment set well above the wall-head (cf. the farmhouse at Inchstelly, near Alves). Single-storey E wing of *c.* 1890 by *J.L. Findlay*, son of J. R. Findlay of Aberlour and originally for the estate office. Crowstepped N gable and richly carved segmental-headed E dormer.

Wide, U-plan STEADING to rear with gabled ends and raised centre, 1887. Converted in 2012–14 by *Ashley Bartlam Partnership* for Walkers Shortbread.

DUNSHUAN, 0.7 km. SW by the Dowans Hotel (*see* above). Late C19, built for the Aberlour estate factor. Platform-piended roof on deep bracketed eaves broken by piended dormers.

*The inscription plaque was later re-carved with the erroneous construction date of 1835.

Crowstepped gables over half the length of the flanks. E door with quasi-bolection moulding.

KINERMONY HOUSE, 1.5 km. SW. Scots Renaissance of 1913–19, likely by *J.L. Findlay*, on an ancient site said to have been occupied by the Knights Templar. Kinermony was also a seat of the Innes family from the early C18. Two storeys and a tall attic over a slightly raised basement, all harled in yellow. Main S front of five bays, the l. two set beneath a steep crowstepped gable. Bolection-moulded ashlar doorpiece in their centre, with corniced sidelights and segmental head. Canted bay window to the l.; stilted, gableted dormerheads on the wall-plate. The N front is generously fenestrated, with a canted bay window on the l. sweeping up to full height.

WALLED GARDEN to the SE, now planted to an extraordinarily high standard. It is among the finest of its kind in N Scotland. – LODGE 100 m. SSW, *c.* 1920, with lugged doorpiece. Bell-cast pyramidal roof with swept dormers.

DAILUAINE DISTILLERY. *See* Carron, p. 500.
EASTER ELCHIES HOUSE. *See* p. 559.
MACALLAN DISTILLERY. *See* p. 560.

2060 COXTON TOWER

1.1 km. SW of Lhanbryde

A comparatively small tower house, very well preserved following restoration by *Law & Dunbar-Nasmith* in 2001. Alexander Innes (†1612) received licence to build in 1571 but his tower was burnt to the ground in 1584. A new 'Cokston Castel' appears on Pont's map of *c.* 1590 and the tower is essentially of that period, with repairs after further sackings in 1635 and 1645. The style is remarkably antiquated, resembling rudimentary towers in the Borders (e.g. Smailholm, early C15) but not a complete anachronism – see, for example, the late C16 tower at Hallbar (Lanarkshire), and Scotstarvit (Fife), which was remodelled in a similarly retrospective style in the 1620s. The tower seems to have been built with an obsessive paranoia of fire: no timber was used in its construction, and even the roof is made of stone. Even more surprisingly, every floor is stone-vaulted, the crown of each floor rotated ninety degrees so that the lateral thrust of each is counteracted by its neighbour directly above or below. It is an elegant and practical solution, and also extremely rare.

Harled, square plan, the walls *c.* 7 m. long and rising tall and sheer to four storeys. Rectangular, chamfered door on the ground floor of the S front. Another door off-centre above it, now reached by a stone stair added *c.* 1846 but originally served by a ladder. Armorial panel above it of *c.* 1587, the top with the initials for Robert Innes of Invermarkie and Alexander

Innes and the bottom with those for Alexander's first and second wives, Janet Reid and Kate Gordon. Quasi-pediment above with the faded date 1644, added when Alexander's grandson, Sir Alexander Innes, was elevated to 2nd Baron of Coxton. Small rectangular, chamfered window to the l. of the entrance; two more above it, all covered by iron grilles. Severe elevations to the N and E, unarticulated except for scant slit-windows and shot-holes. Three more chamfered windows on the W wall, but with stanchions missing. On the upper SE and NW corners, a fat tourelle on corbel rounds with windows under conical stone roofs. Open bartizan in the SW corner with simple merlons and a machicolated corbel base; band of cable moulding with one (originally three) little cannon water spouts. Steeply pitched roof with crowstepped gables and apex chimneystacks. Tall, square chimney in the middle of the S wall-head, much renewed in the mid C19.

The INTERIOR has been unoccupied since *c.* 1867. Each floor consists of only a single room, so the Inneses never had

Coxton Tower.
Engraving by R. W. Billings, 1909

more than three small chambers and a few mural closets at their disposal. Partially subterranean store on the ground floor, doubling as protection for cattle. Late C16 or early C17 door; small shot-holes in the N, E and W walls. In the crown of the vault, a hatch for passing goods up and down – a kind of primitive dumb-waiter – originally fitted with a removable stone slab and once matched on the three floors above. Small first-floor HALL, the entrance secured by another original door and an intact iron yett. Fireplace of *c.* 1820, as in the two rooms above, but with a recess to the l. with window and aumbry. Deeply recessed S window and panel with the arms of Sir Alexander Innes and his second wife, Mary Mackenzie. It must date from after 1647, the year his first wife, Maria Gordon, died.* A staircase winds up from the NE corner, contained entirely within the thickness of the wall. On the second floor, a recessed window in the W wall with square aumbry to the l. Similar S window with shot-hole and fireplace to the l. The height of the third floor comes as a wonderful surprise, the vault tall and pointed as it must support the roof directly on top of it. Narrow rectangular entrances leading into the tourelles, each with windows, shot-holes and a conical vault. More shot-holes in the bartizan, the embrasures splayed internally – another indication of the tower's late date.

No trace of the original courtyard and barmkin. To SSW, the former FORESTER'S LODGE by *A. & W. Reid*, 1867. The estate was sold to William Duff of Dipple in 1714 and held by his successors, the Earls and Duke of Fife, until 1910.

1030 CRAGGANMORE B

Small hamlet developed in the late C19 to support the distillery and Ballindalloch Station.

CRAGGANMORE DISTILLERY (Diageo). Founded in 1869 by John Smith, formerly a manager at Macallan and Glenlivet distilleries. Cragganmore was the first in Speyside to be deliberately sited near a railway stop. Much rebuilt after a fire by *Charles C. Doig*, 1901–2, but again in 1964–7. Doig's quadrangular plan remains, the S arm still incorporating the lower masonry of a MALT BARN and small KILN. E arm with three piended blocks (now a MASH HOUSE and STILL HOUSE), two of them with little glazed lanterns. – Long range of continuously gabled WAREHOUSES to NNW, the N two of *c.* 1869. Next three gables, 1904 by *Doig*; last two (taller and rendered) by *Charles C. Doig & Sons*, 1924–5. Four more at the N end of the drive, 1905 by *Doig*. – WORKMEN'S COTTAGES on the ridge

*See her tomb-slab in the burial ground at Lhanbryde, along with that of Alexander Innes.

to the SW, 1929 by *Doig & Sons*. – Former MANAGER'S HOUSE (now Dunavon), 180 m. E. By *Doig*, 1901.– Former EXCISEMAN'S HOUSE (now Seefeld) to the ESE, *c.* 1916 by *Doig & Sons*. – CRAGGANMORE HOUSE, 100 m. NNE of the main distillery, was also begun *c.* 1869 by John Smith. His house is now the service wing to the E range added *c.* 1885, which is harled with crenellated porch and bay window. Much renewed and altered for Gordon Smith by *Doig*, 1901–3, in a Baronial style with thick round drum tower at the NE corner. Good rainwater goods with drainheads fashioned as gargoyles. A squat drum in the rear wing contains a stair to an ice house. Similar meat house to the l. of it.

Former BALLINDALLOCH STATION, 400 m. NE of the distillery. Built 1923, replacing the station 1863 on the Strathspey Railway. Closed 1965. Low stone building with original signage over the weatherboarded former waiting room. 200 m. NE is the BRIDGE over the Spey by *G. MacFarlane* (engineer), 1863–4, an iron box girder of riveted lattices, *c.* 60.3 m. long. Substantial end piers of rock-faced rubble. On the S approach a substantial former GOODS SHED for the Distillery (now Old Granary). Also *c.* 1863, unusually large (two storeys and eleven bays) so as to secure large amounts of whisky. Converted to flats *c.* 2008.

CRAIGELLACHIE B 2040

Small village on a peninsula at the junction of the Spey and the Fiddich. A suburb was laid out on its hilltop beginning *c.* 1885.

CRAIGELLACHIE CHURCH, Victoria Street. T-plan, the N–S arm built 1870–1 by Miss MacPherson-Grant of Aberlour for her domestic chaplain, Canon Charles Jupp, to minister to the Episcopalians of Speyside (cf. St Margaret's church and Orphanage, Charlestown of Aberlour). NW aisle added by *John Alcock* of Keith in 1902–3; porch and clock tower in the re-entrant angle by *C. C. Doig & Sons*, 1939. Lancets (some with Y-tracery) and bellcote on the S gable.

WAR MEMORIAL, N of the church, by *John Wittet*, 1920–2. Pedestal with segmental pediments. Channelled square column with entasis topped by Celtic cross.

PRIMARY SCHOOL, John Street. Attractive chalet-style by *Brown & Watt*, dated 1900 on the circular turret that is corbelled out from the front and capped by an octagonal timber arcade like a look-out. Big round-arched windows and half-timbered gables.

VILLAGE HALL, John Street. By *C.C. Doig*, 1932. Four-bay gabled rectangle with SW entrance under a depressed segmental head. Original small piended wing to the rear. Diagonally opposite, the former POLICE STATION, 1897–8 by *F.D. Robertson*.

CRAIGELLACHIE HOTEL, Victoria Street. A big establishment by *C.C. Doig*, 1892, with sprawling late C19 and C20 extensions as testament to booming tourism in the heart of whisky country. White harled walls with black margins. Picturesque E front with a pyramidal roof with tall, piended dormers.

In VICTORIA STREET, an attractive terrace of three houses harled with painted margins. Two are early C19, the third (N) late C19 but with no variation in style. 100 m. SSW (off Edward Avenue) is CRAIGELLACHIE LODGE, a simple T-plan of *c.* 1858 renovated in the Baronial style *c.* 1885. Corbelled tourelle on the far l.; two rectangular oriels and a porch with miniature open look-out tower.

107 CRAIGELLACHIE BRIDGE (or TELFORD BRIDGE), 0.4 km. W. By *Thomas Telford*, 1812–15; *William Hazledine*, ironmaster. The oldest surviving large-scale cast-iron bridge in Scotland, and the earliest of Telford's landmark prefabricated lattice-braced designs for spanning widths unsuitable for masonry. It is a triumph both technically and aesthetically, combining beauty and function with remarkable lightness and transparency. The curvature of the arch is uncommonly graceful, as is the gentle humpback to the road deck. Single-span segmental arch over the Spey of four ribs, 45.7 m. long in total, and each composed of five concatenated cross-braces. Upper carriageway supported on slender lozenge-lattice struts. Granite abutments (the N keyed into a cliff) with big circular, crenellated turrets. Restored by *W.A. Fairhurst & Partners* in 1963–4 and closed to vehicles in 1972.

CRAIGELLACHIE DISTILLERY (John Dewar & Sons), Hill Street, 0.3 km. SSE. Founded 1881. Of the original complex built by *Charles C. Doig* in 1890–1, only the KILN (with obligatory pagoda ventilator) and much-altered MALT BARN survive (the latter converted to warehouses in 1968). Major reconstruction of the PRODUCTION BLOCK in 1964–5, including the still house with its three gigantic garage-style doors, entirely glazed.

HAZELWOOD, 2.9 km. ESE. Good villa of c. 1830, likely by *William Robertson* and similar to his Cluny in Forres (*see* p. 640). Three-bay entrance front, the recessed porch framed by a modillioned pediment set on wide pilasters. To the S, two storeys set into a slope with full-height ashlar canted windows and a veranda between them.

BOHARM BURIAL GROUND, 3.3 km. ENE by the A95. Remains of a T-plan church built 1618 at the private expense of James VI and superseded by the church at Mulben (q.v.). W gable of rubble with blocked door and upper window. Rectangular apex bellcote with shaped ball finial and two balusters. – To the E, an early C19 MAUSOLEUM, probably by *William Robertson*, built on the foundations of the Jacobean aisle. Wide crow-stepped gables and diagonal buttresses; pair of W-facing entrance arches with a blind lancet in between. – Six SLABS leaning against the S gable, the third for Alexander Shanks †1768 over an ogee with winged soul and 'memento mori'.

MANSEFIELD, 100 m. SW, was built *c.* 1875 on the site of the former manse of 1723 and incorporates its datestone (with monograms and heraldry) in the central dormer. Large heraldic plaque on the N wall from the former Buchromb House, 2.4 km. SSW (destroyed by fire in 1953).

BRIDGE OF FIDDICH, 0.5 km. ENE. Single segmental span with tooled granite arch ring, 1841.

GAULDWELL CASTLE, 2.1 km. E. Founded in the C12 by the Freskyns of Duffus (q.v.), but the current scant remains suggest a C13 HALL HOUSE similar to Rait Castle (Highland and Islands). Gauldwell was a simple rectangular structure, 38.5 m. by 8.3 m., the former W wall now standing in places to 6.5 m. along with part of the N gable. The flat area to the E was originally a pentagonal courtyard.

William Freskyn founded a CHAPEL and BURIAL GROUND just to the N *c.* 1213. The chapel was small (7.3 m. by 3.7 m.) and superseded by the early C17 church (*see* Burial Ground above).

ARNDILLY HOUSE. *See* p. 467.

CULLEN B *5060*

One of the most attractive planned towns in Moray, founded by Lewis Grant Ogilvy, 5th Earl of Seafield in 1820. It overlooks Cullen Bay, most of the downhill vistas now picturesquely framed by three branches of the disused railway viaduct.

The settlement of 'Invercullen' was chartered as a royal burgh under William I in 1189 and re-confirmed by James II in 1455. By that time, the Old Town extended S from the Castle in a long arc, a single 'long and straggling' street with the church roughly in the centre and with a school, tolbooth, manse and bedehouse (known as Lawtie's Mortifications; *see* below) located nearby. By *c.* 1600, Cullen House and its policies sprawled out to the W, already causing great irritation to the Findlaters; in 1645, it was burnt by Montrose's army. Old Cullen prospered in the second half of the C18 from the manufacture of linen but was 'mean and ill-built' with 'irregular and dirty streets'.* Like the Duke of Gordon at Fochabers (q.v.) in 1776, the 5th Earl of Seafield resolved to clear his policies while simultaneously building a rational, improved town, ENE of the old town. In 1811, *George MacWilliam* was commissioned to make a plan with wide, straight streets and a spacious central square. The plan was altered by *Peter Brown* in 1817 and construction begun in 1820, with modifications by *William Robertson*. Most of the buildings are to his design. The old town was demolished *c.* 1826 leaving behind its fine medieval collegiate church and the incomparable Cullen House.

*Forsyth, *Gazetteer of Scotland* (1803).

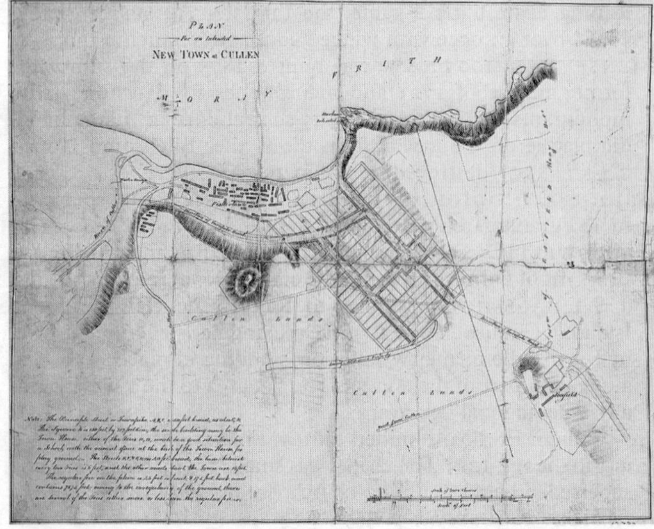

Cullen. Plan for intended new town.
c. 1820

CHURCHES AND CEMETERY

CHURCH HALL, York Place and Seafield Place. 1891–2, as a small church and still occasionally used for services. Broad SW front with a wide five-light window above the entrance, with rather eccentric trefoil-headed tracery, also repeated in the two-light straight-headed windows of the flanks.

CULLEN OLD CHURCH.* Initially a chapel of Fordyce, but achieved parochial status following a petition in 1236. A chaplainry of St Anne was founded *c.* 1536 by Elena Hay and her son, John Duff of Muldavit, and in 1543 a college was established by Alexander Ogilvy of Findlater, Archdeacon Alexander Dick of Glasgow, John Duff of Muldavit and the people of Cullen, which absorbed the chaplainry's endowments. There was probably some reconstruction of at least the E parts of the church at that time.

Although the roofs now give the impression of a two-cell church, with a chancel roof lower than the nave roof, the core is rectangular, and it is uncertain if the E section reflects the extent of the area that served as a chancel. The lateral S aisle was built for the chaplainry in the 1530s and the N aisle added *c.* 1798. With two exceptions the church's fenestration appears to be largely post-medieval, much possibly dating either from works undertaken *c.* 1822 when the town was relocated or from the major restoration of 1885 for the Dowager Countess of Seafield. The lower-roofed E section is of two bays. Its restored E window is of four lights, with intersecting tracery,

*This entry is by Richard Fawcett.

and at the gable apex is what appears to be a medieval canopy head. The S wall has pair of Y-traceried windows, the E one with a large doorway with a roll-moulded surround immediately below it; the W with a blocked and truncated pointed-head doorway beneath. Below the eaves are rectangular heraldic plaques with the arms of Ogilvy and Gordon, in reference to the principal founder of the college and his wife. There is a third plaque between the upper level of timber Y-traceried windows to the W (E of the S aisle), which light the Seafield Loft and which required raised and swept sections of roof to accommodate their greater height; directly below those windows are rectangular two-light windows that lit the area beneath the loft. At an elevated level on the E face of the S aisle is a blocked doorway to a loft, the jambs of which incorporate an inscribed stone. The S wall of the aisle has an echelon grouping of four pointed lights and an image corbel above. Inscriptions on the aisle quoin stones refer to Elena Hay, the founder of the chapel, and offer glory to God. W of the aisle is a late medieval round-arched nave doorway with a filleted roll moulding, the lower part now blocked and the upper part glazed, W of which is a forestair to the W loft. In the W wall is a rectangular doorway below a pair of pointed-arched windows; the gable is surmounted by a birdcage bellcote. The N wall of the nave has a single pointed window. The N aisle has a pointed-arched N doorway below a window of similar form. In the re-entrant angle between the N aisle and chancel, on the site of a smaller structure and forestair to the N loft, is a vestry of 1967.

Internally, the arch into the early C16 S aisle is wide and segmental, on semi-octagonal responds; the E capital has a band of vine trail, the W capital has foliage spiralling around a rod. There are a number of inscriptions relating to the aisle's foundation. Around the aisle's S window rere-arch is a record of the endowment of St Anne's chaplain with 35 acres of land, and the requirement that he was to be of holy life, a good singer, and was to pray for the souls of Elena and her children. Among other inscriptions, on the W respond is the name of the mason who built the aisle, *Robert Moir*, and what appears to be his mark. The SEAFIELD LOFT, against the S wall, E of the 26
S aisle, dominates the interior. It has a twelve-panelled front, eight decorated with roundels containing heraldry, foliage and the date 1602. A Corinthian column at each end supports a full entablature. Beneath the loft are four square piers faced with richly carved timbers said to be from St Anne's Aisle, one dated 18 Ap 1608. There is a GALLERY, presumably of the early C19, over the W end of the nave and extending into the N aisle, the two parts connected by a curved section. Carried on slender quatrefoil cast-iron piers, the wood-grained front has shallow pointed arcading decorated with painted lines and thistles. There are plaster ceilings of polygonal profile throughout but the walls were sadly stripped of plaster in 1967.

FURNISHINGS. SACRAMENT HOUSE. Towards the E end of the N chancel wall, and presumably paid for by the occupants of the adjacent tomb, Alexander Ogilvy and Elizabeth Gordon (who also provided a related sacrament house at their chapel of Deskford (q.v.)). It was possibly partly re-cut in 1877 when re-exposed. Around the rectangular locker is a crocketed ogee arch, above which is a low-relief depiction of angels holding aloft a monstrance. The whole is framed by mouldings carried on polygonal conical corbels; the inscription in a panel at the top can be translated as 'My flesh is meat indeed and my blood is drink indeed. He that eats my flesh and drinks my blood shall live for ever.' – PULPIT at the NE angle with the N aisle. Behind this a MOSAIC, decorated with a cross and sacred monogram, 1960. – STAINED GLASS. Crucifixion in the E window by *J. M. Aiken*, 1933.

24 MONUMENTS. Alexander Ogilvy of Findlater (†1554), the principal founder of the college, and his wife, Elizabeth Gordon. A canopied tomb prominent on the chancel N wall. One of a group of monuments that draw their chief inspiration from the tomb of Bishop John Winchester (†1460) at Elgin Cathedral. The canopy, which has an ogee arch with cusped-cusping and lavish crocketing, rises from a tomb-chest and is flanked by pinnacled buttresses. The arcaded front of the chest has high-relief female figures holding books. Going well beyond the prototype at Elgin, on each side of the tomb itself is a multi-shafted respond capped by pyramidal pinnacles, and there is a cornice formed by a band of tabernacle heads. A striking feature is a pair of classically inspired roundels in the spandrels with vine-trail borders, within which are kneeling figures of Ogilvy and his wife. At the back of the recess is a cartouche framing the inscription, which is held up by angels, flanked by heraldic shields and surmounted by a depiction of God the Father. – In the W wall of the S aisle, a recess with segmental arch and an inscription referring to John Hay, grandfather of Elena Hay, who built the aisle. It contains an EFFIGY that is relatively unusual for being depicted in civilian dress rather than armour. This effigy was removed to Duff House mausoleum in 1790 on the assumption that it represented an apocryphal John Duff of Muldavit who died in 1404, and that date was inserted into the inscription along the top edge of the tomb-chest in the late C18. In fact the effigy presumably represents the John Duff of Muldavit who co-founded both St Anne's chaplainry and the college. Panels at the ends of the tomb-chest and re-set at the back of the arch depict knights on horseback in full chivalric panoply. The tomb was returned to Cullen in 1965–6. – Alexander Innes. N wall of the N aisle. An incised slab depicting an armed figure; originally in the S aisle, it was also moved to Duff House in the C18 and returned to Cullen in 1967. – James Ogilvy, 4th Earl of Findlater and 1st Earl of Seafield, Chancellor of Scotland and signatory to the Act of Union (†1730). Chancel N wall, but originally set at an angle in the chancel's NE corner, where it blocked the

sacrament house; it was relocated in 1877. An inscribed tablet is capped by arms within a pedimented aedicule, all in veined marble. – Flanking memorials to the 7th and 8th Earls of Seafield (†1881 and 1884), each with portrait roundel. – Countess of Seafield (†1761). Chancel E wall. Above the tablet is a pediment with an interrupted cornice supported on consoles. – 11th Earl of Seafield and his Countess (†1915 and 1962). S aisle, E wall. Freestone with portrait busts.

CHURCHYARD. Many TABLE TOMBS, several with complex relief designs in a rural Baroque idiom to their slabs. Set into the churchyard wall to the W of the church is a slab with an angel blowing its trumpet over an as yet unresponsive skeleton.

METHODIST CHURCH, Seatown. By *John Fowlie*, 1905. Round-arched doors and windows.

Former ST MARY, Station Road/Reidhaven Street. Originally a United Presbyterian church of *c.* 1874 but remodelled for the Episcopalians in 1905 by *John Fowlie*. Now a store. Small, cruciform, Gothic. Bellcote added 1918.

Former UNITED FREE CHURCH, Seafield Street. Now Cullen Antiques Centre. By *D. & J.R. McMillan*, 1899–1900; converted 1981. Gothic, with ogee-moulded W door below a four-light Geometrical Dec window and looming three-stage tower to the r. with a short broach spire. Interior floored, but the GALLERY preserved.

Original FREE CHURCH behind, facing Reidhaven Street, built 1844–5 and converted *c.* 1901 into a hall, etc.

CEMETERY, Seaview Place. In a very fine situation overlooking Cullen Bay, opened 1867–8. Cast-iron RAILINGS of 1895, the central gatepiers with crenellated pyramidal capitals.

PUBLIC BUILDINGS

BURGH CROSS, The Square. Essentially of 1872 by *John Miller*, but rebuilding the mercat cross which stood outside the old church and was moved to Castle Hill *c.* 1826. It was carved in 1675 by the master-mason *Daniell Ross*, with additional work of 'building, finishing and perfytting' it by *Lachlan M'Petter*, 'masone of Cullen', in 1695–6. The octagonal shaft with shield is probably of 1675 but how much of the good Victorian work copies the original?* Octagonal with diagonal buttresses extending into long crocketed pinnacles, each housing a little gableted niche. Four cusped ogee arches in the cardinal directions with big crocket finials flanked by small crenellations. Attenuated, faceted dome on top (much restored by *William Robertson*, *c.* 1820), linked to the pinnacles by miniature flying buttresses. – PLAQUE. Medieval, of the Virgin and Child, likely from the Old Church (or its burial ground) and re-set in 1872.

*Ross's original contract from 1675 survives, ordering him to make a cross 'near unto the cross of Banff wt. King or tounes arms', implying that it was originally just a shaft with a simple stepped plinth.

COMMUNITY & RESIDENTIAL CENTRE, Seafield Road. The school of 1876–7. The main gables with stepped tripartite windows under spiked hoodmoulds. Belfry on the NW gable. Piend-roofed S extension (now LIBRARY), 1885.

HARBOUR. A failed attempt to build a harbour was made as early as 1736, when the 5th Earl of Findlater commissioned a plan from *William Adam* for 5 guineas. The 'small but substantial' port commissioned by the 5th Earl of Seafield in 1817 is now used mainly by leisure craft. Original seaward pier on the N by *Thomas Telford*, engineer, built by *William Minto*, 1817–19; extended to its current length by *John Willet* in 1886–7 with a raised parapet on the far end. Its original tapered circular metal light of *c.* 1888 is still *in situ*. *William Robertson* added the long lower quay in 1834, stretching in a curved line from the S and giving the harbour its distinctive wishbone shape. He also inserted the straight inner pier to create a STILLING BASIN, although everything now much refaced in concrete.

RAILWAY VIADUCT. Designed by *P.M. Barnett* for *Blyth & Cunningham*, engineers, in 1884–6, for the Moray Coast Railway between Portsoy (q.v.) and Lossie Junction near Elgin (q.v.). The Earl of Seafield was a director of the Highland Railway and refused to allow his competitors (owned by the Great North of Scotland Railway) to cross the policies of Cullen House, hence the viaduct's meandering – and completely delightful – domination over the town. Its longest section is to the W by the Seatown (*see* below); eight mighty arches of rock-faced rubble. A shorter section of three segmental-headed arches where it crosses North Castle Street, the second arch skewed over the road. A fourth arch was rebuilt and infilled in 1887 after the embankment collapsed. The final part spans Seafield Street with a single segmental arch flanked by pedestrian arches and three further arches E towards Reidhaven Street.

110 TOWN HALL, The Square. By *William Robertson*, 1822–3. Bowed corner of ashlar with shallow, round-headed recesses for the windows at first floor and Seafield coat of arms in the parapet (from a gate at Cullen House). Harled wing of five bays to the l. (originally the Court Room) with minimally advanced ends, also with arched recesses, and windows with floating cornices in the centre. It was originally topped by a pyramidal cupola. Similarly styled extension for library etc. by *John Fowlie*, 1899–1900, originally including a library and restored after a fire by *John J. Meldrum*, 1953–4. Inside the main entrance on the corner, an elliptical stair hall with a badly remodelled imperial staircase, retaining an original Greek key dado and niche with a statue of Venus. Depressed glazed dome above with more Greek key around the base. On the first floor is Robertson's original COUNCIL CHAMBER with curved, panelled doors set in reeded jambs and an excellent open-border ceiling rose. The N wing, stretching up Seafield Street, contained the CULLEN HOTEL, its three central windows on the first floor given thick,

console-bracketed architraves. Four piended dormers added *c.* 1930; five-bay stable court beyond with basket-headed entrance arch, three elliptical bullseyes and a piended, bellcast roof.

CULLEN CASTLE

Castle Hill

The hill, WSW of the town, is a roughly circular mound reputedly used as an Iron Age fort. Many vitrified stones were extracted in the C19. By the mid to late C12 it served as the motte for a castle. Only the wide ditch is still *in situ*, with outer rampart *c.* 1.5 m. high. Destroyed by Edward I in the 'smoke and devastation' of his raid in 1303 but rebuilt, it was here that Elizabeth de Burgh, wife of Robert the Bruce, died in 1327. The centre features a rough enclosure built *c.* 1826 to house the mercat cross (*see* Public Buildings, above). Re-set PLAQUES surrounding it from the C17 and early C18, one of them dated 1688, and with armorials from the Sinclair, Ogilvie and Baird families.

DESCRIPTION

Description begins in SEAFIELD STREET where, moving uphill to the SE, the first part is lined with some of the first houses to be built in the New Town, e.g. Nos. 42–48, the latter dated 1821, and No. 38, which is by *William Robertson*, 1823. THE SQUARE lies beyond. A new parish church was intended for this position from at least *c.* 1811 but since the late C19 the centrepiece has been the Burgh Cross (*see* Public Buildings, above). The square's NE side is not formally closed off but nicely rises uphill, and the SW is tapered to the beginning of Grant Street. Towards the sea, the vista is framed poetically by the arch of the railway viaduct (*see* above) – the one thing that Robertson could never have anticipated, but which strangely complements his own sense of scale. It is impossible to imagine Cullen without it, and a proposal to demolish the viaducts in the mid 1970s was thankfully never carried out. Most of the buildings were designed by *Robertson* between 1822 and 1825. They deploy all of his usual symmetry and equilibrium, recasting his trademark poise for the public arena. The effect is now somewhat diminished – as so often in N Scotland – by the insertion of bus shelters, car parks and a public lavatory. The proportions are broad, the four corners with Seafield Street each anchored by a nicely bowed, pivoted angle; three have good, matching two-storey stone buildings with slightly recessed bows at the corners, the N one still with its original door and fenestration, but the E corner is Robertson's Town Hall and Hotel (*see* Public Buildings). In the NE section of the square, the two-storey former Grammar School (N side, now Aldersyde and Glencoe), built 1821. At the top, the WAR MEMORIAL by *John Wittet*, 1919–20, a large domed octagon with pediments in the cardinal directions and inscription panels between pilasters.

GRANT STREET leads SW off The Square, its l. side flanked by a combined shop and house with another bowed angle under a piended roof, *c.* 1823. Its counterpart on the r. was originally the same, but replaced in 1866–7 by the (former) NORTH OF SCOTLAND BANK by *James Matthews*. Its bowed angle nicely pays homage to its predecessor. Pedimented entrance to The Square. In Grant Street, the BANK OF SCOTLAND (former Union Bank) by *William Henderson*, 1857, its ashlar ground floor with round-arched windows. – At the end of the street, cast-iron GATES to Cullen House (*see* below). Early to mid-C19, the piers Gothic with crenellations and pierced ogival domelets with crocket finials. Restored by *Douglas Forrest* in 1985–6.

Round the corner NORTH CASTLE STREET runs steeply downhill to the viaduct (*see* above), its l. side lined with a good row of nine single-storey cottages, all *c.* 1825. In SOUTH DESKFORD STREET, S of Queen's Drive, another single-storey row known as LAWTIE'S MORTIFICATIONS, first built by *Robertson*, 1824–5, to succeed a bedehouse in the old town endowed for the poor of Cullen by John Lawtie in 1650 and augmented by William Lawtie on his death in 1657. This group fell to ruin and are now as rebuilt by *Moray District Council*, 1995. The inscription plaques re-set in the front are mid C17, with heraldry flanked by scrolls over monograms. Just past them, to the rear of Park House (No. 12), a tall mid-C19 CHIMNEY, originally part of a boat-builders' yard.

SEAFIELD PLACE, along the SE side of the planned town's grid, has several villas and houses of quality. At the S end is the SEAFIELD ESTATE OFFICE (formerly Cathay House, built in 1861 by William Ross, a Provost of Cullen who had made his fortune in Shanghai trading tea and spices). Large, harled, two storeys. Four bay front, the l. wide and advanced with a jinked gable and canted bay window; three gableted dormers through the wall-head to the r. Crenellated porch in the re-entrant angle with a Tudor arch. Further up, opposite the church hall (*see* Churches above), is the MANSE, by *William Robertson*, 1829–30, a neat two-storey house of three bays with piended roof and fine Greek Doric porch. Good coffered ceiling in the entrance hall with plaster rose featuring anthemion and palmette; cantilevered dog-leg staircase beyond it with cast-iron balusters. Next door, WINDYRIDGE, simpler and over a raised basement, built *c.* 1829 for Admiral Sir George Outram, probably by Robertson. His best house, however, is No. 9, at the corner of Reidhaven Street, built *c.* 1834. Again of two storeys and three bays but of rubble with V-channelled quoins and a minimally recessed centre of ashlar containing the pilastered doorpiece with garlanded lintel. Panelled aprons to the windows; those on the first floor pedimented with acroteria. The r. bay window is of *c.* 1880. NORWOOD, next door, is a single storey of *c.* 1840. Roman Doric portico.

SEATOWN, NW of the new town, and overshadowed by the mighty arches of the viaduct (*see* above), is the original fishing village. First documented in 1613, when several families were evicted there by Sir Walter Ogilvy of Findlater. In 1762 there were only twenty-seven houses, but by the mid C19 they numbered over 200. Its plan is pleasantly labyrinthine and developed *ad hoc* as more dwellings were required. The cottages are of the typical kind, three-bay and of one or one and a half storeys with late C19 dormers. Many have margins and quoins painted in pleasing colours. W of the harbour they turn their gables to the sea.

CULLEN HOUSE

1 km. SW

A beautiful and very large house, formerly the ancestral home of the Ogilvy family. The building chronology is extremely complex. The site began as a small accommodation range for the canons of Cullen's collegiate church (*see* p. 516), built *c.* 1543 but likely incorporating an early medieval two-cell range. In 1600, Sir Walter Ogilvy and his wife, Dame Margaret Drummon, began a vast new L-plan tower house to replace their windswept castle at Findlater (q.v.). One arm stretches N while the W was created by adding two additional storeys to the canons' old quarters. Ogilvy was created Lord Ogilvy of Deskford in 1616 and his son became 1st Earl of Findlater in 1638. Another tower was added in the 1660s for the 3rd Earl, whose son became the 1st Earl of Seafield. Plans for a complete reconstruction in a severe Palladian style were submitted by *James Smith* and *Alexander McGill* in 1709, but in the end less ambitious extensions were added to the N and W wings in 1711–14. *James Adam* carried out alterations in the 1760s, as did *John Baxter* in the following decade. Around 1780, the 4th Earl commissioned *Robert Adam* for an entirely new house – roughly coincident with his plans for a new town – but this was never built, nor was a grand remodelling 'in the Saxon style' designed by *James Playfair* in 1788. From 1858 to 1868, the house was much altered by *David Bryce*, who homogenized its disparate parts with his usual extravagant Baronial splendour. By the late C20, the house had much deteriorated and the contents were sold in 1975. *Kit Martin* acquired it in 1982, and from 1982 to 1985 he (along with *Douglas Forrest*) repaired it and divided it vertically into fourteen individual houses – a novel solution for large country houses at that time. In 1987, a fire caused serious damage to the SE corner and W wing, but these were meticulously restored by 1989.

The description of the exterior begins with the WEST COURTYARD. In the main SW angle is the original stair wing of the tower house, still forming the fulcrum of the entire building, as it did in 1600. Single narrow bay of four storeys with a tourelle corbelled out in each corner. The l. is carved with big initials SVO and DMD (for Sir Walter Ogilvy and Dame

Cullen House, perspective view.
Watercolour by D. Bryce, *c.* 1858–61

Margaret Drumon) under rope moulding with cannon water spouts. Original main entrance on the ground floor, crudely truncated and turned into a window in the early C18. Roll-moulded doorpiece flanked by stylized, waisted pilasters with acanthus capitals; heraldic medallions above, said to have been dated either 1602 or 1603 although now completely faded.

The NORTH WING stretches out to the l., the early C17 section of three storeys and five bays (roof heightened in the C18). Most of the sash-and-case windows are Georgian enlargements, the original small square ones suggested by Bryce's stepped hoodmould. Of the five dormerheads, only the second is original to Cullen, with finely carved trails of foliage, Corinthian capitals and winged merhorses. The four others are C17 but have been brought from elsewhere. Standing proud in the centre is Bryce's exuberant, wildly boisterous entrance, carved by *Thomas Goodwillie* in homage to the original. Knobbly pilasters and bolection-moulded doorpiece with rich vines below a heraldic plaque. It is flanked by Goodwillie's delightful sculptures of lion rampants, nearly life-size and looking suitably fearsome.

To the l. of this block is an addition of 1711–14, its gable end sticking out and heavily Baronialized by Bryce. Two-storey tourelle in each corner, corbelled up over bobbin moulding with good carved busts. Big mullioned-and-transomed window on the first floor to light Bryce's new dining room; cable moulding with cannons above and then big conical roofs with fish-scale slates. They are topped, as elsewhere, by Goodwillie's tall statues of, as *The Builder* claimed, 'very strange-looking figures, representing monks, knights, templars, and Augustine canons'.

The WEST WING stretches out at right angles, the early C17 section of seven bays and ending at the internal crowstepped gable. The ground floor was originally the canons' domestic range. Again, the windows were regularized in the C18, with many of the smaller original ones retained as shams. Three fine original dormerheads in the attic depicting Faith (inscribed 'Fayth ye grund of al'), Hope (much re-carved after the fire) and another with missing inscription – but all with excellent C17 detailing. To the W is another extension of 1711–18, originally sitting flush with the rest of the façade but given a Baronial projection by Bryce. Stair-tower in its re-entrant angle with a corbelled square caphouse. Its window is dated 1858 below a sculpture of Father Time (holding a metal scythe) flanked by Youth and Old Age. The far SW gable faces Adam's bridge (*see* below) and was originally very plain, given a big rectangular oriel and two fat tourelles *c.* 1862.

The EAST FAÇADE was re-engineered by Bryce to become a second entrance, and therefore received a needed boost of his Baronial heft. Recessed in the centre is the back of the N wing, three storeys and three bays with more recycled C17 dormerheads. Another spectacular Neo-Jacobean doorway by Goodwillie, largely a copy of the one opposite (but here without the lions).* Four-storey towers are advanced to the l. and r., the l. one inserted 1668 (see the datestone over the S door) with three tiers of windows arranged symmetrically over a nearly windowless basement. The square bartizan and three triangular dormerheads are by Bryce. The r. tower dates from 1711–14, its top storey given a crenellated parapet and two tourelles with ogival domelets by Bryce. His also the stair-turret with conical roof in the main re-entrant angle. Recessed off to the far r. is the gabled end of the dining room, harled by *Kit Martin* after the removal of Victorian accretions. On the far l. of the façade is the back of the original tower house, featuring another early C17 tourelle and charming dormerhead carved with a sun.

The SOUTH FAÇADE overlooks the gorge of the Burn of Cullen and is now a sprawling concatenation of picturesque turrets. On the far r., an elliptical stair-tower of *c.* 1700 attached to the original tower house. It is topped by a big ogival roof, the only authentic one on the property (i.e. not by Bryce). To the l., a very wide bow window over an arcaded basement, inserted by *John Baxter* in 1777–8 for the 4th Earl's drawing room. It was remodelled by Bryce and given his usual mullioned-and-transomed windows, the upper storey made semi-hexagonal below a big ogival faceted roof with weathervane. The five bays on the far l. are the rear of the 1711–14 addition, and the best indication of the plainness of the original building before all of Bryce's changes. Here he left most of the Georgian

*The original doorpiece had two Roman Doric columns supporting a corniced architrave.

masonry intact except for one tourelle and an off-centre stair-turret with a shallow caphouse corbelled out above it.

Extending from the N wing is the former KITCHEN and SERVICE COURT, built *c.* 1765 (usually incorrectly attributed to Playfair). Two-storey U-plan with slightly bellcast piended roofs, most of the stone re-harled in 1982–5. Bellcote on the N façade. Ungainly additions were demolished by Kit Martin in 1983, and it is now divided into six apartments, the old kitchen refitted by *Douglas Forrest* with a gallery floor carried on Tuscan columns.

The INTERIOR of the main house is now divided vertically into seven separate dwellings, preserving the principal interiors. Single-storey square ENTRANCE HALL in the N wing, the walls covered with wooden linenfold panelling. Fireplace on the S wall with blue and white Delft tiles. Large, rectangular STAIR HALL beyond, rising through two full storeys, the fine broad staircase by *James Adam*, 1767–9, with good Neoclassical wrought-iron balusters; ceiling also by him, partially damaged in the fire and then restored. Elaborately carved wooden door dating from 1618 and retaining its original lock and key. At the top of the stairs is the former FIRST SALON, formerly with a sumptuous overmantel carved by *Grinling Gibbons* and a ceiling by Bryce (restored after the fire). Upstairs is the former SECOND SALON, once with a resplendent Jacobean painted ceiling, tragically destroyed in the fire.* It has been replaced by *Robert Orchardson*, 2003–5, with clouds of bubbles and astronauts floating on an acid-yellow ground.

The grand public rooms lay off the first-floor salon. To the W was the DRAWING ROOM, its ceiling of *c.* 1860 destroyed in the fire and now reconstructed. Bryce's two overblown chimneypieces survived the blaze. To the N of the salon lay, first, the former PORTRAIT ROOM (originally the library), with a ceiling of French stuccowork made *c.* 1778–9. Beyond it are the former RUBENS ROOM (originally the breakfast room) and DINING ROOM, both with original Victorian ceilings, heavily geometric with little pendants.

POLICIES. Extensively developed and landscaped in the C18 and extended E after the removal of the old village in the early C19. Of *Thomas White*'s landscape design of 1789 only a small part seems to have been executed. Off the house's W courtyard is the BRIDGE by *William Adam*, 1744–5, spanning the mighty ravine of the Burn of Cullen and serving as the original main axial approach. It is a splendid, Herculean piece of engineering, rendered with a grace that only Adam could have managed.

*The original ceiling was uncovered *c.* 1880 and was once part of a much longer ceiling over a second-floor gallery (truncated by Bryce and turned into a library). It was painted *c.* 1610, the flat part depicting celestial and terrestrial deities (Neptune, Flora, Mercurius and Luna) with attendant cherubim and raised gilt stars, all linked by clouds on a sky-blue ground. On the side coving were later (and more accomplished) paintings of the 'Calydonian Boar Hunt' and 'The Sack of Troy'; on the coved ends, the Royal Arms of Scotland and Charles II.

Tall single arch (*c.* 25.6 m. wide and 19.5 m. tall) with a thick ring of ashlar granite flanked by giant square buttresses with two set-offs. Coursed rubble in the spandrels; damaged dedication plaque on the outer N parapet. The best building in the policies is the GATEWAY at the SE entrance, built for the 5th Earl by *James Adam* in 1767–8. Tall archway with an Ionic pediment bearing the earl's coronet in the tympanum and a lion rampant on the apex with recumbent lions to the sides. It is flanked by screen walls with pedestrian gates under consoled cornices, then linked up to single-storey LODGES (later extended).

The large former WALLED GARDEN (750 m. SSW of house) is by *Playfair*, 1788, with brick walls dotted with short flues. Accompanying pair of cottages to the N, and in the centre of the W side the GARDEN HOUSE by *A. & W. Reid*, 1869. Within the wider landscape, there is on a hilltop 0.9 km. NNW, the TEMPLE OF FAME, an open octostyle Ionic rotunda with a dome, by *William Robertson*, 1821–3, based on designs by *Playfair c.* 1788–9. Its basement served as a tea room.

The quadrangular HOME FARM (0.7 km. WSW) was built over several campaigns in the early to mid C19 and is huge and severe. N front with a central segmental arch below a clock tower, dated 1816 with crenellated parapet and columned bellcote. Corresponding arch on the S arm with doocot tower.

The following ESTATE BUILDINGS are by *William Robertson:* BRUNTOWN HOUSE (1.1 km. NW), *c.* 1825 (the rear later) and the OLD LAUNDRY (100 m. NW), *c.* 1821–2 (converted into a house, 1988). – ICE HOUSE (200 m. SW). Conical, late C18, built into the side of a slope and topped by turf. – MARYWELL COTTAGE (0.8 km. WNW). Likely by *A. & W. Reid*, built 1870 for the keeper of the kennels in the woods to the NE. – Of the other BRIDGES over the Burn of Cullen the best is the graceful, humpbacked IVY BRIDGE (50 m. SSE), built in the late C17 or early C18 on the old main road from Aberdeen to Inverness which ran through the old burgh. It is one of the few in Moray to have survived the Muckle Spate.

Apart from the Adam gateway there are SEATOWN LODGE (900 m. N) – mid-C19 Picturesque, overshadowed by the railway viaduct – and LINTMILL LODGE (850 m. SSE) of *c.* 1870, probably by *A. & W. Reid*.

OLD CULLEN HOUSE, 0.2 km. ENE of Cullen House, by the old church. Said to incorporate the only surviving house from the town of Old Cullen. Elegant, harled U-plan front with pedimented porch by *William Robertson*, *c.* 1827. The house was originally one storey only, raised to two floors and given its low piended roof by *John Fowlie c.* 1899. The interior has wooden carvings from Cullen House, attributed to *Grinling Gibbons's workshop*. – STABLES to the rear, the long N–S arm of the early C18 and likely by *James Smith* and *Alexander McGill*. Slightly taller E–W arm by Robertson, 1822–3.

TOCHIENEAL HOUSE. *See* p. 747.

1050 DALLAS

Planned as a settlement on the Altyre estate (q.v.) in 1799, but officially opened only in 1811. Plots feued for ninety-nine years from Whitsunday 1812.

ST MICHAEL'S PARISH CHURCH, 0.4 km. S. The hamlet of Dolays is first documented in 1203 and the church of 'Dolays Michel' (the 'abode of Michael') in 1226, when it was held by the sub-dean of Elgin Cathedral. It was rebuilt in 1627 and again by *Donald Smith*, baron baillie of Gordonstoun in 1792–4, the bellcote on the W gable carved with the date 1793. Three round-headed windows on the S flank, the l. and r. originally shorter with doors below; these were altered *c.* 1847 when the present entrance was inserted in the far r. bay with its reused Ionic pilasters. Venetian window on the E flank, its centre originally a door to the laird's loft. Split stone forestair in front of it. Former door in the W gable blocked by *A. & W. Reid & Wittet* in 1903–4. Theirs also the short low, N vestry (extended 1934 and 2006–8) and the simple, recast interior with its coomb ceiling and E gallery. – Canted wooden PULPIT, *c.* 1872, formerly in the centre of the S wall.

In the GRAVEYARD, an early C19 WATCH HOUSE with chimney on the W gable. On top, the original lion finial from the war memorial, relocated here *c.* 1927 (*see* below). – Also the MERCAT CROSS, said to have been erected here *c.* 1526 by Robert Reid, priest of Dallas and later Bishop of Orkney. It is among the oldest surviving in Scotland and still in its original position. Weathered cubical base with tall, chamfered and tapered shaft (*c.* 3.7 m. high). Gothic cross on top with stiff-leaf spurs and pierced spandrels, of excellent quality but now very weathered.

Former MANSE (now Kirkton) to W by *John Wittet*, 1904–5.* Centre with a semicircular pediment above the wall-head; gables advanced to the l. and r. with multi-pane glazing in the tops of the windows. – OFFICES by *Donald Smith* (factor of Altyre estate), 1804. Long single storey with detached former poultry house.

The village is a planned settlement in its 'purest' form, consisting of just a single MAIN STREET. WAR MEMORIAL at the S end by *John Wittet*, 1919–21. Pedestal with angle pilasters and segmental pediments; hexagonal shaft above, now topped by a bushy flame finial but originally with lion (*see* watch house above). Halfway along Main Street the HOULDSWORTH INSTITUTE (or Village Hall) by *Wittet*, 1919–21. Large-scale domestic with gabled centre and a piended dormer to the l. and r.

DALLAS LODGE, 1.3 km. WNW. The Dallas (formerly Rhininver) estate was purchased by Sir Robert Gordon of Gordonstoun in 1668. At the end of the C17, his grandson (also Sir Robert,

*Replacing an earlier manse on the same site built 1783–4 by *John Morrison*, clerk to Sir William Gordon of Gordonstoun.

the 3rd Baronet) began to build a large circular steading, a smaller homage to Gordonstoun's Round Square (*see* p. 651) but it was only ever half-completed and the end of the r. arc was given a small house in the C18. From 1899 to 1901, *W.L. Carruthers* converted the building into one of the grandest shooting lodges in Moray. Long, broad crescent in a sweeping curve, the centre with a segmental arch inserted by Carruthers and replacing an early C19 passageway. Single-storey range to the S of it (the best part of the building), its final section rising to two storeys with crowstepped gables and forestair. The curve is terminated and partly obscured at the E end by a substantial two-storey Victorian house, also with crowstepped gables to harmonize. It was partly destroyed by fire in 1971 – probably for the best, as the current skewed proportions nicely emphasize the sweeping circumference to the rear. Inside, the drawing room and dining room have simple Arts and Crafts detailing. Standard Victorian (or C20) elsewhere, but one constantly encounters the delicious curvature of the walls in unexpected ways.

Good group of ESTATE BUILDINGS to the rear, also by *Carruthers* but in a freer Arts and Crafts style. – Ball-finialled GATEPIERS on the S approach, late C18 or early C19. – MULUNDY LODGE, B9010, 1.2 km. NNE. By *Charles C. Doig & Sons*, 1938. Drum turret in the re-entrant angle with good bellcast conical roof and fish-scale slates.

COTS OF RHININVER, 0.7 km. WNW. A surprising survival, built *c.* 1798 for the Cumming Gordons of Altyre (q.v.). Behind the single-storey cottage is a horseshoe-shaped steading (now mostly converted into a house), gracefully bowed around a circular courtyard. Unusual form, clearly following the tradition of Dallas Lodge and Gordonstoun's Round Square (q.v.).

TOR CASTLE, 0.9 km. NNE. Sir Thomas Cuming of Altyre was granted licence to build in 1419 and a fortalice was completed in the mid C15, with enlargements before the mid C17, at which time the castle appears to have been abandoned. A portion of the NW corner survives, a right-angled rubble wall *c.* 9.1 m. high and 2.1 m. thick. A tower in the opposite SE angle was still traceable in 1871, and the entrance and drawbridge originally faced E. Moat infilled in 1955 but still partially visible to S.

DALLAS DHU DISTILLERY 0050

2.3 km. S of Forres

The most complete surviving Victorian distillery in Scotland, in 124
operation from 1899 to 1983 and since 1988 run as a museum (Historic Scotland). Conveniently, it is also one of the smallest. The buildings are mostly plain and utilitarian, of whitewashed rubble, but some of the furnishings approach the level of art.

Dallas Dhu (originally Dallasmore) was designed by *Charles C. Doig* in 1898–9 and his complex remains in its original, pristine state. The layout is the classic Doigian E-plan, the long arm running N–S and parallel to the Highland Railway, where the distillery had its own siding. On the bottom of the E (the S arm) is the long and gabled MALT BARN, two storeys and twelve bays with blocked horizontal windows up top. Much of the ground-level MALTING FLOOR has been converted into a visitor centre and shop, but there are two ELEVATORS on the E for hauling up the barley. In the loft, a CONVEYOR for moving the grain to the STEEPS at the far W end.

To the N is the iconic square MALT KILN with ogee slated roof and louvred pagoda vent on the apex. The area behind the kiln doors can be explored, and above one can see the flues that channelled the peat smoke up to the wire-mesh DRYING FLOOR. To the l. of this, the plain-fronted MILL ROOM with two first-floor windows. Then comes the middle branch of the E, containing the MASH HOUSE with its MASH TUN of 1964 and attached GRIST HOPPER and DRAFF CONVEYOR. The TUN ROOM projects beyond it, slightly lower with a corrugated-iron roof; it was slightly extended in 1964. Inside are six Oregon pine WASH BACKS with ground-floor pipes linked up to the YEAST TANK.

The STILL HOUSE follows, rebuilt after a fire in 1939 to its original external appearance. Two glazed, piended lanterns on the roof ridge; copper, swan-necked WASH STILL and SPIRIT STILL inside, replaced in 1968–9. Then, in the top arm of the E, come the single-storey FILLING STORE and OFFICE – both of unpainted rubble, the latter with a bipartite piended window.

In the adjacent courtyard is a tall, square CHIMNEY for firing the stills, of red brick contrasted with yellow brick quoins. Off to the W is the weatherboarded former COOPERAGE, single-storeyed with a corrugated-iron roof. The BONDED WAREHOUSES stretch beyond it with their five gables: first two bays, 1898; next pair added by Doig in 1901; final two-storey extension on the W, mid C20.

To the N of the complex are the former EXCISE OFFICER'S HOUSE and MANAGER'S HOUSE, the latter (on the r.) with timber porch and ridge tiles. – By the main entrance, two pairs of WORKMEN'S COTTAGES, also 1898. Brick walling on the ground floor; dummy timber framing in the raised centre under a jerkin-ended piended roof. Little weatherboarded, gableted porches.

0050 DALVEY HOUSE

1.4 km ENE of Dyke

A fine Neoclassical house, and a member of the same architectural 'family' as nearby Grange Hall and Invererne (qq.v.).

Dalvey is the second in the series, and in many ways the prettiest. It was built *c.* 1810 for Major Alexander MacLeod of Ullinish, Skye, who acquired the estate from the Grants in 1798 and demolished an existing tower house (shown on Pont's map of *c.* 1590 as Grangehill, as it stood on the former farmland of Pluscarden Priory; Sir Alexander Grant changed its name after his purchase in 1749).

Main S front of two storeys and five bays over a raised basement. The proportions are compact, elegant and suavely classical but in an Adamesque idiom relatively antiquated for its date. Wide, three-bay centre cordoned off by giant-order pilasters under an open pediment with three swagged urn finials.* Balustraded parapet to the l. and r., the ends of the house with narrow pilasters. Perron double stair to a tetrastyle Roman Doric porch with triglyph frieze, the metopes with fans, urns and bucrania (significant for the MacLeods, as their crest features a bull's head); the design of the doorpiece is from Batty Langley's *The Builder's Jewel* (1741). Above this, a Venetian window with Ionic pilasters rising into the bottom of the pediment, as at Invererne. Plain window architraves in the outer bays, all with original twelve-pane glazing.

Substantial NW wing added by *Peter Fulton* in 1897–8, of slightly greyer stone. Five symmetrical bays, again two-storeyed (the raised basement now very high). Wide, minimally advanced centre with end pilasters and an open wall-head pediment – lacklustre homages to the original. Rectangular bay window on the first floor with bowed ends.

The interior is as compact as Grange and Invererne, but the central ENTRANCE HALL was completely remodelled by 92
Fulton in 1897 in masculine Baronial style. High, darkly stained panelled dado; staircase with fat turned balusters and an inglenook-like recess below a ribbed, coved ceiling under the landing.‡ Chimneypiece with fluted, Neo-Jacobean jambs and similar overmantel with broken pediment. The DINING ROOM, W of the hall, is also much remodelled but retains its original plaster ceiling cornice and frieze (again with bucrania) and fittings. The latter were grained *c.* 1897 and given overdoors with good Rococo pastoral scenes, the r. with Chinese pavilions. Also late C19 the sideboard recess (with Corinthian pilasters and swagged bucrania cornice) and chimneypiece with its voluptuous, Adam-inspired foliage. The DRAWING ROOM, E of the hall, is the best indication of the house's original appearance, with beaded panelling, plaster cornice (festooned frieze added *c.* 1928) and original overdoors with Adamesque swags. A wide doorway flanked by Ionic pilasters separates this from the ANTE-ROOM (the early C19 parlour). Faux-Adam overmantel of 1897.

*Unlike Grange and Invererne, Dalvey lacks the curious capitals carved with acanthus jutting out at ninety degrees.

‡In the original house, this had formed part of the library; the staircase of *c.* 1810 was only a narrow rectangular projection off the centre.

Behind the house, a tall square DOOCOT built between 1608 and 1620, likely attached to the barmkin of the original tower house. Crowstepped gables and straight-headed door with chamfered jambs; front roof with a pair of swept flight-holes, all nicely restored in 1996–7. On the SW gable, a plaque with initials for Mark Dunbar (who acquired the estate in 1608) and his wife, Isabel Falconer. Plaque above it for Sir Robert Dunbar and his wife, Christine Learmonth, who owned the Barony of Durris (S) in 1569. It was formerly attached to the Georgian kitchen and re-set here *c.* 1897.

Former HOME FARM to the S of the house, originally quadrangular and built in 1770 for Sir Alexander Grant. Long N arm still *in situ*, the advanced and gabled centre with dated skewputts and a round-headed entrance (now blocked). Former CHAUFFEUR'S COTTAGE in the SE corner, 1904, probably by *W.L. Carruthers & Alexander*. – The DRIVE was originally the main road from Forres to Dyke (qq.v.). Near the middle, a gently humpbacked BRIDGE over the Muckle Burn, rebuilt *c.* 1830 after the floods of 1829. Two segmental arches with crenellated cope and circular end piers added at the end of the C19, likely by Carruthers. – To the NNE, a rustic former GARDENER'S COTTAGE of *c.* 1835. – Neo-Jacobean EAST LODGE of *c.* 1897–8, likely also by Fulton. Channelled, ball-finialled GATEPIERS of *c.* 1749, originally at the ruinous W lodge.

9050

DARNAWAY CASTLE

3.4 km. SSE of Dyke

The ancient seat of of the Earls of Moray. The land, which includes one of the finest forests in Scotland, was held by the Comyn (Cumming) family from the mid C12, but Robert the Bruce forced them to forfeit upon his coronation in 1306. By 1314, the new King had elevated his nephew Thomas Randolph to the earldom of Moray and given him a vast tract of land stretching from the Highlands to modern Perthshire. The first three earls (all members of the Randolph family) started what was to become a large, multi-phase tower house, first documented in 1346. In 1372, the earldom passed to the Dunbars, and it was John Dunbar, the 4th Earl (†1391) who built the Great Hall, which remains the jewel of Darnaway. The Dunbars forfeited in 1429 and after 1455 the earldom became an appanage of the Stewart (now Stuart) family. It was Francis Stewart, the 9th Earl (†1810), who commissioned *Alexander Laing* of Edinburgh to make improvements and additions to the existing house, for which plans were drawn in 1796–7.* In the event the

*The earl also held the estate of Donibristle (Fife), and two of his neighbours there – the Countess of Dysart and the Earl of Morton – had already been Laing's clients.

decision was made in 1801 to demolish all of the tower except the Great Hall, work which was completed between 1802 and 1812.

The new castle is aligned E–W with the late C14 hall jutting out 80
perpendicularly behind. Its style is castellated – the Adam aesthetic pared down to its simplest and most homogeneous form, and exuding a kind of aloof calm. The overall effect is undeniably imposing, but achieved through uniformity rather than architectural sophistication. N front of eleven bays, mostly two-storeyed over raised basement with thick, plain band courses delineating each floor. Crenellated parapet punctuated by tiny dummy tourelles. The three-bay centre is minimally advanced and carried up an additional storey, its first- and second-floor windows Gothic with Y-cusping in the heads. The rest of the windows are straight-headed and topped by lugged hoodmoulds. Entrance in the centre of the *piano nobile*, fronted by a shallow Neo-Tudor porch of 1869–73, with octagonal buttresses and heraldic plaque on the parapet. Contemporary double staircase in front of it with good sculptures of lions at the base. The griffins on the upper landing are by *F. W. Deas*, *c.* 1914, who also added the long, balustraded walls screening the basement. The four-bay flanks are in much the same style and from the centre of the rear the GREAT HALL juts out mightily. Its walls were rebuilt by Laing as a smooth masonry veneer – tall and sheer, with three large Y-traceried and double-transomed lancets on the E and W sides (blind in the middle of the W).* Wide crowstepped gables to the N and S – Laing's final allusions to the tower house that he demolished.

The W SERVICE WING, as laid out by Laing, is a single storey of eight bays. The centre (originally the kitchen) is higher and has a pair of Gothic windows under a piended roof. The three bays to the r. enclose a small service court, originally entered beneath a stocky water tower. Deas converted it into a clock tower *c.* 1912–13, with a broached bottom turning into a pierced, two-light octagon. Good ogival leaded dome on top with little lucarnes. Deas extended Laing's building in 1918–22 with a long screen wall (originally concealing a garage) with channelled quoins and pilaster strips ending in four big circular piers topped by conical capitals. Timber Arts and Crafts GATES between them with some good iron foliage (oakleaf and gilded acorn). At the rear, where the terrain declines sharply (hence the strategic location of the original tower house), the back of the kitchen is joined to the main block by a quadrant link, smoothly bowed and crenellated.

The INTERIOR is very fine. The first floor remains mostly as designed by Laing, with few material changes since 1812. At the centre of the plan on the *piano nobile*, the rectangular

*Laing's original plans called for Lombardic tracery – a preferable solution, but likely not deemed 'Gothic' enough for the hall.

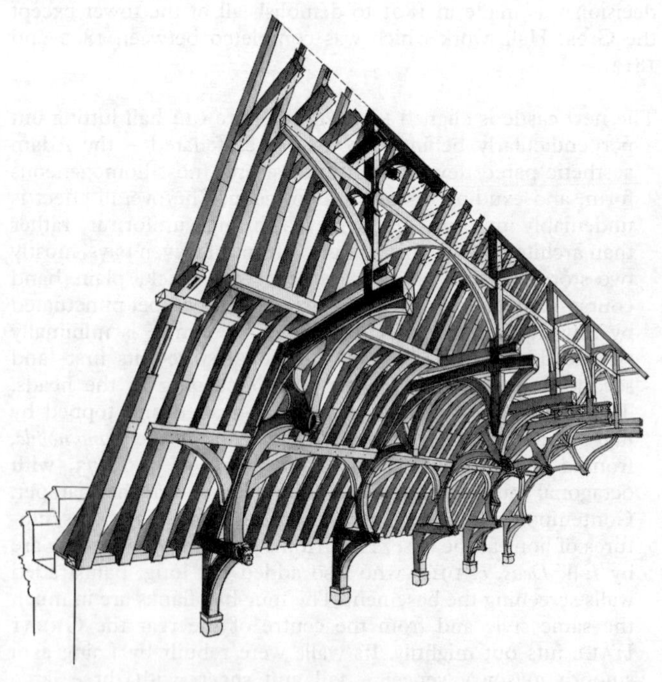

Darnaway Castle, Great Hall, roof.
Drawing by Geoffrey Duke Hay, 1998

ENTRANCE HALL with an open screen of four monolithic sandstone columns and capitals carved with long fronds of acanthus. Chimneypiece on the W wall of rich marble carved with bolection moulding – another allusion to the earlier building. Overmantel flanked by two plaster trails of foliage and flowers, rich and nicely textured. Straight ahead lies the Great Hall (*see* below) but E is the STAIR HALL, rising up two storeys with a pleasant sense of height and spaciousness. Upper ceiling with a central rose and rectangular border with guilloche. Broad, open-well staircase with ornate cast-iron balusters, the central roundels with lions' heads framed by Greek key ornament. A second, mirrored staircase to the W side of the hall has similar detailing and especially crisp plasterwork, while providing much-needed Georgian symmetry with the hall as the fulcrum. To the N is the DINING ROOM (originally the drawing room) with panelled dado and overdoors with corniced architraves. White marble chimneypiece with garlanded urn; fine plaster frieze with tripods and alternating anthemion and palmette. The DRAWING ROOM (originally the dining room) takes up the final bay of the E wing. Plaster frieze with a good procession of swagged garlands, returned at the S end of the room to form an entablature over a distyle Corinthian screen with marble columns. It formerly served as the sideboard recess and the two doors behind led to a closet and butler's pantry. Grey marble chimneypiece on the W wall with engaged, fluted columns and a foliate patera in the centre of the hood.

And so to the splendid GREAT HALL. It has one of the very few medieval timber roofs to have survived in Scotland, and is 55
unique among non-royal castles. Dendrochronology has shown that its timbers were felled in 1387, so the hall must have been built in the final years of the 4th Earl (†1391). Randolph's Hall is thus a full century earlier than the Great Hall at Edinburgh Castle – and also undoubtedly finer, with far fewer historical inaccuracies introduced by restorers.* Laing disassembled the roof and carefully re-erected it on his new walls, although two bays were sacrificed and a few beams truncated in the process. In its reduced state it is of six bays, measuring 26.6 m. by 10.7 m. but was originally approximately 8 m. longer. It is a series of wide, braced Gothic arches, the lower ends 'free-standing' and not connected by tie-beams. These lower horizontal elements are really 'false' hammerbeams, as they do not provide support to a vertical hammer post. But the Darnaway roof was designed before the English hammerbeam roof reached its apogee at the end of the C14, as at Westminster Hall. Here, the roof consists of two tiers, each truss composed of two independent halves. Triangular upper stage made up of an upper and lower (or sleeper) collar with a vertical crown-post. Into this is tenoned a longitudinal butt collar-purlin (or collar-plate) secured by wind-braces. The lower stage is a truncated collar-beam truss with arch braces and angled pendant posts, forming either three broad cusps or (in two cases) four cusps with a vertical pendant post in the centre. The N and S trusses were partly reconstructed by Laing, hence the ogival braces in the centre.

Elsewhere – mostly on the projecting ends of the false hammerbeams – there is a wonderful variety of carved decoration: human figures, crowned kings, beasts of the forest, birds, hunting scenes, a pair of clerics, a sow on hind legs, naturalistic carvings, etc. They are endlessly delightful, and many of them retain tantalizing vestiges of their original polychromy. The third and sixth trusses are enlivened with extra decoration – cusping on the upper collar, quatrefoils on the collar-purlin and cusped tracery in the arch braces. They probably indicate the position of a screens passage and a screen behind the dais, but no record of the layout survives from before the reconstruction. An account from 1793, however, reveals that the hall had a balcony high on the N wall with a 'music gallery' extending to the l. and r.

The hall's floor was raised *c.* 3.6 m. in the late C17 to create a network of vaulted cellars and storage chambers (still *in situ*

*Other comparisons for Darnaway are the roof of the Parliament House, Edinburgh, built by *John Scott* in 1637–9; James IV's great hall at Stirling Castle, removed *c.* 1778; and the smaller House of the Knights of St John in Linlithgow (Lothian), dem. *c.* 1886.

below). The S wall had a massive fireplace and chimney, its position now taken up by one of Laing's big Gothic windows. The broad chimneypiece on the W wall was designed by Laing in 1807, replacing a C14 original. The parquet floor, stained glass (minimalist heraldry) and very high panelled dado all date from *c.* 1870. Surrounding the main door is Laing's original doorpiece from the N façade, a corniced architrave set on high bundles of shafts.

The E re-entrant angle between the Great Hall and the main house is filled by the DUTCH GARDEN, accessed by a wrought-iron GATE by *Robert S. Lorimer*, 1918. Good filigree scrollwork, gilded detailing and overthrow with central roundel featuring the letter 'M'. Overlooking this is a two-storey Arts and Crafts veranda by *Deas* of *c.* 1918, with a canted oriel (originally open but roofed over *c.* 1955).

In front of the castle, a wide, raised TERRACE by Deas with widely spaced balusters. Further balustraded terracing to the E. 125 m. SE of the castle is the REDSTONE, the stone base to the original MARKET CROSS, likely made in 1611 when the medieval village of Darnaway was a burgh of barony. Upper section destroyed.

WALLED GARDEN, 500 m. SE. Built in the late C18, but the fine NE GATE is by *Lorimer & Matthew*, 1927–8. Square gatepiers with stacks of filleted shafts and capitals topped by lithe greyhounds. Wrought-iron gates with two branches of leaves and gilded berries running up the centre. Scrolled overthrow with a heraldic panel and delightful little birds. – GARDENER'S COTTAGE by the W corner, 1926 by *John Wittet*.

STABLES and CARRIAGE HOUSE, 100 m. SSE. Two-storey, seven-bay block, *c.* 1800. Symmetrical N front with big round-headed carriage entrances on the ends. – Former BUTLER'S COTTAGE to the WNW, 1902 by *J. Wittet*. – Former CHAUFFEUR'S COTTAGE further WNW, 1935 by *J. & W. Wittet*.

KENNELS, 900 m. NNE. Five bays by *A. & W. Reid & Melven*, 1878, with long ogival bargeboarding. Kennel runs in front with original cast-iron railings. – Fine KEEPER'S HOUSE just to the SSE in the same style, also 1878 by the Reids.

EAST and WEST LODGES by *J.M. Wardrop*, 1868.* Imposingly large and quasi-Tudor, with bargeboarding rendered as foliate vines and chimneystacks arranged in clusters. Both have highly impressive contemporary GATES and are very rare survivals. Those at the W lodge are very tall and with polished ashlar piers with good Gibbsian banding topped by urns with rich swags of flowers and fruit at their base. Very fine wrought-iron overthrow with rinceau scrolls and quasi-cartouche around a gilded coronet and heavy gates with vertical bars and central roundels with gilded 'M'. The E lodge's gates are lower with four ornate wrought-and cast-iron panels between the piers by *Francis Morton & Co.* each with with gilded coronets

*The design of the E lodge (including the gates) was copied two years later at Donibristle House (Fife).

surrounded by a sunburst of radiating spears and rods (the latter again gilded). Rinceau in the corners.

WHITEMIRE, 1.8 km. WSW has late C19 ESTATE COTTAGES by *A. & W. Reid* and *A. &. W. Reid & Wittet* (*c.* 1887–99). Three have rustic wooden porches. Original fluted pump heads at each end of the street with lion's head spigots. – CONICAVEL, 1.5 km. S was built by the estate for salmon fishermen working on the Findhorn. Six single-storey cottages of the early to mid C19. Most have jerkin-headed gables and stone door canopies.

EARLSMILL HOUSE. *See* Dyke, p. 559.

DAVOCH OF GRANGE *see* GRANGE

DESKFORD *see* KIRKTOWN OF DESKFORD

DIPPLE *see* MOSSTODLOCH

DRUMIN *see* GLENLIVET

DRUMMUIR B 3040

The village grew up E of Drummuir Castle in the mid to late C19, with a station on the Keith & Dufftown Railway from 1864 (dem. 1988, but platform still *in situ*).

DRUMMUIR & BOTRIPHNIE PARISH CHURCH. St Fumac established a preaching outpost here in the C8 or C9. A church dedicated to him was on this site by the mid to late C12 and another followed in 1617 (*see* below). The present church is of 1816–20, likely an early work by *George Angus* of Edinburgh. Very simple, with two round-arched S windows and round-arched doors l. and r. Square windows in the gables and a ball-finialled W bellcote from the old church in Keith (*see* p. 663). Lower session room and vestry added to the E in 1901 by *R.B. Pratt*, who also inserted the Lombardic tracery in the S windows. Good interior also remodelled by Pratt but retaining the original layout and early C19 five-sided gallery carried on Tuscan columns. – Rostrum PULPIT in the Jacobean style, 1901, with pilastered and pedimented backboard.

In the GRAVEYARD, the former SOUTH AISLE of 1617 now serves as a roofless mausoleum. Tablet on the exterior from 1760 recording this as the burial place of the Stuart family 'long before & ever since the Reformation'. – Excellent group of MONUMENTS inside. George Chalmers †1727. Tablet framed by a winged hourglass and putti heads with a bible. Aedicule with two Roman Doric columns, tall pulvinated frieze and broken segmental pediment. Oversized armorial panel in the tympanum. – Anne Gordon †1670 and Katharine Leslie †1667, with a good Latin inscription praising their 'eminent virtues'. Aedicule with two engaged Corinthinanesque columns; decorative frieze with two winged souls. No pediment. – Helen Chalmers †1758 and James Stewart †1807. Crisply lettered aedicule with consoled sill, Ionic columns and pulvinated frieze. Tall, elegantly proportioned pediment.

WAR MEMORIAL. By *R.B. Pratt*, 1920–1, formerly outside Drummuir Hall. Small classical cenotaph.

ST FUMAC'S WELL, 200 m. NE. Circular cavity, 1.4 m. diameter, with ground ledge of C20 stones. St Fumac is said to have bathed here every morning before dressing in green tartan to crawl 'round the bounds of the parish on hands and knees'. A medieval wooden statue of the saint was washed here annually on his feast day until the mid C18, when it was destroyed by the clergy as a token of idolatry.

BOTRIPHNIE HOUSE, SW of the church. The former manse, by *Matthews & Mackenzie*, 1884–6. Pilastered, round-headed entrance with canted bay window to the l. Good, well-preserved interior.

BOTRIPHNIE PRIMARY SCHOOL, 0.5 km. E. Rather raw Gothic by *F.D. Robertson*, 1875, with a short, square tower above the entrance under a truncated bellcast roof. Some carving in the tympana of the entrance and lancet windows to the r. Addition (originally a gymnasium) by *J.D. Corrigall* of Keith, 1905.

DRUMMUIR HALL, E of the school. Boxy, sub-Scots Renaissance by *R.B. Pratt*, 1899–1901. Big round-headed hood to the entrance. Extension to the rear, 2011.

DRUMMUIR CASTLE, 0.4 km. W. One of the most imposing castellated country houses in Moray, begun in 1846–9 by *Mackenzie & Matthews* for Admiral Archibald Duff, who served under Nelson. His ancestor Adam Duff, a merchant of Inverness, acquired the estate in 1621 and the family had previously lived at Mains of Drummuir and Kirkton (*see* below). Neither of these was sufficient for the Admiral, who returned to Drummuir in the mid-1840s and began building on a massive scale. After his death additions were made by *A. & W. Reid*, in 1858 and 1865. Restored with remarkable fidelity by *Douglas Forrest* and *Leslie F. Hunter* for Diageo, 1986–9.

The exterior is a bulwark, mighty but picturesque, built of coursed rubble with ashlar dressings, mostly of three storeys over a raised basement but assymetrical. In plan it is vast, but the repetition of narrow bays lends a surprising compactness. The building's strength derives from its profuse castellation: every wall-head and upper surface is encrusted with crenellated parapets and battlements. On the entrance front, the centre is slightly advanced as a square tower fronted by a substantial porte cochère with Tudor arches on two sides and a third with four-light Gothic tracery, its head with a big six-spoke wheel window. In the parapet, Duff heraldry and the motto, 'Kind Heart Be True And You Shall Never Rue'. Three storeys to the l. of centre with a drum tower at the angle, two to the r. with an octagonal turret, both rising higher than the wall-head. Behind the centre a taller tower with a taller octagonal turret. SERVICE RANGE to the r. by *A. & W. Reid*, 1865, in matching castellated style. Its final bay is two-storeyed with rows of square chimneystacks. Former SERVICE COURT beyond fronted by a segmental arch (widened, 1986–9) and flanked by three ARMORIAL PANELS reset from the C17 parish church (*see* above).

The GARDEN FRONT to the S has a wide, minimally advanced centre with two-storey canted bay window. Three bays to the r., the upper corner with a square turret corbelled out diagonally. The l. section was originally two-storeyed but given an additional floor by the Reids to make it more symmetrical. Thick drum tower on the end as designed by Mackenzie.

Splendid INTERIOR as restored in 1986–9: imposing, urbane and with a superfluity of Gothic detail, beginning with the octagonal VESTIBULE with tierceron vault and quasi-liernes over the windows and big central roundel with a hollow pendant fan-vault, its two tiers composed of open cinquefoil-headed lights. Canopied niches in the corners. Beyond, at the centre of the house, is the spectacular top-lit ENTRANCE 88
HALL surrounded on three storeys by open Tudor arches with decorated spandrels decorated with encircled quatrefoils, the upper ones with Gothic balustrades and at the top a tier of round-headed windows in triplets. The ceiling has pendentive fan-vaults on angel corbels and in the centre is a glazed light with twelve-spoke rosette and quatrefoils in the cardinal directions. The inspiration must be Taymouth Castle (Perth and Kinross). To the r. of the hall, the STAIRCASE with Gothic balustrade and compartmented ceiling with an armorial bosses. The finest room is the DINING ROOM in the SW corner, with dado of cusped ogee arches and two chimneypieces of gleaming Peterhead granite by *MacDonald & Leslie* of Aberdeen. Ribbed ceiling of painted plaster by *Alexander Duffus* of Forres, so convincing that it is easily mistaken for wood, with pendant finials. The wallpaper with Celtic patterns is of 1847, a remarkable survival. The plasterwork of the DRAWING ROOM is again by Duffus but in a decidedly French Rococo style, complemented by the white and gold wallpaper, almost certainly ordered from a French firm, and reproduced in the 1980s. Admiral Duff had clearly spent time in the Parisian *salons*. Voluptuous central rose, very deeply undercut.

HOME FARM STEADING, 0.3 km. NNE. By *William Bruce*, 1858–9, with some modifications by *J. & W. Smith*. Substantial quadrangular plan with Baronial detailing. – Nice LODGE at the entrance by *A. & W. Reid & Wittet*, 1897. A miniature castle, with boisterous crenellations on the parapets. – WALLED GARDEN, 150 m. SE, *c.* 1848 and now very nicely planted. Large canted rectangle with inner walls lined in brick. – On the old farmhouse behind WESTERTON (350 m. WNW), a reset PLAQUE dated 1664 with heraldry and the motto 'Stand Sure'.

KIRKTON HOUSE, 0.6 km. WSW. Seat of the Duffs from the early C18 to the mid C19, and the predecessor to Drummuir Castle. Two-storey E front of five bays, the ground floor built *c.* 1700 (see the Gibbsian surround to its entrance) but with round-headed windows l. and r. in apparently early to mid-C17 frames; they probably come from the church of 1617 (*see* above). First floor and attic added *c.* 1835. Small extension of *c.* 1930 replacing a much longer mid-C19 addition. The S front shows three separate builds E–W: mid C19, *c.* 1930 and two bays of 1996–8, the W one with Venetian window.

MAINS OF DRUMMUIR, 2.7 km. ENE, on the B9115. Small L-plan laird's house of the early to mid C17, and the earliest residence of the Duffs after the estate of Drummuir was purchased in 1621. Three storeys and three bays with crowstepped gables and little coped chimneystacks.* Triangular dormerhead on the l. initialled A.A.D. for Adam Duff (†1682) and his wife, Anne Abercromby, under large fleur-de-lys finial. Dormerhead to the r. carved *c.* 1902 with initials for Thomas Gordon-Duff. Little window on the l. flank; similar one on the r. over reset C17 pediment and blocked double shot-hole. Triangle of three shot-holes to the rear.

MILL OF TOWIE, 3.9 km. NE. A good complex of four C19 buildings. The largest is the double-gabled MILL, its S half early C19 and the N added *c.* 1885–90. Two tall storeys with loft; undershot water wheel in the SW corner by *Barry, Henry & Cook* of Aberdeen. Slightly shorter, two-storey kiln to the SE with narrow, pagoda-louvred cupola. Machinery intact. Original furnace inside the kiln with inverted pyramidal brick chimney above.

4060 ## DRYBRIDGE B

Mid to late C18 hamlet, formerly traversed by three crossings for the Highland Railway between Keith and Portessie. The remaining BRIDGE, N of the hamlet, is a single skewed arch by *Murdoch Paterson*, 1883–4.

BIRKENBUSH, 1.2 km. WSW. Two storeys and three symmetrical bays. Built *c.* 1735, possibly by *James Ogilvie*. The N front has a window in place of its original entrance; large Dutch gable above with a chimney. Late C19 and late C20 wings.

GREENBANK, 1.4 km. SSE. SE of the farmhouse, an early C19 squat cylindrical DOOCOT about 12 m. in circumference with continuous rat ledge. Its conical roof collapsed *c.* 2006.

*The house was remodelled in 1902 to be entered at first-floor level, hence the bad forestair.

WALKERDALES, 0.9 km. WNW. Low, harled house of two storeys, the date 1677 split between its skewputts. Irregular three-bay W front, the off-centre door masked by a porch of *c.* 1900. It has a re-set late C17 heraldic pediment. Three late C19 piended wall-head dormers.

DUFFTOWN B 3040

The original settlement, Kirktown of Mortlach, was likely a missionary centre founded by St Moluag in the late C6 and may have been the location of an early monastic community; three late C11/early C12 bishops are thought to have been based there before Bishop Nectan relocated the see to Aberdeen *c.* 1131. A new planned town was laid out on the hill to the N in 1817, so named for James Duff (the 4th Earl Fife), who financed it as work and accommodation for soldiers returning from the Napoleonic Wars. Dufftown began as a small right-angled cross with a square in the middle and expanded rapidly in the C19. It is now the malt whisky capital of Scotland, famous for its huge concentration of distilleries. As the popular early C20 rhyme goes, 'Rome was built on seven hills, and Dufftown stands on seven stills'.

CHURCHES

Former FREE CHURCH (now Parish Church Hall), Church Street. Of 1849–50 with a slender birdcage bellcote on the S gable, the Gothic W aisle with Dec window and the square tower in the re-entrant angle with a broached stone roof and octagonal spirelet added by *James Souttar*, 1891–2. – STAINED GLASS. W window by *Gordon & Watt* of Aberdeen, 1891–2, paid for by Lord Mount Stephen, a Dufftown native who built the first transcontinental railway in Canada. Large and cloyingly coloured, with foliage and Eucharistic symbols.

MORTLACH PARISH CHURCH, 0.7 km. S.* A fascinating illustration of how a medieval church might be Georgianized and then re-medievalized, first in a full-blooded Gothic Revival idiom so far as the needs of Presbyterian worship would permit, and then in an altogether more restrained and ecclesiologically 'correct' manner. The core is an oriented rectangle of *c.* 27.25 by 8.5 metres, which presumably reflects its C13 plan. A laterally projecting N aisle was added in 1826, by which time the S front had a regular arrangement of four rectangular sash windows between two rectangular doorways. The N aisle was extended in 1876 by *A. Marshall Mackenzie*, when a smaller salient was also thrown out on the S side for the organ and pulpit. A number of features, including the triplet of E lancets, were re-exposed in 1876, and the church's medieval

*This entry is by Richard Fawcett.

characteristics were further emphasized in a restoration by *A. Marshall Mackenzie & Son* in 1930–1. The walls are harled, apart from the entrance front in the N face of the N aisle, where the rubble masonry is exposed; the coped E and W gables probably date from when the church was re-roofed in 1707.

It is the E gable wall that most closely reflects the medieval forms of the church, though most of what is seen there is the result of restorations in 1876 and 1930–1. There are three narrow and widely spaced lancet windows with broadly chamfered reveals, two at the lower level and one above that rises into the gable. At the centre of the S flank is the shallow gabled salient of 1876, which is pierced by three lancets below a quatrefoil in the gable. On each side of the salient is a pair of rectangular windows of 1930, each with three tightly spaced arched lights, and towards the E end of the S face is a restored single lancet window. The W gable wall has a low rectangular three-light window below the W gallery, and a taller arched three-light window above. The N flank is the most complex – and least medieval in appearance – part of the exterior. At the centre is the deeply projecting lateral aisle; towards the outer ends of its N face are the twin entrances to the church, above and between which is an echelon grouping of three lancets within a containing arch, all of 1876. The N gable is surmounted by an octagonal bellcote with a pyramidal stone roof. W of the aisle, the N side of the nave is partly obscured by an enclosed forestair that gives access to the galleries, within which is the church's only medieval doorway; above the forestair is an upper window within an elevated gable. E of the aisle the N side of the church is largely occupied by a three-sided projection housing the minister's entrance and vestry.

The appearance of the interior dates largely from the reordering of 1930–1. Before the restoration of 1876 there had been a horseshoe-shaped gallery focused on a pulpit against the centre of the S wall, and in 1876 greater emphasis was given to the pulpit when the S salient was added to contain the pulpit and a newly permissible organ. The main internal thrust of the 1930 works was to reorientate the interior towards an elevated sanctuary at the E end, while retaining galleries at the W end and in the N aisle; the salient of 1876 was adapted as a war memorial chapel. Within the sanctuary area, and at variance with their external appearance, the widely splayed rere-arches of the restored triplet of E lancets spread so widely that the lower pair are contiguous, and the sill of the upper one is close to the apices of those below. The single lancet towards the E end of the S wall is similarly widely splayed. The only other medieval feature is the N nave doorway, a round-arched opening with a chamfered arris that is now concealed below the stairs to the loft. The interior is covered by boarded and ribbed ceilings of double-pitched profile.

FURNISHINGS. All of 1930–1. – STAINED GLASS. E windows, fine if rather eroded figures of Faith, Hope and Charity, by *Daniel Cottier*, 1876. S side of church, from E to W: David and

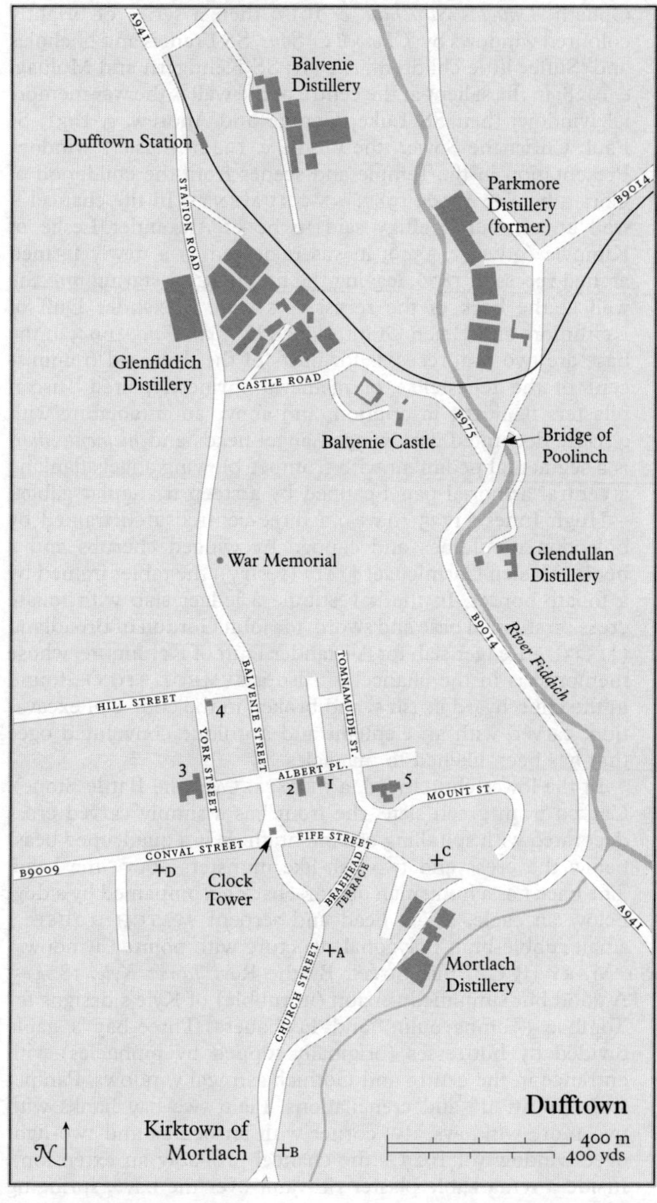

A	Free Church (former)	1	Masonic Hall
B	Mortlach Parish Church	2	Mortlach Memorial Hall
C	St Mary (R.C.)	3	Mortlach Primary School
D	St Michael (Episcopal)	4	Police Station (former)
		5	Stephen Hospital

Goliath, *Douglas Strachan*, *c.* 1917; then a series of brightly coloured windows by *J. Powell & Sons*, SS Francis and Nicholas and 'Suffer little children', *c.* 1931; SS Kentigern and Moluag, *c.* 1928; in the salient at the centre of the wall is the war memorial window; then SS Luke, George and Andrew, *c.* 1931; St Paul, Christ the Sower, the Virgin, *c.* 1942; N aisle E window, Presentation in the Temple and scenes from the childhood of Christ, by *Sax Shaw*, 1987. – MONUMENTS. In the chancel N wall an armoured effigy said to be of Alexander Leslie of Kininvie (q.v.) †*c.* 1549; it was relocated to a newly formed arched recess in 1876, leaving the lion footrest staring into the wall at the back of the recess. – S wall: Alexander Duff of
30 Keithmore and Helen Grant, signed by *John Faid*, 1694; in the base are two oval recesses for busts of the deceased (reminiscent of the fenestellae of medieval shrines); paired Tuscan pilasters flank the inscription, and above an entablature with a frieze decorated with winged angel heads and *memento mori* is a segmental pediment with trumpet-blowing angels flanking a central armorial panel capped by a steep triangular gablet. – Hugh Innes †1733 (nave), a three-centred arch framed by bolection mouldings and capped by winged cherubs and a book. – Helen Carmichael †1417 (vestry), the tablet framed by a foliate border. In the N vestibule a ledger slab with foliate cross on stepped base and sword, for John Gordon of Broadland (†1533). – Ledger slab for Alexander Duff of Keithmore, whose memorial is in the chancel. – Also a SYMBOL STONE, found in the churchyard in 1925, and broken in the course of excavation; carved with an elephant and a unique convoluted ogee that has been likened to manacles.

In the lower churchyard, a CROSS-SLAB (the Battle Stone). Carved from green slate, the front has a simply carved cross decorated with spiralling ornament; there is a quadruped beast below the cross and two fish-like monsters above the head. The back has a huntsman on horseback accompanied by a dog, below an eagle, an ox head and serpent. WATCH HOUSE. a small rubble-built polygonal structure with pointed window.

ST MARY (R.C.), Fife Street. By the Rev. *James Kyle*, 1824–5. A good but simplified version (in rubble) of Kyle's designs for Tombae (Tomnavoulin) and Fochabers. Three-bay S gable divided by buttresses (originally topped by pinnacles) with entrance in the centre and Gothick astragal windows. Parapet with balustrade and crenellations. Plain two-bay flanks with two more windows. NW corner with an oculus and two-light ogee window (of 1927 – the chancel probably an extension). Inside a remarkable plaster rib-vault over the nave, springing from corbels. ALTAR, REREDOS* and PRE-ALTAR by *W.J. Devlin*, 1925. ALTAR PAINTING, Our Lady of the Assumption;

*It replaced a C19 canopy described as 'evocative of the Moorish details of the Brighton Pavilion'.

from the former chapel at Clova (S). – ORGAN by *Conacher & Co. c.* 1878 within an elegant curved loft with a balustrade.

Former SCHOOL of *c.* 1898 and PRESBYTERY *c.* 1826 but completely remodelled (and extended) *c.* 1935. – Good wrought- and cast-iron GATES, 1912.

ST MICHAEL (Episcopal), Conval Street. Simple Gothic by *Ross & Mackintosh*, 1880–1, for Charles Jupp (cf. St Margaret's, Aberlour). Three-bay nave with shallow, slightly lower, chancel. S porch. Big cinquefoil E window. Little timber bell-cote with long, slender faceted roof. N vestry. Open timber kingpost roof and modest original furnishings. – ORGAN by *Conacher & Co., c.* 1876 and originally located at Cullen House (q.v.). Timber case with exposed pipes and a bow in the centre. – STAINED GLASS. E window, *c.* 1880. Enthroned Christ in the centre holding an orb; five surrounding angels playing musical instruments. – (St Michael by *Charles Florence*, 1971). Former PARSONAGE to W, *c.* 1881, probably by *Ross & Mackintosh.*

PUBLIC BUILDINGS

MASONIC HALL, Albert Place. Built 1886–7. Crowstepped gable with crenellated outshot to the r. Rear extension with lantern for a billiard room, 1896.

MORTLACH MEMORIAL HALL, Albert Place. Built 1893–4. Tall N front with two steep gables, the porch with curved braces.

MORTLACH PRIMARY SCHOOL, York Street. 1899–1902 by *Sutherland & Jamieson*. Three gables on the long E front with sub-Venetian tripartite windows. Round-arched porches abutting the centre gable.

Former POLICE STATION, York Street/Hill Street. Dated 1897. By either *D. & J.R. McMillan* or *F.D. Robertson*. Domestic, with rock-faced quoins and exaggerated scrolled skewputts.

STEPHEN HOSPITAL & DUFFTOWN HEALTH CENTRE, Stephen Avenue/Mount Street. By *A. & W. Reid*, 1889–90, like a villa with gabled pavilion wing. Bland later C20 extensions.

WAR MEMORIAL, Balvenie Street. By *A. Marshall Mackenzie & Son*, 1920–1. Slender tapered cross with Art Nouveau angels.

BALVENIE CASTLE

Castle Road

A large and impressive ruin, built in three principal campaigns: 57
mid to late C13, early to mid C15 and then major reconstruction in the mid C16. The site is highly strategic, just above the W bank of the Fiddich on the Huntly–Elgin road via Rothes (qq.v.). Balvenie is now rather tucked away among trees but originally offered commanding views in every direction. It is unusual among Scottish castles in that none of its additions were prompted by destruction or fire, but were rather the result of a natural

evolution dictated by the changing needs of owners over three centuries. It shows the organic transformation of a large, severe and purely military castle into a luxurious, fortified Renaissance palace that was among the most 'modern' of its day.

Balvenie was originally the principal seat of the 'Red' branch of the Comyn (Cumming) earls of Buchan. The first castle was built by either Alexander, the 2nd Earl (†1289) or John, the 3rd Earl (†1308) and appears to have been complete by *c.* 1295. It is a large castle of enclosure, a quadrangle *c.* 48.2 m. by 39.9 m. 'Morhelagh' (or 'Mortlach'), as it was then called, is documented in 1304 and was visited by Edward I of England. In 1308, King Robert the Bruce expelled the Comyns from Scotland and Balvenie passed to the Douglas family. In the early C15 it was owned by John 'The Gross' (due to his vast bulk), later the 7th Earl of Douglas. Either he or his successor made alterations. In 1455, the Douglases were themselves overthrown by King James II and the castle then passed to the Stewart family. It was John Stewart, the 4th Earl of Atholl, who carried out dramatic improvements between 1547 and 1557, resulting in one of the most cosmopolitan domestic spaces in Moray. The castle was purchased by Alexander Duff of Braco in 1687 and in 1722 passed to William Duff, Lord Braco, but he commissioned a new house, located where the Balvenie Distillery now stands (*see* p. 549). The castle was last occupied (by Hanoverian soldiers) in 1746 and restored in 1929 by the *Office of Works* – ironically, the same year that Duff's new Georgian mansion was largely demolished. The castle is now in the care of Historic Scotland.

The approach has always been from the E towards the imposing three-storey E range. Only the S half of the range is C13, clearly indicated by a vertical break in the masonry. Typical of the date, it is composed of large blocks of rubble and is massive and sheer, with three large ruinous windows for the former hall on the second floor. The SE gable was formerly topped by a chimneystack and appears not to have been crowstepped. The N half is as rebuilt by the Earl of Atholl in 1547–57 as the Stewarts' primary residence. It is of smaller blocks of uncoursed rubble with frequent use of pinnings. The ground floor projects slightly forward of the C13 wall to the S, but is made flush at first-floor level by the use of an off-set. The entrance in the l. bay has a roll-moulded, segmental arch with worn sculpture on many of the voussoirs. Oval gunloops to either side and another in the re-entrant angle of the great tower, above which a slender staircase turret is corbelled out (starting very near the ground – another indication of late date). The tower itself is circular and very broad and was originally topped by a tall conical roof with slates. The first floor of the E façade has five rectangular windows (including one the tower) under segmental relieving arches. They were originally shuttered in the lower section and are grooved for glass above; see also the anchors for the metal grilles around them. Roughly over the main entrance, a niche with depressed ogival head surrounded by cable moulding. The second floor was lit by fine bowed oriels with projecting moulded canopies (as at Gordon Castle and the Bishop's House, Elgin) but only their continuously corbelled bases remain. The wall-head contains three heraldic plaques: over the entrance, the royal arms and thistle of Scotland and, to the r., heraldry for the Earls of Atholl and 'I.S.' for John Stewart. Carved in long, faded script below the latter is the family motto, 'FURTH FORTUIN AND FIL THI FATRIS' (or 'Seize your chance and fill your coffers'). Another plaque on the stair-tower with arms for Stewart and his wife, Lady Elizabeth Gordon.

The rest of the enclosure walls are tall but stand to only about two-thirds the height of the E front and are mostly unarticulated. The N wall is built over a long, sloping plinth. Its upper section was rebuilt in the C15 during improvements for the Douglases. The NW corner is buttressed by a rectangular tower, probably C13, that is substantial enough to house a rectangular vaulted chamber (now ruinous) inside. The upper part of the S section of the W wall was also rebuilt in the C15. The SW corner is now a right angle, but a relieving arch and much-renewed masonry show that here too there was a tower with W-facing salient. The S wall also rises from a massive plinth and retains part of a wall-walk above (no battlements). Low drain in the middle of the wall from the former kitchen.

Within the small, rather unpretentious entrance in the mid-C16 part of the E range is a vaulted transe lined with benches and protected by its original double-leaved yett – a very rare survival in Scottish ironwork, where yetts are invariably of one piece (cf. Doune Castle in Central Scotland). To the l. is a narrow, vaulted GUARDROOM with fireplace. The courtyard front of this range is fine and very imposing, the whole length again surviving up to at least three storeys. The two phases are once more clearly defined, although the C13 S section is now as modified by the Douglases. There were formerly two rooms on the ground floor, each with its own door. Both were given vaults in the C15 (now collapsed). The N room was the cellar and has a mural service staircase; the S room was the bakery and retains a good brick-lined, domical oven with round arch and flue. The GREAT HALL lay directly above, accessed via the stair-tower next to the transe (now missing its original conical roof). Now that the hall's floor is gone, there is an uninterrupted view of its fine pointed barrel-vault. The haunches are pierced by higher blocked windows, indicating that this was an insertion by the Douglases. So the C13 hall was evidently unvaulted and lit by two windows on each side, the latter retained for additional light when the new vault was added in the early to mid C15. Gigantic fireplace on the N wall with chimney flue shooting straight up. Above the hall (now with a modern floor), an ACCOMMODATION RANGE originally formed of two chambers. One fireplace for each and another higher on the S gable, showing the floor level of the original garret.

The N half of the E range as reconstructed *c.* 1557 is L-plan to the courtyard with its N jamb only preserved at ground floor but its re-entrant angle taken up by a fine and complete stair-tower, whose upper stage is corbelled out into a square and gabled caphouse. There are three rooms at ground floor, all originally bedrooms. Two were accessed directly from the courtyard, and the N one retains its original vault and two fireplaces. The room in the NE corner is reached via the stair-tower and retains a large latrine; beyond is a shallow passage with a door to (on the l.) a latrine and (on the r.) the stair-turret in the re-entrant angle with the NE round tower. Ahead on the ground floor (in the base of the NE tower) is another bedroom with a fireplace, gunloop and quite unusual pentagonal vault. The first floor has a similar arrangement of rooms, but all have lost their vaults so there is again a thrilling sense of upward expansion. On the N side was a private room, while the middle chamber (in the corner of the L) served as a withdrawing room. Beyond it lies the new HALL (or Dining Room), unexpectedly long as it is carried all the way over the transe and, unusually, equipped with two fireplaces (both original). Three large windows on the S side; in the SE corner, a service stair leading down to the cellar, which was cut through the gable end of the original old hall on the other side. Off the withdrawing chamber is a passage leading to the first-floor bedroom in the NE tower, this one hexagonal and furnished with a fireplace and garderobe. It probably belonged to the earl himself, and may have been further used as a receiving chamber for his innermost circle. The second storey almost certainly contained private apartments for Lady Atholl and her entourage.

The rest of the courtyard was also lined with buildings, but there are now remains only in the SW corner, where the remains of a two-storey building abut the W wall. Built in the C13 with transverse walls forming three compartments. The first and second retain barrel-vaults at ground-floor level (the first one complete and containing a blocked loop at the end). These vaults were added by the Douglases in the C15, allowing a suite of rooms in the first floor (now ruinous), reached by an L-plan staircase. The S range contains more traces of the C15 renovations, including a KITCHEN in the centre with gaping remnants of a flue, and the remains of a brewhouse to the l.

Balvenie was originally surrounded on all four sides by a fine FOSSE, presumably built in the C13 along with the original castle. This has survived only to the S and W, a surprisingly wide channel revetted in stone. It is, rather unusually, separated from the curtain wall by a sloping BERM, *c.* 10.5 m. wide and now covered in grass. On the N side, the fosse has been replaced by a cultivated TERRACE, probably part of a new designed landscape from the mid to late C17. The E side was filled in by the Stewarts as the main approach to their new mansion, destroying the original C13 gatehouse and drawbridge in the process.

DESCRIPTION

The centre is THE SQUARE with the CLOCK TOWER in the middle like a tower house and axially placed at the head of Balvenie Street which runs N. Originally built as the gaol in 1836–9 and (after 1895) the council chambers. Three stages of mixed granite rubble, with dummy shot-holes, tourelles and ogee dome (replacing a squat steeple). Jubilee clock of 1897. Low matching N extension by Morayshire *County Architect*, 1924–5. Around The Square the best building is the former CLYDESDALE BANK by *Mackenzie & Millan*, 1878–80, with a wide pediment. FIFE STREET runs E, originally offering fine views down to the glen below but no houses of special note, except No. 51 (HIGHLAND SPIRIT), its front half built *c.* 1835, two storeys and three bays with piended roof but its similar rear block added by *Mackenzie & Matthews* in 1847 as the North of Scotland Bank. Further on, DULLANBRAE, a house of *c.* 1861, much extended by *A. & W. Reid* *c.* 1876–8 and 1889–93 for George Cowie, the owner of Mortlach Distillery.

CHURCH STREET, S from The Square towards Kirktown of Mortlach, has the former TOWN HALL (now Glenfiddich restaurant) by *R. Duncan* of Huntly, 1879–80. Pedimented central bay. Exuberantly painted. Rear hall converted to a cinema *c.* 1930 (now closed). Further down on the l. is the parish church hall (*see* Churches, above) and a C19 former DRILL HALL (now Community Education Centre). Across the street is WEST PARK, *c.* 1899 and likely by *Charles C. Doig*. It has unusual two-storey rectangular bay windows and a similar central bay above a porch with two square ashlar columns and sweeping roof. Good grids of glazing in the first-floor windows.

At Kirktown of Mortlach, DANESFIELD, NNE of the church, was originally its manse. Neo-Tudor L-plan by *Matthews & Mackenzie*, 1844, incorporating the rectangular manse of 1794 by *George Grant*, minister of Mortlach. PITTYVAICH, 250 m. SSW of the church is a good survival, now under restoration. Four wide bays with crowstepped gables, the l. section originally a three-storey tower built *c.* 1615. It was truncated and given its present first storey in 1724. Small, square window on the front (second from the l.) intact from the early C17.

DISTILLERIES

THE BALVENIE DISTILLERY (William Grant & Sons), 1.6 km. NNE. Founded by William Grant in 1890, three years after Glenfiddich (*see* below) and cheek by jowl with it. Original complex built 1892–3, now much modernized; the two-storey, double-gabled maltings (eleven bays with kiln on the end) is by *Charles C. Doig & Sons*, 1929. – Just beyond them,

WAREHOUSE No. 24 stands on the site of BALVENIE NEW HOUSE, built for William Duff of Braco by *James Gibbs* in 1724–5. It was a fine Neoclassical mansion, and the earliest of its kind in Moray. Converted as the main distillery building, it was demolished in 1929, although its basement remains *in situ*.

Former CONVALMORE DISTILLERY, 1.9 km. N. Built 1893–4 by *Donald MacKay* and much damaged by fire in 1909; rebuilt by *Charles C. Doig*, 1909–12. Typical malt barn with pagoda kiln. Sold to William Grant & Sons in 1990, now part of the vast Glenfiddich/Balvenie complex.

DUFFTOWN DISTILLERY (Diageo), 1.1 km. S. Built as Dufftown-Glenlivet Distillery by *Charles C. Doig*, 1895–6, on the site of an early C19 meal mill. Pagoda kiln in the centre with a long malt barn; still house to the r. under a long, raked gable. – Large complex of WAREHOUSES uphill to the WNW, formerly the site of Pittyvaich Distillery (1974–5; dem. 2002).

THE GLENFIDDICH DISTILLERY (William Grant & Sons), 1.1 km. NNE. Built for William Grant in 1887. Much modernized in recent years, but retaining the original maltings and kiln by *Charles C. Doig*, 1886–7 (Visitors' Centre since 1969). Pagoda ventilator sheathed in copper and topped by a stag; two more pagodas to the NNW with modern spiked ball finials.

GLENDULLAN DISTILLERY (Diageo), 0.8 km. NE. Two separate complexes strung out along the E bank of the Fiddich. Original distillery to the N by *Charles C. Doig*, 1896–8, his classic E-plan with pagoda kiln (closed 1985). Large new production building to the S, 1970–2.

MORTLACH DISTILLERY (Diageo), off Fife Street. The first of Dufftown's 'seven stills', founded in 1823 by George Gordon and James Findlater. Good double-gabled former malt barn by *Charles C. Doig*, 1896, three storeys and fifteen bays. Kiln in the SW corner with pagoda roof ventilator. Another pagoda roof across the road, *c.* 1963. New production complex to the E by *Archial* of Inverness, 2013–14.

Former PARKMORE DISTILLERY, 1.2 km. NNE. Good U-plan complex by *Gordon & MacBey*, 1891–4 (distilling ceased in 1931, but warehouses remain in use). The E arm is the former malt barn, three storeys and eleven bays; kiln at right angle with pagoda roof ventilator. Six bays beyond forming the S arm of the courtyard. – Former MANAGER'S HOUSE (now Rhuvaal) to the N, *c.* 1892, with trussed gables and dormers. – PARKMORE HOUSE, 0.3 km. NNE on the hill, was built *c.* 1897–9 for the brother of the distillery's owner. Big bracketed eaves and bay windows with blocky parapets.

BRIDGE OF POOLINCH, 0.9 km. NE by the entrance to Glendullan Distillery. Single humpback span of rubble over the Fiddich, late C18 (bypassed to the NNW, *c.* 1982). Granite segmental arch-ring with low, gently pointed parapet.

TULLICH HOUSE, 2.7 km. NNE. Good, harled, single-storey villa of *c.* 1835, probably by *William Robertson*.

KEITHMORE, 3.3 km. ESE. Site of a manor house built by Alexander Duff (†1696), who acquired the land from the Marquis of Huntly *c.* 1640.* Former dormerheads re-set in the W wall, the l. with armorial, initials 'A D' and the motto 'VIRTUTE ET OPERA' ('by virtue and industry'). Another monogram to the r. (also originally triangular) with half a rose and the date 1680.

(GLENRINNES LODGE, 1.7 km. SW. Late C19 shooting lodge, probably by *Brown & Watt*, incorporating earlier fabric in the service wing. Scots Renaissance style, harled, with mullioned-and-transomed windows, crowstepped gables, ornate dormerheads and tourelles. Fine rainwater goods with dragon heads, cable-moulded rhones and embossed down-pipes.)

Former GLENRINNES PARISH CHURCH, 7.8 km. SW. By *Matthews & Mackenzie*, 1883–4 to succeed a mission chapel of 1813. Now flats. Of pinned, pink Ben Rinnes granite. Tiny timber bellcote.

GLENFIDDICH LODGE, 7.1 km. SSW. Surprisingly large and rambling single-storey hunting complex by *John Plaw*, *c.* 1790 for the Duke of Gordon, including sawmill and kennels (all now greatly decayed). L-plan with piended roof, the long arm a double pile. S front of nine bays, the third and last minimally advanced.

FORT, Little Conval, 3 km. WSW. Two lines of prehistoric stone ramparts with mounds to the N (total area *c.* 200 m. by 120 m.). Defined by the remains of trenches for wooden palisades. There are at least four lines of enclosure, the innermost marked by a low rubble wall.

DUFFUS 1060

Of the medieval village only the ruinous church remains. The tidy grid-plan village of New Duffus was laid out to its WNW in 1811.

PARISH CHURCH, Hopeman Road. E.E. by *A. & W. Reid*, 1868–9. The SW porch makes a rather awkward transition to octagonal belfry with gableted, louvred lancets and stone spire. Twelve-petal rosette W window.

Pleasant interior with open, raftered ceiling carried on segmental arch-braces with pierced, encircled quatrefoils in the spandrels. Tierceron vault inside the porch.

WAR MEMORIAL. 1920. Octagonal shaft and cross of polished Peterhead granite.

Former ST PETER'S CHURCH, 0.4 km. E, Gordonstoun Road. 22
Even in its ruinous state, one of the most impressive churches

*In the early C19 it was converted into a stable, and a new house (now roofless and used as a barn) was built by William Marshall, factor to the Duke of Gordon.

in Moray. An 'ecclesia' is first recorded on this site in 1174, dedicated to St Peter but apparently founded in the C9 after St Aethan's church at Burghead (*see* p. 492) was destroyed by the Danes. Hugh, Lord Duffus, was buried here in 1226 next to the altar of St Katherine, and in 1269 his successor, Freskin, was buried in the chapel of St Lawrence. Like Duffus Castle (*see* below), the church was damaged by fire in 1298 and King Edward I donated twenty oaks for repairs. By the Reformation, St Peter's consisted of a nave, choir, S porch and W tower with tall spire. The choir and nave were dem. 1730–2 and the nave rebuilt, leaving only the porch and the basement of the W tower.

The PORCH was added by the rector Alexander Sutherland in 1524. Pointed entrance arch with a row of dogtooth in a hollow moulding; hoodmould with paterae and stylized ball-flower. Octopartite rib-vault inside with Sutherland's initials and heraldry on the central boss. Reset between the windows of the S flank is a panel also with Sutherland's initials and heraldry. The apex of the W gable has a birdcage bellcote with pyramidal finials. In front of it is the base of the medieval tower, originally topped by a spire 'four storeys tall'. Splayed base course and long-and-short quoins; skinny lancet on the front topped by a PANEL with Sutherland's coat of arms. The tower base became the Sutherlands' burial aisle and inside has a barrel-vault of rubble voussoirs and LEDGER SLAB for William Sutherland †1626. On the bench next to it, a collection of FRAGMENTS from around the site, including a C13 STOUP (broken in two pieces) and the upper effigy of a praying ecclesiastic, late C15. He has a book tucked under his l. arm.

The E wall stands on the site of the former chancel arch. Straight-headed entrance. Square TABLET to the l. of it with Latin inscription for Alexander Keith †1616, commissioned by his 'dearest' ('charissima') wife, Agnes. Stone forestair to the former LAIRD'S LOFT which had a fireplace inside.

Another door in the centre of the N flank. That side has only two square windows, the l. one set high over a sculpted FRAGMENT of an angel blowing a large trumpet while seated on a sphere. Lower window on the r. topped by a FRAGMENT with heraldry and a pair of faded Sutherland initials.

Inside the S door, to the l., a re-set segmental, roll-moulded PISCINA. On the E gable, two square cupboards at ground level.

S of the porch, the tall MARKET CROSS from the original Kirktown of Duffus, likely mid C14. Square, tapered shaft with chamfered angles, *c.* 4.3 m. high. Worn decorative band near the top and a broken head with missing finial. The big, cubical plinth is original. – Small, rectangular WATCH HOUSE to the E, dated 1830 over its entrance. – Fine TABLE TOMBS, mainly C18, with mortality emblems and inscriptions. Some of the legs have skulls with triangular nose-holes and square teeth, simultaneously primitive and menacing.

DUFFUS CASTLE, 2.3 km. SE. One of the finest motte and bailey castles in Scotland. It now rises amid green farmland, but originally held a very strategic position, surrounded by the brackish waters of Loch Spynie (*see* p. 747). King David I granted the site to Freskin, a Flemish mercenary, *c.* 1140. Giovanni Ferrerio, writing at Kinloss Abbey in the early to mid C16, recorded that David I stayed at Duffus Castle during the summer of 1151. The steep-sided motte originally had a wooden tower with lower bailey encircled by a timber palisade. Freskin's son, William, adopted the title 'de Moravia' ('of Moray') and by *c.* 1200 his family had become the most influential in N Scotland. In the early C13, Bishop Bricius of Elgin Cathedral (q.v.) endowed a chapel here dedicated to the Virgin Mary. Around 1280, Duffus passed to Sir Reginald de Cheyne, 3rd Laird of Inverugie (q.v.), but in 1297 the castle was burnt to the ground by Scottish patriots. Cheyne was granted 200 oaks from Darnaway (q.v.) in 1305 'to rebuild his manor of Dufhous', so the present keep dates from the start of the C14. Around 1355, it passed to the Sutherland family, and it is likely they who rebuilt the ruinous hall complex that survives in the bailey. It was sacked during an uprising in 1452, and again *c.* 1650, when Alexander Sutherland returned from exile with Charles II. He had been elevated to 1st Lord Duffus, and built Duffus House (*see* below) as his new abode. 54

The site is now encircled by a fosse, far too shallow to have been a moat and likely added during landscape improvements in the mid C17. The current approach is from the E, crossing a stone BRIDGE leading to a long, cobbled CAUSEWAY (both built *c.* 1760). A large gate formed the entrance to the BAILEY, enclosing a total of *c.* 6.3 acres. Line of ruined stone buildings along the N wall, some reduced to footings and all less than a storey tall. Excavations in 1984–5 showed that they were built in the mid to late C14. First on the r. is the former KITCHEN, originally 6.5 m. by 3 m., now marked by a solid wall with a drain on the lower l. After this are the low footings of a long, rectangular OUTER HALL. Part of a retaining wall survives a third of the way down, originally supporting the WITHDRAWING CHAMBER. Springers of a barrel-vault below with thin rubble voussoirs. Beyond it are the cellars for three taller chambers – storage and bakehouse, brewhouse, laundry, etc. The taller building next to the keep may have been the chapel.

The bailey stretches out to the S in the form of a long D-shaped curve. Several sections of the CURTAIN WALL are intact, the W side especially high where it traverses the deep ditch encircling the base of the motte. Three of the four original POSTERN gates survive, with chamfered margins to the outside and lintels resting on quadrant corbels. Numerous joist pockets prove that the inner bailey was originally lined with a long complex of support buildings (now no trace above ground). Near the end of the E wall (and flanking the original main gate) is an OVEN built of stone and brick.

The KEEP at the top of the motte is in the form of a large HALL HOUSE, a two-storey rectangular tower that was originally topped by a crenellated parapet (now no trace). Its E side is a mighty swath of rubble with ashlar quoins and a wide, slightly advanced centre. Large, straight-headed entrance off-axis with a chamfered architrave; three skinny lancets around it and a large keyhole-shaped void above it. It originally contained the GUARDS' LOOK-OUT and a row of heraldic panels (now missing). Just inside is a tall two-storey passageway running N–S, with a stone ceiling resting on corbels. To the r. a small GUARDROOM lit by a little window and beyond it a narrow corridor ending in a LATRINE. To the l. are the craggy remains of a straight STAIRCASE leading up to the first storey; when the stairs were intact, the pit underneath served as a PRISON and was accessed via a trap door. Above it (on the far l.) a door led out to the walk on top of the curtain wall. The first floor of the passageway is mostly missing, but over the entrance was a chamber for raising and lowering the portcullis. Part of its substantial encircling arch is still intact, with a high stilted side encased in ashlar. Beyond it to the r. are the remains of a mural fireplace and another far exit onto the curtain wall.

A small arch (reconstructed in the early to mid C20) leads to the interior of the keep, now roofless. To the r., the N wall and much of the NW angle have sheared off and sunk into the slope of the motte. They now jut out like the prow of a ship – all very poetic, but a grave demonstration of the instability of a site which was designed to support only a wooden tower. It features one chute for a former LATRINE and a little flanking passageway lit by a lancet – all now cock-eyed and leaning into the ground. The other three walls of the keep are intact, the joist pockets on the E and W walls showing the height of the original dividing floor. Neither storey was ever vaulted. The ground floor served as the LOWER HALL and was primarily used for storage and servants' accommodation; significant spalling and pink masonry are proof of the castle's destruction *c.* 1645. The GREAT HALL was on the first floor and also contained a few small bedchambers for the laird's household. The W wall has (on the l.) a large mural closet and then a long rectangular window with segmental rere-arch to light the main hall. To the r. are scant remains of the l. jamb of the great chimneypiece (now missing). To the l., the S wall has two windows on the ground floor, their benches and lintels much distorted by subsidence. Above on the first floor are the remains (on the l.) of the spiral staircase winding up to the roof and then two rectangular windows, much of the masonry on the l. now missing. The E wall retains (on the r.) the ruined pointed arch originally leading into the great hall and on the l. corner the rectangular passageway that led to the fallen latrine.

DUFFUS HOUSE (Gordonstoun School), 0.6 km. ESE. A good survival from the original village. The core was built *c.* 1655 by Alexander Sutherland, 1st Lord Duffus, to replace the Castle. Three storeys and four bays aligned E–W, all in lighter stone. Crowstepped E gable with little windows flanking the chimney. Triangular dormers on the wall-head carved for the Dunbar family, who acquired the house *c.* 1712. Rear harled and given channelled quoins by *William Robertson c.* 1835.

Large, double-pile W extension forming an L-plan by *A. & W. Reid*, 1858. Pyramid-roofed tower next to the main entrance; rectangular and canted bay window facing W. – Crowstepped STEADING (to the N) and WEST LODGE also by the Reids, 1875–6. – Channelled GATEPIERS with little lions added to the top.

GLEBE HOUSE, 0.9 km. SW. Built as the manse in 1828–9, likely by *William Robertson*. Two wings forming a U-plan to the rear, partially mid C19. – Former OFFICES to the W, also 1829–9; converted by *Charles C. Doig & Sons*, 1952.

OLD MANSE, 200 m. NE of St Peter's Church. A rare early C18 survival. Two storeys and three bays facing S, from *c.* 1736. Crowstepped extension attached to the E, looking convincingly C17 but built in 1948 and 1952–3.

SCULPTOR'S CAVE, Covesea, 2.3 km. NNE. Carved into the rock are PICTISH SYMBOLS likely to date to the C5 to C7. These include a fish, a crescent and V-rod, stars and a keyhole-shaped carving. The symbols are found near the mouths of the two entrance passages, seemingly marking the transition between outside and in. Within the cave a substantial number of human bones have been found, including remains indicative of decapitation. Late Bronze Age metalwork and Roman coins and jewellery have also been found.

GORDONSTOUN. *See* p. 648.

INVERUGIE HOUSE. *See* p. 662.

DUNDURCAS *see* ROTHES

DUNPHAIL HOUSE 0040

1.6 km. NW of Edinkillie

The land of 'Dovelly' is first documented in the late C12, forming part of the royal hunting forest S of Forres (q.v.). It was principally held by the Comyn (or Cumming) family of Altyre (q.v.), who had built a castle by the mid C13. The estate passed *c.* 1419 to the Dunbars, who constructed a new castle (*see* below).

The nucleus of the present house is by *W.H. Playfair*, completed in 1827–8 for Charles Lennox Cumming-Bruce.* The

*Designs for a new house had been commissioned from *John Baxter* in 1787 – among the first after his completion of Gordon Castle (Fochabers) – and *John Paterson* also made plans in 1817–20.

style is full-blooded Italianate, remarkably well developed for such an early date – and all the more impressive for being the first country house that Playfair designed. The subsequent architectural history is complicated by substantial additions by *Alexander Ross* of Inverness in 1871 and their partial removal in a sensitive remodelling by *Ronald Phillips & Partners* in 1964–6.

On the N front, Playfair's house is a two-storey rectangle of five bays with a wide centre and shallow, platform-piended roof with overhanging eaves on blockish modillions. This was originally fronted by a porte cochère, which Ross removed in 1871 and re-attached to his own large addition on this spot. That was in turn removed in the 1960s and the present porch built, reusing Playfair's original parapet. It has a pair of engaged Roman Doric columns and glazed doors under a broad Neo-Georgian fanlight.

Excellent S façade to the gardens, the main block of three wide bays, regally poised and calm. Advanced ends with tripartite windows on both storeys, originally linked on the ground floor by a wide, round-headed arch. There are now pairs of Roman Doric pilasters, inserted in the 1960s, and a trabeated balcony with Playfair's original balustrade. Little piended roofs over the side bays, all of the eaves again projecting with big cube-like modillions. Off the W flank is a three-stage campanile tower with sundial, datestone and pyramidal roof.

Playfair's original SERVICE WING lay to the E. To the S front it is low, two storeys and seven bays, the ground floor with round-headed windows advanced under a lean-to roof and separated by thick, square buttresses. On the r. a wide single bay with a segmental-headed arch and another parapet; tall tripartite window above it with another piended roof. This was originally topped by another row of glazing with a pyramidal roof and cupola (dem. 1964–6). Towards the N side, the service court was replaced in 1871 with an extension by *Ross*, slightly lower than the main block but in a sympathetic style. Five bays, the former shallow porch in the centre now converted into a round-headed window. Advanced off its l. corner is a block with a trio of windows, originally two-storeyed and designed by Playfair as the kitchen. His house originally ended here, but the service range must have been very quickly found insufficient, as he added a long rectangular KITCHEN COURT beyond it in 1833. To the N, this range is now just a plain screen wall, but it originally had a first storey and roof taller than Ross's addition. All of that was demolished *c.* 1965. At the far end is a single-storey, four-bay building with a platform-piended roof and little coped chimneystack. Two-storey addition behind it with pyramidal roof, also 1833 and originally serving as the LAUNDRY. Towards the garden, the wall of this court had a glasshouse and conservatory (again dem. 1964–6).

The INTERIOR of the house was extensively remodelled in 1964–6, the workmanship good but with little of Playfair remaining beyond the shape and disposition of the rooms. The woodwork, including the stairs and most of the chimneypieces, is by *Jackson & Sons*; the plasterwork is by *J. Brodie & Sons* of Elgin, 1928–32, during renovations under *John Wittet*. A broad HALL spans the depth of the house between porch and garden veranda. It was originally divided into a hall, saloon and boudoir but the partition walls were removed *c*. 1928. Simple wooden panelling with fluted Ionic pilasters; foliate plaster cornice forming two long rectangular panels. Broad dog-leg STAIRCASE on the l. with a wide half-landing. Barley-sugar-twist balusters and square newels with vigorous carved swags and urn finials. Across from it is the former MORNING ROOM, its round-headed arches originally open to the hall but blocked *c*. 1965. Some reused original panelling and pilasters. Circular foliate border around the chandelier; lugged chimneypiece with pulvinated lintel. DRAWING ROOM at the r. end of the hall with shallow coffered panelling on the ceiling. Carved wooden chimneypiece with vigorous acanthus and burgundy marble slips. Excellent BATHROOM in the tower, *c*. 1932 with fixtures and pipes of gleaming metal.

Sumptuous designed LANDSCAPE to the S of the house on two levels, the lower a rough semicircle of lawn straddling the Poldow Burn and emptying into a lake. The gardens were a scene of utter 'ruin and devastation' after the floods of 1829, when the just-completed house was nearly lost. The embankments to the lower section were reinforced with concrete after another flood in 1952, now hidden from the house like a ha-ha. – Hexagonal GAZEBO to the W, early C19.

BRIDGE, 0.4 km. SE. Stilted segmental span over the Poldow Burn, 1818. Two original cast-iron railings on the W with Greek key frieze. Tablet on the E with Latin inscription christening the drive the Via Emilia in honour of Charles Lennox Cumming-Bruce's sister.

MAINS FARM, 0.5 km. NNW. Quadrangular plan of *c*. 1830, probably by Playfair but now much decayed. The farmhouse has a surprisingly large quasi-campanile with big eaves brackets.

SOUTH LODGE, 1.7 km. SE. Crowstepped gables and turret with big conical roof, *c*. 1938 and likely by *Charles C. Doig & Sons*.

DUNPHAIL CASTLE, 0.4 km. NW, on a rocky outcrop. The remains of the Dunbars' early to mid-C15 castle. It was L-plan, consisting of a rectangular main block *c*. 15 m. long and 9.5 m. wide, of which a little of the undercroft survives. NW jamb now very overgrown but with part of an engaged shaft and a slit-window to the W. The NE jamb (added in the early C17 to create a U-plan) is two storeys over a raised basement with N wall intact up to the gable. Pair of rectangular windows with chamfered margins replaced in the mid C17 (see the original lintel on the raised ground floor). Segmental entrance arch on the E wall with a draw-bar hole; unarticulated W wall. The castle was still habitable in the mid C18.

9050

DYKE

Described as a 'municipium' in the mid to late C16, but no record of any civic rights or privileges survives. Formerly a picturesque village but now hemmed in by bad modern housing.

PARISH CHURCH. Fine Georgian rectangle by *James Smith* of Auldearn and *James Smith* of Nairn, dated 1781 on its SW skewputt. Built 'neatly in the stance' of the church of St Andrew, first mentioned in a charter of King William between 1189 and 1199. Symmetrical S elevation of six tall arched windows, the first and last with raised sills to accommodate doors. Corniced birdcage on top of the W gable. Off the E gable, a transverse wing originally built *c.* 1693 as a mausoleum for the Brodie family (see also the late C17 roll-moulded window margin on its E flank) and attached as an aisle to the former church. Its S front was remodelled in the Gothic style by *Matthews & Lawrie* in 1867, the narrower l. gable with a good cast-iron door grille (now blocked). The r. gable has an early to mid-C18 Ionic doorpiece and window with intersecting tracery (also now blocked), but this part much rebuilt in 1948 to create a HALL and VESTRY.

Good, simple interior, renovated 1951–2 but retaining its 1781 layout. Coomb ceiling with kingpost trusses set on raised rafters. – U-plan GALLERY with long canted sides and fielded panelling. – Rare TRIPLE-DECKER PULPIT in the centre of the S wall, with stairs to the l. and r.* Hexagonal upper chamber; below it in the middle, the desk for the precentor to lead the singing. Penitents' box on the bottom, formerly with a bench so that miscreants could sit in full view of the congregation. – MONUMENTS. Walter Kinnaird and Elizabeth Innes, laird and lady of Culbin (SW entrance vestibule). Upper panel with their initials, coats of arms and the year 1613. – In the N vestry wall, a SLAB with Calvary cross and perimeter Latin inscription for Richard Brothy and his wife †1448 (or 1488).

Original GRAVEYARD to the S with C18 and C19 MEMORIALS.‡ – The GATE into the NW extension is the WAR MEMORIAL by *Peter Macgregor Chalmers*, 1920–2. Semicircular arch with powerful gabled overthrow. Sword and laurel wreath in a rectangular niche.

Former FREE CHURCH (now Old Kirk Guest House), 0.7 km. NNE. Early Gothic by *John Rhind*, 1866–7; closed 1941 and

*There are two others at the Garrison Chapel, Fort George (1767), and the Free Church, Lower Gledfield (1848), both Highland and Islands.

‡Rodney's Stone was discovered here in 1781 but is now at Brodie Castle (*see* p. 486).

interior sensitively converted from 1997 by *Mike Guild*. Large S window of five stepped lancets with pierced spandrels. Big gableted bellcote on the S gable and scrolled, crocketed finial on the N. – Former MANSE to the ENE, 1852–3.

PRIMARY SCHOOL. Gothic by *William Mackintosh Sen.*, 1876–7.

ABBOTSHILL BRIDGE, 0.8 km. E. Two segmental spans over the Muckle Burn, *c.* 1830. Arch-rings of rusticated ashlar. Of similar date, the EARLSMILL BRIDGE, 3.1 km. SW.

BERNERA, 0.9 km. NNE. Pretty single-storey cottage, *c.* 1840, with bargeboarding on the porch and dormers. Trellises around the ground-floor windows.

EARLSMILL HOUSE, 3.1 km. SW. By *A. & W. Reid*, *c.* 1865, originally for the factor of Darnaway (q.v.). Two storeys and three wide bays, the centre with a jerkin-headed gable over piended Italianate porch. Wide ashlar pilaster strips on the ends; boldly projecting eaves with deep brackets punctuating the wall-head. Full-height, canted bay window on the E gable. Suavely curved walls inside the drawing room and dining room.

BRODIE CASTLE. *See* p. 480.

DALVEY HOUSE. *See* p. 530.

DARNAWAY CASTLE. *See* p. 532.

EASTER ELCHIES HOUSE 2040

1 km. NNE of Charlestown of Aberlour

Quietly dignified laird's house on land given to the Grant family by the Bishop of Moray in 1543. The two-bay centre of the W front terminates in a crowstepped gable with apex chimneystack. The small stone below its tympanum carries the monogram of John Patrick Grant and is dated 1700, although the house looks fifty years earlier. Bolection-moulded doorpiece to l. of centre and small windows to the two floors above. Outer bays with enlarged ground-floor windows and dormers placed below the wall-head, the bland triangular heads added during enlargements to the house by *A. & W. Reid*, 1856–7 for the Earl of Seafield, who transformed it into a gigantic shooting lodge. The severe, vertical stair-tower on the E front originally culminated in a watch chamber. Stair-turret corbelled out in its NE re-entrant angle, the lower dozen courses of masonry dating from the C17 and the upper section and conical bellcast roof added by the Reids. The original entrance was located just below it.

Since 1961 the house has belonged to the adjacent Macallan Distillery, whose owners restored it in 1979–85 (including the demolition of its Victorian accretions). Extending to the S are two octagonal OFFICE PODS, the first of 1985 by *Michael Laird & Partners*, the second (to an identical plan) by *Wittets*, *c.* 1992. Their centres have shallow platform-piended roofs and faceted skylights and the sides are fully glazed. Out of deference to the main house, the pods are slightly sunk below ground level and the second is canted out at an angle rather than axially aligned.

THE MACALLAN DISTILLERY lies to the W, founded by Alexander Reid in 1823–4 and originally built of wood. Of the stone reconstruction by *Charles C. Doig* from *c.* 1882 to 1894 virtually nothing survives except the double-gabled MALT BARN of 1893 (aligned SSW–NNE) and the footings of two WAREHOUSES. A completely new complex is to be built by *Rogers Stirk Harbour & Partners*, with visitor centre and distillery concealed beneath an undulating green roof.

To the W of the entrance drive, a colossal mass of RACKING WAREHOUSES (2008–12), each hulkingly triple-gabled with brown corrugated walls and green roofs. They dominate the horizon for miles around.

MACALLAN BURIAL GROUND, 0.2 km. S. Scant remains of a pre-Reformation church that fell into ruin *c.* 1760. Only the NW corner survives, part of the walls 3.1 m. high; the church was originally *c.* 19 m. long. – In the SE corner, the ELCHIES MAUSOLEUM of 1715, single storey with a slated pyramidal roof. Wall monument to John Grant †1715, likely carved by *John Faid* of Elgin. Long Latin inscription flanked by two engaged Composite columns. Entablature with undercut ribbon moulding and modillioned cornice. Tall, tomb-like dado with a recumbent skeleton and crossed bones to the l. and r.

5050

EDINGIGHT HOUSE* B

4 km. NW of Knock

The earliest house was built in 1559 after John Innes, the first laird, acquired the land from the abbot of Kinloss. This is represented by the three short bays of the W end of the S front with small rectangular windows on the first floor. There was originally a forestair. The five taller bays to the E date from 1681 for John, the 5th Laird. This part was originally L-plan but the wing was demolished in the mid C19 and the fenestration is now much-altered and regularized. Off-centre door to the garden, formerly beneath a porch; blocked window to the r. of it with chamfered margins. Cavetto skewputts with carved masks to the NW and SE and Innes stars on the SW. The porch on the rear of the E block has an armorial plaque, dated 1559 but carved *c.* 1955. Re-set stone mantelpiece in the drawing room, dated 1681 with initials, heraldry and foliate decoration. It was formerly in the hall on the first floor.

*Until its demolition in 1977, Edingight House referred to the mansion, 0.5 km. SSW, by *A. & W. Reid* *c.* 1885.

EDINKILLIE 0040

Not a village *per se*, but a few buildings in an uncommonly picturesque setting, nestled in a serpentine bend of the Divie with the railway viaduct striding across the horizon.

PARISH CHURCH. Harled preaching-box of 1741–2, built by the masons *Andrew Smith* and *David Maculloch*. It sits in the rectangular footprint of a medieval church, first mentioned in the charters of Bishop Archibald in 1287. Long S elevation, six bays of straight-headed windows with eighteen-pane glazing. Round-headed windows set high in the gables; corniced bellcote on the W restored in 1920. Four-part N wing (including stair wing and vestry) forming a T-plan, some of it added in 1812–13. Key-blocked oculi to the l. and r. inserted by *John Wittet*, 1904–5. Modest Georgian layout within, re-seated in 1811–13 and restored by Wittet. – Tight three-sided GALLERY. – Canted PULPIT (centre of N wall), 1813. Big simple panelling, back-board and canopy. – ORGAN by *Ingram & Co.*, 1940–1. Lattice case. – MEMORIAL (re-set in the vestibule). Festooned helm and the initials M.D. over mortality emblems. Dated 1666 with the Dunbar coat of arms.

BURIAL GROUND with hexagonal early C19 WATCH HOUSE. Faceted roof with ball finial. – Kerbed ENCLOSURE against the W gable, formerly the site of the pre-Reformation RELUGAS BURIAL AISLE. In the middle, a WALL SLAB for Sir Thomas Dick Lauder †1848 (and three children), justly famous for his account of the Moray floods in 1829. – Four C19 PLAQUES for the Urquhart family. Semicircular pediment with fluted shell ornament and gigantic consoles with petalled flowers. – Outside the N wall, the WAR MEMORIAL by *John Wittet*, 1920–1. Rustic aedicule with thick, rock-faced jambs around a block-pedimented niche.

EDINKILLIE HOUSE. The former manse by *John Paterson*, 111
1822–3, and based on his unsuccessful proposals for Dunphail House (q.v). Two-storey butterfly plan with a semi-octagon in the centre of each side (S one larger). Two-bay wings at an angle and single-storey, single-bay wings beyond set parallel to the centre. N entrance in the l. re-entrant angle, the lean-to porch beyond it with rustic columns added by *John Wittet*, 1902.* Pristine garden façade facing the Divie – nothing but twelve-pane glazing (smaller on the first floor) and simple modulation of geometric forms, but immensely satisfying. Inside, the polygonal surfaces outside are expressed as circles, creating unusual spatial relationships. Rounded entrance hall behind the N half-octagon and large circular drawing room to the S. Cantilevered staircase in the W with cast-iron palmette balusters. Nicely bowed hallway on the first floor with circular bedroom in the centre.

*Paterson's original plan shows rustic verandas linked to the outer wings on both sides, but these appear not to have been built.

Crossing the Divie W of the church, a high rubble BRIDGE of
121 1831. To the E the river is crossed by the magnificent VIADUCT built by *Joseph Mitchell* for the Inverness & Perth Junction Railway in 1861–3. Closed 1965 and now pedestrianized as part of the Dava Way. An impressive feat of engineering, and so aesthetically appealing that it is impossible to imagine the landscape without it. Seven high arches of rock-faced rubble, the tall piers very coarse with smooth intrados.

GLENERNEY LODGE, 0.9 km. W. The core is a small early to mid-C19 shooting lodge, built of rubble with projecting eaves and studded gable boards. It now forms the S section of a much longer house, extended N in a similar style by *John Wittet* c. 1910 and again c. 1925–32 by *J. & W. Wittet*. Shallow tetrastyle Roman Doric porch on the E front. Long rear elevation of two storeys and five bays overlooking the idyllic Dorback Burn.

BRAEMORAY LODGE, 4.2 km. SSW. Single-storey shooting lodge of whitewashed plank-and-pole cladding, 1838–9. Veranda to the S and E on rustic columns. L-plan W wing of 1911, partly incorporating an early to mid-C19 core. – SERVICE RANGE to the NNW, c. 1966 in a similar style.

OLD MANSE, 2.3 km. NW. By *John Milne* of Forres, 1877, for Edinkillie Free Church.* Canted, crenellated bay windows.

DUNPHAIL HOUSE. *See* p. 555.

LOGIE HOUSE. *See* p. 691.

1060 ELGIN

INTRODUCTION

The capital of Moray, with a long, complex history and retaining excellent examples of architecture from the C13 and the C17 through to the late C19. The discovery of a carved Pictish cross-slab in the centre of the town (now in the Cathedral graveyard) shows that the area was likely occupied by the C3. By popular tradition, the name 'Elgin' is said to derive from Helgy, a victorious general who overran the area c. 927. A castle on what is now

*The church itself (also by Milne, 1877) was formerly located 0.5 km. SE.

Ladyhill is first documented *c.* 1040 and was later rebuilt in stone, only to be reduced to ruin by Edward I in 1297.

The earliest mention of a burgh proper dates from a charter of King David I, *c.* 1151, and the rights of the burgesses of Elgin (previously granted by David and Malcolm) were re-affirmed by King William the Lion *c.* 1194. In 1224, Elgin was prestigious enough to be selected as the new seat of the bishopric of Moray, and its vast new cathedral begun, among the finest in Scotland. From the C12 to the C14, Elgin – like Edinburgh and many Scottish burghs – consisted of a single long street with closes (or lanes) branching off at right angles. In the C13, this boulevard was known as the *strata communis*, and still forms the backbone of the modern High Street. The parish church of St Giles formed the E boundary of the burgh, which stretched *c.* 0.4 km. to the W up to what is now Gray's Hospital, with the Castle in the approximate centre of the town. The Cathedral and its associated little township were at this time quite separate. The houses were mainly of wood and the town was surrounded by a timber palisade. In 1390, all of Elgin (including the Cathedral and the canons' manses) was burned by Alexander Stewart (Earl of Buchan), much better known by his fearsome nickname, the 'Wolf of Badenoch'. The W section was never rebuilt and by the middle of the C15 the town had pushed to the E – the swollen centre filled by the parish church of St Giles, just as it is now, with its graveyard and adjacent market, market cross, tolbooth and gaol.

The Reformation brought a short period of decline, but the early to mid C17 saw reconstruction on a grand scale, still attested by five buildings of that date. A prominent feature of the 'new' burgh was the use of ground-floor arcaded loggias in the manner of the Veneto and N Italy. The population of Elgin in 1700 was approximately 1,300, and smart houses were built in the early to mid C18 in a trim, classical style. The rest of the century was evidently one of great decline, and in 1783 the town was described as 'a place of little trade and thinly inhabited'.

From *c.* 1820, Elgin began to assume its current form, at last breaking free of its medieval confines. The C13 town plan was broached by construction of Batchen Street and Commerce Street to the S of the High Street and grand-scale public buildings (Anderson's Institution and Gray's Hospital) announced dramatic new wealth and importance. Prosperity continued through the C19, and the S section of the burgh was laid out to rectilinear plan with fine Victorian cottages, houses and villas, many of them the work of the local architects: *William Robertson*, his nephews *A. & W. Reid*, *Thomas Mackenzie*, *Charles C. Doig*, and in the early C20 *John Wittet*. By the start of the C20, Elgin had been completely transformed; but the rest of the century, especially the 1960s and 1970s, brought some dereliction and the inexcusable demolition of fine buildings. The once-elegant shopfronts of the High Street have been badly converted, but the 'bare bones' of extremely fine architecture are all still present: it is not too late for Elgin to rediscover itself.

Elgin Cathedral*

Introduction

One of the most evocatively beautiful of Scotland's ecclesiastical ruins, in a fine setting beside the Lossie, although it required a major local effort, together with the intervention of central government, to bring both building and setting to the condition now seen.

Firm records of a bishop of Moray first occur in the 1120s, but over the following century the see moved between Birnie, Kinneddar (Lossiemouth) and Spynie (qq.v), where it was fixed in 1206. The move to Elgin, which was the secular administrative centre for the area, was authorized by papal mandate on 10 April 1224 and building of the CHURCH was presumably started at once, the land being granted by the king on 19 July of that year. There are references to *Master Gregory* the mason and *Richard* the glazier. As first built it was a cruciform building with a short aisleless E limb, rectangular transepts and an aisled nave of six bays. It is not clear if a central tower was intended from the start, and the pair of W towers, which extended the nave to seven bays, were possibly a slight afterthought. A further addition was a chapel flanking the three E bays of the S nave aisle. In 1242 a new constitution was adopted for the Cathedral clergy, and it was decided that the pattern of worship of Salisbury Cathedral should be followed.

The C15 *Scotichronicon* records damage to the cathedral in 1244 and what must have been a very damaging fire in 1270. The REBUILDING AND EXTENSION after the fire was seized upon as the opportunity for major enhancements. The E limb was extended to seven bays, with broad aisles against all but the two E bays of the presbytery; the E limb appears also to have been heightened. Against the N side an octagonal chapter house was added. Most unusually, the nave was augmented by outer aisles (the S aisle incorporating the existing S chapel), and a porch was added to the W bay of the new S aisle. Between the W towers a new processional doorway was inserted, and the towers themselves heightened by an extra storey.

A THIRD BUILDING CAMPAIGN followed a devastating attack on the Cathedral on 17 June 1390 by Alexander Stewart, Earl of Buchan, the rapacious 'Wolf of Badenoch', in retaliation against Bishop Alexander Bur, who had refused to continue paying for Buchan's protection. There was a further attack by Alexander of the Isles in 1402. Major rebuilding and repair was evidently necessitated, though the process appears to have been protracted and included rebuilding of the central tower, probably by Bishop John Innes (1407–14), insertion of the grand nave W window attributed to Bishop Columba de Dunbar (1422–35) and reconstruction of the windows and vaulting of the chapter house in the time of Bishop Andrew Stewart (1482–1501). The central tower again collapsed *c.* 1506 and had to be rebuilt.

*This entry has been contributed by Richard Fawcett.

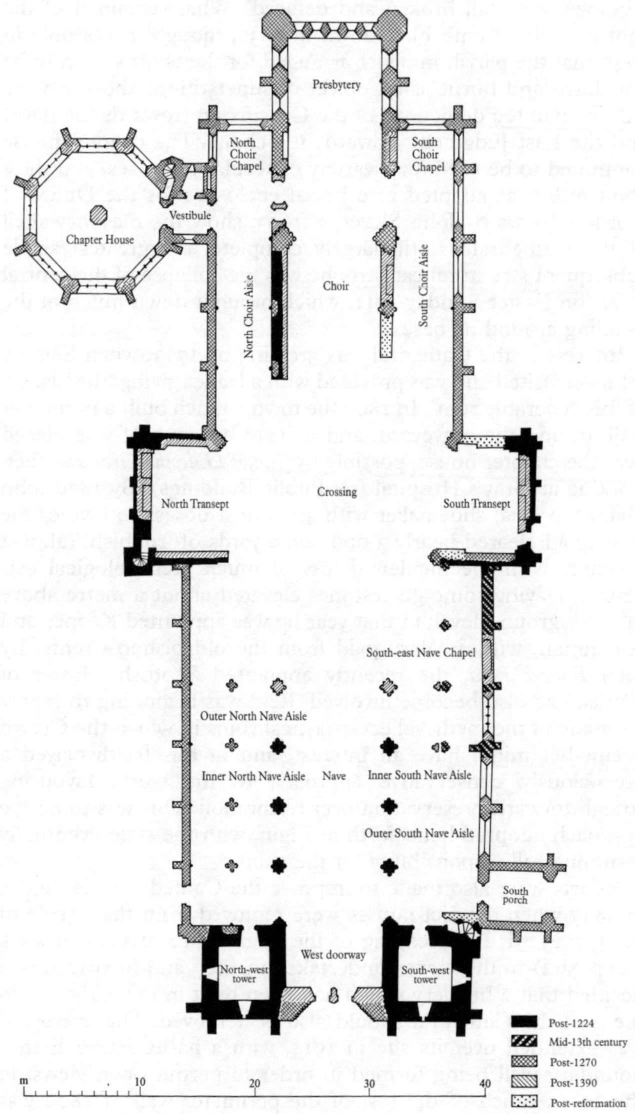

Elgin Cathedral.
Plan

The Cathedral may have been 'cleansed' by the reformers as early as 1561, and the bishop and clergy quickly removed themselves to the parish church of St Giles (*see* Churches below). Six years later, orders were given to remove the lead from the Cathedral's roof, though in 1569 there were thoughts of reinstating it. By 1615 Taylor the 'Water Poet' said that the roofs and windows were 'all broken and defaced'. What remained of the roof over the E limb blew down in 1637, though it was only in 1640 that the parish minister arranged for the choir screen to be cut down and burnt as an object of superstition; above it were still the painted depictions of the Crucifixion (towards the nave) and the Last Judgment (towards the choir). The chapter house continued to be used for a variety of secular purposes, and the S choir aisle was adapted as a burial enclosure for the Dukes of Gordon. Views by John Slezer, *c.* 1693, show the masonry shell of the Cathedral as still largely complete; the greatest single subsequent structural catastrophe was the collapse of the central tower on Easter Sunday 1711, which brought down much of the building around its base.

Interest in the Cathedral was growing by 1773, when Samuel Johnson visited and was provided with a leaflet giving 'the history of this venerable ruin'. In 1809 the town council built a perimeter wall around the graveyard, and in 1816 a new roof was placed over the chapter house, possibly by *James Gillespie Graham*, then working at Gray's Hospital (*see* Public Buildings). By 1826 John Shanks, a local shoemaker with an almost obsessive love of the ruins, had cleared nearly 3,000 cubic yards of 'rubbish' (almost certainly with the incidental loss of much archaeological evidence), leaving some gravestones elevated about a metre above the new ground level; in that year he was appointed Keeper and Watchman, with a salary paid from the old bishop's rents. By then *Robert Reid*, the recently appointed Scottish Master of Works, had also become involved. Reid was beginning to report on many of the medieval ecclesiastical ruins in which the Crown deemed it might have an interest, and in this he displayed a precociously conservative approach to the work, favouring straightforward preservation over restoration. This was to be the approach adopted henceforth at Elgin, with the state eventually assuming full responsibility for the ruins.

Efforts were also made to improve the Cathedral's setting, as in 1847 when derelict houses were removed from the W side of the graveyard. Landscaping of the open space of Cooper Park (*see* p. 592) to the W was undertaken in 1903 and in 1912 it was decided that a brewery which had been built in the early C19 to the E of the Cathedral should also be removed. The graveyard was extended over its site in 1915, with a ha-ha rather than a boundary wall being formed in order to permit open views; in the 1930s much of the rest of the perimeter wall of 1809 was replaced by an iron railing. Also in the 1930s a major campaign of stabilization and consolidation was undertaken, with a further campaign over the last three decades of the C20.

DESCRIPTION

East limb

15 Of the EAST LIMB (CHOIR AND PRESBYTERY) as first built from 1224, in the time of Bishop Andrew de Moravia (1222–42),

the only survivor is the ashlar N wall, which probably extended no further than the three W bays of the present choir, and of which two bays survive in a relatively complete state, the lowest courses on their S side showing extensive fire damage. In the S side, immediately below the later clearstorey, are traces of cut-back arches that indicate there was an internal arcade with wider arches corresponding to a single window in each bay, and with narrower blind arches between; traces of one of those windows may be seen on the outer side of the wall towards the later aisle. This is similar to the design of the E limb of Dornoch Cathedral, started by Bishop Andrew's kinsman Bishop Gilbert de Moravia (1222–45). If the limb rose no higher than that arcading, however, it must have been significantly lower than the transepts and nave from which it projected.

After the fire of 1270 the E limb was rebuilt on an altogether different scale: doubled in length and terminating in a magnificent E FRONT to the central vessel that has two tiers of five lancets. Massive octagonal buttresses at the angles with two bands of blind arches at the lower level, capped by pinnacles with a blind arch and a gablet to each face. Within the E gable is a rose window flanked on each side by a blind arch, with further blind arches at the gable apex. This design is the culmination of a tradition of façade design extending through St Andrews Cathedral, Arbroath Abbey and probably Dryburgh Abbey in Scotland, and also seen in several northern English churches, of which Whitby Abbey is perhaps the finest surviving example. In these the leading characteristic is the superimposed tiers of single lancets, ranging from three in each tier to four at Southwell Minster and five in the W front of Ripon Minster begun *c.* 1233.

The front rises from a deep base course that runs around the whole of the E limb; the windows rest on string courses, and slender shafts rise from between the arches of the lower tier of windows through the upper tier. The shafted reveals of the lower tier of windows are enriched with square flower, and those of the upper tier with dogtooth. One of the most striking features of the front must have been that the lower tier had simple bar tracery, in the form of a circlet above a sub-arch. This is among the earliest documented cases of bar tracery in Scotland, along with the far more ambitious ensemble at Sweetheart Abbey, also of the years after 1270. The tracery of the rose window was replaced after 1390: the stumps of this later tracery show that ultimately there were twelve bowed triangles around its perimeter.

The two narrow unaisled bays of the PRESBYTERY offer a transitional stage of design between the E front and the choir flanks. At the upper level in each bay is a pair of lancets like those in both the E front and the clearstorey to the W. But at the lower level in each bay is a single larger window that was subdivided by Y-tracery, within each part of which was a circlet above a sub-arch i.e. a doubling up of the tracery in the E front. The tracery within the three-bay CHOIR AISLES was replaced

Elgin Cathedral, choir interior.
Engraving by R.W. Billings, 1852

after 1390. It is fully preserved in the middle bay of the S aisle only, and has intersecting arcs within which circlets are set. In spite of the date it is possible that this is a reflection of the late C13 window design. Defining the aisle bays are buttresses with tall chamfered upper stages; at the SE angle they are enriched by gablets. The problems faced by the mason in extending the E limb are seen especially clearly in the retention of the earlier N wall, as a result of which the W half of the N side is blank below the clearstorey, with just a single arch to the N aisle in the bay to its E. By contrast, the S aisle has an arcade, whose piers have triplets of shafts on the cardinal axes, with the leading shafts filleted, and there are alternating shafts and cavettos along the diagonal faces. The minutely detailed arches rise through springer blocks that continue the verticality of the pier into the arch.

Separating the three bays of the choir from the presbytery, between the two surviving arches of the S arcade and in the corresponding position on the N wall, are massive responds that continue the profile of the arcade piers and that are capped by multi-tiered pinnacles above the clearstorey sill. Could these initially have been intended to support a transverse arch that would have demarcated the space of the choir from the presbytery? The wide choir aisles were covered by tierceron-vaulting, which survives over the three E bays of the S aisle and the E bay of the N aisle. The aisle roofs were of unusually low pitch, to avoid introducing a middle storey or making the clearstorey higher than that which already existed in the nave.

The CLEARSTOREY appears to have been designed to conform in its proportions and overall forms, if not in all its details, with that in the nave, an illustration of the wish by masons (more common than is often thought) to have their own work sit in sympathy with earlier work. It has a wall passage behind an arcade that corresponds with the windows on the exterior. Along the S side there is therefore a regular rhythm of two arches and windows in each of the three narrower E bays, but there are three arches and windows in the wider bays further W. Between the slender engaged shafts of the piers are bands of dogtooth. On the N side the pattern is the same up to and including the fourth bay from the E. But over the retained earlier wall, where the wall passage had to be at a slightly higher level, there are differences in the detailing of the inner arches, and there are only two arches in each bay of the choir, with stretches of wall on each side. This suggests that the clearstorey here may have been built in advance of the rest. The clearstorey passage continues across the upper tier of windows in the E wall, above which the rose window must have been fully visible internally, since there is evidence in the masonry for a curved barrel ceiling rising into the roof space.

Chapter house

The CHAPTER HOUSE, projecting from the second bay from the 20
E of the N choir aisle, was also part of the campaign after 1270.
Over the outer face of the door from the aisle, however, are
possible slight traces of a gable, which may suggest that this
was intended as an entrance into the church from the outside
and that therefore the chapter house was started only once the
extension of the E limb was in progress. It is ashlar-built and
octagonal, one of only three of that plan known in Scotland
(cf. Inchcolm, Fife, and Holyrood in Edinburgh, the last
known only through excavation). Its base course is the same
as that of the E limb, and there are slender buttresses at the
angles with gablets. Scarring in the masonry shows that the

windows on seven of the eight faces of the chapter house initally occupied the full width between the buttresses, indicating that they must have contained tracery on a highly ambitious scale. They were reduced as part of the reconstruction by Bishop Andrew Stewart (1482–1501), when the present rather loosely organized tracery of differing designs was introduced. The NE window is almost identical to one in the S nave aisle at Linlithgow St Michael (where it is a secondary insertion). One of these windows was restored in 1904, the others between 1972 and 1986. The roof is of 1987–9.

Between aisle and chapter house is a small vaulted vestibule, and in the E re-entrant angle between it and the chapter house is a turret for a spiral stair to the wall-head. The door into the vestibule from the N choir aisle has engaged shafts carrying capitals with multiple mouldings; the opening was subdivided by a pair of arches carried on a trumeau (now gone), and with an open circlet between the two arches. The doorway from the vestibule to the chapter house was probably even richer, since there is a band of dogtooth between the engaged shafts of the jambs, and the caps have stiff-leaf foliage, albeit of a slightly two-dimensional form. The inner order of the doorway is a late medieval replacement with simple continuous mouldings, which it may be suspected replaced a pair of sub-arches like those of the outer doorway. On the N side of the vestibule a tiny chamber has been added, which contains a fireplace and an elongated basin, suggesting that it had a use in connection with the preparation of the elements for the celebration of Mass.

Within the chapter house, the only area identifiably of the post-1270 campaign is the upper part of the S wall. Above the remodelled inner face of the doorway is a blind arcade of four cusped arches carried on engaged shafts with bands of dogtooth, and within the apex of the wall arch is a further single arch. Otherwise, most of what is now seen is of the time of Bishop Stewart. The walls were thickened on each side of the windows from the level of the sills, with the thickening carried on string courses with corbels at the ends and shafts at the changes in angle, all of which is highly enriched with chunky foliage, figures and beasts. Below the window of the N face, however, a series of trifoliate arches emphasize the seats of the dean and dignitaries. The central pier, which rises from a deep moulded base, is octofoil, with alternating three-quarter shafts and hollows; embodied on its W side is a lectern, with chubby angels supporting a steeply sloping book-rest. The octagonal capital of the pier is decorated with shields bearing the Royal Arms of Scotland and those of Bishop Stewart, together with a number of variants of the *arma Christi* and a depiction of the crucified St Andrew; running between all of these is a band of foliage. The vault, which is essentially of tierceron form adapted to an octagonal plan, may have been inspired by that over the early to mid-C13 decagonal chapter house at Lincoln Cathedral; it may also replicate the form of the original post-1270 vault. The twenty-four bosses of the vault are decorated with depictions of Christ in Majesty, a blessing bishop, the royal arms, Bishop Stewart's arms, the *arma Christi* and a range of human faces and foliage designs.

Transepts

Of the church started in 1224 the S TRANSEPT, which is constructed of irregularly coursed rubble, is the most complete part and gives the best impression of its design. Externally it rises from a double-chamfered base course. The S face is of two stages marked by string courses and divided into three vertical divisions by buttresses without offsets. In the l. bay there is a gabled doorway with the string course stepped over it; the door had three major and two minor shafts set against an angled face in the jambs, leaf forms to the capitals, and massive dogtooth to the central arch order. Above the doorway is a broad vesica-shaped window. The lower windows in the two r. bays have pointed arches, broadly chamfered reveals and hoodmoulds, but in the upper tier the windows are round-arched, demonstrating the interchangeability of arch forms that prevailed at this period; the inner order of the round arches is continuously moulded, while the outer order was carried on nook-shafts with chalice capitals. Early views record that the gable, of which only a fragment remains, had a three-light window, possibly with intersecting tracery, below a pair of niches and a blind trefoil at the apex. Insufficient survives to be able to determine the original forms of the transept's E side with confidence, though early views suggest that it was divided into two parts by a buttress, and that there were again two tiers of windows. Of the transept's W side, only the portion that projected beyond the S nave aisle survives. It was divided into two unequal parts by a buttress. At the lower level there was a single pointed window (now blocked) in the bay next to the aisle, while at the upper level there was a single window in each part similar to the lower windows of the S face. There is no vertical alignment between the two levels of windows. The broken ends of the E and W walls are now braced by C19 buttressing.

Internally, there was a broad blind arch at the lower level on the E side, which presumably framed an altar, and early views appear to show a window within its head. The lower windows of the S and W sides have simply splayed rere-arches, and within the rere-arch of the vesica window above the S door are seats, indicating perhaps the presence of a timber gallery along the W side. At the upper level there is a clearstorey passage that on the S side opens towards the transept through a continuous arcade of alternating round and pointed arches carried on piers or responds with foliate capitals, while on the E and W sides there are single arches corresponding to the windows.

The N TRANSEPT is far less complete, the main survivors being the lower N wall, the NE corner (which stands to almost full height) and part of the W wall. From these, and Slezer's view of 1693, it can be seen that it was very similar to the S transept, with two tiers of windows in three vertical divisions to the N face, and a triplet of windows below a blind trefoil in the gable. Slezer shows all of the windows as round-headed, though his depiction of such minutiae is unreliable. As in the S transept there was a wide blind arch in the E wall but no doorway in the N wall; instead there was a spiral stair at the NW corner, which rises from a higher base course than that below the rest of the transept. Slezer shows that, above a square base, the stair-turret was polygonal. The internal evidence for the original design of the N transept has been confused by the later insertion of tomb-recesses (*see* Monuments below).

Nave

The NAVE is the least complete part of the church. The main physical evidence for the internal elevation of the post – 1224 phase is at the inner E angles of the W towers, where there are the stubs of the two arcade walls; there are also the stumps of the three W arcade piers on each side. From all of this, supplemented by Slezer's views before the final collapse of the central tower, we see that the nave elevations were of two storeys. Elgin is therefore one of the first major Scottish churches – perhaps *the* first – to show a preference for two rather than three storeys; in this it was soon to be followed by the transepts at Pluscarden Priory (Abbey, q.v.) and the nave of Dunblane Cathedral. The arcade piers were basically cruciform with filleted shafts on the cardinal axes and three-quarter shafts in the angles; the bases were of waterholding profile. On the W responds the moulded capitals survive, with an unusually deep vertical face below the abacus and a plain bell. From what can be seen of the earliest roof-line at the junction of the N aisle with the N tower's E wall, the aisle roofs sloped so steeply that

Elgin Cathedral, view from the N.
Drawing by John Slezer, 1693

there would initially have been no space for vaulting over the relatively narrow aisles. Slezer shows that the clearstorey had three windows to each bay, and there was a corresponding arcade on the inner face of the wall; the windows had broadly chamfered external reveals, while the inner arcade had engaged shafts to the jambs.

The CHAPEL added against the three E bays of the S aisle was, like the nave itself, unvaulted. The arcade opening into it was carried on slender quatrefoil piers and responds with filleted shafts separated by hollows, while the arches had multiple filleted rolls alternating with hollows. Within the chapel the bay divisions were marked by transverse arches carried on responds towards the aisle and triple corbels against the outer wall. On the evidence of the blind transverse arch at the E end of the chapel, there was an attractive interplay of intersecting mouldings at the arch springings. The surviving caps are decorated with flattened cabbage-leaf-like foliage.

The main structural changes to the nave after the fire of 1270 were the addition of OUTER AISLES, with a deep PORCH in the W bay of the S aisle. The porch was of two storeys, with access to the upper storey from the aisle. The lower level was covered by two bays of tierceron-vaulting; this would have focused attention on the doorway, which has three engaged orders of shafts and a band of dogtooth to the jambs, moulded caps and a tightly moulded arch that also has an order of dogtooth. Somewhat inexplicably, the doorway is not quite central to the porch, and it is also out of alignment with a blind arch set within the wall arch of the vault. Parts of the walling of the S outer aisle survive and in the fifth bay from the E there is a fragment of a post-1270 window, which has multi-shafted jambs with bands of dogtooth and square flower, comparable with the clearstorey jambs in the E limb. It is not known if the aisle windows of this period contained tracery.

At the same time that the aisles were doubled up, it can be seen from the E sides of the towers that tierceron-vaults were inserted over the existing aisles, and also over the new outer N aisle. It is far from clear, however, how the S outer aisle was covered. In the E chapel, which was absorbed into the new aisle and thus dictated its width, there was clearly no intention to replace the existing transverse arches by vaults. In the aisle bay to its W, however, there is a springing at the level of the transverse arch in the chapel, indicating that a vault was planned in the W bays of the new aisle. But it appears that this plan was aborted and instead the sequence of transverse arches was continued down the whole of the outer aisle. Vaults were eventually inserted over the three W bays, above the level of these arches, and this appears to have been done some time after 1390, since the wall ribs are closely related to the arches of the large four-light aisle windows which replaced some of the earlier openings at this time. Two of those windows survive and one has tracery with circlets of spiralling daggers between pairs of sub-arches. These windows are surmounted by gables, though it is not entirely certain when these were first built, since a surviving fragment of cornice has a band of semi-dogtooth and intersecting arches that might suggest a date after 1270; but it is perhaps more likely that the detailing is a conscious archaism (semi-dogtooth decoration is also found in the late C15 work in the chapter house). If the gables are after 1390, they would possibly best be understood as part of a late medieval taste for lateral gables that also found expression in chapels added to Edinburgh St Giles and Stirling Holy Rude, and that perhaps drew its inspiration from Netherlandish prototypes.

The extent of late medieval work within the body of the nave is uncertain, since so little survives. The W crossing piers and first piers to their W have been completely lost or partly rebuilt. However, the second pier to their W on each side is clearly a late medieval replacement, suggesting that masonry falling from the tower in either 1390 or 1506 necessitated extensive reconstruction at the nave's E end. It was presumably at the same time that the slender piers opening into the SE nave chapel were augmented by additional responds towards the inner aisle.

West end

The W TOWERS, which are built of ashlar, have a different base course from that of the transepts, suggesting that they were not envisaged when work started in the 1220s; nevertheless, they were certainly under construction by the time the nave arcade walls were being built, since the walls and towers are structurally integrated. The towers are walled off from the nave, the only access being a doorway in the E side of each, together with a secondary doorway to the spiral stair at the SE corner of the S tower. The towers are each of four stages. The lowest stages are lit by a single narrow lancet to each external face, and at the second stages there are Y-traceried windows, with those in the N tower having been modified when an intermediate floor was introduced. The third stages, which were probably initially intended as the top ones, are lit by round-arched four-light windows, the lights grouped in two pairs within asymmetrical sub-arches. The buttresses rise sheer through all three of these stages, punctuated by nothing more than the string courses that mark the stages. The top stage of each tower appears to be an addition to the original design from the time of the general increase in scale that was introduced after 1270. On each of the outward faces is an arcade of three arches, the central one framing a single window. At this level the buttresses have chamfered angles and two levels of gablets. In all of this there are some similarities with the free-standing NW bell-tower at Cambuskenneth Abbey, Stirling. The head of the stair projection at the SE angle of the S tower was modified at the same time that the top storeys were added, and was decorated with an arcade of three blind arches on both the E and S faces, with semi-dogtooth decoration to the gablets that frame the arches. The vignette of the Cathedral on Timothy Pont's map of *c.* 1600 suggests that there were low spires over the W towers in their final state. These were presumably of timber and lead, though there is internal evidence that the S tower was to have had a stone spire before the top stage was added, since there is an angled intake of masonry in three of the internal corners.

Internally, the lowest stage of each tower is covered by a quadripartite vault. The stair up to the second stage is now entered from a relocated doorway on its N side, but the original access appears to have been on its E side. The stair has been largely rebuilt and its steps cut from discarded gravestones of medieval and post-medieval date. However, it has already been said that the stair projection was modified after 1270, and a delicately detailed miniature vault over the well must date from that phase. The initial access from the stair to the second stage was to have been at a higher level, through a door in the S wall, and it also seems that the stair was to have continued upwards to a mural passage in the E wall. Since the level of the door which now gives access off the stair is governed by the height of the extrados of the ground-floor vault, this could indicate either that the vault is a product of the post-1270 campaign or that it was intended to reconstruct it at a higher level. The evidence for the C13 arrangements at second-stage level of the N tower has been obscured by the insertion of a barrel-vault and a timber mezzanine floor (the latter now gone), which was presumably carried out after 1390. This room, which is provided with a fireplace, was perhaps intended to accommodate some official concerned with the Cathedral's security. There is individual access to the top stage of each of the towers by way of stairs at the inner W angles. Throughout the upper stages of both towers there are extensive traces of fire damage.

The W FRONT between the towers is now a product of the 14
rebuildings after 1270 and after 1390. The great processional doorway at the centre has jambs with a regular succession of eight orders of three-quarter shafts alternating with cavettos, while the tightly moulded arches have dogtooth and foliage trails in the hollows, all details closely related to those of the extended E limb after 1270. Surmounting the doorway are three gables, an approach to design that represents a development on the triple gables of the W doors at Jedburgh and Arbroath Abbeys. Each gable has an image niche at its centre flanked by cusped forms; those in the central gable are compressed by the penetration into the gable of the arch of the great doorway. In the narrow strip of masonry on each side of the doorway is an image niche, with dogtooth to the shafted jambs, stiff-leaf capitals and stiff-leaf trails to the cusped arches. The closest parallel for the overall form of the doorway is its near contemporary at Glasgow Cathedral, and it is likely that there was initially a similar arrangement of a pair of

sub-arches carried on a trumeau, with blind arches in the tympana of each sub-arch and in the spandrel between them. The innermost element as now seen, however, is clearly of after 1390, consisting of a pair of sub-arches with continuous foliage-decorated mouldings supported on a trumeau, above which is a tympanum with a large central vesica flanked by a pair of censing angels; the vesica presumably once housed a depiction of the Trinity, to whom the Cathedral was dedicated.

The inner face of the doorway also dates from the repairs after 1390. Above the door is a mural passage connecting the towers behind an arcade of four wide arches alternating with five narrow ones, the latter blind except within the arch-heads. This phase also embraced the partial refacing of the upper level of the faces of the towers towards the central vessel of the nave, the oversailing masonry being carried on a pair of blind arches on each side that rose to the same height as the nave arcades. Slight inward curvature of the masonry at the top of this refacing could point to an abandoned intention to add a barrel-vault over the space between the towers. It is possible that, as first built in the final stages of the post-1224 campaign, the upper part of the W front had a rose window with concentric rows of radiating arches and pierced spandrels (cf. the S transept gable of York Minster of *c.* 1240), parts of which were found over the S choir aisle vault in 1936, and for which there is no other likely location. But in the long period of reconstruction after 1390 much of the upper part of the W front was given over to a vast seven-light window, whose arch survives. Its tracery stumps indicate that this had a rose as its centrepiece with twelve bowed triangles around its periphery, like the rose window in the E gable. The window rises into the gable, and around its head an external walkway stepped up on each side and ran across the apex on a foliage-decorated cornice. On this cornice are the royal arms; flanking the window arch are the arms of Moray to the N, while to its S are arms with a pastoral staff thought to be those of Bishop Columba de Dunbar (1422–35).

LITURGICAL FITTINGS

SEDILIA (presbytery). S side, second bay from E, post-1270. Four stalls, stepping up from W to E, originally covered by micro-architectural vaulting, and with gablets punctuated by pinnacles, with square flower decoration to pinnacles and spandrels. – PISCINA. One, badly decayed in the S choir aisle, another badly weathered in the N choir aisle. The piscina in the S transept S wall has a cusped pointed arch with hoodmould. In the transept's E wall, S end, an AUMBRY, with arched head and rebated surround. The aumbry in the N transept's E wall (N end) has a moulded pointed arch carried on engaged shafts (possibly re-set). – Two aumbries in the S outer nave aisle's third bay from E, both with three-centred arches, one with moulded surround, the other rebated for a frame. In the fourth bay a PISCINA, its round-arched recess beneath cut-back gablet.

MONUMENTS

Elgin has retained an unusually fine group of medieval monuments, as well as large numbers of post-medieval monuments, of which only a selection can be mentioned here.

PRESBYTERY. Tomb, N side, third bay from E, steep crocketed gable with semi-dogtooth decoration, recess framed by cinquefoiled arch carried on engaged dogtooth-decorated jambs below trifoliate-headed image niche. As an integral part of the post-1270 extension, this was presumably provided for himself by Bishop Archibald †1298; in this position may it also have been an early example of the use of a tomb as an Easter sepulchre? – In the fourth bay from the E, within the arcade arch, a tomb surmounted by fragments of three arches and gablets punctuated by pinnacles. The tomb was below the two E arches and an entrance to the presbytery from the N aisle is below the W arch, and it thus served as both a tomb and a screen. Thought to have been for Bishop Andrew Stewart †1501. – In front of the presbytery steps, a Tournai marble (?) matrix slab with indent for large rectangular inset.

S CHOIR AISLE. N side E bay: Bishop John Winchester †1460, richly crocketed ogee-arch with cusped cusping rising from a tomb-chest with blind-arcaded front, flanked by pinnacled buttresses with shields at mid-height. The mitred effigy wears mass vestments, carries a pastoral staff and rests his head on a pillow and feet on a lion. On the arch soffit, outline underpainting of censing angels. This design was widely imitated in north-east Scotland. – In the wall behind the stalls, third bay from E, a rectangular recess within a four-centred arch (unusual for Scotland), possibly for Bishop William Tulloch †1482. Within spandrels bowed trifoliate triangles, and within the spandrels of the major cusps and sub-cusps smaller bowed trifoliate triangles or rounded trefoils. The effigy within the recess is clearly earlier and relocated here: bishop in mass vestments carved in mid-relief and set within a trifoliate-headed canopy, flanked by angels and with arms of Scotland and Moray on each side. – Alexander Gordon, 1st Earl of Huntly †1470. Relocated to the centre of the aisle, opposite the presbytery entrance. A headless effigy, most unusual for being represented in secular (parliamentary?) dress rather than armour, and inscription notable for early use of Arabic numerals; otherwise plain tomb-chest decorated with Earl's arms. – Relocated to the third bay from E: William de la Hay of Lochloy †1422, on made-up tomb-chest, an armoured effigy with head on double cushions and feet on lion. – S wall: Henrietta, Duchess of Gordon †1760, signed *P. Scheemaker*. Against an obelisk an amorino holds a draped plaque with the duchess's three-quarter relief portrait, below her coroneted arms.

S TRANSEPT. S wall: tomb-recess with crocketed and multi-cusped ogee arch above a blind-arcaded tomb-chest, flanked by pinnacled buttresses. Shields on the buttresses with arms of Stewart (with a pastoral staff) and Stewart quartering Mar, in reference to Bishop James Stewart †1462. The knight's effigy re-set within the recess bears the arms of Innes on jupon. – Alongside, a tomb-recess of similar design to that of Bishop Winchester in the S choir aisle. Shield on one of the buttresses bears arms of Stewart, possibly for Bishop David Stewart †1476. Within the arch an unidentified knight's effigy.

N TRANSEPT. A dado made up of tomb-chest fronts now runs along much of the N and W walls. In the N wall lower parts of two canopied tombs. In the E recess, a knight's effigy with arms of Dunbar on jupon; in the W recess a badly damaged female (?) effigy with flowing dress. In the W wall a damaged recess with memorial to family of John Dunbar of Bennetfield, latest death recorded 1648.

S NAVE AISLE. – Headless figure of bishop in processional cope (E end), kneeling on draped and cushioned stool; traditionally said to be from the tomb of Bishop John Innes †1414. – Also two monumental figures said to be from the central tower: bishop wearing mitre and cope and with the shaft of his pastoral staff, truncated at knees; headless and legless torso of knight grasping a sword.* – In the S OUTER NAVE AISLE, second bay from E, a STONE COFFIN within the wall thickness.

CHAPTER HOUSE. Among others, several memorials relocated from old St Giles church, e.g. Elizabeth Paterson †1698 and Robert Langlands †1696; two-part aedicular tablet. – NW wall, re-set fragment of memorial to Colin Falconer, erected 1676.

Set into footings at W end of N choir wall, a granite Early Christian CROSS-SLAB. On the face a cross flanked by the Four Evangelists (?) above a panel with four intertwined pellet-decorated beasts. On the back spiralling patterns, double-disc with Z-rod, and crescent with V-rod Pictish symbols, all above stag-hunting scene. It was found close to St Giles church in 1823.

GRAVEYARD. S of Cathedral, MEIKLE CROSS, base and cross-head of uncertain date. Large numbers of C17, C18 and C19 table tombs, upright memorials and ledger slabs (many with *memento mori*), and several enclosures. – Bishop Alexander Douglas †1623 (N boundary wall towards W end), large aedicule flanked by paired Corinthian columns. – E of chapter house, enclosure of John Forsythe †1810, still enclosed by fence and by bars above enclosure. – In SW corner, enclosure with balustraded wall-head and polygonal-headed entrance. – In SE corner enclosures of 1759 and 1775 with fluted pilasters at angles. – On outer face of original E boundary wall, towards

*The Cathedral has a large collection of such stones, which cast invaluable additional light on its architectural history. Most are stored in the Chanter's House.

S end, an incised slab for John Shanks, 'the keeper, and the shower of this Cathedral', †1841.

THE CHANONRY

The CHANONRY surrounded the Cathedral and formed a small township in its own right, bounded by the River Lossie to the E and a long wall *c.* 3.7 m. high and 2 m. thick (mostly destroyed). The Little Cross (*see* p. 453) marked its junction with the royal burgh to the SW. The precinct was originally entered via four gates, but three of these – including the W, or Water, Gate – were removed at the end of the C18. The E gate, known as PANNS PORT, remains, so named for a meadow ('le Pannis') that was first documented in 1566. It is a broad Gothic arch of the early C16, originally with portcullis and a superstructure for its machinery and a guardroom. Its dummy arrow loops and the wide parapet with its big, ledge-like crowsteps were added during restoration in 1857 by the Earl Fife. 100 m. SSW on Pansport Place is the sole remaining fragment of the PRECINCT WALL.

The most important function of the Chanonry was to house the MANSES of the Cathedral dignitaries (dean, precentor, chancellor, etc.), sixteen canons and twenty-two vicars choral. Most of these manses were destroyed (or heavily damaged) in the fires of 1270 and attacks of 1390 and 1402. At the Reformation, most were let out or abandoned and quickly fell into decay; by the mid to late C17, many were 'unjustly dilapidated'. More had disappeared entirely by the end of the C18. NW of the Cathedral is the so-called BISHOP'S HOUSE,* which was, in fact, the PRECENTOR'S MANSE. It was a U-plan with entrance on the N side leading to its central courtyard. Given to Alexander Seton in 1600, in the C19 the house was owned by the Innes family and then the Earl and Countess of Seafield; in 1851 the S and W wings were demolished as they interfered with the new drive to Grant Lodge (*see* p. 592). N wing mostly complete, a three-storey rectangular tower with an early C15 core. Crowstepped gables, each of the steps fashioned as little gablets. Large roll-moulded E window; armorial plaque below for Robert Reid, Abbot of Kinloss (q.v.), and Alexander Lyon, precentor between 1532 and 1541. Attached to the S gable is a narrower stair-tower of the same height, its E skewputt dated 1557. Cavetto corbel below it carved with a good three-faced head. The attached S wing was the hall block, likely built *c.* 1406 and augmented at the end of the C17. Barrel-vaulted cellar now partially sunk below ground. Of the great hall above there is a wide, roll-moulded fireplace in the W wall; lintel decorated with a spiked quatrefoil and heraldry for Bishop John Innes (1407–14). Aumbry to the l. and blocked segmental door to the r. On the N wall are two doors leading to the stair, the upper one blocked with a cannon water spout

*The Bishop's residence was Spynie Palace (q.v.).

to the r. Most of the ruins of this block collapsed *c.* 1888 and against the W wall are large buttresses to shore it up. Between two of them, a re-set section of a bowed oriel (originally on the second floor of the S block) and monogram above with faded date of 1688. In the rear of the N wing, a lofty round-headed carriage arch. One-room stable formerly to the l. of it. In the re-entrant angle above, part of a turret corbelled out over a grotesque sticking out his tongue.

NORTH COLLEGE HOUSE is just to the N, formed from the remains of the DEAN'S MANSE, originally the most important building in the Chanonry. Large, crowstepped L-plan of two storeys and attic, originally built in two sections. Late C15 N wing erected by Dean Gavin Dunbar (1486–1517), containing a vaulted ground floor and large chimneystack and garderobe corbelled out on the rear (N) wall. The W wing was built *c.* 1520 by his successor (also named Gavin Dunbar), its re-carved datestone now re-set on the E gable with the Dunbar motto, 'Ornat fortem prudentia' ('Prudence adorns the brave'). In the main re-entrant angle is a big, full-height bow of ashlar with a semi-conical roof, added by Alexander Robertson in 1858. Corbelled, gabled hood over the door; two pedimented dormers through the wall-head and another pair to the l. and r. Lower T-plan wing to the S (kitchen and service block), also of 1858. The small, Picturesque gate LODGE is of *c.* 1874.

The BIBLICAL GARDEN to the E (N of the cathedral graveyard) probably occupies the site of the Chancellor's and Treasurer's manses. It was opened in 1996 and features specimens of all 110 of the plants mentioned in the Bible.

SOUTH COLLEGE HOUSE on Pansport Place, 150 m. SSE, was the site of the early C16 ARCHDEACON'S MANSE, whose vaulted cellar was filled in when the house was built in two phases (*c.* 1820 and *c.* 1865; converted into flats, 1986). The second and fifth bays are topped by crisp Dutch gables, and over the entrance is a good Gothic wrought- and cast-iron balcony.

Nearby in KING STREET, WINCHESTER HOUSE by *William Robertson*, 1831–2, an attractive but modest classical villa.

ELGIN GREYFRIARS CONVENT*

There were plans for a Franciscan friary in Elgin as early as the 1280s, but it was probably not until the 1480s that an Observant Franciscan friary was established, under the patronage of James IV, and there is a payment to the friars on record in 1494–5. Despite the friary being suppressed in the early stages of the Reformation, in 1559, the buildings survived through other uses. The church was initially adapted to serve as a court of justice and was later used as a meeting place for the burgh's trades. After the site and its buildings had been acquired by Provost William

*This entry has been contributed by Richard Fawcett with advice from Debbie Mays.

King in 1684 the church was used for Episcopalian worship, with the conventual buildings adapted as his house. The church passed out of use in the later C18, but Wood's map of 1828 shows the greater part of all three conventual ranges, as well as the shell of the church, still in place. By the first edition of the Ordnance Survey it was only the W and S ranges that were embodied in the house known as Greyfriars. The Sisters of Mercy bought the site in 1891, and in 1896 the 3rd Marquess of Bute agreed to restore the buildings, to the designs of one of his most favoured architects, the scholarly *John Kinross*. The church was ready for reconsecration in 1898. Work on the conventual buildings followed, but was halted at the time of Lord Bute's death in 1900; it was completed by 1908 for Lord Colum Crichton Stewart. The Sisters vacated the convent in 2010, and in 2014 the buildings are to be taken over by a community of Dominican nuns.

The CHURCH was probably typical of the majority of those built for later medieval mendicant communities in being of unaugmented rectangular plan. It is built of rubble with ashlar dressings, and there are chamfered base courses below the E and W walls. A buttress (restored with a gabled head) against the N wall marks the division between choir and nave. The shell of the church had survived largely complete by the time of Kinross's restoration, with the exception of the upper part of the E wall and the window tracery throughout, though there was sufficient evidence in the remaining stubs for reconstructing the tracery in all but the E window. The principal source of light along the N wall was through five Y-traceried windows, two in the choir and three in the nave. To the W of the buttress there is in addition a pair of superimposed windows to light the rood loft and the altars in front of the screen, the upper window being Y-traceried, and the lower a single light with an ogee-arched head. There appears to have been a similar arrangement of superimposed windows on the line of the screen at the Observant house in Aberdeen, as well as at a number of collegiate churches, including Innerpeffray and Fowlis Easter (Dundee & Angus). A round-arched entrance, presumably for lay-folk, was provided towards the W end of the N wall, and *Kinross* placed a timber porch here on the basis of an existing roof raggle. The W wall had a single four-light window with intersecting tracery, and Kinross replicated this in the E wall, where the window had been of similar dimensions. On the S side space for a Y-traceried window was provided by setting the E range well back from the E end. The only other windows on that side were three single-light ogee-headed openings above the level of the cloister-walk roofs, which lit the W end of the choir, the rood loft and the E end of the nave. There were also small squint-like openings into the church from the E and W ranges, two from the former and one from the latter. There were rectangular doorways with chamfered surrounds opening into the sacristy in the E range, and into the cloister between the choir and nave.

Internally the church must always have been very simple, in keeping with the precepts of the Observant Franciscans, with the only decoration and mouldings being associated with the few furnishings. *Kinross* responded to this aesthetic with great tact, introducing a simply plastered finish to the walls, except for the exposed dressed stonework of the furnishings and window reveals, and he constructed an unribbed timber barrel ceiling of slightly pointed profile that runs without punctuation along the whole space, above a foliate cornice with cresting.

FURNISHINGS. HIGH ALTAR raised on three steps, timber with blind traceried front. – AUMBRY (S wall), late C15 ogee-headed with continuous mouldings, and SEDILIA, restored as a timber-lined recess. SACRAMENT HOUSE (N wall), also late C15, but restored with vine trail to surround and with semi-domed canopy above. – CHOIR STALLS, by *Scott Morton & Co.*, two ranks, with panelled backs capped by tracery and foliate cornice. – SCREEN. Restored as a pair of parallel timber screens defining a passage (?), aligned on the door from the cloister, and capped by a rood loft; based on designs by *David Morton* of *Scott Morton & Co.* The location of the loft had been indicated by a surviving corbel and joist pocket in the S wall. Below the lower N window is a basin within the window rere-arch of uncertain use. The processional entrance to the choir is spanned by an ogee arch with dense sub-articulated reticulation to the tympanum, and is closed by wrought-iron gates. Above the centre of the screen is a painted rood said to have been based on that at Assisi San Damiano, flanked by carved worshipping angels. Towards the nave panelling fronts with traceried heads above the ALTARS on each side of the processional entrance to the choir. These have panelling fronts with foliate muntins. Retables of five painted panels with saints associated with the Order of Our Lady of Ransom (N) and the Franciscan order (S). – PISCINA (nave S wall), late C15 ogee-headed recess with continuous mouldings. Matching PISCINA in the nave N, below the window, restored from a mutilated fragment. – STAINED GLASS. E window by *N.H.J. Westlake*, to designs of *Lord Bute*, Brides of Christ with angels.

CONVENTUAL BUILDINGS, S of the church. Two storeys, with some dormers at the centre of the W range; they are of rubble, with polished pink sandstone dressings and grey Taramount roof slates. The three ranges took as their starting-point the house adapted from the friary's conventual buildings for Provost King. In the course of investigations a painted medieval inscription above the dining-room fireplace was found: 'Nulli Certa Domus' (None Have Fixed Dwellings; a text that was to be repeated above the door in the restored S range). The drawings by *Kinross* make clear that the shell of the W range incorporated what could be retained of the existing buildings, and late medieval windows are evident in the southern parts of both the W and E faces. The E range took as its starting point the stubs projecting from the S flank of the church, while the S range appears to have been built on the foundations of its predecessor.

The W range was designed to contain parlours, kitchens and the refectory at ground-floor level. The refectory at the outer end of the range has retained a painted beam likely to be of medieval origin. This range faces the convent's entrance forecourt, and it was intended to enclose the courtyard more fully by a wing projecting at right angles that would have housed offices including sculleries and a laundry, though no more than a small single-storey offshoot was built. At ground-floor level the E range was designed to contain the sacristy, chapter house, assistant mother's room and novitiate, with an offshoot where a medieval latrine might have been located housing cloakrooms. Both the E and W ranges extended well beyond the S range. Within the latter were planned a recreation room, the mother superior's room and a hall.

The one-, two- and three-light windows are randomly arranged according to the needs of the interiors, with some of the larger windows being deeply set within cavetto mouldings. A number of windows are given greater emphasis: that to the daystair in the E range has a transom, while the windows of the chapter house have trifoliate heads, and the lower windows of a polygonal offshoot in the S re-entrant angle of the W and S ranges have ogee-shaped heads. Above the window of the mother superior's room is a re-set heraldic tablet with the arms of Wallace quartering Lindsay and the initials 'TV' (for Thomas Wallace?). Throughout there is an air of charmingly modest under-statement that gives greater emphasis to details such as the tabernacles in the gables of the chapter house and at the S end of the E range.

The cloister, at the heart of the buildings, took its lead from the surviving evidence, which, in addition to the indications of the locations of the E and W ranges, consisted of a series of corbels and a roof moulding along the S side of the church. The walks were rebuilt with leaded glazing set in timber frames above a stone wall, and they are covered with lead-sheathed lean-to roofs converging on diagonally set arches and buttresses at the angles. In the centre of the garth is a circular well at a crossing of paths.

CHURCHES

ELGIN & FORRES FREE CHURCH, South Street and Hall Place. Built as the United Presbyterian church by *A. W. Bisset*, 1862–4, replacing a chapel of 1807 on the same site. E.E. style with plain lancets. Big N door with central trumeau of basket-headed arches and trefoils in the tympanum; headstops of Philip Melanchthon (the C16 German reformer) and a wild-haired woman, by *Thomas Goodwillie*. Interior truncated 1986–7.

ELGIN BAPTIST CHURCH, Reidhaven Street. 1891–2 by *A. & W. Reid*, replacing a church opened in 1850. E.E. Tripartite

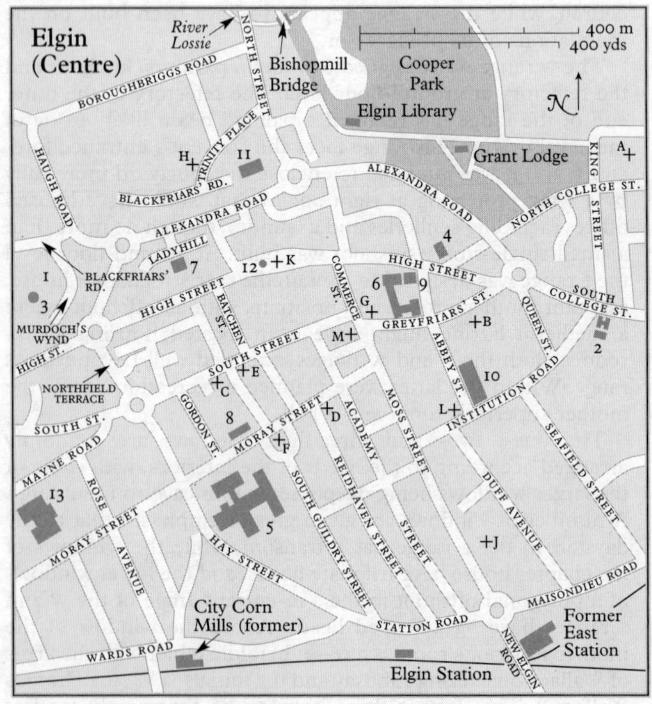

- A Cathedral
- B Elgin Greyfriars
- C Elgin & Forres Free Church
- D Elgin Baptist Church
- E Elgin High Church
- F Elgin South Church (former)
- G Harvest Centre (Elgin City Church)
- H Holy Trinity (Episcopal)
- J St Columba
- K St Giles
- L St Sylvester (R.C.)
- M United Presbyterian Church (former)

- 1 Elgin Castle
- 2 Anderson's Institution
- 3 Duke of Gordon Monument
- 4 Elgin Museum
- 5 Moray College
- 6 Moray Council Headquarters
- 7 Playhouse Cinema
- 8 Police Station
- 9 Sheriff Court
- 10 St Sylvester's Primary School (R.C.)
- 11 Town Hall
- 12 War Memorial
- 13 West End Primary School

front divided by buttresses topped by octagonal shafts and spirelets. Good rosette E window. Subdivided horizontally in 1978–9 and the W gallery blocked.

ELGIN HIGH CHURCH, South Street. By *Thomas Mackenzie*, 1843, as Elgin's first Free Church. Perfunctory Romanesque, with long arched windows. The centre of the N façade advanced and with octagonal pinnacles, formerly with crocketed finials.

N organ chamber by *John Wittet*, 1914, the vestry by *A. & W. Reid*, 1869. The substantial hall facing North Guildry Street, with stepped triple lancets with stiff-leaf is by *A. & W. Reid & Wittet*, 1903–4. Unexpectedly grand interior, mostly of 1843. Panelled ceiling, the moulded ribs with big seaweed bosses. Gothic furnishings, the GALLERY on cast-iron quatrefoil columns, and PULPIT on a dais in front of the ORGAN by *Messrs Scowell*, 1913–14, also with a good Gothic case.

Former ELGIN SOUTH CHURCH, Moray Street and South 41
Guildry Street. Built as the South Free Church by *A. & W. Reid*, 1852–4. Closed since 1999 and now under threat of demolition. An impressive sight in the view down North Guildry Street, where it has a gabled front and square tower ending in an octagonal broach spire. Two-light windows l. and r. of the tower with cusped ogee heads and quatrefoils; angle buttresses with tall crocketed pinnacles and large finials. S wheel window. S VESTRY and HALL by *Charles C. Doig*, 1898.

HARVEST CENTRE (Elgin City Church), Greyfriars Street. Originally a Church of Scotland hall, by *A. & W. Reid & Wittet*, 1896–7. Handsome front with wide crowstepped gable in the centre and tripartite window with a segmental pediment and big thistle finial containing a stylized cartouche. Lower r. wing and to the l. a quadrant corner, both with balustrades.

HOLY TRINITY (Episcopal), Trinity Place. Gothic, but of three distinct builds. Originally a compact Greek cross by *William Robertson*, 1825–6, the gable of its S transept designed as the visual climax to North Street. Octagonal buttresses with tall pinnacles, Perp window and pretty rosette above it and pierced parapet of cusped, pointed arches. The Neo-Tudor porch is later, probably 1852 when *Mackenzie & Matthews* added the E apse with its fine two-light Dec tracery and quatrefoil parapet. Also by them the vestry between chancel and N transept. Nave extended W in 1875 in a similar style. The apse has a tierceron-vault. – REREDOS by *George Gillan* of Forres, 1853. Ornate tracery and end pinnacles with praying angels. – CHOIR STALLS and PEWS. Fleur-de-lys finials. – ORGAN by *Wadsworth Bros* 1881 (restored 1979–80). Big case with exposed blue and gold pipes. – FONT. Stone, octagonal, on a shafted pillar over a wide base. Quatrefoils in the diagonals. COVER, *c.* 1905, with Scots Crown. – STAINED GLASS by *James Ballantine & Son*. – Three in the apse, 1876: Adoration and Baptism; Agony in the Garden and Christ bearing the Cross; the three Maries and Christ appearing to Mary Magdalene. – N transept *c.* 1883. Garden of Gethsemane and the angel and two Maries at the tomb. – W windows, 1880. Crucifixion, Christ the Good Shepherd under an angel, Christ appearing to the Apostles.

HALL to NE, originally the school, by *Mackenzie & Matthews*, 1853–4.

Former PARSONAGE to the SW. A charming design by *William Robertson*, 1825–6, originally single-storeyed but given a first floor *c.* 1869 and Gothicized. Spoiled by the bay window

r. of centre, added 1898. N flank of rubble with a canted timber bay window.

ST COLUMBA, Moss Street/Duff Avenue. By *Peter Macgregor Chalmers*, 1905–6, to serve the growing population in the S of the burgh. Transitional style, externally rather severe, in rock-faced stone. W gable with three lancets with shafts but the W door of the S aisle with a Romanesque arch of three orders with billet moulding and lavishly figured capitals, and round-arched E windows. Good plain interior of bare stone, the nave S arcade of round arches and columns with stylized leaf capitals. Open roof with arch-braced trusses on corbels at clearstorey level. Tall round arches to the crossing and chancel (the W arch barely pointed), simpler arches to the transepts (the N blocked as an organ recess). Chancel and crossing both covered by a barrel ceiling with plain transverse ribs. – PULPIT. The
29 glory of the furnishings and one of the finest survivals of C17 woodwork in N Scotland. It was made for old St Giles church,* is dated 1684 and was carved – as per the surviving contract – by the carpenters *Alexander Moor* and *Philip Buchanan*. Small hexagon, the bottom with fielded panelling and the upper with Ionic angle pilasters. Back-board with excellent engaged Corinthian columns and pulvinated architrave; tester with acanthus frieze and a delightful sun on the intrados. – COMMUNION TABLE and ELDERS' SEATS, richly carved in C17 style to match the pulpit. – SCREENS (transepts). Five light with Dec-Flamboyant tracery. – FONT. Circular, with Primitivist wave pattern on a short, fluted column. – STAINED GLASS. Three bland E windows showing St John the Evangelist, Christ and St Peter. – S aisle lancet, St Michael by *Douglas Strachan*, *c.* 1910. – Central W window by *M.C. Webster* for *Stephen Adam Studio*, 1922–3, in a hybrid Strachan–Tiffany style. Christ in Majesty, Gabriel and Michael, Christ blessing a man in armour.

HALL to the S by *Keith Edwards*, 2009–11. Wide, glazed entrance screen and vertical timber cladding.

36 ST GILES. The parish church, prominently sited on the swollen vesica-shaped area called the Plainstones in the middle of the High Street. The old church was granted by William the Lion to the Bishop of Moray *c.* 1188 but destroyed by Alexander Stuart, the 'Wolf of Badenoch' in 1390 at the same time as his attack on the Cathedral (*see* above). Its successor was taken over by the bishop in the 1560s. Transepts were removed *c.* 1740 during street widening and by 1798 it had become a 'low clumsy misshapen building, at once deforming and incumbering the street'. The chancel was demolished at about that time and the nave finally followed in 1826 (for the pulpit, *see* St Columba). The contest for its replacement brought designs from most of the major architects in Scotland, but in

*When old St Giles was demolished in 1826, the pulpit was bought by the Earl of Fife and moved to Pluscarden Priory. It was returned to Elgin in 1898.

the end the palm went to *Archibald Simpson*. His design, built 1825–8, is already extremely accomplished despite being his first major church commission.* The church is a large and severe Greek temple, with a clever disposition of dual façades that resolves the difficulty of satisfactorily combining a tower and a portico by placing the tower at the E end of the building, in a manner clearly inspired by St Matthew, Brixton, London (C. F. Porden, 1822–4) and copied by John Smith for Aberdeen's North Church (1829–31). This leaves toward the W the substantial hexastyle portico with pediment carried on Greek Doric columns and frieze of large Empire garlands. Three straight-headed doorways, the central one taller. To the E the tower projects from the centre with a first stage as tall as the church with pilasters and another frieze of wreaths. Crowning the clock stage, and most unusual, is a copy of the Choragic Monument of Lysicrates but with columns fully detached – rather than engaged, as on the original – and with Tower of Winds capitals. The windows of the N, S and E flanks are unmoulded rectangles, recessed within the ashlar walls, with thick transoms carved with Greek key.

Spacious interior, remodelled by *Andrew Heiton* in 1893 and again in 2000–1, when pews were replaced by seats in a concert-hall-like arrangement. Shallow coffered ceiling and apse at the E end, flanked by pairs of giant-order pilasters with paterae and egg-and-dart, containing the PULPIT. It is of *c.* 1823 but brought here in 1981 from Newington Parish Church, Edinburgh (now Queen's Hall). Raised high on a Roman Doric column and with slender Corinthian columns supporting the circular domed tester. Cast-iron stair. – U-plan GALLERY with Greek key, the capitals of its columns also carved with vigorous Greek motifs. – ORGAN formerly in the E end, completely reconstructed and moved to the gallery in 1980–1. – STAINED GLASS. Four E windows (two large and two small), 1869–70. Roundels of foliage and biblical verses.

ST SYLVESTER (R.C.), Institution Road. By *Thomas Mackenzie*, 1843–4. Gothic gabled church with attached presbytery at right angles. On the street (S) gable, a four-light, transomed Dec window with lively tracery; square stair-turret in the l. corner with an aborted, truncated spire. SW porch with shafted doorway; flank to the l. with four cusped lancets separated by buttresses. Bright interior, the nave with a braced rafter roof and diagonal joists. Lower chancel with a scissor-brace roof. – GALLERY carried on fine wooden Dec screen. Central arch with quatrefoils in the spandrels. – ORGAN in the gallery by *H. Hilsdon*, 1925. – STAINED GLASS. N (liturgical E) window, 1919. St Sebastian flanked by a missionary and friar.

*In 1826, Simpson had to redraw all of his plans, as a fire in his house in Aberdeen 'completely destroyed' all of his earlier designs.

HALL (originally a school) attached to the E by *George Melven*, 1872. It now has a circular white marble FONT with grey marble colonnettes.

Former UNITED PRESBYTERIAN CHURCH, Moss Street. By *A. & W. Reid*, 1856–8; closed in 1938 (after amalgamation with Elgin South Church) and now a restaurant. A standard gabled box but with good Dec tracery. Square tower embraced at the centre of the front, originally even taller and surmounted by pinnacles but the top removed in 1953, much to the detriment of Elgin's skyline, and only its parapet reused. Inside the vestibule a tierceron-vault. The ribbed ceiling by *Joseph Stuart* survives.

ELGIN CASTLE
Ladyhill

A natural site for defence, it became a stronghold at a very early date. The castle is first mentioned in a charter of Malcolm IV in 1160 and twice in the reign of William the Lion (1165–1214) and served as a royal fortress in the mid to late C12. In the C13, it was held by the Sheriff of Moray and served as a royal residence. Edward I of England occupied it for four days in 1296 and deemed it a 'bon chastell' ('good castle') after receiving the submission of many of his Scottish magnates. It seems to have suffered great damage in 1297, as in 1303 Edward stayed at Thunderton House (*see* p. 600). The building was abandoned by 1455 and may have been in ruins much earlier. The chapel attached to it was dedicated to the Virgin and abandoned after the Reformation.

What remains are a rectangular set of walls (19.6 m. by 10.6 m.) to the ENE of the Duke of Gordon monument (*see* p. 589). They are so fragmentary (with a maximum height of 2.6 m. on the N) that it is impossible to determine their date. The NE angle may have been the foundations of the great tower or (despite the N–S orientation) the chapel. Excavations in 1972–3 revealed some of the outer defences on the N side of the slope, consisting of a stone-based earthen rampart, its exterior revetted with a timber palisade. Footings for the medieval curtain wall behind it.

PUBLIC BUILDINGS AND MONUMENTS

112 ANDERSON'S INSTITUTION, South College Street. By *Archibald Simpson*, 1830–3, as the Elgin Institution for the Support of Old Age and Education of Youth. It is to the town's E end what Gray's Hospital is to the W. It was paid for by the Elgin-born Major-Gen. Anderson, who entered the East India Company as a drummer-boy *c.* 1760 and amassed a large fortune there over the next fifty years. Simple but monumental Greek Revival H-plan of two storeys, the N façade of polished sandstone ashlar with three-bay ends advanced under sharply contoured pediments. Lying-pane glazing, the ground-floor windows with

simple panelled aprons. Nine-bay centre, the middle with paired pilasters flanking a full-height portico with two Ionic columns *in antis*. Reversed block pediment above with a somewhat overwrought statue of Anderson dispensing his largesse: food to a grateful bearded man (on the l.) and a book to a girl (on the r.). Recessed behind it, a thick drum tower encircled by eight square columns with anthemion capitals with saucer dome. Good W elevation, the second and sixth bays slightly advanced with windows sunk in two-storey rectangular panels. Hexastyle portico running between them with unfluted Greek Doric columns.

Connected to the rear is Simpson's former FREE SCHOOL (now Council offices and county archive), connected to the Institution via a narrow service wing. Simple, classical rectangle, now fronted by three S additions by *John Wittet*, 1903 (by when it was the East End School). Four-bay block in the centre with a block pediment and mirrored, five-bay wings to the l. and r. – LODGE to the W, again by Simpson and once serving as the toll cottage for the road to Rothes (q.v.). Fantastical barley-sugar-twist chimneystack.

BRIDGES across the Lossie. The oldest is BOW BRIDGE, Oldmills Road, a single span originally of 1630–5, although the segmental arch-ring rebuilt in 1789. Taking Newmill Road across the river is BREWERY BRIDGE, 1798–1800, with two segmental arches, rubble spandrels with blind oculi in the centre and a band course with coped parapets. The BRIDGE OF SHERIFFMILL, Sheriffmill Road, also with two segmental spans, is of 1803; partially rebuilt, 1829. Arch-rings with voussoirs of dressed ashlar; rubble spandrels with blind oculi. For BISHOPMILL BRIDGE *see* p. 607.

DUKE OF GORDON MONUMENT, Ladyhill. By *William Burn*, 1838–9, in memory of George, the 5th (and last) Duke of Gordon (†1836), and similar to Burn's earlier monument to Lord Melville, in St Andrew's Square, Edinburgh. Tall Tuscan column, 24.1 m. high, on a square pedestal. Inside, a spiral staircase to a domed look-out turret. Originally topped by a lantern, deemed a 'questionable appendage', but augmented in 1854–5 with a colossal statue of the duke by *Thomas Goodwillie* to a design by *Mackenzie & Matthews*. He wears the Chancellor's robes of Marischal College, Aberdeen.

Former DRILL HALL, Cooper Park. *See* Cooper Park, below.

ELGIN ACADEMY. *See* p. 608.

ELGIN MUSEUM, High Street. By *Thomas Mackenzie*, 1841–2, built for the Elgin and Morayshire Literary and Scientific Association. Italianate, deliberately chosen by Mackenzie so as not to compete with Elgin's Grecian public buildings, and of a basilica appearance with a quasi-campanile (formerly the custodian's quarters). Sympathetic single-storey additions by *Matthews & Mackenzie*, 1896 (W) and *A. Marshall Mackenzie & Son*, 1920–1 (E), the latter for a lecture hall. Excellent interior, restored in 2001–3 with its original green and gold colour scheme. The exhibition hall is full-height with alcoves at ground floor and at the N end a fine staircase to the gallery, which is set behind arcading and at the S end projects on square piers with anthemion capitals. Ribbed ceiling and mini-vaults to a clearstorey of small thermal windows.

108 GRAY'S HOSPITAL, Pluscarden Road. Neoclassical juggernaut by *J. Gillespie Graham*, 1815–19, forming the W terminus of the town's main axis. Founded by Dr Alexander Gray, who had amassed a fortune in the East India Company and left £20,000 for its construction in 1808.* Graham's building is huge but simple in plan and execution. Tall, wide rectangle of three storeys, of polished ashlar. E façade of nine bays, each delimited by smooth giant-order pilasters (paired on the ends) and a tetrastyle Doric portico with a blind parapet of bold square and rectangular sunk panels nicely counterbalancing the flourish above of the large dome. This has a tall octagonal base with pilastered, gableted clock faces in the cardinal directions and round-headed windows in the diagonals, supporting a substantial plain drum above with louvred oculi. Above the dome a cupola with a balustrade. The block is two bays deep; attached to the r. flank a rather severe stone wing by *Thomas Turnbull* of Edinburgh, 1936–9, two storeys with flat roof and steel-framed glazing. Behind the centre of the main block, a three-storey, three-bay extension by *John Wittet*, 1906–8. Plain corniced parapet. It is now mostly obscured by the mammoth complex extending to the rear, built in three phases 1992–8 by *Mackie, Ramsay & Taylor*. It is equal parts corporate and clinical, in jointed reconstituted stone blocks. Very much of its date, especially the Mackintosh-inspired motifs of the full-height windows to Pluscarden Road, with their stocky, keystoned segmental pediments. The PLUSCARDEN CLINIC (NW) incorporates what remains of the ELGINSHIRE DISTRICT LUNATIC ASYLUM, the earliest mental facility in Scotland built specifically for paupers. Original block by *Archibald Simpson*, 1832–5, raised to three storeys in 1850; new building, radically enlarged, by *A. & W. Reid*, 1863–6. Two- and three-storey sections with piended roofs and a pediment over the former entrance, much obscured by later additions. – The S gate LODGE, is by *A. & W. Reid*, 1886–7. With a pedimented Doric portico. Extraordinarily old-fashioned for its date. – GATEPIERS at the main entrance, *c.* 1819.

LIBRARY, Cooper Park. *See* Cooper Park, below.

MORAY COLLEGE (University of the Highlands & Islands), Moray Street. Mostly developed after 1971 by *G.R.M. Kennedy & Partners* as Moray Technical College but occupying two earlier educational establishments in the town. The first is the former ELGIN ACADEMY, on the S side of Moray Street, a trim Neoclassical rectangle by *A. & W. Reid*, 1885–6, with pedimented Doric tetrastyle portico. Ends and centre bays of

*He also left £2,000 to be used for 'the reputed old maids in the town' – or, as Shaw pithily put it in 1829, 'the comfort of ten virgins whose hope had departed and whose means were decayed'.

the flanks slightly advanced with channelled pilaster strips. Off the E flank outside, a GATEWAY with a bellcote, brought here in 1906 from the original Academy of 1801 (in Academy Street, now Elgin Youth Café) but dating from its thorough renovation by the *Reids* in 1865–7. The bell was formerly in the tolbooth on High Street (dem. 1843). Opposite, the charming former VICTORIA SCHOOL OF SCIENCE AND ART (now Art Dept), built as the town's Jubilee memorial in 1889–90 by *George Sutherland*. Single-storey, L-plan, with a narrow tower topped by a pyramid roof and porch in the re-entrant angle whose carving is of a fine Richardsonian Romanesque style. Tourelle at the corner. In the gabled wings big radial glazing in the semicircular head, each spoke rendered as a baluster with a little Ionic capital. At the back of the 1970s buildings a LEARNING CENTRE by *LDN Architects*, 2002.

MORAY COUNCIL HEADQUARTERS, High Street. Long, stripped classical box by *John Findlay*, Morayshire County Architect, 1937–8. Built on the site of the Burgh Courthouse (*William Robertson*, 1837–8).* Full-height, recessed centre marked off by a giant post-and-lintel arch frame. The ANNEXE, also in High Street, is a retro-fit by *Bennetts Associates*, 2010–12, of a supermarket built in 1990–1.

PLAYHOUSE CINEMA, City Arms Close. By the cinema specialist *Alister G. MacDonald*, son of Ramsay, 1932. Outside, a hulking dry-dashed box but inside, designed to accommodate 1,100, a splendid Art Deco showpiece in a remarkable state of preservation, including recessed ceiling lights surrounded by stylized petals.

POLICE STATION, Moray Street. By the *Moray & Nairn County Architects*, 1962–3 (architect-in-charge, *Kenneth R. MacKenzie*). Modernist but with traditional trappings, notably the roughly coursed stone facing combined with concrete panels and the comical thistle roof finials.

RAILWAY STATIONS. The present ELGIN STATION, 1988–90, replaced Elgin West Station of 1858 (on the Inverness & Aberdeen Junction Railway). The striking Baronial-style EAST STATION (now offices) in Maisondieu Road was rebuilt for the Great North of Scotland Railway in 1898–1902 by *Patrick M. Barnett*, chief engineer. Drum tower on the far r. corner with cone roof, the door in its base formerly leading to the station agent's house. The platform canopy and interior are preserved, e.g. top-lit former booking hall and screens dividing the waiting rooms. Former ENGINE SHED, 300 m. ENE, off Ashgrove Road. Built 1863. Said to be the oldest surviving in Scotland. Ten bays of arched windows.

ST SYLVESTER'S PRIMARY SCHOOL (R.C.), Abbey Street. By *Michael Rasmussen Associates* of Aboyne, 1991–3. Very low with huge, shallow piended roof, above stone walls to the street.

*Originally the site of the C17 'fine old mansion' of the Andersons of Linkwood. When the house was dem. in 1837, its entrance gatepiers were re-erected at Pitgaveny House (q.v.).

Wide W gable, with a grid of glazing that steps down in the centre.

SHERIFF COURT (and JUSTICE OF THE PEACE COURT), High Street. By *A. & W. Reid*, 1864–5, its stone Neoclassical façade exuding a reassuring sense of municipal efficiency. Two storeys and five bays with a parapet, the middle three slightly advanced and with paired Ionic columns in the upper storey; channelled rustication to the ground floor. Vermiculated quoins. Fine well-preserved courtroom on the ground floor. High, arched windows and fielded panels on the ceiling, the ribs with guilloche. Excellent fan rose in the centre surrounded by cable moulding.

TOWN HALL, Trinity Place. By *Rowand Anderson, Kininmouth & Paul*, 1957–61; extended S and W by the same firm, 1972–5. Two-storey, Modernist and rectilinear. Reinforced concrete frame faced with aggregate panels. On the main N front a central block, its first floor projecting on square columns. Wings recessed to the l. and r. Fine hall interior, suavely revetted in stained timber. Low stage on the W below an angled acoustic board. Long rectangular balcony to each side with three canopies cantilevered out above, the proportions and rhythm perfectly judged. Simple, tiered gallery on the E and long ceiling with original light fixtures. – In the lobby, a cartouche with St Giles, crook and book sculpted by *Thomas Goodwillie*; from the previous Town Hall (*Matthews & Mackenzie*, 1884–5) in Moray Street, destroyed by fire in 1939.

WAR MEMORIAL. *See* p. 594.

WEST END PRIMARY SCHOOL, Mayne Road. The core is by *A. & W. Reid & Melven*, 1874–5, the S wing (originally the infants' department) by *A. & W. Reid*, *c.* 1887, and E front by *John Wittet* in 1903. E-plan with gabled ends to the wings and a semi-octagonal centre with a little spire.

COOPER PARK. Gifted to the town by Sir George Cooper in 1902, but formerly the policies of GRANT LODGE, which was one of the finest villas in Elgin. It became the town's library until 1996 but is now in an appalling state of decay following an arson attack in 2003. The core is a simple but suave rectangular double pile by *Robert Adam*, 1766–8 for Sir Ludovick Grant,* for whom John Adam had worked at Castle Grant (Highland and Islands) in 1749. Robert also made designs for Grant's Moy House (q.v.) from 1759. S front of two storeys and three bays with platform-piended roof and poor modern harling. Windows with simple moulded architraves. The house is now mostly in Victorian guise, following substantial additions in polished ashlar by *A. & W. Reid*, 1849–51 for the Countess of Seafield. Slightly advanced centre flanked by giant-order channelled pilaster strips. Balustraded parapet on top, originally topped by urn finials. Tetrastyle Doric porte cochère. Bad segmental heads to the dormers, *c.* 1902. The

*It is built on the site of an early C17 tower house which the Grants acquired in 1677.

substantial rear wing, 1790–1, is two storeys over a raised basement with piended roof, a singularly uninspired design.* W flank with a canted oriel window on the second storey; window to the l. of it out of alignment with those below. On the E flank, a service court added by the Reids in 1849. Semi-octagonal porch in the centre with rectangular architrave and block pediment over. Four-bay arm off the NE corner, the end (originally a larder) slightly taller with a pyramidal roof. S of the Cathedral on King Street is Grant Lodge's former LODGE, 1851, Picturesque style.

After Cooper's donation the PARK was given a fine new design by *A. Marshall Mackenzie & Son* (dedicated 1903) with a broad thoroughfare to the Cathedral's W front, treating it with all the reverence that it deserves. BOATING POND in the W section (originally a skating pond in the winter), the lower two islands shaped as the British Isles. Off its SW corner, the former WEST LODGE by Mackenzie, 1903, single storey and three bays with projecting eaves. Segmental, gabled porch in the centre carried on four rusticated posts, added *c.* 1918. Just to the ESE is the new ELGIN LIBRARY, its l. section a large and dull double-piended rectangle by *Moray Council*, 1994–6. Glazed rectangular cupola on top. Attached to the r., the Baronial-style former DRILL HALL for the Seaforth Highlanders by *William Reid*, 1904–5.

DESCRIPTION

1. *High Street*

HIGH STREET, the principal road of the medieval burgh, remains 2
the commercial centre of Elgin. Description begins at its W end, at the junction with Alexander Road and Northfield Terrace, an ideal spot to appreciate the axial alignment of Gray's Hospital (*see* Public Buildings, above) and St Giles church (*see* Churches, above) and uphill the Duke of Gordon Monument (*see* Public Buildings, above) by the castle ruins (for High Street W of here, *see* p. 601). The first part of the street is, on the front at least, uneventful, low and two-storeyed, predominantly C19 and principally of interest for a series of diversions into the narrow closes off the N side, where there is fragmentary evidence of the town's earlier buildings. Through the pend of No. 239, for example, the first house on the N side, is a reused lintel dated 1686 with four sets of initials and the insignia of the hammermen (hammer and crown) and tailors (scissors and iron). In the close to the E, a house with a reused early C18 chamfered window margin on the first floor and a pair of cottages with C17 roll-moulded door frames. Through the pend beside No. 229, cottages incorporating a roll-moulded C17 door frame and a re-set marriage lintel dated 1657 with the initials A.F. and I.P. Architecture of quality begins only at

**John Paterson* produced an elegant plan in 1789, including single-storey pavilions and quadrant corridors.

Nos. 187–179, a late C19 group of seven houses best seen as a unified block, despite their altered shopfronts, in polished ashlar. Next, a house of four bays in coursed rubble (formerly harled) with raised long-and-short dressings. Dated 1811 on its central pend. Full-height stair-turrets behind. Then, at the corner of North Street, the Italianate former ROYAL BANK OF SCOTLAND by *A. & W. Reid*, 1856, with canted corner, V-channelled long-and-short quoins, and windows with segmental and triangular pediments. NORTH STREET was laid out in 1821 following the demolition of Calder House (built 1669) and was to have Holy Trinity (*see* Churches, above) at the end of its vista, a view now meanly interrupted by the by-pass.

From here, High Street widens, still following the urban footprint of the early to mid-C13 town, and is gently curved around both sides of St Giles (*see* Churches, above). The flat, open area in front is the 'plainstones', first paved in 1785. Here stood the medieval tolbooth and gaol and successors, finally demolished in 1843. On its site, a monumental FOUNTAIN by *Thomas Mackenzie*, 1845–6, with three tiers of basins and central finial of water-lilies and lotus leaves and the WAR MEMORIAL by *Percy H. Portsmouth*, 1920–1, an ashlar pedestal supporting a bronze figure on top of it wearing toga and helm, his exposed l. thigh and chain-mail pants surprisingly racy for their date. He holds a sword festooned with laurel and a raised torch with victory wreath.

High Street's N side at this point begins with two grotesque 1970s buildings,* but thereafter the façades exhibit Victorian confidence and swagger. They start with premises designed by and for *A. Marshall Mackenzie*, in 1874–5, in good Scots Renaissance style, the l. bay with oriel window and crow-stepped gablet. Three gableted attic dormers have consoles and lions along with Mackenzie's initials, virtuosically carved by *Thomas Goodwillie* and copying those of Ritchie's House of *c.* 1619 which previously stood on the site. Inside – in Mackenzie's former office – a glorious chimneypiece from the original house, dated 1688. Thick, corniced mantel with the initials I.D. and C.V. (for John Donaldson and Catherine Urquhart, who owned Ritchie's House in the late C17) and the Donaldson coat of arms. Console brackets on the ends; caryatids below fashioned as Jacobean balusters with protruding heads and feet. Mackenzie discovered the house's original ground-floor arcade, one of a type once common along High Street. Next is the former ROYAL BANK OF SCOTLAND, a proud Renaissance *palazzo* of 1876–7 by *Peddie & Kinnear*, whose initials are inscribed. Channelled ashlar on the ground floor, the central doorpiece with floridly carved console brackets and a pediment with acroterial anthemion. Dragons and

*Replacements for the Trinity Masonic Lodge and Assembly Rooms by *William Burn*, 1821–2 (dem. 1969) and the North of Scotland Bank by *A. & W. Reid*, 1855–7 (dem. 1966).

sumptuous rinceau on the lintel. In the middle of this block the former ST GILES' BUILDINGS by *R.B. Pratt*, built 1903–4 for A. L. Ramsay & Son as the largest showroom and drapery warehouse in N Scotland; inside were mosaic floors, steam heating, pneumatic tubes for communication between floors, and tea rooms for refreshment. Five bays, the l. one wider and added slightly later; far r. bay narrow with a round-headed, ground-floor window, originally a door. Canted oriel above it with angle shafts shooting past the top and terminating in free-standing spool capitals. First storey with broad segmental showroom windows, the glazing inset with pediments on engaged columns. Over the second bay, a tall faux caphouse with oversized octagonal pinnacle in the SW corner imitating a stair-turret. Good fish-scale slates on the roof. Next door, a house and shop by *A. & W. Reid*, 1883–5, with canted oriels and pilastered windows on the second floor carved with lions' heads. Next is the former BRITISH LINEN BANK, a short-lived return to classicism, originally built 1807 and refronted by *William Robertson* in 1839. Block-modillioned cornice; six garlanded urn finials. Two elliptical-fronted oriels added to the first floor, 1881. The ground floor now gives access to the ST GILES SHOPPING CENTRE, created in 1988–91, which obliterated all of the houses and closes that lay in its wake to the rear of High Street all the way up to the A96. Standard late C20 interior, with an open, two-storey core braced by thick round metal beams. Escalators set diagonally within it. The Centre is to be greatly expanded, with a new façade to High Street, through a joint venture between *Archial* and *Duco Architects*, Edinburgh. Two doors down is the tall former MANCHESTER DRAPERY WAREHOUSE also by *Pratt*, 1904–5, but more Baroque than his St Giles' Buildings, with keyblocked engaged columns and a tall attic storey (originally a workroom for the tailors and haberdashers) with big plain pediment.

And so to TOWER HOUSE, the oldest – and by far the finest – building on the High Street, containing the remains of a house built in the early C17 by Andrew Leslie (merchant and magistrate of Elgin) and his wife, Jean Bonyman. It is a remarkable relic of the post-Jacobean era, consisting of a three-stage rubble tower, its lower two storeys rounded, with a small square caphouse corbelled out above. It is a mighty tower house brought down to a burgh scale. Doorpiece with good bolection moulding. At first floor a datestone of 1634, with coat of arms and the initials A.L. and I.B. Crowstepped gablet on the top; on the wall-head to its l., an original dormerhead (also dated 1634) with consoled sides and thistle finial. Engravings show that, until the early C19, the house continued at least two bays to the r. in the same style, with crowsteps, boisterous window gablets and open arcading along the ground floor. Slightly recessed to the l. of the tower is a three-storey Baronial house added in 1876. Two-storey bowed window with transomed plate glass; rope-moulded cornice on the first floor carved with animals' heads. Semi-conical stone roof fronting

Elgin, High Street, Tower House.
Engraving by R.W. Billings, 1852

a crowstepped gable, harmonizing with the original house. Taller turret in the re-entrant angle topped by a candlesnuffer roof with fish-scale slates. Inside on the second storey, the mantel of an earlier chimneypiece, dated 1629 and again initialled A.L. and I.B.

Opposite, E of St Giles, is the site of the medieval market place, marked by the MUCKLE CROSS. It was first erected *c.* 1635, superseding the medieval cross, but destroyed in 1792 and remade by *Sydney Mitchell*, 1887–8, contemporary with his similar (but larger) cross in Edinburgh. Tall hexagonal base, the angles with composite fluted pilasters topped by water spouts. Semicircular niches in between with bench seats and fluted shells on the little half-domes; round-headed entrance in the W face. In the parapet, St Giles holding a book and pastoral staff with Elgin's town motto, 'SIC ITUR AD ASTRA' ('Thus one goes to the stars'). Granite central shaft with the original C17 lion rampant; 'C.I.' (Charles I) on its shield.

High Street then begins to contract to its original width and the boisterousness starts to abate in a sequence of mid to later C19 Italianate façades, all by *A. & W. Reid*, 1853–5 (No. 95), 1880–1 (Nos. 85–93 with stilted arches to the windows) and 1858 (No. 83). Behind this group in the long and narrow FORSYTH'S CLOSE a two-storey, two-bay late C18 house. Slightly advanced r. side with a pilastered, corniced doorpiece. The close is the first of several in this part of High Street to have been sensitively renewed for housing by the Elgin Fund in 1984. In the close four linked cottages of the early to mid

C19, the middle one slightly taller and of three asymmetric bays with a long window on the l. LOSSIE WYND, the next intersection, was widened to its present form in 1883 and was originally known as Union Street, so on the E corner, UNION BUILDINGS by *John Wittet*, free Classical Revival of 1915–16. Hereafter a grim 1970s interlude of shops within an open arcade, all in wretched dry-dash and opening in the centre into a feeble square. It ends, however, in an excellent group of four early to mid-C18 houses, built of rubble. They are the only survivors of the Early Georgian burgh's architecture. The first (No. 25), three bays of *c.* 1740, originally had only three storeys featuring tall windows with chamfered margins but its attic was added in 1852 with crowstepped gables and three wall-head dormers under ball-finialled gablets. The next house is *c.* 1700, the windows narrow, and its eaves topped by three Dutch-gableted dormers added in 1853. The adjoining pair (Nos. 15 and 17, formerly Masonic Lodge) is of three and five bays, dated 1728 on its l. skewputt. Ground floor regularized by *John P.M. Wright* in 1971, during restoration for the Elgin Fund, with symmetrical segmental arches; twelve-pane glazing on the first and second storeys with crowstepped gables to the flanks. Large keystoned Venetian window in the l. centre.

Behind No. 25 is the fine KILMOLYMOCK CLOSE, restored in 1971, again by *John P.M. Wright*. On its W side, a three-storey, four-bay house of the late C18, surprisingly tall with a gabled attic. Pair of late C18 symmetrical cottages beyond it with a crowstepped gable to the N. Re-set in the wall behind the hedge, a plaque with a pair of affronted beasts, originally located in Thunderton House (*see* p. 600). On the adjoining wall to the l., a plaque dated 1631 with two heraldic crests and the initials G.D. and K.B. Mounted on the reverse wall (down the stairs), a C17 dormerhead with a crown and big dolphin-like consoles on the sides. Similarly, in MASONIC CLOSE, a re-set plaque with three well-preserved heraldic crests for the Seton, Dunbar and Falconer families. Initials A.S. for Alexander Seton, Lord Provost of Elgin 1591–1607 and Chancellor of Scotland 1604–22. Curved scroll with 'Jesus Renue Aright Spirit Wit[hin Me/Us, O] God'. Around the corner, another plaque dated 1688 with monogram in a chaplet, coat of arms and blustery mantelling on top.

Back on High Street, there is then a burst of Baronial with the the EX-SERVICEMEN'S CLUB, built as a villa (St Giles) by *Andrew Heiton*, 1892–4, with a substantial drum tower with conical roof to the entrance and bolection-moulded doorpiece with inscription above. A re-set PLAQUE of 1576 has the doubled initials I.C. for the Cumming of Lochtervandich family, whose house stood on this site from the mid C16. Superb bracket LAMP below it. Next comes the very fine
former BRACO'S BANKING HOUSE, built in 1694 by John 99
Duncan and Margaret Innes. Harled, with crowstepped gables to the flanks. At ground floor is a feature once widespread in the town but now rare: a low arcade of three round-headed arches set on squat columns, each with a quasi-cushion capital

and volutes. Three small windows on the first floor with twelve-pane glazing; windows above carried through the wall-head under original dormerheads with consoled sides. The l. is initialed I.D. and has a thistle finial, the other M.I. with a star and fleur-de-lys. From 1703 to 1722, it served as business premises for William Duff of Braco and Dipple; his town house formerly lay to the W at No. 53 High Street. Restored by *Meldrum & Mantell*, 1975. Set back to its E, Elgin Museum (*see* Public Buildings).

The end of High Street is marked by the LITTLE CROSS of 1733, a re-creation of the original erected in 1402 for Alexander MacDonald, third son of the Lord of the Isles, as penance for having 'spulzied' ('desecrated') the bishop's property. It marked the entrance to the Cathedral Chanonry and the end of its sanctuary wall. Stone shaft with an Ionic capital supporting a blocky, four-sided sundial (now a replica of 1941). The worn early C15 finial is said to depict St Giles on one side and the Virgin and Child on the other. Rounded, four-stepped plinth below. Behind the cross, terminating High Street, an Italianate house of *c.* 1856 by *A. & W. Reid*, with a good, shallow cast-iron balcony but also crowstepped gables. The entrance has a shell tympanum.

Now back along the S side of High Street, which has at this end a concentration of civic buildings, with the Moray Council Headquarters and Sheriff Court (*see* Public Buildings) set back from the street line. Next to the Council offices a wall with four C17 pedimented dormerheads with thistle finials. The second has a little portrait of a man in a ruff and the third is dated 1667. The buildings then stand to the pavement. The first is by *James Jamieson*, 1897–8, after which comes a rebuilding in Jacobean style in 1901 by *J. L. Findlay* (now THE MUCKLE CROSS pub, converted 1997–8). Nos. 42–46 is another merchant's house, dated 1688 on its l. skewputt, of the type already seen at Braco's banking house. Three storeys and five bays, the front formerly harled but now covered in burgundy pebbledash, dating from restoration in 1959. Low, round-headed arcading on the ground floor set on square capitals with primitive volutes. Crowstepped gables to the flanks; roll-moulded architraves to the upper-storey windows. Just inside the pend, a roll-moulded segmental arch showing the exact depth of the shallow loggia that once passed down the High Street. Similar buildings originally stretched to the l. and r. but now the arcade is resumed only at Nos. 50–52, built for Andrew Ogilvie and his wife, Janet Hay, in 1694 (see the r. skewputt). It is only three bays wide, the arcading with corniced imposts over blocky capitals reminiscent of late C12 waterleaf. Six rectangular windows above, slightly enlarged with tooled margins in the early to mid C19. Crowstepped gables to the flanks, the E one with an original roll-moulded window off-centre. Stone-slab roof with two little swept dormers. The original rear wing of the house is still intact past the barrel-vaulted pend. Three short storeys with a crowstepped S gable and two chamfered doorways, one of them originally leading to a scale-and-platt (not spiral) staircase.

The next intersection is COMMERCE STREET, originally known as School Wynd but widened to its present form and renamed in 1856–7. On its E corner is the former MECHANICS' INSTITUTE by *Matthews & Petrie*, 1859. Robust Italianate with entrance keystone carved by *Thomas Goodwillie*. Its counterpart, of comparable style, on the other corner is the former GROSVENOR TEMPERANCE HOTEL, 1857. Halfway up the l. side of Commerce Street is the very grand former ELGIN CLUB (closed 2002), another mini-palazzo by *A. & W. Reid*, 1868–9. Next door, LLOYDS BANK, originally a clothier's shop, by the *Reids c.* 1867. Intact shopfront with fluted columns and lotus-leaf capitals.

Returning to High Street, the architecture increases in size, pretension and expense around St Giles (as on the street's N side). Nos. 76–80 is by *A. & W. Reid*, 1856–8, in full classical mode, with alternating segmental and triangular pediments on the first floor and rusticated quoins. Next door is the former UNION BANK by *Matthews & Petrie*, 1857, the grandest building on this side of the High Street and a hybrid of Palladian and Neo-Baroque ostentation. Giant pilasters and paired windows at first floor with good shell tympana. Its pend is subdivided into five bays by round-headed arches, each with its own groin-vault. Facing the close, an iron lantern with pierced ogival canopy, suspended from the nose ring of a horned and long-suffering bull's head. Next the banal BANK OF SCOTLAND of 1973 and then one wide bay of Gothic fantasy, built *c.* 1883, with stiff-leaf and cable mouldings and two good Dec cast-iron railings. The pend to the l. leads to FIFE ARMS CLOSE, its r. side with a big, bracket-corniced doorpiece of the late C19. Around the corner, re-set high in the rear S gable, a C17 pediment with star finial and the initials B.W.

Next on the High Street is a pair of three-bay shop dwellings of two different builds, the first of *c.* 1890 and the second *c.* 1896 in matching Italianate; surprisingly late for the style. More typical is their neighbour, the former PALACE HOTEL, *c.* 1892, with elliptical oriel windows topped by pediments and segmental-headed dormers. Little mansard roof between with original Gothic railing. A bad concrete swathe of 1970–1 then follows (formerly the site of the Aberdeen Bank founded in the town in 1783) but next to it a shop and house of *c.* 1825, well composed in the style of *William Robertson*, the corner bowed into a slightly recessed quadrant. Twelve-pane windows, the first-floor ones corniced over tight panelled aprons. The pend below leads to the long and paved HARROW INN CLOSE. Its first building on the r. is the former HARROW INN, of the late C18. Above the l. ground-floor window, a marriage stone with four sets of initials, dated 1620 and 1725. More good fragments mounted on the wall opposite. On the bottom, a segmental-headed plaque dated 1776 from the destroyed house of James

Grant of Logie (see his initials, I.G.), formerly located at 114 High Street. Two bulbous fluted columns and the mottos 'Have At You' and 'Stand Fast'. Above it to the r., a worn foliate boss of the C13, likely from one of the aisles in the Cathedral. On top, a marriage stone of 1668 with conjoined monograms and the inscription 'Nulli Certa Domus' (None Have Fixed Dwellings).

Back on the High Street, the next building is the very wide former GORDON ARMS HOTEL (closed 1980), first documented in the late C18. Of two builds, the plainer l. section *c.* 1800. Four storeys and five bays with a panelled, console-bracketed chimney in the middle of the wall-head. Three bays to the r. added in 1888 by *A. & W. Reid* with a full-height canted bay window in the centre and a semicircular, ball-finialed pediment with shell ornament. The shopfront for (and still) BURTON'S is by *A. J. Morrison*, 1935–6, with jet-black marble fascia and Art Deco glazing. The foundation stone for it was laid by Raymond Montague Burton himself (see the dedication on the r. hand side). The final building of note is the former DELMANY PLACE, 1848, with seven wide bays of Renaissance classicism. First-floor windows with panelled aprons and console-bracketed segmental pediments. At the wall-head two wide chimneystacks flanked by gigantic spiralled volutes with trails of foliage, as at St Thomas, Keith and Milton Brodie (qq.v.). The two round-headed arches on the ground floor were inserted by *Mackenzie & Matthews* in 1851 as part of the (vanished) New Market Buildings. Long, barrel-vaulted pend behind, the areas between the pilasters currently bricked up but originally filled with stalls etc. The markets originally ran all the way to South Street (*see* p. 602).

Round the corner in BATCHEN STREET, laid out in 1800, former business premises by *Charles C. Doig*, 1905–6. Five bays, the ends of the upper storeys framed by giant, fluted pilasters. Pedimented central door frame and another on the wall-head with a corniced apex chimneystack. Pierced balustrades to the l. and r. ending in a pair of ball finials. Parallel to the w, off High Street, THUNDERTON PLACE, an important part of the medieval burgh, as evidenced by the first building on the l., THUNDERTON HOUSE, which sits on the site of the manor built between 1303 and 1314 after the damage to the Castle in 1297. Thunderton is referred to in a charter granted by King Robert Bruce to his nephew Thomas Randolph, Earl of Moray, in the first years of the C14. Edward I stayed here on his second pass through Elgin, and it later became the town house of the Earls of Moray, the Dunbars of Westfield and the Lords of Duffus. By the mid to late C15, the house had grown into a courtyard stretching all the way down to the High Street. To this, the Sutherlands added a mighty mansion tower *c.* 1650, originally flanked by the tall caryatids sculptures now in the Elgin Museum. This was ruthlessly demolished during the feuing of the street in 1822, and much of the masonry is now of that date. Thunderton's former glory is best seen in the excellent four dormers on the rear (S) side, carved with monograms of the Duffus, Dunbar, Innes and Mackenzie families. More pedimented dormers are reset in the front walls, along with stone beasts (horses) in the courtyard wall further down.

2. West end of the High Street, Ladyhill and West

The W end of HIGH STREET up to Gray's Hospital is separated from the rest by the late C20 by-pass. Its N side was formerly occupied by long, narrow closes, demolished and replaced with good, competent housing of traditional Scots character in MURDOCH'S WYND and HILL STREET. In the centre of this housing, set back in a garden, are MESSINES and SUVLA COTTAGES, flanking the stairs to the summit of Ladyhill. They are by *J. & W. Wittet*, 1919–20, their scale and symmetry well-judged foils to the monuments that lie behind them, and were the gift of Sir Archibald Williamson (M.P. for Moray and Nairn) to commemorate the end of the First World War. Both have octagonal turrets with a pyramidal roof, and crow-stepped gables. Between the cottages, loggias inside which are re-set C17 dormerheads, one monogrammed K.B. and the other with the Douglas coat of arms. Off Hill Street, now in a sad state of decay, is LADYHILL HOUSE, originally a simple house of 1811 but elaborated in the mid to later C19 by *Thomas Mackenzie* (†1854), and his son *A. Marshall Mackenzie*, who made this their home. They added the full-height bow windows on the ends and the lower E wing, its end also bowed under a conical roof; dormerhead to the l. in C17 style. This is a deliberate aesthetic statement, as Mackenzie – a friend of R.W. Billings and a passionate admirer of Moray antiquities – turned Ladyhill into a repository for *spolia* from Elgin's vanishing architectural past. His son continued this tradition and in front of the E wing is a low addition of 1908, incorporating round-headed arcading from Ritchie's House, which A. Marshall Mackenzie demolished *c.* 1874 for his new office on High Street (*see* p. 594). Four columns (two of them filleted) with voluted capitals; another with spirals of big grape-vine. Pair of square corniced piers with thistle ornament, fleur-de-lys, part of a caryatid, and a hand holding a fan. The NW porch of 1853 has an excellent, aggressively Neo-Norman archway.

The rest of High Street is mostly small mid to later C19 villas, e.g. on the S side FERN HURST of *c.* 1885, formerly the residence of the Provost of Elgin. In its front garden, a pair of original – and extremely rare – late C19 cast-iron PROVOST'S LAMPS with original coloured glass with two angels holding a heraldic panel with the burgh's emblem (St Giles with book and mitre). Uphill to the N in its own grounds is the grandiose MARYHILL HOUSE (now offices for Gray's Hospital), whose core was a medium-sized classical box built for William Young *c.* 1818, extended and given an elaborate facelift by *A. & W. Reid* in 1866–7. Of this date the porch with cable moulding, the canted bays, the balustrades with urns and the segmental pediments of the second-storey windows. Two phalanxes of seven bulbous-headed chimneystacks stride heroically across the rooftop. Bad rear wing of *c.* 1946–8 when a maternity hospital. At the entrance rusticated GATEPIERS with big ball finials.

N of Gray's Hospital (*see* Public Buildings) is WEST ROAD, laid out in 1812 when the first mail coach service was started between Aberdeen and Inverness. An early development was INGLESIDE, N side, of 1816, a subtly resplendent Tudor Gothic cottage of a single storey over a raised basement which shows fully at the rear, where it has a glorious two-storey bow window in the centre, created by the steeply descending site. Inside, the entrance hall has a fine tierceron rib-vault and original doors with blind cusped tracery panelling. Very long three-light window with quasi-Perp tracery under a broad hoodmould; semi-conical piended roof above. A little W is CRAIGIE (No. 19), again single-storeyed to the street. Built *c.* 1908 and probably by *James Newlands*, it is defiantly quirky with walls of crooked and asymmetric gargantuan blocks of rubble, heavy square columns to the doorpiece with anthemion capitals, and bows at the corner with engaged columns carrying vigorously carved capitals. At the rear a heavily buttressed bowed window, off-centre and fashioned as a look-out, and a blocky rusticated loggia with cubic parapet and rounded angle carved like the flanks of a late antique sarcophagus.

The area S of West Road and W of the hospital consists largely of streets of suburban villas. An exception in WITTET
126 DRIVE is No. 31, a Modern Movement bungalow by *J. & W. Wittet*, 1947. Harled single storey of three bays, the entrance covered by a shallow cantilevered canopy. Projecting bay on the l., the window to the r. returned around the corner to part of the N flank. Nearby in PLUSCARDEN ROAD, FLEURS HOUSE (No. 62, now a nursing home), whose core was built for William Young of Burghead by *William Robertson*, 1829. Two-storey and three-bay rectangle over a raised basement; central pilastered doorpiece reached by a flight of steps. Canted bay windows to the l. and r. added *c.* 1842, their lintels linked to form a trabeated loggia. Slightly recessed wing to the r., also *c.* 1842 and originally two-storeyed but raised in the late C19.

3. *South and east of the High Street: South Street to the Cathedral*

SOUTH STREET runs parallel with High Street. Description can begin at its far W end where there are several villas. PARK HOUSE (now offices), on the S side is a symmetrical, platform-piended Georgian box of *c.* 1820, three bays and two storeys over a raised basement. Central corniced doorpiece with two Roman Doric columns reached by a splayed flight of stairs.

Good sunburst ceiling rose in the entrance hall. After some smaller late C19 villas comes HIGHFIELD HOUSE, at the junction with Northfield Terrace, which was built *c.* 1820 as Northfield House, the town residence of Sir Archibald Dunbar. Tall and symmetrical, of two storeys over a raised basement; S front of three bays, the centre wide and slightly advanced under a wall-head pediment. Doorpiece with tall corniced architrave carried on two engaged Roman Doric columns. Big semicircular fanlight with radial glazing. Bad, low annexe to the rear added in 1999–2000; original early C19 carriage house beyond it.

Opposite, the MANSEFIELD HOTEL, so named because it incorporates the former manse of St Giles church by *James McBride*, 1838–40. Its front is to the S and is of two storeys over a tall raised basement; three wide bays under a platform-piended roof. The heritors, much to McBride's chagrin, refused to pay for the entrance portico and eaves cornice so the result is rather austere. Harled modern additions to the rear, fronted on Mayne Road by the original STABLES and COACHHOUSE, which have five Tudor-arched openings (now glazed) at ground floor with twelve-pane windows on the first floor. These were originally two separate buildings fronting a walled courtyard, but now joined by a four-centred entrance arch under a continuous roof. The principal addition is the large MORAY CONFERENCE CENTRE by, 2002. W of the hotel, off Mayne Road, is BRAE BIRNIE, of 1866, also two storeys over a raised basement. Refronted *c.* 1886 with a central pilastered doorpiece and triglyphed architrave with modillioned cornice. Full-height rectangular bay windows advanced to the l. and r. (also late C19), unusually sharp and angular. Simple panelled angle strips flanking the windows; console-bracketed cornice between the floors. Back in South Street, on the N side, off Northfield Terrace, is ST MICHAEL'S, good Arts and Crafts style of 1911–12 by *R. B. Pratt* as the Episcopalian rectory. In snecked, rock-faced rubble and asymmetrically composed with steep roofs on bracketed eaves and mullioned windows.

After this in South Street, nothing else of note except the Free Church and Elgin High Church on the S side (*see* Churches), next to which are the 'centrical and commodious premises' built for the distillers GORDON & MACPHAIL by *Charles C. Doig* in 1894–5, and still serving their original function. Classical Victorian, three storeys, with a canted angle at the corner with Culbard Street and a glazed octagonal turret. Open modillioned pediment on fluted scrolls to each front; alternating smooth and channelled pilaster strips to the l. and r., the shopfronts altered by *Charles James Doig* in 1962. Across the street, a fine quasi-triumphal ARCH, formerly the entrance to the Market Buildings, 1851 by *Mackenzie & Matthews* (*see* p. 600), converted into a shop and warehouse in 1958. Further E, at the corner of Fife Arms Close and set back is the former PICTURE HOUSE by *Sutherland & George*, 1926 (a bingo hall since 1964). One bay wide, with a broad, severe entrance with a massive rectangular architrave under a modillioned cornice and somewhat ungainly mansard roof. To the l. of it is THE LIDO by *J. & W. Wittet*, dated 1927, opened as a 'soda fountain and Palais de Danse', testament to throngs of crowds in search of new entertainment before and after going to the pictures. Stone, with sculpted fascicles in Art Deco style; block pediments above. Diagonally across (at the top of Academy Street), the former (and well-named) GRAND HOTEL by *A. & W. Reid & Wittet*, 1898, a Baronial juggernaut in rock-faced masonry, with excellent, delicate sculpture by of grapevines, ferns, roses and thistle around a central cartouche at the corner and a glazed conical roof turret above. Crowstepped gables to the flanks and one large mullioned-and-transomed window with Gothic lights. At the end, and making the rather awkward transition to Greyfriars Street, the two-storey CHRISTIE'S BUILDINGS (now Yeadon's Booksellers), 1930–1. In each outer bay a narrow basket-headed entrance arch flanked by channelled pilasters under a pediment; key-blocked, glazed oculi above.

A survey of the grid of early to mid-C19 suburban streets to the S of South Street should start at the W end in HAY STREET, formed by Col. Alexander Hay of Westerton in 1822 and feued slowly thereafter. At No. 26 (E side), a handsome two-storey, three-bay house by *A. & W. Reid*, *c.* 1860, originally built for Arthur Duff, sheriff clerk of Elgin (later the manse for the South Church). Channelled quoins and Doric porch with a triglyph architrave and modillion cornice. S of Moray Street, *moderne* FLATS, by *J. & W. Wittet*, 1930s.

In MORAY STREET, running E, after Moray College and the Police Headquarters (*see* Public Buildings), at the next intersection is the former South Church (*see* Churches, above), on an island site at the head of SOUTH GUILDRY STREET. This was formally laid out starting in 1853 and opened in 1858 as the main street from the city centre to the West Station (site of the present station, *see* Public Buildings) and accordingly became a prestigious address, lined with good villas, mostly symmetrical with two storeys and three bays. CARRICK HOUSE (No. 13) by *A. & W. Reid*, is Georgian Survival of 1854, harled, with a lugged, moulded doorpiece. It is followed by two more (Nos. 15 and 17) of very similar style, the first especially good and recessed from the street behind a balustrade. The remaining buildings followed quickly after *c.* 1860, several of them with bold stone doorpieces e.g. Nos. 22–24, Nos. 25–29 and No. 64.

In STATION ROAD, the ROYAL HOTEL, by *A. & W. Reid*, 1864–5. Built as Dalehaple House for James Grant, co-founder of Glen Grant Distillery in Rothes (q.v.); converted to a hotel, *c.* 1887. S front of two storeys and three bays with rusticated quoins, a slightly recessed centre containing a Doric porch and canted bay windows l. and r., their aprons panelled and tilted gently backwards – a decidedly suave touch. The red-roofed

NW addition (originally a billiard room) is by *Charles C. Doig*, *c.* 1892. Inside, an impressive geometric Imperial staircase with arcading on the first-floor landing over a frieze of Vitruvian scroll, and plaster ceiling. Facing the former station in MAISONDIEU ROAD is the former Station Hotel (now LAICHMORAY HOTEL), by *Mackenzie & Matthews*, 1853. Once a very grand Italianate cube of four storeys, broadcasting Elgin's pretension and luxury to travellers but now covered in dry-dash and bereft of its original porte cochère and cast-iron fittings. STABLE BLOCK to the E.

Back N along REIDHAVEN STREET, formed *c.* 1845 and intended as the smartest new suburb of Elgin. However it was owned by the Earl of Seafield, who permitted only single-storey-and-attic cottages to be built on the E side. The first cottage, No. 49, has a strange canted corner corbelled into a glazed gable and a pedimented doorpiece, its capitals with drapery suspended from volutes. By the end of the C19, the W side had been populated by two-storey villas on a grander scale, notably FRAMNAES (No. 28), by *Charles C. Doig*, 1898, with dummy timber framing in the gables and DRUMORE (No. 24), also by Doig, for the minister of Rothes, 1894, with crow-stepped gables, a canted porch in the re-entrant angle and bow window to the l. and canted to r., all with crenellations. GLENCAIRN (No. 20), *c.* 1895, is similar, and no doubt by the same architect, but with C17-style wall-head dormers. Similar houses continue to the end of the street, each one individually detailed. At the head of the street, the Baptist church (*see* Churches, above).

Parallel to the E is ACADEMY STREET, crossing Moray Street, laid out for building *c.* 1821, again mostly with single-storey cottages. N of the junction, E side, the MASONIC TEMPLE by *A. J. Morrison*, 1924, two storeys and five bays of rock-faced rubble, the centre pedimented and framed by giant-order ashlar pilaster strips. Pedimented doorpiece with a thickly channelled, cavetto-moulded round-headed arch.

E again is MOSS STREET, the original thoroughfare to the East Station (*see* Public Buildings) and beyond to Rothes. S of Moray Street, raised above the pavement, is EASTWOOD, early C19, with Doric doorpiece and cast-iron spearhead railings in front. Re-set on the high wall to its S, seven circular and shield-shaped SIGNS, early C20, with fading advertisements for local firms. Further down a well-preserved cast-iron shopfront (Moray Foot Clinic). Also SOUTH VILLA (No. 41), the best in the town, of 1830 by *William Robertson* for the Grants of Elchies, restored *c.* 1950 by *Ashley Bartlam* and latterly his practice's offices. Wide three-bay front, the ends minimally advanced with bracketed anthemion cornices over the windows. In the centre, a semicircular portico with Greek Doric columns and original cast-iron railing. Two-storey canted bays on the flanks, the r. with particularly good cantilevered balcony and taller railing. In the entrance hall, a coffered ceiling and distyle Ionic screen leading to the staircase.

INSTITUTION ROAD, leading E, was laid out 1829–30. On the N side, a pair of matching houses (KINRARA and MORAYBANK) set well back from the street behind gardens. They are by *A. & W. Reid*, *c.* 1845 in the style of their uncle William Robertson, whose practice they had inherited four years earlier. Each is a two-storey, three-bay, platform-piended rectangle with a little central pediment on the wall-head. Doorpieces in the centre, the l. with an anthemion finial and the r. topped by a bracketed balcony with cast-iron anthemion railing. Flanking canted bay windows. Across the street (at the top of Duff Avenue, facing St Sylvester (*see* Churches, above) is AVENUE HOUSE, enlarged from a core of *c.* 1888 by *R.B. Pratt* in 1907–8. Two-storey L-plan, the canted corner with a faceted spire behind a balustrade parapet.

Some other good villas in DUFF AVENUE itself, including ABBEYVALE (E side), formerly St Leonard's, rather stodgy Baronial by *Charles C. Doig*, 1898; later converted to a hotel and now a nursing home. Large, bad extensions to the l. and r. of 1977 and 2003–4. S of this in spacious grounds, THE LODGE, built for Hugh McLean, a tea planter in Malaysia, by *A. & W. Reid*, 1898–9. Single storey and of three bays, in rock-faced rubble, good but quite conventional except for the remarkable corner turret off the r. corner with its tall frieze of blind ellipses and shallow conical roof with fish-scale slates.

Returning to INSTITUTION ROAD, E of Duff Avenue is ABBEYSIDE, a sprawling Baronial *Wunderkind* of *c.* 1875 (converted into a nursing home in 1987). Huge, two-storey L-plan with Dutch gables, 'embossed' Tudor chimney flues and fleur-de-lys pediments above the first-floor windows. Two-storey drum tower in the r. corner with fish-scale-slated ogival dome. Just beyond is THE CROFT, built 1848 for the town clerk and solicitor, Patrick Duff. Two storeys and three bays, the ends slightly advanced under open pediments. Trabeated balcony between them on Greek Doric columns. Diagonally across the street is FRIARS HOUSE, *c.* 1860 by *A. & W. Reid*, two storeys raised over a basement. Doric porch. Two stout ranks of transverse chimneystacks, six on each side. Towards the end, at the corner of Queen Street, is GREYFRIARS HOUSE, 1860, again by the *Reids*. Neo-Jacobean, five bays with an advanced and gabled centre. Finally Anderson's Institution (*see* Public Buildings).

Just S in SEAFIELD STREET, is CRAIGENTORE (formerly Pinefield Villa) by *George Petrie*, 1862, but altered in 1900, probably by *Charles C. Doig*, this phase in lighter ashlar. Canted, crenellated windows in the first and third bays; off-centre advanced porch with panelled door, Ionic pilasters and glazed sidelights.

N of here in SOUTH COLLEGE STREET, on the N side, a fine traditional terrace of houses by *Charles James Doig* of *C. C. Doig & Sons*, designed 1938, completed 1948.

For The Chanonry, *see* p. 579.

4. *North of High Street to the Lossie*

There is much less to explore in the northern town, following extensive later C20 rebuilding in the area either side of the by-pass. The area W of Holy Trinity is dominated by the large but unexceptional premises and warehouses of GORDON & MACPHAIL, distillers. NE of the church in Trinity Road is MORAY HOUSE (Diageo offices) of 1961 after the previous building had been destroyed by a gas explosion. In the stair-tower, stained glass by *Crear McCartney*, incorporating fragments from the original building. The usual luminous colours, immediately recognizable but with jarringly secular content. Four scenes from the distillery industry amid sheaves of barley and fish; swan-neck still in the centre, glowing pink over a roaring fire. Further W on BLACKFRIARS ROAD, below the N side of Ladyhill (*see* p. 601), MANSION HOUSE HOTEL 122
(originally Blackfriarshaugh). It stood near the site of the Dominican friary* and the lodge (1904, fine cusped curvilinear bargeboarding on the gables) probably overlies the area of the nave. The house is on a vast scale, by *A. & W. Reid*, 1850–1, for William Grigor and slightly enlarged and re-clothed in luxurious and quite imaginative Baronial regalia in 1882–3 by *William Kidner* for A.G. Allan (cf. Lesmurdie House, below). It has a tall tower with crenellated parapet set on stepped corbels, as at Kidner's earlier Lesmurdie with a higher round stair-turret. Rear extensions made after the house was converted into a hotel in 1983–4. The interior mostly a sensitive restoration of that date.

5. *Bishopmill*

Elgin's N suburb, beyond the Lossie. A mill was built at 'Bischopsmylnn' *c.* 1203. The first reference to a village of 'Bisaptung' is in 1363. Acquired *c.* 1756 by the Earl of Findlater, by 1771 he was feuing out land for houses. Much expanded in the earlier C20 and since.

Former MISSION HALL, East High Street. Now a showroom. Converted in 1870 from a granary built *c.* 1752. Four round-headed windows on the S flank.

BISHOPMILL BRIDGE, over the Lossie. Iron girder bridge of 1870–1 by *John Willet*, engineer and *James Abernethy*, iron-founder and contractor. It replaced a bridge of 1830–1 by *William Robertson*.

BISHOPMILL PRIMARY SCHOOL, Morriston Road and Duff Place. By *R.B. Pratt*, 1934–5. Large butterfly plan, with a central block fronted originally by a play room with infants' classrooms flanking and long classrooms canted out from it. Cock-eyed SW extension (sports hall) by *Moray Council*, 2007.

*Elgin Blackfriars was established by King Alexander II in 1233–4 and dedicated to St James. Closed before 1570; no remains visible above ground.

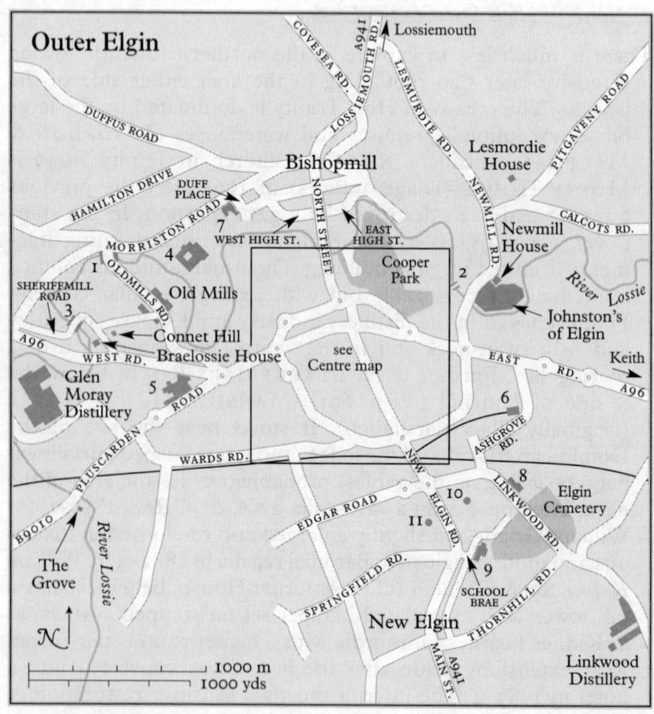

1 Bow Bridge
2 Brewery Bridge
3 Bridge of Sheriffmill
4 Elgin Academy
5 Gray's Hospital
6 Engine Shed (former)
7 Bishopmill Primary School
8 Moray College Technology Centre
9 New Elgin Primary School
10 War Memorial
11 Doocot, Dovecot Park

ELGIN ACADEMY, Morriston Road. By *Aedas Architects*, 2010–12, replacing the Academy of 1967–8. Tall complex of two storeys on a giant L-plan, the ends connected by a huge, smooth quadrant to the rear. To the street, the r. corner is wide and bowed, the first floor (for the library) partially cantilevered; generous glazing with vertical weatherboarding above and below. Asymmetric roof on top, the r. edge segmental and the l. flat, oversailing the rounded façade on pilotis. Full-height atrium to the l. fronted by a screen of glass.

HIGH STREET running E–W was bisected when the new road from Elgin to Lossiemouth was cut through the village centre in 1821. The two parts were spanned by a stone bridge until 1898 when the road was re-routed to its present line. Both parts of the street have some interesting villas built facing the Lossie and Elgin. On East High Street, MILLBANK, by *A. & W. Reid*, *c.* 1845–6, is Neo-Jacobean but DEANSFORD (originally East Neuk) of 1860 is Italianate, with a substantial tetrastyle portico with paired Roman Doric columns. On West High Street, HYTHEHILL (No. 23) is also by the *Reids*, 1851, its single-storey S elevation with a central round-headed niche flanked by canted bay windows.

BRAEMORRISTON HOUSE. Built *c.* 1817 and greatly enlarged by *William Robertson* in 1837 for Capt. Duff of Drummuir (q.v.). Original cottage to the S, single-storeyed and of three bays with gently bowed windows to the flanks. Robertson reorientated it and gave it a sprawling N front, the centre featuring a pedimented, distyle Ionic porch flanked by pairs of apron-panelled windows. Two-storey single pavilions on the ends with pyramidal roofs; three-bay Ionic loggias in front of them topped by balustraded parapets.

N of the centre Nos. 1–55 HARRISON TERRACE of 1947–9 by *John P. M. Wright*, picking up the motif of arcading seen in Elgin High Street. A sensitive design, and one that very few architects of his date would have made.

6. *New Elgin*

Small working-class suburb laid out *c.* 1830, flanking the main road to Rothes (q.v.) and made popular during the railway boom of 1840–50. Originally roughly triangular and separated from the city centre by marshland; now much expanded and a village in its own right.

ELGIN CEMETERY, School Brae. Extended three times and now very large. Original SW section laid out by *Thomas Hutcheon* in 1857–8, with WEST LODGE (Fraser Cottage) with crowstepped gables. Cast-iron Gothic GATEPIERS to the N entrance, spearhead gates and railings. Extended NE, 1877–8, and then SE in 1905–7, the LODGES and a PAVILION by *John Wittet.*

MORAY COLLEGE TECHNOLOGY CENTRE, Linkwood Road. 2002 by *Wittets Architects*.

NEW ELGIN PRIMARY SCHOOL, School Brae. By *A. & R. McCulloch* of Edinburgh, 1904–5. Classrooms with gableted roofs on four sides of a central hall. Windows (bipartite to the N) break the wall-head under little piended roofs. Large extension *c.* 1961.

WAR MEMORIAL, Market Drive and Milnefield Avenue. By *A. J. Morrison*, 1921–2, the carving by *J. R. Henderson* and the statue of a kilted Seaforth Highlander, head bowed over a reversed rifle, by *John Morrison.*

DOOCOT, Dovecot Park (W of New Elgin Road). Small circular, beehive form, mid-C17. Bottle-shaped interior with nesting boxes in concentric rings.

VILLAS AND MANSIONS

BRAELOSSIE HOUSE, Sheriffmill Road, N of the A96. Two-storey, Z-plan Baronial mansion by *A. & W. Reid & Mackenzie*, 1862–3, built for Alexander Lawson, factor to the Earl Fife. It has a very lively, spiky and jagged profile. Four-bay W front, to l. a canted bay window and crowstepped gable and to the r. a three-stage tower with a pyramidal bellcast roof with contrasting tiers of fish-scale slates. Substantial porch in the re-entrant angle. The final bay on the far r., wide and crowstepped, has a glazed tourelle on the corner. Short wing recessed to form a narrow L-plan service court. Three-bay N elevation, the l. slightly advanced and crowstepped. Wide, semi-octagonal bay window with good cast-iron brattishing; narrow two-storey turret with candlesnuffer roof in the re-entrant angle. Inside, an impressive stair hall with open-well wooden staircase and fine barley-twist balusters. Tripartite mullioned-and-transomed window with original stained glass showing Lawson's initials, lion and motto.

CONNET HILL, SW of Braelossie House, is a fine harled, summery villa by *A. Marshall Mackenzie & Son*, 1913. SW front of five bays, the l. flat and two-storeyed under a piended roof. Single-storey triple bay in the centre, the mansard attic with good rectangular flat-roofed dormers. Wide, segmental-fronted pergola in front set on Roman Doric columns; multi-pane glazing and projecting eaves over a striated architrave. The r. bay originally matched the l. but was given an advanced, bowed termination by *J. & W. Wittet* c. 1933 – very suave and swanky, the contour streamlined under a semi-conical piended roof. Flat-roofed porch to the SE also added by the Wittets, cantilevered out over a Roman Doric column.

THE GROVE, 1.7 km. SW, Pluscarden Road. Built *c.* 1830 as Struangrove (now a nursing home). Pilastered, corniced doorpiece and wall-head pediment over a bracketed cornice. Centre and ends defined by broad, panelled pilaster strips.

LESMURDIE HOUSE, 1.3 km. NE off Pitgaveny Road. The original house was a big rubble rectangle built *c.* 1830, still clearly visible from the N. It runs E–W and is two-storeyed, with a piended (now somewhat truncated) roof. Victorian prosperity demanded something far less Spartan, and it was engulfed by two smart new façades and a tower in Scots Baronial style by *William Kidner*, 1880–1, for Charles James Johnston of Newmill (*see* Mills and Distilleries, below). The E front is one storey over a raised basement with a piended, bellcast roof. Five bays, the centre and far r. slightly advanced with crowstepped gables and apex ball finials. Wide bow window in the l. bay with crenellation and the entrance in the second bay under a wide segmental arch. Rising behind, a slated tower with pyramidal roof and clearstorey (formerly to light the billiard room). On the S elevation a porch, which extended originally to form a proper loggia. Recessed behind the second bay, a curiously unassertive three-stage tower with corbelled and crenellated parapet and taller stair-turret. Converted into apartments, 2000–3 by *Wittets Architects*. – NW (off Chandler's Rise) is a small octagonal DOOCOT, *c.* 1830. Two storeys; the lower originally a hen house.

LINKWOOD HOUSE, *see* Linkwood Distillery, below.

MILLS AND DISTILLERIES

Former City Corn Mills, Wards Road. By *Charles C. Doig*, 1912. The usual malting kiln with pyramidal roof and pagoda ventilator. Disused and in poor condition.

Glen Moray Distillery (La Martiniquaise), Bruceland Road. Begun as West Brewery, a C-plan complex built *c.* 1831, converted to Glen Moray-Glenlivet Distillery by *Charles C. Doig*, 1896–7. His work is intact at the S end, two rubble storeys with gabled attic around a central courtyard. S arm (tun room and still house) with tidy row of louvred, piended rectangular cupolas. Original malt barn and kiln in the N arm demolished 1978, replaced with a hulking malt store and dark grains plant, 1979. Tall, soot-stained T-plan with corrugated sides and canted roof. Huge network of warehouses to N, the long double-gabled one on the r. (past the Visitors' Centre) by Doig, 1897. Others mainly of the mid C20. – Single-storey former customs and excise officer's house (now Glen Moray House), also *c.* 1897 by Doig. – The former manager's house (now Hattonhill) is on the summit of Gallow Hill.

Johnston's of Elgin, Newmill Road. A large, good complex 123
for the world-famous manufacturers of wool and cashmere. The firm was founded by Alexander Johnston on this site in 1797 and appropriately christened Newmill.

Newmill House, the family's original residence, lies W of the car park and faces SE. Early C19 core with extensive alterations and additions by *H. M. S. Mackay*, 1865. Harled front of two storeys and seven asymmetric bays. Slightly advanced entrance to the l. of centre, gabled and with an ornate doorcase with shell ornament in the half-dome tympanum. To the r. a canted bay window and three gableted wall-head dormers; two taller bays to the l. with fleur-de-lys-finialled dormerheads. Detached to the l. are two similar bays; they were originally continuous but the centre was destroyed by fire in 1957. Around the corner, facing SW, is a large addition, Garvald House of 1868, also expanded by Mackay around an early C19 core. Two storeys with attic. Four bays, the l. with a canted bay window and long catslide roof above. Advanced third bay with chamfered angles; they are corbelled into squares below the tall corniced parapet with monogram 'CJ'. Tall, wide gable to the r. with full-height canted bay window. Recessed on the far l., another catslide dormer and a low conical end turret with fish-scale-slated roof. – Square gatepiers to the W with pyramidal capitals and spiked ball finials. Making a nearly quadrangular plan with these is the mid to late C19 single-storey L-plan stable and carriage range (now shop and heritage centre). Gableted dormers and a pointed elliptical arch leading to the central courtyard. Inside it, the pend's gable has a doocot.

To the SE (and facing the main entrance), the office, sales room and goods store of 1865 (converted into a shop, 1981, by *Ashley Bartlam Partnership*). It is unexpectedly grand. Two storeys and nine bays, the centre wide, gabled and slightly advanced. Birdcage bellcote on the apex; two tiers of generous twenty-pane glazing to the l. and r. The flanks are a nice burst of Gothic, each with four pointed windows (two on the W later converted into doors) and a quatrefoil in the gable. – Attached to the rear, the single-storey WOOL STORE, 1882. – Forming an L-plan beyond, the two-storey, nine-bay WEAVING SHED, 1847.

Extensive complex of buildings to the S with some earlier mill buildings among C20 additions. – The large harled building is part of the original mill, 1797, with an advanced rectangular WATER TOWER. Three storeys and a solid parapet on big corbels. – Behind it, the long FINISHING MILL of 1861, two-storeyed and with a very wide platform-gabled roof. Birdcage bellcote on the S end. – Beyond it, the original YARN STORE, 1853, of three bays with a wooden gabled porch. – Set perpendicularly across from these, the BOILER HOUSE and two gables of the WEAVING MILL, both 1868. – Behind them, two DYEHOUSES, 1872 and 1870.

LINKWOOD DISTILLERY (Diageo), 2.2 km. SE on Linkwood Road. Founded in 1821 but completely rebuilt by *George Melven* in 1872–4. Of his original complex, the square KILN with pagoda ventilator (blockily pyramidal and inferior to Doig's) and the fourteen-bay, double-gabled former MALT BARN attached to the rear. Major reconstruction of the main production buildings in 1962 and again in 1970–1, some of it demolished for a new STILL HOUSE and TUN ROOM by *Blyth & Blyth* of Edinburgh, 2012–14. – In the SW corner, five bays of piended WAREHOUSES by *A. & W. Reid & Wittet*, 1892–5. – Just NNE of the maltings, the former MANAGER'S HOUSE by *William C. Reid* of Elgin, 1904. Three piended dormers and little block pediment over the entrance. – Former CUSTOMS AND EXCISE OFFICER'S HOUSE (now Dunree), 0.4 km. NW on Linkwood Road. By *Charles C. Doig*, *c.* 1897 with bargeboarded dormerheads. – LINKWOOD HOUSE was built *c.* 1770 for Peter May, factor to the Earl of Findlater but extensively remodelled 1856–61 as the new residence for the distillery owner. The C18 house is on the r., originally two storeys and three bays, the mid-C19 section to its l. noticeably taller, the advanced centre with rounded ground-floor, semicircular window pediment and crowstepped gable with apex chimneystack. – STEADING, 100 m. NNW. By *Matthews & Mackenzie*, 1879–80. Grandiose crowstepped gables, the centre supporting a tall, round bellcote with conical stone roof.

OLD MILLS, Oldmills Road. Early C19, two storeys of whitewashed rubble with a water wheel on the W flank. Attached N, a later C19 kiln with pyramidal-roofed ventilator. – Just to the S, a late C18 GRANARY with ground floor of rubble partially oversailing the lade. First storey with renewed vertical weatherboarding. David I built the 'King's Mills' here in the mid C12, and *c.* 1240 they were granted to the prior of Pluscarden Abbey (q.v.).

ENZIE *see* PORTGORDON

ESSIL *see* GARMOUTH

FINDHORN 0060

The present sleepy village is the third of this name. The first was located *c.* 1.6 km. to the NW and was made a burgh of barony in 1532. It was the most important port in Moray in the C17, when it served as the harbour to Forres (q.v.) and boasted a booming trade with the Continent. The original Findhorn was buried by the Culbin Sands in 1694 and its replacement destroyed by a minor tsunami in 1702. Present village founded soon after, although trade has been non-existent since the early C20.

PARISH CHURCH. The former Free Church by *John Urquhart* of Forres, 1843–4. W front with pedimented, double-pilastered doorpiece; rectangular, louvred bellcote with scroll brackets (cf. the church at Alves) and big mushroom-cap finial. Four-bay flanks, the bottom with rectangular windows and the top with segmental lunettes. Hall off the E gable by *Peter Fulton*, 1907. Simple but pleasing interior as renovated by *John Milne* of Forres, 1872. – U-plan GALLERY, 1844, with plain rectangular panels. Cast-iron columns with lily-leaf capitals. – Wide rectangular PULPIT, 1872, with pointed back-board and two gasoliers. Raised on a platform in 1900.

WAR MEMORIAL, opposite the church. By *Gibb Bros*, masons, 1920–1. Granite obelisk draped with a sheathed cavalry sword.

The HARBOUR (0.4 km. NE on Findhorn Bay) is a simple design comprising two parallel piers, the N one built *c.* 1778 and the S added by *Joseph Mitchell* in 1827–30. On the shore side of the former is the harled QUAY COTTAGE, its lugged and corniced doorpiece inscribed 'James Rose Margaret Simpson 1773'. Opposite the S pier is the JAMES MILNE INSTITUTE with its little clock tower, converted by *John Wittet* in 1921–2 from an early C19 chandlery. Between them sits the MARKET CROSS, an octagonal, ball-finialled shaft of 1979 that reuses the circular base and one plinth course of the original (submerged in 1702). Above it is the CROWN AND ANCHOR INN, its original section of four bays with crowstepped gables and l. skewputt dated 1739. Parallel to the S is the salmon-harled KILVAROCK, a rare survival of a virtually unaltered early to mid-C18 merchant's house. Next is the STATION HOUSE (Nos. 46–48), seven bays of the early to mid C19 with a segmental arch in the centre. So named because from 1860–9 it served as the office and warehouse for the short-lived Findhorn Railway, whose terminus was directly in front. Beyond lies the KIMBERLEY INN with worn l. skewputt dated 1777 and half of a crowstepped gable behind.

ICE HOUSE, N end of the village. Two linked buildings, early C19, for storing salmon before it was shipped to England (cf.

Gollachy (Portgordon) and Tugnet). Partially subterranean under turf-covered mounds. Three chambers in the first section and a single, taller one in the second. Thick stone walls with brick barrel-vaults and rectangular ice chutes.

FINDHORN FOUNDATION, 1.6 km. SE, off B9011. Established as a spiritual community in 1962 and soon expanded with a series of cottages for visitors and residents. The ECO-VILLAGE was begun *c.* 1982, some of the houses self-designed and clad in timber recycled from the spent casks of the Speyside distilleries. Pentagonal UNIVERSAL HALL, by *George Ripley*, built 1974–84, with entrance screen of stained glass and geodesic roof in the auditorium.

4060

FINDOCHTY

B

In 1521 James V granted the lands of 'Fyndacthie' to the Ogilvys of Cullen (q.v.). In 1716, the village was re-founded by a group of fishermen from Fraserburgh (q.v.). Prosperity developed after *c.* 1840, despite competition from Buckie (q.v.).

FINDOCHTY PARISH CHURCH, off Church Street. Built 1861–2 as the United Presbyterian church for a congregation originally of seceders from Rathven. Thrillingly set on a commanding promontory overlooking the sea. The architecture itself cannot – and wisely does not try to – compete. Pristine white harling, S gable with a stone bellcote and steps to the entrance; lancets l. and r.

METHODIST CHURCH, Seaview Road. By *William Hendry* of Buckie, 1914–16, replacing a church on Chapel Street. Economical Gothic with lancets, the W front of rock-faced whinstone contrasted with ashlar and with an abstracted cross finial on a long panelled base – a harbinger of the 1930s. Gabled quasi-transept.

PRIMARY SCHOOL, Burnside Street. 1936, presumably by *James Wood*, Banffshire County Architect. Large E-plan with piended roof and longer central arm, cf. Buckie and Portessie.

WAR MEMORIAL, off School Hill. By *James Wood*, 1920–2, set on a summit overlooking the harbour and the Moray Firth. Tall obelisk of coursed, rock-faced granite.

HARBOUR. Engineered by *C. Brand & Sons* of Glasgow (or *David Stevenson*), 1882–4, in a naturally sheltered site known as Broad Haven. Two piers on the N side forming a long breakwater, the l. side a long narrow L. Short cylindrical leading light on the end of it, *c.* 1903, with entrance just beyond. Diagonal pier added to the S to create a stilling basin, *c.* 1913–14. Further N, a straight jetty off Sterlochy Street, 1901–3. Nearly everything now encased in concrete.

FINDOCHTY CASTLE, 1 km. SW. First documented in 1568, when the castle was transferred from James Ogilvy of Findlater to Thomas Ord. James VI reconfirmed the 'fortalice' as part of Sir Walter Ogilvy's property in 1615. The L-plan building was already in ruins by the mid to late C18. The rectangular main block aligned E–W is *c.* 7.4 m. wide and now mostly destroyed. Some of the N wall remains; the rest is taken up by a ruinous cottage built of stone recycled from the castle. Former W wing intact up to two storeys, of harl-pointed rubble with a large window on the first floor. Just off the NW corner is a small tower (*c.* 5.1 by 3.2 m.), its three sides also carried up two storeys. Remains of a conventional (not crowstepped) gable to the N, originally lit by a small garret window. So the original building likely rose no taller than it does now. Inside the main block, through a narrow doorway in the SW corner* is the former kitchen, barrel-vaulted and with a fireplace (*c.* 1.4 m. wide with a thick, damaged lintel). Adjoining cellar, also barrel-vaulted, with a small window, aumbry and gunloop. Of the former withdrawing room above the kitchen there remain W and S windows, a fireplace and aumbry; the hall to the E has gone but the private chamber in the tower beyond has a W window and a round gunloop in each face.

STRATHLENE HOUSE, 1.6 km. SW. Single-storey rear wing dated 1865 but the S front of 1887, built for William G. Bryson, retired factor to the Earl of Seafield. Five bays, the centre advanced and gabled with two gableted dormers to the r. Good cast-iron sun porch in the re-entrant angle.

FINDRASSIE HOUSE 2060

3.1 km. NW of Elgin

S front of two storeys and three bays in tooled ashlar, begun *c.* 1786 by Abraham Leslie (†1793). Rusticated quoins and lugged, moulded doorpiece with fluted architrave and Gothic fanlight (inserted *c.* 1826). Twelve-pane glazing in the windows, longer on the first floor; harled flanks and rear. Recessed off the W gable is a harled extension by *William Robertson*, built 1826 for Col. Alexander Grant after his retirement from the East India Company. A corresponding E wing with conservatory was demolished *c.* 1945. – Corniced GATEPIERS at the end of the drive, *c.* 1790. Renewed ball finials.

DOOCOT, 250 m. NW. The only vestige of an L-plan tower house built *c.* 1580 by Robert Leslie, half-brother of the 5th Earl of Rothes. Crowstepped lectern (*c.* 5.4 m. by 4.8 m.), now very damaged with a tree growing through the centre. S entrance with lintel dated 1631.

*Tusked masonry in the SW corner shows that there was originally a range to the S, probably a corridor of outbuildings leading up to the kitchen.

3050 # FOCHABERS

The old town of 'Fochoper' is first mentioned *c.* 1150–3 in the charters of King David I and was raised to a free burgh of barony in 1599. It was situated immediately to the SW of Gordon Castle (*see* below) and was described in the mid C18 as a 'place of miserable huts' with 'strumpets who are notorious Thieves'. The present town was contemplated by Alexander, 4th Duke of Gordon, as early as *c.* 1769 and officially opened in 1776. It is a classic example of land improvement that simultaneously cleared the laird's policies while establishing civic order. *John Baxter* designed the plan, consisting of a grid-lined parallelogram running E–W with a large square in the centre. With its unspoilt architecture and four excellent churches, Fochabers is not only among the earliest planned settlements in Moray, but undoubtedly the finest.

CHURCHES

33 BELLIE PARISH CHURCH, The Square. The crown jewel of the town commissioned by the 4th Duke of Gordon *John Baxter*, 1795–8 (*see* Gordon Castle). The proportions are large but coolly rational, with a pristinely monumental symmetry. The church is large, rectangular, five by three bays, in tooled, polished ashlar, two storeys with an elegant platform-piended roof that has slightly bellcast eaves. To The Square it is of five bays, the middle three slightly advanced and fronted by a mighty tetrastyle portico with Roman Doric columns, each with slight entastis, carrying a deep, plain architrave surmounted by a broad pediment with a glazed bullseye in the tympanum. Within the portico three tall doors under round-headed arches; semicircular fanlights with radial glazing. The outer bays have long rectangular ground-floor windows and smaller sixteen-pane glazing across the whole top storey; all in moulded surrounds. Elevated behind the portico a tall cubical clock stage with corner urn finials and then an octagonal belfry with blind and louvred round-headed arches supporting a long faceted spire with three diminishing sets of elliptical oculi on the principal faces. It follows the spire of Baxter's Town House, Peterhead (p. 345) of a decade earlier. The rear is equally handsome, the centre with a full-height bow and square, blind panels on the ground floor. The three windows above them were originally of the same size (cf. Baxter's intact long-and-short margins), rather crudely lengthened in 1835.

The INTERIOR comes as something of a disappointment, due to several reorderings. Its history is more complex than first appears. The pulpit was originally raised high against the flat N wall at the base of the tower, with galleries on three sides (including the S bow) carried on Tuscan columns and reached by the surviving stone stairs from the entrance vestibule. *Archibald Simpson* carried out extensive renovations in 1835–6,

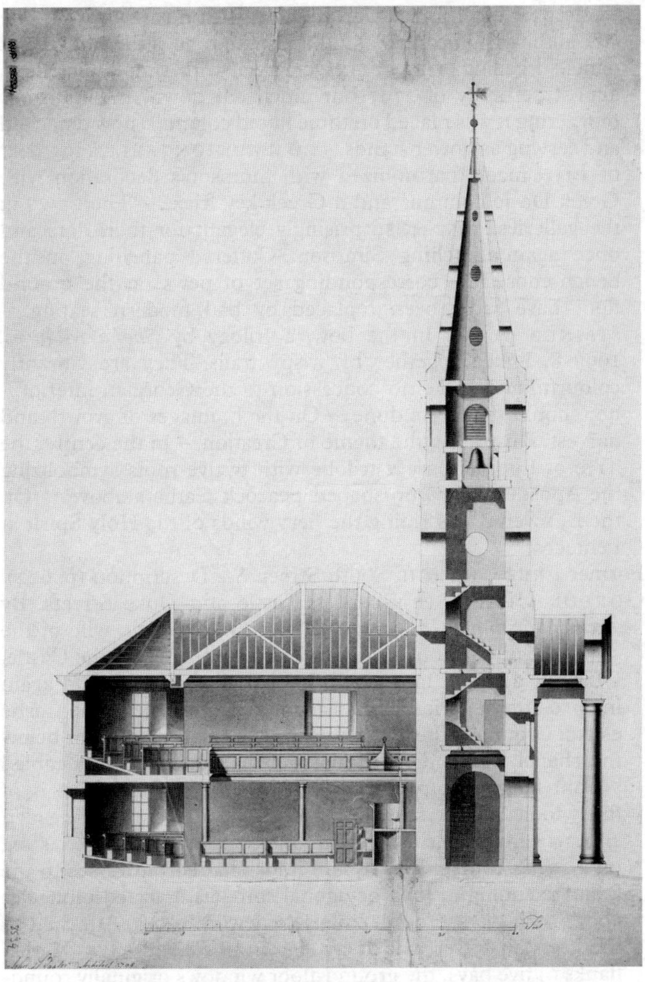

Fochabers, Bellie Parish Church.
Section drawing, 1795

demolishing the S gallery and reorientating the church to place the pulpit in the bow in front of his newly extended windows. The remaining galleries he gave Greek key decoration and encased their cast-iron supports with wooden Greek Doric columns; the galleries originally had canted ends, connecting with the Gordons' private N gallery (reached by an elliptical stair in the tower). Another reorientation followed under *George Bennett Mitchell & Son* in 1952–4, removing the N gallery, straightening the E and W galleries, returning the pulpit to the N and leaving the S bow dominated by an organ which had been installed in 1887. Finally, in 2009, the church was rotated 180 degrees for the third time, the organ removed and a raised chancel formed in the bow, with a rostrum opposite (for audio-visual controls). Of the same time is the ribbed and panelled ceiling. – PULPIT. Octagonal with simple panelling, almost certainly of 1797 but much cut down. In Simpson's reordering it was placed on three fluted columns, now detached and serving as flower stands. – COMMUNION TABLE and FONT of 1931, nicely harmonized with Simpson's decoration with Greek Doric columns and a Greek key frieze. – The PEWS in the galleries, 1952–4, surprisingly elegant for their date and once again matching Simpson. Coffered panelling on the bench-ends. The corresponding set of pews on the ground floor have sadly been replaced by bad modern seating. – STAINED GLASS. In the bow, a trilogy by *Shona McInnes*, 1997–8, linked together by wispy trails. They are vibrantly colourful and make no concession to the Georgian interior – nor should they have done. – On the l., images of growth and harvest, illustrating the theme of Creation. – In the centre, the Tree of Life, its base a trilobe with twelve roots symbolizing the Apostles. Teardrop-shaped peacock feathers above. – On the r., seven doves riding the fiery winds of the Holy Spirit at Pentecost.

Former FREE CHURCH, South Street. *See* Description (p. 622).

GORDON CHAPEL (Episcopal), Castle and Duke Streets. By *Archibald Simpson*, 1832–4, paid for by Elizabeth, wife of the 5th Duke of Gordon, largely as a private chapel for the Castle. Officially adopted into the Episcopal church, 1898 and again in 1950 after a period of disuse following the sale of the Castle estate. Originally there was a school on the ground floor below the chapel. Tall and rather narrow, orientated with its gabled S front facing the parish church in The Square.* This is of finely tooled ashlar, simple and elegant. Shafted, round-headed entrance arch in the centre; three stepped lancets above resting on a string course. Big, square nook-shafted buttresses to the l. and r. ending in long octagonal spirelets. Faceted pinnacles above with giant crocket finials (renewed, 1999). Attached to the l. a stair-tower, added by *Alexander Ross* in 1874. Harled flanks of five bays, the ground-floor windows originally round-headed but made blandly rectangular *c.* 1953 when the bottom storey was converted into a rectory. The gabled NW transeptal projection originally served as the Gordons' private entrance. Triple lancets on the N gable and a glazed cinquefoil above it added by Ross.

The interior was completely remodelled by Ross, including the good Gothic hammerbeam roof with tie-beams, and refurnished. – READING DESK and PULPIT, brass ALTAR RAILS with polychrome rinceau brackets and little gold flowers, and ORGAN by *William Hill & Son*, London. – The nice brass GASOLIERS are *c.* 1893, their branches with leaves. – PAINTED DECORATION on the N chancel wall (now covered by curtains) on canvas; burgundy ground with fleur-de-lys and flowers

*Simpson was to begin his restoration there the following year.

stencilled in gold. On the l., 'I will wash my hands in innocency [*sic*] O Lord' over a sheaf of wheat. On the r., 'And so will I go to the thine altar' with grapevine in the centre. Altar and reredos originally attached to the centre of the wall and further defaced during the Second World War. – FONT (in the lower vestibule). 1779. Marble swagged elliptical bowl with acanthus along the base. Originally in St Andrew's Church, West Dereham (Norfolk); donated by St Mary Coslany, Norwich, after its closure in 1981.

STAINED GLASS. The largest collection of pre-Raphaelite glass in Scotland but surprisingly little known, all commissioned as Gordon memorials. Nine panels by *Edward Burne-Jones* as fabricated by *Morris & Co*. Instead of the usual quarries, each window is surrounded by an outstanding variety of swirling, sinuous foliage. – In the N lancets, 1876–7, the Crucifixion in the centre with a green cross; two mourning 50
angels on the bottom with red wings. Virgin to the l. over the Good Samaritan and on the r. St John and Dorcas tending to a seated woman. Inscription from John 4:10 ('In hoc est charitas . . .'), part of the text excised by Christ's legs. – Rosette above, also 1876–7. Angel in the centre holding a banner. Five angels around him playing musical instruments. In the W wall, the three lancets each have a narrative scene on the bottom and a figure on top, in straight frames against the foliage: Ursula and two women visiting the sick, 1887–8, the saturation of the green foliage especially effective here; Archangel Raphael and an angel leading Enoch, 1904; and St Michael slaying the dragon, 1919. Wonderfully fiery red wings, the texture of the feathers very tactile. – E wall. – Cecilia with Valerian and the angel, 1885; the Good Shepherd over Christ blessing children, 1904. – The r. lancet is by *Crear McCartney*, 1990, St Andrew over Christ calling Andrew and Simon Peter. Uncharacteristic grisaille foliage for a Pluscarden window – an inverted homage to its surroundings. – S window. Christ and the fisherman with wildlife and Spey scenery. 2003 by *Petri Anderson* for *Chapel Studio*. – Re-set in the stair-tower, two armorial windows of *c.* 1805, from Gordon Castle (*see* below). One shows the arms of the 2nd Marquess of Cornwallis, the other of the 4th Duke of Bedford, brothers-in-law to the 5th Duke of Gordon.

Former PRINGLE MEMORIAL CHURCH, High Street. By *D. & J.R. McMillan*, 1898–1900,* opened as the United Free Church, superseding the Free Church on South Street (*see* Description, below). Closed 1947 and converted into the FOLK MUSEUM AND HERITAGE CENTRE, 1984. Big, sturdy Gothic, especially the S façade with four squat lancets in the centre topped by a large four-light Geometric Dec window, lower stair wing to the l. and tall, unstaged SE tower with crenellated parapet, angle pinnacles and broach spire. – Good

*So named after a bequest of £3000 by Alexander Pringle (d. 1896), a successful collector for the board of Inland Revenue.

original timber barrel roof, with transverse ribs set on stone corbels. – STAINED GLASS by *James Garvie & Sons*, 1899. Geometric patterns in the N and S windows, the former with the burning bush.

ST MARY (R.C.), South Street. By *J. Gillespie Graham*, 1826–8, i.e. in advance of Catholic Emancipation, after a design by Bishop *James Kyle*. Perp gabled rectangle orientated N–S, the main façade of gleaming tooled ashlar. Central bay flanked by stepped buttresses rising to panelled, gableted pinnacles with big crocket finials. Double-chamfered entrance arch below a three-light transomed window; pierced balustrade above with apex cross finial. Two-light windows to the l. and r. bays topped by diagonal crenellated parapets and with good angle buttresses on the ends. Long flanks built of mixed rubble, the W side blind and the E with a pair of large, three-light Dec windows. Crowstepped gable to the N. The semi-octagonal N apse was added later. Three two-light windows with curvilinear Dec tracery.

Aisleless interior with four-centred ceiling, two clusters of shafts swept across as transverse ribs. – In the apse, a lavish stone HIGH ALTAR by *Pugin & Pugin c.* 1885 with sumptuous canopies and gables, the central pinnacles above a beautiful marble and copper tabernacle. Carved panels of the Annunciation and Nativity. The SIDE ALTARS with large figures under canopies of the same time. – ORGAN. In the gallery. 1842 by *James Bruce & Co.* Pretty Gothick case. – STAINED GLASS. S wall. One (Crucifixion) is signed by *Mayer & Co.*

Two-storey gabled PRESBYTERY abutting the W flank of the church.

PUBLIC BUILDINGS

115 MILNE'S PRIMARY SCHOOL, E end of High Street. Convincing Neo-Elizabethan extravaganza by *Mackenzie & Matthews*, 1845–6. It was funded by a bequest from Alexander Milne, a former footman at Gordon Castle (*see* below) who was fired from service after refusing to cut and powder his hair. Milne then emigrated to New Orleans and made a vast fortune in property, leaving his native town $100,000 upon his death in 1838. Main N elevation of two storeys and nine bays, E-plan, with the centre advanced as a full-height, attenuated Tudor arch between octagonal buttresses, ending in pinnacles with ogee tops studded with lavish crocketing and a central canopied niche with a statue of Milne holding a book. The wings each have a large canted oriel topped by blind Dec parapets and crenellated pinnacles. The inner bays have ground-floor loggias with Tudor arches, and groin-vaulting inside. They originally led to side entrances (now blocked). First-floor windows with lying-pane glazing and Gothic heads; step-crenellated parapet with octagonal shafts carried on delightful mask corbels. The E and W elevations in a similar collegiate style, both seven bays with a slightly advanced centre, implying a gatehouse. In the

middle of the rear (S) side, a tall square tower with simple louvred tripartite windows. Crenellated finials in the angles like dummy tourelles. Door flanked by shafted pilasters under a pediment. Crenellated parapet.

PUBLIC INSTITUTE, High Street. By *A. Todd Brown* of Keith, 1904–5.

WAR MEMORIAL, far W end of High Street. By *A. Marshall Mackenzie & Son*, 1920–1; carved and built by *William Legge*, Fochabers. Sited on the broad, grassy island in front of the West Lodge to Gordon Castle (*see* below). Grand settings demand a grand scale and this is a Roman Doric column over 8 m. high, with a large, stylized flame finial.

WILSON MEMORIAL, across from the war memorial. By *W. Kirkland Cutlar* of Forres, 1894–5; fabricated by *John Whitehead & Sons*. It commemorates Major Allan Wilson of Fochabers, who died in battle in South Africa in 1893. Hexagonal Gothic fountain with alternating tiers of polished grey (Aberdeen) and red (Peterhead) granite.

DESCRIPTION

HIGH STREET bisects Fochabers in a long straight line W–E. The first building in the town proper (on the l.) is the GORDON ARMS HOTEL, opened 1803, its original block of two storeys and three bays built 1777–9. Doorpiece with two engaged, fluted Doric columns. Across the street, a late C18 house (No. 89) of three bays, the r. given a new shopfront in the early C19 with panelled doors, aproned windows and fleur-de-lys jamb capitals. Protuberant scrolly skewputts. Three houses of *c.* 1800 then follow, displaying the solid, well-proportioned homogeneity that typifies the entire town. After them is the former UNION BANK OF SCOTLAND (now Bank of Scotland), *c.* 1860 and likely by *William Henderson*, their usual architect. High Street then broadens out into THE SQUARE, laid out by *John Baxter* in 1775–6 with the portico and lofty steeple of his new church (*see* above) as the anchor on the S side. He flanks this with two fine mirrored buildings: the MANSE on the r., 1788, and the former TOWN HALL and SCHOOL to the l., *c.* 1792. In front of the church is a grand cast-iron FOUNTAIN of 1878 by *George Smith & Co.* (*Sun Foundry*) of Glasgow, to commemorate the introduction of piped water to Fochabers. Wide octagonal outer basin, a central column with vigorously rendered acanthus leaves, four golden cherubs, each holding an oar and lounging on a horizontal urn with waterspout, two bowls above. The square's remaining sides are lined with late C18 and early C19 houses, mostly two-storeyed and three-bayed, and again with a pleasant uniformity.* No. 18 (in the NW corner) dates from *c.* 1800 and is the best proportioned, now nicely harled in pink with margins painted black. At the

*No. 22 (W side just above High Street) is a late C19 interloper, but incorporating an earlier core.

top of The Square is an exuberant iron LAMP of 1906, with three arms of sinuous scrollwork.

DUKE STREET then extends N to the façade of the Gordon Chapel (*see* Churches, above), directly facing the parish church. Just before it, ST MARGARET'S (the chapel's former parsonage), built 1837–8 around a late C18 core. It is, surprisingly, the work of *William Robertson* – decidedly un-classical with sharp gables and Tudor hoodmoulds. Opposite, THE WHITE HOUSE, late C18, two storeys and three bays with a single-storey service block off the N gable. Two-storey wing added to the rear *c.* 1825 forming an L-plan, its outermost bay enriched with larger windows. Nice circular stair-tower with conical roof in the N re-entrant angle.

High Street continues E from the centre of The Square, including an unassuming three-bay cottage on the S side with the year 1776 carved on the underside of its door lintel. The initials J. A. stand for James Allan, one of the new town's earliest tenementers. On the opposite side, the former ABERDEEN TOWN AND COUNTY BANK by *James Duncan*, 1878. Two storeys of good tooled ashlar with V-channelled quoins. Central door (formerly to the agent's house) with a big cornice on foliate scrolled brackets. Tall first-storey windows (the r. tripartite) with moulded architraves and cornices. Beyond the former Pringle Memorial Church is the WHITE LODGE, built as the Free Church manse by *Alexander Tod*, 1847–9. Two storeys and three bays with harling and contrasting ashlar dressings. Pilastered doorpiece and flanking tripartite windows, all shallowly advanced under a continuous blocking course. Three gableted dormers through the wall-head above. A single-storey former school forms a T-plan to the rear. It is *c.* 1830 and probably by *William Robertson*. Before the addition it was fronted by a tetrastyle colonnade and pediment.

EAST STREET crosses High Street. To the N its vista nicely ends at the former EAST LODGE of Gordon Castle, a fine two-storey octagon with bracketed eaves, gabled outshuts, a pedimented porch and lying-pane glazing. Just in front of it on the W side (and also in MAXWELL STREET), two rows of three ESTATE COTTAGES of *c.* 1890, each with an off-centre door under a catslide wooden canopy. Quatrefoil bargeboarding on the gables, the apex finials now missing. They are of the model type with outbuildings (for washhouse etc.) in the back yards.

SOUTH STREET features some of the town's finest buildings, including St Mary's church (*see* Churches above). W of Westmorland Street and set back is ROSSLYN HOUSE (No. 42), *c.* 1830. Two storeys and three bays of mixed rubble with long, rectangular windows, the ground-floor ones set under shallow relieving arches. Rather unusual glazing with big, square panes. Central porch of *c.* 1840, square with angle pilasters and good Greek key ornament. Next door, part of the former front wall of the original FREE CHURCH (of 1843–4 by *Alexander Tod*) is preserved as the garden wall of KIRKVILLE, a house of *c.* 1800 with pedimented ashlar doorpiece. Inside the drawing room and dining room, original marble slips from chimneypieces designed by *Robert Adam c.* 1770 for Northumberland House, London. The chimneypieces were moved here in 1947 from Syon House but are now at Dipple House (Mosstodloch). Dipple's early C19 painted timber chimneypieces have been given in exchange. S into CHARLOTTE STREET where TIGH-AN-AULT (W side) is an Arts and Crafts house of *c.* 1924 (probably by *J. & W. Wittet*). Rubble walls with broad piended dormers just breaking the wall-head, off-centre doorpiece with a depressed segmental arch and wide crenelle. Largely unrestored interior, the former drawing room with a high panelled dado and good chimneypiece with glazed cabinet in the overmantel.

THE OLD MANSE, off West Street. 1822–3, probably by *William Robertson*. Harled, symmetrical two storeys and three bays over a raised basement. Pilastered doorpiece.

SPEYBANK HOUSE, off West Street. Harled, handsome house of multiple builds. The tall rear section is the original from the early to mid C19.

BELLIE BURIAL GROUND, 2.2 km. NNE. Site of the church dedicated to St Peter, first recorded here in the mid C12, when it was a dependency of Urquhart Priory (*see* p. 754). Abandoned in 1798 for the new parish church (*see* above). All that remains is a flat-gabled fragment of the S wall in the centre of the burial ground, with a memorial to minister William Annand †1699.* Armorial panel with helm and mantling. Around this, to the r. of the church fragment, a horizontal slab for William Saunders †1663, claiming (albeit incorrectly) that he was the first 'pastor' of Bellie after the Reformation and the 'errors of the Roman church'. Latin inscription under a big crest with the initials W. M. A. – Along the S wall, the impressive GORDON MAUSOLEUM by *William Robertson*, 1824–5, a peripteral square colonnade of Ionic columns, each side tetrastyle. One volute of the corner capitals is angled out, just as Vitruvius would have dictated. Raised armorial panels in the centre of the E and W sides with swagged urn finials. Simple rectangular sarcophagi for Jean Christie †1824, wife of the 4th Duke of Gordon, and Adam Gordon †1834. – On the W wall, a pedimented MEMORIAL to George Muirhead †1928, commissioner to the Gordon Richmond estates, and his wife Agnes Clay †1898, both of Speybank House. Two portrait busts, the r. one fine alabaster work by *D. W. Stevenson*.

DUCHESS OF RICHMOND MONUMENT, 3.1 km. ESE, summit of Whiteash Hill. Nestled deep in the forest, although tree felling in 1991–2 reopened spectacular views to the N and NW. Tall rubble pyramidal cairn, about 9 m. high, built 1892 in memory of Frances Harriet, Duchess of Richmond and Gordon †1887.

*Excavations in 2003 revealed that the footings of the wall continued at least another 10 m. to the W. The rectangular manse, rebuilt 1720–8, was located just to the WNW.

OLD SPEY BRIDGE, 0.9 km. NW. A ferry is documented from at least the mid C13, hence the crossing's former name Boat of Bog. The first bridge, allowing the Spey to be crossed on the Inverness to Aberdeen road, was by *George Burn* of Fochabers, 1801–4.* Two of its four arches survive, the rings of hugely channelled ashlar with a big blind oculus in the central spandrel. The others were swept away in 1829 and replaced with a single wooden span by *Archibald Simpson*, 1831–2, in turn reconstructed in cast iron by *James Hoby & Co.* in 1853. Long, segmental arch of three ribs; cruciform lattice grids topped by round-headed arches. Road deck by *James Abernethy & Co.*, 1912. Closed to vehicles 1972. Former TOLL HOUSE on the W bank at Inchberry Road, 1805 by *Burn*, whose initial proposal of a Gothic style was resisted by the duke. Sympathetically extended *c.* 1982.

NEW SPEY BRIDGE just to the N. 1969–72. Two steel box girders by *Scottish Development Department (Roads Division)*.

Former FOCHABERS TOWN STATION (now DOUGLAS LODGE), 1 km. NW across the Spey in Inchberry Place. 1893 by *Murdoch Paterson* for the Highland Railway branch line from Orbliston (*see* Fochabers High Station, Mosstodloch). Converted to dwellings, *c.* 1970. Single-storeyed, the ends with crowstepped gables flanking the columned platform shelter (now glazed).

GORDON CASTLE

1 km. NNE

Until 1952 Gordon Castle was one of the greatest country houses in the north of Scotland but it was then reduced to a disjointed fragment of its once herculean extent – before the demolitions it was the longest domestic façade ever built in Britain, at 250 m. longer even than Wentworth Woodhouse in Yorkshire.

The site, called Bog o' Gight (or Windy Bog), was a defensive stronghold from at least the early C14 with a chapel founded in 1374 dedicated to the Virgin. George Gordon, the 2nd Earl of Huntly, took over the estate in 1449 and built a long, rectangular hall house, evidently completed just before his death in 1501. The 6th Earl carried out a frenzy of additions and improvements, probably beginning *c.* 1586 when this became the Gordons' principal seat – an attempt to distance the family from the turbulence surrounding Huntly Castle (S Aberdeenshire). The earl was created Marquess of Huntly in 1599, a date formerly recorded on the buildings of the castle, proving that his work here ran roughly in tandem with the 'New Warke' at Huntly *c.* 1602.

In 1656, Richard Franck praised the Bog o' Gight for its 'lofty and majestic towers and turrets that storm the air, and seemingly make dents in the very clouds'. That is confirmed by Slezer's drawing of 1672, which shows an ostentatious moated Renaissance palazzo-cum-chateau, reminiscent of Amboise. In fact, the

*The bridge is often mistakenly attributed to *Thomas Telford*. Although Telford submitted a design for consideration, his proposal was rejected.

Gordon Castle.
Engraving by John Slezer, *c.* 1672

drawing represents a conventional, if much tarted-up, Z-plan tower house, with large towers aligned diagonally at the NW and SE corners and a smaller, lower, one at the SW with the hall block in the centre, its core probably late C15 but surrounded by the Marquess's numerous additions. At first floor on the S and W fronts are loggias with arches both trefoiled (W) and round-headed (S). Such features are very unusual in Scottish castles and may have been inspired, as Charles McKean has suggested, by the Gordons' close connections with Spain. An additional building extends N and there was another to the E forming a double pile, of which Slezer depicts the long, faceted roof of its stair-tower. Had it survived, Gordon Castle would now be far better known than Craigievar (Aberdeenshire: South) as the *locus classicus* of Scots Renaissance splendour.

By the mid C18, the castle was in poor condition and Alexander, 4th Duke of Gordon, decided to rebuild on an even more massive scale. *John Adam* provided a design in 1764 (in consultation with the duke's surveyor, *Abraham Roumieu*), but in 1769 the palm went to the lesser-known *John Baxter* of Edinburgh, whose next two decades were consumed with building the new castle as well as the new town of Fochabers. Only the SE tower of the old castle was retained – apparently at the duke's insistence – as a totem of the Gordons' antiquity and power and remodelled to form the centrepiece of Baxter's new symmetrical façade, forty-eight bays in total and *c.* 173 m. from E to W, with the four-storey block incoporating the old tower, flanked by two-storey links to two-storey pavilions and two-storey quadrangles for the stables etc. Completed in 1783, the house was in the rather generic 'Castle Style' popularized by Adam (cf. Darnaway (q.v.)) but the gargantuan scale – and the need to retain the SE tower – perhaps left little room for architectural finesse.

After the 5th (and final) Duke of Gordon died in 1836, the estate was inherited by the 5th Duke of Richmond, Charles Lennox, whose seat (as now) was Goodwood House, West

Sussex. He adopted the name Gordon-Lennox and the 6th Duke became in addition the 1st Duke of Gordon of the second creation. After the 7th and 8th Dukes died in quick succession (in 1928 and 1935), the 9th Duke was forced to sell off the castle to meet double death duties. The building fell into disrepair but was bought back after the Second World War by one of the 7th Duke's grandsons, Lt.-Gen. Sir George Gordon Lennox. As so often in the mid C20, the decision was made to save the building by knocking most of it down in 1952–3. More demolitions followed in 1961–6, when the remaining buildings were restored in large-scale operations by *W. Schomberg Scott*. The Marquess's tower – so carefully preserved by Baxter – survives as an isolated folly; the former E wing and its service court is now free-standing, converted by Scott into a medium-sized country house in its own right; detached to the W is a fragment of the W pavilion and former stable court, now in agricultural use.

The core of the 'Bog of Gight' TOWER is still recognizable as good late C16 work. Six storeys on a square plan, the lower two floors refaced by Baxter in light ashlar to match his additions, of which just one two-storey bay to the l. remains, with rectangular window below a round-headed one at first floor with raised keystone and imposts and a bracketed cornice above that. The S door also remodelled with a roll-moulded, round-headed arch. The tower's upper storeys are browner ashlar, each of the four floors delineated by a string course (the upper one cable-moulded) and originally with rusticated quoins, removed *c.* 1700. Running down the centre is a strip of masonry with a row of Baxter's regularized, twelve-pane windows, replacing the shallow four-storey oriel visible in Slezer's drawing. Crenellated parapet around the top, three of the upper corners with glazed tourelles corbelled out over bands of cable and rope. They are reminiscent of the slightly later (*c.* 1602) glazed oriels lining the top of the Marquess's additions at Huntly. Each is topped by a diagonally set viewing platform with angle crenellations. Flat, rectangular stair-tower in the NW corner, which Slezer shows with a balustrade, no doubt serving a rooftop platform. In the tower's E face two late C16 windows with chamfered margins, a little slit-window and a strip of moulded corbelling, but the E door and the rest dates from alterations by *J. & W. Wittet* in 1970–1, when a large farm court was added to the rear, its footprint following the approximate size of the original tower house and with stout cone-roofed circular tower in the NW corner. Within the court, at the base of the tower remains of a pointed rubble vault, now blocked, associated with the tower's cellar. Also remnants of a spiral staircase to the l., also blocked but accessed via the E door of 1970–1. Inside the tower some corbels at the top for the late C16 vault, two carved as grotesques. Three springers on top for a chamfered rib-vault. The minor C18 fittings in two rooms are almost all that survives of the interiors of Baxter's house.

The present HOUSE, as has been said, is the former E pavilion and service court, its S elevation to the garden showing the stylish but rather plain homogeneity that once characterized Baxter's entire castle. The main part is two storey and seven bays, the central three slightly advanced. Two rows of rectangular windows with moulded architraves, the first-floor ones longer and given raised keystones. Twelve-pane glazing, the three in the upper centre removed by *Archibald Simpson* after a fire in 1827.* Crenellated parapet over a rounded corbel table; platform-piended roof with eight corniced chimneystacks. The W front is nearly identical but was originally attached to a narrow corridor link to the main block, shown by the scarring of the masonry. The central pedimented doorpiece was inserted by Scott. The N façade matches the S but was reconfigured in 1961–5 as the new entrance front, again with pedimented doorpiece. Off to the N are early to mid-C19 GATEPIERS topped by eagles. The interior was first remodelled after the fire by Simpson in 1827 and again by Scott, who re-set in the public rooms four excellent Adam-style chimneypieces, designed by Baxter, retrieved from the destroyed central block. It has a rectangular lobby leading to an octagonal atrium with round-headed arcades, each set on gently canted ashlar piers. The Billiard Room beyond was the Duchess's Sitting Room *c.* 1781 and later the library. A curved staircase of 1965 leads from the hall to a top-lit octagonal Drawing Room, the only domestic interior by Simpson to have survived in Moray. Two pairs of fluted columns with lotus-leaf capitals and curling, gilt fronds of acanthus. White marble chimneypiece with swags and the three Graces on the mantel; doors carved with subtle, attenuated Greek key ornament, Simpson's signature motif.‡ In the Sitting Room to the S, another good chimneypiece with fluted mantel and margents on the jambs.

The crenellated E SERVICE WING is slightly lower, six bays on the N and S fronts with the far end wider and minimally advanced. Round-headed ground floor windows (again with keystones and block imposts), square ones above. Long corbelled cornice below crenellation. In its E wall is an elliptical arch to the court (originally containing larders, a fishhouse and scullery) flanked by glazed, key-blocked oculi and dividing it from an outer court for the bakehouse (dem. *c.* 1952). This outer court is fronted on the S by Simpson's ORANGERY of *c.* 1830, now much decayed but under restoration by *Annie Kenyon Architects (aka)*. Wide, panelled pilasters and full-height windows with lying-pane glazing. At the entrance to the outer court two gatepiers with ball finials of *c.* 1783.

Much less remains of the W WING, which was designed by Baxter as the stables and coachhouse but converted into a

*Part of Simpson's general involvement on the policies and at Fochabers over the next decade (*see* below).

‡ cf. the gallery and pews at Bellie Parish Church, Fochabers (*see* p. 616).

Home Farm by *Schomberg Scott* (with additional work by the *Wittets*, *c.* 1973–4). The E bay retains only the quoin of *Baxter*'s main pavilion, the rest of it dem. *c.* 1962 and replaced by a poor, one-bay facsimile, in breeze block rendered as ashlar, with basket-headed arch entrance. Scott also roofed over the former stable court. Some elliptical arches still *in situ* from the late C18 along with tall, rounded niches (originally the backs of cattle pens) in the S wall.

In the formal garden SE of the orangery is a fine FOUNTAIN, assembled *c.* 1842 from fragments, e.g. the plinth made of four heraldic panels from the C16 to the early C18, one dated 1594. Two coronets, one helm and a collection of Gordon monograms. It sits on four early C19 posts carved with grapevine; small C18 block above carved with masks and supporting a shallow, scalloped basin.

There were extensive formal gardens S of the house in the C18 but these were swept away to create the present parkland setting, probably designed by *Thomas White*, who received payments 1786–90. Of this period is the LAKE, 0.5 km. SW of the house, in the area of the old town of Fochabers, which had been cleared in 1776 when the new town (*see* above) was established. Its fine MARKET CROSS is still *in situ*, undated but probably mid C17. Tall Tuscan column, *c.* 3.3 m. high, with a fragment of jougs still attached. The WALLED GARDENS E of the lake are in two parts. The large kitchen garden was laid out in 1803–4, at *c.* 8.5 acres one of the largest in Scotland. High walls of English bond brickwork. The smaller pleasure garden adjoining to the NW is contemporary and in the middle of its N wall is LAKESIDE HOUSE built in 1800–1 as a pavilion and tea house. The architect was likely *Robert Burn*, who was then building the similar Cairnfield House (q.v.) for the Gordons of that ilk. Much-renewed exterior, its blocky first floor slate-hung. Venetian window to the W; wide, bowed window to the garden with blind sidelights, fluted pilasters and panelled aprons. Below it a French door, originally flanked by glazed vinery and conservatory ranges (dem. *c.* 1965). The interior is inventive, with a good interplay of geometric spaces – one small circular room on each floor inscribed within a cube, the side chambers nicely truncated by bowed walls. Tightly curved, cantilevered E staircase. The GARDEN HOUSE in the N wall of the larger garden was built 1811, also brick, an exceptionally rare material in Moray at this date. Two-storeyed with a wide, canted centre, the first-floor windows with low segmental heads under gently bowed roof-lines, each raised like little 'eyebrows' in the English manner. The garden is being restored to a new design by *Arne Maynard*, 2012.

QUARRY GARDEN, 0.8 km. NE. A magical setting, created in the early C19 from a red sandstone quarry. A huge elliptical concavity with terraced sides, now much decayed. The entrance is spanned by a BRIDGE, early to mid-C19 and in the centre is a former fountain with large circular basin of 1902. On the ridge to the S, foundations of a small hexastyle TEMPLE by *John*

Browne (built *c.* 1825, dem. *c.* 1963). Nearby is a former LODGE of 1825 by *William Robertson* with crenellated parapet and the front gently canted. Later alterations.

The main entrance is the WEST LODGE, 0.9 km. SW. By *Baxter*, 1791–2, theatrically set at the top of a broad triangular island, with curved side walls enhancing the perspective. Everything is to a large scale, but still only a hint of the monumentality that awaited visitors when they reached the castle. The gateway is crenellated with a tall arch in the centre, of polished ashlar, linked by screen walls to lodges, each with a window set in a shallow, round-headed panel. Their lower rear extensions are late C19 (r.) and *c.* 1966 (l.).

GORDON CASTLE FARM, 0.5 km. SE. Large quadrangular mains by *Archibald Simpson*, 1828–9. Its red harling makes it visible from quite a distance. – Former CATTLE COURT parallel to the N, also *c.* 1829 and former KENNELS, 130 m. NNE of *c.* 1803 in red sandstone pinned with slate, somewhat rebuilt in 1843 (now housing).

SWISS COTTAGE, 1.9 km. E. A traditional and charming Swiss chalet built in 1833–5 by the 5th Duke of Gordon, reputedly to persuade his Swiss-born head deer keeper, Jean Pierre Ansermet, to remain under his employ. Nicely restored by *LDN Architects*, 2011–12, and painted a delicious shade of red.

FORRES *0050*

The finest town in Moray. Forres is very likely the 'Varis' mentioned by the Roman cartographer Claudius Ptolemy in the mid C2. There is evidence of an early oval fort on top of Cluny Hill, and the monumental Sueno's Stone – one of the largest and most important Pictish monuments to have survived in Scotland – is proof of this area's importance in the C9 and C10. Forres was made a royal burgh in the reign of King David I and its status renewed by James IV in 1496. From the mid C12, the town was – along with Elgin (q.v.) and Inverness – one of three royal power bases protecting the all-important coastline of the Moray Firth.* A now-vanished castle was established at the W end and a long road (now the High Street) served as the main thoroughfare, with closes branching off at right angles.

Forres was destroyed by Alexander Stewart, the notorious Wolf of Badenoch in 1390 and subsequently rebuilt in timber; most of the houses were again rebuilt in stone in the C16. There was great prosperity from shipping in the C17, and the town had a booming trade with Scandinavia and southern Europe via its harbour at Findhorn (q.v.). Disaster struck in 1694 and the harbour was destroyed; although it was rebuilt, maritime trade

*Nairn was added to the royal burghs *c.* 1190 and Dingwall in 1226/7.

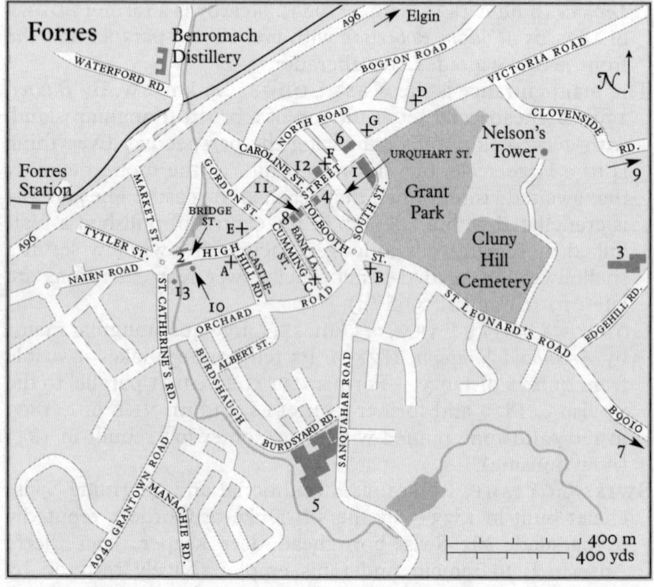

A Castlehill Church (former)
B Congregational Church (former)
C Free Church (former)
D St John (Episcopal)
E St Laurence (Parish Church)
F St Leonard
G St Margaret (R.C.)

1 Anderson's Primary School
2 Castle Bridge
3 Cluny Hill College
4 Falconer Museum
5 Forres Academy
6 Forres House Community Centre & Library
7 Leanchoil Hospital
8 Market Cross
9 Moray Steiner School
10 Thomson Monument, Castle Hill
11 Tolbooth and Courtroom
12 Town Hall
13 War Memorial

never recovered. Agricultural improvement brought renewed vigour in the mid to late C18, when new streets were added and many houses built. The arrival of the railway in 1856 also brought about a new era of wealth, as Forres was the junction of the Inverness & Aberdeen and the Inverness & Perth Junction Railways. Good hotels and the opening of a large hydropathic centre in 1854 made it a thriving tourist destination.

Much of Forres still retains the appearance of a fine, well-appointed Victorian town, with both church and public buildings of distinction and relatively well preserved. The skyline of the burgh – with its three 'towered' anchors of St Leonard's church, the tolbooth and especially the parish church of St Laurence – is among the most picturesque in Scotland.

CHURCHES AND CEMETERY

Former CASTLEHILL CHURCH, High Street. Built as the United Presbyterian church by *John Rhind*, 1870–1; now disused and in very poor condition. Good Dec, the over-large N façade with a five-light window derived from the chapter house of Elgin Cathedral (q.v.). Pierced balustrade above it and square, shafted porches below to the l. and r. Nave of five bays, the clearstorey with two-light, sharply gabled windows breaking into the roof space – a decidedly Continental effect. The church was originally a T-plan, the shallow, slightly lower chancel (with hall and vestry) added by Rhind's brother, *James R. Rhind*, in 1901–2. It has a rose window with Flamboyant tracery – one of the only occurences of that style in N Scotland. – Former MANSE to the rear, by *Rhind*, 1874–6.

Former CONGREGATIONAL CHURCH, Tolbooth Street. By *A. W. Bisset* (†1863), built 1865–7. E.E. box with shafted NW entrance. Royal British Legion Club since 1948.

Former FREE CHURCH, Cumming Street. Heavy, Italianate by *John Urquhart*, 1843–4. Pedimented entrance with four square piers. The missing bellcote resembled those of Urquhart's churches at Alves and Findhorn (qq.v.).

ST JOHN (Episcopal), Victoria Road. The nave is the plain, 38
rectangular church by *Patrick Wilson*, 1839–41. It was among the earliest Episcopal churches in Scotland. From 1842–4 there was a large remodelling by *Thomas Mackenzie*, who added the transepts and apse and encased the façade in the Italianate style. The result still looks tentative and *ad hoc*. S front of ashlar with pediment and rose window flanked by long panels. Three-bay arcaded portico advanced below it; very Tuscan *campanile* to the r., its upper two storeys with open, balustraded arcades and a pyramidal roof with bracketed eaves. Segmental lunettes in the aisle (originally an open arcade) and clearstorey with Lombardic tracery.

Simple interior, mostly as renovated by Mackenzie. Plain, flat walls with upper windows in lugged surrounds below a thick, moulded cornice. Very large coffers on the ceiling, each with a big roundel in the centre. Little dome over the crossing. – WALL PAINTINGS by *William Hole*. Last Supper, 1906–7 (in the apse); Noli me tangere, *c*. 1910 (E transept); Christ blessing children, 1911 (baptistery in the S end). In the transept, Christ and the Canaanite woman by *A.E. Haswell-Miller*, 1937 (copied from one of Hole's illustrations). – STAINED GLASS. Three windows in the apse (Nativity with shepherds, Crucifixion and Ascension), 1869. – S rose window, 1869. Angels in the diagonals.

RECTORY to the E, 1864–5 and also Italianate.

ST LAURENCE, High Street. Excellent Early Gothic by *John
Robertson*, 1902–6, built on the site of the medieval parish 47
church, which had been the seat of the archdeacon of Moray.*

*A church was probably located here since the C9, although the earliest documented building dated from *c*. 1275, erected by King Alexander III in memory of his queen, Margaret of England. This was replaced by a simple, bellcoted Georgian rectangle in 1774–6 (dem. 1904).

The church is very large, rectangular and externally aisleless, but saved from heaviness by its rippling silhouette of spires, which dominate the Forres skyline. Equally fine is the contrast between the rock-faced masonry of the walls and the finely tooled ashlar dressings, flowing like streamlined tubes around the windows and doors. Tall, gabled entrance on the E façade under four-light window with Geometric oculus. Tall, square tower to the r. with another entrance, diagonal buttresses and lofty octagonal stone spire. To the l., a lower tower with faceted, exaggeratedly bellcast roof. Around the corner on the S flank, a tall gable with two-light window in big plate tracery. Then, lower down, three bays of cusped, stepped lancets set in pointed super-arches – an allusion to the transepts at Pluscarden Abbey (q.v.). Row of small lancets below. Tower on the far end with pyramidal roof and another one in the NW corner to complement it. Good octagonal flèche in the middle of the roof ridge.

Spacious INTERIOR, quite restrained but with the same contrasts in masonry as outside. Pointed arcades (N side only) carried on high, smooth columns. Open pine ceiling with A-frame trusses: big, pierced semicircles in the centre over long, four-centred arch-braces. Cusped lights in the spandrels. – GALLERIES. Continuous on the E end, the front nicely curved as a shallow double ogee. On the N, each bay has a semi-elliptical front between the arcades. – COMMUNION TABLE by *Galbraith & Winton*. Polished marble shafts and mistakenly inverted Omega. – Similar octagonal PULPIT by *Hardman, Powell & Co.*, of Caen stone. – Marble FONT by *Stewart McGlashan & Co.* Square top carved with vigorous Romanesque interlace, based on the font at Dryburgh Abbey (Borders). – ORGAN by *E.H. Lawton*, 1905–6.

STAINED GLASS. Fourteen windows by *Douglas Strachan* – a surprising number, and indeed the largest collection of his works in Scotland. Two of them (the Nativity and the one in the baptistery) date from 1931; all the rest were dedicated in 1939. They are outstanding in every way: luminously colourful, with extremely saturated hues and a swirling verve that amplifies their psychogical power. S wall, upper level (E to W): Mary Magdalene and Christ, angel at the empty tomb, supper at Emmaus, Crucifixion, Christ washing the disciples' feet; Christ healing the blind, preaching in the Temple, baptism in the Jordan; Nativity with Magi on the l. and shepherds on the r.; Annunciation flanked by Isaiah's vision and David playing the harp (the latter with especially brilliant colouring). – Single lights on the lower level (E to W): St Ninian; St Laurence (with the Forres coat of arms below); St Columba. Next, six acts of mercy from Matthew 25:35–6: 'I was in prison'; 'I was sick'; 'I was naked'; 'I was a stranger'; 'I was thirsty' (with wonderful blue, green and turquoise); 'I was hungry'. The baptistery window shows 'Suffer the little children'. – Utterly failing to compete are two windows by *Percy Bacon Bros*, 1921–2. W gable: Courage with broken sword, Christ the comforter,

Victory and upper vesica with the burning bush. – E gable: St Peter, Christ as the Good Shepherd and Redeemer, and St Paul.

The CHURCHYARD was cleared of most of its monuments in 1974–5, including its early C19 mort house. Collection of HEADSTONES remaining on the N side. Channelled, corniced GATEPIERS to High Street, *c.* 1776, made for the previous church. Renewed ball finials.

ST LEONARD, High Street. Splendid Dec by *Ross & Macbeth*, 1901–3, as the United Free High Church. Triple-gabled entrance with stiff-leaf shafts and traceried doors; roundels in the spandrels with 'Nec tamen' and dove with olive sprig. Trio of cusped, two-light windows above and then a frieze of diagonal, blind quatrefoils climbing up the gable. To the l., a lower bow (for the gallery stairs) protruding like an apse. On the r. side, a whimsical, rather Viollet-le-Duc-esque tower, its upper stage topped by corbelled octagonal tourelles, gargoyles and crenellated parapet. Tall, octagonal stone spire above it with gableted lucarnes around the base.

Spacious interior on a T-plan with coomb ceiling panelled in squares and octagons. Quasi-hammerbeam braces beneath with long elliptical centres and pierced, cusped lights in the spandrels. – Deep U-plan GALLERY carried on quadruple-shafted piers with colossal stiff-leaf capitals. The front sweeps around in a delicious, sinuous, serpentine arc. – Semi-octagonal wooden PULPIT with cusped panelling and more good stiff-leaf. – Two CHAIRS with crocketed, gableted back-boards. One tympanum carved with the burning bush and the other with spinning mouchettes. – Big canted ORGAN CASE by *Norman & Beard*, 1903 (console removed, 2001). – HALL, 1910–11, also by *Ross & Macbeth*.

ST MARGARET (R.C.), High Street. By *John Wittet*, 1924–7. Little four-bay nave with trefoil-headed lights and stepped pyramidal pinnacles. Slightly lower chancel with St Laurence on the E gable. – Original wooden ALTAR with back-board and small tabernacle. – STAINED GLASS. Roundel of St Margaret (E end); Nativity with Sts Columba and Theresa (nave), bad; Pietà with St John and Mary Magdalene, 1927 (W end). – Original PRESBYTERY to the NW, 1930 by *R.B. Pratt*.

CLUNY HILL CEMETERY, Cluny Hill. A romantic and dream-like setting, nestled in a terraced bowl of the hill and surrounded by thick woodlands. Original (W) section laid out by *John Urquhart* in 1849–50; extensions in 1868–70 and by *Charles C. Doig*, 1884–90 and 1910–12. – Former KEEPER'S LODGE in the SW corner, 1870.

PUBLIC BUILDINGS

Former AGRICULTURAL HALL, Tytler Street. By *A. & W. Reid*, 1867, built as a corn exchange and cattle market by the Forres Agricultural Joint Stock Co. Ltd. Large but simple basilican façade with three attenuated arched windows and chimneystacks on the gable ends. Entrance hoodmould carved by *Thomas Goodwillie* with bull's head (keystone), ram's head and corn sheaf with root vegetables. Good interior with three-sided gallery, cast-iron balustrade and stencilled fascia with a charming procession of animals, birds and wheat.

ANDERSON'S PRIMARY SCHOOL, corner of High Street and South Street. By *William Robertson*, 1823–4, endowed by Jonathan Anderson of Glasgow for education of children from Forres, Kinloss and Rafford (qq.v.). Prim, Neoclassical façade of five bays, the centre minimally advanced with three tall arched panels under a pediment. Above, a Gibbsian steeple with square clock base and tall, octagonal spire – a version of that at Bellie Church, Fochabers (*see* p. 616). Excellent dragon weathervane. Arched boys' and girls' entrances to the l. and r. Ranged out behind them – and completely compromising the building's original proportions – is a long extension by *John Wittet*, built for Forres Academy in 1924–6. Fluted Roman Doric GATEPIERS to High Street with draped urn finials, *c.* 1824.

CASTLE BRIDGE, Bridge Street. By *Peter Fulton*, 1907–8, and engineered by *William Roberts*.* Two segmental arches of channelled ashlar over the Burn of Mosset. Crenellated pepperpots in the four corners; central turret on the N carved with the burgh arms.

CLUNY HILL COLLEGE, off Edgehill Road. Opened as a hydropathic establishment in 1865; now a satellite 'campus' of the Findhorn Foundation (*see* p. 614). Very long and quite dull, the Dutch-gabled original complex begun 1863 by *A. W. Bissett*. Sub-Italianate W wing by *John Forrest*, 1896–7, with further additions in 1905–7 by *Ross & Macbeth*.

Former DRILL HALL, High Street. Now the Territorial Army Centre. By *Charles C. Doig*, 1909–10, with good carving of stag's head and scroll.

120 FALCONER MUSEUM, Tolbooth Street. Fine Graeco-Italianate Renaissance by *A. & W. Reid*, 1868–70, partially built from bequests by Hugh Falconer (renowned botanist, geologist, paleontologist and evolutionary biologist). On the N façade, a tetrastyle Roman Doric portico with triglyph architrave and mutuled cornice. Tripartite window above topped by rosette frieze and pediment with portrait bust of Falconer. Anthemion acroterion above; corniced blocking course with big, garlanded ball finials. The ground floor has semicircular shell ornament with keystones carved as eminent scientists by *Thomas Goodwillie*: Georges Cuvier, Sir Isaac Newton, Edward Forbes, James Watt, etc. Six bays on the W flank, the first floor with two-light pilastered and shafted windows punctuated by spiral nook-shafts. Band course below with Vitruvian scroll.

*Replacing an earlier bridge by *John Smith* of Forres, 1795 (widened in 1823 and rebuilt *c.* 1832 after the Muckle Spate). A bridge on this site is first documented in 1607.

FORRES ACADEMY, Burdsyard Road. By *Alan Reiach, Eric Hall & Partners*, 1969–70. Geometric grid of white panels in black frames. Four-pane windows.

FORRES HOUSE (COMMUNITY CENTRE & LIBRARY), High Street. Brutalist complex by *G. R.M. Kennedy & Partners*, 1972–3.

GRANT PARK, Victoria Road. Formerly the policies of Forres House, gifted to the people of Forres by Sir Alexander Grant in 1922. The house, built *c.* 1810 and much remodelled in 1856 by Sir William Cumming of Altyre (q.v.), sat in the NW corner but burnt down in 1970, its position now marked by a SUNKEN GARDEN designed by *Alistair Sinclair*, *c.* 1972. – For the former EAST LODGE, *see* p. 640.

LEANCHOIL HOSPITAL, St Leonards Road. Designed by *John Rhind* in 1889 and completed after his death by *H. Saxon Snell*, 1892. Large Neo-Jacobean complex on a pavilion plan, the main block with a large pair of shaped gables. Square clock tower above with crenellated parapet and pyramidal roof. Extension on the far r. for a maternity wing, 1939. – L-plan LODGE at the W entrance, 1892, likely also by Rhind.

MARKET CROSS, High Street. By *Mackenzie & Matthews*, 1843–4, on the site of the mercat cross, which was recorded *c.* 1830 as a rather low, hexagonal shaft. Good Dec design of four stages, *c.* 10.7 m. high, with four buttresses on the bottom around a free-standing central pier. On the second stage, the cardinal directions have corbelled empty niches with ogival hoodmoulds; octagonal, crocketed pinnacles in the diagonals connected via little flyers. Fragments of a small wooden Gothic parapet above.

MORAY STEINER SCHOOL, off Clovenside Road. Originally Drumduan, an elegant single-storey villa of *c.* 1830 with fine views over Findhorn Bay. Big, bad alterations in 1911–12 by *W.L. Carruthers & Alexander*, who added the entire first floor and its piended, soffited roof. – OUTBUILDING to the ENE with re-set datestone of 1759 and initials for James Warrand, who sold the estate in 1785.

NELSON'S TOWER, Cluny Hill. By *Charles Stewart*, 1806–12; 106,
restored after a fire by *John Forrest*, 1900. Gothic folly perched *p. 636*
on the highest point of Forres – and one of the earliest monuments in Britain dedicated to Lord Nelson. Tall, three-storey harled octagon with lancets on each face (blind on the ground floor). Spectacular panoramic views from the corbelled, crenellated parapet.

STATION, on the A96. 1955, of red brick with a front-glazed, flat lantern. The rinceau iron brackets on the platform (cast by *P. & W. MacLellan* of Glasgow in 1876) are survivors of the original station, designed by *Joseph Mitchell & Co.* in 1862–3.*

*Once an important junction of the Inverness & Aberdeen and Inverness & Perth Junction Railways.

Forres, Nelson's Tower.
Aquatint by William Daniell, 1821

THOMSON MONUMENT, Castle Hill. See Description, below.

TOLBOOTH, corner of High Street and Tolbooth Street. Good Baronial by *William Robertson*, 1836–40, replicating many of the features of the original tolbooth here. Square tower of three stages, entered on the W via a deeply splayed, round-headed arch. Small windows above under a stepped hoodmould; crenellated parapet with corner tourelles and then a narrower clock stage with tourelles topped by stone candlesnuffers. Very lofty octagonal louvred belfry with fine ogival bellcast roof and gilded weathercock of *c.* 1946. Former COURTROOM to the r. (above the pend) with two lofty arched windows. Two more bays to the High Street, the last gently crowstepped with diagonal square bartizans. Long nine-bay front to Tolbooth Street, the last four formerly the GAOL, built by *John Urquhart* in 1849–50 and replacing an earlier one of *c.* 1720.

Inside, a good open-well, cantilevered staircase with wispy balusters. Inside the courtroom, a coffered ceiling carried on pilasters and stained glass window of St Laurence donated in 1848. Original cells and fittings in the jail.

TOWN HALL, High Street. Originally the Masonic Lodge and Assembly Rooms by *Archibald Simpson*, 1827–9; sold to the Mechanics' Institute in 1855 and long rear hall added by *John Rhind* in 1882–4. From 1899–1901, Simpson's original façade was refronted in spectacular classical fashion by *John Forrest*, broadcasting the full confidence of Forres' prosperity in the Edwardian era.* His *pièces de résistance* are the monolithic,

*Simpson's front had arched recesses with Empire garlands (cf. his church of St Giles, Elgin) and a corniced parapet over four pilasters.

gleaming shafts of polished Peterhead granite which he applied in pairs, running like sentinels down both of his new storeys – columns in the centre and pilasters on the ends, the ground floor Roman Doric and the upper Ionic.

WAR MEMORIAL, SW of Castle Bridge. By *A. Marshall Mackenzie & Son*, 1920–2. Large bronze statue by *Alexander Carrick* of a helmeted Highland soldier standing at ease. Tall pedestal of rock-faced whinstone.

DESCRIPTION

1. Castle Hill and High Street

The Description begins at CASTLE HILL, originally the MOTTE of a royal fortalice built in the mid to late C12 and surrounded by large curtain walls from the C14 (now no trace above ground). A much earlier castle on the site is said to have been destroyed by the Danes *c.* 850 and another is recorded in 966. Pont's map of *c.* 1590 shows a three-storey tower house with stair wing, but by 1654 this had 'almost disappeared'. The rounded cone below (best seen from the W) has been much altered and the top levelled *c.* 1850 to form a park. At the W end the MONUMENT of 1857 to Dr James Thomson, surgeon, †1854 in the Crimean War. Very tall polished Peterhead granite obelisk, *c.* 19.2 m. high, by *Alexander Urquhart* of Elgin.

HIGH STREET leads E, still following the medieval plan established in the C12 with straight road and narrow closes branching off at right angles, as at Elgin (q.v.) and Edinburgh. The centre of the street swells outward in the centre, around the site of the former market and tolbooth. Virtually everything now visible post-dates the late C18, the buildings mostly two- or three-storeyed with a good mix of commercial and domestic, and of particular interest are the surviving Victorian shopfronts.

Outside the park gates (on the r.) is the gabled POST OFFICE with central bellcast dormer, 1910–11 by *Alexander Cattanach* of Kingussie. The former Castlehill Church follows (*see* Churches, above), now in an appalling state of decay. Three houses past Castlehill Road (with its crowstepped gable slightly jutting forward into the street) is No. 154, the oldest known building in Forres. Skewputt on the l. side dated 1668; bolection-moulded doorpiece and a pair of small windows with rounded, pillow-like surrounds. From here, the street opens out to the spectacular sight of St Laurence's church (*see* Churches, above), with the tolbooth beckoning in the distance. A little further down are the former WARDEN'S BUILDINGS, a pair of two-storey mirrored blocks built in 1808 with a fortune made in India. They are suavely proportioned with smoothly bowed corners straddling the lane – an effect that was later copied by *William Robertson* in The Square at Cullen (q.v.). Four bays on each to High Street and the court, the central pivot bowed and slightly recessed. After them is the former LONGVIEW HOTEL, eclectic Scots Renaissance by *John Rhind*, 1881–2, with nicely rambunctious sculpture by *Donald Macleod* of Inverness. Pair of two-storey elliptical oriels topped by big crowstepped gables with heraldic unicorn and lion; two dormers in the centre with C17-style triangular pediments and beasts crawling up the sides. Tourelles in the l. and r. corners with good finials on their conical roofs. On the second floor is a re-set datestone of 1730 from the previous building on the site.

The first house past Cumming Street, *c.* 1835, has a shopfront of 1934 with proto-Art Deco detailing, and here the road begins to widen towards the market cross and tolbooth. Just beyond are two mirrored houses of the late C18, each with a big Dutch nepus gable, the r. one formerly serving as both the North of Scotland Bank and the Town and County Bank, the l. having on the back of its pend a worn plaque carved with the burgh coat of arms, likely mid C17 and discovered during the construction of Castle Bridge (*see* Public Buildings, above). The two houses' dark brown stone is the perfect foil to the
117 gleaming masonry of the splendid BANK OF SCOTLAND, built as the Caledonian Bank by *Mackenzie & Matthews* in 1852–3. Five-bay Palladian palazzo, its ground floor with Roman Doric, pedimented porch and pilastered windows, all with triglyph architraves. First-floor windows topped by alternating triangular and segmental pediments, the capitals of the pilasters with crowned women carved by *Thomas Goodwillie*. Guilloche band course above and then smaller, square windows under a modillion cornice and balustraded parapet. The CLYDESDALE BANK beyond (by *William Robertson*, 1839, originally the British Linen Bank) is tamer, its outer bays minimally advanced with panel-aproned windows on the first floor. The darkly stentorian shopfront by *J. & W. Wittet*, 1938–9, shows just how much – and also, strangely, how little – architectural taste had changed in exactly one century. In the courtyard through the pend, a single-storey gig house and stable building of the early C19.

TOLBOOTH STREET then leads off to the r., its beginning formed into a small square with the regal, cerebral Falconer Museum (*see* Public Buildings, above) in the SE corner. In front is a lead FOUNTAIN of *c.* 1900 with nicely curved leaves on its two main tiers. Across the street is the RED LION HOTEL, originally three separate houses of the late C18, joined into a continuous façade in 1838, the date of its very wide shaped gable on the far r. with little flanking tourelles in genuflection to the tolbooth beyond. Next on the opposite side is the former NEW MARKET by *A. & W. Reid*, 1868–9, sprawling Italianate with pilastered, round-headed windows and three big pediments carried on channelled pilasters. Good cast-iron arcaded shopfronts as remodelled by *A. & W. Reid & Wittet* in 1893 with generous arched openings and little circles in the spandrels. Following this is BOYNE HOUSE, *c.* 1818 with a pilastered and corniced doorpiece, and then – recessed from the street and facing S – the former FREE CHURCH MANSE, *c.* 1845 and likely by *John Urquhart*. Pair of huge Dutch gables on the wall-head; rear extension forming a double pile, 1867. Back on the High Street, the buildings are homogeneous but much lower in quality. About halfway down (Nos. 52–58), the CO-OPERATIVE food store by *Law & Dunbar-Nasmith Partnership*, 1985–6, has jumbo anthemion and palmette railings re-set from the Queens Hotel of *c.* 1818, which it replaced. Nos. 22–24 (early C19) has a good shopfront of *c.* 1896 with Ionic pilasters; at the end of the street is Anderson's Primary School and, stretching beyond it, the pleasant green expanses of Grant Park (*see* Public Buildings, above).

The Description now returns to the W. Across the street and moving W reveals the little St Margaret's church followed by the arrestingly ugly Forres House; further down, St Leonard's church is followed by the Town Hall (*see* Churches or Public Buildings, above). Two buildings down from the Hall is the ROYAL BANK OF SCOTLAND, begun as the National Bank of Scotland by *William Robertson* in 1841 and completed after his death by *Thomas Mackenzie* in 1843 – likely the most restrained Neoclassical work attached to this architect who was to become the paradigmatic practitioner of the Baronial style. Channelled masonry on the ground floor; second and fifth bays minimally advanced under corniced blocking courses. At the corner of Caroline Street is the CARLTON HOTEL, 1900–2 by *Peter Fulton* – a rock-faced, Baronial bulwark with two canted oriels ending in voluted Dutch gables topped by swan-neck pediments. Bowed angle in the l. corner topped by a leaded, finialled dome. A short walk up Caroline Street and then a l. turn leads to HEPWORTH LANE, with four houses (Nos. 1–4) dating from *c.* 1780 to *c.* 1820, all beautifully restored *c.* 1985.

Back on High Street, the other building on the corner (Nos. 69–71) is by *John Urquhart*, 1845–6, its first and sixth bays framed by giant-order pilasters supporting block pediments. Next door to the l., five bays of *c.* 1835 (possibly by *William Robertson*), the l. side with a fine re-set Edwardian glass sign and segmental pediment for the ironmonger Pat Mackenzie. The next building (No. 83) has a nice gilt pestle-and-mortar sign over the door of the mid to late C19; three buildings down (No. 91) dates from *c.* 1835, with a good ashlar front and pediment over the central first-floor window. Three more buildings down (Nos. 101–105) is a combined shop and house of *c.* 1860, the centre dignified by an open pediment with modillion cornice and crowning acroterion. Next door, *c.* 1820 (possibly by *John Paterson*) has rock-faced rustication to the ground floor, a motif then fashionable in Edinburgh's New Town (cf. also Grange Hall, q.v.). The pend entrance leads to a stairwell with good cantilevered staircase and cast-iron teardrop balustrade. The plasterwork on its second-storey ceiling is excellent, and reminiscent of that at Invererne House (q.v.). Central rose with deeply undercut leaves and segmental border with Vitruvian scroll. Acanthus cornice over a frieze of Greek key. More good plasterwork in the two rooms on the first floor. Two houses down High Street (Nos. 117–121) are six bays dating from 1748, the front rendered with false ashlar below a central crowstepped dormer.

2. *East and south of the centre*

There are many fine VILLAS in Forres but only a few can be described here. On RUSSELL PLACE is SEA VIEW (No. 3), built *c.* 1883 by the mason *William Ross*, also a baillie of the burgh. Square tower in the re-entrant angle with a bellcast, pyramidal roof; wonderful, florid bargeboarding on the gables. VICTORIA ROAD continues E from High Street with a string of villas facing Grant Park. On the S side, beyond St John's church and its rectory (*see* Churches, above) is the former EAST LODGE of Forres House, 1858 by *William Lawrie*. Small three bays with pedimented Roman Doric portico and channelled gatepiers with fleur-de-lys-finialled railings. The lane across leads down to ST RONAN'S, big Scots Renaissance of *c.* 1870 with octagonal chimneystacks and mansard roof topped by Gothic brattishing.

Next (and also recessed from the road) is the pink-harled CLUNY, *c.* 1835 and likely by *William Robertson*.* Single storey and three wide bays, the recessed centre with a big, half-modillioned pediment over Doric columns *in antis*. Further down on the l. is the RAMNEE HOTEL, sprawling Arts and Crafts of 1907 with dummy timber-framed gables, crenellated porch and bellcast ogival domelet flanked by dormers (one catslide and two piended). Next comes THE PARK, big crowstepped Baronial of 1877, built for John Burn, the former Provost of Forres. Advanced entrance tower-cum-caphouse with l. turret corbelled out under an attenuated candlesnuffer roof. C17-style triangular dormerheads with beasts climbing up to thistle and rose finials.

ST LEONARDS ROAD runs along the S side of Grant Park and the foot of Cluny Hill, with many good villas silhouetted against the rising woodland. No. 19 (TOWERSIDE) dates from the late C18, two storeys and three bays harled in pink. On the opposite corner (with Alexandra Terrace) is ARDOYNE, *c.* 1890, with stilted gables and parapet fashioned like a miniature aqueduct. Further up on the l., THE ELMS (No. 29), late C18, is now the offices of LDN Architects. Piended two storeys and three bays with a pediment over the centre. Two houses down is RANDOLPH VILLA, *c.* 1866, rather fairytale-like Baronial with a full-height bay window on its crowstepped S gable. Turret with witch's-hat roof and charming round window corbelled out to the l. and r., respectively. A quick

*It is close in appearance to Hazelwood, near Craigellachie (*see* p. 514).

detour up Nelson Road leads to the pleasantly summery CATHKIN, 1905, very broadly piended with a front veranda and thick, glazed round tower on the r. with conical roof. Further down on St Leonards Road is the fine CLUNY BANK HOTEL, *c.* 1885, roughly L-plan with a crenellated Neo-Romanesque porch (including scallop capitals) in the centre. Diagonal square oriels corbelled up on the r. side, and all the gables decorated with wonderful, curvilinear Dec bargeboarding.

Further on, the road is lined with much larger villa-mansions of the early C20. Past Leanchoil Hospital (*see* Public Buildings, above) is NEWBOLD HOUSE (0.7 km.), built by *Peter Fulton* for Col. John Woodcock after he served in India and then made a fortune in tea. Heavy rock-faced Baronial, dated 1893 but actually built 1899–1901, the W porch with a depressed segmental arch carried on monolithic shafts of polished Peterhead granite. They have enormous quasi-stiff-leaf capitals, reminiscent of the Brobdingnagian carving at St Margaret's, Aberlour (*see* p. 503). On the E face, a crenellated bay window and a two-storey bow under conical stone roof. Two C17-style dormers. Stretching to the N, a fine glass conservatory by *Mackenzie & Moncur*. Inside, hollow cast-iron columns of extremely slender shafts with sunburst brackets in the spandrels. LODGE and pepperpot GATEPIERS also by Fulton, the latter carved with imitation fish-scale slates.

CATHAY HOUSE, 0.7 km. further out again, was built by *George Simpson* in 1887–8 for John Kyle, an engineer who had retired from China. Similar to Newbold House but freer, with more convincing Neo-Jacobean detailing. Crenellated E porch with tourelles; rounded three-stage tower behind corbelled into a crowstepped caphouse. Bowed, modillioned window to the r. Similar bay window on the S flank below broken segmental window head with finial; to the l., a corner drum tower with conical roof and Dutch gable with a canted oriel. Another quasi-tower house to the rear with crenellated parapet and open tourelles (both in the centre and the angles). Extending from it, a spectacular cast-iron CONSERVATORY, very probably by *Mackenzie & Moncur* (cf. Newbold House, above), and easily the best in Moray. Glazed arches along the front and tall, coved roof with raised central clearstorey of Paxtonian type. A glazed, gableted corridor links it to the house, and an outer W section was lost *c.* 1971. Kyle filled his house with exotic furnishings, and Cathay must have been the most shining example of Chinoiserie in Moray. These were sold in 1916, but a delightfully Orientalist gasolier remains in the dining room, where the bowed SW corner (set in the base of the drum tower) has the best plasterwork in the house. LODGE by Simpson, 1887–8, its rock-faced, torpedo-like GATEPIERS topped by capitals that come to a sharp point.

KNOCKOMIE HOTEL, 2.1 km. SSW off Grantown Road (A940). English Arts and Crafts villa, built for William Fraser by *W.H. Woodroffe* in 1913–14. Two storeys and three bays, the centre with a chamfered ashlar entrance below an alternating red and grey lintel course. Wide ends advanced and gabled (the l. one very bellcast) with first-floor windows under keystoned, segmental relieving arches. Multi-pane glazing and tall, free-standing chimneystacks facing the centre. Attached to the l. is a three-bay villa of *c.* 1830, also remodelled by Woodroffe. Wide chamfered angle on the l.; piended roof with big soffited eaves and two flat-roofed dormers with a catslide in between. Rear extension with a sympathetic NE front by *Law & Dunbar-Nasmith Partnership*, 1993.

Imposing but cosy ENTRANCE HALL with walls covered in big, square panelling. Cantilevered wooden staircase with diagonal square balusters and cubical newel finials. In the old house, a fielded-panelled segmental ceiling and cast-iron anthemion balustrade.

OTHER BUILDINGS

BENROMACH DISTILLERY (Gordon & MacPhail), 0.6 km. NW, Invererne Road. The smallest distillery in Speyside. By *Charles C. Doig*, 1898–9, to his usual E-plan and very similar to his design at Dallas Dhu (q.v.). Whitewashed MALT BARN in the N arm, unusually tall (three storeys) with twelve bays separated by pilaster strips. Stout, square base of the former KILN to the l. of it, shorn of its pagoda roof *c.* 1975. In the S arm (the bottom of the E), Doig's original single-storey OFFICES and FILLING STORE.

Tall, round CHIMNEY behind the still house, its red brick a fine contrast to the white of the other buildings. – Former DRYING STORE, *c.* 1920, converted into a VISITORS' CENTRE in 1998–9.

BRIDGE OF FINDHORN, 2.6 km. WSW, on the A96. By *Blyth & Blyth* (engineers), 1936–8, and a good example of interwar design.* Long segmental span of three huge steel trusses, each *c.* 91.4 m. long. Big X-lattice girders supporting the ends of the road deck. Concrete abutments with pilaster buttresses.

FINDHORN VIADUCT, 1.7 km. W. By *Joseph Mitchell*, 1856–8, for the Inverness & Aberdeen Junction Railway (ironwork by *William Fairbairn & Sons*, Manchester). Three box spans of wrought iron, *c.* 45.7 m. each. Good channelled masonry on the piers and crisp ashlar pylons with sunken panelling.

SUENO'S STONE, Findhorn Road, 1.2 km. NE. A remarkable example of early medieval carving dating to the C9–C10. The stone is a cross-slab around 6 m. high, carved from sandstone. On the front is an elaborately carved interlaced ring-headed cross with a group of figures below. The back is divided into four panels with almost one hundred individual figures

*It replaced a Gothic suspension bridge by *Capt. Sir Samuel Brown*, 1830–2, which in turn replaced a triple-arched bridge of *c.* 1799 that was destroyed in the floods of 1829.

depicted. The top panel includes figures on horseback, while the panel below contains figures with swords and spears engaged in battle, piles of human heads and decapitated bodies. The next panel includes a canopy or bridge, beneath which are several decapitated bodies, and the final panel shows further human figures. Various interpretations have been proposed for the battle scene represented on the stone. These have revolved around three main ideas: a battle between the Picts and the Scots; Viking conflict with the kings of Pictland/Alba; or a more specific battle in AD 967 at Forres when Dub, son of Máel Choluim, King of Alba, was killed and his body hidden under a bridge at nearby Kinloss.

INVERERNE HOUSE. *See* p. 662.

GARMOUTH 3060

First recorded as a trading centre in 1393. Garmouth (originally Garmach) was elevated to a burgh of barony in 1587 by Robert, 19th Laird of Innes, and – much to the annoyance of the burghers of Elgin – given a harbour, a mercat cross and two annual fairs. The town quickly grew prosperous, and by the end of the C18 it was one of the largest centres for timber trade in Scotland. Its harbour was largely destroyed in the floods of 1829 and never rebuilt. King Charles II landed in Garmouth after returning from exile in Holland and it was here that he was persuaded to sign the Solemn League and Covenant in 1650.

The village plan is labyrinthine and full of very narrow streets – a refreshing change from the usual regularity of Moray's planned settlements. Many of the houses are built of 'clay and bool', a mud-like mixture of mortar, stones and straw.

Former PARISH CHURCH, Church Street. Built as the Free Church by *A. & W. Reid*, 1845; converted into a house by *Martin Archibald*, 1992–3. A handsome classical job, the tall front with attenuated Italianate windows under a stepped, modillioned blocking course. Surprisingly lofty octagonal bell-tower above it. Over the l. and r. bays, vast recumbent consoles reminiscent of their uncle's work at Milton Brodie (q.v.).

GARMOUTH & KINGSTON VILLAGE HALL, Spey Street. Formerly the drill hall, converted from the early C19 Corff House by *Charles C. Doig* in 1905–6.

Former SCHOOL, School Brae. By *A. & W. Reid*, 1874–6, and a surprisingly early example of concrete construction. Contemporary newspapers described how more than 100 tonnes of cement were transported here from London and poured between wooden retaining walls (contractors, *Peter Bisset & Son* of Aberdeen). The result is large and looms over the village, the SE front with big tripartite windows and gables with blind oculi. Gableted bellcote on the r. flank. Low extensions to the rear by *J. & H. Marshall* of Fochabers, 1913.

In the older part of the village, a collection of simple but good buildings dating from the late C18 through the mid C19. At the corner of High Street and Spey Street, the Celtic-cross WAR MEMORIAL, 1920–1, designed by *John Wittet* and carved by *George Garrow* of Elgin. Across from it is THE CROSS, late C18 with V-channelled quoins, and LEMANACRE, with a fine early C19 walled garden and late C18 gatepiers (*ex situ*). Further down Spey Street is EASTFIELD, 1754, its front rendered in yellow and lined as ashlar. Two storeys and five bays, the outer pairs of windows tightly grouped around a wide centre. Shouldered doorpiece with pulvinated architrave and pediment. Beyond it is STAINSON HOUSE, early C18 and likely the oldest surviving building in Garmouth. Two storeys and three wide bays, harled over clay and bool.

Former WATER TOWER, School Brae. Prominently sited on high ground N of the village. Engineered by *Jenkins & Marr*, 1898–1901, to supply Garmouth and Kingston (q.v.). Decommissioned in 1988. Large, circular tower with conical slate roof (now whitewashed and coated in cement). It is one of the earliest examples in Scotland of reinforced concrete, and the partnership had worked on 'concrete and iron net-work foundations' as early as 1887.

Next to it are two large STANDING STONES, possibly the remains of a four-poster STONE CIRCLE of *c.* 1500 B.C. Between them is a recumbent stone split into two, perhaps a cist cover. They were likely part of a much larger monument.*

DELLACHAPLE, Innes Road. The best house in the village. Scots Georgian of *c.* 1820, single storey and three bays over a raised basement. Corniced doorpiece with two Roman Doric columns approached by a splayed flight of steps.

ESSIL BURIAL GROUND, 1 km. S. Partly circular (cf. Dipple, Mosstodloch) and on a pronounced raised mound, suggesting early occupation. A church dedicated to St Peter is first mentioned in the charters of Bishop Bricius between 1208 and 1215; by the mid C14 it was held by the treasurer of Elgin Cathedral (q.v.). The church was extended in 1655–6 but abandoned in 1732 for Speymouth church (Mosstodloch).

Railed, narrow BURIAL ENCLOSURE with PLAQUES for Ann Falconer †1866, Peter Falconer †1848 and family, and James Gordon †1765 and family. They are set within elliptical arches carried on panelled pilasters; corniced blocking courses above. – Parallel behind it is a short, detached WALL FRAGMENT, all that remains of the original church. TABLET on it for Elisbeth Fimester †1770 with 'ME MEN TO MORI' under a curved, semicircular pediment. – Seven TABLE TOMBS to the SE, C17 to C19 and arranged in two rows. Winged souls on the legs and two sets of mortality emblems.

Former SPEY VIADUCT, 0.8 km. ESE. Built for the Moray Coast Railway, 1883–6; closed 1968 and now pedestrianized for the

*The stones' antiquity has occasionally been questioned. Four-poster circles are indeed unusual in Scotland, but there is another example in Moray at Templestone (*see* p. 731).

Speyside Way. Designed by *Blyth & Cunningham* with *Patrick M. Barnett*, GNSR chief engineer; *Blaikie Brothers* of Aberdeen, contractors for ironwork. The constantly meandering course of the Spey demanded prodigious length.* In the centre, a mighty bowstring truss, 101.8 m., of wrought iron with lattice girders, still among the longest single spans in Scotland. Sweeping, segmental curve ending in big panelled, semi-octagonal turrets. Straight triple spans beyond them of 30.5 m., also latticed. Giant rock-faced columns underneath with thick torus capitals of Covennie granite.

GLENFIDDICH *see* DUFFTOWN

GLENLIVET B 1020

A thanage is recorded from the C11 but the site of the medieval village remains unknown. The Distillery is now the principal building, with just a few houses at Bridgend of Glenlivet, where the road crosses the Livet.

Former GLENLIVET PARISH CHURCH, Auchbreck. T-plan, the original section orientated N–S and located to the rear. Built 1825, replacing a timber meeting house of 1736. Lancet windows, some with Y-tracery and transoms inserted in 2004–5 when the church was converted to a house.‡ The S gable originally had just one bullseye, but the conversion added a very long pair of lancets with French doors on the bottom. Large, gabled W aisle added 1878–9, reorientating the church and creating a new entrance. Corbelled octagonal bellcote. Sensitively converted inside, based on a design by *Wittets Architects*. The good timber coomb ceiling and gallery of 1878–9 are intact. In the centre, a big rounded quarter-turn staircase of 2004–5 has treads made out of the former pews. – STAINED GLASS. Four windows by *Charles Florence*, 1956–69. A fifth is now at Glenlivet Distillery (*see* below). (Two others, *c.* 1957–9, are now in store.)

Former MANSE across the road to the SW, built 1825. Symmetrical E front of two storeys and three bays; canted bay window on the r. added by *Thomson*, 1903. Especially good harling. Short two-storey wing, also 1825, forming an L-plan to the rear. – Simple, single-storey STEADING (gig house, stable and byre) to the NNE, also *c.* 1825. Originally U-plan, the short lower arm demolished in the mid C20.

CEMETERY, Bridgend of Glenlivet. Site of the pre-Reformation Chapel of Dounan, the ruins of which were still visible in the late C19.

*Upon completion of the viaduct, the Spey was redirected to flow beneath the central span, but it later broke free to the E channel.

‡Central door inserted in 1878 and blocked *c.* 1965 (now covered by harling).

GLENLIVET PUBLIC HALL, 0.5 km. SE of Bridgend of Glenlivet on the B9008. Designed by *J. Taylor*, the Drumin factor, 1924–5, and given by Capt. Smith Grant of the Distillery. Five-bay piended rectangle with a trussed gable in the centre. Slightly advanced ends linked by a veranda under continuous swept roof.

THE GLENLIVET DISTILLERY (Chivas Brothers). Officially founded by George Smith in 1824 at Upper Drumin (*see* below), and the first distillery in Scotland to be legalized after the Excise Act of 1823. Relocated to the present site in 1858–9 with a large U-plan complex, now mostly modern and much expanded. Present VISITORS' CENTRE built as a second MALT BARN *c.* 1870 and converted *c.* 1980. Two storeys and five bays of flagstone rubble with plain rectangular buttresses. Perpendicular to the N, the vast PRODUCTION BLOCK (including still house and tun room) by *LDN Architects*, 2008–10, formerly occupied by three pagoda kilns. Big rectangle with glazed walls and gables; long raised lantern on the roof ridge with alternating louvres and windows. – Inside the mill room, a STAINED GLASS panel depicting local industry and prehistorical themes by *Charles Florence*, 1965, originally in Glenlivet Parish Church (*see* above).

Behind it (along the main road), the double-gabled N-facing OFFICE, the l. side of *c.* 1880 with ridge tiles and the r. of 1922–4 by *Charles C. Doig & Sons* with segmental hoodmould over the entrance and three bipartite dormers breaking the wall-head to the W. Dry-dashed. To the N are two ranges of WAREHOUSES, among the oldest in Scotland. The first two lower, *c.* 1858, the r. one originally double-gabled and made into one. Then four framed in cast iron with unusual windows with raised Gothic centres and flanking pie-wedge bullseye windows. The first has a rounded gable, the next three pointed and identical, 1880. – Row of workers' COTTAGES in a line to the SW, the first pair and the last one by *Charles C. Doig & Sons*, 1891 and 1902. – OLD DISTILLERY, 0.9 km. SW. Built 1824 but almost completely destroyed by fire in 1858. A ruined cottage (four bays with two gableted dormers) stands on the foundations of the original L-plan OFFICE and EXCISEMAN'S HOUSE.

MINMORE HOUSE HOTEL, 0.4 km. N of the Distillery. Built *c.* 1842 for George Smith and expanded under his son, John Gordon Smith, who inherited in 1871 (cf. Delnabo, S of Tomintoul (*see* p. 750)). Main block of two storeys and three bays, the door (now a window) flanked by late C19 canted bays. Slightly recessed wing to the r., *c.* 1865 with full-height canted bay window by *Charles C. Doig*, 1905–6. Wing to the l. with rear projection also of *c.* 1865, refronted in 1926 by *George Bennett Mitchell* with a broad, two-storey bow.

GLENLIVET HOUSE, 0.5 km. SW of the Distillery. Formerly Blairfindy Lodge, built in the early C19 for shooting on the Glenlivet estate of the Dukes of Gordon. The core is a simple L-plan but in 1905–6 this was given a grand and slightly strange new E front by *A. Marshall Mackenzie & Son*, set at an angle to the original. It is of six bays, the centre with a two-storey porch-tower. There is an earlier extension of *c.* 1890 to the NW. Early C19 U-plan steading and service range, converted 1998–2000. Former DAIRY off the N arm, late C19. Small and square with pyramidal roof.

OLD PACKHORSE BRIDGE, Bridgend of Glenlivet. Built in the early C18 in a fast-running, hairpin curve of the Livet. Two independent hump-back spans, each covered in turf and springing from a rocky outcrop in the centre. Larger semicircular arch on the l., *c.* 8.5 m. wide; segmental one on the r., *c.* 4.8 m. There was originally a third arch on the E bank, damaged in the Muckle Spate and demolished 1830. The knoll to the NE was the site of the medieval DESKIE CASTLE, represented only by a mounded oval earthwork (*c.* 90 m. by 36 m. and 2.5 m. high) with traces of foundation walls on the summit. DOWNAN BRIDGE 300 m. SW, built in 1834, superseded the Old Bridge after the 1829 floods. Broad, segmental rubble span springing from rock abutments (bypassed *c.* 1978).

BRIDGE OF TOMBRECKACHIE, 0.5 km. SE. Segmental rubble span over the Burn of Tervie, early C19. Terminal piers and four pilaster strip buttresses with cushion finials (one missing).

OLD MANSE OF CRAGGAN, 3.6 km. NNW. Built for the Free Church by *A. & W. Reid*, 1852–4. Symmetrical S front of two storeys and three bays; two wide tripartites on the ground floor and three narrow rectangular windows above, all with good original lying-pane glazing. Two piended dormers added in the mid C20.

To the N, the foundations of INVERAVON FREE CHURCH (1852–4 by *John Urquhart*, dem. 1951, the materials used to restore Kirkmichael Parish Church (*see* Tomintoul) after a fire.

MODERATOR'S SEAT, 0.3 km. SSW. Picket-fenced enclosure on the W side of the B9008 with two STONES inscribed 'CLERK'S TABLE' and 'MODERATOR'S SEAT APRIL 1846'. Parishioners worshipped here in a 'moveable' wooden church (built 1846–7) until the church at Craggan opened in 1854.

DRUMIN CASTLE, 1.8 km. NW of the Distillery. On a highly strategic site near the junction of the Avon and Livet. Probably built in the late C14 by Andrew Stewart, the notorious 'Wolf of Badenoch', who was granted the land *c.* 1372 by his father, King Robert II. Sold to the 3rd Earl of Huntly *c.* 1490, but the Gordons had abandoned it in under a century for Blairfindy (*see* below). It was originally a rectangular tower with massively thick (*c.* 2.2–2.8 m.) walls. The W and N walls remain to their four-storey height, the mighty and plain W wall with few windows and fragments of tripartite corbelling along the parapet. The S wall survives to a length of *c.* 11 m. The E wall – originally with separate entrances to the cellar and hall staircases – has vanished. Gutted interior with vaulted ground floor below the former hall, which has a bench-recess. Stone corbels at second, third and attic floors. Large fireplace in the N wall at second floor with segmental head and rounded back. Window loop to the r. of it; entrance to an intramural staircase in the SW corner. The third floor has an inserted fireplace (again on the N) with weathered roll moulding. Narrow latrine entrance to the l. of it and two deep windows on the W wall.

BLAIRFINDY CASTLE, 0.4 km. SE of the Distillery. Once a fine tower house, but now in a poor state. Blairfindy was owned by the Grants (documented as such *c.* 1470), but the present building was completed by John Gordon in 1564 to succeed Drumin (*see* above). Blairfindy protected the pass of Livet from Banffshire into Aberdeenshire. In 1586, the castle passed to the Earls of Huntly, who used it as a hunting seat. During the Civil War, the 2nd Marquess of Huntly was imprisoned here while awaiting his trial and execution in Edinburgh in 1649.

Four-storey L-plan, externally intact up to the wall-head. Main block aligned N–S, the jamb projecting W but shifted slightly S so as to create two re-entrant angles for maximum defence. Seven windows on the S side and part of a chimneystack on the gable (crowsteps now missing). Long E side with two large windows to light the former great hall. Tall chimneystack in the centre of the wall-head; tourelle corbelled out in the NE corner, also roofless but with a window and shot-holes. The sole entrance was in the NW re-entrant angle with its narrow and segmental roll-moulded arch. Heraldic plaque above it dated 1586 with the initials of John and Helen Gordon. Very slender newel stair-turret corbelled up in the angle, the top flanked by a box machicolation to defend the entrance below. It is only four corbels wide.

The interior has gone. A stair from the entrance led up to the first-floor hall and down to the kitchen and cellar, the former with a large arched fireplace and the latter with a service stair up to the hall's SE corner. Both were vaulted and served by a W corridor. The good hall fireplace survives in a depressed segmental arch-frame. Chamber with window in the NW angle, the gaping kitchen flue sweeping up the whole wall to the r. of it.

DOUNE OF DALMORE, 2.1 km. NW of Bridgend of Glenlivet. Remains of a clava ring-cairn, originally with ten orthostats. Three are upright and another three have fallen.

GLENRINNES *see* DUFFTOWN

GORDON CASTLE *see* FOCHABERS

1060

GORDONSTOUN

1.4 km. ENE of Duffus

The land was originally known as Bog o' Plewlands and held by the Ogstoun family from at least the early C13, but renamed in 1638 after the estate was purchased by Sir Robert Gordon, privy councillor to Charles I and vice-chancellor of Scotland. The Innesses of Innermarkie built an L-plan tower house in the mid C16 and a mirror wing was added at the turn of the C17. This was acquired by the Marquess of Huntly in 1616, who reconfigured (or rebuilt) the central tower house while retaining the wings on either side. The centre was mostly demolished in 1728–30 by Sir Robert Gordon, 4th baronet, but he ran out of money and the house was unfinished at his death in 1772; 'great improvements' under his son (†1776) also came to nothing. In 1795 Gordonstoun passed to the Cumming Gordons of Altyre (q.v.) but the house was completely abandoned by *c.* 1823. In 1934 the estate was acquired for the present school, founded by the German educator, Kurt Hahn, and there was a fire in 1941 during temporary military occupation. The preparatory school, formerly at Aberlour House (*see* p. 507), was transferred here in 2004.

The N front is suitably imposing, very broad and well proportioned, and the architect's name remains unknown. Central block of 1728–30 occupying the site of the original tower, two full storeys and an exposed basement below a thick band course. Eight bays wide, all of polished ashlar. Doorpiece in the centre of the basement (dated 1730 on its underside) with paired Corinthian columns and a modillion pediment. To the l. and r. are small, square windows and another door on the far r. with Sir Robert Gordon's painted coat of arms. Multi-pane glazing on the upper floors, nearly twice as long on the first storey. Rusticated quoins on the upper half of the walls and a corniced wall-head with balustrade – originally enclosing a piended roof that was destroyed in a fire in 1941 and never rebuilt. There was a promenade around the roof in the C18 and a stair up to it at the W end.

Abutting to the E and W are the wings retained from the previous house. The E wing is shown attached to the tower on Pont's map of *c.* 1590 but the W wing is later, possibly of after 1616 when the Marquess of Huntly acquired Plewlands. Both were refaced in polished ashlar in 1728–30 and each is two-storeyed and of four bays with a high mansard roof and two early to mid-C19 dormers in C17 style. On the outer corners, a corbelled tourelle with conical roofs and ball finials; channelled quoins below them.

The S façade is essentially similar, except that the material 73
is rubble and the wings project to form a shallow U-plan. Moulded doorpiece in the centre without a pediment. Scarred masonry in E and W bays of the centre block proves that one bay of each wing had to be sacrificed to accommodate this block. On the far r., a segmental barrel-vault (originally the E wing's cellar) was truncated, and the first floor of the re-entrant angles shows that there was internal access at this level. So the wings were originally symmetrical, and the inner roof-line – rather than descending vertically below a canted angle as it does now – came down at the same pitch as it does on the E

and W. The ellipses over the outer first-floor windows (and the blocked window below that on the r.) show the exact span of the original wings before they were truncated. The lost corners must have had more tourelles. Furthermore, a drawing of *c.* 1875 shows that these wings were originally quadrangular with small courts in the centre (now completely roofed over). They were accessed by circular staircases in the angles, still partially *in situ*. At the base of the quoins of the central block are spur walls, which are the beginnings of a grand portico planned by Sir Robert but abandoned after he had run out of money. On the W flank of the house is a re-set heraldic panel for Sir Robert, made by *Joseph Stacey* and signed 'I.S. Magister, Fecit'.

The INTERIOR has been remodelled numerous times (in the early to mid C19, after the fire of 1941 and again in the late C20) but retains a few original features. On the ground floor of the wings are longitudinal barrel-vaults intact from the late C16 and early C17, originally forming a large network of cellar stores for the tower house. The N entrance hall was decorated with copies of Raphael's Sistine frescoes (now lost) and has a dado of reused Gothic panelling from the second Drainie Parish Church (*see* p. 700). The r. entrance on the N façade (now main reception) has a cantilevered quarter-turn staircase of *c.* 1730, the undersides of the treads moulded as ogees. Airy wrought-iron balustrade with scrolls, leaves and tulip blossoms. On the top landing, a re-set C17 doorcase with lugged roll moulding and open segmental pediment carved with an owl. Just off the kitchen is a small dungeon rediscovered in 2002, with a little barrel-vault and former shot-hole converted into an air vent. Square, very claustrophobic chamber *c.* 14.3 m. deep. Elsewhere are two priest holes concealed by trap doors.

GARDEN WALLS. E and W of the wings. In one a fine OVERMANTEL of 1679, re-set from one of the manses in Elgin (*see* p. 579). Thick lintel with the initials W.B. and I.O.; triangular pediment above with monogrammed cartouche and thistle finial. The jambs have delightful lions holding shields. Over the other a DORMERHEAD (also from Elgin) with patera, grapevine and a monogrammed elliptical finial. – WATER TOWER off the E flank, *c.* 1730 with a concave pyramidal roof.

The surrounding LANDSCAPE was created in the early to mid C18 with a long N avenue forming a narrow *allée* of trees to the front of the house. GATEPIERS of *c.* 1900 at the N end, the central pairs with fluted urn finials. The wrought-iron GATES were made *c.* 1951 for Charters House, Sunningdale (Berkshire), and re-erected here *c.* 1975. On the S front there is a very long, narrow CANAL of *c.* 91.4 m., first excavated *c.* 1672 for the 2nd Baronet, Sir Ludovick Gordon, by his factor, *William King*. It simultaneously drained the Bog o' Plewlands and created a long 'runway' to view the house via forced perspective – a very rare surviving example of C17 French practice in Moray.

SW of the house is the extraordinary ROUND SQUARE, a 72
large circular steading begun *c.* 1690 by Sir Robert Gordon, 3rd Baronet. Although built in several phases with *ad hoc* extensions, a circular design was likely always envisaged (cf. Dallas Lodge, q.v.). The result is immensely suave and satisfying. It is composed of alternating sections, the taller ones two-storeyed with crowstepped gables, the intervening segments originally of a single storey and low attic, but most of them raised by the early C19. The building's intended profile was therefore much more jagged and pronounced, as the original low wing to the SSW shows. Elsewhere there is asymmetric, multi-pane glazing, as well as a host of blocked arches, windows and doors; wide circles of catslide dormers in the attic. Main entrance on the N side with five segmental arches, the centre leading to the inner courtyard (two flanking pairs blocked *c.* 1965). Over the inner S door is a re-set painted plaque of *c.* 1627 with heraldry for the Marquess of Huntly and his first wife, Henrietta Stuart.

Just to the N (raised on an artificial mound) is a late C16 beehive DOOCOT, among the earliest in Moray (restored, 1979).* Four stages of thick rubble walls (total circumference, *c.* 19.8 m.), the upper three stepped and with encircling rat ledges. Another DOOCOT lies 0.6 km. NE of the house, formed *c.* 1735 by converting a windmill. Tall, circular tower (circumference, *c.* 15.7 m.) with two diminishing upper stages framed by rat courses.

There are three lodges of note, all built for Lady Florence Gordon Cumming. MICHAEL KIRK LODGE is robust crowstepped Gothic by *Charles C. Doig*, 1902, a copy of the former lodge at Pluscarden Abbey (*see* p. 723). The crowstepped EAST and WEST LODGES are by *A. & W. Reid & Wittet*, *c.* 1898–9, both with rock-faced gatepiers and urn finials like those at the N end of the avenue.‡

Most of the SCHOOL BUILDINGS are bland and utilitarian but
NW of the house is the large ST CHRISTOPHER'S CHAPEL by 53
Murray, Ward & Partners of London, 1965–7. Tall walls of reinforced and channelled concrete, the blank E side with a curved, protruding centre and very slender row of windows. It looks like a giant open book seen in reverse. Polygonal plan behind with seven sides punctuated by vertical tiers of glass. Low, wide W entrance, a rubble wall swept around off the l. to form an open semicircular belfry. Clinical interior very much of its date, with pie-wedge sections of pews facing the E sanctuary. Large, domed oculus above it with radiating ribs dividing the pine ceiling into triangular panels. Canted wall sections around the perimeter sensibly covered in curtains, the centre with an ORGAN case by *Rushworth & Dreaper* of Liverpool, 1967. The PODIUM contains a stone from Drainie Parish Church (*see* p. 700).

*The only other beehive doocot in Moray is at New Elgin (*see* p. 609).

‡Their gates were resited *c.* 1950 to the West and Manachy Lodges at Altyre House (q.v.).

To the SW of the chapel is CUMMING HOUSE, a truncated U-plan by *George Kennedy*, 1939 (originally meant to be quadrangular). Two storeys of dark Canadian cedar weatherboarding, the walls deliberately designed to lean slightly outwards. On the N front, a jettied centre with three-centred open pediment.

32 MICHAEL KIRK, 0.8 km. SE of the house in woodlands.* The chapel is thought to be on the site of the church of Ogstoun, a possession of the Bishops of Moray, which was said to be in ruins in 1677. The present building, a delightful and precociously early example of Gothic revival (or survival?), was erected in 1705 (date on the W gable) as a family mausoleum by Elizabeth Dunbar, widow of Sir Robert Gordon, 3rd Baronet of Gordonstoun, and is an ashlar-built rectangle with four-light E and W windows, and a symmetrical arrangement on the S wall of a door flanked by a single Y-traceried window. These windows were initially unglazed. Blank N wall. The E and W windows rise into the gables, their cusped lights grouped within three intersecting super-arches, with the head of the middle super-arch cut by a large oval; there are three trefoils within the tracery field, one in the oval at the window apex and the others at the heads of the two side super-arches. At arch-springing level of the lights are trifoliate transoms with ogee cusps rising into the light heads, the spandrels of which are carved with foliage (in the W window) or winged angel heads (in the E window). The hollow of the reveal mouldings of the E and W windows and of the S doorway is enriched with relief flowers and stars. Above the S doorway, spandrels are suggested by a shallow recessions.

In 1898–1900 *John Kinross* restored and lavishly furnished the mausoleum as an Episcopalian family chapel for Lady Florence Gordon Cumming, with an elevated sanctuary at the E end. Oak panelling of that date by *Scott Morton* capped by an inscribed cornice terminating at each end with trumpet-blowing angels. It was again restored in 1959, as a non-denominational chapel for the school, when the shallow N shelter was added, the roof replaced and the liturgical arrangements reversed, with a greatly simplified sanctuary and communion table at the W end. – STATUE. St Michael slaying the dragon. Wooden, from a retable of 1900 by *Scott Morton* removed in 1959. – LECTERN, by *Robert Thompson* of Kilburn. – STAINED GLASS, SW window, the Annunciation, *c.* 1900. – MONUMENTS. The interior is dominated by the riotously Baroque monument to the Gordon family, of 1705, on the N wall. The inscription is framed by a lugged architrave which glories in the architectural solecism of having all the elements of a full entablature (with ribbon decoration to the frieze), the cornice of which extends rather surprisingly to form a broken segmental pediment. An armorial tablet with the family's arms flanked by unicorn and wildman supporters rises through the

*This entry is by Richard Fawcett.

pediment, and trumpet-blowing angels rest slightly precariously on the pediment. It was originally opposite the entrance but displaced eastwards to accommodate the monument to the Gordon Cummings of Altyre (deaths recorded from 1749 to 1861 but some of the later inscriptions clearly added); marble tablet within a freestone Corinthian aedicule capped by a broken segmental pediment. – Sir Alexander Penrose Gordon Cumming †1866 (S wall), an elaborate Gothic design with angels flanking the gablet.

CHURCHYARD. The earliest certainly dated gravestone is of 1629, though there is one that is possibly dated 1575. Many C17 and C18 ledger slabs; more recent memorials to Gordonstoun staff. – The N pier of the W gate has an inset carving of a wildman Atlas figure below an Ionic cap that is closely related to one of the supporters on the Gordon monument in the chapel; fragments from gravestones (?) have been set in the S pier. Also in the churchyard, the later medieval OGSTOUN MARKET CROSS. It has a sexfoil head with a square 97
central aperture; a hammer is incised on both faces of the octagonal shaft, and there is a cross-shaped incision on the W face that may be a mason's mark.

GRANGE

B *0060*

So named as it formed the farming manor of Kinloss Abbey (q.v.), first granted in a charter by King William in 1185. By the late C15, the surrounding area was elevated to the barony and regality of Strathisla. Also known as Davoch of Grange.

GRANGE PARISH CHURCH, N of the A95. Built in 1795–6 but standing on a high mound above the N bank of the River Isla, which was first occupied by a Pictish fort and later by a hall and monastic church for Kinloss Abbey. The church is simple and typical of its date, a gabled box with a W bellcote, four arched cross-windows in the S wall and a completely blind N flank where the gallery was placed inside. Two-storey W porch of 1888–9 by *A. & W. Reid*, who also added the vestry and session house to the E. They reorientated the interior, moving the pulpit from the S to the E wall and creating a deep W gallery, carried on four cast-iron columns with fluted capitals, but reusing the C18 panelling. – ORGAN behind the pulpit, 1902–3 by *Wadsworth & Bro.* of Manchester and restored 2007–8. Open rectangular case with good stencilled and painted pipes.

Traces of the former moat still exist on the N and W perimeter. The BURIAL GROUND to the W is the site of the previous church, originally a chapel of ease dedicated to the Virgin, built by Abbot Crystal of Kinloss in 1525. A BURIAL AISLE has a cast-iron GATE of 1816 with cobra-headed finials S of the rear wall of the aisle, a SLAB of 1684 (name submerged in the turf) with big lettering around a heart symbol and two sets of initials. Raised morality emblems on the rear. Set against the burial ground's E end is the former SCHOOL. Late C19 but its centre incorporating a building of 1799 by *Alexander Stronach* of Knock.

Former FREE CHURCH, 0.9 km. NNE. Large gabled rectangle, built 1884 and restored in 1900–1. Now partially ruinous after closure in 1939.

GRANGE HOUSE, 0.3 km. NW, was the manse, built by *Alexander Laing*, 1814–15. Two storeys and five bays, the S front of coursed granite. Kitchen wing at NE corner of 1827 and large S extension by *F.D. Robertson* in 1882–3, forming an L-plan with porch in the re-entrant angle. The Victorian part has a fine interior. Three piended former OFFICES on a detached U-plan, the l. and r. sides by *Thomas Simpson* of Keith, 1811–14. Centre added in the late C19.

KING MEMORIAL HALL, 2.5 km. ESE on the A95. 1925 by *D. & J.R. McMillan*. Large and impressive, the S front raised above a basement, blocky Venetian window above the entrance, and a shaped and crowstepped gable.

BRIDGE OF GRANGE, 0.4 km. W. Single rubble span over the Isla, built 1699 by Alexander Christie 'for the glory of God and the good of the people of Grange'.* Somewhat crudely widened for carriage traffic, 1783.

BRACO, 1.9 km. E. Early C18 core, enlarged in the early C19 and again by *A. & W. Reid* in 1879–80 who incorporated the (renewed) 1711 datestone on the porch amid stepped crenellations and rope moulding. Plaque on the r. flank with festooned helm, inscription and coat of arms for Alexander Duff (†1705) and Margaret Gordon (†1721).‡ Reused dormerhead in the central gable with fleur-de-lys and consoled sides, also 1711.

ISSUEBURN, 2.6 km. SE. A tower house folly, built 2003–9. Quite convincing from a distance.

0060 ## GRANGE HALL

1.1 km. S of Kinloss

An austerely grand but compact house, and the first of a local group that includes Dalvey and Invererne (qq.v.). The former grange of Kinloss Abbey (q.v.) was acquired by the Dunbars in 1567 (cf. Dalvey) but the estate was purchased *c.* 1800 by James Peterkin, who had earned his fortune in Jamaica. He built the present house in 1805. The design is attributed, by tradition, to

*Recorded on a now-lost inscription. The bridge allowed parishioners to cross the river on Sundays to reach the church.

‡Alexander was the brother of William Duff of Dipple, who owned Braco's Banking House in Elgin (*see* p. 597).

William Stark but it seems more probable that this and Dalvey and Invererne were executed by a very competent local mason.

Main S façade of tooled ashlar, two storeys and five bays over a raised basement. The latter has rocky rustication, a motif then fashionable in Edinburgh New Town. The wide central bay is minimally advanced as an implied portico and demarcated by suave pairs of giant-order pilasters; their capitals are carved with long fronds of acanthus with the upper sections pivoted out at ninety degrees, as at Invererne. Pediment above an entablature with a pie-wedge bullseye in the tympanum. Oddly plain and insignificant central window below, whereas Dalvey and Invererne have elegant Venetians; the windows of the l. and r. bays are also unmoulded, now with plate glass inserted by *John Rhind* in 1881. He also added the squat porch with Doric columns, clumsily overlaying the shallow arched recess for the original door. His also the misguided attempt to provide servants' quarters in the attic by adding steep French mansards with pedimented dormers over the outer bays, in place of the low and piended original roof (cf. Invererne and Dalvey). The tripartite and pilastered bay window and garden porch on the W flank are contemporary. The three-bay E flank is plain (and originally harled) with a wide chimneystack flanked by Rhind's dormers. To the rear of the house, a long WING built 1844 for Major Grant Peterkin by *Mackenzie & Matthews*, with roof balustrade and four bays of tall windows over a high raised basement. Italianate stair-tower on the end in ashlar. A wall on the S front screens the former service court E of the house, added 1898–9.

The INTERIOR is among the finest in Moray and superbly well preserved. The public rooms on the ground floor have remained virtually unaltered since 1805, decorated with a panache and verve that go far beyond the usual Adamesque restraint. The large rectangular HALL divides the plan down the centre and is itself divided by a screen of fluted columns, their capitals carved with slender, vertical fronds of acanthus. Excellent entablature above with alternating triglyphs and paterae; guttae and foliate lozenges on the cornice. All of the latter are swept around the rest of the room to form the main frieze. Good rose above the entrance. Beyond the screen, a cantilevered staircase with excellent cast-iron balusters of acanthus. Band of Vitruvian scroll around the landing and then a tall, elliptical cupola with telescoped sides and two tiers of panelling. To the l. of the hall is the PARLOUR with original beaded-panelled doors, dado and window shutters. Plaster frieze with tripods and scrolled garlands, the ground now painted orange-brown. Corniced overdoors similarly treated. White marble chimneypiece carved with flowers and fruit. Original scrolled pelmets and an exuberant chandelier. A double door with console brackets intercommunicates with the identically decorated DRAWING ROOM. Rhind moved the chimneypiece to the E wall when he inserted his bay window and porch, and the original frieze was recreated in the late C19. The DINING ROOM lies on the other side of the hall and is the finest room in the house. Vigorous frieze with urns linked by excellent swags of grapevine, nicely textured. More acanthus and guttae on the cornice; similar friezes over the doors and the consoled frame of the sideboard recess. To the N was the library, converted into a kitchen in 1958.

The STEADING complex (200 m. to the NNW) also dates from *c.* 1805 but has GATEPIERS of the mid C18, likely reused from the previous house.* Hexagonal DOOCOT to the rear, *c.* 1802 (restored 1996–7). Faceted roof with gilded weathercock. – WALLED GARDEN, 250 m. SW, also early C19. – SOUTH LODGE (550 m. S), 1841. Good decorative bargeboarding and apex finials. – NORTH LODGE (500 m. NNW), dated 1858. Much simpler, with central veranda and some Gothic astragals.

1060 HOPEMAN

Grid-plan village founded in 1805 by William Young of Inverugie (cf. Burghead) to house workers for the sandstone quarries at Clashach and Greenbrae. Admiral Archibald Duff of Drummuir began a harbour in 1836 to export the stone and turn Hopeman into a proper fishing port. Fishing profits enabled expansion in the C19 and early C20.

BAPTIST CHURCH, Clark Street. Built 1897–8. Lower S end forming a T-plan by *J. Wittet*, 1922–3 and *J. & W. Wittet*, 1937.

PARISH CHURCH, Farquhar Street. Originally the Free Church, built 1852–4 as a simple T-plan. The centre of the W front has a rather surprising Gothic clock tower added by *J. Wittet* in 1923–4, paid for by Innes Cameron (an Elgin distiller) 'to tell the fisherfolk when to gather mussels'.

The interior is good and unexpectedly spacious, gutted and remodelled by Wittet in 1911–12. Open timber roof, each brace composed of three kingposts with two big open circles in the spandrels. – Long, U-plan GALLERY carried on cast-iron columns. – Canted PULPIT screened off by pierced, round-headed balustrades. – ORGAN. Big rectangular case high on the W wall. – STAINED GLASS. Six good windows by *Dom Martin* of Pluscarden Abbey. In the W wall, Fishers of men and Christ walking on water, 1979. – In the S wall, 'Take up your cross every day' (Luke 9:23) and 'Let the children come to me' (Matthew 19:14), 1991. – In the N wall, Christ's entry into Jerusalem and the Transfiguration, 1980. The former has a lively abstract pattern of hands waving palm fronds. – In the

*An estate plan of *c.* 1750 shows a large mansion with detached pavilions and a larger, ruinous house (probably late C16 or C17) to the N.

upper lights (visible in the gallery), the Evangelists' symbols, a cross and a dove with olive sprig.

HALL off the SE corner by *A. & W. Reid & Wittet*, 1895–6. – Former MANSE at 63 Forsyth Street, 1852–3. Pilastered, pedimented doorpiece with a canted bay window to the l. and r.

MEMORIAL HALL, Farquhar Street. By *A.J. Morrison*, 1924–5. Stepped gable with large tripartite window and high transom. Segmental, keystoned entrance to the r. under triangular pediment.

HARBOUR. Built in two phases, and used for export of both fish and the local sandstone. Original section on the E built by Admiral Duff in 1836–8, narrow and oblong with a long canted arm on the r. The inner pier was originally attached at the top and formed the main entrance. Large extension to the W by *John Willet* of Aberdeen, 1885–8, with L-plan pier forming a large stilling basin. He also extended the N breakwater. – At the bottom of the central quay, an iron CRANE by *Bowser & Cameron* of Glasgow, 1859. Now painted bright red. – ICE HOUSE, 200 m. SSE. Built *c.* 1845 into the slope of the hill and given a surprising – and very charming – Neo-Egyptian entrance. Mighty post-and-lintel door frame with a huge cavetto cornice and stepped blocking course. Cylindrical interior with a conical rubble-vault.

HOPEMAN LODGE, 0.6 km. E, end of Lodge Road. Harled yellow, and with panoramic views of the coast. It began as a single-storey, three-bay house with recessed wings, built 1811–12 by William Young of Inverugie. To this *William Robertson* added a rear extension *c.* 1830 with coachhouse below drawing/dining rooms on the raised ground floor. Extensive alterations in 1911–12 by *R.B. Pratt*, who added the wings, the open-pedimented porch of ashlar, and the entire upper storey. Simple N façade with a plaque of the Gordon-Duff motto, 'Kind hearts be true and ye shall never rue'. The entrance to Robertson's carriage house lay below it (everything blocked up by Pratt).

SHACKLETON HOUSE, Forsyth Street. Formerly The Neuk, by *J. Wittet*, 1909–10, and the only real villa in town. Three-stage, glazed octagonal tower in the r. corner with bellcast, faceted roof and weathervane.

INVERUGIE HOUSE. *See* p. 662.

INCHRORY B 1000

10.7 km. S of Tomintoul

Plain but attractive shooting lodge, the large core dating from 1847 by *Alexander Tod* for the Duke of Richmond. Symmetrical S front of two storeys and three bays. Four-bay rear wing forming an L-plan. Central wing added to the back in 1884. S front extended two bays to the W *c.* 1945 in a similar style; two more bays beyond it with a full-height canted bay window of *c.* 1996.

2060

INNES HOUSE*

2.4 km. NNW of Urquhart

68 Innes was one of several castles built on the marshy banks of Loch Spynie before it was drained in the early C19; it was also protected by the River Lossie, and in former times could only be approached across dry land on its SE side. It is described as a 'mansion', a 'castle', a 'place' (*palatium* – i.e. a courtyard of significant buildings) and 'a tower and fortalice' in late C15 and C16 charters and after 1585 always as 'the Place of Innes'. But the present building is a Renaissance tower house, the result of a very skilful remodelling *c.* 1640–53 by the court architect *William Ayton* for Sir Robert Innes of that ilk, a powerful local magnate. He may have been responding to his father-in-law's Castle Stewart (Highland) and his son-in-law's Craigston (Aberdeenshire: North; *see* p. 132), both built or rebuilt earlier in the C17. The master-mason was *William Ross*. Progress was interrupted by the Civil Wars, in which Sir Robert played a prominent part on the covenanting side, his house reputedly 'all burnt and plundered' by Montrose in February 1645 while under reconstruction. Innes also suffered very severely from a fire in 1739, and afterwards remained unoccupied, perhaps as late as 1754. In 1767 it was sold to the 2nd Earl Fife, who briefly considered an ambitious Gothick remodelling before engaging *James Robertson* in 1768–9 to add service wings, but these were removed before 1870. After Innes was sold *c.* 1912 by the 1st Duke of Fife to Frank Tennant, son of Lord Glenconner, *Walker & Duncan* were engaged in 1914–16 to create a new N entrance forecourt. That is how the house remains.

The PLAN of the tower at Innes is a stepped L, roughly 23 m. long by 18 m. deep, comprising a S and E wing and a large stair-tower in the re-entrant angle. It is unified in appearance and plan, similar to Leslie Castle (South Aberdeenshire; 1661–4) and this, together with accounts between 1640 and 1653 totalling £15,266 Scots, has suggested that Innes is of a single build. But it has now been convincingly shown by Professor Charles McKean that the house evolved through several phases.‡ It began with a small tower house, almost square (9.8 m. by 9.3 m.), corresponding to the angle between the two wings of the present house; this had a turnpike stair

*This entry is by David W. Walker.

‡See Alistair Rowan, 'Innes House, Morayshire' in *Country Life*, 4 November 1976, and Charles McKean, 'The Evolution of Innes House, Moray' in *Proceedings of the Society of Antiquaries of Scotland* 133, 2003.

partly accommodated in a small projection at its NE corner (cf. Scotstarvit, Fife, and Kinnaird, Perth & Kinross) which would originally have risen to a wall-head parapet and an attic cap-house. The walls at ground level are 1.5 m. thick except that on the N side, which contains the kitchen fireplace and which, at 2.1 m. thick, strongly suggests a C15 or earliest C16 date for the tower. Shortly after, a lower S range was added, its basic structure that of the present S wing. Its later date is indicated by its ground floor being at a lower level and its vault on a different arc. Then, probably in the C16, an E range was built, the origin of the present E wing. Its construction allowed for a first-floor hall within the E range, a private apartment in the square tower and a principal bedchamber in the S range, a hierarchical sequence of apartments which had become *de rigueur* for the greater gentry by that time. The missing element of this plan is the main stair. Charles McKean assumed it must have been in the re-entrant angle, as now, while acknowledging that it would have opened into the high end of the great hall, an inherently unlikely arrangement. More probably there was an entrance jamb at the E range's SE, corner with a main stair to the low end of the hall and a turret stair to the upper floors. Thus Innes can be assumed to have developed into a U-plan, with which Pont's sketch in his map of *c.* 1590 appears consistent.

In Ayton's remodelling *c.* 1640–53 the C16 stair was demolished and the present stair-tower, 5.5 m. square and six storeys high, was built into the re-entrant angle of the remaining structure, thus achieving a very compact stepped L-plan format. In its general arrangement the plan remained broadly traditional, the vaulted ground floor consisting of services, with the kitchen still in its original position at the NW corner; the first floor still consisted of three principal apartments and the upper floors of bedchambers. But Ayton's spacious new scale-and-platt stair, remarkably modern for its date and rising right up to second-floor level, had fundamentally transformed the circulation: the principal apartments were no longer entered from one another but individually from the stair landing, and access to the bedchambers had been greatly simplified, the only turnpike being that to the upper floors and the balustraded platform roof of the new tower. When much later – perhaps in the mid C19 – the hall in the E range was converted into the ballroom and its ceiling was raised, there were further consequences for the upper storeys, their floor levels no longer relating to the landings of the stair-tower and being uncomfortably close to the sills of their windows. In the S range the third-floor ceilings were also raised at some point, perhaps to create additional fine bedchambers, but at the cost of reducing height in the attic space.

EXTERIOR. The house is harled pale yellow with stone dressings. Its long E wing and shorter S wing are four storey, with the six-storey stair-tower in the angle between them. This tower contains a door at ground floor, close to the angle with the S wing; at first floor and above the windows rest on string courses, and all are surmounted by triangular or segmental pediments. The door with its architrave and cornice is a reconstruction of 1914–16, when a D-shaped porch (added by *James Robertson* in 1786–9) was removed. In the tower itself – which, on this S side, is two bays broad – the ascent of the great stair within is acknowledged by the way in which the smaller windows on the r. are out of phase with the larger windows on the l. The third-floor windows in the E and S wings break up through the eaves as pedimented dormers (also early C20 restorations, the originals having been removed in the 1840s). The stair-tower rises up into a pierced and pinnacled parapet; at its NW corner a turret is crowned by a conical spirelet. The gabled ends of the wings are two windows wide and have also been pinnacled, those on the E still surviving; those on the S were replaced by sphinxes carved with the date 1677. At attic level the gables are pierced by oval oculi and at the apex are triplets of diagonal chimneystacks. At the N end of the W front is a three-storey canted bay, shown in a perspective of *c.* 1862 but probably earlier, and the attics have gabled dormers, all remodelled in 1914–16. The N entrance front is still substantially original at the upper levels, although partly rebuilt after 1739. In the dormer pediments are the initials of Sir Robert Innes and his wife, Dame Grizzel Stewart, sister of the Earl of Moray. Innes's diptych sundials are similar to those at Heriot's Hospital, where Ayton had been in charge of the works since 1631.

The appearance of the N FORECOURT is now as created by *Walker & Duncan* in 1914–16 when the Tennants transferred the entrance to this side. The designs appear to have been the work of *W.D. Ironside* and his principal assistant, *J.C. Cruickshank*. It was a complete rebuild of the 5th Earl's service court of 1870, when service wings added E and W of the house in 1768–9 by *James Robertson* were removed.* The N entrance to the court is an asymmetrical composition, its roof-line stepped between the gables of the E and W ranges. The low centre block is part of the 1870 works and has a projecting gable with ball finials. Framing it are two archways, that on the r. round-headed and reused from Robertson's wings; the keystone has the 2nd Earl's coronet and monogram; its balustrade is crowned by an eagle. The taller arch on the l. is of 1914–16. Next to the smaller arch a small polygonal former larder or dairy with lunettes, also 1870. The E and W ranges have simple regular fenestration and are harled to match the existing house, their frontal gables non-identical but with chimneystacks answering Ayton's. Within the court, *Walker & Duncan* rebuilt the single-storey hall-corridor running along the N elevation of Ayton's house, its entrance a fine two-storey porch with Roman Doric columns and the Tennant arms. A pediment dated R.P.D. 1755 on the E side of the court was

*A large perspective of Robertson's proposals shows his wings linked to the house by round-headed gateways crowned by balustrades, closely similar to those surviving at Delgatie (*see* p. 157).

found during the remodelling. It has no known connection to Duff family history or to the house and may have been brought from elsewhere.

The INTERIOR is surprisingly simple and possibly it always was. It is now entered through *Walker & Duncan*'s porch into the hall-corridor. A big segmental archway leads through the E wing's middle vault to *Ayton*'s great scale-and-platt stair built around a central square newel. At first floor the hall in the E wing has been heightened as a ballroom. Its original chimneypiece, evidently in the recessed area of the N wall, has long gone, probably during the storm of 1736. As it exists now it is a simple room with a modillion cornice and a mid-Georgian-style chimneypiece which appears to be part of *Walker & Duncan*'s work at its E end. The private apartment within the old tower became the dining room and more recently the drawing room: it is better preserved, its moulded chimneypiece with a heavily swagged lintel and a plaster ceiling frieze both evidently part of the *Ayton* works, but its W-side canted bay is late C18 or early C19. The bedchamber in the S wing is now the library, with a plain C17-style chimneypiece; it has good simple panelling and bookshelves in a late Arts and Crafts manner by Walker & Duncan.

The GARDENS were laid out by the Tennants following the removal of the entrance approach to the N side of the house, and originally designed by *J.C. Cruikshank* of *Walker & Duncan*. A walled ORNAMENTAL GARDEN encloses the house on both flanks, but principally orientated towards the S, with a long axial pathway running from the entrance in the stair-tower. C17 polyhedral SUNDIAL in its centre. SUMMERHOUSE with a conical roof on the W side. The garden layout was altered by *Robert S. Lorimer* in 1918 to accommodate MARK'S GARDEN in memory of Capt. Mark Innes (†1916). Wrought-iron gates, the piers crowned by torchères. In the garden a shrine with cherub's head in bas relief. The Tennants also laid out the ARBORETUM in the SE corner of the park.

The PARKLAND shown in Roy's map of 1747–52 was extended by the 2nd Earl Fife. Lachlan Shaw's *History of the Province of Moray* (1798) describes a 'park of considerable extent . . . groves of full-grown lofty trees, young shooting plantations, verdant fields, and a small winding river, expanded in some places into a lengthened lake, and at others contracted into a neat cascade, decorated by a waving gravel path and several Chinese bridges. The approach to the house bends in a winding course through the grove, and terminates in an open lawn.' There were further alterations by the 4th and 5th Earls. The basic structure of the landscape – some 185 hectares – has remained relatively unaltered, protected by shelter-belts on all sides, but with outlooks towards Ben Rinnes on the S.

COACHHOUSE AND STABLES, 100 m. SW. E range by *William Robertson*, 1830, remodelled by *Walker & Duncan*, who built the W range. Linking walls with ball finials.

HOME FARM, 0.35 km. SSE. Dated 1843. Two-storey courtyard steading with an idiosyncratic Neoclassical S front.

North Lodge, 2.2 km. n. A large Baronial gatehouse in tooled red rubble with polished ashlar dressings, by *A. Marshall Mackenzie* (of *Matthews & Mackenzie*), dated 1872.

Burial ground, 1 km. e. – Capt. Mark Tennant †1916. A tall octagonally shafted cross in granite on an octagonal plinth, raised on a base of four steps. By *Robert S. Lorimer*.

INVERAVON *see* BALLINDALLOCH

0060

INVERERNE HOUSE

1.7 km. nnw of Forres

83 A handsome and quietly dignified house, nicely secluded in a ring of trees. Originally known as Tannachy, it was built by Gen. William Grant in 1818 after his return from the Battle of Waterloo. The architect remains unknown, but Invererne is of the same local group as Dalvey and Grange Hall (qq.v.). s front of two storeys and five bays with thick band course over the raised basement. Broad and minimally advanced centre delimited by pairs of giant-order pilasters, the capitals carved with long fronds of foliage. Their upper sections are pivoted out at a right angle, as at Grange Hall. Open pediment above with three huge swagged urn finials and a glazed oculus in the tympanum. As at Dalvey, a Venetian window with Ionic pilasters just pierces the lower zone of the pediment – an interesting manipulation of space. Central doorpiece also tripartite with continuous entablature and semicircular fanlight with curvilinear glazing. Two-storey extension to the rear, 1888 by *John Milne* of Forres.

Entrance hall running through the centre of the house (as at Dalvey) with transverse arch on Ionic pilasters. Staircase beyond, mostly cantilvered, with good cast-iron balusters. Drawing Room on the l. with beaded panelling on the doors, dado and window shutters. Excellent plasterwork on the rose and frieze with rinceau beneath acanthus. Similar detailing in the Dining Room, the frieze here even finer, with a shield-like procession of medallions. Boldly undercut central rose and gleaming black marble chimneypiece.

Former Home Farm steading, 150 m. wsw. Quadrangular plan, also *c.* 1818 but with many later alterations.

1060

INVERUGIE HOUSE

1.8 km. w of Duffus

By *A. & W. Reid*, 1864, replacing a house of 1807. Peter Mortimer purchased the land in 1852 and contributed freely to the design. Single-storeyed, with platform-piended roof. Elegant elliptical E porch with four Roman Doric columns and pediment. Rectangular bay windows to l. and r. S garden front much wider with a broad, bowed centre and sweeping veranda with trellises.

Interior altered by *R. Carruthers-Ballantyne* in 1936–7, with a surprisingly spacious rectangular stair hall running down the centre. He lowered the ground-floor ceilings to increase headroom on the first floor, hence the bad flat-roofed dormers outside.

At the bottom of the garden (near the line of trees) is CAMUS'S STONE, a standing SLAB of *c.* 1.8 m. said to commemorate Malcolm II's victory over the Danes in the C11. It is, however, likely to be much older, probably of the later Neolithic or early Bronze Age (*c.* 3000–2000 B.C.). On its N face, two carvings of cups with concentric rings.

KEITH B 4050

Keith comprises three parts, and many of its buildings are of local, honey-coloured stone. Old Keith (medieval *Geth*) was situated on the W bank of the Isla, the name first documented in a grant made by King William. Of this, nothing remains but the ruins of Milton Tower, the Old Brig and a tomb from the original church of St Rufus (destroyed) in the Old Graveyard. In 1750, the Earl of Seafield laid out New Keith on a 'barren muir' to the E of the river. It remains a rigid improvement-period grid-plan, bounded by Union Street to the N and Seafield Park in the S. The three main axes of New Keith – Mid Street, Land Street and Moss Street – are crossed by lanes and the sprawling Reidhaven Square. In 1817, the Earl Fife returned to the W bank, laying out Fife Keith on a sparser, more open grid centred on Regent Square. Industry formed the whole: Keith was pre-eminently a textile centre and remains a distillery town.

CHURCHES

HOLY TRINITY (Episcopal), Seafield Avenue. 1882, by *Alexander Ross*. Cruciform, E.E. style, with small gabled transepts (vestry and organ chamber) projecting from the chancel and a semi-detached entrance tower with pyramidal roof. Simple, aisleless nave with lancets. Geometric tracery in the E and W windows. Inside, the chancel arch has capitals carved with mammoth foliage (cf. St Margaret's, Aberlour (*see* p. 503)) continuing to the l. and r. as cornices. Pointed barrel ceiling of pitch-pine. – ALTAR, 1885, by *Ross*, three arches on stumpy marble shafts. – Wooden PULPIT, 1886, and again by Ross. Good Dec panelling and baluastrade. – ORGAN by *Wadsworth Bros*, 1887. – SEABURY CHAIR. C18 mahogany seat on which Primus

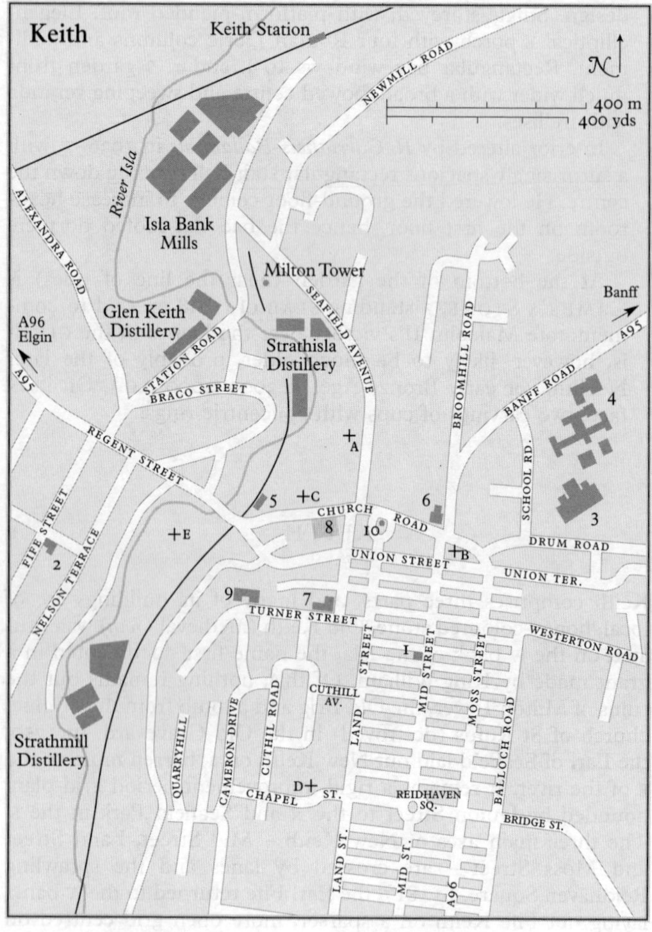

A Holy Trinity (Episcopal)
B Keith North Church
C St Rufus
D St Thomas (R.C.)
E Old Graveyard

1 Burgh Chambers (former)
2 Fife Keith Infant School (former)
3 Junior Primary School
4 Keith Academy
5 Keith Town Station (Keith & Dufftown Railway)
6 Longmore Hall
7 Police Station
8 St Rufus Gardens
9 Turner Memorial Hospital
10 War Memorial

Kilgour sat when Bishop Seabury was consecrated first bishop of the newly independent USA in 1784. – STAINED GLASS. E gable: competent Christ the Good Shepherd, flanked by Moses and St Paul, by *A. Ballantine & Gardiner*, 1896, in memory of the Kynochs, owners of the local woollen mills. – W window a Boer War memorial by *C.E. Kempe*, to Capt. Walter Levinge Thurburn, killed in the relief of Ladysmith, 1900: SS George, Michael (languidly slaying a dragon) and Margaret of Antioch.

NORTH CHURCH, Church Road and Mid Street. Originally the Free Church. 1845, by *A. & W. Reid*. Gothic rectangle of five bays, with narrow lancets, pinnacles and the projecting front supporting a stubby octagonal belfry. Early C20 gallery inside with curved front, the interior restored 1959. – STAINED GLASS. N wall: a red Good Shepherd, early C20. – Two works by *Christian Shaw*: N window of Pentecost, 1992, and S window a fine impressionistic Parable of the Sower, 1995. – In oculus of E wall, a Risen Christ in a blue and silver starburst, 1967.

ST RUFUS, Church Road. 1816–19 by *J. Gillespie Graham*, ideally 37
sited in a spacious churchyard facing the site of its predecessor (*see* Old Graveyard). Imposing Perp, the height of the W tower with pinnacled top, 36.6 m., is perfectly judged and has elaborately decorated clock faces. Large windows with transoms and panel tracery on the flanks and buttresses between. Crenellated wall-heads. E end broad and crowstepped: two windows, now blocked for interior galleries, flanking a shallow porch and large window. Repairs and alterations to E gable by *F.D. Robertson*, 1884–5. Vast interior, the horseshoe gallery on the N, S and E sides on cast-iron clustered shafts and bearing the gilded Seafield arms in the centre. Table, pulpit and dominant organ at the W end in a handsome case, the ORGAN of 1890 by *Nicholson* of Malvern. – SACRAMENT HOUSE. W wall. Mid C16 with swelled balusters flanking the original cavity (now filled by a medallion finial with faded monogram). Upper corners initialled IO for James or John Ogilvy, an occupant of Milton Tower (*see* below).

ST THOMAS (R.C.), Chapel Street. 1830–1 by *William Robertson* 35
for the Rev. Walter Lovi. The grandest and most prominent Catholic church in Moray, imposingly sited above Reidhaven Square. Pedimented and pilastered ashlar façade of three bays, modelled on Santa Maria della Vittoria, Rome, with the side bays topped by extravagant volutes and finials at the ends (cf. Robertson's Milton Brodie (q.v.)); the pediment originally carried statues of St Peter and St Paul (1837). Behind this, a bulbous and faceted copper dome with lunettes, added by *C.J. Ménart*, 1916. Trios of arched windows in the transepts. Belfry and session house/presbytery of two bays added to W of original sanctuary, 1836. The church was repaired and restored by *Oliver Humphries Partners*, 1996. Greek-cross-plan interior, calm and classical, dominated by the central dome, painted dark blue with gold star-burst. Yellow walls with regularly spaced Corinthian pilasters in the nave and sanctuary. – ALTARPIECE (W wall), The Incredulity of St Thomas, 1828, by *François Dubois*, a gift from Charles X of France. It stands in a pedimented aedicule above the HIGH ALTAR of 1916. This has three panels (Madonna and Child flanked by angels) below

a polychromed tabernacle. Two AUMBRIES l. and r. in the same Caen stone and wooden side ALTARS with statue niches. – STAINED GLASS. Central N window, war memorial, 1918, Crucifixion in a heavy architectural surround; corresponding S window of Christ the Good Shepherd. Signed by *J.H. Mauméjean Frères* of Paris – Both are flanked by pairs of limpid windows, 1970s, by *Dom Ninian Sloane* of Pluscarden Abbey. On the N, Our Lady of Aberdeen and St Andrew; on the S, St Margaret of Scotland and Blessed John Ogilvie. In the garden a GAZEBO made from fragments of the original campanile (dem. 1916).

OLD GRAVEYARD, Regent Street. Of the former St Rufus, 1569, demolished 1819, only its platform remains. It was a rectangular church with S projecting steeple, later the town gaol; a plan of 1769 shows the church with eleven separate entrances. Gableted WALL FRAGMENT with fine MEMORIAL to Lady Katherine Rose †1689 and her three sons. Latin inscription on the bottom flanked by engaged Corinthian columns. Ball-finialled aedicule above with coat of arms, hourglass, three winged souls and Katherine's initials with those of her husband, James Strachan. – On SW wall, James Milne of Kinstair (†1771), tall with a pediment, Corinthian columns and superbly inscribed tablet with recumbent skeleton in relief at base (cf. Cuminestown, q.v.). A gilded scroll, 'Arise ye deid and come to judgment', surmounts all.

PUBLIC BUILDINGS

Former BURGH CHAMBERS, Nos. 138–140 Mid Street. Now Moray Access Point. Built as The Institute for various societies, with reading room, billiard room, lecture hall and café, by *F.D. Robertson*, 1885–9. An eclectic surprise, strongly classical, with pedimented centre and segmentally arched, heavily moulded windows on ground floor. Rebuilt by Robertson, 1889, after a fire, with courtroom, council chambers and the addition of a 'renaissance campanile' on the octagonal corner tower that makes the streetscape.

KEITH TOWN STATION, Regent Street and Church Road. Opened 1896 on the Keith & Dufftown Railway. Single-storey weatherboarded waiting room at platform level; detached ticket office to the rear, built into the rising slope. Rebuilt 2002–3 by *Simpson & Wright* of Garmouth, after a fire, to serve the privately run branch line to Drummuir and Dufftown.

LONGMORE HALL, Church Road. 1872–3 by *James Matthews*, presented by William Longmore, banker and distiller. Like a Gothic chapel with W wheel window. N extension of 1964.

POLICE STATION, Turner Street. 1893, by *F.D. Robertson*. Muscular sandstone front with gables. Decorative ridge tiles include 'auld Nick' at the angle.

TURNER MEMORIAL HOSPITAL, Turner Street. 1880 by *F.D. Robertson*. Originally the cottage hospital, a single-storey rubble E-plan with later mansard roof over central portion.

Pavilion-roofed wings added, 1893, for new epidemic wards, also by *Robertson*. Single-storey harled rear additions, 1923, by *Kelly & Nicol*.

WAR MEMORIAL, Church Road, in a suitably grand setting. The Burgh and Parish Memorial, a low chest-like cenotaph of polished ashlar with flanking wall and bronze plaques, 1919, by *George Washington Browne*. Behind, to the 6th Gordon Highlanders, also by *Washington Browne*, 1921, a square ashlar plinth surmounted by a bronze soldier by *Arthur George Walker*, modelled on a local man, Sgt William J. Gordon.

MILTON TOWER
Station Road

The only surviving portion of Milton Castle, begun *c.* 1480 for the Ogilvie family. Ruined square tower, mid C16, with two storeys and garret over vaulted ground floor. Hearth and large aumbry exposed on first floor of S side; inside, vestiges of small square rooms and evidence of at least three remodellings. Tower truncated for road, 1820s; upper vaults were still standing in 1880.

DESCRIPTION

The principal street of the grid-plan town of New Keith is Mid Street, running N–S on a gentle slope, and flanked by the slightly later Moss and Land Streets. Its S end, like all the streets of the grid, is predominantly single-storey cottages. Mid Street bisects REIDHAVEN SQUARE, lying on a gentle slope and crowned at the W by the dome of St Thomas's church (*see* above), nicely framed by the narrowing of Chapel Street. Although it is very large, the square lacks the presence which might have come from enclosing buildings of greater size or poise. In the SE corner, a Neo-Tudor house of *c.* 1860, by and for Robert and William Sim, local distillers. Steep gables and batteries of octagonal chimneystacks.

Continuing N along MID STREET, the street is at first sight slightly too narrow, but it is redeemed by the axial position of the tower of the former Institute (*see* Public Buildings) and by an eclectic clutch of other buildings. The former Seafield Arms Hotel (No. 86) is a solid three storeys and five bays, of 1762, with large hall formerly for district courts; alterations, 1825, by *William Robertson*. Refaced in smooth render lined as ashlar, with late C19 decorative margins over ground- and first-floor windows; corner entrance canted under fanciful corbel. No. 96 is a three-bay late C19 house: central advanced gable with chequer moulding at the apex, cable-moulded door and pilastered dormers with stiff-leaf capitals. Nos. 102–104, of 1879, has a good shopfront (James Annand) and round-headed, central pend entry. The Commercial Hotel, No. 106, was built as Annand's Inn, 1897, plain, with exuberant marble columns and stiff-leaf capitals added to the entrance in the early C20. Further down, the POST OFFICE, of 1912 by *Duncan McMillan* (*D. & J.R. McMillan*), of chunkily rock-faced sandstone but with a whimsical attic storey of a central gable with stepped hoodmould and flanking chimneys. Next, the Burgh Chambers (*see* Public Buildings), then on the other side LLOYDS BANK (previously National Commercial Bank of Scotland) of 1892 with elaborately pierced parapet. At the corner of Bankers Lane, CLYDESDALE BANK, a splendid classical front by *J.D. Corrigall*, 1906–8, dominated by a massive pediment with oculus and swagged tympanum; door with heavily blocked engaged columns topped by palm-decorated volutes. No. 172, in red ashlar sandstone, is Baronial with central oriel window. Finally, the squat ROYAL BANK OF SCOTLAND, 1925, by *Sutherland & George*, sandstone ashlar on a granite plinth.

Mid Street ends with Keith North Church (*see* above) and the ROYAL HOTEL, with delicate leaf moulding at first floor and a date panel the on the chimney-head inscribed DMCM/1883/ARCHT (for *Duncan McMillan*). A fish-scale turret rounds the corner to CHURCH ROAD and the hotel continues for eight more bays, the centre two gabled and slightly advanced for the entrance. Balustraded balcony over. Further down Church Road, the WAR MEMORIAL (*see* Public Buildings) and ST RUFUS GARDENS with a BANDSTAND of 1947 and a ponderous LAMP in pink and grey granite of 1885, moved here from Reidhaven Square in 1933.

To the W, SEAFIELD AVENUE has larger villas, including MILTON LODGE, 1893–4, a substantial Italianate villa, two storeys on an L-plan, in ashlar with elaborate entrance. ISLA BANK HOUSE, 1894–5, a big and Baronial Z-plan villa, has porch with moulded door in one angle, turret and crow steps to gables. LINN HOUSE, 1878–9, presides over STATION ROAD, in a splendid Baronial style. Originally built for the Kynochs; their mill stood just downstream on the site of Glen Keith distillery (*see* Mills and Distilleries). Round corner tower with conical slated roof and a square tower over the door; crowstepped gable and elaborate gablets to W. Restored by *Acanthus Douglas Forrest*, *c.* 1998.

W of the Isla is the sparse grid of FIFE KEITH, laid out in 1817 by Earl Fife. Its locus is REGENT SQUARE, dominated by REGENT HOUSE (Nos. 47–49), a former inn of 1810–20. Five bays with the centre slightly advanced and pedimented in ashlar with columns *in antis*. The rest of the square, as with Reidhaven Square (*see* above), is surprisingly unassuming. REGENT STREET runs E to the river, above which, N of Regent Street, is EARLSMOUNT, of 1869, a thoroughly Baronialized house: crowstepped gables, projecting entrance porch and heavy rope-moulded course on wing; coped chimneys and dated rainwater goods. Below is the OLD BRIG, 1609, the oldest bridge in Moray. Simple segmental arch in tooled granite rubble following a graceful curve over the Isla. Repaired 1724 and 1822. Its function was ceded in 1770 to nearby

UNION BRIDGE, straddling Gaun's Pot, a witches' drowning pool. One segmental arch, lowest order encased in modern concrete; rock-faced ashlar voussoirs and spandrels. Widened in 1816 and given little castellated corner turrets; further enlarged and rebuilt, 1912.

MILLS AND DISTILLERIES

GLEN KEITH DISTILLERY (Chivas Bros), Station Road. Built 1957–60, and so the first distillery in Scotland to open after the late Victorian 'whisky boom'. It stands on the site of a late C18 corn mill. On the r., an L-plan block with glazed lanterns and red chimney. Looming production complex to the l., the far section four-storeyed and rising to a pagoda ventilator with topped by good weathercock.

STRATHISLA DISTILLERY. Very picturesque, and the oldest continuously operating distillery in N Scotland. Founded as Milton Distillery in 1786, but most of the current complex dates from the mid to late C19. Former kiln standing proud with paired pagoda ventilators, *c.* 1872, here placed low and side by side. Water wheel by *James Abernethy & Co.*, 1881, a redundant 'folly' used here to quaint effect. Still house ranged out in front, lower and with two mini-pagodas. Tall, circular brick chimney.

To the N, a U-plan former office block, now mostly converted into a visitors' centre. On the l. gable, two reset fragments from Milton Tower (*see* above), one dated 1695 and the other with coronet and initials for Lady Margaret Oliphant.

STRATHMILL DISTILLERY (Diageo), off Regent Street. By *Charles C. Doig*, 1891–2, opened as Glenisla-Glenlivet and renamed in 1895. It was a substantial rebuild of a distillery opened in 1823 and then converted into a flour mill (Strathisla Mill) in 1838. Of the late C19 complex, the former kiln at the SW end with double pagoda ventilators placed side by side. Long four-gabled warehouses to the N, 1895–8; two more added just to the E by Doig, 1903.

ISLA BANK MILLS, Station Road. Founded 1805 as a flax-dressing station, then developed as major woollen mills; refurbished as business units in the 1990s. Attractive manager's office of two storeys, rubble with ashlar quoins; asymmetric gable and battlemented bay to road, with skews and coped chimneys, 1889. Array of stone weaving sheds with N-facing factory lights.

EDINTORE HOUSE, 4.4 km. S, off B9115. Wide central block of three bays, built 1828. Large ashlar porch in the centre added by *William Robertson c.* 1838, with four pilasters and strips of lying-pane glazing. Pediment above with armorial plaque and datestones, reset by Robertson.

GREENWOOD, 3.6 km. SSE, off A96. Crowstepped L-plan built 1877–8, likely by *A. & W. Reid & Melven.* Crenellated bay windows; octagonal turret in the centre with dummy cruciform arrow slits.

Remains of PITLURG CASTLE, 4.8 km. S. One round tower, mid to late C16, formerly the upper corner of an L- or Z-plan tower house. Two superimposed chambers with segmental barrel-vaults, the lower one in better condition and equipped with gunports. The land was originally held by Kinloss Abbey (q.v.) and passed to the Gordon family in 1539.

1050 KELLAS

Small roadside hamlet, first documented in 1237 when it was held in feu from Bishop Andreas de Moravia (†1242). On a small hillock towards the N end is the WAR MEMORIAL by *John Wittet*, 1920, a Latin cross. Of a pre-Reformation chapel, fragments of two walls remain to the SE (now overgrown). The short, very weathered STANDING STONE was formerly in its burial ground. Opposite, former teacher's house by *A. & W. Reid & Wittet*, 1899, with a tall piended roof and quadrant l. corner corbelled into a square. The former school (1875 by *A. & W. Reid*) is uphill to the rear, also now a house.

94 KELLAS HOUSE, 0.6 km. SW. One of the few Arts and Crafts houses in Moray. Designed by *F. W. Deas* for his cousin, George Christie, and begun in 1913 but not completed until 1921. Sprawling L-plan with gables and flattened chimneystacks, all harled and quite plain – big, simple massing with just a few eccentricities to lend some flavour. Full-height porch on the front with keystoned, elliptical arch; oriel above carved with roses and foliage and then a wide-balustraded parapet. Three bays to the l. with upper oculi and then a substantial bow-ended stair-tower with tall arched windows. Former service wing advanced beyond it, ending in a long bellcast roof. On the garden front, a canted, advanced centre and glazed timber veranda on the l. with Tuscan columns. The E elevation is another L-plan with drum tower (for the service stair) under conical roof, abutting a square bay with mullioned-and-transomed window on the first storey.

Good, well-preserved interior with most of its original fittings. Long rectangular HALL running E–W beneath an elliptical barrel-vault; STAIRCASE in the bow with splat wooden balusters over open circular bases. Long S-facing DRAWING ROOM with chimneypiece of white and coloured Delft tiles under recessed, panelled overmantel. Boudoir attached to the W and divisible by partitions; similar inglenook fireplace with three raised stars on the metal surround. The DINING ROOM has glazed china cabinets in the angles and a moulded cornice carried on clusters of flower petals. Principal BEDROOM on the first floor with chimneypiece of glazed green tiles and mantel with painted swallows.

Pretty harled GATE LODGE, also by Deas. Gabled dormers hung with slates.

KILNMAICHLIE HOUSE B 1030

3.4 km. SSW of Ballindalloch

The barony of 'Kilmaichly' was held by Sir Walter Stewart, the great-grandson of Robert II, in 1490 and is depicted on Robert Gordon's mid-C17 map of Strathavon. The house was purchased by the Grants of Ballindalloch in the mid C18. What survives is a much-modified early C17 house. Long N–S block. An upper storey with crowstepped gables was removed by the Grants, who lowered the roof pitch and gave it new chimneys. Six twelve-pane windows inserted in the W side in the early to mid C19, and from a distance Kilnmaichlie looks like little more than a large Moray farmhouse with strangely spaced bays. Only the three little slit-windows tell that the whole wall is Jacobean. The story is clearer on the E front. Five bays, the second with a square stair-tower with crowstepped caphouse. E skewputts carved with charming little mask corbels. Small windows with chamfered margins, the larger ones C19 insertions. In the SE corner, another mask corbel below the wall-head, originally supporting a bartizan. Late C19 timber porches and early C19 N wing. All now in bad condition.

KINCORTH HOUSE 0060

3.6 km. NW of Forres

Of two phases, and all now decayed. The nucleus of the S front is a two-storey, three-bay house of 1797, its five original Venetian windows with split-Y astragals in the heads. The two dormers and over-large central gable were added 1867–8 by *Alexander Ross*, who built the substantial, two-storey W wing in much redder snecked rubble. W front blandly Gothic, with a blind cinquefoil and corbelled chimney base with dummy arrow loop. – Former ESTATE OFFICE, 100 m. NW. 1878, likely by *Ross & Mackintosh*.

KINGSTON 3060

Small, isolated village at the W mouth of the Spey, founded in 1784 by two timber merchants from Kingston-upon-Hull, Yorkshire. Once a busy industrial centre with seven of the most important shipbuilding yards in Moray. There is eerily little sign of that now, and Kingston's fleeting prosperity ended *c.* 1890 with the advent of iron, steam and steel. A more persistent danger has been the ever-shifting course of the Spey: nearly the entire village was destroyed during the Muckle Spate of 1829, and it remains under threat in the early C21.

Rising up outside the village on the l. is MILLBANK, two storeys and three bays built in 1821. Beyond lies the large, harled DUNFERMLINE HOUSE, early to mid C18 and therefore likely the oldest surviving building in Kingston. First storey added *c.* 1783 with four sets of coped chimneystacks; long E front of nine bays facing the Spey estuary. Along LEIN ROAD, several houses and cottages laid out after 1829 (e.g. Morven, The Yews, Sunnybank and The Bow), all facing S with long gardens ending at the Drainer Burn. The early to mid-C19 SEAVIEW follows, its gable end to the street with skewputts carved as lions' heads.

3040

KININVIE HOUSE B

3.2 km. ESE of Craigellachie

(A tower house, built for the Leslies of Kininvie. Said to be of 1523 but extended in 1610 and remodelled by *William Robertson* in 1840. The result remains convincingly C16 and C17 in style, white-harled. The original part shows at the W end of the garden front as a four-storey tower with the top storey in the attic and a stair jamb with corbelled caphouse. Abutting this, i.e. at the centre of the garden front, the block of 1610, with armorial panels re-set in its walls. The whole of the E wing including the entrance front is of 1840. Small N addition of 1929–30.)

0060

KINLOSS

A sizeable and prosperous town in the Middle Ages, sprawled around the perimeter of the Abbey. Now much smaller, and on the verge of getting swallowed up by the former RAF base.

KINLOSS ABBEY

0.3 km. SE*

19 The Cistercian abbey was founded in 1150 by David I, with monks brought from Melrose; it was itself to be the mother house of abbeys at Culross and Deer (Fife and North Aberdeenshire, q.v.). The extremely fragmentary surviving buildings are largely of the later C12 and earlier C13. Relatively little is recorded of its later architectural history other than that Abbot Adam de Tarras (1389–1414) built an abbot's hall, that a tower was erected by Abbot James Guthrie (1467–81) and that Abbot Robert Reid (1528–53) enlarged the abbot's house in 1537, built a fire-proof

*This entry has been written by Richard Fawcett.

library in 1538 and had extensive painted decoration carried out in 1538–41 by the cantankerous but talented *Andrew Bairhum*. The abbey's spiritual and scholarly life underwent a remarkable late medieval renewal under Abbots Thomas Crystall (1500–28) and Robert Reid. The latter persuaded the Italian humanist scholar Giovanni Ferrerio to come to Scotland to teach the abbey's monks in the 1530s and 40s.

Following the Reformation, Edward Bruce, ancestor of the Earls of Elgin, was made commendator in 1587, and a temporal lordship was created for him in 1601, when he took the title Lord Kinloss. Soon after the Reformation the chapter house was taken over as a parish church. In 1645 the buildings were acquired by Alexander Brodie of Lethen, who in 1650 sold the materials for the construction of the Inverness Citadel, undertaking to apply the money he received to building a new church and manse on a different site (*see* below).

Presumably as a consequence of the sale of its materials in 1650, the abbey's buildings are very poorly preserved, and little more than the broad outline of the church PLAN can be understood. The E limb is one of only two Scottish Cistercian churches (the other is Newbattle) known to have departed from the classic 'Bernardine' plan of a short aisle-less rectangular presbytery immediately flanked by transeptal chapels. That E limb appears to have been of only two bays, with an aisle running the length of each flank, though nothing survives to indicate if those aisles were returned across the E bay as an ambulatory as is thought to have happened at Newbattle. Transepts projected for only one bay on each side of the crossing, with a rectangular chapel on the E side of the S transept, which was walled off from the adjacent aisle (and which was presumably reflected in a similar chapel to the N transept). The aisled nave was probably of seven bays. The cloister was on the S side of the church. The only claustral building that is relatively complete is the sacristy, immediately adjacent to the S transept. The abbot's house projected off the SE corner of the cloister, where it is likely to have adjoined the monastic dormitory or latrine.

The main survivors of the CHURCH are the single S transept chapel, a number of pier fragments and some portions of lower walls. All point to a later C12 date of construction, though insufficient remains to be able to say whether the E limb was aisled from the start. The chapel, which stands to full height apart from its E wall, is entered through an arch with clustered-shaft responds and a complex combination of hollow chamfers and rolls to the arch; there is what appears to be extensive fire damage to the masonry. It is covered by a quadripartite vault with ribs composed of triplets of rolls (the leading roll keeled); there is provision for single disengaged vaulting shafts in the angles, the deep bell-shaped caps and waterholding bases of which survive in a damaged state; it may be noted that the base in the SW corner appears to have been intended for another location, and it now extends into the body of the S

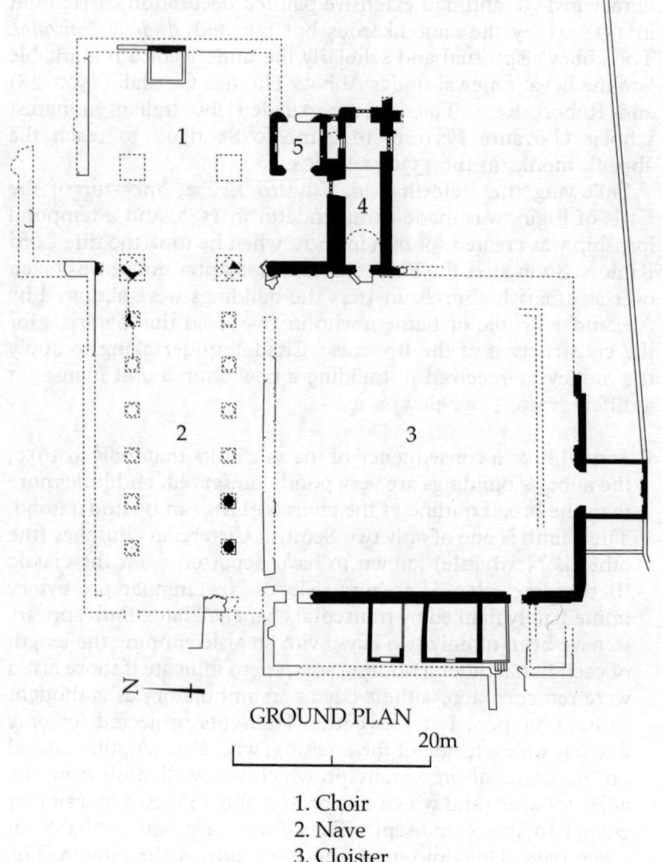

Kinloss Abbey.
Plan

wall. On the N side of the chapel, within the area of the E limb S aisle, there is a vault springer between the two bays; the ribs are of chamfered profile and they are carried on a deep bell-shaped cap. The masonry behind the springer is chamfered back as a result of inappropriate masonry consolidation. In the S wall of the chapel, two arched recesses. The eastern of the two is larger and has a hoodmould, perhaps being intended to hold a PISCINA basin.

The fragments of piers that remain in place on the W side of the crossing and in the nave are all of clustered-shaft form. The crossing piers were evidently composed of sixteen shafts, with the lesser shafts flanking the major cardinal shafts being sharply keeled. There appears to have been a defined crossing from the start, and it was presumably over this crossing that Abbot Guthrie's tower was raised in the later C15. The nave arcade piers were octofoil, and there was evidently alternation between piers in which the cardinal shafts are keeled and those in which it is the diagonal shafts that are keeled. The bases are of either waterholding or double-roll type, all on square sub-bases. Surviving sections of the lower W wall are externally of ashlar, with the bottom chamfer of a base course.

The MONASTIC BUILDINGS are in an extremely fragmentary condition, the most complete part being the room that appears always to have had entrances from both the church and the cloister and thus presumably housed both a SACRISTY (to the E) and LIBRARY (to the W); there is a chamber above its E bay. The sacristy/library is covered by three bays of vaulting defined by heavy transverse arches. The E bay vault is of ribbed quadripartite form, while the other bays are barrel-vaulted, with a groined intersection over the door from the transept. There is a small vaulted closet off the N side of the E bay, which perhaps served as a treasury. The completeness is due to its adaptation as a mortuary chapel in 1910 and the windows and door must date from then; an altar with an arcaded front and what appears to be a relic recess in the mensa remains in place. The chamber over the E bay is covered by a ribbed quadripartite vault carried on shafts, with a single pointed window in its E face, and there is a small barrel-vaulted closet off its E side, like that at the lower level. This chamber would have projected E of the monks' dormitory and, as with the similar provision at Pluscarden (q.v.), it may have been intended as a cell for the abbot.

Running along the entire length of the S face of the sacristy/library, and thus presumably projecting E of the rest of the E range to its S, is evidence of a compartment that was vaulted in four bays, though the wall rib in the E bay has been removed, presumably as part of the 1910 adaptation of the sacristy. This must have been the N wall of the CHAPTER HOUSE and it may be presumed that it was like that at Dundrennan in having three aisles of four bays, since Pennant mentions that there were six piers at the time of his visit in 1769.

The partial footings of the N wall of the cloister, which was also the S wall of the nave, remain in place. A length of the E cloister wall survives against the S transept and sacristy/library; it was enriched with blind arcading, though it is unclear if it was associated with vaulting over the walk. There are also lengths of the S and W cloister walls, which have been retained because of the construction of a number of burial enclosures behind them. The S walk was clearly unvaulted, and there are the corbels and roof moulding of a timber roof. The most striking features of the S wall are two richly decorated early C13 arches. One of these, which appears to have been reconstructed on an enlarged scale as the entrance to a burial enclosure, may have originated as the refectory entrance; it has three orders of engaged shafts supporting a round arch decorated with what seems to have been a form of deeply undercut chevron to the middle order, and with dogtooth to the hoodmould. A short distance to its E is a broad segmental blind arch, also with dogtooth to the hoodmould; in this position it could have framed the lavatory basin, where the monks washed their hands before entering the refectory. Along the W side of the W cloister wall are the wall ribs and supporting corbels of vaulting to the ground floor of the W range, which presumably housed the accommodation of the lay brethren.

The ABBOT'S HOUSE, to the SE of the cloister is now in a precarious state, with the main surviving parts being fragmentary basement vaults, a three-quarter-round stair-tower and a length of wall. It was evidently the product of more than one campaign of construction. The earlier part perhaps survives from the hall built by Abbot Tarras at some time between 1389 and 1414. But most of what is now seen must be the work of Abbot Reid of *c.* 1537. His chamber and oratory were decorated by *Andrew Bairhum*, *c.* 1538, and Reid placed his arms and initials in a panel above the entrance.

MONUMENTS. In the S transept chapel, an INSCRIBED SLAB with a foliate cross-head. Within the area of the chapter house, two monolithic STONE COFFINS. The local post-Reformation preference for TABLE TOMBS is much in evidence across the graveyard; some of those of the C18 within the nave and cloister areas have formalized acanthus borders to the slabs.

BURIAL ENCLOSURES. Within the area of the W range, from N to S: the Davidson enclosure, with a tripartite aedicule, the earliest recorded death being 1821; the Munro enclosure, with a tripartite Corinthian arrangement of tablets, the earliest recorded death being 1764. – Within part of the site of the refectory, the mid-C19 Dunbar enclosure, with a decorative corbel table around the internal wall-head. – To the N of the nave, the Peterkin enclosure, with an aedicular monument for James Peterkin (†1812).

HOME FARM outside the precinct gate with rectangular BARN and GRANARY aligned N–S. Built in the late C18 by Alexander Brodie of Lethen using stone from the abbey. Converted into a house, 2002. Large Italianate STEADING range beyond by *Alexander Ross*, 1870, now overgrown. Big round-headed arch on the W front with thick, rock-faced jambs and keystone carved as a bull's head by *Thomas Goodwillie*.

PARISH CHURCH. More complex than it first appears. The nave came first, built 1764–5 by the mason *David Low*, originally of four bays with round-headed S windows. This replaced a church on the site of 1652–7; from the Reformation until that time, the congregation met in the abbey's former chapter house (*see* above). Large rectangular cross-windows inserted by *William Robertson* in 1829–30. W extension forming a T-plan added by *A. & W. Reid* in 1863–4; small crenellated porch in the re-entrant angle and two lancets on the W flank.

The three-stage tower to the E is also by the Reids, built to commemorate the Grant-Peterkin family of Grange Hall (q.v.). Two-light Dec belfry topped by a step-crenellated parapet. On the rear of the church, a central aisle added by *Alexander Urquhart* of Forres in 1834 to provide additional gallery space. Two low projections are angled out beyond it, formerly the OFFICES for the manse (the core built 1771–5 by *James Anderson* of Forres; much remodelled by *Hugh Garden* and *James Nicol* in 1807).

Plain interior as reorientated and remodelled by the Reids. Canted, panelled wooden ceiling carried on four-centred braces. – Deep E GALLERY with reused Georgian panelling. The N gallery arch is now blocked, with its balustrade exposed. – Hexagonal wooden PULPIT, again *c.* 1765. Fielded panelling and dentilled cornice, now on a truncated base. Wide former back-board, 1883, with Dec gablet and pinnacles. – Octagonal FONT, *c.* 1906. Stiff-leaf over a marble shaft. – ORGAN by *Harrison & Harrison* of Durham, 1879. – STAINED GLASS. Two panels mounted in the NW transept, formerly at St Columba, RAF Kinloss; re-set here in 2012. Toronto window (1996) and Pritchard memorial (1983–4), both by the *Pluscarden Abbey Studio*. – In the tower, a MORT BELL by *John Cowie* of Elgin, inscribed 'Kinglosse 1688', made for the original parish church in the Abbey.

Former MANSE, 150 m. N on Manse Road. By *James Gillespie Graham*, 1819–21, in the same uncharacteristically subdued classical idiom as his manse at Rafford (p. 730). Large two-storey rear wing, much altered by *A. & W. Reid & Melven* in 1877–8.

KINLOSS BARRACKS (Royal Engineers). Formerly RAF Kinloss; handed over to the Army in 2012. Built 1938–9, initially for pilot training in the Second World War and subsequently for operations against Russian ships and submarines. Three runways criss-crossed in a massive capital A. The building layout was similar to Lossiemouth (*see* p. 700), with hangars arranged in a stilted semicircular arc, but most of the original support structures of *c.* 1940 have been demolished. – On the W edge of the base (along the B9011) is LANGCOT HOUSE, a crowstepped villa by *John Forrest*, 1895, formerly used as the commander's house.

BURGIE LODGE, 3.1 km. SE. Unusual harled main block of *c.* 1835, likely by *John Urquhart* of Forres. Two storeys and three bays over a raised basement, the centre recessed between giant-order pilasters of ashlar. Blocking course above it with shallow block pediment stranded in the middle of the wall-head. Rectangular bay windows by *Charles C. Doig & Sons*, 1924.

SEAPARK HOUSE, 0.2 km. W, off the B9011. The land was given to William Ellison and Janet Niven by Walter Reid, the last Abbot of Kinloss in 1574; their tower house was expanded several times in the C17 but pulled down in 1793–4. After *c.* 1800, 'Sea-Park' became the seat of the Dunbar (later

Dunbar Dunbar) family, who built Rothes Glen House (q.v.) as their summer residence.

Once a fine country house, but divided into flats in 1960 and now in poor condition. Main block of *c.* 1805 in a restrained Georgian style, two storeys and three wide bays under a piended roof. Low, square central porch with angle pilasters. The single-storey E and W wings were added *c.* 1834, and the earlier house given crenellated parapets at the same time. The wings end in big, glazed octagonal corner turrets. Further recessed to the E, a much larger wing added *c.* 1842 in similar castellated style, the far r. corners decorated with little tourelles. Glasshouse in the re-entrant angle (enlarged by *Charles C. Doig*, 1903) now in great decay.

To the SE on the main road, a STABLE and CARRIAGE HOUSE complex by *A. & W. Reid*, 1868. Handsome N front anchored by broad, two-storey towers with pyramidal roofs, again with crenellated parapets. Big Tudor arch to the courtyard with faux cross-loops on the jambs.

GRANGE HALL. *See* p. 654.
MILTON BRODIE HOUSE. *See* p. 705.

KINNEDDAR *see* LOSSIEMOUTH

5060 ## KIRKTOWN OF DESKFORD B

A nice small village. A castle was founded by the Sinclairs of Findlater in the late C14 and inherited by the Ogilvy family in 1437. Along with Cullen (q.v.), it became one of their primary seats. Kirktown was raised to a burgh of barony in 1698.

OLD PARISH CHURCH.* Probably built as a chapel to meet the spiritual needs of the Ogilvys. It was within Fordyce parish, and as such belonged to the canons of Aberdeen Cathedral. The church remained in use until St John's (*see* below) was finished in 1872, and survives as a roofless rectangular shell. Most of the openings have always been in the S wall. There were opposed N and S doorways towards the W end, the former later adapted as a window and the latter now blocked. There was also a priest's doorway further E in the S wall, now replaced by a window. At the E end of the S wall, lighting the altar, was a pointed-arched window (now blocked, truncated and lintelled over), with external mouldings of a quarter-roll and hollow, and a roll-moulded segmental-headed rere-arch. A blocked door in the N wall opened towards the castle, where there was perhaps a sacristy. The NW skewputt, which overlooked the castle courtyard, is decorated with a shield.

*This entry is by Richard Fawcett.

Adaptation for Reformed worship introduced galleries at each end, approached by forestairs (since removed); new doorways and windows were rather crudely cut in the S, E and W walls, and the rectangular W gable bellcote added.

The church retains an unusually large number of liturgical fixtures, including a particularly fine SACRAMENT HOUSE, near the E end of the N wall, where its insertion appears to have necessitated blocking a window. It is contained within a rectangular frame decorated with a vine trail, and flanked by miniature buttresses carried on corbels. There is a second vine trail forming an ogee arch around the locker at the middle of the composition, at the head of which is an inscribed scroll with a Latin text that can be translated 'you are my bone and my flesh'; immediately below the locker is a panel with a Latin inscription that can be translated 'I am the living bread that came down from heaven; whoever eats this bread will live for ever. John sixth et cetera'. In the uppermost panel

Kirktown of Deskford, Old Parish Church, sacrament house. Drawing, 1896–7

a pair of angels hold up a monstrance, and at the bottom is a panel with the arms of Alexander Ogilvy and his wife, Elizabeth Gordon, with a text recording their gift: 'This p[rese]nt love[a] ble vark of Sacrame[n]t Hous[e] maid to the hono[u]r and lovi[n]g of God be ane noble man Alexander Ogilvy of that ilk, Elezabet Gordon his spous. The yeir of God, 1551'. Presumably they also provided the very similar sacrament house at Cullen (q.v.). – Two STOUPS mark the locations of the medieval S doors. The basins have been cut back but were within recesses framed by ogee arches with continuous filleted roll-and-hollow mouldings. – AUMBRIES. A rectangular aumbry (?) to the E of the stoup inside the priest's door. Two ogee-headed aumbries in the E wall to S and N of the altar's site; their height above ground level indicates the extent to which levels have risen. – MONUMENTS. Set into the easternmost window arch of the S wall, an incised SLAB for John Murray (†1717). – To the r. of it, Agnes Simpson (†1663) with a long Latin inscription. – In the N wall, an inverted teardrop PLAQUE for the Rev. Walter Ogilvy (†1658).

Former ST JOHN, 0.4 km. SW. By *John Miller*, 1869–72, converted into a house, 2006–7. Cruciform E.E. rectangle, the main W gable with a minimally advanced and pinnacled centre, plate-tracery window with a blind central oculus and birdcage bellcote. Three-light S transept window with intersecting tracery but an unusual arrangement on the N with cross and the letter 'R' for Reidhaven woven into the tracery (cf. Grantown-on-Spey Parish Church (Highland and Islands), also built under the Ogilvys).

TOWER OF DESKFORD, N of the Old Church, and formerly attached to it. The grand tower built by the Ogilvys, probably in the second half of the C16, was a four-storey square topped by a very tall, crowstepped caphouse. Mostly demolished *c.* 1831. Two corner walls of a ground-floor chamber remain, of coursed rubble, 2.3 m. high and 1.4 m. thick. W door under a segmental rere-arch with the springer of a low barrel-vault to the l. The N wall had a central window with ashlar margins and the springer of a higher vault. Plinth of a SW stair-turret, two of its newels probably original. There was a large courtyard surrounded by outbuildings, one portion of it subsumed within the MUCKLE HOOSE, built *c.* 1771. This is two storeys and five bays with some reused C17 chamfered window margins. Polygonal stair-tower added to the rear, *c.* 1998; nice ochre harling. The ground floor has fine wooden panelling reused from Tron Kirk in Edinburgh (closed, 1952) and an excellent stone mantelpiece of *c.* 1580 with thick bolection moulding and deep hollows. It was formerly in an ancillary hall over a suite of service rooms.

DESKFORD HOUSE, 0.3 km. SW of the Tower. The manse of 1871–4 by *John Miller*. The offices are the manse of *c.* 1785–7.

ARDOCH, 0.8 km. N. 1854 for the Earl of Seafield's factor. Two-bay S front with crowstepped gables and ball-finialled, pedimented dormerheads. Re-set in the outbuildings a LINTEL from Ardoch manor house (dem.), dated 1641 with two sets of initials, one of them probably Thomas Ogilvy †1645.

MAINS OF SKEITH, 1 km. SSW. Late C19 farmhouse on the site of a tower house, owned by the Abercrombie family, first documented in the late C15. Re-set is a pedimented dormerhead dated 1687 and late C17 carved mask corbels (or skewputts).

INALTRY CASTLE, 1.6 km. NNE. An overgrown fragment only, probably C13, of a castle once owned by the Ogilvys. Rubble wall aligned E–W, 17.3 m. long and *c.* 3 m. high. Vestiges of the return flanks. Two niches on the N side, one for a chimney flue. Remains of circular hole near the SW corner, part of a projecting latrine turret.

KNOCK B 5050

The small village sprang up at the end of C19 to support the distillery.

KNOCKDHU DISTILLERY (Inver House Distillers). By *Gordon & MacBey*, 1893–4, the NW side long and straight to take advantage of the railway spur to Banff (q.v.) opened in 1859 (closed 1968). Long three-storey malt barn of fourteen bays followed by a square kiln, originally gabled and later given a pagoda ventilator. MASH HOUSE and STILL HOUSE set at a right angle, built 1964 in the footprint of the originals. Piended TUN ROOM with glazed lantern and low, gabled office in front of them; tall, round chimney behind. – Double-gabled WAREHOUSE just to the E, 2011–13. Another trio to the SE, *c.* 1902.

Former UNITED PRESBYTERIAN CHURCH, 2 km. NW. A thatched meeting house was built here for the Anti-Burghers *c.* 1777, rebuilt in 1808 and much extended in 1897. Harled T-plan with tall, broad lancets, the upper arm of 1808. Square W tower with pyramidal roof. Converted into a house, 1989–90.

EDINGIGHT HOUSE. *See* p. 560.

KNOCKANDO 1040

Small Speyside hamlet, now usually referred to as Upper Knockando.

PARISH CHURCH. 1992–3 by *Law & Dunbar-Nasmith Partnership*, after a fire destroyed the previous church. Traditional harled rectangle, but with a tall round SW tower (including louvred upper stage and conical roof) and an E apse for a meeting room, both of them homages to features on the earlier church. Inside, arcade piers of reinforced concrete – STAINED GLASS. Two windows by *Douglas Strachan*, *c.* 1917, were lost in the fire. – W (liturgical E) window by *Andrew Lawson-Johnston*, 1995, with much transparent glass. Two very tall trees with the old church on the bottom l. and the new one on the r. Segmental upper and lower borders with Creation verses. – In the aisles, four small, luminously colourful panels by *Shona McInnes:* S aisle SE, Psalm 85:11 ('Faithfulness springs forth from the Earth'), 1999. The border contains dots and dashes from Morse code; third panel on the S, 2004, Psalm 121:1 with a curlew; fourth panel (on the far r.), 2005, John 15:13 with poppies. – In the N aisle, Philippians 4:7, 2006, with a dipper and marigolds. – Second panel on the S by *Gail Steele*, *c.* 2000, Psalm 23:2 in opalescent glass.

Inside the graveyard's E entrance, three badly weathered PICTISH STONES, two with class I symbols and the other inscribed with C9 or C10 runes. They were relocated here *c.* 1820 from Pulvrenan church and burial ground (1.8 km. ESE). – Former WATCH HOUSE (now chapel). Early C19. Originally furnished with 'a table, an open bible, a snuff mull, pipes and a bowl of whisky'.

CARDHU COUNTRY HOUSE, NE of the church. The manse, by *A. & W. Reid*, 1868–9. Two storeys and three bays, the advanced centre canted on the bottom and corbelled into squares above. Steep gable with an apex chimneystack. T-plan rear wing added during construction. – Large U-plan OFFICES to the NW, 1804.

MARGACH HALL. Long T-plan by *Charles C. Doig*, 1909–10. Scroll-bracketed cornice over the E entrance.

Former STATION, 1.5 km. SE. Built 1896–9 for the Strathspey Railway (closed to passengers 1965). Weatherboarded single storey with pretty upper glazing and ridge-tiled, piended roof. – SIGNAL BOX to W in same style.

KNOCKANDO HOUSE, 2.5 km. ESE. In a serene setting overlooking 'several beautiful windings of the Spey', as it was described in 1791. S-facing laird's house on a shallow U-plan, built 1732 by Ludovic Grant of Castle Grant (Highland and Islands). Finely tooled masonry, despite being of intractable local granite. Main block of two storeys and five bays (later made three), the centre minimally advanced and framed by channelled quoins. Lugged, moulded doorcase with pulvinated architrave and cornice; long round-headed, keystoned window above it. Wall-head pediment with three pineapple finials and a good cartouche with datestone, Grant coat of arms and motto 'Honour and Virtue'. Outer bays with paired oblong windows on the ground floor, the margins intact from 1732.

Single-storey W wing (originally the service block) connected to the centre by a shallow quadrant (best seen from the rear). The E wing (originally a stable and coachhouse) was once identical, much altered by *A. & W. Reid* in 1856–7 and again in 1886–90, when its quadrant was subsumed within a two-storey extension and the house's symmetry lost. Interior largely as remodelled in 1886–90.

DOOCOT, 130 m. E. Fine crowstepped lectern type of the late C17 or early C18, and similar to the one at Leitcheston (*see* p. 725). Two rat ledges.

KNOCKANDO WOOLMILL, 0.9 km. SE. Of international importance, as this is one of the only surviving domestic woollen mills in the world. A 'waulk mill' is first recorded in 1784 and has been in continuous operation since, undergoing gradual expansion as the textile process was mechanized. In 1860, the mill passed to Alexander Smith, who founded 'A. Smith & Son', and this remained the company's name until 1975; its commercial peak was reached in the late C19, as the building fabric will show. In 1976, the site was purchased by the Knockando Woolmill Company, still manufacturing with the original machinery. Buildings beautifully restored by *LDN Architects*, 2009–12.

First on the l. is the small, single-storey SHOP of the late C19, its weatherboarding painted fern green. Next, the MILL HOUSE of *c.* 1910, testament to the owners' new-found prosperity: two storeys of rubble with bargeboarded, timber-gabled dormers. Inside, a surprisingly elegant staircase with alternating cast-iron balusters. Next, THE COTTAGE, early C19, and therefore the oldest building on the site. Harled single storey with corrugated-iron roof; low, square DAIRY later attached to its NE gable. Diagonally across, a small WINTER DRYING SHED clad in corrugated iron with monopitch roof and louvred S window.

Then comes the original late C19 BYRE, converted as the VISITORS' CENTRE in 2010–12. Long, single-storey rectangle running parallel with the earlier buildings. Plain weatherboarding and corrugated roofs; attached to the W gable, a SAWMILL of 1914–15. *LDN*'s extension is attached to the N, with a low-pitch roof and glazed SE face. High front porch with oversailing roof carried on two square posts.

A path leads r. to the MILL itself, early C19 with several later additions. The original single-storey WAULK MILL is rectangular and aligned E–W, of unpainted rubble with a pantile roof. An L-plan was created in the mid C19 by adding a two-storey CARDING and SPINNING MILL, now whitewashed and roofed in corrugated iron. Single-storey lean-to to the S; cast-iron WATER WHEEL of *c.* 1865 on the E flank. Off the N side, a harled, single-storey WEAVING SHED of *c.* 1885, its original gable end washed away in 1945 and rebuilt in brick. Finally, in the re-entrant angle to the SW, a large L-shaped extension added in the late C19. It is weatherboarded, with catslide roofs (taller on the r.) and generous 42-pane glazing. Inside, a host of original Victorian MACHINERY, including two Dobcross LOOMS (by *Hutchinson, Hollingworth & Co.*, Lancashire), dated 1896 and 1899. They are thought to be the oldest looms still in operation.

To the W is the CONSERVATION WORKSHOP by *LDN*, 2010, the only completely new building on the site. Long and gabled with rectangular outshots to the flanks. Skylights facing W.

DISTILLERIES

CARDHU (formerly CARDOW) DISTILLERY (Diageo), 1.2 km. ENE. Founded by the whisky smuggler John Cumming in 1824 with buildings of the 'most straggling and primitive description'.* Rebuilt on the current site by *Charles C. Doig* in 1884–6; much expanded by him in 1896–7 after the distillery was acquired by John Walker & Sons. Two pagoda-roofed KILNS at the top of the complex, the S one of 1884–6 and the N of 1896–7. Ten-bay, double-gabled former MALT BARNS behind each of them. In front on the N, a former malt intake and store room (now with red door), renovated *c.* 1987 as the entrance to a visitors' centre.

Harled, L-plan PRODUCTION BLOCK to the S, built 1960–1 in the footprint of the originals; two-storey OFFICE in the re-entrant angle, late C19. Two sets of WAREHOUSES at the far S end, the upper advanced one by *A. & W. Reid*, 1884, and the second by Doig, 1896. It is triple-gabled and (unusually) three-storeyed. Another warehouse across by Doig, 1905; MANAGER'S HOUSE and CUSTOMS AND EXCISE OFFICER'S HOUSE to the far N, *c.* 1885 and 1894.

Along the N side of the village road, WORKMEN'S COTTAGES of 1900, again by Doig.

KNOCKANDO DISTILLERY (Diageo), 2.1 km. SE. By *Charles C. Doig*, 1898–9, and precociously so: this was the first distillery in Scotland to be wired and lit by electricity. Much expanded in 1904–5, again by Doig; extensively rebuilt and enlarged, 1968–9. Of Doig's first complex, the shorter E portion of the main block, its upper half now harled pink. Original five-bay DISTILLERY OFFICE and EXCISE OFFICE jutting from its NE corner. Looming large to the W are the tall, pagoda-roofed KILN and double-gabled, eleven-bay MALT BARN, both of 1904–5. Doig aligned these axially with the original block – and not according to his usual E-plan – to allow access to the railway in front.

Six continuously gabled WAREHOUSES to the N, 1905 and 1911–13 (also Doig). Line of WORKMEN'S COTTAGES to the W, the S three of *c.* 1899 and the N added 1904. Former MANAGER'S HOUSE and EXCISE OFFICER'S HOUSE up the slope to the N, the l. of 1899 and the r. *c.* 1908.

TAMDHU DISTILLERY (Ian Macleod), 1.4 km. SE. Originally Tamdhu-Glenlivet, built to a 'most modern' and 'scientifically constructed' plan by *Charles C. Doig*, 1896–7. Of his original E-plan complex, the triple-gabled MALTINGS at the N end of the main block, two storeys and twelve bays running E–W. His former KILN is at the W end, now drastically altered and shorn

*See the remains 300 m. to the SE, to the l. of the distillery's main entrance.

of its pagoda top. Major rebuilding in 1973–5, including a new PRODUCTION BLOCK to the S on a large L-plan. Across to the E, a long, graduated range of WAREHOUSES, 1896–7, the triple-gabled one on the far N added by Doig in 1903.

Three blocks of WORKMEN'S COTTAGES on the entrance drive to the N, the r. one the original of 1896–7. Central block added by Doig in 1904; far l. one by *Charles C. Doig & Sons*, 1949. Former CUSTOMS AND EXCISE OFFICER'S HOUSE (now Spey View) by main entrance, 1896–7; former MANAGER'S HOUSE (now Tamdhu House) to the S, of the same date.

KYLNADROCHIT LODGE B 1010

2.3 km. NW of Tomintoul

In free Scots Renaissance style by *G. Mackie Watson*, 1898–1900. It was built for George Smith, a retired minister of Prestonpans but acquired by the 7th Duke of Richmond & Gordon as a shooting lodge after his lodge at The Lecht (q.v.) was destroyed by fire in 1915. Quite plain and sturdy, two storeys, but with a pleasingly asymmetrical entrance front with crowstepped gables and in the centre a shaped gable. Crisp doorpiece with segmental pediment. On the S front a full-height rectangular bay window, again with a shaped gable, and a single-storey bay with crenellation. Good interior. The entrance has an arcaded screen on Ionic supports to the staircase with turned balusters and newels and another arcade on the landing. In the sitting room, recessed, glazed bookshelves and pilastered overmantel with blue tile slips below. The drawing room chimneypiece also with excellent tiles of blue and green flowers. Pulvinated architrave and panelled overmantel with segmental pediment. The dining room chimneypiece manages to look simultaneously C17 and Art Nouveau: lugged, roll-moulded architrave and black marble slips with hard-edged border. Even the lavatory has its original fittings.

Former U-plan STABLES and CARRIAGE HOUSE to N, *c.* 1905, probably by *Watson*.

LAGGAN HOUSE *see* CARRON

THE LECHT B 2010

7.6 km. ESE of Tomintoul

Former MINE. Iron ore was first mined here 1730–7 by the London-based York Buildings Company. The 5th Duke of Richmond reopened operations in 1841 for manganese extraction. It employed sixty-three people at its peak and remains the largest such mine ever worked in Scotland. The ore was crushed and hand-picked before transport by horseback to Portgordon (q.v.) for shipment. Russian manganese soon made the mine unprofitable and it closed in 1847.

The CRUSHING PLANT of 1842 survives, re-roofed *c.* 1980. Tall, two-storey rectangle with segmental openings, the S front with a large entrance and three former windows. Large hatch high on the E gable for loading ore. The W gable originally had a very large overshot water wheel. Gutted interior with joist pockets to the former loft. Stone platform on the W for the 'stamps' that hammered the ore into fine powder.

WELL OF THE LECHT, 0.2 km. WNW. Freshwater spring with a plaque recording that, in 1754, five companies of the 33rd Regiment built this section of ROAD 'from here to the Spey' under the leadership of Col. Lord Charles Hay. This was part of Major Caulfield's military road from Coupar Angus (Perth and Kinross) to Fort George (Highland and Islands) to open up the Highlands after the 1745 Rebellion. *See also* Bridge of Avon, Tomintoul (p. 750).

4060

LETTERFOURIE HOUSE B

1.1 km. ESE of Drybridge

79 One of the largest Georgian houses in Moray, and especially fine and dignified. The lands passed from the Hay family (the Earls of Errol) to the Earls of Huntly in 1476. It remained a Gordon residence until the early to mid C20. James Gordon, 6th Laird, made his fortune in wine in Madeira and retired here with his brother, Alexander, a staunch Jacobite who had fled Scotland after Culloden. Together they commissioned *Robert Adam* for their new house, built 1772–3.

The house, built of pink pinned granite, forms a U-plan on the N entrance front, with a tall, cubical, central block of three bays and three storeys over a sunk basement (cf. Orton and Pitgaveny, qq.v.). It is flanked by single-storey links to two-storey pavilion wings at right angles. In the centre a shallow porch with Corinthian columns. Ashlar band course across the main block and at first floor tall windows with balustraded aprons, moulded margins, consoles and pulvinated architraves. Smaller windows on the second storey and a plain parapet above a cornice masking a low piended roof flanked by blocky longitudinal chimneystacks. The links have shallow pediments in the centre and the pavilions are very plain; the E one was the service wing but the W one originally contained the Catholic chapel below priest's accommodation. Its rear rises tall and sheer with a small projecting wing in the centre and a door in the lower r. re-entrant angle. Two large, round-headed windows in the basement for the chapel itself, the heads with intersecting astragals.

To the garden, the basement is fully exposed, producing an impressive and unexpected verticality while managing – as in all the best of Adam's work – to combine heft with a delicate sense of proportion. The rear of the main block is plain, and now of five bays rather than three. In the centre of the top floor a (blocked) window with a moulded margin with a dated keystone. The links again have advanced centres but no pediments, and the gables of the wings are blind. To the W of the W wing a partially subterranean L-plan passageway leads to the former OUTBUILDINGS with seven barrel-vaulted chambers.

The interior is excellent. High, rectangular ENTRANCE HALL aligned E–W, with a cantilevered STAIRCASE rising the full height of the house with plain square balusters. On the garden front the former DINING ROOM (now a sitting room) with good chimneypiece containing a steel grate made by *James Fraser* of Banff, *c.* 1773, featuring a retractable curved front. Fielded panelled door of dark Spanish mahogany, one of several specially imported by the Gordons. On the first floor, the superb DRAWING ROOM with hand-painted Chinoiserie wallpaper, probably also *c.* 1773, of white flowering branches, lanterns and birds on an aqua-green background. Fine white marble chimneypiece with polished yellow marble infill, again with a beautiful grate by Fraser. The ceiling is the best in the house, painted its original shades of green and white. Large rose in the centre with anthemion and spokes of curled leaves; garlands and bows around the circumference. In the four corners, urns with very delicate rinceau curled around thick flower buds. Thick-textured bows on the long sides. The plasterwork of the landing was remodelled in the early to mid C19. Foliate bracketed cornice and ceiling rose with fern-like fronds. In the LIBRARY another fine chimneypiece. Mantel with garlands and a large urn in the centre; grapevine on the jambs. The former CHAPEL in the W wing has ribbed groin-vaults and fluted pilasters flanking the centre with original painted marbling. MORNING ROOM on the ground floor of the E wing with another good chimneypiece, and a surprisingly grand example also in the former SERVANTS' DINING ROOM in the basement below. Voluted pilasters with attenuated urns; delicate scrollwork on the mantel with a goddess's head.

Early to mid-C19 WATER GARDEN to the S of the house. Two circular basins with fountains, linked by a narrow canal. The large WALLED GARDEN, 450 m. SSE was laid out *c.* 1778. Round-headed, keystoned S entrance arch. Former GARDEN ROOM and ORANGERY in the centre of the N side, now in poor condition.

CRAIGMIN BRIDGE, 0.5 km. WSW. A remarkable and very rare double-decker structure over the Burn of Letterfourie, formerly on the main approach to the house. Late C18, perhaps by *Adam*. The lower arch, springing directly from rocky ravines carries the upper span which has two semicircular arches flanking a mural chamber perched on the crown of the lower arch. Shallow, round-headed niche at the top of the centre. It is possible that the lower bridge pre-dated the house and the second tier was added for horse traffic *c.* 1773.

HOME FARM, 275 m. NNE. Large U-plan complex of 1776, mostly converted in the later C20. Main block has a former granary in the centre. Central gable with birdcage bellcote and Gordon arms in the tympanum with their motto 'Dum sisto vigilo' ('As I stand, I watch').

THE OLD MONASTERY, 0.85 km. ESE. Built 1903–5 as a Catholic chapel with 'retreat house' for monks of Fort Augustus (Highland and Islands). Paid for by Sir Robert Gordon of Letterfourie, who had himself been a novice. Converted to a restaurant *c.* 1979 and now a house. Lancet windows.

2060

LEUCHARS HOUSE

3.4 km. NW of Urquhart

A large, pleasant country villa in Italianate style, built *c.* 1845 for the factor to the Earls Fife, then owners of Innes House (q.v.). The firm was *Mackenzie & Matthews*, their Tuscan style closely resembling Mackenzie's other work in Moray.* In 1948–9, it was rebuilt to its original appearance by *J. & W. Wittet* after a fire. Two storeys of snecked rubble, the front r. gable advanced. Rectangular, pilastered bay window and tripartite round-headed windows above with lying-pane glazing. Square porch in the re-entrant angle with a large ball finial. All of the latter are good ashlar work from the Clashach quarry at Hopeman (q.v.). To the l. of the porch, a timber veranda with trellises of pierced oculi; in the next re-entrant angle behind, a strange and mighty doorpiece with round arch corbelled out over sunken half-ellipses. Behind the house, the service court is bounded by a single-storey quadrant and three-bay piended N wing, both survivors of an earlier house of *c.* 1781. Good fittings inside on the ground floor, including an entrance hall with pilasters and groin-vaults.

Reset DORMERHEAD outside, dated 1583 with coat of arms and the initials I.I. and M.S. (for John Innes and Marhory Strachan). They built the original tower house near this site (shown on Pont's map of *c.* 1590 and dem. mid C19). – Pedestal SUNDIAL with reused caryatid male figure and blocky armorial of the C17. – Former DOOCOT, 100 m. NE. Originally of the circular beehive type, built in the late C16 to serve the tower house. Mostly collapsed *c.* 1970.

*See also the Museum in Elgin, St John's Church in Forres and the former drill hall at Aberlour.

LHANBRYDE

2060

Small village that began to expand in the early to mid C19. Once quite picturesque, but now engulfed by bad modern housing to the N and E.

PARISH CHURCH, 1.8 km. WNW on the B9013. Built 1795–6 as the replacement for St Andrew, Kirkhill (*see* below) and St Bridget (*see* Burial Ground, below), both demolished 1796. The usual Georgian gabled oblong, the main S flank with five round-headed windows. Rounded Y-tracery inserted by *A. & W. Reid & Wittet* in 1898. Theirs also the small E porch, Romanesque E window and bellcote. Later extensions to the rear, including former vestry and hall. Interior as reorientated and renovated in 1898–9, with ribbed coomb ceiling and high GALLERY on the E wall. – Wide, canted PULPIT, altered *c.* 1959 by *J. & W. Wittet*. Octagonal tester with ogival dome. – COMMUNION TABLE by *John Duncan* and *John Scott* of Aberdeen, 1898. Polished Peterhead granite shafts.

LHANBRYDE BURIAL GROUND, St Andrew's Road. On a hillock overlooking the village. Site of the church of St Bridget, first mentioned in the charters of Bishop Bricius between 1208 and 1215. It was demolished in 1796. – Two connected BURIAL ENCLOSURES against the N wall. The l. one has a PLAQUE for James Chalmers †1742 and Helen Leslie †1776, flanked by fluted, fronded pilasters. Tall architrave with mortality emblems; stylized ogee pediment with heraldic crest, two winged souls and a big rosette finial. – Roofless BURIAL AISLE to the SE for the Innes family. In a recess inside, the recumbent stone EFFIGY of a medieval knight, without inscription but likely representing Robert Innes of Monycabok †1547. Full armour with the three stars of Innes on the breastplate, now faded; hands clasped in prayer with sword to the side and a lion beneath his feet. – To the l. of it, a re-set SLAB for Alexander Innes †1612, who began the construction of Coxton Tower (q.v.). Perimeter inscription in Latin and a big armorial crest on the top. On the bottom, a semicircular *memento mori*. – To the r., a SLAB for Maria Gordon †1647, first wife of Sir Alexander Innes, who completed Coxton Tower. Latin dedication and triangular pediment with two coats of arms and a skull.

In the middle of the entrance stairs, the WAR MEMORIAL, by *John Wittet*, 1920. Stocky arch of rock-faced voussoirs around a tablet.

ST ANDREWS BURIAL GROUND, Kirkhill, 2.7 km. WNW. St Andrew's church was first documented in 1426 in a grant confirmation by James I. Demolished in 1796, its stone was used to build the parish church (*see* above). – Tall, roofless BURIAL AISLE for the Leuchars family, marking the E end of the original church. – In front of it, two LEDGER SLABS for Agnes Geddes †1681 and Christian Geddes †1676. – Another further S for Jespar Winchester †1688, James Sim †1658 and Margaret Sim (undated).

To the SSE, a bowstring FOOTBRIDGE over the Lossie by *Newmill Ironworks*, Elgin, 1910–11. Scrolled, V-shaped brackets under the deck.

Former manse, 0.2 km. NNW, completed in 1739 but subsumed into the much expanded KIRKHILL HOUSE by *A. & W. Reid*, *c.* 1870. Two-storey harled front with an advanced, bowed bay under semi-conical piended roof. Gabled bay to the l. and porch in between by *John Wittet*, 1904.

The historic core of the village is ST ANDREW'S ROAD, running straight E–W and then with a gentle curve along the Lhanbryd (or Longhill) Burn. The TENNANT ARMS HOTEL on the N side was built as the Fife Arms Hotel by *Mackenzie & Matthews*, 1854. Neo-Jacobean, the r. end with a semicircular former carriage entrance. The Burial Ground follows, and further on ROSE VILLA, Picturesque style of *c.* 1862 with bargeboarded dormers, and BARRA LODGE, next door, 1851, with a vigorous shell tympanum over the door.

Former STATION (now Station House), 0.3 km. S, across the A96. Simple Italianate, 1858, for the Inverness & Aberdeen Junction Railway (closed, 1964). T-plan with projecting eaves and platform shelter in the S re-entrant angle (now infilled and glazed).

KILCLUAN HOUSE, 1.7 km. NW. Imposing former manse by *William Robertson*, 1825–6. S front of coursed rubble, two tall storeys and three bays over a raised basement. Pilastered, pedimented doorpiece approached by a flight of steps; ground-floor windows to the l. and r. in shallow, round-headed recesses over plain aprons. Piended platform roof with wide end chimneystacks. – U-plan former OFFICES to the NW, 1815 by *Alexander Forteath* (factor to the Earls Fife), for the manse which burnt in 1825.

AA SENTRY BOX, 1.7 km. E, on N side of A69 at Threapland Wood. Standard weatherboarded and gabled design used from 1958 to 1967, of which only seven survive in Scotland.

BLACKHILLS HOUSE, 2.5 km. S. Original house on the l. by *William Robertson*, 1837–8, two storeys and three wide bays with a pilastered, corniced doorpiece. Similar four-bay addition by *A. & W. Reid*, *c.* 1870, and another by *John Wittet*, 1920–1. – PICTISH STONE under a shelter, relocated here *c.* 1913. N face covered with cup marks, one large and the others in irregular diagonal rows. Good double spiral on the E side; crescent and five cup marks on the S. – Large mound SE of the house, originally featuring a watch tower built by the Innes family in the mid C16.

BRIDGE OF CALCOTS, 3.1 km. NW. Two segmental arches over the Lossie, late C18. Blind oculus in the central spandrel.

Former LONGHILL MILL, 1.2 km. N. Built 1891, replacing a corn mill of 1733 destroyed by fire. Converted to residential use by *Ashley Bartlam Partnership*, 2006–10. Two-storey-and-attic T-plan with water wheel (originally overshot) on the S gable. Tall, tapered octagonal ridge vent over the former kiln. It is slated and has a revolving sheet-metal top. Wing off the SE corner, originally piended but now generously glazed. – To the NE, the early to mid-C19 MILLER'S HOUSE.

SHERIFFSTON, 1.7 km. WNW. Early C19 core, much expanded into a Scots Renaissance double pile by *A. & W. Reid*, *c.* 1860.

THATCHED COTTAGE, 1.9 km. SSE, on the B9013. Early to mid C19, and one of the only thatched cottages remaining in N Scotland. Thatch renewed *c.* 1970 and again *c.* 2012.

STANDING STONES, 0.5 km. SE, in field N of Glenesk Cottage (Bogton). Two orthostats (1.8 m. and 1.6 m. high) set 14.7 m. apart, originally forming a stone circle with diameter of *c.* 34 m. The remainder was destroyed *c.* 1810.

LOGIE HOUSE 0050

4.4 km. NNW of Edinkillie

Logie was held by the Comyns (Cummings) of Altyre (q.v.) from 1408. John Cumming became 1st Laird of Logie in 1663 and constructed a sizeable manor house, shown on a mid-C18 estate map as a long, narrow U-plan. This was filled in in the late C18, creating a solid rectangle that forms the nucleus of the present house. It was extended in 1861 by *A. & W. Reid* and in 1924–7 for Sir Alexander Grant, head of the biscuit firm McVitie & Price. This work was done by either *T.P. Marwick & Son* or *John Wittet*, who was then remodelling Dunphail House (q.v.). There were further alterations in 1956, 1961 and again in 1977–9.

Despite the multiple campaigns Logie has a remarkable homogeneity, each architect adopting the restrained Baronial style of the original. The pristine white harling also provides a good sense of continuity. The original laird's house forms the S end of the long E front. It is a three-storey rectangle of three bays, the gables crowstepped but the Jacobean-style gablets above the wall-head dating from 1861. Large 1920s porte cochère advanced in front, its crenellated parapet with angels and heraldic plaques. On the S flank, where the land slopes steeply down to the Findhorn basin, a two-storey, canted bay window, also of the 1920s; little slit-window above it, unmistakable evidence of the C17. The 1860s addition, one storey lower, forms a double pile to the rear of the main block. It also has a two-storey canted bay window on the S front below a crowstepped gable and corner tourelle with candlesnuffer roof. To the garden, this section has C17-style dormerheads and bolection-moulded door in the centre below a long stair window. Square bartizan in the upper l. corner with long pyramidal roof. The three bays to the l. are again 1920s, slightly narrower but otherwise seamless with the Victorian work and with reserved Baronial detailing. More C17-style triangular dormer-heads. At the same time, the SERVICE COURT of 1861 was relocated further N but reusing the original segmental access arch with bolection moulding and stepped lintel. The single-storey former larder and coal store (now the Estate Office) was raised to its current height in 1956 by *W. Ashley Bartlam*, who also built the charming square addition (known as the Apple Room) topped by dome roof with bellcast eaves. Back on the main E front, this part has crowstepped gables and a corbelled tourelle on the r. corner. The three-bay block between this and the main house is the 1920s addition with a taller projection on the l. under a crowstepped gable built to house the service stair. The front wall to the r. of it was brought forward by *Law & Dunbar-Nasmith* in 1977–9 to create a kitchen but re-setting the original crenellated parapet along the wall-head.

The INTERIOR was completely remodelled in 1925–7 in C17 and C18 style, with plasterwork by *J. Brodie & Sons* of Elgin. The ENTRANCE HALL has groin-vaults on pairs of panelled pilasters with acanthus cornices. Cantilevered dog-leg STAIR-CASE at the end with barley-twist balusters; rectangular cornice on its ceiling with elliptical flower border in the centre. The DINING ROOM (originally the Drawing Room) l. of the hall has panelled dado and pairs of fluted pilasters to the canted bay window. Vitruvian scroll on the ceiling and chimneypiece with urns on the jambs. Sitting Room beyond it with white-washed timber chimneypiece with vigorous grapevine rinceaux ending in eagles' heads. The panelled OAK ROOM (r. of the hall) was originally at the front of the house but relocated to the garden side in 1956. Chimneypiece with thick bolection moulding. Further on is the SITTING ROOM (formerly the Dining Room), extended and reorientated in 1977–9. Reused chimneypiece of 1925–6 with engaged Ionic columns and pulvinated mantel. Plaster cornice recreated from the original moulds. On the FIRST FLOOR very exuberant 1920s plaster-work with thick friezes of jumbo foliage, wild and unrestrained in Scots Renaissance style.

To the SSW is a large WALLED GARDEN of the late C18, now very fine after much replanting and rebuilding of dykes and bridges in 2009–12. – On the approach to the house, a single-storey former MOTOR HOUSE by *R. Neish & Forsyth* of Forres, 1939. Tudor arches to the garages. It was meant to have had an upper storey for chauffeur's quarters and tall crowstepped gables with attenuated chimneystacks. Converted to shop and gallery space in 2011–13. – Immediately adjacent is LOGIE STEADING, the former Mains Farm, an impressive complex by *Charles C. Doig & Sons*, 1925–6 (converted for shops and businesses in 1991–2). Long W front with a big four-centred arch in the middle under a blocking course with spiked gablet. Arts and Crafts clock cupola above with a bellcast roof.

Also by Doig & Sons is the NORTH LODGE (0.9 km. NNE), 1926. Good Scots Renaissance with a corbelled bartizan. – The

EAST LODGE (0.6 km. SE), 1891, has a plaque of *c.* 1828 from Relugas House (*see* p. 732).

LOSSIEMOUTH 2070

Lossiemouth is really three separate towns. Seatown, the original settlement, was created in 1698 as a new port for Elgin, replacing one on Loch Spynie which was continually silting up. Half a century later, Elgin Town Council laid out a 'proper' town on a grid-plan, with four main streets stretching W of Seatown. In 1837–9, a new harbour was created in Branderburgh on the NE promontory, and this new settlement soon began to eclipse the original Lossiemouth. Coulard Hill was populated with buildings throughout the late C19 and early C20. At the same time, villas and hotels were laid out on Stotfield Road at the W end of the town, overlooking the Moray Firth and the golf course. Stotfield and Branderburgh finally met in the middle, and Lossiemouth assumed its current form.

The town enjoyed great prosperity as a spa town in the Victorian and Edwardian periods, and from the fishing industry in the mid C19. Its main claim to fame is as the birthplace of James Ramsay MacDonald, Britain's first Labour prime minister.

CHURCHES

BAPTIST CHURCH, King Street. Meagre gabled building of 1868–70 with lancets and bellcote but with a bold N extension by *McLaren Associates* of Edinburgh, 2010.

ST COLUMBA (R.C.), Union Street. Simplified Gothic chapel. 1912–13. Extended 1971.

ST GERARDINE'S HIGH CHURCH, Prospect Terrace. Big, 48
Romanesque Revival by *J.J. Burnet*, 1899–1903. With its red roof tiles and thick, stucco-like harling, it looks like something transported from Florida or southern California. Single-storey nave aligned N–S under a tall, double-pitch gabled roof. Two-stage tower on the S end, its upper section with pairs of round-headed, louvred windows with shafts topped by cushion capitals. Solid, corbelled parapet and stepped pyramidal roof, also tiled. Long porch extending to the W with tall, chamfered round-arched entrance under a niche. Off to the N is a long, seven-bay hall forming an L-plan, added 1929 in a similar style by *Burnet, Son & Dick*.

Harled interior with four round arcades forming a low W aisle, all the ashlar dressings with contrasting lighter and darker accents. Wagon roof of timber, the arch brace to the chancel gouged out with big scallops. N windows with chevron, nail-head and more cushion capitals; E chancel window with interlace, as if from an Anglo-Norman manuscript. – GALLERY in the base of the S tower separated by a tall arch. – Plain, canted

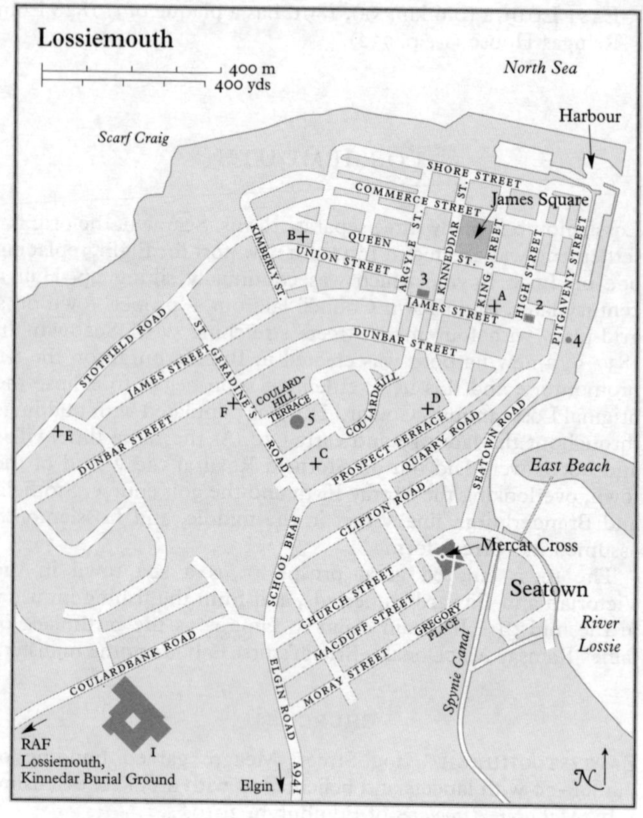

A	Baptist Church	1	High School
B	St Columba (R.C.)	2	Library & Town Hall
C	St Gerardine's High Church	3	Masonic Lodge
D	St James	4	War Memorial
E	St Margaret (Episcopal)	5	Water Reservoir
F	United Free Church		

PULPIT. – FONT with a square alabaster bowl, 1902–3. – STAINED GLASS. Three windows by *Stephen Adam Studio* of Glasgow, 1921–2. Crucifixion and Resurrection (N end); St Gerardine (r. side of the chancel). – In the gallery, Proverbs 31:18 ('Her candle goeth not out by night'), 1924.

Several MEMORIALS relocated here from the former Drainie parish church on the site of the RAF base (*see* below). – In the gallery, a framed wooden PANEL of 1842, commemorating the Stotfield Disaster, when twenty-one sailors were killed by a storm on Christmas Day, 1806. – In the porch, a double

MONUMENT for (on the l.) Alexander Gordon †1741, Margaret Brodie †1734 and children, and (on the r.) Alexander Gordon †1700 and his wife, Isabella King. Underneath are skulls, bones and mortality emblems. Heraldry above flanked by engaged Ionic columns; big urn finials over winged souls, the l. breaking a semicircular pediment.

In the CHURCHYARD, a freestanding COLUMN from the former burial ground at Kinneddar (*see* below). Likely C17, with Corinthian detailing on the capital.

ST JAMES, Prospect Terrace. Originally the United Free High Church. By *A. Marshall Mackenzie*, 1887–8. The main body is the usual gabled Gothic box but with a landmark octagonal SE tower with a spire that has slender lancets at the base, lancets at the belfry and gablets of quatrefoils around the base of the spire.

The church was gutted by fire in 1932, leaving only the tower and outer walls intact. Reconstructed 1932–3 by *George Bennett Mitchell & Son*. The infill of their darker masonry is clearly visible on the main façade above the door with its shafts, stiff-leaf capitals and moulded arch. The large window above is divided into stepped lancets with open spandrels. Plain interior and furnishings of the 1930s reconstruction. – ORGAN. *J.J. Binns, Fitton & Haley*. Tall case with Dec brattishing and four finials. – STAINED GLASS. In the gallery, a huge Miraculous Draught of Fishes by *Charles Florence*, 1971. It is the crowning glory of the church, and the effect from the ground floor is mesmerizing. Large green net with red buoys in the centre and a vortex of fish caught inside. The waves are masterfully conveyed in alternating shades of blue. St James has always been considered the fishermen's church, so the iconography is apt. – In the two N lancets, a pair of saints by *Walter J. Pearce*, 1934. In the SW corner of the CHURCH YARD wall, the datestone from the original Drainie Free Church, 1884.

ST MARGARET (Episcopal), Stotfield Road. 1910–11 by *R.B. Pratt*. Nave and chancel under one roof with a gabled bay on the N side with Y-tracery. Otherwise lancets. NW porch. Simple interior with walls of exposed rock-faced rubble. Kingpost roof of dark oak raised on diagonal struts. – Splendid Gothic FURNISHINGS, mostly *c.* 1900 from the Chapel at Altyre House (q.v.), donated by Lady William Gordon-Cumming, an ardent Episcopalian. Especially good is the PRIE-DIEU, very faithful to the C14, figures in a nodding-ogee niche. Also a charming ORGAN, harmonium-style, by *W. Bell & Co.* – STAINED GLASS. At the base of the E window, a re-set heraldic panel (late C19?) of the Shakespeare coat of arms. – N lancets (St Margaret and St Luke) by the *Pluscarden Abbey* workshop, 1968.

UNITED FREE CHURCH, St Gerardine's Road. By *J. & W. Wittet*, 1937. Single-storey, gabled rectangle of six bays. Four segmental-headed windows to the E flank. Low, polygonal entrance porch on the N with a big trefoil over.

KINNEDDAR BURIAL GROUND, 1.9 km. SW. Site of the oratory established *c.* 934 by St Gerardine, the first Christian missionary to Moray. The church served as the cathedral of Moray under Bishop Richard (1187–1203), who transferred it here from Birnie (q.v.). But from 1207 the cathedral was moved to Spynie (q.v.) and the church reverted to parochial use, superseded by Drainie Parish Church in the mid C17 (*see* RAF Lossiemouth, below). Nothing remains of it or the Bishop's Palace which was extended (or rebuilt) into a castle by Bishop Archibald *c.* 1280 and remained occupied until the late C14. Excavations in 1936 uncovered a large hexagonal complex with a central tower and outer defence walls ringed with small subsidiary towers.

Many fragments of PICTISH STONES have been discovered here, some now in Elgin Museum. The stones suggest an important early Christian centre with royal patronage, probably dating to the C8–C9. – In the SW section, a CROSS of medieval date, probably the mid-C16 MARKET CROSS of the vanished Kirktown of Kinneddar. Plain stone shaft with vestiges of chamfering and stops at the apex; later, spindly iron cross on the top. Cubical pedestal over a two-stepped plinth. – Long walled BURIAL ENCLOSURE on the N, the l. slightly advanced with a moulded door frame and raised long-and-short quoins. Originally divided into four AISLES (now in poor condition).

PUBLIC BUILDINGS

HARBOUR. An unusual L-plan with two long basins clasping the NE corner of the town. The original harbour was established by Elgin Burgh in 1698 and stood at the head of the Lossie (in front of the present Seatown Road) and was engineered by *Peter Brauss*, who carried out Sir William Bruce's plans for supplying Edinburgh with water in 1676. Despite major work in the mid to late C18, this was inadequate by *c.* 1830, especially due to the growing herring industry. The Stotfield & Lossiemouth Harbour Co. commissioned a new harbour in 1837–9 with a long chamber aligned N–S and engineered by *Robert Stevenson & Son*. Breakwater to the N, with extensions in 1845 by *John & Alexander Gibb* and further extensions to the S in 1852–4. The second (or 'new') basin to the W was excavated in 1858–60.

In 1837–9, the Stotfield and Lossiemouth Harbour Co. built the new Branderburgh Harbour at Stotfield Point, now the NE corner of town. *James Bremner* was the engineer. The original basin was extended S in 1852 and W in 1860, creating an L-plan with two long, narrow arms. The harbour was deepened in 1894 and given new walls (and deepened again) in 1937.

TOWN HALL and LIBRARY, High Street. Two separate campaigns. The Town Hall is on the l. and came first. 1884–5 by *Duncan Cameron* of Inverness. Three bays to High Street, the l. and r. slightly advanced and marked by pairs of pilasters. Round-arched windows to the first storey below a boldly projecting, dentilled cornice. On the upper l. corner, a pyramid spire with a clock turret (added 1903 by *J. Wittet*). On the r., a tall blocking course with a segmental centre. The lower, two-storey entrance to the N dates from 1931. The LIBRARY was added by *A. & W. Reid & Wittet*, 1901–4, and funded by a £1,500 gift from Carnegie. It has channelled quoins and a short, corbelled-out clock tower on the corner with a bell-shaped cupola. The interior of the hall has a stage with proscenium arch and W gallery on fluted pilasters. Entrance foyer with good staircase, railing and gate. Inside the library, the roof is supported on big segmental arches and moulded kingposts.

MASONIC LODGE, James Street. 1913–14 by *R. B. Pratt*. Free style with sharp gables, pairs of arched windows and the entrance in a segmental arch with inscription above.

WAR MEMORIAL, Pitgaveny Street. 1921–2 by *Percy Portsmouth* (cf. Elgin). A large work dramatically set into a cliff face opposite the site of the railway station (dem. 1988). High, two-stepped ashlar base enthroning a large bronze figure of Peace and Victory. He is helmeted and holds a sword with a laurel wreath perched on top. Swags of olive across his lap. Two tiers of names inscribed below, with small reliefs of 'Veritas Vincit' and 'Beatae Memoriae' in the bottom corners.

WATER RESERVOIR, Coulardhill Terrace. Disused. *c.* 1928–9 by *Gordon & Co.* of Inverness, engineers. Two concentric concrete circles, the central one raised like a windowless lantern.

DESCRIPTION

The town set out in 1764 by the Elgin Town Council is four very wide streets (Clifton, Church, Macduff and Moray) on a grid-plan criss-crossed by narrow lanes, with a large square on its E side (now GREGORY PLACE). This has the MERCAT CROSS, erected in the same year. Weathered cylindrical shaft, 2.5 m. The upper portion is missing; its appearance is not recorded. Later five-stepped base (also circular) of big blocks. The showiest buildings are concentrated on the N side of the grid along CLIFTON ROAD, beginning with LOSSIEMOUTH HOUSE (No. 33), which was built *c.* 1780 as the dower house for the last Lady Gordon of Gordonstoun. Three storeys and five bays of unpainted harling. Thick bowed stair-tower in the centre with its own roof. A wing (perhaps even earlier than the house) projects from the rear forming an L-plan. Further down on the N side, a three-bay, two-storey house (No. 62) of *c.* 1790. Elegantly poised and balanced, notwithstanding two C20 canted dormers. Harled. Attenuated windows. Two good ball-finialled gatepiers at the entrance. Finally ROCK HOUSE (now a hotel), dated 1789 on its E skewputt. It was built by the grandfather of Empress Eugenie, wife of Napoleon III. Symmetrical five bays; two storeys and attic over a raised basement. Long and short channelled quoins in white. Big sixteen-pane windows. Good moulded doorpiece flanked by lavish late C19 railing. The original fanlight has been reset by the first-floor landing on the cantilevered staircase. In MORAY STREET along the S side of the grid, No. 17 (The Hillocks) was Ramsay MacDonald's home, designed by *J. Wittet*, 1909–10. It was intended for a site on Prospect Terrace (*see* below) but was denied permission, as 'Red bastards don't build up here'. S front of three bays and two storeys, with two tall canted windows breaking the wall-head on the flanks. Later loggia porch of big rusticated blocks. Rear façade to the street.

SEATOWN is the roughly triangular piece of land E of Gregory Place, bounded by the River Lossie and two branches of the Spynie Canal. It was established with housing for the original harbour in 1698, but its current configuration dates from *c.* 1780. A BRIDGE of *c.* 1810 crosses the Spynie Canal, four sluice gates on its S side. Beyond are low, single-storey cottages, mostly of the 1830s and 1840s. They are arranged in long rows, the furthest with their gabled ends to the street. To the E, a FOOTBRIDGE spans the Lossie and gives access to EAST BEACH. Its dunes are not natural, but were created by submerging old railway carriages in the sand. N along SEATOWN ROAD N of Clifton Road where it is open to the river, No. 20 is dated 1629 in faded script on a re-set stone, and so the oldest surviving building in Lossiemouth. Two storeys and five bays of rubble, the shutters now painted a surprising orange. Subtle relieving arch over the lintel of the central ground-floor entrance; another door to the first floor via a dog-leg and later timber porch. Inside, four bays of continuous barrel-vaulting in rubble to the ground floor. Further on, Nos. 14–16, late C18, a pleasant long stone front with a Dutch-gabled centre with a chimney over the former pend. The road then curves N, turning into PITGAVENY STREET below the cliff and the war memorial (*see* above), up to PITGAVENY QUAY, a very fine and long, three-storey complex of offices and warehouses. Two builds, the six N bays (slightly lower in height) of 1851 and the four on the S of *c.* 1860–70. All sensitively restored by *Wittets* from 2004. Bowed SW corner to Commerce Street, its original door now blocked and converted into a window. The first bay was the Harbour Master's Offices, with a scroll-bracketed and corniced entrance. On the r., a rectangular recess for a mural barometer. The second and third bays contain the Fisheries and Community Museum. Then, nine segmental-headed entrances on the ground floor with double-leaf plank doors. Several sunken roundels, purpose-built for storing lifebelts. All else is plain, but the upper windows in the first and third bays have gableted dormers, no doubt signifying the harbour master's authority.

Just behind, on COMMERCE STREET, another mid-C19 warehouse, now converted into a theatre. Basket-headed entrance in the centre.

Now for the later C19 town higher up inland. PROSPECT TERRACE begins at the top of School Brae. Very appropriately named, with sweeping views of the Moray Firth, East Beach, the Lossie, Seatown and Ben Rinnes in the distance, attracting the best of the villas and St Gerardine's church (*see* Churches). Near the E end, just before St James's church (*see* Churches) the comical TOWER HOUSE, *c.* 1897, like a toy fort with a square tower in the centre. Next door HIGHCLIFFE HOUSE, *c.* 1880, a picturesque Italianate cottage but with a very unusual short rectangular tower with a piended roof rising higher than the rest. At the NE end of Prospect Terrace is CRAIGMOUNT. Early C19, painted harl with white margins, it is a tall single storey with full-height canted bays on the front and a recessed central porch under the oversailing roof supported on rustic columns (the originals were Doric – their plinths and capitals remain).

Prospect Terrace becomes HIGH STREET running N. Only the Town Hall and Library at the corner of James Street (*see* Public Buildings) catch the eye. One block W is the singularly unimpressive JAMES SQUARE, attempting to assert itself as the town centre. It is too broad and surrounded by excessively squat buildings. At the SE corner is the Baptist church (*see* Churches), and on the S side are two square piers with big crocketed finials, all that remain of the previous St James's church (built 1880–1 by *Matthews & Mackenzie* and demolished 1966). On the Square's N side, the former REGAL CINEMA of 1939 by *Alexander Cattanach Jun.* Three huge blades, quite Futurist, sweep up the centre of the façade.

STOTFIELD ROAD is Lossiemouth's other premiere address, with expensive villas overlooking the Moray Firth and the golf course, many of which were let to wealthy Londoners. It exudes Edwardian splendour, and begins on a gigantic scale at the corner of ST GERARDINE'S ROAD with the former MARINE HOTEL (now flats) of 1901–3, by *John Wittet* of *A. & W. Reid & Wittet*. Three storeys and five wide bays, the flanks even wider. Nicely contrasted sandstone margins with coursed rubble. Flanking this is the STOTFIELD HOTEL, originally of 1894–5 by *R.B. Pratt* but altered by him in 1901 and subsequently extended, including a square tower with corbelled top to St Gerardine's Road. Across the street is the MORAY GOLF CLUB, Scots Baronial by *A. & W. Reid & Wittet*, 1900–1 but enlarged in 1923 by *R.B. Pratt*. Proceeding further, across from St Margaret's (*see* Churches) is EAST CLIFF, 1884. Five bays and two storeys, the second and third bays recessed and covered by a timber veranda with two tiers of fish-scale tiles. Further again, SKERRY CLIFF, mid and late C19, with crenellations and the porch in a tower with pyramid roof. Also BLUCAIRN (E side) by *F.W. Troup*, 1906–7. Arts and Crafts style with one large gable on the front embracing two storeys and an attic.

The only other area to consider is COULARDBANK ROAD which is primarily post-war but has a cluster of three buildings by *A. & W. Reid* at its E end, beginning with THE WARDENS, formerly the boys' and girls' schools for the General Assembly, 1854. Seven bays, pleasantly broad, the outer wings well advanced and a bit taller. Advanced central porch with a narrow four-centred arch under a steep gable. At its apex, an elegant gabled bellcote with an open lancet. The classrooms stood on either side, each of two bays and divided by a lofty chimneystack. MANSEFIELD was built in 1849 as the manse for the Free Church next door (also 1849, but destroyed by fire in 1886). Single storey over a raised basement; three bays, the outer two with canted windows and simple architraves. Porch with a shaped gable and shield. Across the street is NEWTON COTTAGE, 1855. Simple single storey of three bays, with a fine central entrance under a shallow pediment. It sits on two consoled brackets with lively shell and leaf carving.

COULARD INN, 0.75 km. WSW. A converted farmhouse of *c.* 1830. Probably by *William Robertson*. Symmetrical, three-bay façade of two storeys over a raised basement. Harled with black margins; contrasting plain rubble (much renewed in the late C20) to the basement.

RAF LOSSIEMOUTH, off B9135. Built 1938–9 for training, subsequently for Bomber squadrons. Many Second World War structures (air-raid shelters, hangars and other auxiliary buildings) remain amid later additions. The site of DRAINIE CHURCH (1654–76, dem. 1953) lies within the base. Its manse became the Captain's House. It is by *A. & W. Reid*, 1853–5, the rear steading (RAF Saddle Club) contemporary, with additions to house by the Reids, 1877–8.

CEMETERY, Inchbroom Road, 1.5 km. SSE. Laid out by *Charles C. Doig* in 1900–2. Flanking the central avenue, nearly one hundred War Graves Commission headstones for RAF servicemen killed in the Second World War. *Reginald Blomfield*'s Cross
116 of Sacrifice guards the summit above them.

COVESEA SKERRIES LIGHTHOUSE, off B9040, 3.25 km. WNW. 1844–6 by *Alan Stevenson* (engineer) and *James Smith* (contractor), and with a strong Neo-Egyptian influence. The location is wonderfully atmospheric, rising above the coastline in pristine white grandeur. The impetus for construction was the loss of sixteen ships in Moray Firth in November 1826. Tall circular tower of whitewashed rubble, *c.* 36 m. high, the sea-facing side with a line of six narrow rectangular windows. Upper parapet corbelled out on a frieze of narrow pointed arches. Black domed light on top with an iron beacon, automated in 1984 but deactivated in 2012. Post-and-lintel entrance with cavetto architrave and block pediment inscribed 'In salutem omnium / Northern Lights'. Single-storey, semicircular range wrapping around the back with delightful little chimneystacks topped by flared, inverted copes.

Fine KEEPERS' COTTAGES to the SW, one of Stevenson's earliest designs. Ten-bay range with a pair of minimally advanced windows and doors (the latter styled as miniature temple entrances). Cavetto wall-head cornices topped by stepped blocking courses; more of the square, funnelled chimney flues above.

INCHBROOM HOUSE, 4.4 km. SSE, on the B9103. Harled U-plan, the main block dated 1756 on its r. skewputt. Single-storey E wing added in the late C18; two-storey W wing, early C19 with a rear canted bay window by *A. & W. Reid*, 1872.

INNES LINKS, 5.5 km. SE, Lossiemouth Forest. Emergency COASTAL BATTERY, and the best preserved in Scotland. Built 1940–2 for the anti-invasion defences that ran between Burghead and Cullen (qq.v.). Extensive collection of concrete buildings, virtually unaltered. Two six-gun emplacements, three engine houses, two search-light platforms and two observation posts. Accommodation camp to the SW with twenty-one barrack-hut bases. Complete line of anti-tank cubes along the shore with integral pill-boxes.

MAINS OF MAYEN *see* MAYEN HOUSE

MAYEN HOUSE B 5040

3.3 km. ESE of Milltown of Rothiemay

Moray boasts many country houses with exceptional surroundings, but Mayen's setting could not have been better chosen, nestled in a horseshoe bend of the Deveron with panoramic views of hills, valleys and water.

The house was begun by Major Alexander Duff in 1788 to replace his previous seat (*see* Mains of Mayen, below) and admittedly could never have matched the quality of the landscape. The original core consists of a large near-rectangle, somewhat ponderously cubical but typical of large-scale building in late C18 Morayshire (cf. Pitgaveny, Letterfourie and Orton). Two storeys over a high raised basement, harled with V-channelled quoins of granite. Main E front of three bays, the central door now masked by a gabled porch, added by *A. Marshall Mackenzie* in 1892–3. Simple round-headed window above it. The outer windows, set in shallow, giant-arched recesses, are tripartites on the raised ground floor with wide centres, and simplified Venetian above. Platform-piended roof with two vast longitudinal chimneystacks. Quasi-Venetian dormer in the attic, part of extensive remodelling work by *Acanthus Architects* of Huntly in 1995–6.

Large and rather plain S elevation, originally flat and of only four bays. Canted window in the second bay added by Mackenzie, originally ending at the ground floor but raised to full height in 1996. Two gabled dormers above it of the same date. Wide, partly canted bay to the l. of the chimneystack, all that remains of Mackenzie's extensive addition of 1892–3. It originally formed a huge L-plan and rear service court and extended much further W. The majority of it was demolished in 1995–6 and replaced with two new rear additions. The house was originally flanked by detached wings, recessed from the centre. The S wing was demolished by Mackenzie in 1882, but the N wing (almost certainly the kitchen) is intact. Two storeys and three bays with a piended roof, the windows slightly larger on the first storey. Chimneystack on the roof ridge, deliberately placed off-centre to compensate for foreshortening when the house was seen from a distance.

Interior much remodelled by Mackenzie and restored in 1995–6. Long rectangular entrance hall running down the centre, divided by a pair of Corinthian columns with similar flanking pilasters. Cantilevered staircase at the W end by Mackenzie, of oak and with tight barley-twist balusters. Swag decoration to the ends of the treads. Large Venetian window on the half-landing with geometric glass; round opening above, now covered over but formerly running straight up into a cupola. The ends of the upper landing are flanked by paired round-headed arches resting on three unfluted Corinthian columns. The S side is original and the N renewed.

COACHHOUSE, 150 m. SSE. Substantial quadrangle, 1788. The E arm was ruinous by the early to mid C20 but rebuilt by *Acanthus Architects*, 1995–6.

WALLED GARDEN, NW of the house. Brick, rectangular, built in 1997 and planted to a breathtaking design by *Suki Urquhart*. This is far and away the finest garden in Moray. It is divided into six distinct areas, each with its own theme and character, and converging on a central statue of Apollo. Octagonal GLASSHOUSE in the NW corner with two attached greenhouses.

MAINS OF MAYEN, 0.5 km. WSW, is the predecessor house at Mayen, which Duff purchased in 1785 and subsequently demoted to 'mains' status. The lands were bestowed by King David II on William of Abercromby in the late C14. His descendants, the Abernethy family, were elevated to the Lords Saltoun after 1445 and built the present house in the C17.

It is a large, harled L-plan of three different builds, each two-storeyed with crowstepped gables and slate roofs. The main block runs E–W with a N main front. The plain W section (up to the ridge chimneystack) was built *c.* 1608, the longer portion to the E with a straight-headed doorway in the centre dated 1680 on the heraldic plaque with the initials of Alexander Abernethy and his wife, Jean Halkett, along with the motto '[S]alus per Christum' ('Salvation through Christ'). Above it on the l., a small window and rectangular vent; narrow dormer through the wall-head to the r., also dated 1680 on its plain triangular gablet. The S wing is by *James Matthews*, 1855–7, and a good attempt at harmony, somewhat undone by over-large windows inserted *c.* 1965. Circular drum tower with conical roof in the re-entrant angle, also by Matthews but replacing an earlier (and smaller) turnpike in the same position. Two small, very charming late C17 dormers reused at its base.

MILLTOWN OF ROTHIEMAY B 5040

A pleasant granite village, impressively sited on the Deveron near its confluence with the Isla.

PARISH CHURCH. First built on this site in 1752 to succeed the church cleared with the Kirktown (*see* Rothiemay House, below) but completely reconstructed in 1807. S flank of pinned dark whinstone with round-headed windows with raised keystones and blocked imposts. E door under a semicircular fanlight and birdcage W bellcote with ogival capital and ball finial. Mid-C19 W vestry. In the N wall the late medieval doorpiece of the old church re-set here in 1959 (previously at Rothiemay Castle). Round-headed arch with keystone carved as a winged soul. Stylized flowers and carved faces on the bases of the jambs. Below it the FONT, a weathered octagon, also from the old kirk. Above the door, the former N entrance to the gallery, blocked in 1881–3 when the fine interior was remodelled and re-fitted by *A. & W. Reid*, although retaining the traditional Georgian layout. Segmental panelled timber ceiling with diagonal sarking; transverse ribs carried on alternating stone and wooden corbels. U-plan GALLERY with canted sides, the panelling with blind round-headed arcading set on large brackets. Four cast-iron columns with strapwork around the capitals. – Rectangular wooden PULPIT in the centre of the S wall, also 1881–3. Four ball finials over three panels with nailhead in the centre. Back-board with scrolled side bases and a semicircular pediment. – STAINED GLASS. In the gallery by *Cox, Sons, Buckley & Co.* – W window depicting the *Nunc Dimittis*, *c.* 1881. Simeon stands in a strange Islamic-Gothic church. – E window with Christ as the Good Shepherd, 1887. – Inside the vestibule, a stone TOMB FRAGMENT dated 1672, from the old church. Primitive egg-and-dart along the top.

In the burial ground, a MONUMENT with Latin inscription to Alexander Duff †1816, builder of Mayen House (q.v.). Consoled brackets under a pair of engaged quasi-Corinthian columns; dentilled pediment with a winged soul in the tympanum. Originally with three urn finials, one now missing.

FERGUSON MONUMENT, King George V Memorial Playing Field. By *Kelly & Nicol*, 1907, to commemorate the astronomer James Ferguson †1776, born near Rothiemay in 1710. Rock-faced granite monolith, 3.4 m. high with inverted nailhead on the E face. Dodecagonal base with the signs of the Zodiac carved by *Arthur Taylor*.

The S end of the village is marked by the BRIDGE over the River Deveron, built 1872 by *John Willet* (engineer) and *James Abernethy & Co.* of Aberdeen (founders). Six segmental arches, the middle four of ribbed cast iron and the outer ones narrower with brick voussoirs. Triangular cutwaters reused from the previous bridge of the early to mid C19. On the r. side of the N bank, a former early C19 CORN MILL converted into a house *c.* 1972. Rubble T-plan with rear pyramidal ventilator; original lade and detached mill stones to the S.

In the main street the PRIMARY SCHOOL by *A. & W. Reid*, *c.* 1885, and PUBLIC HALL by *W. L. Duncan*, dated 1920–1. FOUNTAIN in front by *Glenfield & Kennedy* of Kilmarnock in a pedimented surround. Further up on the E side is the hefty Baronial former WEST LODGE to Rothiemay Castle (*see* below), one of the few surviving indicators of its vanished splendour. Across the street is the WAR MEMORIAL cenotaph, 1920–1 and also by Duncan.

ROTHIEMAY HOUSE, 0.6 km. E. By *R. M. Noad*, designed 1962–3 and built 1968, on the site of the sprawling and eclectic Rothiemay Castle which was first recorded in 1465. The manor was granted to Sir William de Abernethy, 3rd Laird of Saltoun, by King David II in 1345. The castle was acquired by William Duff, Lord Braco (subsequently 1st Earl Fife) in 1741 and remained his primary residence after the construction of Duff House, Banff (p. 94) brought so much rancour and heartache. It was extended by the 2nd Earl in 1788–90. By *c.* 1800 the castle had assumed the form of a gargantuan L, the E wing incorporating a Z-plan tower house of the late C15 or early C16. Excavations in 1932 revealed the foundations of a round angle tower in the SE corner. It was demolished in 1964 but its successor incorporates a few fragments, e.g. in the advanced central N wing a C16 yett with intricate interlocking pattern and the late C17 entrance doorpiece in the E re-entrant angle with lugged lintel, pulvinated architrave and good cornice. Inside the vestibule, an ogival aumbry from the first-floor great hall, late C15. GATEPIERS (450 m. NNW of the house), early C19 with Greek key on the architraves.

The N and E boundaries of the grounds are delimited by a CAUSEWAY built by William Duff in 1750–2 carried over the Kirktown Burn by a bridge with a single round arch set on a slight diagonal. The policies were cleared in 1752 by demolishing KIRKTOWN OF ROTHIEMAY. There are some survivals, including foundations of the late medieval CHURCH, 225 m. SSE of the house. 260 m. N is the former MANSE, surrounded by trees. By *John Watson* of Cullen, 1754–5, replacing the manse demolished by Duff. It was converted into a laundry *c.* 1900. – ST PETER'S WELL to the SSE, near the tree line. Rectangular chamber, much rebuilt. Detached lintel in front of it dated 1570, *ex situ* and likely from the castle.

QUEEN MARY'S BRIDGE, S of the site of the church. Single humpback span over the Kirktown Burn, of rubble with a tooled granite arch-ring. Said to be the bridge crossed by Mary Queen of Scots in 1562 as she went to spend a night at Rothiemay Castle, but the masonry is (alas) early to mid-C18. Parapets added by William Duff in 1756.

MAINS OF ROTHIEMAY, 0.3 km. W of Rothiemay House. Quadrangular-plan Home Farm, early to mid-C19 but now much renewed. The KILN BARN is a rare survival, by *William Anderson* for Lord Braco in 1742, but in poor condition (cf. The Bow, Ballindalloch). Long rectangle of rubble, its rear (S) front with a central entrance flanked by skinny rectangular vents. Double-leaf door with hinge in the middle to control the draught for winnowing. Threshing area and granary formerly on the ground-floor interior with drying loft sited above. Circular kiln bowl in the W section where the roof is intact. It is separated by an E gable (formerly internal) with chimneystack on the top.

DOOCOT, 170 m. SW, isolated in a field. Early C18. Unusually large, re-floored by William Duff in 1743. Square plan, each side 8.3 m. and given blind recesses with segmental heads. Two straight-headed doorways on the S face. A painting of 1767 shows the doocot with a steep ogival roof and cupola; this was removed in the early C20. Divided into two chambers, the W side with 456 nesting boxes. Those on the E are now gone, but the original total of *c.* 1300 would have made Rothiemay among the most capacious doocots in N Scotland.

BRIDGE OF MARNOCH, 5.8 km. ENE. *See* p. 287.

MARNOCH LODGE, 5.9 km. ENE. Original harled block of *c.* 1800, two storeys and three bays facing S. A castellated front was formed in the mid to late C19 by adding an advanced ashlar centre topped by a tall crenellated parapet. Small round tourelle in its l. corner. Full-height rectangular bay windows to either side topped by more crenellations. Canted bay window to the E flank; tall addition to the NW, early to mid-C20 with a semi-hexagonal W gable.

WHITESTONES HOUSE, 2.1 km. SW, has in the garden three PICTISH STONES, placed here *c.* 1954. Two are part of the celebrated collection found at Tillytarmont, decorated with crescent (with and without V-rod) and double disc.

RECUMBENT STONE CIRCLE, 0.5 km. NE. One of the largest prehistoric monuments in north-east Scotland. Originally with twelve stones, some of them removed *c.* 1845. Four now remain standing, each *c.* 1.8 m. high with one massive recumbent in the SW weighing nearly 20 tons. Originally, there were probably inner and outer rings, designed as a pair of concentric circles. The recumbent and one of the standing stones display a fine collection of cup marks, a form of Later Neolithic/Early Bronze Age rock art.

MAYEN HOUSE. *See* p. 701.

MILTON BRODIE HOUSE 0060

3.2 km. ENE of Kinloss

Decidedly elegant country villa, and the epitome of summer splendour. The land was owned by Kinloss Abbey (q.v.) from the late C12 and James Dundas, chantor of Moray, built a tower house here *c.* 1587 (shown as 'Windhills' on Pont's map of *c.* 1590). The estate was acquired *c.* 1653 by the Brodies, who in the early C18 demolished every trace of the previous house and replaced it with a laird's mansion. The Georgian U-plan still forms the core, its centre built *c.* 1710 but the wings (for kitchen and service block) added mid to late C18. Between 1835 and 1841 there was an ingenious transformation by *William Robertson*, who reorientated the house and created a dramatic new S front, completely filling the original courtyard. His façade is of seven bays, low and broad and lined with false ashlaring, much of it now overgrown with wisteria. Tetrastyle portico in the centre supported on monolithic columns with good Ionic capitals and sharply corniced architrave. Outer bays slightly advanced and much wider, veneered by Robertson to camouflage the rear gable ends of the house's original wings. Minimally advanced centres with lying-pane glazing (some painted) topped by pediments with angle acroteria and paired apex chimneystacks. Lining the wall-head below are extraordinarily large console brackets.

The chronology explains the main anomaly of the interior, namely four separate staircases – none are centrally located, and each one was originally to serve a free-standing wing. Drawing Room to the l. of the entrance hall with anthemion and egg-and-dart cornice. Dining Room across with open distyle screen of Ionic columns; whitewashed Adam-style chimneypiece with swagged garlands and urns.

SW of the house, the re-set lintel from the former DOOCOT, dated 1769. It was demolished *c.* 1964. – Beyond the walled garden (200 m. SSE of the house), a good octagonal GAZEBO of the mid C18, now in very poor condition. Two storeys with faceted, bellcast roof. Inside the upper chamber, a painted ceiling rose and mural shelf. – GATEPIERS at the S end of the drive, mid C18. Ball finials on pulvinated bases (r. side renewed). – WINDYHILLS COTTAGE, 200 m. NNE. Formerly known as 'The Penitentiary' and incorporating late C17 and C18 fabric (converted into a house, 1993). Long slit-window and some chamfered margins. Worn skewputt possibly dated 1691.

1060

MILTONDUFF

1.5 km. SW of Elgin

DOOCOT, off the village road. Crowstepped lectern type, late C17 or early C18. It is the only survivor of a C17 tower house owned by the Brodies of Lethen.

At PITTENDREICH, 1.75 km. NE, on the B9010 is another DOOCOT. Late C16, square plan (cf. Quarrywood, p. 728). Unusual roof with large flagstones aligned in ridges.

MORTLACH *see* DUFFTOWN

MOSSTODLOCH

3060

The village is bypassed by the A96 and overshadowed by the huge Baxters factory and visitors' centre to the E.

SPEYMOUTH PARISH CHURCH, 1.2 km. N. Built of red sandstone and ruby-harled, hence 'The Red Kirk'. Gabled oblong by *James Ogilvie*, 1732–3, the bellcote rebuilt (and dated) 1763; further enlargement in 1798–9. N aisle by *Alexander Thomson* of Huntly in 1884–5 to form a T-plan. He also enlarged the round-headed windows on the S front, filled them with Y-tracery and inserted the doors to the l. and r. E and W gables with ground-floor windows (the two original entrances to the church) and oculi inserted in 1885. NE re-entrant angle filled by a hall, 2003–4.

Fine interior, refurbished 1884–5 and re-roofed in 1991, but still retaining its original Georgian layout. – Canted U-plan GALLERY with fielded panelling (some original from 1732–3) over stencilled frieze on cast-iron columns. – Good semi-hexagonal PULPIT in the centre of the S wall, 1885, with blind Lombardic tracery. Back-board with Y-tracery and frilly foliate border on top. – PEW-BACK (W wall). A fine survival of 1634, from Dipple church (*see* below). It was 'erecit be' Walter Hay and Lilias Innes, married in 1629. Four black oak panels with conjoined monograms, two coats of arms and a man in a ruff. Rectangular inscription exhorting God to 'renue a right spirit with in me'.

Former MANSE, 0.4 km. N. Built 1735–8; gutted, rebuilt and extended in 1788. Two storeys and five bays with skinny rectangular windows, the wide centre now obscured by a modern glazed porch. Harled with salmon-painted margins. Two-storey piended extension to the rear, late C18.

WAR MEMORIAL, junction of Main Road and B9015. By *A. Marshall Mackenzie & Son*, 1920–1. Square granite column with banded base. Cavetto capital and big flame finial.

DIPPLE BURIAL GROUND, 2 km. S. Within a circular dyke (cf. Essil, Garmouth), likely indicating reuse of a pagan site. The former church of the Holy Ghost (first recorded in the charter of Bishop Bricius between 1208 and 1214) was abandoned for Speymouth church in 1732 and nothing now survives above ground. – Roofless BURIAL AISLE with ogee cornice, early C18. – On the W wall, an aediculed TABLET for the two wives of John Scot (Marjory Stuart †1696 and Euphemia Gordon †1709) and four children. Long Latin inscription; crude semicircular pediment with mortality emblems.

DIPPLE HOUSE, 1.6 km. S. L-plan front of the early C19, probably by *Alexander Tod.* Canted bay windows and gables with ball-and-spike finials. Inside, two rooms have good chimneypieces by *Robert Adam*, *c.* 1775, originally for Northumberland House, London (dem. 1874). White marble with fluted pilasters and yellow marble accents. Large swagged urn with rams' heads under egg-and-dart; winged trumpeter with scrolled vines and husks. They were formerly at Kirkville, Fochabers (*see* p. 622). – Square DAIRY to S with pyramidal roof, early to mid C19.

STATION HOUSE, 2.9 km. SW near Orbliston. Originally Fochabers High Station by *Joseph Mitchell* for the Inverness & Aberdeen Junction Railway, 1858 (closed, 1964).* Handsome front to the platform with recessed veranda on cast-iron Roman Doric columns. Advanced gabled ends, the l. formerly the office and the r. with a clock.

STYNIE FARMHOUSE, 1 km. NNE. Symmetrical two storeys and three bays, early C19 and of very high quality. Harled with long-and-short channelled quoins. Minimally advanced centre with pilastered, corniced doorpiece and pediment on the wall-head. Corniced ground-floor windows to the l. and r.

TROCHELHILL, 2.1 km. SW. Harled L-plan front of 1861–3 with tall wall-head chimneystack and fanlit porch in the re-entrant angle. Big gable on the E flank.

OLD SPEY BRIDGE. *See* p. 624.

0060

MOY HOUSE

2.3 km. NW of Forres

One of the greatest architectural losses in Moray after it was ravaged by fire in 1995. John Campbell of Cawdor purchased the land from the Bishop of Moray in 1579, and the C17 'auld house' was acquired by Major George Grant in 1733. Its nucleus was rebuilt by his nephew Sir Ludovic Grant of Grant in 1762–3 to a design by *John Adam*, shortly after his work at Castle Grant (Highland and Islands). An earlier plan by his brother Robert had been rejected, but either way this is the earliest Adam building in the county, which makes its loss all the more regrettable. The mason and overseer was *Collen Williamson*, who later supervised construction of the White House in Washington D.C.

The gutted and roofless central block still retains its austere dignity. Ashlar W front of three storeys and five bays, cherry-cocked ashlar with V-channelled quoins. Narrow, slightly recessed centre with entrance fronted by two Roman Doric columns (formerly supporting the roof of the porch). Venetian window above with engaged Ionic columns and very thick (almost manneristic) pulvinated architraves. Its keystone is carved as a primitive mask corbel – not a choice that Adam

*Name changed to Orbliston Station in 1893 when a spur of the Highland Railway began service to Fochabers Town Station (*see* p. 624).

would have ever allowed. The E elevation was, surprisingly, the most important approach to the house, used by the majority of visitors after they had crossed the Findhorn via ferry.* It is a symmetrical U-plan, Adam's work in the centre almost uncompromisingly severe: long, straight and again of five bays. Central door with cornice and thin Ionic columns; enlarged first-floor window above it to accommodate a balcony. The shorter, three-bay wings are earlier, likely designed by Williamson in 1752 to flank the original C17 house. Bolection-moulded doorpieces in the re-entrant angles and chamfered window margins – unexpectedly sensitive gestures to continuity. Attached to the N and S are two-storey, single-bay wings by *Alexander Ross* of 1870, the former now completely gutted. Grand, V-channelled gatepiers beyond the S one and then a three-bay former service building, still with piended roof.

Former STABLES and CARRIAGE HOUSES, 300 m. NNE, also in very poor condition. Quadrangular plan of *c.* 1780, possibly by *Williamson*. Long S front of nine bays with wide, pedimented ends. Large octagonal cupola over the entrance with very bell-cast roof. – ICE HOUSE by the S end of the drive, *c.* 1769. Partially subterranean round chamber with rectangular door frame.

Former BURIAL GROUND, 100 m. SSE, on a roughly oval plan. Site of Moy Parish Church, closed in 1618 after uniting with Dyke (*see* p. 558).

MULBEN 3050

Scrappy crossroads hamlet.

Former BOHARM FREE CHURCH, SE of the cross-roads. Built 1857 and altered in 1898 by *F.D. Robertson*; converted to dwellings, 1975. S gable with wide, tapered buttress and bellcote. Four lancets to the flanks. – Former MANSE to the r., 1863 and also modified by Robertson.

Former BOHARM PARISH CHURCH, 1.3 km. SW. Closed in 1974 and now decayed. Simple harled, gabled rectangle with round-headed windows, built 1792–5 to replace the C17 church (*see* Craigellachie). E porch and W vestry by *William Robertson*, 1828; W birdcage bellcote by *Matthews & Mackenzie*, 1883. S aisle with wheel window forming a T-plan, 1898–9 by *John Alcock*.

PUBLIC HALL. 1923. Pedimented N doorpiece. Outside, WAR MEMORIAL, by *Alexander Smart* of Keith, 1920. Rough Huntly granite obelisk.

*Ferry service is documented at Broom of Moy (0.8 km. SSE) from the mid C15. The river was bridged *c.* 1799, after which carriage traffic could approach Moy from the W.

Former STATION, 0.4 km. NE. 1858 for the Inverness & Aberdeen Junction Railway, probably by *Joseph Mitchell*. Between the station-master's house and office wing a canopied platform shelter with cast-iron columns and bracketed eaves (cf. Orton, Rothes).

BOHARM HOUSE, 1.3 km. SW. Formerly the parish manse, built 1811. Two storeys of tooled granite over a tall raised basement. On the SW front, a door with radial fanlight and canopy over large brackets, reused from the former Rothiemay Castle (q.v.). Windows to the l. and r. aligned strangely close to the centre. Conventional, symmetrical fenestration above and below; piended rear wing added *c.* 1840. – Grand rusticated GATEPIERS of the late C18, with fluted cornices and draped ball finials (*ex situ*, originally located in Forres (q.v.)). – In one range of the STEADING (mid-C18), a chimneypiece of *c.* 1880 from Rothiemay Castle. Wild fronds of foliage.

MAINS OF MULBEN, 0.6 km. N. Good survival of a late C17 laird's house, and very similar to the one at Easter Elchies (q.v.). Tall crowstepped T-plan, built 1696 by Ludovic Grant (1st Baronet) and Janet Brodie. Pair of triangular dormerheads with their initials re-set on the SE gable. NW wing added *c.* 1880, when most of the interior was renovated. One large, simple stone fireplace *in situ* from the C17.

BOAT O' BRIG, 3.6 km. WNW. An ancient crossing over the Spey. The E bank was the site of a HOSPITAL and CHAPEL dedicated to St Nicholas, founded by Muriel de Pulloc in the early C13 and operated by Elgin Cathedral 'for the reception of poor travelers'. Its ruins were mostly demolished to make way for a suspension bridge by *Capt. Sir Samuel Brown*, 1829–30.* Present BRIDGE of 1956 by Banff County Council, a single bowed span of trussed steel. Unusually grand TOLL COTTAGE at the E end of 1830 by *William Robertson*, with pedimented tetrastyle portico on unfluted Greek Doric columns. Just to the N, the VIADUCT by *Joseph Mitchell*, 1856–8, for the Inverness & Aberdeen Junction Railway. Six ashlar arches on the W bank and one on the E, the abutments with pilasters and sunken panelling. Its plate-girder span over the river was replaced with steel lattice trusses by *William Roberts*, engineer, 1905–6.

127 AUCHROISK DISTILLERY (Diageo), 2.1 km. WNW. 1973–4 by *Westminster Design Associates*, originally for Justerini & Brooks. The best C20 distillery in north-east Scotland, complemented by beautifully spare landscaping. The whole is a network of crisply defined, well-articulated forms. The gables are sharp – asymmetric and jagged or unexpectedly extended or truncated – but still graceful. Sheer flanks everywhere, often rising two or three storeys without windows. Good, stark contrast in tone between the harled white walls of the buildings and their black roofs.

*See also his destroyed bridge outside Forres (*see* p. 642). The medieval bridge was replaced *c.* 1680 by ferry service, hence Boat o' Brig.

Main PRODUCTION BLOCK in the centre with low TUN ROOM topped by demi-gabled skylights. Circular YEAST HOUSE in front of it with a tall conical roof; L-plan MASH HOUSE far to the rear, taller and with massively swept roofs.

GLENTAUCHERS DISTILLERY (Chivas Brothers), 2.3 km. ESE. Built 1896–8 by *John Alcock* for James Buchanan on the classic E-plan, construction supervised by *Charles C. Doig*. Of this, the E half (seven bays) of the double-gabled MALT BARNS and two adjacent pagoda-roofed KILNS remain. Early C20 TUN ROOM free-standing to the E, its first storey oversailing. MASH HOUSE, TUN ROOM and STILL HOUSE completely rebuilt in 1965–6. – Nine piended WAREHOUSES to the W, continuously gabled on the N.

AUCHLUNKART HOUSE. *See* p. 471.

NEW SPYNIE *see* QUARRYWOOD

NEWMILL B 4050

Dour grid-plan village established *c.* 1759 by the Earls Fife as a rival to New Keith (q.v.) but too isolated to meet with much success. The focal point is the CLOCK TOWER in The Square, 123
a war memorial of 1922–3 by *F.D. Robertson*. Four stages, the clock stage over a band of corbelled rope moulding and with crowstepped gablets above and then a pagoda-like cupola with a ball finial on a spike.

Former PARISH CHURCH, 0.4 km. NE. 1870–1; now a house. Lancets and rosette E window. Gableted W bellcote. Re-set datestone of 1663 with initials of George and Margaret Gordon, from Glengarrick Castle, which stood on this site but had vanished by the mid to late C18. – Former MANSE (now Glengerrack House) to the NNE, a large T-plan of 1878. SE face with long round-headed window over cantilevered cornice and two small glazed port holes. Canted bay window to the r.

ORTON HOUSE 3050

5.8 km. NE of Rothes

(A tall severe Neoclassical cube of three storeys and three bays over a raised basement (cf. Pitgaveny and Letterfourie, qq.v.) built in 1786 for Hon. Arthur Duff, son of the 1st Earl Fife. Mixed pinned granite rubble with V-channelled ashlar quoins; lugged window architraves on the ground floor and corniced on the first. The projecting, pedimented centre bay is by *Mackenzie & Matthews*, 1847–8 with Doric testrastyle porte cochère. N and S are single-storey, two-bay wings by *William*

Robertson, 1826, each smoothly bowed at the ends and with tripartite windows with engaged Roman Doric columns flanking the central light. Large rear wing with a piended roof forming an L-plan, again likely by Robertson. Substantial two- and three-storey rear additions by *Peddie & Washington Browne*, 1904–5 for John and Margaret Wharton Duff.)

The N and S lodges (800 m. NNW and 400 m. S of the house) retain GATEPIERS of *c.* 1786 with Gibbsian banding. – DOOCOT, 700 m. SSE. Late C18, cylindrical, with conical slate roof of *c.* 1900. Intact wooden potence and nesting boxes.

The Wharton Duff MAUSOLEUM, 1.6 km. NE, has a superbly atmospheric setting that was once the site of a Romanesque chapel dedicated to the Virgin. Tall, Gothic, steeply gabled. By *Matthews & Mackenzie*, 1844. Fine entrance with tall pointed arch subdivided by double arches on a trumeau; huge blind quatrefoil above with dedicatory inscription in Latin. ST MARY'S, 175 m. NNW, is of 1854–5 by *Matthews & Mackenzie* around a late C18 core, with diamond chimneystacks and a canted bay window on the E gable. Extended in similar style by *Meldrum & Mantell*, 1998–9. ST MARY'S COTTAGE, 300 m. SW, is a charming Gothic *cottage orné* by *Matthews & Mackenzie*, 1851–4.

PADDOCKHAUGH *see* BIRNIE

2060

PITGAVENY HOUSE

3.3 km. NE of Elgin

The land belonged to the bishopric of Moray in the Middle Ages and is first mentioned in a charter (as 'Petgony') in 1497. In 1765, the estate was purchased by James Brander, who made his fortune in Portugal shipping citrus fruit to London's markets. He built the present house in 1776 – a vast Neoclassical cube rising tall and sheer, similar to the central blocks of Letterfourie and Orton (qq.v.). The architect's name is unrecorded but he was an accomplished follower of the Adam tradition at its most austerely elegant.

Main SW front of tooled ashlar, three storeys over a semi-sunk basement. Five bays with V-channelled long-and-short quoins; first floor with longer, eighteen-pane windows, wilfully accentuating the building's height and severity. The centre is minimally advanced under a pediment, its tympanum with an oculus inscribed with Brander's initials and the date 1776. Corniced blocking course to the l. and r. with ball finials; double piended roof. Renewed pedimented, Roman Doric doorpiece in the centre, resited to an ungainly new front porch *c.* 1870. This was demolished during substantial restorations by *Law & Dunbar-Nasmith Partnership* in 1991–3 that have returned the house to its original appearance.

The flanks are of coursed rubble, originally meant to be harled. Outer windows placed close to the ends; blank masonry in the middle strongly indicates that pavilions (or corridors to pavilions) were anticipated. An unsigned drawing commissioned by John Brander in the late C18 or early C19 shows that wings with huge Venetian windows were at one point considered – perhaps an acknowledgment that the house's severity needed to be softened, as at Letterfourie. Rectangular SERVICE WING to the rear dated 1870, a two-storey piended rectangle with single-storey corridor linking it to the main house. The wing was given two more upper storeys by *Charles C. Doig* in 1912, which were removed in 1991–3, along with a large annexe in the re-entrant angle between house and wing.

The INTERIOR is well appointed and has very lofty ceilings, with public rooms on the *piano nobile* in typical Georgian fashion. Rectangular ENTRANCE HALL with bracketed cornice and sunburst rose; full-height STAIR HALL beyond, rising up with a thrilling sense of spaciousness. Cantilevered open-well staircase and plaster ceiling high above with large central fan and swagged garland frieze. DINING ROOM (originally a PARLOUR) to the l. of the hall with dado rail, fielded panelled window shutters and bracketed cornice. White marble chimneypiece with a fluted mantel, central garland and husks on the jambs. Original marble slips and cast-iron grate of *c.* 1870, when the buffet recess was added. Former DRAWING ROOM on the first floor with more good carpentry and plaster frieze with anthemion linked by wispy trails of foliage. White marble chimneypiece with fluted jambs and mantel, all inset with strips of polished yellow marble. It is virtually identical to the fireplace in the drawing room at Letterfourie, suggesting either direct Adam involvement or else standardization by him for an elite clientele. A BEDROOM has a fire-grate intact from *c.* 1776, a rare survival with attenuated urns and scrolls. It is the most Adam-esque object in the house.

In front of the door, an uninscribed STONE said to mark the site of Bothganowan (or Bothnagowan), the smith's bothy where Macbeth murdered Duncan in 1040. – Former GATE-PIERS (200 m. NNW), at the original entrance off the old road from Elgin to Lossiemouth. Thick V-channelling and ball finials, *c.* 1776. – A second set (500 m. SSW) on the new road laid out *c.* 1820. Also late C18, with fluted architraves and big swagged urn finials. They were brought here from the Elgin house of the Andersons of Linkwood (dem. 1837).

HOME FARM, 200 m. SSW. Likely the location of the C17 house at Pitgaveny, built by either the Innes family or the Brodies of Lethen (who owned the estate 1630 to 1747). U-plan laid out in the mid to late C18. Two-storey, crowstepped STABLE BLOCK (now the Estate Office) added in the centre, *c.* 1890. – Off the NW corner, a circular HORSE-GANG MILL of the mid to late C18, now roofless. – Near it, a circular late C17 or early C18 DOOCOT.

Continuous rat ledge and conical roof. – The SW entrance to the lower WALLED GARDEN has a re-set C17 bolection-moulded doorpiece, a relic of the Brodies' original tower house.

1050 PLUSCARDEN

A collection of buildings in a sublime location, nestled between two tree-covered hills.

PLUSCARDEN ABBEY*

Delightfully located in the valley of the Black Burn, Pluscarden was one of three Scottish priories of the rather obscure Valliscaulian order of monks, who drew inspiration for their way of life from both the Cistercians and the Carthusians. It was founded by King Alexander II *c.* 1230 or 1231, the same years as the two other Scottish foundations for the order, at Ardchattan (Argyll) and Beauly (Highland and Islands).

The PLAN of the church consisted of a three-bay aisleless E limb which was initially fully occupied by the presbytery, a crossing surmounted by a low and probably unfinished tower, transepts each with a two-bay E chapel aisle, and a nave with a single aisle, on the S side, adjacent to the cloister. The only significant additions to this plan is an early C16 sacristy on the N side of the choir. In 1454 the priory was united with the Benedictine house of Urquhart and made dependent on Dunfermline Abbey. In 1457 it was said the buildings had been in poor repair for sixty years, which perhaps suggests that it had suffered along with Elgin Cathedral in either 1390 or 1402, in the onslaughts by the Earl of Buchan or Alexander of the Isles. Major fire damage of the stonework is still in evidence, especially in the transepts. Extensive repairs and modifications were subsequently carried out. At the Reformation, in 1560, Lord Seton was appointed steward, and in 1565 it was granted to one of his sons (the future Earl of Dunfermline), for whom it was erected into a lordship in 1587.

After passing through various hands, in 1709 the estates were acquired by William Duff of Dipple, father of the 1st Earl Fife. By then only the shell of the E limb and transepts of the church survived to the wall-head, along with much of the S aisle S wall. The nave may have been lost soon after the Reformation, with other parts dismantled to provide stone for repairs to Elgin Parish Church in 1682. The shell of the E claustral range also survived; it had housed a sequence of

*This entry is by Richard Fawcett, with thanks to Stephen Holmes and Br Paschal Downs OSB.

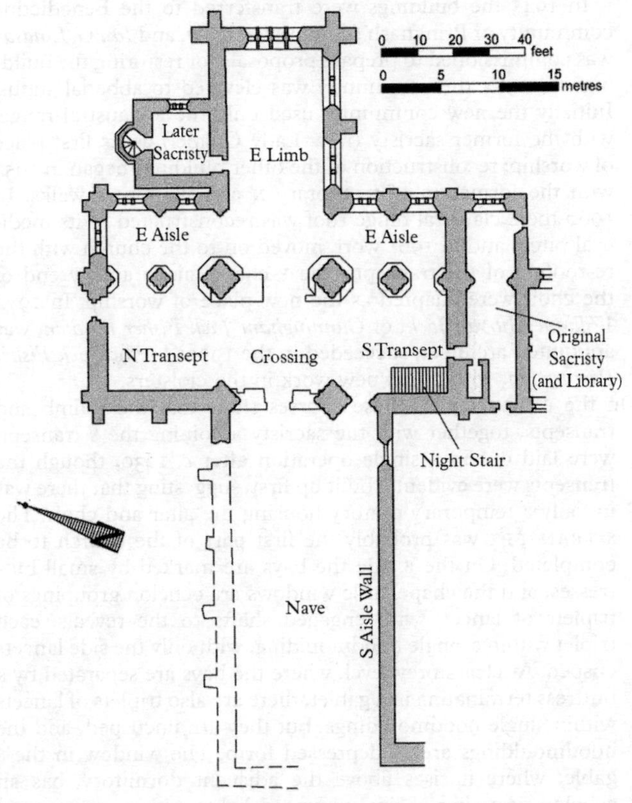

Pluscarden Abbey Church.
Plan

sacristy and library, chapter house, parlour and warming room, with the dormitory at first-floor level. Sections of the S and W inner walls of the cloister survived, together with fragments to the S and SE of the E range that may have formed part of the prior's house and latrine block. Extents of the precinct wall also remained in place, with the best stretches to the E and N of the church, the latter with the remains of a gatehouse. In 1821, the 4th Earl Fife had the E claustral range re-roofed, and the warming room was adapted for Presbyterian worship. In 1898 the estates were sold to the 3rd Marquess of Bute, a Catholic convert. Restoration of the buildings was initiated under the direction of his favoured architect *John Kinross* (cf. Elgin Greyfriars Convent, p. 580, and Chapeltown of Glenlivet), but was halted at Lord Bute's death in 1900. In 1914 the estate passed to his third son, Lord Colum Crichton-Stuart, who sold everything at Pluscarden except the priory and a small amount of land, and who hoped to re-establish monastic life on the site.

In 1945 the buildings were transferred to the Benedictine community of Prinknash (Gloucestershire), and *Ian G. Lindsay* was commissioned to prepare proposals for restoring the buildings. In 1974 the community was elevated to abbatial status. Initially the new community used only the E claustral range, with the former sacristy (now Lady Chapel) as its first place of worship; reconstruction of the other buildings began in 1953 with the formation of temporary N and W cloister walks. In 1960 the E claustral range roof was reconstructed to its medieval pitch, and in 1961 work moved on to the church with the re-roofing of the transepts; the E chapel aisles and W end of the choir were adapted as the new place of worship. In 1972 *William Murray Jack*, of *Cunningham Jack Fisher Purdom*, was appointed architect, succeeded in the 1990s by the *Jack Fisher Partnership*, with much new work in the cloisters.

On the EXTERIOR the base courses show that the E limb and transepts, together with the sacristy adjoining the S transept, were laid out in a single operation after *c.* 1230, though the transepts were evidently built up first, suggesting that there was initially a temporary oratory housing the altar and choir. The S TRANSEPT was probably the first part of the church to be completed. On the E side the bays are marked by small buttresses, and the chapel aisle windows are echelon groupings of triplets of lancets with engaged shafts to the reveals, each triplet within a single hoodmoulding, with only the side lancets cusped. At clearstorey level, where the bays are separated by a buttress terminating in a gablet, there are also triplets of lancets within single hoodmouldings, but they are uncusped, and the hoodmouldings are of depressed form. The window in the S gable, where it rises above the adjacent dormitory, has an echelon grouping of five uncusped lights within a depressed arch (an arrangement comparable with the much taller S transept gable window at Dryburgh Abbey (Borders)); at the apex of the gable is a blind trefoiled bowed triangle. The lower part of the transept W face is abutted by the E cloister walk and the S nave aisle; the unbuttressed upper part has three single lancets, their hoodmouldings connected by a string course.

The bays of the N TRANSEPT are demarcated on the E, N and S sides by tall buttresses rising up to gablets; all have chamfered angles to their upper parts apart from that between the E clearstorey bays. The E chapel windows have restored three-light intersecting tracery, while each bay of the E clearstorey has a pair of cusped single-light windows with the hoodmouldings connected by a string course. On the W side the N bay has a tall lancet, the S bay a Y-traceried window. The N wall is a fine composition, perhaps partly inspired by the S transept at Elgin Cathedral. At the lower level, towards the E, is a door with a depressed rounded arch in which the complex mouldings simply emerge from the broadly splayed jambs. Above that, and resting on a string course, is a row of three equally spaced pointed single-light windows. Above another string course are three taller single-light windows, the middle one of which is cusped and rises to a lesser height than the others to accommodate a large circular window that rises well into the gable and which may have contained radiating tracery originally (cf. Elgin Cathedral's W front). At the apex of the gable is a blind encircled quatrefoil.

The CROSSING TOWER rises no higher than the surrounding roofs, and terminates in a parapet carried on a corbel table. The exposed spandrels, which are pierced by trefoils with projecting spurs between the lobes, are partly infilled, and there are only narrow slit openings. Saddleback roof with gables to E and W.

The bays of the EAST LIMB are articulated by buttresses of 13
a similar form to those in the N transept, the chamfered angles of the upper parts rising sheer to gablets below the wall-head corbel table. Almost the entire width between the buttresses was initially given over to vast windows, the arches of which are still in evidence in the N, E and S walls. Above the E window is a large vesica, with a trefoil within a triangle near the gable apex. The windows above the transept aisles were curtailed as bowed triangles, and on the S side tracery with three encircled cinquefoils has been reinstated. Most of the window arches have been blocked, presumably after 1457, with smaller windows formed within the blocking, a modification that has some parallels in the W window at Sweetheart Abbey (Dumfries and Galloway), and in the S windows intersecting tracery has been reinstated. Within the great E window arch, however, there are four lancets with continuous mouldings below a three-light window with cusped intersecting tracery. Along the N flank, the provision of corbels and a roof moulding within the later blocking indicate that there was to have been a tall lean-to structure on this side, E of the transept chapel aisle, and the small Y-traceried windows above the roof moulding are set high within the blocked arches. Whatever was to have been built there was superseded by a square sacristy and treasury block in the middle bay; this has a polygonal stair-turret on its N side, and a restored three-light window with a circlet of uncusped spiralling daggers on its E side. Heraldry shows this to have been built by the last pre-Reformation prior of the house, Alexander Dunbar (1529–60).

Of the NAVE there are the fire-damaged stumps of the N and S walls of the central vessel where they adjoined the transepts, along with the lower part of the S aisle wall, and the displaced bases of the W door. Although the evidence is no longer entirely clear, on the S side the squat E respond of the arcade is raised above a fragment of wall and it may be assumed that the choir stalls were initially set against that wall, indicating that the monks' choir extended from the crossing into the nave as first built, possibly with a choir for lay brethren in the W bays. On the aisleless N side, the E reveal of a large window probably dates from post-1457. The provision of an adjacent arched opening (now blocked) in the W face of the N transept, and of what appears to be a roof moulding below the window above that opening, may suggest that there was once a proposal to have a short armpit aisle here. The W door bases make provision for jambs with at least four orders of triplet shafts separated by smaller shafts.

INTERIOR. Although the E arcades of the two TRANSEPTS are badly fire-damaged (presumably caused in either 1390 or 1402) and have been blocked by walls since 1961, it can be seen that their construction must have been started soon after the priory's foundation in 1230. The outer responds of both arcades, which must have been built along with the outer walls of the transepts, consist of sequences of three-quarter rolls and projections that are chamfered back. The central pier of the S arcade and the SE crossing pier employ combinations of the same elements, suggesting that they were built soon afterwards. But the N transept arcade pier differs in being of clustered-shaft form, and appears to be slightly later. The S transept was thus evidently the first part to be carried up to any height, perhaps because it was structurally continuous with the E claustral range, which would have been one of the first conventual buildings to be erected.

Pluscarden Abbey, interior of north transept.
Engraving by R.W. Billings, 1852

As completed, the E elevations of the transepts offer two fascinating approaches to the problem of combining two-storey elevations with vaulted aisles. The 1220s and 30s were a period when solutions to this problem were being widely explored, as at Southwell Minster (Nottinghamshire) and Pershore Abbey (Worcestershire). At the upper level of the S transept the bays are demarcated by a slender triplet of wall-shafts, which rises from a string course a short way above arcade level. In each bay three arches rise from that string course: at the centre is a tall arch of depressed two-centred form that frames the clearstorey window, and on each side is a lower pointed arch that runs in front of the wall passage. This pattern of arches tends to reduce the visual impact of the area of blank wall that corresponds to the roof over the aisles, where there would have been a triforium in a church with three storeys. The treatment of the upper level in the N transept is very different. There is again a string course above arcade level, but in this case the two cusped single-light windows in each bay are simply framed internally by arches of the same form, which rise from that string course; once again there is little sense of the blank wall corresponding to the aisle roof being a dead area, though this is achieved by different means from those seen in the S transept.

Within the chapels there are differences of detailing, but the most significant one is that in the S transept the bays are demarcated by a broad transverse arch rather than by a rib, and there is an attractive interpenetration of ribs and arch at this point. Within the main body of the S transept the broad night stair rises against the W wall; at its head the arch of the dormitory door was supported by a shaft on each side (now lost). Adjacent to the base of this stair is the heavily restored sacristy door. The two W windows above the stair are linked by a lower arch like those flanking the inner arches on the E clearstorey. The S respond of the arch into the S nave aisle is of clustered-shaft form, suggesting construction only moved on to that part around the same time that the main body of the N transept was under construction. Within the S gable there is an inner skin of mullions rising from a stepped string course, and corresponding to the mullions of the window externally.

The greatest fire damage must have been to the CROSSING piers, which have been encased in masonry. The E and W tower arches have been largely blocked by inserted walls, but with a lower arch formed within the E arch. These walls, which were probably intended to brace the tower, presumably indicate that by the later C15 the monastic choir had been moved from the nave into the E limb. The wall in the E arch appears to have served as a pulpitum, and it has a stair within its thickness on the N side.

As first built, the EAST LIMB must have been an architecturally splendid and light-filled space. Traces of the vaulting that covered it are evident in cut-back springers between the window arches and the E corners. The wall ribs followed a steeper curve than the windows that they otherwise closely framed. The form of the vaulting is unclear, but was perhaps of tierceron form, as was provided over the aisles at Elgin Cathedral after 1270. Stumps of the original bar tracery of two of the blocked windows on the N side show that it was of the type with two sub-arches, each containing a pair of single lights and a circlet, and with a third circlet between the sub-arches. Both this and the type with three circlets within a bowed triangle in the W bay are found in what were probably the earliest examples of bar tracery in Britain, at Westminster Abbey, of the 1240s. But the earliest documented Scottish examples of bar tracery are of post-1270 at Elgin Cathedral and Sweetheart Abbey and such a date is perhaps most likely for Pluscarden. Presumably the tracery of the lost great E window was a permutation on the theme of the side windows (cf. the E window of Sweetheart Abbey). The vaulting was removed presumably after 1457, following damage *c.* 1390 or 1402, at the same time as the partial blocking of the windows. After that date there may have been a pointed or rounded timber barrel ceiling, as is known to have existed at Elgin Cathedral. The present almost flat boarded ceiling dates from 1982. The N SACRISTY is entered through a polygonal-headed doorway, the vault boss again with the arms of Dunbar, flanked by a king and St Andrew.

MONASTIC BUILDINGS. The similarity of the base course along the E face of the E CLAUSTRAL RANGE to that below the E limb and transepts of the church shows that it is essentially of the second quarter of the C13. However, it owes part of its present strictly rectangular plan and some of its external detailing to restoration in the 1820s. The two-storey block adjoining the S end of the transept originally contained the sacristy (and library) on the ground floor. It projects as far E as the chapel aisle, and has an unframed triplet of lights to the sacristy itself, with a smaller triplet recessed within a depressed arch at the upper level, where the wall face is slightly set back; there is also a smaller window to a closet at the upper level. Within its gable is a window with a circlet of spiralling daggers, with a smaller circlet at the apex. To its S, along the ground floor of the E range , in the first, second and fifth bays are simple three-light windows within depressed arches, while in the third and fourth bays are a wide cusped arch and a Y-traceried bowed triangle respectively, both above a stretch of wall provided with corbels for a lean-to roof. At first-floor level restored single-light and two-light windows alternate. Projecting E from this range's S end were substantial ranges above vaulted substructures, which presumably housed a prior's lodging and the monastic latrine.

Towards the cloister the round-arched door from the cloister into the SACRISTY is of two orders, with the outer order carried on shafts. The provision of an entry from the cloister as well as from the church may indicate that, as at many Cistercian houses, the W part of this chamber was used as a library, with a timber partition between the two parts. The W bay is partly given over to a small cell below the upper part of the night stair in the transept. The main space is covered by quadripartite vaulting, with a tighter rhythm of bays in the E portion, where it projects beyond the E wall of the adjacent range; that E portion is demarcated from the W bays by an arch with five-shafted responds. An arched opening cut through the N wall looks into the transept chapel. The sacristy was presumably put to other uses when the C16 sacristy was built (*see* above); it now serves as the community's Lady Chapel.

As usual, the frontispiece to the CHAPTER HOUSE is the 17
most impressive feature within the E cloister walk. Beyond an inner order with engaged shafts, the round-arched door has ten alternating minor and major shafts against angled jambs; a trumeau carries sub-arches that follow the arc of the main arch. These sub-arches are reflected in a Y-traceried window on each side of the door. The chapter house itself is of a type that was particularly favoured in Scotland, having four compartments of quadripartite vaulting carried on a central pier; as was common, it is entirely contained within the body of the range. The details of the chamber are strikingly refined. The pier has eight major filleted shafts alternating with eight lesser filleted shafts, with only the lesser shafts having caps. The main element of each rib emerges without break from the major shafts of the pier, while the caps of the lesser shafts support the outer elements of the ribs. In the way that the shafts are transformed into ribs there is perhaps something of the same spirit that is to be seen in the chapter house vestibule at Chester Cathedral. A date around the second quarter of the C13 is confirmed by the stiff-leaf foliage of the vault bosses. On the W side of the chamber the intermediate vault springer, which has evidently been damaged, rises between the two door arches; between the doors and the windows are trifoliate-headed recesses.

The PARLOUR is entered through a round-arched doorway with engaged shafts; it is covered by two bays of quadripartite vaulting. The round-arched door into the WARMING HOUSE is essentially the same as that into the sacristy/library. This chamber occupies the three S bays of the E range, and its six compartments of quadripartite vaulting are carried on octagonal piers from which the ribs emerge without any break at capital level. It is now used as the refectory, with a kitchen walled off in the two S bays on the W side. A timber pulpit has been formed within the N window embrasure on the E side, and there is a doorway towards the E end of the S wall that may have connected with the prior's lodging, though its polygonal head is recent. The only feature at first floor to be mentioned here is the rib-vaulted chamber above the sacristy, which has a small barrel-vaulted closet on its N side. Now known as the Prior's Chapel, could this have been the prior's chamber before a self-contained lodging was built at the outer end of the range? There is a similar chamber and closet at Kinloss Abbey.

The door into the REFECTORY, in the S cloister walk, is similar to the N transept door, with the arch mouldings emerging from broad splays in the jambs. The E end of the S claustral range was reconstructed in 1982 by *William Murray Jack*. Reconstruction of the E cloister walk followed in 1986. In 1994 the claustral W range was rebuilt as St Benedict's men's guesthouse to the designs of *Colin Fisher* of the *Jack Fisher Partnership*; the N and W cloister walks were rebuilt in 2008 to the designs of *Fisher* and *Angus McGhie*. In the N CLOISTER WALK is the round-arched door from the S nave aisle. It had five orders of alternating major and minor shafts (all now lost) against angled jambs, with a moulded inner order. The outer order of the arch is embellished with projecting fleurs-de-lys, which appear to be simply blocked out and may have been intended to be more finely finished.

FURNISHINGS. – SACRAMENT HOUSE in N wall of presbytery, made up of two disparate parts, above the locker and within a triangular gablet, two somewhat summarily represented kneeling angels hold a monstrance. – SEDILIA in middle bay on S side of presbytery, damaged but with remains of miniature vaulting over seats as at Elgin; its position demonstrates that the presbytery initially occupied the whole of the E limb. – HIGH ALTAR, in W bay of E limb, from dissolved abbey of Fort Augustus. – STATUE of Our Lady of Pluscarden by *A.J. Oakley*. – ROOD, in the E crossing arch, polychrome and gilt full-relief figures of Virgin and St John flanking crucifixion, early C20 German, from Convent of the Holy Cross, Haywards Heath, West Sussex. – LADY CHAPEL REREDOS, carved and painted censing angels flanking tabernacle, by *Oakley*. – CRUCIFIX by *David Clayton*. – REFECTORY. Holy water STOUP at entrance, possibly from St Bride's in Glenfruin. – C16 STATUE of St Anne from the convent of Fernham. – ICON, St Andrew's altar, S transept, painted by a nun of the Mount of Olives *c.* 2000. – Oak CHEST of boarded construction; complex flamboyant tracery within crocketed ogee arches, set against arcaded background. Probably French, early C16.

WALL PAINTINGS. Although now very fragmentary, an important survival. Descriptions by Charles Cordiner of 1788 record them when they were more complete, though his interpretations may be questioned. – E CROSSING ARCH: St John (of the Apocalypse?) accompanied by eagle, gazing up to the sun and moon and stars; kneeling figure (perhaps a donor). – SE TRANSEPT CHAPEL: St John the Baptist. – SACRISTY (now Lady Chapel): life-sized Apostles and Evangelists; the Woman clothed with the Sun and Christ in Majesty; St John and the Virgin; small tracery designs on the arch between the second and third bays from the E. – STAINED GLASS. A fine feature of the church, principally the work of members of the community, and relying largely on strongly coloured formalized or abstract designs worked either in traditional leaded techniques or *dalle-de-verre*. The following are by *Br Gilbert Taylor*: – CHOIR, E window, Christ our Eucharist, 1983. N TRANSEPT, E chapels, Visitation, 1965; Four Evangelist symbols and Agnus Dei, 1985; Virgin and Child, 1960. – W wall, St Benedict and St Gregory, 1988; St Peter, St Patrick, St Margaret, Celtic saints, 1992. – S TRANSEPT, gable, Alpha and Omega, 1982. – By *Sadie McLellan*, 1964–7, the N transept N windows, vibrantly coloured forms representing the gifts of the Spirit and culminating in the Woman clothed with the Sun in the top rose. – SACRISTY (Lady Chapel), City of God and monk's journey, by *Dom Ninian Sloane*, 1958–60, and *Br Gilbert Taylor*, 1960; St Andrew, by *Crear McCartney*, 1957. – MEMORIALS. N TRANSEPT, a number of incised slabs, including William of Birnie †1480 and James Wyatt †1515. 51

PRIORY LODGE, by the main entrance. By *James McBride*, 1820–1.* Y-tracery and crowstepped gables with apex crosses, the entrance with a blind trefoil. Three diamond chimneystacks in the centre. NE addition of *c.* 1984 disturbing the original cruciform plan.

PARISH CHURCH, 0.7 km. ESE. The former Free Church by *A. & W. Reid & Wittet*, 1898. Fine Gothic style echoing many of the Abbey's features.‡ Paired lancets in the nave and two-light Dec windows in the transepts. Big three-light tracery in the W gable with *roue tournante* of large mouchettes. Square two-stage SW tower with moulded, round-headed entrance. Solid parapet with angle waterspouts; octagonal lead spire on a louvred wooden base, 1960, replacing the red-tiled original. Transverse former hall off the E gable. Original pine interior with ribbed coomb ceiling carried on semicircular braces. – Canted Gothic PULPIT flanked by SCREEN WALLS (front one now removed). – STAINED GLASS. Over the pulpit, luminous symbols of the Evangelists by *Crear McCartney*, 1963.

WAR MEMORIAL. 1918–19 by *John Wittet*. Large triangular cairn of rustic, rough-hewn boulders quarried at Heldon Hill.

Former MANSE to the W (now Cowiesburn House), built *c.* 1830 in the Gothic strain of *William Robertson*; rear extension added *c.* 1848.

Former SCHOOL, 1.3 km. ESE. By *A. & W. Reid & Melven*, 1874–5. Multi-gabled with fleur-de-lys finials over the two entrances.

PICTISH STONE, 4.5 km. E, Upper Manbeen. Class I symbols, now eroding badly: 'fish monster' with dog head on the r. and tail fin to the l. Mirror and comb below. Top defaced by modern initials.

* The design was later copied at the Michael Kirk Lodge, Gordonstoun (*see* p. 651).

‡ The congregation had previously met in the E cloister walk but was forced to vacate when the Duke of Fife sold to the Marquis of Bute.

4060

PORTESSIE

A fishing village, now almost undifferentiated from the eastern end of Buckie.

METHODIST CHURCH, Chancellor Road. By *W. Beddoes Rees* of Cardiff, 1912–13, succeeding a chapel of 1866–7. Good free Gothic in dark Newton freestone. Galleried interior.

PRIMARY SCHOOL, School Road. 1936–8 by *James Wood*, Banffshire County Architect (cf. Buckie and Findochty).

3060

PORTGORDON

B

Planned village, founded *c.* 1794–7 by Alexander, 4th Duke of Gordon (cf. Fochabers and Tomintoul (qq.v.)).

Former ENZIE FREE CHURCH, 1.8 km. SSW. Known as the 'Cocked Hat Kirk'. Of 1844, but disused from 1946, converted as a grain store and now roofless. Neo-Tudor; box bellcote with long pyramidal finial. – VESTRY by *Bruce & Sutherland*, 1885–6. – STAINED GLASS. Fragments in the E window by *Bruce & McClery*, 1914.

KIRKWOOD HOUSE to the W is the manse, built 1847–8. The rear wing, originally one storey but heightened in 1890–1 has a range beyond of 1898 by *James Perry* of Buckie.

ENZIE PARISH CHURCH, High Street East. The former hall for Enzie Free Church (*see* above) by *D. & J. R. McMillan*, 1901–2. Lancets and a bellcote. – STAINED GLASS. N windows, by *Edward Copland* of Aberdeen, 1902.

METHODIST CHURCH, Gordon Street. 1874. Dark whinstone with round-arched windows.

HARBOUR. An important centre for grain export in the early to mid C19, eclipsed *c.* 1880 by Buckpool and Buckie (qq.v.) and now virtually disused. Originally of 1804, of which the E pier is *in situ*. Rebuilt and enlarged to its current form by *D. & T. Stevenson*, engineers, 1870–4. Rough rectangle with stilling basin on the E between two rubble jetties (now with a slipway). BAROMETER, in a fine pedimented niche on Harbour Head. By *Hay & Lyall* of Aberdeen, 1859.

In the middle of GORDON SQUARE, the WAR MEMORIAL, Celtic cross by *John Wittet*, 1920–1, and ORAN HOUSE, a handsome villa of *c.* 1878 with mullioned windows and big canted oriel window. Its early to mid-C19 rear wing was built as a chandlery.

MORAY CREMATORIUM, Broadley, 2.5 km. S. Built as Enzie Parish Church by *Bruce & Sutherland*, 1885–7. E front with fine rose window but ugly porch of 1998–9 when it was converted. The chancel has been reduced to a recess and the furnishings rearranged and remodelled. – ORGAN by *Wadsworth Bros*, 1889.

Former GOLLACHY ICE HOUSE, 0.5 km. NE. Early C19, harled with turf-covered roof.

LEITCHESTON FARM, 1.8 km. SSE, off the A98. Fine earlier C17 lectern-type DOOCOT with crowstepped sides. Very unusual internal arrangement of four compartments with small inter-connecting doorways. Associated with Leitcheston, a laird's house founded by the Gordons *c.* 1630.

PORTGORDON MALTINGS, 1.1 km. SSW. Large complex of 1978–9 with three later extensions. Big cylindrical towers with conical roofs.

Former RAILWAY BRIDGE, 0.9 km. NE. Two semicircular arches over the Burn of Gollachy, *c.* 1886 by *P.M. Barnett* for the Moray Coast Railway.

PORTKNOCKIE B 4060

Cliff-top village, founded in 1677 by fishermen from Cullen (q.v.). The herring industry brought about expansion from the mid C19 and until *c.* 1930 the harbour was among the most important on the Moray Firth. Most of Portknockie has the single-storey cottages usual for the C19 coastal villages.

CHURCH OF CHRIST, Seafield Street and Falconer Terrace. 1902, built as a Baptist hall. Sharply pointed entrance arch and lancets.

PORTKNOCKIE PARISH CHURCH, Church Street and Hill Street. Built 1860–1 as the United Presbyterian Free Church from 1869 to 1942. Bellcote on the S gable and nice octofoil-tracery S window inserted *c.* 1899, when the interior was remodelled by *D. & J.R. McMillan*; the gallery probably of that date. Other furnishings mostly later. A few doors E is the former FREE CHURCH HALL (Youth Centre) of 1888, formerly harled and with raised long-and-short margins and quoins. Split forestair to the S door.

Former SEAFIELD PARISH CHURCH (Kirk House), 450 m. SSE, outside the town. By *William Robertson*, 1838, as a chapel of ease for Portknockie and Seatown, Cullen (q.v.). Converted into a house, 1971–2. The usual gabled box with straight-headed Neo-Tudor windows and porch. The bellcote has a good cresting of miniature bartizans and arrowslits. Former manse (now CULANE) to the S, built *c.* 1839.

Former FISHERMEN'S HALL, Patrol Place. Built *c.* 1820 as a coal store, managed by the Society of Fishermen, who adopted it as their hall, *c.* 1842. Restored 2002. Now a house. Two-storeyed with forestair to the upper room.

PRIMARY SCHOOL, Bridge Street, 1876 for Rathven School Board. Long single-storey E front with three minimally advanced gables, all with blind triple lancets in the tympana. The former SCHOOLHOUSE in King Edward Terrace is 1883–4.

HARBOUR. Built 1886–90, surprisingly late, with slight expansions in 1896 and 1925–6. Superior natural position, roughly circular and with rather sheer cliffs of *c.* 15.2 m. to three sides. Principal pier on the N side, an L-plan with forked outshot to the W. Two parallel quays to the S, both aligned N–S and forming two basins (the outer one a stilling pool). One entrance in the break of the W arm. Now largely encased in concrete.

WAR MEMORIAL, Bridge Street/Park Street. 1923. Polished grey granite column with a pensive statue of Victory.

BOW FIDDLE ROCK, NE off Patrol Road. A natural Gothic stone arch *c.* 52 m. high, hollowed out by the sea. Just to the N of the village a low bank cuts off a small area of headland, *c.* 70 m. by 15 m., known as 'Green Castle'. Excavation has shown the site was occupied in the Pictish period from the C7–C9 by a PROMONTORY FORT and was defended by an elaborate timber-laced rampart that enclosed a number of timber buildings.

4060 PRESHOME B

An inconspicuous place, 3 km. SSE of Portgordon.

ST GREGORY (R.C.). Built 1788–90 and the first post-Reformation Catholic church in Scotland to openly declare its identity, thanks to the influence of the Duke of Gordon. Largely paid for by James and Alexander Gordon of Letterfourie (q.v.).* Built in the garden of an existing presbytery, the church may have been designed by *Fr John Reid*, its first priest, who was educated at the Scots College in Rome and was a keen admirer of architecture. The masons were *William Logie* and *Alexander Milne*. Harled with stone dressings, the broad W façade is an amalgam of Italian Baroque and Scots Georgian. Five bays with arched windows, the centre three minimally advanced and the middle window stepped up under a gable swept up to a pediment with a cross. Entrances in the centre and flanking bays to gallery stair-towers which have finials and low piended roofs. The rest is plain, rather barn-like, with a semi-octagonal chancel added by *P.P. Pugin* in 1896 with Lombardic windows N and S. He redecorated the lofty interior (restored 1989–90) and renewed the nave ceiling. Walls stencilled in brilliant colours, with liberal use of gold. The ceiling of the apse is painted blue with gold stars; encaustic tiles to the sanctuary. Galleries were also removed at the end of the C19.

FURNISHINGS. Mostly by Pugin, executed by *R.L. Boulton & Sons* in extravagant style, notably the HIGH ALTAR of Caen stone and marble containing a tabernacle with quartz-studded

*Their monument and coat of arms for the gable were never carried out.

door with praying angels above and canopied reredos, and the SANCTUARY RAILS with polished marble shafts and pierced Dec tracery. Two excellent large CANOPIES for the side altars with pinnacles and crocketed arches over statues of the Virgin and St Francis de Sales. – ALTAR PAINTING. St Gregory, after Carracci's in San Gregorio Magno al Celio, Rome. Given by the 7th Earl of Findlater, who commissioned it for his drawing room at Cullen House (q.v.), its inclusion strongly resisted by Pugin. – ORGAN. *c.* 1820 by *James Bruce* for *Wood, Small & Co.* Ornate Dec case, the central pinnacle nearly touching the ceiling. – MEMORIALS. Bishop James Kyle †1869. Brass, with an angel holding a plaque with Gothic script. Similar memorial to Canon John James Kyle †1917.

CHAPEL HOUSE, E, is the former presbytery. Designed in 1830 by Bishop *James Kyle,* who had been consecrated Vicar Apostolic of the Northern District in 1828, but his plans drawn and amended by *William Robertson*. The library retains its fittings and it was here that Bishop Kyle amassed the 'Preshome Letters', of 30,000 documents relating to the Scottish Catholic Church (now in the Scottish Catholic Archives, Edinburgh). The LAUNDRY is late C18 and probably one of the pavilion wings for the second presbytery on the site. The first presbytery was a cottage built *c.* 1697 for Thomas Nicholson (†1718), the first post-Reformation Catholic Bishop of Scotland.

QUARRYWOOD 1060

Named for a long-vanished castle, but known as New Spynie after the construction of the church.

SPYNIE PARISH CHURCH. Built 1735–6 to replace the church at Spynie itself (q.v.). Simple T-plan, the S flank of four bays. The pointed arch of the l. door is probably C16 and reused from the previous church. Shorter, straight-headed entrance on the r. also reused, but with the jambs inverted. Little window above it with a sill formerly dated 1691. In the centre, the former minister's door was blocked in the early C19 and is now flanked by two rectangular windows inserted 1803–5. Scars of their smaller predecessors to the l. and r.; ogee-headed SUNDIAL between them of 1740. W bellcote dated 1723, reused from Spynie and topped by pyramidal finials; the BELL by *Michael Burgerhuys*, 1637, is said to have been given by Bishop Guthrie. The N aisle has a large, convincingly Neo-Georgian, window by *John Wittet*, 1905. Delightfully unspoilt interior, with plaster coomb ceiling and segmental stone arch to the N aisle. Remodelled in 1803–5, including the E and W GALLERIES and the semi-hexagonal PULPIT with pilastered back-board and tester. They all have fielded panelling and little dentilled cornices.

SPYNIE KIRK HOUSE, WSW of the church. Former manse by *William Robertson*, 1840–1. Harled, symmetrical S front of two storeys and three bays with big piended roof on projecting eaves. Corniced, pilastered doorpiece in the centre; windows with lying-pane glazing, longer on the ground floor.

DOOCOT, 150 m. WSW in a housing development. The only vestige of Quarrelwood Castle, built on the S shore of Loch Spynie by the Sutherland family in the late C15.* The doocot is harled and nearly square, probably late C16. Crowstepped gables; heavy roof of overlapping stone slabs, supported internally (cf. Pittendreich, p. 706) by masonry arches.

ARDGILZEAN HOUSE, 1.5 km. SW. Large, rock-faced villa, likely by *A. & W. Reid & Wittet* and dated 1897 on its semicircular dormerhead. Wide, gabled ends flanking a slightly recessed round entrance arch. Fine carpentry inside.

THE OAKWOOD, 1.3 km. SSE on the edge of the wood by the A96. A rare survival of part of a café and motel complex, built 1932–5 in a rustic North American style by its proprietors, *Dougal* and *Andrew Duncan*. Closed in 1994 and now a showroom. Original front section with a piended, ridge-tiled roof (originally thatched) and triangular dormers inset with coloured glass. Two-storey rear extension (1935) with chunky log-cabin cladding in lozenge patterns and a naïve sunburst on the W side. Inside, an A-frame timber roof over the former tea room and dance floor, and Art Deco glass in old bar and ballroom. A caretaker's bungalow also survives but the long row of chalets to the E was demolished *c.* 1985. Also lost are the original petrol pumps painted to resemble trees and topped by lights fashioned as burning bushes.

QUARRY WOOD HENGE (or 'DANISH CAMP'), 1.1 km. SSE of the church in the woods. Neolithic. An external bank and internal ditch enclose a sub-oval area with diameter of *c.* 47 m. Overgrown but generally well preserved. Entrance in the W defined by a causeway *c.* 4 m. wide; two boulders in the SW sector. These sites are thought to have been used for ceremonial gatherings in the Later Neolithic or Early Bronze Age (*c.* 2500–2000 B.C.).

0050

RAFFORD

'Ruffus' is first documented in the early C13, when it was already the main settlement on the road S of Forres (q.v.). The present village is split into upper and lower sections.

PARISH CHURCH, off Kirkside. Good Perp by *J. Gillespie Graham*, 1824–6, well sited on a hill encircled by trees. Wide, three-bay

*It replaced a hall house of *c.* 1333 built by Sir Robert Lauder, justiciar of north Scotland.

rectangle with a tall tower projecting from the centre of the S gable. The door has a crocketed ogival hoodmould with big finial; good faceted dummy lanterns to the l. and r. raised up on long shafts. Similar crocketed pinnacles corbelled out above around a pierced parapet. The W flank has three two-light windows between buttresses with double set-offs and bushy crocketed pinnacles. The three similar windows in the E flank were added by *P. Macgregor Chalmers* in 1907 along with an hexagonal NE vestry (dem. 1995 and the whole flank given a dull, single-storey HALL with rubble screen wall). Lofty interior, completely remodelled by Chalmers and reoriented to the N. He demolished the gallery, but reused its panelling for the dado, and this accounts for the strangely bare S wall, with only a small round-headed arch of 1907 to the tower vestibule. Timber ceiling, the centre a wide segmental arch carried on tie-beams with kingposts. Flat sides with quadrant arch braces linked to stone corbels, each pierced by a quatrefoil.

FURNISHINGS. 1907, all with curvilinear tracery. – STAINED GLASS. Large N (liturgical E) window by *A.L. Moore & Son*, 1920–1, a memorial to Major Harold B. Galloway †1915, who built Blervie House (q.v.). Christ blessing children, in the Garden of Gethsemane, and as the light of the world, all under Gothic canopies. Three angels on the bottom holding a memorial scroll. – BELL (tower). 1567, from the church in the burial ground.

BURIAL GROUND, 200 m. S. Site of the medieval church, first documented in a charter of *c.* 1209 and assigned to the subchanter of Elgin Cathedral (q.v.). Apparently dedicated to St Maelrubha (†722), the church was rebuilt in 1754, measured *c.* 20.1 m. by 6.1 m. and was largely dem. 1827. The base of its E gable is incorporated in the W wall of the early C19 MORT HOUSE, which has a N doorpiece with reused chamfered jambs (likely C17) and simple fireplace inside. – The wall continues N to form the rear of another BURIAL AISLE, the quoins and door frame with long-and-short V-channelling. – Coped BURIAL ENCLOSURE for the Dunbar Brodie family by the main entrance. Rectangular doorpiece with reused C17 roll moulding; re-set STONE to the r. dated 1649 with the initials R.D. and I.C.

VILLAGE HALL, Lower Rafford, 1 km. SE. Former Free Church by *A. & W. Reid*, 1885–9; converted 1949–50.* E.E., the W gable with a simple shafted doorway flanked by little lancets. Seven-petal rosette window above and then a gableted bellcote. Bad SW extension, 1997–8, when the ceiling was lowered and the gallery blocked.

WAR MEMORIAL, Church Terrace. By *John Wittet*, 1920–1. Channelled obelisk of pink granite topped by a four-leaf ball finial.

*Replacing the original Free Church on the same site by *John Urquhart* of Forres, 1843–4 (dem. *c.* 1887).

RONGAI HOUSE, 175 m. SSE of the church. Built as the manse by *J. Gillespie Graham*, 1817–18. Symmetrical main block of two storeys and three bays, harled over a raised basement. Good, competent solidity (cf. Kinloss manse, q.v.). Corniced, pilastered doorpiece in the centre approached by a flight of steps; rear wing forming a T-plan, *c.* 1840.

OLD SCHOOL HOUSE, near the burial ground. By *A. & W. Reid*, 1844, one of their very earliest commissions; L-plan S extension by *A. & W. Reid & Wittet*, 1899. Further S is the mid-C19 OLD STEADING, built on a nearly quadrangular plan. Converted *c.* 1980. Re-set in its NE gable, a medieval carving of a head (likely C15) with dramatic almond-shaped eyes. Pupils crudely gouged in later.

BLERVIE CASTLE, 1.5 km. NE. In a commanding hilltop position, long exploited for its strategic and defensive advantages. According to several chronicles, Blervie was the place where a band of enraged Moray men assassinated King Malcolm I in 954. A castle ('Ulern') is first documented on the site in 1221, and in 1263 the Exchequer ordered Alexander Comyn, Earl of Buchan, to repair and garrison it in preparation for invasion by King Haco of Norway. The Comyns retained ownership for at least another century and a half but by *c.* 1567 Blervie had passed to the Dunbars, who built the present – and greatly decayed – tower house. It was besieged by the Marquis of Huntly in 1646 and in 1724 sold to William Duff, 1st Earl Fife. His son, Capt. Ludovic Duff (†1811), demolished most of the hall block *c.* 1774, reusing the stone to build his new residence (*see* Blervie Mains House, below). Most of the NW tower collapsed during a storm in 2005. The fabric remains in a perilous state.

The remains are mid to late C16, consisting of part of the central block and the ruins of the NW tower. The castle was originally five-storeyed and is usually said to have been on a Z-plan, although there is no evidence of another diagonal tower and it may well have been L-plan from the start. Its appearance closely resembled Burgie Tower (q.v.) and the two are almost certainly the work of the same architect. The ruined hall block in the centre was originally square and is now roofless, with the W wall and part of the N wall intact. The centre of its ground floor is now filled by farm buildings, first inserted in the early C19. Of the first-floor hall, the W wall retains a good, straight-headed chimneypiece, formerly dated 1598.* Mighty jogged architrave across the top with fragments of cornice; segmental arch above it, likely from an earlier chimneypiece. Window to the l. with the remains of a segmental barrel-vault; two doors to the r. to the NW tower block, the second blocked in the C17. Part of a window (the l. jamb and sill) beyond it. STAIR-TOWER above it, originally winding up to the battlements and caphouse (dem. *c.* 1774). As at Burgie,

*Now extremely faint, and usually erroneously reported as 1398.

it is corbelled on an inverted conical base in the re-entrant angle. Five rectangular slit-windows on its N face.

Of the NW TOWER only the E wall and parts of the N and S return walls are intact, originally containing one bedroom on each floor. The lower half is filled with debris from the collapse, although one elliptical gunloop can be seen on the S.

BLERVIE MAINS HOUSE, 0.8 km. NNE. Good, persuasive Georgian, built 1776 by Capt. Ludovic Duff, son of the 1st Earl Fife, from stone from Blervie Castle (q.v.). SW front of two storeys and five bays in squared, cherry-pointed rubble with V-channelled quoins; centre minimally advanced under a stilted attic gable with chimneystack. Unusually attractive skewputts with lipped scrolls (the l. one dated), the ends with a row of dogtooth and nautilus shells towards the flanks. Single-storey, off-centre addition to the rear, early to mid C19. Good open-well, cantilevered staircase inside with treads reused from the castle (likely late C17, with thick moulded risers truncated in 1776 and the undersides then re-moulded). In the drawing room a late C19 timber chimneypiece from an Edinburgh house. Rams' heads on the jambs; rinceau on the lintel with eagles' heads on the ends. One of the attic bedrooms has a fine bolection-moulded chimneypiece, another relic from the castle.

LITTLE BLERVIE, 1.8 km SE. Very successful rustic-contemporary fusion by *McKenzie Strickland Associates*, 2010–11. Broad, shallow-gabled rectangle with boldly projecting eaves carried on square posts. The S side is a curtain of glass punctuated by Glulam struts; the N is revetted in larch. Open, full-height interior in the S half, nicely blurring the lines between indoors and out.

LADY DUFF'S TOMB, 0.7 km. NNW of Rafford. Moated mound, almost certainly the site of a Pictish fort. The partially subterranean tomb in the centre is early C19 and now overgrown.

TEMPLESTONE, 1.2 km. NE. To the NE of a steading, a four-poster stone setting. It is unusual both in the smallness of the stones and that they form the corners of a rectangle (not a circle), *c.* 3.5 m. by 2.7 m. This type of stone setting probably dates to the Early to Middle Bronze Age and others of its type have been found to be associated with cremation burial.

ALTYRE HOUSE. *See* p. 461.

BLERVIE HOUSE. *See* p. 479.

RATHVEN B 4060

An important village in the Middle Ages, originally the centre of its own parish but now virtually a satellite of Buckie (q.v.). A leper hospital founded in the early C13 later served as an alms or bede-house (rebuilt 1634; dem. 1886).

PARISH CHURCH, Main Road. Built 1794 to replace the church in the burial ground (*see* below). Birdcage W bellcote, round-arched window with keystones and block imposts in the W gable and four in the S flank, the l. one divided by a transom in 1932 when the N windows were inserted by *R.M. Fulton* of Buckie and the interior reordered. The pulpit – in the usual Georgian arrangement – had been in the centre of the S side with U-plan gallery opposite; the W gallery is part of the original, now facing the PULPIT of 1932. – ORGAN behind the pulpit by *Wadsworth Bros*, 1908. – STAINED GLASS. N windows by *James Nicol* of *George Donald & Sons*, 1932. – S windows (Adoration and Ascension) by *Nathaniel Bryson*, 1908. – Under the gallery, Christ with the wise virgins, brilliantly coloured, by *Gordon M. Webster*, 1936. – VESTRY by *John Miller*, 1874. – HALL by *Simpson & Wright*, 2011–13.

BURIAL GROUND, Main Road. The medieval church of St Peter, first recorded in 1224–6, was a dependency of the collegiate church in Cullen (Old Church, q.v.). The former S aisle survives, the jamb of its entrance dated 1612 with dedicatory Latin inscription. It became the RANNAS AISLE in 1798, its walls heightened and tall pointed barrel-vault inserted. Stone slab roof. Inside, MEMORIAL (also *c.* 1798) for Andrew Hay of Rannas †1789, tracing his genealogy back to the early C15. Large triple-shafted Gothic arch around it.

OLD SCHOOLHOUSE, E of the church. Built 1798, harled, of domestic appearance with some original windows. Five bays at ground floor, the l. two originally with porches. Single-storey wing by *John Miller*, 1862. E addition, 2013.

RATHVEN HOUSE, 0.5 km. SE. The former manse, by *John Miller*, 1868–70.

9040

RELUGAS

On high ground between the confluence of the Findhorn and Divie rivers.

The house, by *Ashley Bartlam Partnership*, replaced one that was largely built by Sir Thomas Dick Lauder, author of the account of the floods of 1829, who acquired Relugas in 1808 (dem. *c.* 1958). A few fragments survive, e.g. the former arch to the garden and service court with a plaque containing the initials of Lauder and his wife, and a curious Neo-Romanesque belfry. Late C18 GATEPIERS with thick V-channelled rustication and attenuated urn finials. The LODGE is a good (and surprisingly late) stab at Scots Renaissance with crowsteps, re-entrant drum tower and catslide dormers to the rear, 1950–1.

The policies were landscaped in a picturesque style with walks through the woods and including the dramatic

Randolph's Leap on the Findhorn. Doune of Relugas, 100 m. E of the house, is an ancient vitrified fort, on a wooded knoll in a bend of the Divie. Oval summit aligned NW–SE and surrounded by ruinous drystone wall over revetment and fragments of a rampart (*c.* 5.5 m. wide by 1.5 m. high). Ditch enclosure (*c.* 5.5 m. wide by 2 m. deep) with external bank to the NW, N and NE. Fragments of Roman pottery were discovered in the early to mid C19.

Bridge of Logie, 0.2 km. NNE. High, single span across the Divie, 1783 – one of the few to survive the floods of 1829. Segmental arch-ring abutted directly against the rock.

Daltulich Bridge, 1.8 km. SW. High, graceful single span over the Findhorn, *c.* 1792 (total width, 21.9 m.). Arch-ring with slender dressed voussoirs.

ROTHES 2040

First recorded in 1189 and 1198, when Peter de Polloc, 'Lord of Rothayes', was the witness to several charters. He built a castle on a strategic promontory near the Spey in the early C13, which then became the seat of the Leslie family *c.* 1288. Although the Leslies were elevated to Earls of Rothes *c.* 1457, the settlement – presumably a cluster of buildings below the castle – was never elevated to a burgh.

The present town was laid out by James Ogilvy, 3rd Earl of Seafield in 1766, one of many such planned villages in Moray. The earliest houses straddled the Burn of Rothes with short spurs leading off of it to the N and S. Despite much expansion, the town is still bisected by the Burn and retains its original form of a St Andrew's cross. Rothes was little more than a crofting village until the mid C19, when the arrival of the distilleries gave it a new industrial townscape.

CHURCHES AND CEMETERY

PARISH CHURCH, High Street and Seafield Square. Built 1781–4 to succeed the old church (*see* Burial Ground) and Dundurcas church (*see* below). Simple Georgian T-plan, plain rubble walls (de-harled in 1954) with four tall round-arched windows in the N flank with lattice glazing and an apsidal-ended S aisle, the door in its bow converted into a window in 1887. Set against the E gable a four-stage ashlar clock tower by *A. & W. Reid*, 1870, with pyramidal roof. SE vestry of 1813. The interior was renovated in 1886–7 by *Alexander Smith* of Cullen (the Earl of Seafield's estate architect) and *Andrew Thomson* of Keith, but retained the traditional Georgian layout. U-plan gallery with long canted angles, facing the PULPIT against the N wall.

– STAINED GLASS (in the apse) by *Shona McInnes*, 2009, based on Proverbs 3:6. At the top, Ben Aigan with autumnal leaves and a cross overlooking the town of Rothes (with malt kiln, parish church and part of High Street). Below centre, the waters of the Spey over chalice and grain.

Former UNITED FREE CHURCH, High Street. Disused and in poor condition. Large, E.E. style, 1898–1900 by *George Sutherland* (*Sutherland & Jamieson*). Long cusped lancets in the centre of the E front above the gabled portal. Good big SE tower with broach spire. Lancets in the S flank. Coomb wooden ceiling (with arch braces) and gallery intact inside.

ROTHES BURIAL GROUND, Burnside Street. Site of St Laurence, built *c.* 1554 and deeded to the Hospital of St. Nicholas at Boat o' Brig (q.v.).* Pulled down 1780. The roofless LESLIE AISLE stands just E of the church site. Probably late C18. A slab for Alexander Leslie traces his lineage back to George Leslie, 1st Earl of Rothes (†1490). Ornate TOMBSTONE for James Leslie †1576, son of the 3rd Earl of Rothes and the church's 'rector' from 1563. One of the finest C16 monuments in Moray. Skilled heraldic carving and good Gothic script. Perimeter inscription with 'heir lyis ane nobil man / Mastir James Leslie persone of rothes brother g / ermane of George erle / umquhil of the same quha deyit i ye lord ye xiii of / octobir a[nno] d[omi]ni 1586'. Armorial panel below (two lions rampant and two sleeves with three buckles) surrounded by the initials W.I.L. Incised skull underneath with bone in jaw over scrolls with 'reme[m]ber ye death' and 'resurgat'.

PUBLIC BUILDINGS

GRANT HALL, New Street. By *R.B. Pratt*, 1897–1900. Severe E front of rock-faced rubble, three bays and two storeys raised on a tall plinth. Corbelled semi-octagonal buttresses at the angles and in the centre buttresses carried up into pepperpot pinnacles flanking a gable. Gabled entrance below with a moulded, round-headed arch dying into wide chamfers. There were originally turrets over the outer buttresses and a central cupola. Single-storey wing to the r. and longer wing down Dominies Lane.

ROTHES PRIMARY SCHOOL, Green Street. By *John Wittet*, 1915–18. Large, square plan around a central court, single-storeyed with piended roofs. Baroque-style arched pediments for the entrances breaking through the eaves. Two gables in the centre and a cupola. Similar W elevation. – N annexe for technical classes (now NURSERY SCHOOL), 1908. Single-storey gabled T-plan of three wide bays. It was associated with the previous school of 1875.

*It replaced a C13 CHAPEL and GRAVEYARD, said to have been located near Chapel Hill (0.4 km. S of the Castle).

Rothes Castle

Off High Street

On a hilltop controlling an important medieval trade route along the Spey valley, with commanding views of the countryside and Ben Aigan. The 'house of Rothayes' is documented in the late C12 and King William the Lion instructed Peter de Polloc to build a castle there *c.* 1200. The Leslies moved to Rothes from Garioch (South Aberdeenshire) *c.* 1288 and adopted it as their family seat, becoming the Earls of Rothes *c.* 1457. King Edward I lodged at the 'manner house of Rothays' in 1296, the night after his visit to Elgin Castle (q.v.). Abandoned by the Leslies *c.* 1620 the castle was burnt by villagers in 1662, claiming that it harboured thieves and vagabonds. Much of the remaining masonry would have been quarried for building the new town in 1766. All that stands now is one stretch of the E CURTAIN WALL, 21.1 m. long and between 6 and 7 m. high. Roughly coursed masonry with rubble infill, probably early C13. Tall and slightly curved foundation plinth to the E. Inside, the remains at first floor of a tall window embrasure with half of a round arch. Also the remains of an AUMBRY. At the N end is the beginning of the N curtain wall with vestiges of another first-floor window; springing of a barrel-vault in the re-entrant angle with rubble infill above.

Grass-covered depressions mark the location of the former KEEP, said to have been a four-storey hall house. Rounded ditch to SW, originally a dry MOAT traversed by a drawbridge.

A CHAPEL dedicated to Our Lady of Grace was also built in the C13. Said to have been located 0.4 km. S (near Chapel Hill) and abandoned in 1555 for the parish church (*see* Burial Ground).

DESCRIPTION

NEW STREET runs N–S in the town's upper half, laid out in the late C18 and mostly rebuilt in the mid to late C19, with the customary one- and two-storey cottages. Towards the N end the SEAFIELD ARMS HOTEL, built as the Plough Inn *c.* 1855 but its centre reconfigured by *R.B. Pratt* in 1897 with a ball-finialled gable surrounding a glazed oculus and windows under semicircular hoodmoulds. Rear block of the same date. Diagonally opposite, the former manager's house (No. 68) for Glen Grant Distillery, 1898 by *Charles C. Doig*. Grander than its neighbours, finialled gablets breaking through the eaves. At the next intersection to the S, opposite Grant Hall (*see* Public Buildings), the much larger former STATION HOTEL, 1898–1901 by *George Sutherland* (*Sutherland & Jamieson*) with fronts to New Street and School Terrace and the entrance on the chamfered corner with a round-headed entrance arch, corbelled out above into a canted window with an octagonal turret and faceted roof.

SE across the Spey is SEAFIELD SQUARE, running NE from the junction of New Street and High Street by the parish church. This was not, unlike most planned towns in Moray, part of the original plan, but assumed its current form in the early to mid C19. W of the church, a house of *c.* 1852 enlivened by *A.J. Sharp* in 1901, e.g. the semicircular pediments over the first-floor windows. Next door is the former CITY OF GLASGOW BANK, *c.* 1859, coolly proficient in grey ashlar. Just beyond, in the square's garden, the mercat-cross-style WAR MEMORIAL by *John Wittet*, 1920–1.* Tall pedestal with fluted pilasters and swan-neck pediments to each side, and an Ionic column with a unicorn.

The long, straight HIGH STREET was called Old Street until the end of the C19. The first house on the E side after the parish church is the finest in Rothes, dated 1858 on its r. skewputt. Two storeys and four bays with a tooled sandstone front. The l. bay is a slightly recessed quadrant. Then follows a good terrace (Nos. 8–16), also mid to late C19. Across the street is the former United Free Church (*see* Churches, above) with its central gable and tall tower and spire. Further down on that side, the villa-style former CALEDONIAN BANK, late C19, with a good ashlar front of three bays separated by channelled pilaster strips, with canted bays and a central wall-head gable with acroterion. Further S again, SPEY VILLA (originally Glen Spey Villa), built 1881 for James Stuart, who three years later began construction of Glen Spey Distillery behind (*see* Distilleries, below) in 1884. Gabled porch in the centre with round-headed, roll-moulded door. Quasi-crocket finial to this and the gable and dormers.

ROTHES HOUSE, off Manse Brae. Originally the parish manse. By *William Robertson*, 1839–41, after a design by *John Smith*. That explains the slightly incoherent plan, so out of keeping with Robertson's usual hyper-rationality, and the gabled style. Round-headed entrance porch with stepped parapet. Slightly advanced l. bay with chamfered angles corbelled into squares.

GLEBE HOUSE, 0.8 km. S. The former Free Church manse, designed by *Alexander McWatt*, minister, in 1848–9. Splendid hilltop setting. T-plan with symmetrical E front of tooled rubble, two storeys and three bays with a shallow piended roof. Central porch with moulded architrave and pilaster strips. – Former STEADING and GIG HOUSE to SW by *John Masson* of Rothes, *c.* 1850.

DISTILLERIES

The whisky industry was already thriving in Rothes in 1734, when a Mr Waters was active as a 'Gauger' of casks. One of the peculiarities of the town is that its distilleries are tucked away from the main road and difficult to see.‡

*Originally at the N end of town but placed here in 1993.

‡The unattractive (and very visible) building complex at the NE corner of Rothes is not a distillery, but a biomass energy plant and animal feed processing unit, opened 2013 on the site of an early C20 evaporation works.

GLEN GRANT DISTILLERY (Campari), off Elgin Road. The earliest in Rothes. Built 1840–1 and enlarged in 1865 with alterations by *A. & W. Reid*, 1883. Most of the production block has been rebuilt, the STILL HOUSE dating from 1973–4. Rectangular courtyard in the middle of the complex with an open E end. On its W side, the OFFICES of 1840, given a Baronial front by *Charles C. Doig* in 1900–1. On the N side, a crowstepped former WAREHOUSE, two storeys of the late C19, with a wide canted façade added *c.* 1962. Doorpiece with bolection moulding; parapet with crenellated corners. Across from it (S side), the former MALT BARN of 1840, now dry-dashed and missing its third storey. Seven bays with small horizontal windows. Off to the E, WAREHOUSES by Doig, *c.* 1897. Three storeys and six bays, diagonally gabled to the N (along the entrance drive).

The VISITORS' CENTRE is the converted stables and coach-house (1887, by the Reids) for Glengrant House, built for the distillery's owner, Major John Grant, in 1884–5. It was a fine Baronial villa, inexcusably demolished in 1993.

GLENROTHES DISTILLERY (Berry Bros & Rudd), Burnside Street. Originally built by *A. & W. Reid & Melven*, 1878–9. The KILN (disused) dates from an expansion by *Charles C. Doig* in 1896–7, doubling the first maltings and kiln formerly located to the W. Obligatory pyramidal ogee roof with pagoda ventilator. Attached (on the site of Doig's maltings), a cavernous STILL HOUSE by *R.J. Walker & Smith*, 1979–80. Two tall storeys with a wide gambrel attic; nine bays, the eighth with a gigantic, segmental entrance arch. High first floor lined with segmental-headed windows. Sixteen WAREHOUSES along the N side of the Burn of Rothes. MANAGER'S HOUSE (now Glendoonie) to the E on Burnside Street. By Doig, 1894. Further down, the former CUSTOMS AND EXCISE OFFICER'S HOUSE (now Craiglynn) by Doig, 1897–8. Good rock-faced Baronial.

GLEN SPEY DISTILLERY (Diageo), off High Street. Built 1884–5 on the site of an old corn mill, probably by *Hugh J. Mackenzie* of Elgin. The site is nestled against the base of the hill and overlooked by the castle ruins. Much Victorian masonry remains, but little of interest survived a fire in 1920 and reconstruction of the production buildings in 1969–70. Original rubble MALT BARN (now a racking warehouse) running N–S, three storeys and eleven bays with two pilaster buttresses on the flanks. Three-gabled front to the N, the centre narrow and raised to create a capital W. – Three sets of piended WAREHOUSES to the NW, N and E (by the main entrance), one added by *Charles C. Doig* in 1898.

SPEYBURN DISTILLERY (Inver House), 1.2 km. NNW, North Road. Built as Speyburn-Glenlivet Distillery by *Charles C. Doig*, 1896–7. Located in a scenic but narrow ravine, hence its uncharacteristically compact design. Former MALT BARN at the W end, three-storeyed and uncommonly tall. Conventional floor maltings could never have fitted in the available space, so Doig was forced to build upwards instead of out. Seven bays with segmental-headed windows, the ground-floor ones very lofty. Square DRYING KILN to the E with an unusual arrangement of two DRYING FLOORS, superimposed on top of one another so as to make the most of the spatial constraints. Pyramidal ogee roof above with pagoda apex ventilator.

Tall single-storey-and-attic STILL HOUSE set perpendicular to the E, two bays with piended, louvred ridge vents. – Four bays of gabled WAREHOUSES beyond, the W half to be converted into a BOILER ROOM and TUN ROOM by *Ken Mathieson Architectural Design*, 2013. – On the slope to the WNW, the former MANAGER'S HOUSE (now SPEYBURN HOUSE), *c.* 1915. Two bays with gableted dormers breaking the eaves.

DUNDURCAS CHURCH, 3.1 km. NE. On a beautiful site overlooking a haugh and the Woods of Knockmore beyond the Spey. Rebuilt in 1748–53 by *John Chalmers*, mason, probably on the medieval footprint,* but superseded in 1782 by the churches at Rothes and Boharm (qq.v.) and its roof removed, reportedly to stop 'an insane preacher' from holding services for dissenters. It is a fairly simple gabled rectangle, 15.6 m. by 8.1 m. with sharp E and W gables and a birdcage bellcote (of 1701, for the previous church). S front of six bays with chamfered, straight-headed doors flanking a pair of windows and with small, square windows at each end, the l. now blocked. The E and W fronts have doors with a window over, the E one very attenuated, on the N flank just two outer windows matching those on the S, of which the lintel of the r. one is dated 1760. This refers to repairs by *Patrick Grant* (mason). Exposed rubble interior. – Memorial slab for David Dalrymple †1747 and Elspet Cumming †1743, 'a Gentle Woman of Probity & Goodnefs'. Ogival pediment dated 1748 with two winged souls, hand on open book, and initials.

The GRAVEYARD is a roughly circular mound, suggesting use from a very early date and with a slight ditch to the SW, probably indicating that it was a fortified site in pagan times. – Just inside the main gate, a TABLET dated 1822 with Latin inscription commemorating the building of the dyke to prevent the 'impertinent intrusion of sheep and cattle'. Fluted pilasters and pediment inset with a triangular gablet.

AIKENWAY CASTLE, 2.1 km. NNE. On a steep, flat-topped promontory surrounded by the Spey on three sides. It was occupied by the Earls of Rothes in the late C15. Just two fragments of the original building survive, *c.* 1.6 m. high and forming part of a circular stair-tower. Barmkin wall reduced to footings and mostly overgrown.

OLD STATION HOUSE, 5.1 km. NE, B9015. Formerly Orton Junction Station on the Inverness & Aberdeen Junction Railway

*Dedicated to Our Lady of Grace and first mentioned in 1244. It was later annexed to the Hospital at Rathven. Dundurcas evidently became quite wealthy before the Reformation, generating 'a certain amount' of revenue for Kinloss Abbey (q.v.).

where it joined the Morayshire Railway branch from Rothes. By *Joseph Mitchell*, 1860. L-plan, with stationmaster's house to S and offices etc. behind. Platform shelter in the re-entrant angle, its canopy on cast-iron Roman Doric columns.

AUCHINROATH HOUSE. *See* p. 470.
BOAT O' BRIG. *See* p. 710.
ORTON HOUSE. *See* p. 711.

ROTHES GLEN HOUSE 2050

4.1 km. NNW of Rothes

A sumptuous Baronial mansion by *Ross & Macbeth*, built 1892–4 as the summer residence for Edward and Phoebe Dunbar-Dunbar of Seapark House, Kinloss (*see* p. 677). It replaced a house called Birchfield (built 1869–71, also by *Alexander Ross*) after it was destroyed by fire.

Main SE entrance front of two storeys and five bays, broadly symmetrical around a slightly advanced centre. Doorpiece with Neo-Jacobean waisted pilasters and chamfered angles to the l. and r.; caphouse corbelled out above with a pair of tourelles under candlesnuffer roofs. They flank a crowstepped gable with a coat of arms and scroll with 'Sub Spe' (a play of words on 'hope' and the River Spey). Diagonal bartizan on the far l. and drum tower on the far r. under conical roof, the latter with excellent wrought-iron finial. Behind this front, set back on the NE elevation, is a magnificent four-storey tower with a first-floor canted oriel corbelled out over acanthus. Crenellated parapet on top with cannon water spouts and three open tourelles; round stair-tower sweeping up the r. side, protruding at the top as a circular turret with a conical bellcast roof. The rest of this front and that to the garden are more conventional, with crowstepped gables and dormerheads. Fine rainwater goods throughout, many of the upper spouts rendered as dragons.

The INTERIOR was restored to a high standard from 2004 to 2013. Triple-arched Gothic screen in the entrance hall carried on bundled piers. Staircase behind with cast-iron balustrade and filigree wrought-iron work, all top-lit by a coved ceiling with etched and tinted glass. Italian mosaic floor below, the design strangely taking no account of the staircase and piers. The principal rooms (Drawing Room, Sitting Room, Ballroom and Dining Room) all have strapwork ceilings in geometric patterns. Good Carrara marble chimeypieces in the Drawing Room and Sitting Room.

Former STABLES and CARRIAGE HOUSE, 200 m. SSW. 1873, probably by *Alexander Ross* (now dwellings). Quadrangular plan with segmental courtyard entrance; gable above with plaque showing the Dunbar-Dunbars' initials. Long, slender clock tower on top with good Gothic brattishing.

ROTHIEMAY HOUSE *see* MILLTOWN OF ROTHIEMAY

SCALAN COLLEGE *see* CHAPELTOWN OF GLENLIVET

2060

SPYNIE

A church dedicated to the Holy Trinity is first documented at Spynie in 1187. In *c.* 1207, it was important enough to be elevated to a cathedral by Pope Innocent III, as instigated by Bishop Bricius of Moray (1203–22). The episcopal palace was begun at the same time, succeeding the seats of the see at Birnie (q.v.) and Kinneddar (Lossiemouth). However, its dignity was short-lived, as the episcopal seat was moved again – for the final time – to Elgin in 1224, by order of Pope Honorius III. The church then became the parish church, serving as the ninth prebend for the new Cathedral at Elgin. A settlement rapidly grew up around it, bolstered by trade revenues from a harbour on the tidal Loch Spynie and its proximity to the bishops' residence, which remained at Spynie Palace (q.v.) and was connected to Elgin via the River Lossie. The 'old toun' was elevated to a free burgh of barony in 1451 and a burgh of regality in 1452. By the mid C16 the harbour had become too shallow and the principal port was transferred to Findhorn (q.v.). Spynie was burnt by Montrose in 1645 and the Palace abandoned in 1690 after the abolition of the bishopric.

BURIAL GROUND. Site of the cathedral church which became parochial in 1224. It remained in use after the Reformation but was demolished in 1736 when New Spynie church was built (*see* Quarrywood). Excavations in 1924 revealed foundations of a surprisingly small and unassuming rectangular building, *c.* 22.6 m. by 10.7 m. The E gable was built of stone, the rest evidently of clay.

Impressive collection of late C17 and C18 MONUMENTS, among the best in Moray. – BURIAL ENCLOSURE towards the NE corner with a long TABLET to Samuel Tulloch †1706 and family, with Latin inscription over three conjoined monograms. The four exterior walls have CARVINGS of 'Tyme Fleeth', 'Conquer Eternal[ly]', 'Mynd Mortalit[y]' and a chilling 'Death Pursueth' with a skeleton firing a bow and arrow. – To the WSW, a beautiful CONSECRATION CROSS carved for the cathedral in the early C13. Large, round medallion with eight spurs of faded stiff-leaf, mounted on a shaft and base of 1907. The top may have been reused as a mercat cross from the mid C15. – Adjacent BURIAL AISLE for the Leslies of Findrassie House (q.v.), dated 1766 on its lintel. On the exterior E wall are four medieval BODY STONES, likely C13, with traces of stiff-leaf roundels similar to the consecration cross.

Inside are two early medieval SLABS, again probably C13. The l. is incised with a rudimentary Jerusalem cross, the r. with a sword. – Among the Leslie monuments, a SLAB (to the l. of the door) for Isobel Leslie †1688 with perimeter inscription and large carvings of heraldry and skull and crossbones. Similar one to the r. for Margaret Aeyton †1714. Excellent MONUMENT for Abraham Leslie †1793 with two fluted Corinthian columns and big fronds of acanthus on the capitals. Also a mounted SLAB with long Latin inscription for Robert Leslie †1588 (son of George Leslie, 4th Earl of Rothes) and his wife, Janet Elphinstone.

Roofless former MORT HOUSE to the W, early C19 with angle pilasters. Entrance overlying the former W gable of the church; interior lined with stone shelves for burials. – By the graveyard wall, James Ramsay MacDonald †1937, former prime minister and resident of Lossiemouth (q.v.), and family. Marble slab, carved with 'Passed to where beyond these voices there is peace'.

SPYNIE PALACE. The grandest surviving bishop's palace in Scotland, and one of the finest medieval monuments in the country. It was the principal residence and fortress of the bishops of Moray from the early C13 to the end of the C17, making it the oldest continuously occupied episcopal palace in Britain, despite a temporary abolition of the bishopric between 1638 and 1661. Bishop Colin Falconer (1680–6) seems to have been the last official to occupy the palace before the final abolition in 1690, when Spynie was annexed to the Crown. Abandoned, it quickly fell into disuse and in 1728 it was already a site of 'great wast and embezilment'. The ruins passed to the state in 1973 and major excavations between 1986 and 1994 have greatly enhanced our understanding of the palace's history and original appearance.

The present palace is at least the third set of buildings on the site. A group of wooden structures (likely a hall, private chapel and kitchen) was built after the move from Kinneddar (*see* Lossiemouth), surrounded by a palisade and rectangular ditch. These were replaced (and augmented) in stone throughout the C13. Beginning in the early to mid C14, there was then a grand reconstruction in stone, resulting in a large square complex (*c.* 44 m. by 49 m.) with a proper curtain wall to surround it. Only a few features of this rebuilding survive the new programme of work which began again in the late C14 and operated more or less continuously until the early C16, by which point the palace had adopted the appearance it has today.

DESCRIPTION begins with the fragmentary SOUTH RANGE, which incorporates C14 masonry but was much remodelled in the early C15. Nothing remains of the W half except a diagonal section of wall (re-erected in 1991) which is attached to the much later David's Tower (*see* below). It follows the line of the C14 curtain wall, which was similarly canted out. The E half of this range housed the chapel at first floor (hence its E–W orientation) and also originally contained the main entrance. The gate is still partly *in situ* on the l. (see its chamfered l. jamb), the rest blocked with mortared rubble in the early to mid C15 when a new gatehouse was created on the E side (*see* below). There were originally three lancets in the upper wall for the chapel, one arch of which is still visible on the r. The central one was blocked *c.* 1450 when the chapel was remodelled and the outer windows were made into narrow, oblong openings with ogee lintel (the l. one still intact). Inside, the chapel has gone but walls still retain C15 plaster (most of it covering the blocked central window). The remodelled window to the r. has narrow, splayed embrasures set within a broad, low segmental rere-arch. Next to the l. window, i.e. close to the site of the altar, is a trefoil-headed PISCINA. The ground floor is described in an inventory of 1607 as a cattle byre and stable. Also in the C15, the S range was given a two-storey GALLERY facing the courtyard, traced by the flash-line on the former W gable and a beam socket and two corbels on the E wall.

The SE TOWER housed the sacristy and palace officials. It is square and projects rather awkwardly. Its N and E walls stand to their full five-storey height, the S and W to *c.* 1.8 m. The ground and first floors are C14, contemporary with the S curtain wall, but at the base of the N and S sides are large mid-C16 gunloops inserted by Bishop Patrick Hepburn, with fat elliptical embrasures to give the gunmen a full field of fire, and in the N and E sides of the first floor the plain splayed arrowslits have been converted in the late C15 into shot-holes of inverted keyhole form, among the earliest found in Scotland.* Over them are scant indications of the springing of a groin-vault, demolished in the late C15 when the upper three storeys were built. They had timber floors carried on stone corbels. Over the E wall-head are seven corbels from the original machicolated parapet; in the SE corner, traces of a slightly recessed turret.

The EAST RANGE also retains much C14 masonry but the GATEHOUSE was inserted in the early to mid C15 – more defensible than its predecessor on the S and also much more imposing. Remains of a pointed entrance arch in the centre (most of the voussoirs now missing) with rectangular buttresses to the l. and r. Diamond turrets corbelled out above, joined by two little basket-headed arches resting on a corbel. Murder holes in the soffits and two observation slits just below. Over the arch is an ARMORIAL PANEL with crozier, most likely containing the heraldry of Bishop John of Winchester (1435–60), the king's master of works.‡ The design is strongly connected with developments in northern England, cf. the

*The earliest documented examples are in England, invented *c.* 1380 with the advent of hand guns. The earliest Scottish examples are nearly a century later.

‡He was also responsible for additions to Linlithgow Palace (Lothian) and the castles at Inverness and Urquhart (Invernesshire).

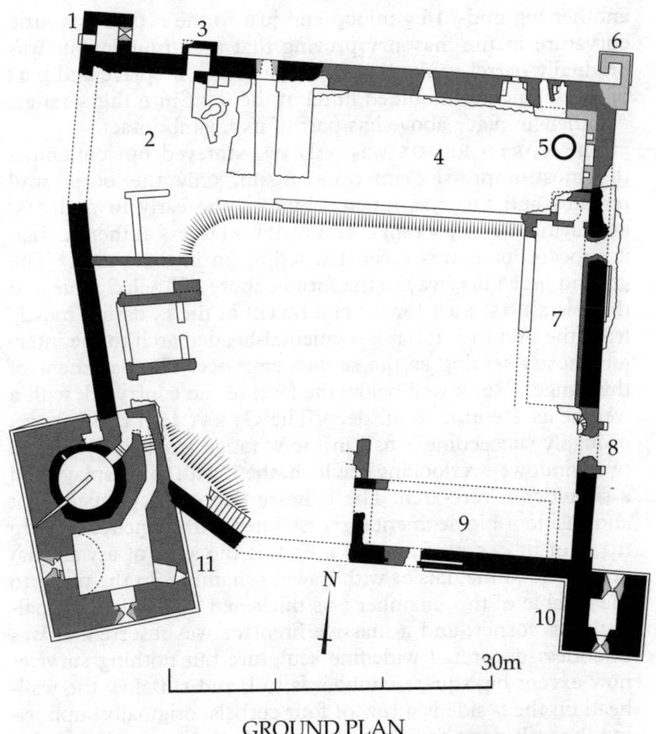

Spynie Palace.
Ground-floor plan

three-storey gatehouse at Middleham Castle, Yorkshire (late C14), and at Langley Castle, Northumberland (*c.* 1350). Grooves along the top show that there was once a timber superstructure. Inside the thickness of the arch is the original slot for the portcullis. The interior of the range has gone but to the l. of the gate is the bottom of a spiral staircase, originally leading up to the former GUARD CHAMBER, with remains of a small fireplace in its NE corner and two windows for them to survey the interior for intruders. The area to the N contained domestic accommodation. At the far N end of the E wall is another big mid-C16 gunloop and just to the r. of it is a little curvature in the masonry proving that the ground floor was originally barrel-vaulted. In the N gable is a fireplace and part of the segmental-moulded lintel of the door into the N range. Another fireplace above has part of its l. jamb intact.

The NORTH RANGE was only two-storeyed but contained the most impressive interiors. Again, only the outer wall remains and this was much rebuilt in the early to mid C15, overlaying the C14 N range, and its N wall is less authentic than it appears for it was reconstructed again in the 1960s.* The ground here falls away to the former shore of Loch Spynie and there is a POSTERN (or WATER GATE) at the l., dating mostly from the mid C16. It has a segmental-headed arch to the interior, mostly serving as the service entrance. The basement of this range is sunk well below the level of the courtyard, with a well at its E end, *c.* 8 m. deep. The GREAT HALL lay above, probably succeeding a hall in the W range (*see* below). It had two windows overlooking the loch, the l. with thick splays and a shouldered rere-arch. The r. has a depressed, cusped light and inside a big segmental recess lined with benches. Just to the r. of it, *c.* 5 m. from the E end, is the spur of a wall that once divided the dais or withdrawing chamber. In the mid C16 the E gable of this chamber was thickened to stabilize the palace's NE corner, and a massive fireplace was inserted. It was doubtless decorated with fine sculpture but nothing survives now except big square cupboards to l. and r. Below the wall-head on the N side is a row of four corbels, originally supporting the wall-posts for the hall roof. A flash-line on the E gable shows that it was steeply pitched. It was probably constructed between 1410 and 1438 (and probably featured authentic hammer-beams). The screens passage occupied the W bay of the hall and the alcove in its W end may have been a timber staircase to a gallery. The W part of the N range was divided into two chambers, now featuring an early C15 KILN. At the NW corner is a four-storey C14 TOWER. The small size of the rooms suggests that it housed senior domestic staff. There is a spur of masonry on the S wall where the tower was attached to the W curtain. Original entrance on the S (at courtyard level) blocked in the C19 when the tower was converted into a doocot. A metal spiral staircase of *c.* 1990 leads up to what was originally the door to the WALL-WALK over the N range. Another C16 gunloop low down in the E wall, outside the N curtain and facing the postern gate.

The N half of the WEST RANGE is lost but to the S the C14 curtain wall remains intact, its first floor originally featuring three Dec windows. The centre of these (best seen from the exterior) has survived, although lowered in height. It was of two lights and featured a foiled oculus – the ostentation likely

*Of the ten joist sockets in the hall floor, eight were replaced by holes that are far too small. The two head corbels were not re-set at the same level, and anyway probably faced each other on opposite sides of the hall.

indicating that this was the position of the original great hall. Later, the first floor was split into two levels to make a kitchen: the lower part of the S window blocked and given a fireplace (burnt masonry) and the upper section (formerly the head of the Dec window) converted into a chamfered rectangle. The rest of the range was replaced in the early to mid C15 by two new buildings. The l. is sunk slightly below courtyard level and retains the springer of a segmental barrel-vault. The r. side is separated by a narrow passageway running E–W, and is of two storeys with part of its S wall surviving to full height. There was a barrel-vaulted cellar with a partition wall running down the centre; above it, a pair of two (originally four) rectangular windows with chamfered margins and segmental rere-arches. Big stone corbels showing the levels of the original floor and roof.

And so finally to the mighty DAVID'S TOWER, rising up in all its bulwark-like solidity at the palace's SW corner. Except for the basement (*see* below), it dates entirely from the mid to late C15, begun by Bishop David Stewart (1462–76) and finished by his successor, Bishop William Tulloch (1477–82).* It is of five stages, 19 m. by 13.5 m. and *c.* 22 m. high, with sheer, flat rubble walls and big long-and-short ashlar quoins. Double-stepped plinth on the bottom, the S and W sides with large gunloops inserted by Bishop Hepburn in the C16 (cf. the SE tower). He also remodelled the windows (see the strip of masonry running down the centre with enlarged, chamfered margins), and so he carved his coat of arms over the first floor. Stewart's heraldry sits to the r. with the royal arms of Scotland over.‡ Large traces of the original harling, now very faded; on the wall-head, traces of three round corner towers with many corbels still *in situ*. They were originally tripartite and filleted. The N face of the tower retains some small windows – the only original ones surviving from the late C15, unmodified by Hepburn – and a small door that served as a service entrance. Strange, minimally recessed section of masonry stretching above it, and then the remains of the N gable of the caphouse.

The entrance to the tower's basement is a low door in the NE corner. The lobby within has a strange shape, with stairs splitting off in two directions – likely evidence that the basement of a C14 round tower was retained when the new tower was built on top. At the end of the r. passageway, a circular CELLAR (*c.* 5.3 m. in diameter) with a depressed domical vault of rubble. One narrow ventilation hole to the SW and part of a partition wall, all probably C14. Although usually referred to as a prison cell, the room was identified as a SALT HOUSE in the 1607 inventory and it may always have been used to store meat. The room to the l. of the lobby is large and

*The closest known parallel is the huge tower added to the bishop's castle in Glasgow between 1426 and 1446.

‡Tulloch's arms are all the way near the top, showing that he completed the original work.

barrel-vaulted, probably the original WINE CELLAR. Two original windows to the S and W converted into gunloops; trap door in the SE corner for passing goods up to the first floor. There are now ten sculptural FRAGMENTS on display including string courses, lintels and two pieces of Dec tracery (one of them probably the original from the W range).

The principal entrance, however, was at first floor on the E side. Each storey originally consisted of a single large room, 12.5 m. by 6.8 m., with the E side occupied by a series of mural chambers (likely for bedrooms). They were barrel-vaulted and stacked one on top of the other but the vaults collapsed in the late C18 and only those at second and fourth floor have been reconstructed to give an impression of the original layout. There is now a thrilling sense of upward movement ending in open sky. The ENTRANCE LOBBY had stairs to the r. (modern concrete replacements) and a barrel-vaulted GUARD CHAMBER to the l. Small chamber beyond it with a trap door to the wine cellar. The lower floor served as the HALL. The chimneypiece is a poor modern reconstruction. Depressed segmental relieving arch above it and windows to the l. and r. lined with benches. Narrow door on the N side (renewed) leading to a steep staircase down to the service door. A spiral stair winds up the NE corner, past a door onto the W curtain walk with an entresol chamber beyond it. The second floor is similarly arranged but less grand. Joist pockets show the position of the original floor; off-centre on the W wall is a robbed fireplace with more modern surrounds. On the third floor (described as a 'mid chalmer' in the 1607 inventory), the floor of the E mural chambers has been reconstructed, with springers of the original barrel-vault curling over. Original chimneypiece intact on the N side with rich bolection moulding – a hint of the opulence that once lay below. There is another in the W wall of the fourth floor. This storey also retains the springers of its slightly pointed barrel-vault. The rere-arches of the N and S windows still echo the main vault's original profile. On the E side, the central mural chamber likely served as the bishop's private ORATORY, and its lower window was blocked to accommodate an altar and retable. Its piscina would have drained directly into the latrine chute. The fifth floor in part of the roof space was lit by dormers (now lost). Substantial remains of the N and S crowstepped gables, the latter also with remnants of a large fireplace. The upper roof accommodated a garret, as shown by the two corbels (one a reused grotesque) and the plain window opening high on the N wall. From here, stairs led up to the WALL-WALK which surrounded the roof, and whose vanished parapet was carried on a row of corbels. The turnpike stair originally ended in the caphouse.

In the late Middle Ages, the area to the S of the palace contained extensive gardens and orchards as well as a large complex of 'kaitspalls' or tennis courts. A cobbled road led down to the cathedral church (*see* Burial Ground, above). The shallow lagoon to the NE, below the escarpment on which the palace stands, is all that remains of Loch Spynie. This was a tidal inlet that separated from the Moray Firth *c.* 1480 and then became a large fresh-water reservoir. Numerous attempts were made in the C14–C18 to recover the land for farming, but it was not finally drained until 1808–12, when a system of canals was built by *Thomas Telford* (overseen by the engineer *Thomas Hughes*). The Spynie Canal, N of the palace, is 10 km. long from here to Lossiemouth. The Innes Canal, E of the Lossie, is part of the same scheme.

Spynie House, 400 m. SSW of the Palace. Early to mid-C19 core, much enlarged and Baronialized by *Charles C. Doig*, 1895–6. Harled, crowstepped, L-plan, the S gable with a canted bay. Rounded entrance in the re-entrant angle with bolection-moulded doorpiece under stepped rope moulding; faux cap-house corbelled above with C17-style triangular dormerhead. Long N wing ending in a drum tower with inverted crenellations and big conical roof.

THOMSHILL *see* BIRNIE

TOCHIENEAL HOUSE B 5060

1.9 km. SSE of Cullen

Late C18 but enlarged and reorientated *c.* 1832 for John Wilson, the Earl of Seafield's factor, probably by *William Robertson*, who was working on Cullen House. Three-bay N front, one storey with bowed Greek Doric porch. Platform piended roof with corniced longitudinal chimneys. The twelve-pane windows with stone margins are quintessential Robertson. Basement exposed on the flanks and rear, the rear itself has three storeys. A covered footbridge in the centre links to a single-storey wing said to have been built as a schoolroom. Re-harled to a good shade of yellow, 2009–10 by *Mantell Ritchie*. Simple, elegant interior. Cantilevered, dog-leg staircase in the centre. Good cast-iron basket grates in the attic room, and kitchen stove and oven in the basement, all probably from the *Banff Foundry*.

Gardener's Cottage, late C19, and converted 2011–13 by *Mantell Ritchie*.

TOMBAE *see* TOMNAVOULIN

TOMINTOUL B 1010

Small, remote, improvement village in the Cairngorms, founded by Alexander, 4th Duke of Gordon. *Thomas Milne* began surveying in 1775 and drew the final plans *c.* 1777; the first tenants occupied their feus in 1780. There was little growth until the early to mid C19, and Queen Victoria wrote in 1853 that Tomintoul was 'the most tumble-down, poor looking place I ever saw'. The rise of tourism and sport in the C19 and C20 (fishing, shooting and skiing) brought many improvements.

PARISH CHURCH, Main Street. Moray's only example of the so-called Parliamentary churches, built following the 1823 Act for Building Additional Places of Worship in isolated Highland communities. *Thomas Telford* was the general superintendent of the project, but the actual design of the buildings was carried out by one of his surveyors, *William Thomson*. His economical T-plan 'Standard Church' was adopted in 1825 and Tomintoul's model built in 1826–7. Altered by *John Robertson* of Inverness, 1899–1900. Of that date the porch and Gothic windows of the main (W) front with Geometric tracery and buttresses with long pinnacles. Original stumpy birdcage bellcote on the N gable. In the Tudor-headed windows of the aisle curvilinear Perp tracery by Robertson. Low vestry in the N re-entrant angle, 1900. The interior was completely renovated and recast by Robertson in Gothic style. Flat panelled ceiling on broad Tudor-arched trusses with traceried spandrels springing from wooden clustered shafts. Two lacy arch braces also over the E aisle. – Gothic FURNISHINGS by *James Garvie & Sons*, *c.* 1900, except the REREDOS of 1911, carved with the Finding in the Temple, the Risen Christ and the Good Shepherd. – ORGAN by *E.F. Walcker & Co.*, 1903.

Former MANSE to the N, also 1826 and one of *Telford*'s two 'approved' designs for Parliamentary manses, executed by *James Smith*. Single-storey U-plan front of five bays with a piended roof. Rear wing of 1894 and late C20 canted bay windows flanking the door.

OUR LADY AND ST MICHAEL (R.C.), Main Street. By *George Mathewson* of Dundee, 1837–8, replacing a church of 1788. Tall, Greek cross plan with lancets; the presbytery is the E arm. Original entrance front to the W with pointed door and dedication stone in a granite surround and large, solid bellcote at the apex with gablets. S porch added 1939 when the interior was reordered and the REREDOS moved from the arched E recess to the N transept. Marble base with three Perp panels; tall central niche above with two octagonal Dec canopies. Panels to the l. and r. with sculptures of the Garden of Gethsemane and Resurrection. Original flat ribbed ceiling, with octagonal star pattern and large foliate boss in the centre. W gallery with Tudor arches on wooden quatrefoil piers. – ST MICHAEL'S CENTRE to the S. Originally the school, built *c.* 1842, converted into a convent in 1880 (closed *c.* 1967). Long rectangle with intact mid-C19 core, but S wing and N porch by *John Wittet*, 1919–21. Chapel also by Wittet, with round-headed windows and slightly lower, semi-octagonal apse.

Former FREE CHURCH (or Dalvrecht Kirk), 4.8 km. NNW. 1843–4. Renovated 1900 and converted into a house after 1943. Whitewashed flanks with four lancets. Slightly advanced centre on the N gable with pointed entrance and open platform bellcote with spike finial. Coomb ceiling inside supported on wooden piers with faux marbling and bell capitals.

Former MANSE to NNW, also 1843–4, of rubble with three spiked eaves. Piended rear wings added in 1900 to form a U-plan.

Former KIRKMICHAEL PARISH CHURCH, 5.9 km. NNW. The pre-Reformation chapel dedicated to St Michael was held as a mensal church by the Bishops of Moray. The new kirk of 1747 was already in a 'lamentable condition' by 1794 and completely reconstructed in 1804–7. Restored after a fire by *A. Cattanach Jun.*, 1950–1, but closed *c.* 2003 and to be converted into a house by *CM Design*, 2013–14. Simple rectangle with birdcage bellcote. Round-headed windows, the Y-tracery of 1951. E porch and NW vestry, 1907. Re-set in the E gable a mask CORBEL of the late C15 or early C16.

Some well-executed C19 HEADSTONES of local slate. – Near the graveyard's centre the early medieval ST MICHAEL'S CROSS, *c.* 1.5 m. high with shaft 30 cm. wide. Plain with a cup in the centre of the cross-bar. It was likely retained and used until *c.* 1560 as a mercat cross for the long-vanished Kirktown of Michael.

KIRKMICHAEL HOUSE, 0.7 km. SE. 1866–8 by *Alexander Tod,* to replace the manse of 1825 destroyed by fire. Superb hilltop situation with panoramic views of the Avon valley. SW front of two storeys and three bays, the ends wide with canted bay windows and narrow, round-headed glazing in the gables. Two wings form a U-plan to the rear.

DESCRIPTION. A grid-plan village but only since the early to mid C20. There was originally only the unusually broad MAIN STREET. It runs N–S and ends at the former entrance to the military road, which linked Tomintoul to the road from The Lecht (q.v.) to the Bridge of Avon. Midway is the large and pleasantly proportioned SQUARE. This was the only area that contained any buildings in the late C18. The surrounding buildings are (as usual) too small but dominating the W side is the GORDON ARMS HOTEL, opened *c.* 1838 but rebuilt in 1898–9. Two and half storeys with a rare double-floored attic; five bays, the r. wide and gabled with a tall canted bay window. There was originally fine bargeboarding on the gables. In the square's centre a grand painted cast-iron FOUNTAIN by the *Lion Foundry* of Kirkintilloch, 1915, with two iron steps, lions' head waterspouts to the basins and stone classical female bearing an urn on her head. At the SE corner, the RICHMOND HOTEL of 1858, expanded in 1895 by *Charles C. Doig*, who built the semi-octagonal CLOCK TOWER with faceted roof on the opposite corner in the same year.

BRIDGE OF AVON (formerly Bridge of Campdalemore), 2.5 km. NW. Engineered by *Major William Caulfeild* in 1754 as part of the military road from Strathspey up and over The Lecht (*see* p. 685).* Two unequal segmental spans of 14.9 m. and 7.1 m., the l. arch higher and wider to cross the Avon's main channel. Smaller relief arch to the r., rebuilt in 1831 after the original was destroyed in the floods of 1829. Triangular cutwaters. Bypassed since 1990.

Former BRIDGE OF BROWN, 4.9 km. WNW. Segmental rubble arch over the Burn of Lochy, built 1734 and now in poor condition. Closed 1979–80. New bridge just to the S.

BRIDGE OF CONGLASS, 0.8 km. ENE. Single segmental rubble span over the Conglass Water, *c.* 1830 and incorporating earlier fabric.‡ Pilastered buttresses on the ends terminating in inverted cushion capitals.

BALLANTRUAN FARMHOUSE, 6.9 km. NNW. Mid C18, a typical two-storey and three-bay house with unpretentious Georgian trappings inside, e.g. fielded panelling in the l. room, originally fronting an alcove with box beds. Dentilled cornice along the top. Two angled cupboards opposite and ceiling with well-finished wooden joists.

CROUGHLY, 2.7 km. NNE. W-facing house of three builds, the original part (now the three-bay centre) a single storey built by James Gordon of Croughly after marriage in 1760. Slightly later wings form a U-plan to the rear, their E gables with paired flight-holes. A three-bay house was attached to the N gable *c.* 1812.

DELNABO, 1.9 km. SSW. Site of a medieval manor house, long occupied by the Grant family and the final refuge of George Gordon (2nd Marquis of Huntly) before his execution in 1649. Now a large shooting lodge, its two-storey SE front of 1891–2 by *Charles C. Doig* in unaggressive Baronial, for Col. John George Smith, owner of the Glenlivet Distillery (*see* p. 646). Large extension *c.* 1935, with NE front in a blandly similar style. Square entrance in the re-entrant angle with anachronistic classical doorpiece and harled two-storey crenellated tower both *c.* 1991, with a large rear tourelle and candlesnuffer roof.

Long U-plan STEADING and CARRIAGE HOUSE complex to SW. Early to mid-C19 core, the centre converted into GARAGES by *Charles C. Doig & Sons*, 1925.

RUTHVEN, 3.8 km. NNW. Handsome U-plan farmhouse of coursed granite rubble, *c.* 1832.

INVERLOCHY, 6.4 km. NNW, of similar type and date.

STRATHAVON LODGE, 3.8 km. NNW. S front of two storeys and three bays, late C19. Wide ends with canted bay windows and round-headed windows in the gables. Bracketed eaves.

*The replacement to a smaller bridge of 1736–8 by the mason *Alexander Fraser*.

‡The previous bridge, erected by the fourth Duke of Gordon in the late C18 and repaired 1819, was seriously damaged in the floods of 1829.

Extended in the early C20 and late C20, all in a similar style. STEADING and KENNELS behind.

INCHRORY. *See* p. 657.

TOMNAVOULIN B 2020

Small roadside hamlet in Glenlivet, with a former SCHOOL, built by the 6th Duke of Richmond in 1861, former MISSION HALL built 1892–3 by *William Smith* of Dufftown as a chapel of ease to Inveravon Free Church, and WAR MEMORIAL, a Celtic cross of 1921.

TAMNAVULIN DISTILLERY (United Spirits). Built in 1965–6, mothballed in 1995, reopened 2007. A surprisingly good, clean design with harled walls, light-green roofs and jinked asymmetric gables. Two large blocks of tripled-gabled warehouses to the NE. To the NNE a former CARDING MILL, built *c.* 1840 and restored in 1984–5 as visitor's centre (now disused). Two storeys and six bays of good sturdy rubble with lying-pane glazing. Cast-iron undershot water wheel on the SW gable.

BRIDGE OF LIVET, 0.5 km. N. Good rubble span of *c.* 16.8 m., built *c.* 1788 by the 4th Duke of Gordon. Segmental, slightly hump-backed arch-ring over the Livet. Bypassed since *c.* 1976.

At TOMBAE, 0.75 km. SE, is the former CHURCH OF THE INCARNATION (R.C.). A Catholic priest served this area from at least 1745. The present building by *John Gall* of Aberdeen, 1827–9, superseded a 'mass house' built *c.* 1788 at Kinakyle, 1.3 km. SSE (badly damaged by the floods of 1829 and now vanished). Tall sham-Gothic façade of tooled pink granite, unexpectedly facing away from the road and instead cutting a very fine – and amazingly public – figure across the Livet valley, demonstrating the extent of Catholic confidence and Gordon protection before Emancipation. It is one of the three examples in Moray of *James Kyle's* standardized Catholic façade design (cf. also St Mary, Dufftown and St Mary, Fochabers). Interior also remodelled by Bishop Kyle in 1843–4 with assistance from *Rev. Walter Lovi*. Full-blown Gothic Revival, achieved not via its décor but – for once in Moray – through its architecture. The entirety is rib-vaulted, the centre springing from octagonal cast-iron piers with capitals of Dec seaweed fronds. Narrower aisles with sharply pointed vaults set on similar corbels. Recessed chancel. Kyle's restoration created a space between the chancel and NE gable, first used as a Presbytery (until 1871) and then a school (until 1902). – CHAPEL HOUSE is the presbytery built in 1872. SE is the former SCHOOL of 1903.

TOMBAE FARMHOUSE, 425 m. SE of church. The symmetrical S front, of two storeys and three bays, is *c.* 1785 and was formerly the home of James Gordon, the priest who built the church. – Substantial U-plan mid-C19 STEADING attached to the W, well restored in 1985–6. Of this date, though looking deceptively mid C19, is a circular CURING KILN with stone conical roof.

3060 TUGNET

On the E side of the Spey estuary.

SCOTTISH DOLPHIN CENTRE. Formerly a large salmon-fishing complex, the catches made by netting the river mouth. Developed by the Gordon estate, and built over several campaigns in the late C18, it originally employed over 150 workers. Main elevation to the S with the former DWELLING-HOUSE BLOCK on the r. Two storeys and five bays of coursed rubble, built 1772 (likely by *John Baxter*). Keystoned, elliptical arch in the centre with block imposts; wall-head chimneystack above with wide base and swept sides. To the l. and r., shorter single-bay wings extending to the rear and forming a quadrangular plan. Central courtyard lined with former cottages, cooperage, stables and stores. Stone forestair in the SE corner.

Former FISH HOUSE (Museum and Wildlife Centre) to W, built 1783. Single-storey U-plan abutting the square's W gable and forming a narrower rectangular court. Four-bay S elevation with dated keystone on its blocked arch. Massive double wall-head chimney to the W with two brick stacks, for the salmon boilers. Inside the former BOILER HOUSE (now café), an intact timber wheel and hoisting tackle.

Former ICE HOUSE to W of the fish house. By far the largest surviving in the United Kingdom. Built 1830 after its predecessor was destroyed in the floods of 1829; last used in 1968 and converted to a museum, 1981. Here, salmon were packed to await transport to London and Edinburgh. Three long chambers with turf-covered roofs and continuous segmental gables running E–W. Four square, louvred openings, originally serving as ice chutes. Wide S entrance on lower ground, its lintel recarved *c.* 1975 and now erroneously reading 1630. Low entrance passage leading to five subterranean chambers, each with a high, stilted barrel-vault lined in brick. Straight-headed doorways in between.

Former STATION, 1.3 km. SE off the B9104. Opened as Fochabers Station by the Great North of Scotland Railway, 1886. Closed 1968. Piended, weatherboarded rectangle with recessed centre. A rare survival of what was once a smart rural station.

At BOGMOOR, 2.3 km. SSE, the former SCHOOL built *c.* 1845 with another bay added *c.* 1876. Of red sandstone pinned with slate, and originally with excellent bargeboarding. To be converted into a house by *CM Design*, 2013–14. 175 m. S, No. 22, THE MUIR, is a rare C19 rustic cottage with tree-trunk posts to its porch, vertical weatherboarding and scalloped eaves valence.

NE of the village is the former DALLACHY AIRFIELD, built as an RAF station in 1942–3 and closed in 1945. Two huge runways and two-storey control tower still *in situ*.

TYNET 3060

3.4 km. SSW of Portgordon

ST NINIAN'S CHAPEL (R.C.). An unassuming building of national importance, as the earliest surviving post-Reformation Catholic church in Scotland and one of the best-preserved examples of clandestine architecture in Britain, sensitively restored by *Orphoot & Lindsay* in 1949–51. It succeeded the chapel at Chapelford (*see* below), abandoned in 1728, after which worship was conducted in a changing rotation of barns. The nucleus is the 'dwelling of a poor woman' donated by the Laird of Tynet in 1755, for which Father Godman made a short extension disguised as a sheep barn, reasoning that 'if we may expect any humanity or sympathy they will be ashamed to put us from a sheep-cot, especially when there is incomparably better of that kind in the country'. It is still just as easily mistaken for a long, low steading. Along the S front, eight windows with twelve-pane glazing, enlarged to their present size in 1787 when the chapel was renovated, the thatch roof replaced with slates and the ball finial added to the W gable. W door blocked *c.* 1859 when straight-headed doorways were inserted in the S front's second and far E bays, the latter for a sacristy created inside. On the N side, one original tiny window of 1755, the others enlarged.

Plain, whitewashed interior, only slightly less self-effacing than the outside, with coomb ceiling. The W vestibule was created *c.* 1902 and contains the baptistery with railing of flat balusters. The nave entrance has a good reused mid-C18 doorpiece with Corinthian columns. Chancel arch of reeded pilasters, 1787; of the same date the appropriately simple hexagonal PULPIT with fielded panels and tester and COMMUNION RAIL with turned balusters. – BENCHES. *c.* 1859. – HIGH ALTAR (now in the sacristy). *c.* 1902. Gothic with marble shafts. The post-Vatican II ALTAR is *c.* 1965 of plain stone blocks. Above it a DOVE suspended from a roundel with angels of *c.* 1923. The dove is said to have come from the chapel at Chapelford. – FONT (baptistery). With a baluster pillar; behind it a MONSTRANCE with Annunciation under a broken segmental pediment.

ST NINIAN'S CEMETERY, Chapelford, 1.75 km. SE. The first chapel, a dependency of Urquhart Priory (*see* p. 754), was here by the C13. It fell into decay but was repaired (and enlarged to a cruciform plan) in 1687–8 as probably the first post-Reformation Catholic church in Scotland. Desecrated and abandoned after the death of the 2nd Duke of Gordon in

1728 (*see* St Ninian's Chapel, above). No trace remains. – The MORTUARY CHAPEL by *W.G. Brander*, 1955–6, has the chapel's 1687 datestone re-set and re-set TOMBSTONES (S wall) commemorating four Catholic priests †1718–1828. – DAWSON MAUSOLEUM. By *Reginald Fairlie*, 1939. Single-storey octagon of snecked rubble with a faceted, slightly bellcast roof. – TABLE STONE for Anna Gordon and Adam Gordon †1695, who 'by deuotion mad his frequent flights and sheus desire to be with heauenly lights'. Cross on the bottom with mortality emblems.

2060 URQUHART

A village developed here in the C12, and was made a burgh of barony and regality *c.* 1535. It was attached to Urquhart Priory, founded for Benedictines by King David I *c.* 1124 as a cell of Dunfermline Abbey (Fife). The priory was vacated in 1454 after Pope Nicholas V united it with Pluscarden Priory (q.v.). The village was laid out in its present form *c.* 1784 by James Duff, 2nd Earl Fife, who acquired the surrounding land in 1777.

Former FREE CHURCH, E end of Main Street. Built 1844 by *A. & W. Reid* from the stone of St Margaret's church in the burial ground (*see* below); converted into a house in 2002–4. Simple Romanesque with attenuated windows and gableted W bellcote. Shallow E projection of 1907–8 by *John Wittet*.

Former PARISH CHURCH, off Meft Road, 0.6 km. NNW. On a 'high eminence' chosen by James Duff, 5th Earl Fife, for visibility from Innes House (q.v.). Rather grand Tudor Gothic by *Alexander Reid*, 1842–3; converted by *Colin Keir* from 1990 and now a guest house.* Six tall, two-light Perp windows with ogee heads above the transoms (the outer ones blind). Buttresses between. S front with minimally advanced centre in ashlar, including a window under ogee hoodmould. Diagonal buttresses extending into an English-looking tower with crenellated top and pinnacles (crocketed finials removed after a storm in 1953). Short chancel with stepped triple lancets by *Alexander Ross & Son*, 1930–1; vestry in the NE re-entrant angle by the same.

Inside the vestibule, a cusped geometric lierne vault with knobbly foliage bosses. – MONUMENT for Alexander Tod †1760 and family (reused from the original church in the burial ground). Aedicule with engaged Ionic columns and large winged soul in a segmental pediment. Console-bracketed base with protruding panel of skull and crossbones.

*Reid's design was heavily indebted to unused plans drawn up by his uncle, *William Robertson*, in 1837 for the parish church in Drumnadrochit (Highland and Islands).

BURIAL GROUND, Station Road. Site of St Margaret's church, first recorded in 1234. It was replaced *c.* 1659 and demolished 1844 (*see* former parish church, above). Near the centre, a short piece of wall is probably a fragment. – On its S face, a TABLET to the Rev. Alexander Gadderar †1714, with long Latin inscription giving his biography. Fronded pilasters to the sides; trefoiled pediment with bible, hourglass and two angels playing long trumpets. – In the kerbed ENCLOSURE next to the main entrance, a PLAQUE for Elizabeth Tod †1781, George Gilzean †1784 and family. Moulded ogee arch on top over an angel with abstractly striated wings.

ST MARGARET'S HALL, Station Road. Former Free Church schoolhouse of 1845. – STAINED GLASS. Two windows from the former Free Church (*see* above), 1907–8. Christ holding chalice and raising his r. hand in benediction. Also a roundel with the Crown of Victory, formerly in the oculus over the pulpit. – STONE SLAB. C13, and likely the only surviving fragment of Urquhart Priory. Latin wheel cross in low relief with shaft and base incised below. Dog-tooth around three sides.

MAIN STREET, the historic core, has its E end terminated by the former Free Church (*see* above). On the N side, at the corner of Meft Road, the VILLAGE HALL of 1923–4, by *Charles C. Doig & Sons* with later additions. Good original interior with A-frame roof and curved braces. Outside, the WAR MEMORIAL cross by *J. R. Henderson*, 1921. Further E is the set-back OLD SCHOOLHOUSE by *A. & W. Reid*, 1846–55, with ball-and-spike-finialled gables and clusters of square, corniced chimneystacks. The school formerly attached to the W was demolished 1971. Further down, and even more recessed is ST MARGARET'S, built as the Free Church manse in 1846, altered by the *Reids* in 1865 and prettily modernized in 1894. Single storey and three bays with a canted bay window. Two dormers poking up, their gables (and the central porch) with iron finials.

GLEBE HOUSE, W end of Main Street. The parish manse by *Alexander Forteath*, the Earl Fife's factor, 1821–2. Symmetrical two storeys and three bays over raised basement, harled and nicely proportioned. Canted bay windows l. and r. by *A. Marshall Mackenzie,* 1874. His also the half-octagon on the E gable. – WALLED GARDEN to SSW, early C19. The door lintel carved with 'IHS' likely came from Urquhart Priory. – Small, square DOOCOT in the S corner with pyramidal roof. It is built of clay and bool (cf. Garmouth, q.v.).

STANDING STONES, 1.4 km. N, in the NW angle of crossroads by Innesmill. Five stones ranging from 1.1 to 1.7 m. high, the two tallest in the SE. They originally formed a stone circle *c.* 34 m. in diameter of at least twelve stones. Another stone lies fallen to the NNE, *ex situ*.

LEUCHARS HOUSE. *See* p. 688.

GLOSSARY

Numbers and letters refer to the illustrations (by John Sambrook) on pp. 768-775

ABACUS: flat slab forming the top of a capital (3a).

ACANTHUS: classical formalized leaf ornament (3b).

ACCUMULATOR TOWER: *see* Hydraulic power.

ACHIEVEMENT: a complete display of armorial bearings (i.e. coat of arms, crest, supporters and motto).

ACROTERION: plinth for a statue or ornament on the apex or ends of a pediment; more usually, both the plinth and what stands on it (4a).

ADDORSED: descriptive of two figures placed back to back.

AEDICULE (*lit.* little building): architectural surround, consisting usually of two columns or pilasters supporting a pediment.

AFFRONTED: descriptive of two figures placed face to face.

AGGREGATE: *see* Concrete, Harling.

AISLE: subsidiary space alongside the body of a building, separated from it by columns, piers or posts. Also (Scots) projecting wing of a church, often for special use, e.g. by a guild or by a landed family whose burial place it may contain.

AMBULATORY (*lit.* walkway): aisle around the sanctuary (q.v.).

ANGLE ROLL: roll moulding in the angle between two planes (1a).

ANSE DE PANIER: *see* Arch.

ANTAE: simplified pilasters (4a), usually applied to the ends of the enclosing walls of a portico (q.v.) *in antis*.

ANTEFIXAE: ornaments projecting at regular intervals above a Greek cornice, originally to conceal the ends of roof tiles (4a).

ANTHEMION: classical ornament like a honeysuckle flower (4b).

APRON: panel below a window or wall monument or tablet.

APSE: semicircular or polygonal end of an apartment, especially of a chancel or chapel. In classical architecture sometimes called an *exedra*.

ARABESQUE: non-figurative surface decoration consisting of flowing lines, foliage scrolls etc., based on geometrical patterns. Cf. Grotesque.

ARCADE: series of arches supported by piers or columns. *Blind arcade* or *arcading*: the same applied to the wall surface. *Wall arcade*: in medieval churches, a blind arcade forming a dado below windows. Also a covered shopping street.

ARCH: Shapes *see* 5c. *Basket arch* or *anse de panier* (basket handle): three-centred and depressed, or with a flat centre. *Nodding*: ogee arch curving forward from the wall face. *Parabolic*: shaped like a chain suspended from two level points, but inverted.
Special purposes. *Chancel*: dividing chancel from nave or crossing. *Crossing*: spanning piers at a crossing (q.v.). *Relieving* or *discharging*: incorporated in a wall to relieve superimposed weight (5c). *Skew*: spanning responds not diametrically opposed. *Strainer*: inserted in an opening to resist inward pressure. *Transverse*: spanning a main axis (e.g. of a vaulted space). *See also* Jack arch, Overarch, Triumphal arch.

ARCHITRAVE: formalized lintel, the lowest member of the classical entablature (3a). Also the moulded frame of a door or window (often borrowing the profile of a classical architrave). For *lugged* and *shouldered* architraves *see* 4b.

ARCUATED: dependent structurally on the arch principle. Cf. Trabeated.

ARK: chest or cupboard housing the tables of Jewish law in a synagogue.

ARRIS: sharp edge where two surfaces meet at an angle (3a).

ASHLAR: masonry of large blocks wrought to even faces and square edges (6d). *Broached ashlar* (Scots): scored with parallel lines made by a narrow-pointed chisel (broach). *Droved ashlar*: similar but with lines made by a broad chisel.

ASTRAGAL: classical moulding of semicircular section (3f). Also (Scots) glazing-bar between window panes.

ASTYLAR: with no columns or similar vertical features.

ATLANTES: *see* Caryatids.

ATRIUM (plural: atria): inner court of a Roman or C20 house; in a multi-storey building, a toplit covered court rising through all storeys. Also an open court in front of a church.

ATTACHED COLUMN: *see* Engaged column.

ATTIC: small top storey within a roof. Also the storey above the main entablature of a classical façade.

AUMBRY: recess or cupboard, especially one in a church, to hold sacred vessels used for the Mass.

BAILEY: *see* Motte-and-bailey.

BALANCE BEAM: *see* Canals.

BALDACCHINO: freestanding canopy, originally fabric, over an altar. Cf. Ciborium.

BALLFLOWER: globular flower of three petals enclosing a ball (1a). Typical of the Decorated style.

BALUSTER: pillar or pedestal of bellied form. *Balusters*: vertical supports of this or any other form, for a handrail or coping, the whole being called a *balustrade* (6c). *Blind balustrade*: the same applied to the wall surface.

BARBICAN: outwork defending the entrance to a castle.

BARGEBOARDS (corruption of 'vergeboards'): boards, often carved or fretted, fixed beneath the eaves of a gable to cover and protect the rafters.

BARMKIN (Scots): wall enclosing courtyard attached to a tower house.

BARONY: *see* Burgh.

BAROQUE: style originating in Rome *c.*1600 and current in England *c.*1680–1720, characterized by dramatic massing and silhouette and the use of the giant order.

BARROW: burial mound.

BARTIZAN: corbelled turret, square or round, frequently at an angle (8a).

BASCULE: hinged part of a lifting (or bascule) bridge.

BASE: moulded foot of a column or pilaster. For *Attic* base *see* 3b. For *Elided* base *see* Elided.

BASEMENT: lowest, subordinate storey; hence the lowest part of a classical elevation, below the piano nobile (q.v.).

BASILICA: a Roman public hall; hence an aisled building with a clerestory.

BASTION: one of a series of defensive semicircular or polygonal projections from the main wall of a fortress or city.

BATTER: intentional inward inclination of a wall face.

BATTLEMENT: defensive parapet, composed of *merlons* (solid) and *crenelles* (embrasures) through which archers could shoot (8a); sometimes called *crenellation*. Also used decoratively.

BAY: division of an elevation or interior space as defined by regular vertical features such as arches, columns, windows etc.

BAY LEAF: classical ornament of overlapping bay leaves (3f).

BAY WINDOW: window of one or more storeys projecting from the face of a building. *Canted*: with a straight front and angled sides. *Bow window*: curved. *Oriel*: rests on corbels or brackets and starts above ground level; also the bay window at the dais end of a medieval great hall.

BEAD-AND-REEL: *see* Enrichments.

BEAKHEAD: Norman ornament with a row of beaked bird or beast heads usually biting into a roll moulding (1a).

BEE-BOLL: wall recess to contain a beehive.

BELFRY: chamber or stage in a tower where bells are hung. Also belltower in a general sense.

BELL CAPITAL: *see* 1b.

BELLCAST: *see* Roof.

BELLCOTE: bell-turret set on a roof or gable. *Birdcage bellcote*: framed structure, usually of stone.

BERM: level area separating a ditch from a bank on a hillfort or barrow.

BILLET: Norman ornament of small half-cylindrical or rectangular blocks (1a).

BIVALLATE: of a hillfort: defended by two concentric banks and ditches.

BLIND: *see* Arcade, Baluster, Portico.

BLOCK CAPITAL: *see* 1a.

BLOCKED: columns etc. interrupted by regular projecting blocks (*blocking*), as on a Gibbs surround (4b).

BLOCKING COURSE: course of stones, or equivalent, on top of a cornice and crowning the wall.

BÖD: *see* Bü.

BOLECTION MOULDING: covering the joint between two different planes (6b).

BOND: the pattern of long sides (*stretchers*) and short ends (*headers*) produced on the face of a wall by laying bricks in a particular way (6e).

BOSS: knob or projection, e.g. at the intersection of ribs in a vault (2c).

BOW WINDOW: *see* Bay window.

BOX FRAME: timber-framed construction in which vertical and horizontal wall members support the roof. Also concrete construction where the loads are taken on cross walls; also called *cross-wall construction*.

BRACE: subsidiary member of a structural frame, curved or straight. *Bracing* is often arranged decoratively, e.g. quatrefoil, herringbone. *See also* Roofs.

BRATTISHING: ornamental crest, usually formed of leaves, Tudor flowers or miniature battlements.

BRESSUMER (*lit.* breast-beam): big horizontal beam supporting the wall above, especially in a jettied building.

BRETASCHE (*lit.* battlement): defensive wooden gallery on a wall.

BRICK: *see* Bond, Cogging, Engineering, Gauged, Tumbling.

BRIDGE: *Bowstring*: with arches rising above the roadway which is suspended from them. *Clapper*: one long stone forms the roadway. *Roving*: *see* Canal. *Suspension*: roadway suspended from cables or chains slung between towers or pylons. *Stay-suspension* or *stay-cantilever*: supported by diagonal stays from towers or pylons. *See also* Bascule.

BRISES-SOLEIL: projecting fins or canopies which deflect direct sunlight from windows.

BROACH: *see* Spire and 1c.

BROCH (Scots): circular tower-like structure, open in the middle, the double wall of dry-stone masonry linked by slabs forming internal galleries at varying levels; found in W and N Scotland and mostly dating from between 100 B.C. and A.D. 100.

BÜ or BÖD (Scots, esp. Shetland; *lit.* booth): combined house and store.

BUCRANIUM: ox skull used decoratively in classical friezes.

BULLSEYE WINDOW: small oval window, set horizontally (cf. Oculus). Also called *oeil de boeuf*.

BURGH: formally constituted town with trading privileges. *Royal Burghs*: monopolized foreign trade till the C17 and paid duty to the Crown. *Burghs of Barony*: founded by secular or ecclesiastical barons to whom they paid duty on their local trade. *Police Burghs*: instituted after 1850 for the administration of new centres of population and abolished in 1975. They controlled planning, building etc.

BUT-AND-BEN (Scots, *lit.* outer and inner rooms): two-room cottage.

BUTTRESS: vertical member projecting from a wall to stabilize it or to resist the lateral thrust of an arch, roof or vault (1c, 2c). A *flying buttress* transmits the thrust to a heavy abutment by means of an arch or half-arch (1c).

CABLE or ROPE MOULDING: originally Norman, like twisted strands of a rope.

CAMES: *see* Quarries.

CAMPANILE: freestanding belltower.

CANALS: *Flash lock*: removable weir or similar device through which boats pass on a flush of water. Predecessor of the *pound lock*: chamber with gates at each end allowing boats to float from one level to another. *Tidal gates*: single pair of lock gates allowing vessels to pass when the tide makes a level. *Balance beam*: beam projecting horizontally for opening and closing lock gates. *Roving bridge*: carrying a towing path from one bank to the other.

CANDLE-SNUFFER ROOF: conical roof of a turret (8a).

CANNON SPOUT: *see* 8a.

CANTILEVER: horizontal projection (e.g. step, canopy) supported by a downward force behind the fulcrum.

CAPHOUSE (Scots): small chamber at the head of a turnpike stair, opening onto the parapet walk (8a). Also a chamber rising from within the parapet walk.

CAPITAL: head or crowning feature of a column or pilaster; for classical types *see* 3a; for medieval types *see* 1b.

CARREL: compartment designed for individual work or study, e.g. in a library.

CARTOUCHE: classical tablet with ornate frame (4b).

CARYATIDS: female figures supporting an entablature; their male counterparts are *Atlantes* (*lit.* Atlas figures).

CASEMATE: vaulted chamber, with embrasures for defence, within a castle wall or projecting from it.

CASEMENT: side-hinged window. Also a concave Gothic moulding framing a window.

CASTELLATED: with battlements (q.v.).

CAST IRON: iron containing at least 2.2 per cent of carbon, strong in compression but brittle in tension; cast in a mould to required shape, e.g. for columns or repetitive ornaments. *Wrought iron* is a purer form of iron, with no more than 0.3 per cent of carbon, ductile and strong in tension, forged and rolled into e.g. bars, joists, boiler plates; *mild steel* is its modern equivalent, similar but stronger.

CATSLIDE: *see* 7.

CAVETTO: concave classical moulding of quarter-round section (3f).

CELURE or CEILURE: enriched area of roof above rood or altar.

CEMENT: *see* Concrete.

CENOTAPH (*lit.* empty tomb): funerary monument which is not a burying place.

CENTRING: wooden support for the building of an arch or vault, removed after completion.

CHAMBERED TOMB: Neolithic burial mound with a stone-built chamber and entrance passage covered by an earthen barrow or stone cairn.

CHAMFER (*lit.* corner-break): surface formed by cutting off a square edge or corner. For types of chamfers and *chamfer stops see* 6a. *See also* Double chamfer.

CHANCEL: E end of the church containing the sanctuary; often used to include the choir.

CHANTRY CHAPEL: often attached to or within a church, endowed for the celebration of Masses principally for the soul of the founder.

CHECK (Scots): rebate.

CHERRY-CAULKING or CHERRY-COCKING (Scots): decorative masonry technique using lines of tiny stones (*pins* or *pinning*) in the mortar joints.

CHEVET (*lit.* head): French term for chancel with ambulatory and radiating chapels.

CHEVRON: V-shape used in series or double series (later) on a Norman moulding (1a). Also (especially when on a single plane) called *zigzag*.

CHOIR: the part of a church E of the nave, intended for the stalls of choir monks, choristers and clergy.

CIBORIUM: a fixed canopy over an altar, usually vaulted and supported on four columns; cf. Baldacchino.

CINQUEFOIL: *see* Foil.

CIST: stone-lined or slab-built grave.

CLACHAN (Scots): a hamlet or small village; also, a village inn.

CLADDING: external covering or skin applied to a structure, especially a framed one.

CLEARSTOREY: uppermost storey of the nave of a church, pierced by windows. Also high-level windows in secular buildings.

CLOSE (Scots): courtyard or passage giving access to a number of buildings.

CLOSER: a brick cut to complete a bond (6e).

CLUSTER BLOCK: *see* Multi-storey.

COADE STONE: ceramic artificial stone made in Lambeth 1769–*c.*1840 by Eleanor Coade (†1821) and her associates.

COB: walling material of clay mixed with straw.

COFFERING: arrangement of sunken panels (coffers), square or polygonal, decorating a ceiling, vault or arch.

COGGING: a decorative course of bricks laid diagonally (6e). Cf. Dentilation.

COLLAR: *see* Roofs and 7.

COLLEGIATE CHURCH: endowed for the support of a college of priests, especially for the saying of masses for the soul(s) of the founder(s).

COLONNADE: range of columns supporting an entablature. Cf. Arcade.

COLONNETTE: small column or shaft.

COLOSSAL ORDER: *see* Giant order.

COLUMBARIUM: shelved, niched structure to house multiple burials.

COLUMN: a classical, upright structural member of round section with a shaft, a capital and usually a base (3a, 4a).

COLUMN FIGURE: carved figure attached to a medieval column or shaft, usually flanking a doorway.

COMMENDATOR: receives the revenues of an abbey *in commendam* ('in trust') when the position of abbot is vacant.

COMMUNION TABLE: table used in Protestant churches for the celebration of Holy Communion.

COMPOSITE: *see* Orders.

COMPOUND PIER: grouped shafts (q.v.), or a solid core surrounded by shafts.

CONCRETE: composition of *cement* (calcined lime and clay), *aggregate* (small stones or rock chippings), sand and water. It can be poured into *formwork* or *shuttering* (temporary frame of timber or metal) on site (*in-situ* concrete), or *pre-cast* as components before construction. *Reinforced*: incorporating steel rods to take the tensile force. *Prestressed*: with tensioned steel rods. Finishes include the impression of boards left by formwork (*board-marked* or *shuttered*), and texturing with steel brushes (*brushed*) or hammers (*hammer-dressed*). *See also* Shell.

CONDUCTOR (Scots): down-pipe for rainwater; *see also* Rhone.

CONSOLE: bracket of curved outline (4b).

COPING: protective course of masonry or brickwork capping a wall (6d).

COOMB OR COMB CEILING (Scots): with sloping sides corresponding to the roof pitch up to a flat centre.

CORBEL: projecting block supporting something above. *Corbel course:* continuous course of projecting stones or bricks fulfilling the same function. *Corbel table*: series of corbels to carry a parapet or a wall-plate or wall-post (7). *Corbelling*: brick or masonry courses built out beyond one another to support a chimney-stack, window etc. For *continuous* and *chequer-set* corbelling see 8a.

CORINTHIAN: *see* Orders and 3d.

CORNICE: flat-topped ledge with moulded underside, projecting along the top of a building or feature, especially as the highest member of the classical entablature (3a). Also the decorative moulding in the angle between wall and ceiling.

CORPS-DE-LOGIS: the main building(s) as distinct from the wings or pavilions.

COTTAGE ORNÉ: an artfully rustic small house associated with the Picturesque movement.

COUNTERSCARP BANK: low bank on the downhill or outer side of a hillfort ditch.

COUR D'HONNEUR: formal entrance court before a house in the French manner, usually with flanking wings and a screen wall or gates.

COURSE: continuous layer of stones etc. in a wall (6e).

COVE: a broad concave moulding, e.g. to mask the eaves of a roof. *Coved ceiling*: with a pronounced cove joining the walls to a flat central panel smaller than the whole area of the ceiling.

CRADLE ROOF: *see* Wagon roof.

CREDENCE: shelved niche or table, usually beside a piscina (q.v.), for the sacramental elements and vessels.

CRENELLATION: parapet with crenelles (*see* Battlement).

CRINKLE-CRANKLE WALL: garden wall undulating in a series of serpentine curves.

CROCKETS: leafy hooks. *Crocketing* decorates the edges of Gothic features, such as pinnacles, canopies etc. *Crocket capital*: *see* 1b.

CROSSING: central space at the junction of the nave, chancel and transepts. *Crossing tower*: above a crossing.

CROSS-WINDOW: with one mullion and one transom (qq.v.).

CROWN-POST: *see* Roofs and 7.

CROWSTEPS: squared stones set like steps, especially on a crowstepped gable (7, 8a).

CRUCKS (*lit.* crooked): pairs of inclined timbers (*blades*), usually curved, set at bay-lengths; they support the roof timbers and, in timber buildings, also support the walls. *Base*: blades rise from ground level to a tie-or collar-beam which supports the roof timbers. *Full*: blades rise from ground level to the apex of the roof, serving as the main members of a roof truss. *Jointed:* blades formed from more than one timber; the lower member may act as a wall-post; it is usually elbowed at wall-plate level and jointed just above. *Middle*: blades rise from halfway up the walls to a tie-or collar-beam. *Raised*: blades rise from halfway up the walls to the apex. *Upper*: blades supported on a tie-beam and rising to the apex.

CRYPT: underground or half-underground area, usually below the E end of a church. *Ring crypt*: corridor crypt surrounding the apse of an early medieval church, often associated with chambers for relics. Cf. Undercroft.

CUPOLA (*lit.* dome): especially a small dome on a circular or polygonal base crowning a larger dome, roof or turret. Also (Scots) small dome or skylight as an internal feature, especially over a stairwell.

CURSUS: a long avenue defined by two parallel earthen banks with ditches outside.

CURTAIN WALL: a connecting wall between the towers of a castle. Also a non-load-bearing external wall applied to a C20 framed structure.

CUSP: *see* Tracery and 2b.

CYCLOPEAN MASONRY: large irregular polygonal stones, smooth and finely jointed.

CYMA RECTA and CYMA REVERSA: classical mouldings with double curves (3f). Cf. Ogee.

DADO: the finishing (often with panelling) of the lower part of a wall in a classical interior; in origin a formalized continuous pedestal. *Dado rail*: the moulding along the top of the dado.

DAGGER: *see* Tracery and 2b.

DEC (DECORATED): English Gothic architecture *c.* 1290 to *c.* 1350. The name is derived from the type of window tracery (q.v.) used during the period.

DEMI- or HALF-COLUMNS: engaged columns (q.v.) half of whose circumference projects from the wall.

DENTIL: small square block used in series in classical cornices (3c). *Dentilation* is produced by the projection of alternating headers along cornices or string-courses.

DIAPER: repetitive surface decoration of lozenges or squares flat or in relief. Achieved in brickwork with bricks of two colours.

DIOCLETIAN or THERMAL WINDOW: semicircular with two mullions, as used in the Baths of Diocletian, Rome (4b).

DISTYLE: having two columns (4a).

DOGTOOTH: E.E. ornament, consisting of a series of small pyramids formed by four stylized canine teeth meeting at a point (1a).

DOOCOT (Scots): dovecot. When freestanding, usually *Lectern* (rectangular with single-pitch roof) or *Beehive* (circular, diminishing towards the top).

DORIC: *see* Orders and 3a, 3b.

DORMER: window projecting from the slope of a roof (7). *Dormer head*: gable above a dormer, often formed as a pediment (8a).

DOUBLE CHAMFER: a chamfer applied to each of two recessed arches (1a).

DOUBLE PILE: *see* Pile.

DRAGON BEAM: *see* Jetty.

DRESSINGS: the stone or brickwork worked to a finished face about an angle, opening or other feature.

DRIPSTONE: moulded stone projecting from a wall to protect the lower parts from water. Cf. Hoodmould, Weathering.

DRUM: circular or polygonal stage supporting a dome or cupola. Also one of the stones forming the shaft of a column (3a).

DRY-STONE: stone construction without mortar.

DUN (Scots): small stone-walled fort.

DUTCH or FLEMISH GABLE: *see* 7.

EASTER SEPULCHRE: tomb-chest, usually within or against the N wall of a chancel, used in Holy Week ceremonies for reservation (entombment) of the sacrament after the mass of Maundy Thursday.

EAVES: overhanging edge of a roof; hence *eaves cornice* in this position.

ECHINUS: ovolo moulding (q.v.) below the abacus of a Greek Doric capital (3a).

EDGE RAIL: *see* Railways.

EDGE-ROLL: moulding of semi-circular section or more at the edge of an opening.

E.E. (EARLY ENGLISH): English Gothic architecture *c.* 1190–1250.

EGG-AND-DART: *see* Enrichments and 3f.

ELEVATION: any face of a building or side of a room. In a drawing, the same or any part of it, represented in two dimensions.

ELIDED: used to describe a compound feature, e.g. an entablature, with some parts omitted. Also, parts of, e.g., a base or capital, combined to form a larger one.

EMBATTLED: with battlements.

EMBRASURE: splayed opening in a wall or battlement (q.v.).

ENCAUSTIC TILES: earthenware tiles fired with a pattern and glaze.

EN DELIT: stone laid against the bed.

ENFILADE: reception rooms in a formal series, usually with all doorways on axis.

ENGAGED or ATTACHED COLUMN: one that partly merges into a wall or pier.

ENGINEERING BRICKS: dense bricks, originally used mostly for railway viaducts etc.

ENRICHMENTS: the carved decoration of certain classical mouldings, e.g. the ovolo with *egg-and-dart*, the cyma reversa with *waterleaf*, the astragal with *bead-and-reel* (3f).

ENTABLATURE: in classical architecture, collective name for the three horizontal members (architrave, frieze and cornice) carried by a wall or a column (3a).

ENTASIS: very slight convex deviation from a straight line, used to prevent an optical illusion of concavity.

ENTRESOL: mezzanine floor subdividing what is constructionally a single storey, e.g. a vault.

EPITAPH: inscription on a tomb or monument.

EXEDRA: *see* Apse.

EXTRADOS: outer curved face of an arch or vault.

EYECATCHER: decorative building terminating a vista.

FASCIA: plain horizontal band, e.g. in an architrave (3c, 3d) or on a shopfront.

FENESTRATION: the arrangement of windows in a façade.

FERETORY: site of the chief shrine of a church, behind the high altar.

FESTOON: ornamental garland, suspended from both ends. Cf. Swag.

FEU (Scots): land granted, e.g. by sale, by the *feudal superior* to the *vassal* or *feuar*, on conditions that usually include the annual payment of a fixed sum of *feu duty*. Any subsequent proprietor of the land becomes the feuar and is subject to the same obligations.

FIBREGLASS (or glass-reinforced polyester (GRP)): synthetic resin reinforced with glass fibre. GRC: glass-reinforced concrete.

FIELD: *see* Panelling and 6b.

FILLET: a narrow flat band running down a medieval shaft or along a roll moulding (1a). It separates larger curved mouldings in classical cornices, fluting or bases (3c).

FLAMBOYANT: the latest phase of French Gothic architecture, with flowing tracery.

FLASH LOCK: *see* Canals.

FLATTED: divided into apartments. Also with a colloquial (Scots) meaning: 'He stays on the first flat' means that he lives on the first floor.

FLÈCHE or SPIRELET (*lit.* arrow): slender spire on the centre of a roof.

FLEURON: medieval carved flower or leaf, often rectilinear (1a).

FLUSHWORK: knapped flint used with dressed stone to form patterns.

FLUTING: series of concave grooves (flutes), their common edges sharp (arris) or blunt (fillet) (3).

FOIL (*lit.* leaf): lobe formed by the cusping of a circular or other shape in tracery (2b). *Trefoil* (three), *quatrefoil* (four), *cinquefoil* (five) and *multifoil* express the number of lobes in a shape.

FOLIATE: decorated with leaves.

FORE-BUILDING: structure protecting an entrance.

FORESTAIR: external stair, usually unenclosed.

FORMWORK: *see* Concrete.

FRAMED BUILDING: where the structure is carried by a framework – e.g. of steel, reinforced concrete, timber – instead of by load-bearing walls.

FREESTONE: stone that is cut, or can be cut, in all directions.

FRESCO: *al fresco*: painting on wet plaster. *Fresco secco*: painting on dry plaster.

FRIEZE: the middle member of the classical entablature, sometimes ornamented (3a). *Pulvinated frieze* (*lit.* cushioned): of bold convex profile (3c). Also a horizontal band of ornament.

FRONTISPIECE: in C16 and C17 buildings the central feature of doorway and windows above linked in one composition.

GABLE: peaked external wall at end of double-pitch roof. For types *see* 7. Also (Scots): whole end wall of whatever shape. *Pedimental gable*: treated like a pediment.

GADROONING: classical ribbed ornament like inverted fluting that flows into a lobed edge.

GAIT or GATE (Scots): street, usually with a prefix indicating use, direction or destination.

GALILEE: chapel or vestibule usually at the W end of a church enclosing the main portal(s).

GALLERY: a long room or passage; an upper storey above the aisle of a church, looking through arches to the nave; a balcony or mezzanine overlooking the main interior space of a building; or an external walkway.

GALLETING: small stones set in a mortar course.

GAMBREL ROOF: *see* 7.

GARDEROBE: medieval privy.

GARGOYLE: projecting water spout, often carved into human or animal shape. For cannon spout *see* 8.

GAUGED or RUBBED BRICKWORK: soft brick sawn roughly, then rubbed to a precise (gauged) surface. Mostly used for door or window openings (5c).

GAZEBO (jocular Latin, 'I shall gaze'): ornamental lookout tower or raised summer house.

GEOMETRIC: English Gothic architecture *c.* 1250–1310. *See also* Tracery. For another meaning, *see* Stairs.

GIANT or COLOSSAL ORDER: classical order (q.v.) whose height is that of two or more storeys of the building to which it is applied.

GIBBS SURROUND: C18 treatment of an opening (4b), seen particularly in the work of James Gibbs (1682–1754).

GIRDER: a large beam. *Box*: of hollow-box section. *Bowed*: with its top rising in a curve. *Plate*: of I-section, made from iron or steel plates. *Lattice*: with braced framework.

GLACIS: artificial slope extending out and downwards from the parapet of a fort.

GLAZING-BARS: wooden or sometimes metal bars separating and supporting window panes.

GLAZING GROOVE: groove in a window surround into which the glass is fitted.

GNOMON: vane or indicator casting a shadow onto a sundial.

GRAFFITI: *see* Sgraffito.

GRANGE: farm owned and run by a religious order.

GRC: *see* Fibreglass.

GRISAILLE: monochrome painting on walls or glass.

GROIN: sharp edge at the meeting of two cells of a cross-vault; *see* Vault and 2b.

GROTESQUE (*lit.* grotto-esque): wall decoration adopted from Roman examples in the Renaissance. Its foliage scrolls incorporate figurative elements. Cf. Arabesque.

GROTTO: artificial cavern.

GRP: *see* Fibreglass.

GUILLOCHE: classical ornament of interlaced bands (4b).

GUNLOOP: opening for a firearm (8a).

GUSHET (Scots): a triangular or wedge-shaped piece of land or the corner building on such a site.

GUTTAE: stylized drops (3b).

HALF-TIMBERING: archaic term for timber-framing (q.v.). Sometimes used for non-structural decorative timberwork.

HALL CHURCH: medieval church with nave and aisles of approximately equal height. Also (Scots C20) building for use as both hall and church, the double function usually intended to be temporary until a separate church is built.

HAMMERBEAM: *see* Roofs and 7.

HARLING (Scots, *lit.* hurling): wet dash, i.e. a form of roughcasting in which the mixture of aggregate and binding material (e.g. lime) is dashed onto a wall.

HEADER: *see* Bond and 6e.

HEADSTOP: stop (q.v.) carved with a head (5b).

HELM ROOF: *see* 1c.

HENGE: ritual earthwork with a surrounding ditch and outer bank.

HERM (*lit.* the god Hermes): male head or bust on a pedestal.

HERRINGBONE WORK: *see* 6e (for brick bond). Cf. Pitched masonry.

HEXASTYLE: *see* Portico.

HILLFORT: Iron Age earthwork enclosed by a ditch and bank system.

HIPPED ROOF: *see* 7.

HOODMOULD: projecting moulding above an arch or lintel to throw off water (2b, 5b). When horizontal often called a *label.* For label stop *see* Stop.

HORIZONTAL GLAZING: with panes of horizontal proportions.

HORSEMILL: circular or polygonal farm building with a central shaft turned by a horse to drive agricultural machinery.

HUNGRY-JOINTED: *see* Pointing.

HUSK GARLAND: festoon of stylized nutshells (4b).

HYDRAULIC POWER: use of water under high pressure to work machinery. *Accumulator tower*: houses a hydraulic accumulator which accommodates fluctuations in the flow through hydraulic mains.

HYPOCAUST (*lit.* underburning): Roman underfloor heating system.

IMPOST: horizontal moulding at the springing of an arch (5c).

IMPOST BLOCK: block between abacus and capital (1b).

IN ANTIS: *see* Antae, Portico and 4a.

INDENT: shape chiselled out of a stone to receive a brass. Also, in restoration, new stone inserted as a patch.

INDUSTRIALIZED or SYSTEM BUILDING: system of manufactured units assembled on site.

INGLENOOK (*lit.* fire-corner): recess for a hearth with provision for seating.

INGO (Scots): the reveal of a door or window opening where the stone is at right angles to the wall.

INTERCOLUMNATION: interval between columns.

INTERLACE: decoration in relief simulating woven or entwined stems or bands.

INTRADOS: *see* Soffit.

IONIC: *see* Orders and 3c.

JACK ARCH: shallow segmental vault springing from beams, used for fireproof floors, bridge decks etc.

JAMB (*lit.* leg): one of the vertical sides of an opening. Also (Scots) wing or extension adjoining one side of a rectangular plan making it into an L-, T- or Z-plan.

JETTY: the projection of an upper storey beyond the storey below. In a stone building this is achieved by corbelling. In a timber-framed building it is made by the beams and joists of the lower storey oversailing the wall; on their outer ends is placed the sill of the walling for the storey above.

JOGGLE: the joining of two stones to prevent them slipping by a notch in one and a projection in the other.

KEEL MOULDING: moulding used from the late C12, in section like the keel of a ship (1a).

KEEP: principal tower of a castle.

KENTISH CUSP: *see* Tracery.

KEY PATTERN: *see* 4b.

KEYSTONE: central stone in an arch or vault (4b, 5c).

KINGPOST: *see* Roofs and 7.

KNEELER: horizontal projecting stone at the base of each side of a gable to support the inclined coping stones (7).

LABEL: *see* Hoodmould and 5b.

LABEL STOP: *see* Stop and 5b.

LACED BRICKWORK: vertical strips of brickwork, often in a contrasting colour, linking openings on different floors.

LACING COURSE: horizontal reinforcement in timber or brick to walls of flint, cobble etc.

LADE (Scots): channel formed to bring water to a mill; mill-race.

LADY CHAPEL: dedicated to the Virgin Mary (Our Lady).

LAIGH or LAICH (Scots): low.

LAIR (Scots): a burial space reserved in a graveyard

LAIRD (Scots): landowner.

LANCET: slender single-light, pointed-arched window (2a).

LANTERN: circular or polygonal windowed turret crowning a roof or a dome. Also the windowed stage of a crossing tower lighting the church interior.

LANTERN CROSS: churchyard cross with lantern-shaped top.

LAVATORIUM: in a religious house, a washing place adjacent to the refectory.

LEAN-TO: *see* Roofs.

LESENE (*lit.* a mean thing): pilaster without base or capital. Also called *pilaster strip*.

LIERNe: *see* Vault and 2c.

LIGHT: compartment of a window defined by the mullions.

LINENFOLD: Tudor panelling carved with simulations of folded linen.

LINTEL: horizontal beam or stone bridging an opening.

LOFT: gallery in a church. *Organ loft*: in which the organ, or sometimes only the console (keyboard), is placed. *Laird's loft, Trades loft* etc. (Scots): reserved for an individual or special group. *See also* Rood (loft).

LOGGIA: gallery, usually arcaded or colonnaded along one side; sometimes freestanding.

LONG-AND-SHORT WORK: quoins consisting of stones placed with the long side alternately upright and horizontal, especially in Saxon building.

LOUVRE: roof opening, often protected by a raised timber structure, to allow the smoke from a central hearth to escape. *Louvres*: overlapping boards to allow ventilation but keep the rain out.

LOWSIDE WINDOW: set lower than the others in a chancel side wall, usually towards its W end.

L-PLAN: *see* Tower house and 8b.

LUCARNE (*lit.* dormer): small gabled opening in a roof or spire.

LUCKENBOOTH (Scots): lock-up booth or shop.

LUGGED ARCHITRAVE: *see* 4b.

LUNETTE: semicircular window or blind panel.

LYCHGATE (*lit.* corpse-gate): roofed gateway entrance to a churchyard for the reception of a coffin.

LYNCHET: long terraced strip of soil on the downward side of prehistoric and medieval fields, accumulated because of continual ploughing along the contours.

MACHICOLATIONS (*lit.* mashing devices): series of openings between the corbels that support a projecting parapet through which missiles can be dropped (8a). Used decoratively in post-medieval buildings.

MAINS (Scots): home farm on an estate.

MANOMETER or STANDPIPE TOWER: containing a column of water to regulate pressure in water mains.

MANSARD: *see* 7.

MANSE: house of a minister of religion, especially in Scotland.

MARGINS (Scots): dressed stones at the edges of an opening. 'Back-set margins' (RCAHMS) are actually set forward from a rubble wall to act as a stop for harling (q.v.). Also called *rybats*.

MARRIAGE LINTEL (Scots): door or window lintel carved with the initials of the owner and his wife and the date of building work, only coincidentally of their marriage.

MATHEMATICAL TILES: facing tiles with the appearance of brick, most often applied to timber-framed walls.

MAUSOLEUM: monumental building or chamber usually intended for the burial of members of one family.

MEGALITHIC: the use of large stones, singly or together.

MEGALITHIC TOMB: massive stonebuilt Neolithic burial chamber covered by an earth or stone mound.

MERCAT (Scots): market. The *Mercat Cross* of a Scottish burgh was the focus of market activity and local ceremonial. Most examples are post-Reformation with heraldic or other finials (not crosses).

MERLON: *see* Battlement.

MESOLITHIC: Middle Stone Age, in Britain *c.* 5000 to *c.* 3500 B.C.

METOPES: spaces between the triglyphs in a Doric frieze (3b).

MEZZANINE: low storey between two higher ones or within the height of a high one, not extending over its whole area.

MILD STEEL: *see* Cast iron.

MISERICORD (*lit.* mercy): shelf on a carved bracket placed on the underside of a hinged choir stall seat to support an occupant when standing.

MIXER-COURTS: forecourts to groups of houses shared by vehicles and pedestrians.

MODILLIONS: small consoles (q.v.) along the underside of a Corinthian or Composite cornice (3d). Often used along an eaves cornice.

MODULE: a predetermined standard size for co-ordinating the dimensions of components of a building.

MORT-SAFE (Scots): device to secure corpse(s): either an iron frame over a grave or a building where bodies were kept during decomposition.

MOTTE-AND-BAILEY: C11 and C12 type of castle consisting of an earthen mound (motte) topped by a wooden tower within or adjoining a bailey, an enclosure defended by a ditch and palisade, and also, sometimes, by an inner bank.

MOUCHETTE: *see* Tracery and 2b.

MOULDING: shaped ornamental strip of continuous section; *see* Cavetto, Cyma, Ovolo, Roll.

MULLION: vertical member between window lights (2b).

MULTI-STOREY: five or more storeys. Multi-storey flats may form a *cluster block*, with individual blocks of flats grouped round a service core; a *point block*, with flats fanning out from a service core; or a *slab block*, with flats approached by corridors or galleries from service cores at intervals or towers at the ends (plan also used for offices, hotels etc.). *Tower block* is a generic term for a high multi-storey building.

MULTIVALLATE: of a hillfort: defended by three or more concentric banks and ditches.

MUNTIN: *see* Panelling and 6b.

MUTULE: square block under the corona of a Doric cornice.

NAILHEAD: E.E. ornament consisting of small pyramids regularly repeated (1a).

NARTHEX: enclosed vestibule or covered porch at the main entrance to a church.

NAVE: the body of a church W of the crossing or chancel, often flanked by aisles (q.v.).

NEOLITHIC: New Stone Age in Britain, *c.* 3500 B.C. until the Bronze Age.

NEWEL: central or corner post of a staircase (6c). For Newel stair *see* Stairs.

NIGHT STAIR: stair by which religious entered the transept of their church from their dormitory to celebrate night offices.

NOGGING: *see* Timber-framing.

NOOK-SHAFT: shaft set in the angle of a wall or opening (1a).

NORMAN: *see* Romanesque.

NOSING: projection of the tread of a step (6c). *Bottle nosing*: half round in section.

NUTMEG: medieval ornament with a chain of tiny triangles placed obliquely.

OCULUS: circular opening.

OEIL DE BOEUF: *see* Bullseye window.

OGEE: double curve, bending first one way and then the other, as in an *ogee* or *ogival arch* (5c). Cf. Cyma recta and Cyma reversa.

OPUS SECTILE: decorative mosaic-like facing.

OPUS SIGNINUM: composition flooring of Roman origin.

ORATORY: a private chapel in a church or a house. Also a church of the Oratorian Order.

ORDER: one of a series of recessed arches and jambs forming a splayed medieval opening, e.g. a doorway or arcade arch (1a).

ORDERS: the formalized versions of the post-and-lintel system in classical architecture. The main orders are *Doric*, *Ionic* and *Corinthian*. They are Greek in origin

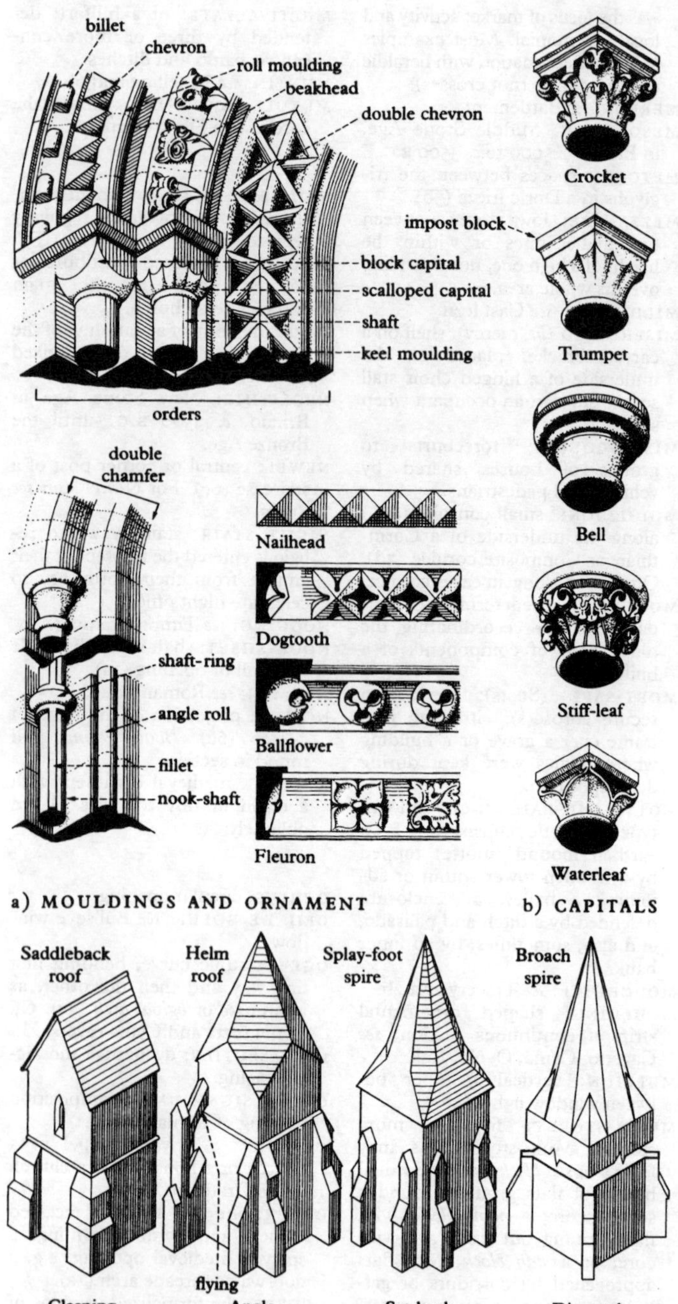
billet
chevron
roll moulding
beakhead
double chevron
block capital
scalloped capital
shaft
keel moulding
orders
double chamfer
shaft-ring
angle roll
fillet
nook-shaft
Nailhead
Dogtooth
Ballflower
Fleuron
impost block
Crocket
Trumpet
Bell
Stiff-leaf
Waterleaf
a) MOULDINGS AND ORNAMENT
b) CAPITALS
Saddleback roof
Helm roof
Splay-foot spire
Broach spire
flying
Clasping
Angle
Set-back
Diagonal
c) BUTTRESSES, ROOFS AND SPIRES

FIGURE 1: MEDIEVAL

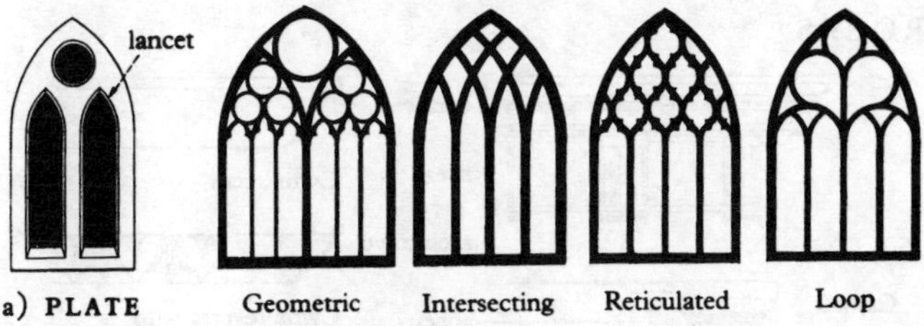

lancet

a) PLATE TRACERY

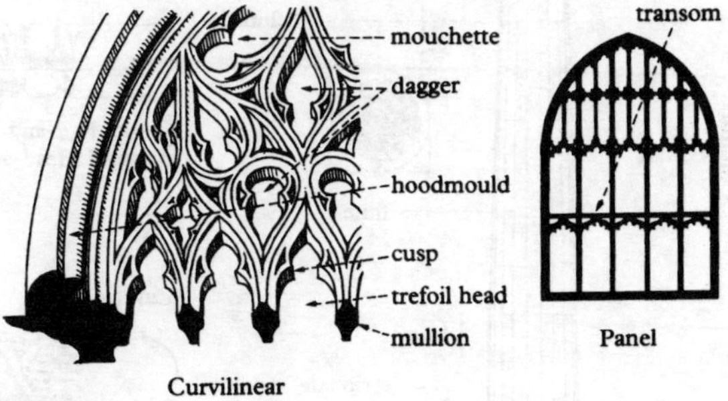

Geometric Intersecting Reticulated Loop

mouchette
dagger
hoodmould
cusp
trefoil head
mullion

Curvilinear

transom

Panel

b) BAR TRACERY

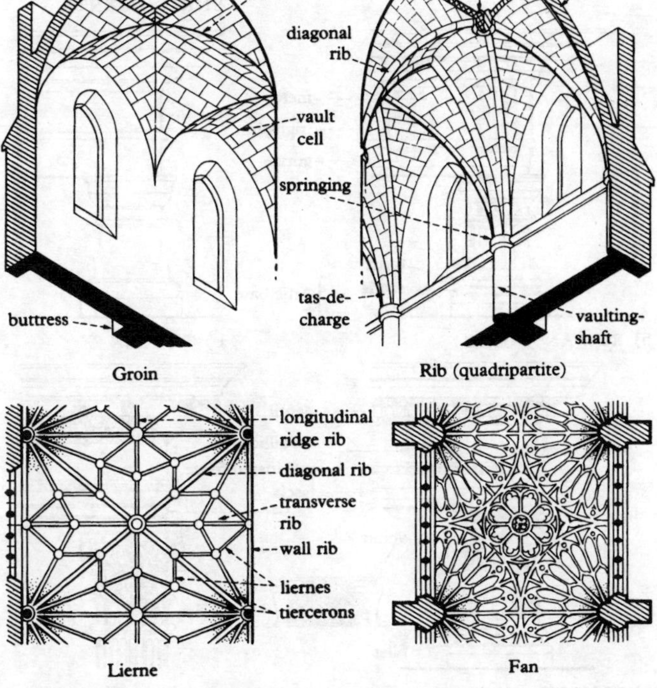

FIGURE 2: MEDIEVAL

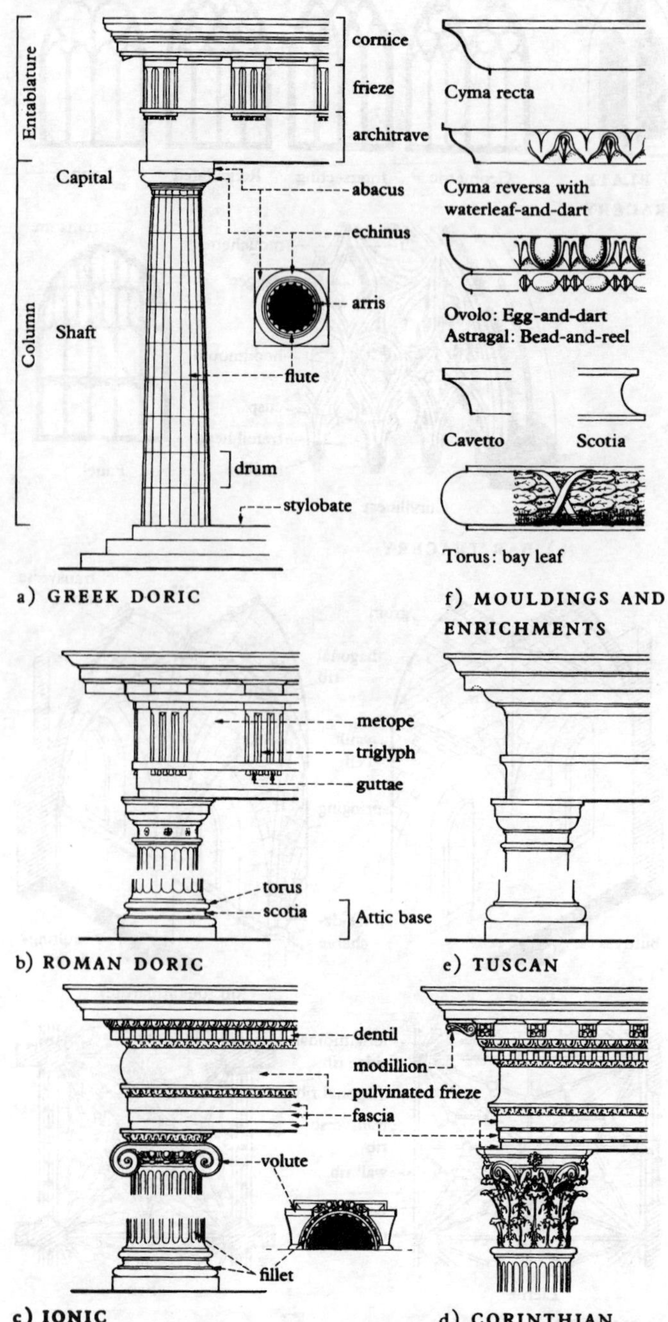
ORDERS
Entablature
cornice
frieze
architrave
Capital
abacus
echinus
arris
Column
Shaft
flute
drum
stylobate
a) GREEK DORIC
Cyma recta
Cyma reversa with waterleaf-and-dart
Ovolo: Egg-and-dart
Astragal: Bead-and-reel
Cavetto
Scotia
Torus: bay leaf
f) MOULDINGS AND ENRICHMENTS
metope
triglyph
guttae
torus
scotia
Attic base
b) ROMAN DORIC
e) TUSCAN
dentil
modillion
pulvinated frieze
fascia
volute
fillet
c) IONIC
d) CORINTHIAN

FIGURE 3: CLASSICAL

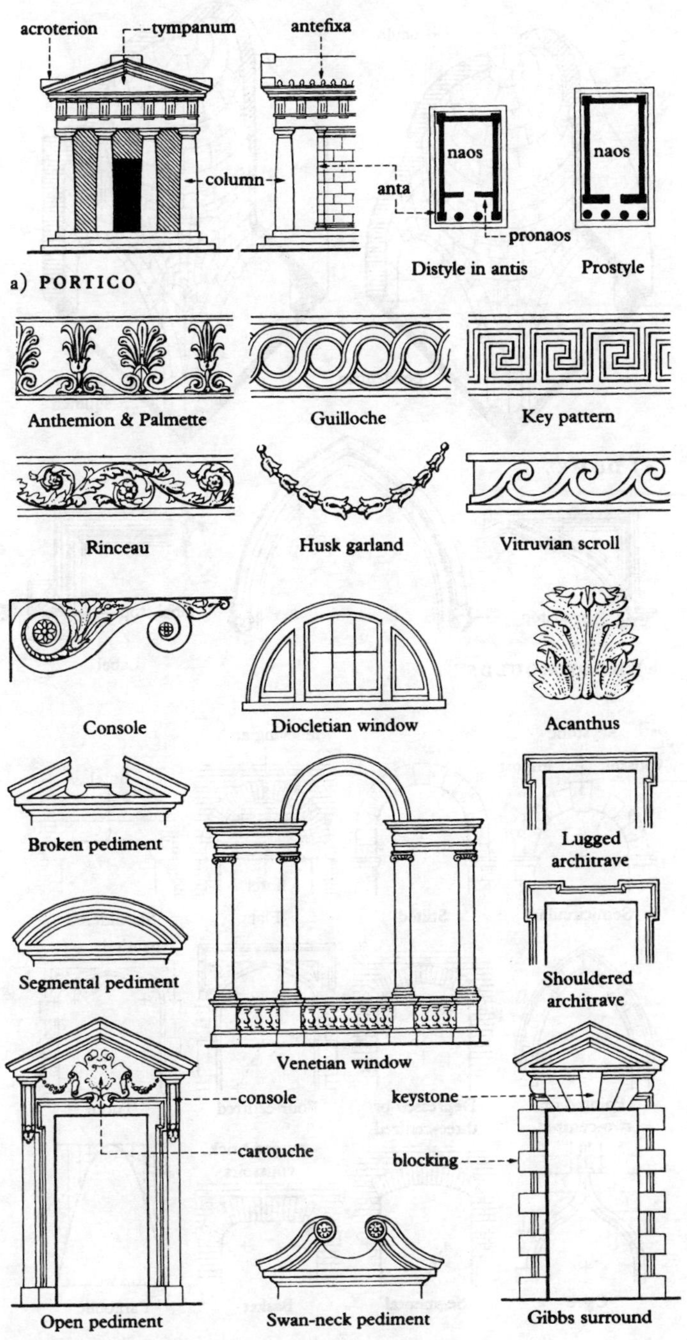
acroterion
tympanum
antefixa
column
anta
naos
naos
pronaos
Distyle in antis
Prostyle
a) PORTICO
Anthemion & Palmette
Guilloche
Key pattern
Rinceau
Husk garland
Vitruvian scroll
Console
Diocletian window
Acanthus
Broken pediment
Lugged architrave
Shouldered architrave
Segmental pediment
Venetian window
console
cartouche
keystone
blocking
Open pediment
Swan-neck pediment
Gibbs surround
b) ORNAMENTS AND FEATURES

FIGURE 4: CLASSICAL

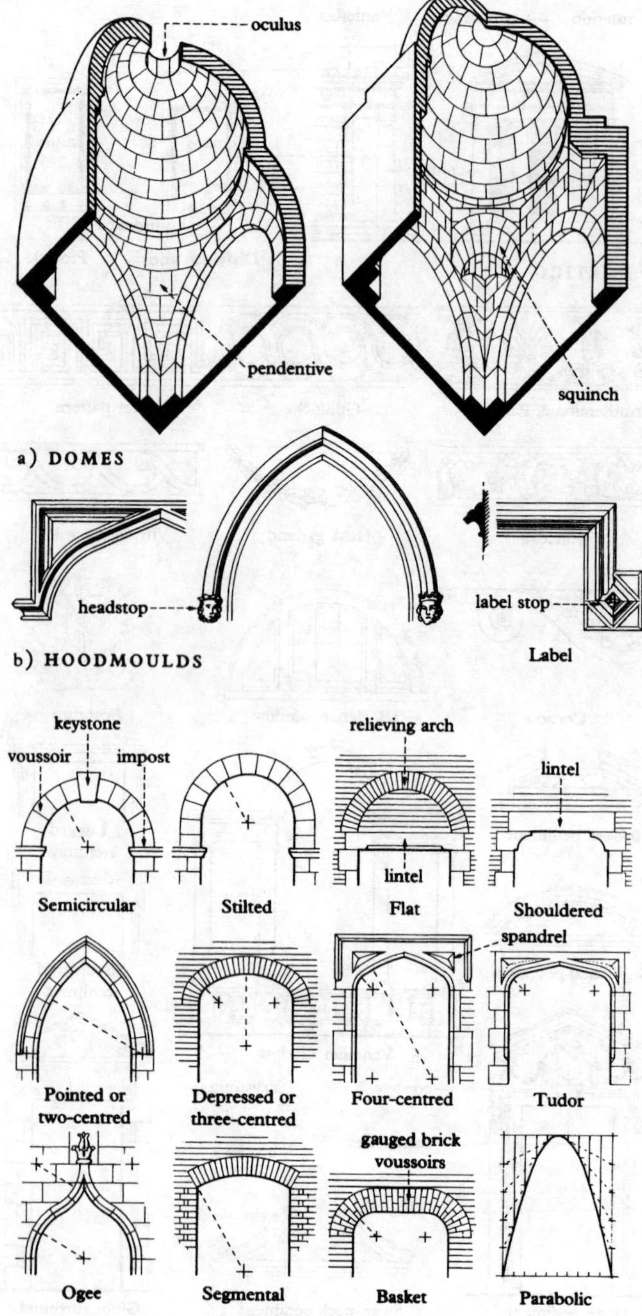

FIGURE 5: CONSTRUCTION

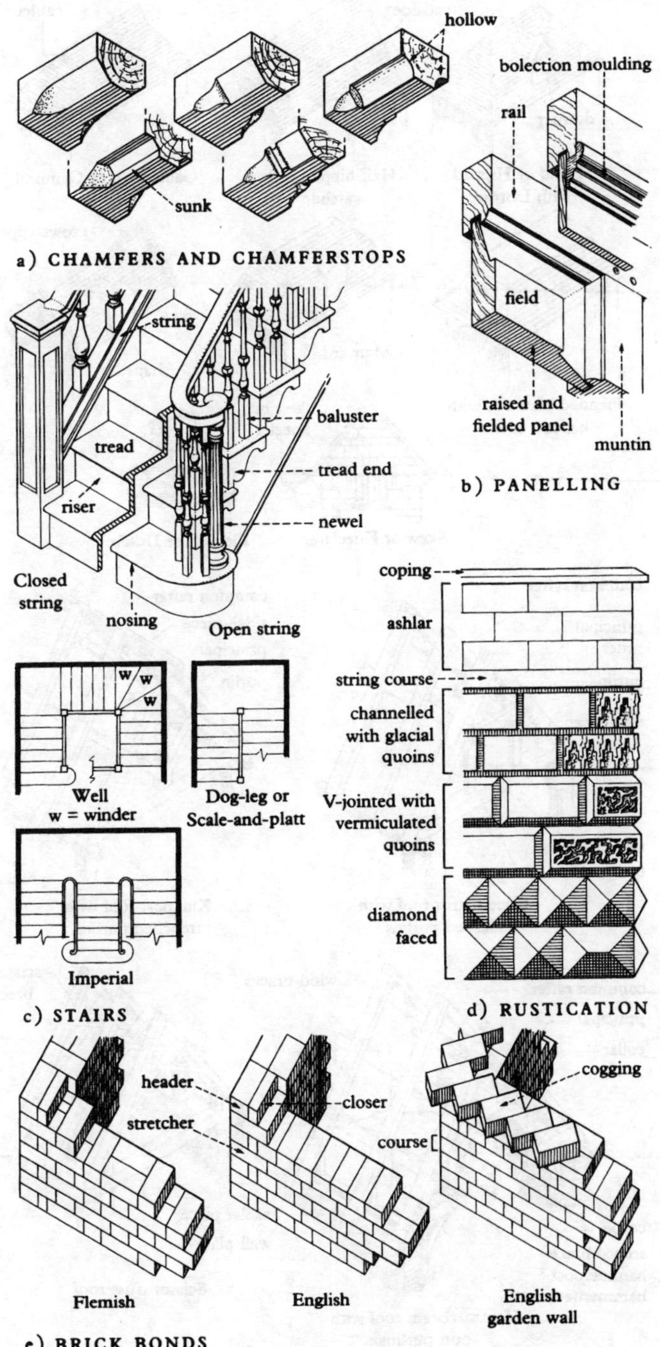

FIGURE 6: CONSTRUCTION

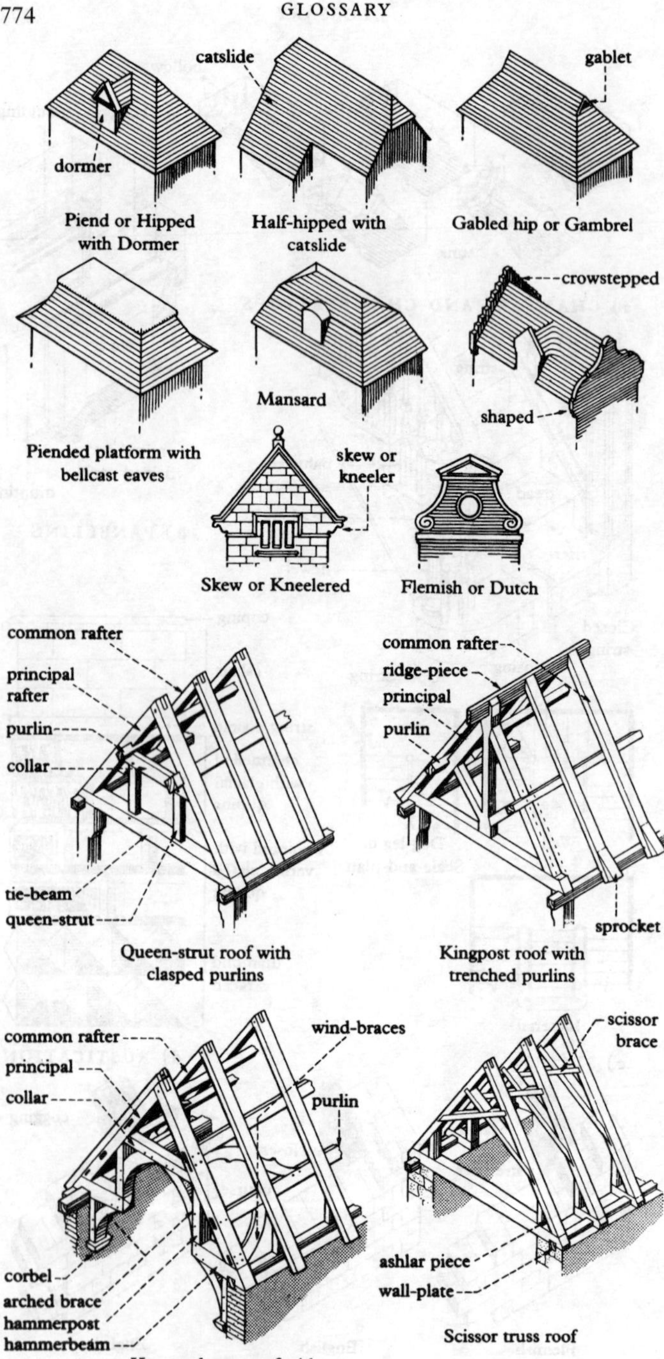
catslide
gablet
dormer
Piend or Hipped with Dormer
Half-hipped with catslide
Gabled hip or Gambrel
crowstepped
Mansard
shaped
Piended platform with bellcast eaves
skew or kneeler
Skew or Kneelered
Flemish or Dutch
common rafter
principal rafter
purlin
collar
tie-beam
queen-strut
Queen-strut roof with clasped purlins
common rafter
ridge-piece
principal
purlin
sprocket
Kingpost roof with trenched purlins
common rafter
principal
collar
wind-braces
purlin
corbel
arched brace
hammerpost
hammerbeam
Hammerbeam roof with butt purlins
scissor brace
ashlar piece
wall-plate
Scissor truss roof

FIGURE 7: ROOFS AND GABLES

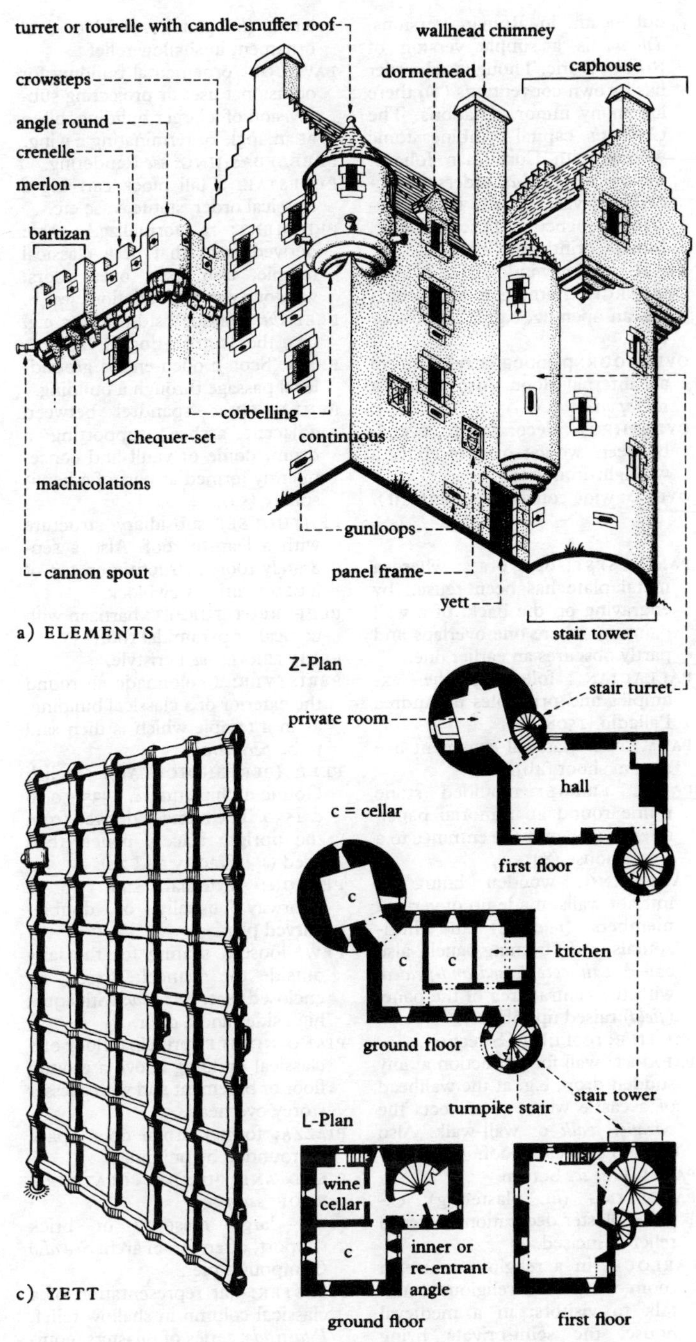
turret or tourelle with candle-snuffer roof
crowsteps
angle round
crenelle
merlon
bartizan
corbelling
chequer-set
machicolations
cannon spout
wallhead chimney
dormerhead
caphouse
continuous
gunloops
panel frame
yett
stair tower
a) ELEMENTS
Z-Plan
stair turret
private room
hall
c = cellar
first floor
c
c
c
kitchen
ground floor
stair tower
turnpike stair
L-Plan
wine cellar
c
inner or re-entrant angle
ground floor
first floor
b) FORMS
c) YETT

FIGURE 8: THE TOWER HOUSE

but occur in Roman versions. *Tuscan* is a simple version of Roman Doric. Though each order has its own conventions (3), there are many minor variations. The *Composite* capital combines Ionic volutes with Corinthian foliage. *Superimposed orders*: orders on successive levels, usually in the upward sequence of Tuscan, Doric, Ionic, Corinthian, Composite.

ORIEL: *see* Bay window.

OVERARCH: framing a wall which has an opening, e.g. a window or door.

OVERDOOR: painting or relief above an internal door. Also called a *sopraporta.*

OVERTHROW: decorative fixed arch between two gatepiers or above a wrought-iron gate.

OVOLO: wide convex moulding (3f).

PALIMPSEST: of a brass: where a metal plate has been reused by engraving on the back; of a wall painting: where one overlaps and partly obscures an earlier one.

PALLADIAN: following the examples and principles of Andrea Palladio (1508–80).

PALMETTE: classical ornament like a palm shoot (4b).

PANEL FRAME: moulded stone frame round an armorial panel, often placed over the entrance to a tower house (8a).

PANELLING: wooden lining to interior walls, made up of vertical members (*muntins*) and horizontals (*rails*) framing panels: also called *wainscot. Raised-and-fielded*: with the central area of the panel (*field*) raised up (6b).

PANTILE: roof tile of S section.

PARAPET: wall for protection at any sudden drop, e.g. at the wallhead of a castle where it protects the *parapet walk* or wall-walk. Also used to conceal a roof.

PARCLOSE: *see* Screen.

PARGETING (*lit.* plastering): exterior plaster decoration, either in relief or incised.

PARLOUR: in a religious house, a room where the religious could talk to visitors; in a medieval house, the semi-private living room below the solar (q.v.).

PARTERRE: level space in a garden laid out with low, formal beds.

PATERA (*lit.* plate): round or oval ornament in shallow relief.

PAVILION: ornamental building for occasional use; or projecting subdivision of a larger building, often at an angle or terminating a wing.

PEBBLEDASHING: *see* Rendering.

PEDESTAL: a tall block carrying a classical order, statue, vase etc.

PEDIMENT: a formalized gable derived from that of a classical temple; also used over doors, windows etc. For variations *see* 4b.

PEEL (*lit.* palisade): stone tower, e.g. near the Scottish-English border.

PEND (Scots): open-ended ground-level passage through a building.

PENDENTIVE: spandrel between adjacent arches, supporting a drum, dome or vault and consequently formed as part of a hemisphere (5a).

PENTHOUSE: subsidiary structure with a lean-to roof. Also a separately roofed structure on top of a C20 multi-storey block.

PEPPERPOT TURRET: bartizan with conical or pyramidal roof.

PERIPTERAL: *see* Peristyle.

PERISTYLE: a colonnade all round the exterior of a classical building, as in a temple which is then said to be *peripteral.*

PERP (PERPENDICULAR): English Gothic architecture *c.* 1335–50 to *c.* 1530. The name is derived from the upright tracery panels then used (*see* Tracery and 2a).

PERRON: external stair to a doorway, usually of double-curved plan.

PEW: loosely, seating for the laity outside the chancel; strictly, an enclosed seat. *Box pew*: with equal high sides and a door.

PIANO NOBILE: principal floor of a classical building above a ground floor or basement and with a lesser storey overhead.

PIAZZA: formal urban open space surrounded by buildings.

PIEND AND PIENDED PLATFORM ROOF: *see* 7.

PIER: large masonry or brick support, often for an arch. *See also* Compound pier.

PILASTER: flat representation of a classical column in shallow relief. *Pilastrade*: series of pilasters, equivalent to a colonnade.

PILE: row of rooms. *Double pile*: two rows thick.

PILLAR: freestanding upright member of any section, not conforming to one of the orders (q.v.).

PILLAR PISCINA: *see* Piscina.

PILOTIS: C20 French term for pillars or stilts that support a building above an open ground floor.

PINS OR PINNINGS (Scots): *see* Cherry-caulking.

PISCINA: basin for washing Mass vessels, provided with a drain; set in or against wall to S of an altar or freestanding (*pillar piscina*).

PITCHED MASONRY: laid on the diagonal, often alternately with opposing courses (*pitched and counterpitched* or herringbone).

PIT PRISON: sunk chamber with access from above through a hatch.

PLATE RAIL: *see* Railways.

PLATEWAY: *see* Railways.

PLATT (Scots): platform, doorstep or landing. *Scale-and-platt stair*: *see* Stairs and 6c.

PLEASANCE (Scots): close or walled garden.

PLINTH: projecting courses at the foot of a wall or column, generally chamfered or moulded at the top.

PODIUM: a continuous raised platform supporting a building; or a large block of two or three storeys beneath a multi-storey block of smaller area.

POINT BLOCK: *see* Multi-storey.

POINTING: exposed mortar jointing of masonry or brickwork. Types include *flush*, *recessed* and *tuck* (with a narrow channel filled with finer, whiter mortar). *Bag-rubbed*: flush at the edges and gently recessed in the middle. *Ribbon*: joints formed with a trowel so that they stand out. *Hungry-jointed*: either with no pointing or deeply recessed to show the outline of each stone.

POPPYHEAD: carved ornament of leaves and flowers as a finial for a bench end or stall.

PORTAL FRAME: C20 frame comprising two uprights rigidly connected to a beam or pair of rafters.

PORTCULLIS: gate constructed to rise and fall in vertical gooves at the entry to a castle.

PORTE COCHÈRE: porch large enough to admit wheeled vehicles.

PORTICO: a porch with the roof and frequently a pediment supported by a row of columns (4a). A portico *in antis* has columns on the same plane as the front of the building. A *prostyle* porch has columns standing free. Porticoes are described by the number of front columns, e.g. tetrastyle (four), hexastyle (six). The space within the temple is the *naos*, that within the portico the *pronaos*. *Blind portico*: the front features of a portico applied to a wall.

PORTICUS (plural: porticūs): subsidiary cell opening from the main body of a pre-Conquest church.

POST: upright support in a structure.

POSTERN: small gateway at the back of a building or to the side of a larger entrance door or gate.

POTENCE (Scots): rotating ladder for access to doocot nesting boxes.

POUND LOCK: *see* Canals.

PREDELLA: in an altarpiece, the horizontal strip below the main representation, often used for subsidiary representations.

PRESBYTERY: the part of a church lying E of the choir where the main altar is placed. Also a priest's residence.

PRESS (Scots): cupboard.

PRINCIPAL: *see* Roofs and 7.

PRONAOS: *see* Portico and 4a.

PROSTYLE: *see* Portico and 4a.

PULPIT: raised and enclosed platform for the preaching of sermons. *Three-decker*: with reading desk below and clerk's desk below that. *Two-decker*: as above, minus the clerk's desk.

PULPITUM: stone screen in a major church dividing choir from nave.

PULVINATED: *see* Frieze and 3c.

PURLIN: *see* Roofs and 7.

PUTHOLES or PUTLOG HOLES: in wall to receive putlogs, the horizontal timbers which support scaffolding boards; not always filled after construction is complete.

PUTTO (plural: putti): small naked boy.

QUARRIES: square (or diamond) panes of glass supported by lead strips (*cames*); square floor-slabs or tiles.

QUATREFOIL: *see* Foil.

QUEEN-STRUT: *see* Roofs and 7.

QUILLONS: the arms forming the cross-guard of a sword.

QUIRK: sharp groove to one side of a convex medieval moulding.

QUOINS: dressed stones at the angles of a building (6d).

RADBURN SYSTEM: pedestrian and vehicle segregation in residential developments, based on that used at Radburn, New Jersey, U.S.A., by Wright and Stein, 1928–30.

RADIATING CHAPELS: projecting radially from an ambulatory or an apse (*see* Chevet).

RAFTER: *see* Roofs and 7.

RAGGLE: groove cut in masonry, especially to receive the edge of a roof-covering.

RAIL: *see* Panelling and 6b.

RAILWAYS: *Edge rail*: on which flanged wheels can run. *Plate rail*: L-section rail for plain unflanged wheels. *Plateway*: early railway using plate rails.

RAISED AND FIELDED: *see* Panelling and 6b.

RAKE: slope or pitch.

RAMPART: defensive outer wall of stone or earth. *Rampart walk*: path along the inner face.

RATCOURSE: projecting string-course on a doocot to deter rats from climbing to the flight holes.

REBATE: rectangular section cut out of a masonry edge to receive a shutter, door, window etc.

REBUS: a heraldic pun, e.g. a fiery cock for Cockburn.

REEDING: series of convex mouldings, the reverse of fluting (q.v.). Cf. Gadrooning.

RENDERING: the covering of outside walls with a uniform surface or skin for protection from the weather. *Lime-washing*: thin layer of lime plaster. *Pebble-dashing*: where aggregate is thrown at the wet plastered wall for a textured effect. *Roughcast*: plaster mixed with a coarse aggregate such as gravel. *Stucco*: fine lime plaster worked to a smooth surface. *Cement rendering*: a cheaper substitute for stucco, usually with a grainy texture.

REPOUSSÉ: relief designs in metalwork, formed by beating it from the back.

REREDORTER (*lit.* behind the dormitory): latrines in a medieval religious house.

REREDOS: painted and/or sculptured screen behind and above an altar. Cf. Retable.

RESPOND: half-pier or half-column bonded into a wall and carrying one end of an arch. It usually terminates an arcade.

RETABLE: painted or carved panel standing on or at the back of an altar, usually attached to it.

RETROCHOIR: in a major church, the area between the high altar and E chapel.

REVEAL: the plane of a jamb, between the wall and the frame of a door or window.

RHONE (Scots): gutter along the eaves for rainwater: *see also* Conductor.

RIB-VAULT: *see* Vault and 2c.

RIG (Scots): a strip of ploughed land raised in the middle and sloped to a furrow on each side; early cultivation method (runrig) usually surrounded by untilled grazing land.

RINCEAU: classical ornament of leafy scrolls (4b).

RISER: vertical face of a step (6c).

ROCK-FACED: masonry cleft to produce a rugged appearance.

ROCOCO: style current between *c.* 1720 and *c.* 1760, characterized by a serpentine line and playful, scrolled decoration.

ROLL MOULDING: medieval moulding of part-circular section (1a).

ROMANESQUE: style current in the C11 and C12. In England often called Norman. *See also* Saxo-Norman.

ROOD: crucifix flanked by representations of the Virgin and St John, usually over the entry into the chancel, painted on the wall, on a beam (*rood beam*) or on top of a *rood screen* or pulpitum (q.v.) which often had a walkway (*rood loft*) along the top, reached by a *rood stair* in the side wall. *Hanging rood*: cross or crucifix suspended from roof.

ROOFS: For the main external shapes (hipped, gambrel etc.) *see* 7. *Helm* and *Saddleback*: *see* 1c. *Lean-to*: single sloping roof built against a vertical wall; also applied to the part of the building beneath. *Bellcast*: sloping roof slightly swept out over the eaves.
Construction. *See* 7.
Single-framed roof: with no main trusses. The rafters may be fixed

to the wall-plate or ridge, or longitudinal timbers may be absent altogether.

Double-framed roof: with longitudinal members, such as purlins, and usually divided into bays by principals and principal rafters.

Other types are named after their main structural components, e.g. *hammerbeam*, *crown-post* (*see* Elements below and 7).

Elements. *See* 7.

Ashlar piece: a short vertical timber connecting an inner wall-plate or timber pad to a rafter.

Braces: subsidiary timbers set diagonally to strengthen the frame. *Arched braces*: curved pair forming an arch, connecting wall or post below with a tie- or collar-beam above. *Passing braces*: long straight braces passing across other members of the truss. *Scissor braces*: pair crossing diagonally between pairs of rafters or principals. *Wind-braces*: short, usually curved braces connecting side purlins with principals; sometimes decorated with cusping.

Collar or *collar-beam*: horizontal transverse timber connecting a pair of rafter or cruck blades (q.v.), set between apex and the wall-plate.

Crown-post: a vertical timber set centrally on a tie-beam and supporting a collar purlin braced to it longitudinally. In an open truss lateral braces may rise to the collar-beam; in a closed truss they may descend to the tie-beam.

Hammerbeams: horizontal brackets projecting at wall-plate level like an interrupted tie-beam; the inner ends carry *hammerposts*, vertical timbers which support a purlin and are braced to a collar-beam above.

Kingpost: vertical timber set centrally on a tie-or collar-beam, rising to the apex of the roof to support a ridge piece (cf. Strut).

Plate: longitudinal timber set square to the ground. *Wall-plate*: along the top of a wall to receive the ends of rafters; cf. Purlin.

Principals: pair of inclined lateral timbers of a truss. Usually they support side purlins and mark the main bay divisions.

Purlin: horizontal longitudinal timber. *Collar purlin* or *crown plate*: central timber which carries collar-beams and is supported by crown-posts. *Side purlins*: pairs of timbers placed some way up the slope of the roof, which carry common rafters. *Butt* or *tenoned purlins* are tenoned into either side of the principals. *Through purlins* pass through or past the principal; they include *clasped purlins*, which rest on queenposts or are carried in the angle between principals and collar, and *trenched purlins* trenched into the backs of principals.

Queen-strut: paired vertical, or near-vertical, timbers placed symmetrically on a tie-beam to support side purlins.

Rafters: inclined lateral timbers supporting the roof covering. *Common rafters*: regularly spaced uniform rafters placed along the length of a roof or between principals. *Principal rafters*: rafters which also act as principals.

Ridge, ridge piece: horizontal longitudinal timber at the apex supporting the ends of the rafters.

Sprocket: short timber placed on the back and at the foot of a rafter to form projecting eaves.

Strut: vertical or oblique timber between two members of a truss, not directly supporting longitudinal timbers.

Tie-beam: main horizontal transverse timber which carries the feet of the principals at wall level.

Truss: rigid framework of timbers at bay intervals, carrying the longitudinal roof timbers which support the common rafters. *Closed truss*: with the spaces between the timbers filled, to form an internal partition.

See also Cruck, Wagon roof.

ROPE MOULDING: *see* Cable moulding.

ROSE WINDOW: circular window with tracery radiating from the centre. Cf. Wheel window.

ROTUNDA: building or room circular in plan.

ROUGHCAST: *see* Rendering.

ROUND (Scots): bartizan, usually roofless.

ROVING BRIDGE: *see* Canals.

RUBBED BRICKWORK: *see* Gauged brickwork.

RUBBLE: masonry whose stones are wholly or partly in a rough state. *Coursed*: coursed stones with rough faces. *Random*: uncoursed stones in a random pattern. *Snecked*: with courses broken by smaller stones (snecks).

RUSTICATION: *see* 6d. Exaggerated treatment of masonry to give an effect of strength. The joints are usually recessed by V-section chamfering or square-section channelling (*channelled rustication*). *Banded rustication* has only the horizontal joints emphasized. The faces may be flat, but can be *diamond-faced*, like shallow pyramids, *vermiculated*, with a stylized texture like worm-casts, and *glacial* (frost-work), like icicles or stalactites.

RYBATS (Scots): *see* Margins.

SACRAMENT HOUSE: safe cupboard in a side wall of the chancel of a church and not directly associated with an altar, for reservation of the sacrament.

SACRISTY: room in a church for sacred vessels and vestments.

SADDLEBACK ROOF: *see* 1c.

SALTIRE CROSS: with diagonal limbs.

SANCTUARY: part of church at E end containing high altar. Cf. Presbytery.

SANGHA: residence of Buddhist monks or nuns.

SARCOPHAGUS: coffin of stone or other durable material.

SARKING (Scots): boards laid on the rafters to support the roof covering.

SAXO-NORMAN: transitional Romanesque style combining Anglo-Saxon and Norman features, current *c.* 1060–1100.

SCAGLIOLA: composition imitating marble.

SCALE-AND-PLATT (*lit.* stair and landing): *see* Stair and 6c.

SCALLOPED CAPITAL: *see* 1a.

SCARCEMENT: extra thickness of the lower part of a wall, e.g. to carry a floor.

SCARP: artificial cutting away of the ground to form a steep slope.

SCOTIA: a hollow classical moulding, especially between tori (q.v.) on a column base (3b, 3f).

SCREEN: in a medieval church, usually at the entry to the chancel; *see* Rood (screen) and Pulpitum. A *parclose screen* separates a chapel from the rest of the church.

SCREENS or SCREENS PASSAGE: screened-off entrance passage between great hall and service rooms or between the hall of a tower house and the stair.

SCRIBE (Scots): to cut and mark timber against an irregular stone or plaster surface.

SCUNTION (Scots): reveal.

SECTION: two-dimensional representation of a building, moulding etc., revealed by cutting across it.

SEDILIA (singular: sedile): seats for clergy (usually for a priest, deacon and sub-deacon) on the S side of the chancel.

SEPTUM: dwarf wall between the nave and choir.

SESSION HOUSE (Scots): a room or separate building for meetings of the minister and elders who form a kirk session. Also a shelter by the church or churchyard entrance for an elder collecting for poor relief, built at expense of kirk session.

SET-OFF: *see* Weathering.

SGRAFFITO: decoration scratched, often in plaster, to reveal a pattern in another colour beneath. *Graffiti*: scratched drawing or writing.

SHAFT: vertical member of round or polygonal section (1a, 3a). *Shaft-ring*: at the junction of shafts set *en délit* (q.v.) or attached to a pier or wall (1a).

SHEILA-NA-GIG: female fertility figure, usually with legs apart.

SHELL: thin, self-supporting roofing membrane of timber or concrete.

SHEUGH (Scots): a trench or open drain; a street gutter.

SHOULDERED ARCH: *see* 5a.

SHOULDERED ARCHITRAVE: *see* 4b.

SHUTTERING: *see* Concrete.

SILL: horizontal member at the bottom of a window-or door-frame; or at the base of a timber-framed wall into which posts and studs are tenoned.

SKEW (Scots): sloping or shaped stones finishing a gable upstanding from the roof. *Skewputt*: bracket at the bottom end of a skew. *See* 7.

SLAB BLOCK: *see* Multi-storey.

SLATE-HANGING: covering of overlapping slates on a wall. *Tile-hanging* is similar.

SLYPE: covered way or passage leading E from the cloisters between transept and chapter house.

SNECKED: *see* Rubble.

SOFFIT (*lit.* ceiling): underside of an arch (also called *intrados*), lintel etc. *Soffit roll*: medieval roll moulding on a soffit.

SOLAR: private upper chamber in a medieval house, accessible from the high end of the great hall.

SOPRAPORTA: *see* Overdoor.

SOUNDING-BOARD: *see* Tester.

SOUTERRAIN: underground stone-lined passage and chamber.

SPANDRELS: roughly triangular spaces between an arch and its containing rectangle, or between adjacent arches (5c). Also non-structural panels under the windows in a curtain-walled building.

SPERE: a fixed structure screening the lower end of the great hall from the screens passage. *Spere-truss*: roof truss incorporated in the spere.

SPIRE: tall pyramidal or conical feature crowning a tower or turret. *Broach*: starting from a square base, then carried into an octagonal section by means of triangular faces; *splayed-foot*: a variation of the broach form, found principally in the south-east of England, in which the four cardinal faces are splayed out near their base, to cover the corners, while oblique (or intermediate) faces taper away to a point (1c). *Needle spire*: thin spire rising from the centre of a tower roof, well inside the parapet: when of timber and lead often called a *spike*.

SPIRELET: *see* Flèche.

SPLAY: of an opening when it is wider on one face of a wall than the other.

SPRING OR SPRINGING: level at which an arch or vault rises from its supports. *Springers*: the first stones of an arch or vaulting-rib above the spring (2c).

SQUINCH: arch or series of arches thrown across an interior angle of a square or rectangular structure to support a circular or polygonal superstructure, especially a dome or spire (5a).

SQUINT: an aperture in a wall or through a pier, usually to allow a view of an altar.

STAIRS: *see* 6c. *Dog-leg stair* or (Scots) *Scale-and-platt stair*: parallel flights rising alternately in opposite directions, without an open well. *Flying stair*: cantilevered from the walls of a stairwell, without newels; sometimes called a *geometric* stair when the inner edge describes a curve. *Turnpike* or *newel stair*: ascending round a central supporting newel (8b); also called a *spiral stair* or *vice* when in a circular shaft, a *winder* when in a rectangular compartment. (Winder also applies to the steps on the turn.) *Well stair*: with flights round a square open well framed by newel posts. *See also* Perron.

STAIR TOWER: full-height projection from a main block (especially of a tower house) containing the principal stair from the ground floor (8a).

STAIR TURRET: turret corbelled out from above ground level and containing a stair from one of the upper floors of a building, especially a tower house (8a).

STALL: fixed seat in the choir or chancel for the clergy or choir (cf. Pew). Usually with arm rests, and often framed together.

STANCHION: upright structural member, of iron, steel or reinforced concrete.

STANDPIPE TOWER: *see* Manometer.

STEADING (Scots): farm building or buildings; generally used for the principal group of buildings on a farm.

STEAM ENGINES: *Atmospheric*: worked by the vacuum created when low-pressure steam is condensed in the cylinder, as developed by Thomas Newcomen. *Beam engine*: with a large pivoted beam moved in an oscillating fashion by the piston. It may drive a flywheel or be *non-rotative*. *Watt* and *Cornish*: single-cylinder; *compound*: two cylinders; *triple expansion*: three cylinders.

STEEPLE: tower together with a spire, lantern or belfry.

STIFFLEAF: type of E.E. foliage decoration. *Stiffleaf capital*: *see* 1b.

STOP: plain or decorated terminal to mouldings or chamfers, or at the end of hoodmoulds and labels (*label stop*), or stringcourses (5b, 6a); *see also* Headstop.

STOUP: vessel for holy water, usually near a door.

STRAINER: *see* Arch.

STRAPWORK: decoration like interlaced leather straps, late C16 and C17 in origin.

STRETCHER: *see* Bond and 6e.

STRING: *see* 6c. Sloping member holding the ends of the treads and risers of a staircase. *Closed string*: a broad string covering the ends of the treads and risers. *Open string*: cut into the shape of the treads and risers.

STRINGCOURSE: horizontal course or moulding projecting from the surface of a wall (6d).

STUCCO: decorative plasterwork. *See also* Rendering.

STUDS: subsidiary vertical timbers of a timber-framed wall or partition.

STUGGED (Scots): of masonry hacked or picked as a key for rendering; used as a surface finish in the C19.

STUPA: Buddhist shrine, circular in plan.

STYLOBATE: top of the solid platform on which a colonnade stands (3a).

SUSPENSION BRIDGE: *see* Bridge.

SWAG: like a festoon (q.v.), but representing cloth.

SYSTEM BUILDING: *see* Industrialized building.

TABERNACLE: safe cupboard above an altar to contain the reserved sacrament or a relic; or architectural frame for an image or statue.

TABLE STONE or TABLE TOMB: memorial slab raised on freestanding legs.

TAS-DE-CHARGE: the lower courses of a vault or arch which are laid horizontally (2c).

TENEMENT: holding of land, but also applied to a purpose-built flatted block.

TERM: pedestal or pilaster tapering downward, usually with the upper part of a human figure growing out of it.

TERRACOTTA: moulded and fired clay ornament or cladding.

TERREPLEIN: in a fort the level surface of a rampart behind a parapet for mounting guns.

TESSELLATED PAVEMENT: mosaic flooring, particularly Roman, made of *tesserae*, i.e. cubes of glass, stone or brick.

TESTER: flat canopy over a tomb or pulpit, where it is also called a *sounding-board*.

TESTER TOMB: tomb-chest with effigies beneath a tester, either freestanding (tester with four or more columns), or attached to a wall (*half-tester*) with columns on one side only.

TETRASTYLE: *see* Portico.

THERMAL WINDOW: *see* Diocletian window.

THREE-DECKER PULPIT: *see* Pulpit.

TIDAL GATES: *see* Canals.

TIE-BEAM: *see* Roofs and 7.

TIERCERON: *see* Vault and 2c.

TIFTING (Scots): mortar bed for verge slates laid over gable skew.

TILE-HANGING: *see* Slate-hanging.

TIMBER-FRAMING: method of construction where the structural frame is built of interlocking timbers. The spaces are filled with non-structural material, e.g. *infill* of wattle and daub, lath and plaster, brickwork (known as *nogging*) etc., and may be covered by plaster, weatherboarding (q.v.) or tiles.

TOLBOOTH (Scots; *lit.* tax booth): burgh council building containing council chamber and prison.

TOMB-CHEST: chest-shaped tomb, usually of stone. Cf. Table tomb, Tester tomb.

TORUS (plural: tori): large convex moulding, usually used on a column base (3b, 3f).

TOUCH: soft black marble quarried near Tournai.

TOURELLE: turret corbelled out from the wall (8a).

TOWER BLOCK: *see* Multi-storey.

TOWER HOUSE (Scots): for elements and forms *see* 8a, 8b. Compact fortified house with the main hall raised above the ground and at least one more storey above it. A medieval Scots type continuing well into the C17 in its modified forms: *L-plan* with a jamb at one corner; *Z-plan* with a jamb at each diagonally opposite corner.

TRABEATED: dependent structurally on the use of the post and lintel. Cf. Arcuated.

TRACERY: openwork pattern of masonry or timber in the upper part of an opening. *Blind* tracery is tracery applied to a solid wall. *Plate tracery*, introduced *c.* 1200, is the earliest form, in which shapes are cut through solid masonry (2a).

Bar tracery was introduced into England *c.* 1250. The pattern is formed by intersecting moulded ribwork continued from the mullions. It was especially elaborate during the Decorated period (q.v.). Tracery shapes can include circles, *daggers* (elongated ogee-ended lozenges), *mouchettes* (like daggers but with curved sides) and upright rectangular *panels*. They often have *cusps*, projecting points defining lobes or *foils* (q.v.) within the main shape: *Kentish* or *split-cusps* are forked.

Types of bar tracery (*see* 2b) include *geometric(al)*: *c.* 1250–1310, chiefly circles, often foiled; *Y-tracery*: *c.* 1300, with mullions branching into a Y-shape; *intersecting*: *c.* 1300, formed by interlocking mullions; *reticulated*: early C14, net-like pattern of ogee-ended lozenges; *curvilinear*: C14, with uninterrupted flowing curves; *loop*: *c.* 1500–45, with large uncusped loop-like forms; *panel*: Perp, with straight-sided panels, often cusped at the top and bottom.

TRANSE (Scots): passage.

TRANSEPT: transverse portion of a cruciform church.

TRANSITIONAL: generally used for the phase between Romanesque and Early English (*c.* 1175–*c.* 1200).

TRANSOM: horizontal member separating window lights (2b).

TREAD: horizontal part of a step. The *tread end* may be carved on a staircase (6c).

TREFOIL: *see* Foil.

TRIFORIUM: middle storey of a church treated as an arcaded wall passage or blind arcade, its height corresponding to that of the aisle roof.

TRIGLYPHS (*lit.* three-grooved tablets): stylized beam-ends in the Doric frieze, with metopes between (3b).

TRIUMPHAL ARCH: influential type of Imperial Roman monument.

TROPHY: sculptured or painted group of arms or armour.

TRUMEAU: central stone mullion supporting the tympanum of a wide doorway. *Trumeau figure*: carved figure attached to it (cf. Column figure).

TRUMPET CAPITAL: *see* 1b.

TRUSS: braced framework, spanning between supports. *See also* Roofs.

TUMBLING or TUMBLING-IN: courses of brickwork laid at right angles to a slope, e.g. of a gable, forming triangles by tapering into horizontal courses.

TURNPIKE: *see* Stairs.

TUSCAN: *see* Orders and 3e.

TUSKING STONES (Scots): projecting end stones for bonding with an adjoining wall.

TWO-DECKER PULPIT: *see* Pulpit.

TYMPANUM: the surface between a lintel and the arch above it or within a pediment (4a).

UNDERCROFT: usually describes the vaulted room(s) beneath the main room(s) of a medieval house. Cf. Crypt.

UNIVALLATE: of a hillfort: defended by a single bank and ditch.

VAULT: arched stone roof (sometimes imitated in timber or plaster). For types *see* 2c.

Tunnel or *barrel vault*: continuous semicircular or pointed arch, often of rubble masonry.

Groin vault: tunnel vaults intersecting at right angles. *Groins* are the curved lines of the intersections.

Rib vault: masonry framework of intersecting arches (ribs) supporting *vault cells*, used in Gothic architecture. *Wall rib* or *wall arch*: between wall and vault cell. *Transverse rib*: spans between two walls to divide a vault into bays. *Quadripartite* rib vault: each bay has two pairs of diagonal ribs dividing the vault into four triangular cells. *Sexpartite* rib vault: most often used over paired bays, has an extra pair of ribs springing from between the bays. More elaborate vaults may include *ridge-ribs* along the crown of a vault or bisecting the bays; *tiercerons*: extra decorative ribs springing from the corners of a bay; and *liernes*: short decorative ribs in the crown of a vault, not linked to any springing point. A *stellar* or *star* vault has liernes in star formation.

Fan vault: form of barrel vault used in the Perp period, made up of halved concave masonry cones decorated with blind tracery.

VAULTING-SHAFT: shaft leading up to the spring or springing (q.v.) of a vault (2c).

VENETIAN or SERLIAN WINDOW: derived from Serlio (4b). The motif is used for other openings.

VERMICULATION: *see* Rustication and 6d.

VESICA: oval with pointed ends.

VICE: *see* Stair.

VILLA: originally a Roman country house or farm. The term was revived in England in the C18 under the influence of Palladio and used especially for smaller, compact country houses. In the later C19 it was debased to describe any suburban house.

VITRIFIED: bricks or tiles fired to a darkened glassy surface. *Vitrified fort*: built of timber-laced masonry, the timber having later been set on fire with consequent vitrification of the stonework.

VITRUVIAN SCROLL: classical running ornament of curly waves (4b).

VOLUTES: spiral scrolls. They occur on Ionic capitals (3c). *Angle* volute: pair of volutes, turned outwards to meet at the corner of a capital.

VOUSSOIRS: wedge-shaped stones forming an arch (5c).

WAGON ROOF: with the appearance of the inside of a wagon tilt; often ceiled. Also called *cradle roof*.

WAINSCOT: *see* Panelling.

WALLED GARDEN: in C18 and C19 Scotland, combined vegetable and flower garden, sometimes well away from the house.

WALLHEAD: straight top of a wall. *Wallhead chimney*: chimney rising from a wallhead (8a). *Wallhead gable*: gable rising from a wallhead.

WALL MONUMENT: attached to the wall and often standing on the floor. *Wall tablets* are smaller with the inscription as the major element.

WALL-PLATE: *see* Roofs and 7.

WALL-WALK: *see* Parapet.

WARMING ROOM: room in a religious house where a fire burned for comfort.

WATERHOLDING BASE: early Gothic base with upper and lower mouldings separated by a deep hollow.

WATERLEAF: *see* Enrichments and 3f.

WATERLEAF CAPITAL: Late Romanesque and Transitional type of capital (1b).

WATER WHEELS: described by the way water is fed on to the wheel. *Breastshot*: mid-height, falling and passing beneath. *Overshot*: over the top. *Pitchback*: on the top but falling backwards. *Undershot*: turned by the momentum of the water passing beneath. In a *water turbine*, water is fed under pressure through a vaned wheel within a casing.

WEALDEN HOUSE: type of medieval timber-framed house with a central open hall flanked by bays of two storeys, roofed in line; the end bays are jettied to the front, but the eaves are continuous.

WEATHERBOARDING: wall cladding of overlapping horizontal boards.

WEATHERING: or SET-OFF: inclined, projecting surface to keep water away from the wall below.

WEEPERS: figures in niches along the sides of some medieval tombs. Also called *mourners*.

WHEEL HOUSE: Late Iron Age circular stone dwelling; inside, partition walls radiating from the central hearth like wheel spokes.

WHEEL WINDOW: circular, with radiating shafts like spokes. Cf. Rose window.

WROUGHT IRON: *see* Cast iron.

WYND (Scots): subsidiary street or lane, often running into a main street or gait (q.v.).

YETT (Scots, *lit.* gate): hinged openwork gate at a main doorway, made of iron bars alternately penetrating and penetrated (8c).

Z-PLAN: *see* Tower house and 8b.

INDEX OF ARCHITECTS AND ARTISTS

Entries for partnerships and group practices are listed after entries for a single name.

INDEX OF PLACES

Principal references are in **bold** type; demolished buildings are shown in *italic*.

(A) = Aberdeenshire North; (M) = Moray. [B] indicates places in the county of Banffshire before 1975 (see p. xv above).